Henry D. Thoreau

Countee Cullen

D. H. Lawrence

Charles Dickens

Jonathan Swift

Daniel Defoe

G. Bernard Shaw

Phillis Wheatley

Stephen Crane

Langston Hughes

Bret Harte

Henry W. Longfellow

oscar wilde

Thornton Wilder

Edgar A Poe

Ernest Hemingway

J. Austen

Sinclair Lewis

Herman Melville

R Eddy

Ivan Turgenev

A Bradstreet

T. S. Eliot

Jack London

Thomas Hardy

MACMILLAN LITERATURE SERIES

# APPRECIATING LITERATURE

## SIGNATURE EDITION

## TEACHER'S ANNOTATED EDITION

**GLENCOE/McGRAW-HILL**
A Macmillan/McGraw-Hill Company
Mission Hills, California

# Macmillan Literature Series

SIGNATURE EDITION

## TABLE OF CONTENTS

# Student's Edition

 ake literature the heart of your Language Arts program with *Macmillan Literature Series,* Signature Edition.

**The Unit Preview**

1 provides a frame of reference for the selection

2 offers a springboard for classroom discussion

3 opens students' minds to learning about themselves through the experiences of others

**Before each selection, students will find**

1 a brief biography of the author and notes on the author's contributions to literature

2 a purpose-setting question that links the students' experiences to concepts in the selection

PEARL BUCK
1892–1973

Buck was born in West

Virginia but grew up in

China. Many of her works,

such as *The Good Earth*,

take place in China.

The stories by this Nobel

Prize recipient create

better understanding

among people.

# Student's Edition

 From Beowulf to James Michener, from Emily Dickinson to Dante, *Macmillan Literature Series* presents the most thought-provoking classic and contemporary selections, crossing periods, cultures, and genres. Selections were chosen and organized in response to surveys of 5,200 English teachers.

## STUDENTS BECOME ACTIVE READERS THROUGH STUDY AND RESPONSE ACTIVITIES.

After each selection, a three-part questioning strategy leads students through various levels of thinking:

1   Recalling: students recall literal facts.
2   Interpreting: students apply critical thinking skills.
3   Extending: students explore selection ideas.

*Challenge and Viewpoint* activities encourage different types of response.

*Comparing Activities* encourage students to look at literature in new ways.

## SPEAKING AND LISTENING HANDBOOK *Grades 7–12*

Includes lessons on how to present orally, listen effectively, and interact in collaborative learning activities.

## THINKING SKILLS HANDBOOK *Grades 7–12*

Provides lessons on how to apply higher order thinking skills.

## READING AND STUDY SKILLS HANDBOOK *Grades 7–10*

Lessons reinforce the skills essential to demonstrating comprehension.

### BENJAMIN FRANKLIN
### 1706–1790

Franklin educated himself by reading widely. He published his first essay as a teenager. He moved penniless from Boston to Philadelphia, where he became a civic leader.

# Student's Edition

 riting assignments challenge students at different levels. At the end of selections, students have a choice of two different writing assignments—an analytical composition about the selection or a creative writing project.

The *Writing About Literature Handbook* encourages writing about the selections.

## The Research Paper Casebook
*Grades 11–12*
Guides students through the specific steps needed to produce a successful research paper.

EVALUATE STUDENT PROGRESS WITH UNIT REVIEWS AND ACTIVITIES TO ENSURE COMPREHENSION.

The *Model for Active Reading* and follow-up activities help students extract meaning and enjoyment from the selections in each unit.

*Literary Skills Reviews* and *Themes Reviews* reinforce the unit lessons.

## Student's Resources
## Lessons in Active Learning
In the Student Resources handbooks at the back of the Student's Edition are guides for independent learning and evaluation.

ROBERT FROST

1874–1963

•

Frost is closely identified

with New England even

though he was born in

San Francisco and moved

to New Hampshire as a

child. He received many

honors, including four

Pulitzer Prizes.

# Teacher's Annotated Edition

IT IS MORE THAN JUST A PLANNING TOOL!
IT IS A PRACTICAL GUIDE WITH
TIME-SAVING FEATURES.

Every feature in the Teacher's Annotated Edition can be immediately used and applied in the classroom.

On-the-page annotations

1   provide on-the-spot help in directing class discussion
2   include ideas that can be shared with students of various abilities
3   save time for busy teachers rather than demand more time

**INTRODUCE STUDENTS TO GREAT LITERATURE WITH EFFECTIVE PREREADING STRATEGIES.**

Lead students into the literature with the help of these prereading features:

1   *At a Glance* summarizes major developments on the page; teachers can see "what happens where" without having to read the entire selection.

2   *Literary Options* lists the most obvious literary elements associated with the selection allowing teachers to focus on one or more dominant elements or techniques.

3   *Thematic Options* lets teachers select one or more themes to focus on in the teaching of the selection.

GWENDOLYN
BROOKS
1917 –

Brooks was the first black

woman to win a Pulitzer

Prize. She began writing

poetry that was quite

traditional, but in her

later work she often uses

free verse and open forms.

# Teacher's Annotated Edition

eyed-to-text annotations highlight passages in the selection for the teacher. Similar to marginal notes that any teacher keeps, these annotations

1 give insight about the passage and its relation to the selection as a whole

2 enrich class discussion

3 are brief enough to be used while teaching

These keyed-to-text annotations include literary elements, background, vocabulary, paraphrases, reading skills, and response journal.

*Response Journal* offers suggestions for student writing about a specific passage in a selection.

*Reflecting on the Selection* suggests overview questions that allow students to respond in general before beginning a detailed post-selection analysis.

*Guided Reading* questions address thinking skills and check students' comprehension page by page, helping prepare them for end-of-selection study questions.

CHALLENGE STUDENTS WITH ACTIVITIES AND REVIEWS THAT DEVELOP THEIR THINKING SKILLS AS THEY RESPOND TO LITERATURE.

Unit teaching notes offer activities for the *Model for Active Reading* feature in the student text.

*Answers to themes review* help to encourage class discussion.

*Answers* to end-of-selection questions appear on the Teacher's Annotated Edition page, so there's no more juggling separate answer keys.

*Annotations* at the beginning of each Student's Resources handbook explain the philosophy, structure, or application of the lessons.

ANTON CHEKHOV

1860–1904

•

Chekhov was the grandson

of a Russian serf. While

at medical school he

began to write, launching

a brilliant literary career.

# Teacher's Annotated Edition

PROVISION FOR EVALUATION AND WRITING
ABOUT LITERATURE TEACH STUDENTS SKILLS TO
HELP THEM IN ALL CURRICULUM AREAS.

 n-the-page *Suggestions for Critiques* of the two-part composition assignments suggested in the student text save you time in assessing student writing.

It is easy to assess student achievement with a variety of reviews and checkpoints:

1   Selection End: three-level study questions feature recall, interpretation, and extension.

2   Unit End: Literary Skills Review encourages students to look at literature in a broad context.

## WILLIAM SHAKESPEARE
### 1564–1616

•

Shakespeare, poet and

playwright, is said to be

the world's favorite author.

No other writer's plays

have been produced so

often and read so widely

all over the world.

# Teacher's Classroom Resources

THE LESSON PLAN BOOKLETS—
PREREADING, READING, RESPONDING,
AND EVALUATING—BRING IT ALL
TOGETHER.

hese booklets in the Teacher's Classroom Resources specify when to use each component while teaching a selection.

1   One-page lesson plans begin with clearly stated objectives.

2   Each lesson plan lists materials and activities by lesson elements: *Prereading, Reading and Response, Composition, Closure and Transfer, Reteaching, Enrichment and Extension, and Evaluation.*

The *Macmillan Literature Series* Lesson Plans make teaching manageable by providing step-by-step management of each and every component.

UNIT BOOKLETS HELP STUDENTS BECOME ACTIVE READERS AND IN-DEPTH THINKERS.

For teaching each selection, teachers will find in the Unit Booklets:

A *Teaching Chart* to identify features in the Student's Edition, Teacher's Annotated Edition, and Teacher's Classroom Resources (including Overhead Transparencies) for use before, during, and after reading a selection.

*Teaching Notes*

1   Author notes to help teachers provide additional background and context for the selection.

2   A Statement of Theme or Main Idea and Synopsis.

3   Motivation suggestions to engage students' interest before reading.

4   Words in Glossary to show teachers the selection words that appear in the Glossary in the Student's Edition.

5   Additional Projects to help students work in a novel, often nonverbal, way to further explore the selection.

A *Prereading Vocabulary blackline master* to introduce and provide practice with difficult words from the selection using various strategies.

A *Reading Guide blackline master* to keep less-able readers focused on the selection and help them note key points as they read.

A *Check Test blackline master* to give teachers a quick sense of students' grasp of the selection on a literal level.

A *Writing Process Guide blackline master* to help students complete the analytical composition assignments in the Student's Edition.

A *Selection Test blackline master* including vocabulary test items to help teachers evaluate the students' understanding.

TEACHER'S
CLASSROOM
RESOURCES
These resources offer
everything a teacher
needs for planning and
teaching lessons for
Grades 6–12.

# Teacher's Classroom Resources

THE LITERATURE IS MADE ACCESSIBLE
TO ALL THE STUDENTS.

*Literary Skills* and *Active-Learning Guides* provide opportunities for students to become actively involved with literary terms and elements as well as reinforcement of *Student's Resources Lessons in Active Learning*.

An *Answer Key booklet* is a quick reference that provides answers and guidelines for evaluation.

*Overhead Transparencies* provide an alternative medium for instruction while students are actively involved with great literature.

*Teacher's Professional Resources booklet* contains helpful articles about the teaching of literature.

*Models of Student Writing* cover twelve types of writing and exemplify the writing process and the teacher's evaluation of that process.

Additional Teaching Materials complete a comprehensive literature program.

*Macmillan Literature Series Test Generator* provides individual test items that can be selected from the computer data bank so that tests can be customized.

*Macmillan Literature Novel and Drama Guides* enable students to apply independently their literary and vocabulary skills.

*The Macmillan Literature Series Video Library* supports classroom instruction and brings literature to life by showing how to integrate videotapes with reading.

*The Macmillan Literature Series Audiotapes* expand students' literary experiences with outstanding presentations and active reader comments.

MARK TWAIN
1835–1910

Mark Twain, who was

born Samuel Clemens,

did not just write a story.

He told it. His mastery

of American speech and

his ability to spin a yarn

are unsurpassed.

# Scope and Sequence

## MACMILLAN LITERATURE SERIES

All the components fit together to make MACMILLAN LITERATURE SERIES,
Signature Edition, a comprehensive language arts program.

| Reading and Literary Skills | Discovering Literature | Introducing Literature | Enjoying Literature | Understanding Literature | Appreciating Literature | American Literature | English Literature with World Masterpieces | World Literature |
|---|---|---|---|---|---|---|---|---|
| allegory | | | | | | 181, 936 | 56, 120, 287, 290, 893 | |
| alliteration | | 219, 274, 598 | 224, 282, 628, 630, 646 | 195, 720, 724, 730 | 200, 788, 792 | 131, 936 | 18, 26, 430, 996, 1020 | |
| allusion | | 430, 598 | 453, 646 | 487, 724 | 200, 792 | 29, 936 | 276, 285, 286, 656, 1020 | |
| analogy | | | | | 332, 792 | 39, 936 | 1020 | |
| antagonist | | | | | 792 | 665, 936 | 1020 | |
| assonance | | | 227, 646 | 195, 720, 724 | 192, 788, 792 | 131, 937 | 430, 996, 1020 | |
| atmosphere | | 131, 172, 598 | 92, 165, 646 | 75, 304, 724 | 58, 792 | 148–149 | 225, 756, 1020 | |
| audience | | 47, 289, 322, 598 | 25, 297, 330, 486, 646 | 233, 261, 327 | 263, 353 | 68 | 236 | |
| autobiography, biography | | 21, 289, 295, 303, 333, 598 | 11, 297, 304, 312, 646 | 234, 240, 245, 251, 716, 724 | 264, 270, 277, 346, 792 | 58, 244, 937 | 365, 498, 1021 | |
| ballad, song | | | | 171, 724 | 225, 792 | 7, 12–14, 170–171, 236–238, 286 | 5, 49, 52, 55, 141, 143, 266, 313, 366, 372, 394–395, 554, 651, 804, 1021 | |
| blank verse | | | | 356, 724 | 196, 491, 793 | 123, 937 | 165, 277, 285, 286, 1021 | |
| cause and effect | | 72, 479, 598 | 47, 318, 341, 494, 646 | | | | | |
| character | | 105, 171, 368, 404, 434, 447, 498, 574, 598 | 67, 77, 430, 462, 468, 496, 566, 622, 624, 646 | 53, 63, 145, 157, 326–327, 374, 428, 613, 708, 724 | 44, 134, 432, 512, 612, 772, 793 | 114, 323, 339, 710, 937 | 78, 225, 502, 510, 640, 701, 712, 724, 731, 904, 913, 1021 | |
| characterization | | 95, 109, 170, 404, 434, 498, 532, 574, 598 | 67, 85, 160, 406, 430, 622, 624, 646, 647 | 40, 47, 613, 725 | 39, 793 | 323, 512, 600–601, 937 | 78, 79, 104, 698, 712, 724, 819, 1021–1022 | |
| chronological order | | 72, 308, 599 | 47, 159, 318, 332, 647 | | | | | |
| Classicism | | | | | | 101, 937 | 311–313, 1022 | |
| climax | | 65, 172, 308, 332, 404, 599 | 41, 166, 430, 647 | 10, 273, 326, 427, 725 | 20, 448, 793 | 323, 711, 937 | 224, 711, 1022, 1028 | |
| comedy | | | 349, 350, 647 | 293, 725 | 353, 384, 793 | 665, 667 | 132–133, 242–243, 313, 569, 913, 1022 | |
| comparison/contrast | | 143, 519, 599 | 211, 647 | 708 | 345, 346 | 92, 896–897 | 986 | |
| concrete language | | 235, 599 | 238, 647 | 277, 725 | 320 | | | |
| conflict | | 79, 85, 170, 308, 330, 404, 451, 508, 599 | 52, 165, 430, 647 | 26, 33, 273, 326, 427, 458, 592, 725 | 28, 134, 448, 491, 793 | 323, 365–366, 938 | 224, 701, 1022, 1028 | |
| consonance | | | | 720 | 192, 788 | 131, 938 | 430, 996, 1022 | |
| description | | 289, 312, 327, 599 | 297, 323, 333, 648 | 240, 725 | 794 | 92, 311, 938 | 1023 | |
| details | | 100, 138, 202, 282, 312, 406, 599 | 73, 96, 212, 290, 291, 292, 323, 432, 434, 618, 648 | 69, 158, 240 | 58, 103, 174, 296, 320 | 92, 150 | 42, 78, 79, 104 | |
| dialogue | | 45, 161, 171, 341, 355, 600 | 22, 189, 344, 349, 364, 642, 648 | 33, 273, 293, 326, 726 | 309, 354, 382, 794 | 665, 939 | 52, 476, 933, 1023 | |
| drama | | 44, 341, 404, 592, 594, 600 | 22, 349, 364, 430, 432, 433, 640, 642, 648 | 293, 726 | 353, 354, 794 | 665, 710–711, 753, 939 | 144–145, 236, 242, 391, 826, 1023 | |
| dramatic monologue | | | | | 235, 794 | 414, 419, 939 | 502, 507, 1023 | |
| elegy | | | | | | 261 | 38, 274, 366, 371, 498, 1024 | |
| epic | | | | 433, 726 | 225, 576, 794 | 939 | 5, 8, 120, 277, 285, 351, 786, 820, 1024, 1027 | |
| essay | | 21, 289, 317, 600 | 11, 297, 318, 323, 327, 331, 648 | 263, 273, 277, 280, 285, 726 | 290, 296, 309, 313, 319, 325, 339, 346, 794 | 664, 939 | 228, 332, 339, 461, 466, 1024 | |
| exposition (in plot) | | | | 10, 273, 326, 427, 726 | 20, 296, 448, 794 | 323, 710, 848, 939 | 224, 711, 1024, 1028 | |
| fable | | 145, 455, 600 | 471, 649 | 114, 727 | 90, 795 | 303, 939–940 | 732, 1024 | |

| Reading and Literary Skills | Discovering Literature | Introducing Literature | Enjoying Literature | Understanding Literature | Appreciating Literature | American Literature | English Literature with World Masterpieces | World Literature |
|---|---|---|---|---|---|---|---|---|
| fact vs. opinion | | 334 | 342, 343, 651 | | | | | |
| falling action | | | | 10, 273, 326, 427, 727 | 20, 448, 795 | 323, 711 | 224, 711, 1024, 1028 | |
| figurative language | | 273, 601 | 245, 247, 248, 282, 628, 630, 649, 650, 651, 654 | 63, 196, 727 | 201, 289, 346, 788, 795 | 164, 940 | 140, 177, 448, 1024–1025 | |
| figure of speech | | 601 | 649 | 196, 727 | 177, 201, 209, 211, 213, 219, 249, 795 | 164, 220, 940 | 140, 448, 1025 | |
| foil | | | | | 795 | 600–601, 940 | 903 | |
| folk literature | | 413, 461, 601 | 469, 471, 486, 649 | 75 | 575, 644 | 7, 12–14, 70, 170, 236, 426 | 49, 52, 55, 103, 554, 641, 651, 804, 827, 1025, 1027 | |
| foot | | | | 185, 727 | 795 | 123, 940 | 119, 165, 540, 940, 1025 | |
| foreshadowing | | 91, 172, 369, 508, 601 | 57, 130, 160, 458, 566, 649 | 26, 639, 727 | 20, 795 | 810, 940 | 18, 1025 | |
| frame | | | | 126, 727 | 90, 664, 795 | 298, 613, 940 | 57, 1025 | |
| free verse | | | 260, 649 | 727 | 198, 246, 260, 795 | 260–261, 265, 404, 413, 426, 940 | 232, 563, 656, 1025 | |
| hero, protagonist | | 466, 601 | 449, 650 | 433, 467, 726 | 460, 568, 576, 606, 794, 798 | 323, 665, 711, 944 | 5, 146, 224, 351, 433, 436, 861, 1029, 1031 | |
| heroic couplet | | | | | | 87, 170, 941 | 291, 352, 438, 1025 | |
| imagery, sensory language | | 16, 233, 274, 498, 601 | 7, 238, 282, 628, 650 | 196, 199, 277, 399, 428, 728, 731 | 75, 205, 249, 320, 346, 796 | 32, 34, 92, 132, 164, 227, 274, 404, 413, 426, 574, 941 | 177, 246, 286, 652, 687, 1025–1026 | |
| Imagism | | | | | | 401–402, 404, 409, 413, 427, 450, 783, 941 | | |
| inferring | | 100, 138, 170, 203, 283, 472, 601 | 73, 96, 213, 292, 406, 650 | 290 | 350 | 536 | 384 | |
| irony | | 178, 602 | 189, 650 | 145, 428, 728 | 129, 133, 416, 612, 784, 796 | 391, 474, 496, 941 | 225, 640, 1026 | |
| literal language | | | | 63, 196, 728 | 796 | 164, 942 | 177 | |
| local color | | | | 40, 728 | 167, 796 | 311, 315, 334, 340, 395 | | |
| lyric poetry | | 271, 602 | 275, 650 | 208, 222, 730 | 177, 222, 231, 249, 796 | 286–287, 942 | 8, 38, 110, 557, 1026 | |
| main idea | | 317, 324 | 327, 335, 634 | 114, 285 | 90, 780 | 323, 534, 947 | 698, 764, 1031 | |
| metaphor | | 243, 602 | 247, 628, 630, 650 | 63, 203, 720, 728 | 213, 215, 217, 289, 788, 796 | 39, 164, 942 | 140, 242, 448, 893, 996, 1026 | |
| meter | | | | 185, 728 | 192, 796 | 122–123, 215, 942 | 119, 165, 501, 540, 563, 1026 | |
| Middle English | | | | | | | 40, 56–57, 96–97, 1026 | |
| mock-epic | | | | | | 286 | 351, 439, 1026 | |
| Modernism | | | | | | 401–405, 409, 421, 429, 442, 446, 450, 459, 464, 489, 540, 545, 575, 666–667, 758, 767, 942 | 563–565, 651, 655, 683 | |
| mood | | 131 | 92 | 729 | 58, 383, 774, 797 | 148–149, 621 | 165, 177, 225, 756, 1027 | |
| myth/legend | | 413, 422, 602 | 439, 440, 650–651 | 439 | 575–580, 794 | 7 | 103, 827, 877, 1026, 1027 | |
| narration | | 169, 209, 308, 324, 602 | 297, 318, 332, 651 | 729 | 225, 296, 797 | 113, 844, 942 | 1027 | |
| narrative poetry | | 258, 264, 602 | 273, 651 | 162, 222, 730 | 177, 222, 225, 249, 797 | 286, 942 | 38, 553, 557, 1027 | |
| narrator | | 115, 126, 532, 602 | 107, 120, 550, 651 | 85, 729 | 75, 612, 797 | 319, 333, 753, 942 | 553, 689, 716, 1027 | |
| Naturalism | | | | | | 311, 396, 399, 942 | 487, 541, 545, 1027 | |
| nonfiction | | 21, 289, 308, 312, 317, 322, 586, 588, 603 | 10, 297, 318, 323, 327, 330, 634, 636, 651 | 233, 729 | 263, 346, 786, 797 | 58, 244, 664 | 228, 332, 339, 365, 461, 498 | |
| novel | | 91, 485, 603 | 501, 651 | 491, 729 | 611, 612, 797 | 114, 156, 395, 943 | 313, 321, 391, 514, 665, 894, 1027–1028 | |
| Old English | | | | | | | 3, 5, 40–41, 1028 | |
| onomatopoeia | | 228, 603 | 234, 628, 630, 651 | 188, 720, 729 | 200, 788, 797 | 131, 436, 943 | 431, 996, 1028 | |

# Scope and Sequence

The heart of your language arts program.

| Reading and Literary Skills | Discovering Literature | Introducing Literature | Enjoying Literature | Understanding Literature | Appreciating Literature | American Literature | English Literature with World Masterpieces | World Literature |
|---|---|---|---|---|---|---|---|---|
| oral tradition | | 216, 341, 418, 603 | 349 | 433 | 579 | 7, 14, 943 | 5, 18, 49, 52, 55, 804, 820, 862, 1028 | |
| oratory | | | | | 331 | 65, 68–69, 96, 255, 943 | 225 | |
| parallelism | | | | 195, 729 | 194, 331, 346, 797 | 84, 943 | 1028 | |
| parody | | | | | | 566, 943 | 323, 338, 1028 | |
| personification | | | 248, 628, 630, 651 | 201, 720, 729 | 209, 788, 798 | 220, 943 | 448, 996, 1028 | |
| persuasion | | 322, 336, 603 | 297, 330, 344, 652 | 263, 280, 729 | 326, 798 | 84, 943 | 1028 | |
| plot | | 57, 65, 404, 532, 572, 603 | 41, 47, 52, 57, 63, 157, 430, 458, 501, 566, 581, 620, 624, 652 | 10, 26, 138, 145, 151, 273, 427, 592, 704, 729–730 | 20, 104, 134, 448, 612, 770, 798 | 323, 794, 943 | 224, 391, 514, 639–640, 698, 711, 725, 731, 750, 827, 1028 | |
| point of view | | 115, 126 | 107, 120, 157, 550, 652 | 85, 94, 109, 145, 151, 509, 565, 712, 730 | 75, 82, 86, 134, 612, 776, 798 | 333, 384, 613, 943–944 | 689, 698, 716, 731, 1029 | |
| predicting outcomes | | 91, 204, 369, 508 | 57, 214, 566, 620 | 26, 639, 727 | 20, 795 | 810, 940 | 1025 | |
| purpose | | 47, 289, 295, 322, 604 | 25, 297, 305, 652 | 233, 273, 277, 280, 285, 718 | 263, 277, 290, 313, 346, 786 | 69, 83 | 990 | |
| Realism | | | | | | 310–311, 367, 388, 395–396, 399, 666, 669, 944 | 487, 488, 545, 563, 1029 | |
| resolution | | 65, 172, 604 | 41, 167, 620, 653 | 10, 273, 326, 427, 730 | 20, 798 | 323, 711 | 224, 711, 1028, 1029 | |
| rhyme | | 16, 221, 604 | 7, 228, 628, 653 | 187, 356, 720, 725, 730 | 192, 239, 250, 260, 261, 798, 799 | 131, 170, 286, 552, 944 | 119, 430, 996, 1029 | |
| rhyme scheme | | | 228, 653 | 187, 730 | 239, 241, 799 | 170, 945 | 119, 458 | |
| rhythm | | 16, 225, 274, 604 | 7, 231, 282, 628, 630, 653 | 185, 356, 720 | 177, 192, 196, 260, 261, 491, 788, 799 | 87, 122–123, 170, 215, 228, 265, 426, 436, 758, 945 | 57, 119, 165, 258, 327, 352, 439, 501, 540, 554, 563, 684, 996, 1029, 1030 | |
| rising action | | | | 10, 273, 326, 427, 730 | 20, 799 | 323, 711, 945 | 224, 711, 1028 | |
| romance | | | | | 579, 799 | 156, 945 | 49, 353, 441, 894 | |
| Romanticism | | | | | | 101, 119, 132, 437, 567, 570, 628, 666, 945 | 366, 372, 376, 387, 389–391, 394–395, 408, 432–433, 442, 487, 1029 | |
| satire | | | | | 663, 722, 799 | 483, 548, 945 | 242, 243, 295, 312, 331, 340, 732, 894, 903, 1030 | |
| setting | | 131, 169, 186, 404, 532, 605 | 92, 101, 157, 164, 349, 430, 502, 581, 624, 653 | 69, 75, 145, 304, 428, 509, 710, 731 | 58, 68, 134, 383, 612, 774, 799 | 148–149, 323, 945 | 225, 514, 640, 698, 756, 1030 | |
| short story | | 13, 53, 576, 605 | 4, 31, 624, 653 | 1, 145, 158, 159, 731 | 1, 149, 153, 166, 174, 799 | 323, 945–946 | 565, 698, 1030 | |
| simile | | 240, 605 | 245, 628, 630, 654 | 63, 202, 487, 720, 727, 731 | 211, 289, 788, 799 | 39, 164, 946 | 140, 820, 996, 1024, 1025, 1030 | |
| skimming and scanning | | 49, 604, 605 | 27, 653, 654 | 185 | | 123, 945 | | |
| soliloquy | | | | 399, 731 | 512, 799 | 946 | 145, 165, 612, 1030 | |
| sonnet | | | | | 236, 239, 241, 799, 800 | 392, 394, 946 | 114, 119, 139, 251, 274, 396, 442, 1030 | |
| speaker | | | 279, 654 | 175, 177, 720, 731 | 178, 181, 249, 788, 800 | 946 | 116, 165, 557, 996 | |
| stage directions and staging | | 45, 341, 385, 605 | 22, 349, 365, 642, 654 | 293, 304, 326–327, 430, 731 | 354, 383, 432, 465, 536, 800 | 665, 669, 710, 946 | 236, 1030 | |
| stanza | | 16, 252, 605 | 7, 258, 654 | 161, 171, 731 | 177, 239, 241, 800 | 170–171, 552, 946 | 55, 127, 371, 406, 438, 439, 458, 883, 1021, 1031 | |
| stream of consciousness | | | | | | 403–404, 575, 582–583, 639, 946 | 563, 565, 725, 731, 1028, 1031 | |

# Scope and Sequence

The heart of your language arts program.

| Reading and Literary Skills | Discovering Literature | Introducing Literature | Enjoying Literature | Understanding Literature | Appreciating Literature | American Literature | English Literature with World Masterpieces | World Literature |
|---|---|---|---|---|---|---|---|---|
| style | | 47 | 25 | 233, 277, 731 | 263, 800 | 3, 23, 384, 464, 496, 772–773, 946 | 243, 246, 277, 285, 286, 653, 683, 752, 1031 | |
| symbol | | | 287 | 436 | 114, 134, 173, 219, 782, 800 | 190–191, 650–651, 902–903, 947 | 376, 382, 383, 640, 650, 717, 992, 1031 | |
| theme | | 145, 156, 174, 178, 186, 200, 209, 267, 269, 342, 368, 371, 404, 605 | 4, 7, 139, 145, 157, 276, 277, 279, 282, 287, 350, 366, 430, 502, 654 | 114, 118, 126, 145, 157, 188, 327, 428, 540, 714, 731 | 90, 98, 134, 536, 612, 780, 800 | 323, 384, 534, 650–651, 710–711, 904–905, 947 | 225, 514, 698, 764, 994, 1031 | |
| thesis statement | | 317, 324, 606 | 327, 335, 618, 654 | 285, 702 | 339, 769, 800 | 894 | 984 | |
| tone | | | | | 82, 134, 178, 186, 263, 778, 800 | 474, 870, 947 | 246, 265, 285, 312, 640, 658, 676, 756, 1002, 1031 | |
| topic sentence | | 322, 331, 606 | 305, 335, 655 | 285, 703 | 769 | | | |
| total effect | | 178, 186, 200, 277, 323, 404, 532 | 157, 178, 211, 285, 331, 430, 581, 628 | 127, 220, 222, 227, 286, 427, 540, 668 | 134, 247, 253, 346, 459, 569, 605, 661, 734, 790 | 306, 908–909 | 224–225, 639, 998 | |
| tragedy | | | 350, 655 | 293, 331, 731 | 353, 462, 568, 800 | 665 | 133, 146, 224, 313, 826, 861, 1031 | |
| Transcendentalism | | | | | | 154–155, 260, 947 | | |
| word choice | | 47, 238 | 25, 243, 655 | 181, 728, 731 | 178, 181, 249, 800 | 211 | 395, 502, 554, 569, 651, 663, 679, 683, 756 | |

| Composition Skills | Discovering Literature | Introducing Literature | Enjoying Literature | Understanding Literature | Appreciating Literature | American Literature | English Literature with World Masterpieces | World Literature |
|---|---|---|---|---|---|---|---|---|
| ANALYTICAL (Students are asked to write about the following literary genres, techniques, elements, and terms.) | | | | | | | | |
| autobiography, biography | | 295, 586 | 305, 634 | 240, 245, 251, 257, 716 | 270, 277, 281 | 64 | | |
| character | | 105, 115, 156, 174, 369, 447, 472, 574 | 67, 77, 107, 270, 365, 468, 622 | 40, 47, 53, 63, 109, 126, 145, 157, 429, 669, 706, 708 | 39, 44, 52, 154, 460, 570, 662, 772 | 211, 339, 441, 512 | 41, 79, 103, 726, 731 | |
| comparison/contrast | | 265, 369 | 67 | 63, 669, 708 | 52, 570, 662, 772 | 29, 39, 95, 391, 496, 588, 605, 621, 632, 896–897 | 127, 269, 507, 650, 701, 893, 913, 937, 951, 986 | |
| diction and sentence structure | | | | | | 171, 827 | 249 | |
| drama | | 45, 405, 592 | 23, 431, 640 | | 383 | 711 | 225, 640 | |
| figures of speech | | | | 205 | 114, 117 | 220 | | |
| imagery | | 233, 240 | 238, 247, 628 | 216 | 207, 213, 251 | 227 | 143 | |
| irony | | | | | 129, 784 | 391 | 351 | |
| nonfiction | | 295, 312, 586 | 305, 323, 328, 634 | 262, 273, 277, 280, 285, 289, 718 | 296, 309, 320, 323, 326, 332, 339, 349, 786 | 180, 244, 844, 853, 900–901 | 231, 339, 465, 705, 990 | |
| plot | | 57, 72, 85, 126, 167, 279, 443, 461, 572 | 41, 52, 243, 273, 620 | 26, 138, 151, 704 | 28, 770 | 113, 583 | 764 | |
| poetry | | 218, 269, 277, 281, 580 | 225, 234, 285, 289, 628 | 167, 173, 178, 205, 212, 215, 217, 225, 226, 720 | 181, 194, 198, 206, 215, 217, 227, 230, 233, 235, 239, 255, 788 | 134, 273, 287, 387, 413, 420, 426, 449, 463, 779, 906–907 | 452, 527, 537, 545, 646, 671, 679, 685, 996 | |
| point of view | | | | 85, 94, 151, 178, 712 | 75, 776 | 801 | | |
| purpose | | | | 245, 257, 280, 285 | 270 | 653, 660, 853 | 339, 990 | |
| review of a book or drama | | 45, 405, 533, 592 | 23, 431, 582, 640 | | | | | |
| setting | | 131, 182 | 92, 167, 482 | 69, 75, 80, 710 | 58, 68, 774 | 324 | | |
| symbol | | | | | 114, 117, 345, 782 | 333, 627, 832, 840, 902–903 | 431, 501, 667, 688, 724, 992 | |
| theme | | 145 | 189 | 114, 118, 157, 540, 714 | 90, 99, 108, 780 | 124, 475, 535, 810, 904–905 | 285, 756, 803, 873, 994 | |
| tone | | | | | 86, 154, 289, 778 | 305 | 656 | |
| total effect | | | 189, 628 | 145, 429, 540, 669, 722 | 141, 167, 259, 570, 735, 790 | 149, 637, 651, 908–909 | 225, 640, 998 | |

# Scope and Sequence

MACMILLAN LITERATURE SERIES

The heart of your language arts program.

| Composition Skills | Discovering Literature | Introducing Literature | Enjoying Literature | Understanding Literature | Appreciating Literature | American Literature | English Literature with World Masterpieces | World Literature |
|---|---|---|---|---|---|---|---|---|
| CREATIVE (Students are asked to create the following kinds of written materials.) | | | | | | | | |
| anecdote | | | | 126 | 270 | 588 | | |
| aphorisms | | | | | | 64 | | |
| article | | | | 145 | 108, 114, 606 | | | |
| description | | 156, 182, 216, 265, 269, 312, 447, 466, 472, 477 | 67, 77, 92, 273, 323, 462, 482, 493 | 69, 75, 94, 151, 205, 216, 277, 289 | 58, 68, 99, 117, 141, 192, 206, 207, 251, 320, 323, 383 | 45, 92, 118, 149, 191, 339, 366, 463, 475, 512, 621, 660 | 41, 103, 294, 406, 431, 527, 545 | |
| dialogue | | 150, 423, 443 | 243, 468 | 109 | 20, 52, 570 | 711 | 933 | |
| diary, journal entry | | 105 | 52, 582 | 33, 47, 262 | 133 | 29, 252, 651 | 305, 711, 756 | |
| drama | | 45, 126, 369, 594 | 23, 189, 431, 468, 642 | 138, 304 | 75 | 420, 711 | 507, 861, 877, 913 | |
| essay | | 295, 312, 322 | 305, 323, 328 | 273, 280, 285 | 296, 309, 326, 339, 349 | 171, 180, 844, 869 | 231, 339, 705 | |
| fable | | 145, 455 | 139 | 118 | 90 | 305 | | |
| figurative language, imagery | | | 238 | 63 | 213, 217 | 220, 387 | 143, 342, 667 | |
| narrative, story | | 14, 72, 115, 174, 279, 308, 451, 461, 576 | 5, 107, 167, 624 | 53, 80, 85, 151, 157, 225, 429, 540 | 150, 281, 309 | 449, 482, 496, 613 | 286, 514, 724, 893 | |
| opinion | | | | 245, 280 | 129 | 69, 353, 653 | | |
| persuasion | | 238, 322 | 365 | 280 | 44, 167, 326, 332 | 39, 84, 605 | | |
| poem | | 131, 218, 226, 233, 240, 257, 277, 281, 582 | 229, 265, 275, 279, 285, 630 | 167, 215, 217, 226, 327 | 181, 183, 186, 194, 198, 213, 215, 227, 230, 233, 235, 239, 244, 251, 255, 259 | 273, 413, 426, 459, 552, 765 | 127, 646, 650, 656, 662, 671, 679, 683, 825, 937 | |
| point of view | | | | 173, 178, 669 | 309 | 113 | 685, 873 | |
| setting | | | 92, 487 | 304 | 68, 320 | 333, 637 | | |
| sketch | | | | 240, 251, 487 | 270 | 118, 211, 324 | 365, 701 | |
| speech | | | | 114 | 44, 332, 460 | 257, 420, 827 | 225, 507 | |

| Vocabulary Skills | Discovering Literature | Introducing Literature | Enjoying Literature | Understanding Literature | Appreciating Literature | American Literature | English Literature with World Masterpieces | World Literature |
|---|---|---|---|---|---|---|---|---|
| analogies | | 182, 317 | 73, 328 | 262 | 154, 309, 662 | 287, 560, 660 | 469, 501, 925, 937, 961 | |
| antonyms | | 135, 150, 447 | 156, 232, 449 | 26, 114, 157 | 114, 296, 332 | 39, 124, 366, 601, 711 | 286, 358, 540, 764, 913, 955 | |
| connotation/denotation | | | 453 | 213 | 200 | 149, 211 | | |
| context clues | | 22, 95, 201 | 11, 86, 365, 458, 581 | 85 | 99, 150, 320 | | | |
| dialect | | 238 | 102 | 126, 210 | 606 | 324 | 640 | |
| dictionary | | 80 | 58, 482 | | | | | |
| etymology | | 267, 385, 477 | 260, 318 | 75, 151, 487 | 39, 270, 339, 460 | 14, 92, 420, 773, 785 | 97, 305, 873 | |
| glossary | | 138 | 96 | | | | | |
| jargon, technical words, slang | | 369 | 305 | 181, 728 | 735 | 512 | | |
| pronunciation key | | 303 | 393 | | | | | |
| sentence completions | | 65, 115, 161, 186, 265, 279, 461 | 47, 227 | 273 | 44, 133, 326 | 29, 87, 535, 651 | 861 | |
| synonyms | | 14, 58, 107, 221, 295 | 5, 41, 130, 312 | 10, 40, 245 | 20, 75, 345 | 22, 64, 455, 832 | 89, 231, 331, 481, 650, 929 | |
| thesaurus | | 252 | 179 | | | | | |
| word choice | | 252 | 179 | 185, 251, 280 | 129, 188, 200, 227, 232, 289, 735 | 80, 171, 227, 257, 366, 512, 563 | 371, 431, 679 | |
| word development, invention | | | | 190 | 167, 246, 270, 339 | 273 | 903 | |

Glencoe/McGraw-Hill
A Macmillan/McGraw-Hill Company
15319 Chatsworth Street
Mission Hills, California 91345

# APPRECIATING LITERATURE

## SIGNATURE EDITION

**GLENCOE/McGRAW-HILL**
A Macmillan/McGraw-Hill Company
Mission Hills, California

Send all inquiries to:
Glencoe/McGraw-Hill
15319 Chatsworth Street
P.O. Box 9509
Mission Hills, CA 91395-9509

Pupil's Edition ISBN 0-02-635071-8/10
Teacher's Annotated Edition ISBN 0-02-635072-6/10

1 2 3 4 5 6 7 8 9   97 96 95 94 93 92 91

## ACKNOWLEDGMENTS

Grateful acknowledgment is given authors, publishers, and agents for permission to reprint the following copyrighted material. Every effort has been made to determine copyright owners. In the case of any omissions, the Publisher will be pleased to make suitable acknowledgments in future editions.

**Teresa Palomo Acosta**

TERESA PALOMO ACOSTA: "Two Sentences for Gabriela Mistral" is reprinted by permission of the author.

**Agenzia Letteraria Internaziale**

ITALO CALVINO: "The Enchanted Garden" from *Difficult Loves*. Copyright 1949 by Guilio Einaudi editore, Torino. Copyright © 1958 by Guilio Einaudi s.p.a., Torino. By permission of the publisher.

**Samuel Allen**

SAMUEL ALLEN: "To Satch." Reprinted by permission of Samuel Allen.

**Rudolfo A. Anaya**

RUDOLFO A. ANAYA: "A Chicano in China" is excerpted from *A Chicano in China*. © 1986 by the University of New Mexico Press, Albuquerque, NM 87131. All rights reserved. Reprinted by permission of the author.

**Isaac Asimov**

ISAAC ASIMOV: "The Eureka Phenomenon" from *The Left Hand of the Election*. Copyright © 1971 by Mercury Press, Inc. Reprinted by permission of Isaac Asimov.

**Brandt & Brandt Literary Agents, Inc.**

STEPHEN VINCENT BENÉT: "By the Waters of Babylon" from *The Selected Works of Stephen Vincent Benét*. Published by Holt, Rinehart & Winston, Inc. Copyright 1937, by Stephen Vincent Benét. Copyright renewed © 1964 by Thomas C. Benét, Stephanie B. Mahin and Rachel Benét Lewis.
LESLIE NORRIS: "Shaving." Copyright © 1977 by Leslie Norris. The preceding selections were reprinted by permission of Brandt & Brandt Literary Agents, Inc.

**Curtis Brown, Ltd.**

HANSON W. BALDWIN: "R.M.S. Titanic." Published in *Harper's Magazine*, January, 1934. Copyright © 1933 by Harper and Row, Publishers, Inc. Copyright © renewed 1961. Reprinted by permission of Curtis Brown, Ltd., New York.

**Curtis Brown Group Limited**

DORIS LESSING: "Through the Tunnel," from *The Habit of Loving*. Copyright © Doris Lessing 1957. Reprinted by permission of Curtis Brown Ltd., London, on behalf of Doris Lessing.

(pp. 457–466) from *The Spirit of St. Louis*. Copyright 1953 by Charles Scribner's Sons; copyright renewed 1981 by Anne Morrow Lindbergh. (New York: Charles Scribner's Sons, 1953.)
EDITH WHARTON: "April Showers" from *The Collected Short Stories of Edith Wharton*. Copyright © 1968 William R. Tyler.
The preceding selections were reprinted by permission of Charles Scribner's Sons, an imprint of Macmillan Publishing Company.

**The Society of Authors**
JOHN GALSWORTHY: "Quality" from *Caravan*. Reprinted by permission of The Society of Authors as the literary representative of the Estate of John Galsworthy.

**Twayne Publishers, Inc.**
CLAUDE MCKAY: "Spring in New Hampshire" from *The Selected Poems of Claude McKay*. Copyright 1981 by Twayne Publishers, Inc. Reprinted by permission of Twayne Publishers, a division of G. K. Hall & Co., Boston.

**The University of Nebraska Press**
WILLA CATHER: "The Sentimentality of William Tavener" from *Willa Cather's Collected Short Fiction, 1892–1912* (Rev. Ed.) with introduction by Mildred R. Bennett, edited by Virginia Faulkner. Copyright © 1965, 1970 by the University of Nebraska Press. Reprinted by permission of University of Nebraska Press.

**Viking Penguin, Inc.**
PHILIP BOOTH: "First Lesson" from *Letter from a Distant Land*. Copyright © 1957 by Philip Booth.
MAXINE KUMIN: "400-Meter Freestyle" from *Our Ground Time Here Will Be Brief*. Copyright © 1957, 1958, 1959, 1960, 1961 by Maxine Kumin.
SAKI: "The Open Window" from *The Complete Short Stories of Saki*. Copyright 1930 by The Viking Press, Inc. Copyright renewed 1958 by The Viking Press, Inc.
JOHN STEINBECK: *The Pearl*. Copyright 1945 by John Steinbeck. Copyright renewed 1973 by Elaine Steinbeck, Thom Steinbeck, and John Steinbeck IV.
The preceding selections were reprinted by permission of Viking Penguin, Inc.

**George Weidenfeld & Nicolson Ltd.**
HEINRICH BÖLL: "The Laugher" from *Absent Without Leave and Other Stories*, translated by Leila Vennewitz. Reprinted by permission of George Weidenfeld & Nicolson Ltd.

**Wesleyan University Press**
JAMES WRIGHT: "A Blesssing" from *The Branch Will Not Break*. Copyright © 1961 by James Wright. This poem first appeared in *Poetry*. Reprinted by permission of Wesleyan University Press.

# CREDITS

**Illustration Credits:**
Cover: David Frampton
Jan Brett, 284, 285, 286, 287. Debbi Chabrian, 156, 161, 165. David Chestnutt, 56–57. Lorraine Epstein, 116. John Freas, 242–243. Donald Gates, 70, 72, 73. Phil Huling, 85. Bob Masheris, 79. Michael McNelly, xiv-1, 106–107, 262–263, 336–337. Hima Pamoedjo, 42, 231. Winslow Pels, 610–611, 667, 669, 672–673, 674, 678–679, 683, 684, 686, 689, 692, 695, 699, 701, 703, 706, 707, 710–711, 714, 718, 720–721, 723, 727, 728, 731, 732. Jan Sterrett, 152. Carol Wald, 60, 61, 66. Larry Winborg, 120–121. Richard Williams, xiv-1, 5, 7, 9, 12, 15, 16–17. Ed Young, 610–611, 615, 618–619, 622–623, 624, 626, 631, 634, 638, 642–643, 645, 646, 647, 649, 651, 654–655, 657.

**Photo Credits:** © Paul Agresti, 210–211. © Clara Aich, 180. © America Hurrah Antiques, 25, 26. ART RESOURCE: 131; The Bridgeman Art Library, 238. © Jerry Bauer, 45. THE BETTMANN ARCHIVE, INC.: 76, 262–3C, 307, 613. Bibliothèque Nationale, Paris 574–5C, 586, 595. BLACK STAR: © Herman J. Kokojan, xii, 262–3B, 317B; © Vernon Merritt, 329B; © Charles Moore, 329T; © Norman Myers, 294, 298. Courtesy of THE BODLEIAN LIBRARY, Oxford: Ms Douce 383, folio 16, 576 detail; 577; 579 detail 581 detail; Ms Rawlinson, Q.b.6, folio 60, 583TR; ibid., folio 56v, 587TR; ibid., folio 397, 599TR. © BBC, London, 467. © THE BRIDGEMAN ART LIBRARY: Courtesy of the Trustees of the British Museum, 574–5T; Faringdon Collection Trust, Buscot Park, Faringdon Berks, 224. © The British Library: xiv, 591, 603. The Cleveland Museum of Art: anonymous gift, 126. © James H. Carmichael, 228–9. BRUCE COLEMAN: © John Shaw, 49. © COLOUR LIBRARY INTERNATIONAL (USA) LTD.: x, 176–7C, 184–5, 197, 218, 240, 252. CULVER PICTURES, INC.: 2, 21, 40, 59, 69, 83, 104, 118, 124, 142, 189T, C, 202T, BC, B, 203T, B, 222T, C, B, 232, 248T, 268C, 291, 293, 297, 302, 306, 321, 324, 327, 340, 347, 384, 385. © Dr. E.R. Degginger, APSA, 212. Einstein Archives, 268TR. MARY EVANS PICTURE LIBRARY: 352–3T, 463. E.T. ARCHIVE: Garrick Club, 195. © Jim Finlayson, Polaroid Print, 102, 170. © FOCUS ON SPORTS, 273. © Films Incorporated, 144, 147. By permission of the Folger Shakespeare Library, 189B, 462, 464. © Al Francekevich, 176–7B, 182–3. © Denis Gibier, 100. © Elizabeth Glasgow, 32–3. THE GRANGER COLLECTION: 53, 130, 155, 179B, 190, 236B, 282, 322, 461, 574–5B, 663. Courtesy Harper & Row, 178T. © Courtesy of the Hefner Gallery, 311. © Deborah Hoffman, 265. © Michael Holford, 578. THE IMAGE BANK: © Harald Sund, 220–21; © Art Kane, 358; © A. Kerstitch, 97; © Jane Latta, 611–12; © Ken Lax, 254–5. Trustees of the Lambeth Palace Library, 582. Library of Congress: Matthew Brady Collection, 342–3. Courtesy Little, Brown & Co., 135. THE METROPOLITAN MUSEUM OF ART: Gift of Arthur A. Houghton, Jr., 1970, 88. MONKMEYER PRESS PHOTO: © Tom McKirchy, 193; © Stephen Y. Mori, 115; © David Muench, 36–7; © Hugh Rogers, 234B. New Directions, 271. THE NEW YORK PUBLIC LIBRARY: Picture Collection, 247C; Schomburg Collection, Photo by James Latimore Allen, 201B, 223B. © The New York Times, 237B. Nicosia, Boston, 223TC. PHOTO RESEARCHERS, INC.: © Douglas Faulkner, 93; © Jim Goodwin, 317T; © Stephen J. Kraseman, 204; © Laurence Lowry/Rapho, 176–7B; 216; © Leonard Lee Rue, 256–7. © P.H. Polk, 233. © PRIMETIME TELEVISION: xiii, 352B, 357, 360L, C, R, 362T, B, 373T, B, 377T, B, 381T, B. THE STOCK MARKET: Ed Goldfarb, 208. Stratford Shakespeare Festival, Canada: © Robert C. Ragsdale, A.R.P.S., 470L, R, 471, 476, 482, 499, 503, 508, 517, 523, 528, 546, 555, 562. © Martha Swope: American Shakespeare Festival, Stratford, Conn., 352C, 386L, C, R, 387, 393, 401, 407, 414, 420, 425, 440, 446, 449, 455, 458. © Bill Thompson, 111, 163. TIME-LIFE © TIME INC.: © Robert W. Kelley, 329; © Arthur Tress, 138. University of Oxford, Museum of the History of Science, 268. UPI/BETTMANN NEWSPHOTOS, 246. © Thomas Victor, 168. AP/WIDE WORLD PHOTOS: 268, 274; Evalyn Shapiro, 202TC. WOODFIN CAMP & ASSOCIATES: © Mike Maple, 318.

vii

# A LETTER TO THE STUDENT

To appreciate is to understand and admire the value of something. If someone saves a life or performs some other heroic action, we can appreciate the action because we know how valuable it is to the community and because we understand the circumstances that made the action so difficult. If we read a great work of literature, we can appreciate it if we realize its value to ourselves and if we understand the elements that make it work.

The key to appreciating literature is *thinking* about what you read. Many different skills are involved in thinking about literature, most of which you have already been using for years. When you compare characters, contrast settings, analyze point of view, infer outcomes, you are using specific thinking skills that help you understand what makes literature what it is.

To help you sharpen your literary thinking skills, *Appreciating Literature* gives you both great literature to think about and an organized way to think about it. After each selection, you will find three kinds of Study Questions. These questions will focus your thoughts on *recalling* the details of the selection, *interpreting* the meaning of those details, and *extending* the meaning of those details into your own experience. Special feature sections will help you think about a writer's vocabulary, a particular literary element, and what you do when you yourself write about literature.

Near the back of this book you will find a special section called "Student's Resources: Lessons in Active Learning." The handbooks that make up this section are practical guides for responding to literature by speaking, thinking, reading and studying, and writing. Each handbook lesson is designed to help you grow as an active, independent reader and thinker, to help you take charge of your own learning.

The American writer Ernest Hemingway once said that, in order to begin writing a story or a novel, he tried to write "one true sentence." *Appreciating Literature* is designed to help you think about what makes a sentence "true"—what qualities make literature genuine, what qualities make it great, what qualities make it last forever.

# CONTENTS

## THE SHORT STORY

**PREVIEW: THE SHORT STORY** *1*

*Contents* ix

---

The selections in Appreciating Literature *were carefully chosen. The annotations in this column indicate the literary skill or element that each selection illustrates.*

............ Plot development
..................... Conflict
.............. Characterization
Round and dynamic characters
......... Character motivation
...... Setting and atmosphere
........... Change of setting

...... First-person point of view
..... Limited third-person; tone
...... Omniscient point of view

.................... Stated theme
............... Implied theme
............... Implied theme
............. Review of theme

..................... Symbol
..................... Symbol
..................... Symbol

.............. Situational irony
................. Verbal irony

# POETRY

**PREVIEW: POETRY**  *177*

x  *Contents*

........ Imagery: sight, smell
............ Personification
.................. Simile
............... Metaphor
.......... Implied metaphor
.......... Extended metaphor
................. Symbolism
.......... Review of imagery
.......... Review of imagery

LITERARY FOCUS: **Types of Poetry**  222

*Narrative Poetry*

................... Ballad
.......... Historical narrative
.......... Modern narrative

*Lyric Poetry*

................. Lyric: joy
............. Lyric: inspiration
............... Lyric: regret

*Dramatic Poetry*

.......... Dramatic monologue

LITERARY FOCUS: **Patterns in Poetry**  236

........ Shakespearean sonnet
.......... Petrarchan sonnet
............. Concrete poetry
.......... Experimental form

LITERARY FOCUS: **The Total Effect**  247

MODEL FOR ACTIVE READING

A variety of poems demonstrating the interaction of literary elements and techniques in poetry

**ACTIVE READING: Hearing a Poem**  260

**REVIEW: POETRY**  261

# NONFICTION

# DRAMA

*Contents*  xiii

# THE KING ARTHUR LEGEND

# THE NOVEL

# STUDENT'S RESOURCES

## LESSONS IN ACTIVE LEARNING ...............................738

*Contents* **xv**

Related blackline masters in *Teacher's Classroom Resources.*

Instruction and literature-based activities for oral/aural skills. Students may use lessons with *any* selection.

Definition, example, explanation for each skill plus procedures for application to literature. Students may use lessons with *any* selection.

Focused instruction on skills most essential to extracting meaning and demonstrating mastery. Students may use handbook as *constant* reference.

Composition assignments throughout the text refer to these lessons, which reinforce prewriting, writing, and revising skills.

*The Short Story*

# PREVIEW:
# THE SHORT STORY

*The story . . . must spring from an impression or perception . . . pressing enough to have made the writer write. . . . It should magnetize the imagination and give pleasure. . . .*

—Elizabeth Bowen

We read stories for a number of reasons. We read stories for the pleasure of recognizing familiar experiences and feelings; we read stories to escape into unfamiliar places and times. Most of all, we read stories because they stimulate our imaginations. By increasing our capacity to imagine, they make our lives larger.

All these reasons come into play as we read fiction because stories themselves are so very different. Some are full of action and adventure. Others, more subdued, look closely at the small moments that illuminate ordinary lives. Some stories reassure us with familiar truths; others startle us with new ideas. However, every good story is made up of the same basic elements—events, persons, places, images, and ideas. Every author combines these raw materials for a particular purpose: to communicate his or her "pressing" perception of the world, to show us something we have never seen in quite the same way before.

The stories on the following pages are arranged so that we can examine each of the elements that make up a story: plot, character, setting, point of view, theme, symbol, and irony. In the final group of stories, we will look at how these elements come together in each work to produce a total effect, the author's special vision of life. Once you have learned what an author does in writing a story, you will be able to read any story with greater satisfaction and to discover the pressing perception that made its author write.

*The Short Story* **1**

PREVIEW

Ask students what they like to read and why. Encourage students to say why they like novels better than poetry, for instance, or nonfiction better than fiction. Lead to a discussion of the short story, and point out that as they read the stories in this unit, they will see that some writers, such as Heinrich Böll in "The Laugher," approach their subjects with humor, while others, such as Arthur Conan Doyle in "The Red-Headed League," depend on plot, setting, and suspense for their impact. To some, such as Anton Chekhov in "The Woman Who Had No Prejudices" and John Galsworthy in "Quality," characterization gives the story its special meaning.

While different writers use different approaches, all of the stories in the unit have a theme, or message, to convey. The story's theme might be an astute observation of human nature or an idea about morals or ethics, but it is usually the center around which the rest of the story revolves. Mention that, as they read the selections in this unit, students will have the opportunity to examine the short story's components in depth by reading some excellent examples of this genre.

## AT A GLANCE

- Dr. Watson calls upon Sherlock Holmes, who has another visitor, Jabez Wilson.
- Wilson is described as stout, red-faced, elderly, and red-haired.

## LITERARY OPTIONS

- plot structure
- foreshadowing
- characterization

## THEMATIC OPTIONS

- value of observation and reasoning
- appearance and reality
- solving problems

### 1 POINT OF VIEW

The story is told from Watson's first-person point of view. Watson's limited information permits Doyle to keep the reader in suspense.

### 2 PLOT: EXPOSITION

The exposition begins when the three men get together and Holmes identifies Watson.

### 3 FORESHADOWING

Holmes's remark that life is more extraordinary than imagination suggests that Wilson's case will be unusual.

# LITERARY FOCUS: Plot, Character, and Setting

Sir Arthur Conan Doyle (1859–1930), a Scottish physician practicing in England, began to write detective stories to occupy his spare time. The product of this hobby was the brilliant detective hero Sherlock Holmes, whom Conan Doyle modeled on one of his own medical school instructors.

■ Can you figure out the solution to this mystery *before* Sherlock Holmes does?

*Sir Arthur Conan Doyle*

# The Red-Headed League

**1** I had called upon my friend, Mr. Sherlock Holmes, one day in the autumn of last year, and found him in deep conversation with a very stout, florid-faced, elderly gentleman, with fiery red hair. With an apology for my intrusion, I was about to withdraw, when Holmes pulled me abruptly into the room and closed the door behind me. "You could not possibly have come at a better time, my dear Watson," he said, cordially.

"I was afraid that you were engaged."

"So I am. Very much so."

"Then I can wait in the next room."

**2** "Not at all, Watson. Mr. Wilson, I would like you to meet Dr. Watson, my partner, friend, and helper in many of my most successful cases."

The stout gentleman half rose from his chair and gave a bob of greeting, with a quick, little, questioning glance from his small, fat-encircled eyes.

"Try the settee,"[1] said Holmes, relapsing into his armchair, and putting his finger tips together, as was his custom when in judicial moods. "I know, my dear Watson, that you share my love of all that is bizarre and outside the conventions and humdrum routine of everyday life. You have shown your relish for it by the enthusiasm which has prompted you to chronicle, and, if you will excuse my saying so, somewhat to embellish so many of my own little adventures."

"Your cases have indeed been of the greatest interest to me," I observed.

"You will remember that I remarked the other day, just before we went into the very simple problem presented by Miss Mary Sutherland, **3** that for strange effects and extraordinary combinations we must go to life itself, which is always far more daring than any effort of the imagination."

"A proposition which I took the liberty of doubting."

"You did, doctor, but none the less you must come round to my view, for otherwise I shall keep on piling fact upon fact on you, until your reason breaks down under them and acknowledges me to be right. Now, Mr. Jabez[2] Wilson here has been good enough to call upon me this morning, and to begin a narrative which pro-

---

1. **settee** [se tē′]: medium-sized sofa.

2. **Jabez** [jā′bez]

**2**  *The Short Story*

## GUIDED READING

### LITERAL QUESTION

**1a.** How does Holmes introduce Dr. Watson to Mr. Wilson? (He refers to Watson as his partner, friend, and helper.)

### INFERENTIAL QUESTION

**1b.** What can you infer about the relationship of Holmes and Watson based on the detective's remarks to Wilson and Watson? (They are close friends; they have shared interests; they work well together; they respect and understand each other.)

mises to be one of the most singular which I have listened to for some time. You have heard me remark that the strangest and most unique things are very often connected not with the larger but with the smaller crimes, and occasionally, indeed, where there is room for doubt whether any positive crime has been committed. As far as I have heard, it is impossible for me to say whether the present case is an instance of crime or not, but the course of events is certainly among the most singular that I have ever listened to. Perhaps, Mr. Wilson, you would have the great kindness to recommence your narrative. I ask you, not merely because my friend, Dr. Watson, has not heard the opening part, but also because the peculiar nature of the story makes me anxious to have every possible detail from your lips. As a rule, when I have heard some slight indication of the course of events, I am able to guide myself by the thousands of other similar cases which occur to my memory. In the present instance I am forced to admit that the facts are, to the best of my belief, unique.''

The portly client puffed out his chest with an appearance of some little pride, and pulled a dirty and wrinkled newspaper from the inside pocket of his greatcoat. As he glanced down the advertisement column, with his head thrust forward, and the paper flattened out upon his knee, I took a good look at the man, and endeavored, after the fashion of my companion, to read the indications which might be presented by his dress or appearance.

I did not gain very much, however, by my inspection. Our visitor bore every mark of being an average, commonplace British tradesman, obese, pompous, and slow. He wore rather baggy gray shepherd's check trousers, a not overclean black frock coat, unbuttoned in the front, and a drab waistcoat with a heavy, brassy Albert chain,[3] and a square pierced bit of metal dangling down as an ornament. A frayed top hat and a faded brown overcoat with a wrinkled velvet collar lay upon a chair beside him. Altogether, look as I would, there was nothing remarkable about the man save his blazing red head, and the expression of extreme chagrin and discontent upon his features.

Sherlock Holmes's quick eye took in my occupation, and he shook his head with a smile as he noticed my questioning glances. ''Beyond the obvious facts that he has at some time done manual labor, that he takes snuff, that he is a Freemason,[4] that he has been in China, and that he has done a considerable amount of writing lately, I can deduce nothing else.''

Mr. Jabez Wilson started up in his chair, with his forefinger upon the paper, but with his eyes upon my companion. ''How, in the name of good fortune, did you know all that, Mr. Holmes?'' he asked. ''How did you know, for example, that I did manual labor? It's as true as gospel, for I began as a ship's carpenter.''

''Your hands, my dear sir. Your right hand is quite a size larger than your left. You have worked with it, and the muscles are more developed.''

''Well, the snuff, then, and the Freemasonry?''

''I won't insult your intelligence by telling you how I read that, especially as, rather against the strict rules of your order, you use an arc-and-compass breastpin.''

''Ah, of course, I forgot that. But the writing?''

''What else can be indicated by that right cuff so very shiny for five inches, and the left one with the smooth patch near the elbow where you rest it upon the desk?''

''Well, but China?''

''The fish that you have tattooed immediately above your right wrist could only have been done in China. I have made a small study of tattoo marks, and have even contributed to the literature of the subject. That trick of staining the

---

3. **Albert chain:** watch chain named after Prince Albert (1819–1861), the husband of England's Queen Victoria (1819–1901).

4. **Freemason:** member of a secret fraternal order. The emblem of the group is the arc-and-compass, which, as Holmes notes, should always be concealed.

---

## GUIDED READING

### LITERAL QUESTIONS

**1a.** How does Holmes usually ''guide'' himself to solve a mystery? (He refers to the thousands of similar cases that he remembers.)

**2a.** What does Holmes deduce about Wilson from observation? (He deduces that Wilson has done manual labor, takes snuff, is a Freemason, has been in China, and has done a great deal of writing recently.)

### INFERENTIAL QUESTIONS

**1b.** Why does Doyle have Holmes explain his usual method of solving a case? (Doyle wants to impress the reader with the uniqueness of this particular case and Holmes's range of experience.)

**2b.** What does the reader learn about Sherlock Holmes, detective, from his ability to deduce facts about Wilson? (Holmes is very observant and has excellent powers of reasoning and deduction.)

■ Holmes continues to explain his deductions about Wilson.
■ Watson reads the advertisement for a new member of the Red-Headed League.
■ Mr. Wilson describes his assistant, Vincent Spaulding, who works for half wages and has strange habits.

**1 PLOT: NARRATIVE HOOK**

With Watson's reading of the advertisement, the basic conflict of the story is introduced: the mystery of the bizarre Red-Headed League.

**2 CHARACTERIZATION**

Watson is confused, but Holmes's behavior conveys his amusement and suggests that he has already begun to solve the case.

**3 FORESHADOWING**

Holmes finds Spaulding's willingness to work for half wages uncommon and, possibly, significant.

---

fishes' scales of a delicate pink is quite peculiar to China. When, in addition, I see a Chinese coin hanging from your watch chain, the matter becomes even more simple.''

Mr. Jabez Wilson laughed heavily. ''Well, I never!'' said he. ''I thought at first that you had done something clever, but I see that there was nothing in it, after all.''

''I begin to think, Watson,'' said Holmes, ''that I make a mistake in explaining. '*Omne ignotum pro magnifico,*'[5] you know, and my poor little reputation, such as it is, will suffer shipwreck if I am so candid. Can you not find the advertisement, Mr. Wilson?''

''Yes, I have got it now,'' he answered, with his thick, red finger planted halfway down the column. ''Here it is. This is what began it all. You just read it for yourself, sir.''

I took the paper from him, and read as follows:

To the Red-Headed League:

On account of the bequest of the late Ezekiah[6] Hopkins, of Lebanon, Pa., U.S.A., there is now another vacancy open which entitles a member of the League to a salary of four pounds a week for purely nominal services. All red-headed men who are sound in body and mind, and above the age of twenty-one years, are eligible. Apply in person on Monday, at eleven o'clock, to Duncan Ross, at the offices of the League, 7 Pope's Court, Fleet Street.

''What on earth does this mean?'' I ejaculated, after I had twice read over the extraordinary announcement.

Holmes chuckled, and wriggled in his chair, as was his habit when in high spirits. ''It is a little off the beaten track, isn't it?'' said he. ''And now, Mr. Wilson, off you go at scratch,[7] and tell

---

5. *Omne ignotum pro magnifico:* Latin for ''Every mysterious thing seems greater than it really is.''
6. **Ezekiah** [ez'ə ki'ə]
7. **at scratch:** from the beginning.

**4** *The Short Story*

---

us all about yourself, your household, and the effect which this advertisement had upon your fortunes. You will first make a note, doctor, of the paper and the date.''

''It is *The Morning Chronicle* of April 27, 1890. Just two months ago.''

''Very good. Now, Mr. Wilson?''

''Well it is just as I have been telling you, Mr. Sherlock Holmes,'' said Jabez Wilson, mopping his forehead; ''I have a small pawnbroker's business at Coburg Square, near the City.[8] It's not a very large affair, and of late years it has not done more than just give me a living. I used to be able to keep two assistants, but now I only keep one; and I would have a job to pay him, but that he is willing to come for half wages, so as to learn the business.''

''What is the name of this obliging youth?'' asked Sherlock Holmes.

''His name is Vincent Spaulding, and he's not such a youth, either. It's hard to say his age. I should not wish a smarter assistant, Mr. Holmes; and I know very well that he could better himself, and earn twice what I am able to give him. But, after all, if he is satisfied, why should I put ideas in his head?''

''Why indeed? You seem most fortunate in having an employee who comes under the full market price. It is not a common experience among employers in this age. I don't know that your assistant is not as remarkable as your advertisement.''

''Oh, he has his faults, too,'' said Mr. Wilson. ''Never was such a fellow for photography. Snapping away with a camera when he ought to be improving his mind, and then diving down into the cellar like a rabbit into its hole to develop his pictures. That is his main fault; but, on the whole, he's a good worker. There's no vice in him.''

''He is still with you, I presume?''

''Yes, sir. He and a girl of fourteen, who does

---

8. **the City:** the center of downtown London.

---

**LITERAL QUESTIONS**

**1a.** What is being sought in the newspaper advertisement? (The advertisement is for a red-headed man sound in body and mind who wants to earn money by doing nominal work.)

**2a.** In what ways is Vincent Spaulding an unusual employee? (Although an older man, he works for half wages, and his on-the-job photography makes him spend time in the cellar.)

**INFERENTIAL QUESTIONS**

**1b.** What seems unusual about the advertisement? (The qualification of red-headedness is odd; it is also unusual to offer money for ''purely nominal services.'')

**2b.** Why do you think Doyle lets the reader know about Spaulding's unusual qualities? (They may play an important role later in the story.)

**1 PLOT DEVELOPMENT**

As Wilson recounts the events, we learn that Spaulding is the one who brought the important advertisement to his attention.

**2 CHARACTERIZATION**

Wilson "gobbles up the bait," quick to show interest in the possibility of easy money. His eagerness suggests that he may be gullible and shortsighted.

a bit of simple cooking, and keeps the place clean—that's all I have in the house, for I am a widower, and never had any family. We live very quietly, sir, the three of us; and we keep a roof over our heads, and pay our debts, if we do nothing more.

**1** "The first thing that put us out was that advertisement. Spaulding, he came down into the office just this day eight weeks, with this very paper in his hand, and he says:

"'I wish to the Lord, Mr. Wilson, that I was a red-headed man.'

"'Why that?' I asks.

"'Why,' says he, 'here's another vacancy on the League of the Red-headed Men. It's worth quite a little fortune to any man who gets it, and I understand that there are more vacancies than there are men, so that the trustees are at their **2** wits' end what to do with the money. If my hair would only change color, here's a nice little crib[9] all ready for me to step into.'

"'Why, what is it, then?' I asked. You see,

---

9. **crib:** easy job or position.

*The Red-Headed League*  **5**

---

## GUIDED READING

### LITERAL QUESTION

**1a.** What does Spaulding tell Wilson about the vacancy in the League of Red-Headed Men? (He says it is worth a little fortune and there were more vacancies than there were men who qualified.)

### INFERENTIAL QUESTION

**1b.** What is suspicious about Spaulding's description of the vacancy? (It is strange that a trivial job could be worth "a little fortune" and that there could be a shortage of red-haired applicants for such an easy job.)

- Spaulding encourages Wilson to apply to the Red-Headed League.
- Spaulding accompanies Wilson when he goes to make application.
- Spaulding pushes through the crowd to get Wilson into the office.

**1 CHARACTERIZATION**

Wilson's admission that he doesn't know what is going on helps to explain his gullibility.

**2 PLOT DEVELOPMENT**

Wilson's need for money provides the motivation for him to apply for the advertised position.

**3 CHARACTERIZATION**

Wilson's vanity concerning the "rich tint" of his hair also impels him to participate in the strange adventure.

**4 SETTING AND STYLE**

Wilson describes the scene of Fleet Street "choked with red-headed folk" in a memorable simile: "Pope's Court looked like a coster's orange barrow."

**5 FORESHADOWING**

Spaulding's ease in getting Wilson through the crowd is a clue that the assistant may be involved in an important, but unexplained, way.

---

1 Mr. Holmes, I am a very stay-at-home man, and as my business came to me instead of my having to go to it, I was often weeks on end without putting my foot over the doormat. In that way I didn't know much of what was going on outside, and I was always glad of a bit of news.

"'Have you never heard of the League of the Red-headed Men?' he asked, with his eyes open.

"'Never.'

"'Why, I wonder at that, for you are eligible yourself for one of the vacancies.'

"'And what are they worth?' I asked.

"'Oh, merely a couple of hundred a year, but the work is slight, and it need not interfere very much with one's other occupations.'

2 "'Well, you can easily think that that made me prick up my ears, for the business has not been over-good for some years, and an extra couple of hundred would have been very handy.

"'Tell me all about it,' said I.

"'Well,' said he, showing me the advertisement, 'you can see for yourself that the League has a vacancy, and there is the address where you should apply for particulars. As far as I can make out, the League was founded by an American millionaire, Ezekiah Hopkins, who was very peculiar in his ways. He was himself red-headed, and he had a great sympathy for all red-headed men; so, when he died, it was found that he had left his enormous fortune in the hands of trustees, with instructions to apply the interest to the providing of easy berths to men whose hair is of that color. From all I hear it is splendid pay, and very little to do.'

"'But,' said I, 'there would be millions of red-headed men who would apply.'

"'Not so many as you might think,' he answered. 'You see it is really confined to Londoners, and to grown men. This American had started from London when he was young, and he wanted to do the old town a good turn. Then, again, I have heard it is no use your applying if your hair is light red, or dark red, or anything but real bright, blazing, fiery red. Now, if you

cared to apply, Mr. Wilson, you would just walk in; but perhaps it would hardly be worth your while to put yourself out of the way for the sake of a few hundred pounds.'

3 "Now, it is a fact, gentlemen, as you may see for yourself, that my hair is of a very full and rich tint, so that it seemed to me that, if there was to be any competition in the matter, I stood as good a chance as any man that I had ever met. Vincent Spaulding seemed to know so much about it that I thought he might prove useful, so I ordered him to put up the shutters for the day, and to come right away with me. He was very willing to have a holiday, so we shut the business up, and started off for the address that was given us in the advertisement.

"I never hope to see such a sight as that again, Mr. Holmes. From north, south, east, and west every man who had a shade of red in his hair had tramped into the City to answer the ad-
4 vertisement. Fleet Street was choked with red-headed folk, and Pope's Court looked like a coster's orange barrow.[10] I should not have thought there were so many in the whole country as were brought together by that single advertisement. Every shade of color they were— straw, lemon, orange, brick, Irish setter, liver, clay; but, as Spaulding said there were not many
5 who had the real vivid flame-colored tint. When I saw how many were waiting I would have given it up in despair; but Spaulding would not hear of it. How he did it I could not imagine, but he pushed and pulled and butted until he got me through the crowd, and right up the steps which led to the office. There was a double stream upon the stair, some going up in hope, and some coming back dejected; but we wedged in as well as we could, and soon found ourselves in the office."

"Your experience has been a most entertaining one," remarked Holmes, as his client paused

---

10. **coster's orange barrow:** fruit vendor's bin of oranges.

---

## GUIDED READING

**LITERAL QUESTIONS**

**1a.** What does Spaulding say to encourage Wilson to apply for the position? (He tells him that the vacancy is worth a couple of hundred dollars a year for little work. He says that Wilson meets the requirements especially well.)

**2a.** How does Spaulding get Wilson to the head of the line? (He pushes and pulls through the crowd.)

**INFERENTIAL QUESTIONS**

**1b.** Why are Spaulding's remarks especially effective with Wilson? (He knows that Wilson needs money; also, Wilson is vain about his bright red hair.)

**2b.** What do you think is unusual about Spaulding's maneuvers? (He appeared to have some special ability to get Wilson ahead of other applicants.)

AT A GLANCE

The red-headed interviewer disqualifies the other applicants, congratulates Wilson on filling the vacancy, and pulls Wilson's hair "to be sure it is real."

1 FORESHADOWING

The bareness of the office and the unexplained preference for Wilson's candidacy hint that things are not what they seem.

2 THEME

The interviewer's apparent concern with checking the reality behind the appearance contrasts with Wilson's willingness to accept unusual circumstances at face value.

and refreshed his memory with a huge pinch of snuff. "Pray continue your very interesting statement."

"There was nothing in the office but a couple of wooden chairs and a deal table, behind which sat a small man, with a head that was even redder than mine. He said a few words to each candidate as he came up, and then he always managed to find some fault in them which would disqualify them. Getting a vacancy did not seem to be such a very easy matter, after all. However, when our turn came, the little man was much more favorable to me than to any of the others, and he closed the door as we entered, so that he might have a private word with us.

"'This is Mr. Jabez Wilson,' said my assistant, 'and he is willing to fill a vacancy in the League.'

"'And he is admirably suited for it,' the other answered. 'He has every requirement. I cannot recall when I have seen anything so fine.' He took a step backward, cocked his head on one side, and gazed at my hair until I felt quite bashful. Then suddenly he plunged forward, wrung my hand, and congratulated me warmly on my success.

"'It would be injustice to hesitate,' said he. 'You will, however, I am sure, excuse me for taking an obvious precaution.' With that he seized my hair in both his hands, and tugged until I yelled with the pain. 'There is water in your eyes,' said he, as he released me, 'I perceive that all is as it should be. But we have to be careful, for we have twice been deceived by wigs and once by paint. I could tell you tales of cobbler's wax[11] which would disgust you with human nature.'

"He stepped over to the window, and shouted through it at the top of his voice that the vacancy was filled. A groan of disappointment came up

---

11. **cobbler's wax:** sticky substance with which shoemakers treat thread.

*The Red-Headed League* 7

LITERAL QUESTION

**1a.** What "precaution" does the interviewer take after declaring Wilson qualified for the job? (He pulls Wilson's red hair to make sure it is real.)

INFERENTIAL QUESTION

**1b.** What lesson might be learned from the interviewer's statement that he has been deceived by wigs, wax, and paint? (that everything is not always what it seems to be)

AT A GLANCE

- Spaulding volunteers to watch the shop while Wilson works.
- Ross tells Wilson that he cannot leave the building while on the job.
- The job is copying the *Encyclopedia Britannica*.

**1 CHARACTERIZATION**

Once again, Wilson lets the ever-helpful Vincent Spaulding remove an "obstacle" for him.

**2 FORESHADOWING**

Ross's emphatic order that Wilson remain in the building adds to the air of strangeness and mystery surrounding the unusual job.

from below, and the folk all trooped away in different directions, until there was not a red head to be seen except my own and that of the manager.

"'My name,' said he, 'is Mr. Duncan Ross, and I am myself one of the pensioners upon the fund left by our noble benefactor. Are you a married man, Mr. Wilson? Have you a family?'

"I answered that I had not.

"His face fell immediately.

"'Dear me!' he said, gravely, 'that is very serious indeed! I am sorry to hear you say that. The fund was, of course, for the propagation and spread of the red-heads as well as for their maintenance. It is exceedingly unfortunate that you should be a bachelor.'

"My face lengthened at this, Mr. Holmes, for I thought that I was not to have the vacancy after all; but, after thinking it over for a few minutes, he said that it would be all right.

"'In the case of another,' said he, 'the objection might be fatal, but we must stretch a point in favor of a man with such a head of hair as yours. When shall you be able to enter upon your new duties?'

"'Well, it is a little awkward, for I have a business already,' said I.

"'Oh, never mind about that, Mr. Wilson!' said Vincent Spaulding. "I shall be able to look after that for you.'

"'What would be the hours?' I asked.

"'Ten to two.'

"Now a pawnbroker's business is mostly done of an evening, Mr. Holmes, especially Thursday and Friday evenings, which is just before pay-day, so it would suit me very well to earn a little **1** in the mornings. Besides, I knew that my assistant was a good man, and that he would see to anything that turned up.

"'That would suit me very well,' said I. 'And the pay?'

"'Is four pounds a week.'

"'And the work?'

"'Is purely nominal.'

"'What do you call purely nominal?'

**8** *The Short Story*

"'Well, you have to be in the office, or at least in the building, the whole time. If you leave, you forfeit your whole position forever. The will is very clear upon that point. You don't comply with the conditions if you budge from the office during that time.'

"'It's only four hours a day, and I should not think of leaving,' said I.

**2** "'No excuse will avail,' said Mr. Duncan Ross. 'Neither sickness nor business nor anything else. There you must stay, or you lose your billet.'[12]

"'And the work?'

"'Is to copy out the *Encyclopedia Britannica*. There is the first volume of it in that press.[13] You must find your own ink, pens, and chair. Will you be ready tomorrow?'

"'Certainly,' I answered.

"'Then, good-by, Mr. Jabez Wilson, and let me congratulate you once more on the important position which you have been fortunate enough to gain.' He bowed me out of the room, and I went home with my assistant, hardly knowing what to say or do, I was so pleased at my own good fortune.

"Well, I thought over the matter all day, and by evening I was in low spirits again for I had quite persuaded myself that the whole affair must be some great hoax or fraud, though what its object might be I could not imagine. It seemed altogether past belief that anyone could make such a will, or that they would pay such a sum for doing anything so simple as copying out the *Encyclopedia Britannica*. Vincent Spaulding did what he could to cheer me up, but by bedtime I had reasoned myself out of the whole thing. However, in the morning I determined to have a look at it anyhow, so I bought a penny bottle of ink, and with a quill pen and seven sheets of foolscap paper,[14] I started off for Pope's Court.

---

12. **billet:** job.
13. **press:** cupboard.
14. **foolscap paper:** writing paper.

*GUIDED READING*

**LITERAL QUESTION**

**1a.** What are two problems that threaten Wilson's getting the job? (Wilson is unmarried; he would have to leave his own business to do the work.)

**INFERENTIAL QUESTION**

**1b.** Why don't the quick solutions to these "problems" make Wilson suspicious? (It demonstrates how naïve and gullible Wilson is.)

the room for an instant, for I was not sure when he might come, and the billet was such a good one, and suited me so well, that I would not risk the loss of it.

"Eight weeks passed away like this, and I had written about Abbots and Archery and Armor and Architecture and Attica, and hoped with diligence that I might get on to the B's before very long. It cost me something in foolscap, and I had pretty nearly filled a shelf with my writings. And then suddenly the whole business came to an end."

"To an end?"

2

"Yes, sir. And no later than this morning. I went to my work as usual at ten o'clock, but the door was shut and locked, with a little square of cardboard hammered on to the middle of the panel with a tack. Here it is, and you can read for yourself."

He held up a piece of white cardboard about the size of a sheet of note paper. It read in this fashion:

---

THE RED-HEADED LEAGUE
IS DISSOLVED
OCTOBER 9, 1890

---

Sherlock Holmes and I surveyed this curt announcement and the rueful face behind it, until the comical side of the affair so completely overtopped every other consideration that we both burst out into a roar of laughter.

3

"I cannot see that there is anything very funny," cried our client, flushing up to the roots of his flaming head. "If you can do nothing better than laugh at me, I can go elsewhere."

"No, no," cried Holmes, shoving him back into the chair from which he had half risen. "I really wouldn't miss your case for the world. It is most refreshingly unusual. But there is, if you will excuse my saying so, something just a little

1

"Well, to my surprise and delight, everything was as right as possible. The table was set out ready for me, and Mr. Duncan Ross was there to see that I got fairly to work. He started me off upon the letter A, then he left me; but he would drop in from time to time to see that all was right with me. At two o'clock he bade me good-day, complimented me upon the amount that I had written, and locked the door of the office after me.

"This went on day after day, Mr. Holmes, and on Saturday the manager came in and planked down four golden sovereigns[15] for my week's work. It was the same next week, and the same the week after. Every morning I was there at ten, and every afternoon I left at two. By degrees Mr. Duncan Ross took to coming in only once of a morning, and then, after a time, he did not come in at all. Still, of course, I never dared to leave

---

15. **sovereigns** [sov′rənz]: gold coins worth one pound each at the time of the story.

*The Red-Headed League*  9

---

- Wilson learns that "Ross" has given a false name and a bogus forwarding address.
- At Holmes's request Wilson describes his assistant, mentioning an acid splash on Spaulding's forehead.
- Holmes asks if Spaulding's ears are pierced; they are.

### 1 PLOT DEVELOPMENT

Complication and confusion mounts as Wilson seeks to track down his vanished employers.

### 2 THEME

Holmes suggests that, in reality, the issues involved in the case may be more important than they appear.

### 3 CHARACTERIZATION

Holmes's careful reasoning process leads him to ask questions that center upon Spaulding.

### 4 FORESHADOWING

Holmes's movement in his chair and his statement and question are clues that he may know something about Spaulding.

---

funny about it. Pray, what steps did you take when you found the card upon the door?"

**1** "I was staggered, sir. I did not know what to do. Then I called at the offices round, but none of them seemed to know anything about it. Finally, I went to the landlord, who is an accountant living on the ground floor, and I asked him if he could tell me what had become of the Red-headed League. He said that he had never heard of any such body. Then I asked him who Mr. Duncan Ross was. He answered that the name was new to him.

" 'Well,' said I, 'the gentleman at No. 4.'

" 'What, the red-headed man?'

" 'Yes.'

" 'Oh,' said he, 'his name was William Morris. He was a solicitor,[16] and was using my room as a temporary convenience until his new premises were ready. He moved out yesterday.'

" 'Where could I find him?'

" 'Oh, at his new offices. He did tell me the address. Yes, 17 King Edward Street, near St. Paul's.'[17]

"I started off, Mr. Holmes, but when I got to that address it was a manufactory of artificial kneecaps, and no one in it had ever heard of either Mr. William Morris or Mr. Duncan Ross."

"And what did you do then?" asked Holmes.

"I went home to Saxe-Coburg Square, and I took the advice of my assistant. But he could not help me in any way. He could only say that if I waited I should hear by post. But that was not quite good enough, Mr. Holmes. I did not wish to lose such a place without a struggle; so, as I have heard that you were good enough to give advice to poor folk who were in need of it, I came right away to you."

"And you did very wisely," said Holmes. "Your case is an exceedingly remarkable one, and I shall be happy to look into it. From what you have told me I think that it is possible that

---

16. **solicitor:** British attorney who handles legal matters but does not appear in court.
17. **St. Paul's:** famous London cathedral.

**10** *The Short Story*

---

**2** graver issues hang from it than might at first sight appear."

"Grave enough!" said Mr. Jabez Wilson. "Why I have lost four pounds a week."

"As far as you are personally concerned," remarked Holmes, "I do not see that you have any grievance against this remarkable league. On the contrary, you are, as I understand, richer by some thirty pounds, to say nothing of the minute knowledge which you have gained on every subject that comes under the letter A. You have lost nothing by them."

"No, sir. But I want to find out about them, and who they are, and what their object was in playing this prank—if it was a prank—upon me. It was a pretty expensive joke for them, for it cost them two-and-thirty pounds."

"We shall endeavor to clear up these points for you. And, first, one or two questions, Mr. **3** Wilson. This assistant of yours who first called your attention to the advertisement—how long had he been with you?"

"About a month then."

"How did he come?"

"In answer to an advertisement."

"Was he the only applicant?"

"No, I had a dozen."

"Why did you pick him?"

"Because he was handy, and would come cheap."

"At half wages, in fact?"

"Yes."

"What is he like, this Vincent Spaulding?"

"Small, stout-built, very quick in his ways, no hair on his face, though he's not short of thirty. Has a white splash of acid upon his forehead."

**4** Holmes sat up in his chair in considerable excitement. "I thought as much," said he. "Have you ever observed that his ears are pierced for earrings?"

"Yes sir. He told me that a gypsy had done it for him when he was a lad."

"Hum!" said Holmes, sinking back in deep thought. "He is still with you?"

---

## GUIDED READING

### LITERAL QUESTION

**1a.** What does Holmes do after Wilson mentions the acid scar on Spaulding's forehead? (Holmes sits up in his chair, acts excited, and asks if Spaulding's ears are pierced.)

### INFERENTIAL QUESTION

**1b.** What do Holmes's reactions suggest? (Holmes may know who Spaulding is from previous indirect encounters.)

"Oh, yes, sir; I have only just left him."

"And has your business been attended to in your absence?"

"Nothing to complain of, sir. There's never very much to do of a morning."

"That will do, Mr. Wilson. I shall be happy to give you an opinion upon the subject in the course of a day or two. Today is Saturday, and I hope that by Monday we may come to a conclusion."

"Well, Watson," said Holmes, when our visitor had left us, "what do you make of it all?"

"I make nothing of it," I answered, frankly. "It is a most mysterious business."

"As a rule," said Holmes, "the more bizarre a thing is, the less mysterious it proves to be. It is your commonplace, featureless crimes which are really puzzling, just as a commonplace face is the most difficult to identify. But I must be prompt over this matter."

"What are you going to do, then?" I asked.

"To smoke," he answered. "It is quite a three-pipe problem, and I beg that you won't speak to me for fifty minutes." He curled himself up in his chair, with his thin knees drawn up to his hawk-like nose, and there he sat with his eyes closed and his black clay pipe thrusting out like the bill of some strange bird. I had come to the conclusion that he had dropped asleep, and indeed was nodding myself, when he suddenly sprang out of his chair with the gesture of a man who has made up his mind, and put his pipe down upon the mantelpiece.

"Sarasate[18] plays at the St. James's Hall this afternoon," he remarked. "What do you think, Watson? Could your patients spare you for a few hours?"

"I have nothing to do today. My practice is never very absorbing."

"Then put on your hat and come. I am going through the City first, and we can have some lunch on the way. I observe that there is a good deal of German music on the program, which is rather more to my taste than Italian or French. It is introspective, and I want to introspect. Come along!"

We traveled by the Underground[19] as far as Aldersgate; and a short walk took us to Saxe-Coburg Square, the scene of the singular story which we had listened to in the morning. It was a poky, little, shabby-genteel place, where four lines of dingy, two-storied brick houses looked out into a small railed-in enclosure, where a lawn of weedy grass and a few clumps of faded laurel-bushes made a hard fight against a smoke-laden and uncongenial atmosphere. Three gilt balls[20] and a brown board with JABEZ WILSON in white letters, upon a corner house, announced the place where our red-headed client carried on his business. Sherlock Holmes stopped in front of it with his head on one side, and looked it all over, with his eyes shining brightly between puckered lids. Then he walked slowly up the street, and then down again to the corner, still looking keenly at the houses. Finally he returned to the pawnbroker's, and, having thumped vigorously upon the pavement with his stick two or three times, he went up to the door and knocked. It was instantly opened by a bright-looking, clean-shaven young fellow, who asked him to step in.

"Thank you," said Holmes, "I only wished to ask you how you would go from here to the Strand."[21]

"Third right, fourth left," answered the assistant, promptly, closing the door. "Smart fellow, that," observed Holmes, as we walked away. "He is, in my judgment, the fourth smartest man in London, and for daring, I am not sure that he has not a claim to be third. I have known something of him before."

---

18. **Sarasate** [saʹrə saʹtē]: Pablo de Sarasate (1844–1908), a Spanish violinist.

19. **Underground:** London subway.
20. **Three gilt balls:** three gold-colored balls, the sign of a pawnbroker's shop.
21. **the Strand:** major London street.

*The Red-Headed League* **11**

**AT A GLANCE**

- Holmes meditates, then invites Watson to a concert.
- They visit Wilson's shop where Holmes thumps his stick on the pavement and asks Spaulding for directions.
- Holmes calls Spaulding smart and says he knows something of him.

**1 CHARACTERIZATION**

Holmes's confidence in his reasoning abilities earns the reader's trust that he will solve the case.

**2 INTERPRETING**

Holmes is suggesting that this case will be easy to solve precisely because it seems so bizarre.

**3 CHARACTERIZATION**

Although Holmes appears to be napping, in reality he is in thoughtful contemplation of the case.

**4 SETTING**

Words like "poky," "shabby-genteel," "dingy," and "weedy" convey the lack of prosperity and activity on the street where Wilson's shop is.

**5 FORESHADOWING**

Holmes's assessment of Spaulding as daring and smart implies that Holmes knows who he is from previous experience and that he will be a formidable adversary.

## GUIDED READING

### LITERAL QUESTIONS

**1a.** What does Watson think is happening when he sees Holmes sitting in a chair with his eyes closed? (He thinks that Holmes has fallen asleep.)

**2a.** What reason does Holmes give Spaulding for knocking on the shop door? (Holmes says that he needs directions.)

### INFERENTIAL QUESTIONS

**1b.** What do you think he is actually doing while he is closing his eyes? (He is using his reasoning ability to try to solve the case.)

**2b.** What do you think is the real reason Holmes knocks on the door? (He wants to get a look at Spaulding to see if he is the man Holmes suspects he is.)

## 1 POINT OF VIEW

Holmes's refusal to explain his actions restricts the reader to Watson's limited understanding, thereby heightening the suspense.

## 2 READING SKILLS: COMPARISON/CONTRAST

The road behind Wilson's establishment, with its "stream of commerce flowing in a double tide," "hurrying swarm of pedestrians," and "fine shops," contrasts sharply with "the faded and stagnant square" previously described.

## 3 FORESHADOWING

Holmes's careful attention to apparently trivial details suggests that the street will be important to future actions.

"Evidently," said I, "Mr. Wilson's assistant counts for a good deal in this mystery of the Red-headed League. I am sure that you inquired your way merely in order that you might see him."

"Not him."

"What then?"

"The knees of his trousers."

"And what did you see?"

"What I expected to see."

1 "Why did you beat the pavement?"

"My dear doctor, this is a time for observation, not for talk. We are spies in an enemy's country. We know something of Saxe-Coburg Square. Let us now explore the parts which lie behind it."

The road in which we found ourselves as we turned round the corner from the retired Saxe-Coburg Square presented as great a contrast to it as the front of a picture does to the back. It was one of the main arteries which convey the traffic of the City to the north and west. The roadway was blocked with the immense stream of commerce flowing in a double tide inward and out-

2 ward, while the footpaths were black with the hurrying swarm of pedestrians. It was difficult to realize, as we looked at the line of fine shops and stately business premises, that they really abutted on the other side upon the faded and stagnant square which we had just quitted.

"Let me see," said Holmes, standing at the corner, and glancing along the line, "I should like just to remember the order of the houses here. It is a hobby of mine to have an exact knowledge of London. There is Mortimer's, the tobacconist, the little newspaper shop, the Coburg branch of the City and Suburban Bank, the Vegetarian Restaurant, and McFarlane's carriage-building depot. That carries us right on to the other block. And now, doctor, we've done our work, so it's time we had some play. A sandwich and a cup of coffee, and then off to violinland, where all is sweetness and delicacy and harmony, and there are no red-headed clients to vex us with their conundrums."[22]

---

22. **conundrums** [kə nun'drəmz]: puzzling problems.

12    *The Short Story*

## GUIDED READING

### LITERAL QUESTION

**1a.** What information does Holmes share with Watson about the case? (He tells him only that he was looking at the knees of Spaulding's trousers and that they must explore the area behind the pawnbroker's shop.)

### INFERENTIAL QUESTION

**1b.** Why is it important to the reader that Doyle use Watson's point of view during the investigation? (Because Watson does not understand what Holmes is thinking and Holmes won't tell him, Watson's limited point of view maintains the suspense.)

My friend was an enthusiastic musician, being himself not only a very capable performer, but a composer of no ordinary merit. All the afternoon he sat in the stalls[23] wrapped in the most perfect happiness, gently waving his long, thin fingers in time to the music, while his gently smiling face and his languid, dreamy eyes were as unlike those of Holmes, the sleuth-hound, Holmes, the relentless, keen-witted, ready-handed criminal agent, as it was possible to conceive. In his singular character the dual nature alternately asserted itself, and his extreme exactness and astuteness represented, as I have often thought, the reaction against the poetic and contemplative mood which occasionally predominated in him. The swing of his nature took him from extreme languor to devouring energy; and, as I knew well, he was never so truly formidable as when, for days on end, he had been lounging in his armchair amid his improvisations and his black-letter editions. Then it was that the lust of the chase would suddenly come upon him, and that his brilliant reasoning power would rise to the level of intuition, until those who were unacquainted with his methods would look askance at him as on a man whose knowledge was not that of other mortals. When I saw him that afternoon so enwrapped in the music at St. James's Hall, I felt that an evil time might be coming upon those whom he had set himself to hunt down.

"You want to go home, no doubt, doctor," he remarked, as we emerged.

"Yes, it would be as well."

"And I have some business to do which will take some hours. This business at Coburg Square is serious."

"Why serious?"

"A considerable crime is in contemplation. I have every reason to believe that we shall be in time to stop it. But today being Saturday rather complicates matters. I shall want your help tonight."

"At what time?"

"Ten will be early enough."

"I shall be at Baker Street[24] at ten."

"Very well. And, I say, doctor, there may be some little danger, so kindly put your army revolver in your pocket." He waved his hand, turned on his heel, and disappeared in an instant among the crowd.

I trust that I am not more dense than my neighbors, but I was always oppressed with a sense of my own stupidity in my dealings with Sherlock Holmes. Here I had heard what he had heard, I had seen what he had seen, and yet from his words it was evident that he saw clearly not only what had happened, but what was about to happen, while to me the whole business was still confused and grotesque. As I drove home to my house in Kensington I thought over it all from the extraordinary story of the red-headed copier of the *Encyclopedia* down to the visit to Saxe-Coburg Square, and the ominous words with which he had parted from me. What was this nocturnal expedition, and why should I go armed? Where were we going, and what were we to do? I had the hint from Holmes that this smooth-faced pawnbroker's assistant was a formidable man—a man who might play a deep game. I tried to puzzle it out, but gave it up in despair, and set the matter aside until night should bring an explanation.

It was a quarter past nine when I started from home and made my way across the Park, and so through Oxford Street to Baker Street. Two hansoms[25] were standing at the door, and, as I entered the passage, I heard the sound of voices from above. On entering his room I found Holmes in animated conversation with two men, one of whom I recognized as Peter Jones, the

---

23. **stalls:** theater seats located on the ground floor close to the stage.

24. **Baker Street:** street on which Holmes lived.
25. **hansoms:** two-wheeled horse carriages.

AT A GLANCE
- At the concert Watson describes the two sides of Holmes's character.
- Afterward, Holmes says that he thinks they will be in time to stop a crime.
- Watson agrees to meet Holmes at ten with his revolver.
- Later that evening, Watson meets Holmes and two men.

### 1 CHARACTERIZATION

Watson describes the dual nature of Holmes's personality: Oscillating between the worlds of logic and poetry, Holmes seems not entirely at home in either.

### 2 CHARACTERIZATION

Watson's reference to Holmes's "brilliant reasoning power" and the respect others have for him bolsters the reader's admiration and confidence in the detective's abilities.

### 3 FORESHADOWING

Holmes's instructions that Watson bring his revolver suggest there may be serious danger ahead.

### 4 POINT OF VIEW

Watson's self-styled "stupidity" limits the reader's understanding and maintains suspense about what the detective is thinking and what will happen.

---

## GUIDED READING

### LITERAL QUESTIONS

**1a.** According to Watson's description of Holmes's habits, what usually follows a period of contemplation for the detective? (Holmes usually has a great deal of energy and gets into the "lust of the chase.")

**2a.** What questions does Watson ask himself about the case and about Holmes's instructions? (What is the evening expedition? Why should he go armed? Where are they going? What will they do?)

### INFERENTIAL QUESTIONS

**1b.** What do Watson's words suggest about the value of relaxation to Holmes? (A period of relaxation prepares Holmes to use extraordinary energy to solve a case.)

**2b.** What do you infer about Watson's attitude toward Holmes when, despite his questions, he follows Holmes's instructions? (Watson has great trust and confidence in Holmes.)

- Police agent Peter Jones and Mr. Merryweather are with Holmes.
- Holmes says that the game has high stakes: money for Merryweather, who is a bank director, and a criminal for Jones.
- They reach the street behind Wilson's shop.

### 1 BACKGROUND

A "wild-goose chase" was a follow-the-leader game played on horseback in Elizabethan England, but the term has commonly come to mean a chase for something like a wild goose that cannot be caught.

### 2 CHARACTERIZATION

Jones's somewhat condescending manner toward Holmes ("has the makings of a detective") suggests Jones's own limited understanding of Holmes's gifts.

### 3 PLOT DEVELOPMENT

Jones's description of John Clay as a remarkable, much-wanted criminal contributes to the excitement.

### 4 POINT OF VIEW

Because Holmes is not communicative, the reader's understanding remains limited to what Watson knows.

### 5 FORESHADOWING

Holmes's decision to bring Jones along because he is "brave as a bulldog" and "tenacious as a lobster" gives the reader a clue that those qualities will be needed soon.

official police agent, while the other was a long, thin, sad-faced man, with a very shiny hat and oppressively respectable frock coat.

"Ha! our party is complete," said Holmes, buttoning up his pea jacket, and taking his heavy hunting crop from the rack. "Watson, I think you know Mr. Jones, of Scotland Yard?[26] Let me introduce you to Mr. Merryweather, who is to be our companion in tonight's adventure."

"We're hunting in couples again, doctor, you see," said Jones, in his consequential way. "Our friend here is a wonderful man for starting a chase. All he wants is an old dog to help him do the running down."

**1** "I hope a wild goose may not prove to be the end of our chase," observed Mr. Merryweather, gloomily.

"You may place considerable confidence in Mr. Holmes, sir," said the police agent, loftily. "He has his own little methods, which are, if he **2** won't mind my saying so, just a little too theoretical and fantastic, but he has the makings of a detective in him. It is not too much to say that once or twice, as in that business of the Sholto murder and the Agra treasure,[27] he has been more nearly correct than the official force."

"Oh, if you say so, Mr. Jones, it is all right," said the stranger, with deference. "Still, I confess that I miss my bridge games. It is the first Saturday night for seven-and-twenty years that I have not had my bridge."

"I think you will find," said Sherlock Holmes, "that you will play for a higher stake tonight than you have ever done yet, and that the play will be more exciting. For you, Mr. Merryweather, the stake will be some thirty thousand pounds; and for you, Jones, it will be the man upon whom you wish to lay your hands."

"John Clay, the murderer, thief, smasher,[28]

---

26. **Scotland Yard:** headquarters of the London police.
27. **Sholto . . . treasure:** references to an earlier Holmes story, "The Sign of the Four."
28. **smasher:** person who passes counterfeit money.

and forger. He's a young man, Mr. Merryweather, but he is at the head of his profession, and I **3** would rather have my bracelets[29] on him than on any criminal in London. He's a remarkable man, is young John Clay. His grandfather was a royal duke, and he himself has been to Eton and Oxford.[30] His brain is as cunning as his fingers, and though we meet signs of him at every turn, we never know where to find the man himself. He'll crack a crib[31] in Scotland one week, and be raising money to build an orphanage in Cornwall the next. I've been on his track for years, and have never set eyes on him yet."

"I hope that I may have the pleasure of introducing you tonight. I've had one or two little turns also with Mr. John Clay, and I agree with you that he is at the head of his profession. It is past ten, however, and quite time that we started. If you two will take the first hansom, Watson and I will follow in the second."

**4** Sherlock Holmes was not very communicative during the long drive, and lay back in the cab humming the tunes which he had heard in the afternoon. We rattled through an endless labyrinth of gas-lit streets until we emerged into Farringdon Street.

"We are close there now," my friend remarked. "This fellow Merryweather is a bank director, and personally interested in the matter. **5** I thought it as well to have Jones with us also. He is not a bad fellow, though an absolute imbecile in his profession. He has one positive virtue. He is as brave as a bulldog, and as tenacious as a lobster if he gets his claws upon anyone. Here we are, and they are waiting for us."

We had reached the same crowded thoroughfare in which we had found ourselves in the morning. Our cabs were dismissed, and, following the guidance of Mr. Merryweather, we

---

29. **bracelets:** handcuffs.
30. **Eton and Oxford:** Eton is an exclusive private preparatory school near London; Oxford is one of England's most famous universities.
31. **crack a crib:** break into a building.

---

## GUIDED READING

**LITERAL QUESTIONS**

**1a.** How does Jones describe John Clay? (He says he is a murderer, thief, counterfeiter, and forger; he is remarkable, of royal birth, and educated; he is cunning and difficult to catch. Clay is the criminal Jones most wants.)

**2a.** With what words does Holmes describe police agent Jones? (He says he is an "absolute imbecile" in his profession but "brave" and "tenacious.")

**INFERENTIAL QUESTIONS**

**1b.** From Jones's description of Clay, what do you infer about the upcoming encounter with Clay? (It could be extremely dangerous; it could be difficult to catch Clay.)

**2b.** Why do you think Holmes brings Jones along? (Holmes has already done the reasoning, so he doesn't need a good detective. Jones's bravery and tenacity, however, will be helpful.)

passed down a narrow passage and through a side door, which he opened for us. Within, there was a small corridor, which ended in a very massive iron gate. This also was opened, and led down a flight of winding stone steps, which terminated at another formidable gate. Mr. Merryweather stopped to light a lantern, and then conducted us down a dark, earth-smelling passage, and so, after opening a third door, into a huge vault, or cellar, which was piled all round with crates and massive boxes.

"You are not very vulnerable from above," Holmes remarked, as he held up the lantern and gazed about him.

"Nor from below," said Mr. Merryweather, striking his stick upon the flags which lined the floor. "Why, dear me, it sounds quite hollow!" he remarked, looking up in surprise.

"I must really ask you to be a little more quiet," said Holmes, severely. "You have already imperiled the whole success of our expedition. Might I beg that you would have the

goodness to sit down upon one of those boxes, and not to interfere?"

The solemn Mr. Merryweather perched himself upon a crate, with a very injured expression upon his face, while Holmes fell upon his knees upon the floor, and, with the lantern and a magnifying lens, began to examine minutely the cracks between the stones. A few seconds sufficed to satisfy him, for he sprang to his feet again, and put his glass in his pocket.

"We have at least an hour before us," he remarked; "for they can hardly take any steps until the good pawnbroker is safely in bed. Then they will not lose a minute, for the sooner they do their work the longer time they will have for their escape. We are at present, doctor—as no doubt you have divined—in the cellar of the City branch of one of the principal London banks. Mr. Merryweather is the chairman of directors, and he will explain to you that there are reasons why the more daring criminals of London should take a considerable interest in this cellar at present."

"It is our French gold," whispered the director. "We have had several warnings that an attempt might be made upon it."

"Your French gold?"

"Yes. We had occasion some months ago to strengthen our resources and borrowed, for that purpose, thirty thousand napoleons[32] from the Bank of France. It has become known that we have never had occasion to unpack the money, and that it is still lying in our cellar. The crate upon which I sit contains two thousand napoleons packed between layers of lead foil. Our reserve of bullion[33] is much larger at present than is usually kept in a single branch office, and the directors have had misgivings upon the subject."

"Which were very well justified," observed

---

32. **thirty thousand napoleons:** French gold coins, worth about $1,200,000 today.
33. **bullion** [bool'yən]: gold.

---

AT A GLANCE

- They follow Merryweather into a crate-filled bank vault.
- Merryweather is startled that the floor sounds hollow.
- Holmes scolds Merryweather for making noise and says they have an hour's wait.
- Merryweather says that the crates contain borrowed French gold.

### 1 PLOT DEVELOPMENT

The hollow sound hints that the crime involves a tunnel beneath the bank. Holmes's statement that noise may have imperiled their success adds to the tension.

### 2 THEME

This passage suggests the value of close observation. Here Holmes is looking for loose stones to determine if an entrance has already been prepared to the bank vault.

### 3 PLOT DEVELOPMENT

The motivation for a possible robbery attempt is now clear, as Merryweather speaks of the French gold.

---

## GUIDED READING

### LITERAL QUESTIONS

**1a.** What does Holmes examine with his magnifying glass after Merryweather sits down? (He studies the cracks between the stones of the floor.)

**2a.** What is stored in the crates in the cellar? (The crates contain borrowed French gold.)

### INFERENTIAL QUESTIONS

**1b.** What might Holmes be looking for? (He may be trying to determine if the criminals have prepared an entrance to the vault and, if so, where it is.)

**2b.** What crime do you think Clay has planned? (Clay is about to break into the bank from a tunnel below to steal the gold that is stored there.)

Holmes. "And now it is time that we arranged our little plans. I expect that within an hour matters will come to a head. In the meantime, Mr. Merryweather, we must put the screen over that dark lantern."

"And sit in the dark?"

"I am afraid so. I had brought a pack of cards in my pocket, and I thought that, as we were a *partie carrée,*[34] you might have your bridge games after all. But I see that the enemy's preparations have gone so far that we cannot risk the presence of a light. And, first of all, we must choose our positions. These are daring men, and though we shall take them at a disadvantage, they may do us some harm unless we are careful. I shall stand behind this crate, and do you conceal yourself behind those. Then when I flash a light upon them, close in swiftly. If they fire, Watson, have no compunction about shooting them down."

I placed my revolver, cocked, upon the top of the wooden case behind which I crouched. Holmes shot the slide across the front of his lantern, and left us in pitch darkness—such an absolute darkness as I have never before experienced. The smell of hot metal remained to assure us that the light was still there, ready to flash out at a moment's notice. To me, with my nerves worked up to a pitch of expectancy, there was something depressing and subduing in the sudden gloom, and in the cold, dank air of the vault.

"They have but one retreat," whispered Holmes. "That is back through the house into Saxe-Coburg Square. I hope that you have done what I asked you, Jones?"

"I have an inspector and two officers waiting at the front door."

"Then we have stopped all the holes. And now we must be silent and wait."

What a time it seemed! From comparing notes afterwards it was but an hour and a quarter, yet it appeared to me that the night must have almost

---

34. **partie carrée** [pär tē′ kä rā′]: French for "party of four," the number needed to play some card games.

gone, and the dawn be breaking above us. My limbs were weary and stiff, for I feared to change my position; yet my nerves were worked up to the highest pitch of tension, and my hearing was so acute that I could not only hear the gentle breathing of my companions, but I could distinguish the deeper, heavier in-breath of the bulky Jones from the thin, sighing note of the bank director. From my position I could look over the case in the direction of the floor. Suddenly my eyes caught the glint of a light.

At first it was but a lurid spark upon the stone pavement. Then it lengthened out until it became a yellow line, and then, without any warning or sound, a gash seemed to open and a hand appeared; a white, almost womanly hand, which felt about in the center of the little area of light. For a minute or more the hand, with its writhing fingers, protruded out of the floor. Then it was withdrawn as suddenly as it appeared, and all was dark again save the single lurid spark which marked a chink between the stones.

Its disappearance, however, was but momentary. With a rending, tearing sound, one of the

---

- A stone turns over, and Clay pulls himself into the cellar, followed by a companion.
- Holmes grabs Clay; his companion dives back down the hole.
- Holmes knocks down Clay's pistol and tells Clay his friend will be caught at the pawnshop door.

**1 PLOT: CLIMAX**

The prevention of the bank robbery and capture of Clay provide the climax of the story.

**2 CHARACTERIZATION**

The two masters compliment each other; although on opposite sides of the law, they respect each other's abilities and cleverness.

broad, white stones turned over upon its side, and left a square, gaping hole, through which streamed the light of a lantern. Over the edge there peeped a clean-cut, boyish face, which looked keenly about it, and then, with a hand on either side of the aperture, drew itself shoulder-high and waist-high, until one knee rested upon the edge. In another instant he stood at the side of the hole, and was hauling after him a companion, lithe and small like himself, with a pale face and a shock of very red hair.

**1** "It's all clear," he whispered. "Have you the chisel and the bags? Great Scott! Jump, Archie, jump, and I'll swing for it!"

Sherlock Holmes had sprung out and seized the intruder by the collar. The other dived down the hole, and I heard the sound of rending cloth as Jones clutched at his skirts. The light flashed upon the barrel of a revolver, but Holmes's hunting crop came down on the man's wrist, and the pistol clinked upon the stone floor.

"It's no use, John Clay," said Holmes blandly. "You have no chance at all."

"So I see," the other answered, with the ut-most coolness. "I fancy that my pal is all right, though I see you have got his coattails."

**2** "There are three men waiting for him at the door," said Holmes.

"Oh, indeed! You seem to have done the thing very completely. I must compliment you."

"And I you," Holmes answered. "Your red-headed idea was very new and effective."

"You'll see your pal again presently," said Jones. "He's quicker at climbing down holes than I am. Just hold out while I fix the derbies."[35]

"I beg that you will not touch me with your filthy hands," remarked our prisoner, as the handcuffs clattered upon his wrists. "You may not be aware that I have royal blood in my veins. Have the goodness, also, when you address me always to say 'sir' and 'please.'"

"All right," said Jones, with a stare and a snigger. "Well, would you please, sir, march upstairs, where we can get a cab to carry your highness to the police station?"

---

35. **derbies:** handcuffs.

*The Red-Headed League* **17**

---

## GUIDED READING

### LITERAL QUESTION

**1a.** What does Sherlock Holmes do to avoid being hurt by Clay? (He surprises Clay and grabs him by the collar; he knocks his pistol out of his hand.)

### INFERENTIAL QUESTION

**1b.** From Holmes's capture of Clay, what do you infer about the detective's physical capabilities? (He is quick, brave, and probably somewhat athletic.)

- Clay goes with the detective.
- Merryweather thanks Holmes, who declares that he enjoyed settling accounts with Clay.
- Holmes explains to Watson the object of the advertisement and the reason Clay took the job.
- Holmes observed that the cellar was behind the pawnshop and adjoined the bank.

## 1 PLOT: FALLING ACTION

The conversation between Holmes and Merryweather and Holmes's explanation of his solution make up the falling action of the story.

## 2 CHARACTERIZATION

Holmes's explanation of what was "perfectly obvious" to him confirms his extraordinary reasoning powers.

## 3 THEME

Holmes knew from the start that Spaulding was not what he seemed to be because of the unusual conditions of his employment with Wilson.

## 4 PLOT DEVELOPMENT

The reader can now recognize how Doyle provided clues that led to the conclusion of the story.

## 5 THEME

Holmes explains his use of reasoning and careful observation to determine the location of the cellar in Wilson's pawnshop and the state of Spaulding's knees.

---

"That is better," said John Clay, serenely. He made a sweeping bow to the three of us, and walked quietly off in the custody of the detective.

1 "Really, Mr. Holmes," said Mr. Merryweather, as we followed them from the cellar, "I do not know how the bank can thank you or repay you. There is no doubt that you have detected and defeated in the most complete manner one of the most determined attempts at bank robbery that has ever come within my experience."

"I have had one or two little scores of my own to settle with Mr. John Clay," said Holmes. "I have been at some small expense over this matter, which I shall expect the bank to refund, but beyond that I am amply repaid by having had an experience which is in many ways unique, and by hearing the very remarkable narrative of the Red-headed League."

2 "You see, Watson," he explained, in the early hours of the morning, as we sat over a glass of whiskey-and-soda in Baker Street, "it was perfectly obvious from the first that the only possible object of this rather fantastic business of the advertisement of the League, and the copying of the *Encyclopedia*, must be to get this not over-bright pawnbroker out of the way for a number of hours every day. It was a curious way of managing it, but, really, it would be difficult to suggest a better. The method was no doubt suggested to Clay's ingenious mind by the color of his accomplice's hair. The four pounds a week was a lure which must draw him, and what was it to them, who were playing for thousands? They put in the advertisement, one rogue has the temporary office, the other rogue incites the man to apply for it, and together they manage to secure his absence every morning in the week. 3 From the time that I heard of the assistant having come for half wages, it was obvious to me that he had some strong motive for securing the situation."

"But how could you guess what the motive was?"

"Had there been women in the house, I should have suspected a mere vulgar intrigue. That, however, was out of the question. The man's business was a small one, and there was nothing in his house which could account for such elaborate preparations and such an expenditure as they were at. It must, then, be something out of the house. What could it be? I thought of the assistant's fondness for photography, and his trick of vanishing into the cellar. The cellar! There was the end of this tangled clue. Then I made inquiries as to this mysterious assistant, and found that I had to deal with one of the coolest and most daring criminals in London. He was doing something in the cellar—something which took many hours a day for months on end. What could it be, once more? I could think of nothing save that he was running a tunnel to some other building.

5 "So far I had got when we went to visit the scene of action. I surprised you by beating upon the pavement with my stick. I was ascertaining whether the cellar stretched out in front or behind. It was not in front. Then I rang the bell, and, as I hoped, the assistant answered it. We have had some skirmishes, but we had never set eyes upon each other before. I hardly looked at his face. His knees were what I wished to see. You must yourself have remarked how worn, wrinkled, and stained they were. They spoke of those hours of burrowing. The only remaining point was what they were burrowing for. I walked round the corner, saw the City and Suburban Bank abutted on our friend's premises, and felt that I had solved my problem. When you drove home after the concert, I called upon Scotland Yard, and upon the chairman of the bank directors, with the result that you have seen."

"And how could you tell that they would make their attempt tonight?"

---

## GUIDED READING

### LITERAL QUESTIONS

**1a.** What does Holmes say to Watson about the League advertisement? (He says that it was "perfectly obvious" that the object was to get Wilson out of the pawnshop.)

**2a.** What were specific clues that helped Holmes solve the case? (the willingness of Spaulding to work for half wages, the smallness of Wilson's business, Spaulding's habit of going to the cellar, and the worn knees)

### INFERENTIAL QUESTIONS

**1b.** What do those words tell you about Holmes? (He has superior reasoning powers; events that puzzle other people seem clear to him.)

**2b.** With these clues in mind, how would the story have been different if Holmes had been the narrator? The reader would have understood the significance of each clue as it was presented, and there would have been no suspense.)

"Well, when they closed their League offices, that was a sign that they cared no longer about Mr. Jabez Wilson's presence—in other words, that they had completed their tunnel. But it was essential that they should use it soon, as it **might be discovered, or the bullion might be removed. Saturday would suit them better than any other day, as it would give them two days for their escape. For all these reasons I expected them to come tonight."**

"You reasoned it out beautifully," I exclaimed, in unfeigned admiration. "It is so long a chain, and yet every link rings true."

"It saved me from ennui,"[36] he answered,

yawning. "Alas! I already feel it closing in upon me. My life is spent in one long effort to escape **from the commonplaces of existence. These little problems help me to do so."**

"And you are a benefactor of the race," said I.

He shrugged his shoulders. "Well, perhaps, after all, it is of some little use," he remarked. *"L'homme c'est rien—l'oeuvre c'est tout,"*[37] as Gustave Flaubert[38] wrote to George Sand."[39]

---

37. **L'homme . . . tout** [lôm sä rē aɴ' lœv'rə sä tōō]: French for "Man is nothing; his work is everything."
38. **Gustave Flaubert** [gōōs täv' flō bār']: French novelist (1821–1880).
39. **George Sand** [zhôrzh sänd]: pen name of Amandine Dupin, French novelist (1804–1876).

---

36. **ennui** [än'wē]: boredom.

---

## STUDY QUESTIONS

### Recalling

1. What conclusions does Holmes draw about Jabez Wilson's past activities? Upon what evidence does Holmes base these conclusions?
2. What does Wilson think the Red-Headed League is? What does it turn out to be?
3. List the clues that enable Holmes to solve the mystery of the Red-Headed League.
4. Describe the bank robbers' plan, and explain what Holmes does to foil it.

### Interpreting

5. What evidence supports Holmes's conclusion that Jabez Wilson is "none too bright"?
6. Prove that Holmes is a better observer than Watson. In what other ways are they different?
7. Would you have liked the story better if Holmes had explained his reasoning at each stage of the investigation? Why or why not?

### Extending

8. What satisfactions do you think people draw from reading detective stories?

## VIEWPOINT

We can often increase our pleasure in a work of literature by consulting the opinion of an expert on the author's writing. Throughout this book in each section titled "Viewpoint," you will find a quotation about the author and selection you have read; most of these quotations come from literary critics or the authors themselves. Each quotation is followed by questions asking you to consider the opinion in light of your own reaction to the work.

Sherlock Holmes is probably the world's best-known detective. One writer explains the special appeal of Conan Doyle's hero in the following way:

> The name of the great sleuth has become an international symbol of all that is estimable [admirable],. . . romantic and glamorous in the pursuit and detection of crime.
> — H. Haycroft, *Sherlock Holmes's Greatest Cases*

■ In what ways does Holmes prove himself to be an "estimable" sleuth in this story? What might be "glamorous" about Holmes and his work?

*The Red-Headed League* **19**

## LITERARY FOCUS

### Plot Development

- *exposition:* meeting
- *narrative hook:* advertisement
- *rising action:* Wilson's story
- *climax:* arrest
- *falling action:* Holmes's explanation
- *resolution:* remarks about boredom

### Foreshadowing

Holmes remarks: "for strange effects we must go to life itself"; "the strangest and most unique things are very often connected not with the large but with the smaller crimes"

## VOCABULARY

1. (d) unusual
2. (c) slight
3. (a) bordered
4. (a) bizarre
5. (b) persistent

---

## LITERARY FOCUS

### Plot Development

The **plot** is the sequence of events in a story. It usually follows the pattern below.

In the **exposition** the author introduces the story's characters, setting, and situation to us. The **narrative hook** is the point at which the author catches our attention and establishes the basic conflict that the story will eventually resolve. The narrative hook marks the beginning of the **rising action,** which adds complications to the story.

The rising action leads up to the **climax,** the point of our greatest involvement in the story. The climax usually indicates the way in which the story's conflict will be solved. The **falling action** reveals the outcome of the climax, and the **resolution** brings the story to a satisfying and logical conclusion.

### Thinking About Plot Development

■ In "The Red-Headed League" the narrative hook is Watson's reading of the advertisement for the league (page 4). Make a chart identifying the other parts of the plot, filling in the events that represent the: (a) exposition, (b) rising action, (c) climax, (d) falling action, and (e) resolution.

### Foreshadowing

Many authors use clues known as **foreshadowing** to prepare their readers for later developments in the plot. These clues can take the form of minor incidents or statements that suggest later developments. Foreshadowing increases our involvement in any story, but it is particularly effective in a mystery like "The Red-Headed League." Such clues enable the alert reader to feel like the detective who eventually unravels the mystery.

### Thinking About Foreshadowing

■ In "The Red-Headed League" find two clues in the first three pages of the story that indicate that Holmes will eventually solve the mystery.

## VOCABULARY

### Synonyms

A **synonym** is a word that has the same or nearly the same meaning as another word. For example, *envy* and *jealousy* are synonyms. The words in capital letters are from "The Red-Headed League." Choose the word that is *nearest* the meaning of each word in capitals, *as the word is used in the story.* Write the number of each item and the letter of your choice on a separate sheet.

1. SINGULAR:  (a) definite  (b) exciting  (c) one  (d) unusual
2. NOMINAL:  (a) cautious  (b) pretended  (c) slight  (d) useless
3. ABUTTED:  (a) bordered  (b) bounded  (c) covered  (d) screened
4. GROTESQUE:  (a) bizarre  (b) foolish  (c) insane  (d) imaginary
5. TENACIOUS:  (a) bold  (b) persistent  (c) eager  (d) objectionable

## COMPOSITION

### Evaluating a Response to a Story

■ Write an evaluation of "The Red-Headed League." First decide whether or not you liked the story. Then explain your response, considering the following questions: Does the story arouse your interest at the beginning? What questions does it raise that you want to see answered? Does it sustain your interest and lead toward a logical solution? Support your opinions with specific examples from the story. *For help with this assignment, see Lesson 1 in the Writing About Literature Handbook at the back of this book.*

### Writing Dialogue

■ A friend has misplaced something important— for example, a favorite record or tape. Write the dialogue for a conversation in which your friend explains the problem and asks you for help. Like a detective, you ask a series of logical questions that lead your friend to remember where he or she left the missing object. Be sure to distinguish clearly between your two speakers.

---

## COMPOSITION: GUIDELINES FOR EVALUATION

### EVALUATING A RESPONSE TO A STORY

**Objective**

To evaluate "The Red-Headed League" as a story

**Guidelines for Evaluation:**

- suggested length: 3–4 paragraphs
- should clearly state writer's opinion about the story's effectiveness
- should support the opinion by discussing how Doyle arouses interest, creates suspense and resolves the story

### WRITING DIALOGUE

**Objective**

To construct a dialogue between two characters attempting to locate a misplaced item

**Guidelines for Evaluation**

- suggested length: 150–400 words
- should include one character who clearly states the problem and one character who addresses the problem

Dorothy Canfield Fisher (1879–1958) was born in Kansas but spent most of her adult life on a farm in Vermont. In a career that spanned over fifty years, Fisher wrote short stories and a number of novels that drew on her experience of life in rural New England. Like "The Bedquilt," most of her fiction reflects her understanding of the families who worked hard to make the land productive.

■ How can an unexpected act of artistic creation change a person's self-perception?

*Dorothy Canfield Fisher*

# The Bedquilt[1]

**1**    Of all the Elwell family Aunt Mehetabel[2] was certainly the most unimportant member. It was in the New England days, when an unmarried woman was an old maid at twenty, at forty was everyone's servant, and at sixty had gone through so much discipline that she could need no more in the next world. Aunt Mehetabel was sixty-eight.

   She had never for a moment known the pleasure of being important to anyone. Not that she was useless in her brother's family; she was expected, as a matter of course, to take upon herself the most tedious and uninteresting part **2** of the household labors. On Mondays she accepted as her share the washing of the men's shirts, heavy with sweat and stiff with dirt from the fields and from their own, hard-working bodies. Tuesdays she never dreamed of being allowed to iron anything pretty or even interesting, like the baby's white dresses or the fancy aprons of her young-lady nieces. She stood all day pressing out a tiresome, monotonous succession of dishcloths and towels and sheets.

In preserving time[3] she was allowed to have none of the pleasant responsibility of deciding when the fruit had cooked long enough, nor did she share in the little excitement of pouring the sweet-smelling stuff into the stone jars. She sat in a corner with the children and stoned cherries incessantly, or hulled strawberries until her fingers were dyed red to the bone.

   The Elwells were not consciously unkind to their aunt—they were even in a vague way fond of her; but she was so utterly insignificant a **3** figure in their lives that they bestowed no thought whatever on her. Aunt Mehetabel did not resent this treatment; she took it quite as unconsciously as they gave it. It was to be expected when one was an old-maid dependent in a busy family. She gathered what crumbs of comfort she could from their occasional careless kindnesses and tried to hide the hurt which even yet pierced her at her brother's rough joking. In the winter, when they all sat before the big hearth, roasted apples, drank mulled[4] cider, and teased the girls about their beaux[5] and the boys about

---

1. **Bedquilt:** bedcover made of two layers of cloth that are stuffed with fiber and stitched together in patterns.
2. **Mehetabel** [me het′ə bel]

3. **preserving time:** time when fruit is harvested and some of the crop is cooked and put up in jars.
4. **mulled** [muld]: spiced and heated.
5. **beaux** [bō]: French for "boyfriends."

*The Bedquilt*   **21**

- Her one pleasure in life is making quilts.
- She creates an elaborate design and longs to execute it.
- Finally, she asks for and receives permission from Sophia to make the quilt.

**1 CHARACTERIZATION**

Mehetabel's shyness and low opinion of herself are part of a lifelong pattern.

**2 STYLE: WORD CHOICE**

Use of the adjective *tepid* shows that even Mehetabel's one accomplishment brings her only lukewarm satisfaction and fulfillment.

**3 PLOT: NARRATIVE HOOK**

Mehetabel's idea is the spark that ignites the story. Its genesis is described in religious terms, suggesting its greatness and its powerful impact on Mehetabel.

**4 INTERNAL CONFLICT**

Mehetabel struggles to allow herself to make the magnificent quilt she has imagined.

**5 CHARACTERIZATION**

Childlike, Mehetabel feels she must ask permission to begin work; her inability to communicate makes this simple act an ordeal.

---

their sweethearts, she shrank into a dusty corner with her knitting, happy if the evening passed without her brother saying, with a crude sarcasm, ''Ask your Aunt Mehetabel about the beaux that used to come a-sparkin'[6] her!'' or, ''Mehetabel, how was't when you was in love **1** with Abel Cummings?'' As a matter of fact, she had been the same at twenty as at sixty—a quiet, mouselike little creature, too timid and shy for anyone to notice or to raise her eyes for a moment and wish for a life of her own.

Her sister-in-law, a big hearty housewife who ruled indoors with as autocratic a sway as did her husband on the farm, was rather kind in an absent, offhand way to the shrunken little old woman, and it was through her that Mehetabel was able to enjoy the one pleasure of her life. Even as a girl, she had been clever with her needle in the way of patching bedquilts. More than that she could never learn to do. The garments which she made for herself were the most lamentable affairs, and she was humbly grateful for any help in the bewildering business of put- **2** ting them together. But in patchwork she enjoyed a tepid importance. She could really do that as well as anyone else. During the years of devotion to this one art, she had accumulated a considerable store of quilting patterns. Sometimes the neighbors would send over and ask ''Miss Mehetabel'' for such and such a design. It was with an agreeable flutter at being able to help someone that she went to the dresser, in her bare little room under the eaves, and extracted from her crowded portfolio the pattern desired.

**3** She never knew how her great idea came to her. Sometimes she thought she must have dreamed it; sometimes she even wondered reverently, in the phraseology of the weekly prayer meeting, if it had not been ''sent'' to her. She never admitted to herself that she could have thought of it without other help; it was too great, too ambitious, too lofty a project for her

---

6. **a-sparkin':** slang for ''sparking,'' or courting.

**22**   *The Short Story*

---

humble mind to have conceived. Even when she finished drawing the design with her worn fingers, she gazed at it incredulously, not daring to believe that it could indeed be her handiwork. At first it seemed to her only like a lovely but quite unreal dream. She did not think of putting it into execution—so elaborate, so complicated, so beautifully difficult a pattern could be only for the angels in heaven to quilt. But so curiously does familiarity accustom us even to very wonderful things that, as she lived with this **4** astonishing creation of her mind, the longing grew stronger and stronger to give it material life with her nimble old fingers.

She gasped at her daring when this idea first swept over her and put it away as one does a sinfully selfish notion, but she kept coming back to it again and again. Finally, she said compromisingly to herself that she would make one ''square,'' just one part of her design, to see how it would look. Accustomed to the most complete **5** dependence on her brother and his wife, she dared not do even this without asking Sophia's permission. With a heart full of hope and fear thumping furiously against her old ribs, she approached the mistress of the house on churning day,[7] knowing with the innocent guile of a child that the country woman was apt to be in a good temper while working over the fragrant butter in the cool cellar.

Sophia listened absently to her sister-in-law's halting, hesitating petition. ''Why, yes, Mehetabel,'' she said, leaning far down into the huge churn for the last golden morsels—''why, yes, start another quilt if you want to. I've got a lot of pieces from the spring sewing that will work in real good.'' Mehetabel tried honestly to make her see that this would be no common quilt, but her limited vocabulary and her emotion stood between her and expression. At last Sophia said, with a kindly impatience, ''Oh,

---

7. **churning day:** day on which the farm's cream is whipped, or churned, into butter.

---

## GUIDED READING

**LITERAL QUESTIONS**

**1a.** How does Mehetabel react when neighbors come to borrow quilt patterns from her? (With an ''agreeable flutter,'' she gets them what they have asked for.)

**2a.** Where does Mehetabel think the idea for the original quilt pattern comes from? (She thinks she must have dreamed it or it was ''sent'' to her.)

**INFERENTIAL QUESTIONS**

**1b.** How do you think Mehetabel really feels when neighbors request her help? (It is the only time she has a sense of importance and self-esteem; she enjoys being useful in this way.)

**2b.** What does her inability to credit herself with originality tell you about Mehetabel? (Her self-esteem is so low that she does not believe she can have such a wonderful, creative idea.)

there! Don't bother me. I never could keep track of your quiltin' patterns, anyhow. I don't care what pattern you go by."

With this overwhelmingly, although unconsciously, generous permission, Mehetabel **[1]** rushed back up the steep attic stairs to her room and in a joyful agitation, began preparation for the work of her life. It was even better than she hoped. By some heaven-sent inspiration she had invented a pattern beyond which no patchwork quilt could go.

**[2]** She had but little time from her incessant round of household drudgery for this new and absorbing occupation, and she did not dare sit up late at night lest she burn too much candle. It was weeks before the little square began to take on a finished look, to show the pattern. Then Mehetabel was in a fever of impatience to bring it to completion. She was too conscientious to shirk even the smallest part of her share of the work of the house, but she rushed through it with a speed which left her panting as she climbed to the little room. This seemed like a radiant spot to her as she bent over the innumerable scraps of cloth which already in her imagination ranged themselves in the infinitely diverse pattern of her masterpiece. Finally she could wait no longer and one evening ventured to bring her work down beside the fire where the family sat, hoping that some good fortune would give her a place near the tallow candles on the mantelpiece. She was on the last corner of the square, and her needle flew in and out with inconceivable rapidity. No one noticed her, a fact which filled her with relief, and by bedtime she had but a few more stitches to add.

As she stood up with the others, the square fluttered out of her trembling old hands and fell on the table. Sophia glanced at it carelessly. "Is that the new quilt you're beginning on?" she asked with a yawn. "It looks like a real pretty pattern. Let's see it." Up to that moment Mehetabel had labored in the purest spirit of disinterested devotion to an ideal: but as Sophia **[3]** held her work toward the candle to examine it and exclaimed in amazement and admiration, she felt an astonished joy to know that her creation would stand the test of publicity.

"Land sakes!" ejaculated her sister-in-law, looking at the many-colored square. "Why, Mehetabel Elwell, where'd you git that pattern?"

"I made it up," said Mehetabel quietly, but with utterable pride.

"No!" exclaimed Sophia incredulously. "*Did* you! Why, I never see such a pattern in my life. Girls, come here and see what your Aunt Mehetabel is doing."

The three tall daughters turned back reluctantly from the stairs. "I don't seem to take much interest in patchwork," said one listlessly.

**[4]** "No, nor I neither!" answered Sophia. "But a stone image would take an interest in this pattern. Honest, Mehetabel, did you think of it yourself? And how under the sun and stars did you ever git your courage up to start in a-making it? Land! Look at all those tiny, squinchy little seams! Why, the wrong side ain't a thing *but* seams!"

The girls echoed their mother's exclamations, and Mr. Elwell himself came over to see what they were discussing. "Well, I declare!" he said, looking at his sister with eyes more approving than she could ever remember. "That beats old Mis' Wightman's quilt that got the blue ribbon so many times at the county fair."

Mehetabel's heart swelled within her, and tears of joy moistened her old eyes as she lay that night in her narrow, hard bed, too proud and excited to sleep. **[5]** The next day her sister-in-law amazed her by taking the huge pan of potatoes out of her lap and setting one of the younger children to peeling them. "Don't you want to go on with that quiltin' pattern?" she said. "I'd kind o' like to see how you're goin' to make the grapevine design come out on the corner."

By the end of summer the family interest had risen so high that Mehetabel was given a little stand in the sitting room where she could

*The Bedquilt* **23**

AT A GLANCE

- Mehetabel works on her design, and the family members admire her work.
- Mehetabel feels proud.
- The next day Sophia tells her to work on the quilt instead of peeling potatoes.

## 1 FORESHADOWING

By calling it "the work of her life," Fisher suggests that the quilt may play a crucial role in Mehetabel's life.

## 2 INTERNAL CONFLICT

Although she wants to work on the quilt, Mehetabel's frugality and conscientiousness leave her little time to sew.

## 3 THEME

For the first time, Mehetabel revels in the joy that comes from her own creativity.

## 4 STYLE: FIGURATIVE LANGUAGE

Sophia's statement that even a stone image would be interested in the quilt colorfully emphasizes her admiration of the quilt pattern.

## 5 PLOT: RISING ACTION

Sophia's admiration for the quilt leads her to change her thoughtless treatment of Mehetabel.

## GUIDED READING

### LITERAL QUESTION

**1a.** How does Sophia first see Mehetabel's square? (It falls onto the table when Mehetabel stands up.)

### INFERENTIAL QUESTION

**1b.** Why is this moment the end of Mehetabel's laboring "in the purest spirit of disinterested devotion to an ideal"? (Because from that moment on her work is subject to public scrutiny and she will be aware of potential and actual approval.)

AT A GLANCE

- Mehetabel's life now has meaning.
- When Mehetabel joins in conversation, people listen; strangers come to see her quilt.
- When Mehetabel finishes the quilt five years later, it is taken at once to the county fair.

## 1 THEME

The transformation has begun: Her creativity gives Mehetabel's life new purpose. The comparison of Mehetabel to a priestess suggests the importance she attaches to her work.

## 2 SETTING

This passage reflects the story's nineteenth-century New England locale, where it was a great honor to gain the approval of the minister, who was usually the best-educated person in the neighborhood.

## 3 CHARACTERIZATION

Mehetabel's new-found "status" causes a change in her behavior: She sits up straight, joins in conversation, and wins more respect from the children.

## 4 EXTERNAL CONFLICT

Mehetabel's serious illness represents a major setback and tests her persistence.

## 5 INTERNAL CONFLICT

Mehetabel is torn between her delight in having her quilt shown at the fair and her sadness in its immediate loss.

---

keep her pieces and work in odd minutes. She almost wept over such kindness, and resolved firmly not to take advantage of it by neglecting her work, which she performed with a fierce thoroughness. But the whole atmosphere of her world was changed. Things had a meaning now. Through the longest task of washing milk pans there rose the rainbow of promise of her variegated work. She took her place by the little table and put the thimble on her knotted, hard finger with the solemnity of a priestess performing a sacred rite.

She was even able to bear with some degree of dignity the extreme honor of having the minister and the minister's wife comment admiringly on her great project. The family felt quite proud of Aunt Mehetabel as Minister Bowman had said it was work as fine as any he had ever seen, "and he didn't know but finer!" The remark was repeated verbatim[8] to the neighbors in the following weeks when they dropped in and examined, in a perverse silence, some astonishingly difficult tour de force[9] which Mehetabel had just finished.

The family, especially, plumed[10] themselves on the slow progress of the quilt. "Mehetabel has been to work on that corner for six weeks, come Tuesday, and she ain't half done yet," they explained to visitors. They fell out of the way of always expecting her to be the one to run on errands, even for the children. "Don't bother your Aunt Mehetabel," Sophia would call. "Can't you see she's got to a ticklish place on the quilt?"

The old woman sat up straighter and looked the world in the face. She was part of it at last. She joined in the conversation and her remarks were listened to. The children were even told to mind her when she asked them to do some service for her, although this she did but seldom,

---

8. **verbatim** [ver bā′tim]: Latin for "in exactly the same words."
9. **tour de force** [tōōr′də fôrs′]: French for "feat of great strength or skill."
10. **plumed** [plōomd]: felt pride for.

---

the habit of self-effacement being too strong.

One day some strangers from the next town drove up and asked if they could inspect the wonderful quilt which they had heard of, even down in their end of the valley. After that such visitations were not uncommon, making the Elwell's house a notable object. Mehetabel's quilt came to be one of the town sights, and no one was allowed to leave the town without having paid tribute to its worth. The Elwells saw to it that their aunt was better dressed than she had ever been before, and one of the girls made her a pretty little cap to wear on her thin white hair.

A year went by and a quarter of the quilt was finished; a second year passed and half was done. The third year Mehetabel had pneumonia and lay ill for weeks and weeks, overcome with terror lest she die before her work was completed. A fourth year and one could really see the grandeur of the whole design; and in September of the fifth year, the entire family watching her with eager and admiring eyes, Mehetabel quilted the last stitches in her creation. The girls held it up by the four corners, and they all looked at it in a solemn silence. Then Mr. Elwell smote one horny hand within the other and exclaimed, "By ginger! That's goin' to the county fair!" Mehetabel blushed a deep red at this. It was a thought which had occurred to her in a bold moment, but she had not dared to entertain it. The family acclaimed the idea, and one of the boys was forthwith dispatched to the house of the neighbor who was chairman of the committee for their village. He returned with radiant face. "Of course he'll take it. Like's not it may git a prize, so he says; but he's got to have it right off, because all the things are goin' tomorrow morning."

Even in her swelling pride Mehetabel felt a pang of separation as the bulky package was carried out of the house. As the days went on, she felt absolutely lost without her work. For years it had been her one preoccupation; and she could not bear even to look at the little stand,

---

## GUIDED READING

### LITERAL QUESTIONS

**1a.** How has the "whole atmosphere" of Mehetabel's world changed? (Things have meaning now. When she does her chores, she is looking forward to working on the quilt.)

**2a.** In what new ways do people treat Mehetabel now? (They listen to her; they tell the children to mind her; strangers come to see the quilt; the family sees that she wears better clothes.)

### INFERENTIAL QUESTIONS

**1b.** What does Mehetabel's experience demonstrate about the effect of work on someone's life? (Having a worthwhile project to do can make you feel happier and can make tedious work more bearable.)

**2b.** Why do people treat her differently from before? (They admire what she has done; they are anxious to help her complete the quilt since she is bringing honor to the family.)

An appliqué quilt made in Massachusetts c. 1860.

- Her brother offers Mehetabel a ride to the fair; she has never been more than six miles away.
- Excited, she cannot sleep the night before her trip.
- That evening she returns tired but blissful.

### 1 CHARACTERIZATION

Because of her limited experience, Mehetabel cannot envision her quilt at the fair and she is unable to feel satisfaction from this accomplishment.

### 2 STYLE: ANALOGY

The comparison of a visit to the county fair to "a ride in a golden chariot up to the gates of heaven" conveys her great excitement as well as the poignant narrowness of her life up to that point.

### 3 RESPONSE JOURNAL

Ask the students to describe an event in their lives about which they were so excited that they could not sleep the night before.

now quite bare of the litter of scraps which had **1** lain on it so long. One of the neighbors, who took the long journey to the fair, reported that the quilt was hung in a place of honor in a glass case in "Agricultural Hall." But that meant little to Mehetabel's utter ignorance of all that lay outside of her brother's home. The family noticed the old woman's depression, and one day Sophia said kindly, "You feel sort o' lost without the quilt, don't you, Mehetabel?"

"They took it away so quick!" she said wistfully. "I hadn't hardly had one real good look at it myself."

Mr. Elwell made no comment, but a day or two later he asked his sister how early she could get up in the morning.

"I dun'no'. Why?" she asked.

"Well, Thomas Ralston has got to drive clear to West Oldton to see a lawyer there, and that is four miles beyond the fair. He says if you can git up so's to leave here at four in the morning he'll drive you over to the fair, leave you there for the day, and bring you back again at night."

**2** Mehetabel looked at him with incredulity. It was as though someone had offered her a ride in a golden chariot up to the gates of heaven. "Why, you can't *mean* it!" she cried, paling with the intensity of her emotion. Her brother laughed, a little uneasily. Even to his careless indifference this joy was a revelation of the narrowness of her life in his home. "Oh, 'tain't so much to go to the fair. Yes, I mean it. Go git your things ready, for he wants to start tomorrow morning."

**3** All that night a trembling, excited old woman lay and stared at the rafters. She who had never been more than six miles from home in her life was going to drive thirty miles away—it was like going to another world. She who had never seen anything more exciting than a church supper was to see the county fair. To Mehetabel it was like making the tour of the world. She had never dreamed of doing it. She could not at all imagine what it would be like.

Nor did the exhortations of the family, as they bade goodbye to her, throw any light on her confusion. They had all been at least once to the scene of gaiety she was to visit; and as she tried to eat her breakfast, they called out conflicting advice to her till her head whirled. Sophia told her to be sure to see the display of preserves. Her brother said not to miss inspecting the stock, her nieces said the fancywork[11] was the only thing worth looking at, and her nephews said she must bring them home an account of the races. The buggy drove up to the door, she was helped in, and her wraps tucked about her. They all stood together and waved goodbye to her as she drove out of the yard. She waved back, but she scarcely saw them. On her return home that evening she was very pale, and so tired and stiff that her brother had to lift her out bodily, but her lips were set in a blissful smile. They crowded around her with thronging questions until Sophia pushed them all aside, telling them Aunt Mehetabel was too tired to speak until she had had her supper. This was eaten in an enforced silence on the part of the

___
11. **fancywork:** ornamental needlework.

## GUIDED READING

### LITERAL QUESTION

**1a.** Why, according to Mehetabel, does she feel so lost without the quilt? (She says that they took it away so quickly that she hardly had time to look at it.)

### INFERENTIAL QUESTION

**1b.** Why do you think Mehetabel needs more time to look at the quilt? (Mehetabel's new sense of self-worth is so tied up with her grand project that it may seem fragile and endangered without the physical presence of the object.)

children, and then the old woman was helped into an easy chair before the fire. They gathered about her, eager for news of the great world, and Sophia said, "Now, come, Mehetabel, tell us all about it!"

Mehetabel drew a long breath. "It was just perfect!" she said. "Finer even than I thought. They've got it hanging up in the very middle of a sort o' closet made of glass, and one of the lower corners is ripped and turned back so's to show the seams on the wrong side."

"What?" asked Sophia a little blankly.

"Why, the quilt!" said Mehetabel in surprise. "There are a whole lot of other ones in that room but not one that can hold a candle to it, if I do say it who shouldn't. I heard lots of people say the same thing. You ought to have heard what the women said about that corner, Sophia. They said—well, I'd be ashamed to *tell* you what they said. I declare if I wouldn't!"

Mr. Elwell asked, "What did you think of that big ox we've heard so much about?"

"I didn't look at the stock," returned his sister indifferently. "That set of pieces you gave me, Maria, from your red waist, come out just lovely!" she assured one of her nieces. "I heard one woman say you could 'most smell the red silk roses."

"Did any of the horses in our town race?" asked young Thomas.

"I didn't see the races."

"How about the preserves?" asked Sophia.

"I didn't see the preserves," said Mehetabel calmly. "You see, I went right to the room where the quilt was, and then I didn't want to leave it. It had been so long since I'd seen it. I had to look at it first real good myself, and then I looked at the others to see if there was any that could come up to it. And then the people begun comin' in, and I got so interested in hearin' what they had to say I couldn't think of goin' anywheres else. I ate my lunch right there, too; and I'm glad as can be I did, too. For what do you think?"—she gazed about her with kindling eyes. "While I stood there with a sandwich in one hand, didn't the head of the hull concern come in and open the glass door and pin 'First Prize' right in the middle of the quilt!"

There was a stir of congratulation and proud exclamation. Then Sophia returned again to the attack. "Didn't you go to see anything else?" she queried.

"Why, no," said Mehetabel. "Only the quilt. Why should I?"

She fell into a reverie, where she saw again the glorious creation of her hand and brain hanging before all the world with the mark of highest approval on it. She longed to make her listeners see the splendid vision with her. She struggled for words; she reached blindly after unknown superlatives. "I tell you it looked like—" she said; and paused, hesitating. Vague recollections of hymn-book phraseology came into her mind, the only form of literary expression she knew; but they were dismissed as being sacrilegious, and also not sufficiently forcible. Finally, "I tell you it looked real *well*!" she assured them—and sat staring into the fire, on her tired old face the supreme content of an artist who had realized his ideal.

---

## STUDY QUESTIONS

### Recalling

1. Describe Aunt Mehetabel's life before she begins work on the bedquilt.

2. Describe how Mehetabel creates the design for the bedquilt. Why is she reluctant to start working on it?

3. How long does it take Mehetabel to finish the

---

AT A GLANCE

- After supper, when family members urge Mehetabel to tell about the fair, she describes how the quilt is displayed.
- She watched it receive first prize.
- Although Mehetabel struggles to explain, she cannot adequately express the satisfaction of an artist who has achieved her goal.

1 CHARACTERIZATION

Mehetabel is so humble that she feels she would be boasting if she repeats the compliments that her quilt received.

2 CONFLICT

At the fair Mehetabel resolves the conflict between her own desires and those of others by doing exactly what *she* wants to do.

3 PLOT: CLIMAX

Mehetabel's presence at the fair when her quilt receives first prize is the climax of the story.

4 THEME

Having seen her quilt at the fair, Mehetabel is now able to experience a deep sense of fulfillment from her creation.

REFLECTING ON THE STORY

Do you think a single accomplishment can really produce an overall change in an individual's self-confidence? (Most students will probably feel that an achievement can change an individual's life if it is very satisfying and, especially, if it is recognized by others.)

STUDY QUESTIONS

1. dependent on brother; does menial chores
2. inspiration; thinks it's too complicated for her small talents
3. 5 years; they compliment her; give her place to work; run her errands

4. She sees it win 1st prize.
5. can't describe design; can't express her feelings about the fair; through her quilt
6. becomes assertive; feels worthwhile; gains sense of purpose
7. summarizes change in Mehetabel
8. Answers will vary; elicit examples from various fields.

## VIEWPOINT

- *surface:* drab, hard working, not pleasurable
- *hidden:* her creativity and eventual satisfaction

## LITERARY FOCUS

1. family's ill treatment of her *vs.* her inability to object
2. low self-esteem *vs.* creative expression; caused by shyness plus family's ignoring and looking down at her
3. *external:* gains family's respect;
   *internal:* gains sense of worth

---

bedquilt? Find three ways in which her family changes its treatment of her during this time.
4. What happens to Mehetabel and her bedquilt at the fair?

### Interpreting

5. Find two examples of Mehetabel's inability to express herself in words. How *does* she express herself?
6. In what ways does Mehetabel's own personality change because of her work on the bedquilt? Explain how this work gives meaning to her life.
7. What does the last sentence in the story mean?

### Extending

8. Mention examples of your own work that you found satisfying. Do you think such work can change someone's life? Why or why not?

## VIEWPOINT

Dorothy Canfield Fisher once gave this explanation of her own creative impulse to write:

It is to try with all one's might to understand that part of human life which does not lie visibly on the surface.

■ How might Mehetabel's life be described by someone who knows only its surface — her actions and words? What hidden part of her life does this story enable us to see?

## LITERARY FOCUS

### External and Internal Conflict

At the heart of a good plot lies a **conflict** of some kind: a struggle between two opposing forces. An **external conflict** occurs between a character and some outside force. That force may be nature. For instance, a woman may face a conflict with nature as she tries to sail a boat through a dense fog. The opposing force may be another person. For instance, two characters may engage in an argument or competition. The struggle may be against a social system or some other institution. For example, a man may fight against an unjust law. Finally, a character may fight against fate, or circumstances that cannot be changed. For instance, a character may struggle against the irreversible progress of a disease.

An **internal conflict**, on the other hand, occurs within a character's own mind. A character may experience conflicting emotions — for example, being proud about a new job and frightened about its responsibilities. A character may have to choose between opposing goals: for example, between saving money for college and buying a much-needed car. A character may face a moral dilemma: for instance, telling the truth even if it will hurt someone else.

Many stories involve both external and internal conflict. A man involved in an external conflict against an unjust law may also experience an internal conflict over whether the struggle is worth the effort. Whatever form it takes, the conflict is usually resolved by the story's end.

### Thinking About External and Internal Conflict

1. What external conflicts does Aunt Mehetabel experience with her family?
2. What conflicts occur within Aunt Mehetabel? What causes them?
3. How are the external and internal conflicts in the story resolved?

## COMPOSITION

### Writing About Plot

■ Explain how the events and conflicts in "The Bedquilt" prepare you for the change that occurs in Mehetabel. First describe the change that occurs in Mehetabel's personality between the beginning and end of the story. Then show how the events of the story bring about this change in her. *For help with this assignment, see Lesson 2 in the Writing About Literature Handbook at the back of this book.*

### Writing an Interview

■ Interview a person with an interesting hobby or special skill. You want to find out how your interviewee developed this interest, what special skills are required to pursue it, and why the activity is a satisfying one. Take notes during the conversation, and use these notes to write a coherent record of the interview. You can follow question-and-answer form as you write. Be sure to begin by telling who your interviewee is and what he or she does.

28    *The Short Story*

---

## COMPOSITION: GUIDELINES FOR EVALUATION

### WRITING ABOUT PLOT

**Objective**
To follow the shifts in Mehetabel's character

**Guidelines for Evaluation**
- suggested length: three to five paragraphs
- should contrast her character at the beginning and end of the story
- should clearly show with examples from the story how and why the shift occurs

### WRITING AN INTERVIEW

**Objective**
To examine a person's sense of accomplishment

**Guidelines for Evaluation**
- suggested length: 500–800 words
- should describe a person's skill or hobby, presenting specific facts about it
- should make clear why the person finds satisfaction in this activity
- should take the form of questions and answers

Navaho author Juanita Platero began her literary collaboration with Californian Siyowin Miller in 1929. Since then Platero and Miller have written a novel, *The Winds Erase Your Footprints,* as well as a number of stories. Like the following story, most of their works explore the relationship between Navaho culture and the contemporary industrial world.

■ What happens when a person falls out of harmony with his or her cultural background?

*Juanita Platero and Siyowin Miller*

# Chee's Daughter

1 The hat told the story, the big, black, drooping Stetson.[1] It was not at the proper angle, the proper rakish angle for so young a Navaho.[2] There was no song, and that was not in keeping either. There should have been at least a humming, a faint, all-to-himself "he he he heya," for it was a good horse he was riding, a slender-legged, high-stepping buckskin[3] that would race the wind with light knee-urging. This was a day for singing, a warm winter day, when the touch of the sun upon the back belied the snow high on distant mountains.

Wind warmed by the sun touched his high-boned cheeks like flicker feathers, and still he rode on silently, deeper into Little Canyon, until the red rock walls rose straight upward from the stream bed and only a narrow piece of blue sky hung above. Abruptly the sky widened where the canyon walls were pushed back to make a wide place, as though in ancient times an angry stream had tried to go all ways at once.

---

1. **Stetson:** famous brand name for men's hats, especially the kind worn by cowboys.
2. **Navaho** [nav′ə hō′]: largest Indian tribe in the United States. The Navaho live in Arizona, New Mexico, and Utah and are known for their skill in weaving and making silver jewelry.
3. **buckskin:** yellowish-gray horse.

2 This was home—this wide place in the canyon—levels of jagged rock and levels of rich red earth. This was home to Chee, the rider of the buckskin, as it had been to many generations before him.

He stopped his horse at the stream and sat looking across the narrow ribbon of water to the bare-branched peach trees. He was seeing them each springtime with their age-gnarled limbs transfigured beneath veils of blossom pink; he was seeing them in autumn laden with their yellow fruit, small and sweet. Then his eyes searched out the indistinct furrows of the fields beside the stream, where each year the corn and beans and squash drank thirstily of the overflow from summer rains. Chee was trying to outweigh today's bitter betrayal of hope by gathering to himself these reminders of the integrity of the land. Land did not cheat! His mind lingered deliberately on all the days spent here in the sun caring for the young plants, his songs to the earth and to the life springing from it—". . . In the middle of the wide field. . . Yellow Corn Boy. . . He has started both ways. . ." then the 3 harvest and repayment in full measure. Here was the old feeling of wholeness and of oneness with the sun and earth and growing things.

*Chee's Daughter* 29

AT A GLANCE

- Although he is riding a good horse on a warm winter day, there is something "not right" about the young Navaho's manner as he returns to his home in Little Canyon.
- Feeling betrayed, Chee reminds himself of the integrity of the land.

LITERARY OPTIONS

- direct and indirect characterization
- theme
- internal and external conflict

THEMATIC OPTIONS

- roots and traditions
- harmony with nature
- patience in pursuing a goal

1 **INDIRECT CHARACTERIZATION**

The angle of the young Navaho's hat and his failure to sing on a warm winter day reveal he is troubled.

2 **SETTING**

Chee's home with a stream and "rich red earth" between "levels of jagged rock" has been home to generations of Navahos whose values and traditions have sprung from their life in the valley.

3 **THEME**

The values of Chee's people, whose livelihood has come from agriculture, stress oneness with the land.

## GUIDED READING

### LITERAL QUESTION

**1a.** What does Chee remember as he sits looking across the stream? (He remembers the peach trees laden with blossoms and with fruit; he remembers the days he has spent farming the furrows where corn, beans, and squash grow.)

### INFERENTIAL QUESTION

**1b.** Why might Chee spend time just looking at the land and remembering? (He feels discouraged and disappointed about something, and he probably hopes that his memories of the land will give him renewed strength and encouragement.)

- Chee rides to the family compound.
- By their behavior, he knows that his family has heard the news that his wife has died.
- Chee thinks of his three-year-old daughter, who follows him everywhere.

**1 INDIRECT CHARACTERIZATION**

Chee's smile at the sight of his daughter's small hogan reveals his great love of her.

**2 POINT OF VIEW**

By using limited third-person narration, the authors reveal only Chee's thoughts. Readers are not given any information beyond what Chee knows.

**3 INDIRECT CHARACTERIZATION**

The child's instinctive affection for her father reveals his nature as a loving, nurturing father who has done his best in his wife's absence.

Chee urged the buckskin toward the family compound where, secure in a recess of overhanging rock, was his mother's dome-shaped hogan,[4] red rock and red adobe like the ground on which it nestled. Not far from the hogan was the half-circle of brush like a dark shadow against the canyon wall—corral for sheep and goats. Farther from the hogan, in full circle, stood the horse corral made of heavy cedar branches sternly interlocked. Chee's long thin lips curved into a smile as he passed his daughter's tiny hogan squatted like a round Pueblo[5] oven beside the corral. He remembered the summer day when together they sat back on their heels and plastered wet adobe all about the circling wall of rock and the woven dome of piñon twigs. How his family laughed when the Little One herded the bewildered chickens into her tiny hogan as the first snow fell.

Then the smile faded from Chee's lips and his eyes darkened as he tied his horse to a corral post and turned to the strangely empty compound. "Someone has told them," he thought, "and they are inside weeping." He passed his mother's deserted loom on the south side of the hogan and pulled the rude wooden door toward him, bowing his head, hunching his shoulders to get inside.

His mother sat sideways by the center fire, her feet drawn up under her full skirts. Her hands were busy kneading dough in the chipped white basin. With her head down, her voice was muffled when she said, "The meal will soon be ready, Son."

Chee passed his father sitting against the wall, hat over his eyes as though asleep. He passed his older sister, who sat turning mutton ribs on a crude wire grill over the coals, noticed

---

4. **hogan:** Navaho house made with logs and adobe, which is red clay like earth.
5. **Pueblo** [pweb′lō]: referring to Indian tribes of the southwestern United States who live in villages made of adobe and stone. Pueblo Indians taught the Navaho to grow crops.

tears dropping on her hands: "She cared more for my wife than I realized," he thought.

Then because something must be said sometime, he tossed the black Stetson upon a bulging sack of wool and said, "You have heard, then." He could not shut from his mind how confidently he had set the handsome new hat on his head that very morning, slanting the wide brim over one eye: he was going to see his wife, and today he would ask the doctors about bringing her home; last week she had looked so much better.

His sister nodded but did not speak. His mother sniffled and passed her velveteen sleeve beneath her nose. Chee sat down, leaning against the wall. "I suppose I was a fool for hoping all the time. I should have expected this. Few of our people get well from the coughing sickness.[6] But *she* seemed to be getting better."

His mother was crying aloud now and blowing her nose noisily on her skirt. His father sat up, speaking gently to her.

Chee shifted his position and started a cigarette. His mind turned back to the Little One. At least she was too small to understand what had happened, the Little One who had been born three years before in the sanitarium where his wife was being treated for the coughing sickness, the Little One he had brought home to his mother's hogan to be nursed by his sister, whose baby was a few months older. As she grew fat-cheeked and sturdy-legged, she followed him about like a shadow; somehow her baby mind had grasped that of all those at the hogan who cared for her and played with her, he—Chee—belonged most to her. She sat cross-legged at his elbow when he worked silver at the forge; she rode before him in the saddle when he drove the horses to water; often she lay wakeful on her sheep pelts until he stretched out for the night in the darkened hogan and she could snuggle warm against him.

Chee blew smoke slowly, and some of the

---

6. **coughing sickness:** tuberculosis.

---

## GUIDED READING

### LITERAL QUESTIONS

**1a.** What does Chee say is the reason that his family is not outside when he gets home? (He says that "someone has told them and they are inside weeping.")

**2a.** What are some of the things that Chee and his daughter have done together? (They built her small hogan; she watched him work at the silver forge; she has ridden with him; she has snuggled against him at night.)

### INFERENTIAL QUESTIONS

**1b.** What can you infer about the feelings of Chee's mother, father, and sister toward his wife? (Their sadness indicates that they cared deeply for her.)

**2b.** What kind of a father do you think Chee is? (He appears to be a very loving, caring father who spends a great deal of time with his small daughter.)

sadness left his dark eyes as he said, "It is not as bad as it might be. It is not as though we are left with nothing."

Chee's sister arose, sobs catching in her throat, and rushed past him out the doorway. Chee sat upright, a terrible fear possessing him. For a moment his mouth could make no sound. Then: "The Little One! Mother, where is she?"

His mother turned her stricken face to him. "Your wife's people came after her this morning. They heard yesterday of their daughter's death through the trader at Red Sands."

Chee started to protest, but his mother shook her head slowly. "I didn't expect they would want the Little One either. But there is nothing you can do. She is a girl child and belongs to her mother's people; it is custom."

Frowning, Chee got to his feet, grinding his cigarette into the dirt floor. "Custom! When did my wife's parents begin thinking about custom? Why, the hogan where they live doesn't even face the east!"[7] He started toward the door. "Perhaps I can overtake them. Perhaps they don't realize how much we want her here with us. I'll ask them to give my daughter back to me. Surely, they won't refuse."

His mother stopped him gently with her outstretched hand. "You couldn't overtake them now. They were in the trader's car. Eat and rest, and think more about this."

"Have you forgotten how things have always been between you and your wife's people?" his father said.

That night, Chee's thoughts were troubled—half-forgotten incidents became disturbingly vivid—but early the next morning he saddled the buckskin and set out for the settlement of Red Sands. Even though his father-in-law, Old Man Fat, might laugh, Chee knew that he must talk to him. There were some things to which Old Man Fat might listen.

Chee rode the first part of the fifteen miles to Red Sands expectantly. The sight of sandstone buttes[8] near Cottonwood Spring reddening in the morning sun brought a song almost to his lips. He twirled his reins in salute to the small boy herding sheep toward many-colored Butterfly Mountain, watched with pleasure the feathers of smoke rising against tree-darkened western mesas[9] from the hogans sheltered there. But as he approached the familiar settlement sprawled in mushroom growth along the highway, he began to feel as though a scene from a bad dream was becoming real.

Several cars were parked around the trading store, which was built like two log hogans side by side, with red gas pumps in front and a sign across the tar-paper roofs: *Red Sands Trading Post—Groceries Gasoline Cold Drinks Sandwiches Indian Curios.* Back of the trading post an unpainted frame house and outbuildings squatted on the drab, treeless land. Chee and the Little One's mother had lived there when they stayed with his wife's people. That was according to custom—living with one's wife's people—but Chee had never been convinced that it was custom alone which prompted Old Man Fat and his wife to insist that their daughter bring her husband to live at the trading post.

Beside the post was a large hogan of logs, with brightly painted pseudo-Navaho[10] designs on the roof—a hogan with smoke-smudged windows and a garish blue door which faced north to the highway. Old Man Fat had offered Chee a hogan like this one. The trader would build it if he and his wife would live there and Chee would work at his forge, making silver jewelry where tourists could watch him. But Chee had asked instead for a piece of land for a cornfield and help in building a hogan far back from the highway

---

8. **buttes** [būts]: isolated hills with steep sides and flat tops.
9. **mesas** [mā′səz]: high plateaus.
10. **pseudo-Navaho** [sōō′dō]: imitation Navaho.

*Chee's Daughter* **31**

---

7. **east:** By Navaho custom the door of a house should face east.

**1 PLOT: NARRATIVE HOOK**

The chief conflict in the story becomes apparent when Chee learns that his wife's people have taken his Little One.

**2 THEME**

Chee's mother reminds him that, according to custom, his daughter must stay with her mother's family. Chee's family respects Navaho custom, even if it brings them unhappiness.

**3 SETTING**

Old Man Fat's hogan, with "pseudo-Navaho designs on the roof" and its "garish" blue door, facing, untraditionally, north, contrasts sharply with the natural, traditional adobe hogan of Chee's parents.

**4 THEME**

Chee wants to maintain the Navaho tradition of living from the land, and had rejected his father-in-law's commercialism.

---

## GUIDED READING

### LITERAL QUESTIONS

**1a.** In what ways do Chee's in-laws follow custom? (They have taken their daughter's girl child to live with them; they had insisted that Chee and his wife live with them when they were first married.)

**2a.** As Chee approaches the trading store, how does his mood change? (He begins to feel as if a scene from a nightmare is coming true.)

### INFERENTIAL QUESTIONS

**1b.** Chee believes strongly in following tradition and custom. Why does he not respect his wife's people for doing so? (He suspects they use "custom" to suit their purposes.)

**2b.** From this reaction what can you infer about Chee's feelings during the time that he and his wife had lived with Old Man Fat? (Chee was not happy living at the trading store. Just seeing it brings back unpleasant memories.)

- Chee sees Old Man Fat's wife weaving while tourists watch.
- He sees the Little One, who runs to Chee's embrace.
- Old Man Fat asks Chee angrily if he has come to spoil their business.

## 1 SETTING

Old Man Fat's hogan is a commercial establishment, in sharp contrast to the peaceful, natural hogan of Chee's parents.

## 2 INDIRECT CHARACTERIZATION

The interaction between daughter and father shows her love for him and tells the reader that he is a kind and loving father.

## 3 DIRECT CHARACTERIZATION

The authors tell the reader directly that Chee's father-in-law is fat, indolent, and now very angry.

and a corral for the sheep he had brought to this marriage.

A cold wind blowing down from the mountains began to whistle about Chee's ears. It flapped the gaudy Navaho rugs which were hung in one long bright line to attract tourists. It swayed the sign *Navaho Weaver at Work* beside the loom where Old Man Fat's wife sat hunched in her striped blanket, patting the colored thread of a design into place with a wooden comb. Tourists stood watching the weaver. More tourists stood in a knot before the hogan where the sign said: *See Inside a Real Navaho Home 25¢*.

Then the knot seemed to unravel as a few people returned to their cars; some had cameras; and there against the blue door Chee saw the Little One standing uncertainly. The wind was plucking at her new purple blouse and wide green skirt; it freed truant strands of soft dark hair from the meager queue[11] into which it had been tied with white yarn.

"Isn't she cunning!" one of the women tourists was saying as she turned away.

_____
11. **queue** [kū]: braid.

Chee's lips tightened as he began to look around for Old Man Fat. Finally he saw him passing among the tourists collecting coins.

Then the Little One saw Chee. The uncertainty left her face, and she darted through the crowd as her father swung down from his horse. Chee lifted her in his arms, hugging her tight. While he listened to her breathless chatter, he watched Old Man Fat bearing down on them, scowling.

As his father-in-law walked heavily across the graveled lot, Chee was reminded of a statement his mother sometimes made: "When you see a fat Navaho, you see one who hasn't worked for what he has."

Old Man Fat was fattest in the middle. There was indolence in his walk even though he seemed to hurry, indolence in his cheeks so plump they made his eyes squint, eyes now smoldering with anger.

Some of the tourists were getting into their cars and driving away. The old man said belligerently to Chee, "Why do you come here? To spoil our business? To drive people away?"

"I came to talk with you," Chee answered,

## GUIDED READING

### LITERAL QUESTION

**1a.** What are the tourists doing at Old Fat's hogan? (They are paying to watch Old Fat's wife weave and admiring Little One.)

### INFERENTIAL QUESTION

**1b.** From this information, why do you think Old Man Fat is anxious to have Chee's daughter live with him? (He wants to exploit her as a tourist attraction in order to make more money.)

AT A GLANCE

- Chee suggests to Old Man Fat that they share the care of the child, since his family's crops have been good.
- Scornful, Old Man Fat boasts that he and his wife eat food from cans.
- Chee recognizes the old argument between himself and his wife's family, who consider themselves "progressive."

trying to keep his voice steady as he faced the old man.

1   "We have nothing to talk about," Old Man Fat blustered and did not offer to touch Chee's extended hand.

"It's about the Little One." Chee settled his daughter more comfortably against his hip as he weighed carefully all the words he had planned to say. "We are going to miss her very much. It wouldn't be so bad if we knew that *part* of each year she could be with us. That might help you too. You and your wife are no longer young people and you have no young ones here to depend

2 upon." Chee chose his next words remembering the thriftlessness of his wife's parents, and their greed. "Perhaps we could share the care of this little one. Things are good with us. So much snow this year will make lots of grass for the sheep. We have good land for corn and melons."

Chee's words did not have the expected effect. Old Man Fat was enraged. "Farmers, all of you! Long-haired farmers! Do you think everyone must bend his back over the short-handled hoe in order to have food to eat?" His tone changed as he began to brag a little. "We not on-

ly have all the things from cans at the trader's, but when the Pueblos come past here on their way to town, we buy their salty jerked mutton,[12] young corn for roasting, dried sweet peaches."

Chee's dark eyes surveyed the land along the highway as the old man continued to brag about being "progressive." *He* no longer was tied to

3 the land. He and his wife made money easily and could *buy* all the things they wanted. Chee realized too late that he had stumbled into the old argument between himself and his wife's parents. They had never understood his feeling about the land—that a man took care of his land and it in turn took care of him. Old Man Fat and his wife scoffed at him, called him a Pueblo farmer, all during that summer when he planted and weeded and harvested. Yet they ate the green corn in their mutton stews, and the chili paste from the fresh ripe chilis, and the tortillas from the cornmeal his wife ground. None of this working and sweating in the sun for Old Man Fat, who talked proudly of his easy way of liv-

---

12. **jerked mutton:** strips of lamb dried and preserved in the sun, often called "jerky."

*Chee's Daughter*   **33**

1 **INDIRECT CHARACTERIZATION**

Old Man Fat's remark and failure to touch Chee's hand show that Old Man Fat does not like his son-in-law.

2 **DIRECT CHARACTERIZATION**

Through Chee's thoughts the authors tell the reader directly that his wife's parents are thriftless and greedy.

3 **THEME**

Conflicting values: Chee accepts the traditional Navaho belief in the importance of the land; Old Man Fat considers himself progressive because he has rejected tradition and operates in a cash society.

## GUIDED READING

### LITERAL QUESTION

**1a.** How does Old Man Fat react when Chee tells him that his family's land will yield plenty of food for the Little One? (He becomes very angry and denounces farmers.)

### INFERENTIAL QUESTION

**1b.** Why does Old Man Fat become so upset with farmers? (Farming is hard work, and Old Man Fat has rejected the traditional way of life because he is lazy. He may also feel threatened by Chee's success.)

- Chee offers to bring goods to the Little One; Old Man Fat tells him to stay away.
- At home, Chee questions the wisdom of traditional values; without his daughter, life seems meaningless.
- Chee herds sheep through "endless" days.

### 1 THEME

Chee's wife had accepted the traditional values and gone with him to live upon the land, which would never fail them.

### 2 INTERNAL CONFLICT

Chee struggles between his strong desire to ride away with his daughter and his knowledge that custom and law would require her return.

### 3 EXTERNAL CONFLICT

The conflict between Chee and his father-in-law continues as Old Man Fat rejects Chee's offer to bring food and clothing to his daughter.

### 4 STYLE: IMAGERY

The authors' appeal to the senses of smell ("the oily fragrance of chili powder," "coffee boiling") and sight ("a half of mutton hanging by the door;" "bright strings of chili") conveys the wealth of supplies in the comfortable hogan.

### 5 INTERNAL CONFLICT

Chee questions the Navaho traditions, wondering if the old statement, "Take care of the land and it will take care of you," remains true in changing times.

---

ing—collecting money from the trader who rented this strip of land beside the highway, collecting money from the tourists.

**1** Yet Chee had once won that argument. His wife had shared his belief in the integrity of the earth, that jobs and people might fail one, but the earth never would. After that first year she had turned from her own people and gone with Chee to Little Canyon.

Old Man Fat was reaching for the Little One. "Don't be coming here with plans for my daughter's daughter," he warned. "If you try to make trouble, I'll take the case to the government man in town."

**2** The impulse was strong in Chee to turn and ride off while he still had the Little One in his arms. But he knew his time of victory would be short. His own family would uphold the old custom of children, especially girl children, belonging to the mother's people. He would have to give his daughter up if the case were brought before the headman of Little Canyon, and certainly he would have no better chance before a strange white man in town.

He handed the bewildered Little One to her grandfather who stood watching every movement suspiciously. Chee asked, "If I brought you a few things for the Little One, would that be making trouble? Some velvet for a blouse, or some of the jerky she likes so well . . . this summer's melon?"

Old Man Fat backed away from him. "Well," he hesitated, as some of the anger disappeared from his face and beads of greed shone in his **3** eyes. "Well," he repeated. Then as the Little One began to squirm in his arms and cry, he said, "No! No! Stay away from here, you and all your family."

The sense of his failure deepened as Chee rode back to Little Canyon. But it was not until he sat with his family that evening in the hogan, while the familiar bustle of meal preparing went on about him, that he began to doubt the wisdom of the things he'd always believed. He

**34**  *The Short Story*

---

**4** smelled the coffee boiling and the oily fragrance of chili powder dusted into the bubbling pot of stew; he watched his mother turning round crusty fried bread in the small black skillet. All around him was plenty—a half of mutton hanging near the door, bright strings of chili drying, corn hanging by the braided husks, cloth bags of dried peaches. Yet in his heart was nothing.

He heard the familiar sounds of the sheep outside the hogan, the splash of water as his father filled the long drinking trough from the water barrel. When his father came in, Chee could not bring himself to tell a second time of the day's happenings. He watched his wiry, soft-spoken father while his mother told the story, saw his father's queue of graying hair quiver as he nodded his head with sympathetic exclamations.

**5** Chee's doubting, acrid thoughts kept forming: Was it wisdom his father had passed on to him, or was his inheritance only the stubbornness of a long-haired Navaho resisting change? Take care of the land and it will take care of you. True, the land had always given him food, but now food was not enough. Perhaps if he had gone to school, he would have learned a different kind of wisdom, something to help him now. A schoolboy might even be able to speak convincingly to this government man whom Old Man Fat threatened to call, instead of sitting here like a clod of earth itself—Pueblo farmer indeed. What had the land to give that would restore his daughter?

In the days that followed, Chee herded sheep. He got up in the half-light, drank the hot coffee his mother had ready, then started the flock moving. It was necessary to drive the sheep a long way from the hogan to find good winter forage. Sometimes Chee met friends or relatives who were on their way to town or to the road camp where they hoped to get work; then there was friendly banter and an exchange of news. But most of the days seemed endless; he could not walk far enough or fast enough from his

---

## GUIDED READING

### LITERAL QUESTIONS

**1a.** How does Old Man Fat respond when Chee asks if he can bring some things to his daughter? (After a moment's hesitation Old Man Fat tells Chee to stay away.)

**2a.** What does Chee begin to question after he returns home without his daughter? (He begins to question the wisdom of the ancient beliefs of his people; in particular, remaining close to the land.)

### INFERENTIAL QUESTIONS

**1b.** Although Old Man Fat is greedy, why does he tell Chee not to bring things for his daughter? (When the Little One squirms and begins to cry, Old Man Fat recognizes that she wants to go with her father and he wants to break the bond between them.)

**2b.** Why does Chee have these questions? (He does not know how the land can provide a way for him to get his daughter back.)

memories of the Little One or from his bitter
**1** thoughts. Sometimes it seemed his daughter
trudged beside him, so real he could almost hear
her footsteps—the muffled pad-pad of little feet
in deerhide. In the glare of a snowbank he would
see her vivid face, brown eyes sparkling. Mingling with the tinkle of sheep bells he heard her
laughter.

When, weary of following the small sharp
hoof marks that crossed and recrossed in the
snow, he sat down in the shelter of a rock, it was
only to be reminded that in his thoughts he had
forsaken his brotherhood with the earth and sun
and growing things. If he remembered times
when he had flung himself against the earth to
rest, to lie there in the sun until he could no
longer feel where he left off and the earth began,
it was to remember also that now he sat like an
alien against the same earth; the belonging together was gone. The earth was one thing and
he was another.

It was during the days when he herded sheep
that Chee decided he must leave Little Canyon.
Perhaps he would take a job silversmithing for
one of the traders in town. Perhaps, even though
he spoke little English, he could get a job at the
road camp with his cousins; he would ask them
about it.

Springtime transformed the mesas. The
peach trees in the canyon were shedding
fragrance and pink blossoms on the gentled
wind. The sheep no longer foraged for the
yellow seeds of chamiso[13] but ranged near the
hogan with the long-legged new lambs, eating
tender young grass.

Chee was near the hogan on the day his cousins rode up with the message for which he
**2** waited. He had been watching with mixed emotions while his father and his sister's husband
cleared the fields beside the stream.

"The boss at the camp says he needs an extra

---

13. **chamiso** [chə mē′sō]: desert shrub.

hand, but he wants to know if you'll be willing
to go with the camp when they move it to the
other side of the town?'' The tall cousin shifted
his weight in the saddle.

The other cousin took up the explanation.
"The work near here will last only until the new
cutoff beyond Red Sands is finished. After that,
the work will be too far away for you to get back
here often.''

That was what Chee had wanted—to get away
from Little Canyon—yet he found himself not so
interested in the job beyond town as in this new
cutoff which was almost finished. He pulled a
blade of grass, split it thoughtfully down the
center, as he asked questions of his cousins.
Finally he said: "I need to think more about this.
If I decide on this job, I'll ride over.''

Before his cousins were out of sight down
the canyon, Chee was walking toward the fields,
a bold plan shaping in his mind. As the plan
began to flourish, wild and hardy as young
tumbleweed, Chee added his own voice softly to
the song his father was singing: ''. . . In the middle of the wide field . . . Yellow Corn Boy . . .
I wish to put in.''
**3** Chee walked slowly around the field, the rich
red earth yielding to his footsteps. His plan depended upon this land and upon the things he
remembered most about his wife's people.

Through planting time Chee worked zealous-
ly and tirelessly. He spoke little of the large new
field he was planting, because he felt so strongly
that just now this was something between him-
**4** self and the land. The first days he was ever
stooping, piercing the ground with the pointed
stick, placing the corn kernels there, walking
around the field and through it, singing, ''. . . His
track leads into the ground . . . Yellow Corn
Boy . . . his track leads into the ground.'' After
that, each day Chee walked through his field
watching for the tips of green to break through;
first a few spikes in the center and then more
and more, until the corn in all parts of the field
was above ground. Surely, Chee thought, if he

*Chee's Daughter* **35**

- Chee considers leaving home.
- Chee learns about a cutoff. Chee devises a plan.
- He plants a large new field and watches the plants grow.

**1 INDIRECT CHARACTERIZATION**

By relating Chee's ever-present thoughts about his daughter, the authors show the depth of his love for her.

**2 CONFLICT**

Because he feels alienated from the land, Chee can only watch as others begin the traditional task of clearing the fields, a task in which he normally would have joined.

**3 THEME**

Chee turns to the land to seek a solution to his problem.

**4 INDIRECT CHARACTERIZATION**

Chee is singing; he is happy, he has a plan, and he feels at peace as he works hard on the land.

## GUIDED READING

### LITERAL QUESTIONS

**1a.** What is the information, given to Chee by his cousins, that he finds most interesting? (He is most interested in the new cutoff beyond Red Sands.)

**2a.** Upon what does Chee's plan depend? (It depends upon the land and upon what he remembers about his wife's family.)

### INFERENTIAL QUESTIONS

**1b.** Why do you think that Chee finds that information so interesting? (Old Man Fat's hogan is at Red Sands. Chee may feel that the cutoff will reduce Old Man Fat's tourist business.)

**2b.** What do you think Chee remembers about his wife's family that may help him get his daughter back? (He probably remembers that they are very greedy and lazy. They will probably not cope well with economic hardship.)

- Convinced that the land will not forsake him, Chee plants and cultivates his crops.
- At summer's end Chee puts bulging packs on his ponies and rides over to find Red Sands Trading Post closed, as he expected.

**1 INDIRECT CHARACTERIZATION**

Chee's hard, patient work shows that he has returned to trusting the land that he loves.

**2 STYLE: PERSONIFICATION**

The comparison of the corn plants to people who "waved green arms" and "bent to embrace" reflects Chee's happy mood and reinforces the Navaho sense of oneness with the land.

sang the proper songs, if he cared for this land faithfully, it would not forsake him now, even though through the lonely days of winter he had betrayed the goodness of the earth in his thoughts.

1     Through the summer Chee worked long days, the sun hot upon his back, pulling weeds from around young corn plants; he planted squash and pumpkin; he terraced[14] a small piece of land near his mother's hogan and planted carrots and onions and the moisture-loving chili. He was increasingly restless. Finally he told his family what he hoped the harvest from this land would bring him. Then the whole family waited with him, watching the corn: the slender graceful

2 plants that waved green arms and bent to embrace each other as young winds wandered through the field, the maturing plants flaunting their pollen-laden tassels in the sun, the tall and sturdy parent corn with new-formed ears and a froth of purple, red, and yellow corn beards against the dusty emerald of broad leaves.

Summer was almost over when Chee slung the bulging packs across two pack ponies. His

---

14. **terraced:** made land on a hillside suitable for farming by dividing it into a series of flat steps.

**36**    *The Short Story*

mother helped him tie the heavy rolled pack behind the saddle of the buckskin. Chee knotted the new yellow kerchief about his neck a little tighter, gave the broad black hat brim an extra tug, but these were only gestures of assurance and he knew it. The land had not failed him. That part was done. But this he was riding into? Who could tell?

When Chee arrived at Red Sands, it was as he had expected to find it—no cars on the highway. His cousins had told him that even the Pueblo farmers were using the new cutoff to town. The barren gravel around the Red Sands Trading Post was deserted. A sign banged against the dismantled gas pumps: *Closed until further notice.*

Old Man Fat came from the crude summer shelter built beside the log hogan from a few branches of scrub cedar and the sides of wooden crates. He seemed almost friendly when he saw Chee.

"Get down, my son," he said, eyeing the bulging packs. There was no bluster in his voice today, and his face sagged, looking somewhat saddened, perhaps because his cheeks were no longer quite full enough to push his eyes upward at the corners. "You are going on a journey?"

Chee shook his head. "Our fields gave us so

AT A GLANCE

- Chee claims that he has extra produce to sell to the trader.
- Old Man Fat admits that they are not doing well.
- Old Man Fat's wife says that they have sold their brass bed.

**1 INDIRECT CHARACTERIZATION**

Chee's claim that he has come to sell to the trader reveals his cleverness: He will be canny and indirect in dealing with Old Man Fat.

**2 STYLE: IMAGERY**

Repetition of the word *corn* and detailed description of the colors provide the reader with a sense of the abundance of the supplies.

1 much this year, I thought to sell or trade this to the trader. I didn't know he was no longer here."

Old Man Fat sighed, his voice dropping to an injured tone. "He says he and his wife are going to rest this winter; then after that he'll build a place up on the new highway."

Chee moved as though to be traveling on, then jerked his head toward the pack ponies. "Anything you need?"

"I'll ask my wife," Old Man Fat said as he led the way to the shelter. "Maybe she has a little money. Things have not been too good with us since the trader closed. Only a few tourists come this way." He shrugged his shoulders. "And with the trader gone—no credit."

Chee was not deceived by his father-in-law's unexpected confidences. He recognized them as a hopeful bid for sympathy and, if possible, something for nothing. Chee made no answer. He was thinking that so far he had been right about his wife's parents: their thriftlessness had left them with no resources to last until Old Man Fat found another easy way of making a living.

Old Man Fat's wife was in the shelter working at her loom. She turned rather wearily when her husband asked with noticeable deference if she would give him money to buy supplies. Chee surmised that the only income here was from his mother-in-law's weaving.

She peered around the corner of the shelter at the laden ponies, and then she looked at Chee. "What do you have there, my son?"

Chee smiled to himself as he turned to pull the pack from one of the ponies, dragged it to the 2 shelter where he untied the ropes. Pumpkins and hard-shelled squash tumbled out, and the ears of corn—pale yellow husks fitting firmly over plump ripe kernels, blue corn, red corn, yellow corn, many-colored corn, ears and ears of it—tumbled into every corner of the shelter.

"Yooooh," Old Man Fat's wife exclaimed as she took some of the ears in her hands. Then she glanced up at her son-in-law. "But we have no money for all this. We have sold almost everything we own—even the brass bed that stood in the hogan."

Old Man Fat's brass bed. Chee concealed his amusement as he started back for another pack. That must have been a hard parting. Then he stopped, for, coming from the cool darkness of the hogan was the Little One, rubbing her eyes as though she had been asleep. She stood for a moment in the doorway, and Chee saw that she was

*Chee's Daughter* **37**

---

**LITERAL QUESTION**

**1a.** What does Chee claim is the reason he has brought his produce to Red Sands? (He says that they have had a good harvest, and he hoped to sell the excess to the trader.)

**INFERENTIAL QUESTION**

**1b.** What is the real reason Chee has come? (He thinks that Old Man Fat and his wife are having a hard time and hopes he can bargain for the Little One based on their need for the supplies.)

- The Little One runs toward Chee.
- When Chee admits that he wants something other than money, Old Man Fat says they will not give the child up for food.
- Chee offers to leave the supplies.
- When her grandparents see Little One as just another mouth to feed, they agree to give her up.
- Chee rides off singing with his daughter before him in the saddle.

**1 PLOT DEVELOPMENT**

Because of his impatience, Chee creates an obstacle when he indicates too soon that he wants his daughter instead of money for the food.

**2 INDIRECT CHARACTERIZATION**

This final salvo reveals Chee's intelligence: His careful words help the greedy in-laws to see Little One as someone with whom they will have to share their bounty.

**3 PLOT: CLIMAX**

When the old woman decides that the Little One can go, the external conflict faced by Chee is happily resolved.

REFLECTING ON THE STORY

What are the values by which Chee lives? (Possible answers include that he values tradition, a life in harmony with nature, hard labor, a oneness with the land, and love of one's child.)

---

dirty, barefoot, her hair uncombed, her little blouse shorn of all its silver buttons. Then she ran toward Chee, her arms outstretched. Heedless of Old Man Fat and his wife, her father caught her in his arms, her hair falling in a dark cloud across his face, the sweetness of her laughter warm against his shoulder.

**1** It was the haste within him to get this slow waiting game played through to the finish that made Chee speak unwisely. It was the desire to swing her before him in the saddle and ride fast to Little Canyon that prompted his words. "The money doesn't matter. You still have something...."

Chee knew immediately that he had overspoken. The old woman looked from him to the corn spread before her. Unfriendliness began to harden in his father-in-law's face. All the old arguments between himself and his wife's people came pushing and crowding in between them now.

Old Man Fat began kicking the ears of corn **2** back onto the canvas as he eyed Chee angrily. "And you rode all the way over here thinking that for a little food we would give up our daughter's daughter?"

Chee did not wait for the old man to reach for the Little One. He walked dazedly to the shelter, rubbing his cheek against her soft dark hair, and put her gently into her grandmother's lap. Then he turned back to the horses. He had **3** failed. By his own haste he had failed. He swung into the saddle, his hand touching the roll behind it. Should he ride on into town?

Then he dismounted, scarcely glancing at Old Man Fat, who stood uncertainly at the corner of the shelter, listening to his wife. "Give me a hand with this other pack of corn, Grandfather," Chee said, carefully keeping the small bit of hope from his voice.

Puzzled, but willing, Old Man Fat helped carry the other pack to the shelter, opening it to find more corn as well as carrots and round, pale

yellow onions. Chee went back for the roll behind the buckskin's saddle and carried it to the entrance of the shelter, where he cut the ropes and gave the canvas a nudge with his toe. Tins of coffee rolled out, small plump cloth bags; jerked meat from several butcherings spilled from a flour sack; and bright red chilis splashed like flames against the dust.

"I will leave all this anyhow," Chee told them. "I would not want my daughter nor even you old people to go hungry."

Old Man Fat picked up a shiny tin of coffee, then put it down. With trembling hands he began to untie one of the cloth bags—dried sweet peaches.

The Little One had wriggled from her grandmother's lap, unheeded, and was on her knees, digging her hands into the jerked meat.

"There is almost enough food here to last all winter." Old Man Fat's wife sought the eyes of her husband.

Chee said, "I meant it to be enough. But that **2** was when I thought you might send the Little One back with me." He looked down at his daughter noisily sucking jerky. Her mouth, both fists, were full of it. "I am sorry that you feel you cannot bear to part with her."

Old Man Fat's wife brushed a straggly wisp of gray hair from her forehead as she turned to look at the Little One. Old Man Fat was looking too. And it was not a thing to see. For in that moment **3** the Little One ceased to be their daughter's daughter and became just another mouth to feed.

"And why not?" the old woman asked wearily.

Chee was settled in the saddle, the barefooted Little One before him. He urged the buckskin faster, and his daughter clutched his shirtfront. The purpling mesas flung back the echo: "...My corn embrace each other. In the middle of the wide field...Yellow Corn Boy embrace each other."

---

## *GUIDED READING*

### LITERAL QUESTIONS

**1a.** In his impatience what does Chee reveal that causes his in-laws to become angry with him? (He reveals that he wants his daughter in exchange for the food.)

**2a.** What does Chee say when Old Man Fat's wife declares there is almost enough food to last all winter? (He says that he meant it to be enough for the two of them.)

### INFERENTIAL QUESTIONS

**1b.** What causes Chee to become impatient and reveal his real motive for coming? (His love for his daughter is so great that when he sees her, he speaks without thinking.)

**2b.** What do Chee's words help Old Man Fat's wife realize? (She realizes they will have to buy more food if they want to keep Little One.)

## STUDY QUESTIONS

### Recalling

1. Why does Chee's daughter go to live with his in-laws?
2. Explain the "old argument" that stands between Chee and his wife's family.
3. What steps does Chee take to bring his daughter home? Explain how he finally succeeds.

### Interpreting

4. Find four or five details in the story that illustrate Chee's feeling of oneness with nature.
5. What differences are there between Chee's home and that of Old Man Fat? How do these differences reflect the conflict between the two men?
6. What conflict does Chee experience within himself after his meeting with his father-in-law? Explain how the ending of the story helps to resolve this conflict.

### Extending

7. What is this story saying about the relationship between a person's roots and his or her identity?

## VIEWPOINT

The anthropologist Alfonso Ortiz interprets the Navaho attitude toward the land in this way:

> The Navahos believe that evil and suffering occur when man gets out of harmony with his environment.

■ Is this attitude expressed in "Chee's Daughter"? Why or why not?

## LITERARY FOCUS

### Direct and Indirect Characterization

Authors use **direct characterization** when they make direct statements about their characters' personalities. We can accept as the truth an author's direct statement that a character is gentle or intelligent. In addition, authors frequently use the technique of **indirect characterization** to reveal their characters' personalities through their thoughts, words, and actions, or through the comments of other characters. Indirect characterization requires us to interpret a character's behavior to decide what that character is like.

### Thinking About Characterization

■ Describe Old Man Fat's personality. What do the authors directly tell us about him? What do his words and actions reveal about him?

## VOCABULARY

### Word Origins

The origin and history of a word is called its **etymology**. You can find a word's etymology in a dictionary by reading the information that is usually given in brackets [ ] just before or after the definitions. A dictionary would print the etymology for the word *canyon* as follows:

**can-yon** (kan′yən) *n.* [Spanish *cañón* tube, gorge, going back to Latin *canna* reed, cane. See CANE.]
— *Macmillan Dictionary*

This entry tells us that the word comes from a Spanish word and earlier from a Latin word.

If you look up *pumpkin* in a dictionary, you can trace its origins back to the Middle French word *pompon*, the Latin *pepo*, and, earliest of all, the Greek *pepon*, which means "cooked by the sun."

Look up the etymologies of the following words from "Chee's Daughter," and write what you find out about their history.

1. adobe
2. butte
3. hogan
4. tortilla
5. melon
6. mesa
7. pueblo
8. squash
9. chili
10. Navaho

## COMPOSITION

### Writing About Character

■ Describe the character of Chee as it is revealed by both direct and indirect characterization. First tell what the authors directly say about Chee. Then explain what is indirectly revealed by Chee's actions, words, thoughts, and feelings, and the words of others.

### Writing a Letter

■ Imagine that you are a tourist visiting Old Man Fat's trading post. Write a letter to a good friend describing what you have seen. Decide how you as a tourist feel about the post, and describe it so that your reader can share your perception of it.

*Chee's Daughter* **39**

## STUDY QUESTIONS

1. Navaho custom
2. traditional agrarian values *vs.* "progressive" scorn for land and custom
3. appeals to in-laws' greed with offer of food
4. finds comfort in surveying fields after wife's death; believes land will care for him; believes earth will provide way of winning child back; appreciates bountiful harvest
5. *Chee:* peaceful, orderly traditional hogan; *Old Man Fat:* "imitation" Navaho dwelling at trading post; traditional values *vs.* commercialism and greed
6. desire to take daughter *vs.* breaking tradition and the law; wins daughter by being true to values
7. Roots are a source of strength.

## VIEWPOINT

Yes; in-laws' greed reflected in their squalid lives; Chee's family lives in harmony and prosperity

## LITERARY FOCUS

greedy; lazy; authors say there was "indolence" in his walk; his own words show that he is selfish, weak, and arrogant

## VOCABULARY

1. Spanish from Arabic *at-toba,* brick
2. French from Old French *buter,* to thrust against
3. Navaho *qoghan,* house
4. Spanish diminutive of *torta,* cake
5. Middle English from Old French from Late Latin *melo* from Latin *melopepo* from Greek *melopepon,* apple-shaped melon
6. Spanish from Latin *mensa,* table
7. Spanish from Latin *populus,* people
8. native American *askootasquash,* fleshy fruit of the gourd family
9. Mexican from Nahuatl *chilli,* dried red pepper
10. Spanish from native American, *Navahu,* great fields

---

## COMPOSITION: GUIDELINES FOR EVALUATION

### WRITING ABOUT CHARACTER

#### Objective
To write a character study

#### Guidelines for Evaluation
- suggested length: three to five paragraphs
- should cite examples of what the *authors* say about Chee
- should cite examples in which Chee's character is revealed through thoughts, words, and actions

### WRITING A LETTER

#### Objective
To write a description of the trading post; to convey the writer's attitude toward it

#### Guidelines for Evaluation
- suggested length: three to five paragraphs
- should describe the post in detail
- should use language and details that make clear the writer's attitude

AT A GLANCE

- Strong-willed Hester is a Mid-western farmer's wife whose husband, William, usually follows her advice.
- William respects his wife but is a silent, hard man with his sons and neighbors.

LITERARY OPTIONS

- characterization
- conflict
- tone

THEMATIC OPTIONS

- appearance and reality
- family relations
- importance of memories

**1 DIRECT CHARACTERIZATION**

Cather uses direct statements to tell us that Hester is a strong, executive woman.

**2 CONFLICT**

This particular passage may suggest that Cather is preparing us for a conflict with unexpected turns.

**3 TONE**

Cather continues to use terse language to round out and reflect the character of William Tavener.

**4 CONFLICT**

Hester's method of indulging her sons without her husband's knowledge is evidence of the external conflict between them; it further fuels the image of Hester as strong-willed.

Willa Cather (1873–1947) was a poet, short story writer, and Pulitzer Prize–winning novelist. She grew up in Nebraska, and although she spent much of her adult life in cities, she never lost her sense of the American landscape. In works like *My Ántonia,* her most popular novel, and the following story, Cather recalls both the hardships and the satisfactions of life on the frontier.

■ How can one brief conversation change a relationship, even a long-time one, forever?

*Willa Cather*

# The Sentimentality of William Tavener

It takes a strong woman to make any sort of success of living in the West, and Hester undoubtedly was that. When people spoke of William Tavener as the most prosperous farmer in McPherson County, they usually added that his 1 wife was a "good manager." She was an executive woman, quick of tongue and something of an imperatrix.[1] The only reason her husband did not consult her about his business was that she did not wait to be consulted.

It would have been quite impossible for one man, within the limited sphere of human action, to follow all Hester's advice, but in the end William usually acted upon some of her suggestions. When she incessantly denounced the "shiftlessness" of letting a new threshing machine[2] stand unprotected in the open, he eventually built a shed for it. When she sniffed contemptuously at his notion of fencing a hog corral with sod walls, he made a spiritless beginning on the structure—merely to "show his tem-

per," as she put it—but in the end he went off quietly to town and bought enough barbed wire to complete the fence. When the first heavy rains came on, and the pigs rooted down the sod wall and made little paths all over it to facilitate their ascent, he heard his wife relate with relish the story of the little pig that built a mud house, 2 to the minister at the dinner table, and William's gravity never relaxed for an instant. Silence, indeed, was William's refuge and his strength.

William set his boys a wholesome example to respect their mother. People who knew him very well suspected that he even admired her. 3 He was a hard man towards his neighbors, and even towards his sons: grasping, determined, and ambitious.

There was an occasional blue day about the house when William went over the store bills, but he never objected to items relating to his wife's gowns or bonnets. So it came about that 4 many of the foolish, unnecessary little things that Hester bought for her boys, she had charged to her personal account.

One spring night Hester sat in a rocking chair by the sitting-room window, darning socks. She

---

1. **imperatrix** [im′pə ra′triks]: female emperor or commander.
2. **threshing machine:** machine that separates grain from worthless plant matter.

*GUIDED READING*

**LITERAL QUESTIONS**

**1a.** What words describe Hester? What words describe William? (Hester is strong, quick of tongue, a good manager, an executive woman, and an imperatrix. William is silent, hard, grasping, determined, and ambitious.)

**2a.** How does William usually react to Hester's personal purchases? (He never objects.)

**INFERENTIAL QUESTIONS**

**1b.** In view of these traits, what do you think domestic life is like for Hester and William? (There are probably many small battles of will, with very little real communication between them.)

**2b.** What does William's attitude towards Hester's personal purchases suggest about his feeling for her? (his unexpressed feelings of tenderness toward his wife) rocked violently and sent her long needle vigorously back and forth over her gourd,[3] and it took only a very casual glance to see that she was wrought up over something. William sat on the other side of the table reading his farm paper. If he had noticed his wife's agitation, his calm, clean-shaven face betrayed no sign of concern. He must have noticed the sarcastic turn of her remarks at the supper table, and he must have noticed the moody silence of the older boys as they ate. When supper was but half over, little Billy, the youngest, had suddenly pushed back his plate and slipped away from the table, manfully trying to swallow a sob. But William Tavener never heeded ominous forecasts in the domestic horizon, and he never looked for a storm until it broke.

After supper the boys had gone to the pond under the willows in the big cattle corral, to get rid of the dust of plowing. Hester could hear an occasional splash and a laugh ringing clear through the stillness of the night, as she sat by the open window. She sat silent for almost an hour reviewing in her mind many plans of attack. But she was too vigorous a woman to be much of a strategist, and she usually came to her point with directness. At last she cut her thread and suddenly put her darning down, saying emphatically:

"William, I don't think it would hurt you to let the boys go to that circus in town tomorrow."

William continued to read his farm paper, but it was not Hester's custom to wait for an answer. She usually divined his arguments and assailed them one by one before he uttered them.

"You've been short of hands all summer, and you've worked the boys hard, and a man ought use his own flesh and blood as well as he does his hired hands. We're plenty able to afford it, and it's little enough our boys ever spend. I don't see how you can expect 'em to be steady and hard workin', unless you encourage 'em a little. I never could see much harm in circuses, and our boys have never been to one. Oh, I know Jim Howley's boys get drunk an' carry on when they go, but our boys ain't that sort, an' you know it, William. The animals are real instructive, an' our boys don't get to see much out here on the prairie. It was different where we were raised, but the boys have got no advantages here, an' if you don't take care, they'll grow up to be greenhorns."

Hester paused a moment, and William folded up his paper, but vouchsafed no remark. His sisters in Virginia had often said that only a quiet man like William could ever have lived with Hester Perkins. Secretly, William was rather proud of his wife's "gift of speech," and of the fact that she could talk in prayer meeting as fluently as a man. He confined his own efforts in that line to a brief prayer at Covenant meetings.

Hester shook out another sock and went on.

"Nobody was ever hurt by goin' to a circus. Why, law me! I remember I went to one myself once, when I was little. I had most forgot about it. It was over at Pewtown, an' I remember how I had set my heart on going. I don't think I'd ever forgiven my father if he hadn't taken me, though that red clay road was in a frightful way after the rain. I mind they had an elephant and six poll parrots, an' a Rocky Mountain lion, an' a cage of monkeys, an' two camels. My! but they were a sight to me then!"

Hester dropped the black sock and shook her head and smiled at the recollection. She was not expecting anything from William yet, and she was fairly startled when he said gravely, in much the same tone in which he announced the hymns in prayer meeting:

"No, there was only one camel. The other was a dromedary."[4]

---

3. **gourd** [gōord]: hard, inedible fruit. Hester places the gourd inside a sock to make darning easier.

4. **dromedary** [drom´ə der´ē]: camel with one hump, native to North Africa.

*The Sentimentality of William Tavener* **41**

**1 STYLE: METAPHOR**

A farmer's activities depend upon the weather. Cather uses meteorological metaphors to convey the atmosphere of conflict in the Taveners' home.

**2 VOCABULARY: DIALECT**

Cather writes the conversation to indicate the way that a midwestern farm family of that era might speak: Words such as *workin'* and *ain't* are liberally sprinkled in, adding more personality to the characters.

**3 POINT OF VIEW**

The omniscient point of view enables the reader to see most events through Hester's eyes but also allows the reader to know about William's secret pride in his wife.

**4 THEME**

William startles Hester and the reader by breaking the silence to correct his wife's story.

## GUIDED READING

**LITERAL QUESTION**

**1a.** What indications at the supper table show William that the rest of his family is upset about something? (Hester makes sarcastic remarks; the boys are moody and silent; little Billy leaves the table on the brink of tears.)

**INFERENTIAL QUESTION**

**1b.** What does William's failure to respond tell you about him? (He is accustomed to dealing with family discontent only when he can ignore it no longer.)

## 1 CHARACTERIZATION

William shows a vulnerability in admitting that he deceived his own father; his admission elicits an unusual defense of his behavior from Hester. Both are shown directly to be round characters with contradictory personality traits.

## 2 STYLE: TONE

Hester's sympathetic response to William's childhood escapade is a breakthrough; after years of being his adversary, she is finally "on his side" again.

## 3 POINT OF VIEW

The narrator juxtaposes descriptions of external events with Hester's thoughts. Hester's movement of her chair closer to William not only shows her interest in what he is saying but also symbolizes the growing emotional closeness she is feeling for her husband.

## 4 THEME

Before this discussion their relationship had been antagonistic. Their struggle over family issues had compromised their intimacy.

COME TO THE CIRCUS

She peered around the lamp and looked at him keenly.

"Why, William, how come you to know?"

William folded his paper and answered with some hesitation, "I was there, too."

Hester's interest flashed up. "Well, I never, William! To think of my finding it out after all these years! Why, you couldn't have been much bigger'n our Billy then. It seems queer I never saw you when you was little, to remember about you. But then you Back Creek folks never have anything to do with us Gap people. But how come you to go? Your father was stricter with you than you are with your boys."

"I reckon I shouldn't 'a gone," he said slowly, "but boys will do foolish things. I had done a good deal of fox hunting the winter before, and **1** Father let me keep the bounty⁵ money. I hired Tom Smith's Tap to weed the corn for me, an' I slipped off unbeknownst to Father an' went to the show."

Hester spoke up warmly: "Nonsense, William! It didn't do you no harm, I guess. You was always worked hard enough. It must have been a big sight for a little fellow. That clown must have just tickled you to death."

William crossed his knees and leaned back in his chair.

"I reckon I could tell all that fool's jokes now. Sometimes I can't help thinkin' about 'em in meetin' when the sermon's long. I mind I had on a pair of new boots that hurt me like the mischief, but I forgot all about 'em when that fellow rode the donkey. I recall I had to take them boots off as soon as I got out of sight o' town, and walked home in the mud barefoot."

**2** "O poor little fellow!" Hester ejaculated, drawing her chair nearer and leaning her elbows on the table. "What cruel shoes they did use to make for children. I remember I went up to Back Creek to see the circus wagons go by. They came down from Romney, you know. The circus men stopped at the creek to water the animals, an' the elephant got stubborn an' broke a big limb off the yellow willow tree that grew there by the tollhouse porch, an' the Scribners were 'fraid as death he'd pull the house down. But this much I saw him do; he waded in the creek an' filled his trunk with water and squirted it in at the window and nearly ruined Ellen Scribner's pink lawn dress that she had just ironed an' laid out on the bed ready to wear to the circus."

"I reckon that must have been a trial to Ellen," chuckled William, "for she was mighty prim in them days."

**3** Hester drew her chair still nearer William's. Since the children had begun growing up, her conversation with her husband had been almost wholly confined to questions of economy and expense. Their relationship had become purely a business one, like that between landlord and ten- **4** ant. In her desire to indulge her boys she had unconsciously assumed a defensive and almost hostile attitude towards her husband. No debtor ever haggled with his usurer⁶ more doggedly than did Hester with her husband in behalf of her sons. The strategic contest had gone on so long that it had almost crowded out the memory

---

5. **bounty:** reward. Farmers paid bounties to anyone who killed animals that destroyed farm property.

6. **usurer** [ū'zhər ər]: person who lends money at a high rate of interest.

## GUIDED READING

### LITERAL QUESTIONS

**1a.** What causes Hester to look at William "keenly"? (By correcting a detail in her story, William suggests that he was at the same circus.)

**2a.** What two pairs of financial/business terms does Cather use to describe the couple's past relationship? (She uses *landlord* and *tenant, debtor* and *usurer*.)

### INFERENTIAL QUESTIONS

**1b.** What do you predict will be William's final response to Hester's request that he let the boys go to the circus? (After reminiscing about many subjects with his wife, William will allow the boys to attend the circus.)

**2b.** By casting Hester as *tenant* and *debtor*, what does Cather suggest about the dynamics of the relationship? (Hester is an intelligent woman who feels subordinate to her husband.)

of a closer relationship. This exchange of confidences tonight, when common recollections took them unawares and opened their hearts, had all the miracle of romance. They talked on and on; of old neighbors, of old familiar faces in the valley where they had grown up, of long forgotten incidents of their youth—weddings, picnics, sleighing parties and baptizings. For years they had talked of nothing else but butter and eggs and the prices of things, and now they had as much to say to each other as people who meet after a long separation.

When the clock struck ten, William rose and went over to his walnut secretary[7] and unlocked it. From his red leather wallet he took out a ten-dollar bill and laid it on the table beside Hester.

"Tell the boys not to stay late, an' not to drive the horses hard," he said quietly, and went off to bed.

Hester blew out the lamp and sat still in the dark a long time. She left the bill lying on the **table where William had placed it. She had a painful sense of having missed something, or lost something; she felt that somehow the years had cheated her.**

The little locust trees that grew by the fence were white with blossoms. Their heavy odor floated in to her on the night wind and recalled a night long ago, when the first whippoorwill[8] of

---

7. **secretary:** kind of desk.
8. **whippoorwill** [hwip′ər wil′]: North American bird whose call sounds like its name.

the spring was heard, and the rough, buxom girls of Hawkins Gap had held her laughing and struggling under the locust trees, and searched in her bosom for a lock of her sweetheart's hair, which is supposed to be on every girl's breast when the first whippoorwill sings. Two of those same girls had been her bridesmaids. Hester had been a very happy bride. She rose and went softly into the room where William lay. He was sleeping heavily, but occasionally moved his hand before his face to ward off the flies. Hester went into the parlor and took the piece of mosquito net from the basket of wax apples and pears that her sister had made before she died. One of the boys had brought it all the way from Virginia, packed in a tin pail, since Hester would not risk shipping **so precious an ornament by freight. She went back to the bedroom and spread the net over William's head. Then she sat down by the bed and listened to his deep, regular breathing until she heard the boys returning. She went out to meet them** and warn them not to waken their father.

"I'll be up early to get your breakfast, boys. Your father says you can go to the show." As she handed the money to the eldest, she felt a sudden throb of allegiance to her husband and said sharply, "And you be careful of that, an' don' waste it. Your father works hard for his money."

The boys looked at each other in astonishment and felt that they had lost a powerful ally.

---

## STUDY QUESTIONS

### Recalling

1. What specific personality traits are Hester and William described as having at the beginning of the story?
2. Briefly summarize the passage on page 42 that describes Hester and William's relationship.

According to this passage, why is their conversation about the circus unusual for them?
3. What does Hester do before she goes to bed? What does she tell the boys?

### Interpreting

4. Why do you think William gives Hester the money for the circus?

*The Sentimentality of William Tavener* **43**

---

- Hester and William share memories, and he gives her money for the boys to go to the circus.
- Hester, sitting alone in the dark, feels that she has missed something.
- Next day, Hester instructs the boys to be careful with William's money.

### 1 PLOT: CLIMAX

After William goes to bed, Hester realizes that she has missed a closeness with her husband in all the years that she has taken an antagonistic stance toward him.

### 2 STYLE: TONE

Cather uses lyrical, sensuous images to symbolize Hester's past happiness.

### 3 FALLING ACTION

Hester covers William. She realizes that William's sharing of his experiences has prompted her to become tender and caring toward him—qualities she has recently reserved for her sons.

### REFLECTING ON THE STORY

What do you think may be the future relationship between Hester and William? (Possible answer: They may be able to communicate better.)

### STUDY QUESTIONS

1. Hester: "an executive woman, quick of tongue"; William: "hard, determined, ambitious"
2. a purely business one; rarely spoke of anything personal
3. covers William with net; they should be careful with William's money at the circus
4. his memories stir warm feelings

**5.** She is reminded of their former closeness; the marriage has lost warmth and intimacy.

**6.** Hester's allegiance shifts from her sons to her husband.

**7.** William has a tender side, which he normally hides.

**8.** sharp contrast to ordinary everyday life; appeals to all the senses

## LITERARY FOCUS

### Flat and Round Characters
- Both are round.
- *William:* tough but reveals sensitive side; *Hester:* tough-minded but an indulgent mother

### Static and Dynamic Characters
Hester changes more because she actually discovers something about her husband.

## VOCABULARY

**1.** (c) agitation
**2.** (c) assailed
**3.** (c) fluently
**4.** (a) prosperous
**5.** (c) allegiance

---

**5.** In what way does her conversation with William make Hester realize that she had "lost something"? What had she lost?

**6.** By the end of the story, how have the relationships among the family members changed?

**7.** What do you think the story's title means?

### Extending

**8.** Why might a childhood trip to the circus be memorable to an adult, as it is for William in this story?

## LITERARY FOCUS

### Flat and Round Characters

Depending on how much information we are given about them, characters can be either flat or round. **Flat characters** seem very simple, as if they could be summed up with only one or two personality traits. On the other hand, **round characters** have many different and sometimes even contradictory personality traits. Because they are **complex**, or many-sided, round characters are capable of doing and saying surprising things. In this sense they are like people in real life.

### Thinking About Flat and Round Characters

■ Are William and Hester flat or round characters? Prove your answer with examples of their behavior in the story.

### Static and Dynamic Characters

Besides being either flat or round, characters can be either static or dynamic. **Static characters** remain the same throughout the story. **Dynamic characters,** in contrast, change and develop, often because of something that happens to them in the course of the story. Such a change, in fact, can be the most important event in the story.

### Thinking About Static and Dynamic Characters

■ In "The Sentimentality of William Tavener" who do you think changes more, William or Hester? Explain.

## VOCABULARY

### Sentence Completions

Each of the following sentences contains a blank with four possible choices for completing the sentence. All of the choices come from "The Sen-

---

timentality of William Tavener." Choose the word that completes each sentence correctly and that uses the word *as the word is used in the story.* Write the number of each item and the letter of your choice on a separate sheet.

**1.** His _____ was obvious from the way his hands shook and his voice rose.
(a) gravity    (c) agitation
(b) shiftlessness    (d) directness

**2.** The mayor _____ the new highway plan, noting that it was too costly.
(a) heeded    (c) assailed
(b) continued    (d) announced

**3.** Denise has a talent for languages: She can converse _____ in French, Spanish, and German.
(a) incessantly    (c) fluently
(b) emphatically    (d) occasionally

**4.** Frank hopes that his new invention will finally make him _____.
(a) prosperous    (c) grasping
(b) wholesome    (d) defensive

**5.** Holly is loyal: Her _____ never wavers.
(a) silence    (c) allegiance
(b) recollection    (d) astonishment

## COMPOSITION

### Writing About Character

■ Compare and contrast the characters of William and Hester. You may want to consider the following: (a) their backgrounds, (b) their personalities as revealed in direct comments by the author, (c) their relationships with their sons, and (d) their feelings toward each other. *For help with this assignment, see Lesson 3 in the Writing About Literature Handbook at the back of this book.*

### Writing a Persuasive Speech

■ Imagine that you are William Tavener's youngest son, Billy. Write a brief speech that you believe will persuade your father to let you go to the circus. In writing your speech, explain why you want to see the circus, and try to answer some of the objections you think your father will raise. Be sure to write a speech that is appropriate to a young boy.

---

## COMPOSITION: GUIDELINES FOR EVALUATION

### WRITING ABOUT CHARACTER

**Objective**
To study character through the use of comparison and contrast

**Guidelines for Evaluation**
- suggested length: four to six paragraphs
- should list character traits of both William and Hester
- should point out the similarities and differences between the two characters

### WRITING A PERSUASIVE SPEECH

**Objective**
To write a persuasive speech based on facts and opinions

**Guidelines for Evaluation**
- suggested length: three to five paragraphs
- should clearly state Billy's desire to go to the circus
- should use facts to overcome William's possible objections
- should use style appropriate to young boy

Max Apple (born 1941) has published a novel, a one-act play, and two well-received collections of short stories. In the following short story he examines the effects of an untimely death upon the two survivors.

■ As you read, decide why you think Jessica is acting the way she does.

*Max Apple*

# Bridging

### I

1 At the Astrodome, Nolan Ryan is shaving the corners. He's going through the Giants in order. The radio announcer is not even mentioning that by the sixth the Giants haven't had a hit. The K's mount on the scoreboard. Tonight Nolan passes the Big Train and is now the all-time strikeout king. He's almost as old as I am and he still throws nothing but smoke. His fastball is an aspirin; batters tear their tendons lunging for his curve. Jessica and I have season tickets, but tonight she's home listening and I'm in the basement of St. Anne's Church watching Kay Randall's fingertips. Kay is holding her hands out from her chest, her fingertips on each other. Her fingers move a little as she talks and I can hear her nails click when they meet. That's how close I'm sitting.

2 Kay is talking about "bridging"; that's what her arched fingers represent.

"Bridging," she says, "is the way Brownies become Girl Scouts. It's a slow steady process. It's not easy, but we allow a whole year for bridging."

Eleven girls in brown shirts with red bandannas at their neck are imitating Kay as she talks. They hold their stumpy chewed fingertips out and bridge them. So do I.

I brought the paste tonight and the stick-on gold stars and the thread for sewing buttonholes.

"I feel a little awkward," Kay Randall said on the phone, "asking a man to do these errands . . . but that's my problem, not yours. Just bring the supplies and try to be at the church meeting room a few minutes before seven."

I arrive a half hour early.

3 "You're off your rocker," Jessica says. She begs me to drop her at the Astrodome on my way to the Girl Scout meeting. "After the game, I'll meet you at the main souvenir stand on the first level. They stay open an hour after the game. I'll be all right. There are cops and ushers every five yards."

She can't believe that I am missing this game to perform my functions as an assistant Girl Scout leader. Our Girl Scout battle has been going on for two months.

*Bridging* **45**

---

AT A GLANCE

- The narrator has season tickets to the Houston Astros, but he is discussing Brownies with Scout leader Kay Randall.
- His daughter Jessica is home listening to the baseball game they could have attended.

LITERARY OPTIONS

- characterization
- symbol
- point of view

THEMATIC OPTIONS

- surviving the loss of a loved one
- independence
- withdrawal vs. activism

**1 POINT OF VIEW**

By using baseball jargon (*shaving, K's*), the unnamed narrator immediately establishes a casual, conversational tone.

**2 SYMBOL**

Because of the title, the reader, knowing that the concept of bridging will probably be very significant, pays special attention to Kay Randall's description.

**3 CHARACTERIZATION**

Jessica's first words reveal her forthrightness, stubborn independence, and assertiveness in dealing with her father.

---

## GUIDED READING

### LITERAL QUESTION

**1a.** What does Jessica say to the narrator's decision to pass up the game? (She tells him he's off his rocker.)

### INFERENTIAL QUESTION

**1b.** What is unusual about their relationship? (Traditional roles are reversed: He attends Girl Scouts, while she wants to go to the ballgame.)

- When Jessica had agreed to go to the first meeting, the narrator had volunteered to be an assistant Scout leader.
- Jessica wants to be "let alone" by the Scouts, her therapist, and her father—all of whom are trying to help her get over her mother's death.

## 1 POINT OF VIEW

The narrator describes Jessica's actions without interpreting them to himself or to others; thus his reference to her bracing herself for "destruction" causes the reader to be aware of her vulnerability behind a tough façade.

## 2 SYMBOL

The narrator may mean that Jessica will not "bridge" the distance between herself and other girls and that by refusing to "connect" with them, she may really be refusing to cope with the loss of her mother.

## 3 POINT OF VIEW

As this discussion shows, the narrator is preoccupied throughout the story with worry over Jessica.

## 4 STYLE: ANALOGY

Because baseball is real to him, the narrator uses the game to contrast his and Jessica's grief, mutual dependency, and inability to escape from Kay's Scout jargon (bridging) and Sharon's psychiatric jargon (separation anxiety).

## 5 CHARACTERIZATION

Whatever the reason—grief, guilt, sensitivity, his own dependency, or desire to be comforted—the narrator permits Jessica to stay home.

---

"Girl Scouts is stupid," Jessica says. "Who wants to sell cookies and sew buttons and walk around wearing stupid old badges?"

When she agreed to go to the first meeting, I was so happy I volunteered to become an assistant leader. After the meeting, Jessica went directly to the car the way she does after school, after a birthday party, after a ball game, after anything. A straight line to the car. No jabbering with girlfriends, no smiles, no dallying, just right to the car. She slides into the back seat, belts in, and braces herself for destruction. It has already happened once.

I swoop past five thousand years of stereotypes and accept my assistant leader's packet and credentials.

"I'm sure there have been other men in the movement," Kay says, "we just haven't had any in our district. It will be good for the girls."

Not for my Jessica. She won't bridge, she won't budge.

"I know why you're doing this," she says. "You think that because I don't have a mother, Kay Randall and Girl Scouts will help me. That's crazy. And I know that Sharon is supposed to be like a mother too. Why don't you just leave me alone."

Sharon is Jessica's therapist. Jessica sees her twice a week. Sharon and I have a meeting once a month.

"We have a lot of shy girls," Kay Randall tells me. "Scouting brings them out. Believe me, it's hard to stay shy when you're nine years old and you're sharing a tent with six other girls. You have to count on each other, you have to communicate."

I imagine Jessica zipping up her sleeping bag, mumbling good night to anyone who first says it to her, then closing her eyes and hating me for sending her out among the happy.

"She likes all sports, especially baseball," I tell my leader.

"There's room for baseball in scouting," Kay says. "Once a year the whole district goes to a

**46**    *The Short Story*

game. They mention us on the big scoreboard."

"Jessica and I go to all the home games. We're real fans."

Kay smiles.

"That's why I want her in Girl Scouts. You know, I want her to go to things with her girlfriends instead of always hanging around with me at ball games."

"I understand," Kay says. "It's part of bridging."

With Sharon the term is "separation anxiety." That's the fastball, "bridging" is the curve. Amid all their magic words I feel as if Jessica and I are standing at home plate blindfolded.

While I await Kay and the members of Troop III, District 6, I eye St. Anne in her grotto and St. Gregory and St. Thomas. Their hands are folded as if they started out bridging, ended up praying.

In October the principal sent Jessica home from school because Mrs. Simmons caught her in spelling class listening to the World Series through an earphone.

"It's against the school policy," Mrs. Simmons said. "Jessica understands school policy. We confiscate radios and send the child home."

"I'm glad," Jessica said. "It was a cheap-o radio. Now I can watch the TV with you."

They sent her home in the middle of the sixth game. I let her stay home for the seventh too.

The Brewers are her favorite American League team. She likes Rollie Fingers, and especially Robin Yount.

"Does Yount go in the hole better than Harvey Kuenn used to?"

"You bet," I tell her. "Kuenn was never a great fielder but he could hit three hundred with his eyes closed."

Kuenn is the Brewers' manager. He has an artificial leg and can barely make it up the dugout steps, but when I was Jessica's age and the Tigers were my team, Kuenn used to stand at the plate, tap the corners with his bat, spit some tobacco juice, and knock liners up the alley.

---

## GUIDED READING

### LITERAL QUESTION

**1a.** How does Jessica behave after the first Scout meeting? (She goes directly to the car without chatting or smiling.)

### INFERENTIAL QUESTION

**1b.** Do you think this is just shyness on her part? (Jessica is shy but also solitary. She knows what she likes and prefers not to be sociable.)

She took the Brewers' loss hard.

"If Fingers wasn't hurt they would have squashed the Cards, wouldn't they?"

I agreed.

"But I'm glad for Andujar."

We had Andujar's autograph. Once we met him at a McDonald's. He was a relief pitcher then, an erratic right-hander. In St. Louis he improved. I was happy to get his name on a napkin. Jessica shook his hand.

One night after I read her a story, she said, "Daddy, if we were rich could we go to the away games too? I mean, if you didn't have to be at work every day."

"Probably we could," I said, "but wouldn't it get boring? We'd have to stay at hotels and eat in restaurants. Even the players get sick of it."

"Are you kidding?" she said. "I'd never get sick of it."

**1** "Jessica has fantasies of being with you forever, following baseball or whatever," Sharon says. "All she's trying to do is please you. Since she lost her mother she feels that you and she are alone in the world. She doesn't want to let anyone or anything else into that unit, the two of you. She's afraid of any more losses. And, of course, her greatest worry is about losing you."

"You know," I tell Sharon, "that's pretty much how I feel too."

"Of course it is," she says. "I'm glad to hear you say it."

Sharon is glad to hear me say almost any-
**2** thing. When I complain that her $100-a-week fee would buy a lot of peanut butter sandwiches, she says she is "glad to hear me expressing my anger."

"Sharon's not fooling me," Jessica says. "I know that she thinks drawing those pictures is supposed to make me feel better or something. You're just wasting your money. There's nothing wrong with me."

"It's a long, difficult, expensive process," Sharon says. "You and Jessica have lost a lot. Jessica is going to have to learn to trust the world

again. It would help if you could do it too."

So I decide to trust Girl Scouts. First Girl Scouts, then the world. I make my stand at the meeting of Kay Randall's fingertips. While Nolan
**3** Ryan breaks Walter Johnson's strikeout record and pitches a two-hit shutout, I pass out paste and thread to nine-year-olds who are sticking and sewing their lives together in ways Jessica and I can't.

## II

Scouting is not altogether new to me. I was a Cub Scout. I owned a blue beanie and I remember
**4** very well my den mother, Mrs. Clark. A den mother made perfect sense to me then and still does. Maybe that's why I don't feel uncomfortable being a Girl Scout assistant leader.

We had no den father. Mr. Clark was only a photograph on the living room wall, the tiny living room where we held our monthly meetings. Mr. Clark was killed in the Korean War. His son John was in the troop. John was stocky but Mrs. Clark was huge. She couldn't sit on a regular chair, only on a couch or a stool without sides. She was the cashier in the convenience store beneath their apartment. The story we heard was that Walt, the old man who owned the store, felt sorry for her and gave her the job. He was her landlord too. She sat on a swivel stool and rang up the purchases.

We met at the store and watched while she locked the door; then we followed her up the steep staircase to her three-room apartment. She carried two wet glass bottles of milk. Her body took up the entire width of the staircase. She passed the banisters the way semi trucks[1] pass each other on a narrow highway.

We were ten years old, a time when everything is funny, especially fat people. But I don't remember anyone ever laughing about Mrs. Clark. She had great dignity and character. So

---

1. **semi truck:** large vehicle consisting of a trailer at the rear with several sets of wheels, supported and towed by a tractor truck at the head.

*Bridging* **47**

## AT A GLANCE

- The narrator wants to get Jessica to do things with others.
- Sharon, their family therapist, discusses interdependency with the narrator.

**1 CONTRAST**

The reader is shown an example of Jessica's behavior and then Sharon's interpretation; Apple uses this device to increase the reader's sympathy for the child—struggling on her own, surrounded by "sympathetic" adults.

**2 CHARACTERIZATION**

Jessica is not alone in rebelling against therapeutic help; although he is less opposed than she, the narrator clearly has his doubts too.

**3 SYMBOL**

The narrator uses paste and thread—both objects that join things together—to suggest the contrast between the connected lives of the Girl Scouts and the fragmented world of Jessica and himself.

**4 ANECDOTE**

The narrator's anecdote helps explain why he became a Girl Scout assistant leader. Mrs. Clark may have taught him something about coping with a spouse's death.

## GUIDED READING

### LITERAL QUESTION

**1a.** What does Sharon say that Jessica is going to have to learn to do? (trust the world)

### INFERENTIAL QUESTION

**1b.** What do you think Sharon means? (that Jessica has to stop being afraid that she will lose everything she loves)

- Mrs. Clark, the narrator's den mother, had dignity. Her husband had died a war hero.
- Jessica refuses to go on a field trip.
- The narrator admires Kay. They talk over coffee.

## 1 DIALOGUE

Apple frequently uses father-daughter dialogues to show their relationship and relative willingness to "bridge."

## 2 CHARACTERIZATION

When her father gets his first merit badge for promptness, Jessica shows her sophisticated sense of humor by suggesting he "wear it to work."

## 3 READING SKILLS: CONTRAST

Whereas John Clark was able to explain his father's death, Jessica cannot explain her mother's death.

did John. I didn't know what to call it then, but I knew John was someone you could always trust.

She passed out milk and cookies, then John collected the cups and washed them. They didn't even have a television set. The only decoration in the room that barely held all of us was Mr. Clark's picture on the wall. We saw him in his uniform and we knew he died in Korea defending his country. We were little boys in blue beanies drinking milk in the apartment of a hero. Through that aura I came to scouting. I wanted Kay Randall to have all of Mrs. Clark's dignity.

When she took a deep breath and then bridged, Kay Randall had noticeable armpits. Her wide shoulders slithered into a tiny rib cage. Her armpits were like bridges. She said "bridging" like a mantra,[2] holding her hands before her for about thirty seconds at the start of each meeting.

"A promise is a promise," I told Jessica. "I signed up to be a leader, and I'm going to do it with you or without you."

"But you didn't even ask me if I liked it. You just signed up without talking it over."

"That's true; that's why I'm not going to force you to go along. It was my choice."

"What can you like about it? I hate Melissa Randall. She always has a cold."

"Her mother is a good leader."

"How do you know?"

"She's my boss. I've got to like her, don't I?" I hugged Jessica. "C'mon, honey, give it a chance. What do you have to lose?"

"If you make me go I'll do it, but if I have a choice I won't."

Every other Tuesday, Karen, the fifteen-year-old Greek girl who lives on the corner, babysits Jessica while I go to the Scout meetings. We talk about field trips and how to earn merit badges. The girls giggle when Kay pins a promptness badge on me, my first.

---

2. **mantra:** in Hinduism, a chanted sacred text thought to possess mystical effectiveness.

Jessica thinks it's hilarious. She tells me to wear it to work.

Sometimes when I watch Jessica brush her hair and tie her ponytail and make up her lunch kit I start to think that maybe I should just relax and stop the therapy and the scouting and all my not-so-subtle attempts to get her to invite friends over. I start to think that, in spite of everything, she's a good student and she's got a sense of humor. She's barely nine years old. She'll grow up like everyone else does. John Clark did it without a father; she'll do it without a mother. I start to wonder if Jessica seems to the girls in her class the way John Clark seemed to me: dignified, serious, almost an adult even while we were playing. I admired him. Maybe the girls in her class admire her. But John had that hero on the wall, his father in a uniform, dead for reasons John and all the rest of us understood.

My Jessica had to explain a neurologic disease she couldn't even pronounce. "I hate it when people ask me about Mom," she says. "I just tell them she fell off the Empire State Building."

### III

Before our first field trip I go to Kay's house for a planning session. We're going to collect wildflowers in East Texas. It's a one-day trip. I arranged to rent the school bus.

I told Jessica that she could go on the trip even though she wasn't a troop member, but she refused.

We sit on colonial furniture in Kay's den. She brings in coffee and we go over the supply list. Another troop is joining ours so there will be twenty-two girls, three women, and me, a busload among the bluebonnets.[3]

"We have to be sure the girls understand that the bluebonnets they pick are on private land and that we have permission to pick them. Oth-

---

3. **bluebonnets:** plants having clusters of blue flowers, found in Texas and surrounding regions.

---

## GUIDED READING

### LITERAL QUESTIONS

**1a.** When was the narrator first introduced to scouting? (as a young Cub Scout)

**2a.** How does Jessica respond when invited to go on a field trip? (She refuses to go.)

### INFERENTIAL QUESTIONS

**1b.** Why does scouting have a special "aura" for him? (His childhood experiences with Mrs. Clark, in the shadow of her dead, war-hero husband's picture, left a strong impression on him.)

**2b.** Why does she choose this course? (She doesn't want to socialize; she doesn't want to share her father.)

**1 CHARACTERIZATION**

Like the narrator, Kay feels lonely, and like him she also seems unready to make any "first moves."

**2 CHARACTERIZATION**

The narrator can be realistic: He does not let his loneliness distort his perception of Kay.

**3 SYMBOL**

Jessica's continuing attachment to baseball symbolizes her refusal to let go of her grief and her father. Conversely, his attachment to the game decreases as he allows other people and experiences into his life.

erwise they might pick them along the roadside, which is against the law."

I imagine all twenty-two of them behind bars for picking bluebonnets and Jessica laughing while I scramble for bail money.

I keep noticing Kay's hands. I notice them as she pours coffee, as she checks off the items on the list, as she gestures. I keep expecting her to bridge. She has large, solid, confident hands. When she finishes bridging I sometimes feel like clapping the way people do after the national anthem.

"I admire you," she tells me. "I admire you for going ahead with Scouts even though your daughter rejects it. She'll get a lot out of it indirectly from you."

Kay Randall is thirty-three, divorced, and has a Bluebird[4] too. Her older daughter is one of the stubby-fingered girls, Melissa. Jessica is right; Melissa always has a cold.

Kay teaches fifth grade and has been divorced for three years. I am the first assistant she's ever had.

"My husband, Bill, never helped with Scouts," Kay says. "He was pretty much turned off to everything except his business and drinking. When we separated I can't honestly say I missed him; he'd never been there. I don't think the girls miss him either. He only sees them about once a month. He has girlfriends, and his business is doing very well. I guess he has what he wants."

"And you?"

She uses one of those wonderful hands to move the hair away from her eyes, a gesture that **1** makes her seem very young.

"I guess I do too. I've got the girls, and my job. I'm lonesome, though. It's not exactly what I wanted."

We both think about what might have been as we sit beside her glass coffeepot with our lists

___

4. **Bluebird:** member of the youngest (6–8-year-olds) of the Camp Fire organization.

**50** *The Short Story*

of sachet supplies. If she was Barbra Streisand and I Robert Redford and the music started playing in the background to give us a clue and there was a long close-up of our lips, we might just fade into middle age together. But Melissa called **2** for Mom because her mosquito bite was bleeding where she scratched it. And I had an angry daughter waiting for me. And all Kay and I had in common was Girl Scouts. We were both smart enough to know it. When Kay looked at me before going to put alcohol on the mosquito bite, our mutual sadness dripped from us like the last **3** drops of coffee through the grinds.

"You really missed something tonight," Jessica tells me. "The Astros did a double steal. I've never seen one before. In the fourth they sent Thon and Moreno together, and Moreno stole home."

She knows batting averages and won-lost percentages too, just like the older boys, only they go out to play. Jessica stays in and waits for me.

During the field trip, while the girls pick flowers to dry and then manufacture into sachets, I think about Jessica at home, probably beside the radio. Juana, our once-a-week cleaning lady, agreed to work on Saturday so she could stay with Jessica while I took the all-day field trip.

It was no small event. In the eight months since Vicki died I had not gone away for an entire day.

I made waffles in the waffle iron for her before I left, but she hardly ate.

"If you want anything, just ask Juana."

"Juana doesn't speak English."

"She understands, that's enough."

"Maybe for you it's enough."

"Honey, I told you, you can come; there's plenty of room on the bus. It's not too late for you to change your mind."

"It's not too late for you either. There's going to be plenty of other leaders there. You don't have to go. You're just doing this to be mean to me."

## GUIDED READING

### LITERAL QUESTION

**1a.** What does the narrator realize about himself and Kay? (They have too little in common.)

### INFERENTIAL QUESTION

**1b.** Why does he feel this way? (He knows they are both lonely but feels that their mutual need is not enough of a basis for a relationship.)

I'm ready for this. I spent an hour with Sharon steeling myself. "Before she can leave you," Sharon said, "you'll have to show her that you can leave. Nothing's going to happen to her. And don't let her be sick that day either."

Jessica is too smart to pull the "I don't feel good" routine. Instead she becomes more silent, more unhappy looking than usual. She stays in her pajamas while I wash the dishes and get ready to leave.

I didn't notice the sadness as it was coming upon Jessica. It must have happened gradually in the years of Vicki's decline, the years in which I paid so little attention to my daughter. There were times when Jessica seemed to recognize the truth more than I did.

As my Scouts picked their wildflowers, I remembered the last outing I had planned for us. It was going to be a Fourth of July picnic with some friends in Austin. I stopped at the bank and got $200 in cash for the long weekend. But when I came home Vicki was too sick to move and the air conditioner had broken. I called our friends to cancel the picnic; then I took Jessica to the mall with me to buy a fan. I bought the biggest one they had, a 58-inch oscillating model that sounded like a hurricane. It could cool 10,000 square feet, but it wasn't enough.

Vicki was home sitting blankly in front of the TV set. The fan could move eight tons of air an hour, but I wanted it to save my wife. I wanted a fan that would blow the whole earth out of its orbit.

I had $50 left. I gave it to Jessica and told her to buy anything she wanted.

"Whenever you're sad, Daddy, you want to buy me things." She put the money back in my pocket. "It won't help." She was seven years old, holding my hand tightly in the appliance department at J. C. Penney's.

I watched Melissa sniffle even more among the wildflowers, and I pointed out the names of various flowers to Carol and JoAnne and Sue and Linda and Rebecca, who were by now used to me and treated me pretty much as they treated Kay. I noticed that the Girl Scout flower book had very accurate photographs that made it easy to identify the bluebonnets and buttercups and poppies. There were also several varieties of wild grasses.

We were only 70 miles from home on some land a wealthy rancher long ago donated to the Girl Scouts. The girls bending among the flowers seemed to have been quickly transformed by the colorful meadow. The gigglers and monotonous singers on the bus were now, like the bees, sucking strength from the beauty around them. Kay was in the midst of them and so, I realized, was I, not watching and keeping score and admiring from the distance but a participant, a player.

JoAnne and Carol sneaked up from behind me and dropped some dandelions down my back. I chased them; then I helped the other leaders pour the Kool-Aid and distribute the Baggies and the name tags for each girl's flowers.

My daughter is home listening to a ball game, I thought, and I'm out here having fun with nine-year-olds. It's upside down.

When I came home with dandelion fragments still on my back, Juana had cleaned the house and I could smell the taco sauce in the kitchen. Jessica was in her room. I suspected that she had spent the day listless and tearful, although I had asked her to invite a friend over.

"I had a lot of fun, honey, but I missed you."

She hugged me and cried against my shoulder. I felt like holding her the way I used to when she was an infant, the way I rocked her to sleep. But she was a big girl now and needed not sleep but wakefulness.

"I heard on the news that the Rockets signed Ralph Sampson," she sobbed, "and you hardly ever take me to any pro basketball games."

"But if they have a new center things will be different. With Sampson we'll be contenders. Sure I'll take you."

"Promise?"

"Promise." I promise to take you everywhere, my lovely child, and then to leave you. I'm learning to be a leader.

*Bridging* **51**

## AT A GLANCE

- The narrator enjoys the field trip.
- Jessica greets him tearfully when he returns.
- He promises to take her to a basketball game. Inwardly he also promises to lead her out of her dependency.

### 1 CONFLICT

Both father and daughter realize they are engaged in a contest of wills over their mutual dependency.

### 2 CONTRAST

Perhaps Jessica has always had less hope and a surer grasp of "reality" than her father.

### 3 PLOT: RESOLUTION

In less than the year Kay said it sometimes takes to bridge, the narrator has emerged from his mourning and is ready to lead his daughter out of her grief and toward independence.

### REFLECTING ON THE STORY

What does the narrator need to bridge before he can help Jessica? (He needs to bridge the distance between the insular world of their grief and the outside world.)

## GUIDED READING

### LITERAL QUESTIONS

**1a.** What does Sharon say the narrator has to show Jessica? (He has to show her that he can leave.)

**2a.** What is the narrator's silent promise to his daughter? (to take her everywhere and then to leave her)

### INFERENTIAL QUESTIONS

**1b.** Why is this so? (She needs to see that he is not afraid that something bad will happen to either one of them while they are apart all day long, so that she'll believe it too.)

**2b.** What does he mean? (He can show her the way to recovery, but she must independently choose to follow.)

1. Vicki, narrator's dead wife; Jessica, his daughter; Kay, Girl Scout troop leader; Sharon, Jessica's therapist
2. died of rare neurological disease eight months before
3. narrator at Girl Scout meeting; Jessica at home listening to baseball game
4. "I know why you're doing this."
5. Jessica refuses to go and doesn't want her father to go; father, determined to go without Jessica, knows she must become independent.
6. Interest in baseball might keep her father close to her.
7. Literal meaning: transition from status as Brownies to status as Girl Scouts; symbolic meaning: difficult transition from Jessica's frightened dependence on father to mature relationship
8. *Same relationship*—father may not be strong enough to resist Jessica's fears and emotions about losing him; *different relationship*—by actions like field trip, father will foster Jessica's independence.
9. Love does what is necessary for a person, even if it hurts temporarily. Opinions will vary.

VIEWPOINT

*Artifacts*—Astrodome, therapist, earphones, TV, peanut-butter sandwiches, taco sauce, convenience store, Empire State Building, and so forth. Through reference to these items, Apple establishes a contemporary American setting.

## STUDY QUESTIONS

### Recalling

1. How is each of the following characters related to the story narrator: Vicki, Jessica, Kay, Sharon?
2. What happened to Vicki?
3. At the beginning of the story, where is the narrator? Where is Jessica?
4. What does Jessica say to her father about his attempts to help her get over her mother's death?
5. Summarize the different attitudes of Jessica and the narrator toward the Girl Scout field trip.

### Interpreting

6. Jessica's interest in and knowledge about baseball is unusual for a nine-year-old. Suggest a reason for her interest that is not related to a simple love of the game.
7. Explain the literal and symbolic meanings of the word *bridging* in this story.
8. Make a prediction about Jessica's relationship with her father a year or two from the time of the story. Will it be the same or different? If it will be the same, why? If different, in what way? Support your prediction with references to the story.

### Extending

9. The therapist suggested that Jessica's father show his daughter "tough love." What is tough love? Do you think it is helpful in some situations? Why or why not?

## VIEWPOINT

A critic in the *Atlantic Monthly* called attention to a characteristic of Apple's writing style that makes the world in which his stories are set seem very familiar to readers:

Fast food and the fast buck, TV game shows and the Astrodome: . . . these artifacts of American life . . . strike Max Apple . . . as signs of life, and he writes about them with mischievous wit and generosity. . . .

- Find at least ten examples of "artifacts of American life" in "Bridging." Explain what kind of setting the author establishes through the use of these artifacts.

## COMPOSITION

### Writing About Characters' Relationships

- The death of Vicki results in the development of a very close relationship between the narrator (Vicki's husband) and Jessica (her daughter). Compare and contrast Jessica's and the narrator's feelings about the relationship. First state your perception of Jessica's feeling. Cite evidence from the story upon which your perception is based. Cite words, thoughts, and actions of Jessica and other story characters. Then state your perception of the narrator's feeling about the relationship, supporting your statement with similar citations from the story. Finally state your opinion about the feelings of each character. Which character has the more realistic, psychologically healthier feeling about the relationship, Jessica or her father? Support your opinion with convincing facts, reasons, and examples.

### Writing Dialogue

- Imagine that Jessica's father has taken a vacation—without Jessica. He is driving through the Southwest and gets a flat tire on a Navaho reservation. Chee (from the story "Chee's Daughter," page 29) has been working on his land and sees that Jessica's father is in trouble. He offers to help change the tire. As the two men work, they have a conversation. Write a dialogue in which the two men talk to each other. Plan the content of the dialogue by thinking about these questions: What two important things do the men have in common? How does each man feel about the relationship he has with his daughter? Are their attitudes similar or different? Do either or both men have problems with the relationship? As a model for the form of the dialogue you write, use either the dialogue in "Bridging" or the dialogue in one of the plays in this book.

## COMPOSITION: GUIDELINES FOR EVALUATION

### WRITING ABOUT CHARACTERS' RELATIONSHIPS

#### Objective
To analyze and evaluate characters' feelings

#### Guidelines for Evaluation
- suggested length: three paragraphs
- should describe Jessica's feelings, then the narrator's feelings
- should state which feelings are more valid

### WRITING DIALOGUE

#### Objective
To write a dialogue between characters

#### Guidelines for Evaluation
- suggested length: one to two pages
- should bring out similarities between the two men (death of wife; responsibility for daughter); different cultures
- should be written in dialogue form

Born in Maine but raised in Nevada, Walter Van Tilburg Clark (1909–1971) is famous for his stories and novels about the American West. *The Ox-Bow Incident,* his best-known novel, concerns the attempt of settlers to maintain a system of justice in the middle of the western wilderness. In "Why Don't You Look Where You're Going?" he examines the behavior of people in the vast and isolated sea.

■ Have you ever had a close call? How can a near-accident affect a person?

*Walter Van Tilburg Clark*

# Why Don't You Look Where You're Going?

1   White as a sainted leviathan,[1] but too huge for even God to have imagined it, the liner played eastward easily. It swam at a much greater speed than appeared, for it was alone in open ocean, and there were only the waves to pass.

Everyone on board was comfortable, even satisfied. The sea was a light summer one, still blue, although the sun was far gone toward the mountain range of fog on the horizon astern.[2] Its swelling, and the rippling of the swells, could not give the slightest motion to the vessel, whose long hulk glanced through it as through
2   warm and even air. The sense of well-being in the passengers was made firm by the knowledge that their fate was somebody else's responsibility for the next three days. There was nothing an ordinary mortal could do about a ship like this; it was as far out of his realm as the mechanics of heaven. He could talk about it as he might about one of the farther galaxies, in order to experience the almost extinct pleasure of awe, but he

could not do anything about it, and what was even more comfortable, he could not be expected to do anything about it.

Even the crew shared this un-Olympian[3]
3   calm, for the liner was a self-sufficient creature who, once put upon her course, pursued it independently, with gently rhythmic joy. The wheel took care of itself; the fuel sped upon quick wires; the warm and supple steel joints rose and fell, self-oiled to perfect limberness. More like a white Utopian[4] city than any the earth will ever bear, she parted the subservient waters and proceeded.

A school of flying fish, which looked like dragonflies from the upper deck, broke water for an instant and fled back, no more than a brief proof of the pace of the liner.

The tall man in the gray topcoat stopped his circumambulation and peered toward the smoke of dusk rising out of the ocean. The woman in

---

1. **leviathan** [li vī′ə thən]: huge sea monster.
2. **astern** [ə sturn′]: to the stern, or the rear of a ship.

3. **un-Olympian** [un ō lim′pē ən]: unlike the gods of Greek mythology who lived on Mount Olympus; here, powerless.
4. **Utopian** [ū tō′pē ən]: having social and political perfection.

*Why Don't You Look Where You're Going?*   **53**

---

AT A GLANCE

■ The passengers on a huge, powerful ocean liner are comfortable and have a sense of well-being.
■ The liner is a "self-sufficient" creature; even the crew feel as if they have relinquished responsibility for their own safety.

LITERARY OPTIONS

■ setting and atmosphere
■ characterization
■ plot

THEMATIC OPTIONS

■ dependence and self-reliance
■ heroism

1 **SETTING**

The setting is an ocean liner at sea; it is depicted in magnificent terms, emphasizing its size, power, and speed.

2 **SETTING/ATMOSPHERE**

The passengers have relinquished responsibility for their own safety, so complex and powerful is the liner upon which they move through the water.

3 **PERSONIFICATION AND THEME**

Clark gives unusual qualities to this mighty liner, calling it a "self-sufficient creature" that has been put on "her course," which is pursued "independently" with "rhythmic joy." He reinforces the idea of passengers putting their safety in someone else's hands.

## GUIDED READING

**LITERAL QUESTION**

**1a.** What words does Clark use to describe the ship? (He calls it a "sainted leviathan," a "self-sufficient creature," and a "white Utopian city.")

**INFERENTIAL QUESTION**

**1b.** Why do you think Clark emphasizes the magnificent proportions of the ship? (He wants to support the idea of the liner as a powerful haven of safety in an otherwise alien environment.)

- The tall man points out something on the distant horizon.
- A crowd of passengers gather and peer at the object.
- Each passenger wants to be first to identify the object.

### 1 PLOT: NARRATIVE HOOK

The action begins when the tall man sees an unidentified object on the horizon.

### 2 CHARACTERIZATION

Clark does not give the passengers names; instead, he uses descriptive phrases such as "stout, mustached" man and "tall man," thus depersonalizing them.

### 3 POINT OF VIEW

The story is told from an omniscient point of view. Although each passenger asserts his or her individuality, Clark repeatedly speaks of the passengers as thinking, feeling, and reacting as a *group*.

### 4 SETTING/ATMOSPHERE

Description of the ship as a "gliding city" crowded with "curious people" conveys the fear of loss of individuality that motivates each person to compete in trying to identify the object.

---

white flannel paused impatiently beyond him.

**1** "What's that?" he asked.

"What?"

"There, ahead. No, a little more to the right. Like a log or something. See?"

"No."

"Well, look. There." He leaned over the rail and pointed.

"No. Oh, yes. Seaweed, I suppose."

"No, that wouldn't show; not so far. It sticks up."

The man's gesture drew other passengers to the rail. A boy in a white jacket was moving through them, clinking a musical triangle and intoning, "First call to dinner, first call to dinner," but they were impressed by the pointing finger and remained at the rail.

**2** "What is it?" asked the stout, mustached man in linen knickers.

"I don't know," said the tall man, not looking around because his discovery was so small on the darkening sea.

"There's something, though," he added, and pointed again.

The other passengers also leaned over and peered hopefully. Those too far along to have heard the tall man's explanation looked at the sea vaguely, then at the people who were nearer the tall man, then at the sea again.

"He says there's something," the fat man informed them.

Then, "Oh, yes, I see it now." He pointed also. "There. See it? Still too far away to tell what it is, though." He appeared to think for a moment, and produced an original idea.

"We ought to pass it pretty close," he said, protruding his lower lip and puckering his mouth as a sign that he was considering carefully. "Pretty close, I should say, as we're going now."

The passengers exclaimed gratefully, and were able to look intelligent when they returned to peering. They felt better. Anybody could see by their backs that they felt better, much more

**3** decisive. As landsmen they were grateful for the discovery. Other walkers, coming to the side of the vessel, asked questions and were almost told what the fat man had said. But there was never any citation of authority or any admission of the pioneering of the tall man. The reputation for discovery was not easy to resign.[5]

The latecomers remained until the entire rail was lined, and the number of the gathering excited each individual in it; the expected event attained mythological proportions.

This scene was reënacted on the other three decks, although the watchers were fewer because the decks were closed and all the watching had to be done from portholes. Children jumped up and down behind their parents, inquiring in exasperated crescendos. Occasionally a beleaguered father or mother offered an unsatisfactory explanation, or held a child up to see

**4** that there was only water. The entire starboard[6] wall of the gliding city was crowded with curious people, and their curiosity was toughened by their desire to be first in stating the nature of the discovery. Since the discovery had already been made, it was now accounted common property, and recognition of the object seemed more important. The first idle speculation died, as meriting scorn; most of the watchers were quiet and intent.

The young man with the fine blond hair left the rail and returned almost at once with a victorious air and a pair of binoculars. These he fixed to his eyes, turned upon the focal point, and began to manipulate with nimble fingers. At once others whose cabins were close also got binoculars. They appeared determined, as if to say the original inspiration was not what mattered here, but the use made of it. Those who either had no binoculars or had to go too far to get them divided their attention between the

---

5. **The reputation . . . resign:** No one wanted to admit that he or she had not made the discovery.
6. **starboard:** right side of a ship.

---

## GUIDED READING

**LITERAL QUESTIONS**

**1a.** What do the passengers do after the tall man first points to the object? (They gather along the rail to identify it.)

**2a.** What does the young man with blond hair contribute to the event? (He brings a pair of binoculars.)

**INFERENTIAL QUESTIONS**

**1b.** Why do you think the passengers are so curious about the object? (Crossing the ocean on a ship, passengers become bored with the view of the endless sea; sighting an object on the horizon breaks the monotony of the voyage.)

**2b.** How do you think the other passengers feel toward the man with the binoculars? (They are probably envious that he is first to use binoculars; they also see him as a source of information.)

ocean off the starboard bow[7] and the blond young man, who had taken on the shining aspect of the clairvoyant. They watched his face minutely for signs of recognition and were affected by his slightest movement. He bore their worship grandly, almost with an air of not suspecting it.

"What is it?" they asked.

"I can't make it out yet." He continued to adjust the binoculars.

When he ceased fingering and held the glasses steadily, they asked again, "What is it?" and "Can you see it now?"

"Yes," he said, "I think I can." But he withheld the information, as one who will not be pressed into a hasty, and therefore possibly erroneous, conclusion. He fingered the binoculars just the perfect trifle more. Even the tall man in the gray coat abandoned his scrutiny and turned a tanned and bony face, drawn by staring, toward the blond young man.

The object was now close enough so that its location could be clearly marked by everyone at the moments when it appeared on the crest of a billow and balanced before beginning the long, gentle descent into the concealing trough. It might have been a great, triangular fin, if it had been much closer.

"Whatever it is, it had better look out. We're going right for it."

The fat man's suggestion that it might be a portion of the superstructure of a derelict caused a pleasant worry.

"I've heard," said a man with spectacles and a checkered cap over a big nose, "I've heard they're often heavy enough below water to sink a good large boat." He spoke with quiet joy.

The tall man, who had been thinking about the fat man's suggestion, snorted.

"What part?" he challenged.

But, although the fat man was not insensible of the challenge, it was neglected because the blond young man had become signally rigid behind his binoculars.

He overplayed his pause, however, and a square, masculine young woman said factually and loudly, "It's a boat," and held her glasses a moment longer before lowering them to accept adulation in person.

"Yes," admitted the young man. "I was just going to say it's a boat." He added, "That thing that sticks up is a sail, a kind of triangular sail," and felt that his remark justified his lowering his glasses also and looking around.

By now the boat was near enough so that the pace of the liner made it appear to draw nearer very rapidly. Since it was known to be a boat, and everyone could see it lay directly in the path of the liner, the guesses about what a small boat could be doing in mid-ocean gave way to irritation because it was doing nothing to save itself.

"We'd make matchwood of it," stated the fat man angrily.

"It would go to the bottom," declared the young man violently, "to the bottom, like a plummet."

The masculine young lady disagreed. "Not to the bottom; it would reach a level of suspension[8] much sooner. The water is over three thousand feet deep here."

The other passengers rebuked her heartlessness with silence.

"Well, I do wish he'd wake up. I wish he'd get out of the way," complained the matron whose twin six-year-olds were extending her by their attempts to see over and under the rail. The passengers warmed to her humanity, and, understanding that the young woman was quelled, all leaned over the rail and stared anxiously ahead.

High overhead the whistle of the liner hissed and squealed abortively, and then settled into a long, mournful, gigantic moo.

Immediately a man appeared in the small

---

7. **bow** [bou]: forward part of a ship.

8. **level of suspension**: depth at which an object stops sinking.

*Why Don't You Look Where You're Going?* **55**

**AT A GLANCE**

- Various individuals conjecture about the distant object. Finally a young woman identifies the object as a boat.

- The passengers are upset because the boat is in danger of being obliterated by their liner.

**1 TONE**

The narrator describes the behavior and feelings of the passengers—here, for example, of the young man—in sarcastic and condescending terms.

**2 CHARACTERIZATION**

Clark's brief description of actions conveys insight into the personalities of the anonymous passengers. Most of them tend to dramatize relatively trivial actions in order to inflate their own importance.

**3 PLOT: RISING ACTION**

The suggestion that the ocean liner could sink the small sailboat adds a serious complication to the story.

**4 STYLE: ONOMATOPOEIA**

Clark comically appeals to the sense of sound as the reader hears the whistle "hiss," "squeal," and—most impressively—issue a "long, mournful, gigantic moo."

---

## GUIDED READING

**LITERAL QUESTION**

**1a.** How do some of the passengers feel about the small boat when they realize it is directly in their course? (They feel angry.)

**INFERENTIAL QUESTION**

**1b.** How do you explain their reaction? (With no control over the liner, they cannot help the small boat. Because they don't want to see it sunk, they feel angry that the pilot is not yet taking evasive action.)

AT A GLANCE

- Startled, the man in the small boat works frantically.
- The little boat moves safely out of the way.
- Its pilot shakes his fist at the liner; the passengers feel relief.

## 1 PLOT: CLIMAX

The pilot overcomes the forces of the ocean and moves the small boat safely out of the way of the liner.

## 2 THEME

The passengers are relieved; vicariously, they have experienced the danger and overcome the obstacle along with the boat's courageous pilot.

boat. The liner was so close upon him that the passengers could see him look up startled. He became very active. He leaned over, stood up, disappeared behind the boxlike cabin, and reappeared almost at once. He was working rapidly with his hands, glancing up frequently without stopping his work. The passengers knew he was frightened. Then the triangular sail swung slowly across the boxlike cabin, slatted[9] idly two, three, four times, and slowly filled out like a breathing chest. The man, energetic as a jumping jack, worked at the rail for an instant, then threw himself aft,[10] slipped the noose from the tiller,[11] and projected himself, chest and shoulders, against the bar. The sail flapped limp again,

1 but only once, and suddenly drew a deep breath. The little boat heeled over until it was nearly awash,[12] slithered along at a dogwalk[13] during the ascent of one billow, then perfectly bit in and skittered off toward safety.

Four times the height of his sail above him, the bow of the liner passed over the tiny man in his cockpit, and left him valiantly awash, bobbing under four three-hundred-foot tiers of fascinated eyes. They could see that he had no hat, that he wore a black beard, and that his pants were held up by a knotted rope. He braced the tiller with a knee, raised both fists over his 2 head, and shook them at the liner. The passengers were immensely relieved. The women laughed, and the men leaned far over the rail to

---

9. **slatted:** flapped.
10. **aft:** toward the rear of a ship.
11. **tiller:** lever, or bar, used to turn the rudder and steer a boat.

12. **heeled . . . awash:** leaned to one side until it nearly went under.
13. **at a dogwalk:** slowly.

**56** *The Short Story*

## GUIDED READING

### LITERAL QUESTION

**1a.** What does the pilot of the sailboat do as the liner passes by him? (He shakes his fists at the ocean liner.)

### INFERENTIAL QUESTION

**1b.** What does this action tell you about how he feels and why he feels this way? (He apparently feels angry at the ocean liner because he was frightened by its unexpected threat and the degree of effort he had to expend.)

They leaned over farther and farther to watch the little boat as it diminished. Why don't you look where you're going? That was good. That was conceit for you; a man who didn't **2** count himself less than he was worth. "Everybody's out of step but Johnny," sang the young man with the blond hair. He sang it at the man in the little boat, who was obviously too far away to hear, but everybody else appreciated it; they leaned back and looked at the young man with many kinds of grins and smiles to appreciate it, and quickly leaned over the rail again to watch.

The stern of the little boat said to them, *"The Flying Dutchman*[16]*—Rockport—Me."* They became silent and watched the puppet of a bearded man sit to his tiller and labor earnestly to navigate the wake of the liner. A great many of them unconsciously went farther and farther aft, to keep *The Flying Dutchman* in sight. The stern of the liner was crowded, and all the faces were serious and fixed.

When the little man was far enough astern to feel secure and had his boat properly angled into the heave of the wake, he underwent a change of heart. The watchers could just see him, yet everybody recognized that he was standing up **3** again and waving. Every face brightened spontaneously, and the afterdeck[17] blossomed windily with hands, handkerchiefs, hats, and caps.

The fat man bellowed astoundingly through the trumpet of his hands, "Good luck, sailor!"

"'Why don't you look where you're going?'" he repeated gruffly. "'Why don't you look where you're going?' That's good."

The masculine young lady stood with her hands on the rail and peered wistfully under the Andes[18] of the cloud bank where the tiny, black triangle of sail was only now and then visible, getting less so.

shout at him between cupped hands. They saw that he was shouting also; his mouth was wide open and his teeth showed in his beard. Everyone became silent and listened. But there was such a rush of white water back from the stem,[14] and the wind wuthered[15] so in the railing, that the man appeared to be trying to free his jaw from a cramp, making no sound. He addressed them continuously and energetically, but not until the liner had nearly drawn its whole length by did a wind flaw bring up his voice with an item of his lecture. The passengers aft repeated it with glee; indeed they wriggled with glee at it, their bodies and their faces.

**1**
   "He said, 'Why don't you look where you're going?'"
   Everyone was charmed.

---

14. **stem:** front edge of the boat.
15. **wuthered** [woᵵһ′ərd]: blew with a roaring sound.

---

16. *The Flying Dutchman:* The boat is named for a legendary ghost ship.
17. **afterdeck:** deck at the rear of a ship.
18. **Andes** [an′dēz]: South American mountain range; here, clouds massed to resemble peaks.

*Why Don't You Look Where You're Going?* **57**

## AT A GLANCE

- The passengers are delighted to hear the pilot shout, "Why don't you look where you're going?"
- They read the name of the little boat: *The Flying Dutchman.*
- When the pilot stands up and waves, the passengers wave back.

**1** **THEME**

Having identified with the pilot of the sailboat and having enjoyed the vicarious thrill of his escape to safety, the passengers admire him for his plucky courage and audacity in yelling at the huge liner.

**2** **SETTING/ATMOSPHERE**

Since the danger to the sailboat is over, the atmosphere on the liner shifts from tension to lightheartedness.

**3** **PLOT: RESOLUTION**

Identifying with the pilot as a hero and admiring his self-reliance, the passengers wave enthusiastically at him.

**REFLECTING ON THE STORY**

What qualities of the sailboat pilot do the passengers admire? (Possible answers include his courage, his defiance toward the liner, and his self-reliance.)

---

## *GUIDED READING*

### LITERAL QUESTION

**1a.** What do the passengers hear the sailboat pilot shouting? ("Why don't you look where you're going?")

### INFERENTIAL QUESTION

**1b.** Why are they so delighted to hear those words? (Each, trying to escape anonymity, has identified with the self-reliant sailor and is proud of his audacious view that the big ship should be the one to look out.)

## STUDY QUESTIONS

### Recalling

1. *liner:* "too huge for even God to have imagined it"; *passengers:* "comfortable, even satisfied"
2. Someone sees mysterious object; passengers gather and speculate; woman identifies boat.
3. when it is almost on top of him; steers out of the way
4. "Why don't you look where you're going?"; they're charmed.
5. They could relax and depend on others without feeling guilty.
6. Their lack of names takes away their individuality and makes them seem basically alike; the sailor has a distinct identity.
7. ■ People want to feel important.
   ■ They had nothing else to do.
8. asserts the rights of the individual, no matter how small
9. It is rare but so valuable that even conformists applaud it.

### VIEWPOINT

■ Passengers seem out of place in natural surroundings.
■ The sailor, contending with the sea, has earned his place there.

### LITERARY FOCUS

■ *Setting:* huge ocean liner moving through the water on a warm, sunny day
■ *Atmosphere:* easygoing, complacent
■ *Details:* The liner, a "white Utopian city" moving through "subservient waters," contrasts with the small boat's struggle, just as the sheltered passengers contrast with the self-reliant sailor.

## STUDY QUESTIONS

### Recalling

1. What does Clark say about the liner and the mood of its passengers at the story's beginning?
2. Trace the sequence of events and interactions as the passengers identify the small boat.
3. When does the man in the boat notice the liner? What does he do to avoid a crash?
4. What does the man call out to the passengers as he leaves? How do they react to what he says?

### Interpreting

5. Why might the liner's passengers feel "comfortable" about the fact that the ship's operation was "somebody else's responsibility"?
6. What effect does Clark create by using descriptions rather than names to identify his characters? Why is it significant that the only item given an actual name is *The Flying Dutchman*?
7. What point about human nature is made by the way the passengers compete over discovering the tiny boat? Why might they spot the boat long before the bearded man notices their liner?
8. What is the significance of the story's title?

### Extending

9. What do you think this story may be saying about the meaning and value of individuality?

## VIEWPOINT

A review in the *New Yorker* magazine pointed out that many of Walter Van Tilburg Clark's stories revolve around a contrast between the natural and the human worlds. The review described a collection of Clark's stories as follows:

> A series of sweeping panoramas of land and sea and sky, in which birds and animals appear by right while the people who turn up from time to time are only strays.

■ In what ways is this description appropriate to "Why Don't You Look Where You're Going?" Would you call *all* the people in this story "strays"? Why or why not?

## LITERARY FOCUS

### Setting and Atmosphere

The **setting** of a story is the time and place in

which the events of the story occur. An author usually describes the setting early in the narrative, using several vivid details to lead us directly into the world of the story.

In many stories the setting simply provides a background for the plot and characters. However, in some stories the choice of setting can actually influence the plot and characters. For example, a story that takes place in a modern American suburb is likely to be about events and people quite different from those we would meet in a story set on an ancient battlefield.

The setting often creates an **atmosphere,** or mood, that colors the entire story. The atmosphere may be exotic or homey, colorful or bleak, forbidding or comforting, intimate or grand, placid or exciting, and so on. Recognizing a story's atmosphere often helps us to understand the story's characters and action.

### Thinking About Setting and Atmosphere

■ Describe the setting and the general atmosphere of "Why Don't You Look Where You're Going?" What details and comments about the ocean, the two boats, and the characters' moods create this atmosphere?

## COMPOSITION

### Writing About Setting

■ Explain the function of the setting as it is presented in the first three paragraphs of "Why Don't You Look Where You're Going?" First describe the setting. Then explain how the setting influences what happens in the story and helps us to understand the very different behavior of the passengers on the liner and the man in the boat.

### Describing an Object

■ Have someone else choose an object for you to describe from a gradually decreasing distance. Write your description in three or four different stages. Begin your description from a great distance, when you can barely see the object. (Your partner should not tell you anything about it.) Then, as you gradually move closer, describe the object in greater and greater detail. End by identifying the object for your reader.

---

## COMPOSITION: GUIDELINES FOR EVALUATION

### WRITING ABOUT SETTING

**Objective**

To show how setting functions within the story

**Guidelines for Evaluation**
■ suggested length: three to five paragraphs
■ should identify details that describe the setting in first three paragraphs
■ should use examples to show how setting influences events and characters

### DESCRIBING AN OBJECT

**Objective**

To describe an object from a changing perspective

**Guidelines for Evaluation**
■ suggested length: three to four paragraphs
■ should describe an object as seen at four distances
■ should convey the features at each point
■ should use descriptive language to create a picture of object before its identity is clear

Poet, novelist, and short story writer, Stephen Vincent Benét (1898–1943) was the son and grandson of high-ranking Army officers. He was greatly interested in American history, and many of his writings use fantasy and folklore to explore themes from America's past. Benét's highly imaginative works include *John Brown's Body,* a Pulitzer Prize–winning narrative poem about the Civil War.

■ We live in an age of technology beyond the understanding of most of us. Is it possible that technology has advanced beyond human control?

*Stephen Vincent Benét*

# By the Waters of Babylon

1   The north and the west and the south are good hunting ground, but it is forbidden to go east. It is forbidden to go to any of the Dead Places except to search for metal and then he who touches the metal must be a priest or the son of a priest. Afterwards, both the man and the metal must be purified. These are the rules and the laws; they are well made. It is forbidden to cross the great river and look upon the place that was the Place of the Gods—this is most strictly forbidden. We do not even say its name though we know its name. It is there that spirits live, and demons—it is there that there are the ashes of the Great Burning. These things are forbidden—they have been forbidden since the beginning of time.

2   My father is a priest; I am the son of a priest. I have been in the Dead Places near us, with my father—at first, I was afraid. When my father went into the house to search for the metal, I stood by the door and my heart felt small and weak. It was a dead man's house, a spirit house. It did not have the smell of man, though there were old bones in a corner. But it is not fitting that a priest's son should show fear. I looked at the bones in the shadow and kept my voice still.

Then my father came out with the metal—a good, strong piece. He looked at me with both eyes but I had not run away. He gave me the metal to hold—I took it and did not die. So he knew that I was truly his son and would be a priest in my time. That was when I was very young—nevertheless, my brothers would not have done it, though they are good hunters. After that, they gave me the good piece of meat and the warm corner by the fire. My father watched over me—he was glad that I should be a priest. But when I boasted or wept without a reason, he punished me more strictly than my brothers. That was right.

After a time, I myself was allowed to go into the dead houses and search for metal. So I learned the ways of those houses—and if I saw bones, I was no longer afraid. The bones are light and old—sometimes they will fall into dust if you touch them. But that is a great sin.

I was taught the chants and the spells—I was taught how to stop the running of blood from a wound and many secrets. A priest must know many secrets—that was what my father said. If the hunters think we do all things by chants and spells, they may believe so—it does not hurt them. I was taught how to read in the old books and how to make the old writings—that was

*By the Waters of Babylon*   **59**

---

- When he grows older, he asks to go on a journey; his father grants permission.
- Fasting and waiting for signs, he sees an eagle, three deer, and a white fawn, all going east.

**1 THEME**

Living in a society with limited understanding, the narrator values and yearns for knowledge.

**2 STYLE: METAPHOR**

By contrasting the physical pain of the purification ceremony with his spirit (a cool stone), the author conveys the narrator's courage and a strength of spirit, as well as his figurative way of looking at the world.

**3 CONFLICT**

By contrasting the narrator's straightforward gaze with his shaky voice, Benét suggests the boy's internal conflict as he courageously faces his fear of the forbidden.

hard and took a long time. My knowledge made me happy—it was like a fire in my heart. Most of all, I liked to hear of the Old Days and the stories of the gods. I asked myself many questions that I could not answer, but it was good to ask them. At night, I would lie awake and listen to the wind—it seemed to me that it was the voice of the gods as they flew through the air.

We are not ignorant like the Forest People— our women spin wool on the wheel, our priests wear a white robe. We do not eat grubs from the tree, we have not forgotten the old writings, although they are hard to understand. Nevertheless, my knowledge and my lack of knowledge burned in me—I wished to know more. When I was a man at last, I came to my father and said, "It is time for me to go on my journey. Give me your leave."

He looked at me for a long time, stroking his beard, then he said at last, "Yes. It is time." That night, in the house of the priesthood, I asked for and received purification. My body hurt but my spirit was a cool stone. It was my father himself who questioned me about my dreams.

He bade me look into the smoke of the fire and see—I saw and told what I saw. It was what I have always seen—a river, and, beyond it, a great Dead Place and in it the gods walking. I have always thought about that. His eyes were stern when I told him—he was no longer my father but a priest. He said, "This is a strong dream."

"It is mine," I said, while the smoke waved and my head felt light. They were singing the Star song in the outer chamber and it was like the buzzing of bees in my head.

He asked me how the gods were dressed and I told him how they were dressed. We know how they were dressed from the book, but I saw them as if they were before me. When I had finished, he threw the sticks three times and studied them as they fell.

"This is a very strong dream," he said. "It may eat you up."

"I am not afraid," I said and looked at him with both eyes. My voice sounded thin in my ears but that was because of the smoke.

He touched me on the breast and the forehead. He gave me the bow and the three arrows.

"Take them," he said. "It is forbidden to travel east. It is forbidden to cross the river. It is forbidden to go to the Place of the Gods. All these things are forbidden."

"All these things are forbidden," I said, but it was my voice that spoke and not my spirit. He looked at me again.

"My son," he said. "Once I had young dreams. If your dreams do not eat you up, you may be a great priest. If they eat you, you are still my son. Now go on your journey."

I went fasting, as is the law. My body hurt but not my heart. When the dawn came, I was out of sight of the village. I prayed and purified myself, waiting for a sign. The sign was an eagle. It flew east.

Sometimes signs are sent by bad spirits. I waited again on the flat rock, fasting, taking no food. I was very still—I could feel the sky above me and the earth beneath. I waited till the sun was beginning to sink. Then three deer passed in the valley, going east—they did not wind me or see me. There was a white fawn with them—a very great sign.

I followed them, at a distance, waiting for what would happen. My heart was troubled

---

**GUIDED READING**

**LITERAL QUESTIONS**

**1a.** What does his father tell the boy about his dream? (He tells him that it is a strong dream that may eat him up.)

**2a.** What does the narrator do as he leaves on his journey? (He fasts and waits for signs.)

**INFERENTIAL QUESTIONS**

**1b.** What do these words reveal about the reason that it is forbidden to travel east? (The people fear that they will be killed if they go to the Place of the Gods.)

**2b.** What can we infer about the narrator's attitude toward his journey? (He takes the journey very seriously. He expects to be guided by powers outside of himself. He respects the supernatural.)

about going east, yet I knew that I must go. My head hummed with my fasting—I did not even see the panther spring upon the white fawn. But, before I knew it, the bow was in my hand. I shouted and the panther lifted his head from the fawn. It is not easy to kill a panther with one arrow but the arrow went through his eye and into his brain. He died as he tried to spring—he rolled over, tearing at the ground. Then I knew I was meant to go east—I knew that was my journey. When the night came, I made my fire and roasted meat.

It is eight suns' journey to the east and a man passes by many Dead Places. The Forest People are afraid of them but I am not. Once I made my fire on the edge of a Dead Place at night and, next morning, in the dead house, I found a good knife, little rusted. That was small to what came afterward but it made my heart feel big. Always when I looked for game, it was in front of my arrow, and twice I passed hunting parties of the Forest People without their knowing. So I knew my magic was strong and my journey clean, in spite of the law.

Toward the setting of the eighth sun, I came to the banks of the great river. It was half-a-day's journey after I had left the god-road—we do not use the god-roads now for they are falling apart into great blocks of stone, and the forest is safer going. A long way off, I had seen the water through trees but the trees were thick. At last, I came out upon an open place at the top of a cliff. There was the great river below, like a giant in the sun. It is very long, very wide. It could eat all the streams we know and still be thirsty. Its name is Ou-dis-sun, the Sacred, the Long. No man of my tribe had seen it, not even my father, the priest. It was magic and I prayed.

Then I raised my eyes and looked south. It was there, the Place of the Gods.

How can I tell what it was like—you do not know. It was there, in the red light, and they were too big to be houses. It was there with the red light upon it, mighty and ruined. I knew that in another moment the gods would see me. I covered my eyes with my hands and crept back into the forest.

Surely, that was enough to do, and live. Surely it was enough to spend the night upon the cliff. The Forest People themselves do not come near. Yet, all through the night, I knew that I should have to cross the river and walk in the places of the gods, although the gods ate me up. My magic did not help me at all and yet there was a fire in my bowels, a fire in my mind. When the sun rose, I thought, "My journey has been clean. Now I will go home from my journey." But, even as I thought so, I knew I could not. If I went to the Place of the Gods, I would surely die, but, if I did not go, I could never be at peace with my spirit again. It is better to lose one's life than one's spirit, if one is a priest and the son of a priest.

Nevertheless, as I made the raft, the tears ran out of my eyes. The Forest People could have killed me without fight, if they had come upon me then, but they did not come. When the raft was made, I said the sayings for the dead and painted myself for death. My heart was cold as a frog and my knees like water, but the burning in my mind would not let me have peace. As I pushed the raft from the shore, I began my death song—I had the right. It was a fine song.

AT A GLANCE
- Uneasy about going east, the narrator is reassured when he kills a panther.
- He is the first man of his tribe to see the river Ou-dis-sun.
- Certain he will die, he makes a raft and pushes off from the shore.

**1 CONFLICT**

The narrator sees the panther's quick death as a sign, resolving his inner conflict over continuing into the forbidden area.

**2 STYLE: PERSONIFICATION**

Comparing the river to a hungry giant conveys the narrator's feelings about the river's immensity and power.

**3 SETTING**

Benét conveys the almost magical quality of the ruins of the Place of the Gods, as seen at sunset.

**4 CONFLICT**

The narrator's inner conflict becomes a choice between risking physical death and accepting the death of his spirit.

**5 STYLE: FIGURATIVE LANGUAGE**

To express the narrator's terror, Benét skillfully uses similes (cold as a frog, knees like water) that would occur naturally within the limited experience of a primitive society.

## GUIDED READING

### LITERAL QUESTIONS

**1a.** After he gives the name of the great river, what does the narrator say about it? (He says that no member of his tribe has ever seen it.)

**2a.** What is the reason that the narrator can never be at peace with his spirit if he does not go to the Place of the Gods? (As priest and son of a priest, he believes that it is better to lose one's life than one's spirit.)

### INFERENTIAL QUESTIONS

**1b.** If that is the case, how do you think he may have learned about the river? (He and other priests have probably learned about it from the old books and from legends.)

**2b.** What qualities does this explanation show that the narrator possesses? (He has great courage and willingness to die; he has a sense of the honor and responsibility of priesthood.)

- John sings his death song.
- He paddles near to the Place of the Gods; when his raft turns over, he swims ashore.
- The ground does not burn; he knows that it is a great Dead Place, not an enchanted island.

## 1 READING SKILLS: SEQUENCE

In his death song, John reviews—in chronological order—his daring actions: going to the Dead Places, taking the metal, killing the panther, traveling east to the great river, and journeying to the Place of the Gods.

## 2 STYLE: PERSONIFICATION

Benét builds on the earlier personification of the river as a hungry giant by having John explain the strong mid-river currents as that giant's pulling the raft in his hands.

## 3 STYLE: METAPHOR

Again, Benét uses the limitations of a hunting society in John's description of his useless knowledge (a squirrel's heap of winter nuts and small and naked as a new-hatched bird).

## 4 SETTING

John at last reaches the Place of the Gods and describes it—in clear unadorned language—as a place vastly different from its portrayal in the myths and superstitions of his people. Most important, it is a real place, with some familiar features (It felt like ground underfoot), not an "enchanted" land.

---

"I am John, son of John," I sang. "My people are the Hill People. They are the men.
I go into the Dead Places but I am not slain.
I take the metal from the Dead Places but I am not blasted.
I travel upon the god-roads and am not afraid.

1 E-yah! I have killed the panther, I have killed the fawn!
E-yah! I have come to the great river. No man has come there before.
It is forbidden to go east, but I have gone, forbidden to go on the great river, but I am there.
Open your hearts, you spirits, and hear my song.
Now I go to the Place of the Gods, I shall not return.
My body is painted for death and my limbs weak, but my heart is big as I go to the Place of the Gods!"

All the same, when I came to the Place of the Gods, I was afraid, afraid. The current of the 2 great river is very strong—it gripped my raft with its hands. That was magic, for the river itself is wide and calm. I could feel evil spirits about me, in the bright morning; I could feel their breath on my neck as I was swept down the stream. Never have I been so much alone—I tried to think of my knowledge, but it was a 3 squirrel's heap of winter nuts. There was no strength in my knowledge any more and I felt small and naked as a new-hatched bird—alone upon the great river, the servant of the gods.

Yet, after a while, my eyes were opened and I saw. I saw both banks of the river—I saw that once there had been god-roads across it, though now they were broken and fallen like broken vines. Very great they were, and wonderful and broken—broken in the time of the Great Burning when the fire fell out of the sky. And always the current took me nearer to the Place of the Gods, and the huge ruins rose before my eyes.

I do not know the customs of rivers—we are the People of the Hills. I tried to guide my raft with the pole but it spun around. I thought the

**62** *The Short Story*

river meant to take me past the Place of the Gods and out into the Bitter Water of the legends. I grew angry then—my heart felt strong. I said aloud, "I am a priest and the son of a priest!" The gods heard me—they showed me how to paddle with the pole on one side of the raft. The current changed itself—I drew near to the Place of the Gods.

When I was very near, my raft struck and turned over. I can swim in our lakes—I swam to the shore. There was a great spike of rusted metal sticking out into the river—I hauled myself up upon it and sat there, panting. I had saved my bow and two arrows and the knife I found in the Dead Place but that was all. My raft went whirling downstream toward the Bitter Water. I looked after it, and thought if it had trod me under, at least I would be safely dead. Nevertheless, when I had dried my bowstring and restrung it, I walked forward to the Place of the Gods.

4 It felt like ground underfoot; it did not burn me. It is not true what some of the tales say, that the ground there burns forever, for I have been there. Here and there were the marks and stains of the Great Burning, on the ruins, that is true. But they were old marks and old stains. It is not true either, what some of our priests say, that it is an island covered with fogs and enchantments. It is not. It is a great Dead Place—greater than any Dead Place we know. Everywhere in it there are god-roads, though most are cracked and broken. Everywhere there are the ruins of the high towers of the gods.

How shall I tell what I saw? I went carefully, my strung bow in my hand, my skin ready for danger. There should have been the wailings of spirits and the shrieks of demons, but there were not. It was very silent and sunny where I had landed—the wind and the rain and the birds that drop seeds had done their work—the grass grew in the cracks of the broken stone. It is a fair island—no wonder the gods built there. If I had come there, a god, I also would have built.

---

## GUIDED READING

### LITERAL QUESTIONS

**1a.** When he feels alone, what does John try to think of? (He tries to think of his knowledge.)

**2a.** Compare the legends and the priest's stories about the Place of the Gods. (Some legends portrayed it as a place where the ground burned forever; some priests thought it was a foggy, enchanted island.)

### INFERENTIAL QUESTIONS

**1b.** Why is it unable to help him? (As all explorers and pioneers, he must learn firsthand about his new environment.)

**2b.** Why do you think such different stories arose? (When dealing with the unknown, some people fear it and make it worse than reality; others idealize it and make it better than reality.)

How shall I tell what I saw? The towers are not all broken—here and there one still stands, like a great tree in a forest, and the birds nest high. But the towers themselves look blind, for the gods are gone. I saw a fish hawk, catching fish in the river. I saw a little dance of white butterflies over a great heap of broken stones and columns. I went there and looked about me—there was a carved stone with cut-letters, broken in half. I can read letters but I could not understand these. They said UBTREAS. There was also the shattered image of a man or a god. It had been made of white stone and he wore his hair tied back like a woman's. His name was ASHING, as I read on the cracked half of a stone. I thought it wise to pray to ASHING, though I do not know that god.

How shall I tell what I saw? There was no smell of man left, on stone or metal. Nor were there many trees in that wilderness of stone. There are many pigeons, nesting and dropping in the towers—the gods must have loved them, or, perhaps, they used them for sacrifices. There are wild cats that roam the god-roads, green-eyed, unafraid of man. At night they wail like demons but they are not demons. The wild dogs are more dangerous, for they hunt in a pack, but them I did not meet till later. Everywhere there are the carved stones, carved with magical numbers or words.

I went North—I did not try to hide myself. When a god or a demon saw me, then I would die, but meanwhile I was no longer afraid. My hunger for knowledge burned in me—there was so much that I could not understand. After a while, I knew that my belly was hungry. I could have hunted for my meat, but I did not hunt. It is known that the gods did not hunt as we do—they got their food from enchanted boxes and jars. Sometimes these are still found in the Dead Places—once, when I was a child and foolish, I opened such a jar and tasted it and found the food sweet. But my father found out and punished me for it strictly, for, often, that food is death. Now, though, I had long gone past what was forbidden, and I entered the likeliest towers, looking for the food of the gods.

I found it at last in the ruins of a great temple in the mid-city. A mighty temple it must have been, for the roof was painted like the sky at night with its stars—that much I could see, though the colors were faint and dim. It went down into great caves and tunnels—perhaps they kept their slaves there. But when I started to climb down, I heard the squeaking of rats, so I did not go—rats are unclean, and there must have been many tribes of them, from the squeaking. But near there, I found food, in the heart of a ruin, behind a door that still opened. I ate only the fruits from the jars—they had a very sweet taste. There was drink, too, in bottles of glass—the drink of the gods was strong and made my head swim. After I had eaten and drunk, I slept on the top of a stone, my bow at my side.

When I woke, the sun was low. Looking down from where I lay, I saw a dog sitting on his haunches. His tongue was hanging out of his mouth; he looked as if he were laughing. He was a big dog, with a gray-brown coat, as big as a wolf. I sprang up and shouted at him but he did not move—he just sat there as if he were laughing. I did not like that. When I reached for a stone to throw, he moved swiftly out of the way of the stone. He was not afraid of me; he looked at me as if I were meat. No doubt I could have killed him with an arrow, but I did not know if there were others. Moreover, night was falling.

I looked about me—not far away there was a great, broken god-road, leading North. The towers were high enough, but not so high, and while many of the dead-houses were wrecked, there were some that stood. I went toward this god-road, keeping to the heights of the ruins, while the dog followed. When I had reached the god-road, I saw that there were others behind him. If I had slept later, they would have come upon me asleep and torn out my throat. As it

*By the Waters of Babylon* **63**

- He sees towers, carved stones, statues, pigeons, cats, and dogs.
- Going north to find knowledge, he looks for food in a large building.
- Waking from a long sleep, he sees a dog watching him; the dog follows him north.

**1 SETTING**

The carved stones, the columns, and the lettering indicate that the inhabitants of the Great Place belonged to a civilization much more developed than John's.

**2 STYLE: REPETITION**

The repetition of the question "How shall I tell what I saw?" emphasizes his incredulity before the awesome remains of the destroyed culture.

**3 FORESHADOWING**

John's reference to the wild dogs hints that they will pose another obstacle to his journey.

**4 RESPONSE JOURNAL**

Ask students to select an object that is common to our culture (a television set, an automobile, a pair of jeans, etc.) and describe it from the point of view of someone from another culture who has never before seen it.

**5 CONFLICT**

John faces physical danger from a pack of hungry, wild dogs who are ready to attack him.

## GUIDED READING

### LITERAL QUESTION

**1a.** What kinds of animals does John see? (He sees birds, butterflies, cats, dogs, and rats.)

### INFERENTIAL QUESTION

**1b.** Why do you think animals are there but no sign of gods or men? (Apparently what John describes as the Great Burning has destroyed the gods or people who lived there.)

- When the dogs rush him, John shuts a door in their faces.
- John climbs stairs and enters rooms of riches; he sees washing and cooking places, but their "magic" is gone.
- At night, he makes a fire and sleeps; then he awakens to hear whisperings.

1 **CHARACTERIZATION**

John reveals his intelligence, resourcefulness, and self-reliance as he finds a door to close against the wild dogs' attack.

2 **THEME**

John's reverence for knowledge causes him to appreciate the rooms and to admire the wisdom of the god who lived in this place.

3 **SETTING**

In describing the opulence of the apartment, John continues to rely upon the belief in magic that he learned as a member of the Hill People—in spite of the fact that the inhabitant of the rooms had needs and implements not unfamiliar to John.

4 **CONFLICT**

John faces two conflicts: the external danger of the wild dogs, and his inner conflict between superstitious fear and a wish for knowledge.

was, they were sure enough of me; they did not hurry. When I went into the dead-house, they kept watch at the entrance—doubtless they thought they would have a fine hunt. But a dog cannot open a door and I knew, from the books, that the gods did not like to live on the ground but on high.

I had just found a door I could open when the dogs decided to rush. Ha! They were surprised when I shut the door in their faces—it was a good door, of strong metal. I could hear their foolish baying beyond it but I did not stop to answer them. I was in darkness—I found stairs and climbed. There were many stairs, turning around till my head was dizzy. At the top was another door—I found the knob and opened it. I was in a long small chamber—on one side of it was a bronze door that could not be opened, for it had no handle. Perhaps there was a magic word to open it but I did not have the word. I turned to the door in the opposite side of the wall. The lock of it was broken and I opened it and went in.

Within, there was a place of great riches. The god who lived there must have been a powerful god. The first room was a small anteroom—I waited there for some time, telling the spirits of the place that I came in peace and not as a robber. When it seemed to me that they had had time to hear me, I went on. Ah, what riches! Few, even, of the windows had been broken—it was all as it had been. The great windows that looked over the city had not been broken at all though they were dusty and streaked with many years. There were coverings on the floors, the colors not greatly faded, and the chairs were soft and deep. There were pictures upon the walls, very strange, very wonderful—I remember one of a bunch of flowers in a jar—if you came close to it, you could see nothing but bits of color, but if you stood away from it, the flowers might have been picked yesterday. It made my heart feel strange to look at this picture—and to look at the figure of a bird, in some hard clay, on a

table and see it so like our birds. Everywhere there were books and writings, many in tongues that I could not read. The god who lived there must have been a wise god and full of knowledge. I felt I had right there, as I sought knowledge also.

Nevertheless, it was strange. There was a washing-place but no water—perhaps the gods washed in air. There was a cooking-place but no wood, and though there was a machine to cook food, there was no place to put fire in it. Nor were there candles or lamps—there were things that looked like lamps but they had neither oil nor wick. All these things were magic, but I touched them and lived—the magic had gone out of them. Let me tell one thing to show. In the washing-place, a thing said "Hot" but it was not hot to the touch—another thing said "Cold" but it was not cold. This must have been a strong magic but the magic was gone. I do not understand—they had ways—I wish that I knew.

It was close and dry and dusty in their house of the gods. I have said the magic was gone but that is not true—it had gone from the magic things but it had not gone from the place. I felt the spirits about me, weighing upon me. Nor had I ever slept in a Dead Place before—and yet, tonight, I must sleep there. When I thought of it, my tongue felt dry in my throat, in spite of my wish for knowledge. Almost I would have gone down again and faced the dogs, but I did not.

I had not gone through all the rooms when the darkness fell. When it fell, I went back to the big room looking over the city and made fire. There was a place to make fire and a box with wood in it, though I do not think they cooked there. I wrapped myself in a floor-covering and slept in front of the fire—I was very tired.

Now I tell what is very strong magic. I woke in the midst of the night. When I woke, the fire had gone out and I was cold. It seemed to me that all around me there were whisperings and voices. I closed my eyes to shut them out. Some will say that I slept again, but I do not think that

---

## GUIDED READING

**LITERAL QUESTION**

**1a.** What does John describe in the apartment? (He describes coverings on the floor, pictures, a washing place with things that said "Hot" and "Cold," a cooking place, and a place to make fire.)

**INFERENTIAL QUESTION**

**1b.** What do you think these objects are? (carpets, paintings, sink and faucets, stove, fireplace)

I slept. I could feel the spirits drawing my spirit out of my body as a fish is drawn on a line.

Why should I lie about it? I am a priest and the son of a priest. If there are spirits, as they say, in the small Dead Places near us, what spirits must there not be in that great Place of the Gods? And would not they wish to speak? After such long years? I know that I felt myself drawn as a fish is drawn on a line. I had stepped out of my body—I could see my body asleep in front of the cold fire, but it was not I. I was drawn to look out upon the city of the gods.

It should have been dark, for it was night, but it was not dark. Everywhere there were lights—lines of light—circles and blurs of light—ten thousand torches would not have been the same. The sky itself was alight—you could barely see the stars for the glow in the sky. I thought to myself "This is strong magic" and trembled. There was a roaring in my ears like the rushing of rivers. Then my eyes grew used to the light and my ears to the sound. I knew that I was seeing the city as it had been when the gods were alive.

That was a sight indeed—yes, that was a sight: I could not have seen it in the body—my body would have died. Everywhere went the gods, on foot and in chariots—there were gods beyond number and counting and their chariots blocked the streets. They had turned night to day for their pleasure—they did not sleep with the sun. The noise of their coming and going was the noise of many waters. It was magic what they could do—it was magic what they did.

I looked out of another window—the great vines of their bridges were mended and the god-roads went east and west. Restless, restless, were the gods and always in motion! They burrowed tunnels under rivers—they flew in the air. With unbelievable tools they did giant works—no part of the earth was safe from them, for, if they wished for a thing, they summoned it from the other side of the world. And always, as they labored and rested, as they feasted and made love, there was a drum in their ears—the pulse of the giant city, beating and beating like a man's heart.

Were they happy? What is happiness to the gods? They were great, they were mighty, they were wonderful and terrible. As I looked upon them and their magic, I felt like a child—but a little more, it seemed to me, and they would pull down the moon from the sky. I saw them with wisdom beyond wisdom and knowledge beyond knowledge. And yet not all they did was well done—even I could see that—and yet their wisdom could not but grow until all was peace.

Then I saw their fate come upon them and that was terrible past speech. It came upon them as they walked the streets of their city. I have been in the fights with the Forest People—I have seen men die. But this was not like that. When gods war with gods, they use weapons we do not know. It was fire falling out of the sky and a mist that poisoned. It was the time of the Great Burning and the Destruction. They ran about like ants in the streets of their city—poor gods, poor gods! Then the towers began to fall. A few escaped—yes, a few. The legends tell it. But, even after the city had become a Dead Place, for many years the poison was still in the ground. I saw it happen, I saw the last of them die. It was darkness over the broken city and I wept.

All this, I saw. I saw it as I have told it, though not in the body. When I woke in the morning, I was hungry, but I did not think first of my hunger for my heart was perplexed and confused. I knew the reason for the Dead Places but I did not see why it had happened. It seemed to me it should not have happened, with all the magic they had. I went through the house looking for an answer. There was so much in the house I could not understand—and yet I am a priest and the son of a priest. It was like being on one side of the great river, at night, with no light to show the way.

Then I saw the dead god. He was sitting in his chair, by the window, in a room I had not

*By the Waters of Babylon*  65

- John feels the spirits draw his spirit out of his body.
- He sees lights, "chariots," and bridges at night; he hears roaring and sees the gods in motion.
- When he sees the destruction of the city by war, he weeps.
- Searching the house, he sees a dead god.

**1 STYLE: IMAGERY**

Through John's wondering eyes and troubled ears, the reader shares in the sights and sounds of the city before its destruction: *circles and blurs of light, glow in the sky,* and *roaring in my ears like the rushing of rivers.*

**2 SETTING**

John's vision of the incredible nighttime activities of the city leads him to an understanding of the level of knowledge possessed by its former inhabitants.

**3 CHARACTERIZATION**

John's description of the "poor gods" shows by indirect characterization his growing sensitivity and compassion for the inhabitants of the lost civilization.

**4 THEME**

John, who seeks and values knowledge, cannot comprehend its limitations; he feels sure that knowledge can prevent such destruction as he has witnessed.

## *GUIDED READING*

### LITERAL QUESTIONS

**1a.** How does John explain his ability to view the city at night? (He says that the spirits drew his spirit from his body.)

**2a.** What is it that John cannot understand about the gods who had so much wisdom and knowledge? (He cannot understand why they could not have prevented their own destruction.)

### INFERENTIAL QUESTIONS

**1b.** How do you think John is able to see the life of the past? (He may be dreaming, but he definitely is seeing sights of which he has no experience. As a member of a priest's family, he may have psychic powers.)

**2b.** What do you think Benét is telling the reader about wisdom and knowledge? (Though they can create wonderful things and lead to peace, if not properly controlled, they can also lead to destruction.)

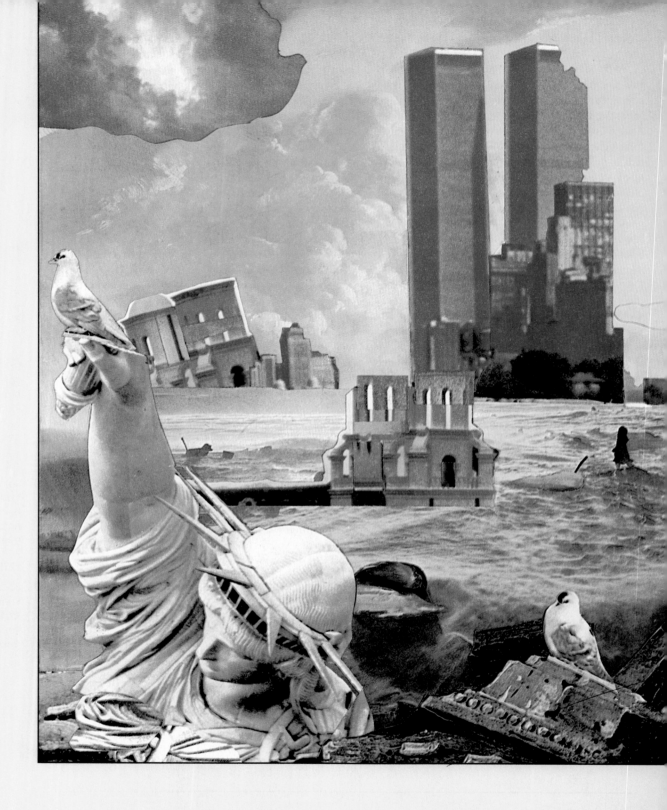

entered before and, for the first moment, I thought that he was alive. Then I saw the skin on the back of his hand—it was like dry leather. The room was shut, hot and dry—no doubt that had kept him as he was. At first I was afraid to approach him—then the fear left me. He was sitting looking out over the city—he was dressed in the clothes of the gods. His age was neither young nor old—I could not tell his age. But there was wisdom in his face and great sadness. You could see that he would have not run away. He had sat at his window, watching his city die—then he himself had died. But it is better to lose one's life than one's spirit—and you could see from the face that his spirit had not been lost. I knew, that, if I touched him, he would fall into dust—and yet, there was something unconquered in the face.

That is all of my story, for then I knew he was a man—I knew then that they had been men, neither gods nor demons. It is a great knowledge, hard to tell and believe. They were men—they went a dark road, but they were men. I had no fear after that—I had no fear going home, though twice I fought off the dogs and once I was hunted for two days by the Forest People. When I saw my father again, I prayed and was purified. He touched my lips and my breast, he said, "You went away a boy. You come back a man and a priest." I said, "Father, they were men! I have been in the Place of the Gods and seen it! Now slay me, if it is the law—but still I know they were men."

He looked at me out of both eyes. He said, "The law is not always the same shape—you have done what you have done. I could not have done it in my time, but you come after me. Tell!"

I told and he listened. After that, I wished to tell all the people but he showed me otherwise. He said, "Truth is a hard deer to hunt. If you eat too much truth at once, you may die of the truth. It was not idly that our fathers forbade the Dead Places." He was right—it is better the truth should come little by little. I have learned that, being a priest. Perhaps, in the old days, they ate knowledge too fast.

Nevertheless, we make a beginning. It is not for the metal alone we go to the Dead Places now—there are the books and the writings. They are hard to learn. And the magic tools are broken—but we can look at them and wonder. At least, we make a beginning. And, when I am chief priest we shall go beyond the great river. We shall go to the Place of the Gods—the place newyork—not one man but a company. We shall look for the images of the gods and find the god ASHING and the others—the gods Lincoln and Biltmore and Moses. But they were men who built the city, not gods or demons. They were men. I remember the dead man's face. They were men who were here before us. We must build again.

---

## STUDY QUESTIONS

### Recalling

1. What position does John hold among the Hill People? What privileges and responsibilities arise from this position?
2. List two reasons that John gives for setting out on his journey to the Place of the Gods.

3. Describe three things that John notices on his first day in the Place of the Gods.
4. What does John finally realize about the gods? When does he reach this understanding?

### Interpreting

5. Contrast the life of the Hill People with the lives of those who had lived in the Place of the Gods.

*By the Waters of Babylon* **67**

- John realizes that the inhabitants of the city were men, not gods.
- He tells his father what he has learned.
- Now they go to the Dead Places for books; when John is chief priest, they will go to the Place of the Gods, which is New York.
- John resolves to build again.

### 1 PLOT: CLIMAX

The climax of the story occurs when John realizes that men, not gods, built the city and caused the destruction of their own civilization.

### 2 THEME

With a wisdom perhaps greater than that of the destroyed civilization, John's father warns about the dangers of knowledge that a society cannot control.

### REFLECTING ON THE STORY

Do you think that John's people will be able to reconstruct the advanced civilization without making the mistakes that destroyed it? (They will probably be more cautious than their predecessors, and so have a greater chance of surviving.)

### STUDY QUESTIONS

1. son of a priest; visits sacred places; learns secrets
2. desire for knowledge; has vision
3. tall buildings; wild dogs; "god roads" on land and across the river; statue labeled *ASHING*; building marked *UBTREAS*
4. they were humans; when he sees the dead man
5. *Place of the Gods:* inhabitants of New York City; *Hill People:* primitive hunting society after destruction of the civilized world

6. *Ou-di-sun:* Hudson River; *Bitter Water:* Atlantic Ocean; *ASHING:* George Washington; *UBTREAS:* Subtreasury Building (now known as Federal Hall National Memorial); the building with the starry ceiling is Grand Central.

7. People used knowledge irresponsibly.

8. No. Our surprise at seeing our own world in ruins makes an impact.

9. Technology has the potential for harm as well as good.

### VIEWPOINT

*Babylon:* place where Hill People live; *Zion:* Place of the Gods; John identifies with his ancestors as the Jews did with Zion.

### LITERARY FOCUS

1. Before his journey John is ignorant and confused. His discovery that the "gods" were men matures him.

2. Myths and legends enshroud the place; John's visit reveals it as a modern city built and destroyed by humans. Benét was commenting about power and responsibility.

### COMPARING STORIES

1. ■ "League": External conflict; Holmes solves mystery; foils robbery.
   ■ "Bedquilt": External conflict; family gains respect for Mehetabel, who solves her internal conflict and gains self-respect.

2. ■ "Chee": Losing daughter makes him question faith; earth provides a means for her return.
   ■ "Tavener": Hester allows sons to become more important than husband; reminiscing reunites them.

3. ■ "Why Don't You": Ocean liner confronts small sailboat; man outmaneuvers liner, symbolizing victory for individualism.
   ■ "Babylon": Tribesman confronts ruins of advanced society and gains insight into knowledge and power.

6. What do the references to "Ou-di-sun," "Bitter Water," and "Ashing" mean to modern readers? Explain the meaning of at least two other such references in the story.

7. What does John mean when he says, "Perhaps in the old days they ate knowledge too fast"?

8. Do you think the story would have been more effective if the identity of the Place of the Gods had been revealed earlier in the story? Why or why not?

**Extending**

9. What might John's warning about those who "ate knowledge too fast" mean for our own time?

### VIEWPOINT

The title of this story was taken from Psalm 137 in the Bible. In this psalm the Israelites, who had been taken captive by the Babylonians, lament their exile from their homeland, which they refer to as "Zion":

> By the waters of Babylon,
> there we sat down and wept,
> when we remembered Zion.

■ What is "Babylon" and what is "Zion" in Benét's story? In what way might the last lines of the story express the same feelings that this psalm expresses?

### LITERARY FOCUS

**Change of Setting**

Many stories include more than one setting. A **change of setting** usually signals an important development in the story and often helps to bring about other changes—for example, in the action and characters.

A character's *perception* of the setting can also change as the character acquires more information about it. A place that seemed friendly, for example, can turn out to be dangerous, or a place that had seemed alien can turn out to be familiar. Furthermore, a change in *our* perception of the setting affects our overall response to the story.

**Thinking About Change of Setting**

1. Explain how John's visit to the Place of the Gods leads to a change in his character.

2. How does John's visit to the Place of the Gods change his—and your—perception of it? What did you feel when you realized where John was and who the gods actually were?

### COMPOSITION

**Writing About Setting**

■ How does the setting in "By the Waters of Babylon" reveal Benét's purpose? First decide what Benét's purpose was in writing this story. Then explain how that purpose is revealed in the contrast between the story's two settings: John's home and the Place of the Gods. *For help with this assignment, see Lesson 4 in the Writing About Literature Handbook at the back of this book.*

**Describing a Place**

■ Imagine a character who lives at a time other than our own but has been transported into our time. First make your character's identity clear to the reader. Then describe a well-known place—for example, the Statue of Liberty—from the perspective of your character, who is completely unfamiliar with it. Your readers should be able to identify the place by the end of your description.

### COMPARING STORIES

1. In both "The Red-Headed League" and "The Bedquilt" the main character successfully resolves a conflict and wins the admiration of others for his or her achievement. Compare the kinds of conflicts that the characters resolve in these two stories and the very different achievements of the characters who resolve them.

2. "Chee's Daughter" and "The Sentimentality of William Tavener" both present characters who lose touch with an important value and then recover what they had lost. Compare the stories. Explain why the characters lose touch with important values, and tell how they recover them.

3. "Why Don't You Look Where You're Going?" and "By the Waters of Babylon" each presents a confrontation between a technologically advanced world and a simpler one. Compare the confrontations in the two stories. What is the result of this confrontation in each story?

---

## COMPOSITION: GUIDELINES FOR EVALUATION

### WRITING ABOUT SETTING

**Objective**

To relate the setting of story to its purpose

**Guidelines for Evaluation**

■ suggested length: three to five paragraphs
■ should state Benét's purpose
■ should contrast John's home and place of the gods
■ should explain how contrasting these settings helps Benét accomplish his purpose

### DESCRIBING A PLACE

**Objective**

To create a character from another time and describe a place from that person's perspective

**Guidelines for Evaluation**

■ suggested length: three to five paragraphs
■ should create a character from either the past or the future
■ should describe a well-known place through the point of view of the character

# LITERARY FOCUS: *Point of View and Tone*

Born into a family of traveling actors, Edgar Allan Poe (1809–1849) was orphaned at an early age and raised by a wealthy Virginian family. He later attended West Point but abandoned his military career for the life of a professional writer. In his musical poetry and in tales of terror like ''The Cask of Amontillado,'' Poe created works memorable for their imaginative power.

■ Have you ever felt like getting even with someone—and imagined trying to do it? What was the result?

*Edgar Allan Poe*

# The Cask of Amontillado[1]

1   The thousand injuries of Fortunato[2] I had borne as best I could; but when he ventured upon insult, I vowed revenge. You, who so well know the nature of my soul, will not suppose, however, that I gave utterance to a threat. *At length* I would be avenged; this was a point definitively settled—but the very definitiveness with which it was resolved precluded the idea of risk. I must not only punish, but punish with impunity. A wrong is unredressed when retribution overtakes its redresser. It is equally unredressed when the avenger fails to make himself felt as such to him who has done the wrong.

It must be understood that neither by word nor deed had I given Fortunato cause to doubt my good will. I continued, as was my wont, to smile in his face, and he did not perceive that my smile *now* was at the thought of his immolation.[3]

2   He had a weak point—this Fortunato—although in other regards he was a man to be respected and even feared. He prided himself on his connoisseurship in wine. Few Italians have the true virtuoso spirit.[4] For the most part their enthusiasm is adopted to suit the time and opportunity—to practice imposture[5] upon the British and Austrian millionaires. In painting and gemmary[6] Fortunato, like his countrymen, was a quack—but in the matter of old wines he was sincere. In this respect I did not differ from him materially; I was skillful in the Italian vintages myself, and bought largely whenever I could.

3   It was about dusk, one evening during the supreme madness of the carnival season,[7] that I encountered my friend. He accosted me with excessive warmth, for he had been drinking much. The man wore motley.[8] He had on a tight-fitting parti-striped dress, and his head was surmounted by the conical cap and bells. I was so

---

1. **Amontillado** [ə män′tə lä′dō]: pale, dry Spanish sherry, or wine, to which herbs and other ingredients are added.
2. **Fortunato** [fôr′chōō nä′tō]
3. **immolation** [im′ə lä′shən]: complete destruction.

4. **virtuoso** [vur′chōō ō′sō] **spirit**: great appreciation for the arts; here, the art of wine-tasting.
5. **imposture** [im pos′chər]: deception.
6. **gemmary** [jem′ə rē]: knowledge of jewels and stones.
7. **carnival season:** colorful festival that precedes Lent, the six-week period of self-denial observed by many Christians.
8. **motley** [mot′lē]: multi-colored (*parti-striped*) costume for a clown or jester.

*The Cask of Amontillado* **69**

## AT A GLANCE

- The narrator vows revenge on Fortunato.
- Fortunato's weakness is his pride in his knowledge of wine.
- During carnival the narrator meets Fortunato, who has been drinking and is dressed like a clown.

## LITERARY OPTIONS

- point of view
- style
- setting

## THEMATIC OPTIONS

- manipulation of weakness
- revenge
- insanity

### 1 POINT OF VIEW

Since Poe uses the first-person point of view, the reader's knowledge of character and events is limited to information the narrator, Montresor, chooses to reveal.

### 2 THEME

Patiently plotting his revenge, the narrator recognizes his opponent's weakness as an area for manipulation.

### 3 SETTING

The setting at dusk ''during the supreme madness of the carnival season,'' when Fortunato, ironically dressed for good times, has been drinking, provides an ideal atmosphere for a story of manipulation and revenge.

---

## GUIDED READING

**LITERAL QUESTION**

**1a.** What does the narrator claim is Fortunato's one weakness? (his pride in his connoisseurship in wine)

**SELECTION FOR PRACTICE IN ACTIVE READING**

(TCR 5, p. 55)

**INFERENTIAL QUESTION**

**1b.** What does the narrator mean by calling it a weakness? (It is the one means by which he can get revenge.)

- The narrator says he wants Luchesi to assess his Amontillado.
- Fortunato denies Luchesi's expertise and offers to go to the vaults with the narrator.
- They go to the narrator's empty house.

### 1 CHARACTERIZATION

The narrator's apparent friendliness to Fortunato reveals, through indirect characterization, his ability to deceive and manipulate.

### 2 THEME

The narrator understands Fortunato's pride well enough to know that mention of a rival connoisseur will manipulate Fortunato into doing precisely what he, the narrator, wants.

### 3 CHARACTERIZATION

The costumes show by indirect characterization the role each is to play: Fortunato is dressed as a clown; the avenger is masked in black.

### 4 CHARACTERIZATION

Again, in indirect characterization, the narrator reveals skillful manipulation of his servants, and his satisfaction with this ability.

1 pleased to see him that I thought I should never have done wringing his hand.

I said to him, "My dear Fortunato, you are luckily met. How remarkably well you are looking today! But I have received a pipe[9] of what passes for Amontillado, and I have my doubts."

"How?" said he. "Amontillado? A pipe? Impossible! And in the middle of the carnival!"

"I have my doubts," I replied; "and I was silly enough to pay the full Amontillado price without consulting you in the matter. You were not to be found, and I was fearful of losing a bargain."

"Amontillado!"

"I have my doubts."

"Amontillado!"

"And I must satisfy them."

"Amontillado!"

2 "As you are engaged, I am on my way to Luchesi. If anyone has a critical turn, it is he. He will tell me—"

"Luchesi cannot tell Amontillado from sherry."[10]

"And yet some fools will have it that his taste is a match for your own."

"Come, let us go."

"Whither?"

"To your vaults."

"My friend, no; I will not impose upon your good nature. I perceive you have an engagement. Luchesi—"

"I have no engagement—come."

"My friend, no. It is not the engagement, but the severe cold with which I perceive you are afflicted. The vaults are insufferably damp. They are incrusted with niter."[11]

"Let us go, nevertheless. The cold is merely nothing. Amontillado! You have been imposed upon. And as for Luchesi, he cannot distinguish sherry from Amontillado."

---

9. **pipe:** large barrel.
10. **sherry:** here, a sweet sherry, unlike the dry Amontillado.
11. **niter** [nī'tər]: nitrate salt deposit.

**70** *The Short Story*

3 Thus speaking, Fortunato possessed himself of my arm. Putting on a mask of black silk, and drawing a *roquelaure*[12] closely about my person, I suffered him to hurry me to my palazzo.[13]

There were no attendants at home; they had absconded to make merry in honor of the time. I 4 had told them that I should not return until the morning, and had given them explicit orders not to stir from the house. These orders were sufficient, I well knew, to insure their immediate disappearance, one and all, as soon as my back was turned.

I took from their sconces two flambeaux,[14] and giving one to Fortunato, bowed him through several suites of rooms to the archway that led into the vaults. I passed down a long and winding staircase, requesting him to be cautious as he followed. We came at length to the foot of

---

12. *roquelaure* [rō kə lôr']: knee-length cloak.
13. **palazzo** [pə lat'sō]: large home or palace.
14. **from their . . . flambeaux** [flam bō']: from their holders two flaming torches.

## GUIDED READING

### LITERAL QUESTIONS

**1a.** How does the narrator get Fortunato to accompany him? (He suggests that he has made a mistake about the Amontillado and then urges Fortunato not to go with him.)

**2a.** What has the narrator done to insure that no one else is at home? (He has told his servants that they are not to leave the house, knowing that they will disobey him.)

### INFERENTIAL QUESTIONS

**1b.** Why does Fortunato accompany him? (Fortunato's pride makes him want to disclose an error in the narrator's judgment, and he does not want his rival Luchesi to taste the wine.)

**2b.** What does this arrangement suggest about the narrator's encounter with Fortunato? (It has been carefully planned.)

the descent, and stood together on the damp ground of the catacombs[15] of the Montresors.[16]

The gait of my friend was unsteady, and the bells upon his cap jingled as he strode.

"The pipe," said he.

"It is farther on," said I; "but observe the white webwork which gleams from these cavern walls."

He turned toward me, and looked into my eyes with two filmy orbs that distilled the rheum of intoxication.

"Niter?" he asked at length.

"Niter," I replied. "How long have you had that cough?"

"Ugh! ugh! ugh!—ugh! ugh! ugh!—ugh! ugh! ugh!—ugh! ugh! ugh!—ugh! ugh! ugh!"

My poor friend found it impossible to reply for many minutes.

"It is nothing," he said, at last.

"Come," I said, with decision, "we will go back; your health is precious. You are rich, respected, admired, beloved; you are happy, as once I was. You are a man to be missed. For me it is no matter. We will go back; you will be ill, and I cannot be responsible. Besides, there is Luchesi—"

"Enough," he said; "the cough is a mere nothing; it will not kill me. I shall not die of a cough."

"True—true," I replied; "and, indeed, I had no intention of alarming you unnecessarily—but you should use all proper caution. A draft of this Medoc will defend us from the damps."

Here I knocked off the neck of a bottle which I drew from a long row of its fellows that lay upon the mold.

"Drink," I said, presenting him the wine.

He raised it to his lips with a leer. He paused and nodded to me familiarly, while his bells jingled.

"I drink," he said, "to the buried that repose around us."

"And I to your long life."

He again took my arm, and we proceeded.

"These vaults," he said, "are extensive."

"The Montresors," I replied, "were a great and numerous family."

"I forget your arms."[17]

"A huge human foot d'or, in a field azure; the foot crushes a serpent rampant whose fangs are embedded in the heel."[18]

"And the motto?"

*Nemo me impune lacessit.*[19]

"Good!" he said.

The wine sparkled in his eyes and the bells jingled. My own fancy grew warm with the Medoc. We had passed through walls of piled bones, with casks and puncheons[20] intermingling, into the inmost recesses of the catacombs. I paused again, and this time I made bold to seize Fortunato by an arm above the elbow.

"The niter!" I said; "see, it increases. It hangs like moss upon the vaults. We are below the river's bed. The drops of moisture trickle among the bones. Come, we will go back ere it is too late. Your cough—"

"It is nothing," he said; "let us go on. But first, another draft of the Medoc."

I broke and reached him a flagon of De Grâve. He emptied it at a breath. His eyes flashed with a fierce light. He laughed and threw the bottle upwards with a gesticulation I did not understand.

I looked at him in surprise. He repeated the movement—a grotesque one.

"You do not comprehend?" he said.

"Not I," I replied.

---

17. **arms:** coat-of-arms, a family emblem usually with symbolic pictures and a motto.
18. **foot d'or . . . heel:** The Montresor emblem is a golden foot on a blue background. The foot is crushing a snake that is rising against it and biting the heel.
19. *Nemo . . . lacessit:* Latin for "No one attacks me without being punished."
20. **puncheons** [pun′chənz]: large wine barrels.

*The Cask of Amontillado* **71**

---

15. **catacombs:** underground cemetery made up of rooms and passages with recesses in the walls for tombs. Wine is kept here because of the low temperatures and the darkness.
16. **Montresors** [mon′trā zôrz′]

## AT A GLANCE

- After Fortunato coughs, the narrator flatters him and urges that they go back.
- They drink Medoc.
- The narrator describes his family arms and motto.

### 1 SETTING

The underground family catacombs, their darkness intensified by contrast with the "white webwork" of niter, provide an ominous setting.

### 2 THEME

The narrator, outwardly urging Fortunato to go back, appeals to his victim's pride, thereby manipulating him.

### 3 IRONY

Poe uses verbal irony when the narrator, who seeks revenge, offers a toast to Fortunato's long life.

### 4 SYMBOL

The image of the serpent biting the foot that is crushing it symbolizes revenge. It is not clear whether the narrator identifies with the foot or the serpent, since the two are locked in fatal combat.

---

## GUIDED READING

### LITERAL QUESTION

**1a.** How does the narrator convince Fortunato to drink wine as they go through the catacombs? (He says that it will protect Fortunato from the dampness.)

### INFERENTIAL QUESTION

**1b.** What do you think is the real reason that the narrator keeps urging alcohol on Fortunato? (He knows he can better manipulate Fortunato if the latter's mental processes have been compromised by alcohol.)

## AT A GLANCE

- When Fortunato asks if the narrator is a mason, he shows him a trowel he has under his cloak.
- Beyond a deep crypt they see another less spacious one.

### 1 STYLE: IMAGERY

The descriptive images allow the reader to smell the foul air as well as to see the glowing torch.

### 2 RESPONSE JOURNAL

Ask the students to describe a setting that creates an atmosphere of happiness, fear, loneliness, or sadness. Remind them to include imagery that appeals to several senses.

"Then you are not of the brotherhood."

"How?"

"You are not of the masons."[21]

"Yes, yes," I said, "yes, yes."

"You? Impossible! A mason?"

"A mason," I replied.

"A sign," he said.

"It is this," I answered, producing a trowel[22] from beneath the folds of my *roquelaure*.

"You jest," he exclaimed, recoiling a few paces. "But let us proceed to the Amontillado."

"Be it so," I said, replacing the tool beneath the cloak, and again offering him my arm. He leaned upon it heavily. We continued our route in search of the Amontillado. We passed through a range of low arches, descended, passed on, and, descending again, arrived at a deep crypt, in which the foulness of the air caused our flambeaux rather to glow than flame.

At the most remote end of the crypt there appeared another less spacious. Its walls had been lined with human remains, piled to the vault overhead, in the fashion of the great catacombs of Paris. Three sides of this interior crypt were still ornamented in this manner. From the fourth the bones had been thrown down, and lay promiscuously upon the earth, forming at one point a mound of some size. Within the wall thus exposed by the displacing of the bones, we perceived a still interior recess, in depth about four feet, in width three, in height six or seven. It seemed to have been constructed for no especial use within itself, but formed merely the interval between two of the colossal supports of the roof of the catacombs, and was backed by one of their circumscribing walls of solid granite.

It was in vain that Fortunato, uplifting his dull torch, endeavored to pry into the depth of the recess. Its termination the feeble light did not enable us to see.

---

21. **masons:** Freemasons, a secret fraternal order; also, another name for bricklayers.
22. **trowel:** bricklayer's tool; also, a symbol of the Freemasons.

## GUIDED READING

### LITERAL QUESTION

**1a.** What problem does Fortunato encounter when he tries to look into the recess to find the Amontillado? (He cannot see into it by the dim light of his torch.)

### INFERENTIAL QUESTION

**1b.** Why do you think that the narrator claims to have stored the wine in such a remote place? (He wants Fortunato to enter the recess.)

"Proceed," I said; "herein is the Amontillado. As for Luchesi—"

"He is an ignoramus," interrupted my friend, as he stepped unsteadily forward, while I followed immediately at his heels. In an instant he had reached the extremity of the niche, and finding his progress arrested by the rock, stood stupidly bewildered. A moment more and I had fettered him to the granite. In its surface were two iron staples, distant from each other about two feet, horizontally. From one of these depended a short chain, from the other a padlock. Throwing the links about his waist, it was but the work of a few seconds to secure it. He was too much astounded to resist. Withdrawing the key I stepped back from the recess.

**1** "Pass your hand," I said, "over the wall; you cannot help feeling the niter. Indeed it is *very* damp. Once more let me *implore* you to return. No? Then I must positively leave you. But I must first render you all the little attentions in my power."

"The Amontillado!" ejaculated my friend, not yet recovered from his astonishment.

"True," I replied; "the Amontillado."

As I said these words I busied myself among the pile of bones of which I have before spoken. Throwing them aside, I soon uncovered a quan-**2** tity of building stone and mortar. With these materials and with the aid of my trowel, I began vigorously to wall up the entrance of the niche.

I had scarcely laid the first tier of the masonry when I discovered that the intoxication of Fortunato had in a great measure worn off. The earliest indication I had of this was a low moaning cry from the depth of the recess. It was *not* the cry of a drunken man. There was then a long and obstinate silence. I laid the second tier, and the third, and the fourth; and then I heard the **3** furious vibrations of the chain. The noise lasted for several minutes, during which, that I might hearken to it with the more satisfaction, I ceased my labors and sat down upon the bones. When at last the clanking subsided, I resumed the

trowel, and finished without interruption the fifth, the sixth, and the seventh tier. The wall was now nearly upon a level with my breast. I again paused, and holding the flambeaux over the masonwork, threw a few feeble rays upon the figure within.

**4** A succession of loud and shrill screams, bursting suddenly from the throat of the chained form, seemed to thrust me violently back. For a brief moment I hesitated—I trembled. Unsheathing my rapier,[23] I began to grope with it about the recess; but the thought of an instant reassured me. I placed my hand upon the solid fabric of the catacombs, and felt satisfied. I reapproached the wall. I replied to the yells of him who clamored. I reechoed—I aided—I surpassed them in volume and in strength. I did this, and the clamorer grew still.

It was now midnight, and my task was drawing to a close. I had completed the eighth, the

---

23. **rapier** [rā′pē ər]: double-edged sword.

*The Cask of Amontillado* **73**

**AT A GLANCE**

- When Fortunato enters the recess, the narrator chains him to the wall and begins to brick up the entrance.
- Fortunato moans, is silent, and then frantically vibrates the chain.
- When Fortunato screams, Montresor screams louder than his victim.

**1 STYLE: IMAGERY**

The reader feels the dampness of the niter as Poe's imagery paints a scene of horror.

**2 PLOT: CLIMAX**

When the narrator chains Fortunato to the wall and begins to brick up the opening, the reader suspects how the quarrel will be resolved.

**3 POINT OF VIEW**

Montresor's delight in the struggles of his imprisoned adversary reveals that the narrator is inhuman and insane.

**4 STYLE: IMAGERY**

Poe conveys Fortunato's recognition of his fate by allowing the reader to hear his "loud and shrill screams."

## GUIDED READING

### LITERAL QUESTIONS

**1a.** What does Fortunato find when he enters the niche in search of the Amontillado? (nothing but a wall of granite)

**2a.** What does Montresor do when Fortunato begins to scream? (He trembles and gropes about the recess with his rapier.)

### INFERENTIAL QUESTIONS

**1b.** Why does he find only that? (There never was any Amontillado. Montresor's claim that he had purchased some is a fabrication used to entrap Fortunato.)

**2b.** How do you explain these actions? (He worries that Fortunato's screams may be heard and considers killing him with the rapier; however, the solidity of the catacomb wall reassures him.)

- As Montresor starts to place the last stone, Fortunato begs to be freed.
- Montresor puts the last stone in and replaces the pile of bones.
- For fifty years no mortal has disturbed the bones.

**1 POINT OF VIEW**

The revelation that the events occurred fifty years ago, Montresor's lack of remorse, and his insanity render the story even more horrifying.

**REFLECTING ON THE STORY**

Why do you think Montresor never reveals what Fortunato has done to invite his revenge? (Possible answers are that he does not remember, that he knows it was not really serious, or that the revenge has become more important than the slight that prompted it.)

**STUDY QUESTIONS**

1. Fortunato has insulted him.
2. in the street; the Montresor family catacombs
3. tempts him to sample wine
4. chains him to wall; bricks up entry
5. suggests that his reasons are not valid
6. Montresor: suggests villain; Fortunato: suggests fool
7. He is convinced he is justified. Yes—vengeance has two requirements: victim must know perpetrator; avenger must never be punished.
8. Students may suggest that evil is often more interesting to read about than virtue. Also, tales of horror can be fun as long as you know they are fictional.

**VIEWPOINT**

No—Fortunato is portrayed as a foolish victim. We learn that the murder was committed fifty years before.

---

ninth, and the tenth tier. I had finished a portion of the last and the eleventh; there remained but a single stone to be fitted and plastered in. I struggled with its weight; I placed it partially in its destined position. But now there came from out the niche a low laugh that erected the hairs upon my head. It was succeeded by a sad voice, which I had difficulty in recognizing as that of the noble Fortunato. The voice said:

"Ha! ha! ha!—he! he!—a very good joke indeed—an excellent jest. We will have many a rich laugh about it at the palazzo—he! he! he!—over our wine—he! he! he!"

"The Amontillado!" I said.

"He! he! he!—he! he! he!—yes, the Amontillado. But is it not getting late? Will not they be awaiting us at the palazzo—the Lady Fortunato and the rest? Let us be gone."

"Yes," I said, "let us be gone."

"*For the love of God, Montresor.*"

"Yes," I said, "for the love of God."

But to these words I hearkened in vain for a reply. I grew impatient. I called aloud:

"Fortunato!"

No answer. I called again:

"Fortunato!"

No answer still. I thrust a torch through the remaining aperture and let it fall within. There came forth in return only a jingling of the bells. My heart grew sick—on account of the dampness of the catacombs. I hastened to make an end of my labor. I forced the last stone into its position; I plastered it up. Against the new masonry I **1** reerected the old rampart of bones. For the half of a century no mortal has disturbed them. *In pace requiescat!*[24]

---

24. *In pace requiescat* [in päch′ā′ rāk′wē es′kät′]: Latin for "Rest in peace."

**STUDY QUESTIONS**

**Recalling**

1. According to Montresor, why must Fortunato be punished?
2. Where does the story begin, and where does the action move to?
3. Explain how Montresor persuades Fortunato to come with him.
4. What does Montresor do to Fortunato in the vault?

**Interpreting**

5. The narrator, Montresor, does not tell us much about the injuries Fortunato has done to him. What might this omission indicate about Montresor?
6. Both Montresor and Fortunato wear costumes. How is each man's apparel appropriate to his character and his role in the story?
7. What is Montresor's attitude toward his own actions in this story? At the end has he achieved the revenge he spoke about in the first paragraph? Why or why not?

**Extending**

8. Poe's tales of terror have been very popular for over a century. Why do you think stories like "The Cask of Amontillado" appeal to readers?

**VIEWPOINT**

One literary critic has suggested that "The Cask of Amontillado" allows the reader to witness an upsetting event at a distance

without requiring us to be "there," without . . . invoking our pity.

— E. H. Davidson, *Selected Writings of Edgar Allan Poe*

- Do you think that the story arouses any pity for Fortunato? Why or why not? How do the last two sentences of the story help to set the reader at a distance from its events?

## LITERARY FOCUS

### First-Person Point of View

**Point of view** is the relationship between the storyteller and the story. Another name for the storyteller is the **narrator.** In a story told from the **first-person point of view,** the narrator is one of the characters and relates events in which he or she was involved. Stories told from the first-person point of view are often especially vivid because their narrators are so close to the action. However, these stories usually offer a very limited view of the truth since they cannot reveal things that the narrator does not know—for example, the thoughts of other characters; similarly, a first-person narrator may not fully understand the events in the story.

In some first-person stories we cannot even be sure that the narrator is entirely truthful. Such a storyteller is called an **unreliable narrator,** a narrator who in some way distorts the truth. Stories with unreliable narrators often include evidence that the narrator is hiding the truth or is mentally unbalanced. In reading a story with a first-person narrator, we should first decide whether the narrator seems to be reliable or not; if the narrator seems unreliable, we should always question his or her account of the story's events.

### Thinking About First-Person Point of View

1. Is Montresor a reliable or an unreliable first-person narrator? Give evidence to support your opinion.
2. Would this story be more effective if it were told from a different point of view—for example, from that of Fortunato or a police investigator? Why or why not?

### Imagery

**Imagery** is the descriptive language that writers use to make people, places, objects, and experiences especially vivid to their readers. Imagery appeals to our five senses of sight, sound, smell, taste, and touch. For example, a writer might intensify a description of a race with images that let us see the runners' straining muscles, hear their pounding feet, and smell the freshly cut grass in the field next to the track. In "The Cask of Amontillado" Edgar Allan Poe uses sense imagery to heighten the effect of his tale.

### Thinking About Imagery

1. In the catacombs scene find vivid images that refer to three *different* senses.
2. What is the effect of the sound images Poe uses in the final paragraphs of the story?

## VOCABULARY

### Synonyms

A **synonym** is a word that has the same or nearly the same meaning as another word. For example, *leap* and *jump* are synonyms. The words in capital letters are from "The Cask of Amontillado." Choose the letter of the word that is *nearest* the meaning of each word in capitals, *as the word is used in the story.* Write the number of each item and the letter of your choice on a separate sheet.

1. REDRESS: (a) cancel (b) forgive (c) clothe (d) set right
2. DISTILLED: (a) blinded (b) removed (c) concentrated (d) protected
3. RECESS: (a) break (b) peak (c) niche (d) low point
4. PRECLUDED: (a) added (b) contained (c) concealed (d) prevented
5. FETTERED: (a) captured (b) chained (c) attracted (d) misled

## COMPOSITION

### Writing About Point of View

■ Explain why the point of view used by Poe in "The Cask of Amontillado" is effective. First describe the personality of Montresor. Then describe the things Montresor chooses to tell us and to leave out. Finally explain how Montresor's point of view affects the impact of the story. *For help with this assignment, see Lesson 5 in the Writing About Literature Handbook at the back of this book.*

### Writing a Radio Play

■ Imagine that two scientists are exploring an old castle. While wandering through a maze of tunnels beneath the castle, they make a startling discovery. Write a radio play about their experience. Include dialogue for the two scientists as well as several vivid sound effects.

*The Cask of Amontillado* **75**

### First-Person Point of View

1. unreliable; lies to Fortunato, feels no horror in his act, seems unbalanced
2. No. This version gives us the best insight into Montresor's madness.

### Imagery

1. *hearing:* jingling bells on cap; *sight:* gleaming webwork; *touch:* dampness
2. create a chilling image of Fortunato's unseen condition

## VOCABULARY

1. (d) set right
2. (c) concentrated
3. (c) niche
4. (d) prevented
5. (b) chained

## COMPOSITION: GUIDELINES FOR EVALUATION

### WRITING ABOUT POINT OF VIEW

#### Objective
To tell why the use of an unreliable narrator is effective

#### Guidelines for Evaluation
- suggested length: three to five paragraphs
- should present character sketch of Montresor
- should cite specific examples illustrating that Montresor is an unreliable narrator
- should explain the effect the narrator's point of view has on story's impact

### WRITING A RADIO PLAY

#### Objective
To write a radio play that conveys a story through dialogue and sound effects

#### Guidelines for Evaluation
- suggested length: 400–700 words
- should create two characters and dialogue for each
- should create an imaginative situation
- should use sound effects to heighten imagery

LITERARY OPTIONS

- point of view
- tone
- characterization

THEMATIC OPTIONS

- reality vs. artistic ambitions
- family relations

**1 POINT OF VIEW**

Immediately Wharton establishes a double point of view. We see the novel through Theodora's loving eyes: we also sense that the third-person narrator views Theodora's clichéd writing more critically.

**2 THEME**

Wharton contrasts Theodora's romantic novel with her real life of hard work and responsibility.

Most of the novels and short stories that Edith Wharton (1862–1937) wrote were about wealthy characters. One of her novels—*The Age of Innocence*—won the Pulitzer Prize in 1921. Wharton departs from her usual subject matter in the following story about a seventeen-year-old girl who aspires to become "known in literature."

■ The author might have taken the title of this story from the old saying "April showers bring May flowers." In your opinion does the saying apply to this story or not?

*Edith Wharton*

# April Showers

1 "But Guy's heart slept under the violets on Muriel's grave."

It was a beautiful ending; Theodora had seen girls cry over last chapters that weren't half as pathetic. She laid her pen aside and read the words over, letting her voice linger on the fall of the sentence; then, drawing a deep breath, she wrote across the foot of the page the name by which she had decided to become known in literature—Gladys Glyn.

Downstairs the library clock struck two. Its muffled thump sounded like an admonitory knock against her bedroom floor. Two o'clock! 2 and she had promised her mother to be up early enough to see that the buttons were sewn on Johnny's reefer,[1] and that Kate had her cod-liver oil[2] before starting for school!

Lingeringly, tenderly she gathered up the pages of her novel—there were five hundred of them—and tied them with the blue satin ribbon that her Aunt Julia had given her. She had meant to wear the ribbon with her new dotted muslin on Sundays, but this was putting it to a nobler use. She bound it round her manuscript, tying the ends in a pretty bow. Theodora was clever at making bows, and could have trimmed hats beautifully, had not all her spare moments been given to literature. Then, with a last look at the precious pages, she sealed and addressed the package. She meant to send it off next morning to the *Home Circle*. She knew it would be hard to obtain access to a paper which numbered so many popular authors among its contributors, but she had been encouraged to make the venture by something her Uncle James had said the last time he had come down from Boston.

He had been telling his brother, Doctor Dace, about his new house out at Brookline. Uncle James was prosperous, and was always moving into new houses with more "modern improvements." Hygiene was his passion, and he migrated in the wake of sanitary plumbing.

"The bathrooms alone are worth the money," he was saying, cheerfully, "although it

---

1. **reefer:** short, heavy jacket.
2. **cod-liver oil:** unpleasant-tasting liquid rich in vitamins A and D.

**76** *The Short Story*

---

LITERAL QUESTION

**1a.** How does Theodora tie up the pages of her novel? (with a blue satin ribbon)

INFERENTIAL QUESTION

**1b.** Why does Theodora do this? (The novel is precious to her and worthy of the special ribbon Aunt Julia had given her.)

**1** *is* a big rent. But then, when a man's got no children to save up for—'' he glanced compassionately round Doctor Dace's crowded table ''—and it *is* something to be in a neighborhood where the drainage is A-one. That's what I was telling our neighbor. Who do you suppose she is, by the way?'' He smiled at Theodora. ''I rather think that young lady knows all about her. Ever hear of Kathleen Kyd?''

Kathleen Kyd! The famous ''society novelist,'' the creator of more ''favorite heroines'' than all her predecessors put together had ever turned out, the author of *Fashion and Passion*, *An American Duchess*, *Rhona's Revolt*. Was there any intelligent girl from Maine to California whose heart would not have beat faster at the mention of that name?

''Why, yes,'' Uncle James was saying, ''Kathleen Kyd lives next door. Frances G. Wollop is her real name, and her husband's a dentist. She's a very pleasant, sociable kind of woman; you'd never think she was a writer. Ever hear how she began to write? She told me the whole story. It seems she was a saleswoman in a store, working on starvation wages, with a mother and a consumptive[3] sister to support. Well, she wrote a story one day, just for fun, and sent it to the *Home Circle*. They'd never heard of her, of course, and she never expected to hear from them. She did, though. They took the story and passed their plate for more. She became a regular contributor and eventually was known all over the country. Now she tells me her books bring her in about ten thousand a year.[4] Rather more than you and I can boast of, eh, John? Well, I hope *this* household doesn't contribute to her **2** support.'' He glanced sharply at Theodora. ''I don't believe in feeding youngsters on sentimental trash; it's like sewer gas—doesn't smell bad, and infects the system without your knowing it.''

---

3. **consumptive:** afflicted with tuberculosis.
4. **ten thousand a year:** at the time, a great deal of money.

Theodora listened breathlessly. Kathleen Kyd's first story had been accepted by the *Home Circle*, and they had asked for more! Why should Gladys Glyn be less fortunate? Theodora had done a great deal of novel reading—far more than her parents were aware of—and felt herself competent to pronounce upon the quality of her own work. She was almost sure that ''April Showers'' was a remarkable book. If it lacked Kathleen Kyd's lightness of touch, it had an emotional intensity never achieved by that brilliant writer. Theodora did not care to amuse her readers; she left that to more frivolous talents. Her aim was to stir the depths of human nature, and **3** she felt she had succeeded. It was a great thing for a girl to be able to feel that about her first novel. Theodora was only seventeen; and she remembered, with a touch of retrospective compassion, that George Eliot[5] had not become famous till she was nearly forty.

No, there was no doubt about the merit of ''April Showers.'' But would not an inferior work have had a better chance of success? Theodora recalled the early struggles of famous authors, the notorious antagonism of publishers and editors to any new writer of exceptional promise. Would it not be wiser to write the book down to the average reader's level, reserving for some later work the great ''effects'' into which she had thrown all the fever of her imagination? The thought was sacrilege! Never would she lay hands on the sacred structure she had reared; never would she resort to the inartistic expedient of modifying her work to suit the popular taste. Better obscure failure than a vulgar triumph. The great authors never stooped to such concessions, and Theodora felt herself included in their ranks by the firmness with which she rejected all thought of conciliating an unappreciative public. The manuscript should be sent as it was.

---

5. **George Eliot** (1819–1880): pen name of Mary Ann Evans, distinguished English novelist.

*April Showers* **77**

- Theodora's Uncle James talks about the romantic author Kathleen Kyd, inspiring Theodora.
- Theodora is proud of her work and expects it to be recognized.
- For a while she considers bringing her novel down to a more common level but discards the idea.

**1 SETTING**

Uncle James's ''compassionate'' glance around the ''crowded'' table suggests that the Dace family may be financially hard-pressed.

**2 THEME**

Although Uncle James directs his remarks about how ''sentimental trash'' can harm young people at Theodora, he is unaware that she has already been infected.

**3 CHARACTERIZATION**

Theodora's comparison of herself to George Eliot shows her naive self-confidence.

## GUIDED READING

### LITERAL QUESTION

**1a.** What is Uncle James's opinion of romantic novels? (He calls them ''sentimental trash'' that ''infects the system.'')

### INFERENTIAL QUESTION

**1b.** How can you tell that Uncle James's opinion has no effect on Theodora? (Right after his admonition, she dreams of following in Kyd's footsteps.)

- Next morning, Theodora wakes up late to find her chores undone.
- Her father chides her gently, and she apologizes.
- She apologizes to her invalid mother.
- With fame she would win her family's approval and buy them things they need.

### 1 THEME

The "ominous thump" of the clock striking nine seems to separate Theodora's dreaming from the demands of her real life.

### 2 STYLE: DRAMATIC IRONY

Theodora is totally unaware that her day is really composed of "the lesser obligations of life."

### 3 POINT OF VIEW

The narrator relates Theodora's fantasies, both of her own success and of her family's comfort. The reader is expected to see that Theodora's daydreams are unlikely to come true.

### 4 STYLE: VERBAL IRONY

Theodora's father is not above making a little fun of Theodora, as his gently ironic question shows.

### 5 TONE

The melodramatic terms in which Theodora thinks about her life both reveal and mock her romanticism.

She woke with a start and a heavy sense of apprehension. The *Home Circle* had refused "April Showers"! No, that couldn't be it; there **1** lay the precious manuscript, waiting to be posted. What was it, then? Ah, that ominous thump below stairs—nine o'clock striking! It was Johnny's buttons!

She sprang out of bed in dismay. She had been so determined not to disappoint her mother about Johnny's buttons! Mrs. Dace, helpless from chronic rheumatism, had to entrust the care of the household to her eldest daughter; and Theodora honestly meant to see that Johnny had his full complement of buttons, and that Kate and **2** Bertha went to school tidy. Unfortunately, the writing of a great novel leaves little time or memory for the lesser obligations of life, and Theodora usually found that her good intentions matured too late for practical results.

Her contrition was softened by the thought that literary success would enable her to make up for all the little negligences of which she was guilty. She meant to spend all her money on her **3** family; and already she had visions of a wheeled chair for her mother, a fresh wallpaper for the doctor's shabby office, bicycles for the girls, and Johnny's establishment at a boarding school where sewing on his buttons would be included in the curriculum. If her parents could have guessed her intentions, they would not have found fault with her as they did; and Doctor Dace, on this particular morning, would not have looked up to say, with his fagged,[6] ironical air:

**4** "I suppose you didn't get home from the ball till morning?"

Theodora's sense of being in the right enabled her to take the thrust with a dignity that would have awed the unfeeling parent to fiction.

"I'm sorry to be late, father," she said.

Doctor Dace, who could never be counted on to behave like a father in a book, shrugged his shoulders impatiently.

_____

6. **fagged:** weary; tired.

**78** *The Short Story*

"Your sentiments do you credit, but they haven't kept your mother's breakfast warm."

"Hasn't mother's tray gone up yet?"

"Who was to take it, I should like to know? The girls came down so late that I had to hustle them off before they'd finished breakfast, and Johnny's hands were so dirty that I sent him back to his room to make himself decent. It's a pretty thing for the doctor's children to be the dirtiest little savages in Norton!"

Theodora had hastily prepared her mother's tray, leaving her own breakfast untouched. As she entered the room upstairs, Mrs. Dace's patient face turned to her with a smile much harder to bear than her father's reproaches.

"Mother, I'm *so* sorry—"

"No matter, dear. I suppose Johnny's buttons kept you. I can't think what that boy does to his clothes!"

Theodora sat the tray down without speaking. It was impossible to own to having forgotten Johnny's buttons without revealing the cause **5** of her forgetfulness. For a few weeks longer she must bear to be misunderstood; then—ah, then if her novel were accepted, how gladly would she forget and forgive! But what if it were refused? She turned aside to hide the dismay that flushed her face. Well, then she would admit the truth—she would ask her parents' pardon, and settle down without a murmur to an obscure existence of mending and combing.

She had said to herself that after the manuscript had been sent, she would have time to look after the children and catch up with the mending; but she had reckoned without the postman. He came three times a day; for an hour before each ring she was too excited to do anything but wonder if he would bring an answer this time, and for an hour afterward she moved about in a leaden stupor of disappointment. The children had never been so trying. They seemed to be always coming to pieces, like cheap furniture; one would have supposed they had been put together with bad glue. Mrs. Dace worried

## GUIDED READING

### LITERAL QUESTION

**1a.** How does Dr. Dace chide his daughter? (He asks, "I suppose you didn't get home from the ball till morning?")

### INFERENTIAL QUESTION

**1b.** Do you think Dr. Dace is truly angry with Theodora? Why or why not? (No—he softens his criticism with humor. He loves her and is used to—if tired of—her dreamy, neglectful ways. He knows she means well.)

**1** herself ill over Johnny's tatters, Bertha's bad marks at school, and Kate's open abstention from cod-liver oil; and Doctor Dace, coming back late from a long round of visits to a fireless office with a smoky lamp,[7] called out furiously to know if Theodora would kindly come down and remove the "East, West, home's best" that hung above the empty grate.

In the midst of it all, Miss Sophy Brill called. It was very kind of her to come, for she was the busiest woman in Norton. She made it her duty to look after other people's affairs, and there was not a house in town but had the benefit of her personal supervision. She generally came when things were going wrong, and the sight of her bonnet on the doorstep was a surer sign of calamity than a crepe bow[8] on the bell. After she left, Mrs. Dace looked very sad, and the doctor punished Johnny for warbling down the entry:

> "Miss Sophy Brill
> Is a bitter pill!"

while Theodora, locking herself in her room, resolved with tears that she would never write another novel.

**2** The week was a long nightmare. Theodora could neither eat nor sleep. She was up early enough, but instead of looking after the children and seeing that breakfast was ready, she wandered down the road to meet the postman, and came back wan and empty-handed, oblivious of her morning duties. She had no idea how long the suspense would last; but she didn't see how authors could live if they were kept waiting more than a week.

Then suddenly, one afternoon—she never quite knew how or when it happened—she found herself with a *Home Circle* envelope in her hands, and her dazzled eyes flashing over a wild dance of words that wouldn't settle down and make sense.

---

7. **smoky lamp:** kerosene, or oil-burning, lamp.
8. **crepe bow:** bow of black fabric displayed as a sign of mourning.

"Dear Madam:" (They called her *Madam!* And then; yes, the words were beginning to fall into line now.) "Your novel, 'April Showers,' has been received, and we are glad to accept it on the usual terms. A serial on which we were counting for immediate publication has been delayed by the author's illness, and the first chapters of 'April Showers' will therefore appear in our midsummer number. Thanking you for favoring us with your manuscript, we remain," and so forth.

Theodora found herself in the wood beyond the schoolhouse. She was kneeling on the ground, brushing aside the dead leaves and pressing her lips to the little bursting green things that pushed up eager tips through last year's decay. **3** It was spring—spring! Everything was crowding toward the light and in her own heart hundreds of germinating hopes had burst into sudden leaf. She wondered if the thrust of those little green fingers hurt the surface of the earth as her springing raptures hurt—yes, actually hurt!—her hot, constricted breast! She looked up through interlacing boughs at a tender, opaque blue sky full of the coming of a milky moon. She seemed enveloped in an atmosphere of loving comprehension. The brown earth throbbed with her joy, the treetops trembled with it, and a sudden star broke through the branches like an audible "I know!"

Theodora, on the whole, behaved very well.

*April Showers* 79

---

## GUIDED READING

**LITERAL QUESTION**

**1a.** After Theodora gets the good news, what does she feel bursting in her own heart? (hundreds of germinating hopes)

**INFERENTIAL QUESTION**

**1b.** Why is the language of this passage significant? (It echoes the exaggerated, overly-romantic prose typical of the kind of writing Theodora does and admires.)

AT A GLANCE

- Theodora is famous in Norton.
- When the magazine finally appears, Theodora is shocked to discover that the "April Showers" it includes is not her novel.
- She travels to Boston, head-quarters of the magazine, to solve the puzzle.

**1 CHARACTERIZATION**

Doctor Dace seems to cover up his emotions with humor; his whistling and sarcasm are indi-rect expressions of his proud, happy feelings.

**2 VOCABULARY: CONCRETE LANGUAGE**

To give an impression of the headiness of Theodora's tri-umph, Wharton offers concrete examples of the worshipful way peers and the other townspeople treat her.

**3 PLOT: CLIMAX**

Wharton keeps the suspense high by letting the audience discover the truth through Theodora's horrified eyes.

**4 PLOT: FALLING ACTION**

Theodora has evidently reacted to her awful discovery by leaving Norton and returning in a daze; obviously she has found out more bad news about her novel.

---

1 Her mother cried, her father whistled and said he supposed he must put up with grounds in his coffee now, and be thankful if he ever got a hot meal again; while the children took the most deafening and harassing advantage of what seemed a sudden suspension of the laws of na-ture.

Within a week everybody in Norton knew that Theodora had written a novel, and that it was coming out in the *Home Circle*. On Sundays, 2 when she walked up the aisle, her friends dropped their prayer books and the soprano sang false in her excitement. Girls with more pin money than Theodora had ever dreamed of cop-ied her hats and imitated her way of speaking. The local paper asked her for a poem; her old school teachers stopped to shake hands and grew shy over their congratulations; and Miss Sophy Brill came to call. She had put on her Sunday bonnet and her manner was almost abject. She ventured, very timidly, to ask her young friend how she wrote, whether it "just came to her," and if she had found that the kind of pen she used made any difference; and wound up by beg-ging Theodora to write a sentiment in her album.

Even Uncle James came down from Boston to talk the wonder over. He called Theodora a "sly baggage," and proposed that she should give him her earnings to invest in a new patent grease-trap company. From what Kathleen Kyd had told him, he thought Theodora would probably get a thousand dollars for her story. He concluded by suggesting that she should base her next ro-mance on the subject of sanitation, making the heroine nearly die of sewer gas poisoning be-cause her parents won't listen to the handsome young doctor next door, when he warns them that their plumbing is out of order. That was a subject that would interest everybody, and do a lot more good than the sentimental trash most women wrote.

At last the great day came. Theodora had left an order with the bookseller for the midsummer number of the *Home Circle* and before the shop

was open she was waiting on the sidewalk. She clutched her precious paper and ran home with-out opening it. Her excitement was almost more than she could bear. Not heeding her father's call to breakfast, she rushed upstairs and locked her-self in her room. Her hands trembled so that she could hardly turn the pages. At last—yes, there it was: "April Showers."

The paper dropped from her hands. What name had she read beneath the title? Had her emotion blinded her?

3 "April Showers, by *Kathleen Kyd*."

Kathleen Kyd! Oh, cruel misprint! Oh, das-tardly typographer! Through tears of rage and disappointment Theodora looked again; yes, there was no mistaking the hateful name. Her glance ran on. She found herself reading a first paragraph that she had never seen before. She read farther. All was strange. The horrible truth burst upon her: *It was not her story!*

She never knew how she got back to the sta-4 tion. She struggled through the crowd on the platform, and a gold-banded arm pushed her into the train just starting for Norton. It would be dark when she reached home; but that didn't matter—nothing mattered now. She sank into her seat, closing her eyes in the vain attempt to shut out the vision of the last few hours; but minute by minute memory forced her to relive it; she felt like a rebellious schoolchild dragged forth to repeat the same detested "piece."

Although she did not know Boston well, she had made her way easily enough to the *Home Circle* building; at least, she supposed she had, since she remembered nothing till she found her-self ascending the editorial stairs as easily as one does incredible things in dreams. She must have walked very fast, for her heart was beating fu-riously, and she had barely breath to whisper the editor's name to a young man who looked out at her from a glass case, like a zoological speci-men. The young man led her past other glass cases containing similar specimens to an inner

---

## GUIDED READING

### LITERAL QUESTIONS

**1a.** How soon does everyone in Norton find out about her novel? (within a week)

**2a.** What does Theodora discover as soon as she sees the magazine? (It contains a different "April Showers.")

### INFERENTIAL QUESTIONS

**1b.** Why does the news travel so fast? (It is a small town, and everyone knows everyone else and much of their business as well.)

**2b.** What do you think happened? (Perhaps the mag-azine editors liked her title and used it for the novel that they really wanted to publish.)

enclosure which seemed filled by an enormous presence. Theodora felt herself enveloped in the presence, submerged by it, gasping for air as she sank under its rising surges.

Gradually fragments of speech floated to the surface. " 'April Showers?' Mrs. Kyd's new serial? *Your* manuscript, you say? You have a letter from me? The name, please? Evidently some unfortunate misunderstanding. One moment." And then a bell ringing, a zoological specimen ordered to unlock a safe, her name asked for again, the manuscript, her own precious manuscript, tied with Aunt Julia's ribbon, laid on the table before her, and her outcries, her protests, her interrogations, drowned in a flood of bland apology: "An unfortunate accident—Mrs. Kyd's manuscript received the same day—extraordinary coincidence in the choice of a title—duplicate answers sent by mistake—Miss Dace's novel hardly suited to their purpose—should of course have been returned—regrettable oversight—accidents would happen—sure she understood."

The voice went on, like the steady pressure of a surgeon's hand on a shrieking nerve. When it stopped she was in the street. A cab nearly ran her down, and a car bell jangled furiously in her ears. She clutched her manuscript, carrying it tenderly through the crowd, like a live thing that had been hurt. She could not bear to look at its soiled edges and the ink stain on Aunt Julia's ribbon.

The train stopped with a jerk and she opened her eyes. It was dark, and by the windy flare of gas on the platform she saw the Norton passengers getting out. She stood up stiffly and followed them. A warm wind blew into her face the fragrance of the summer woods, and she remembered how, two months earlier, she had knelt among the dead leaves, pressing her lips to the first shoots of green. Then for the first time she thought of home. She had fled away in the morning without a word, and her heart sank at the thought of her mother's fears. And her father—how angry he would be! She bent her

head under the coming storm of his derision.

The night was cloudy, and as she stepped into the darkness beyond the station a hand was slipped in hers. She stood still, too weary to feel frightened, and a voice said, quietly:

"Don't walk so fast, child. You look tired."

"Father!" Her hand dropped from his, but he recaptured it, and drew it through his arm. When she found voice, it was to whisper, "You were at the station?"

"It's such a good night I thought I'd stroll down and meet you."

Her arm trembled against his. She could not see his face in the dimness, but the light of his cigar looked down on her like a friendly eye, and she took courage to falter out: "Then you knew—"

"That you'd gone to Boston? Well, I rather thought you had."

They walked on slowly, and presently he added, "You see, you left the *Home Circle* lying in your room."

How she blessed the darkness and the muffled sky! She could not have borne the scrutiny of the tiniest star.

"Then mother wasn't very much frightened?"

"Why, no, she didn't appear to be. She's been busy all day over some toggery[9] of Bertha's."

Theodora choked. "Father, I'll—" She groped for words, but they eluded her. "I'll do things—differently; I haven't meant—" Suddenly she heard herself bursting out: "It was all a mistake, you know—about my story. They didn't want it; they won't have it!" and she shrank back involuntarily from his impending mirth.

She felt the pressure of his arm, but he didn't speak, and she figured his mute hilarity. They moved on in silence. Presently he said:

"It hurts a bit just at first, doesn't it?"

"O Father!"

_____

9. **toggery:** clothes.

*April Showers*  **81**

## AT A GLANCE

- In Boston she learns that the letter was sent to her by mistake: Kyd's manuscript with the same title had actually been accepted.
- Her sympathetic father meets her at the station; he had seen the magazine.

**1 STYLE: METAPHOR**

Wharton uses words suggesting someone drowning (*submerged, gasping for air*) to describe Theodora's sense of being overwhelmed.

**2 STYLE: SIMILE**

Wharton conveys Theodora's excruciating suffering by comparing the editor's voice to a "surgeon's hand on a shrieking nerve."

**3 READING SKILLS: CONTRAST**

Wharton effectively contrasts Theodora's present pain with her past happiness by returning her to the scene of her triumph.

**4 STYLE: SIMILE**

Wharton's comparison of Dr. Dace's cigar to a "friendly eye" makes the audience aware of the possibility that his reaction may surprise and comfort his daughter.

## GUIDED READING

**LITERAL QUESTION**

**1a.** How does her father explain his appearance at the station? (He says it was such a good night he thought he'd take a stroll.)

**INFERENTIAL QUESTION**

**1b.** What is his real reason? (He realized that she would need sympathy when she came home.)

- Her father explains that he had a similar experience: He wrote a novel in his youth.

## REFLECTING ON THE STORY

What do you think Theodora's experience teaches her? (She has learned to weather disappointment, to value her father, and to temper her daydreams with a sense of reality.)

## STUDY QUESTIONS

1. Gladys Glyn, Theodora's pen name; Kathleen Kyd, society novelist; Doctor Dace, Theodora's father; *Home Circle,* the paper to which Theodora submitted her novel; *April Showers,* the title of Theodora's novel
2. taking care of her family
3. elated—story accepted; disappointed, angry—story not hers
4. Kathleen Kyd's manuscript was received the same day, had the same title.
5. her father; ambition to write, novel rejected
6. overconfident; first paragraph of story, paragraphs beginning "Theodora listened breathlessly," "No, there was no doubt"
7. She felt guilty but thought literary success would make up for neglect. Opinions will vary.
8. "April showers," rejection; "May flowers," more realistic expectations
9. *Possible answer:* Continue with writing but don't lose touch with realities.

## LITERARY FOCUS

### Limited Third-Person Point of View
1. narrator reveals only the thoughts of Theodora; refers to her in third person; reveals information not known by her
2. Possible answer: less suspenseful if editor's thoughts are known earlier

### Tone
basically sympathetic; somewhat critical; amused

---

He stood still, and the gleam of his cigar showed a face of unexpected participation.

"You see I've been through it myself."

"You, Father? You?"

"Why, yes. Didn't I ever tell you? I wrote a novel once. I was just out of college, and didn't want to be a doctor. No; I wanted to be a genius, so I wrote a novel."

The doctor paused, and Theodora clung to him in a mute passion of commiseration. It was as if a drowning creature caught a live hand through the murderous fury of the waves.

"Father—O Father!"

"It took me a year—a whole year's hard work; and when I'd finished it the public wouldn't have it, either; not at any price and that's why I came down to meet you, because I remembered my walk home."

---

## STUDY QUESTIONS

### Recalling
1. Identify the following characters and names in the story: Gladys Glyn, Kathleen Kyd, Doctor Dace, *Home Circle,* "April Showers."
2. What should Theodora have been doing while she was writing "April Showers"?
3. Describe and explain the different feelings Theodora has when she receives the letter from *Home Circle* and then when she reads "April Showers" in the midsummer number of the paper.
4. When Theodora goes to Boston, what explanation is she given for the confusion over her story?
5. Who is waiting for Theodora when she returns from Boston? What reason does he give for being there?

### Interpreting
6. Which of these words describes Theodora's attitude toward herself as a writer at the beginning of the story: humble, unsure, overconfident? Cite evidence from the story to support your choice.
7. How would you characterize Theodora's feelings about neglecting her responsibilities at home? Was she right to feel this way? Explain what you mean.
8. What experiences of Theodora's can be described as "April showers"? What "May flowers" might they bring?

### Extending
9. What would you advise Theodora to do—continue with her writing or not? Explain your thinking.

## LITERARY FOCUS

### Limited Third-Person Point of View

In a story written from a **limited third-person point of view**, the narrator reveals the thoughts and feelings of only one story character, often the main character. The narrator refers to this character by name or as "he" or "she" and lets readers know everything that this character thinks and feels. The narrator may even allow readers to know more about that character than the character knows.

### Thinking About Limited Third-Person Point of View
1. What evidence in "April Showers" indicates that the story has been told from the limited third-person point of view?
2. Would this story have been more or less interesting if the narrator had revealed the thoughts of characters besides Theodora?

### Tone

In any piece of writing, **tone** is the attitude the author takes toward the subject. We often think of tone as something that can be heard—for example, a tone of voice. *Written* words also express tone. The tone of a story may be serious or lighthearted, restrained or moving, frightening or uplifting.

### Thinking About Tone
■ How would you describe the tone of "April Showers"? Is Wharton critical of Theodora or sympathetic to her? Is she touched or amused by Theodora's experiences? Support your opinion with examples from the story.

Anton Chekhov (1860–1904) launched one of the world's most brilliant literary careers from rather unlikely beginnings. The grandson of a Russian serf, a peasant who was not free but was bound to the land, Chekhov graduated from medical school and became a practicing physician. However, he also began to write and publish stories during his university days. Later, he turned his hand to drama, producing before his early death a handful of memorable plays.

■ Can we ever predict with any certainty how another person will react in a situation?

*Anton Chekhov*

# The Woman Who Had No Prejudices

Maxim Kuzmich Salyutov[1] was tall, broad-shouldered and thickset. His build might safely be termed athletic. His strength was remarkable. He used to bend twenty-kopeck pieces,[2] pull up young trees by the roots, lift weights with his teeth, and swear that there wasn't a man on earth who would dare fight him. He was bold and brave. He had never been known to fear anything. People, on the contrary, were afraid of him and used to turn pale when he was angry. Men and women used to shriek and turn red when he shook hands with them: it hurt! It was impossible to listen to his fine baritone,[3] as it used to drown everything out. The strength of the man! I've never known anything like it!

And this wondrous, superhuman, ox-like strength turned into nothing at all—was like a mere crushed rat—when Maxim Kuzmich pro-posed to Elena Gavrilovna.[4] Maxim Kuzmich turned pale, turned crimson, trembled and hadn't the strength to lift a chair when the time came to force "I love you" from his big mouth. His strength deserted him and his big body turned into a big, empty vessel.

He proposed at the skating rink. She fluttered along the ice, light as a feather, while he trembled and grew numb and whispered as he chased after her. Suffering was written all over his face. His nimble, agile legs bent under him and tangled themselves up when they had to inscribe an intricate monogram on the ice. He feared a refusal, you think? No, Elena Gavrilovna loved him and yearned for his offer of heart and hand. A pretty little brunette, she was ready to burn up with impatience at any moment. He was already thirty years old, his rank wasn't high, he didn't have much money, but he was so handsome and witty and spry! He was a good dancer, a fine shot. Nobody rode horseback better than he.

1. **Maxim Kuzmich Salyutov**
[mak sēm′ kōōz mēch′ sal ū′tof]
2. **twenty-kopeck** [kō′pek] **pieces:** A kopeck is one one-hundredth of a rouble, the basic monetary unit in Russia.
3. **baritone:** moderately deep male voice.

4. **Elena Gavrilovna** [il yē′na gav rēl′ōv na]

*The Woman Who Had No Prejudices* **83**

- Maxim proposes but thinks his origin gives him no right to.
- Her parents consent to the marriage.
- Still, Maxim is tormented.
- He allows himself to be blackmailed to protect his secret but ends up revealing it to Elena on their wedding night.

## 1 CONFLICT

Maxim faces an internal conflict that his physical strength cannot overcome: He wants to tell Elena the truth but fears rejection.

## 2 THEME

Maxim knows that it is important to be completely honest with his future wife, but he hasn't yet had sufficient courage to be so.

## 3 CONFLICT

Maxim experiences an external conflict with a certain friend, who blackmails him.

## 4 POINT OF VIEW

The omniscient point of view allows Chekhov to contrast everyone's assumption about the couple's happiness with the reality of Maxim's misery.

Once, when he and she were out walking, he jumped across a ditch which any English jumper would have had trouble in clearing.

How could one help loving such a man!

And he knew that he was loved. He was sure of it. But one thought tormented him. This thought stifled his brain; it made him rage and weep; he couldn't eat, drink, or sleep because of it. It poisoned his life. He vowed his love, but while he did so the thought stirred in his brain and hammered at his temples.

"Be my wife!" he said to Elena Gavrilovna. "I love you! Madly! Wildly!"

**1** And at the same time he was thinking,

"Have I the right to be her husband? No, I haven't! If she knew of my origin, if someone were to tell her about my past, she'd slap my face. Disgraceful, miserable past! She's high-born, rich, and cultured, and she'd spit on me if she knew the kind of creature I am!"

When Elena Gavrilovna threw herself on his neck and vowed her love for him, he didn't feel happy.

The thought had poisoned everything. Returning home from the skating rink, he bit his lips and thought,

**2** "I'm a scoundrel. If I were an honorable man, I would have told her everything, everything! I ought to have let her into my secret before I proposed. But I didn't, and that makes me a good-for-nothing, a scoundrel!"

Elena Gavrilovna's parents gave their consent to her marriage to Maxim Kuzmich. They liked the athlete: he was respectful to them and they had high hopes for his future as an official. Elena Gavrilovna was in seventh heaven. She was happy. The poor athlete, however, was far from happy. Up until the wedding itself he was tormented by the same thought that had tormented him when he proposed.

**3** He was also tormented by a certain friend who knew his past as well as the palm of his hand. He had to give the friend almost all his salary.

"Blow me to dinner at The Hermitage," the friend would say, "or else I'll tell everyone. And lend me twenty-five roubles."

Poor Maxim Kuzmich grew thin and peaked. His cheeks became sunken, the veins in his fists became prominent. The thought was making him ill. If it hadn't been for the woman he loved, he would have shot himself.

"I'm a scoundrel, a good-for-nothing," he thought. "I must have it out with her before the wedding. Let her go ahead and spit on me."

But he didn't have it out with her before the wedding. He wasn't brave enough.

And the thought that he would have to part with the woman he loved, after he had had it out with her, was more horrible, to his mind, than all other thoughts.

The wedding evening came. The young couple **4** were married and congratulated and everyone marveled at their happiness. Poor Maxim Kuzmich received congratulations, drank, danced, and laughed, but felt terribly unhappy. "I'll make myself have it out with her, swine that I am! The marriage service has been performed, but it's still not too late! We still can part."

And he had it out with her.

When the longed-for hour arrived and the bridal pair were led into the bedroom, conscience and honor took their own. Pale and trembling, not remembering their new relationship, hardly breathing, Maxim Kuzmich went up to her timidly, took her by the hand, and said,

"Before we belong...to each other, I must...have something out with you."

"What's the matter, Max? You're...pale! You've been pale and silent all these past days. Are you ill?"

"I...must tell you all, Lelya...Let's sit down...I must amaze you. I must poison your happiness, but what can I do? Duty comes first. I'm going to tell you about my past."

Lelya opened her eyes wide and smiled.

"Well, tell me. Only quickly, please. And don't tremble like that."

## GUIDED READING

### LITERAL QUESTIONS

**1a.** What is the information that Maxim is afraid to tell Elena? (He is afraid to tell her about his past.)

**2a.** Why doesn't Maxim tell his secret to Elena before the wedding? (He isn't brave enough.)

### INFERENTIAL QUESTIONS

**1b.** What does Maxim assume will be Elena's reaction to the information? (He apparently assumes that, because she comes from an upper-class background, she will despise him.)

**2b.** Why do you think he is finally able to tell her his secret? (They are alone, they are committed to each other, and he knows he cannot wait any longer.)

1 "I was b-b-born in Tam . . . Tam . . . bov.[5] My parents were of low birth and terribly poor . . . I'll tell you what kind of pig I am . . . You'll be horrified. Wait . . . You'll see . . . I was a beggar . . . When I was a little boy, I used to sell apples . . . pears . . ."

"You?"

2 "You're horrified? But darling, that's not the worst. Oh, how unhappy I am! You'll curse me when you know!"

"But what?"

"When I was twenty, I was . . . was . . . forgive me! Don't send me away! I was . . . a clown in a circus!"

"You? A clown?"

Salyutov, expecting a slap on the cheek, covered his pale face with his hands. He was on the verge of fainting.

"You . . . a clown?"

And Lelya fell off the couch, jumped up and began running around the room.

What was the matter with her? She seized her stomach. Laughter (hysteria?) rang out and filled the bedroom.

3 "Ha-ha-ha! You were a clown? You? Maxinka . . . Darling! Do a trick! Prove that you were one! Ha-ha-ha! Darling!"

She ran up to Salyutov and threw her arms around him.

"Do something! Dearest! Darling!"

"Are you laughing, wretched woman? Do you despise me?"

"Do something! Can you walk the tight rope? Go on!"

4 She covered her husband's face with kisses, nestled against him, fawned on him. She didn't seem to be angry. Happy, comprehending none of this, he granted his wife's request.

He walked over to the bed, counted three, and stood with his legs in the air, his forehead resting on the edge of the bed.

"Bravo, Max! *Bis!* [6] Ha-ha! Darling! More!"

Max swayed slightly, sprang from this position on to the floor and began walking on his hands.

In the morning Lelya's parents were greatly surprised.

"Who's that pounding upstairs?" they asked each other. "The newlyweds are still asleep. The servants must be up to something. What a racket they're making! The wretches!"

Papa went upstairs but found no servants there.

The noise, to his great surprise, was coming from the newlyweds' room. He stood by the door, shrugged his shoulders and opened it a crack. He looked into the bedroom, gave a start, and almost died of astonishment: Maxim Kuzmich was standing in the middle of the bedroom and performing the most desperate somersaults in the air; Lelya was standing beside him, applauding. Both their faces were shining with joy.

---

5. **Tam . . . bov:** Tambov, a city in western Russia.

6. *Bis* [bēs]: French for "Bravo! Again!"

*The Woman Who Had No Prejudices*   **85**

## AT A GLANCE

- Maxim confesses that he was born poor and that he had been a beggar and a clown.
- Throwing her arms around Maxim, Elena asks him to prove he was a clown by doing a trick.
- The next morning Papa finds Maxim performing somersaults as Elena and Maxim beam with joy.

1 **CHARACTERIZATION**

Maxim's stuttering and calling himself a pig reveal by indirect characterization his nervousness and low self-esteem.

2 **THEME**

Maxim's internal conflict is resolved when he finds the courage to trust his wife and confess.

3 **PLOT: CLIMAX**

When Elena laughs and throws her arms around Maxim, the reader knows that Maxim's past will create no conflict between them.

4 **CHARACTERIZATION**

Chekhov's portrayal of tenderness and love, conveyed by words like *nestled* and *fawned,* reveals the unexpected complexity of the characters.

**REFLECTING ON THE STORY**

Is this a humorous story or a serious one? (Possible answers include that it is humorous, that it is serious, that it is both, and that it makes a serious point in a humorous way.)

## GUIDED READING

**LITERAL QUESTIONS**

**1a.** How does Elena react when Maxim tells her that he has been a clown? (She laughs, runs around the room, hugs and kisses him, and asks him to do a trick for her.)

**2a.** When Elena's father finds the newlyweds, what expression do Elena's and Maxim's faces reflect? (They are beaming with joy.)

**INFERENTIAL QUESTIONS**

**1b.** From Elena's earlier reasons for loving Maxim, why is her reaction not surprising? (Because she loves him for his athletic skills like shooting, dancing, and riding, she might also be expected to love him for doing clown's acrobatics.)

**2b.** What do you think is the source of this emotion for Maxim and for Elena? (He is at last relieved of his fear, and she is delighted by his talents.)

1. tall; thickset; handsome; strong; athletic
2. He used to be a beggar and a circus clown.
3. on their wedding night; fearfully
4. with great delight
5. feels inferior; is honest
6. Humorous: The secret is not serious. Touching: The characters obviously love each other.
7. tender; takes emotional reality of characters more seriously
8. Love requires trust.
9. Until Maxim trusts Elena enough to be honest, he is unhappy.

LITERARY FOCUS

1. Elena's tolerance; their love for each other; story's title
2. Maxim's anxiety creates suspense; his confession is surprising and humorous.

COMPARING STORIES

- "Cask": unreliable narrator; an unstable aristocrat; deceptively calm; like close observer
- "April": limited third-person; more mature than Theodora, reader recognizes Theodora's immaturity
- "Prejudices": omniscient narrator; intelligent; sophisticated; with sense of humor; like detached, sympathetic observer

## STUDY QUESTIONS

### Recalling

1. Mention five or six details in the physical description of Maxim.
2. Why does Maxim doubt that he has "the right" to be Elena's husband?
3. When and how does Maxim finally tell Elena his secret?
4. How does Elena respond to Maxim's secret?

### Interpreting

5. What might Maxim's deep embarrassment about his secret tell us about his character? What does his inability to hide his secret from Elena reveal about him?
6. Why is the outcome of the story both humorous *and* touching?
7. How would you describe the author's attitude toward Maxim and Elena? What do you think the last line reveals about this attitude?
8. A serious point can often be made *more* effectively with humor. What serious point about human relationships does Chekhov use humor to make in this story?

### Extending

9. In one of Chekhov's plays, a character says, "You must trust and believe in people...or life becomes impossible." How might this statement apply to what happens in "The Woman Who Had No Prejudices"?

## LITERARY FOCUS

### Omniscient Point of View

A story told from the **omniscient point of view** is told by an all-knowing narrator, one who stands outside the story and looks into the minds of all its characters. The omniscient narrator is usually identified with the author of the story; therefore, we can trust everything that this narrator tells us.

### Thinking About Omniscient Point of View

1. What hints does Chekhov's omniscient narrator give us throughout the story that the ending will be happy?
2. Why do you think the omniscient narrator does *not* tell us Maxim's secret but instead lets us find it out at the same time as Elena?

## COMPOSITION

### Writing About Tone

■ Describe Chekhov's tone in "The Woman Who Had No Prejudices," and explain how his selection of details creates that tone. In discussing details, you may want to consider (a) descriptions of characters, (b) events of the plot, and (c) Chekhov's choice of language. *For help with this assignment, see Lesson 6 in the Writing About Literature Handbook at the back of this book.*

### Writing a Plot Outline

■ Write a plot outline for a suspenseful short story in which the main character hides a secret from someone else. Follow the plot structure outlined on page 20: Describe the character's situation, and indicate the events that are your narrative hook, rising action, climax, falling action, and resolution.

## COMPARING STORIES

■ "The Cask of Amontillado," "April Showers," and "The Woman Who Had No Prejudices" all concern people in highly emotional circumstances. Each, however, is told from a different point of view. Choose two or more stories and compare their impacts on you. Did you feel more like an observer or a participant? Explain how the point of view of each story made you feel this way. Describe your mental picture of the narrator of each story.

---

## COMPOSITION: GUIDELINES FOR EVALUATION

### WRITING ABOUT TONE

**Objective**

To examine Chekhov's tone in the story

**Guidelines for Evaluation**

- suggested length: 3–6 paragraphs
- should characterize the author's tone
- should cite details relating to character, plot, and language

### WRITING A PLOT OUTLINE

**Objective**

To write a plot outline for a suspenseful story

**Guidelines for Evaluation**

- suggested length: 300 words
- should introduce a main character with a secret
- should place character in a specific situation
- should list incidents that lead to climax
- should describe the climax and a resolution

# LITERARY FOCUS: Theme

Photograph © 1982 by Jill Krementz

William Saroyan (1908–1981) was born of Armenian immigrants in Fresno, California. First known as a writer of short stories, he later won acclaim as a playwright and was offered (but did not accept) the Pulitzer Prize for his play *The Time of Your Life*. In addition, his works include novels and a number of autobiographical books.

■ Not everyone receives the same moral from a fable. What do you think Saroyan learns from his Grandmother's story? What about you?

*William Saroyan*

# The Shepherd's Daughter

It is the opinion of my grandmother, God bless her, that all men should labor, and at the table, a moment ago, she said to me: You must learn to do some good work, the making of some item useful to man, something out of clay, or out of wood, or metal, or cloth. It is not proper for a young man to be ignorant of an honorable craft. Is there anything you can make? Can you make a simple table, a chair, a plain dish, a rug, a coffee pot? Is there anything you can do?

And my grandmother looked at me with anger.

I know, she said, you are supposed to be a writer, and I suppose you are. You certainly smoke enough cigarettes to be anything, and the whole house is full of the smoke, but you must learn to make solid things, things that can be used, that can be seen and touched.

There was a king of the Persians,[1] said my grandmother, and he had a son, and this boy fell in love with a shepherd's daughter. He went to his father and he said, My lord, I love a shepherd's daughter, and I would have her for

_____
1. **Persians:** people of Persia, an ancient empire located in the areas now known as Iran and Iraq.

my wife. And the king said, I am king and you are my son and when I die you shall be king, how can it be that you would marry the daughter of a shepherd? And the son said, My Lord, I do not know but I know that I love this girl and would have her for my queen.

The king saw that his son's love for the girl was from God, and he said, I will send a message to her. And he called a messenger to him and he said, Go to the shepherd's daughter and say that my son loves her and would have her for his wife. And the messenger went to the girl and he said, The king's son loves you and would have you for his wife. And the girl said, What labor does he do? And the messenger said, Why, he is the son of the king; he does no labor. And the girl said, He must learn to do some labor. And the messenger returned to the king and spoke the words of the shepherd's daughter.

The king said to his son, The shepherd's daughter wishes you to learn some craft. Would you still have her for your wife? And the son said, Yes, I will learn to weave straw rugs. And the boy was taught to weave rugs of straw, in patterns and in colors and with ornamental

*The Shepherd's Daughter* **87**

---

## AT A GLANCE

- The narrator's grandmother starts to tell him a Persian fable.
- A Persian prince learns rug weaving so that a shepherd's daughter will marry him.

## LITERARY OPTIONS

- theme
- frame story

## THEMATIC OPTIONS

- value of work
- power of love

### 1 THEME

The narrator's grandmother insists that he learn to make concrete objects as opposed to intangible literary works.

### 2 FRAME STORY

By telling this tale within a tale, the grandmother hopes to convince her grandson of the benefits of honest labor.

---

## GUIDED READING

### LITERAL QUESTION

**1a.** What does the narrator's grandmother say about his work? (that he must learn to make solid, useful items)

### INFERENTIAL QUESTION

**1b.** What do these remarks reveal about the grandmother's opinion of writing? (that it is not worthwhile because its products are neither tangible nor useful)

Detail from a Persian manuscript, ca. 1525.
The Metropolitan Museum of Art, New York,
Gift of Arthur A. Houghton, Jr.

**88**  *The Short Story*

designs, and at the end of three days he was making very fine straw rugs, and the messenger returned to the shepherd's daughter, and he said, These rugs of straw are the work of the king's son.

And the girl went with the messenger to the king's palace, and she became the wife of the king's son.

One day, said my grandmother, the king's son was walking through the streets of Bagdad,[2] and he came upon an eating place which was so clean and cool that he entered it and sat at a table.

This place, said my grandmother, was a place of thieves and murderers, and they took the king's son and placed him in a large dungeon where many great men of the city were being held, and the thieves and murderers were killing the fattest of the men and feeding them to the leanest of them, and making sport of it. The king's son was of the leanest of the men, and it was not known that he was the son of the king of the Persians, so his life was spared, and he said to the thieves and murderers, I am a weaver of straw rugs and these rugs have great value. And they brought him straw and asked him to weave and in three days he weaved three rugs, and he said, Carry these rugs to the palace of the king of

the Persians, and for each rug he will give you a hundred gold pieces of money. And the rugs were carried to the palace of the king, and when the king saw the rugs he saw that they were the work of his son and he took the rugs to the shepherd's daughter and he said, These rugs were brought to the palace and they are the work of my son who is lost. And the shepherd's daughter took each rug and looked at it closely and in the design of each rug she saw in the written language of the Persians a message from her husband, and she related this message to the king.

And the king, said my grandmother, sent many soldiers to the place of the thieves and murderers, and the soldiers rescued all the captives and killed all the thieves and murderers, and the king's son was returned safely to the palace of his father, and to the company of his wife, the little shepherd's daughter. And when the boy went into the palace and saw again his wife, he humbled himself before her and he embraced her feet, and he said, My love, it is because of you that I am alive, and the king was greatly pleased with the shepherd's daughter.

Now, said my grandmother, do you see why every man should learn an honorable craft?

I see very clearly, I said, and as soon as I earn enough money to buy a saw and a hammer and a piece of lumber I shall do my best to make a simple chair or a shelf for books.

---

2. **Bagdad:** ancient Persian city, located in what is now Iraq.

---

## STUDY QUESTIONS

### Recalling

1. What is the narrator's profession? In his grandmother's opinion, what should he be doing instead?

2. In what way does the grandmother attempt to make her point to the narrator?

3. Explain how the king's son wins the hand of the shepherd's daughter and how he engineers his own rescue from the den of thieves. What is the moral of the story, according to the narrator's grandmother?

4. At the end of the story, what does the narrator promise his grandmother he will do?

*The Shepherd's Daughter* **89**

- After marrying the shepherd's daughter, the prince is captured by thieves.
- The prince tricks the thieves into carrying to the palace rugs in which a message is woven.
- The shepherd's daughter interprets the message, and the prince is rescued.
- The narrator promises to make something "useful" after he earns money to buy tools.

**1 THEME**

The fable demonstrates the practical benefits of the prince's honorable craft: If he had remained a shiftless king's son, he would not have been able to save himself.

**2 FRAME STORY**

The point of view shifts from the fable back to the original frame. Out of respect, amusement, and affection for his grandmother, the narrator gently tells her that he will do as she wishes as soon as it is practical for him to do so.

**REFLECTING ON THE STORY**

Why does his grandmother tell the narrator a fable? (She wants to use a story—his own weapon as a writer—to convince him of the truth of her opinions about honest work.)

**STUDY QUESTIONS**

1. writer; working at a craft
2. tells him a tale
3. by learning to weave; weaves rugs containing secret messages; that everyone should learn an honorable craft
4. make a chair or bookshelf as soon as he earns enough money

**5.** ■ amusement, affection
   ■ No—he believes writing is an honorable craft.
**6.** intelligence, ingenuity; writes his story in the rugs
**7.** Yes—stories can enrich people's lives.

## VIEWPOINT

In order to buy the things needed to practice carpentry, he will have to earn a living writing.

## LITERARY FOCUS

### Stated Theme
"It is not proper for a young man to be without an honorable craft."

### Frame Story
The prince's craft saves his life.

---

### Interpreting

5. What do you think the narrator feels toward his grandmother? Do you think he accepts her opinion of the kind of work he does? Why or why not?
6. Besides the craft that he learns, what other talents and abilities enable the king's son to win his freedom from the thieves? In what ways might these talents make the king's son resemble the narrator?

### Extending

7. Would you argue that writing is also "an honorable craft" producing "solid things, things that can be used"? Why or why not?

## VIEWPOINT

One commentator on Saroyan writes that "The Shepherd's Daughter" is

> . . . an Oriental fable which Saroyan recounts with fitting simplicity but concludes with a whimsical wink to his reader.
> — H. K. Floan, *William Saroyan*

■ In what way is the narrator's promise to his grandmother at the end of the story a "whimsical wink"?

## LITERARY FOCUS

### Stated Theme

The **theme** is the main idea, the insight about life and human experience that an author expresses in a work. This idea may be a general truth about life or an exploration of a special way of looking at life. The theme of a work is a complete idea and should be expressed in a complete sentence. It may be stated directly in the work or may be implied in the other elements of the work. No matter what form it takes, the theme lies at the very center of a work and ties all aspects of the work together to express the author's insight.

A story has a **stated theme** when its author expresses the work's main idea directly. For example, Dorothy's statement in *The Wizard of Oz* that "there's no place like home" plainly tells us the theme of the work: Everything we might want can be found "at home"—within ourselves.

### Thinking About the Stated Theme

■ What is the stated theme of "The Shepherd's Daughter"? Be sure to look for a complete sentence that states the story's theme and takes the narrator's viewpoint into account.

### Frame Story

Many stories that state their themes directly do so by using a device called a frame. A **frame story** is really two stories, or a story within a story. Often, one person in the frame, or "outer" story, imagines or tells the "inner" story. In *The Wizard of Oz,* for instance, Dorothy's experience in Kansas serves as the frame for her dream about Oz. Very often the story's theme is stated in the frame, and this theme is worked out in more detail in the inner story.

### Thinking About the Frame Story

■ Explain how the story about the king's son develops the theme stated in the frame of "The Shepherd's Daughter."

## COMPOSITION

### Writing About Theme

■ Show how Saroyan illuminates his theme, or main idea, in "The Shepherd's Daughter." First write a sentence that expresses the story's theme. Then explain how Saroyan develops that theme through the title, plot, characters, setting, and narrator of his story. In discussing the elements of the story, be sure to write about both the frame and the grandmother's fable. *For help with this assignment, see Lesson 7 in the Writing About Literature Handbook at the back of this book.*

### Writing a Fable

■ A **fable** is a short tale that presents a lesson in story form. This lesson is often called a **moral.** Starting with the words *Once upon a time there was . . . ,* write a fable illustrating one of the following morals or one of your own choice.

a. Practice what you preach.
b. Slow and steady wins the race.
c. Don't put off for tomorrow what you can do today.
d. Beauty is in the eye of the beholder.
e. All that glitters is not gold.

90    *The Short Story*

---

## COMPOSITION: GUIDELINES FOR EVALUATION

### WRITING ABOUT THEME

**Objective**
To show how theme is developed

**Guidelines for Evaluation**
■ suggested length: five to eight paragraphs
■ should state the theme of story
■ should show how theme is developed through the title, plot, character, setting, point of view
■ refer to frame and inner story in explanation

### WRITING A FABLE

**Objective**
To write a fable illustrating a moral

**Guidelines for Evaluation**
■ suggested length: four to eight paragraphs
■ should present one or more characters and create a situation
■ should illustrate a particular stated moral
■ should use simple language

Doris Lessing was born in Persia in 1919, grew up in Rhodesia (now Zimbabwe), and has spent most of her adult life in England. She began writing seriously at a very young age and now ranks as one of the major writers of our time. Lessing often writes about personal and social turmoil and about the growth of individuals in a changing and often hostile environment.

■ Have you ever felt compelled to do something, maybe even something dangerous, to prove a point? What happened?

*Doris Lessing*

# Through the Tunnel

1     Going to the shore on the first morning of the vacation, the young English boy stopped at a turning of the path and looked down at a wild and rocky bay, and then over to the crowded beach he knew so well from other years. His mother walked on in front of him, carrying a bright striped bag in one hand. Her other arm, swinging loose, was very white in the sun. The boy watched that white, naked arm, and turned his eyes, which had a frown behind them, toward the bay and back again to his mother. When she felt he was not with her, she swung around. "Oh, there you are, Jerry!" she said. She looked impatient, then smiled. "Why, darling, would you rather not come with me? Would you rather—" She frowned, conscientiously worrying over what amusements he might secretly be longing for, which she had been too busy or too careless to imagine. He was very familiar with that anxious, apologetic smile. Contrition sent him running after her. And yet, as he ran, he looked back over his shoulder at the wild bay; and all morning, as he played on the safe beach, he was thinking of it.

    Next morning, when it was time for the routine of swimming and sunbathing, his mother said, "Are you tired of the usual beach, Jerry? Would you like to go somewhere else?"

    "Oh, no!" he said quickly, smiling at her out of that unfailing impulse of contrition—a sort of chivalry. Yet, walking down the path with her, he blurted out, "I'd like to go and have a look at those rocks down there."

3     She gave the idea her attention. It was a wild-looking place, and there was no one there; but she said, "Of course, Jerry. When you've had enough, come to the big beach. Or just go straight back to the villa,[1] if you like." She walked away, that bare arm, now slightly reddened from yesterday's sun, swinging. And he almost ran after her again, feeling it unbearable that she should go by herself, but he did not.

    She was thinking. Of course he's old enough to be safe without me. Have I been keeping him too close? He mustn't feel he ought to be with me. I must be careful.

    He was an only child, eleven years old. She was a widow. She was determined to be neither possessive nor lacking in devotion. She went worrying off to her beach.

_____
1. **villa:** a summer house.

*Through the Tunnel*   **91**

## AT A GLANCE

- An English boy and his mother vacation at the seashore.
- The wild, rocky bay attracts Jerry.
- The mother realizes his need for independence and allows him to go to the bay alone.

## LITERARY OPTIONS

- implied theme
- style
- characterization

## THEMATIC OPTIONS

- growth and risk
- dependence and independence
- overcoming obstacles.

### 1 SETTING

The setting provides a meaningful context for the events about to unfold. The French shoreline, with its civilized beach, lies next to a wild, rocky bay.

### 2 CHARACTERIZATION

Jerry feels guilty for lagging behind but is fascinated by the rocky bay.

### 3 PLOT: CONFLICT

The disparity between the mother's thoughts and her words mirrors Jerry's conflict between wanting to please his mother and going off on his own.

## GUIDED READING

### LITERAL QUESTIONS

**1a.** Why does the boy almost run after his mother? (He felt it unbearable that she should go alone.)

**2a.** What words describe Jerry? What words describe his mother? (Jerry: *contrite, chivalric;* Mother: *conscientious, anxious, apologetic*)

### INFERENTIAL QUESTIONS

**1b.** What do you think keeps the boy from following his mother? (Desire for independence and new experience is stronger than his need for the comfort and safety he feels with his mother.)

**2b.** How would you describe Jerry's relationship with his mother? (He is careful not to hurt her; he is loving but guarded.)

- Jerry swims far out in the bay.
- He joins a group of local, older boys.
- The boys dive through a gap in the big rock to get to the other side, and Jerry tries to join them.

### 1 IMAGERY

Lessing's images of the sea, at once terrifying and exciting, represent the real world.

### 2 STYLE: METAPHOR

As Jerry begins to "distance" himself emotionally from his mother, she also diminishes in size, becoming "a speck of yellow."

### 3 CHARACTERIZATION

The contrast between Jerry's distress and the boys' impassive gaze emphasizes Jerry's naiveté.

### 4 THEME

The black, looming wall of rock resembles the difficult challenge Jerry faces in establishing his independence.

As for Jerry, once he saw that his mother had gained her beach he began the steep descent to the bay. From where he was, high up among red-brown rocks, it was a scoop of moving bluish green fringed with white. As he went lower, he saw that it spread among small promontories and inlets of rough, sharp rock, and the crisping, lapping surface showed stains of purple and darker blue. Finally, as he ran sliding and scraping down the last few yards, he saw an edge of white surf and the shallow, luminous movement of water over white sand, and, beyond that, a solid, heavy blue.

He ran straight into the water and began swimming. He was a good swimmer. He went out fast over the gleaming sand, over a middle region where rocks lay like discolored monsters under the surface, and then he was in the real sea—a warm sea where irregular cold currents from the deep water shocked his limbs.

When he was so far out that he could look back not only on the little bay but past the promontory that was between it and the big beach, he floated on the buoyant surface and looked for his mother. There she was, a speck of yellow under an umbrella that looked like a slice of orange peel. He swam back to shore, relieved at being sure she was there, but all at once very lonely.

On the edge of a small cape that marked the side of the bay away from the promontory was a loose scatter of rocks. Above them, some boys were stripping off their clothes. They came running, naked, down to the rocks. The English boy swam toward them, but kept his distance at a stone's throw. They were of that coast; all of them were burned smooth dark brown and speaking a language he did not understand. To be with them, of them, was a craving that filled his whole body. He swam a little closer; they turned and watched him with narrowed, alert dark eyes. Then one smiled and waved. It was enough. In a minute, he had swum in and was on the rocks beside them, smiling with a desperate, nervous supplication. They shouted cheerful greetings at him; and then, as he preserved his nervous, uncomprehending smile, they understood that he was a foreigner strayed from his own beach, and they proceeded to forget him. But he was happy. He was with them.

They began diving again and again from a high point into a well of blue sea between rough, pointed rocks. After they had dived and come up, they swam around, hauled themselves up, and waited their turn to dive again. They were big boys—men, to Jerry. He dived, and they watched him; and when he swam around to take his place, they made way for him. He felt he was accepted and he dived again, carefully, proud of himself.

Soon the biggest of the boys poised himself, shot down into the water, and did not come up. The others stood about, watching. Jerry, after waiting for the sleek brown head to appear, let out a yell of warning; they looked at him idly and turned their eyes back toward the water. After a long time, the boy came up on the other side of a big dark rock, letting the air out of his lungs in a spluttering gasp and a shout of triumph. Immediately the rest of them dived in. One moment, the morning seemed full of clattering boys; the next, the air and the surface of the water were empty. But through the heavy blue, dark shapes could be seen moving and groping.

Jerry dived, shot past the school of underwater swimmers, saw a black wall of rock looming at him, touched it, and bobbed up at once to the surface, where the wall was a low barrier he could see across. There was no one visible; under him, in the water, the dim shapes of the swimmers had disappeared. Then one, and then another of the boys came up on the far side of the barrier of rock, and he understood that they had swum through some gap or hole in it. He plunged down again. He could see nothing through the stinging salt water but the blank rock. When he came up, the boys were all on the diving rock, preparing to attempt the feat again.

## GUIDED READING

### LITERAL QUESTIONS

**1a.** In what words does the narrator describe the rocks and water where Jerry first swims? *(rocks like discolored monsters, a warm sea where irregular cold currents . . . shocked his limbs)*

**2a.** When the biggest boy doesn't surface from his dive, how does Jerry's response differ from that of the other boys? (Jerry yells a warning; the boys direct an "idle" look at Jerry and return their attention to the water.)

### INFERENTIAL QUESTIONS

**1b.** What do the rocks and undercurrents in the bay where Jerry swims with ease imply? (While Jerry is reveling in the "real sea," potential danger and the unpredictable await him.)

**2b.** What can you infer from these opposite reactions? (The boys, practiced divers, regard Jerry as an inconsequential, brief intrusion in their activity.)

AT A GLANCE

- Jerry fails to swim through the rock and feels ashamed.
- Desperately, he shouts some French words at the older boys to hold their attention.
- The boys dive again.

**1 STYLE: SIMILE**

Jerry feels his need for acceptance as both disfiguring and permanent.

**2 CHARACTERIZATION**

Jerry uses the only French words he knows to hold the attention of the older boys. He has a history of acknowledging shame over failure by clowning.

And now, in a panic of failure, he yelled up, in English, "Look at me! Look!" and he began splashing and kicking in the water like a foolish dog.

They looked down gravely, frowning. He knew the frown. At moments of failure, when he clowned to claim his mother's attention, it was with just this grave, embarrassed inspection that she rewarded him. Through his hot shame, feeling the pleading grin on his face like a scar that he could never remove, he looked up at the group of big brown boys on the rock and shouted,

"*Bonjour! Merci! Au revoir! Monsieur, monsieur!*"² while he hooked his fingers round his ears and waggled them.

Water surged into his mouth; he choked, sank, came up. The rock, lately weighted with boys, seemed to rear up out of the water as their weight was removed. They were flying down past him, now, into the water; the air was full of

---

2. *Bonjour . . . monsieur:* meaningless display of commonly known French words: "Hello! Thank you! Good-by! Sir, sir!"

*Through the Tunnel* **93**

---

## GUIDED READING

### LITERAL QUESTION

**1a.** What does Jerry do when he fails to follow the boys? (He clowns for their attention—yelling, splashing, waggling his ears—and feels shame.)

### INFERENTIAL QUESTION

**1b.** What does the incongruence between Jerry's behavior and feelings reveal about him? (He is in transition between childhood and adolescence, belonging neither with his mother nor with the big boys.)

**1 IMAGERY**

Lessing describes the familiar in vivid and happy colors; she bestows threatening, angry images on the unfamiliar.

**2 CHARACTERIZATION**

Jerry's ambivalence toward his mother is shown by his being both defiant and beseeching.

**3 IMAGERY**

The goggles temporarily transform the underwater world from frightening to approachable.

**4 VOCABULARY: DENOTATION**

Lessing chooses words denoting smallness (minute, tiny) to suggest that Jerry's fear is ebbing.

falling bodies. Then the rock was empty in the hot sunlight. He counted one, two, three. . . .

At fifty, he was terrified. They must all be drowning beneath him, in the watery caves of the rock! At a hundred, he stared around him at the empty hillside, wondering if he should yell for help. He counted faster, faster, to hurry them up, to bring them to the surface quickly, to drown them quickly—anything rather than the terror of counting on and on into the blue emptiness of the morning. And then, at a hundred and sixty, the water beyond the rock was full of boys blowing like brown whales. They swam back to the shore without a look at him.

He climbed back to the diving rock and sat down, feeling the hot roughness of it under his thighs. The boys were gathering up their bits of clothing and running off along the shore to another promontory. They were leaving to get away from him. He cried openly, fists in his eyes. There was no one to see him, and he cried himself out.

It seemed to him that a long time had passed, and he swam out to where he could see his mo-**1** ther. Yes, she was still there, a yellow spot under an orange umbrella. He swam back to the big rock, climbed up, and dived into the blue pool among the fanged and angry boulders. Down he went, until he touched the wall of rock again. But the salt was so painful in his eyes that he could not see.

He came to the surface, swam to shore, and went back to the villa to wait for his mother. Soon she walked slowly up the path, swinging **2** her striped bag, the flushed, naked arm dangling beside her. "I want some swimming goggles," he panted, defiant and beseeching.

She gave him a patient, inquisitive look as she said casually, "Well, of course, darling."

But now, now, now! He must have them this minute, and no other time. He nagged and pestered until she went with him to a shop. As soon as she had bought the goggles, he grabbed them from her hand as if she were going to claim them

for herself, and was off, running down the steep path to the bay.

Jerry swam out to the big barrier rock, adjusted the goggles, and dived. The impact of the water broke the rubber-enclosed vacuum, and the goggles came loose. He understood that he must swim down to the base of the rock from the surface of the water. He fixed the goggles tight and firm, filled his lungs, and floated, face **3** down on the water. Now he could see. It was as if he had eyes of a different kind—fish eyes that showed everything clear and delicate and wavering in the bright water.

Under him, six or seven feet down, was a floor of perfectly clean, shining white sand, rippled firm and hard by the tides. Two grayish shapes steered there, like long, rounded pieces of wood or slate. They were fish. He saw them nose toward each other, poise motionless, make a dart forward, swerve off, and come around again. It was like a water dance. A few inches **4** above them the water sparkled as if sequins were dropping through it. Fish again—myriads of minute fish, the length of his fingernail, were drifting through the water, and in a moment he could feel the innumerable tiny touches of them against his limbs. It was like swimming in flaked silver. The great rock the big boys had swum through rose sheer out of the white sand—black, tufted lightly with greenish weed. He could see no gap in it. He swam down to its base.

Again and again he rose, took a big chestful of air, and went down. Again and again he groped over the surface of the rock, feeling it, almost hugging it in the desperate need to find the entrance. And then, once, while he was clinging to the black wall, his knees came up and he shot his feet out forward and they met no obstacle. He had found the hole.

He gained the surface, clambered about the stones that littered the barrier rock until he found a big one, and, with this in his arms, let himself down over the side of the rock. He dropped, with the weight, straight to the sandy floor.

*GUIDED READING*

**LITERAL QUESTION**

**1a.** How does Jerry approach his mother to ask for goggles? ("Defiant and beseeching," he pesters his mother until she agrees to buy them immediately.)

**INFERENTIAL QUESTION**

**1b.** What does Jerry's behavior indicate about his character? (His urgency and belligerent manner show that he is distancing himself from his mother.)

Clinging tight to the anchor of stone, he lay on his side and looked in under the dark shelf at the place where his feet had gone. He could see the hole. It was an irregular, dark gap; but he could not see deep into it. He let go of his anchor, clung with his hands to the edges of the hole, and tried to push himself in.

He got his head in, found his shoulders jammed, moved them in sidewise, and was inside as far as his waist. He could see nothing ahead. Something soft and clammy touched his mouth; he saw a dark frond moving against the grayish rock, and panic filled him. He thought of octopuses, of clinging weed. He pushed himself out backward and caught a glimpse, as he retreated, of a harmless tentacle of seaweed drifting in the mouth of the tunnel. But it was enough. He reached the sunlight, swam to shore, and lay on the diving rock. He looked down into **1** the blue well of water. He knew he must find his way through that cave, or hole, or tunnel, and out the other side.

First, he thought, he must learn to control his breathing. He let himself down into the water with another big stone in his arms, so that he could lie effortlessly on the bottom of the sea. He counted. One, two, three. He counted steadily. He could hear the movement of blood in his chest. Fifty-one, fifty-two. . . . His chest was hurting. He let go of the rock and went up into the air. He saw that the sun was low. He rushed **2** to the villa and found his mother at her supper. She said only, ''Did you enjoy yourself?'' and he said, ''Yes.''

All night the boy dreamed of the water-filled cave in the rock, and as soon as breakfast was over he went to the bay.

**3** That night, his nose bled badly. For hours he had been underwater, learning to hold his breath, and now he felt weak and dizzy. His mother said, ''I shouldn't overdo things, darling, if I were you.''

That day and the next, Jerry exercised his lungs as if everything, the whole of his life, all

that he would become, depended upon it. Again his nose bled at night, and his mother insisted on his coming with her the next day. It was a torment to him to waste a day of his careful self- **4** training, but he stayed with her on that other beach, which now seemed a place for small children, a place where his mother might lie safe in the sun. It was not his beach.

He did not ask for permission, on the following day, to go to his beach. He went before his mother could consider the complicated rights and wrongs of the matter. A day's rest, he discovered, had improved his count by ten. The big boys had made the passage while he counted a hundred and sixty. He had been counting fast, in **5** his fright. Probably now, if he tried, he could get through that long tunnel, but he was not going to try yet. A curious, most unchildlike persistence, a controlled impatience, made him wait. In the meantime, he lay underwater on the white sand, littered now by stones he had brought down from the upper air, and studied the entrance to the tunnel. He knew every jut and corner of it, as far as it was possible to see. It was as if he already felt its sharpness about his shoulders.

He sat by the clock in the villa when his mother was not near, and checked his time. He was incredulous and then proud to find he could hold his breath without strain for two minutes. The words *two minutes*, authorized by the clock, brought close the adventure that was so necessary to him.

In another four days, his mother said casually one morning, they must go home. On the day before they left, he would do it. He would do it if it killed him, he said defiantly to himself. But two days before they were to leave—a day of triumph when he increased his count by fifteen— his nose bled so badly that he turned dizzy and had to lie limply over the big rock like a bit of seaweed, watching the thick red blood flow onto the rock and trickle slowly down to the sea. He was frightened. Supposing he turned dizzy in

*Through the Tunnel* **95**

AT A GLANCE
- Jerry practices for days holding his breath under water.
- When Jerry can hold his breath for at least two minutes, he decides he is ready for the tunnel.

**1 THEME**

Jerry knows instinctively that he must pass through the tunnel to become independent.

**2 CHARACTERIZATION**

By not probing him about his activities, Jerry's mother is also ''letting go.''

**3 THEME**

Jerry must undergo physical and mental pain to prove himself.

**4 SYMBOLISM**

Jerry sees the beach as a symbol of childhood.

**5 THEME**

Jerry's behavior continues to grow more adult.

## GUIDED READING

### LITERAL QUESTIONS

**1a.** What was Jerry doing on the day when his mother asked if he enjoyed himself? (He surfaced from the tunnel entrance in a panic and lay counting on the ocean floor until his chest hurt.)

**2a.** How does Jerry view the beach? (It seems a place for small children—it is not his beach.)

### INFERENTIAL QUESTIONS

**1b.** Why can Jerry not tell his mother about his extraordinary day of panic and pain? (He must grapple with the challenge alone in order to protect his fragile emotional distance from his mother.)

**2b.** What does his changed view signify? (Jerry, a character in transition, no longer identifies with the children or the small beach.)

- Frightened by the physical challenge of the tunnel, Jerry almost postpones his attempt for another year.
- Immediately after, he decides that it is now or never.

## 1 THEME

Jerry must choose: risk swimming the tunnel or give up his chance to grow into someone he respects.

the tunnel? Supposing he died there, trapped? Supposing—his head went around in the hot sun, and he almost gave up. He thought he would return to the house and lie down, and next summer, perhaps, when he had another year's growth in him—*then* he would go through the hole.

But even after he had made the decision, or thought he had, he found himself sitting up on the rock and looking down into the water; and he knew that now, this moment, when his nose had only just stopped bleeding, when his head was still sore and throbbing—this was the moment when he would try. If he did not do it now, he never would. He was trembling with fear that he would not go; and he was trembling with horror at that long, long tunnel under the rock, under the sea. Even in the open sunlight, the barrier rock seemed very wide and very heavy; tons of rock pressed down on where he

**96**  *The Short Story*

## GUIDED READING

### LITERAL QUESTION

**1a.** When does Jerry make the final decision to attempt the swim? (He decides to make the swim right after he thinks he will postpone it a year.)

### INFERENTIAL QUESTION

**1b.** In what sense is this decision prompted by fear? (Jerry is afraid that if he does not make the swim now he may be too afraid and will back out later.)

would go. If he died there, he would lie until one day—perhaps not before next year—those big boys would swim into it and find it blocked.

He put on his goggles, fitted them tight, tested the vacuum. His hands were shaking. Then he chose the biggest stone he could carry and slipped over the edge of the rock until half of him was in the cool, enclosing water and half in the hot sun. He looked up once at the empty sky, filled his lungs once, twice, and then sank fast to the bottom with the stone. He let it go and began to count. He took the edges of the hole in his hands and drew himself into it, wriggling his shoulders in sidewise as he remembered he must, kicking himself along with his feet.

Soon he was clear inside. He was in a small rockbound hole filled with yellowish-gray water. The water was pushing him up against the roof. The roof was sharp and pained his back. He pulled himself along with his hands—fast, fast—and used his legs as levers. His head knocked against something; a sharp pain dizzied him. Fifty, fifty-one, fifty-two. . . . He was without light, and the water seemed to press upon him with the weight of rock. Seventy-one, seventy-two. . . . There was no strain on his lungs. He felt like an inflated balloon, his lungs were so light and easy, but his head was pulsing.

He was being continually pressed against the **1** sharp roof, which felt slimy as well as sharp. Again he thought of octopuses, and wondered if the tunnel might be filled with weed that could tangle him. He gave himself a panicky, convulsive kick forward, ducked his head, and swam. His feet and hands moved freely, as if in open water. The hole must have widened out. He thought he must be swimming fast, and he was frightened of banging his head if the tunnel narrowed.

**2** A hundred, a hundred and one. . . . The water paled. Victory filled him. His lungs were beginning to hurt. A few more strokes and he would be out. He was counting wildly; he said a hundred and fifteen, and then, a long time later, a

hundred and fifteen again. The water was a clear jewel-green all around him. Then he saw, above his head, a crack running up through the rock. Sunlight was falling through it, showing the clean, dark rock of the tunnel, a single mussel shell, and darkness ahead.

He was at the end of what he could do. He looked up at the crack as if it were filled with air and not water, as if he could put his mouth to it to draw in air. A hundred and fifteen, he heard himself say inside his head—but he had said that long ago. He must go on into the blackness ahead, or he would drown. His head was swelling, his lungs cracking. A hundred and fifteen, a hundred and fifteen pounded through his head, and he feebly clutched at rocks in the dark, pulling himself forward, leaving the brief space of sunlit water behind. He felt he was dying. He was no longer quite conscious. He struggled on in the **3** darkness between lapses into unconsciousness. An immense, swelling pain filled his head, and then the darkness cracked with an explosion of green light. His hands, groping forward, met nothing; and his feet, kicking back, propelled him into the open sea.

He drifted to the surface, his face turned up to the air. He was gasping like a fish. He felt he would sink now and drown; he could not swim the few feet back to the rock. Then he was clutching it and pulling himself up onto it. He lay face down, gasping. He could see nothing but a red-veined, clotted dark. His eyes must have burst, he thought; they were full of blood. He tore off his goggles and a gout of blood went into the sea. His nose was bleeding, and the blood had filled the goggles.

He scooped up handfuls of water from the cool, salty sea, to splash on his face, and did not know whether it was blood or salt water he tasted. After a time, his heart quieted, his eyes cleared, and he sat up. He could see the local boys diving and playing half a mile away. He did not want them. He wanted nothing but to get back home and lie down.

*Through the Tunnel* **97**

## GUIDED READING

**LITERAL QUESTIONS**

**1a.** How does Jerry measure his and the other boys' time under water? (He counts.)

**2a.** How does Jerry feel about seeing the local boys playing after his victory? (He does not want to be with them.)

**INFERENTIAL QUESTIONS**

**1b.** What can you infer about Jerry from his practice of counting? (Lacking the big boys' instincts, he chooses the certainty of numbers.)

**2b.** What might this feeling imply about his accomplishment? (He has a more mature attitude than before: he no longer needs the company and approval of the local boys.)

**AT A GLANCE**

- Jerry returns to the villa and announces that he can stay under water for two minutes.
- He has met the challenge and no longer needs to go to the bay.

**1 PLOT: FALLING ACTION**

Jerry's success in his test affirms his growing independence. He no longer needs to be with the older boys.

**2 DIALOGUE**

Jerry's mother is still protective. Jerry is quietly proud—even nonchalant.

REFLECTING ON THE STORY

Why is going to the bay no longer important to Jerry? (He no longer needs to prove himself.)

STUDY QUESTIONS

1. wild and isolated
2. She doesn't want to be too protective or possessive.
3. joins them; dives with them; when they leave, cries on the rock
4. must find hole, needs goggles, must learn how to hold breath; gets mother to buy goggles, practices holding breath
5. He's exhausted; he has a nosebleed; his head is bruised.
6. ■ to prove his courage
   ■ His fear will prevent him next year.
7. Yes—he is no longer afraid.
8. He becomes more independent.
9. He had achieved his goal.
10. by taking a courageous action

VIEWPOINT

Growth comes as a result of going beyond limitations

---

1 In a short while, Jerry swam to shore and climbed slowly up the path to the villa. He flung himself on his bed and slept, waking at the sound of feet on the path outside. His mother was coming back. He rushed to the bathroom, thinking she must not see his face with bloodstains, or tearstains, on it. He came out of the bathroom and met her as she walked into the villa, smiling, her eyes lighting up.

"Have a nice morning?" she asked, laying her hand on his warm brown shoulder a moment.

2 "Oh, yes, thank you," he said.

"You look a bit pale." And then, sharp and anxious, "How did you bang your head?"

"Oh, just banged it," he told her.

She looked at him closely. He was strained; his eyes were glazed-looking. She was worried. And then she said to herself, Oh, don't fuss! Nothing can happen. He can swim like a fish.

They sat down to lunch together.

"Mummy," he said, "I can stay under water for two minutes—three minutes, at least." It came bursting out of him.

"Can you, darling?" she said. "Well, I shouldn't overdo it. I don't think you ought to swim any more today."

She was ready for a battle of wills, but he gave in at once. It was no longer of the least importance to go to the bay.

---

**STUDY QUESTIONS**

**Recalling**
1. How is the bay that Jerry notices on the first day of his vacation different from the beach that he normally visits?
2. Why does Jerry's mother agree to let him go to the inlet?
3. Find the details that show Jerry's efforts to be accepted by the older boys and the details that reveal his frustration as they desert him.
4. What obstacles must Jerry overcome in his attempt to swim through the tunnel? How does he overcome them?
5. Describe Jerry's physical condition after his swim.

**Interpreting**
6. Why does Jerry want to swim the tunnel? Why is it so important to him to complete the swim this year rather than wait until next year?
7. Does his attitude toward the tunnel change in any way from the beginning to the end of the story? Explain.
8. In what ways does Jerry's attitude toward his mother change from the beginning to the end of the story?

9. Why does Jerry feel at the end of the story that "it was no longer of the least importance to go to the bay"?

**Extending**
10. In what way might each of us have a desire to pass "through the tunnel"?

**VIEWPOINT**

One book about Doris Lessing notes that her stories allow readers to experience

what it is like to be alive...in the ordinary way of being young and then not so young and then old, and of discovering along the way things about living that cannot be understood until they are felt.

— D. Brewster, *Doris Lessing*

■ What did you discover about living in Jerry's attempt to swim through the tunnel?

**LITERARY FOCUS**

**Implied Theme**

The **theme** is the main insight about human experience that an author expresses in a work. While some writers present us with direct statements of their themes, most writers prefer to imply their themes in their works. An **implied theme** is one that is gradually revealed to the reader through the other elements of the work. Because the theme is a complete idea, it should be stated in a complete sentence. We can usually find a story's implied theme by asking the following questions:

- What ideas about life does the story's *title* suggest?
- What do the particular *events* and *conflicts* reveal about life in general?
- What might these particular *characters* with these personality traits tell us about people in general?
- What view of the world do the *setting* and its details offer us?
- What does seeing the events and characters from this particular *point of view* tell us about life?
- Was the author's *purpose* in putting these elements together to say something about life in general or to present one special sort of person and view of life?

**Thinking About Implied Theme**

1. What ideas about life might be implied by the title, "Through the Tunnel"?
2. What ideas about human experience might be implied by Jerry's age and his relationships with his mother and the older boys?
3. Explain why it is so important for Jerry to swim the tunnel. What does his need to swim the tunnel reveal about life in general?

## VOCABULARY

**Using Context Clues**

You can often discover a word's general meaning from its **context,** or the words around it. For example, in the following passage from "Through the Tunnel," the context provides clues to the meaning of the word *possessive:*

> She was thinking....Have I been keeping him too close?...She was determined to be neither *possessive* nor lacking in devotion.

The passage connects *possessive* with the idea of "keeping him too close." In addition, the combina-

tion of *"neither...nor"* suggests that *possessive* is the opposite of *lacking in devotion* and probably means something like "overly devoted."

Each of the sentences below comes from "Through the Tunnel." Find the meaning of each of the *italicized* words in these sentences by studying its context. Check your answer in the Glossary at the back of the book or in a dictionary. Then use the word in a sentence of your own. Make sure that your use of the word corresponds to its use in the story.

1. Water *surged* into his mouth; he choked, sank, came up.
2. Fish again — *myriads* of minute fish, the length of his fingernail, were drifting through the water....
3. Again and again he *groped* over the surface of the rock, feeling it, almost hugging it in the desperate need to find the entrance.
4. Something soft and clammy touched his mouth; he saw a dark *frond* moving against the grayish rock....He pushed himself out backward and caught a glimpse...of a harmless tentacle of seaweed drifting in the mouth of the tunnel.
5. He gave himself a panicky, *convulsive* kick forward, ducked his head, and swam.

## COMPOSITION

**Writing About Theme**

■ Show how "April Showers" and "Through the Tunnel" have similar themes. First express the theme of each story. Then point out as many similarities as you can find between these themes.

**Writing with Sensory Language**

■ Writers use **sensory language,** language that appeals to one or more of the five senses of sight, hearing, smell, taste, and touch, to help readers imagine the scenes that they are describing. For example, in "Through the Tunnel" Doris Lessing creates a vivid picture of Jerry's vision under water when she says that "...the water sparkled as if sequins were dropping through it." Choose a place that is special to you, and describe it in a paragraph using sensory language. Use a number of vivid details that appeal to more than one of the five senses, and end by expressing your main impression of the place.

*Through the Tunnel* **99**

## COMPOSITION: GUIDELINES FOR EVALUATION

### WRITING ABOUT THEME
**Objective**
To find similarities between the themes of two stories

**Guidelines for Evaluation**
- suggested length: three to five paragraphs
- should identify themes of "April Showers" and "Through the Tunnel"
- should list the similarities between themes

### WRITING WITH SENSORY LANGUAGE
**Objective**
To create an impression of a place by using sensory language

**Guidelines for Evaluation**
- suggested length: one paragraph
- should use words that appeal to the various senses
- should include vivid details
- should convey writer's overall impression

AT A GLANCE

- Young friends Giovannino and Serenella play along a railroad track.
- Giovannino announces that a train is coming.

LITERARY OPTIONS

- theme
- setting

THEMATIC OPTIONS

- anxiety and foreboding
- friendship
- social differences

**1 SETTING**

Giovannino and Serenella, playmates, make up games as they go along the railroad tracks adjacent to the seaside.

**2 THEME**

Serenella, almost anticipating Giovannino's thoughts and ready for any adventure, is a perfect friend.

**3 CHARACTERIZATION**

The dialogue quickly reveals the dynamics of their friendship: He provides ideas, which she easily understands and readily accepts.

Italian writer Italo Calvino (1923–1985) produced several novels and short story collections, many of which have been translated into English. In the following story he invites readers to share the adventures of a young girl and boy on one unusual day.

■ Calvino has been called a writer of fantasy, and his works are said to have a fairy-tale quality. What characteristics, if any, has this story in common with the fairy tales and fantasies you know?

*Italo Calvino*

# The Enchanted Garden

**1** Giovannino[1] and Serenella[2] were strolling along the railroad tracks. Below was a scaly sea of somber, clear blue; above, a sky lightly streaked with white clouds. The railroad tracks were shimmering and burning hot. It was fun going along the tracks, there were so many games to play—he balancing on one rail and holding her hand while she walked along on the other, or else both jumping from one sleeper[3] to the next without ever letting their feet touch the stones in between. Giovannino and Serenella had been out looking for crabs, and now they had decided to explore the railroad tracks as far as **2** the tunnel. He liked playing with Serenella, for she did not behave as all the other little girls did, forever getting frightened or bursting into tears at every joke. Whenever Giovannino said, "Let's go there," or "Let's do this," Serenella followed without a word.

Ping! They both gave a start and looked up. A telephone wire had snapped off the top of the pole. It sounded like an iron stork shutting its beak in a hurry. They stood with their noses in the air and watched. What a pity not to have seen it! Now it would never happen again.

**3** "There's a train coming," said Giovannino. Serenella did not move from the rail. "Where from?" she asked.

Giovannino looked around in a knowledgeable way. He pointed at the black hole of the tunnel, which showed clear one moment, then misty the next, through the invisible heat haze rising from the stony track.

"From there," he said. It was as though they already heard a snort from the darkness of the tunnel, and saw the train suddenly appear, belching out fire and smoke, the wheels mercilessly eating up the rails as it hurtled toward them.

"Where shall we go, Giovannino?"

There were big gray aloes[4] down by the sea, surrounded by dense, impenetrable nettles,[5]

---

1. **Giovannino** [jō vä nē′nō]
2. **Serenella** [se re ne′lä]
3. **sleeper:** wood beam used to connect and support the rails; crosstie.

4. **aloes** [al′ōz]: plants having fleshy leaves with spines along the edges.
5. **nettles:** prickly or stinging plants.

**100** *The Short Story*

---

## GUIDED READING

**LITERAL QUESTION**

**1a.** What happened to the telephone wire? (It snapped off the top of the pole.)

**INFERENTIAL QUESTION**

**1b.** Why is it a pity that the children did not see it? (They think it is a pity because they are out for a day of adventures, using all their senses, and this would have been an unusual and interesting sight.)

they always had that uncomfortable feeling that they had no right to any of this, and might be chased out at any moment.

They scrambled out of the water, and there beside the swimming pool they found a Ping-Pong table. Instantly Giovannino picked up the paddle and hit the ball, and Serenella, on the other side, was quick to return his shot. And so they went on playing, though giving only light taps at the ball, in case someone in the villa heard them. Then Giovannino, in trying to parry a shot that had bounced high, sent the ball sailing away through the air and smack against a gong hanging in a pergola.[8] There was a long, somber boom. The two children crouched down behind a clump of ranunculus.[9] At once two menservants in white coats appeared, carrying big trays; when they had put the trays down on a round table under an orange-and-yellow-striped umbrella, off they went.

Giovannino and Serenella crept up to the table. There was tea, milk, and sponge cake. They had only to sit down and help themselves. They poured out two cups of tea and cut two slices of cake. But somehow they did not feel at all at ease, and sat perched on the edge of their chairs, their knees shaking. And they could not really enjoy the tea and cake, for nothing seemed to have any taste. Everything in the garden was like that: lovely but impossible to enjoy properly, with that worrying feeling inside that they were only there through an odd stroke of luck, and the fear that they'd soon have to give an account of themselves.

Very quietly they tiptoed up to the villa. Between the slits of a Venetian blind they saw a beautiful shady room, with collections of butterflies hanging on the walls. And in the room was a pale little boy. Lucky boy, he must be the owner of this villa and garden. He was stretched out on a chaise longue,[10] turning the pages of a large book filled with figures. He had big white hands and wore pajamas buttoned up to the neck, though it was summer.

As the two children went on peeping through the slits, the pounding of their hearts gradually subsided. Why, the little rich boy seemed to be sitting there and turning the pages and glancing around with more anxiety and worry than their own. Then he got up and tiptoed around, as if he were afraid that at any moment someone would come and turn him out, as if he felt that that book, that chaise lounge, and those butterflies framed on the wall, the garden and games and tea trays, the swimming pool and paths, were only granted to him by some enormous mistake, as if he were incapable of enjoying them and felt the bitterness of the mistake as his own fault.

The pale boy was wandering about his shady

---

8. **pergola** [pur′gə lə]: garden shelter made of branches or latticework covered with shrubs or vines.
9. **ranunculus** [rə nən′kyə ləs]: buttercups.

10. **chaise longue** [shāz′ lông′]: chair with a seat long enough to support the sitter's legs.

**102** *The Short Story*

## GUIDED READING

### LITERAL QUESTION

**1a.** In what way is the little rich boy glancing around in his room? (with more anxiety and worry than the two children)

### INFERENTIAL QUESTION

**1b.** Why do you think he is behaving in this way? (For some reason he is not comfortable in his environment. He is as unsatisfied as they are.)

while up the hillside ran a rambling hedge with thick leaves but no flowers. There was still no sign of the train; perhaps it was coasting, with the engine cut off, and would jump out at them all of a sudden. But Giovannino had now found an opening in the hedge. "This way," he called.

1 The fence under the rambling hedge was an old bent rail. At one point it twisted about on the ground like the corner of a sheet of paper. Giovannino had slipped into the hole and already half vanished.

"Give me a hand, Giovannino."

They found themselves in the corner of a garden, on all fours in a flower bed, with their hair full of dry leaves and moss. Everything was quiet; not a leaf was stirring.

"Come on," said Giovannino, and Serenella nodded in reply.

There were big old flesh-colored eucalyptus trees and winding gravel paths. Giovannino and Serenella tiptoed along the paths, taking care not to crunch the gravel. Suppose the owners appeared now?

2 Everything was so beautiful: sharp bends in the path and high, curling eucalyptus leaves and patches of sky. But there was always the worrying thought that it was not their garden, and that they might be chased away any moment. Yet not a sound could be heard. A flight of chattering sparrows rose from a clump of arbutus[6] at a turn in the path. Then all was silent again. Perhaps it was an abandoned garden?

But the shade of the big trees came to an end, and they found themselves under the open sky facing flower beds filled with neat rows of petunias and convolvulus, and paths and balustrades[7] and rows of box trees. And up at the end of the garden was a large villa with flashing windowpanes and yellow-and-orange curtains.

---

6. **arbutus** [är bu′tus]: trees or shrubs having dark green leaves and white or pinkish flowers.
7. **convolvulus** [kən väl′vyə ləs]: morning glories; **balustrades**: railings supported by upright posts.

And it was all quite deserted. The two children crept forward, treading carefully over the gravel: Perhaps the windows would suddenly be flung open, and angry ladies and gentlemen appear on the terraces to unleash great dogs down the paths. Now they found a wheelbarrow standing near a ditch. Giovannino picked it up by the handles and began pushing it along: It creaked like a whistle at every turn. Serenella seated herself in it and they moved slowly forward, Giovannino pushing the barrow with her on top, along the flower beds and fountains.

Every now and then Serenella would point to a flower and say in a low voice, "That one," and Giovannino would put the barrow down, pluck it, and give it to her. Soon she had a lovely bouquet.

Eventually the gravel ended and they reached an open space paved in bricks and mortar. In the middle of this space was a big empty rectangle: a swimming pool. They crept up to the edge; it was lined with blue tiles and filled to the brim with clear water. How lovely it would be to swim in!

"Shall we go for a dip?" Giovannino asked Serenella. The idea must have been quite dangerous if he asked her instead of just saying, "In we go!" But the water was so clear and blue, and Serenella was never afraid. She jumped off the barrow and put her bunch of flowers in it. They were already in bathing suits, since they'd been out for crabs before. Giovannino plunged in—not from the diving board, because the splash would have made too much noise, but from the edge of the pool. Down and down he went with his eyes wide open, seeing only the blue from the tiles and his pink hands like goldfish; it was not the same as under the sea, full of shapeless green-black shadows. A pink form appeared above him: Serenella! He took her hand and they swam up to the surface, a bit anxiously. No, there was no one watching them at all. But it was not so nice as they'd thought it would be;

*The Enchanted Garden* 101

- The children slip through a hedge into a garden.
- Giovannino gives Serenella a ride and picks flowers for her.
- They find a swimming pool and go for a dip.

### 1 SETTING

With almost dreamlike ease Giovannino and Serenella slip through a hole in a hedge into a garden—the "enchanted garden."

### 2 PLOT: NARRATIVE HOOK

At any time they could be driven from this beautiful garden formed out of sharp bends, curling leaves, and patches of sky.

### 3 SETTING

The beauty of the place is marred by the children's anxiety and precautions lest they be caught.

## GUIDED READING

### LITERAL QUESTIONS

**1a.** What does Giovannino ask Serenella about the pool? ("Shall we go for a dip?")

**2a.** After Giovannino takes her hand, how do he and Serenella swim up to the surface? (anxiously)

### INFERENTIAL QUESTIONS

**1b.** Why does his asking the question suggest danger? (He is giving her a chance to be a part of the decision, so he must consider the idea serious.)

**2b.** Why do they feel this way? (They realize they are trespassing and are nervous about being caught.)

# MACMILLAN LITERATURE SERIES

## SIGNATURE EDITION

### DISCOVERING LITERATURE

### INTRODUCING LITERATURE

### ENJOYING LITERATURE

### UNDERSTANDING LITERATURE

### APPRECIATING LITERATURE

### AMERICAN LITERATURE

### ENGLISH LITERATURE
WITH WORLD MASTERPIECES

### WORLD LITERATURE

room furtively, touching with his white fingers the edges of the cases studded with butterflies; then he stopped to listen. The pounding of Giovannino and Serenella's hearts, which had died down, now got harder than ever. Perhaps it was the fear of a spell that hung over this villa and garden and over all these lovely, comfortable things, the residue of some injustice committed long ago.

Clouds darkened the sun. Very quietly Giovannino and Serenella crept away. They went back along the same paths they had come, stepping fast but never at a run. And they went through the hedge again on all fours. Between the aloes they found a path leading down to the small, stony beach, with banks of seaweed along the shore. Then they invented a wonderful new game: a seaweed fight. They threw great handfuls of it in each other's faces till late in the afternoon. And Serenella never once cried.

---

## STUDY QUESTIONS

### Recalling

1. What were Giovannino and Serenella doing before they entered the garden? Why do they go into the garden?
2. List in chronological order the actions of the two children as they move from the corner of the garden just inside the hedge to the villa.
3. The children were enjoying themselves outside the garden. Do they enjoy themselves as much once they are inside it? Find statements in the story that support your answer.
4. Describe the appearance and actions of the person Giovannino and Serenella see when they look inside the villa.
5. When do the children leave the garden?

### Interpreting

6. Giovannino tells Serenella that a train is coming. Do you think there really is a train? Explain why you think that.
7. Why do the two children feel so uneasy about being in the garden?
8. Find a statement near the end of the story that suggests why the garden might be enchanted.
9. What does the children's final action on the beach suggest?

### Extending

10. If you could talk to Italo Calvino about this story, what questions would you ask? What comments would you make?

## VIEWPOINT

The Italian critic Renato Barilli has called attention to a characteristic of Calvino's writing style:

Calvino's preoccupation with the precise observation and description of *things*—objects, plants, and actions . . .

■ Find at least three examples of Calvino's precise description in this story. Identify the sense to which each appeals.

## LITERARY FOCUS

### How Story Details Help Reveal Theme

The **theme** is the main idea of a short story or other literary work, an insight about some aspect of human life and experience that an author wants to convey to readers. Most stories have an **implied theme,** which the author gradually reveals through the artful use of details. In this story Calvino deals with the following aspect of human life: the imaginative world of childhood and the reality of the adult world.

### Thinking About Story Details and Theme

1. Which details does the author provide as he discusses these aspects of human life?
2. State the theme of this story in a sentence or two.

*The Enchanted Garden* **103**

AT A GLANCE
- The children watch the pale boy.
- They creep away.
- Back at the shore they invent a new game—a seaweed fight.

**1 THEME**
The narrator suggests that something is not right about the place—a "residue of some injustice."

### REFLECTING ON THE STORY

What do you think the "residue of some injustice" refers to? (Perhaps the discrepancy between the luxury of the villa and the poverty of people like Giovannino and Serenella is unjust.)

### STUDY QUESTIONS

1. looking for crabs, playing games on the railroad tracks; to get out of the path of an oncoming train
2. walking along the gravel paths, pushing Serenella in a wheelbarrow, picking flowers, swimming, playing Ping-Pong, having tea
3. No—they fear they will be caught. ("Suppose the owners appeared now?")
4. pale little boy; reading, tiptoeing around, listening
5. after seeing the boy
6. Nothing indicates that a train actually appeared.
7. Possible answers: They know that poor people do not belong there; also, the garden and villa could represent the world of adults.
8. "the residue of some injustice committed long ago"
9. pleasure in their own world and in each other
10. Possible question: What does the garden represent?

### VIEWPOINT
Sample descriptions: the telephone wire—sound; hedge—sight; Giovannino's swim underwater—sight

### LITERARY FOCUS
1. ■ the games on the railroad tracks, the imagined train, the exploration of the garden, the wild seaweed fight—all details suggesting the innocence, joy, and imagination of childhood
   ■ the hedge and fence around the garden; the formality of the garden; uneasiness, the villa and its furnishings (especially the framed butterflies) and sickly boy, the "injustice committed long ago"—all details suggesting the realities of the adult world
2. Children live in a world whose freedom, innocence, and wonder conflict with the sad realities of the adult world.

## AT A GLANCE

- The narrator attends a banquet in London, honoring a Lieutenant-General Scoresby.
- A clergyman friend of the narrator calls the general "an absolute fool."

## LITERARY OPTIONS

- point of view
- humor
- characterization

## THEMATIC OPTIONS

- chance
- appearance and reality
- human fallibility

### 1 POINT OF VIEW

The first-person narrator seems to feel an exaggerated hero worship for Scoresby.

### 2 DIALOGUE

With one line the clergyman deflates the image of Scoresby. The contrast between this trenchant comment and the narrator's overblown praise is funny.

Samuel L. Clemens (1835–1910), better known by the pen name of Mark Twain, grew up near the Mississippi River in Missouri. An early taste for adventure led him to work as a riverboat pilot and later as a prospector and journalist in the western United States. Twain's experiences on the frontier helped him develop a knack for spinning yarns, or tall tales, a talent that brought him his first fame as a writer. He later built on this reputation with his classic novels, *The Adventures of Tom Sawyer* and *The Adventures of Huckleberry Finn*. Much of the greatness of Twain's work comes from his inventiveness and keen eye for human frailty.

■ Is it better for a person to be lucky or smart?

*Mark Twain*

# Luck

It was at a banquet in London in honor of one of the two or three conspicuously illustrious English military names of this generation. For reasons which will presently appear, I will withhold his real name and titles and call him Lieutenant-General Lord Arthur Scoresby, Y.C., K.C.B.,[1] etc., etc., etc. What a fascination there is in a renowned name! There sat the man, in actual flesh, whom I had heard of so many thousands of times since that day, thirty years before, when his name shot suddenly to the zenith from a Crimean battlefield,[2] to remain forever celebrated. It was food and drink to me to look, and look, and look at that demigod; scanning, searching, noting: the quietness, the reserve, the noble gravity of his countenance; the simple honesty that expressed itself all over him; the sweet unconsciousness of his greatness—unconsciousness of the hundreds of admiring eyes fastened upon him, unconsciousness of the deep, loving, sincere worship welling out of the breasts of those people and flowing toward him.

The clergyman at my left was an old acquaintance of mine—clergyman now, but had spent the first half of his life in the camp and field and as an instructor in the military school at Woolwich.[3] Just at the moment I have been talking about a veiled and singular light glimmered in his eyes and he leaned down and muttered confidentially to me—indicating the hero of the banquet with a gesture:

"Privately—he's an absolute fool."

This verdict was a great surprise to me. If its subject had been Napoleon, or Socrates, or Solomon,[4] my astonishment could not have been greater. Two things I was well aware of: that the Rev-

---

1. **Y.C., K.C.B.:** abbreviations for British honorary titles.
2. **Crimean** [krĭ mē′ən] **battlefield:** Southern Russia was the scene of the Crimean War (1853–1856) fought by England, France, and Turkey against Russia.

3. **Woolwich** [wu′lich]: the Royal Military Academy near London.
4. **Napoleon . . . Solomon:** great leaders from different periods of history. Napoleon (1769–1821) was a French general and emperor; Socrates (469–399 B.C.), a Greek philosopher; Solomon, a king of Israel in the tenth century B.C.

**104** *The Short Story*

## GUIDED READING

### LITERAL QUESTION

**1a.** How does the narrator react when the clergyman says that Scoresby is a fool? (He is greatly surprised.)

### INFERENTIAL QUESTION

**1b.** Why does he react in that fashion? (He has heard for thirty years how great Scoresby is; his fascination in seeing Scoresby and his exaggerated view of Scoresby's heroism indicate that he accepts the popular view of Scoresby.)

erend was a man of strict veracity and that his judgment of men was good. Therefore I knew, beyond doubt or question, that the world was mistaken about his hero: he *was* a fool. So I meant to find out, at a convenient moment, how the Reverend, all solitary and alone, had discovered the secret.

Some days later the opportunity came, and this is what the Reverend told me:

"About forty years ago I was an instructor in the military academy at Woolwich. I was present in one of the sections when young Scoresby underwent his preliminary examination. I was touched to the quick with pity, for the rest of the class answered up brightly and handsomely, while he—why, dear me, he didn't know *any-thing*, so to speak. He was evidently good, and sweet, and lovable, and guileless; and so it was exceedingly painful to see him stand there, as serene as a graven image, and deliver himself of answers which were veritably miraculous for stupidity and ignorance. All the compassion in me was aroused in his behalf. I said to myself, when he comes to be examined again he will be flung over, of course; so it will be simply a harmless act of charity to ease his fall as much as I can. I took him aside and found that he knew a little of Caesar's history[5]; and as he didn't know anything else, I went to work and drilled him like a galley-slave[6] on a certain line of stock questions concerning Caesar which I knew would be used. If you'll believe me, he went through with flying colors on examination day! He went through on that purely superficial "cram," and got compliments too, while others, who knew a thousand times more than he, got plucked. By some strangely lucky accident—an accident not likely to happen twice in a cen-

tury—he was asked no question outside of the narrow limits of his drill.

"It was stupefying. Well, all through his course I stood by him, with something of the sentiment which a mother feels for a crippled child; and he always saved himself—just by miracle, apparently.

"Now, of course, the thing that would expose him and kill him at last was mathematics. I resolved to make his death as easy as I could; so I drilled him and crammed him, and crammed him and drilled him, just on the line of questions which the examiners would be most likely to use, and then launched him on his fate. Well, sir, try to conceive of the result: to my consternation, he took the first prize! And with it he got a perfect ovation in the way of compliments.

"Sleep? There was no more sleep for me for a week. My conscience tortured me day and night. What I had done I had done purely through charity, and only to ease the poor youth's fall. I never had dreamed of any such preposterous results as the thing that had happened. I felt as guilty and miserable as Frankenstein.[7] Here was a wooden-head whom I had put in the way of glittering promotions and prodigious responsibilities, and but one thing could happen: he and his responsibilities would all go to ruin together at the first opportunity.

"The Crimean War had just broken out. Of course there had to be a war, I said to myself. We couldn't have peace and give this donkey a chance to die before he is found out. I waited for the earthquake. It came. And it made me reel when it did come. He was actually gazetted to a captaincy in a marching regiment! Better men grow old and gray in the service before they climb to a sublimity like that. And who could ever have foreseen that they would go and put such a load of responsibility on such green[8] and

5. **Caesar's** [sē′zərz] **history:** the record of the military campaigns of Julius Caesar (100–44 B.C.), Roman general and statesman.
6. **galley-slave:** one of many slaves needed to row a ship in ancient and medieval times.

7. **Frankenstein** [frang′kən stīn′]: doctor who creates a monster in the novel by Mary Shelley.
8. **green:** inexperienced.

*Luck* 105

AT A GLANCE
- The clergyman tells that he, as an instructor, tutored the ignorant Scoresby.
- Through luck, Scoresby did well on the examination and won first prize in mathematics.
- Scoresby was given a captaincy in the Crimean War.

1 THEME
The narrator's complete trust in the clergyman's honesty and judgment suggests that Scoresby, contrary to all appearances, is indeed a fool.

2 POINT OF VIEW
The first-person point of view for the inner story reveals information about Scoresby that the narrator of the outer story does not know.

3 CHARACTERIZATION
The reader might question the judgment of one who spends a vast amount of time tutoring someone he expects to fail and is disappointed at a successful result of his "cramming."

4 SATIRE
The clergyman's choice of simile *(as guilty and miserable as Frankenstein)* and metaphor *(wooden-head)* conveys Twain's satiric view of the military.

## GUIDED READING

**LITERAL QUESTIONS**

**1a.** How does Scoresby perform after he has been tutored by the instructor? (Scoresby does very well, receiving compliments and a prize.)

**2a.** How does the narrator feel when Scoresby wins the mathematics prize? (He cannot sleep because his conscience bothers him.)

**INFERENTIAL QUESTIONS**

**1b.** Why do you think Scoresby succeeded? (He may have been incredibly lucky, or he may have been shrewd enough to fool people into thinking him intelligent.)

**2b.** Why is he so upset? (He feels that it will be his fault if Scoresby is given responsibilities that he cannot meet.)

- To "protect the country," the narrator joins Scoresby's regiment.
- Scoresby's repeated blunders are interpreted as signs of genius.
- Scoresby is promoted until he replaces the regimental colonel in battle.

**1 STYLE: HUMOR**

The narrator's exaggeration ("I thought my hair would turn white") and the absurdity of his following the inept Scoresby into battle add to the light-hearted humor of the story.

**2 READING SKILLS: CAUSE AND EFFECT**

The clergyman believes that because Scoresby was considered a genius all his actions were regarded as brilliant strokes of genius.

**3 THEME**

The clergyman's exaggerated reactions to Scoresby's blunders and the folly of the general convey Twain's skepticism regarding human judgment.

inadequate shoulders? I could just barely have stood it if they had made him a cornet;[9] but a captain—think of it! I thought my hair would turn white.

"Consider what I did—I who so loved repose and inaction. I said to myself, I am responsible to the country for this, and I must go along with him and protect the country against him as far as I can. So I took my poor little capital that I had saved up through years of work and grinding economy, and went with a sigh and bought a cornetcy[10] in his regiment, and away we went to the field.

"And there—oh, dear, it was awful. Blunder?— why, he never did anything *but* blunder. But, you see, nobody was in on the fellow's secret. Everybody had him focused wrong, and necessarily misinterpreted his performance every time. Consequently they took his idiotic blunders for inspirations of genius. They did, honestly! His mildest blunders were enough to make a man in his right mind cry; and they did make me cry—and rage and rave, too, privately. And the thing that kept me always in a sweat of apprehension was the fact that every fresh blunder he made increased the luster of his reputation! I kept saying to myself, he'll get so high that when discovery does finally come it will be like the sun falling out of the sky.

"He went right along up, from grade to grade, over the dead bodies of his superiors, until at last, in the hottest moment of the battle of —— down went our colonel, and my heart jumped into my mouth, for Scoresby was next in rank! Now for it, said I; we'll all land in Sheol[11] in ten minutes, sure.

"The battle was awfully hot; the allies were steadily giving way all over the field. Our regi-

---

9. **cornet:** lowest commissioned officer rank in the British cavalry.
10. **bought a cornetcy:** At the time of the story, a soldier in the British army could buy a commission.

11. **Sheol** [shē′ōl]: in the Bible, an underground land of the dead.

## GUIDED READING

**LITERAL QUESTION**

**1a.** What keeps the narrator in a "sweat of apprehension"? (He is upset because each of Scoresby's blunders increases Scoresby's reputation and leads to further promotions.)

**INFERENTIAL QUESTION**

**1b.** Why does this bother him so much? (He is sure that Scoresby's luck will end, and Scoresby and the clergyman will be responsible for a major catastrophe.)

AT A GLANCE

- Scoresby's absurd charge over a hill surprises a Russian army that flees through its own line.
- The allies win, and Scoresby is decorated on the field.
- Because he confused his right and his left hand, he becomes known as a military genius.

ment occupied a position that was vital; a blunder now must be destruction. At this crucial moment, what does this immortal fool do but detach the regiment from its place and order a charge over a neighboring hill where there wasn't a suggestion of an enemy! 'There you go!' I said to myself; 'this *is* the end at last.' ''

"And away we did go, and were over the shoulder of the hill before the insane movement could be discovered and stopped. And what did we find? An entire and unsuspected Russian army in reserve! And what happened? We were eaten up? That is necessarily what would have happened in ninety-nine cases out of a hundred. But no; those Russians argued that no single regiment would come browsing around there at such a time. It must be the entire English army, and that the sly Russian game was detected and blocked; so they turned tail, and away they went, pellmell, over the hill and down into the field, in wild confusion, and we after them; they themselves broke the solid Russian center in the field,

2 and tore through, and in no time there was the most tremendous rout you ever saw, and the defeat of the allies was turned into a sweeping and splendid victory! Marshal Canrobert[12] looked on, dizzy with astonishment, admiration, and delight; and sent right off for Scoresby, and hugged him, and decorated him on the field in presence of all the armies!

"And what was Scoresby's blunder that time?
3 Merely the mistaking his right hand for his left—that was all. An order had come to him to fall back and support our right; and, instead, he fell *forward* and went over the hill to the left. But the name he won that day as a marvelous military genius filled the world with his glory, and that glory will never fade while history books last.

"He is just as good and sweet and lovable and unpretending as a man can be, but he doesn't

---

12. **Marshal Canrobert** [kan rō bãr´]: François Certain Canrobert (1809–1895), the highest-ranking French officer in the Crimean War.

*Luck* 107

1 THEME

Scoresby's stupidity in ordering the charge over the hill is so extreme that the Russian army believes there must be more than meets the eye. In other words, the Russians *should* have taken the appearance for the reality.

2 PLOT: CLIMAX

The climax of the story occurs when Scoresby's greatest blunder leads to a major victory.

3 READING SKILLS: FACT VS. OPINION

Although the general opinion is that Scoresby is a brilliant military genius, the fact is that he is so stupid that he does not know his right hand from his left.

## GUIDED READING

### LITERAL QUESTION

**1a.** What does the Russian reserve army think is happening when Scoresby leads his troops over the hill? (They think the entire English army has discovered their strategy and is attacking.)

### INFERENTIAL QUESTION

**1b.** What is Twain implying about military victories? (He is implying that they do not necessarily depend upon superior strategy or ability but may result from chance or luck.)

## 1 READING SKILLS: CAUSE AND EFFECT

By contrasting Scoresby's reputation as a "shining soldier" with the blunders that have "littered his whole military life," Twain is suggesting that luck, not ability, causes success.

### REFLECTING ON THE STORY

Does luck make a success less admirable? Explain. (Possible answers: Yes, a lucky success may not be based on one's ability; no, even a person's talents can be viewed as a matter of luck.)

### STUDY QUESTIONS

1. a great military hero
2. tutored him; won a prize
3. felt responsible; routing the Russian army
4. his mistakes always turn out well
5. the narrator admires him; the clergyman thinks him a fool.
6. tutored him; poor judgment of others
7. no, makes use of opportunity; the clergyman; does things he regrets
8. success depends on luck; stated; "the very best thing in all this world that can befall a man is to be born lucky"
9. envy of less successful; elusiveness of success

### COMPARING STORIES

"Daughter": Success depends on the practice of a craft; skill. "Tunnel": Success comes from careful preparation. "Luck": Success is matter of chance.

---

know enough to come in when it rains. Now that is absolutely true. He is the supremest fool in the universe; and until half an hour ago nobody knew it but himself and me. He has been pursued, day by day and year by year, by a most phenomenal and astonishing luckiness. He has been a shining soldier in all our wars for a generation; he has littered his whole military life with blunders, and yet has never committed one that

didn't make him a knight or a baronet or a lord or something. Look at his breast; why, he is just clothed in domestic and foreign decorations. Well, sir, every one of them is the record of some shouting stupidity or other; and, taken together, they are proof that the very best thing in all this world that can befall a man is to be born lucky. I say again, as I said at the banquet, Scoresby's an absolute fool."

---

## STUDY QUESTIONS

### Recalling

1. What is the narrator's first impression of Scoresby at the banquet?
2. What did the clergyman do to help Scoresby in school, and how did Scoresby benefit from this aid?
3. Why did the clergyman accompany Scoresby to the war? What incident in the war made Scoresby a hero?
4. According to the clergyman, what is the real reason for Scoresby's fame?

### Interpreting

5. How does the narrator's first impression of Scoresby contrast with the clergyman's opinion of the hero?
6. In what ways did the clergyman help create Scoresby's "luck"? What other factors helped Scoresby to succeed?
7. Do you think that Scoresby is indeed "an absolute fool"? Why or why not? Who else in the story might be considered a fool? Explain.
8. What theme does Twain present in "Luck"? Is this theme directly stated, or is it implied? Explain.

### Extending

9. Why do you think people often regard success and failure as matters of luck?

## COMPOSITION

### Writing About Theme

■ Explain how Mark Twain develops his theme, or main idea, in "Luck." First write a sentence that expresses the theme of "Luck." Then show how Twain illuminates this theme through the story's title, plot, characters, point of view, and tone. *For help with this assignment, see Lesson 7 in the Writing About Literature Handbook at the back of this book.*

### Writing a Newspaper Article

■ Imagine that you are a war correspondent writing a story about Scoresby. First explain who Scoresby is and describe a situation to which he must respond. (You can use an incident from the story or make up one of your own.) Then write a detailed account of his behavior in that situation and the results of his actions. Be sure to indicate if luck affected his success.

## COMPARING STORIES

■ "The Shepherd's Daughter," "Through the Tunnel," and "Luck" all focus on a character's success in the face of great danger or difficult obstacles. For two or more of the stories, compare and contrast the view of success presented in each story. In each case, consider how the view of success is related to the theme of the story.

---

## COMPOSITION: GUIDELINES FOR EVALUATION

### WRITING ABOUT THEME

**Objective**
To show how the theme is developed in story

**Guidelines for Evaluation**
- suggested length: five to eight paragraphs
- should express theme
- should show how title, plot, characters, tone, and point of view help develop theme

### WRITING A NEWSPAPER ARTICLE

**Objective**
To write about Scoresby from the point of view of a war correspondent

**Guidelines for Evaluation**
- suggested length: five to six short paragraphs
- should identify Scoresby
- should describe a military situation, action, and outcome
- should indicate if luck affected the outcome

# LITERARY FOCUS: *Symbolism*

Nobel Prize winner John Galsworthy (1867–1933) wrote of an England awakening to the need for improvement in the lives of its working-class people. Galsworthy helped to promote this cause with plays, novels, and stories like "Quality" depicting the struggle of the "little man" against economic forces beyond his control.

■ Do you think it is true that in contemporary society people no longer value craftsmanship? Why?

## AT A GLANCE

- The narrator knows Gessler as his father's bootmaker.
- Gessler Brothers have two shops; in the window are fine boots.
- Gessler calls making boots an art.

## LITERARY OPTIONS

- symbol
- characterization
- theme

## THEMATIC OPTIONS

- devotion to excellence
- individual vs. society
- idealism vs. materialism

*John Galsworthy*

# Quality

1     I knew him from the days of my extreme youth, because he made my father's boots; inhabiting with his elder brother two little shops let into one, in a small bystreet—now no more, but then most fashionably placed in the West End.[1]

    That tenement had a certain quiet distinction; there was no sign upon its face that he made for any of the Royal Family—merely his own German name of Gessler Brothers; and in the window a few pairs of boots. I remember that it always troubled me to account for those 2 unvarying boots in the window, for he made only what was ordered, reaching nothing down,[2] and it seemed so inconceivable that what he made could ever have failed to fit. Had he bought them to put there? That, too, seemed inconceivable. He would never have tolerated in 3 his house leather on which he had not worked himself. Besides, they were too beautiful—the pair of pumps, so inexpressibly slim, the patent

leathers with cloth tops, making water come into one's mouth, the tall brown riding boots with marvelous sooty glow, as if, though new, they had been worn a hundred years. Those pairs could only have been made by one who saw before him the Soul of Boot—so truly were they prototypes incarnating the very spirit of all footgear. These thoughts, of course, came to me later, though even when I was promoted to him, at the age of perhaps fourteen, some inkling haunted me of the dignity of himself and brother. For to make boots—such boots as he made—seemed to me then, and still seems to me, mysterious and wonderful.

    I remember well my shy remark, one day, while stretching out to him my youthful foot:

    "Isn't it awfully hard to do, Mr. Gessler?"

    And his answer, given with a sudden smile from out of the sardonic redness of his beard: "Id is an Ardt!"

    Himself, he was a little as if made from leather, with his yellow crinkly face, and crinkly reddish hair and beard, and neat folds slanting down his cheeks to the corners of his mouth, and his guttural and one-toned voice; for leather

---

1. **the West End:** area of London that contains the theater district and many fine shops.
2. **reaching nothing down:** keeping no goods on reserve.

*Quality* **109**

## 1 POINT OF VIEW

The first-person narrator is someone who has known the bootmaker for many years and can therefore provide intimate personal insight into his character.

## 2 CHARACTERIZATION

Gessler's failure to maintain a stock, his making only what is ordered, and his insistence that he himself work on the leather all suggest an unwillingness to compromise standards.

## 3 RESPONSE JOURNAL

Ask students to write a description of someone they know who enjoys and takes pride in his or her work.

---

## GUIDED READING

**LITERAL QUESTION**

**1a.** How does the narrator describe the decision that he is old enough to get boots from Gessler? (He speaks of being "promoted to him.")

**INFERENTIAL QUESTION**

**1b.** How do the narrator's words convey his opinion of Gessler? (By speaking of his purchase of boots from Gessler in terms of being "promoted," he conveys his feeling that it is an honor to have Gessler's boots.)

- The narrator describes the Gessler brothers.
- It is not possible to buy their boots often—they last so long.
- One day he tells Gessler that his last pair of boots creaked.

## 1 CHARACTERIZATION

His elder brother's deference to Gessler shows by indirect characterization that the younger brother dominates the business.

## 2 STYLE: SIMILE

The simile comparing Gessler's shop to a church conveys the narrator's sense of awe and respect for Gessler.

## 3 CHARACTERIZATION

The narrator's sense of Gessler's total dedication to bootmaking is conveyed by his imagining that Gessler awakens from "some dream of boots."

## 4 THEME

The description of Gessler's almost romantic examination of the boot he has previously crafted portrays his dedication to his work and his devotion to its product.

## 5 VOCABULARY: DIALECT

Galsworthy's re-creation of the broken speech of the German immigrant enables the reader to imagine Gessler more fully and to sympathize with him.

is a sardonic substance, and stiff and slow of purpose. And that was the character of his face, save that his eyes, which were gray-blue, had in them the simple gravity of one secretly possessed by the Ideal. His elder brother was so very like him—though watery, paler in every way, with a great industry—that sometimes in the early days I was not quite sure of him until the interview **1** was over. Then I knew that it was he, if the words, "I will ask my brudder," had not been spoken; and that, if they had, it was his elder brother.

When one grew old and wild and ran up bills, one somehow never ran them up with Gessler Brothers. It would not have seemed becoming to go in there and stretch out one's foot to that blue iron-spectacled glance, owing him for more than— say—two pairs, just the comfortable reassurance that one was still his client.

For it was not possible to go to him very often—his boots lasted terribly, having something beyond the temporary—some, as it were, essence of boot stitched into them.

**2** One went in, not as into most shops, in the mood of: "Please serve me, and let me go!" but restfully, as one enters a church; and, sitting on the single wooden chair, waited—for there was never anybody there. Soon, over the top edge of that sort of well—rather dark, and smelling soothingly of leather—which formed the shop, there would be seen his face, or that of his elder brother, peering down. A guttural sound, and the tip-tap of bast slippers[3] beating the narrow wooden stairs, and he would stand before one without coat, a little bent, in leather apron, with **3** sleeves turned back, blinking—as if awakened from some dream of boots, or like an owl surprised in daylight and annoyed at this interruption.

And I would say: "How do you do, Mr. Gessler? Could you make me a pair of Russian leather boots?"

---

3. **bast slippers:** slippers made from a woody fiber.

Without a word he would leave me, retiring whence he came, or into the other portion of the shop. And I would continue to rest in the wooden chair, inhaling the incense of his trade. Soon he would come back, holding in his thin, veined hand a piece of gold-brown leather. With eyes fixed on it, he would remark: "What a beaudiful biece!" When I, too, had admired it, he would speak again. "When do you wand dem?" And I would answer: "Oh! As soon as you conveniently can." And he would say: "Tomorrow fordnighd?" Or if he were his elder brother: "I will ask my brudder!"

Then I would murmur: "Thank you! Good morning, Mr. Gessler." "Goot morning!" he would reply, still looking at the leather in his hand. And as I moved to the door, I would hear the tip-tap of his bast slippers restoring him, up the stairs, to his dream of boots. But if it were some new kind of footgear that he had not yet **4** made me, then indeed he would observe ceremony—divesting me of my boot and holding it long in his hand, looking at it with eyes at once critical and loving, as if recalling the glow with which he had created it, and rebuking the way in which one had disorganized this masterpiece. Then, placing my foot on a piece of paper, he would two or three times tickle the outer edges with a pencil and pass his nervous fingers over my toes, feeling himself into the heart of my requirements.

I cannot forget that day on which I had occasion to say to him: "Mr. Gessler, that last pair of town walking boots creaked, you know."

He looked at me for a time without replying, as if expecting me to withdraw or qualify the statement, then said:

**5** "Id shouldn'd 'ave greaked."

"It did, I'm afraid."

"You goddem wed before dey found demselves?"

"I don't think so."

At last he lowered his eyes, as if hunting for

---

## GUIDED READING

### LITERAL QUESTION

**1a.** Why is the narrator not able to buy boots from Gessler very often? (Gessler's boots last for a long time.)

### INFERENTIAL QUESTION

**1b.** What does this fact tell you about the boots? (They are very well made and of good quality leather.)

AT A GLANCE

- Gessler tells the narrator to send the boots back.
- On a later occasion the narrator goes into the Gessler shop wearing a pair of boots made by a large firm.
- Gessler predicts that the large firms will destroy his business.
- The narrator orders many boots.

**1 SYMBOL**

Gessler's remark shows that he thinks of boots as living things; to him they symbolize a whole system of values, not just the means by which he supports himself.

**2 PLOT: NARRATIVE HOOK**

Gessler's prediction that the large firms that sell inferior boots will destroy his living is the narrative hook that introduces the story's central conflict between the individual craftsman and the large enterprise.

**3 THEME**

Because of the excellent quality of Gessler's boots, his customers cannot purchase boots very often. Use of the word *terribly* conveys the narrator's ironic distress over the high quality that would otherwise be an asset.

memory of those boots, and I felt sorry I had mentioned this grave thing.

"Zend dem back!" he said; "I will look at dem."

A feeling of compassion for my creaking boots surged up in me, so well could I imagine the sorrowful long curiosity of regard which he would bend on them.

"Zome boods," he said slowly, "are bad from birdt. If I can do noding wid dem, I dake dem off your bill."

Once (once only) I went absent-mindedly into his shop in a pair of boots bought in an emergency at some large firm's. He took my order without showing me any leather, and I could feel his eyes penetrating the inferior integument[4] of my foot. At last he said:

"Dose are nod my boods."

The tone was not one of anger, nor of sorrow, not even of contempt, but there was in it something quiet that froze the blood. He put his hand down and pressed a finger on the place where the left boot, endeavoring to be fashionable, was not quite comfortable.

"Id 'urds you dere," he said. "Dose big virms 'ave no self-respect. Drash!" And then, as if something had given way within him, he spoke long and bitterly. It was the only time I ever heard him discuss the conditions and hardships of his trade.

"Dey get id all," he said, "dey get id by advertisement, nod by work. Dey dake it away from us, who lofe our boods. Id gomes to this— bresently I haf no work. Every year id gets less— you will see." And looking at his lined face I saw things I had never noticed before, bitter things and bitter struggle—and what a lot of gray hairs there seemed suddenly in his red beard!

As best I could, I explained the circumstances of the purchase of those ill-omened boots. But his face and voice made so deep an impression that during the next few minutes I ordered many pairs. Nemesis[5] fell! They lasted more terribly than ever. And I was not able conscientiously to go to him for nearly two years.

When at last I went I was surprised to find

---

4. **integument** [in teg′yə mənt]: natural covering or hide; here, the narrator's boot.

5. **Nemesis** [nem′ə sis]: Greek goddess of vengeance.

*Quality* **111**

---

## GUIDED READING

### LITERAL QUESTION

**1a.** How does Gessler respond when the narrator wears a pair of boots made by a large firm? (He does not show the narrator any leather; he stares at the boots; he shows where they hurt; he says the large firms take away his work.)

### INFERENTIAL QUESTION

**1b.** What do you think is Gessler's mood as he makes this response? (He appears to be despondent about the future of his business.)

AT A GLANCE

- The Gesslers sell one of their shops.
- Months later, Gessler's brother dies.
- He himself ages markedly, but his boots are better than ever.

**1 SYMBOL**

Gessler's devotion to an excellence that most people do not seek symbolizes the struggle of the individual to maintain personal values in conflict with society's demands.

**2 READING SKILLS: COMPARISON AND CONTRAST**

The narrator's contrast of Gessler with the man he was earlier demonstrates the personal price Gessler is paying to maintain the quality of his work.

---

that outside one of the two little windows of his shop another name was painted, also that of a bootmaker—making, of course, for the Royal Family. The old familiar boots, no longer in dignified isolation, were huddled in the single window. Inside, the now contracted well of the one little shop was more scented and darker than ever. And it was longer than usual, too, before a face peered down, and the tip-tap of the bast slippers began. At last he stood before me, and gazing through those rusty iron spectacles, said:

"Mr. ——, isn't it?"

"Ah! Mr. Gessler," I stammered, "but your **1** boots are really *too* good, you know! See, these are quite decent still!" And I stretched out to him my foot. He looked at it.

"Yes," he said, "beople do nod wand good boods, id seems."

To get away from his reproachful eyes and voice I hastily remarked: "What have you done **2** to your shop?"

He answered quietly: "Id was too exbensif. Do you wand some boods?"

I ordered three pairs, though I had only wanted two, and quickly left. I had, I do not know quite what feeling of being part, in his mind, of a conspiracy against him; or not perhaps so much against him as against his idea of boot. One does not, I suppose, care to feel like that; for it was again many months before my next visit to his shop, paid, I remember, with the feeling: "Oh! well, I can't leave the old boy—so here goes! Perhaps it'll be his elder brother!"

For his elder brother, I knew, had not character enough to reproach me, even dumbly.

And, to my relief, in the shop there did appear to be his elder brother, handling a piece of leather.

"Well, Mr. Gessler," I said, "how are you?"

He came close, and peered at me.

"I am breddy well," he said slowly, "but my elder brudder is dead."

And I saw that it was indeed himself—but how aged and wan! And never before had I heard him mention his brother. Much shocked, I murmured: "Oh! I am sorry!"

"Yes," he answered, "he was a good man, he made a good bood; but he is dead." And he touched the top of his head, where the hair had suddenly gone as thin as it had been on that of his poor brother, to indicate, I suppose, the cause of death. "He could nod ged over losing de oder shop. Do you wand any boods?" And he held up the leather in his hand: "Id's a beaudiful biece."

I ordered several pairs. It was very long before they came—but they were better than ever. One simply could not wear them out. And soon after that I went abroad.

It was over a year before I was again in London. And the first shop I went to was my old **2** friend's. I had left a man of sixty, I came back to one of seventy-five, pinched and worn and tremulous, who genuinely, this time, did not at first know me.

"Oh! Mr. Gessler," I said, sick at heart; "how splendid your boots are! See, I've been wearing this pair nearly all the time I've been abroad; and they're not half worn out, are they?"

He looked long at my boots—a pair of Russian leather, and his face seemed to regain steadiness. Putting his hand on my instep, he said:

"Do dey vid you here? I 'ad drouble wid dat bair, I remember."

I assured him that they had fitted beautifully.

"Do you wand any boods?" he said. "I can make dem quickly; id is a slack dime."

I answered: "Please, please! I want boots all round—every kind!"

"I will make a vresh model. Your food must be bigger." And with utter slowness, he traced my foot, and felt my toes, only once looking up to say:

"Did I dell you my brudder was dead?"

To watch him was painful, so feeble had he grown; I was glad to get away.

---

## GUIDED READING

**LITERAL QUESTIONS**

**1a.** What reason does Gessler give for the loss of the second shop? (He says that it is too expensive to keep.)

**2a.** When the narrator returns to visit Gessler after a year abroad, what does he order from the bootmaker? (He orders every kind of boot.)

**INFERENTIAL QUESTIONS**

**1b.** What does this sale tell you about Gessler's business? (Apparently his prediction has come true, and former customers are buying their boots somewhere else.)

**2b.** What do you think is his motive for ordering boots that he doesn't need? (He feels sorry for the old man and wants to give him as much business as possible.)

I had given those boots up, when one evening they came. Opening the parcel, I set the four pairs out in a row. Then one by one I tried them on. There was no doubt about it. In shape and fit, in finish and quality of leather, they were the best he had ever made me. And in the mouth of one of the town walking boots I found his bill. The amount was the same as usual, but it gave me quite a shock. He had never before sent it in till quarter day.[6] I flew downstairs, and wrote a check, and posted it at once with my own hand.

A week later, passing the little street, I thought I would go in and tell him how splendidly the new boots fitted. But when I came to where his shop had been, his name was gone. Still there, in the window, were the slim pumps, the patent leathers with cloth tops, the sooty riding boots.

I went in, very much disturbed. In the two little shops—again made into one—was a young man with an English face.

"Mr. Gessler in?" I said.

He gave me a strange, ingratiating look.

"No, sir," he said, "no. But we can attend to anything with pleasure. We've taken the shop over. You've seen our name, no doubt, next door. We make for some very good people."

"Yes, yes," I said; "but Mr. Gessler?"

_____

6. **quarter day:** one of four days spaced evenly throughout the year for billing and payment.

"Oh!" he answered; "dead."

"Dead! But I only received these boots from him last Wednesday week."

"Ah," he said; "a shockin' go. Poor old man starved 'imself."

"Good God!"

"Slow starvation, the doctor called it! You see he went to work in such a way! Would keep the shop on, wouldn't have a soul touch his boots except himself. When he got an order, it took him such a time. People won't wait. He lost everybody. And there he'd sit, goin' on and on—I will say that for him—not a man in London made a better boot! But look at the competition! He never advertised! Would 'ave the best leather, too, and do it all 'imself. Well, there it is. What could you expect with his ideas?"

"But starvation——!"

"That may be a bit flowery, as the sayin' is—but I know myself he was sittin' over his boots day and night, to the very last. You see I used to watch him. Never gave 'imself time to eat; never had a penny in the house. All went in rent and leather. How he lived so long I don't know. He regular let his fire go out. He was a character. But he made good boots."

"Yes," I said, "he made good boots."

And I turned and went out quickly, for I did not want that youth to know that I could hardly see.

_____

## STUDY QUESTIONS

### Recalling

1. What evidence does the narrator provide of the high quality of Mr. Gessler's boots?
2. Why do the Gessler brothers lose their other shop? How does this loss affect each brother?
3. According to the new owner of the shop, why does Mr. Gessler's business fail?
4. What happens to Mr. Gessler?

### Interpreting

5. Prove from two or three of his own statements that Mr. Gessler's feeling for his work and his boots goes beyond the desire to make a living.
6. Why does Mr. Gessler refuse to lower his standards even when he loses his other shop?
7. Do you think the story is saying that Mr. Gessler was foolish to sacrifice so much for his craft? Why or why not?

*Quality* **113**

**8.** individual craftsmanship vs. mass production and merchandising; beauty and integrity vs. materialism

**9.** Yes, but there are not many; few people are willing to suffer for and pay for true quality.

## VIEWPOINT

He is a simple shopkeeper. His spiritual qualities—love of his craft and commitment to excellence—make him heroic.

## LITERARY FOCUS

**1.** He represents quality.

**2.** struggle to retain values in the face of widespread mediocrity and cynicism

## VOCABULARY

**1.** (d) praising
**2.** (a) certainty
**3.** (c) shrill
**4.** (c) humor
**5.** (a) dressing
**6.** (a) scorn
**7.** (a) lucky
**8.** (c) expanded
**9.** (c) firm
**10.** (d) sardonic

---

**8.** Beyond the individual story of Mr. Gessler's failure in business, what larger conflict is "Quality" all about?

### Extending

**9.** Do you think people like Mr. Gessler still exist today? Explain.

## VIEWPOINT

A critic writing about John Galsworthy made this comment about the unlikeliness of his heroes:

> Galsworthy's heroes were never of the smoothly-parted hair type whose victories claim the limelight of so many stage sets.
> — R. H. Mottram, *John Galsworthy*

■ Why does Mr. Gessler initially seem an unlikely sort of hero? What attributes eventually make him heroic?

## LITERARY FOCUS

### Symbol

A **symbol** is any object, person, place, or experience that means more than what it is. A symbol has a literal meaning of its own but also represents something larger than itself. For example, a nation's flag is a symbol in a larger sense of the nation itself.

The larger meaning of a symbol often grows from the symbol's actual attributes. For instance, we use the eagle as a symbol of America because, as a high-flying, powerful bird, the eagle represents the freedom and strength we associate with this country.

Writers often use symbols to represent ideas or qualities in terms that their readers can understand. A symbol makes what is being symbolized seem more real to us—more vivid, more interesting, or more moving.

On the literal level "Quality" is the touching story of the life and death of a bootmaker. However, the story also gives Mr. Gessler and his devotion to his craft a larger symbolic meaning.

### Thinking About Symbols

**1.** What symbolic connections might there be between the title of the story and Mr. Gessler?

**2.** What do you think is the larger symbolic meaning of Mr. Gessler's devotion to his bootmaking?

**114**   *The Short Story*

---

## VOCABULARY

### Antonyms

**Antonyms** are words that have opposite or nearly opposite meanings. *Break* and *mend* are antonyms. The words in capitals come from "Quality." Choose the letter of the word that is *most nearly the opposite* of each word in capitals *as the word is used in the story.*

**1.** REBUKING:   (a) turning   (b) scolding
(c) expressing   (d) praising

**2.** INKLING:   (a) certainty   (b) question
(c) outline   (d) hint

**3.** GUTTURAL:   (a) harsh   (b) low   (c) shrill   (d) soft

**4.** GRAVITY:   (a) dignity   (b) honor   (c) humor
(d) weight

**5.** DIVESTING:   (a) dressing   (b) spending
(c) releasing   (d) inserting

**6.** COMPASSION:   (a) scorn   (b) pity   (c) sympathy
(d) weakness

**7.** ILL-OMENED:   (a) lucky   (b) cheap   (c) agreeable
(d) abominable

**8.** CONTRACTED:   (a) reduced   (b) lowered
(c) expanded   (d) constructed

**9.** TREMULOUS:   (a) shaky   (b) huge   (c) firm
(d) whining

**10.** INGRATIATING:   (a) witty   (b) kindly   (c) insincere
(d) sardonic

## COMPOSITION

### Writing About Symbol

■ Explain how Mr. Gessler's boots serve as a symbol that helps to reveal his character. First discuss the qualities—physical and otherwise—that Mr. Gessler and his boots share. Then explain what Mr. Gessler's devotion to his boots shows about his character. *For help with this assignment, See Lesson 8 in the Writing About Literature Handbook at the back of this book.*

### Writing a Feature Article

■ Imagine that you are a journalist writing a feature article about the loss of Mr. Gessler's business and his death. Be sure to answer the questions "Who?" "What?" "When?" "Where?" and "Why?" for your readers. End by commenting on the meaning of Mr. Gessler's death.

---

## COMPOSITION: GUIDELINES FOR EVALUATION

### WRITING ABOUT SYMBOL

**Objective**
To interpret a literary symbol

**Guidelines for Evaluation**
■ suggested length: two to three paragraphs
■ should cite the qualities shared by Mr. Gessler and his boots
■ should explain how the boots represent an ideal

### WRITING A FEATURE ARTICLE

**Objective**
To write an article about an event

**Guidelines for Evaluation**
■ suggested length: two to three paragraphs
■ should describe Mr. Gessler's fate
■ should answer five "W" questions
■ should conclude with interpretation of the implications of his death

A native of San Leandro, California, Toshio Mori (1910–1980) drew upon his Japanese American heritage for many of his stories. As he did in "Abalone, Abalone, Abalone," Mori often wrote of people who find endless fascination in the beauty of the natural world.

■ Why do you think a person collects rocks or shells or souvenirs? Do you have a collection of something?

*Toshio Mori*

# Abalone,[1] Abalone, Abalone

Before Mr. Abe went away I used to see him quite often at his nursery.[2] He was a carnation grower just as I am one today. At noontime I used to go to his front porch and look at his collection of abalone shells.

They were lined up side by side against the side of his house on the front porch. I was curious as to why he bothered to collect them. It was a lot of bother polishing them. I had often seen him sit for hours on Sundays and noon hours polishing each one of the shells with the greatest of care. Of course I knew these abalone shells were pretty. When the sun strikes the insides of these shells it is something beautiful to behold. But I could not understand why he continued collecting them when the front porch was practically full.

He used to watch for me every noon hour. When I appeared he would look out of his room and bellow, "Hello, young man!"

"Hello, Abe-*san*,"[3] I said. "I came to see the abalone shells."

Then he came out of the house and we sat on the front porch. But he did not tell me why he collected these shells. I think I have asked him dozens of times but each time he closed his mouth and refused to answer.

"Are you going to pass this collection of abalone shells on to your children?" I said.

"No," he said. "I want my children to collect for themselves. I wouldn't give it to them."

"Why?" I said. "When you die?"

Mr. Abe shook his head. "No. Not even when I die," he said. "I couldn't give the children what I see in these shells. The children must go out for themselves and find their own shells."

"Why, I thought this collecting hobby of abalone shells was a simple affair," I said.

"It is simple. Very simple," he said. But he would not tell me further.

For several years I went steadily to his front porch and looked at the beautiful shells. His collection was getting larger and larger. Mr. Abe sat and talked to me and on each occasion his hands were busy polishing the shells.

"So you are still curious?" he said.

"Yes," I said.

One day while I was hauling the old soil from the benches and replacing it with new soil I

---

1. **Abalone** [ab′ə lō′nē]: edible marine mollusk with an ear-shaped shell that is lined with mother-of-pearl.
2. **nursery:** place where plants are raised for sale.
3. **Abe-*san*** [a′ba san′]: Mister Abe. *San* is a term of respect in Japanese and is added to a name as a suffix.

*Abalone, Abalone, Abalone* **115**

**GUIDED READING**

**LITERAL QUESTION**

**1a.** What is the narrator's repeated question to Abe? (He wants to know why Abe collects the abalone shells.)

**INFERENTIAL QUESTION**

**1b.** Why doesn't Abe tell why he collects the shells? (Abe cannot transfer his sense of beauty—the narrator must find and experience it for himself.)

- The narrator finds a shell in his greenhouse and while cleaning and polishing it discovers its unique beauty.
- Exclaiming that he finally understands, he brings the shell to Abe.

## 1 THEME

Through the work and close attention of polishing, the narrator discovers the beauty of an individual shell and, thereby, the reason for collecting.

## 2 SYMBOLISM

Like a rainbow, the shell symbolizes nature's ever-changing, unpredictable beauty.

## 3 THEME

Abe advises the narrator to avoid reducing the "reason" to words. The most valuable experiences, Mr. Abe implies, need simply to be felt.

found an abalone shell half buried in the dust between the benches. So I stopped working. I dropped my wheelbarrow and went to the faucet and washed the abalone shell with soap and water. I had a hard time taking the grime off the surface.

After forty minutes of cleaning and polishing the old shell it became interesting. I began polishing both the outside and the inside of the shell. I found after many minutes of polishing I could not do very much with the exterior side. It had scabs of the sea which would not come off by scrubbing and the surface itself was rough and hard. And in the crevices the grime stuck so that even with a needle it did not become clean.

**1** But on the other side, the inside of the shell, the more I polished the more luster I found. It had me going. There were colors which I had not seen in the abalone shells before or anywhere else. The different hues, running berserk in all directions, coming together in harmony. I guess **2** I could say they were not unlike a rainbow which men once symbolized. As soon as I thought of this I thought of Mr. Abe.

**116** *The Short Story*

I remember running to his place, looking for him, "Abe-*san*!" I said when I found him. "I know why you are collecting the abalone shells!"

He was watering the carnation plants in the greenhouse. He stopped watering and came over to where I stood. He looked me over closely for awhile and then his face beamed.

**3** "All right," he said. "Do not say anything. Nothing, mind you. When you have found the reason why you must collect and preserve them, you do not have to say anything more."

"I want you to see it, Abe-*san*," I said.

"All right. Tonight," he said. "Where did you find it?"

"In my old greenhouse, half buried in the dust," I said.

He chuckled. "That is pretty far from the ocean," he said, "but pretty close to you."

At each noon hour I carried my abalone shell and went over to Mr. Abe's front porch. While I waited for his appearance I kept myself busy polishing the inside of the shell with a rag.

One day I said, "Abe-*san*, now I have three shells."

"Good!" he said. "Keep it up!"

## GUIDED READING

### LITERAL QUESTION

**1a.** When does the shell become interesting to the narrator? (after he spends forty minutes cleaning and polishing it)

### INFERENTIAL QUESTION

**1b.** Why does the shell become interesting after the narrator has worked on it? (The cleaning reveals the shell's hidden beauty, and the narrator has invested personal effort.)

"I have to keep them all," I said. "They are very much alike and very much different."

"Well! Well!" he said and smiled.

That was the last I saw of Abe-*san*. Before the month was over he sold his nursery and went back to Japan. He brought his collection along and thereafter I had no one to talk to at the noon hour. This was before I discovered the fourth abalone shell, and I should like to see Abe-*san* someday and watch his eyes roll as he studies me whose face is now akin to the collectors of shells or otherwise.

---

## STUDY QUESTIONS

### Recalling

1. What does the narrator think at first about abalone shells and Mr. Abe's devotion to his collection?

2. What questions does the narrator ask Mr. Abe about his collection? How does Mr. Abe answer him?

3. Describe the sequence of the narrator's actions and responses when he finds the abalone shell near his greenhouse.

### Interpreting

4. Why does Mr. Abe insist that his children find their own shells?

5. The narrator compares the abalone shell to a rainbow. In what ways might the shell and a rainbow be similar?

6. What do you think the narrator learns from his experience with Mr. Abe and from collecting the abalone shells?

7. What do you think the abalone shells might symbolize in this story?

### Extending

8. Do you think that this story could apply equally well to *any* kind of collection, or is there something special and different about the abalone shells? Explain.

## VIEWPOINT

William Saroyan has said about his fellow Californian Toshio Mori:

He can see through a human being to the strange, comical, melancholy truth that changes a fool into a great solemn hero.

■ Some people might regard Mr. Abe's devotion to his shell collection as slightly foolish. What truth dignifies his odd behavior?

## COMPOSITION

### Writing About Symbol

■ Explain how Mori uses abalone shells to reveal his theme in "Abalone, Abalone, Abalone." First state the story's theme in a single complete sentence. Then explain how this theme is illuminated by (a) the particular physical attributes of abalone shells as they are described in the story and (b) the devotion of Mr. Abe and the narrator to their collections of these shells. *For help with this assignment, see Lesson 8 in the Writing About Literature Handbook at the back of this book.*

### Describing a Symbol

■ Write about something that has a special symbolic meaning for you. You might write about a gift from someone you love, an award of which you are proud, or a souvenir from a place you visited. First describe the object, and then explain what it symbolizes for you.

## COMPARING STORIES

■ Both "Quality" and "Abalone, Abalone, Abalone" give special meaning to a character's devotion to a rather humble activity. Mr. Gessler finds his ideal in making fine boots; Mr. Abe, in collecting seashells. What does each story say about the effect of such devotion on a person's life? What extra qualities do boots take on for Mr. Gessler? What extra qualities do abalone shells take on for Mr. Abe?

*Abalone, Abalone, Abalone* **117**

## AT A GLANCE

Abe moves back to Japan, and the narrator feels he has come to resemble Abe and others who appreciate special beauty.

## REFLECTING ON THE STORY

How did finding an abalone shell change the narrator's attitude toward Abe? (In discovering the value of what seemed a foolish hobby, the narrator deepens his understanding of Abe's perceptiveness.)

## STUDY QUESTIONS

1. wonders why Mr. Abe collects them
2. why he collects them; doesn't say
3. cleans and polishes the shell
4. The reward is in the process of discovery.
5. iridescent colors; beauty
6. to look for hidden beauty
7. beauty and perfection of nature
8. On surface they appear ordinary, yet each one is unique.

## VIEWPOINT

His effort gives shells their value.

## COMPARING STORIES

■ "Quality": Gessler's devotion makes him heroic but also destroys him; boots embody his ideal of excellence.
■ "Abalone": Abe's devotion shows his sensitive side; shells represent his ideal of beauty and individuality.

---

## COMPOSITION: GUIDELINES FOR EVALUATION

### WRITING ABOUT A SYMBOL

**Objective**

To show how theme is realized through symbolism

**Guidelines for Evaluation**

- suggested length: two to three paragraphs
- should state the theme
- should describe an abalone shell in detail
- should explain what the shell represents

### DESCRIBING A SYMBOL

**Objective**

To identify and describe something of personal symbolic significance

**Guidelines for Evaluation**

- suggested length: two to three paragraphs
- should identify and describe something that holds symbolic meaning
- should explain the significance and symbolism

Katherine Mansfield (1888–1923) was born in Karori, a small village near Wellington, New Zealand, but she spent most of her adult life in London. As a child she attended the village school in Karori, which was attended by all the children in the vicinity—those from comfortable homes as well as those from poor ones. It is this experience that she draws upon in "The Doll's House."

■ How do children usually react to differences in their families' wealth and social position? How do the children in this story react?

*Katherine Mansfield*

# The Doll's House

When dear old Mrs. Hay went back to town after staying with the Burnells she sent the children a doll's house. It was so big that the carter and Pat carried it into the courtyard, and there it stayed, propped up on two wooden boxes beside the feed-room door. No harm could come of it; it was summer. And perhaps the smell of paint would have gone off by the time it had to be taken in. For, really, the smell of paint coming from that doll's house ("Sweet of old Mrs. Hay, of course; most sweet and generous!")—but the smell of paint was quite enough to make any one seriously ill, in Aunt Beryl's opinion. Even before the sacking was taken off. And when it was. . . .

There stood the doll's house, a dark, oily, spinach green, picked out with bright yellow. Its two solid little chimneys, glued onto the roof, were painted red and white, and the door, gleaming with yellow varnish, was like a little slab of toffee. Four windows, real windows, were divided into panes by a broad streak of green. There was actually a tiny porch, too, painted yellow, with big lumps of congealed paint hanging along the edge.

But perfect, perfect little house! Who could possibly mind the smell? It was part of the joy, part of the newness.

"Open it quickly, some one!"

The hook at the side was stuck fast. Pat pried it open with his penknife, and the whole house front swung back, and—there you were, gazing at one and the same moment into the drawing room and dining room, the kitchen and two bedrooms. That is the way for a house to open! Why don't all houses open like that? How much more exciting than peering through the slit of a door into a mean little hall with a hatstand and two umbrellas! That is—isn't it?—what you long to know about a house when you put your hand on the knocker. Perhaps it is the way God opens houses at dead of night when He is taking a quiet turn with an angel. . . .

"O-oh!" The Burnell children sounded as though they were in despair. It was too marvelous; it was too much for them. They had never

**118**   *The Short Story*

seen anything like it in their lives. All the rooms were papered. There were pictures on the walls, painted on the paper, with gold frames complete. Red carpet covered all the floors except the kitchen; red plush chairs in the drawing room, green in the dining room; tables, beds with real bedclothes, a cradle, a stove, a dresser with tiny plates and one big jug. But what Kezia liked more than anything, what she liked frightfully, was the lamp. It stood in the middle of the dining room table, an exquisite little amber lamp with a white globe. It was even filled all ready for lighting, though, of course, you couldn't light it. But there was something inside that looked like oil, and that moved when you shook it.

The father and mother dolls, who sprawled very stiff as though they had fainted in the drawing room, and their two little children asleep upstairs, were really too big for the doll's house. They didn't look as though they belonged. But the lamp was perfect. It seemed to smile at Kezia, to say, "I live here." The lamp was real.

The Burnell children could hardly walk to school fast enough the next morning. They burned to tell everybody, to describe, to—well—to boast about their doll's house before the school bell rang.

"I'm to tell," said Isabel, "because I'm the eldest. And you two can join in after. But I'm to tell first."

There was nothing to answer. Isabel was bossy, but she was always right, and Lottie and Kezia knew too well the powers that went with being eldest. They brushed through the thick buttercups at the road edge and said nothing.

"And I'm to choose who's to come and see it first. Mother said I might."

For it had been arranged that while the doll's house stood in the courtyard they might ask the girls at school, two at a time, to come and look. Not to stay to tea, of course, or to come traipsing through the house. But just to stand quietly in the courtyard while Isabel pointed out the beauties, and Lottie and Kezia looked pleased. . . .

But hurry as they might, by the time they had reached the tarred palings of the boys' playground the bell had begun to jangle. They only just had time to whip off their hats and fall into line before the roll was called. Never mind. Isabel tried to make up for it by looking very important and mysterious and by whispering behind her hands to the girls near her, "Got something to tell you at playtime."

Playtime came and Isabel was surrounded. The girls of her class nearly fought to put their arms round her, to walk away with her, to beam flatteringly, to be her special friend. She held quite a court under the huge pine trees at the side of the playground. Nudging, giggling together, the little girls pressed up close. And the only two who stayed outside the ring were the two who were always outside, the little Kelveys. They knew better than to come anywhere near the Burnells.

For the fact was, the school the Burnell children went to was not at all the kind of place their parents would have chosen if there had been any choice. But there was none. It was the only school for miles. And the consequence was all the children in the neighbourhood, the Judge's little girls, the doctor's daughters, the storekeeper's children, the milkman's, were forced to mix together. Not to speak of there being an equal number of rude, rough little boys as well. But the line had to be drawn somewhere. It was drawn at the Kelveys. Many of the children, including the Burnells, were not allowed even to speak to them. They walked past the Kelveys with their heads in the air, and as they set the fashion in all matters of behavior, the Kelveys were shunned by everybody. Even the teacher had a special voice for them, and a special smile for the other children when Lil Kelvey came up to her desk with a bunch of dreadfully common-looking flowers.

They were the daughters of a spry, hard-working little washerwoman, who went about from house to house by the day. This was awful

*The Doll's House* **119**

- The Burnell children love the house—little Kezia likes the lamp.
- Oldest sister Isabel gets to tell schoolmates about the house, and she will choose the first pair to visit it.
- The outcast Kelveys are shunned.

**1 CHARACTERIZATION**

Kezia expresses a child's wonder at the lamp that looks so real and seems "to smile."

**2 SYMBOL**

A line must be drawn for the little visitors; while the doll's house is open to outsiders, the Burnells' house is not.

**3 THEME**

Isabel's "court," with Lil and Else standing outside, illustrates the spectrum of privilege and status.

**4 BACKGROUND**

Circumstances force some blurring of the lines between the classes—but not in the case of the Kelveys.

## GUIDED READING

### LITERAL QUESTIONS

**1a.** What invitation will not be extended to the girls who come to see the doll house? (They may not "stay to tea" or "come traipsing through the house.")

**2a.** How is the mother of the Kelveys described? (as a "spry, hardworking little washerwoman" who went about from house to house by the day)

### INFERENTIAL QUESTIONS

**1b.** What does this imply about the Burnell household? (It is not a particularly friendly place.)

**2b.** What influence might Mrs. Kelvey's status have on the way the Kelveys are treated? (They are probably ignored because they are poor.)

- Mr. Kelvey is presumed to be in jail.
- Lil and her little sister Else, who always clings to her, are meanly dressed.
- Days pass, children visit, the doll house is famous.

## 1 IRONY

There are parallels between the Kelveys' clothes—which make them seem ludicrous—and the red and white chimneys, green paint, red plush chairs, and real bedclothes that enhance the doll's house.

## 2 READING SKILLS: COMPARISON AND CONTRAST

As one skilled in looking important, Isabel is not as astonished by the marvel of illusion as Kezia. She is also less genuine than her younger sister.

enough. But where was Mr. Kelvey? Nobody knew for certain. But everybody said he was in prison. So they were the daughters of a washerwoman and a jailbird. Very nice company for other people's children! And they looked it. Why Mrs. Kelvey made them so conspicuous was hard to understand. The truth was they were dressed in "bits" given to her by the people for whom she worked. Lil, for instance, who was a stout, plain child, with big freckles, came to school in a dress made from a green art-serge tablecloth of the Burnells', with red plush sleeves from the Logans' curtains. Her hat, perched on top of her high forehead, was a grown-up woman's hat, once the property of Miss Lecky, the postmistress. It was turned up at the back and trimmed with a large scarlet quill. What a little guy she looked! It was impossible not to laugh. And her little sister, our Else, wore a long white dress, rather like a nightgown, and a pair of little boy's boots. But whatever our Else wore she would have looked strange. She was a tiny wishbone of a child, with cropped hair and enormous solemn eyes—a little white owl. Nobody had ever seen her smile; she scarcely ever spoke. She went through life holding on to Lil, with a piece of Lil's skirt screwed up in her hand. Where Lil went our Else followed. In the playground, on the road going to and from school, there was Lil marching in front and our Else holding on behind. Only when she wanted anything, or when she was out of breath, our Else gave Lil a tug, a twitch, and Lil stopped and turned round. The Kelveys never failed to understand each other.

Now they hovered at the edge; you couldn't stop them listening. When the little girls turned round and sneered, Lil, as usual, gave her silly, shamefaced smile, but our Else only looked.

And Isabel's voice, so very proud, went on telling. The carpet made a great sensation, but so did the beds with real bedclothes, and the stove with an oven door.

When she finished Kezia broke in. "You've forgotten the lamp, Isabel."

**120**   *The Short Story*

"Oh, yes," said Isabel, "and there's a teeny little lamp, all made of yellow glass, with a white globe that stands on the dining room table. You couldn't tell it from a real one."

"The lamp's best of all," cried Kezia. She thought Isabel wasn't making half enough of the little lamp. But nobody paid any attention. Isabel was choosing the two who were to come back with them that afternoon and see it. She chose Emmie Cole and Lena Logan. But when the others knew they were all to have a chance, they couldn't be nice enough to Isabel. One by one they put their arms round Isabel's waist and walked her off. They had something to whisper to her, a secret. "Isabel's *my* friend."

Only the little Kelveys moved away forgotten; there was nothing more for them to hear.

Days passed, and as more children saw the doll's house, the fame of it spread. It became the one subject, the rage. The one question was, "Have you seen Burnells' doll's house? Oh, ain't it lovely!" "Haven't you seen it? Oh, I say!"

## GUIDED READING

### LITERAL QUESTION

**1a.** What does the author say about the relationship between the Kelvey girls? (They "never failed to understand each other.")

### INFERENTIAL QUESTION

**1b.** Why do you think the girls have this kind of understanding? (Since they are virtual outcasts, they need each other even more than siblings usually do.)

Even the dinner hour was given up to talking about it. The little girls sat under the pines eating their thick mutton sandwiches and big slabs of johnnycake spread with butter. While always, as near as they could get, sat the Kelveys, our Else holding onto Lil, listening too, while they chewed their jam sandwiches out of a newspaper soaked with large red blobs. . . .

"Mother," said Kezia, "can't I ask the Kelveys just once?"

"Certainly not, Kezia."

"But why not?"

"Run away, Kezia; you know quite well why not."

At last everybody had seen it except them. On that day the subject rather flagged. It was the dinner hour. The children stood together under the pine trees, and suddenly, as they looked at the Kelveys eating out of their paper, always by themselves, always listening, they wanted to be horrid to them. Emmie Cole started the whisper.

"Lil Kelvey's going to be a servant when she grows up."

"O-oh, how awful!" said Isabel Burnell, and she made eyes at Emmie.

Emmie swallowed in a very meaning way and nodded to Isabel as she'd seen her mother do on those occasions.

"It's true—it's true—it's true," she said.

Then Lena Logan's little eyes snapped. "Shall I ask her?" she whispered.

"Bet you don't," said Jessie May.

"Pooh, I'm not frightened," said Lena. Suddenly she gave a little squeal and danced in front of the other girls. "Watch! Watch me! Watch me now!" said Lena. And sliding, gliding, dragging one foot, giggling behind her hand, Lena went over to the Kelveys.

Lil looked up from her dinner. She wrapped the rest quickly away. Our Else stopped chewing. What was coming now?

"Is it true you're going to be a servant when you grow up, Lil Kelvey?" shrilled Lena.

Dead silence. But instead of answering, Lil only gave her silly, shamefaced smile. She didn't seem to mind the question at all. What a sell for Lena! The girls began to titter.

Lena couldn't stand that. She put her hands on her hips; she shot forward. "Yah, yer father's in prison!" she hissed, spitefully.

This was such a marvelous thing to have said that the little girls rushed away in a body, deeply, deeply excited, wild with joy. Someone found a long rope, and they began skipping. And never did they skip so high, run in and out so fast, or do such daring things as on that morning.

In the afternoon Pat called for the Burnell children with the buggy and they drove home. There were vistors. Isabel and Lottie, who liked visitors, went upstairs to change their pinafores. But Kezia thieved out at the back. Nobody was about; she began to swing on the big white gates of the courtyard. Presently, looking along the road, she saw two little dots. They grew bigger, they were coming toward her. Now she could see that one was in front and one close behind. Now she could see that they were the Kelveys.

*The Doll's House*   **121**

AT A GLANCE

- Kezia asks her mother if she can invite the Kelveys but is rebuffed.
- Everyone sees the doll house but the Kelveys.
- Kezia avoids visitors and spots the Kelveys.

**1 PLOT: CONFLICT**

Kezia's questions conflict with the status quo. Her attitude suggests that she may reveal more humaneness than other members of her family.

**2 STYLE: IMAGERY**

Lena, sliding and gliding toward the Kelveys, evokes the image of a snake moving in to strike.

**3 RESPONSE JOURNAL**

Have students respond to the girls' feelings and behavior following Lena's attack on the Kelveys.

**4 VOCABULARY: WORD CHOICE**

The phrase "thieved out at the back" implies that Kezia's nonconformity is the equivalent of criminal behavior in her constricted world.

## GUIDED READING

### LITERAL QUESTION

**1a.** What did the little girls think of Lena's taunt, "Yah, yer father's in prison"? (It was such a marvelous thing to say.)

### INFERENTIAL QUESTION

**1b.** In what sense is this cruel taunt "marvelous"? (It is bold and goes beyond the girls' everyday level of cruelty toward the Kelveys. It seems to be something the other girls wish they'd had the nerve to say.)

- Kezia nervously invites the Kelveys to see the doll house.
- After some coaxing they agree, but Aunt Beryl soon discovers them.
- The Kelveys are shooed away, and Kezia is reprimanded by the sour aunt.
- The girls reflect on their adventure; Else says she saw the lamp.

**1 PLOT: CONFLICT**

As opportunity comes, Kezia wavers, then decides to cross the line between "her kind" and the Kelveys.

**2 PLOT: RISING ACTION**

Lil, breathing hard, and Else, scarcely breathing, view the doll's house for an enormous moment.

**3 PLOT: CLIMAX**

Aunt Beryl's outburst represents the story's high point.

**REFLECTING ON THE STORY**

What do Else's comment and smile signify? (Possible answers: Else, unaffected by social lines, is satisfied; like the perfect lamp that smiled at Kezia, Else smiles.)

---

**1** Kezia stopped swinging. She slipped off the gate as if she were going to run away. Then she hesitated. The Kelveys came nearer, and beside them walked their shadows, very long, stretching right across the road with their heads in the buttercups. Kezia clambered back on the gate; she had made up her mind; she swung out.

"Hullo," she said to the passing Kelveys.

They were so astounded that they stopped. Lil gave her silly smile. Our Else stared.

"You can come and see our doll's house if you want to," said Kezia, and she dragged one toe on the ground. But at that Lil turned red and shook her head quickly.

"Why not?" asked Kezia.

Lil gasped, then she said, "Your ma told our ma you wasn't to speak to us."

"Oh, well," said Kezia. She didn't know what to reply. "It doesn't matter. You can come and see our doll's house all the same. Come on. Nobody's looking."

But Lil shook her head still harder.

"Don't you want to?" asked Kezia.

Suddenly there was a twitch, a tug at Lil's skirt. She turned round. Our Else was looking at her with big, imploring eyes; she was frowning; she wanted to go. For a moment Lil looked at our Else very doubtfully. But then our Else twitched her skirt again. She started forward. Kezia led the way. Like two little stray cats they followed across the courtyard to where the doll's house stood.

**2** "There it is," said Kezia.

There was a pause. Lil breathed loudly, almost snorted; our Else was still as a stone.

"I'll open it for you," said Kezia kindly. She undid the hook and they looked inside.

"There's the drawing room and the dining room, and that's the—"

"Kezia!"

Oh, what a start they gave!

"Kezia!"

It was Aunt Beryl's voice. They turned round.

**122** *The Short Story*

At the back door stood Aunt Beryl, staring as if she couldn't believe what she saw.

**3** "How dare you ask the little Kelveys into the courtyard?" said her cold, furious voice. "You know as well as I do, you're not allowed to talk to them. Run away, children, run away at once. And don't come back again," said Aunt Beryl. And she stepped into the yard and shooed them out as if they were chickens.

"Off you go immediately!" she called, cold and proud.

They did not need telling twice. Burning with shame, shrinking together, Lil huddling along like her mother, our Else dazed, somehow they crossed the big courtyard and squeezed through the white gate.

"Wicked, disobedient little girl!" said Aunt Beryl bitterly to Kezia, and she slammed the doll's house to.

The afternoon had been awful. A letter had come from Willie Brent, a terrifying, threatening letter, saying if she did not meet him that evening in Pulman's Bush, he'd come to the front door and ask the reason why! But now that she had frightened those little rats of Kelveys and given Kezia a good scolding, her heart felt lighter. That ghastly pressure was gone. She went back to the house humming.

When the Kelveys were well out of sight of Burnells', they sat down to rest on a big red drainpipe by the side of the road. Lil's cheeks were still burning; she took off the hat with the quill and held it on her knee. Dreamily they looked over the hay paddocks, past the creek, to the group of wattles where Logan's cows stood waiting to be milked. What were their thoughts?

Presently our Else nudged up close to her sister. But now she had forgotten the cross lady. She put out a finger and stroked her sister's quill; she smiled her rare smile.

"I seen the little lamp," she said, softly.

Then both were silent once more.

---

## GUIDED READING

**LITERAL QUESTION**

**1a.** What does Kezia do for the Kelveys? (shows them the doll's house.)

**INFERENTIAL QUESTION**

**1b.** How is Kezia different from the rest of her family? (They are superficial and obsessed with social status. She alone shows a spark of humanity.)

## STUDY QUESTIONS

### Recalling

1. What was the reaction of Isabel, Lottie, and Kezia to the doll house Mrs. Hay sent them? What did Kezia like most about the doll house?
2. Why were the three children so excited about getting to school the day after the doll house arrived?
3. Who were the only two children not invited to see the doll house? Why?
4. In what way was Kezia's attitude toward the Kelveys different from that of her sisters and the other children at school?
5. Summarize what happens in the story from the point when Kezia sees the Kelveys coming along the road to the end of the story.

### Interpreting

6. Which characters did you like most? Which characters did you like least? Explain your answers by referring to details of the story.
7. The lamp in the doll house is an important symbol in this story. Whom or what does it stand for?
8. What inference can you make about the author's attitude toward considering neighbors inferior? Support your inference with evidence from the story.

### Extending

9. Discuss what this story has to do with setting examples. Explain how readers can apply what the author says to their own lives.

1. overwhelmed, excited, thrilled; the lamp on the dining room table
2. anxious to boast about doll's house to other children
3. Lil and Else Kelvey; parents and children consider them inferior because mother is washerwoman and father rumored to be in prison.
4. wants to invite Kelveys to see the doll's house
5. Kezia invites the Kelveys into the yard; at Else's urging they go in, and Kezia shows them doll's house; Aunt Beryl shoos Kelveys out of yard and berates Kezia; Else recalls that she "seen the little lamp."
6. Answers and supporting reasons will vary: *like most*—Kezia, Lil, and Else Kelvey, Mrs. Hay; *like least*—Isabel, Lena Logan, Aunt Beryl, Mrs. Burnell
7. Lamp may represent Kezia's kindness to Lil and Else Kelvey.
8. Answers will vary with students' experiences, maturity, and perceptiveness.
9. Aunt Beryl and Mrs. Burnell set poor examples for the Burnell children; Isabel's behavior toward Lil and Else sets an example for the other girls. Suggestions for applications to life will vary.

# LITERARY FOCUS: Irony

Known throughout the world by the pen name of O. Henry, William Sydney Porter (1862–1910) began his writing career in the last decade of his life. He went on to produce hundreds of short stories and became most famous for his ingenious habit of ending his tales with a surprising twist.

■ Money can't buy love, they say—or can it?

*O. Henry*

# Mammon[1] and the Archer[2]

Old Anthony Rockwall, retired manufacturer and proprietor of Rockwall's Eureka Soap, looked out the library window of his Fifth Avenue mansion and grinned. His neighbor to the right—the aristocratic clubman,[3] G. Van Schuylight Suffolk-Jones—came out to his waiting motorcar, wrinkling a contumelious nostril, as usual, at the Italian renaissance sculpture[4] of the soap palace's front elevation.

"Stuck-up old statuette of nothing doing!" commented the ex-Soap King. "The Eden Musée'll get that old frozen Nesselrode[5] yet if he don't watch out. I'll have this house painted red, white, and blue next summer and see if that'll make his Dutch nose turn up any higher."

And then Anthony Rockwall, who never cared for bells, went to the door of his library and shouted "Mike!" in the same voice that had once chipped off pieces of the welkin[6] on the Kansas prairies.

"Tell my son," said Anthony to the answering menial, "to come in here before he leaves the house."

When young Rockwall entered the library the old man laid aside his newspaper, looked at him with a kindly grimness on his big, smooth, ruddy countenance, rumpled his mop of white hair with one hand and rattled the keys in his pocket with the other.

"Richard," said Anthony Rockwall, "what do you pay for the soap that you use?"

Richard, only six months home from college, was startled a little. He had not yet taken the measure of this sire of his, who was as full of unexpectednesses as a girl at her first party.

"Six dollars a dozen, I think, dad."

"And your clothes?"

"I suppose about sixty dollars, as a rule."

"You're a gentleman," said Anthony, de-

---

1. **Mammon:** wealth personified and regarded as an evil influence.
2. **the Archer:** Cupid, the Roman god of love. He is pictured as a winged boy with a bow and arrow that he shoots at lovers.
3. **clubman:** person who spends much time at exclusive private clubs.
4. **Italian renaissance** [ren'ə säns'] **sculpture:** sculpture in the style developed in Italy from the fourteenth through the sixteenth century.
5. **Eden Musée'll** [mū zā'] **. . . Nesselrode:** Rockwall means that his neighbor is as cold and stiff as a statue in a museum. Nesselrode is a dessert made of a mixture of custard, candied fruits, and nuts.

6. **welkin:** sky.

124   *The Short Story*

cidedly. "I've heard of these young bloods spending $24 a dozen for soap, and going over the hundred mark for clothes. You've got as much money to waste as any of 'em, and yet you stick to what's decent and moderate. Now I use the old Eureka—not only for sentiment, but it's the purest soap made. Whenever you pay more than 10 cents a cake for soap you buy bad perfumes and labels. But 50 cents is doing very well for a young man in your generation, position and condition. As I said, you're a gentleman. They say it takes three generations to make one. They're off. Money'll do it as slick as soap grease. It's made you one. By hokey! it's almost made one of me. I'm nearly as impolite and disagreeable and ill-mannered as these two old knickerbocker gents[7] on each side of me that can't sleep of nights because I bought in between 'em."

"There are some things that money can't accomplish," remarked young Rockwall, rather gloomily.

"Now, don't say that," said old Anthony, shocked. "I bet my money on money every time. I've been through the encyclopedia down to Y looking for something you can't buy with it; and I expect to have to take up the appendix next week. I'm for money against the field. Tell me something money won't buy."

"For one thing," answered Richard, rankling a little, "it won't buy one into the exclusive circles of society."

"Oho! won't it?" thundered the champion of the root of evil. "You tell me where your exclusive circles would be if the first Astor[8] hadn't had the money to pay for his steerage[9] passage over?"

Richard sighed.

"And that's what I was coming to," said the old man, less boisterously. "That's why I asked you to come in. There's something going wrong with you, boy. I've been noticing it for two weeks. Out with it. I guess I could lay my hands on eleven million within twenty-four hours, besides the real estate. If it's your liver,[10] there's the *Rambler* down in the bay, coaled, and ready to steam down to the Bahamas in two days."

"Not a bad guess, dad; you haven't missed it far."

"Ah," said Anthony, keenly; "what's her name?"

Richard began to walk up and down the library floor. There was enough comradeship and sympathy in this crude old father of his to draw his confidence.

"Why don't you ask her?" demanded old Anthony. "She'll jump at you. You've got the money and the looks, and you're a decent boy. Your hands are clean. You've got no Eureka soap on 'em. You've been to college, but she'll overlook that."

"I haven't had a chance," said Richard.

"Make one," said Anthony. "Take her for a walk in the park, or a straw ride, or walk home with her from church. Chance! Pshaw!"

"You don't know the social mill, dad. She's part of the stream that turns it. Every hour and minute of her time is arranged for days in advance. I must have that girl, dad, or this town is a blackjack swamp forevermore. And I can't write it—I can't do that."

"Tut!" said the old man. "Do you mean to tell me that with all the money I've got you can't get an hour or two of a girl's time for yourself?"

"I've put it off too late. She's going to sail for Europe at noon day after tomorrow for a two years' stay. I'm to see her alone tomorrow evening for a few minutes. She's at Larchmont[11] now at her aunt's. I can't go there. But I'm allowed to

---

7. **knickerbocker** [nik′ər bok′ər] **gents:** residents of New York City, especially descendants of the early Dutch settlers.
8. **Astor:** name of a society family whose ancestors became wealthy in the early American fur trade.
9. **steerage:** the type of ship accommodations often used by immigrants.

10. **liver:** The liver has often been confused with the heart, especially as the supposed center of the emotions.
11. **Larchmont:** exclusive suburb north of New York City.

*Mammon and the Archer* **125**

AT A GLANCE
- Reassured by his son's spending habits, Anthony claims that money can buy anything; Richard says it cannot buy entry into society.
- Richard confirms his father's guess that he is in love.
- He will have only a few moments alone with "her" the next evening.

1 SYMBOL

Rockwall sees the choice of soaps as a moral indicator—a symbol of whether his son wastes wealth in foolish purchases or is moderate in his spending, like a true gentleman.

2 CONFLICT

The external conflict between Anthony and his son involves their disagreement about whether money can buy everything.

3 CHARACTERIZATION

Anthony's words reveal by indirect characterization his straightforwardness, his loving concern for his son, and his ability to recognize that his son is troubled.

## GUIDED READING

### LITERAL QUESTIONS

**1a.** Why are Anthony's two neighbors unable to sleep at night, according to Anthony? (He says they cannot sleep because he bought the house in between theirs.)

**2a.** Why can't Richard propose to the girl he loves? (He says that he has waited too long, and now she is about to leave for two years abroad.)

### INFERENTIAL QUESTIONS

**1b.** Why are the neighbors upset about this? (Gentlemen who inherit money rather than having had to work for it think they represent the true culture and resent the uncultured, newly wealthy such as Anthony.)

**2b.** Why do you think Richard waited? (He feels inferior to the girl and her family, who, like Anthony's neighbors, represent the socially accepted families of older wealth.)

## AT A GLANCE

- Richard will be with his love briefly in a cab going to the theater.
- Anthony defends the power of money; Aunt Ellen praises love.
- His aunt gives Richard his mother's ring.

## 1 IRONY

The suggestion that money should be worshiped as a source of good is ironic in a story whose title refers to money as a source of evil.

## 2 TONE

Anthony's use of slang like "knock money" and his description of the rules of society not being "bucked for a yard" maintain the lighthearted, humorous tone of the story.

*Fifth Avenue,* 1919, Childe Hassam. The Cleveland Museum of Art, Anonymous Gift.

meet her with a cab at the Grand Central Station tomorrow evening at the 8:30 train. We drive down Broadway to Wallack's at a gallop, where her mother and a box party[12] will be waiting for us in the lobby. Do you think she would listen to a declaration from me during that six or eight minutes under those circumstances? No. And what chance would I have in the theater or afterward? None. No, dad, this is one tangle that your money can't unravel. We can't buy one minute of time with cash; if we could, rich people would live longer. There's no hope of getting a talk with Miss Lantry before she sails."

---

12. **box party:** group of people sharing a box at the theater.

**126** *The Short Story*

"All right, Richard, my boy, said old Anthony, cheerfully. "You may run along down to your club now. I'm glad it ain't your liver. But don't forget to burn a few punk sticks in the joss house to the great god Mazuma[13] from time to time. You say money won't buy time? Well, of course, you can't order eternity wrapped up and delivered at your residence for a price, but I've seen Father Time get pretty bad stone bruises on his heels when he walked through the gold diggings."

That night came Aunt Ellen, gentle, sentimental, wrinkled, sighing, oppressed by wealth, in to Brother Anthony at his evening paper, and began discourse on the subject of lovers' woes.

"He told me all about it," said Brother Anthony, yawning. "I told him my bank account was at his service. And then he began to knock money. Said money couldn't help. Said the rules of society couldn't be bucked for a yard by a team of ten millionaires."

"Oh, Anthony," sighed Aunt Ellen, "I wish you would not think so much of money. Wealth is nothing where a true affection is concerned. Love is all-powerful. If he only had spoken earlier! She could not have refused our Richard. But now I fear it is too late. He will have no opportunity to address her. All your gold cannot bring happiness to your son."

At eight o'clock the next evening Aunt Ellen took a quaint old gold ring from a moth-eaten case and gave it to Richard.

"Wear it tonight, nephew," she begged. "Your mother gave it to me. Good luck in love she said it brought. She asked me to give it to you when you had found the one you loved."

Young Rockwall took the ring reverently and tried it on his smallest finger. It slipped as far as the second joint and stopped. He took it off and stuffed it into his vest pocket, after the manner of man. And then he phoned for his cab.

---

13. **burn . . . Mazuma:** burn incense in the temple of the god of money.

## GUIDED READING

### LITERAL QUESTION

**1a.** What adverb describes Anthony's mood after his discussion with Richard? *(cheerfully)*

### INFERENTIAL QUESTION

**1b.** Why is the use of this word surprising? (Anthony has appeared to be very concerned about his son's problem with romance. Because that problem is unresolved, it is surprising that Anthony's mood appears to be one of cheer.)

At the station he captured Miss Lantry out of the gabbing mob at eight-thirty-two.

"We mustn't keep mamma and the others waiting," said she.

"To Wallack's Theater as fast as you can drive!" said Richard, loyally.

They whirled up Forty-second to Broadway, and then down the white-starred lane that leads from the soft meadows of sunset to the rocky hills of morning.[14]

At Thirty-fourth Street young Richard quickly thrust up the trap[15] and ordered the cabman to stop.

"I've dropped a ring," he apologized, as he climbed out. "It was my mother's, and I'd hate to lose it. I won't detain you a minute—I saw where it fell."

In less than a minute he was back in the cab with the ring.

But within that minute a crosstown car had stopped directly in front of the cab. The cabman tried to pass to the left, but a heavy express wagon cut him off. He tried the right and had to back away from a furniture van that had no business to be there. He tried to back out, but dropped his reins and swore dutifully. He was blockaded in a tangled mess of vehicles and horses.

One of those street blockades had occurred that sometimes tie up commerce and movement quite suddenly in the big city.

"Why don't you drive on?" said Miss Lantry, impatiently. "We'll be late."

Richard stood up in the cab and looked around. **[1]** He saw a congested flood of wagons, trucks, cabs, vans and street cars filling the vast space where Broadway, Sixth Avenue, and Thirty-fourth Street cross one another as a twenty-six-

---

14. **white-starred lane . . . morning:** a fanciful reference to Broadway, the famous New York street that is lined at one point with brightly lit theaters (*white-starred*) and runs from northwest (*sunset*) to southeast (*morning*).
15. **trap:** sliding window between the front and back seats in a cab.

---

inch maiden fills her twenty-two-inch girdle. And still from all the cross streets they were hurrying and rattling toward the converging point at full speed, and hurling themselves into the straggling mass, locking wheels and adding their **[2]** drivers' imprecations to the clamor. The entire traffic of Manhattan seemed to have jammed itself around them. The oldest New Yorker among the thousands of spectators that lined the sidewalks had not witnessed a street blockade of the proportions of this one.

"I'm very sorry," said Richard, as he resumed his seat, "but it looks as if we are stuck. They won't get this jumble loosened up in an hour. It was my fault. If I hadn't dropped the ring we—"

"Let me see the ring," said Miss Lantry. "Now that it can't be helped, I don't care. I think theaters are stupid, anyway."

At 11 o'clock that night somebody tapped lightly on Anthony Rockwall's door.

"Come in," shouted Anthony, who was in a red dressing gown, reading a book of piratical adventures.

**[3]** Somebody was Aunt Ellen, looking like a gray-haired angel that had been left on earth by mistake.

"They're engaged, Anthony," she said, softly. "She has promised to marry our Richard. On their way to the theater there was a street blockade, and it was two hours before their cab could get out of it.

"And oh, Brother Anthony, don't ever boast **[4]** of the power of money again. A little emblem of true love—a little ring that symbolized unending and unmercenary affection—was the cause of our Richard finding his happiness. He dropped it in the street, and got out to recover it. And before they could continue the blockade occurred. He spoke to his love and won her there while the cab was hemmed in. Money is dross[16] compared with true love, Anthony."

"All right," said old Anthony. "I'm glad the

---

16. **dross** [drôss]: worthless or waste matter.

*Mammon and the Archer* **127**

AT A GLANCE

- In the cab with Miss Lantry, Richard drops the ring and asks the cabman to stop a moment.
- A huge traffic jam develops, and Richard shows Miss Lantry the ring.
- Aunt Ellen tells Anthony that Richard has won his bride.

**1 SETTING**

The story occurs in New York City at the turn of the century, a time and place in which such a monumental traffic jam could occur.

**2 READING SKILLS: TOPIC SENTENCE**

The topic sentence occurs toward the end of this paragraph describing the traffic jam: "The entire traffic of Manhattan seemed to have jammed itself around them."

**3 POINT OF VIEW**

O. Henry's decision to narrate the story from an omniscient point of view permits the reader to jump from the young couple in the cab back to Anthony's mansion.

**4 THEME**

Aunt Ellen feels that she has won the argument concerning the relative power of money and love.

---

## GUIDED READING

**LITERAL QUESTIONS**

**1a.** Why does Richard request that the cabman stop? (He has dropped the ring and wants to retrieve it.)

**2a.** After the couple become engaged, what does Aunt Ellen tell Anthony about the power of money? (She says that it is worthless compared with true love.)

**INFERENTIAL QUESTIONS**

**1b.** Why do you think that is, or is not, an accident? (It appears to be an accident. Richard orders the cab to go quickly to the theater, and he seems sincere in his apology to Miss Lantry.)

**2b.** How do you expect Anthony to reply? (Because he has stated earlier his belief in the power of money, the reader expects him to argue with her.)

- Anthony, glad his son has what he wants, repeats his statement that he would spare no expense.
- The next day a man named Kelly comes to collect money for creating the traffic jam.
- Anthony asks Kelly if he saw a naked archer—Cupid—in the traffic jam.

## 1 PLOT: CLIMAX

The climax occurs when the reader learns that Anthony has hired someone to create the traffic jam. Both romance and money have led to Richard's success.

## 2 SITUATIONAL IRONY

The reader expects until the last paragraphs of the story that love proved to be more important than money; the surprise knowledge that money bought the traffic jam provides situational irony.

### REFLECTING ON THE STORY

Do you think that Anthony will take credit for the traffic jam? Why or why not? (Some students might think he will not jeopardize his son's happiness by telling; others, that he will want to prove he is right about money.)

### STUDY QUESTIONS

1. retired soap manufacturer
2. looks at him "with a kindly grimness"; that money can buy time
3. the woman he loves is leaving
4. she thinks the ring caused the delay; Anthony paid for the traffic jam.
5. wants to preserve illusion; he is kind
6. humor, cleverness, generosity; yes; perhaps—seems to share Anthony's values
7. Mammon: wealth as evil; Archer: Cupid; wealth cooperated with love

---

boy has got what he wanted. I told him I wouldn't spare any expense in the matter if—''

"But Brother Anthony, what good could your money have done?"

"Sister," said Anthony Rockwall. "I've got my pirate in a devil of a scrape. His ship has just been scuttled, and he's too good a judge of the value of money to let drown. I wish you would let me go on with this chapter."

The story should end here. I wish it would as heartily as you who read it wish it did. But we must go to the bottom of the well for truth.

The next day a person with red hands and a blue polka-dot necktie, who called himself Kelly, called at Anthony Rockwall's house, and was at once received in the library.

"Well," said Anthony, reaching for his checkbook, "it was a good bilin' of soap.[17] Let's see—you had $5,000 in cash."

"I paid out $300 more of my own," said Kelly. "I had to go a little above the estimate. I got the express wagons and cabs mostly for $5; but the trucks and two-horse teams mostly raised me to $10. The motormen wanted $10, and some of the loaded teams $20. The cops struck me hardest—$50 I paid two, and the rest $20 and $25.

---

17. **good bilin' of soap:** great boiling, or lathering up, of soap; in other words, tremendous turmoil.

---

But didn't it work beautiful, Mr. Rockwall? I'm glad William A. Brady[18] wasn't onto that little outdoor vehicle mob scene. I wouldn't want William to break his heart with jealousy. And never a rehearsal, either! The boys was on time to the fraction of a second. It was two hours before a snake could get below Greeley's statue.''[19]

"Thirteen hundred—there you are, Kelly," said Anthony, tearing off a check. "Your thousand, and the $300 you were out. You don't despise money, do you, Kelly?"

"Me?" said Kelly. "I can lick the man that invented poverty."

Anthony called Kelly when he was at the door.

"You didn't notice," said he, "anywhere in the tie-up, a kind of a fat boy without any clothes on shooting arrows around with a bow did you?"

"Why, no," said Kelly, mystified. "I didn't. If he was like you say, maybe the cops pinched him before I got there."

"I thought the little rascal wouldn't be on hand," chuckled Anthony. "Good-by, Kelly."

---

18. **William A. Brady** (1863–1950): theatrical producer.
19. **Greeley's statue:** monument at Broadway and Thirty-fourth Street in New York City honoring Horace Greeley (1811–1872), an American journalist.

---

### STUDY QUESTIONS

**Recalling**

1. What is Anthony Rockwall's background?
2. Find statements that reveal Anthony's feelings for his son. Explain the disagreement about money between father and son.
3. Why is Richard downcast at the beginning of the story?
4. How does Aunt Ellen think Richard's engagement came about? What really happened?

**Interpreting**

5. Why do you think Anthony does not tell Aunt Ellen that he arranged the traffic jam? What does his silence tell us about him?
6. What are Anthony's good qualities? Do you think the narrator wants us to like Anthony? To agree with his opinions? Why or why not?
7. Explain what the story's title means and how it is appropriate to the story.

**128** *The Short Story*

8. Do you think that O. Henry is arguing that money can buy everything? Why or why not?

## VIEWPOINT

Like many of O. Henry's stories, "Mammon and the Archer" is a light-hearted version of the standard plot of "boy meets girl." However, as one writer has noted:

O. Henry usually made his . . . stories illustrate some more or less serious theme.
— A. Voss, *The American Short Story*

■ What serious theme might O. Henry be illustrating in "Mammon and the Archer"?

## LITERARY FOCUS

### Situational Irony

**Irony** is a contrast between appearance and reality. **Situational irony** is a form of irony that occurs when we expect one outcome but find that the opposite happens. An example of this sort of irony might involve a situation in which a wealthy old woman promises her nephew that he will inherit her "greatest treasure" and, instead of a fortune, bequeaths him a pampered elderly cat. Like many other O. Henry stories, "Mammon and the Archer" ends with a twist of situational irony.

### Thinking About Situational Irony

1. Explain how the ending of "Mammon and the Archer" represents a contrast between expectation and reality.
2. How would the effect of the story change if we had known about Anthony's scheme all along?

## VOCABULARY

### Precise Verbs

Good writers try to use precise verbs rather than vague verbs. They also try to vary their verbs.

The following sentences all come from "Mammon and the Archer." The blank in each sentence could be filled by the verb *said*, a word that any writer may use often in a story containing dialogue. However, O. Henry manages to find a number of interesting and more precise substitutes for *said*. Without looking back at the story, select a verb for each blank. Be prepared to explain why you think

your choice fits into the sentence. Finally, go back to the story to discover the choices that O. Henry himself made.

1. Anthony . . . went to the door of his library and _____ "Mike!"
   (a) screamed        (c) shouted
   (b) whispered       (d) remarked
2. "Oho! won't it?" _____ the champion of the root of evil.
   (a) argued          (c) commented
   (b) asked           (d) thundered
3. "Oh Anthony," _____ Aunt Ellen, "I wish you would not think so much of money."
   (a) chattered       (c) howled
   (b) sighed          (d) moaned
4. "I've dropped a ring," he _____, as he climbed out.
   (a) apologized      (c) giggled
   (b) sobbed          (d) complained
5. "I thought the little rascal wouldn't be on hand," _____ Anthony.
   (a) called          (c) snarled
   (b) hissed          (d) chuckled

## COMPOSITION

### Writing About Irony

■ Discuss O. Henry's use of irony in "Mammon and the Archer." You may want to consider the following questions as you prepare to write: How does O. Henry's use of irony contribute to the story's humor? How does his use of irony support the story's theme, or central idea? *For help with this assignment, see Lesson 9 in the Writing About Literature Handbook at the back of this book.*

### Supporting an Opinion

■ Choose one of the following quotations about money, and explain why you either agree or disagree with it. If necessary, interpret the statement. Be sure to support your opinion thoroughly.

a. A fool and his money are soon parted.
b. Money doesn't grow on trees.
c. Money talks.
d. Money is the root of all evil.
e. Money can't buy love.

*Mammon and the Archer*  **129**

## COMPOSITION: GUIDELINES FOR EVALUATION

### WRITING ABOUT IRONY

#### Objective

To illustrate how irony adds humor and supports theme

#### Guidelines for Evaluation

- suggested length: three to four paragraphs
- should explain how surprise ending represents situational irony
- should explain why this irony is funny
- should explain how irony expresses theme

### SUPPORTING AN OPINION

#### Objective

To write an argument supporting an opinion

#### Guidelines for Evaluation

- suggested length: three to four paragraphs
- should interpret quotation
- should state writer's opinion
- should present logical argument that supports or undercuts quotation

- Framton Nuttel, in the country on retreat, visits Mrs. Sappleton.
- He is received by her niece, who begins to relate a tragedy related to an open window.

LITERARY OPTIONS

- verbal irony
- characterization

THEMATIC OPTIONS

- appearance vs. reality
- human frailty

**1 CHARACTERIZATION**

Framton Nuttel, ridiculous name and all, is immediately portrayed as a nervous man, obsessed with superficial conventions.

**2 READING SKILLS: MAKING INFERENCES**

His sister's comments imply that Framton is nervous, gloomy, and antisocial.

**3 FORESHADOWING**

The niece's earnest questioning indicates that some interesting information about her aunt may be forthcoming—and Framton's unfamiliarity with the family may be significant.

Hector Hugh Munro (1870–1916), more commonly known by the pen name of Saki, was raised in England but traveled widely. He served with the police force in Burma, wrote dispatches from Russia as a foreign correspondent, and died under German sniper fire during World War I. England, however, provides the setting for most of his stories, which are brief, witty and end in an unexpected way.

■ Have you ever wanted to play a joke on someone just for the fun of it? What did you do?

*Saki*

# The Open Window

"My aunt will be down presently, Mr. Nuttel," said a very self-possessed young lady of fifteen. "In the meantime you must try and put up with me."

Framton Nuttel endeavored to say the correct something which should duly flatter the niece of the moment without unduly discounting the aunt that was to come. Privately he doubted more than ever whether these formal visits on a succession of total strangers would do much towards helping the nerve cure which he was supposed to be undergoing.

"I know how it will be," his sister had said when he was preparing to migrate to this rural retreat; "You will bury yourself down there and not speak to a living soul, and your nerves will be worse than ever from moping. I shall just give you letters of introduction to all the people I know there. Some of them, as far as I can remember, were quite nice."

Framton wondered whether Mrs. Sappleton, the lady to whom he was presenting one of the letters of introduction, came into the nice division.

"Do you know many of the people round here?" asked the niece, when she judged that they had had sufficient silent communion.

"Hardly a soul," said Framton. "My sister was staying here, at the rectory,[1] you know, some four years ago, and she gave me letters of introduction to some of the people here."

He made the last statement in a tone of distinct regret.

"Then you know practically nothing about my aunt?" pursued the self-possessed young lady.

"Only her name and address," admitted the caller. He was wondering whether Mrs. Sappleton was in the married or widowed state. An undefinable something about the room seemed to suggest masculine habitation.

"Her great tragedy happened just three years ago," said the child; "that would be since your sister's time."

"Her tragedy?" asked Framton. Somehow in this restful country spot tragedies seemed out of place.

"You may wonder why we keep that window wide open on an October afternoon," said the niece, indicating a large French window[2] that opened on to a lawn.

---

1. **rectory:** house of a clergyman.
2. **French window:** floor-length hinged window that opens outward.

---

*GUIDED READING*

LITERAL QUESTION

**1a.** Does Framton think formal visiting will help his nerve cure? (He doubts it will help.)

INFERENTIAL QUESTION

**1b.** What does Framton's opinion of visiting suggest about his attitude toward strangers? (He is uneasy around them.)

"It is quite warm for the time of the year," said Framton; "but has that window got anything to do with the tragedy?"

"Out through that window, three years ago to a day, her husband and her two young brothers went off for their day's shooting. They never came back. In crossing the moor³ to their favorite snipe-shooting⁴ ground they were all three engulfed in a treacherous piece of bog.⁵ It had been that dreadful wet summer, you know, and places that were safe in other years gave way suddenly without warning. Their bodies were never recovered. That was the dreadful part of it." Here the child's voice lost its self-possessed note and became falteringly human. "Poor aunt always thinks that they will come back some day, they and the little brown spaniel that was lost with them, and walk in at that window just as they used to do. That is why the window is kept open every evening till it is quite dusk. Poor dear aunt, she has often told me how they went out, her husband with his white waterproof coat over his arm, and Ronnie, her youngest brother, singing, 'Bertie, why do you bound?' as he always did to tease her, because she said it got on her nerves. Do you know, sometimes on still, quiet evenings like this, I almost get a creepy feeling that they will all walk in through that window—"

She broke off with a little shudder. It was a relief to Framton when the aunt bustled into the room with a whirl of apologies for being late in making her appearance.

"I hope Vera has been amusing you?" she said.

"She has been very interesting," said Framton.

"I hope you don't mind the open window," said Mrs. Sappleton briskly. "My husband and brothers will be home directly from shooting,

___

3. **moor:** area of open, often marshy land.
4. **snipe-shooting:** Snipe is a popular game bird.
5. **bog:** marsh.

and they always come in this way. They've been out for snipe in the marshes today, so they'll make a fine mess over my poor carpets. So like you menfolk, isn't it?"

She rattled on cheerfully about the shooting and the scarcity of birds, and the prospects for duck in the winter. To Framton it was all purely horrible. He made a desperate but only partially successful effort to turn the talk on to a less ghastly topic. He was conscious that his hostess was giving him only a fragment of her attention, and her eyes were constantly straying past him to the open window and the lawn beyond. It was certainly an unfortunate coincidence that he

*Fresh Widow,* Marcel Duchamp, 1920.

Museum of Modern Art, NY

*The Open Window* **131**

**AT A GLANCE**

- The niece relates that three years ago, her three uncles went through the open window and never returned.
- She says her aunt keeps the window open, imagining they will come back.

**1 CHARACTERIZATION**

The niece's remark and shudder reveal her flair for drama. She has enjoyed her tale and is awaiting its effects on the hapless listener.

**2 VERBAL IRONY**

Vera has been more than "interesting"—she has told a tale eerie enough to unsettle her nervous visitor exceedingly.

**3 CHARACTERIZATION**

Framton looks perfectly ridiculous as he fights his mounting terror in an effort to observe social amenities.

___

## GUIDED READING

**LITERAL QUESTION**

**1a.** How does Framton feel when Mrs. Sappleton enters? (He is relieved.)

**INFERENTIAL QUESTION**

**1b.** How does the aunt soon add to Framton's horror? (Her matter-of-fact cheerfulness about her husband's return verifies her niece's dreadful story.)

## AT A GLANCE

- On schedule, the muddy hunters and their spaniel return.
- Framton, terrified, flees.
- Vera explains Framton's flight with another invented story.

### 1 CHARACTERIZATION

Framton's assumption that his ailments interest others reveal how self-absorbed he is.

### 2 PLOT: CLIMAX

Aided by Vera's horrified reaction, Framton is frightened by the incredible appearance of "ghosts."

### 3 THEME

Vera has gauged her nervous victim well. Framton is a very amusing figure as he beats a hasty retreat.

### 4 VERBAL IRONY

As far as Framton was concerned, he *had* seen a ghost.

### 5 VERBAL IRONY

Vera, whose name means "truth," creates very entertaining—if false—stories when she finds the opportunity to do so.

### REFLECTING ON THE STORY

Is the story primarily funny or frightening? Explain. (Students who find the story funny should cite the comic descriptions of Nuttel and Vera's clever victimization of him. Students who find the story frightening should cite the ways in which Vera makes her story seem plausible to us.)

---

should have paid his visit on this tragic anniversary.

"The doctors agree in ordering me complete rest, and absence of mental excitement, and avoidance of anything in the nature of violent physical exercise," announced Framton, who labored under the tolerably widespread delusion that total strangers and chance acquaintances are hungry for the least detail of one's ailments and infirmities, their cause and cure. "On the matter of diet they are not so much in agreement," he continued.

"No?" said Mrs. Sappleton, in a voice which only replaced a yawn at the last moment. Then she suddenly brightened into alert attention—but not to what Framton was saying.

"Here they are at last!" she cried. "Just in time for tea, and don't they look as if they were muddy up to the eyes!"

Framton shivered slightly and turned towards the niece with a look intended to convey sympathetic comprehension. The child was staring out through the open window with dazed horror in her eyes. In a chill shock of nameless fear Framton swung round in his seat and looked in the same direction.

In the deepening twilight three figures were walking across the lawn towards the window. They all carried guns under their arms, and one of them was additionally burdened with a white coat hung over his shoulders. A tired brown spaniel kept close at their heels. Noiselessly they neared the house, and then a hoarse young voice chanted out of the dusk: "I said, Bertie, why do you bound?"

Framton grabbed wildly at his stick and hat. The hall door, the gravel drive, and the front gate were dimly noted stages in his headlong retreat. A cyclist coming along the road had to run into the hedge to avoid imminent collision.

"Here we are, my dear," said the bearer of the white mackintosh,[6] coming in through the window; "fairly muddy, but most of it's dry. Who was that who bolted out as we came up?"

"A most extraordinary man, a Mr. Nuttel," said Mrs. Sappleton; "could only talk about his illness, and dashed off without a word of goodby or apology when you arrived. One would think he had seen a ghost."

"I expect it was the spaniel," said the niece calmly. "He told me he had a horror of dogs. He was once hunted into a cemetery somewhere on the banks of the Ganges[7] by a pack of pariah[8] dogs, and had to spend the night in a newly-dug grave with the creatures snarling and grinning and foaming just above him. Enough to make any one lose their nerve."

Romance at short notice was her specialty.

---

6. **mackintosh:** raincoat worn in England, named for the inventor Charles Macintosh (1766–1843).
7. **Ganges** [gan'jēz]: river in northern India.
8. **pariah** [pə ri'ə]: outcast; here, wild.

---

## STUDY QUESTIONS

### Recalling

1. Why is Framton visiting the countryside?
2. How does Vera explain the fact that the window is left open? What is the real explanation?
3. Why does Framton rush from the house? How does Vera explain his departure to her aunt?

### Interpreting

4. What traits in Framton's personality might make him accept Vera's story?
5. Explain how the way in which Vera presents her story to Framton makes it seem more believable.
6. What effect did Vera's first story have on you? What about her *second* story?

---

## STUDY QUESTIONS

1. He's undergoing a nerve cure.
2. ■ The aunt thinks her missing husband and brothers will return.
   ■ The weather is warm.
3. ■ The men return.
   ■ She says he was afraid of the dog.
4. nervousness; vulnerability
5. She is convincing.
6. evoked sympathy; amusement

7. What word other than *romance* could you apply to Vera's activities? Why do you think the narrator chose this word?

### Extending

8. Give another example of the power of the imagination. Do you think everyone is susceptible to the power of suggestion? Explain.

## LITERARY FOCUS

### Verbal Irony

**Verbal irony** occurs when someone says one thing but means the opposite. Verbal irony is usually humorous, but it can also make a serious point.

In "The Open Window," for example, the narrator says that Vera began to speak to Framton "when she judged that they had had sufficient silent communion." This statement is ironic because it describes an awkward silence between two strangers as "silent communion"—something that happens only between close friends. The statement also makes an important point about each character: Framton is too wrapped up in his own ailments to notice the long pause while Vera has enough initiative to break it.

### Thinking About Verbal Irony

1. Look up the meaning of the name Vera. How might Saki's choice of this name be an example of verbal irony?
2. In what way is the story's last line ironic?
3. Find two other ironic statements in the story.

## VOCABULARY

### Sentence Completions

Each of the following sentences contains a blank with four possible words for completing the sentence. All of the choices come from "The Open Window." Write the letter of the word that completes each sentence correctly and that uses the word *as the word is used in the story.*

1. Since Jim was a poor swimmer, Ann _____ his warning about the rough surf.
   (a) discounted        (c) underwent
   (b) unraveled         (d) bolted

2. European storks _____ to Africa each fall.
   (a) indicate          (c) filter
   (b) unleash           (d) migrate

3. Paul suffered from the _____ that he was Napoleon.
   (a) habitation        (c) delusion
   (b) exaggeration      (d) position

4. Mr. Randall, who had always been healthy, dreaded the _____ of old age.
   (a) infirmities       (c) benefits
   (b) divisions         (d) devotions

5. Black clouds meant that rain was _____.
   (a) sufficient        (c) moping
   (b) imminent          (d) desperate

## COMPOSITION

### Writing About a Story's Conclusion

■ Evaluate the effect of the "double" ending of "The Open Window." Begin by discussing how you responded to the first appearance of the hunters. Then explain how you responded when you realized the truth. Finally discuss whether you liked the way the story ended.

### Writing a Diary Entry

■ Imagine that you are either Framton or Vera writing in your diary hours after the events in "The Open Window" have taken place. Relate your reactions to these events from the point of view of your character. Be sure to stay within the personality of the character, and try to echo the way the character speaks in the story.

## COMPARING STORIES

■ Both "Mammon and the Archer" and "The Open Window" have endings that surprise the reader for opposite reasons. O. Henry presents a seemingly ordinary occurrence—Richard's engagement—and shows that it came about in an extraordinary way. On the other hand, Saki presents a seemingly extraordinary event—the appearance of the "ghostly" hunters—and reveals that it is a perfectly ordinary occurrence after all. Which sort of surprise did you prefer, and why?

7. mischief; lying; suggests it is amusing
8. Students may offer personal examples of being caught up in an illusion—for example, watching a horror movie.

1. truth; name contrary to behavior
2. Vera's stories are romantic in that they're colorful and untrue.
3. Mrs. Sappleton's hope that Vera has been "amusing"; the comment that Nuttel looked as if "he had seen a ghost"

### VOCABULARY

1. (a) discounted
2. (d) migrate
3. (c) delusion
4. (a) infirmities
5. (b) imminent

### COMPARING STORIES

Students should:

- demonstrate knowledge of the events leading to each ending
- discuss feelings provoked by the endings
- state a preference for one story over the other

---

## *COMPOSITION: GUIDELINES FOR EVALUATION*

### WRITING ABOUT A STORY'S CONCLUSION

#### Objective
To state a personal response to story's ending

#### Guidelines for Evaluation
- suggested length: one to three paragraphs
- should state initial response to hunter's return and reaction to the truth
- should express an opinion about the ending

### WRITING A DIARY ENTRY

#### Objective
To write a diary entry from the point of view of a character

#### Guidelines for Evaluation
- suggested length: three to four paragraphs
- should be written in first person
- should describe what character believes has transpired
- should use language of the assumed character

The annotations in the Pupil's Edition that accompany this story bring to students' attention each of the elements of the short story along with various techniques of fiction. Review the eight steps under "Reminders for Active Reading of Short Stories" (page 134), and have students tell how each has been illustrated in one or two of the stories they have studied. Then have students apply each of the eight reminders to Norris' story, by pointing to specific passages in the story and notations in the text.

# LITERARY FOCUS: *The Total Effect*

Most people recognize that writing a story is a creative act. Just as important, *reading* a story demands creative, active thinking. As we read any story, we think about what is happening, why it happens, and what it means. We notice and interpret clues about the plot, characters, setting, point of view, tone, and theme of the story, along with its possible uses of irony and symbol. When we have finished, we find that we have put these clues together into an interpretation of the story. In a sense, we have taken the author's words and *re*created the story that he or she originally imagined.

Because reading a story is an imaginative act, different people will make somewhat different observations as they read. However, an active reader will keep in mind the following basic points.

## Reminders for Active Reading of Short Stories

1. The **title** of a story can be a clue to its theme.
2. The **plot** will usually unfold in several stages: exposition, narrative hook, rising action, climax, falling action, and resolution. A conflict of some kind sets in motion this whole process. Suspense builds interest in the plot as it unfolds.
3. **Characters** can be directly or indirectly portrayed and can be flat or round, static or dynamic.
4. The **setting** creates the story's atmosphere, and can help reveal the characters and theme of the story.
5. **Point of view** concerns the relationship between the narrator and the story. The author's **tone** expresses an attitude toward the story's characters and events.
6. The **theme** may be stated directly, or it may be implied in the other elements of the story.
7. Objects, persons, places, and events in the story may have both literal and **symbolic** meaning.
8. A story may include situational or verbal **irony**, which creates a contrast between appearance and reality.

## Model for Active Reading

On the following pages you will see how a careful reader kept the elements of fiction in mind while reading "Shaving," a short story by Leslie Norris. The reader's observations about the story appear as marginal notations. Each notation includes a page reference for further information on the item in question. Read "Shaving" alone first purely for your own enjoyment. Then read it again with the marginal notations. The process shown in this model can guide your reading of the final stories in this unit.

Poet and short story writer Leslie Norris (born 1921) grew up in a mining town in Wales, a country on the western coast of Great Britain. He now lives and teaches in England. His stories have appeared in such American publications as the *New Yorker* and the *Atlantic Monthly*. Like ''Shaving,'' many of Norris' stories portray young people at moments when their lives are about to change.

■ How do any of us know when we have grown up? What does ''maturity'' mean to you?

AT A GLANCE
■ On the way home from an April football game, Barry realizes he is growing up and that he has an identity.
■ He sees an old friend, Jackie Bevan, talking to a girl.

LITERARY OPTIONS
■ characterization
■ imagery
■ symbol

THEMATIC OPTIONS
■ taking responsibility
■ growth and change
■ adolescence

*Leslie Norris*

# Shaving

Earlier, when Barry had left the house to go to the game, an overnight frost had still been thick on the roads, but the brisk April sun had soon dispersed it, and now he could feel the spring warmth on his back through the thick tweed of his coat. His left arm was beginning to stiffen up where he'd jarred it in a tackle, but it was nothing serious. He flexed his shoulders against the tightness of his jacket and was surprised again by the unexpected weight of his muscles, the thickening strength of his body. A few years back, he thought, he had been a small, unimportant boy, one of a swarming gang laughing and jostling to school, hardly aware that he possessed an identity. But time had transformed him. He walked solidly now, and often alone. He was tall, strongly made, his hands and feet were adult and heavy, the rooms in which all his life he'd moved had grown too small for him. Sometimes a devouring restlessness drove him from the house to walk long distances in the dark. He hardly understood how it had happened. Amused and quiet, he walked the High Street among the morning shoppers.

He saw Jackie Bevan across the road and remembered how, when they were both six years old, Jackie had swallowed a pin. The flustered teachers had clucked about Jackie as he stood there, bawling, cheeks awash with tears, his nose wet. But now Jackie was tall and suave, his thick, pale hair sleekly tailored, his gray suit enviable. He was talking to a girl as golden as a daffodil.

''Hey, hey!'' called Jackie. ''How's the athlete, how's Barry boy?''
He waved a graceful hand at Barry.

*Shaving* **135**

Title (p. 99): The title may relate to the story's plot and reveal its theme.

Setting (p. 58): The time of year in which a story takes place is often significant.

Direct characterization (p. 39): The author describes Barry's physical appearance and his attitude toward his recent growth.

## GUIDED READING

**LITERAL QUESTIONS**

**1a.** When does the story take place? (April)

**2a.** How does Barry walk now? (solidly, often alone)

**INFERENTIAL QUESTIONS**

**1b.** What significance do you think the season might have in the story? (Like spring, adolescence is a time of growth, change, and promise.)

**2b.** Barry has changed recently. What does the author suggest is the nature of such changes? (He has become strong and independent.)

"Come and talk to Sue," he said.

Barry shifted his bag to his left hand and walked over, forming in his mind the answers he'd make to Jackie's questions.

"Did we win?" Jackie asked. "Was the old Barry Stanford magic in glittering evidence yet once more this morning? Were the invaders sent hunched and silent back to their hovels in the hills? What was the score? Give us an epic account, Barry, without modesty or delay. This is Sue, by the way."

"I've seen you about," the girl said.

"You could hardly miss him," said Jackie. "Four men, roped together, spent a week climbing him—they thought he was Everest.[1] He ought to carry a warning beacon, he's a danger to aircraft."

"Silly," said the girl, smiling at Jackie. "He's not much taller than you are."

She had a nice voice too.

"We won," Barry said. "Seventeen points to three, and it was a good game. The ground was hard, though."

He could think of nothing else to say.

"Let's all go for a frivolous cup of coffee," Jackie said. "Let's celebrate your safe return from the rough fields of victory. We could pour libations[2] all over the floor for you."

"I don't think so," Barry said. "Thanks. I'll go straight home."

"Okay," said Jackie, rocking on his heels so that the sun could shine on his smile. "How's your father?"

"No better," Barry said. "He's not going to get better."

"Yes, well," said Jackie, serious and uncomfortable, "tell him my mother and father ask about him."

"I will," Barry promised. "He'll be pleased."

Barry dropped the bag in the front hall and moved into the room which had been the dining room until his father's illness. His father lay in the white bed, his long body gaunt, his still head scarcely denting the pillow. He seemed asleep, thin blue lids covering his eyes, but when Barry turned away he spoke.

"Hullo, Son," he said. "Did you win?"

His voice was a dry, light rustling, hardly louder than the breath which carried it. Its sound moved Barry to a compassion that almost unmanned him, but he stepped close to the bed and looked down at the dying man.

"Yes," he said. "We won fairly easily. It was a good game."

---

1. **Everest:** Mount Everest, the highest mountain in the world, located in the Himalayan mountain range between Nepal and Tibet.
2. **pour libations** [lī bā′shənz]: Jackie is referring to an ancient Greek ritual in which a victorious warrior poured wine onto the ground as an offering of thanks to the gods.

**136** *The Short Story*

Indirect characterization (p. 39): *Dialogue* reveals character traits of Jackie and Barry.

Exposition (p. 20): The story so far has presented information about Barry. We now learn an important fact about his family.

Setting (p. 68): The change of setting from outdoors to the sickroom changes the story's *atmosphere*.

## GUIDED READING

### LITERAL QUESTION

**1a.** How does Barry react to his father's question? (His compassion almost "unmans" him.)

### INFERENTIAL QUESTION

**1b.** What does this response reveal about Barry? (His feelings about his father override his feelings of triumph.)

His father lay with his eyes closed, inert, his breath irregular and shallow.

"Did you score?" he asked.

"Twice," Barry said. "I had a try in each half."

He thought of the easy certainty with which he'd caught the ball before his second try; casually, almost arrogantly he had taken it on the tips of his fingers, on his full burst for the line, breaking the full-back's tackle. Nobody could have stopped him. But watching his father's weakness he felt humble and ashamed, as if the morning's game, its urgency and effort, was not worth talking about. His father's face, fine-skinned and pallid, carried a dark stubble of beard, almost a week's growth, and his obstinate, strong hair stuck out over his brow.

"Good," said his father, after a long pause. "I'm glad it was a good game."

Barry's mother bustled about the kitchen, a tempest of orderly energy.

"Your father's not well," she said. "He's down today, feels depressed. He's a particular man, your father. He feels dirty with all that beard on him."

Barry filled a glass with milk from the refrigerator. He was very thirsty.

"I'll shave him," he said.

His mother stopped, her head on one side.

"Do you think you can?" she asked. "He'd like it if you can."

"I can do it," Barry said.

He washed his hands as carefully as a surgeon. His father's razor was in a blue leather case, hinged at the broad edge and with one hinge broken. Barry unfastened the clasp and took out the razor. It had not been properly cleaned after its last use and lather had stiffened into hard yellow rectangles between the teeth of the guard. There were water-shaped rust stains, brown as chocolate, on the surface of the blade. Barry removed it, throwing it in the wastebin. He washed the razor until it glistened, and dried it on a soft towel, polishing the thin handle, rubbing its metal head to a glittering shine. He took a new blade from its waxed envelope, the paper clinging to the thin metal. The blade was smooth and flexible to the touch, the little angles of its cutting clearly defined. Barry slotted it into the grip of the razor, making it snug and tight in the head.

The shaving soap, hard, white, richly aromatic, was kept in a wooden bowl. Its scent was immediately evocative and Barry could almost see his father in the days of his health, standing before his mirror, thick white lather on his face and neck. As a little boy Barry had loved the generous perfume of the soap, had waited for his father to

Round character (p. 44): Barry's character is complicated by the *internal conflict* he feels.

Narrative hook (p. 20): Because of the story's *title*, we expect that Barry's shaving of his father will make up the main action.

Rising action (p. 20): Barry prepares to shave his father. Attention to these small acts and objects builds *suspense*.

*Shaving* 137

AT A GLANCE

■ Humbled by his father's losing struggle with death, Barry says little about his own victory.

■ Hoping to lift his father's depression, Barry makes elaborate preparations to shave him.

## GUIDED READING

### LITERAL QUESTIONS

**1a.** How are Barry's father's face and hair described? (His face is pallid, fine-skinned; his hair is obstinate and strong.)

**2a.** What does Barry first do with the razor? (He washes, dries, and polishes it.)

### INFERENTIAL QUESTIONS

**1b.** How does this combination of weakness and strength represent Barry's view of his father? (He remembers his strength, sees his sensitivity and weakness.)

**2b.** Why do you think Barry prepares so carefully? (He knows that he is to perform an important adult ritual; also, since his father is "particular," he will appreciate the care Barry is taking.)

Remembering his father's meticulous shaving ritual, Barry scours the shaving cup that is older than he is.

lift the razor to his face, for one careful stroke to take away the white suds in a clean revelation of the skin. Then his father would renew the lather with a few sweeps of his brush, one with an ivory handle and the bristles worn, which he still used.

His father's shaving mug was a thick cup, plain and serviceable. A gold line ran outside the rim of the cup, another inside, just below the lip. Its handle was large and sturdy, and the face of the mug carried a portrait of the young Queen Elizabeth II,[3] circled by a wreath of leaves, oak perhaps, or laurel. A lion and unicorn[4] balanced precariously above her crowned head, and the Union Jack,[5] the Royal Standard,[6] and other flags were furled each side of the portrait. And beneath it all, in small black letters, ran the legend: "Coronation June 2nd 1953." The cup was much older than Barry. A pattern of faint translucent cracks, fine as a web, had worked itself haphazardly, invisibly almost, through the white glaze. Inside, on the bottom, a few dark bristles were lying, loose and dry. Barry shook them out, then held the cup in his hand, feeling its solidness. Then he washed it ferociously, until it was clinically clean.

Symbol (p. 114): The special connection to the past gives the shaving cup *symbolic meaning.*

3. **Queen Elizabeth II** (born 1926): Queen of Great Britain since 1953.
4. **lion and unicorn:** These animals are shown on the Royal Arms, the emblem of the British monarchy.
5. **Union Jack:** national flag of Great Britain.
6. **Royal Standard:** flag of British royalty.

**138** *The Short Story*

## GUIDED READING

### LITERAL QUESTIONS

**1a.** What does Barry recall about his father's shaving? (the clean revelation of skin)

**2a.** Besides ornaments, what is on the glaze? (a haphazard pattern of faint cracks)

### INFERENTIAL QUESTIONS

**1b.** How might this memory relate to his present feelings? (He hopes to renew his father, perhaps to stroke away illness as easily as beard.)

**2b.** Why, given his father's health, might Barry notice these cracks? (They are signs of age and dwindling strength, haphazard like fate.)

Methodically he set everything on a tray, razor, soap, brush, towels. Testing the hot water with a finger, he filled the mug and put that, too, on the tray. His care was absorbed, ritualistic. Satisfied that his preparations were complete, he went downstairs, carrying the tray with one hand.

His father was waiting for him. Barry set the tray on a bedside table and bent over his father, sliding an arm under the man's thin shoulders, lifting him without effort so that he sat against the high pillows.

"By God, you're strong," his father said. He was as breathless as if he'd been running.

"So are you," said Barry.

"I was," his father said. "I used to be strong once."

He sat exhausted against the pillows.

"We'll wait a bit," Barry said.

"You could have used your electric razor," his father said. "I expected that."

"You wouldn't like it," Barry said. "You'll get a closer shave this way."

He placed the large towel about his father's shoulders.

"Now," he said, smiling down.

The water was hot in the thick cup. Barry wet the brush and worked up the lather. Gently he built up a covering of soft foam on the man's chin, on his cheeks and his stark cheekbones.

"You're using a lot of soap," his father said.

"Not too much," Barry said. "You've got a lot of beard."

His father lay there quietly, his wasted arms at his sides.

"It's comforting," he said. "You'd be surprised how comforting it is."

Barry took up the razor, weighing it in his hand, rehearsing the angle at which he'd use it. He felt confident.

"If you have prayers to say..." he said.

"I've said a lot of prayers," his father answered.

Barry leaned over and placed the razor delicately against his father's face, setting the head accurately on the clean line near the ear where the long hair ended. He held the razor in the tips of his fingers and drew the blade sweetly through the lather. The new edge moved light as a touch over the hardness of the upper jaw and down to the angle of the chin, sliding away the bristles so easily that Barry could not feel their release. He sighed as he shook the razor in the hot water, washing away the soap.

"How's it going?" his father asked.

"No problem," Barry said. "You needn't worry."

It was as if he had never known what his father really looked like.

Verbal irony (p. 133): The father's reference to praying—different from Barry's light joke—emphasizes the seriousness of the situation.

*Shaving* 139

AT A GLANCE

- Barry carefully arranges the shaving tools and assures his father that the customary method presents no problem.
- The shaving progresses smoothly.

## GUIDED READING

### LITERAL QUESTION

**1a.** How does Barry's father expect to be shaved? (with an electric shaver)

**2a.** What does Barry do as he takes up the razor? (rehearses how he will hold it)

### INFERENTIAL QUESTION

**1b.** What does Barry's choice of the razor suggest about him? (He is caring, painstaking, and sensitive to his father's needs.)

**2b.** What might Barry be thinking and feeling as he performs this adult shaving ritual? (He may be affirming his confidence in his abilities. He may also perceive the action as comforting to his father.)

- As Barry rediscovers his father's face, he feels protective love.
- His father recognizes Barry's strength and competence and hands his authority to Barry.
- Barry cleans and puts away the shaving tools.

He was discovering under his hands the clear bones of the face and head, they became sharp and recognizable under his fingers. When he moved his father's face a gentle inch to one side, he touched with his fingers the frail temples, the blue veins of his father's life. With infinite and meticulous care he took away the hair from his father's face.

"Now for your neck," he said. "We might as well do the job properly."

"You've got good hands," his father said. "You can trust those hands, they won't let you down."

Barry cradled his father's head in the crook of his left arm, so that the man could tilt back his head, exposing the throat. He brushed fresh lather under the chin and into the hollows alongside the stretched tendons. His father's throat was fleshless and vulnerable, his head was a hard weight on the boy's arm. Barry was filled with unreasoning protective love. He lifted the razor and began to shave.

"You don't have to worry," he said. "Not at all. Not about anything."

He held his father in the bend of his strong arm and they looked at each other. Their heads were very close.

"How old are you?" his father said.

"Seventeen," Barry said. "Near enough seventeen."

"You're young," his father said, "to have this happen."

"Not too young," Barry said. "I'm bigger than most men."

"I think you are," his father said.

He leaned his head tiredly against the boy's shoulder. He was without strength, his face was cold and smooth. He had let go all his authority, handed it over. He lay back on his pillow, knowing his weakness and his mortality, and looked at his son with wonder, with a curious humble pride.

"I won't worry then," he said. "About anything."

"There's no need," Barry said. "Why should you worry?"

He wiped his father's face clean of all soap with a damp towel. The smell of illness was everywhere, overpowering even the perfumed lather. Barry settled his father down and took away the shaving tools, putting them by with the same ceremonial precision with which he'd prepared them: the cleaned and glittering razor in its broken case; the soap, its bowl wiped and dried, on the shelf between the brush and the coronation mug; all free of taint. He washed his hands and scrubbed his nails. His hands were firm and broad, pink after their scrubbing. The fingers were short and strong, the little fingers slightly crooked, and soft dark hair grew on the backs of his hands and his fingers just above the knuckles. Not long ago they had been small bare hands, not very long ago.

**140**   *The Short Story*

**Tone** (p. 82). *Cradled, vulnerable,* and *unreasoning protective love* express the author's *attitude* toward Barry, his father, and the act of shaving.

**Climax** (p. 20): The climax points toward the resolution of the story's *conflicts*.

**Falling action** (p. 20): As Barry puts away the instruments, the story winds to a close.

**Theme** (p. 98): This reference to Barry's childhood underlines his recognition of how he has changed.

## GUIDED READING

### LITERAL QUESTIONS

**1a.** What does Barry do before shaving his father's neck? (cradles his head in his arm)

**2a.** What is Barry's reply to "You're young to have this happen"? ("Not too young, I'm bigger than most men.")

### INFERENTIAL QUESTIONS

**1b.** What change does this mark in the father-son relationship? (Barry is now the protective, parental figure. The father is the trusting, dependent child figure.)

**2b.** What does the father's reply "I think you are" mean? (He means that Barry, catapulted into adult responsibilities, is stronger and more compassionate than many adults.)

Barry opened wide the bathroom window. Already, although it was not yet two o'clock, the sun was retreating and people were moving briskly, wrapped in their heavy coats against the cold that was to come. But now the window was full in the beam of the dying sunlight, and Barry stood there, illuminated in its golden warmth for a whole minute, knowing it would soon be gone.

---

## STUDY QUESTIONS

### Recalling

1. In the beginning of the story, what do we learn about Barry's appearance and athletic skill? What do we learn about his father's health?

2. Why does Barry shave his father? List Barry's various preparations for this act.

3. Retell the conversation Barry has with his father while shaving him. What does Barry's father say at the end of their talk?

4. According to the narrator, what has Barry's father "handed over"? What does Barry do when he leaves his father's room?

### Interpreting

5. Why do you think Barry cleans the shaving instruments after the shaving until they are "free of taint"?

6. What may the cracked shaving cup and the setting sun each symbolize?

7. Why do you think the story points several times to the difference between Barry as a child and Barry at present? In what various ways is Barry now "bigger than most men"?

8. At the beginning of the story, Barry and his father each know that the older man is dying. What further understanding does each come to as Barry shaves his father?

### Extending

9. Explain why trivial actions or words sometimes help us to see important changes in our lives, as the shaving incident does for Barry and his father in this story.

## VIEWPOINT

Many of Leslie Norris' stories focus on people at crucial moments in their lives. As one writer said about another Norris story:

Norris compresses the turning points of a lifetime into his story beautifully.
— M. Levin, *New York Times*

■ What does a single brief encounter in "Shaving" reveal about the changes that are occurring in Barry's life as a result of his father's illness? Do you think the story would have been more effective if it had shown Barry and his father in several different situations?

## COMPOSITION

### Writing About the Total Effect

■ Discuss the total effect of "Shaving." Begin by describing the story's overall impact on you. Then explain how Norris uses plot, character, setting, point of view and tone, theme, symbol, and irony to create that overall effect. *For help with this assignment, see Lesson 12 in the Writing About Literature Handbook at the back of this book.*

### Describing a Process

■ Describe a familiar process such as running a race, making a shelf, washing a car, or frying an egg. First describe your preparations, including your materials. Then describe the process step by step. Be sure to use concrete sensory details to make the description as vivid as possible.

*Shaving* **141**

AT A GLANCE

■ In the bathroom Barry stands in golden sunlight, knowing that it will soon be gone.

REFLECTING ON THE STORY

In what way is Barry's shaving his father both a beginning and an end? (It represents the end of Barry's childhood and foreshadows the end of his father's life. It signifies the beginning of adulthood for Barry.)

STUDY QUESTIONS

1. tall, strong, successful; is seriously ill
2. ■ He's ill.
   ■ cleans razor; gets soap and mug; places items on tray
3. talk about son's strength, joke; won't worry about anything
4. his authority; washed instruments and stood in the setting sun's light
5. attempt to stave off death
6. cup: father's life; sun: end of son's youth
7. shows transition into manhood; accepts father's mortality
8. Father sees his son's maturity; son acknowledges his love of his father.
9. They catch us off guard; enable us to be affected.

VIEWPOINT

a son assuming a parent's role; no, would have lessened impact

---

## COMPOSITION: GUIDELINES FOR EVALUATION

### WRITING ABOUT TOTAL EFFECT

**Objective**

To demonstrate how literary elements create total effect

**Guidelines for Evaluation**

■ suggested length: five to ten paragraphs
■ should express writer's reaction
■ should explain how plot, character, setting, point of view, tone, theme, symbol, irony add up to a general feeling about the story

### DESCRIBING A PROCESS

**Objective**

To describe a familiar process in vivid detail

**Guidelines for Evaluation**

■ suggested length: one to three paragraphs
■ should identify the process
■ should describe preparations and materials
■ should describe each step of the process

Ambrose Bierce (1842–1914) served with the Union, or Northern, army during the Civil War and earned many citations for bravery in battle. His experience in the war was reflected in a number of his short stories. Like ''An Occurrence at Owl Creek Bridge,'' Bierce's most famous story, many of these stories capture the emotional intensity of people exposed to mortal danger.

■ Has a bad dream ever seemed real to you, even when you awakened?

*Ambrose Bierce*

# An Occurrence at Owl Creek Bridge

## I

A man stood upon a railroad bridge in northern Alabama, looking down into the swift water twenty feet below. The man's hands were behind his back, the wrists bound with a cord. A rope loosely encircled his neck. It was attached to a stout cross-timber above his head, and the slack fell to the level of his knees. Some loose boards laid upon the sleepers[1] supporting the metals of the railway supplied a footing for him and his executioners—two private soldiers of the Federal army,[2] directed by a sergeant who in civil life may have been a deputy sheriff. At a short remove upon the same temporary platform was an officer in the uniform of his rank, armed. He was a captain. A sentinel at each end of the bridge stood with his rifle in the position known as ''support,'' that is to say, vertical in front of the left shoulder, the hammer resting on the forearm thrown straight across the chest—a formal and unnatural position, enforcing an erect carriage of the body. It did not appear to be the duty of these two men to know what was occurring at the center of the bridge; they merely blockaded the two ends of the foot plank which traversed it.

Beyond one of the sentinels, nobody was in sight; the railroad ran straight away into a forest for a hundred yards, then, curving, was lost to view. Doubtless there was an outpost farther along. The other bank of the stream was open ground—a gentle acclivity topped with a stockade of vertical tree trunks, loopholed for rifles, with a single embrasure through which protruded the muzzle of a brass cannon commanding the bridge. Midway of the slope between bridge and fort were the spectators—a single company of infantry in line, at ''parade rest,'' the butts of the rifles on the ground, the barrels inclining slightly backward against the right shoulder, the hands crossed upon the stock. A lieutenant stood at the right of the line, the point of his sword upon the ground, his left hand resting upon his right. Excepting the group of four at the center of the bridge, not a man moved. The company faced the bridge, staring stonily,

---
1. **sleepers:** railroad ties.
2. **Federal army:** Union army of the North.

142   *The Short Story*

motionless. The sentinels, facing the banks of the stream, might have been statues to adorn the bridge. The captain stood with folded arms, silent, observing the work of his subordinates, but making no sign. Death is a dignitary who when he comes announced is to be received with formal manifestations of respect, even by those most familiar with him. In the code of military etiquette silence and fixity are forms of deference.

The man who was engaged in being hanged was apparently about thirty-five years of age. He was a civilian, if one might judge from his habit, which was that of a planter. His features were good—a straight nose, firm mouth, broad forehead, from which his long, dark hair was combed straight back, falling behind his ears to the collar of his well-fitting frock coat. He wore a mustache and pointed beard, but no whiskers; his eyes were large and dark gray, and had a kindly expression which one would hardly have expected in one whose neck was in the hemp.[3] Evidently this was no vulgar assassin. The liberal military code makes provision for hanging many kinds of persons, and gentlemen are not excluded.

The preparations being complete, the two private soldiers stepped aside and each drew away the plank upon which he had been standing. The sergeant turned to the captain, saluted, and placed himself immediately behind that officer, who in turn moved apart one pace. These movements left the condemned man and the sergeant standing on the two ends of the same plank, which spanned three of the crossties of the bridge. The end upon which the civilian stood almost, but not quite, reached a fourth. This plank had been held in place by the weight of the captain; it was now held by that of the sergeant. At a signal from the former, the latter would step aside, the plank would tilt, and the condemned man go down between two ties. The

_____
3. **hemp:** noose; hemp is a fiber from which rope is made.

3 arrangement commended itself to his judgment as simple and effective. His face had not been covered nor his eyes bandaged. He looked a moment at his "unsteadfast footing," then let his gaze wander to the swirling water of the stream racing madly beneath his feet. A piece of dancing driftwood caught his attention and his eyes followed it down the current. How slowly it appeared to move! What a sluggish stream!

He closed his eyes in order to fix his last thoughts upon his wife and children. The water, touched to gold by the early sun, the brooding mists under the banks at some distance down the stream, the fort, the soldiers, the piece of drift— all had distracted him. And now he became conscious of a new disturbance. Striking through the thought of his dear ones was a sound which he could neither ignore nor understand, a sharp, distinct, metallic percussion like the stroke of a blacksmith's hammer upon the anvil; it had the same ringing quality. He wondered what it was, and whether immeasurably distant or near by—it seemed both. Its recurrence was regular, but as slow as the tolling of a death knell. He awaited each stroke with impatience and—he knew not why—apprehension. The intervals of 4 silence grew progressively longer; the delays became maddening. With their greater infrequency the sounds increased in strength and sharpness. They hurt his ear like the thrust of a knife; he feared he would shriek. What he heard was the ticking of his watch.

He unclosed his eyes and saw again the water below him. "If I could free my hands," he thought, "I might throw off the noose and spring 5 into the stream. By diving I could evade the bullets and, swimming vigorously, reach the bank, take to the woods, and get away home. My home, thank God, is as yet outside their lines; my wife and little ones are still beyond the invader's farthest advance."

As these thoughts, which have here to be set down in words, were flashed into the doomed

*An Occurrence at Owl Creek Bridge* **143**

## AT A GLANCE

- The prisoner, a thirty-five-year-old planter, awaits death.
- He thinks of his family and of escape.

### 1 PLOT: FORESHADOWING

The details of the scene culminate in the introduction of death, the story's prime antagonist.

### 2 TOTAL EFFECT

Bierce uses the third-person point of view like a camera, first giving a wide-angle sweep of the scene, then zooming in to a closeup of the protagonist, who is an unlikely criminal.

### 3 POINT OF VIEW

The point of view shifts from objective to limited third-person when it focuses on the prisoner's perceptions.

### 4 ATMOSPHERE

His tension is so great that the ticking of a watch hammers like an anvil in the ear of the prisoner.

### 5 THEME

Although death seems certain, the prisoner does not accept it and plots survival.

## GUIDED READING

**LITERAL QUESTIONS**

**1a.** How does Bierce ironically describe the military code's "provision for hanging"? (It is liberal, because gentlemen are not exempt.)

**2a.** Why does the prisoner close his eyes? (to focus his last thoughts on his family)

**INFERENTIAL QUESTIONS**

**1b.** In what way might death be compared to this code? (No distinctions of class, or otherwise, exempt one from death.)

**2b.** What does this detail tell us about him? (His family is most important to him.)

- The army sergeant steps off the plank.
- The planter is a Southerner determined to help the Confederate cause.
- He learns of a Union stockade at Owl Creek Bridge.
- Anyone caught interfering with railroads or railroad bridges will be hanged by the Union Army.

**1 READING SKILLS: SEQUENCE OF EVENTS**

Out of chronological order, Part II flashes back to a time before the events depicted in Part I. The setting is Farquhar's plantation home.

**2 PLOT: EXPOSITION**

We learn why Peyton is to hang: He attacked the bridge in order to share in the excitement of war—from which he had felt excluded.

**3 CHARACTERIZATION**

Peyton is humorous and courageous, and believes himself able to assess a military situation quickly.

*Films Incorporated, from An Occurrence at Owl Creek Bridge by Ambrose B[...]*

man's brain rather than evolved from it, the captain nodded to the sergeant. The sergeant stepped aside.

## II

Peyton Farquhar[4] was a well-to-do planter of an old and highly respected Alabama family. Being a slave owner and like other slave owners a politician, he was naturally an original secessionist[5] and ardently devoted to the Southern cause. Circumstances of an imperious nature, which it is unnecessary to relate here, had prevented him from taking service with the gallant army which had fought the disastrous campaigns ending with the fall of Corinth,[6] and he chafed under the inglorious restraint, longing for the release of his energies, the larger life of the soldier, the opportunity for distinction. That opportunity, he felt, would come, as it comes to all in war time. Meanwhile he did what he could. No service was too humble for him to perform in aid of the South, no adventure too perilous for

---

4. **Peyton Farquhar** [pā′tən fär′kwər]
5. **secessionist:** supporter of the secession, or separation, of the Southern states from the Union.
6. **fall of Corinth:** defeat of the Confederate army near Corinth, Mississippi, in 1862.

**144** *The Short Story*

---

him to undertake if consistent with the character of a civilian who was at heart a soldier, and who in good faith and without too much qualification assented to at least a part of the frankly villainous dictum that all is fair in love and war.

One evening while Farquhar and his wife were sitting on a rustic bench near the entrance to his grounds, a gray-clad soldier rode up to the gate and asked for a drink of water. Mrs. Farquhar was only too happy to serve him with her own white hands. While she was fetching the water her husband approached the dusty horseman and inquired eagerly for news from the front.

"The Yanks are repairing the railroads," said the man, "and are getting ready for another advance. They have reached the Owl Creek bridge, put it in order, and built a stockade on the north bank. The commandant has issued an order, which is posted everywhere, declaring that any civilian caught interfering with the railroad, its bridges, tunnels, or trains will be summarily hanged. I saw the order."

"How far is it to the Owl Creek bridge?" Farquhar asked.

"About thirty miles."

"Is there no force on this side the creek?"

"Only a picket post[7] half a mile out, on the railroad, and a single sentinel at this end of the bridge."

"Suppose a man—a civilian and student of hanging—should elude the picket post and perhaps get the better of the sentinel," said Farquhar, smiling, "what could he accomplish?"

The soldier reflected. "I was there a month ago," he replied. "I observed that the flood of last winter had lodged a great quantity of driftwood against the wooden pier at this end of the bridge. It is now dry and would burn like tow."

The lady had now brought the water, which the soldier drank. He thanked her ceremonious-

---

7. **picket post:** group of soldiers stationed outside a camp to guard the army from a surprise attack.

---

## GUIDED READING

**LITERAL QUESTIONS**

**1a.** What are Peyton's politics in this war? (He is a secessionist.)

**2a.** What does the soldier say could be accomplished at the bridge? (Because both the wooden supports of the bridge and some driftwood lodged against them are very dry, the bridge would burn easily.)

**INFERENTIAL QUESTIONS**

**1b.** How would you expect him to feel about the Union troops? (He would want to try to thwart them in some way.)

**2b.** What can you infer about why Peyton is to be hanged? (He went to the bridge, thirty miles away, and was captured while trying to burn it.)

ly, bowed to her husband, and rode away. An hour later, after nightfall, he repassed the plantation, going northward in the direction from which he had come. He was a Federal scout.[8]

### III

As Peyton Farquhar fell straight downward through the bridge he lost consciousness and was as one already dead. From this state he was awakened—ages later, it seemed to him—by the pain of a sharp pressure upon his throat, followed by a sense of suffocation. Keen, poignant agonies seemed to shoot from his neck downward through every fiber of his body and limbs. These pains appeared to flash along well-defined lines of ramification and to beat with an inconceivably rapid periodicity. They seemed like streams of pulsating fire heating him to an intolerable temperature. As to his head, he was conscious of nothing but a feeling of fullness—of congestion. These sensations were unaccompanied by thought. The intellectual part of his nature was already effaced; he had power only to feel, and feeling was torment. He was conscious of motion. Encompassed in a luminous cloud, of which he was now merely the fiery heart, without material substance, he swung through unthinkable arcs of oscillation, like a vast pendulum. Then all at once, with terrible suddenness, the light about him shot upward with the noise of a loud plash; a frightful roaring was in his ears, and all was cold and dark. The power of thought was restored; he knew that the rope had broken and he had fallen into the stream. There was no additional strangulation; the noose about his neck was already suffocating him and kept the water from his lungs. To die of hanging at the bottom of a river!—the idea seemed to him ludicrous. He opened his eyes in the darkness and saw above him a gleam of light, but how distant, how inaccessible! He was still sinking, for

8. **Federal scout:** a spy for the Union army of the North.

the light became fainter and fainter until it was a mere glimmer. Then it began to grow and brighten, and he knew that he was rising toward the surface—knew it with reluctance, for he was now very comfortable. "To be hanged and drowned," he thought, "that is not so bad; but I do not wish to be shot. No; I will not be shot; that is not fair."

He was not conscious of an effort, but a sharp pain in his wrist apprised him that he was trying to free his hands. He gave the struggle his attention, as an idler might observe the feat of a juggler, without interest in the outcome. What splendid effort!—what magnificent, what superhuman strength! Ah, that was a fine endeavor! Bravo! The cord fell away; his arms parted and floated upward, the hands dimly seen on each side in the growing light. He watched them with a new interest as first one and then the other pounced upon the noose at his neck. They tore it away and thrust it fiercely aside, its undulations resembling those of a water snake. "Put it back, put it back!" He thought he shouted these words to his hands, for the undoing of the noose had been succeeded by the direst pang that he had yet experienced. His neck ached horribly; his brain was on fire; his heart, which had been fluttering faintly, gave a great leap, trying to force itself out at his mouth. His whole body was racked and wrenched with an insupportable anguish! But his disobedient hands gave no heed to the command. They beat the water vigorously with quick, downward strokes, forcing him to the surface. He felt his head emerge; his eyes were blinded by the sunlight; his chest expanded convulsively, and with a supreme and crowning agony his lungs engulfed a great draught of air, which instantly he expelled in a shriek!

He was now in full possession of his physical senses. They were, indeed, preternaturally keen and alert. Something in the awful disturbance of his organic system had so exalted and refined them that they made record of things never before perceived. He felt the ripples upon his face

*An Occurrence at Owl Creek Bridge* **145**

- Peyton is tricked by a Federal scout.
- The scene shifts to the bridge where Peyton is hanged.
- He regains consciousness in the stream.
- He tears off his bonds and surfaces.

**1 POINT OF VIEW**

Bierce uses the omniscient point of view to inform the reader that Peyton has been duped: His visitor was actually a Union spy.

**2 POINT OF VIEW**

Here, the point of view again shifts from omniscient to limited third-person narration, which intensifies our awareness of Peyton's thoughts and emotions.

**3 TOTAL EFFECT**

Most of the action occurs in Part III of the story. Having expected Peyton to die, we are startled and thrilled by the possibility that he may survive.

**4 THEME**

Peyton's struggle to survive is so instinctive that, initially, he is not even aware of it.

**5 PLOT: CONFLICT**

Peyton's mind seeks death as a release from pain, but his body instinctively struggles toward painful life.

---

## GUIDED READING

### LITERAL QUESTION

**1a.** How are Peyton's senses described, when he rises out of the water? (They are "preternaturally keen and alert.")

### INFERENTIAL QUESTION

**1b.** In addition to "something in the awful disturbance of his organic system," what could have caused Peyton's heightened awareness? (danger and the fear of death)

**1 DETAILS**

Peyton's heightened perceptions seem to allow him to see the world in microscopic detail.

**2 STYLE: REPETITION**

The preparations for a shooting echo the cold, military formality of the preparations for hanging.

**3 TOTAL EFFECT**

As in a dream, objects are distorted and move in slow motion.

---

and heard their separate sounds as they struck. He looked at the forest on the bank of the stream, saw the individual trees, the leaves and the veining of each leaf—saw the very insects upon them: the locusts, the brilliant-bodied flies, the gray spiders stretching their webs from twig to twig. He noted the prismatic colors in all the dewdrops upon a million blades of grass. The humming of the gnats that danced above the eddies of the stream, the beating of the dragonflies' wings, the strokes of the water spiders' legs, like oars which had lifted their boat—all these made audible music. A fish slid along beneath his eyes and he heard the rush of its body parting the water.

He had come to the surface facing down the stream; in a moment the visible world seemed to wheel slowly round, himself the pivotal point, and he saw the bridge, the fort, the soldiers upon the bridge, the captain, the sergeant, the two privates, his executioners. They were in silhouette against the blue sky. They shouted and gesticulated, pointing at him. The captain had drawn his pistol, but did not fire; the others were unarmed. Their movements were grotesque and horrible, their forms gigantic.

Suddenly he heard a sharp report and something struck the water smartly within a few inches of his head, spattering his face with spray. He heard a second report, and saw one of the sentinels with his rifle at his shoulder, a light cloud of blue smoke rising from the muzzle. The man in the water saw the eye of the man on the bridge gazing into his own through the sights of the rifle. He observed that it was a gray eye and remembered having read that gray eyes were keenest, and that all famous marksmen had them. Nevertheless, this one had missed.

A counterswirl had caught Farquhar and turned him half round; he was again looking into the forest on the bank opposite the fort. The sound of a clear, high voice in a monotonous singsong now rang out behind him and came across the

water with a distinctness that pierced and subdued all other sounds, even the beating of the ripples in his ears. Although no soldier, he had frequented camps enough to know the dread significance of that deliberate, drawling, aspirated chant; the lieutenant on shore was taking a part in the morning's work. How coldly and pitilessly—with what an even, calm intonation, presaging and enforcing tranquillity in the men—with what accurately measured intervals fell those cruel words:

"Attention, company!...Shoulder arms!... Ready!...Aim!...Fire!"

Farquhar dived—dived as deeply as he could. The water roared in his ears like the voice of Niagara,[9] yet he heard the dulled thunder of the volley and, rising again toward the surface, met shining bits of metal, singularly flattened, oscillating slowly downward. Some of them touched him on the face and hands, then fell away, continuing their descent. One lodged between his collar and neck; it was uncomfortably warm and he snatched it out.

As he rose to the surface, gasping for breath, he saw that he had been a long time under water; he was perceptibly farther downstream—nearer to safety. The soldiers had almost finished reloading; the metal ramrods flashed all at once in the sunshine as they were drawn from the barrels, turned in the air, and thrust into their sockets. The two sentinels fired again, independently and ineffectually.

The hunted man saw all this over his shoulder; he was now swimming vigorously with the current. His brain was as energetic as his arms and legs; he thought with the rapidity of lightning.

"The officer," he reasoned, "will not make that martinet's error[10] a second time. It is as easy

---

9. **Niagara:** a great flood. Niagara Falls is a large waterfall on the border between Canada and the United States.
10. **martinet's error:** error of a person in authority, usually in the military, who follows rules very strictly.

---

## GUIDED READING

**LITERAL QUESTION**

**1a.** When he first sees the soldiers, how do they and their movements look? (Their forms are gigantic; their movements, grotesque and horrible.)

**INFERENTIAL QUESTION**

**1b.** Why do they look this way? (Farquhar's perceptions are distorted.)

- A wave, caused by a cannon-ball splashing near him, washes him ashore.
- He travels all day through wilderness, then follows a wide road lighted by strange stars.

**1 PLOT: SUSPENSE**

Bierce keeps the reader in suspense by introducing a new life-threatening situation as soon as Peyton escapes from the previous one.

**2 CHARACTERIZATION**

Peyton, a civilian, prides himself on his military knowledge: He anticipates the army's tactics and assesses their weaponry.

**3 STYLE: IMAGERY**

Interwoven with realistic details of execution and manhunt, images of nature, unearthly light, and sound evoke the beauty of natural and spiritual worlds.

**4 SETTING**

Here, as throughout Part III, a scene of apparent serenity and beauty is revealed as menacing and dangerous.

---

to dodge a volley as a single shot. He has probably already given the command to fire at will. God help me, I cannot dodge them all!''

**1** An appalling plash within two yards of him was followed by a loud, rushing sound, *diminuendo,*[11] which seemed to travel back through the air to the fort and died in an explosion which stirred the very river to its deeps! A rising sheet of water, which curved over him, fell down upon him, blinded him, strangled him! The cannon had taken a hand in the game. As he shook his head free from the commotion of the smitten water, he heard the deflected shot humming through the air ahead, and in an instant it was cracking and smashing the branches in the forest beyond.

**2** ''They will not do that again,'' he thought; ''the next time they will use a charge of grape.[12] I must keep my eye upon the gun; the smoke will apprise me—the report arrives too late; it lags behind the missile. That is a good gun.''

Suddenly he felt himself whirled round and round—spinning like a top. The water, the banks, the forests, the now distant bridge, fort, and men—all were commingled and blurred. Objects were represented by their colors only; circular horizontal streaks of color—that was all he saw. He had been caught in a vortex and was being whirled on with a velocity of advance and gyration which made him giddy and sick. In a few moments he was flung upon the gravel at the foot of the left bank of the stream—the southern bank—and behind a projecting point which concealed him from his enemies. The sudden arrest of his motion, the abrasion of one of his hands on the gravel, restored him, and he wept with delight. He dug his fingers into the sand, threw it over himself in handfuls, and audibly blessed it. It looked like diamonds, rubies, emeralds; he could think of nothing beautiful which it did not

resemble. The trees upon the bank were giant garden plants; he noted a definite order in their arrangement, inhaled the fragrance of their **3** blooms. A strange, roseate light shone through the spaces among their trunks and the wind made in their branches the music of aeolian harps.[13] He had no wish to perfect his escape— was content to remain in that enchanting spot until retaken.

A whiz and rattle of grapeshot among the branches high above his head roused him from his dream. The baffled cannoneer had fired him a random farewell. He sprang to his feet, rushed up the sloping bank, and plunged into the forest.

All that day he traveled, laying his course by the rounding sun. The forest seemed interminable; nowhere did he discover a break in it, not even a woodman's road. He had not known that he lived in so wild a region. There was something uncanny in the revelation.

By nightfall he was fatigued, footsore, famishing. The thought of his wife and children urged him on. At last he found a road which led him in what he knew to be the right direction. It was as wide and straight as a city street, yet it seemed untraveled. No fields bordered it, no dwelling anywhere. Not so much as the barking of a dog suggested human habitation. The black bodies of the trees formed a straight wall on both sides, terminating on the horizon in a point, like a diagram in a lesson in perspective. Overhead, as **4** he looked up through this rift in the wood, shone great golden stars looking unfamiliar and grouped in strange constellations. He was sure they were arranged in some order which had a secret and malign significance. The wood on either side was full of singular noises, among which—once, twice, and again—he distinctly heard whispers in an unknown tongue.

His neck was in pain and lifting his hand to it

---

11. *diminuendo* [də min′ū en′dō]: gradually quieting.
12. **charge of grape:** cluster of grapeshot, or small iron pellets used for ammunition.

13. **aeolian** [ē ō′lē ən] **harps:** stringed musical instruments that produce harmonic chords when struck by the wind.

---

## GUIDED READING

**LITERAL QUESTION**

**1a.** What is unusual about the road he finds? (It is like a city street, but it is in a wilderness and untraveled.)

**INFERENTIAL QUESTION**

**1b.** How realistic do the details of the road and surrounding forest seem? (more dreamlike than real) he found it horribly swollen. He knew that it had a circle of black where the rope had bruised it. His eyes felt congested; he could no longer close them. His tongue was swollen with thirst; he relieved its fever by thrusting it forward from between his teeth into the cold air. How softly the turf had carpeted the untraveled avenue—he could no longer feel the roadway beneath his feet!

Doubtless, despite his suffering, he had fallen asleep while walking, for now he sees another scene—perhaps he has merely recovered from a delirium. He stands at the gate of his own home. All is as he left it, and all bright and beautiful in the morning sunshine. He must have traveled the entire night. As he pushes open the gate and passes up the wide white walk, he sees a flutter of female garments; his wife, looking fresh and cool and sweet, steps down from the veranda to meet him. At the bottom of the steps she stands waiting, with a smile of ineffable joy, an attitude of matchless grace and dignity. Ah, how beautiful she is! He springs forward with extended arms. As he is about to clasp her, he feels a stunning blow upon the back of the neck; a blinding white light blazes all about him with a sound like the shock of a cannon—then all is darkness and silence!

1    Peyton Farquhar was dead; his body, with a broken neck, swung gently from side to side beneath the timbers of the Owl Creek bridge.

---

## STUDY QUESTIONS

### Recalling

1. When and where does "An Occurrence at Owl Creek Bridge" take place? As it opens, what is happening on the bridge?
2. What do we learn in Part II of the story about Peyton Farquhar's personality and his background?
3. Briefly retell the events of Peyton's "escape" in Part III.
4. What happens to Peyton, according to the last sentence of the story?

### Interpreting

5. Use three or four details to show how Bierce creates suspense when Peyton Farquhar is standing on the bridge in Part I.
6. Did you suspect before you read the last sentence that Peyton was only imagining his escape? Why or why not?
7. What do you think the story might be saying about the relationship between the mind and reality?

### Extending

8. Why do you think people's perceptions are often intensified during crises?

## VIEWPOINT

Many of Ambrose Bierce's stories end with a surprising revelation, but as one writer has noted about "An Occurrence at Owl Creek Bridge":

> Withholding the information here is not trickery, but a logical, calculated end to shock the reader with the realization that he has been witnessing a life-and-death struggle of some poignancy. . . .
> — R. A. Wiggins, *Ambrose Bierce*

■ Explain how withholding the information about Peyton's death makes his struggle seem more poignant, or moving.

## LITERARY FOCUS

### Elements of the Short Story

Every story that we read weaves together a number of elements—plot, character, setting, point of view, theme, and sometimes irony and symbolism. In reading a story we enter the world of its setting and are caught up in its plot and characters. Our reactions to these events and people are governed by the tone of the narrator, and this tone usually indicates to us whether the meaning of the story goes

*An Occurrence at Owl Creek Bridge*  **149**

1. Part 2; It would have begun with the visit of the Union Spy. This more conventional order would be less effective, since we would not be as caught up in Peyton's fate.
2. ■ He is a soldier at heart; his personality motivates his actions.
   ■ perhaps
3. ■ Part 1: bridge, appropriate for hanging and "escape"
   ■ Part 2: Peyton's home, appropriate for background
   ■ Part 3: Peyton's mind, appropriate because of fantasized escape
4. ■ No
   ■ when Peyton hears the watch ticking
   ■ that the visitor is a spy; that Peyton is dead
5. ■ bridge: separation between life and death; situation: treachery of the imagination or the instinct for survival
6. ■ could also justify his death
   ■ Yes—it is unexpected.
7. ■ Imagination can create its own reality; life and death are a hairbreadth apart.

## VOCABULARY

1. fullness
2. destroyed
3. breath
4. mixed together
5. endless

---

beyond literal appearances to the levels of symbol and irony. The theme, the central idea of the story and the point that it makes about life, is the product of all the other elements of the story.

### Thinking About the Elements of the Short Story

1. **Plot:** If the plot of "An Occurrence at Owl Creek Bridge" had followed normal chronological order, which section would it have begun with? Do you think the story would be more effective if it had followed this order? Why or why not?
2. **Character:** What do we know about Peyton Farquhar's character? How important do you think his individual personality is in this story? Do you think the "events" of the story could have happened to anyone?
3. **Setting:** What is the setting of each section of the story? How is each setting appropriate to what is happening in each part?
4. **Point of View:** As the story opens, does the narrator seem to know anything about Peyton Farquhar? When does the narrator enter Peyton's mind? What does the narrator tell us that Peyton could not know?
5. **Symbolism:** What might the bridge in the story symbolize? Is Peyton Farquhar's situation symbolic in any way? Explain.
6. **Irony:** We learn that Peyton "assented to at least a part of that villainous dictum that all is fair in love and war." Explain the irony of this statement. Is the ending of the story ironic? Why or why not?
7. **Theme:** What does this story say about the power of the imagination? About the relationship between life and death?

## VOCABULARY

### Using Context Clues

You can often find clues to the meaning of an unfamiliar word from its **context,** the words that surround it. In the following example from "The Occurrence at Owl Creek Bridge," context clues help to clarify the meaning of the word *percussion*.

> Striking through the thought of his dear ones was a sound which he could neither ignore nor understand, a sharp, distinct, metallic *percussion* like the stroke of a blacksmith's hammer upon the anvil. . . .

The words around *percussion* tell us that the word refers to the sound of something beating rhythmically.

The following sentences all come from "An Occurrence at Owl Creek Bridge." Find the meaning of each of the *italicized* words in these sentences by studying its context. Check your answer in the Glossary at the back of the book or in a dictionary. Then use the word in a sentence of your own. Make sure that your use of the word corresponds to its use in the story.

1. As to his head, he was conscious of nothing but a feeling of fullness—of *congestion*.
2. The intellectual part of his nature was already *effaced*; he had power only to feel.
3. . . .his chest expanded convulsively, and with a supreme and crowning agony his lungs engulfed a great *draught* of air. . . .
4. Suddenly he felt himself whirled round and round . . . .The water, the banks, the forests, the now distant bridge, fort, and men—all were *commingled* and blurred.
5. The forest seemed *interminable*; nowhere did he discover a break in it, not even a woodman's road.

## COMPOSITION

### Writing About Suspense

■ Bierce builds the tension of "An Occurrence at Owl Creek Bridge" with a series of suspenseful situations. Find and describe two specific scenes that increase the tension in the story. First relate what happens to Peyton in each scene and his reactions to these events. Then explain why each scene is suspenseful and what each one adds to the story as a whole. Finally point out any clues that the events in the scene are taking place in Peyton's mind.

### Creating Suspense with Details

■ Write a short narrative of a vivid and suspenseful dream. Describe the dream with many realistic sensory details so that the reader shares in the dreamer's sensations, just as we share in Peyton Farquhar's feelings. The end of the narrative should reveal that everything happened in a dream.

---

## COMPOSITION: GUIDELINES FOR EVALUATION

### WRITING ABOUT SUSPENSE

**Objective**

To analyze how suspense is created through specific scenes in story

**Guidelines for Evaluation**

■ suggested length: three to five paragraphs
■ should cite two scenes that heighten story's tension
■ should explain why the scenes are suspenseful
■ should note clues that suggest the events are imaginary

### CREATING SUSPENSE WITH DETAILS

**Objective**

To relate a dream with realistic sensory details

**Guidelines for Evaluation**

■ suggested length: two to four paragraphs
■ should contain realistic sensory details that create suspense
■ should use the first-person point of view
■ should reveal that the narrative was a dream

Born in Germany, Nobel Prize–winning novelist Heinrich Böll (1917–1985) began his writing career after the end of World War II. Many of his novels and short stories treat seriously the problems of postwar German society. However, occasionally, as in "The Laugher," his work presents a somewhat lighter view of modern life.

■ Can a person laugh or cry or express some other strong emotion without feeling anything inside?

*Heinrich Böll*

# The Laugher

When someone asks me what business I am in, I am seized with embarrassment: I blush and stammer, I who am otherwise known as a man of poise. I envy people who can say: I am a bricklayer. I envy barbers, bookkeepers and writers the simplicity of their avowal, for all these professions speak for themselves and need no lengthy explanation, which I am constrained to reply to such questions: I am a laugher. An admission of this kind demands another, since I have to answer the second question: "Is that how you make your living?" truthfully with "Yes." I actually do make a living at my laughing, and a good one too, for my laughing is—commercially speaking—much in demand. I am a good laugher, experienced, no one else laughs as well as I do, no one else has such command of the fine points of my art. For a long time, in order to avoid tiresome explanations, I called myself an actor, but my talents in the field of mime and elocution are so meager that I felt this designation to be too far from the truth: I love the truth, and the truth is: I am a laugher. I am neither a clown nor a comedian. I do not make people gay, I portray gaiety: I laugh like a Roman emperor, or like a sensitive schoolboy, I am as much at home

2 in the laughter of the seventeenth century as in that of the nineteenth, and when occasion demands I laugh my way through all the centuries, all classes of society, all categories of age: it is simply a skill which I have acquired, like the skill of being able to repair shoes. In my breast I harbor the laughter of America, the laughter of Africa, white, red, yellow laughter—and for the right fee I let it peal out in accordance with the director's requirements.

I have become indispensable; I laugh on records, I laugh on tape, and television directors treat me with respect. I laugh mournfully, moderately, hysterically; I laugh like a streetcar conductor or like a helper in the grocery business; laughter in the morning, laughter in the evening, nocturnal laughter and the laughter of twilight. In short: wherever and however laughter is required—I do it.

It need hardly be pointed out that a profession of this kind is tiring, especially as I have also—this is my specialty—mastered the art of infectious laughter; this has also made me indispensable to third- and fourth-rate comedians, who are scared—and with good reason—that their audiences will miss their punch lines, so I spend

*The Laugher* **151**

## GUIDED READING

### LITERAL QUESTIONS

**1a.** What people does the narrator envy? (bricklayers, barbers, bookkeepers, writers)

**2a.** To whom is the narrator indispensable? (third- and fourth-rate comedians)

### INFERENTIAL QUESTIONS

**1b.** Why does he envy these people? (Their usefulness is apparent; his is not.)

**2b.** Why do you think he finds this part of his job "especially" tiring? (It is hard enough to laugh on cue, but to stimulate others to laugh is even more difficult.)

- In nightclubs he leads the laughs and saves comedy acts.
- Besieged by demands for his skills, he is too exhausted to laugh off duty.

## 1 POINT OF VIEW

The laugher does not see the humor of his situation. Throughout, the limitations of the first-person point of view achieve comic effect.

most evenings in night clubs as a kind of discreet claque,[1] my job being to laugh infectiously during the weaker parts of the program. It has to be carefully timed: my hearty, boisterous laughter must not come too soon, but neither must it come too late, it must come just at the right spot: at the prearranged moment I burst out laughing, the whole audience roars with me, and the joke is saved.

_____

1. **claque** [klak]: person or group hired to applaud or laugh at a performance.

**152**   *The Short Story*

1   But as for me, I drag myself exhausted to the checkroom, put on my overcoat, happy that I can go off duty at last. At home I usually find telegrams waiting for me: "Urgently require your laughter. Recording Tuesday," and a few hours later I am sitting in an overheated express train bemoaning my fate.

I need scarcely say that when I am off duty or on vacation I have little inclination to laugh: the cowhand is glad when he can forget the cow, the bricklayer when he can forget the mortar, and carpenters usually  have doors at home which

## GUIDED READING

### LITERAL QUESTION

**1a.** What is "urgently required" of the narrator, according to the telegram? (his laughter)

### INFERENTIAL QUESTION

**1b.** Why might such telegrams make the narrator "bemoan" his fate? (He is weary of having to laugh on demand.)

don't work or drawers which are hard to open. Confectioners[2] like sour pickles, butchers like marzipan,[3] and the baker prefers sausage to bread; bullfighters raise pigeons for a hobby, boxers turn pale when their children have nosebleeds: I find all this quite natural, for I never laugh off duty. I am a very solemn person, and people consider me—perhaps rightly so—a pessimist.

During the first years of our married life, my wife would often say to me: "Do laugh!" but since then she has come to realize that I cannot grant her this wish. I am happy when I am free to relax my tense face muscles, my frayed spirit, in

---

2. **Confectioners:** those who make pastries, candies, or other sweets.
3. **marzipan** [mär′zə pan′]: sweet dessert made of almond paste, sugar, and egg whites.

profound solemnity. Indeed, even other people's laughter gets on my nerves, since it reminds me too much of my profession. So our marriage is a quiet, peaceful one, because my wife has also forgotten how to laugh: now and again I catch her smiling, and I smile too. We converse in low tones, for I detest the noise of the night clubs, the noise that sometimes fills the recording studios. People who do not know me think I am taciturn. Perhaps I am, because I have to open my mouth so often to laugh.

I go through life with an impassive expression, from time to time permitting myself a gentle smile, and I often wonder whether I have ever laughed. I think not. My brothers and sisters have always known me for a serious boy.

So I laugh in many different ways, but my own laughter I have never heard.

---

## STUDY QUESTIONS

### Recalling

1. Describe what the narrator does for a living, and mention at least three of his specific skills.
2. How does the narrator behave when he is off duty?
3. What does the narrator tell us about his personality?

### Interpreting

4. Why does the narrator "bemoan" his fate when he goes to each new job? Do you think his attitude toward his work is different from that of other workers? Why or why not?
5. What distinction do you think the laugher draws in the last sentence between laughing in many ways and hearing his own laughter?
6. What parts of the story do you think are deliberately exaggerated? What is the effect of this exaggeration?

### Extending

7. What do we reveal about ourselves in our laughter?

## VIEWPOINT

A reviewer in the *New York Times* described Böll's position among other German writers in these terms:

Böll is generally acknowledged as...the man who looks for authentic humanity in a society thriving on ersatz [an artificial substitute].

— J. P. Bauke

■ Explain how the laugher's profession enables Böll to make fun of the artificiality of modern life.

## LITERARY FOCUS

### The Single Effect

A century and a half ago, Edgar Allan Poe defined the short story as a narrative that can be read in a single sitting and that produces *a single effect* on its reader. In the case of Poe's own stories—for example, "The Cask of Amontillado"—this single effect is often a chilling one.

*The Laugher* **153**

The laugher, solemn by nature, never laughs when he is off duty.

### 1 THEME

Since genuine laughter is spontaneous, not forced, the narrator cannot laugh "off duty," even at his wife's request.

### REFLECTING ON THE STORY

Do you think the author was laughing when he wrote this story? (Answers will vary; some may think that the author is making a serious point, while others may find that the laugher's exaggeration, solemnity, and self-importance are comic.)

### STUDY QUESTIONS

1. He laughs; imitates any type of laughter; can prompt others; times laughs perfectly.
2. He is solemn.
3. He is pessimistic.
4. ■ finds work exhausting
   ■ Answers will vary; some may think most workers dislike their work, while others will describe those who integrate their life and work.
5. distinguishes between spontaneous laughter and "bought" laughter
6. narrator's solemnity; seems ludicrous
7. attitudes toward life

### VIEWPOINT

The story suggests that people have lost touch with their authentic feelings.

1. "I am a good laugher"; "I never laugh off duty"; "I am happy when I am free to relax . . . in profound solemnity."

2. Most students will probably find it amusing because of the ludicrous contrast between the laugher's personality and profession.

## VOCABULARY

1. (d) true : false
2. (a) bind : bound
3. (c) carpenter : wood
4. (b) cheerful : optimist
5. (c) label : name

---

In Heinrich Böll's "The Laugher" everything the narrator tells us points to the ironic contrast between his personality and his profession.

### Thinking About a Story's Single Effect

1. Find three statements in the story that emphasize the irony of the narrator's situation.
2. Irony is often funny, but it can also be very serious. Did you find the narrator's predicament primarily amusing or serious? Why?

## VOCABULARY

### Analogies

**Analogies** are comparisons that point out relationships between items. In vocabulary tests, analogies are usually written as two pairs of words; the words in the first pair are always related to each other in the *same* way as those in the second pair. For example, in the analogy SWEET : SOUR : : LIGHT : DARK, the relationship between each pair of words is that of *opposites.*

Many different kinds of relationships can be used to form analogies. For example, the words in each pair might be synonyms (LOOK : GLANCE) or different grammatical forms of the same word (WRITE : WROTE). An adjective might be related to the noun it describes (GRACEFUL : DANCER), or a user might be related to the material being used (SCULPTOR : MARBLE).

The capitalized words in the analogies below appear in the story. Complete the analogies by choosing the pair of words that are related in the same way as the pair in capital letters.

1. AVOWAL : DENIAL : :
   (a) branch : tree     (c) trade : bargain
   (b) cure : health     (d) true : false

2. CONSTRAIN : CONSTRAINED : :
   (a) bind : bound     (c) enforce : punish
   (b) complain : cross     (d) feel : pain

3. BRICKLAYER : MORTAR : :
   (a) nurse : physician     (c) carpenter : wood
   (b) cook : restaurant     (d) teacher : student

4. SOLEMN : PESSIMIST : :
   (a) joy : emotion     (c) quiet : taciturn
   (b) cheerful : optimist     (d) serious : frivolous

5. DESIGNATION : TITLE : :
   (a) fiction : fact     (c) label : name
   (b) office : job     (d) walk : run

## COMPOSITION

### Writing About Character and Tone

■ Because "The Laugher" is told in the first person, the tone of the story directly reflects the personality of the central character, the narrator. Describe the narrator's personality, and explain how his personality creates the tone. Begin by considering that the narrator describes himself as a very solemn person and a pessimist. Find two or three quotations from the story that bear out this description. Then identify additional traits in the narrator's personality. Finally briefly summarize the tone of the story.

### Writing a Monologue

■ Imagine that, like the laugher, you practice an unusual profession. For example, you might be a person who is hired to agree with people, to cheer at baseball games, or to taste new foods. Describe your skills and the various things your work requires you to do. List both the advantages and drawbacks of your profession, and indicate your overall attitude toward it.

---

## COMPOSITION: GUIDELINES FOR EVALUATION

### WRITING ABOUT CHARACTER AND TONE

**Objective**

To describe a character's personality and explain its effect on the tone of the story

**Guidelines for Evaluation**

- suggested length: three to five paragraphs
- should describe the laugher's personality, using quotations from the story
- should describe the story's tone

### WRITING A MONOLOGUE

**Objective**

To describe an unusual profession

**Guidelines for Evaluation**

- suggested length: three to five paragraphs
- should create a character with an unusual profession
- should describe the job and the writer's feelings about the work

A native of a small fishing village in Maine, Sarah Orne Jewett (1849–1909) never wrote of far-flung places. Instead, her stories and novels focus on the land and people she grew up among. Her motto was the French writer Flaubert's famous statement that one should write about everyday life as if one were writing history itself.

■ Ordinary experiences can be filled with significance, if we look for it. Think of a special day in your life. What details, even the ordinary ones, do you remember?

*Sarah Orne Jewett*

# The Hiltons' Holiday

## I

There was a bright, full moon in the clear sky, and the sunset was still shining faintly in the west. Dark woods stood all about the old Hilton farmhouse, save down the hill, westward, where lay the shadowy fields which John Hilton, and his father before him, had cleared and tilled with much toil—the small fields to which they had given the industry and even affection of their honest lives.

John Hilton was sitting on the doorstep of his house. As he moved his head in and out of the shadows, turning now and then to speak to his wife, who sat just within the doorway, one could see his good face, rough and somewhat unkempt, as if he were indeed a creature of the shady woods and brown earth, instead of the noisy town. It was late in the long spring evening, and he had just come from the lower field as cheerful as a boy, proud of having finished the planting of his potatoes.

"I had to do my last row mostly by feelin'," he said to his wife. "I'm proper glad I pushed through, an' went back an' ended off after supper. 'Twould have taken me a good part o' tomorrow mornin', an' broke my day."

"'Tain't no use for ye to work yourself all to pieces, John," answered the woman, quickly. "I declare it does seem harder than ever that we couldn't have kep' our boy; he'd been comin' fourteen years old this fall, most a grown man, and he'd work right 'longside of ye now the whole time."

"'Twas hard to lose him; I do seem to miss little John," said the father, sadly. "I expect there was reasons why 'twas best. I feel able an' smart to work; my father was a girt[1] strong man, an' a monstrous worker afore me. 'Tain't that; but I was thinkin' myself to-day what a sight o' company the boy would ha' been. You know, small's he was, how I could trust him to leave anywheres with the team, and how he'd beseech to go with me wherever I was goin'; always right in my tracks I used to tell 'em. Poor little John, for all he was so young he had a great deal o' judgment; he'd ha' made a likely man."

The mother sighed heavily as she sat within the shadow.

"But then there's the little girls, a sight o'

---

1. **girt:** dialect expression for "great."

*The Hiltons' Holiday* **155**

**AT A GLANCE**

- After finishing his potato planting, John Hilton chats with his wife in the doorway.
- Although it is late evening, John has only just come in from work.

**LITERARY OPTIONS**

- interaction of elements
- characterization
- setting

**THEMATIC OPTIONS**

- new experiences
- family love
- rural and town life

**1 SETTING**

Within the description of the setting, Jewett ties the family's history directly to the farm and reveals the Hiltons' respect for hard work and love of the land.

**2 INTERACTION OF ELEMENTS**

The simile *as if he were indeed a creature of the shady woods* places John firmly within the context of the peaceful landscape; the comparison with the "noisy town" foreshadows his trip.

**3 STYLE: DIALECT**

The dialect that John and his wife use reinforces the rural Maine setting where they live.

## GUIDED READING

**LITERAL QUESTION**

**1a.** What has John just finished doing? (He has just finished planting potatoes in the lower field.)

**INFERENTIAL QUESTION**

**1b.** Besides pride, what feeling does finishing his planting evoke in John? (He feels sorrow because his young son, who had formerly helped him, has died.)

- They comment on how their daughter, Katy, helps John, as Susan Ellen helps her mother.
- The girls are at a neighbor's house visiting the new teacher.
- The parents discuss the girls' futures.

**1 INTERACTION OF ELEMENTS**

The plot exposition reveals the girls' personalities and suggests how their differences help to define the relationships between family members.

**2 CHARACTERIZATION**

John's anxiety about his daughters' lateness reveals his tender-hearted concern for them.

**3 READING SKILLS: COMPARISON/CONTRAST**

Throughout the story, the omniscient narrator compares and contrasts the two sisters to develop their individual characteristics, move the plot forward, and reflect changes in their attitudes.

help an' company,'' urged the father, eagerly, as if it were wrong to dwell upon sorrow and loss. ''Katy, she's most as good as a boy, except that she ain't very rugged. She's a real little farmer, she's helped me a sight this spring; an' you've got Susan Ellen, that makes a complete little housekeeper for ye as far as she's learnt. I don't see but we're better off than most folks, each on us having a workmate.''

''That's so, John,'' acknowledged Mrs. Hilton, wistfully, beginning to rock steadily in her straight splint-bottom chair. It was always a good sign when she rocked.

''Where be the little girls so late?'' asked their father. '''Tis gettin' long past eight o'clock. I don't know when we've all set up so late, but it's so kind o' summer-like an' pleasant. Why, where be they gone?''

''I've told ye; only over to Becker's folks,'' answered the mother. ''I don't see myself what keeps 'em so late; they beseeched me after supper till I let 'em go. They're all in a dazzle with the new teacher; she asked 'em to come over. They say she's unusual smart with 'rethmetic, but she has a kind of gorpen look to me. She's goin' to give Katy some pieces for her doll, but I told Katy she ought to be ashamed wantin' dolls' pieces, big as she's gittin' to be. I don't know's she ought, though; she ain't but nine this summer.''

''Let her take her comfort,'' said the kind-hearted man. ''Them things draws her to the teacher, an' makes them acquainted. Katy's shy with new folks, more so'n Susan Ellen, who's of the business kind. Katy's shy-feelin' and wishful.''

''I don't know but she is,'' agreed the mother slowly. ''Ain't it sing'lar how well acquainted you be with that one, an' I with Susan Ellen? 'Twas always so from the first. I'm doubtful sometimes our Katy ain't one that'll be like to get married—anyways not about here. She lives right with herself, but Susan Ellen ain't nothin' when she's alone, she's always after company; all the boys is waitin' on her a'ready. I ain't afraid but she'll take her pick when the time

**LITERAL QUESTION**

**1a.** How do the Hiltons characterize their daughters? (Whereas Susan Ellen is sociable and already has boys trailing after her, Katy is shy, solitary, and has dreams that may not include marriage.)

**INFERENTIAL QUESTION**

**1b.** What might cause Mrs. Hilton to feel closer to Susan Ellen than to Katy? (She may feel closer to Susan Ellen because the girl's interests and personality suggest that she will follow in her mother's domestic footsteps, whereas Katy's interests and personality suggest another destiny.)

comes. I expect to see Susan Ellen well set-tled—she feels grown up now—but Katy don't care one mite 'bout none o' them things. She wants to be rovin' out o' doors. I do believe she'd stand an' hark to a bird the whole fore-noon.''

"Perhaps she'll grow up to be a teacher," suggested John Hilton. "She takes to her books more'n the other one. I should like one on 'em to be a teacher same's my mother was. They're good girls as anybody's got.''

"So they be," said the mother, with unusual gentleness, and the creak of her rocking chair was heard, regular as the ticking of a clock. The night breeze stirred in the great woods, and the sound of a brook that went falling down the hill-side grew louder and louder. Now and then one could hear the plaintive chirp of a bird. The moon glittered with whiteness like a winter moon, and shone upon the low-roofed house un-til its small windowpanes gleamed like silver, and one could almost see the colors of a bloom-ing bush of lilac that grew in a sheltered angle by the kitchen door. There was an incessant sound of frogs in the lowlands.

"Be you sound asleep, John?" asked the wife presently.

"I don't know but what I was a'most," said the tired man, starting a little. "I should laugh if I was to fall sound asleep right here on the step; 'tis the bright night, I expect, makes my eyes feel heavy, an' 'tis so peaceful. I was up an' dressed a little past four an' out to work. Well, well!'' and he laughed sleepily and rubbed his eyes. "Where's the little girls? I'd better step along an' meet 'em.''

"I wouldn't just yet; they'll get home all right, but 'tis late for 'em certain. I don't want 'em keepin' Mis' Becker's folks up neither. There, le's wait a few minutes," urged Mrs. Hilton.

"I've be'n a-thinkin' all day I'd like to give the child'n some kind of a treat," said the father, wide awake now. "I hurried up my work 'cause

## 4

I had it so in mind. They don't have the oppor-tunities some do, an' I want 'em to know the world, an' not stay right here on the farm like a couple o' bushes.''

"They're a sight better off not to be so full o' notions as some is," protested the mother, suspi-ciously.

"Certain," answered the farmer; "but they're good, bright child'n, an' commencin' to take a sight o' notice. I want 'em to have all we can give 'em. I want 'em to see how other folks does things.''

"Why, so do I"—here the rocking chair stopped ominously—"but so long's they're con-tented—''

"Contented ain't all in this world; hopper-toads may have that quality an' spend all their time a-blinkin'. I don't know's bein' contented is all there is to look for in a child. Ambition's somethin' to me.''

"Now you've got your mind on to some plot or other." (The rocking chair began to move again.) "Why can't you talk right out?''

"'Tain't nothin' special," answered the good man, a little ruffled; he was never prepared for his wife's mysterious powers of divination. "Well there, you do find things out the master! I only thought perhaps I'd take 'em to-morrow, an' go off somewhere if 'twas a good day. I've been promisin' for a good while I'd take 'em to Top-ham Corners; they've never been there since they was very small.''

"I believe you want a good time yourself. You ain't never got over bein' a boy." Mrs. Hil-ton seemed much amused. "There, go if you want to an' take 'em; they've got their summer hats an' new dresses. I don't know o' nothin' that stands in the way. I should sense it better if there was a circus or anythin' to go to. Why don't you wait an' let the girls pick 'em some strawberries or nice ros'berries, and then they could take an' sell 'em to the stores?''

John Hilton reflected deeply. "I should like to get me some good yellow-turnip seed to plant

## GUIDED READING

### LITERAL QUESTIONS

**1a.** What does John want Katy to be? (He wants her to become a teacher like his mother was.)

**2a.** What is John's purpose in finishing his planting that day? (He wants to take tomorrow off and visit Topham Corners with his daughters.)

### INFERENTIAL QUESTIONS

**1b.** What does John's intention suggest about him? (It suggests that perhaps he, too, wanted to know the larger world.)

**2b.** Why does he feel being content on the farm is not enough for his daughters? (He wants them to know the world and to do important things in the future.)

- The girls arrive home and describe the teacher's party.
- They all go to bed.
- John wakes late and begins his chores while planning their day.

**1 SETTING**

The girls' entrance shows them to be as comfortable in their surroundings as their parents are.

**2 CHARACTERIZATION**

Jewett characterizes Katy directly by describing a trait of hers and indirectly by describing where she sits.

**3 PLOT: RISING ACTION**

In discussing the proposed trip, Mrs. Hilton so mildly disagrees with her husband that the girls remain unaware of his plan.

**4 INTERACTION OF ELEMENTS**

The actions of the Hiltons (getting up early) characterize them as hard working and are interwoven with the setting (birds, foxes, and squirrels) to emphasize the interaction between them and the land.

---

late. I ain't more'n satisfied with what I've been gettin' o' late years o' Ira Speed. An' I'm goin' to provide me with a good hoe; mine's gettin' wore out an' all shackly.[2] I can't seem to fix it good.''

"Them's excuses," observed Mrs. Hilton, with friendly tolerance. "You just cover up the hoe with somethin', if you get it—I would. Ira Speed's so jealous he'll remember it of you this twenty year, your goin' an' buyin' a new hoe o' anybody but him.''

"I've always thought 'twas a free country," said John Hilton, soberly. "I don't want to vex Ira neither; he favors us all he can in trade. 'Tis difficult for him to spare a cent, but he's as honest as daylight.''

At this moment there was a sudden sound of young voices, and a pair of young figures came out from the shadow of the woods into the moon-lighted open space. An old cock crowed loudly from his perch in the shed, as if he were a herald of royalty. The little girls were hand in hand, and a brisk young dog capered about them as they came.

"Wa'n't it dark gittin' home through the woods this time o' night?'' asked the mother, hastily, and not without reproach.

"I don't love to have you gone so late; mother an' me was timid about ye, and you've kep' Mis' Becker's folks up, I expect," said their father, regretfully. "I don't want to have it said that my little girls ain't got good manners.''

"The teacher had a party," chirped Susan Ellen, the elder of the two children. "Goin' home from school she asked the Grover boys, an' Mary an' Sarah Speed. An' Mis' Becker was real pleasant to us: she passed round some cake, an' handed us sap sugar on one of her best plates, an' we played games an' sung some pieces too. Mis' Becker thought we did real well. I can pick out most of a tune on the cabinet organ; teacher says she'll give me lessons.''

---

2. **shackly:** dialect expression for ''ramshackle,'' or falling apart.

"I want to know, dear!" exclaimed John Hilton.

"Yes, an' we played Copenhagen,[3] an' took sides spellin', an' Katy beat everybody spellin' there was there.''

Katy had not spoken, she was not so strong as her sister, and while Susan Ellen stood a step or two away addressing her eager little audience, Katy had seated herself close to her father on the doorstep. He put his arm around her shoulder, and drew her close to his side, where she stayed.

"Ain't you got nothin' to tell, daughter?'' he asked, looking down fondly, and Katy gave a pleased little sigh for answer.

"Tell 'em what's goin' to be the last day o' school, and about our trimmin' the schoolhouse,'' she said, and Susan Ellen gave the program in most spirited fashion.

"'Twill be a great time," said the mother, when she had finished. "I don't see why folks want to go trapesin' off to strange places when such things is happenin' right about 'em." But the children did not observe her mysterious air. "Come, you must step yourselves right to bed.''

They all went into the dark, warm house, the bright moon shone upon it steadily all night, and the lilac flowers were shaken by no breath of wind until the early dawn.

---

**II**

The Hiltons always waked early. So did their neighbors, the crows and song-sparrows and robins, the light-footed foxes and squirrels in the woods. When John Hilton waked, before five o'clock, an hour later than usual because he had sat up so late, he opened the house door and came out into the yard, crossing the short green turf hurriedly as if the day were too far spent for any loitering. The magnitude of the plan for taking a whole day of pleasure confronted him ser-

---

3. **Copenhagen:** game in which the players join hands in a circle.

---

## GUIDED READING

**LITERAL QUESTIONS**

**1a.** What is John's excuse for going to Topham Corners? (He is going to buy yellow-turnip seed and a new hoe.)

**2a.** What does Susan Ellen say they did at the party? (They ate cake and sap sugar, played games, sang songs, tried the organ, and had a spelling bee.)

**INFERENTIAL QUESTIONS**

**1b.** Why would such an expedition make Ira Speed jealous? (He runs the local store and would not like the Hiltons' spending money elsewhere.)

**2b.** How do the girls' interests and accomplishments at the party reflect their parents' opinion of them? (Susan Ellen is interested in food and playing the organ—both domestic, whereas Katy wins the spelling bee and is interested in decorating the schoolhouse—both associated with scholarship.)

iously, but the weather was fair, and his wife, whose disapproval could not have been set aside, had accepted and even smiled upon the great project. It was inevitable now that he and the children should go to Topham Corners. Mrs. Hilton had the pleasure of waking them, and telling the news.

In a few minutes they came frisking out to talk over the great plans. The cattle were already fed, and their father was milking. The only sign of high festivity was the wagon pulled out into the yard, with both seats put in as if it were Sunday; but Mr. Hilton still wore his everyday clothes, and Susan Ellen suffered instantly from disappointment.

"Ain't we goin', father?" she asked, complainingly, but he nodded and smiled at her, even though the cow, impatient to get to pasture, kept whisking her rough tail across his face. He held his head down and spoke cheerfully, in spite of this vexation.

**1** "Yes, sister, we're goin' certain, an' goin' to have a great time, too." Susan Ellen thought that he seemed like a boy at that delightful moment, and felt new sympathy and pleasure at once. "You go an' help mother about breakfast an' them things; we want to get off quick's we can. You coax mother now, both on ye, an' see if she won't go with us."

"She said she wouldn't be hired to," responded Susan Ellen. "She says it's goin' to be hot, an' she's laid out to go over an' see how her aunt Tamsen Brooks is this afternoon."

The father gave a little sigh; then he took heart again. The truth was that his wife made light of the contemplated pleasure, and, much as **2** he usually valued her companionship and approval, it was sure that they should have a better time without her. It was impossible, however, not to feel guilty of disloyalty at the thought. Even though she might be completely unconscious of his best ideals, he only loved her and the ideals the more, and bent his energies to satisfying her indefinite expectations. His wife

still kept much of that youthful beauty which Susan Ellen seemed likely to reproduce.

An hour later the best wagon was ready, and the great expedition set forth. The little dog sat apart, and barked as if it fell entirely upon him to voice the general excitement. Both seats were in the wagon, but the empty place testified to Mrs. Hilton's unyielding disposition. She had wondered why one broad seat would not do, but John Hilton meekly suggested that the wagon **3** looked better. The little girls sat on the back seat dressed alike in their Sunday hats of straw with blue ribbons, and their little plaid shawls pinned neatly about their small shoulders. They wore gray thread gloves, and sat very straight. Susan Ellen was half a head the taller, but otherwise, from behind, they looked much alike. As for their father, he was in his Sunday best—a plain black coat, and a winter hat of felt, which was heavy and rusty-looking for that warm early-summer day. He had it in mind to buy a new straw hat at Topham, so that this with the turnip seed and the hoe made three important reasons for going.

"Remember an' lay off your shawls when you get there, an' carry them over your arms," **4** said the mother, clucking like an excited hen to her chickens. "They'll do to keep the dust off your new dresses goin' and comin'. An' when you eat your dinners don't get spots on you, an' don't point at folks as you ride by, an' stare, or they'll know you came from the country. An' John, you call into Cousin Ad'line Marlow's an' see how they all be, an' tell her I expect her over certain to stop a while before hayin'. It always eases her phthisic⁴ to git up here on the highland, an' I've got a new notion about doin' over her best-room carpet sence I see her that'll save rippin' one breadth. An' don't come home all wore out; an', John, don't you go an' buy me no kickshaws⁵ to fetch home. I ain't a child, an' you

---

4. **phthisic** [tiz′ik]: tuberculosis or asthma.
5. **kickshaws:** toys or trinkets.

AT A GLANCE

- Mrs. Hilton wakes the girls and tells them of the day's plans.
- John feels guilty about being pleased that his wife is not going.
- Mrs. Hilton reminds them what to do as they sit ready to leave.

**1 POINT OF VIEW**

The omniscient narrator reveals the thoughts of each character and so shows the strengthening of ties among family members.

**2 CHARACTERIZATION**

John becomes a more complex and rounded character when he admits to himself he does not want his wife to accompany them on the trip and then feels guilty for having such thoughts.

**3 READING SKILLS: COMPARISON/CONTRAST**

The comparison of the two girls illustrates how their parents treat them equally (same clothes, both in back seat), although aware of the differences in their personalities.

**4 STYLE: PROSE RHYTHM**

Jewett reinforces the domestic image of Mrs. Hilton as a clucking hen by having her issue a set of instructions connected by several *an's* that make the rhythm of her speech seem choppy.

---

## GUIDED READING

### LITERAL QUESTIONS

**1a.** Why is Susan Ellen worried when she finds her father milking the cow? (Because he is not dressed up, she is afraid that they are not going to town.)

**2a.** What clothes do the Hiltons wear to go to town? (They dress in their Sunday best.)

### INFERENTIAL QUESTIONS

**1b.** What causes her to feel sympathy and pleasure at his words? (He seems younger to her and ready for a good time; his attitude means she will have fun, too.)

**2b.** What does their clothing reflect about their attitude toward the trip? (It shows that the trip has a special meaning for them, perhaps because it is completely out of the ordinary.)

- John and the girls finally leave as Mrs. Hilton watches.
- They stop to greet people along the way.
- Susan Ellen asks questions; Katy silently enjoys the changing setting.
- Katy wants to go to Topham Academy as her grandmother did.

**1 CHARACTERIZATION**

Her perceptive realization that, unlike her husband, she is unable to be a child again, makes Mrs. Hilton feel lonely and left out of the day's adventure.

**2 STYLE: WORD CHOICE**

Jewett's choice of the word *inconsiderately* reveals that the trip will be seen through the girls' eagerly impatient eyes.

**3 CHARACTERIZATION**

Although Katy enjoys seeing new and strange sights, a glimpse of familiar flowers along the road is reassuring.

**4 PLOT: RISING ACTION**

Katy's flash of insight that she too will attend Topham Academy shows how her strong ties to the past will influence her future; the insight both makes the day special and strengthens her ties to the family.

ain't got no money to waste. I expect you'll go, like's not, an' buy you some kind of a foolish boy's hat; do look an' see if it's reasonable good straw, an' won't splinter all off round the edge. An' you mind, John—''

''Yes, yes, hold on!'' cried John, impatiently; then he cast a last affectionate, reassuring look at her face, flushed with the hurry and responsibility of starting them off in proper shape. ''I wish you was goin' too,'' he said, smiling. ''I do so!'' Then the old horse started, and they went out at the bars, and began the careful long descent of the hill. The young dog, tethered to the lilac bush, was frantic with piteous appeals; the little girls piped their eager good-bys again and again, and their father turned many times to look back and wave his hand. As for their mother, she stood alone and watched them out of sight.

There was one place far out on the high road where she could catch a last glimpse of the wagon, and she waited what seemed a very long time until it appeared and then was lost to sight again behind a low hill. ''They're nothin' but a pack o' child'n together,'' she said aloud, and then felt lonelier than she expected. She even stooped and patted the unresigned little dog as she passed him, going into the house.

The occasion was so much more important than anyone had foreseen that both the little girls were speechless. It seemed at first like going to church in new clothes, or to a funeral; they hardly knew how to behave at the beginning of a whole day of pleasure. They made grave bows at such persons of their acquaintance as happened to be straying in the road. Once or twice they stopped before a farmhouse, while their father talked an inconsiderately long time with someone about the crops and the weather and even dwelt upon town business and the doings of the selectmen,[6] which might be talked of at any time. The explanations that he gave of

---

6. **selectmen:** board of officers elected to run municipal affairs in many New England towns.

their excursion seemed quite unnecessary. It was made entirely clear that he had a little business to do at Topham Corners, and thought he had better give the little girls a ride; they had been very steady at school, and he had finished planting, and could take the day as well as not. Soon, however, they all felt as if such an excursion were an everyday affair, and Susan Ellen began to ask eager questions, while Katy silently sat apart enjoying herself as she never had done before. She liked to see the strange houses, and the children who belonged to them; it was delightful to find flowers that she knew growing all along the road, no matter how far she went from home. Each small homestead looked its best and pleasantest, and shared the exquisite beauty that early summer made, shared the luxury of greenness and floweriness that decked the rural world. There was an early peony or a late lilac in almost every dooryard.

It was seventeen miles to Topham. After a while they seemed very far from home, having left the hills far behind, and descended to a great level country with fewer tracts of woodland, and wider fields where the crops were much more forward. The houses were all painted, and the roads were smoother and wider. It had been so pleasant driving along that Katy dreaded going into the strange town when she first caught sight of it, though Susan Ellen kept asking with bold fretfulness if they were not almost there. They counted the steeples of four churches, and their father presently showed them the Topham Academy, where their grandmother once went to school, and told them that perhaps some day they would go there too. Katy's heart gave a strange leap; it was such a tremendous thing to think of, but instantly the suggestion was transformed for her into one of the certainties of life. She looked with solemn awe at the tall belfry, and the long rows of windows in the front of the academy, there where it stood high and white among the clustering trees. She hoped that they were going to drive by, but something

---

## GUIDED READING

**LITERAL QUESTIONS**

**1a.** Why does John stop along the way? (He stops to talk to friends about farming and politics.)

**2a.** What is different about the physical setting as they approach the town? (The land becomes level with fewer woods, the crops are further along, the houses are painted, and the roads are wider and smoother.)

**INFERENTIAL QUESTIONS**

**1b.** What does this behavior suggest about his standing in the community? (He is an important member whose opinions are sought after.)

**2b.** What does this difference suggest about the area where the Hiltons live? (It has been more recently settled than Topham; it is also less traveled; because it is higher, the weather is cooler; also, fewer wealthy people live there.)

AT A GLANCE
- John wants the girls to impress the townspeople.
- A stranger's smile eases Katy's fears.
- John points out Judge Masterson's house and recounts the friendship between the judge and his mother.
- John speaks proudly about his mother.

**1 CHARACTERIZATION**

John reveals his insecurity at being a country person in town by warning the girls to appear pretty to impress the "best people."

**2 SYMBOL**

The elderly lady's smile symbolizes the warm, friendly atmosphere that the Hiltons encounter in Topham.

**3 INTERACTION OF ELEMENTS**

John's story of how the relationship between his mother and the judge has affected his life also reveals to the girls that their family has some social standing in Topham; thus the plot reinforces the day's importance for them.

---

forbade her taking the responsibility of saying so.

Soon the children found themselves among the crowded village houses. Their father turned to look at them with affectionate solicitude.

**1** "Now sit up straight and appear pretty," he whispered to them. "We're among the best people now, an' I want folks to think well of you."

"I guess we're just as good as they be," remarked Susan Ellen, looking at some innocent passers-by with dark suspicion, but Katy tried indeed to sit straight, and folded her hands prettily in her lap, and wished with all her heart to be

**2** pleasing for her father's sake. Just then an elderly woman saw the wagon and the sedate party it carried, and smiled so kindly that it seemed to Katy as if Topham Corners had welcomed and received them. She smiled back again as if this hospitable person were an old friend, and entirely forgot that the eyes of all Topham had been upon her.

"There, now we're coming to an elegant house that I want you to see; you'll never forget it," said John Hilton. "It's where Judge Masterson lives, the great lawyer; the handsomest house in the county, everybody says."

"Do you know him, father?" asked Susan Ellen.

"I do," answered John Hilton, proudly. "Him and my mother went to school together in their young days, and were always called the two best scholars of their time. The judge called

**3** to see her once; he stopped to our house to see her when I was a boy. An' then, some years ago —you've heard me tell how I was on the jury, an' when he heard my name spoken he looked at me sharp, and asked if I wa'n't the son of Catharine Winn, an' spoke most beautiful of your grandmother, an' how well he remembered their young days together."

"I like to hear about that," said Katy.

"She had it pretty hard, I'm afraid, up on the old farm. She was keepin' school in our district when father married her—that's the main reason

*The Hiltons' Holiday* **161**

---

**GUIDED READING**

**LITERAL QUESTION**

**1a.** Why does John take the girls past Judge Masterson's house? (The judge is a great lawyer, owns the most handsome house in the county, and was a friend of John's mother.)

**INFERENTIAL QUESTION**

**1b.** Why does Susan Ellen want to know if John knows the judge? (She perceives that such an acquaintance would give her status within the town.)

The Hiltons' Holiday **T-161**

**1 READING SKILLS: COMPARISON/CONTRAST**

The comparison of the girls' attitudes toward their father's story about his mother reflects their different attitudes toward the past, their father, and the future.

**2 SETTING**

Judge Masterson's house shows both his position within the community and his wealth; the new setting also introduces the girls to the way the rich live.

**3 CHARACTERIZATION**

The judge's speech, which contains no dialect, and his excellent manners indicate that he is more sophisticated than John; however, his relationship with John's mother implies she also had these traits.

**4 CHARACTERIZATION**

By impulsively kissing the judge's cheek, Katy reveals a compassion toward people, and an innate sense of quality.

---

I backed 'em down when they wanted to tear the old schoolhouse all to pieces,'' confided John Hilton, turning eagerly. ''They all say she lived longer up here on the hill than she could anywhere, but she never had her health. I wa'n't but a boy when she died. Father an' me lived alone afterward till the time your mother come; 'twas a good while, too; I wa'n't married so young as some. 'Twas lonesome, I tell you; father was plumb discouraged losin' of his wife, an' her long sickness an' all set him back, an' we'd work all day on the land an' never say a word. I s'pose 'tis bein' so lonesome early in life that makes me so pleased to have some nice girls growin' up around me now.''

**1** There was a tone in her father's voice that drew Katy's heart toward him with new affection. She dimly understood, but Susan Ellen was less interested. They had often heard this story before, but to one child it was always new and to the other old. Susan Ellen was apt to think it tiresome to hear about her grandmother, who, being dead, was hardly worth talking about.

''There's Judge Masterson's place,'' said their father in an everyday manner, as they turned a **2** corner, and came into full view of the beautiful old white house standing behind its green trees and terraces and lawns. The children had never imagined anything so stately and fine, and even Susan Ellen exclaimed with pleasure. At that moment they saw an old gentleman, who carried himself with great dignity, coming slowly down the wide, box-bordered path toward the gate.

''There he is now, there's the judge!'' whispered John Hilton, excitedly, reining his horse quickly to the green roadside. ''He's goin' downtown to his office; we can wait right here an' see him. I can't expect him to remember me; it's been a good many years. Now you are goin' to see the great Judge Masterson!''

There was a quiver of expectation in their hearts. The judge stopped at his gate, hesitating a moment before he lifted the latch, and glanced up the street at the country wagon with its two prim little girls on the back seat, and the eager man who drove. They seemed to be waiting for something; the old horse was nibbling at the fresh roadside grass. The judge was used to being looked at with interest, and responded now with a smile as he came out to the sidewalk, and unexpectedly turned their way. Then he suddenly lifted his hat with grave politeness, and came directly toward them.

''Good morning, Mr. Hilton,'' he said. ''I am very glad to see you, sir,'' and Mr. Hilton, the little girls' own father, took off his hat with equal courtesy, and bent forward to shake hands.

Susan Ellen cowered and wished herself away, but little Katy sat straighter than ever, with joy in her father's pride and pleasure shining in her pale, flower-like little face.

**3** ''These are your daughters, I am sure,'' said the old gentleman, kindly, taking Susan Ellen's limp and reluctant hand; but when he looked at Katy, his face brightened. ''How she recalls your mother!'' he said with great feeling. ''I am glad to see this dear child. You must come to see me with your father, my dear,'' he added, still looking at her. ''Bring both little girls, and let them run about the old garden; the cherries will soon be getting ripe,'' said Judge Masterson, hospitably. ''Perhaps you will have time to stop this afternoon as you go home?''

''I should call it a great pleasure if you would come and see us again some time. You may be driving our way, sir,'' said John Hilton.

''Not very often in these days,'' answered the old judge. ''I thank you for the kind invitation. I should like to see the fine view again from your hill westward. Can I serve you in any way while you are in town? Good-by, my little friends!''

Then they parted, but not before Katy, the shy Katy, whose hand the judge still held un- **4** consciously while he spoke, had reached forward as he said good-by, and lifted her face to kiss him. She could not have told why, except that she felt drawn to something in the serious, worn face. For the first time in her life the child

---

## GUIDED READING

**LITERAL QUESTIONS**

**1a.** How has his lonely early life shaped John's family views? (He is pleased to have the girls around him.)

**2a.** Why is the judge's greeting warmer for Katy than for Susan Ellen? (Katy reminds him of his old friend, her grandmother.)

**INFERENTIAL QUESTIONS**

**1b.** What effect does it have on his ambitions for his daughters? (As a result, he wants them to have more education than he did as well as more pleasure and less hardship and loneliness.)

**2b.** What traits of Katy make her resemble her grandmother and how does this resemblance affect the judge? (Katy looks like her and has the same frail health and interest in education. He sees Katy as a kind of continuation of his old friend's life.)

had felt the charm of manners; perhaps she owned a kinship between that which made him what he was, and the spark of nobleness and purity in her own simple soul. She turned again and again to look back at him as they drove away.

"Now you have seen one of the first gentlemen in the country," said their father. "It was worth comin' twice as far—" But he did not say any more, nor turn as usual to look in the children's faces.

In the chief business street of Topham a great many country wagons like the Hiltons' were fastened to the posts, and there seemed to our holiday-makers to be a great deal of noise and excitement.

"Now I've got to do my errands, and we can let the horse rest and feed," said John Hilton. "I'll slip his headstall right off, an' put on his halter. I'm goin' to buy him a real good treat o' oats. First we'll go an' buy me my straw hat; I feel as if this one looked a little past to wear in Topham. We'll buy the things we want, an' then we'll walk all along the street, so you can look in the windows an' see the han'some things, same's your mother likes to. What was it mother told you about your shawls?"

"To take 'em off an' carry 'em over our arms," piped Susan Ellen, without comment, but in the interest of alighting and finding themselves afoot upon the pavement the shawls were forgotten. The children stood at the doorway of a shop while their father went inside, and they tried to see what the Topham shapes of bonnets were like, as their mother had advised them; but everything was exciting and confusing, and they could arrive at no decision. When Mr. Hilton came out with a hat in his hand to be seen in a better light, Katy whispered that she wished he would buy a shiny one like Judge Masterson's; but her father only smiled and shook his head, and said that they were plain folks, he and Katy. There were dry goods for sale in the same shop, and a young clerk who was measuring linen kindly pulled off some pretty labels with gilded edges and gay pictures, and gave them to the little girls, to their exceeding joy. He may have had small sisters at home, this friendly lad, for he took pains to find two pretty blue boxes besides, and was rewarded by their beaming gratitude.

It was a famous day; they even became used to seeing so many people pass. The village was full of its morning activity, and Susan Ellen gained a new respect for her father, and an increased sense of her own consequence, because even in Topham several persons knew him and called him familiarly by name. The meeting with an old man who had once been a neighbor seemed to give Mr. Hilton the greatest pleasure. The old man called to them from a house doorway as they were passing, and they all went in. The children seated themselves wearily on the wooden step, but their father shook his old friend eagerly by the hand, and declared that he was delighted to see him so well and enjoying the fine weather.

"Oh, yes," said the old man, in a feeble, quavering voice, "I'm astonishin' well for my age. I don't complain, John, I don't complain."

They talked long together of people whom they had known in the past, and Katy, being a little tired, was glad to rest, and sat still with her hands folded, looking about the front yard. There were some kinds of flowers that she never had seen before.

"This is the one that looks like my mother," her father said, and touched Katy's shoulder to remind her to stand up and let herself be seen. "Judge Masterson saw the resemblance; we met him at his gate this morning."

"Yes, she certain does look like your mother, John," said the old man, looking pleasantly at Katy, who found that she liked him better than at first. "She does, certain; the best of young folks is, they remind us of the old ones. 'Tis nateral to cling to life, folks say, but for me, I git impatient at times. Most everybody's gone now, an' I want to be goin'. 'Tis somethin' before me, an' I want to have it over with. I want to be there

*The Hiltons' Holiday*  **163**

---

**AT A GLANCE**

- The Hiltons descend on Topham's chief business street.
- Mr. Hilton buys a new hat and a clerk gives the girls gifts.
- Susan Ellen is impressed with how people greet her father in town.
- John introduces them to an old neighbor who has moved to town.

**1 SETTING**

Topham's main street mirrors the holiday atmosphere that the Hiltons have created among themselves.

**2 ATMOSPHERE**

The kind clerk reflects the friendly atmosphere the girls encounter in town.

**3 INTERACTION OF ELEMENTS**

The characterization of Susan Ellen as a person aware of social position interacts with plot developments (her father's encounters with the townspeople) to emphasize Jewett's theme that new experiences can strengthen relationships.

**4 THEME**

As he becomes increasingly aware during the trip of her physical and emotional resemblance to his mother, John's pride in Katy solidifies, and when outsiders (his old neighbor and the judge) verify his perception, he feels the day to be special.

---

## GUIDED READING

**LITERAL QUESTION**

**1a.** What do the girls do when their father goes inside the shop? (They try to see the bonnets, so they can tell their mother about them.)

**INFERENTIAL QUESTION**

**1b.** Why does the excitement make them indecisive? (Unused to dealing with a variety of sights and sounds, they cannot filter their impressions quickly enough to make a decision.)

- When John asks what Mrs. Hilton would like, Susan Ellen suggests a pepper box.
- As they pass a photographer's, John decides a picture would be an excellent memento of the day.
- They reach home at nightfall.

**1 READING SKILLS: COMPARISON/CONTRAST**

The excitement of town and the Hiltons' holiday mood is contrasted with the old man's loneliness, something the girls find difficult to accept.

**2 PLOT: CLIMAX**

The climax of the story and of the Hiltons' holiday occurs when they have their picture taken; it captures their enjoyment at its height.

**3 SYMBOL**

Because it captures the girls at "their brightest and best," the photograph becomes a symbol of the joy and closeness of that day. John, however, realizes that the girls will appreciate the photograph's significance only later.

**4 THEME**

Mrs. Hilton's observation that the girls have grown older and taller, shows that she realizes how the day has brought emotional growth and stronger family ties that she had no part in developing.

---

'long o' the rest o' the folks. I expect to last quite a while though; I may see ye couple o' times more, John.''

John Hilton responded cheerfully, and the children were urged to pick some flowers. The old man awed them with his impatience to be gone. There was such a townful of people about him and he seemed as lonely as if he were the last survivor of a former world. Until that moment they had felt as if everything was just beginning.

''Now I want to buy somethin' pretty for your mother,'' said Mr. Hilton, as they went soberly away down the street, the children keeping fast hold of his hands. ''By now the old horse will have eat his dinner and had a good rest, so pretty soon we can jog along home. I'm goin' to take you round by the academy, and the old North meeting house where Dr. Barstow used to preach. Can't you think o' somethin' that your mother 'd want?'' he asked suddenly, confronted by a man's difficulty of choice.

''She was talkin' about wantin' a new pepper box, one day; the top o' the old one won't stay on,'' suggested Susan Ellen, with delightful readiness. ''Can't we have some candy, father?''

''Yes, ma'am,'' said John Hilton, smiling and swinging her hand to and fro as they walked. ''I feel as if some would be good myself. What's all this?'' They were passing a photographer's doorway with its enticing array of portraits. ''I do declare!'' he exclaimed, excitedly, ''I'm goin' to have our pictures taken; 'twill please your mother more'n a little.''

This was, perhaps, the greatest triumph of the day, except the delightful meeting with the judge; they sat in a row, with the father in the middle, and there was no doubt as to the excellence of the likeness. The best hats had to be taken off because they cast a shadow, but they were not missed, as their owners had feared. Both Susan Ellen and Katy looked their brightest and best; their eager young faces would forever shine there; the joy of the holiday was mirrored

in the little picture. They did not know why their father was so pleased with it; they would not know until age had dowered[7] them with the riches of association and remembrance.

Just at nightfall the Hiltons reached home again, tired out and happy. Katy had climbed over into the front seat beside her father, because that was always her place when they went to church on Sundays. It was a cool evening, there was a fresh sea wind that brought a light mist with it, and the sky was fast growing cloudy. Somehow the children looked different; it seemed to their mother as if they had grown older and taller since they went away in the morning, and as if they belonged to the town now as much as to the country. The greatness of their day's experience had left her far behind, the day had been silent and lonely without them, and she had had their supper ready, and been watching anxiously, ever since five o'clock. As for the children themselves they had little to say at first—they had eaten their luncheon early on the way to Topham. Susan Ellen was childishly cross, but Katy was pathetic and wan. They could hardly wait to show the picture, and their mother was as much pleased as everybody had expected.

''There, what did make you wear your shawls?'' she exclaimed a moment afterward, reproachfully. ''You ain't been an' wore 'em all day long? I wanted folks to see how pretty your new dresses was, if I did make 'em. Well, well! I wish more'n ever now I'd gone an' seen to ye!''

''An' here's the pepper box!'' said Katy, in a pleased, unconscious tone.

''That really is what I call beautiful,'' said Mrs. Hilton, after a long and doubtful look. ''Our other one was only tin. I never did look so high as a chiny[8] one with flowers, but I can get us another any time for every day. That's a proper

---

7. **dowered**: endowed.
8. **chiny**: china.

---

## GUIDED READING

**LITERAL QUESTIONS**

**1a.** Why does John decide to have their photograph taken? (It will be an excellent present for Mrs. Hilton and will help them all remember the day.)

**2a.** What is Mrs. Hilton's response to the presents? (She likes them but chides the girls for leaving their shawls on in the photograph and mentions the need for an ''everyday'' pepper box.)

**INFERENTIAL QUESTIONS**

**1b.** Why does he think the girls will be pleased with the photograph in the future? (As they get older, they will appreciate the special day and what it symbolizes—their introduction to the world and the strong ties they had with their father.)

**2b.** What does she mean that she ''never did look so high as a chiny one with flowers''? (The china pepper box is for someone fancier than she is and represents the town culture.)

- John admits he forgot to buy the hoe and turnip seeds.
- Mrs. Hilton admits the trip was good for the girls.
- John reveals his pride in the girls.

## 1 THEME

John's pride in the girls emphasizes Jewett's theme that strong ties develop through special experiences.

### REFLECTING ON THE STORY

How did the Hiltons' holiday change its participants? (Susan Ellen gains respect for her father and social standing; Katy feels strong ties to her grandmother and increased sympathy and respect for her father; John's ties with both girls become stronger.)

### STUDY QUESTIONS

1. *Katy:* helps with farm work; not very rugged; *Susan Ellen:* good housekeeper
2. to broaden their experience
3. judge's house, town; judge, old man
4. It's a lasting memory.
5. John's love for learning mirrored in Katy; Susan Ellen like mother
6. ■ judge: Susan cowered, Katy sat up straight; represents contact with world;
   ■ old man: both are awed; represents end of life
7. ■ They gain an appreciation of each other and the world.
   ■ John: pride in daughters; Katy: pleasing father; Susan: gains respect for father
   ■ Katy is most affected by meeting the judge.
8. New experiences can change views.

### VIEWPOINT

- All the experiences in town
- The experiences are new; they deepen family relationships.

hat, as good as you could have got, John. Where's your new hoe?'' she asked, as he came toward her from the barn, smiling with satisfaction.

"I declare to Moses If I didn't forget all about it,'' meekly acknowledged the leader of the great excursion. ''That an' my yellow-turnip seed, too; they went clean out o' my head, there was so many other things to think of. But 'tain't no sort o' matter; I can get a hoe just as well to Ira Speed's.''

His wife could not help laughing. "You an' the little girls have had a great time. They was full o' wonder to me about everythin', and I expect they'll talk about it for a week. I guess we was right about havin' 'em see somethin' more o' the world.''

''Yes,'' answered John Hilton, with humility,

''yes, we did have a beautiful day. I didn't expect so much. They looked as nice as anybody, and appeared so modest an' pretty. The little girls will remember it perhaps by an' by. I guess they won't never forget this day they had 'long o' father.''

It was evening again, the frogs were piping in the lower meadows, and in the woods, higher up the great hill, a little owl began to hoot. The sea air, salt and heavy, was blowing in over the country at the end of the hot, bright day. A lamp was lighted in the house, the happy children were chatting together, and supper was waiting. The father and mother lingered for a moment outside and looked down over the shadowy fields; then they went in, without speaking. The great day was over, and they shut the door.

### STUDY QUESTIONS

#### Recalling

1. Near the beginning of the story, how does John describe each of his daughters?
2. Why does John want to take the girls on a holiday?
3. What do John and the girls see on their holiday, and whom do they meet?
4. Why does the photograph stand out as the greatest triumph of the day?

#### Interpreting

5. Explain how the differences between John and his wife are reflected in their daughters. Cite evidence from the story to support your answer.
6. Contrast the girls' reactions to their meeting with Judge Masterson with their response to the old neighbor. What does each encounter add to the day's experience?
7. Why does the outing become "so much more important than anyone had foreseen"? What does it mean to John, to Katy, and to Susan Ellen? Whom do you think it affects the most?

#### Extending

8. At the end of the day, Mrs. Hilton thought that the girls looked "as if they had grown older and taller." Why might an experience like the Hiltons' holiday have such an effect on someone?

### VIEWPOINT

One writer has noted Sarah Orne Jewett's belief that

...the trivial and commonplace can be significant and important.
— A. Voss, *The American Short Story*

■ What "trivial and commonplace" things become "significant and important" in "The Hiltons' Holiday"? Why?

### LITERARY FOCUS

#### Interaction of Elements

We can look at a story in terms of its individual elements: plot, character, setting, point of view, tone, theme, and, in some cases, symbolism and irony. However, a good story is more than the sum of its individual elements. For a story to be successful, these elements must *interact,* or work together, to create a unified whole that produces its own unique effect on the reader.

In "The Hiltons' Holiday" these elements are closely interwoven. For example, the local color, or special regional features, of the Maine setting contributes to our picture of the characters as well. In addition, the changes in setting form an important part of the story's plot.

### Thinking About the Interaction of a Story's Elements

1. Explain how the changes in setting in "The Hiltons' Holiday" determine the events of the plot.
2. How do the characters reflect the setting?
3. Identify the story's point of view. Find two or three places where the narrator's revelations of different characters' thoughts help create a sense of the day's importance.
4. How do the relationships among the characters help to reveal the theme of this story? State the theme, the larger point about life in general that the story makes.
5. Explain how the photograph serves as a symbol of the Hiltons' holiday. In what way does the photograph express the story's theme?

### VOCABULARY

#### Prefixes

A **prefix** is a word part which, when placed before a root word, changes that word's meaning. For example, the words *disapproval* and *rediscover* both begin with prefixes. *Disapproval* attaches the prefix *dis-,* meaning "not," to the root word *approval.* The prefix therefore changes the meaning of *approval* to its opposite. In *rediscover,* the prefix *re-* means "back or again," and the meaning of the word becomes "to discover again."

The following words are taken from "The Hiltons' Holiday." In each case, write the prefix and its meaning, the root word and its meaning, and the meaning of the complete word.

1. impossible
2. unyielding
3. disloyalty
4. reassuring
5. inconsiderately

#### Noun-Forming Suffixes

A word part attached to the end of a base word is called a **suffix.** Certain suffixes, when attached to root words, change them into nouns. For example, adding the suffix -*ness* to the adjective *gentle* changes it into the noun *gentleness.*

All of the following words are taken from the story, and all are nouns ending with suffixes. For each word, identify the root word and its part of speech (verb or adjective); then identify the noun-forming suffix.

1. festivity
2. excitement
3. greenness
4. suggestion
5. remembrance

Do the same with ten more nouns in the story.

### COMPOSITION

#### Writing About the Total Effect

■ Discuss the total effect of "The Hiltons' Holiday." First describe the story's overall impact on you. Then explain how Jewett uses plot, character, setting, point of view and tone, theme, and symbol to create that impact. *For help with this assignment, see Lesson 12 in the Writing About Literature Handbook at the back of this book.*

#### Writing an Advertisement

■ Imagine that your hometown is eager to attract tourists during the vacation season. Write an advertisement about some aspect of your town that will appeal to out-of-town visitors.

### COMPARING STORIES

1. Both "Shaving" and "The Hiltons' Holiday" show how a commonplace event brings about an important change in relationships between fathers and children. What is that change in each story? What brings it about?
2. Both "An Occurrence at Owl Creek Bridge" and "The Laugher" reverse our expectations in some way and are therefore ironic. What is the irony in each story? How does point of view help to create irony in each story? What is the effect of the irony in each story: Is it startling, irritating, moving, or amusing?

*The Hiltons' Holiday* **167**

### LITERARY FOCUS

1. The adventure begins when the setting changes from farm to town.
2. The Hiltons' lives are limited by the farm, which also makes them simple, solid, hard-working characters.
3. omniscient narrator; meeting Judge and seeing Topham Academy
4. The Hiltons' perceptions of one another change as the day goes on: Sharing experiences strengthens ties.
5. The photograph captures their emotions: It's a reminder of the closeness and excitement they feel.

### VOCABULARY

#### Prefixes

1. *im:* not; *possible:* capable of being done;
2. *un:* not; *yielding:* surrendering
3. *dis:* lack of; *loyalty:* allegiance
4. *re:* again; *assure:* affirm
5. *in:* not; *consider:* regard

#### Noun-forming Suffixes

1. *festive* (adj.) + *ity*
2. *excite* (verb) + *ment*
3. *green* (adj.) + *ness*
4. *suggest* (verb) + *ion*
5. *remember* (verb) + *ance*

## COMPOSITION: GUIDELINES FOR EVALUATION

### WRITING ABOUT THE TOTAL EFFECT

**Objective**

To write an essay describing the total effect of a story

**Guidelines for Evaluation**

■ suggested length: three to five paragraphs
■ should state overall impact of the story
■ should explain how the literary elements contribute to the story's total effect

### WRITING AN ADVERTISEMENT

**Objective**

To write a persuasive advertisement

**Guidelines for Evaluation**

■ suggested length: one to three paragraphs
■ should be written in a persuasive selling style

American writer James Purdy (born 1923) was born in Ohio and studied at the University of Chicago as well as at universities in Mexico and Spain. He is known chiefly for his novels but has also published collections that include short stories and plays. In the following story Purdy portrays a turning point in the relationship between a boy and his grandfather.

■ "Wishing will make it so" are lyrics of an old song. Do you agree with this sentiment? Will the boy in "Home by Dark" find the words true or untrue?

*James Purdy*

# Home by Dark

Every day his grandfather bought him a new toy of a cheap kind, and a little racing car made out of chocolate. The boy ate the racing car slowly and almost dutifully as he and his grandfather sat on the immense porch and talked about how the birds know when to leave for the South.

"Have we ever been South?" the boy asked his grandfather, after he had finished the chocolate racing car and wiped his hands carefully on his cowboy handkerchief.

"No," the old man said. "Not since your parents died."

"Why don't we go?" the young boy said.

"There would be no reason to," the old man replied.

The birds that had been twittering on the huge lawn that surrounded the great white house in which he lived with his grandfather suddenly rose together in a flock as if hearing an inaudible signal, and disappeared into a clump of trees far off.

"There they all go," the boy told his grandfather.

"There they go," the old man repeated.

"Are you glad they're gone?" the young boy wondered.

"They're not really gone. Not South," the old man told the boy. "It isn't time yet—it's only July."

"Oh, I knowed they hadn't gone South," the boy told his grandfather. "I saw them yesterday do it. They practice like this all day long. They twitter and twitter and twitter, then they all get silent and then *zoom*, they all fly off like they knowed it was time."

"*Knew*," the grandfather corrected.

"Yes, *knew*," the boy nodded, and put his hand gently on his grandfather's hand.

"Birds are really strange creatures," the old man admitted. "They remember always where to go, where to build their nests, where to return to. . . ." He shook his head.

**168** *The Short Story*

---

## GUIDED READING

### LITERAL QUESTION

**1a.** What does the grandfather buy the boy every day? (a cheap toy and a racing car made of chocolate)

### INFERENTIAL QUESTION

**1b.** Why do you think the grandfather buys this candy? (He may be trying in a small way to make up for the boy's great loss of his parents. It is the simple, loving gesture of a man who really has no concrete way to "make things right.")

"They know to go South when it's cold," the boy agreed. "Except the sparrows. They stay all winter, poor little fellows. They are tough. They don't have no more feathers than the other birds, yet they stay right on, don't they?"

The grandfather nodded.

"Maybe, though, they *do* have more feathers and we can't see them," the boy added, thinking.

"That could be," the old man told his grandson, and he brought his cane up now painfully, and then pressed down with it with his hand.

The boy waited a little for his grandfather to say something more, and the old man, sensing the boy's need for words, said: "Did you like your chocolate racing car?"

"It was sweet and bitter and sweet all at the same time, and then at the very end it was soapy."

"Soapy?" the grandfather wondered.

The boy nodded.

"Well, then there was something wrong with it," the old man complained faintly.

"No," the boy said airily. "That's the way the sweet and the bitter get after you have them both together. See," he said pulling on his grandfather's cane a little, "after you taste the sweet you taste the bitter and after you taste the sweet again you taste the sweet and the bitter, and it's only soapy for a second!"

"I see," the grandfather nodded.

"And then it's all sweet!" The boy laughed, and he jumped up and down on the porch steps, making strange little sounds imitating nobody knew what.

"And I lost a tooth!" the boy told his grandfather.

"Cook told me," the old man informed him.

"Tonight when I go to bed, I am going to put it under my pillow and when I wake up in the morning do you know what is going to be under where I slept all night?"

The grandfather smiled and shook his head.

"A pot of gold," the boy told him.

"What will you do with it?" the grandfather asked.

"I might turn into a bird and go South then," the boy told him.

"But you wouldn't want to leave your old granddad and Cook," the grandfather chided.

The boy thought a moment and said, "I would fly back for supper."

"Well, it will be interesting to see your pot of gold tomorrow," the old man agreed.

"You really think I will get it then?" the boy asked.

"All wishes like that come true," the grandfather said somewhat gravely. "It's because they're a . . . a *pure* wish."

"A *pure* wish?" the boy wondered, scratching his nose. "What's that?"

"Well, like pure candy; you've had that, you know."

The boy shook his head.

"Your chocolate racing car is pure candy," the grandfather said, unsure this was so, and no conviction in his voice.

"Oh," the boy answered.

"All you really wished for, you see," the grandfather explained, "was to have your wish come true. You really hadn't thought what you would do with your wish and your pot of gold."

"Yes," the boy agreed, but his attention wandered.

"So tonight when you go to sleep you must just think that you want the pot of gold, and that is all you want. And don't wish for it too hard, you know."

"No?" the boy raised his voice.

"Not too hard. That would frighten the good fairy away."

"The good fairy?" the boy wondered.

"Yes. Who did you think brought your pot of gold?"

"I thought," the boy felt his way. "I thought . . . somebody dead."

*Home by Dark*　**169**

- The pair discusses birds and the taste of the chocolate car.
- The boy announces he has lost a tooth. He will put it under his pillow and receive a pot of gold.
- They discuss wishes.
- The boy is hoping "someone dead" will bring his gold.

## 1 CHARACTERIZATION

The grandfather, sensitive to the boy's need for talk, asks about the candy; the boy analyzes the candy but innocently talks about life.

## 2 DIALOGUE

The grandfather does not yet perceive that the boy's wish to go South reflects a deeper yearning: his need for his parents.

## GUIDED READING

### LITERAL QUESTIONS

**1a.** According to the narrator, why does the grandfather ask the boy if he liked the chocolate racing car? (He recognizes the boy's "need for words.")

**2a.** Who did the child think brought the magical pot of gold? ("somebody dead")

### INFERENTIAL QUESTIONS

**1b.** What does a "need for words" mean? (It means that the boy needs to participate in conversation, to share his feelings.)

**2b.** To whom is the boy probably referring? (his dead parents)

- The grandfather says the good fairy brings the gold.
- It is an hour before bedtime, and the boy asks again about going South.
- The grandfather says that memories prevent him from going South.
- The boy doubts he will get the pot of gold.

**1 CONFLICT**

The grandfather wants to avoid this painful issue—his memories of the boy's parents—while the boy needs to have his answer now.

**2 SYMBOL**

"Gold" evokes mutual excitement, but the childish jet sounds suggest that the boy associates the gold with flying South, where the grandfather says he "would never go."

"What?" the old man said, and he moved his cane again so that now it pointed down to the grass where the birds had gathered in a flock.

"Cook didn't really tell me who did bring it," the boy said, studying the confusion on his grandfather's face.

"Yes," the old man said absently, and then looking at his grandson he said, "well, it's really the good fairy, I expect. Don't you know about her?"

The boy shook his head.

"Well, she is the one who's supposed to bring the gold." And the old man laughed rather loudly.

"Do you believe in her?" the boy asked.

"The good fairy?" the old man said, and he began to laugh again, but stopped. "Yes, I do," he said after a pause and with a sleepy serious expression.

The grandfather fished his heavy gold watch out of his vest pocket and looked at its face.

"Seven P.M.," he said.

"Seven P.M.," the boy repeated. "One hour to bedtime."

"That's right," the grandfather said, and he put his hand on the boy's head.

"Why don't you want to go South?" the young boy wondered, suddenly.

"Well," the old man stirred in his chair. "Memories, I suppose, you know." But then looking at his grandson he knew the boy did *not* know, and he said, "It's a long story."

"You don't remember why?" the boy asked.

"When you're older I will talk about it," the old man began. "You see there's so much explanation to it, and well, I'm very old, and it tires me out when I make long explanations."

**1** "What is *explanation*—just telling everything, then?"

"Yes," the old man smiled. "And if I told you why I don't want to go South why we'd be here for days!"

"But we are anyhow!" the boy exclaimed.

"We're always just standing and sitting and standing and talking here or watching the birds."

The old man was silent.

"Ain't we?" the boy said.

"Well, if I was a bird I would *never* go South," the old man spoke almost as if to himself.

The boy waited and then when his grandfather said no more he told him: "I would always come home at dark, I think, if I was a bird."

**2** "Yes, sir, *tomorrow*," the old man's voice sounded, taking on warmth, "you'll have your pot of gold!"

"Hurray!" the small boy shouted, and he ran around the old man's chair making sounds now that were those of a jet.

"What will you buy me tomorrow?" the boy asked his grandfather.

"But tomorrow you will have your own pot of gold!" the grandfather told his grandson. "You'll be rich!"

"Will I then?" the boy wondered.

**170** *The Short Story*

## GUIDED READING

### LITERAL QUESTIONS

**1a.** Why doesn't the grandfather want to go South? (memories)

**2a.** When does the grandfather say he will talk about the "memories . . . the long story"? (when the boy is older)

### INFERENTIAL QUESTIONS

**1b.** What is he thinking of? (It would make him sad to relive his memories of the boy's parents by visiting those southern places.)

**2b.** Why won't the grandfather talk about them now? (He wants to wait for a time when the boy is better able to understand. At that point it may also be less painful for the grandfather to talk about them.)

"Don't you believe you'll have it?" the old man interrogated.

"No," the boy said softly.

"But you must believe," the grandfather warned him.

"Why?" the boy asked, looking closely into his grandfather's face.

"You must always believe in one thing, that one thing."

"What is *that one thing?*" the boy asked, an almost scared look on his face.

"Oh, it's hard to say," the old man admitted failure again.

"Not like going South now, don't tell me again," the boy complained.

"No, this is even harder to explain than going South, but I will try to tell you."

The old man drew his grandson closer to him and arranged the collar of the boy's shirt. He said: "There is always one thing a person believes and wants to believe even if he doesn't believe it."

"Ahem," the boy said, standing on only one leg.

"Do you see?" the old man asked, his face soft and smiling.

"Yes," the boy replied, his voice hard.

"All right, then," the old man went on. "There is this one thing you want and you want it more than anything in the world. You see?"

"Like the birds knowing where to fly, you mean?" the boy was cautious.

"Yes," the old man doubted this, and then said, "but more like your pot of gold."

"Oh," the boy replied.

"You want this one thing, and you have to go on believing in it, no matter what."

"Well, what is the thing?" the boy smiled broadly now, showing the place in his mouth where he had lost his tooth, which was a front one.

"Only the person who knows can tell!" the grandfather said loudly as though this were a joke now.

"But am I old enough to know?" the boy said, puzzled and surprised.

"You're old enough and you should tell me now," the grandfather encouraged him.

"So," the boy paused, screwing his eyes shut, and he stood first on one foot and then on another. "I would like my father and mother both to be alive again, and all of us, including you, living South."

The old man opened his mouth and closed it again.

"Isn't that the right answer?" the boy said, worried.

"Yes, of course," the old man hurriedly agreed.

"You don't act like it was the right answer," the boy complained.

"Well, it is, anyhow. The only thing was—I was thinking about wishes that are about the future, you see."

"Oh," the boy was disappointed. Then in a kind of querulous voice he said, "My wish wasn't the future?"

"It's so hard to explain," the grandfather laughed, and he roughed up the boy's hair.

"Well," the boy said, "let's talk about things we can tell each other."

The grandfather laughed.

The light was beginning to die slowly in the trees, and a full rounded moon began to show in the near distance.

Suddenly the boy said *Oh* in a scared voice.

"What is it?" the grandfather was concerned.

"I think I lost my tooth," the boy said.

"You did?" the grandfather was even more alarmed now than the boy.

"I did, I lost it." He felt suddenly in his pockets.

"When we were talking about the birds, you know, I throwed my hand out . . . and the tooth must have been in my hand."

"You *threw* your hand out. Well, then it's in the grass," the grandfather said.

*Home by Dark*  **171**

- The grandfather advises the boy always to believe in "one thing."
- The boy thinks the wish is for his parents to return.
- Grandfather says the wish should be about the future.
- The boy discovers he has lost his tooth.

**1 CHARACTERIZATION**

The fact that the boy has lost his front tooth—the first one to go—indicates that he is about six and that he's testing his most cherished dream for the first time.

**2 THEME**

The old man's loss for words tells the boy the painful truth about the death of his parents—that wishing cannot bring them back.

**3 PLOT: RISING ACTION**

The boy can't find the tooth—that has come to represent his dream—his parents' return.

---

## GUIDED READING

**LITERAL QUESTIONS**

**1a.** What does the grandfather tell the boy? (that he must always believe in one thing)

**2a.** How does the grandfather react when the boy voices his dream about his parents? (He opens his mouth and closes it again; he agrees hurriedly.)

**INFERENTIAL QUESTIONS**

**1b.** Why can't the old man tell the youngster exactly what his belief or dream should be? (because it is a personal dream constructed of personal hopes that are the boy's alone)

**2b.** Why does the old man react this way? (The boy has surprised him. He did not expect the child to make such a profound wish. He expected a wish about the future.)

**AT A GLANCE**

- The boy bemoans his lost tooth; they search in vain.
- The grandfather tries to cheer him up.

**1 CHARACTERIZATION**

The boy's comment that the tooth was very little reflects his dawning realization that his dream had small chance of coming true.

**2 IRONY**

The grandfather expresses hope about the tooth while the boy seems resigned to letting go of his dream.

**3 PLOT: CLIMAX**

The grandfather sees the depth of the boy's awareness, and the boy faces the finality of death.

---

"Yes," the boy agreed.

The old man got out of his chair and his grandson helped him silently down the twelve steps that led to the long walk about which extended the immense lawn where the tooth had been thrown.

They searched patiently in the long grass, which had needed cutting for some time. **1** "It was such a little tooth," the boy said, as though he realized this fact for the first time.

The old man could not bend over very far, but his eyes, which were still keen, looked sharply about him for the tooth.

"Oh, what shall I ever do!" the boy said suddenly.

"But it will turn up!" the old man cried, but there was the same note of disappointment and fear in his voice, which, communicating itself to the boy, caused the latter to weep.

"You mustn't cry," the grandfather was stern. "It won't do at all!"

"But the pot of gold and all!" the boy cried.

"It doesn't matter at all," the grandfather said, and he touched the boy on the face.

"But you told me it did," the boy wept now.

"I told you *what?*" the old man said.

"You told me there was just that one thing you should want to believe in."

**2** "But you've only lost your tooth," the old man replied. "And we'll find it. It isn't lost forever. The gardener will find it when he comes."

"Oh, I'm afraid not," the boy said, wandering about now picking up the grass by the handfuls, looking and watching about him in the fading light.

"If we only hadn't let Cook take the flashlight we might locate it with that," the grandfather said, a few minutes later, when the light was quite gone.

The boy now just stood in one place staring down at the grass.

"I think we'll have to give up the search for tonight," the grandfather finally said.

**172** *The Short Story*

"But this is the only night I can have my wish!" the boy cried "This is the ONLY night."

"Nonsense," the grandfather told him. "Not true at all."

"But it is, it is," the boy contradicted his grandfather, gravely.

**3** "How do you know?" the grandfather wondered.

"My mother told me," the boy said.

"But you don't . . . you don't remember her!" the grandfather stared into the growing dark.

"She told me in my sleep," the boy said, his voice plain, unemphatic.

The grandfather looked at his grandson's face but the dark hid it and its expression from him.

"Let's go up the steps now," the grandfather told him.

The small boy helped the old man up the twelve steps, and at the last one the old man laughed, making fun of his fatigue.

"Don't ever get old now, don't you ever do that," he laughed.

The grandfather sat down heavily in the chair, his cane thrown out as though commanding something, or somebody.

"We'll find your tooth tomorrow, or we'll all be hanged," the grandfather said cheerily. "And we won't let Cook take our flashlight again, will we?"

The boy did not answer. He stood as he stood every night beside his grandfather, looking out over the western sky, tonight half-seeing the red harvest moon rise.

"I will buy you something different tomorrow," the grandfather said, "so that it will be a real surprise. Do you hear?"

The boy said yes.

"You're not crying now," the grandfather said. "That's good."

The boy nodded.

"I'm glad you're brave too, because a boy should not cry, really, no matter even. . . . Well, he should never cry."

---

## GUIDED READING

**LITERAL QUESTION**

**1a.** How does the boy know that this is the only night he can have his wish? (He says his mother told him in his sleep.)

**INFERENTIAL QUESTION**

**1b.** Why does he say that his mother spoke in his dream? (The lost tooth is tied to the lost idea of getting his mother back.)

"But I don't know what to believe in now," the boy said in a dry old voice.

"Fiddlesticks," the old man said. "Now come over here and sit on my lap and I will talk to you some more."

The boy moved slowly and sat down on his grandfather's lap.

"Ouch," the grandfather said playfully when he felt how heavy the boy was.

"Just the two of us," the old man said. "Just the two of us here, but we're good friends, aren't we. Good, good old friends."

He pushed the boy's head tight against his breast so he would not hear the sounds that came out now like a confused and trackless torrent, making ridiculous the quiet of evening, and he closed his own eyes so that he would not see the moon.

---

## STUDY QUESTIONS

### Recalling

1. Find a statement near the story beginning that explains why the boy lives with his grandfather.
2. List in order the subjects the boy and his grandfather discuss up to the point when the boy accidentally throws away his tooth.
3. How do the boy and his grandfather differ in their feelings about going South? Refer to each character's words that express their feelings.
4. What is the one thing the boy says he wants to believe?
5. When the boy accidentally throws away his tooth, how does he react? What is the grandfather's reaction?

### Interpreting

6. Do you think the boy acts and speaks the way real children do, or do you think he is unconvincing? Give details from the story that explain your opinion.
7. At what point does the mood of this story change dramatically? What was the mood before this point? What does it become?

8. Do you think the boy would have agreed with the words quoted in the introduction before he threw away his tooth? Would he agree with the words after that incident? Give reasons for your answer.

### Extending

9. If the boy in this story were a friend of yours, what would you tell him about disappointments like his?

## COMPARING STORIES

1. "Shaving," "The Hiltons' Holiday," and "Home by Dark" show how a commonplace event brings about an important change in relationships between adults and children. What is that change in each story? What brings it about?
2. Both "An Occurrence at Owl Creek Bridge" and "The Laugher" reverse our expectations in some way and are therefore ironic. What is the irony in each story? How does point of view help to create irony in each story? What is the effect of the irony in each story: Is it startling, irritating, moving, or amusing?

Home by Dark 173

*Home by Dark* **173**

### AT A GLANCE

- The grandfather tries to reinforce the close, loving bond between them.
- The boy weeps.

### REFLECTING ON THE STORY

Why does the old man shut out the crying and the moon? (Possible answers: His guard against sorrow is to hold back tears and time; the boy and the moon represent change.)

### STUDY QUESTIONS

1. "Not since your parents died."
2. the birds going South; the boy's missing tooth and the pot of gold the fairy will bring for it; the necessity of belief
3. The boy wants to go; grandfather does not.
4. his father and mother alive, living in the South with them
5. boy, scared and upset; grandfather, more alarmed
6. like real children; *details*—boy's use of ungrammatical speech, his naiveté; his imitation of a jet; his frequent questions; his weeping
7. when the boy accidentally throws his tooth away; before, pleasant, homey, mildly humorous; after, foreboding
8. before loss of tooth—yes, because his grandfather assured him of the importance of believing in something; after loss—probably not, because he will not get his wish
9. *Possible answers:* Disappointments are a part of life; disappointments are often balanced by fulfillment.

### COMPARING STORIES

1. "Shaving": Barry's passage into manhood—shaving; "Holiday": new appreciation for each other—trip to town; "Home": wishing on lost tooth reveals painful truths for grandfather and grandson
2. ■ "Bridge": startling—Peyton dies: We are confined to Peyton's point of view until the end.

■ "Laugher": amusing—disparity between occupation and personality. The humorless laugher tells us directly about his situation, where another narrator would be less comical.

As you read the stories in this unit, try to increase the students' awareness of details by focusing on one or two details in each work and asking what they mean. Ask them to find other examples of significant details in the stories mentioned in this essay ("The Red-Headed League," "By the Waters of Babylon," and "An Occurrence at Owl Creek Bridge") and to explain why they are significant.

You will find among the materials for this unit in your *Teacher's Classroom Resources* the related blackline master Significant Details in Short Stories.

# ACTIVE READING

## Significant Detail

At the beginning of "The Red-Headed League," we find the great detective Sherlock Holmes and his friend Dr. Watson looking at the same person, Jabez Wilson. Yet Holmes and Watson see different things. Watson attempts to "read" Wilson from his face and clothes, but Watson is not a good reader. All he can see is an "average commonplace" Englishman who has "nothing remarkable" about him except for his bright red hair. Holmes, however, deduces from a few significant details that Jabez Wilson "has at some time done manual labor, that he takes snuff, that he is a Freemason, that he has been in China, and that he has done a considerable amount of writing lately...." Amazing? Not to Sherlock Holmes.

As readers we can be as dull as Watson or as keen as Holmes. The difference lies in our ability to see—and enjoy—the details that make up plot, character, and setting. Without life-giving details we would have only a dry summary or sketch of a story. With them we have the pleasure of reading. Moreover, the details can have significance.

In "By the Waters of Babylon" Stephen Vincent Benét puts the reader somewhat in the position of a detective. The young narrator, John, is a good observer, yet all he sees are fragments that he can only dimly interpret. From these fragments, however, we as readers can reconstruct and recognize the civilization that bewilders John. When John says of the water faucets, "a thing said 'Hot'... another thing said 'Cold,'" Benet makes us see and *feel* how the everyday objects we take for granted have been hard won for us by our ancestors and how we might lose them. We could summarize the story in a few sentences; it is the details that turn it into a moving experience.

Let us look at another example of another story's brilliant use of detail. In "An Occurrence at Owl Creek Bridge" Bierce's sharp use of sensory detail creates an intense sense of reality. Think of the "shining bits of metal, singularly flattened" yet "uncomfortably warm," that surround Peyton in the river. He notices the details and then realizes what they mean: that these pieces of metal are spent bullets. This detail allows us to share Farquhar's experience—to *feel* it—at the same time that we sense that there is a strange, almost dreamlike intensity about it. Our ability to see the significance of such small things is the secret of our pleasure in reading.

# REVIEW:
# THE SHORT STORY

## Guide for Studying the Short Story

As you read short stories, review the following guide in order to appreciate how an author creates a fictional world.

### Plot, Character, and Setting

1. What kinds of **conflict** does the story present?
2. What is the **exposition**? What event is the **narrative hook**? What complications form the **rising action**?
3. What event is the **climax**? Does the **resolution** logically follow the conflict and climax?
4. What does the author **directly tell** about the characters? What does the author **indirectly show** through their words and actions?
5. Are the characters **round** or **flat**? **Static** or **dynamic**?
6. When and where does the story take place?
7. What **details** are used to describe the **setting**? What **atmosphere** is created by these details?
8. Does the setting change during the story?

### Point of View and Tone

1. Does the author use the **first-person point of view**, in which a character tells the story?
2. Does the author reveal the thoughts of only one character through **limited third-person point of view**?
3. Does the author reveal the thoughts of several characters through **omniscient point of view**?
4. What is the author's **tone**?

### Theme

1. Is the **theme**, or central idea, directly **stated**?
2. If the theme is not stated directly, what theme is **implied** by the story's other elements?

### Symbol and Irony

1. Is an object, place, person, or experience in the story given **symbolic** meaning?
2. Does the story include **situational irony**? Does it include **verbal irony**?

*The Short Story* **175**

### REVIEW

Have students read the list of elements of the short story in the unit review. Make sure that students understand them. Tell students that although each of the stories in this unit contains many of the elements listed in the review, the relative importance of each element in a particular selection depends on the author's approach.

The questions in the Guide for Reading the Short Story appear with write-on lines, in blackline master form, among the materials for this unit in your *Teacher's Classroom Resources*.

176 *Poetry*

# PREVIEW:
# POETRY

*A poem . . . begins in delight and ends in wisdom.*
—Robert Frost

Like other forms of literature, poetry concerns real life, but it distills that life to its essence. Poetry is the most concentrated form of literature: It makes every moment, every word, every syllable count.

This concentration is what distinguishes poetry from prose, the form of writing that we read in short stories, novels, and newspapers. While prose runs from margin to margin down the page, each line of poetry stops in a particular place because of the poet's desire to create a particular effect. While prose falls into groups of logically linked sentences and paragraphs, poetry is arranged into lines and groups of lines known as **stanzas**, which are created by patterns of sight and sound as well as by logic. Poetry is also more musical and fanciful than prose: Where prose recreates the familiar rhythms of everyday speech, poetry gives words unaccustomed wings.

A poem simultaneously stirs our senses and makes us think. It can make our inner ears hum with its sound effects. Its sensory **images** dazzle our imaginations with sights, aromas, tastes, and textures. **Figures of speech** may lift the poem above literal fact to an imaginative plane where connections between seemingly unrelated things suddenly become plausible. These sound effects, images, and figures of speech can in turn touch our emotions and make us see the world as the poet wants us to see it—if only for a moment.

In the following pages we will examine the various formal elements that create meaning in a poem—the poem's speaker, sounds, imagery, and figurative language. In addition, we will look at different kinds of poetry—**narrative**, **lyric**, and **dramatic**—as well as examine poems that are **traditional** and **experimental** in form. Finally, we will see how these elements come together to create the poem's total effect— that special combination of delight and wisdom that we experience in seeing the world transformed, however fleetingly.

*Poetry* **177**

After reading the Preview, ask students to name and discuss poems they have already read and enjoyed. The following questions should be considered:

- What distinguishes poetry from prose?
- How is reading poetry different from reading prose?
- How is poetry's effect on the reader different from the effect of prose?
- Is it always immediately apparent whether a work of literature is poetry or prose? Why or why not?

These are not easy questions and do not have a single right answer; students should respond to them freely and imaginatively. Students might be asked to keep these questions in mind in reading, discussing, and writing about the unit; they may find that, as they explore poetry further, their opinions will change.

Remind students that in many ways poetry is the most personal form of literature. Because of their varying experiences and personalities, different people may respond in very different ways to the same poem. However, each individual interpretation must begin with evidence from the poem itself; everything we say about a poem must be based on the poem's particular words, images, and sounds.

# *LITERARY FOCUS: Speaker and Tone*

Every poem has a **speaker**, or **voice**, that addresses us. That speaker may be the poet or may be a character whom the poet has invented. Sometimes the speaker may even be an animal or an inanimate object. In poetry anyone and anything can speak—from grandfathers to grand pianos. We should therefore put together a mental image of the speaker whenever we read a poem.

The words of a poem tell us a great deal about the speaker. They often tell us whether the speaker is male or female, young or old, sophisticated or naive. Above all, the words of a speaker communicate a particular **tone**, or attitude toward the subject and audience of the poem. The words of the poem express the feelings of the speaker about what is happening in the poem, whether they are feelings of excitement, grief, amusement, confusion, or a combination of several emotions. As you meet the speakers created by the following poets, try to imagine who they are, what they are like, and what they are feeling.

**William Stafford** (born 1914) grew up in the Midwest. He now lives and teaches in Oregon. Stafford has written a number of books, including *Traveling Through the Dark*, for which he won the National Book Award for Poetry. In "Fifteen" Stafford's speaker vividly recalls a brief experience from his youth.

■ In what ways can being treated as older than you are be both an asset and a drawback?

© Rollie McKenna

**Sylvia Plath** (1932–1963) was born in Boston, Massachusetts, and graduated from Smith College. She later studied in England, where she met and married the British poet Ted Hughes. The bulk of her work has been published after her early and tragic death. Her publications include *Ariel, Crossing the Water,* and *Winter Trees.* Like the poem "Mirror," Plath's works often invest unusual speakers with personality and passion.

■ What aspects of aging are attractive to you? Which, if any, do you fear?

**178** *Poetry*

**James Wright** (1927–1980) was born in Ohio and grew up near the steel mills on the Ohio River. In high school he was enrolled in a vocational training program until two teachers recognized his writing talent. His *Collected Poems* won the Pulitzer Prize for Poetry in 1972. In "A Blessing" Wright's speaker relates a joyous encounter with the natural world.

■ What conditions are necessary for a person to feel at one with nature? Have you ever felt this way? When and where?

**Gwendolyn Brooks** (born 1917) spent her childhood on Chicago's South Side, which serves as the background for many of her poems. She first began writing at the age of seven and by thirteen was a published poet. She won the Pulitzer Prize for her second collection of poetry, *Annie Allen,* about a black girl's growing up. As she does in "The Bean Eaters," Brooks often writes about the effects of poverty on people's lives.

■ What memories of your youth do you think you will treasure in old age? What mementos do you think will be of special value to you?

## AT A GLANCE

- The adult speaker recalls his discovery, at fifteen, of an overturned motorcycle.
- At first, the boy imagines riding off to the road's end.
- Instead, he helps the injured owner, who says "good man" and roars away.

## LITERARY OPTIONS

- speaker
- symbol
- imagery

## THEMATIC OPTIONS

- childhood fantasies vs. adult realities
- growth and learning
- time and memory

## SPEAKER

Appearing three times in the poem, the refrain "I was fifteen" lodges the action within the speaker's dual sensibility: that of a fifteen-year-old and an adult (ll. 5, 10, 15).

## IMAGERY

The speaker's sophisticated imagery *(shiny flanks, demure headlights / fringed)* supports the fact that he is now a grown man (ll. 7−9).

## SYMBOL

The bridge where the speaker experiences a tremble may symbolize the transition from childhood to adulthood (ll. 14−15).

## MAIN IDEA

The word *Thinking,* in its placement, meaning, and slow rhythm, drags the boy from childhood toward mature, reflective adulthood (l. 16).

## REFLECTING ON THE POEM

Why does the speaker think the incident is important? (Possible answers may include that it marks a critical step in his development into an adult.)

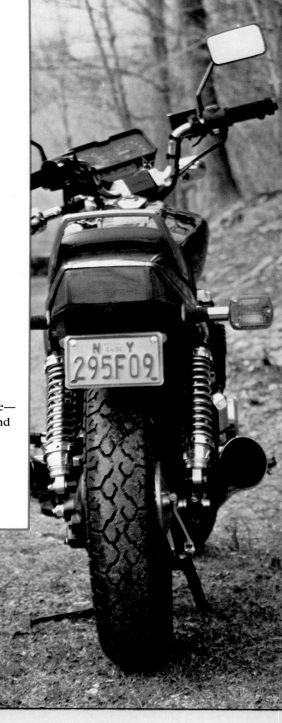

*William Stafford*

# Fifteen

South of the bridge on Seventeenth[1]
I found back of the willows one summer
day a motorcycle with engine running
as it lay on its side, ticking over
5   slowly in the high grass. I was fifteen.

I admired all that pulsing gleam, the
shiny flanks, the demure headlights
fringed where it lay; I led it gently
to the road, and stood with that
10  companion, ready and friendly. I was fifteen.

We could find the end of a road, meet
the sky on out Seventeenth. I thought about
hills, and patting the handle got back a
confident opinion. On the bridge we indulged
15  a forward feeling, a tremble. I was fifteen.

Thinking, back farther in the grass I found
the owner, just coming to, where he had flipped
over the rail. He had blood on his hand, was pale—
I helped him walk to his machine. He ran his hand
20  over it, called me good man, roared away.

I stood there, fifteen.

_____

1. **Seventeenth:** name of a street or avenue.

# STUDY QUESTIONS

## Recalling

1. Explain where and how the boy discovers the motorcycle. How old is he at the time?
2. What does the boy imagine doing with the motorcycle, and what does he do instead? What does he see in the grass?
3. What had happened to the bike's owner? What does he say to the boy before roaring away?

## Interpreting

4. What words in the poem make the motorcycle seem like a living creature?
5. What word does the speaker apply to the motorcycle after he discovers what has happened to the owner? Why do you think he uses this word?
6. Why is the boy's age important? In what ways is the boy different from the motorcyclist?
7. Show how the boy acts both like a child and an adult. What do you think he learns from this incident?

## Extending

8. What aspects of life do daydreams dwell on? What aspects of life do they leave out?

## LITERARY FOCUS

### The Speaker of a Poem

Every poet addresses us through a **speaker** of some kind—a person (or sometimes an animal or object) that utters the words of the poem. Unlike the person who brings a singing telegram, the speaker of a poem does more than deliver the poet's message: The speaker is also a part of that message. Therefore, one of the first things we should do when we read a poem is identify the speaker and decide what he, she, or it is like.

In many poems the speaker is the poet, who may speak in order to share a current experience or recall a poignant memory. On the other hand, poets often invent speakers very different from themselves in order to explore new ways of looking at life. Such speakers may or may not share the poet's opinions and concerns. Some poems may contain several speakers who talk to each other, rather than directly addressing the reader. Finally, in some poems the speakers may not be human at all. They may be animals or even objects that momentarily spring to life.

The words used by the speaker of a poem tell us a great deal about that speaker's identity, personality, and feelings. This information can help us to understand the poem's meaning more fully, and it can also add to our enjoyment of the poem.

### Thinking About the Speaker

1. Briefly describe the speaker as a boy. Prove from his choice of words that the speaker is now considerably older than he was at the time of the incident with the motorcycle.
2. What other differences can you find between the speaker as a boy and at present?

## COMPOSITION

### Writing About the Speaker of a Poem

■ In a paragraph describe the attitude of the adult speaker in "Fifteen" toward the incident he relates in the poem. In particular, explain why that incident might be important enough for the speaker to remember it.

### Writing a Poem About the Past

■ Write a short poem in which an older person looks back on an incident from his or her childhood. You may write as yourself, or you may invent an older speaker. Be sure that you make clear the difference between your speaker at present and the child who is involved in the incident.

*Fifteen* **181**

## STUDY QUESTIONS

1. by chance; near a bridge; fifteen
2. taking a long, exciting ride; looks for the owner; injured rider
3. was thrown from the bike and knocked unconscious; "good man"
4. *pulsing flanks; demure; companion*
5. *machine;* realizes it's dangerous
6. between childhood and adulthood; younger, less realistic
7. ■ child: wants to take something that doesn't belong to him; sees motorcycle as friendly
   ■ adult: looks for, helps owner; recognizes motorcycle's danger
   ■ learns that adult freedom brings frightening responsibility
8. *dwell on:* pleasure, excitement; *leave out:* responsibilities

## LITERARY FOCUS

1. ■ half child, half adult
   ■ Language is more sophisticated; repetition of "I was fifteen" implies a perspective of many years
2. sees the incident as a step toward maturity; aware of responsibility

---

## COMPOSITION: GUIDELINES FOR EVALUATION

### WRITING ABOUT THE SPEAKER

**Objective**

To identify the attitude of a speaker toward an incident described in a poem

**Guidelines for Evaluation**

- suggested length: one paragraph
- should identify the attitude of the adult speaker in "Fifteen" toward the incident described
- should suggest why the incident was important

### WRITING A POEM ABOUT THE PAST

**Objective**

To write a poem about insight gained in retrospect

**Guidelines for Evaluation**

- suggested length: five to fifteen lines
- should describe a childhood incident from a later perspective
- should reveal the differences between the speaker as a child and at present

*Sylvia Plath*

# Mirror

I am silver and exact. I have no preconceptions.[1]
Whatever I see I swallow immediately
Just as it is, unmisted by love or dislike.
I am not cruel, only truthful—
5  The eye of a little god, four-cornered.
Most of the time I meditate on the opposite wall.
It is pink, with speckles. I have looked at it so long
I think it is a part of my heart. But it flickers.
Faces and darkness separate us over and over.

10  Now I am a lake. A woman bends over me,
Searching my reaches[2] for what she really is.
Then she turns to those liars, the candles or the moon.
I see her back, and reflect it faithfully.
She rewards me with tears and an agitation of hands.
15  I am important to her. She comes and goes.
Each morning it is her face that replaces the darkness.
In me she has drowned a young girl, and in me an old woman
Rises toward her day after day, like a terrible fish.

---

1. **preconceptions:** ideas formed beforehand.
2. **reaches:** depths.

**182**  *Poetry*

## STUDY QUESTIONS

### Recalling

1. List five qualities that the speaker associates with itself.
2. What does the woman do every day with regard to the speaker? According to the speaker, what is she searching for?
3. What has been "drowned" in the speaker? What rises in its place?

### Interpreting

4. What details reveal the speaker's identity?
5. In what ways are the candles and moon "liars"? How does the speaker contrast these things to itself?
6. What is happening every day to the woman? Why does she react as she does when she looks at the speaker?
7. The speaker says that it is "not cruel, only truthful." Do you think the last two lines are "not cruel, only truthful"? Explain.

### Extending

8. Do you think people place too much emphasis on the way they look? Why or why not?

## COMPOSITION

### Writing About a Fictional Speaker

■ Describe the appearance and personality of the speaker in "Mirror." Begin by explaining what the speaker is and what it looks like. Then describe the speaker's personality traits. Using examples from the poem, explain which of the speaker's personality traits make it seem human. Finally point out those aspects of the speaker's personality that seem inhuman.

### Writing as an Object

■ Choose an inanimate object that you use often, and write a short poem in which that object talks about itself and you. Be sure to make the object's identity clear and to write from the special viewpoint of that object.

*Mirror*  **183**

STUDY QUESTIONS

1. truthfulness; lack of cruelty; acceptance; silverness; exactness
2. looks into it; "what she really is"
3. a young girl; an old woman
4. title; descriptions of itself
5. Their dim light makes the woman seem more attractive. It tells the truth.
6. She's growing older. Her reflection reveals more and more traces of age.
7. Answers will vary. *Not cruel:* The mirror has no emotions. *Cruel:* It expresses a subjective and brutal opinion.
8. Answers should state the student's opinion and give reasons for it.

## COMPOSITION: GUIDELINES FOR EVALUATION

### WRITING ABOUT A FICTIONAL SPEAKER

**Objective**
To describe the speaker of a poem

**Guidelines for Evaluation**
- suggested length: three paragraphs
- should state that the speaker is a mirror
- should describe the personality of the speaker, using traits that imply human/inhuman qualities

### WRITING AS AN OBJECT

**Objective**
To write a short poem from the point of view of an inanimate object

**Guidelines for Evaluation**
- suggested length: one to two stanzas
- should have a familiar inanimate object as its speaker
- should provide identifying details
- should describe the writer from the object's view

### James Wright

# A Blessing

Just off the highway to Rochester, Minnesota,
Twilight bounds softly forth on the grass.
And the eyes of those two Indian ponies
Darken with kindness.
5 They have come gladly out of the willows
To welcome my friend and me.
We step over the barbed wire into the pasture
Where they have been grazing all day, alone.
They ripple tensely, they can hardly contain their happiness
10 That we have come.
They bow shyly as wet swans. They love each other.
There is no loneliness like theirs.
At home once more,
They begin munching the young tufts of spring in the darkness.
15 I would like to hold the slenderer one in my arms,
For she has walked over to me
And nuzzled my left hand.
She is black and white,
Her mane falls wild on her forehead,
20 And the light breeze moves me to caress her long ear
That is delicate as the skin over a girl's wrist.
Suddenly I realize
That if I stepped out of my body I would break
Into blossom.

*A Blessing* **185**

AT A GLANCE
- The speaker and a friend watch two ponies grazing in a pasture.
- Although they love each other, the speaker senses the ponies are lonely.
- When one pony nuzzles him the speaker experiences intense joy.

LITERARY OPTIONS

- tone
- figurative language

THEMATIC OPTIONS

- communion with nature
- love and companionship

TONE

Gentle sounds and images establish the speaker's sympathetic and tender tone (l. 2).

PERSONIFICATION

To set up the interchange between the speaker and the ponies, Wright gives the animals human qualities: Their eyes "Darken with kindness," they "welcome," "love each other," and are lonely (ll. 4, 6, 11, 12).

METAPHOR AND MAIN IDEA

The image of himself as a blossoming flower conveys the speaker's intensely joyful response to nature (ll. 22–24).

REFLECTING ON THE POEM

What effect does the experience with the ponies have on the speaker? (Possible answers may include that he feels at one with nature, that the boundaries between humans and nature seem surmountable.)

STUDY QUESTIONS

1. at twilight; a Minnesota pasture
2. enter pasture; show affection
3. The pony nuzzles his hand; the speaker caresses the pony's ear.
4. "if I stepped out of my body I would break / Into blossom"
5. ability to feel love, shyness
6. ■ lines 1–5: identifies with the twilight; line 20: breeze moves him
   ■ He is a human being with an intellectual awareness of the experience.
7. He feels ecstasy. His being human creates a boundary between himself and the horses.
8. Answers may suggest less complicated affections, connection to more basic needs and feelings.

## LITERARY FOCUS

1. ■ feels love; admiration; awe
   ■ title; description of pony
2. The speaker feels "blessed" by his experience. His tone combines affection, happiness, and quiet reverence.

## STUDY QUESTIONS

### Recalling

1. When and where does the incident take place?
2. What do the speaker and his friend do when they see the two ponies? How do the ponies act toward the humans and toward each other?
3. Describe what occurs between the speaker and the slenderer pony in lines 15–21.
4. What does the speaker realize at the end of the poem?

### Interpreting

5. What human qualities does the speaker give to the ponies?
6. Find several places in the poem in which the speaker makes himself seem like a part of the natural world. How is he also separate from it?
7. What emotion do you think the phrase "break/ Into blossom" expresses? Why would the speaker have to step out of his body in order to break into blossom?

### Extending

8. What do you think we can experience from close contact with animals that we may miss in our contacts with other humans?

## LITERARY FOCUS

### Tone

The **tone** of a poem is the attitude the speaker expresses toward the subject matter and audience of the poem. We normally think of tone as the emotion we express with our voices and add to the words that we speak. A writer, on the other hand, must rely entirely on the written word to express emotion. The tone of a poem may express any emotion—for example, sympathy, anger, joy, sorrow, amusement, or solemnity. It may even combine several different feelings or shift from one emotion to another.

In a poem, as in any piece of writing, the tone is created chiefly by the author's word choices and sentence structure. For example, short sentences can create a breathless, excited tone. If we read carefully, we can hear the tone and sense the feelings running through the words of any poem.

### Thinking About Tone

1. In "A Blessing" what is the attitude of the speaker toward the slenderer pony? What words or images express that attitude?
2. Describe the tone of the poem and the attitude of the speaker toward his experience. Does the tone combine several different emotions? Explain.

## COMPOSITION

### Writing About a Title

■ Explain how the title "A Blessing" captures the experience described in Wright's poem. First describe the speaker's experience in the poem, and explain what it means to him. Then explain how the poem's title is appropriate to that experience. Finally, indicate the ways in which the title actually adds to the meaning of the speaker's experience.

### Writing with Unusual Verbs

■ In "A Blessing" James Wright uses a number of vivid and unusual verbs: the twilight "bounds," the ponies "ripple," the speaker "would break/ Into blossom." Write a short poem describing an animal engaged in an action. Try to use verbs that are not usually associated with that animal.

## COMPOSITION: GUIDELINES FOR EVALUATION

### WRITING ABOUT A TITLE

**Objective**
To analyze the title of a poem

**Guidelines for Evaluation**
■ suggested length: three paragraphs
■ should describe the speaker's experience and perceptions
■ should explain how the title emphasizes the nature of the experience

### WRITING WITH UNUSUAL VERBS

**Objective**
To write a poem using vivid and unusual verbs

**Guidelines for Evaluation**
■ suggested length: one stanza
■ should describe an animal in action
■ should use verbs not usually associated with the animal described

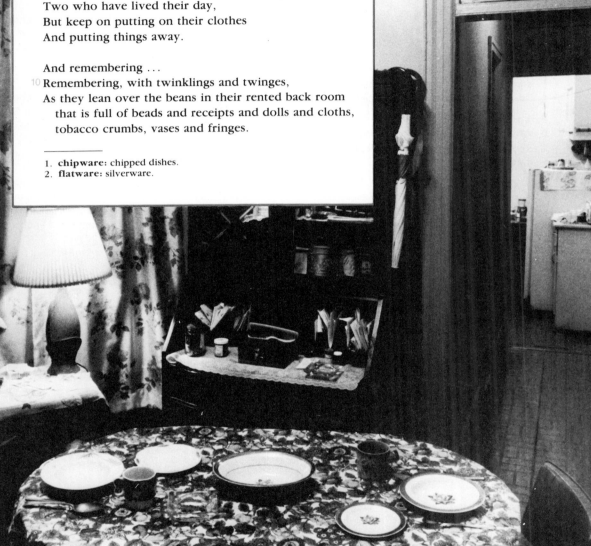

*Gwendolyn Brooks*

# The Bean Eaters

They eat beans mostly, this old yellow pair.
Dinner is a casual affair.
Plain chipware[1] on a plain and creaking wood,
Tin flatware.[2]

5 Two who are Mostly Good.
Two who have lived their day,
But keep on putting on their clothes
And putting things away.

And remembering ...
10 Remembering, with twinklings and twinges,
As they lean over the beans in their rented back room
   that is full of beads and receipts and dolls and cloths,
   tobacco crumbs, vases and fringes.

---

1. **chipware:** chipped dishes.
2. **flatware:** silverware.

## AT A GLANCE

An old couple eat a dinner of beans in their rented room filled with mementos and memories.

## LITERARY OPTIONS

- imagery
- main idea

## THEMATIC OPTIONS

- time and memory
- poverty and wealth

## IMAGERY

Brooks uses the bric-a-brac the couple have collected to describe their domestic history and to suggest their richer, or fuller, past (ll. 3–4, 12–13).

## MAIN IDEA

By describing how the couple remember the past "with twinklings and twinges" the poet subtly contrasts their past happiness with their present existence (l. 10).

## REFLECTING ON THE POEM

Describe the speaker's feelings about the old couple. (Possible answers may include that she seems to mix respect and tenderness for them with sadness and quiet anger at their poverty.)

## STUDY QUESTIONS

1. eat mostly beans; use plain chipware; creaking wood table
2. putting on clothes; eating beans; remembering; putting things away
3. beads; receipts; dolls; cloths
4. They are poor—they eat beans "mostly" and live in one room.
5. The word *twinklings* suggests happy memories; and the objects in their room suggest full lives.
6. universality
7. affectionate; sympathetic; quietly sad
8. Souvenirs keep the past alive. They may arouse happiness, sorrow, regret, anger.

### VOCABULARY

1. ■ beans; chipware; beads
   ■ General nouns like *food* would make the images less vivid.
2. Answers should list objects that are the inexpensive and natural remains of a simple life.

### COMPARING POEMS

1. ■ "Fifteen": older speaker, reflective tone
   ■ "Mirror": inanimate object, analytical tone
   ■ "Blessing": young speaker, reverent tone
   ■ "Bean Eaters": omniscient speaker, distanced sympathy
2. ■ "Fifteen": The speaker's delight and excitement give the bike a seductive character.
   ■ "Mirror": The mirror's analytical tone makes it seem cold.
   ■ "Blessing": The speaker's emotions are projected onto ponies.

## STUDY QUESTIONS

### Recalling

1. List three details used by the speaker to describe the dinner of the couple in the poem.
2. What activities of the old couple are described in stanzas 2 and 3?
3. List four of the items that fill the "rented back room" of the couple.

### Interpreting

4. Use examples from the poem to explain how the speaker makes the couple's economic status clear.
5. Can you find any evidence of happiness in their lives? Explain.
6. What effect does the speaker create by not giving the old people individual names?
7. Describe the speaker's tone: Is it, for example, admiring, pitying, angry, curious, or unfeeling? Does it combine several feelings?

### Extending

8. Why do you think people hold onto souvenirs of the past? What various emotions might such mementos arouse?

## VOCABULARY

### Specific and Concrete Nouns

Specific and concrete nouns refer to particular persons, places, and things that can be clearly pictured. For example, *bean* is a specific concrete noun that refers to a particular kind of food; *food* itself is a general noun. Specific and concrete nouns are important in all writing but are especially crucial in poetry. By piling up a series of specific and concrete nouns, Gwendolyn Brooks quickly paints a vivid picture of the life of the old couple in "The Bean Eaters."

1. Find three examples of Brooks's use of specific and concrete nouns in "The Bean Eaters." Substitute a general noun for one of these words, and describe the effect of this substitution.
2. Add more nouns to the list in lines 12–13 of the old couple's possessions. Be sure to choose nouns that are specific, concrete, *and* appropriate to the old people.

## COMPARING POEMS

1. For two or more of the poems in this section—"Fifteen," "Mirror," "A Blessing," and "The Bean Eaters "—describe the attitude of the speaker to the passage of time. Be sure to identify the speaker in each and to describe the tone of the poem.
2. Several of the poems in this section give human qualities to nonhuman things. For two or more of these poems, explain how the speaker's identity and tone help create these qualities. In each case what effect does the poet achieve?

# LITERARY FOCUS: *The Sound of Poetry*

The world is alive with sound. Birds warble and whistle, truck engines grumble, and human chatter fills the air with its own noises. Even when we read silently, we "listen" to the sounds of the letters and words we see. Poets are particularly sensitive to the sounds of language. They know that the music of a poem is much more than a pleasant background or decoration to the poem's meaning: The sound of a poem intensifies and often creates its meaning.

Poets have a number of sound effects at their disposal. The following poets are particularly inventive in their use of these sound effects.

**Emily Dickinson** (1830–1886) spent her whole life in the town of Amherst, Massachusetts. Disappointed by early rejection of her poetry, she vowed never to have her work published. It was only after her death that her sister found over 1,700 poems scribbled on scraps of paper and hidden in Dickinson's room. As she does in "I Like to See It Lap the Miles," Dickinson often finds striking sound effects to suit her highly original way of looking at life.

■ Have you ever encountered a machine that seemed to have human qualities? What qualities did it have?

**Robert Burns** (1759–1796) grew up on a poor farm in Ayrshire, Scotland. He began to write poetry at a young age and eventually became known as Scotland's national poet. "My Heart's in the Highlands" is an example of Burns's gift for using traditional Scottish tunes in his poetry.

■ Have you ever felt a special bond with a particular place?

**William Shakespeare** (1564–1616) was born in the town of Stratford in England. In his early twenties he left Stratford for London, where he became known as an actor and playwright. His plays and poems have made him the best-known author of the English-speaking world. The speech "Tomorrow, and Tomorrow, and Tomorrow," an excerpt from the play *Macbeth,* demonstrates Shakespeare's use of rhythm to create a dramatically powerful utterance.

■ If you were a close friend of the speaker of this poem, what might you say to help him to change his grim view of the world?

**William Carlos Williams** (1883–1963), born in Rutherford, New Jersey, eventually settled in his home town to practice his twin professions, pediatrics and poetry. He once said, ''Anything that the poet can lift from its dull bed by force of imagination becomes his material. Anything.'' ''Winter Trees'' uses the rhythms of everyday speech to describe a familiar scene in a fresh and imaginative way.

■ In what ways does the predictability of nature provide comfort to human beings? Can you think of an example from your own life?

**Alexander Pope** (1688–1744), the son of a prosperous London businessman, was left a hunchback by a childhood illness. Educated at home, he began to write poetry at the age of eleven and eventually became the most influential poet of his day, a time concerned with setting clear standards for art and literature. In ''Sound and Sense'' he clearly states—and ingeniously demonstrates—his opinions about poetry.

■ What is the effect when the sound of a poem dominates its sense? When its meaning overpowers its sound?

*Emily Dickinson*

# I Like to See It Lap the Miles

I like to see it lap the Miles—
And lick the Valleys up—
And stop to feed itself at Tanks—
And then—prodigious step

5 Around a Pile of Mountains—
And supercilious[1] peer
In Shanties—by the sides of Roads—
And then a Quarry pare

To fit its sides
10 And crawl between
Complaining all the while
In horrid—hooting stanza—
Then chase itself down Hill—

And neigh like Boanerges[2]
15 Then—prompter than a Star
Stop—docile and omnipotent
At its own stable door—

---

1. **supercilious:** proud, arrogant.
2. **Boanerges** [bō′ə nur′jēz]: booming preacher.
Christ referred to the apostles John and James as
"Boanerges," or "sons of thunder."

---

## STUDY QUESTIONS

### Recalling
1. According to lines 1–2, what does "it," the subject of the poem, "lap" and "lick"?
2. Name three places to which "it" travels. What words describe its movements in these places?
3. What sounds does "it" make?
4. Where and how does "it" finally stop?

### Interpreting
5. What is the real identity of the thing described in this poem? What is its "horrid—hooting stanza"?

What is it really doing when it stops at its own "stable door"?
6. What human or animal qualities does the speaker give to the subject of the poem? What impression do they create of the subject?
7. Describe the speaker's attitude toward the subject.

### Extending
8. Why do you think people often attribute the qualities of living creatures to machines?

*I Like to See It Lap the Miles*　**191**

The speaker describes a train as if it were a horse or a giant.

- rhythm
- figurative language

- the imagination
- machinery vs. nature

By describing the train like a living thing (e.g., it *licks, feeds, peers*), the poet makes it less mechanical and, therefore, more appealing (ll. 2, 3, 6).

The speaker's choice of descriptive adjectives (*prodigious, supercilious, docile and omnipotent*) shows her awe of and amusement at the train (ll. 4, 6, 16).

By introducing a dash after "And then" in the first stanza, the poet starts to slow the pace of the poem as well as that of the train (l. 4).

How does the poet use the pace of the poem to mirror its action? (The poem starts out fast, slows down at mountains, picks up downhill, and slows to a stop.)

1. the miles; the valleys
2. "feeds" itself at tanks; "step[s]" around mountains; "chase[s] itself" down a hill
3. complains; hoots; neighs
4. at the door of its stable; docile and omnipotent
5. a train; its whistle; pulling in at a station
6. the ability to step, peer, complain; an animal with a will of its own
7. fascination; amusement
8. makes them seem less forbidding

**Rhythm**

- regular iambic
- begins at a fast pace; slows down in stanzas 2 and 3; picks up speed at the end of stanza 3; slows to stop at last two lines
- The odd punctuation creates unexpected halts and spurts.

**Slant Rhyme**

- *up, step* (lines 2, 4); *peer, pare* (lines 6, 8); *while, Hill* (lines 11, 13); *Star, door* (lines 15, 17)
- All the instances of slant rhyme help to connect the poem's lines and create patterns within them.

## LITERARY FOCUS

### Rhythm

The word *rhythm* comes from a Greek word meaning "flow" and refers to any repeated pattern. In a poem the **rhythm** is the pattern of beats created by the syllables and stresses of the words in each line.

In some poems the pattern of beats is regular and predictable. For example, the following lines by the Elizabethan poet Ben Jonson use a regular rhythm in which the stressed syllables, which are marked ´, alternate with the unstressed syllables, which are marked ‿ :

Queen and huntress, chaste and fair,
Now the sun is laid to sleep.

When the rhythm follows such a strict pattern, the poem is said to have a definite **meter.** By contrast many modern poems use an irregular and free-flowing rhythm in which the beats do not follow a consistent pattern. For example, each of the following lines from William Stafford's "Fifteen" seems to have its own rhythm:

I found back of the willows one summer
day a motorcycle with engine running...

The rhythm of a poem often echoes its sense, or meaning. For example, a poem about a military band is likely to march in regular meter, while a poem about a dragonfly would probably zip and halt unpredictably. Stressed syllables slow down a line, and unstressed syllables quicken its movement. Punctuation and stanza breaks can also affect the rhythm of a poem.

### Thinking About Rhythm

- Read Dickinson's poem out loud, and note the syllables and accents in each line. Does the poem follow a regular rhythm or an irregular one? What other qualities can you hear in the rhythm: When does it speed up and slow down? How does the punctuation affect the rhythm?

### Slant Rhyme

Words **rhyme** when they repeat the same sound. **Slant rhyme** is a type of rhyme that occurs when two words repeat similar, but not identical, sounds. Slant rhymes are created between words that have the same vowel sounds but different consonants, as in *meek* and *neat;* this type of slant rhyme is known as **assonance.** Slant rhymes also occur when words have the same consonants but not the same vowel sounds, as in *pat* and *pit;* this type of slant rhyme is known as **consonance.** Some slant rhymes combine assonance and consonance, for example, *painter* and *tinder,* or *enchanted* and *repented.*Other terms for slant rhyme are **approximate rhyme, off rhyme, near rhyme,** and **half rhyme.**

Slant rhyme was not popular in poetry until this century; in fact, Emily Dickinson was often criticized for her use of it. Slant rhyme can be very effective in poetry because it snaps us to attention, surprising us with the hint of an echo when we expect a more obvious rhyme.

### Thinking About Slant Rhyme

- Find three examples of slant rhyme in "I Like to See It Lap the Miles," and explain what each rhyme adds to the poem.

## COMPOSITION

### Writing About Rhythm and Rhyme

- Explain how Dickinson's use of rhythm and rhyme suits her subject in "I Like to See It Lap the Miles." Be sure to describe both the rhythm and rhyme of the poem. Then explain how the rhythm and rhyme are particularly appropriate to the behavior of the poem's subject.

### Writing a Description with Rhythm

- Write a poem that describes a machine as if it were a human being or an animal. Pay special attention to the appearance, sounds, and actions of the machine. Use a rhythm that suits the movement of the machine you are describing.

192    *Poetry*

## COMPOSITION: GUIDELINES FOR EVALUATION

### WRITING ABOUT RHYTHM AND RHYME

**Objective**

To analyze the use of rhythm and rhyme in a poem

**Guidelines for Evaluation**

- suggested length: one to three paragraphs
- should identify the subject of the poem as a train
- show how the poem's rhythm and rhyme reflect a train's characteristics

### WRITING DESCRIPTION WITH RHYTHM

**Objective**

To write a rhythmic poem describing a machine as a living creature

**Guidelines for Evaluation**

- suggested length: one to three stanzas
- should describe a machine, giving it human or animal qualities
- should use a rhythm suggested by the characteristic movement of the machine

*Robert Burns*

# My Heart's in the Highlands[1]

My heart's in the Highlands, my heart is not here,
My heart's in the Highlands a-chasing the deer,
A-chasing the wild deer and following the roe[2]—
My heart's in the Highlands, wherever I go!

5 Farewell to the Highlands, farewell to the North,
The birthplace of valor, the country of worth!
Wherever I wander, wherever I rove,
The hills of the Highlands forever I love.

Farewell to the mountains high covered with snow,
10 Farewell to the straths[3] and green valleys below,
Farewell to the forests and wild-hanging woods,
Farewell to the torrents and loud-pouring floods!

My heart's in the Highlands, my heart is not here,
My heart's in the Highlands a-chasing the deer,
15 A-chasing the wild deer and following the roe—
My heart's in the Highlands, wherever I go!

---

1. **Highlands:** hilly regions in Scotland.
2. **roe:** small deer found in Europe and Asia.
3. **straths:** wide river beds.

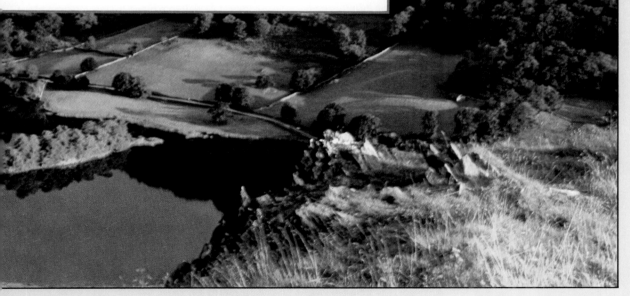

### AT A GLANCE

Celebrating their beauty, the speaker lovingly says goodbye to his native Scottish Highlands.

### LITERARY OPTIONS

- repetition and parallelism
- rhythm
- rhyme

### THEMATIC OPTIONS

- love of home
- responding to nature
- loss and regret

### REPETITION

The three words the speaker repeats the most *(heart, Highlands, and Farewell)* engrave his sense of love and loss not only on his memory but on the reader's as well.

### PARALLELISM

Burns uses a special kind of parallelism, in which the second part of a line contrasts with the first, to emphasize the speaker's contrasting emotions (ll. 1, 13).

### RHYTHM

The poem's rhythm suggests a song written in three-quarter, or waltz, time. This strong, regular rhythm sweeps the reader along with the speaker's emotions.

### RHYME

Burns's use of end rhymes (e.g., *here/deer; roe/go*) enhances the rhythm, adds to the poem's songlike quality, and makes the poem more memorable.

### REFLECTING ON THE POEM

Why does the speaker feel so intensely about the Scottish Highlands? (Possible answers may include that he misses them with the special nostalgia many people feel for their native land.)

STUDY QUESTIONS

1. in the Scottish Highlands; wild deer
2. his love for the Highlands
3. mountains; riverbeds; valleys; woods and forests
4. ■ its wildness and the valor and worth of its people
   ■ It is his home.
5. carries Highlands in his heart everywhere
6. love, joy, sadness, nostalgia
7. Nostalgia is pleasant in that it involves a loving memory. It is unpleasant in that it reminds us of the inability to recover something lost. It is good when it enriches the present, and it is bad when it prevents us from living in the present.

## LITERARY FOCUS

1. *My Heart's in the Highlands, Highlands, farewell;* create pattern and heighten emotion
2. ■ first stanza: lines 1, 3, 5, 6, 7, 9–12
   ■ sample answer: "My heart is in the Highlands rather than being here." The unparallel revision is less forceful and more conventional.

## STUDY QUESTIONS

### Recalling

1. According to the speaker, where is his heart, and what is it chasing?
2. What does the speaker say will stay the same no matter where he travels?
3. List four things to which the speaker bids farewell.

### Interpreting

4. What qualities of the region seem most important to the speaker? Why do you think he feels the way he does about the Highlands?
5. What consolation might the speaker find in the last line? Explain.
6. Does the poem express one emotion, or does it mix several different emotions? Explain.

### Extending

7. *Nostalgia* means "pleasant pain." Explain how nostalgia can be both pleasant and painful. In what ways might nostalgia for a place be good? In what ways might it be bad?

## LITERARY FOCUS

### Repetition and Parallelism

Poets often create special effects in their poems with **repetition,** which is the repeated use of sounds, words, phrases, lines, or even stanzas. Repetition increases the importance of the items that are repeated. It also helps to tie the work together into a unified whole. In addition, repetition has an emotional appeal: It creates the reassuring sense that we are returning to something familiar.

When a line or stanza is repeated in a poem, it is called a **refrain,** a term also used in music to refer to repeated portions of a melody. In general, all forms of repetition add to a poem's musical quality.

**Parallelism** is the placement of related ideas in parallel, or similar, structures. Julius Caesar's famous statement "I came, I saw, I conquered" is an example of parallelism because it is composed of three parallel clauses consisting of the pronoun *I* and a past-tense verb. Like repetition, parallelism gives extra emphasis to the items that are arranged in the parallel structures and helps to tie a work together.

### Thinking About Repetition and Parallelism

1. What words and lines are repeated in "My Heart's in the Highlands"? How do these repetitions add to the emotional force of the poem?
2. Where does Burns use parallelism in "My Heart's in the Highlands"? Rewrite one of these lines so that it is no longer parallel. Have you changed the poem for better or for worse? Explain.

## COMPOSITION

### Writing About the Sound of a Poem

■ Discuss the ways in which Burns's poem resembles a song. First point out examples of Burns's use of such songlike qualities as rhyme, repetition, and regular rhythm in "My Heart's in the Highlands." Then explain the ways in which the songlike qualities of Burns's poem add to its impact.

### Writing a Poem of Farewell

■ Write a short poem of no more than eight lines bidding farewell to a place that is very important to you. Before you write, picture the place and think of what it means to you. Begin several lines of your poem with the words *Farewell to . . . ,* and follow this phrase with some specific, vivid details. Use repetition in other places as well, and try to follow a regular meter and rhyme.

## COMPOSITION: GUIDELINES FOR EVALUATION

### WRITING ABOUT THE SOUND OF A POEM

**Objective**
To analyze the songlike quality of a poem

**Guidelines for Evaluation**
■ suggested length: one to two paragraphs
■ should cite examples of rhyme, regular rhythm, or other songlike qualities
■ should explain how these qualities add to the poem's impact

### WRITING A POEM OF FAREWELL

**Objective**
To write a poem of farewell

**Guidelines for Evaluation**
■ suggested length: eight lines or less
■ should bid farewell to a familiar place
■ should begin several lines with "Farewell to," followed by specific features of the place
■ should have regular meter and rhyme

*William Shakespeare*

# Tomorrow, and Tomorrow, and Tomorrow

Tomorrow, and tomorrow, and tomorrow,
Creeps in this petty pace from day to day,
To the last syllable of recorded time;
And all our yesterdays have lighted fools
5 The way to dusty death. Out, out, brief candle!
Life's but a walking shadow, a poor player
That struts and frets his hour upon the stage
And then is heard no more. It is a tale
Told by an idiot, full of sound and fury
10 Signifying nothing.

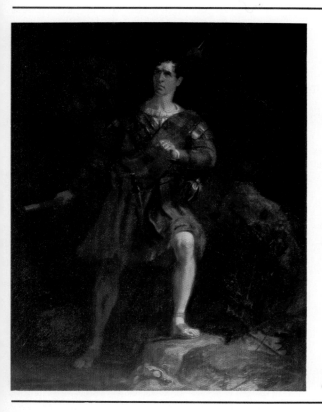

*Charles Kemble as Macbeth*, Andrew Morton,
(1802–1845).

*Tomorrow, and Tomorrow, and Tomorrow* **195**

## AT A GLANCE

Macbeth expresses his bitter view of human life as boring, short, pathetic, and senseless.

## LITERARY OPTIONS

- blank verse
- imagery
- figurative language

## THEMATIC OPTIONS

- life and death
- time

## BLANK VERSE

Speaking in blank verse enables Macbeth to express his thoughts in rhythms close to those of everyday speech; blank verse heightens the intimacy of Macbeth's meditation.

## IMAGERY

Macbeth emphasizes his despair by likening life to a light that is easily extinguished ("Out, out, brief candle!") and envisioning death as the darkness that endures (l. 5).

## MAIN IDEA AND METAPHOR

By comparing life to a "tale told by an idiot," Macbeth portrays human experience as a meaningless, if frenetic, activity (ll. 8–10).

## REFLECTING ON THE POEM

What is it about life that makes it seem meaningless to Macbeth? (Possible answers may include that he perceives it as tedious and brief and that it leads to the emptiness of death.)

1. *tomorrow; day to day; his hour; recorded time; all our yesterdays*
2. "dusty death"
3. *a walking shadow; a bad actor; a meaningless tale told by an idiot*
4. creates a sense of days passing, one by one, all the same; view of time passing slowly
5. dying
6. slowly; "petty pace"
7. He places little value on life, which is a brief and tedious journey toward death.
8. A tragedy creates the feeling that life is meaningless.

## VIEWPOINT

- Days creep "to the last syllable of recorded time."
- "all our yesterdays"

## LITERARY FOCUS

1. ■ exactly: lines 4, 7, 8
   ■ altered: lines 1–3, 5–6, 9–10
   ■ Line 1 creates a striking beginning; lines 2–3 slow the pace; line 5 emphasizes the brevity of life; line 6 emphasizes "life"; line 9 slows the pace for the finale.
2. Blank verse makes the speech creep along and adds to its fatalistic tone.

## STUDY QUESTIONS

### Recalling

1. List five references to time in these lines.
2. According to Macbeth, the speaker of these lines, what waits at the end of "all our yesterdays"?
3. To what three things does Macbeth compare life in lines 6–10?

### Interpreting

4. What is the effect of the repetition of the word *tomorrow*? What view does it express of the future?
5. In line 5 Macbeth is referring to more than putting out a candle. What is he really talking about?
6. What is Macbeth's view of time: Does it pass too quickly or too slowly? Give evidence from the poem.
7. What value does Macbeth place on life, according to these lines? What relationship does he see between life and death?

### Extending

8. In the play Macbeth utters these words just after learning of his wife's death. Why might someone respond to tragic news as Macbeth does in this speech?

## VIEWPOINT

One critic sees the character of Macbeth as a man whose actions have led him to lose his belief in everything:

> His cynicism is general: it is not his own life, but Life, which has come to have no meaning.

> — J. Holloway, *Twentieth Century Interpretations of Macbeth*

■ Explain how this statement might be applied to Macbeth's "Tomorrow" speech. Point out those places in the speech that show that Macbeth is speaking about life in general.

## LITERARY FOCUS

### Blank Verse

**Blank verse** consists of any number of unrhymed lines that are each ten syllables long with a stress on every other syllable. Another name for this verse form is **unrhymed** (therefore "blank") **iambic pentameter**. An **iamb** is a unit of rhythm made up of an unstressed syllable followed by a stressed syllable. The words *con fuse* and *re peat* are both iambs.

Blank verse seems more like prose than most other verse forms. It does not rhyme, it is not usually written in stanzas, and it is very close to the natural rhythms of the English language. Although based on carefully counted syllables and beats, blank verse usually flows very naturally when it is written well. Because of its natural, free-flowing quality, blank verse is very popular among writers of English, accounting for over half of all the poetry written in English.

### Thinking About Blank Verse

1. Count the number of stressed and unstressed syllables in each line of this excerpt from *Macbeth*. Where does Shakespeare follow the pattern of iambic pentameter exactly? Where does he alter the pattern? What might his reasons be in each case?
2. How does the use of a regular rhythm affect the tone of this speech? Do you think the use of blank verse adds to or detracts from the emotion of Macbeth's response to his wife's death? Explain.

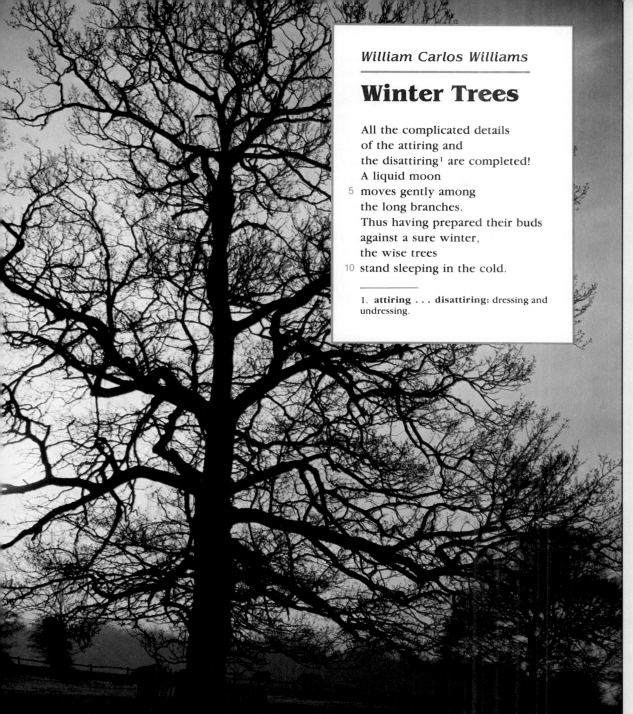

## William Carlos Williams

# Winter Trees

All the complicated details
of the attiring and
the disattiring[1] are completed!
A liquid moon
5  moves gently among
the long branches.
Thus having prepared their buds
against a sure winter,
the wise trees
10  stand sleeping in the cold.

---

1. **attiring . . . disattiring:** dressing and undressing.

1. attiring and disattiring of trees
2. *liquid; moves gently*
3. winter; sleeping
4. change from fall to winter
5. dressing, undressing; usually applied to people; suggests the growth and loss of leaves
6. Sap freezes, natural processes slow down in winter. The tree "knows" how to survive winter.
7. Students may feel either that such humanization is false because it is sentimental or that it is truthful because it creates an awareness of shared similarities.

## LITERARY FOCUS

1. three; slows flow, emphasizes words preceding and following breaks
2. ■ "details / of the attiring and / the disattiring": slows flow, focuses on important nouns
   ■ "among / the long branches": slows movement, highlights individual words and phrases

## STUDY QUESTIONS

### Recalling

1. According to lines 1–3, what are completed?
2. What words does the speaker use to describe the moon?
3. According to the speaker, what have the trees prepared for, and what are they doing now?

### Interpreting

4. What natural process is actually being described in the poem?
5. What do the words *attiring* and *disattiring* mean? Why are these unusual words to apply to trees? Why might these words be appropriate to the trees in the poem?
6. In what sense might a tree sleep? In what ways might a tree be wise?

### Extending

7. Do you think giving human qualities to nonhuman things creates a false picture of nature? Why or why not?

## LITERARY FOCUS

### Free Verse

**Free verse** is poetry that does not follow a regular, predictable pattern of rhythm, line length, or rhyme. Free verse is a relatively recent form of poetry; poets first broke from traditional forms to write free verse in the nineteenth century.

In free verse the lines may vary in their lengths and may end in unusual places. For example, lines may break between subjects and their verbs. In determining the lengths of lines, the writer of free verse considers such questions as how the lines look on the page, how they sound when they are read, and, especially, how the breaks at the ends of the lines affect the poem's meaning and flow. The writer of free verse must therefore be sensitive to the natural rhythms and pauses of language.

### Thinking About Free Verse

1. How many sentences does "Winter Trees" contain? Williams separates his subjects and verbs on different lines of poetry. How do these breaks affect the flow of the poem?
2. Read "Winter Trees" out loud. Find two other unusual line breaks in the poem, and explain how each affects the flow and movement of the poem.

## COMPOSITION

### Writing About Poetry and Prose

■ Discuss the resemblance of "Winter Trees" to both poetry and prose. First list the principal qualities that differentiate poetry and prose. Then explain how "Winter Trees" exemplifies some of the traits of poetry and some of the traits of prose.

### Writing Free Verse

■ Using free verse, write a poem about a change of seasons. Do not actually name the seasons. Instead, choose details that make the time of year clear to your reader. Pay particular attention to your line breaks and the way in which they affect the poem's meaning and flow.

## COMPOSITION: GUIDELINES FOR EVALUATION

### WRITING ABOUT POETRY AND PROSE

**Objective**

To identify the elements of poetry and prose that appear in "Winter Trees"

**Guidelines for Evaluation**

- suggested length: two to three paragraphs
- should list characteristics of poetry: controlled line breaks, rhyme, rhythm
- should list characteristics of prose: unbroken lines, natural speech

### WRITING FREE VERSE

**Objective**

To write a poem in free verse

**Guidelines for Evaluation**

- suggested length: one to two stanzas
- should be written in free verse
- should describe aspects of a seasonal change without explicitly identifying the change
- should contain the qualities of free verse

## Alexander Pope

# Sound and Sense

True ease in writing comes from art, not chance,
As those move easiest who have learned to dance.
'Tis not enough no harshness gives offense,
The sound must seem an echo to the sense.
5 Soft is the strain[1] when Zephyr[2] gently blows,
And the smooth stream in smoother numbers[3] flows;
But when loud surges lash the sounding shore,
The hoarse, rough verse should like the torrent roar;
When Ajax[4] strives some rock's vast weight to throw,
10 The line too labors, and the words move slow;
Not so, when swift Camilla[5] scours the plain,
Flies o'er the unbending corn, and skims along the main.
Hear how Timotheus'[6] varied lays[7] surprise,
And bid alternate passions fall and rise!

---

1. **strain:** passage of music or poetry.
2. **Zephyr:** the west wind. Zephyrus was the mythological god of the west wind.
3. **numbers:** poetic meter.
4. **Ajax:** legendary Greek warrior famed for his strength.
5. **Camilla:** mythological queen who could run so swiftly that she could pass over a field of grain without bending the stalks or over a sea without getting her feet wet.
6. **Timotheus:** Greek musician and poet.
7. **lays:** songs or ballads.

## STUDY QUESTIONS

### Recalling

1. According to line 1, what produces "True ease in writing"? What two things does the speaker require of poetry in lines 3 and 4?
2. According to lines 7–8, how should poetry portray "loud surges"? According to lines 9–10, how should poetry describe the labor of Ajax?

### Interpreting

3. What does "True ease in writing" mean? How is "art" the opposite of "chance"?

4. In what ways is writing comparable to dancing?
5. Explain how the sounds of the words in line 7 echo the sense, or meaning, of the line. How does the rhythm in lines 9 and 10 help these lines to practice what they preach?
6. In general, do you think Pope's poem shows that he can follow his own advice? Explain with examples.

### Extending

7. In your own experience would you agree that true ease in doing something always comes from hard work and discipline? Explain.

*Sound and Sense* **199**

**AT A GLANCE**

Pope sets forth his ideals regarding the close relationship between the sound and meaning of a poem.

**LITERARY OPTIONS**

- onomatopoeia
- alliteration

**THEMATIC OPTIONS**

- art and the imagination
- ideals

**ONOMATOPOEIA**

Pope's examples of onomatopoeia (*harshness, echo, smooth, lash, skims*) demonstrate the connection between sound and sense (ll. 3, 4, 6, 7, 12).

**ALLITERATION**

Alliteration ("soft is the strain," "smooth stream") connects sound with meaning (ll. 5, 6).

**REFLECTING ON THE POEM**

In your own words, express the advice Pope was offering to the poets of his day. (The sounds of a poem should support its meaning.)

**STUDY QUESTIONS**

1. skill and care; no harshness; sound should echo sense
2. with hoarse, rough verse; with slow-moving lines
3. ability to write gracefully and effectively; art—done with skill; chance—done haphazardly
4. expresses emotion; has form; requires skill
5. Line 7 contains full, harsh vowel sounds. In lines 9–10 one-syllable words slow the pace.
6. Yes—it contains carefully rhymed and metered lines whose sounds echo their meanings.
7. Students may cite personal activities that require practice.

## Onomatopoeia and Alliteration

1. ■ blows: sounds like moaning wind
   ■ hoarse, rough: harsh combination
   ■ roar: Vowels and consonants resonate.
2. ■ "The sound must seem": initial / internal; creates echo
   ■ "the smooth stream": initial / internal; creates flowing effect
   ■ "But when loud surges lash": initial / internal; echoes waves
   ■ "swift Camilla scours": initial/internal; echoes scouring and suggests swiftness
3. sounds convey meaning, echo sense

## Allusions

1. references to Zephyr and Ajax
2. Students may argue that the unfamiliarity poses obstacles or that it stimulates the joy of discovery.

## VOCABULARY

1. ordinary: *soft, loud;* formal: *surges, labors*
2. suggests force of the ocean

## COMPARING POEMS

1. ■ "Miles"—regular rhythm, slant rhyme, onomatopoeia, alliteration
   ■ "Highlands"—rhyme, alliteration, repetition, onomatopoeia, regular meter
   ■ "Tomorrow"—slant rhyme, rhythm, repetition, onomatopoeia, alliteration, variations on regular meter
   ■ "Trees"—internal rhyme, slant rhyme, alliteration, free verse
   ■ "Sound"—rhyme, rhythm, onomatopoeia; alliteration; follows regular meter with some variation
2. ■ "Miles": regular rhythm, slant / full rhymes suggest the train's sound and movement of train
   ■ "Highlands": rhymes, repetition create a melody conveying nostalgia

---

## LITERARY FOCUS

### Onomatopoeia and Alliteration

**Onomatopoeia** [on′ə mat′ə pē′ə] is the use of a word whose sound mimics or suggests its meaning. For example, the word *buzz* actually sounds like what it means—the noise made by a bee. The word *clop* imitates the hollow slap of hooves on hard surfaces. Onomatopoeia both reinforces the meaning of a poem and adds to its musical quality.

**Alliteration,** another special sound effect, is the repetition of consonant sounds within a short space. Usually alliteration occurs at the beginning of words, as in the sentence "The *b*ee *b*rushed the *b*lossom and then *b*uzzed away." Such alliteration is called **initial alliteration.** A more subtle form of alliteration, called **internal alliteration,** occurs within, rather than at the beginning of, words. Both internal and initial alliteration can be found in the sentence, "The *Ch*inese in*ch*worm *ch*ewed through the pea*ch*."

Wherever it occurs, alliteration adds to the musical quality of a poem by creating echoes among its sounds. Alliteration also adds to the meaning and unity of a poem by connecting its words and ideas.

### Thinking About Onomatopoeia and Alliteration

1. Find three examples of onomatopoeia in "Sound and Sense," and explain how the sound of each word mimics its meaning.
2. Find four examples of initial and internal alliteration in "Sound and Sense." Describe the effect of each.
3. Explain how Pope's use of onomatopoeia and alliteration in "Sound and Sense" supports the poem's overall meaning.

### Allusions

An **allusion** is a reference to a work of literature or to a well-known person, place, or event from history. Writers who use allusions expect their audiences to recognize the original source of the allusion. Among the most popular sources of allusions are the Bible and the Greek and Roman myths.

An allusion serves as a kind of shorthand, a brief reference to a well-known idea, situation, or picture that needs no further explanation. For example, Pope adds a striking picture to "Sound and Sense"

**200** *Poetry*

---

when he refers to Camilla, a mythological queen so fleet of foot that she could run over the ocean's waves without getting her feet wet.

### Thinking About Allusions

1. Using the footnotes, identify two other allusions in "Sound and Sense."
2. Do these allusions add to or detract from your enjoyment of the poem? Explain.

## VOCABULARY

### Word Choice and Connotation

**Word choice** is a writer's particular selection of language in any work. Often referred to as **diction,** word choice strongly influences the tone of a poem and our impression of its speaker.

An important factor in word choice is connotation. Several words may have the same general **denotation,** or literal meaning. However, their **connotations**—the associations we have for these words—may differ a great deal. For example, *flood* and *torrent* have the same basic literal meaning, but *torrent* sounds more formal, and it also creates a more violent picture than *flood*. Pope chose *torrent* in "Sound and Sense" in order to create a particular impression that *flood* would not create.

### Thinking About Word Choice

1. Find two of Pope's words that could be used in ordinary conversation. Find two that sound more formal.
2. Why do you suppose Pope chose the word *surges* instead of *waves* in line 7?

## COMPARING POEMS

1. Compare the use of sound in any two or more of the poems in this section: "I Like to See It Lap the Miles," "My Heart's in the Highlands," "Tomorrow, and Tomorrow, and Tomorrow," "Winter Trees," and "Sound and Sense." What sound devices (rhythm, rhyme, repetition, parallelism, onomatopoeia, alliteration) does each poem use? Does it use a regular meter or free verse?
2. Choose any two or more poems from this section, and explain how the sound of each poem echoes its sense. Which of the two echoes its sense more effectively? Why?

---

■ "Tomorrow": round, mournful vowel sounds convey melancholy
■ "Trees": short lines highlight individual words; phrases
■ "Sound": onomatopoeia; alliteration imitates things described

# LITERARY FOCUS: *Imagery, Figurative Language*

Language is like modeling clay: It can be shaped in many ways to create many different impressions. We often make a conscious attempt to mold language whenever we have something special to say. Of all the forms of literature, poetry molds and stretches language the most. Poets use **images**—concrete details that appeal to the senses—to create vivid impressions of their subjects. They also stretch words beyond their literal meanings by using **figurative language**, or figures of speech, which are unusual comparisons that embroider or exaggerate the literal facts to make a special point. The following poets all create striking impressions with images and figures of speech.

**Alfred, Lord Tennyson** (1809–1892) was born into the large family of an English minister. He eventually became the most celebrated poet of Victorian England and was named poet laureate. In "The Eagle" Tennyson creates a starkly powerful picture of a majestic creature.

■ Can you think of examples from the human and natural worlds where size and power are not related? Who do you know that seems to possess a noble strength?

**Walt Whitman** (1819–1892), who was born and raised on Long Island, New York, worked as a printer, teacher, and editor before deciding to write full-time. He also served as a nurse during the Civil War, and many of his poems—like "Cavalry Crossing a Ford"—reflect his war experience. His famous collection of poems, *Leaves of Grass,* established Whitman as a daring pioneer who broke with traditional poetic forms.

■ What are the dangers and the benefits of looking at a situation with a detached point of view?

**Claude McKay** (1889–1948) was born in Jamaica in the British West Indies and later studied at Tuskegee Institute in Alabama. He is best known for his *Songs of Jamaica* and *Harlem Shadows.* In "Spring in New Hampshire" he makes vibrant imagery convey emotion.

■ People can feel trapped from both inside and outside. How is the speaker in this poem trapped?

**Amy Lowell** (1874–1925), a member of a distinguished Massachusetts family, advanced the use of free verse in American literature. A Pulitzer Prize-winning poet, Lowell spearheaded the Imagist movement, which emphasized the use of "hard clear" visual images and precise language in poetry. Lowell put these principles into practice in such poems as "Solitaire."

■ When has your imagination taken you on an exciting journey? In what way did your surroundings add to your mental adventure?

**Karl Shapiro** (born 1913) became deeply interested in poetry as a high school student. His preoccupation with poetry eventually gained him a Pulitzer Prize for a series of poems he composed while fighting in the Pacific during World War II. Shapiro's poetry has changed over the years from a traditional to a more experimental style. In "Manhole Covers" he experiments with images, line lengths, and even time periods, jumping from ancient times into the future.

■ What ordinary object in everyday life do you find beautiful? What about it might future generations find attractive?

**Vachel Lindsay** (1879–1931) believed that poems should not simply be read but should be performed. A number of his works have been set to music. Like "An Indian Summer Day on the Prairie," many of his poems pulsate with strong rhythms and intense images.

■ When you think of the sun at dawn, midday, and dusk, what images do you see when you close your eyes?

**Emily Dickinson** (1830–1886) spent much of her life in her father's house in Amherst, Massachusetts. She created a whole poetic world from her observations of people and nature. Most of her short, untitled poems were published after her death. In "It Sifts from Leaden Sieves" she uses exact images and unusual figures of speech to create a visual riddle for the reader.

■ According to the speaker of this poem, is nature considered a deliberate or a haphazard force? Why?

**202** *Poetry*

**Robert Frost** (1874–1963), another poet identified with New England, was actually born in San Francisco but moved to New Hampshire as a child. Frost spent some time in England, where he first gained recognition for his poetry. He returned to the United States and received many honors during his lifetime, including four Pulitzer Prizes. In "A Hillside Thaw" he demonstrates his ability to transform an ordinary rural scene with fresh language.

■ Considering his choice of images, do you think the speaker is more artistic or scientific in his view of the world? Which are you?

**Robert Browning** (1812–1889) grew up in a London suburb. In 1846 he eloped with the celebrated poet Elizabeth Barrett, and the pair went to live in Italy, where Browning devoted himself to his semi-invalid wife. Known for the gallery of dramatic characters who speak in his works, Browning also used jarring sounds and startling images in poems such as "My Star."

■ Have you ever experienced something as extraordinary that a friend experienced as quite ordinary? How did the difference in reactions make you feel?

**Gabriela Mistral** (1889–1957) was the first Latin American writer to win the Nobel Prize for Literature (1945). Born in Vicuna, Chile, Lucila Godoy Alcayaga, a schoolteacher, won the Chilean prize for poetry in 1914. She adopted the pen name Gabriela Mistral, derived from the names of the Archangel Gabriel and the "mistral" wind of southern France.

■ How would you describe the relationship between the human and natural worlds in Mistral's poem?

**Teresa Palomo Acosta** (born 1949) is a native of McGregor, Texas, and now lives in Austin. In 1986 she won the University of Arizona's National Chicano Short Story Contest. From *Passing Time,* Acosta's collection of poems, "Two Sentences for Gabriela Mistral" expresses Acosta's admiration for the power of Mistral's poetry.

■ What might move a poet to write a tribute to another poet?

*Poetry* **203**

Initially the eagle stands motionless on a crag above the sea; then he plunges down.

## LITERARY OPTIONS

- imagery
- contrast

## THEMATIC OPTIONS

- responses to nature
- greatness

## PERSONIFICATION

By personifying the eagle ("He clasps the crag with crooked hands"), the poet suggests that the bird has a humanlike mind and tenacity (l. 1).

## IMAGERY

The speaker's images place the eagle above most of the natural world ("Close to the sun," "Ringed with the azure world," "The wrinkled sea beneath him"), thus creating a sense of the bird's majesty (ll. 2, 3, 4).

## CONTRAST

The description of the majestic eagle as motionless *(clasps, stands, watches)* lays the groundwork for a startling contrast: the simile that depicts the bird as falling suddenly and precipitously "like a thunderbolt" (ll. 1, 3, 5, 6).

## REFLECTING ON THE POEM

Why do you think the poet describes the eagle in such heroic terms? (Possible answers may include that the poet loves nature in general and has a particular fascination for this majestic, fierce-looking, and independent bird.)

*Alfred, Lord Tennyson*

# The Eagle

He clasps the crag with crooked hands,
Close to the sun in lonely lands,
Ringed with the azure[1] world, he stands.

The wrinkled sea beneath him crawls;
5  He watches from his mountain walls,
And like a thunderbolt he falls.

---

1. **azure:** sky-blue.

**204** *Poetry*

## STUDY QUESTIONS

### Recalling

1. Where is the eagle in stanza 1? What is he doing?
2. What does the eagle watch in stanza 2?
3. What does the eagle do in the last line? To what is he compared?

### Interpreting

4. What words in the poem make the eagle seem like a statue or part of the rocky landscape? Explain how this picture of the eagle adds to the impact of the last line.
5. How does the poem convey the eagle's solitude? How does it convey his strength?
6. What other traits does the poem give to the eagle? What words suggest these traits?

### Extending

7. The eagle was the military standard of the Roman Empire and is the national emblem of the United States. What qualities make the eagle appropriate in these roles? What other things might the eagle be used to represent?

## VIEWPOINT

Noted writer Louis Untermeyer points out that Tennyson did not sacrifice accuracy to beauty in writing poetry:

Delicate and romantic though most of Tennyson's poetry is, much of it is...graphic as well as graceful. In six lines he captures not only the exact look but the dramatic power of the eagle.

— The Paths of Poetry

■ Do you think that "The Eagle" is a "graceful" poem? Why or why not? Explain how the poem both portrays the eagle's appearance exactly and brings out the bird's dramatic power.

## LITERARY FOCUS

### Imagery

In literature an **image** is a picture or sensation that is created with words. Although the word *image* most often suggests a visual picture, it can also refer to other sensory experiences such as sound, touch, taste, smell, and movement. For example, in describing a campfire, you might talk about not only its bright darting flames but also its snapping sound, glowing warmth, and pungent smell, as well as the smoky taste it gives your food.

A poem's **imagery** is its collection of such images. A poem may be dominated by one central image or may consist of a series of different images. As we read a poem, its images remind us of our own sensory experiences and draw us into the poet's words. Imagery also engages our emotions. As pictures, sounds, and other sensory experiences erupt in our minds, the emotions we associate with these experiences erupt as well. For example, in a poem about the Fourth of July, the images of whizzing fireworks, marching bands, picnics, and bright summer mornings may evoke excitement, anticipation, patriotism, or any other emotions associated with Independence Day.

### Thinking About Imagery

1. To which sensations (sight, hearing, touch, smell, taste, movement) do Tennyson's various images appeal? Does one sensation predominate?
2. Why is the image of the eagle in the last line a fitting end to the poem?

*The Eagle*  **205**

# Cavalry Crossing a Ford

A line in long array where they wind betwixt green islands,
They take a serpentine[1] course, their arms flash in the sun—hark to
    the musical clank,
Behold the silvery river, in it the splashing horses loitering stop to
    drink,
Behold the brown-faced men, each group, each person a picture,
    the negligent rest on the saddles,
5 Some emerge on the opposite bank, others are just entering the
    ford—while,
Scarlet and blue and snowy white,
The guidon flags[2] flutter gayly in the wind.

---

1. **serpentine:** winding.
2. **guidon flags:** military pennants.

## STUDY QUESTIONS

### Recalling

1. Where does the poem take place? What action is described in the poem?
2. List three things that the speaker sees. What sounds does he hear?
3. What is the last thing the speaker mentions?

### Interpreting

4. Prove that the speaker is physically far away from the procession.
5. Why might the sound of armaments be called "musical"? In what sense might this image be ironic? Do you think the word *gayly* is inappropriate in a war poem? Why or why not?
6. Which details in the poem do not seem warlike? Which details do? Is the overall mood of the poem peaceful or warlike? Happy or sad? Explain.
7. What point about war do you think Whitman is making in this poem?

## COMPOSITION

### Writing About a Poem's Structure and Meaning

■ Explain how the structure of this poem suits its meaning. First use specific examples to show how the poem moves from an overall view of the procession to a series of separate images. Then explain how this approach fits the poem's subject.

### Writing a Description of Movement

■ Write a poem of at least six lines describing the movement of a large group. You may describe this movement from any angle—above, below, the side—and from any distance. Be sure to use images of color, sound, and motion in your poem. If you choose, you may describe the movement of one of the following: (a) a flock of migrating birds, (b) a marching band, (c) a water ballet team, (d) a handful of helium balloons, (e) autumn leaves blown by the wind, (f) two opposing teams of basketball players, (g) a school of dolphins.

---

## LITERARY OPTIONS

- imagery
- free verse

## THEMATIC OPTIONS

- war
- individuals and groups

## IMAGERY

The speaker paints a relaxed and beguiling portrait of the troop, describing a "musical clank" and the "silvery river" (ll. 2, 3).

## FREE VERSE

The naturalness of the verse line emphasizes the relaxed nature of the scene and creates a casual, reflective tone.

## REFLECTING ON THE POEM

What does Whitman seem to think of war? (Possible answers may include that a sometimes casual human surface may hide its very grim reality.)

## STUDY QUESTIONS

1. at a river ford; soldiers and horses crossing
2. sees: men, weapons, river; hears: weapons clanking, splashing water
3. flags waving in wind
4. has panoramic view, cannot hear men talking
5. musical: resembles bells; ironic: weapons kill; *gayly:* unusual but sometimes appropriate to war—also creates irony
6. not warlike: green islands, musical clank, silvery river; warlike: soldiers, flashing arms; mood: peaceful, happy
7. War's horrors are perpetrated by ordinary people.

---

**SELECTION FOR PRACTICE IN ACTIVE READING**

(TCR 5, p. 63)

---

## COMPOSITION: GUIDELINES FOR EVALUATION

### WRITING ABOUT POEM'S STRUCTURE AND MEANING

**Objective**

To analyze relationship between structure and meaning in a poem

**Guidelines for Evaluation**

- suggested length: one to two paragraphs
- should show that the poem moves from overall view to a series of separate images
- should explain how the structure fits the meaning

### WRITING A DESCRIPTION OF MOVEMENT

**Objective**

To write a poem describing the movement of a group

**Guidelines for Evaluation**

- suggested length: one to two stanzas
- should have a moving group as a subject
- should present the subject from specific vantage point
- should contain images of color, sound, motion
- should reveal the speaker's attitude

Claude McKay

# Spring in New Hampshire
(To J.L.J.F.E.)

Too green the springing April grass,
   Too blue the silver-speckled sky,
For me to linger here, alas,
   While happy winds go laughing by,
5  Wasting the golden hours indoors,
Washing windows and scrubbing floors.

Too wonderful the April night,
   Too faintly sweet the first May flowers,
The stars too gloriously bright,
10   For me to spend the evening hours,
When fields are fresh and streams are leaping,
Wearied, exhausted, dully sleeping.

---

## STUDY QUESTIONS

### Recalling

1. Where and when does the poem take place? How do you know?
2. List five details of spring that the speaker notices.
3. What does the speaker do indoors, and how does the speaker feel about these activities? What specific words in the poem describe these feelings?

### Interpreting

4. To what various senses do the poem's images of spring appeal? What emotional effect does McKay create by repeating the word *too* in these images?
5. Describe the speaker's tone in presenting the outdoor scenes, and contrast that with the one the speaker uses for the indoor scenes. Use specific words from the poem.
6. What might the poem be saying about the difference between the natural world and human life?

### Extending

7. Why might a beautiful sight make someone unhappy? Name some situations in which beauty could cause both sorrow and joy.

## COMPOSITION

### Writing About Contrasting Images

■ "Spring in New Hampshire" develops several contrasts: between day and night, between indoors and outdoors, and between the world of nature and the daily life of the speaker. First describe the emotional effect of the poem. Then explain how these various contrasts contribute to that effect.

### Writing a Description with Contrasts

■ In a poem or short prose piece describe an outdoors scene from the point of view of someone who must stay indoors. Your speaker should express his or her feelings about not being able to go outside. Use strongly contrasting images.

*Spring in New Hampshire* **207**

### LITERARY OPTIONS

- imagery
- contrast

### THEMATIC OPTIONS

- natural beauty
- regret

### IMAGERY

The poet uses images of light to describe the "silver-speckled" spring days and "bright" nights and enhance their natural appeal (ll. 2, 9).

### READING SKILLS: CONTRAST

Heavy words describe the speaker's indoor life (*scrubbing, dully sleeping*) in contrast to the lighthearted fresh fields and leaping streams he longs to enjoy (ll. 6, 11–12).

### REFLECTING ON THE POEM

What are the differences between the two worlds in the poem? (One answer would be that the natural world is more fulfilling than the world encumbered by life's responsibilities.)

### STUDY QUESTIONS

1. New Hampshire, spring; title
2. green grass, blue sky, happy winds, bright stars, flowers
3. washes windows, scrubs floors, a waste of time; *wasting the golden hours*
4. sight, hearing, touch, smell; emphasizes speaker's loss
5. outdoors: *gay, happy, sweet;* indoors: *glum, wasting, dully*
6. The natural world is more beautiful and fulfilling.
7. ■ inability to enjoy it
   ■ Students may share own experiences.

---

## COMPOSITION: GUIDELINES FOR EVALUATION

### WRITING ABOUT CONTRASTING IMAGES

**Objective**

To explain how contrasting images create a poem's emotional effect

**Guidelines for Evaluation**

- suggested length: two to three paragraphs
- should describe the poem's emotional effect
- should identify contrasting images and explain how contrasts create impact

### WRITING WITH CONTRASTS

**Objective**

To write a description using strong contrasts

**Guidelines for Evaluation**

- suggested length: one to two paragraphs or stanzas
- should describe outdoors scene from the viewpoint of one confined indoors
- should express strong feelings by contrasting images of indoors and outdoors

At night, while others sleep, the speaker imagines being in other times and places.

## LITERARY OPTIONS

- personification
- imagery

## THEMATIC OPTIONS

- journeys of imagination
- individualism

## PERSONIFICATION

Personifying her mind, or imagination, enables the poet to make its activities visually concrete as it "begins to peek and peer," "plays at ball," and "shakes wrought dice-cups" (ll. 3–5).

## IMAGERY

The poem's detailed visual imagery is surrealistically vivid, appropriately evoking the brilliance of a dream. Note, for example, the "blue Chinese gardens" (l. 4) and the "broken flutings of white pillars" (l. 6).

## SPEAKER

The speaker may feel a little superior to the "good folk" who only sleep while she indulges her vivid imagination (l. 10).

## REFLECTING ON THE POEM

Why might the poet believe that her imaginings are superior to the dreams of the other city-dwellers? (Possible answers may include that as an artist she is more in control of her fantastic dreams and may deliberately steer them to the exotic and unconventional.)

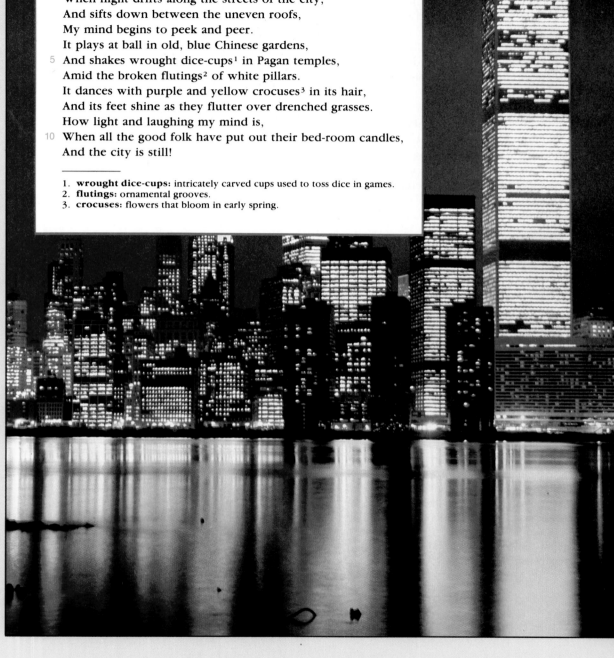

*Amy Lowell*

# Solitaire

When night drifts along the streets of the city,
And sifts down between the uneven roofs,
My mind begins to peek and peer.
It plays at ball in old, blue Chinese gardens,
5  And shakes wrought dice-cups[1] in Pagan temples,
Amid the broken flutings[2] of white pillars.
It dances with purple and yellow crocuses[3] in its hair,
And its feet shine as they flutter over drenched grasses.
How light and laughing my mind is,
10  When all the good folk have put out their bed-room candles,
And the city is still!

---

1. **wrought dice-cups:** intricately carved cups used to toss dice in games.
2. **flutings:** ornamental grooves.
3. **crocuses:** flowers that bloom in early spring.

## STUDY QUESTIONS

### Recalling

1. When and where does the speaker's mind begin its activities?
2. List four places to which the speaker's mind travels and four things that it does.
3. According to line 10, what is everyone else doing?

### Interpreting

4. Since the speaker's mind is not literally traveling, what mental activity is actually being described in the poem?
5. Why do you think the speaker uses images of exotic faraway places to describe what her mind does? What makes each of these images vivid?
6. How is the speaker different from the other "good folk"? How might the poem's title refer to this difference? What else could it mean?

### Extending

7. Do you think the minds of creative people work differently from the minds of other people? Explain. Can creativity be taught, or is it something a person is born with?

## LITERARY FOCUS

### Personification

**Personification** is a figure of speech in which an animal, object, or idea is given human qualities. The thing that is personified might speak, feel emotions, and even assume a human appearance. In some cases it may have its own personality and perform a number of human activities. For example, a television set may complain to its owner about the fact that it has blown a tube. In other cases the personification can be as fleeting as a single image. For instance, we use personification when we say that the sky looks angry or that justice is blind.

Personification has been used in literature since earliest times. It became especially popular during the Middle Ages, when medieval morality plays, intended to teach lessons, presented qualities such as "Love" and "Good Sense" as human characters. Personification can be very dramatic, and writers often use it to bring vivid life to a work.

### Thinking About Personification

■ Explain how Lowell's speaker uses personification in portraying her mind in "Solitaire." What specific human features does her mind take on?

*Solitaire* **209**

## STUDY QUESTIONS

1. at night in the city
2. palaces, gardens, temples, ruins, meadows; peeks and peers, plays at ball, shakes dice-cups, dances
3. sleeping
4. process of fantasizing
5. These images convey the impression that thoughts are varied and fascinating. Concrete details make these images vivid.
6. stays awake while others sleep; suggests speaker is *solitary* and unique; possibly compares the speaker's mental game to the card game solitaire
7. Answers will vary. Some may feel that creativity is a gift given to a few. Others may feel that everyone is creative.

## LITERARY FOCUS

Her mind sees, plays, dances, and laughs; it has an exuberant personality.

*Karl Shapiro*

# Manhole Covers

The beauty of manhole covers—what of that?
Like medals struck by a great savage khan,[1]
Like Mayan calendar stones,[2] unliftable, indecipherable,
Not like old electrum,[3] chased and scored,[4]
5  Mottoed and sculptured to a turn,
But notched and whelked[5] and pocked and smashed
With the great company names:
Gentle Bethlehem,[6] smiling United States.[7]
This rustproof artifact[8] of my street,
10  Long after roads are melted away, will lie
Sidewise in the grave of the iron-old world,
Bitten at the edges,
Strong with its cryptic American,
Its dated beauty.

---

1. **khan:** ruler of the Mongolian empire in Asia during the Middle Ages.
2. **Mayan [mī′ən] calendar stones:** The Mayan tribes of Central America used stones to record the passage of time. The Mayans' highly developed civilization declined after the arrival of the Europeans in the Americas during the sixteenth century.
3. **electrum:** alloy made of gold and silver and used for coins.
4. **chased and scored:** engraved and grooved.
5. **whelked:** marked with spirals.
6. **Bethlehem:** Bethlehem Steel, large American steel company.
7. **United States:** U.S. Steel.
8. **artifact:** object made by human labor; also, a product of a past civilization.

## STUDY QUESTIONS

### Recalling

1. To what two things does Shapiro compare manhole covers? To what ancient civilizations do these images refer?
2. List the unusual adjectives Shapiro uses to describe the manhole covers in line 6.
3. According to lines 9–14, how will the manhole cover become different from its surroundings as time goes by? What sort of beauty will the manhole cover have then?

### Interpreting

4. What physical qualities in manhole covers does the poem emphasize? What words in the poem suggest these qualities?
5. In what way will the manhole cover become a "rustproof artifact"? To what earlier images in the poem is this image connected?
6. Explain the meaning of the last two lines.
7. For what different reasons are the manhole covers beautiful to the speaker?

### Extending

8. Why might commonplace objects like manhole covers become mysterious and beautiful from the perspective of the future?

## LITERARY FOCUS

### Similes

A **simile** is a figure of speech that directly compares two apparently unlike things. Most similes use the word *like* or *as* to link the two items. A simile draws attention to some characteristic that the two otherwise dissimilar items have in common. For example, Tennyson's "Eagle" concludes with the simile "And like a thunderbolt he falls." This figure of speech brings together two unlike things— an eagle and a flash of lightning. However, the eagle and lightning have something in common: sudden dramatic movement and breathtaking power.

### Thinking About Similes

■ Find one simile in "Manhole Covers," and point out the differences between the two items compared by the simile. What common trait do these items share?

*Manhole Covers* **211**

## STUDY QUESTIONS

1. calendar stones and medals; Mayans and Mongolians
2. *notched, whelked, pocked, smashed*
3. ■ It will endure while they crumble.
   ■ cryptic, dated
4. ■ heaviness, texture, and durability
   ■ *unliftable, notched, rustproof*
5. will be enduring evidence of our civilization; Mongolian and Mayan artifacts
6. The manhole cover will then become ancient, indecipherable, and therefore beautiful.
7. their various designs; their durability; their role as evidence of American civilization
8. They will be unfamiliar, no longer commonplace and utilitarian.

## LITERARY FOCUS

- Similes: "Like medals struck,"; "Like Mayan calendar stones"
- Differences: The manhole covers are utilitarian, while the medals are decorative and the calendar stones have religious or scientific significance.
- Common traits: manhole covers and medals are embossed and durable; the manhole covers and calendar stones are heavy, durable, and marked with writing.

*Vachel Lindsay*

# An Indian Summer Day on the Prairie

*In the Beginning*
The sun is a huntress young,
The sun is red, red joy,
The sun is an Indian girl,
Of the tribe of the Illinois.

*Mid-morning*
5　The sun is a smoldering fire,
That creeps through the high gray plain,
And leaves not a bush of cloud
To blossom with flowers of rain.

*Noon*
The sun is a wounded deer,
10　That treads pale grass in the skies,
Shaking his golden horns,
Flashing his baleful[1] eyes.

*Sunset*
The sun is an eagle old;
There in the windless west,
15　Atop of the spirit-cliffs
He builds him a crimson nest.

―――――――――
1. **baleful:** threatening.

# STUDY QUESTIONS

## Recalling

1. Where and when does the poem take place?
2. How is the poem divided? To what time does each stanza refer?
3. Name the thing or things to which the sun is compared in each stanza.

## Interpreting

4. Explain how the image of the sun in each stanza fits the time of day being described in the stanza.
5. Trace the change in mood of the poem from beginning to end. Explain how the verbs and adjectives—especially the colors—in each stanza add to its mood.
6. Explain how rhythm and rhyme add to the impact of the poem. Why do you think Lindsay chose to use such strong sound effects in a poem about a silent landscape?

## Extending

7. The sun has fascinated people since earliest times. Why do you think the sun has often been assigned human or animal features?

# LITERARY FOCUS

## Metaphor

A **metaphor** is a figure of speech that connects two basically dissimilar items through some striking similarity. For example, "Paul's mind is an open book" is a metaphor. It does not mean that Paul walks around with pages flapping on his head but rather that his thoughts can be known almost as easily as the contents of an open book.

Often metaphors make us see the similarity between two things for the first time. For example, the metaphor "Her gown is a butterfly's wing" connects two things that do not seem to have much in common at first. However, we can imagine how both the dress and the butterfly's wing might be delicate, smooth, and full of pattern and color. Once the metaphor brings the two things together, we can find the similarities that connect them.

When they are unusual, metaphors can lend dramatic power to a piece of writing. They can also help us to see the world in a new way by expressing fresh and startling connections among the things around us.

## Thinking About Metaphor

■ Identify the metaphor in the first line of each stanza in "An Indian Summer Day on the Prairie." What qualities connect the two things in each metaphor? Which one of these metaphors seems most unusual to you, and why?

# COMPOSITION

## Writing About Imagery

■ Trace the progression in the imagery of "An Indian Summer Day on the Prairie." First identify the major differences between the images in the first and last stanzas. Then show how the images in the two middle stanzas lead gradually from the first set of images to the last set.

## Writing with Metaphors

■ Write a poem of a few stanzas showing the changes in a natural scene over a period of time. Begin each stanza with the words, "The sky (or wind or snow or mountain) is a _____," and complete each line with a different word. Be sure to use images of light, color, and the natural landscape to make the changes in your scene clear.

---

## COMPOSITION: GUIDELINES FOR EVALUATION

### WRITING ABOUT IMAGERY

**Objective**

To analyze the progression of images in a poem

**Guidelines for Evaluation**

- suggested length: one to two paragraphs
- should identify and contrast images in first and last stanzas
- should identify images in second and third stanzas and explain how these form transition from the first to the final images

### WRITING WITH METAPHORS

**Objective**

To create metaphors that describe a change in nature

**Guidelines for Evaluation**

- suggested length: three to five stanzas
- should describe changes in natural scene over time
- should include stanza beginning with different metaphors
- should contain images of light, color, landscape

---

STUDY QUESTIONS

1. during Indian summer (a short period in autumn); across the western prairie
2. into four stanzas; dawn, mid-morning, noon, sunset
3. stanza 1: Indian huntress, joy; stanza 2: smoldering fire; stanza 3: wounded deer; stanza 4: aged eagle
4. ■ The young girl's ruddy skin evokes color of sun at dawn.
   ■ The fire suggests growing heat.
   ■ The wounded deer suggests the ferociousness and desperation of unbearable heat. The old eagle suggests the sun's sinking.
5. ■ stanza 1—joyful mood: vibrant *red, young*
   ■ stanza 2—foreboding mood: *creeps, smoldering, gray*
   ■ stanza 3—angry mood: *baleful, wounded, shaking, golden*
   ■ stanza 4—resigned mood: *old, windless, crimson*
6. Rhyme and rhythm create a hypnotic, chantlike quality. The striking sound devices express the intensity of the landscape.
7. Sample answer: Because the sun is so important to life on earth, people have needed to imagine it in more tangible, familiar terms.

## LITERARY FOCUS

- stanza 1: "huntress young"; youth, color
- stanza 2: "smoldering fire"; heat
- stanza 3: "wounded deer"; pain, anger
- stanza 4: "eagle old"; end of life
- Answers will vary; perhaps the wounded deer is the most unusual, least explicable comparison.

# It Sifts from Leaden Sieves[1]

It sifts from Leaden Sieves—
It powders all the Wood.
It fills with Alabaster[2] Wool
The Wrinkles of the Road—

5 It makes an Even Face
Of Mountain, and of Plain—
Unbroken Forehead from the East
Unto the East again—

It reaches to the Fence—
10 It wraps it Rail by Rail

Till it is lost in Fleeces—
It deals Celestial Vail[3]

To Stump, and Stack—and Stem—
A Summer's empty Room—
15 Acres of Joints,[4] where Harvests were,
Recordless, but for them—

It Ruffles Wrists of Posts
As Ankles of a Queen—
Then stills its Artisans—like Ghosts—
20 Denying they have been—

---

1. **Sieves:** utensils with many tiny openings, used to strain liquids or fine particles.
2. **Alabaster:** fine-grained, translucent white stone often used for statues.
3. **deals . . . Vail:** throws a veil.
4. **Joints:** seams, lines.

## STUDY QUESTIONS

### Recalling

1. What images describe what "it" does to the wood and the road in stanza 1?
2. What words describe the mountain and plain in stanza 2?
3. Explain how "it" decorates the fence and the place "where harvests were" in stanzas 3 and 4.
4. How does "it" bring its activities to a close in stanza 5?

### Interpreting

5. Identify "it," and explain what is actually happening in this poem. What are the leaden sieves? Why might "it" be described as sifting?
6. Explain how three other images that Dickinson uses to describe "its" activities are appropriate to the subject.

7. In what way is the word *Artisans* in line 19 appropriate to what is happening in the poem?
8. What effect does Dickinson create by never directly saying what "it" is? Would you have preferred the poem if she had been more direct? Explain.

### Extending

9. Why do you think a scene like the one in this poem is often described as if it were a work of art?

## VIEWPOINT

One writer suggests that Emily Dickinson's best writing relies on kinesthesia, or the image of motion:

> The most impressive imagery in Emily Dickinson's poems is undoubtedly kines-

thetic [relating to movement] rather than visual or auditory [relating to sound], and although she does ... invent some marvelous images of these latter sorts, they are likely, in her best poems to be associated with images of motion ... and rest.

—R. Chase, *Emily Dickinson*

■ Where does Dickinson use images of motion in "It Sifts from Leaden Sieves"? Where does she use images of rest? Why are images of motion and rest especially appropriate for this poem?

## LITERARY FOCUS

### Implied Metaphor

An **implied metaphor** is a metaphor in which the connection between two items is suggested rather than directly expressed in the form "A is B." For example, poet Edith Sitwell's phrase "The pale silken ribbons of rain" is an implied metaphor that suggests the ribbonlike qualities of rain without expressing that likeness directly.

The implied metaphor has both advantages and disadvantages. The implied metaphor, "silken ribbons of rain," is more subtle than the direct metaphor, "The streams of rain were silken ribbons." Because it is more subtle, an implied metaphor can sometimes slip by the reader. At its best, however, the implied metaphor creates a delicate web of connections that we accept almost without thinking about the art of the weaver who made them.

### Thinking About Implied Metaphor

1. Because Dickinson does not name her subject, her poem is full of implied metaphors. How many can you find in the first stanza? What items are being equated in each metaphor?
2. Change one of these metaphors into a direct metaphor. Which form do you prefer? Why?

## COMPOSITION

### Writing About Two Poems

■ Compare Dickinson's "It Sifts from Leaden Sieves" with her poem "I Like to See It Lap the Miles" (page 191). First show what is similar in each speaker's treatment of her subject. Then explain how the poems differ in their use of sound effects and imagery.

### Writing a Riddle Poem

■ Write a brief poem in which the subject is an unnamed "it," as Emily Dickinson does in "It Sifts from Leaden Sieves." Using vivid descriptions, point out the details of your subject's appearance and behavior without actually saying what "it" is. However, be sure to give your readers enough clues to enable them to identify "it" by the end of the poem.

## VIEWPOINT

- motion: images of snow falling
- rest: images of snow stopping;
- Falling snow creates an image of stillness.

## LITERARY FOCUS

1. 
   - line 1: snow, sifted flour; skies, sieves
   - line 2: snow, powder
   - line 3: snow, alabaster, wool
   - line 4: road, cloth, skin
2. Students should understand that direct metaphors have diminished impact.

## COMPOSITION: GUIDELINES FOR EVALUATION

### WRITING ABOUT TWO POEMS

**Objective**

To compare and contrast two poems by same author

**Guidelines for Evaluation**

- suggested length: two paragraphs
- should point out similarities in treatment of subjects (for example, the use of implied metaphors)
- should identify differences in imagery and sound devices

### WRITING A RIDDLE POEM

**Objective**

To write a poem in which subject is implied

**Guidelines for Evaluation**

- should refrain from naming its subject
- should provide vivid details that allow reader to identify the subject

*Robert Frost*

# A Hillside Thaw

To think to know the country and not know
The hillside on the day the sun lets go
Ten million silver lizards out of snow!
As often as I've seen it done before
5 I can't pretend to tell the way it's done.
It looks as if some magic of the sun
Lifted the rug that bred them on the floor
And the light breaking on them made them run.
But if I thought to stop the wet stampede,
10 And caught one silver lizard by the tail,
And put my foot on one without avail,
And threw myself wet-elbowed and wet-kneed
In front of twenty others' wriggling speed,—
In the confusion of them all aglitter,
15 And birds that joined in the excited fun
By doubling and redoubling song and twitter,
I have no doubt I'd end by holding none.

It takes the moon for this. The sun's a wizard
By all I tell; but so's the moon a witch.
20 From the high west she makes a gentle cast
And suddenly, without a jerk or twitch,
She has her spell on every single lizard.
I fancied when I looked at six o'clock
The swarm still ran and scuttled just as fast.
25 The moon was waiting for her chill effect.
I looked at nine; the swarm was turned to rock
In every lifelike posture of the swarm,

Transfixed on mountain slopes almost erect.
Across each other and side by side they lay.
30 The spell that so could hold them as they were
Was wrought through trees without a breath of storm
To make a leaf, if there had been one, stir.
It was the moon's: she held them until day,
One lizard at the end of every ray.
35 The thought of my attempting such a stay!

## STUDY QUESTIONS

### Recalling

1. According to lines 2–3, what does the sun do?
2. In stanza 1 what does the speaker try to do and with what result?
3. To what human figures does the speaker liken the sun and moon in lines 18–19?
4. According to lines 20–22, what does the moon succeed in doing?
5. Summarize the scene the speaker sees at nine o'clock.

### Interpreting

6. Explain what is actually happening in the poem. To what does "this" in line 18 refer?
7. What picture does Frost create in the metaphor in line 3? Why is this metaphor both appropriate and unusual?
8. In what way does the speaker contrast the work of the sun and the moon? How does he contrast his own power with that of these heavenly bodies?
9. Find four references to magic in the poem. What do these references add to the poem? What magic has the poet himself created in his description of this ordinary event?

## LITERARY FOCUS

### Extended Metaphor

An **extended metaphor** is a metaphor that is carried through several lines of a poem or is even sustained through an entire poem.

An extended metaphor allows the poet to investigate in depth the similarities between the items in a metaphor. For example, a poet might use an extended metaphor to develop a connection between the phases of a human life and the seasons of the year. A successful extended metaphor often gives us a rich, rounded, and fresh perspective on the subject being described. It stretches our imaginations as well, challenging us to recognize and accept the many connections the poet has made.

### Thinking About Extended Metaphor

1. Explain the extended metaphor in "A Hillside Thaw." What various things does the metaphor connect?
2. What new perspective does this metaphor add to your view of the natural event described in the poem?

## COMPOSITION

### Writing About Poetry

■ Show how Frost uses poetic technique to convey his meaning in "A Hillside Thaw." First explain what the poem means. Then show how Frost's speaker, word choice, tone, and use of sound, imagery, and figurative language express this meaning. *For help with this assignment, see Lesson 11 in the Writing About Literature Handbook at the back of this book.*

### Creating an Extended Metaphor

■ Write a short poem or prose piece in which you create a metaphor and extend it throughout the entire work. Choose items that lend themselves to such a comparison. For example, you might describe the sky filled with stars as a populous city, or you might compare the growth of a child to the growth of a plant. Be sure to present the similarities between the items.

1. releases lizards from snow
2. imagines stopping lizards; fails
3. sun, wizard; moon, witch
4. casts a spell over the lizards
5. The lizards have turned to rock.
6. Snow melts in the sun and re-freezes in the moonlight.
7. Melting snow is seen as a multitude of lizards. The metaphor is appropriate because the rivulets imitate lizards' movements. The metaphor is unusual because lizards live in a hot, dry climate.
8. sun / wizard: creates lizards out of snow; moon / witch: casts spell that freezes them; speaker: powerless
9. references to magic: lines 6, 18, 19, 22; add a sense of wonder to ordinary event

### LITERARY FOCUS

1. The extended metaphor compares rivulets of melting snow to lizards, the sun to a wizard, and the moon to a witch. The metaphor connects natural processes and magic.
2. It endows an ordinary event with a magical quality.

## COMPOSITION: GUIDELINES FOR EVALUATION

### WRITING ABOUT POETRY

**Objective**

To analyze how poetic techniques convey meaning

**Guidelines for Evaluation**

- suggested length: two to three paragraphs
- should explain the meaning of the poem
- should analyze how poet conveys meaning and discuss what each poetic technique contributes to the poem

### CREATING AN EXTENDED METAPHOR

**Objective**

To write an extended metaphor

**Guidelines for Evaluation**

- suggested length: one to three stanzas / paragraphs
- should compare two items using an extended metaphor
- should present similarities between items

The poet describes a star that seems to sparkle for him alone, since others cannot see it.

## LITERARY OPTIONS

- symbolism
- main idea

## THEMATIC OPTIONS

- uniqueness of the individual
- artistic imagination

## SYMBOLISM

The star that erratically hurls its luminous red and blue rays may symbolize the speaker's intuitive flashes of perception and artistic ability (ll. 3–6).

## WORD CHOICE

Browning's use of an unusual word, *dartles* (l. 9), to describe the star's sparkling suggests both the star's uniqueness and the poet's special ability to respond to it.

## MAIN IDEA

The speaker feels superior to others, even if they have a "world" and he has only a "star," because he sees the star in a way special to himself alone (ll. 12–13).

## REFLECTING ON THE POEM

What is special about the star in the poem? (Possible answers may include that it has revealed itself to the speaker, who is the only one able to see it.)

---

**SELECTION FOR PRACTICE IN ACTIVE READING**

(TCR 5, p. 64)

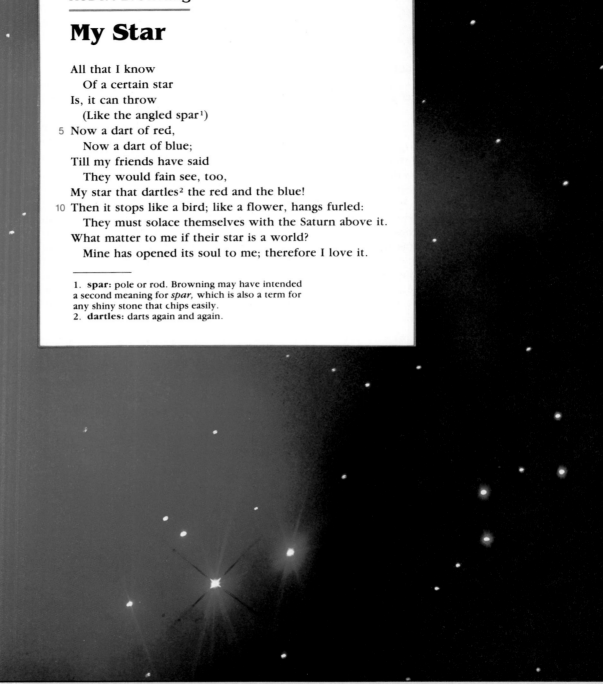

*Robert Browning*

# My Star

All that I know
   Of a certain star
Is, it can throw
   (Like the angled spar[1])
5 Now a dart of red,
   Now a dart of blue;
Till my friends have said
   They would fain see, too,
My star that dartles[2] the red and the blue!
10 Then it stops like a bird; like a flower, hangs furled:
   They must solace themselves with the Saturn above it.
What matter to me if their star is a world?
   Mine has opened its soul to me; therefore I love it.

---

1. **spar:** pole or rod. Browning may have intended a second meaning for *spar,* which is also a term for any shiny stone that chips easily.
2. **dartles:** darts again and again.

## STUDY QUESTIONS

### Recalling

1. What does the speaker's star do in the first six lines of the poem?
2. According to lines 7–8, do his friends see his star?
3. To what two things does the speaker compare his star in line 10?
4. According to the last line, how does the speaker feel about his star, and why does he feel this way?

### Interpreting

5. What qualities make the speaker's star special to him? Why do you think he prefers his star to "the world" his friends see?
6. In what way does the speaker's connection to his star set him apart from other people? What might the speaker mean when he says that his star has "opened its soul" to him?

### Extending

7. Can you think of other things that might inspire the sort of affection the speaker feels for his star? Why might people develop such feelings?

## LITERARY FOCUS

### Symbolism

A **symbol** is a figure of speech in which an object, place, person, or experience means more than what it is. A symbol, therefore, is both itself and something more than itself. For example, on one level a diploma is a piece of paper. However, on another level it symbolizes the achievement, hard work, satisfactions, and difficulties of the graduating student.

A symbol may also mean different things to different people. For example, while a hearth may be only a fireplace to some people, to others it may stand for family life or security or some happy memory. We all have private symbols that are full of meaning from our own experiences—associations that are unique to each of us.

The use of symbols in a literary work is called **symbolism**. We can recognize symbolism in literature when something takes on a meaning far beyond the importance of the individual item itself.

### Thinking About Symbolism

1. How does Browning give the star special significance in his poem?
2. What things do you think the speaker's star might symbolize?

*My Star*  **219**

## STUDY QUESTIONS

1. throws out darts of red and blue
2. no
3. a bird; a flower
4. He loves it because it has opened its soul to him.
5. its ability to throw out colors, his special ability to see it; prefers the star because it is personal and private
6. The star allows him to see beauty others cannot. The star has revealed its beauty to him alone.
7. Answers will vary. Students may suggest old, beloved possessions or places.

## LITERARY FOCUS

1. only the speaker sees it
2. Possible answers: a loved one; a place whose beauty is unrecognized; a poem that no one else likes

## COMPARING POEMS

1. Answers should cite two or more poems, describe these poems as if they were paintings, and explain which of these imaginary paintings the student prefers. Answers will vary, but the following are examples:

- Tennyson's "Eagle" or Whitman's "Cavalry Crossing a Ford" might be very realistic, almost literal renderings of their subjects.
- Some students might picture "Manhole Covers" as a collage that mixes images of manhole covers with images of ancient civilizations.

2. Answers should

- cite two or more poems, perhaps "Solitarie," "Manhole Covers," "An Indian Summer Day on a Prairie," "It Sifts from Leaden Sieves," "A Hillside Thaw," "My Star"

- explain how each poem transforms a scene or event through figurative language
- identify the forms of figurative language used, such as similes, metaphors, (including implied and extended), personification, and symbol
- state which transformation the student prefers, and give reasons for this preference

- simile
- main idea

- the power of love
- the power of art

### SIMILE

The speaker's similes involve the magical taming of treacherous elements in the natural world (ll. 3–4).

### MAIN IDEA

The speaker's song soothes the person she is singing to, erasing for her the cruelty and evil she feels is present in life (ll. 5–6).

### REFLECTING ON THE POEM

According to the speaker, what is the power of love or art? (It can erase evil or cruelty in us and in the outside world.)

### STUDY QUESTIONS

1. all evil, all cruel things
2. gulch, bramble—smooth as beloved's forehead; lion—gentle as eyelids
3. great love, serenity when she sings; "on earth all evil ends"; "for me all cruel things end"
4. When speaker sings to beloved, world seems transformed; brings inner peace
5. lines 2 and 6; images in lines 3, 4, 7, and 8 also hyperbolic; to underscore intensity of emotion
6. stanza 1: smoothness vs. jaggedness and roughness; stanza 2: gentleness and smallness vs. power and potential violence; highlights transforming power of love
7. Music may heighten present emotion or temporarily create false emotional state; usually temporary.

---

### Gabriela Mistral

## Serenity

When I am singing to you,
on earth all evil ends:
as smooth as your forehead
are the gulch and the bramble.

5  When I am singing to you,
for me all cruel things end:
as gentle as your eyelids,
the lion with the jackal.

## Suavidades

Cuando yo te estoy cantando,
en la Tierra acaba el mal:
todo es dulce por tus sienes:
la barranca, el espinar.

5  Cuando yo te estoy cantando,
se me acaba la crueldad:
suaves son, como tus párpados,
¡la leona y el chacal!

### STUDY QUESTIONS

#### Recalling

1. In stanzas 1 and 2 what things end when the speaker sings?
2. What happens to the gulch and the bramble in the first stanza and the lion with the jackal in the second?

#### Interpreting

3. What are the speaker's feelings for the person she is addressing? Which images in particular express these feelings?

4. How does the title relate to the poem's overall meaning?
5. Where in the poem does the poet use hyperbole, or exaggeration? Why do you think she employs this literary device?
6. Describe Mistral's use of contrasting images. How does their use strengthen the emotion of the poem?

#### Extending

7. Discuss the power of music to alter one's emotional state. Are these effects usually lasting or temporary? Explain your answer.

220  *Poetry*

LITERARY OPTIONS

- imagery
- speaker

THEMATIC OPTIONS

- art and the imagination
- childhood

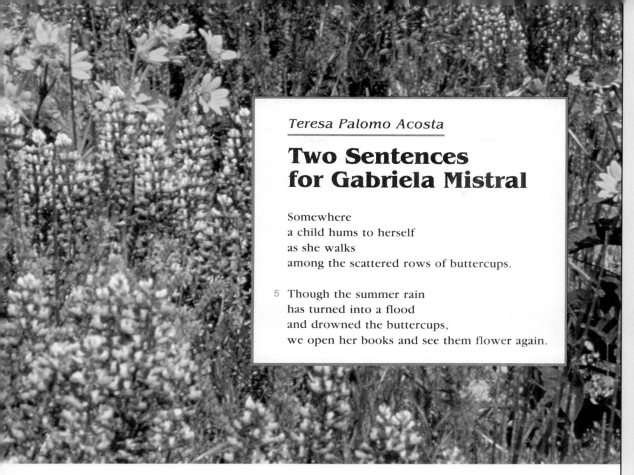

*Teresa Palomo Acosta*

# Two Sentences for Gabriela Mistral

Somewhere
a child hums to herself
as she walks
among the scattered rows of buttercups.

5 Though the summer rain
has turned into a flood
and drowned the buttercups,
we open her books and see them flower again.

## IMAGERY

The speaker's images in the first sentence *(hums, buttercups)* create a simple, evocative picture of childhood (ll. 1–4).

## SPEAKER

In the second sentence the speaker turns from Mistral's childhood to her own more turbulent present, in which adult cares have "drowned" childhood's innocent pleasures.

## MAIN IDEA

Just as the speaker can imaginatively enter into Mistral's childhood in the first stanza, so in the second stanza Mistral's poetry can make the speaker's adult world magically reflower.

## REFLECTING ON THE POEM

According to the speaker, what is the power of Mistral's poetry? (It has the power to restore beauty that has been wiped away.)

## STUDY QUESTIONS

**Recalling**

1. What two actions does the child take? Where does she take them?
2. Into what does the summer rain turn? What effect does this change have on the landscape?
3. According to Acosta what happens when we open Mistral's books?

**Interpreting**

4. Acosta suggests that Mistral's work has several qualities. Describe these qualities, and give evidence to support your answer.

5. Contrast the images in lines 2–4 with those in lines 5–7. In addition to their literal meaning, what figurative meaning might be given to lines 5–7?
6. Explain the use of the word *flower* in line 8. How does it relate the second stanza to the first?

## COMPARING POEMS

■ Consider the poems in this section. On the basis of their imagery, visualize as paintings two or more of these poems. Describe the colors and images in each "painting," and tell which one you prefer and why.

*Two Sentences for Gabriela Mistral* **221**

## STUDY QUESTIONS

1. hums and walks; *among the scattered . . . buttercups*
2. a flood; drowns the buttercups
3. We see the buttercups flower again.
4. Work is vivid, upbeat, alive, graceful *(child, buttercups)*; work also is hopeful, restorative (last line).
5. lines 2–4: pleasant, happy (humming child, lovely natural setting); lines 5–7: unpleasant and unhappy (destruction, loss); loss of childhood or happiness; Mistral's poetry
6. suggests that opening Mistral's books can bring her work back to life; relates restorative power of poetry to image of buttercups

## COMPARING POEMS

Answers will vary—should visualize two or more poems as paintings, describing color and other images in each.

# LITERARY FOCUS: *Types of Poetry*

Although all poetry shares certain common traits, poems can be divided into three basic categories. **Narrative poems** tell stories. More concentrated than short stories, narrative poems focus on the crucial parts of an experience. **Lyric poems** reveal private feelings. Most lyric poems are short and are marked by intense emotion and musical language. **Dramatic poems**, like plays, present characters speaking to themselves, to each other, or to the reader. Dramatic poems often contain other dramatic elements such as dialogue and setting. As the work of the following poets shows, these categories often overlap.

**Edgar Allan Poe** (1809–1849), born to a family of actors, established himself as an important figure on the American literary scene with his short stories and poetry. However, his personal life was full of conflict and sadness. In ''Eldorado'' he tells of a quest for an ideal world.

■ Which do you think is the more effective approach—setting several small specific goals or one large general goal? Why?

**George Gordon, Lord Byron** (1788–1824), one of the most dashing figures in all literature, was a handsome British aristocrat who won early fame as a poet. Byron was also a strong advocate of personal liberty. He died in Greece on his way to join the fight to free that country from Turkish domination. ''The Destruction of Sennacherib'' vividly portrays a different sort of combat, one in which victory comes not through battle but through divine intervention.

■ What is the basic story line of Byron's poem? Who are the opponents? With whom do you side?

**Robert Frost** (1874–1963) worked as a teacher, farmer, and journalist before writing poetry full-time. He became the most famous American poet of his era, praised by President Kennedy for his ''battle to illuminate the nature of man and the world in which he lives.'' In ''The Tuft of Flowers'' Frost finds a delicate link between human nature and the natural world.

■ How can temporary solitude actually increase your sense of closeness with other people? With Nature?

**William Wordsworth** (1770–1850) was born in the beautiful Lake District of northern England. He led the Romantic movement in literature, which reawakened interest in the importance of nature and human feeling. His belief that poetry is the "spontaneous overflow of powerful emotions," is shown in poems like "My Heart Leaps Up."

■ What feelings do you now have that you hope you will never outgrow?

**Samuel Allen** (born 1917) has practiced law, as well as teaching literature and writing poetry. Allen, who is a native of Ohio and sometimes uses the pen name of Paul Vesey, has had work published in *American Negro Poetry* and *Beyond the Blues*. In "To Satch" he pays tribute to the famous pitcher LeRoy Robert "Satchel" Paige.

■ Who in recent years have you considered a hero? What is it about yourself that draws you to this person?

**Mari Evans**, musician, writer, educator, former television host and producer, has taught and read at universities and colleges across the country. Her poems usually express some dimension of the Black experience. Like much of her work, "If There Be Sorrow" captures complex emotions with simple language.

■ According to the speaker of this poem, there is often a price to pay for reaching your goal. Have you ever paid this price?

**Frank Horne** (1899–1974) was a prize-winning athlete during college and went on to become a prize-winning poet. A practicing physician, he actively participated in the civil rights movement of the 1950s and 1960s. In "To James" Horne draws on his knowledge of athletics to create a lively, driving dramatic poem.

■ Would you like to have the speaker of this poem for a parent or a coach? Why or why not?

*Poetry* **223**

*Edgar Allan Poe*

# Eldorado[1]

Gaily bedight,[2]
A gallant knight,
In sunshine and in shadow,
Had journeyed long,
5    Singing a song
In search of Eldorado.

But he grew old—
This knight so bold—
And o'er his heart a shadow
10    Fell, as he found
No spot of ground
That looked like Eldorado.

And, as his strength
Failed him at length,
15 He met a pilgrim shadow—
"Shadow," said he,
"Where can it be—
This land of Eldorado?"

"Over the Mountains
20    Of the Moon,
Down the Valley of the Shadow,
Ride, boldly ride,"
The shade replied,—
"If you seek for Eldorado!"

---

1. **Eldorado:** mythical land full of gold and jewels, sought but never found by the early Spanish explorers of America.
2. **bedight:** dressed, equipped.

Detail from *The Prince Enters the Briar Wood,* Sir Edward Burne-Jones (1833–1898). Faringdon Collection Trust, Buscot Park, Faringdon, Berks.

**224**  *Poetry*

## STUDY QUESTIONS

### Recalling

1. What words describe the knight in the first stanza? What does he seek?
2. According to stanza 2, how does the knight change during his quest, and why?
3. Whom does the knight meet, and what does this being tell the knight?

### Interpreting

4. Why do you think no place looks like Eldorado to the knight?
5. What do you think the "Mountains of the Moon" and the "Valley of the Shadow" actually mean?
6. What do the shadow's words reveal about the knight's chances for finding Eldorado?
7. The word *shadow* appears in each stanza. How does its meaning change from the beginning to the end of the poem? How might this change be related to the quest for Eldorado?
8. Why is "Eldorado" a fitting name for what the knight seeks? What might Eldorado symbolize?

### Extending

9. What can a person gain — and lose — by pursuing a goal like Eldorado? Do you think everyone has an Eldorado of his or her own?

## LITERARY FOCUS

### Narrative Poetry

A **narrative poem** tells a story in verse. However, because poetry is more concentrated than prose, a narrative poem may not follow the recognizable plot structure and sequence of events we usually see in prose narratives. The poet who tells a story is usually more concerned with creating a vivid and complete emotional effect. Therefore, a narrative poem may focus only on the most meaningful parts of a story. In reading narrative poetry we often accept jumps of time, space, and logic that we might find difficult to understand in more "realistic" prose narratives.

Long narrative poems with heroic subjects are known as **epics**. The best-known epics include the *Iliad* and *Odyssey* by the Greek poet Homer, the *Aeneid* by the Latin poet Virgil, the *Divine Comedy* by the Italian poet Dante, and *Paradise Lost* by the British poet John Milton.

One of the most popular forms of narrative poetry is the **ballad**, a short narrative with a definite pattern of rhythm and rhyme. **Folk ballads** or **popular ballads** are usually anonymous; they circulate by word of mouth for generations in a particular region before they are written down. **Literary ballads** are written by poets to imitate folk ballads. Poe's "Eldorado" is an example of such a ballad.

### Thinking About Narrative Poetry

1. Retell the story presented in "Eldorado." Who is the main character, what is his problem, and how is it resolved?
2. What elements in the poem make it different from a short story? What jumps in time, space, and logic does the narrative make?

## STUDY QUESTIONS

1. *gaily bedight, gallant;* a place called Eldorado
2. grows older, disillusioned; because he does not find Eldorado
3. pilgrim shadow; Eldorado lies "Over the Mountains / Of the Moon, / Down the Valley of the Shadow"
4. He seeks something unattainable.
5. mountains, nonexistent place; valley, death
6. may find it after death
7. ■ Stanza 1: The shadow is not metaphoric; it is simply a shade cast; the knight is optimistic at this point.
   ■ Stanza 2: The shadow becomes a metaphor for sadness, as knight begins to lose hope.
   ■ Stanza 3: The shadow refers to a ghost, adding a sense of foreboding.
   ■ Stanza 4: The shadow becomes a symbol for death; the knight discovers that his quest is for death.
8. Eldorado was a mythical land never found. It could symbolize love, happiness, or perfection.
9. One may gain an incentive but lose satisfaction of pursuing a goal that can be reached. Answers will vary.

## LITERARY FOCUS

1. The main character, the knight, searches for a place called Eldorado; youth and optimism fade, and he realizes he will not find Eldorado until death.
2. ■ The poem relies on symbol, metaphor, and sound devices rather than plot, character, and setting
   ■ The phrase *he grew old* conveys that time has passed; the phrase *journeyed long* suggests different settings.

# The Destruction of Sennacherib[1]

The Assyrian came down like the wolf on the fold,[2]
And his cohorts[3] were gleaming in purple and gold;
And the sheen of their spears was like stars on the sea,
When the blue wave rolls nightly on deep Galilee.

5   Like the leaves of the forest when Summer is green,
That host with their banners at sunset were seen:
Like the leaves of the forest when Autumn hath blown,
That host on the morrow lay withered and strown.[4]

For the Angel of Death spread his wings on the blast,[5]
10  And breathed in the face of the foe as he passed;
And the eyes of the sleepers waxed[6] deadly and chill,
And their hearts but once heaved, and forever grew still!

And there lay the steed with his nostril all wide,
But through it there rolled not the breath of his pride;
15  And the foam of his gasping lay white on the turf,
And cold as the spray of the rock-beating surf.

And there lay the rider distorted and pale,
With the dew on his brow, and the rust on his mail:
And the tents were all silent, the banners alone,
20  The lances unlifted, the trumpet unblown.

And the widows of Ashur[7] are loud in their wail,
And the idols are broke in the temple of Baal;[8]
And the might of the Gentile,[9] unsmote by the sword,
Hath melted like snow in the glance of the Lord!

---

1. **Sennacherib** [sə nak′ər ib]: King of Assyria from 705 to 681 B.C. According to the Bible, when he led his troops in a siege of Jerusalem an angel swept over his camp and left him and thousands of his troops dead.
2. **fold:** flock of sheep.
3. **cohorts:** soldiers.
4. **strown:** strewn, or scattered.
5. **blast:** wind.
6. **waxed:** became.
7. **Ashur:** Assyria.
8. **Baal:** god of the ancient Assyrians.
9. **Gentile:** one who is not a Jew; here, Sennacherib, the Assyrian.

During their siege of Jerusalem, the Angel of Death destroys the sleeping Assyrians.

## LITERARY OPTIONS

- narrative poetry
- simile

## THEMATIC OPTIONS

- divine power dominates human power
- destruction of evil

## NARRATIVE POETRY

The poet starts thirteen lines with the word *And*. This repetition helps to convey the driving, inexorable movement of the narrative—even as an army drives forward, or as divine power accomplishes its objective.

## MAIN IDEA

The last two lines summarize the speaker's interpretation of his narrative: Human might, especially when it is evil, has no chance against divine intervention (ll. 23–24).

## SIMILE

Similes contrast the might of a foe that comes down "like the wolf on the fold" with the obliteration of that same foe, defeated by the Lord and "melted like snow" (ll. 1, 24).

## REFLECTING ON THE POEM

How does the speaker show his feelings toward Sennacherib? (Possible answers may include that he compares the Assyrian to a wolf, refers to his army as foes, and exults in their defeat.)

# STUDY QUESTIONS

## Recalling

1. What words describe the Assyrian king and his army in stanza 1?
2. According to stanza 3, who visits the Assyrian camp during the night? What does this being do, and what effect does this action have on the sleeping Assyrians?
3. What picture do stanzas 4 and 5 paint of the Assyrians' horses? The soldiers?
4. What, according to the last two lines, has "melted" the Assyrian might?

## Interpreting

5. What impression of the Assyrian army do the images in stanza 1 create? Find two images that dramatize the change in that army.
6. What point do the last two lines make about the difference between human and divine power?
7. What is the attitude of the speaker of the poem toward the destruction of Sennacherib? Is he detached, or does he sympathize with one side? Give specific evidence.
8. Describe the rhythm in this poem. How is the rhythm appropriate to the story that the poem tells?

## Extending

9. What makes this story a good subject for a narrative poem? Do you think it would work equally well as a short story? Why or why not?

# VOCABULARY

## Vivid Modifiers and Nouns

Much of the effect of "The Destruction of Sennacherib" comes from Byron's bold combinations of **nouns** and **modifiers**—especially adjectives and participles. Many of the modifiers and nouns in this poem are common words, but they create strong images of color, sensation, and movement. For example, "And his cohorts were gleaming in purple and gold" paints in a few words the dazzling scene of an ancient battalion decked out in rich armor that shines in the setting sun.

Byron intensifies the power of his modifiers by using them in unexpected ways. The word *gleaming,* for example, does not usually refer to human beings. Similarly, in the line "And the eyes of the sleepers waxed deadly and chill," *chill* is an unexpected and striking adjective to use in describing eyes.

■ Choose three modifiers and three nouns from "The Destruction of Sennacherib," and create new combinations that are as unusual and vivid as Byron's original choices. You might, for example, combine *gold* and *snow,* or *silent* and *wave.* Once you have chosen your nouns and their modifiers, write a sentence for each pair, making your images as vivid as possible.

# COMPOSITION

## Writing About Poetry

■ Write an essay of two or three paragraphs about Byron's use of poetic techniques to convey his meaning in "The Destruction of Sennacherib." First explain what the poem means. Then explain how the poem's speaker, sound, imagery, and figurative language express this meaning. *For help with this assignment, see Lesson 11 in the Writing About Literature Handbook at the back of this book.*

## Writing a Narrative Poem

■ Write a brief poem about a gripping historical or current event. Focus on the main events of the story, and make your poem as exciting as possible with vivid details of color, sound, and action. Try to use rhyme and regular rhythm as you write.

STUDY QUESTIONS

1. wolves
2. Angel of Death; breathes in the face of the foe, causes death
3. horses—proud in life, died painfully; soldiers—distorted, pale
4. "glance of the Lord"
5. The army is vast, powerful, and fierce. Dramatizing the change are images contrasting summer and autumn leaves and gleaming armor and rusty mail.
6. Divine power is far greater.
7. sympathetic; compares Assyrians to wolves; calls army foe
8. The strong, galloping rhythm evokes speed and attack.
9. The narrative contains conflict, action, and a resolution; answers should state opinion and give reasons.

## VOCABULARY

Possible answers: withered wings; chill sheen; pale sword

---

# COMPOSITION: GUIDELINES FOR EVALUATION

## WRITING ABOUT POETRY

### Objective

To analyze how poetic techniques convey meaning

### Guidelines for Evaluation

- suggested length: two to three paragraphs
- should begin by explaining the poem's meaning
- should describe poem's use of speaker, sound, imagery, and figurative language
- should show how these elements convey meaning

## WRITING A NARRATIVE POEM

### Objective

To write a narrative poem

### Guidelines for Evaluation

- suggested length: three to four stanzas
- should describe a historical or current event
- should use details of color, sound, action
- should convey mood using rhythm and rhyme

*Robert Frost*

# The Tuft of Flowers

I went to turn the grass once after one
Who mowed it in the dew before the sun.

The dew was gone that made his blade so keen
Before I came to view the leveled scene.

5 I looked for him behind an isle of trees;
I listened for his whetstone[1] on the breeze.

But he had gone his way, the grass all mown,
And I must be, as he had been,—alone,

"As all must be," I said within my heart,
10 "Whether they work together or apart."

But as I said it, swift there passed me by
On noiseless wing a bewildered butterfly,

Seeking with memories grown dim o'er night
Some resting flower of yesterday's delight.

15 And once I marked his flight go round and round,
As where some flower lay withering on the ground.

And then he flew as far as eye could see,
And then on tremulous wing came back to me.

I thought of questions that have no reply,
20 And would have turned to toss the grass to dry;

---

1. **whetstone:** stone wheel used for sharpening a blade.

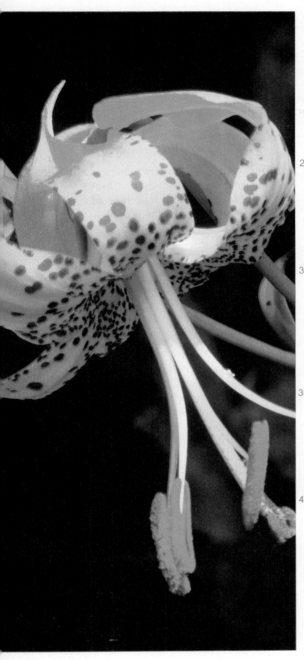

But he turned first, and led my eye to look
At a tall tuft of flowers beside a brook,

A leaping tongue of bloom the scythe had spared
Beside a reedy brook the scythe had bared.

25 The mower in the dew had loved them thus,
By leaving them to flourish, not for us,

Nor yet to draw one thought of ours to him,
But from sheer morning gladness at the brim.

The butterfly and I had lit upon,
30 Nevertheless, a message from the dawn,

That made me hear the wakening birds around,
And hear his long scythe whispering to the ground,

And feel a spirit kindred to my own;
So that henceforth I worked no more alone;

35 But glad with him, I worked as with his aid,
And weary, sought at noon with him the shade;

And dreaming, as it were, held brotherly speech
With one whose thought I had not hoped to reach.

"Men work together," I told him from the heart,
40 "Whether they work together or apart."

*The Tuft of Flowers*  **229**

The Tuft of Flowers  **T-229**

- The speaker sees a butterfly discover an unmowed tuft of flowers.
- He perceives that he, the butterfly, and the other worker are united in their love of nature.

## SYMBOLISM

The tuft of flowers symbolizes the beauty of nature which, if appreciated ("loved"), unites all living things (l. 25).

## IMAGERY

Images of renewal reflect the speaker's new-found kinship with other living things and nature ("a message from the dawn," "wakening birds") (ll. 30–31).

## MAIN IDEA

The last two lines summarize the speaker's own flight from isolation and despair to community and hope.

## REFLECTING ON THE POEM

What does the speaker discover? (Possible answers may suggest that because a common feeling for nature unites them, the butterfly and the two workers share a kinship and that the worker is not alone.)

1. turning grass in a field; another worker; mown the field
2. He says to himself that all men work alone.
3. butterfly; a flower; tuft of flowers
4. because of "sheer morning gladness"
5. ■ "Men work together."
   ■ The mower who had preceded him
6. ■ The speaker feels lonely.
   ■ Everyone is essentially isolated.
7. His first words reveal isolation from others; his last words reveal a sense of closeness to all living things.
8. All living things share a love of beauty. Message: We are never completely alone.
9. People can be brought together by a closeness to nature.
10. Thoughts and feelings can be revealed through actions. Wordless communication is better in that it can be more direct. It is limited in that it is not specific or detailed.

## VIEWPOINT

The speaker and mower are separated by time and space. People and nature are separated by human beings' attempts to control nature.

## STUDY QUESTIONS

### Recalling

1. What is the speaker doing in the beginning of the poem? Who has preceded him? What has the earlier worker done to the field?
2. What does the speaker say in lines 9–10? To whom does he speak?
3. What passes the speaker in the field? What does this creature seem to be looking for, and what does it finally find?
4. According to the speaker, why has the other worker left this one thing?
5. What does the speaker say in the last two lines of the poem? To whom does he speak this time?

### Interpreting

6. Describe the speaker's feelings in the first ten lines of the poem. What does he mean in lines 9–10?
7. Contrast the statement in lines 9–10 with the speaker's words at the end of the poem. What do these lines mean? What has made the speaker change his mind?
8. Why might the speaker feel a kinship with the butterfly and the other worker? What message do they communicate to him?
9. What is the poem saying about the relationship between one person and another and between people and nature?

### Extending

10. Explain how communication can take place without words. In what way is wordless communication better than speech? In what way is it more limited than speech?

## VIEWPOINT

One writer has noted Robert Frost often examines the barriers that separate people:

To Frost...barriers serve as a framework for mutual understanding and respect. It is because of barriers that we understand each other, and, far from striving to tear them down...Frost insists on recognizing them.
— M. Montgomery, "Robert Frost and His Use of Barriers," *Robert Frost: A Collection of Critical Essays*

■ In "The Tuft of Flowers" what separates one person from another? What separates people from nature? How do such barriers add to the impact of the last lines of the poem?

## COMPOSITION

### Writing About a Narrative Poem

■ Explain how "The Tuft of Flowers" gives importance to an apparently insignificant event. First relate the experience that this poem narrates. Then explain why this event is significant to the speaker, and point out a few specific images and statements that make it important.

### Writing a Narrative Poem

■ Write a narrative poem about an experience in which you arrive on a scene after someone else has left it. For example, you might walk into an empty but chaotic locker room or into an old deserted house that shows what its former inhabitants were like. Decide what "message" you see in the traces left by other person(s).

## COMPOSITION: GUIDELINES FOR EVALUATION

### WRITING ABOUT A NARRATIVE POEM

**Objective**

To show how poem gives importance to seemingly insignificant event

**Guidelines for Evaluation**

- suggested length: two paragraphs
- should begin by relating events in the poem
- should explain the importance of events to speaker
- should cite images and statements from the poem

### WRITING A NARRATIVE POEM

**Objective**

To write poem that conveys message through traces left by someone

**Guidelines for Evaluation**

- suggested length: three to six stanzas
- should describe a place recently deserted
- should show how a message is revealed by traces left by others
- should convey the impact of the message

**William Wordsworth**

# My Heart Leaps Up

My heart leaps up when I behold
  A rainbow in the sky:
So was it when my life began;
So is it now I am a man;
5 So be it when I shall grow old,
  Or let me die!
The Child is father of the Man;
And I could wish my days to be
Bound each to each by natural piety.

## STUDY QUESTIONS

### Recalling

1. What makes the speaker's heart leap up? How long has he felt this way?
2. According to line 7, how is "the Child" connected to "the Man"?
3. What hope does the speaker express in lines 8–9 about the days of his life?

### Interpreting

4. Describe the emotion expressed by the speaker in the poem's opening.
5. What does the metaphor in line 7 mean?
6. Define the word *piety*. What do you think "natural piety" means in this poem?
7. According to this poem, what should we preserve from our childhood?

### Extending

8. Do you think people's childhood acts and feelings should influence their adult lives? Why or why not?

## LITERARY FOCUS

### Lyric Poetry

   A **lyric poem** is a brief, often musical expression of the speaker's emotion. In ancient Greece, lyric poems were performed by individual poets who sang of private feelings and accompanied themselves on stringed instruments called lyres. Although poets no longer actually sing their own lyric poems, we still apply the term *lyrics* to the words of songs, and we still label as *lyric* any poem that is at heart an expression of feeling.

   Beyond expressing emotion in a few lines, lyric poetry follows no set pattern. Many lyric poems describe a particular thing—a sunset, a face, a memory—that stirs the speaker's feelings. Some offer insights about human nature or about the place of human beings in the world. Most lyric poems use imaginative figures of speech and musical language. However, whatever form it takes, a lyric poem is a unified expression of feeling that allows the reader to share in the emotion that "sings" in its lines.

### Thinking About Lyric Poetry

1. What emotion lies at the heart of this poem and holds it together? What figures of speech express this feeling most vividly?
2. Find examples of the musical devices—such as rhyme, regular rhythm, repetition—that make this lyric poem songlike.

*My Heart Leaps Up*   **231**

---

*Samuel Allen*

# To Satch[1]

Sometimes I feel like I will never stop
Just go forever
Till one fine morning
I'll reach up and grab me a handful of stars
5  And swing out my long lean leg
And whip three hot strikes burning down the heavens
And look over at God and say
How about that!

---

1. **Satch:** nickname for LeRoy Robert Paige (1905–1982), famous major league baseball pitcher.

## STUDY QUESTIONS

**Recalling**

1. How does the speaker feel, according to lines 1–2?
2. What will he do on one fine morning?
3. What will he say then, and to whom will he say it?

**Interpreting**

4. Satchel Paige pitched in the major leagues well into his middle age—a very unusual feat. How do these facts fit the speaker of this poem? How does the poem make Paige seem legendary?
5. Where in the poem does the speaker exaggerate? What feeling about life does he express by exaggerating?
6. The form of this poem is one long sentence that rolls on and on. In what way does the poem's form match its content?

**Extending**

7. Why do you think people often look for legends in real-life persons?

232   *Poetry*

## VOCABULARY

**Colloquial Language**

**Colloquial language** is the language of informal conversation. We use colloquial language constantly when we speak but much more rarely when we write. In "To Satch" Samuel Allen consistently writes in a colloquial style—beginning with the poem's title, which uses an informal nickname of the poem's subject instead of his formal name, LeRoy Robert Paige. In "To Satch" Allen's use of such colloquial expressions as "grab me" (instead of "take") and "whip" (instead of "throw") add to the zest of the poem. They make us hear the voice of a real person, almost as if he were standing right in front of us.

■ Find three more examples of colloquial language in "To Satch." Then retitle the poem "To LeRoy Robert Paige," and rewrite a few of its lines using a more formal, less conversational style. Read both versions out loud. What are the advantages and disadvantages of each?

*Mari Evans*

# If There Be Sorrow

If there be sorrow
let it be
for things undone . . .
undreamed
5    unrealized
       unattained
to these add one:
Love withheld . . .
. . . restrained

LITERARY OPTIONS

- lyric poetry
- poetic form

THEMATIC OPTIONS

- regrets for things undone
- unfulfilled love

LYRIC POETRY

The speaker's quiet but heartfelt regret makes this poem a poignant expression of emotion.

POETIC FORM

Three consecutive one-word lines mirror the implied meagerness of the speaker's life (ll. 4, 5, 6). They also create a reticent, restrained tone.

REFLECTING ON THE POEM

What emotions does the speaker express? (She expresses disappointment and regret.)

STUDY QUESTIONS

1. things undone, undreamed, unrealized, unattained
2. love withheld
3. ■ *undone:* cause regret; *undreamed:* deprives life of excitement; *unrealized:* results in disappointment; *unattained:* causes bitterness
   ■ Withheld love is also something "undone," but it involves not acknowledging something that already exists.
4. most important—most specific cause for sorrow
5. regret and disappointment; stresses feeling of emptiness
6. Doing nothing causes regret; taking action makes life richer.

---

## STUDY QUESTIONS

### Recalling
1. For what things should there be sorrow, according to lines 1–6?
2. What in particular does the poem add to this list?

### Interpreting
3. Explain why each of the things listed in lines 3–6 can cause sorrow. How is the cause for sorrow mentioned in lines 8–9 similar to these others? How is it different from them?
4. In your opinion, are the speaker's last two lines an afterthought, or do they express the most important feeling in the poem? Explain.
5. What emotions does the poem convey? What emotional effect does Evans create by repeating the prefix *un-* four times in a short poem?

### Extending
6. Why might people feel that it is better to make mistakes than it is to do nothing?

## COMPOSITION

### Writing About Form in Poetry
■ Describe the effect of Mari Evans' unusual punctuation and line breaks in "If There Be Sorrow." In preparing to write, answer the following questions: Where does Evans use punctuation, and where does she omit it? Why does she break lines where she does? Why are some lines much shorter than others? Then indicate whether you think these devices add to or detract from the emotion expressed in "If There Be Sorrow." Support your opinion with examples and explanations.

### Writing About Emotions
■ Write a short poem expressing an emotion without specifically naming the emotion. You might describe something that stirs happiness or regret or anger, using words that convey that feeling without directly telling what it is. Try to unify your poem by using parallel constructions.

*If There Be Sorrow*   **233**

---

## COMPOSITION: GUIDELINES FOR EVALUATION

### WRITING ABOUT FORM IN POETRY
**Objective**
To analyze how punctuation and line breaks create poetic effects

**Guidelines for Evaluation**
- suggested length: two to three paragraphs
- should answer the four stated questions
- should state whether these devices convey emotion
- should give reasons and examples

### WRITING ABOUT EMOTIONS
**Objective**
To write poem that expresses emotion

**Guidelines for Evaluation**
- suggested length: five to ten lines
- should convey emotion without naming it
- should provide details describing the cause of the emotion

# To James

Do you remember
How you won
That last race...?
How you flung your body
5 At the start...
How your spikes
Ripped the cinders
In the stretch...
How you catapulted
10 Through the tape...
Do you remember...?
Don't you think
I lurched with you
Out of those starting holes...?
15 Don't you think
My sinews tightened
At those first
Few strides...
And when you flew into the stretch
20 Was not all my thrill
Of a thousand races
In your blood...?
At your final drive
Through the finish line
25 Did not my shout
Tell of the

Triumphant ecstasy
Of victory...?
Live
30 As I have taught you
To run, Boy—
It's a short dash
Dig your starting holes
Deep and firm
35 Lurch out of them
Into the straightaway
With all the power
That is in you
Look straight ahead
40 To the finish line
Think only of the goal
Run straight
Run high
Run hard
45 Save nothing
And finish
With an ecstatic burst
That carries you
Hurtling
50 Through the tape
To victory...

---

- The speaker addresses a young athlete, reliving the athlete's recent victory in a race.
- The speaker tells his listener to live his life much as he ran his race.

## LITERARY OPTIONS

- dramatic poetry
- extended metaphor

## THEMATIC OPTIONS

- life as an endurance race
- confronting challenges

## DRAMATIC POETRY

- The poet creates a speaker and a listener, an older man and boy (perhaps his son), as well as a dramatic situation: the moment after a well-run race. The speaker indicates that he intimately shared James's experience during the race and so is entitled to remind him of the connections between the race and life itself.

## EXTENDED METAPHOR

Beginning in line 29, the speaker launches an extended metaphor in which he compares the physical act of running to an approach to living: Prepare well, be sure of your goals, and give it your all.

## REFLECTING ON THE POEM

What might the speaker mean in the final line when he refers to "victory"? (Answers will vary. Some students may feel that the speaker means achieving your life goals and triumphing over obstacles; others may point to the satisfaction of having lived a good life, if not necessarily a triumphant one.)

# STUDY QUESTIONS

## Recalling

1. List three details from the race as recalled by the speaker. In what ways did he share in his listener's experience?
2. Whom does the speaker address in this poem? In what line of the poem is this made clear?
3. In lines 29–32, to what does the speaker compare life? List five pieces of advice about living that he offers his listener.

## Interpreting

4. The speaker gives several descriptions of running a race. What details does he repeat? How is each description different, and what point does each one make?
5. Describe the relationship between the speaker and his listener. What is the speaker's attitude toward his listener?
6. Explain the comparison the speaker makes beginning in line 29. What attitude is the speaker telling his listener to take toward each part of life?
7. Do you agree with the speaker's advice? Why or why not?

## Extending

8. Why do you think people often compare life to an athletic contest? What aspects of living does such a comparison emphasize? What aspects does it leave out?

# LITERARY FOCUS

## Dramatic Poetry

A **dramatic poem** is a type of poem that uses one or several of the techniques associated with drama. All dramatic poems present characters, often in tense situations, who speak to silent listeners, to themselves, or directly to the reader.

We can often find several elements of drama in a dramatic poem. Some dramatic poems establish their characters in vivid settings and show them engaged in action. In some cases two or more characters speak to one another, allowing readers to "eavesdrop" like members of a theater audience. However, most dramatic poems concentrate on the character of one speaker, leaving the reader to fill in the other theatrical effects that would be supplied in a play. For example, dramatic poems do not always specify the circumstances in which the character speaks; readers are free to imagine such details.

One of the most popular forms of dramatic poetry is the **dramatic monologue**, which presents only one speaker who addresses a silent listener. A dramatic monologue usually occurs at a crucial moment in the speaker's life, often a point of conflict. The speaker of a dramatic monologue reveals something important about himself or herself; in many dramatic monologues the speakers tell more about themselves than they may realize.

## Thinking About Dramatic Poetry

■ Explain how "To James" demonstrates the qualities of a dramatic monologue.

# COMPOSITION

## Writing About a Dramatic Poem

■ Describe a specific situation in which "To James" could be spoken. First describe the speaker as he reveals himself in the poem. Then identify a specific time, place, and set of circumstances in which this speaker might address his listener in the words of the poem. Use quotations from the poem to explain why your situation is appropriate. End by explaining how the situation you describe would add to the impact of the poem.

## Writing a Dramatic Poem

■ Write a short dramatic poem in which a character of your own invention speaks to a listener. Before you write, be sure you have a clear picture of your character, his or her listener, and the situation in which your character is speaking. You may want to show your character in a moment of action, tension, or conflict of some kind. Be sure that your poem clearly reveals the personality of your character.

# COMPARING POEMS

■ Choose one narrative, one lyric, and one dramatic poem from the poems in this section: "Eldorado," "The Destruction of Sennacherib," "The Tuft of Flowers," "My Heart Leaps Up," "To Satch," "If There Be Sorrow," and "To James." For each poem explain how the categories *narrative, lyric,* and *dramatic* overlap. For example, does "To James" include narrative and lyric qualities?

*To James* **235**

## *COMPOSITION: GUIDELINES FOR EVALUATION*

### WRITING ABOUT A DRAMATIC POEM

**Objective**

To explain a specific situation in which a dramatic poem is spoken

**Guidelines for Evaluation**

- suggested length: one to two paragraphs
- should begin by describing the speaker
- should identify time, place, circumstances in which the poem could be spoken

### WRITING A DRAMATIC POEM

**Objective**

To reveal character and situation through a dramatic monologue

**Guidelines for Evaluation**

- suggested length: ten to fifteen lines
- should be spoken by one person to a silent listener
- should contain details that reveal the character of the speaker

# *LITERARY FOCUS: Patterns in Poetry*

Poems, like houses, can differ very much in design and construction. Some poems are like traditional houses. They follow a recognizable pattern, even a familiar one that has been used by many other poems. For example, every **sonnet** follows a predetermined pattern made up of a specified number of lines of a specified length with a specified rhyme scheme. However, poems following traditional patterns may vary widely in the raw materials—the speakers, subjects, images, and sounds—with which they fill in these patterns.

Other poems are like free-form houses. They seem to sprawl across the page without a recognizable structure. However, like free-form buildings, such poems contain hidden "girders" of meaning, subtle patterns of sound and image that give form to their apparent formlessness. The patterns and structures of such poems are simply less obvious than those of more traditional poems.

Although they chose very different forms, all of the poets in the following section have built into their poems patterns and structures that hold these poems together.

**William Shakespeare** (1564–1616) is probably the best-known author in the English language. Shakespeare wrote his plays and poems at a time in which writers worked within certain prescribed patterns. Shakespeare's greatness lies in his unequaled mastery of both form and content, mastery he demonstrates in the sonnet "Shall I Compare Thee to a Summer's Day?"

■ In what ways is art "bigger than life"? In what ways do you think it is smaller?

**Elinor Wylie** (1885–1928) was raised in Philadelphia and Washington, D.C., and began writing poetry in her teens. Wylie's work is often celebrated for its precise vocabulary and vivid imagery, as well as for her experimentation with pattern. In "Puritan Sonnet" she shows the skill with which she can fit modern language and ideas to the constraints of a traditional form.

■ How does the saying "Less is more" apply to this poem? When, in your own experience, has this proved true?

**236** *Poetry*

**Maxine Kumin** (born 1925) has taught and lectured at a number of distinguished universities. A winner of the Pulitzer Prize for Poetry in 1973, she describes her craft in these terms: ". . . in the process of writing, . . . as you pound and hammer the poem into shape and into form, the order—the marvelous informing order—emerges from it." In "400-Meter Freestyle" Kumin "hammers" a poem into an unconventional shape uniquely suited to her subject.

■ Have you ever taken part in or seen an athletic event in which someone expended more energy than necessary and did poorly or lost? How might pacing have changed the outcome?

**Lawrence Ferlinghetti** (born 1920) is famous for his role as the founder of City Lights Books in San Francisco, the first paperback bookstore in the United States and a haven for experimental writers. In the 1950s Ferlinghetti led the Beats, a group of writers and other artists who broke away from traditional artistic forms and conventional themes.

■ The speaker of "Constantly risking absurdity" describes the dangers of writing poetry. How might these same dangers apply to other creative endeavors such as song-writing, acting, or painting?

*William Shakespeare*

# Shall I Compare Thee to a Summer's Day?

Shall I compare thee to a summer's day?
Thou art more lovely and more temperate.[1]
Rough winds do shake the darling buds of May,
And summer's lease hath all too short a date.
5  Sometime too hot the eye of heaven shines,
And often is his gold complexion dimmed;
And every fair[2] from fair sometime declines,
By chance, or nature's changing course, untrimmed:[3]
But thy eternal summer shall not fade
10  Nor lose possession of that fair thou ow'st,[4]
Nor shall Death brag thou wand'rest in his shade
When in eternal lines to time thou grow'st.
    So long as men can breathe or eyes can see,
    So long lives this, and this gives life to thee.

---

1. **temperate**: moderate, mild.
2. **fair**: beauty.
3. **untrimmed**: stripped.
4. **ow'st**: owns, possesses.

Detail from *The Blessed Damozel,* 1878, Dante Gabriel Rossetti. Fogg Art Museum, Cambridge, Massachusetts.

## STUDY QUESTIONS

### Recalling

1. According to line 2, in what two ways is the person addressed in the poem superior to a summer's day?
2. According to lines 7-8, what often happens to beauty? For what two reasons?
3. According to lines 9-10, in what specific ways is the person addressed in the poem superior to summer?
4. What boast will Death be unable to make about the subject, according to the speaker?
5. According to lines 13-14, what will give the person addressed in the poem life, and how long will that life last?

### Interpreting

6. What does the speaker mean by the phrase "thy eternal summer" in line 9?
7. What is the speaker's attitude toward time? Does it pass quickly or slowly? Is it a positive, negative, or neutral force? Support your answer with examples from the poem.
8. Describe the speaker's feelings for the person addressed in the poem.

### Extending

9. In what ways could great literature be said to "conquer" death?

## LITERARY FOCUS

### The Shakespearean Sonnet

A **sonnet** is a lyric poem of fourteen lines. It is almost always written in iambic pentameter (see page 196) and usually follows very strict patterns of stanza divisions and rhymes.

The **Shakespearean** or **English sonnet** is one of two major types of sonnets. Borrowed from an earlier Italian poetry form, the Shakespearean sonnet was developed in England in the early sixteenth century and was later made famous by Shakespeare. The Shakespearean sonnet consists of three **quatrains,** or four-line stanzas, followed

by a **couplet,** or pair of rhyming lines. The Shakespearean sonnet also follows a strict rhyme scheme usually written as *abab, cdcd, efef, gg.* That is, in each quatrain the first line rhymes with the third, and the second line rhymes with the fourth. The couplet ends the poem with a new rhyme.

The divisions in the sonnet give structure to its ideas as well as to its shape and sound. For example, each quatrain usually presents a series of problems or arguments, and the couplet expresses the poet's conclusion about the subject. In Shakespeare's sonnets the final couplet often provides a direct and memorable statement of the poem's central idea.

### Thinking About Shakespearean Sonnets

1. Explain how "Shall I Compare Thee to a Summer's Day?" conforms to the pattern described for the number of lines, arrangement of stanzas, and rhyme scheme of the Shakespearean sonnet.
2. What divisions of thought do you find in this sonnet? Referring to specific lines, show whether these divisions follow the pattern often used by Shakespearean sonnets.

## COMPOSITION

### Writing About Poetry

■ Show how Shakespeare's poetic techniques reveal the meaning of his sonnet "Shall I Compare Thee to a Summer's Day?" In particular you should consider Shakespeare's use of speaker, sound, imagery, figurative language, and pattern to express his meaning. *For help with this assignment, see Lesson 11 in the Writing About Literature Handbook at the back of this book.*

### Writing a Poem with a Comparison

■ Write a brief poem in which you address a person directly, comparing that person to a season or a particular type of weather. Your choice of comparison and your diction should make clear your attitude toward the person you are addressing in the poem.

## STUDY QUESTIONS

1. more lovely and temperate
2. fades; by chance or aging
3. Subject will always be young, and beauty will never fade.
4. that the subject "wand'rest in his shade"
5. poem; as long as there are people to read it
6. unchanging beauty; sweet temperament
7. feels it passes quickly; negative force that diminishes beauty
8. admiration, desire to immortalize
9. Literature lives long after the author's death.

## LITERARY FOCUS

1. consists of fourteen lines; iambic pentameter; three quatrains followed by rhyming couplet; rhyme scheme: *abab, cdcd, efef, gg*
2. ■ Lines 1-8 describe the person to whom the sonnet is addressed and present arguments showing why the subject is lovelier than summer.
   ■ Lines 9-12 argue that these qualities will never fade or die.
   ■ Lines 13-14 clinch the argument by saying that the poem will give immortality to the person addressed.
   ■ This organization is common to Shakespearean sonnets. The three quatrains state and support an idea; the final couplet provides a new, memorable perspective on it.

## COMPOSITION: GUIDELINES FOR EVALUATION

### WRITING ABOUT POETRY

**Objective**

To analyze how meaning is conveyed through poetic techniques

**Guidelines for Evaluation**

■ suggested length: three to five paragraphs
■ should demonstrate how poetic techniques are used to convey meaning in Shakespeare's sonnet
■ should analyze literary elements (speaker, sound, imagery, figurative language, pattern)

### WRITING A POEM WITH A COMPARISON

**Objective**

To write a poem with a comparison

**Guidelines for Evaluation**

■ suggested length: five to fifteen lines
■ should be addressed directly to a person
■ should make extended comparison between this person and a season or type of weather
■ should reveal the speaker's attitude

The speaker announces that she dislikes a lush, rich scene; she prefers a spare, almost chill landscape of pale skies, bare fields, and monotones.

## LITERARY OPTIONS

- Petrarchan sonnet
- visual imagery

## THEMATIC OPTIONS

- the beauty of austerity
- responding to nature

## IMAGERY

The poet draws a precise picture of the kind of landscape she prefers: "pearly monotones," "Bare hills," "cold silver on a sky of slate," "thin blue or snowy gray" (ll. 4, 6, 9).

## MAIN IDEA

The speaker states the main idea simply and directly as befits her "Puritan" heritage: "I love the look, austere, immaculate, /Of landscapes drawn in pearly monotones" (ll. 3–4).

## PETRARCHAN SONNET

After the octave (ll. 1–8) describes the spare landscape that the speaker loves, the sestet extends the landscape in time, envisioning its passage through all the seasons of the year (ll. 9–14).

## REFLECTING ON THE POEM

In what way might the strict order of the Petrarchan sonnet be appropriate to the ideas Wylie expresses? (Students should note that the strict order and visible structure of the sonnet could be said to mirror the spare, clear lines of the landscape the speaker prefers.)

*Elinor Wylie*

# Puritan Sonnet

Down to the Puritan marrow of my bones
There's something in this richness that I hate.
I love the look, austere, immaculate,
Of landscapes drawn in pearly monotones.
5 There's something in my very blood that owns
Bare hills, cold silver on a sky of slate,
A thread of water, churned to milky spate[1]
Streaming through slanted pastures fenced with stones.

I love those skies, thin blue or snowy gray,
10 Those fields sparse-planted, rendering meager sheaves;
That spring, briefer than apple-blossom's breath,
Summer, so much too beautiful to stay,
Swift autumn, like a bonfire of leaves,
And sleepy winter, like the sleep of death.

_____
1. **spate:** sudden downpour.

## STUDY QUESTIONS

### Recalling

1. What does the speaker of this poem hate? In contrast, what does she love, according to lines 3–4?
2. Name five specific landscape features singled out by the speaker in lines 6–8. What adjectives does she associate with them?
3. What particular colors does the speaker mention throughout the poem?
4. What special quality does the speaker assign to each season in lines 11–14?

### Interpreting

5. What does *Puritan* mean, and what associations does the word have?
6. In what way do Wylie's color images fit the picture of the Puritan?
7. What common traits can you find in the various things preferred by the speaker in lines 3–10? Do these qualities seem appropriate to the word *Puritan*? Why or why not?
8. What view of life does the poem present?

### Extending

9. Does this poem persuade you to prefer gray days and bare landscapes? If so, why? If not, how would you answer Wylie?

## LITERARY FOCUS

### The Petrarchan Sonnet

The **Petrarchan** [pe trärk'ən] **sonnet** is the forerunner of the Shakespearean sonnet. Also called the **Italian sonnet,** it is a form of lyric poetry that was developed in thirteenth-century Italy and took its name from its most famous practitioner, the Italian poet Francesco Petrarch (1304–1374). The word *sonnet* is derived from the Italian *sonnetto,* which means "little song"; in fact, the Petrarchan sonnet was originally meant to be sung to musical accompaniment.

Like the Shakespearean sonnet, the Petrarchan sonnet is fourteen lines long and follows a strict rhyme scheme. However, both its stanza divisions and its rhyme scheme differ from those of the Shakespearean sonnet.

The Petrarchan sonnet is usually divided into two stanzas. The first stanza is eight lines long and is called the **octave;** the second stanza is six lines long and is called the **sestet**. The rhyme scheme of the octave can be represented as *abba abba;* that is, lines 1, 4, 5, and 8 rhyme, as do lines 2, 3, 6, and 7. The sestet follows a different rhyme scheme, usually represented as *cdecde,* although some sonnets may alter this pattern.

As in the Shakespearean sonnet, the form of the Petrarchan sonnet structures the ideas in the poem. The octave usually presents a situation, an idea, or a question, and the sestet provides a resolution, a comment, or an answer.

### Thinking About the Petrarchan Sonnet

1. Explain how Wylie's sonnet follows the stanza and rhyme patterns of the Petrarchan sonnet.
2. In what ways are the ideas presented in Wylie's octave and sestet similar? In what ways are they different?

*Puritan Sonnet* **241**

## AT A GLANCE

The speaker admiringly tracks a swimmer's economic movements at the beginning of a 400-meter free-style race.

### LITERARY OPTIONS

- concrete poetry
- onomatopoeia

### THEMATIC OPTIONS

- physical achievements
- confronting challenges

### ONOMATOPOEIA

The speaker uses words whose sound corresponds to their sense, making the reader see (catapults) and hear (cracks) the swimmer (l. 1).

### CONCRETE POETRY

The pattern of long horizontal lines of equal length connected at alternate ends by short vertical lines suggests the back-and-forth progress of a swimmer.

### WORD CHOICE

Just as the swimmer is economical in his movements, so the poet uses a number of short, sharp words ("wrist cock to heel snap") (l. 21).

### CONCRETE POETRY

The undulating words at alternate ends of succeeding lines (his, him) may mirror the swimmer's kicking feet and the splashes they make in the water (ll. 22–24, 26–28).

*Maxine Kumin*

# 400-Meter Freestyle

THE GUN full swing the swimmer catapults and crac

5  feet away onto that perfect glass he catches
a
n
d
throws behind him scoop after scoop cunningly movi
10

water back to move him forward. Thrift is his wonderf
s
15  e
c
ret; he has schooled out all extravagance. No musc
20

ples without compensation wrist cock to heel snap
h
i
s
25  mobile mouth that siphons in the air that nurtur

at  half  an  inch  above  sea  level  so  to  spea

242   *Poetry*

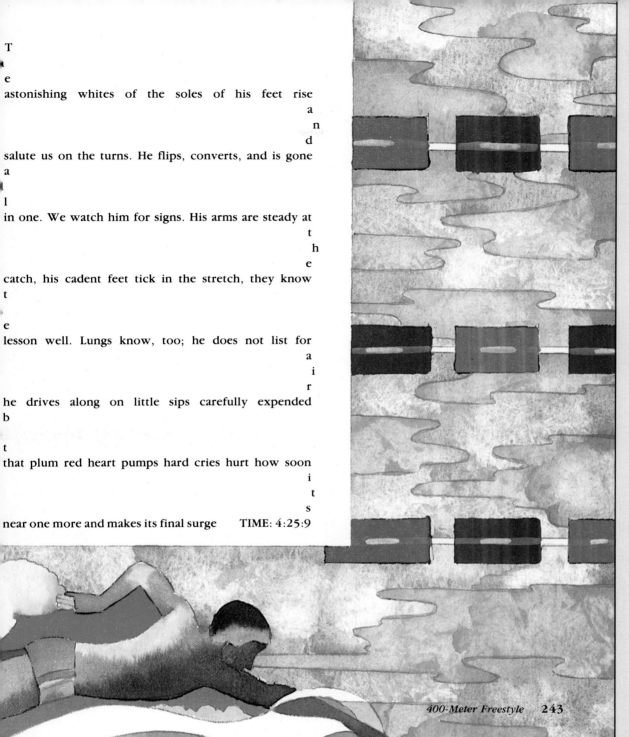

T
  e
astonishing whites of the soles of his feet rise

                                       a

                                       n

                                       d
salute us on the turns. He flips, converts, and is gone

a

l
in one. We watch him for signs. His arms are steady at

                                       t

                                       h

                                       e
catch, his cadent feet tick in the stretch, they know

t

e
lesson well. Lungs know, too; he does not list for

                                       a

                                       i

                                       r
he drives along on little sips carefully expended

b

t
that plum red heart pumps hard cries hurt how soon

                                       i

                                       t

                                       s
near one more and makes its final surge     TIME: 4:25:9

*400-Meter Freestyle*   243

## AT A GLANCE

The swimmer passes the stretch easily and makes a final surge, finishing the race in 4:25:9.

## REFLECTING ON THE POEM

What qualities of the swimmer impress the speaker? (The speaker is interested in the swimmer's economic movements, his drive and expertise, and the way he looks as he moves.)

1. 400-meter freestyle swimming race; with the swimmer's dive into water upon hearing the starting gun
2. thrift
3. catapults, scoops water, cocks wrists, snaps feet, kicks, siphons in air, flips body; his heart
4. four minutes, twenty-five and nine-tenths seconds
5. marks abruptness of the start and finish
6. economy of movement; expertise; drive; appearance as he moves
7. ■ catapulting into water; muscles rippling; siphoning air; feet rising; flipping; kicking
   ■ These images maintain the poem's strong momentum.
8. Each is quick, efficient.
9. Answers should state and support the student's opinion about whether the poem evokes the feeling of a race and should explain which aspects of the race the student would focus on.

## LITERARY FOCUS

1. ■ horizontal lines of even length; connected end to end by three-letter words printed vertically
   ■ The poem moves back and forth across the page, imitating the swimmer's movement as he swims laps.
2. This form takes extra effort to decipher and to connect the lines, just as the swimmer makes a special effort in turning after each lap.

## STUDY QUESTIONS

### Recalling
1. What athletic event does the poem describe? How does it begin?
2. What is the swimmer's "wonderful secret"?
3. Name five specific actions that the swimmer takes in the course of the event. What "cries hurt" toward the end of the event?
4. What is the swimmer's time?

### Interpreting
5. For what reason do you think Kumin capitalizes the words at the beginning and end of the poem?
6. Which of the swimmer's qualities seem to interest the speaker most?
7. Find six images of motion in the poem. What effect do these images have on the poem's momentum?
8. Explain how the swimmer's movements demonstrate his understanding of his "wonderful secret."

### Extending
9. How well do you think this poem describes the experience of an athletic contest? What aspects of such an event would you focus on?

## LITERARY FOCUS

### Concrete Poetry
A **concrete poem** is a poem that, above everything else, stresses the visual appearance of the words and lines on the page. Concrete poems create pictures on the page by experimenting with punctuation, line lengths, even with the way in which the poem's words are spelled and typed.

Somewhat more difficult to read than conventional poems, concrete poems are meant to startle readers out of the habit of reading words *only* for their meanings. Concrete poems do have meanings, but they remind us that words affect us by the way they look and sound, as well as by what they mean.

Concrete poetry is a very recent form of poetry, and many people believe that it is more closely allied with the visual arts than with literature. However, concrete poetry is poetry, and despite its playfulness it has a serious purpose. It reminds us that all poetry affects us on other levels than purely rational thought.

### Thinking About Concrete Poetry
1. Describe the special visual effects achieved by Kumin in "400-Meter Freestyle." In what ways does the poem's shape mirror its subject matter?
2. In what way might the act of reading "400-Meter Freestyle" require the same kind of concentration shown by the swimmer in the poem?

## COMPOSITION

### Writing About Verbs
■ Describe the effect of Kumin's choice of verbs in "400-Meter Freestyle." First consider the verbs that convey exactly the swimmer's physical movements. Then decide the effect of verbs such as *schooled* that go beyond purely physical description.

### Writing a Concrete Poem
■ Write a concrete poem of your own in which the layout of the words and lines on the page expresses the poem's content. If you like you may write about one of the following activities and objects: (a) a pole-vaulting contest, (b) a roller-coaster ride, (c) a leaping kangaroo, (d) a tennis match, (e) a butterfly, or (f) a fingerprint.

## COMPOSITION: GUIDELINES FOR EVALUATION

### WRITING ABOUT VERBS
**Objective**
To analyze the way a poet uses verbs to create effect

**Guidelines for Evaluation**
■ suggested length: two paragraphs
■ should cite verbs that precisely describe the swimmer's physical movements
■ should analyze the effect of these verbs
■ should summarize the overall effect of verb choices in poem

### WRITING A CONCRETE POEM
**Objective**
To write a concrete poem

**Guidelines for Evaluation**
■ suggested length: one page
■ should use unusual punctuation, line lengths, line placement, and spelling to create a picture or pattern on the page
■ should have a visual appearance that imitates the movement or qualities of its subject

Lawrence Ferlinghetti

# Constantly risking absurdity

Constantly risking absurdity
                              and death
            whenever he performs
                        above the heads
5                                     of his audience
        the poet like an acrobat
                    climbs on rime
                        to a high wire of his own making
    and balancing on eyebeams
10                                above a sea of faces
                paces his way
                        to the other side of day
        performing entrechats[1]
                        and sleight-of-foot tricks
15      and other high theatrics
                        and all without mistaking
            any thing
                    for what it may not be
        For he's the super realist
20                                who must perforce[2] perceive
            taut truth
                        before the taking of each stance or step
    in his supposed advance
                        toward that still higher perch
25  where Beauty stands and waits
                    with gravity
                            to start her death-defying leap
        And he
                a little charleychaplin man
30                                who may or may not catch
            her fair eternal form
                        spreadeagled in the empty air
            of existence

---

1. **entrechats** [onˈtrə shaˈ]: complicated leaps in ballet in which the dancer's
legs crisscross several times.
2. **perforce:** of necessity.

**AT A GLANCE**

The poet is described as an acrobat who takes risks in order to capture Beauty.

**LITERARY OPTIONS**

- free verse
- extended metaphor

**THEMATIC OPTIONS**

- the artistic imagination
- visions and ideals

**FREE VERSE**

The poet conveys his thoughts in a single, extended "sentence" that has no punctuation throughout its entire length and ends without a period. The absence of conventional punctuation helps create a feeling of suspense appropriate to the image of the poet as tightrope walker.

**EXTENDED METAPHOR**

Throughout the entire poem Ferlinghetti develops a metaphor equating the poet with an acrobat: He "climbs . . . to a high wire of his own making," performs "high theatrics," and hopes to catch fellow acrobat Beauty (ll. 7–8, 15, 30).

**EXPERIMENTATION WITH FORM**

The back-and-forth physical layout of this poem suggests the tentative movement of a high-wire artist stepping back and forth carefully and "balancing on eyebeams" (l. 9).

**REFLECTING ON THE POEM**

What "risks" does Ferlinghetti take in this poem? (Ferlinghetti's risks include the absence of punctuation, the depiction of the poet as a comic figure, and verbal stunts like "sleight-of-foot tricks.")

## STUDY QUESTIONS

1. absurdity; death
2. acrobat
3. climbs on "rime"; balances on eyebeams; performs entrechats
4. beauty; catch her; not assured
5. ■ comic; bumbling; endearing
   ■ Beauty is grave, fair, bold.
   ■ suggests poets strive, sometimes ridiculously or fatally, to attain ideal of beauty
6. Readers must stretch imagination, mind to comprehend poem's meaning.
7. ■ One who portrays things as they are.
   ■ creates things beyond reality; creates heightened realism
8. Poet must risk absurdity, failure in quest for truth / beauty; poetry must challenge poet and readers.
9. Poets may risk meaninglessness in struggle to be original. Their incentive is the hope of attaining truth / beauty.

## LITERARY FOCUS

■1. lines wander, vary in length, have no regular meter / rhyme scheme, begin lower case. Punctuation is omitted, words invented.
2. Many lines have three iambic feet, end rhymes, internal rhymes.
3. imitates acrobat by performing tricks with words, rhyme, meter

## VOCABULARY

line 9: *eyebeam;* line 14: *sleight-of-foot;* line 29: *charleychaplin*

## STUDY QUESTIONS

### Recalling

1. What two things does the poet constantly risk, according to the speaker?
2. To what sort of performer is the poet compared?
3. Name at least three feats of the poet-performer.
4. What partner stands and waits for the poet-performer on the "still higher perch"? What will the poet try to do with this partner? Is he assured of success?

### Interpreting

5. What picture of the poet does Ferlinghetti create by calling him "a little charleychaplin man"? Contrast this image with that of Beauty in lines 25–26. What does this contrast suggest about the relationship between a poet and art?
6. In what senses does a poet perform "above the heads of his audience"?
7. Define *realist.* Since *super* means both "above" and "to a greater degree," what two ideas about poetry does Ferlinghetti suggest when he says that the poet is a "super realist"?
8. What ideas about the role of the poet and of poetry does this poem express?

### Extending

9. *Absurdity* means "meaninglessness." In what sense does any poet risk being absurd? What might be the poet's incentives for taking such a risk?

## LITERARY FOCUS

### Free Verse and Experimentation with Form

**Free verse** is poetry that follows no strict patterns of meter, rhyme, line length, or stanza arrangement (see page 198). A poet who writes in free verse often experiments with all of these various features of poetry but does not put them together in any consistent pattern. In contrast with the traditional patterns and forms of poetry written before the twentieth century, experimentation with free verse is typical of much modern poetry.

Modern poems may combine very short stanzas with very long ones or may have no stanzas at all. Rhymes may appear out of nowhere and then vanish just as unpredictably. A line marching along with a

regular rhythm might be followed by one with a totally offbeat rhythm. In modern poems lines might or might not begin with capital letters; some might line up on the left margin, and others might wander all over the page. The poet's experimentation may also extend to spelling, punctuation, and grammar.

Although many modern poems do not follow any set pattern, they must, like all poems, communicate some idea or feeling to the reader. Poets experiment with free verse because it allows them to squeeze and stretch poetry until it fits whatever it is they have to say.

### Thinking About Experimentation with Form

1. Find instances in "Constantly risking absurdity" of Ferlinghetti's unconventional approach to poetic form.
2. Can you find any instances of pattern—such as regular rhythm, rhyme, or repetition?
3. In what way does Ferlinghetti's experimentation suit the message of his poem?

## VOCABULARY

### Inventive Language

In describing what a poet does, Ferlinghetti uses, combines, and even spells words inventively, performing his own witty balancing act for us. Some of his verbal stunts work clever variations on familiar expressions, as in "sleight-of-foot tricks."

1. Find three examples of Ferlinghetti's inventiveness with language in "Constantly risking absurdity," and describe the effect of each.
2. Try to invent two or three words of your own by combining familiar words in a new way.

## COMPARING POEMS

1. Compare the overall patterns of any two of the poems in this section: "Shall I Compare Thee to a Summer's Day?" "Puritan Sonnet," "400-Meter Freestyle," and "Constantly risking absurdity." Does each poem follow a traditional or an experimental format? What internal patterns of rhyme, rhythm, and so forth can you find in each?
2. Several of the poems in this section are concerned with the function of art. Compare two of these poems, pointing out both the similarities and differences in their views of art.

## COMPARING POEMS

1. Answers should cite two poems and include examples of the following points:
   ■ "Summer's Day": traditional Shakespearean sonnet; three iambic quatrains followed by couplet; *abab, cdcd, efef, gg*
   ■ "Puritan": traditional Petrarchan sonnet; fourteen iambic lines divided into octave / sestet; *abbaabba, cdecde*
   ■ "400-Meter": experimental; evokes subject; no regular rhythm
   ■ "absurdity": irregular, experimental free verse; lines scattered across page
   ■ Students should state preference and give reasons.

2. Answers should cite two poems dealing with role of art / artist: "Summer's Day" portrays artist as being able to immortalize subject in art, and "absurdity" portrays artist as slightly ridiculous figure who risks failure striving to attain truth and beauty in art.

# LITERARY FOCUS: *The Total Effect*

Because poetry is so concentrated, a good poem can affect us more intensely than any other work of literature. A good poem reaches us on several different levels: It feeds our senses, stirs our emotions, and fires our imaginations. It makes us see, hear, feel, and think at the same time. The total effect of a poem, therefore, is rich and exciting—a special union of technique and substance, of artful form and heartfelt meaning.

The following poets combine form and substance to create powerful and moving poems.

**Ted Hughes** (born 1930) grew up in England, attended Cambridge University, and later married the American poet Sylvia Plath. Although he has also written juvenile literature, he is best known for his brooding poems. As he does in "Wind," Hughes often focuses on the harsh and disturbing side of the natural world.

■ Have you ever been fascinated by something, but, at the same time, frightened by it? When? Where?

**Philip Booth** (born 1925) has won many prizes for his poetry. Born in New Hampshire, he makes his permanent residence in Maine and has become known as the poet of the Maine coast. In "First Lesson" Booth describes a special relationship with the sea.

■ Do you think people learn better when they are under pressure or when they are relaxed? Why?

**Richard Wilbur** (born 1921) grew up in rural New Jersey. He wrote his first poetry while serving in the armed forces during World War II. Over the years Wilbur's poems have brought him many prizes, including the National Book Award and the Pulitzer Prize, as well as international recognition. Wilbur often uses traditional forms in new and unpredictable ways, as he does in "Boy at the Window."

■ To a small child how can losing a prized object be like losing a friend?

**Edna St. Vincent Millay** (1892–1950) published her first major poem while still in college. A colorful character, she was active in both artistic and political circles and became, as one writer said, "her own legend." Millay is known for her lyrical poems as well as for her striking use of imagery. She once said of her writing, "I see things with my own eyes just as if they were the first eyes that ever saw, and then I set about to tell, as best I can, just what I see."

■ The speaker in "The Fawn" wants badly to be accepted by the wild animal she encounters. Do you view her desire as reasonable or unreasonable? As understandable?

Photograph © 1982 by Jill Krementz

**May Swenson** (born 1919) grew up in Utah as the eldest child of Swedish immigrant parents. A resident of New York since her graduation from college, Swenson has written plays and prize-winning poems. Her work is known for its vivid imagery as well as for its often playful experimentation with line arrangements and punctuation, characteristics that can be seen in "By Morning."

■ In what ways can a change of weather bring with it promise and a profound change of attitude? Has this ever happened to you?

**248**   *Poetry*

## The Total Effect

When you first look at a painting, your eyes sweep the entire work. Then as you look more closely, you begin to notice the fine detail—specific colors, lines, and shapes. Finally you can step back once again and take in the work as a whole, but this time with a fuller appreciation for it as an integrated work of art.

Similarly, when you read a poem, you should first experience the poem as a whole. You should read it twice: first out loud and then silently, letting its sounds and images sweep over you. Then you can focus on the details, study the techniques, and grasp the poet's ideas. Finally, after you understand the poem's individual parts, you can read it once again as a whole and appreciate its total effect.

In analyzing a poem, it helps to take into account its individual features: its speaker, sounds, images, figures of speech, type, and use of pattern. The same poem may produce different responses in different readers. However, an active reader will always consider the following points in the process of understanding a poem.

## Reminders for Active Reading of Poetry

1. The **title** will point out the poet's main idea or concern.
2. Every poem is presented through a **speaker** of some kind. The speaker may or may not be a human being and may or may not be the poet. The poem's **choice of words** should be appropriate to the speaker.
3. The **sound** of a poem—its use of rhythm, rhyme, assonance, consonance, repetition, parallelism, and onomatopoeia—should suit the poem's subject and contribute to its effect.
4. **Imagery** should make the poem appeal to the senses of the reader. **Figures of speech**—such as personification, simile, metaphor, and symbol—should add new levels of meaning to the poem.
5. A **narrative poem** tells a story. A **lyric poem** expresses an emotion. A **dramatic poem** presents a character in a specific situation.
6. Poems can follow **traditional patterns** or can be **experimental** in format.

## Model for Active Reading

The following poem, "Wind" by Ted Hughes, shows how an alert reader approaches poetry. The reader's observations about the poem appear as marginal notations. Each notation includes a page reference for further information on the item in question. Read "Wind" first for your own pleasure. Then read it again with the marginal notations. The process shown in this model can guide you as you read other poems.

*Poetry* **249**

- All night and next day, violent winds assault a house and surrounding fields.
- The speaker stands in awe outside at noon, then retreats to his fire where he and his companion sit transfixed.

## LITERARY OPTIONS

- total effect
- imagery
- figurative language

## THEMATIC OPTIONS

- nature's power
- human ineffectuality

## REFLECTING ON THE POEM

How would you feel if you were in the speaker's house? (Answers will vary. Most students will probably expect to be uneasy, but some may expect to be excited.)

*Ted Hughes*

# Wind

This house has been far out at sea all night,
The woods crashing through darkness, the booming hills,
Winds stampeding the fields under the window
Floundering black astride and blinding wet

5 Till day rose; then under an orange sky
The hills had new places, and wind wielded
Blade-like, luminous black and  emerald,
Flexing like the lens of a mad e,

At noon I scaled along the house-side as far as
10 The coal-house door. Once I looked up—
Through the brunt wind that dented the balls of my eyes
The tent of the hills drummed and strained its guyrope,[1]

The fields quivering, the skyline a grimace,
At any second to bang and vanish with a flap:
15 The wind flung a magpie away and a black-
Back gull bent like an iron bar slowly. The house

Rang like some fine green goblet in the note
That any second would shatter it. Now deep
In chairs, in front of the great fire, we grip
20 Our hearts and cannot entertain book, thought,

Or each other. We watch the fire blazing,
And feel the roots of the house move, but sit on,
Seeing the window tremble to come in,
Hearing the stones cry out under the horizons.

---

1. **guyrope:** one of the ropes supporting a tent.

**Implied metaphor** (p. 215): *Stampeding* implies a connection between the wind and wild horses.

**Rhyme** (p. 192) and **Rhythm** (p. 192): *Sky* and *eye* are true end rhymes; *wielded* and *emerald* are slant rhymes. The poem's rhythm is irregular, echoing the storm.

**Narrative poetry** (p. 225): "Wind" tells a story. Like a lyric poem, it also expresses strong emotion, and like a dramatic poem, it presents a speaker in a tense situation.

**Imagery** (p. 205): These lines contain vivid images of sight, sound, and motion.

**Simile** (p. 211): The house is directly compared to a goblet.

**Personification** (p. 209): The window and stones are made to seem like living creatures.

## STUDY QUESTIONS

### Recalling

1. Where has the speaker's house been all night, according to the first stanza? What were the winds doing to the fields during the night?
2. In the second stanza what is the wind compared to? What has the wind done to the fields?
3. What does the speaker do at noon? Describe how the wind felt to him then.
4. What things does the speaker say he and his companion "cannot entertain" as they sit in their chairs? What do they do instead?

### Interpreting

5. Briefly describe what is actually happening in the poem.
6. How does the speaker feel about the wind? Is it a friendly, neutral, or menacing force? Is the speaker drawn to this force in any way? How do you know?
7. Why do you think the speaker and his companion "sit on" even when they "feel the roots of the house move"?

### Extending

8. What conflicting reactions might people experience to violence in nature?

## COMPOSITION

### Writing About Sound and Imagery

■ Show how Hughes uses sound effects and imagery in "Wind" to convey the violence of a wind storm. Be sure to refer to specific sound effects (rhyme, rhythm, assonance, consonance, onomatopoeia, alliteration) and sense images as you write.

### Writing a Poem Describing an Event

■ Write a short poem in which a speaker describes a storm or other exciting natural event in which he or she is still involved. Be sure to use the present tense and to include vivid details that convey the power of this event. Try especially to include sound effects that help place the reader in the middle of the speaker's experience.

## COMPOSITION: GUIDELINES FOR EVALUATION

### WRITING ABOUT SOUND AND IMAGERY

**Objective**

To analyze the way the poem uses sound effects and imagery to create an effect

**Guidelines for Evaluation**

- suggested length: one to three paragraphs
- should explain which sound effects Hughes uses
- should explain what sense images are used
- should show how each helps convey the storm's violence

### WRITING A POEM DESCRIBING AN EVENT

**Objective**

To write a poem about an exciting natural event

**Guidelines for Evaluation**

- suggested length: five to fifteen lines
- should be written in the form of a poem
- should describe the speaker's experience of natural event
- should be written in the present tense, using vivid imagery to convey the force of the event

A loving father turns a lesson about how to float into a lesson about living.

## LITERARY OPTIONS

- total effect
- extended metaphor

## THEMATIC OPTIONS

- understanding natural forces
- trust
- surviving adversity

## REPETITION

Note how, throughout the poem, the speaker repeats the word *lie* with various adverbs (*back, out, up*) to communicate the comforting lesson of letting go to his daughter (ll. 1, 4, 10).

## TOTAL EFFECT

Just as the sea and her father hold the daughter, so the end rhymes at the beginning and end of the poem hold the father's words together (ll. 1, 3, 5, 11, 13, 15).

## EXTENDED METAPHOR

At the end of the poem, the father lets go of his daughter, permitting the sea to hold her and help her survive. The father turns this situation into a metaphor for living: Trust yourself and life, and you will not sink or be swept away by adversity (ll. 12–15).

## REFLECTING ON THE POEM

Why is this lesson called the *first* lesson? (Although there is much more to learn about swimming and about life, learning to trust the element in which you are immersed is the keystone to survival.)

*Philip Booth*

# First Lesson

Lie back, daughter, let your head
be tipped back in the cup of my hand.
Gently, and I will hold you. Spread
your arms wide, lie out on the stream
5  and look high at the gulls. A dead-
man's-float is face down. You will dive
and swim soon enough where this tidewater
ebbs to the sea. Daughter, believe
me, when you tire on the long thrash
10  to your island, lie up, and survive.
As you float now, where I held you
and let go, remember when fear
cramps your heart what I told you:
lie gently and wide to the light-year
15  stars, lie back, and the sea will hold you.

## STUDY QUESTIONS

### Recalling

1. To whom is the speaker talking? Where are they as he speaks?
2. What instructions does the speaker give in lines 1–5? How will he help his listener? In lines 6–8 what does he promise that she will do "soon enough"?
3. What advice does the speaker offer his listener in lines 9–10 for when she tires "on the long thrash"? What should she remember when she is afraid?

### Interpreting

4. On the literal level, what is the speaker teaching his listener in the poem?
5. Find examples in the poem of both positive and negative references to the sea. On which note, positive or negative, does the poem end?
6. What words are repeated in the poem? Why do you think these words are important?
7. What larger lesson about life might the speaker be trying to teach his listener? Explain the larger significance of the poem's last two lines, especially of the image "wide to the light-years/stars."

### Extending

8. In what senses might the sea be both a positive and negative force?

## LITERARY FOCUS

### The Total Effect

The **total effect** of a poem is the poem's overall impact on the reader. We experience a poem not only by understanding its ideas but also by becoming acquainted with its speaker, hearing its sounds, responding to its images, sensing its emotions, and appreciating its format and use of patterns. Understanding how the various parts of the poem work does not reduce the poem to a group of ideas, sounds, and images. Rather, it draws us further into the poem, for the more we look at a good poem, the more we find. We can never understand a poem *enough*; we can only understand it *better*.

### Thinking About the Total Effect

1. Describe the speaker's tone in "First Lesson": For example, is it impersonal, comforting, excited, or frightened? Explain how Booth's use of sound, especially rhyme and repetition, creates this tone. What words are repeated, and how does this repetition add to the poem's meaning?
2. Explain how the poem's images of sight, touch, and motion contribute to its emotional effect.
3. Describe the poem's overall impact on you as a reader. How does Booth produce this impact?

*First Lesson* **253**

## STUDY QUESTIONS

1. his daughter; standing in the ocean near the shore
2. lines 1–5: lie back, spread arms wide, look up at gulls; will hold her; lines 6–8: dive, swim
3. lines 9–10: "lie up" and "survive" when she tires; lie back and let the sea hold her up
4. to float on her back
5. *Positive:* She will soon swim, and the sea will support her. *Negative:* The speaker mentions the dead man's float; she may tire or become afraid. The poem ends on a positive note.
6. *lie back, will hold you, gently;* offer reassurance
7. She should relax and let the flow of life carry her rather than struggling. She will survive if she looks optimistically to the future ("light-year / stars").
8. *Positive:* The sea supports many forms of life. *Negative:* The sea can be fierce and destructive.

## LITERARY FOCUS

1. ■ comforting tone; rhythm, rhyme, repetition—all soothing
   ■ The repetitions *lie back, lie up, I will hold you* reinforce the comforting tone.
2. ■ sight: *gulls; light-year stars;* touch: daughter's head cupped in father's hands; fear gripping heart; motion: *long thrash*
   ■ The contrast of soothing and frightening images intensifies the poem's emotional effect.
3. Possible answer: The poem has a reassuring effect. Booth uses all poetic elements to create this effect: The speaker is a father comforting his daughter; the sounds are soothing; the images are primarily reassuring.

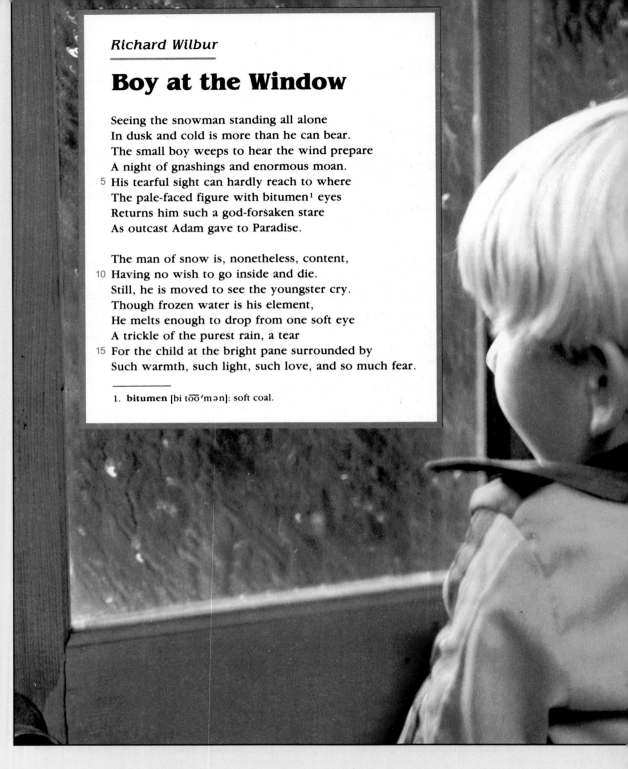

*Richard Wilbur*

# Boy at the Window

Seeing the snowman standing all alone
In dusk and cold is more than he can bear.
The small boy weeps to hear the wind prepare
A night of gnashings and enormous moan.
5 His tearful sight can hardly reach to where
The pale-faced figure with bitumen[1] eyes
Returns him such a god-forsaken stare
As outcast Adam gave to Paradise.

The man of snow is, nonetheless, content,
10 Having no wish to go inside and die.
Still, he is moved to see the youngster cry.
Though frozen water is his element,
He melts enough to drop from one soft eye
A trickle of the purest rain, a tear
15 For the child at the bright pane surrounded by
Such warmth, such light, such love, and so much fear.

---

1. **bitumen** [bi tōō′mən]: soft coal.

## STUDY QUESTIONS

### Recalling

1. What does the boy see, and what does he do? For what reason?
2. To what does line 8 liken the snowman's stare?
3. According to lines 9–10, how does the snowman feel about being outside and why?
4. For whom does the snowman drop a tear?

### Interpreting

5. In the first stanza what impression does the boy have of the snowman? What do lines 9–10 show about the accuracy of that impression?
6. What is the snowman's impression of the boy? Why might this impression move even a snowman to tears?
7. Contrast the boy's emotional state and attitude toward life with the snowman's.

### Extending

8. Why might childhood be full of fear as well as warmth and love?

## COMPOSITION

### Writing About Poetry

■ Explain how Wilbur uses the techniques of poetry to express his meaning in "Boy at the Window." First explain what the poem means. Then show how Wilbur uses speaker, word choice, tone, sound, imagery, and figurative language to express his meaning. *For help with this assignment, see Lesson 11 in the Writing About Literature Handbook at the back of this book.*

### Writing a Poem from Contrasting Perspectives

■ Write a poem of two stanzas contrasting the perspective of a human being with that of an object. In your first stanza the human being should observe and respond to the object; in your second stanza the object should in turn observe and respond to the human being. Be sure to use language appropriate to person and object in each stanza.

*Boy at the Window*　**255**

1. snowman standing alone outside on a cold evening; cries because he feels sorry for snowman
2. the "god-forsaken" stare Adam turned on Paradise
3. He is content; he would melt indoors.
4. the boy at the window
5. The boy thinks the snowman is sad and lonely; he is actually content.
6. He is touched by the boy's sadness; the boy's sadness contrasts with the comfort of his life.
7. ■ boy: frightened, sad, unhappy about natural order of things
   ■ snowman: calm, content with things as they are
8. Possible answers: Children feel powerless and weak; they often project their own feelings onto others.

---

## COMPOSITION: GUIDELINES FOR EVALUATION

### WRITING ABOUT POETRY

**Objective**

To explain how poetic techniques convey meaning

**Guidelines for Evaluation**

- suggested length: three to five paragraphs
- should summarize poem's meaning
- should describe poem's use of speaker, sound, imagery, and figurative language
- should explain how these elements are appropriate to the poem's meaning

### WRITING A POEM FROM CONTRASTING PERSPECTIVES

**Objective**

To reveal two different perspectives in a poem

**Guidelines for Evaluation**

- suggested length: two stanzas
- should present a person observing and responding to an object in first stanza
- should present the object observing and responding to the person in the second stanza

- Chancing upon a sleeping fawn, the charmed speaker wants desperately to be accepted by the beautiful wild animal.
- To her disappointment, however, the fawn awakens and flees.

### LITERARY OPTIONS

- imagery
- main idea

### THEMATIC OPTIONS

- natural beauty
- relationships between humans and animals

### IMAGERY

The speaker's loving descriptions of the deer create an impression of delicacy (polished cleft small ebony hooves) and charming awkwardness (leaping and stumbling) (ll. 5, 21).

### MAIN IDEA

The speaker longs to be one with the natural world and not feared by its creatures ("A part of the forest, seen without surprise") (l. 18). However, the fawn's flight from the speaker makes this unity impossible.

### SPEAKER

The speaker is not certain whether it is instinctive fear of anything strange or a sense of her human fear (of rejection) that sends the young animal crashing into the woods (ll. 19–23).

### REFLECTING ON THE POEM

What answer do you think the speaker would prefer to the question she asks in the last stanza? (Students may say that the speaker would prefer that the fawn be alarmed, as he might be at any unexpected sight in the forest, human or natural.)

---

*Edna St. Vincent Millay*

# The Fawn

There it was I saw what I shall never forget
And never retrieve.
Monstrous and beautiful to human eyes, hard to believe,
He lay, yet there he lay,
5  Asleep on the moss, his head on his polished cleft small ebony hooves,
The child of the doe, the dappled child of the deer.

Surely his mother had never said, "Lie here
Till I return," so spotty and plain to see
On the green moss lay he.
10  His eyes had opened; he considered me.

I would have given more than I care to say
To thrifty ears, might I have had him for my friend
One moment only of that forest day:

Might I have had the acceptance, not the love
15  Of those clear eyes;
Might I have been for him the bough above
Or the root beneath his forest bed,
A part of the forest, seen without surprise.

Was it alarm, or was it the wind of my fear lest he depart
20  That jerked him to his jointy knees
And sent him crashing off, leaping and stumbling
On his new legs, between the stems of the white trees?

STUDY QUESTIONS

1. fawn; in the forest
2. lines 14–15: to be accepted;
   lines 16–18: a bough or root—
   part of the forest
3. jumps up and runs away; is
   alarmed or senses her fear
4. ■ She calls the fawn "monstrous" because he looks
   exotic and unusual to her.
   The effect of this word is
   startling.
   ■ She finds it hard to believe
   that the fawn is so strange
   and beautiful and so near.
5. ■ Possibilities for painting:
   earthy forest colors, slender forms, soft moss, details of branches and
   fawn's body
   ■ The fawn's youth is suggested by language such
   as *small, jointy knees, new
   legs, child.*
6. awe, delight, and then regret
7. ■ because of the animal's
   innocence
   ■ Animals instinctively flee
   from unfamiliar creatures.

## STUDY QUESTIONS

### Recalling

1. What unforgettable sight does the speaker see? Where does she see this sight?
2. According to lines 14–15, what does the speaker want from this creature? According to lines 16–18, what things would she like to be for him?
3. What does the creature do when he sees the speaker? What reasons does she suggest for his behavior?

### Interpreting

4. Why might the speaker describe the creature as "Monstrous"? What effect does this word create? Why does the speaker find the sight "hard to believe"?
5. If you were to paint a picture of the creature and his surroundings based on Millay's words, what colors, shapes, and details would you include? What words suggest the creature's youth?
6. What mixed emotions does this experience stir in the speaker?

### Extending

7. Why do you think a human being would want so much to be accepted by a wild animal? Why is such acceptance rare?

*The Fawn*  **257**

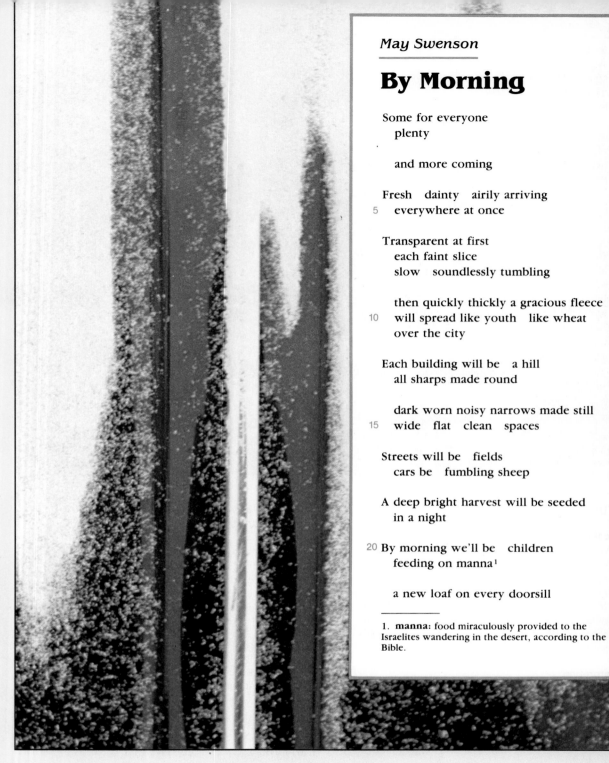

An overnight snowfall magically transforms a cityscape into a bucolic scene.

## LITERARY OPTIONS

- imagery
- figurative language

## THEMATIC OPTIONS

- nature and civilization
- transformations and renewals

## IMAGERY

The speaker's delicate, unusual images (for example, *faint* instead of *thin*) create a softening effect, just as the snow softens the cityscape, blurring distinctions and turning angles into curves. The very lightness of the imagery also mirrors the apparent weightlessness of the snow.

## FIGURATIVE LANGUAGE

A number of the speaker's metaphors and similes refer to food, implying that snow nourishes our spiritual life (ll. 10, 18, 22).

## MAIN IDEA

Snow miraculously renews people's innocence (ll. 20, 21).

## REFLECTING ON THE POEM

According to the poem, what is nourishing about the snow? (Its beauty and cleanness seem to turn the world into an innocent, lovelier place, and this transformation cheers and renews us.)

*May Swenson*

# By Morning

Some for everyone
    plenty

and more coming

Fresh   dainty   airily arriving
5   everywhere at once

Transparent at first
    each faint slice
    slow   soundlessly tumbling

    then quickly thickly a gracious fleece
10   will spread like youth   like wheat
    over the city

Each building will be   a hill
    all sharps made round

    dark worn noisy narrows made still
15   wide   flat   clean   spaces

Streets will be   fields
    cars be   fumbling sheep

A deep bright harvest will be seeded
    in a night

20 By morning we'll be   children
    feeding on manna[1]

    a new loaf on every doorsill

---

1. **manna:** food miraculously provided to the Israelites wandering in the desert, according to the Bible.

## STUDY QUESTIONS

### Recalling

1. What place is being transformed in "By Morning"? During what time of day does this transformation happen?
2. In lines 4–8 what adjectives and adverbs describe what is arriving? To what two things is it likened in line 10?
3. What will the buildings become? What will happen to the "sharps" and the "narrows"? The streets and the cars?
4. According to lines 21–22, what will be found on every doorsill?

### Interpreting

5. What natural occurrence is Swenson actually describing? How do you know?
6. Give three examples of Swenson's fanciful use of images and figures of speech. Why might the phenomenon she describes inspire such language?
7. Into what type of landscape is the scene being transformed in lines 12–19? Describe the speaker's attitude toward this change. Why do you think she feels as she does?
8. What serious idea does the biblical allusion to "manna" add to the poem? What does the idea of nourishment add?

### Extending

9. In describing a scene like the one in "By Morning," what fanciful terms might you use?
10. Why might people who are normally cut off from nature be restored by an event like the one described in the poem?

## COMPOSITION

### Writing About Poetry

■ Discuss the total effect of "By Morning." First describe the poem's overall impact on you. Then discuss how Swenson uses speaker, sound, imagery, figurative language, and format to create that effect. In particular, discuss how Swenson's unusual placement of words, spaces, and lines adds to the poem's overall effect.

### Writing a Poem About a Transformation

■ Write a poem that describes the gradual but complete transformation of some person, place or object. For example, you might describe a bud opening up into a flower or a stylishly dressed person being soaked by a downpour. Experiment with the spacing of words so that the appearance of your poem on the page is appropriate to the change it describes.

## COMPARING POEMS

1. Compare and contrast the attitudes toward nature expressed in two or more of the poems in this section: "Wind," "First Lesson," "Boy at the Window," "The Fawn," and "By Morning." How does the poet's use of speaker, sound, imagery, and other poetic techniques contribute to the view of nature presented in the poem?
2. Of the poems in this section, which had the greatest impact on you? Which had the least impact? Referring to speaker, sound, imagery, and other poetic techniques, explain why each poem affected you as it did.

*By Morning*   **259**

## STUDY QUESTIONS

1. a city; during night
2. ■ fresh, dainty, transparent, faint, slow, airily, soundlessly
   ■ It is likened to youth and wheat.
3. hills; sharps: round; narrows: wide; streets: fields; cars: sheep
4. loaf of manna
5. snowfall; images *(fleece)* describing snow
6. ■ "Each building will be a hill."
   ■ "Streets will be fields"
   ■ "A new loaf on every doorsill"
   ■ Snow transforms appearances fancifully.
7. A clean and rural landscape; welcomes change because it makes surroundings beautiful
8. ■ The snowfall is needed and welcome.
   ■ that nature refreshes and feeds us spiritually
9. Answers will vary. They should include fanciful items to describe a snowfall or similar transformation.
10. It brings them into contact with nature's beauty and power to transform life.

## COMPARING POEMS

1. Answers should
   ■ cite two poems concerned with nature
   ■ describe attitude toward nature presented in each
   ■ explain the use of poetic techniques in each
2. Answers should
   ■ single out poems having greatest impact / least impact
   ■ defend choices by describing effect of poetic techniques such as speaker, tone, sound devices, imagery, figurative language, and form

## COMPOSITION: GUIDELINES FOR EVALUATION

### WRITING ABOUT POETRY

**Objective**

To explain how poet uses poetic techniques to create impact

**Guidelines for Evaluation**

■ suggested length: three to five paragraphs
■ should describe the poem's overall impact
■ should describe the use of poetic elements such as speaker, sound, imagery, figurative language
■ should show how these add to poem's impact

### WRITING A POEM ABOUT TRANSFORMATION

**Objective**

To write a poem describing a transformation

**Guidelines for Evaluation**

■ suggested length: five to fifteen lines
■ should describe the gradual but complete transformation of a person, place, or thing
■ should be experimental in format
■ should use poetic elements

Encourage the students to read the poems in this unit aloud; you might try reading some if not all of the poems out loud in class. You could ask students how their voices might bring out the special qualities in each poem. Colloquial or conversational poems, like those by Robert Frost or "To Satch" by Samuel Allen, might lend themselves especially well to classroom readings, as might the driving rhythm of "An Indian Summer Day on the Prairie" by Vachel Lindsay or "The Destruction of Sennacherib" by Lord Byron. Students might also enjoy trying out different speakers for the same poem, just as the essay on Hearing a Poem describes how two different speakers might read "I Like to Hear It Lap the Miles." For example, consider asking students to read "Fifteen" as if the speaker were a young man and then as if he were much older. You might ask students to read "To James" as if the speaker were James's coach and then as if the speaker were James's father. More experimental poems, such as "400-Meter Freestyle," "Constantly risking absurdity," or "By Morning," might present enjoyable challenges to students to find vocal equivalents for the playful or inventive qualities of the poem as it appears on the page.

You will find among the materials for this unit in your *Teacher's Classroom Resources* the related blackline master Hearing a Poem.

# ACTIVE READING

### Hearing a Poem

A poem's real life begins when we give it a voice. Of course, we need to understand what the words, phrases, and sentences of the poem mean. But the poem becomes much more enjoyable when we can hear it as well—when we can imagine that its words, phrases, and sentences are being spoken by a living voice that pauses at certain points, speeds up at others, grows loud, grows soft, rises, falls.

Of course, two different people reading the same poem may hear two different voices. For example, how would you read the following lines from Dickinson's "I Like to See It Lap the Miles"? "Complaining all the while/In horrid—hooting stanza—/Then chase itself down Hill—" Do the dashes make you imagine a breathless, halting speaker? Does the regular meter make you hear the onrushing movement of the thing the speaker is describing? Do you hear a hoot on "hooting"? And what sort of person do you hear speaking to you? One who describes her subject with a dry, quiet wit? Or one who enjoys pulling out the stops and imitating her subject? Whomever we hear, listening closely to the voice of a poem helps us to enjoy the whole work more.

Rhythm and rhyme give poetry an exciting pulsing voice that distinguishes it from everyday speech. However, a poem's rhythm and rhyme should enhance and not drown out its meaning. Wordsworth's lovely "My Heart Leaps Up," for example, is written in fairly strict iambic rhythm with definite end rhymes. Emphasizing the poem's rhythm and rhyme overpowers the delicacy and wonder that the speaker feels; ignoring the rhythm and rhyme turns the poem into prose. Instead, we should imagine that the speaker speaks quietly but with an underlying excitement that makes him unconsciously echo the rhythm of his own heartbeat.

A free verse poem such as "A Blessing" by James Wright has its own special voice. It follows no strict rhythm and rhyme and is conversational, but it is not *merely* conversational; it too has something extra that sets it apart from prose. We know that the experience described in the poem is important to the poet-speaker because he calls his poem "A Blessing." As he realizes how important it is, a thrill goes through him and surges into the poem's last lines: "Suddenly I realize/That if I stepped out of my body I would break/Into blossom." The dramatic change in line length makes us hear a catch in the speaker's voice and lets us share his excitement. The poem soars from the printed page and breaks into life.

# REVIEW: POETRY

## Guide for Studying Poetry

The following guide will help you to recognize the types of poetry and the techniques a poet uses to join form and meaning.

### Speaker and Tone

1. Who or what is the poem's **speaker**? In what ways are the poet's **word choices** appropriate to that speaker?
2. What **tone** does the speaker use throughout the poem?

### Sound of Poetry

1. What pattern can you find in the poem's **rhythm**? Does it have a regular **meter**?
2. What **rhymes** can you find in the poem? If the poem contains end rhymes, what is its rhyme scheme? If the poem does not rhyme, is it written in **blank verse** or **free verse**?
3. Does the poem contain **repetition** or **parallelism**?
4. What examples can you find of **alliteration** and **onomatopoeia**?

### Imagery and Figurative Language

1. What vivid **images** does the poem contain?
2. What examples can you find of **personification**?
3. What **similes** directly compare dissimilar items?
4. What **metaphors** equate dissimilar items? Which of these metaphors are **implied**? Which, if any, are **extended**?
5. What **symbols** can you find?

### Types of Poetry

1. What events in the poem form a **narrative**?
2. What personal emotions does the poet express in a **lyric**?
3. What character or characters speak within the poem to make it **dramatic**? What situation makes the character or characters speak?

### Patterns in Poetry

1. What **pattern** does the poem follow in its length, stanzas, line length, meter, and rhyme scheme? Is the poem's pattern a **traditional** one, such as the **Shakespearean** or **Petrarchan sonnet**?
2. Where does the poem depart from traditional patterns in stanza arrangement, line length, capitalization, and punctuation?

**REVIEW**

Refer to the unit review, Guide for Studying the Techniques and Types of Poetry. These questions may be used in several ways:

- They may be used to direct students' attention in reading each selection in turn. Students might simply keep the questions in mind as they read, or they might write brief answers to the questions.
- The questions may be used as an aid to analyzing and understanding selections that students find especially difficult. The gradual, systematic consideration of separate poetic elements and forms can allow students to penetrate even seemingly impenetrable poems.
- The questions may be used as a basis for discussion after the class has read a selection. As the review questions are organized by section, students might consider only those questions on topics they have already studied, or students might consider all the questions, in preparation for the topics to be studied later.
- The questions may be used as a review after students have completed all the selections, allowing the class to pull together the various poetic elements and forms they have considered and helping them grasp the similarities and differences among the selections.

The questions in the Guide for Reading Poetry appear with write-on lines, in blackline master form, among the materials for this unit in your *Teacher's Classroom Resources*.

262    *Nonfiction*

# PREVIEW:
# NONFICTION

*. . .facts must be manipulated; some must be brightened; others shaded; yet, in the process, they must never lose their integrity.*

—Virginia Woolf

**Nonfiction** is factual prose writing that includes biography, autobiography, and essays. Unlike fiction, nonfiction is rooted in fact; it observes and comments on people who actually lived and events that really happened.

A work of nonfiction, however, does more than relate facts. Through the particular choice of facts, their arrangement, and interpretation, and through the skillful use of language, authors of nonfiction communicate their own opinions and reveal their own personalities.

An author of a work of nonfiction usually writes for a very definite **purpose** and **audience.** The author wants to communicate a particular opinion or thought; that is his or her purpose. The opinion or thought may be packaged so that it informs readers, entertains them, or moves them to some action. The author may be writing for an audience of experts or of casual readers. The author's **tone,** or attitude toward the subject, usually indicates the purpose and audience he or she had in mind in writing the work. In addition, the work's **title** and overall **style**—the author's choice and arrangement of words—may reveal the author's purpose in a piece of nonfiction.

The following nonfiction selections fall into two groups. The first contains biographical and autobiographical writings—works that present information about the lives of their subjects. The second contains narrative, descriptive, persuasive, and expository essays.

*Nonfiction* **263**

# LITERARY FOCUS: *Biography, Autobiography*

The story of a person's life written by someone other than the subject is a **biography.** Whether full length or merely a short sketch, a good biography is concerned with presenting both the facts of the subject's life and the meaning behind those facts.

The biographer gathers information by studying letters, diaries, and other firsthand documents connected with the subject. However, a good biography is more than the sum of its facts: The biographer's interpretation of this information is as crucial as the original research. Two biographies of the same person may by very different because of the different purpose, audience, and tone of each. Most important, a good biography brings its subject to life with interesting, telling incidents, vivid details, and sensitive portrayals of personality and psychology.

The story of a person's life written by that person is an **autobiography.** Research is usually less important in preparing an autobiography than it is in biography. What is important in autobiography is firsthand experience, as the author relates events from memory and interprets those events with insights provided by time.

People often write autobiographies in order to put their lives into perspective: to understand the past, both its problems and its achievements, and acknowledge the events and people that shaped their lives. Some people—for example, public or controversial figures—also write autobiographies to explain and justify their actions. In reading an autobiography, we should be alert to the author's purpose—whether that purpose is to justify a life, to find the truth, or to do both.

**264**   *Nonfiction*

A writer and a mathematician, Banesh Hoffmann (1906–1986) taught for many years at Queens College of the City University of New York. He has written about the nature of gravity, relativity, and the quantum theory. Hoffman worked with Albert Einstein at Princeton University and has completed two books about his colleague and friend.

■ To many people Albert Einstein is a name synonymous with "genius," a person beyond the reach of ordinary humans. Where did Einstein get his ideas? Where do you get yours?

*Banesh Hoffmann*

# My Friend, Albert Einstein

1 He was one of the greatest scientists the world has ever known, yet if I had to convey the essence of Albert Einstein in a single word, I would choose *simplicity*. Perhaps an anecdote will help. Once, caught in a downpour, he took off his hat and held it under his coat. Asked why, he explained, with admirable logic, that the rain would damage the hat, but his hair would be none the worse for its wetting. This knack for going instinctively to the heart of a matter was the secret of his major scientific discoveries—this and his extraordinary feeling for beauty.

I first met Albert Einstein in 1935, at the famous Institute for Advanced Study in Prince-
2 ton, N.J. He had been among the first to be invited to the Institute, and was offered *carte blanche*[1] as to salary. To the director's dismay, Einstein asked for an impossible sum: it was far too *small*. The director had to plead with him to accept a larger salary.

I was in awe of Einstein, and hesitated before

approaching him about some ideas I had been working on. When I finally knocked on his door, a gentle voice said, "Come"—with a rising inflection that made the single word both a welcome and a question. I entered his office and found him seated at a table, calculating and smoking his pipe. Dressed in ill-fitting clothes, his hair characteristically awry, he smiled a warm welcome. His utter naturalness at once set me at ease.

As I began to explain my ideas, he asked me to write the equations on the blackboard so he
3 could see how they developed. Then came the staggering—and altogether endearing—request: "Please go slowly. I do not understand things quickly." This from Einstein! He said it gently, and I laughed. From then on, all vestiges of fear were gone.

Einstein was born in 1879 in the German city of Ulm. He had been no infant prodigy; indeed, he was so late in learning to speak that his parents feared he was a dullard. In school, though his teachers saw no special talent in him, the signs were already there. He taught himself

---

1. **carte blanche** [kärt′ blänch′]: French for "blank check"; unrestricted freedom of action.

*My Friend, Albert Einstein* **265**

- Rejected by academics, Einstein pursued independent research.
- When he was in his twenties, Einstein's genius burst forth in two seemingly contradictory theories about light.
- Einstein, who was deeply religious, said, "Ideas come from God."

## 1 BIOGRAPHICAL SKETCH

Academic failure and rejection did not deter Einstein from his commitment to science.

## 2 THEME

Einstein introduces two revolutionary theories, proposing the compatibility of seemingly extreme opposites.

## 3 VOCABULARY: WORD CHOICE

The literal meaning of *worry* here, "to seize by the throat with the teeth," indicates the intensity of Einstein's commitment to solving problems.

## 4 BIOGRAPHICAL SKETCH

While many people argue the incompatibility between scientific and religious views, Einstein perceived no separation.

## 5 RESPONSE JOURNAL

Ask students to cite or create their own credos—or mottoes—and illustrate them with personal anecdotes.

---

calculus, for example, and his teachers seemed a little afraid of him because he asked questions they could not answer. At the age of 16, he asked himself whether a light wave would seem stationary if one ran abreast of it. From that innocent question would arise, ten years later, his theory of relativity.[2]

**1** Einstein failed his entrance examinations at the Swiss Federal Polytechnic School, in Zurich, but was admitted a year later. There he went beyond his regular work to study the masterworks of physics on his own. Rejected when he applied for academic positions, he ultimately found work, in 1902, as a patent examiner in Berne,[3] and there in 1905 his genius burst into fabulous flower.

**2** Among the extraordinary things he produced in that memorable year were his theory of relativity, with its famous offshoot, $E = mc^2$ (energy equals mass times the speed of light squared), and his quantum theory of light.[4] These two theories were not only revolutionary, but seemingly contradictory: the former was intimately linked to the theory that light consists of waves, while the latter said it consists somehow of particles. Yet this unknown young man boldly proposed both at once—and he was right in both cases, though how he could have been is far too complex a story to tell here.

Collaborating with Einstein was an unforgettable experience. In 1937, the Polish physicist Leopold Infeld and I asked if we could work with him. He was pleased with the proposal, since he had an idea about gravitation waiting to be worked out in detail. Thus we got to know not merely the man and the friend, but also the professional.

---

2. **theory of relativity:** Einstein's theory concerning the relationship among matter, energy, space, time, and gravitation.
3. **Berne:** city in Switzerland.
4. **quantum [kwon'təm] theory of light:** Originally set forth by the German physicist Max Planck (1858–1947), quantum theory states that radiant energy like light is transmitted in separate units, rather than in a continuous stream.

**266** *Nonfiction*

---

**3** The intensity and depth of his concentration were fantastic. When battling a recalcitrant problem, he worried it as an animal worries its prey. Often, when we found ourselves up against a seemingly insuperable difficulty, he would stand up, put his pipe on the table, and say in his quaint English, "I will a little tink" (he could not pronounce "th"). Then he would pace up and down, twirling a lock of his long, graying hair around his forefinger.

A dreamy, faraway and yet inward look would come over his face. There was no appearance of concentration, no furrowing of the brow—only a placid inner communion. The minutes would pass, and then suddenly Einstein would stop pacing as his face relaxed into a gentle smile. He had found the solution to the problem. Sometimes it was so simple that Infeld and I could have kicked ourselves for not having thought of it. But the magic had been performed invisibly in the depths of Einstein's mind, by a process we could not fathom.

**4** Although Einstein felt no need for religious ritual and belonged to no formal religious group, he was the most deeply religious man I have known. He once said to me, "Ideas come from God," and one could hear the capital "G" in the reverence with which he pronounced the word. On the marble fireplace in the mathematics building at Princeton University is carved, in the original German, what one might call his scientific credo: **5** "God is subtle, but he is not malicious." By this Einstein meant that scientists could expect to find their task difficult, but not hopeless: the Universe was a Universe of law, and God was not confusing us with deliberate paradoxes[5] and contradictions.

Einstein was an accomplished amateur musician. We used to play duets, he on the violin, I at the piano. One day he surprised me

---

5. **paradoxes:** A paradox is anything that is itself seemingly inconsistent or contradictory. Some paradoxes, although apparently absurd, ultimately prove true.

---

## *GUIDED READING*

### LITERAL QUESTIONS

**1a.** Why did Einstein's two theories formulated in 1905 startle the science community? (His ideas were revolutionary and seemingly contradictory.)

**2a.** What is Hoffmann's interpretation of Einstein's credo? (The scientist's job is difficult, not hopeless: "the Universe [is] a Universe of law"; God does not confuse us.)

### INFERENTIAL QUESTIONS

**1b.** What do you think those controversial theories imply about Einstein? (He had the imagination to see beyond widely accepted concepts and the confidence to disagree with the most respected scientists of his time.)

**2b.** What might Einstein's credo suggest about him? (Although a genius, Einstein worked hard; he regarded the universe as orderly and ultimately understandable.)

by saying Mozart[6] was the greatest composer of all. Beethoven[7] "created" his music, but the music of Mozart was of such purity and beauty one felt he had merely "found" it—that it had always existed as part of the inner beauty of the Universe, waiting to be revealed.

It was this very Mozartean simplicity that most characterized Einstein's methods. His 1905 theory of relativity, for example, was built on just two simple assumptions. One is the so-called principle of relativity, which means, roughly speaking, that we cannot tell whether we are at rest or moving smoothly. The other assumption is that the speed of light is the same no matter what the speed of the object that produces it. You can see how reasonable this is if you think of agitating a stick in a lake to create waves. Whether you wiggle the stick from a stationary pier, or from a rushing speedboat, the waves, once generated, are on their own, and their speed has nothing to do with that of the stick.

Each of these assumptions, by itself, was so plausible as to seem primitively obvious. But together they were in such violent conflict that a lesser man would have dropped one or the other and fled in panic. Einstein daringly kept both—and by so doing he revolutionized physics. For he demonstrated they could, after all, exist peacefully side by side, provided we gave up cherished beliefs about the nature of time.

Science is like a house of cards, with concepts like time and space at the lowest level. Tampering with time brought most of the house tumbling down, and it was this that made Einstein's work so important—and controversial. At a conference in Princeton in honor of his 70th birthday, one of the speakers, a Nobel Prize-winner, tried to convey the magical quality of Einstein's achievement. Words failed him, and with a shrug of helplessness he pointed to

_____
6. **Mozart** [mōt′särt]: Wolfgang Amadeus Mozart (1756–1791), Austrian composer.
7. **Beethoven** [bā′tō′vən]: Ludwig van Beethoven (1770–1827), German composer.

his wristwatch, and said in tones of awed amazement, "It all came from this." His very ineloquence made this the most eloquent tribute I have heard to Einstein's genius.

We think of Einstein as one concerned only with the deepest aspects of science. But he saw scientific principles in everyday things to which most of us would give barely a second thought. He once asked me if I had ever wondered why a man's feet will sink into either dry or completely submerged sand, while sand that is merely damp provides a firm surface. When I could not answer, he offered a simple explanation.

It depends, he pointed out, on *surface tension*, the elastic-skin effect of a liquid surface. This is what holds a drop together, or causes two small raindrops on a windowpane to pull into one big drop the moment their surfaces touch.

When sand is damp, Einstein explained, there are tiny amounts of water between grains. The surface tensions of these tiny amounts of water pull all the grains together, and friction then makes them hard to budge. When the sand is dry, there is obviously no water between grains. If the sand is fully immersed, there is water between grains, but no water *surface* to pull them together.

This is not as important as relativity; yet there is no telling what seeming trifle will lead an Einstein to a major discovery. And the puzzle of the sand does give us an inkling of the power and elegance of his mind.

Einstein's work, performed quietly with pen-

Three views of Albert Einstein (page 268). *Above right,* posing for a formal portrait at the age of fourteen in Germany; *center,* caught at an informal moment; *below right,* with his daughter, being sworn in as American citizens in 1940. *Background,* a blackboard with some of Einstein's mathematical notations regarding the theory of relativity.

*My Friend, Albert Einstein* **267**

---

AT A GLANCE

- The theory of relativity rests on violently opposing assumptions.
- Einstein challenged cherished beliefs about the nature of time.
- Einstein saw the scientific principles behind everyday events, explaining how surface tension makes damp sand firm.

**1 PURPOSE**

Noting Einstein's preference for Mozart characterizes the scientist as one who explored the physical nature of the world to discover its inner beauty.

**2 BIOGRAPHICAL SKETCH**

Einstein's assumptions that revolutionize physics also demonstrate two essential aspects of his nature, simplicity and commitment.

**3 STYLE: SIMILE**

This comparison illustrates the impact of Einstein's discovery on other scientists and on heretofore inviolable "laws" of physics.

**4 AUDIENCE**

The reference to "most of us" implies that Hoffmann's audience includes both nonscientists and scientists like himself.

**5 MAIN IDEA**

The example of the sand is a variation on the theme of simplicity within the complex: Hoffmann points out that simple matters could lead to major breakthroughs for Einstein.

---

## GUIDED READING

**LITERAL QUESTION**

**1a.** Where does Hoffmann say Einstein saw scientific principles? (in simple, everyday things to which most of us would not give a second thought)

**INFERENTIAL QUESTION**

**1b.** What do you think Einstein's concern with simple phenomena revealed about him? (His curiosity and appreciation remained always alive, unlimited, and motivating, encompassing both "seeming trifles" and "major discoveries.")

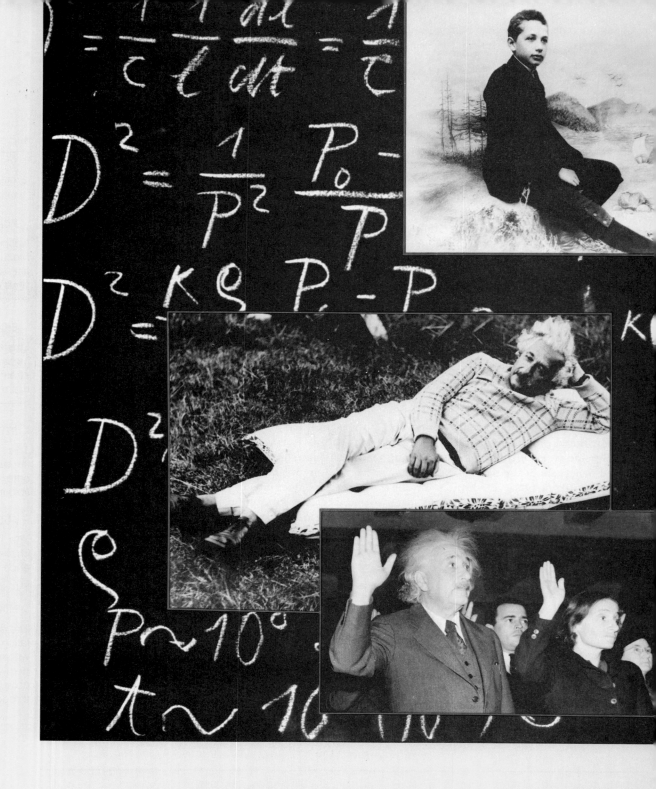

cil and paper, seemed remote from the turmoil of everyday life: But his ideas were so revolutionary they caused violent controversy and irrational anger. Indeed, in order to be able to award him a belated Nobel Prize, the selection committee had to avoid mentioning relativity, and pretend the prize was awarded primarily for his work on the quantum theory.

Political events upset the serenity of his life even more. When the Nazis[8] came to power in Germany, his theories were officially declared false because they had been formulated by a Jew. His property was confiscated, and it is said a price was put on his head.

When scientists in the United States, fearful that the Nazis might develop an atomic bomb, sought to alert American authorities to the danger, they were scarcely heeded. In desperation, they drafted a letter which Einstein signed and sent directly to President Roosevelt. It was this act that led to the fateful decision to go all-out on the production of an atomic bomb—an endeavor in which Einstein took no active part.

---

8. **Nazis:** the National Socialist party, which came to power in Germany in 1933 and ruled until 1945 under the leadership of Adolf Hitler.

---

_1_ When he heard of the agony and destruction that his $E = mc^2$ had wrought, he was dismayed beyond measure, and from then on there was a look of ineffable sadness in his eyes.

There was something elusively whimsical about Einstein. It is illustrated by my favorite anecdote about him. In his first year in Princeton, on Christmas Eve, so the story goes, some children sang carols outside his house. Having finished, they knocked on his door and explained they were collecting money to buy Christmas _2_ presents. Einstein listened, then said, ''Wait a moment.'' He put on his scarf and overcoat, and took his violin from its case. Then, joining the children as they went from door to door, he accompanied their singing of ''Silent Night'' on his violin.

How shall I sum up what it meant to have known Einstein and his works? Like the Nobel Prize-winner who pointed helplessly at his watch, I can find no adequate words. It was akin to the revelation of great art that lets one see what was formerly hidden. And when, for example, I walk on the sand of a lonely beach, I am reminded of his ceaseless search for cosmic simplicity— and the scene takes on a deeper, sadder beauty.

## STUDY QUESTIONS

### Recalling

1. Mention three of the intellectual achievements that Hoffmann cites as proof of Einstein's brilliance.
2. Find two instances in which Hoffmann presents the personal side of Einstein as a warm, friendly man.
3. What part did Einstein play in the development of the atomic bomb? What was his reaction to the use of it?

### Interpreting

4. What did the Nobel Prize winner speaking about Einstein mean when he pointed to his watch and said, "It all came from this"?
5. Contrast the intellectual and the personal sides of Einstein. Explain how both sides of Einstein reveal a kind of simplicity.

### Extending

6. Many people believe that great people become less admirable when their quirks are revealed. Is this true for Einstein? Why or why not?

_My Friend, Albert Einstein_  **269**

VIEWPOINT

It conveys his modesty and thoughtfulness.

## LITERARY FOCUS

1. descriptions of meeting; working with him; his reverence for God; his feelings about music; his response to the bomb
2. *walk in rain:* reveals simple logic; *conversation about wet sand:* shows ability to make discoveries about everyday things; *joining carolers:* impulsiveness, enjoyment of simple pleasures

## VOCABULARY

*credit:* belief someone will pay; *credence:* belief; *credible:* believable; *incredible:* unbelievable; *credulous:* too willing to believe; *discredit:* destroy belief in

1. *explanare,* to make flat or level: to make clear
2. *flectere,* to bend: change in loudness or pitch
3. *statio,* position: standing still
4. *collaborare,* to work together: working together
5. *eloquens,* speaking out: vividly expressive
6. *confiscare,* to put in a chest or treasury: seized by authority

## COMPARING BIOGRAPHIES

1. Answers will vary but should offer reasons for students' preferences.
2. Hoffman relates anecdotes, facts, or memories of Einstein and then comments on them. Mathabane conveys his feelings by relating the impressions and questions and feelings that occurred to him as the events he describes occurred.

# VIEWPOINT

Albert Einstein changed the way people think about space and time, matter and energy. However, he also wrote to a young student:

Do not worry about your difficulties with mathematics; I can assure you that mine are still greater.

■ In what ways does this remark fit the character that Hoffmann affectionately describes?

# LITERARY FOCUS

## Biographical Sketch

A **biographical sketch** is an informal, intimate picture of a person's life. Rather than concentrating like a standard biography on the important events of the subject's life, a biographical sketch focuses on the subject's personality. A biographical sketch may include fewer facts than a formal biography because it is assumed that the reader already knows something about the subject. Instead, the biographical sketch offers several incidents that create a vivid, candid impression of the subject.

One of the most useful tools a writer can use in a biographical sketch is the **anecdote**, a brief, often entertaining account of something the subject said or did. An anecdote—like the one Hoffmann tells us about Einstein's bareheaded walk in the rain—can bring a subject's personality to life in a few quick strokes.

### Thinking About the Biographical Sketch

1. What parts of Hoffmann's biography could have been written only by someone who knew Einstein personally?
2. List three anecdotes that Hoffmann uses, and explain the aspect of Einstein's personality that each anecdote reveals.

# VOCABULARY

## Latin Roots

The **root** is the most basic part of a word. Various words can be formed from the same root when different prefixes and suffixes (see page 167) are attached to it. For example, both *export* and *portable* are built on the root *-port-* from the Latin word *portare*, which means "to carry."

In Hoffmann's essay the word *credo*, meaning "a belief," is itself originally a Latin word meaning "I believe." When combined with various prefixes and suffixes, *credo* also serves as the root for a number of other English words, including *credit, credence, credible, incredible, credulous,* and *discredit.* How is the meaning of each of these words related to the idea of belief? Find at least three other words based on the word *credo.*

Look up the Latin origins for each of the following words from "My Friend, Albert Einstein." Write the definition for each word, and then write a sentence of your own using each word.

1. explained
2. inflection
3. stationary
4. collaborating
5. eloquent
6. confiscated

# COMPOSITION

## Writing About Biography

■ What is Hoffmann's purpose in writing about Albert Einstein, and how does he accomplish this purpose? Cite specific facts, details, and incidents that Hoffmann uses in his portrait of Einstein. *For help with this assignment, see Lesson 10 in the Writing About Literature Handbook at the back of this book.*

## Writing a Biographical Sketch with Anecdotes

■ Write a description of someone whom you know well, using two or three anecdotes to give your reader insight into your subject's character. Be sure to choose events that clearly illustrate important traits in your subject's personality.

# COMPARING BIOGRAPHY AND AUTOBIOGRAPHY

1. "My Friend, Albert Einstein," a biographical sketch, concentrates on revealing Einstein's personality. The selection from *Kaffir Boy,* an autobiography, presents significant events in the author's life. Compare the two selections. Which kind of nonfiction do you prefer to read? Why?
2. Both Mark Mathabane and Banesh Hoffmann write with intensity about the people and events they describe. Compare the ways in which these two writers convey their feelings and their attitudes to the reader.

---

# COMPOSITION: GUIDELINES FOR EVALUATION

## WRITING ABOUT BIOGRAPHY

### Objective

To identify Hoffmann's purpose and explain how he achieves his goal

### Guidelines for Evaluation

- suggested length: three to four paragraphs
- should state that Hoffmann wants to give reader insights into Einstein's genius, personality
- should describe Einstein's personality traits
- should cite facts, details, and anecdotes

## WRITING A BIOGRAPHICAL SKETCH WITH ANECDOTES

### Objective

To present picture of someone's personality

### Guidelines for Evaluation

- suggested length: three to four paragraphs
- should describe subject's personality traits
- should use at least two anecdotes to illustrate these traits

Mark Mathabane (born 1960) grew up poor in South Africa under the apartheid system. In the following excerpt from his autobiographical book, *Kaffir Boy*, Mathabane recounts some of his experiences as a child and youth in Alexandra, a black ghetto in Johannesburg, South Africa.

■ Have books opened worlds to you the way they did for the author of the following selection?

*Mark Mathabane*

# from **Kaffir¹ Boy**

To learn to express my thoughts and feelings effectively in English became my main goal in life. I saw command of the English language as the crucial key with which to unlock doors leading into that wonderful world of books revealed to me through the reading of Robert Louis Stevenson's gripping tale of buried treasure, mutiny on the high seas, one-legged seamen and the old sea song that I could recite even in my dreams:

> Fifteen men on a dead man's chest
> Yo-ho-ho, and a bottle of rum.

My heart ached to explore more such worlds, to live them in the imagination in much the same way as I lived the folktales of my mother and grandmother. I reasoned that if I somehow kept improving my English and ingratiated Mrs. Smith by the fact, then possibly she would give me more books like *Treasure Island* each time Granny took me along. Alas, such trips were few and far between. I could not afford to skip school

---

1. **Kaffir** [kaf'ər]: member of a Bantu-speaking tribe of South Africa. The term is often used scornfully.

regularly; and besides, each trip did not yield a book. But I clung to my dream.

A million times I wondered why the sparse library at my tribal school did not carry books like *Treasure Island*, why most of the books we read had tribal points of view. I would ask teachers and would be told that under the Bantu Education Law black children were supposed to acquire a solid foundation in tribal life, which would prepare them for a productive future in their respective homelands. In this way the dream of Dr. Verwoerd,² prime minister of South Africa and the architect of Bantu Education, would be realized, for he insisted that "the native child must be taught subjects which will enable him to work with and among his own people; therefore there is no use misleading him by showing him the green pastures of European society, in which he is not allowed to graze. Bantu Education should not be used to create imitation whites."

---

2. **Dr. Verwoerd** [fər vŭrt']: Hendrik Frensch Verwoerd (1901–1966); South African leader largely responsible for the policy of apartheid [ə pärt'hāt], or separation of the races.

*Kaffir Boy* **271**

**AT A GLANCE**

■ Mathabane's goal is to learn to express himself in English.
■ He is told that books like *Treasure Island* are not made available to black children—under Bantu Law they were to concentrate on tribal life.

**LITERARY OPTIONS**

■ purpose
■ characterization
■ point of view

**THEMATIC OPTIONS**

■ seeking change
■ turning disadvantages into assets
■ attaining a goal

**1 CHARACTERIZATION**

Mathabane's heart and mind yearn for knowledge; his means are hard work and pleasing others.

**2 BACKGROUND**

Mathabane describes the social and political climate in South Africa that determine a "suitable" education for blacks.

---

## GUIDED READING

**LITERAL QUESTION**

**1a.** To what subjects is the "native child" restricted in South Africa? (subjects that enable the child to work with and among his or her own people)

**INFERENTIAL QUESTION**

**1b.** Why might this be a discouraging reality for the narrator? (He dreams of exploring fantastic, exciting worlds—places of imagination far removed from the practicalities of Bantu tribal life.)

- The narrator rereads the few English books he acquires, severs his ties with gangs, and does exceptionally well in school.
- He prefers mythology to books like Booker T. Washington's autobiography.

## 1 THEME

Through books he learns about different realities that he explored in his imagination.

## 2 CHARACTERIZATION

Mathabane makes thorough use of his available resources, engaging his mind completely to explore new possibilities.

## 3 PURPOSE

Not only does Mathabane tell us about his own story, he also tells about the obstacles all blacks must overcome in South Africa for an education.

## 4 POINT OF VIEW

Mathabane finds the quest for the Golden Fleece more inspiring than Booker T. Washington's patient ascent to success. Washington's struggles as a former slave seem "unsettlingly familiar" to the author.

## 5 CHARACTERIZATION

Individuality came naturally to Mathabane, for whom even writing upside down felt normal.

---

**1** How I cursed Dr. Verwoerd and his law for prescribing how I should feel and think. I started looking toward the Smiths to provide me with the books about a different reality. Each day Granny came back from work around five in the afternoon, I would be the first to meet her at the gate, always with the same question, "Any books for me today?" Many times there weren't any. **2** Unable to read new English books on a regular basis, I reread the ones I had over and over again, till the pages become dogeared. With each reading each book took on new life, exposed new angles to the story, with the result that I was never bored.

My bleak vocabulary did not diminish my enthusiasm for reading. I constantly borrowed Mr. Brown's pocket-size dictionary to look up meanings of words, and would memorize them like arithmetic tables and write them in a small notebook. Sometimes I would read the dictionary. My pronunciation was appalling, but I had no way of finding out. I was amazed at the number of words in the English language, at the fact that a word could have different shades of meaning, or that certain words looked and sounded alike and yet differed greatly in meaning. Would I ever be able to learn all that?

• • •

After severing my ties with gangs, I had more time for my studies and books. I continued my above-average work, and was soon promoted to Standard Four, with the highest marks in the class. Teachers began forecasting great things for me: some said I would make a good teacher, others maintained that I had the brains to become a **3** doctor. But all these predictions depended upon one thing—money. I was fast arriving at the point where many a black child, eager to continue learning, had to drop out because parents could not afford school fees, books and uniforms. I tried not to dwell on it. "Learn as much as you can, while the opportunity is still there," became my motto.

Though tribal indoctrination was still the focus of our curriculum in Standard Four, a few new and challenging subjects were introduced. In literature, we read a Tsonga[3] translation of Booker T. Washington's[4] autobiography, *Up from Slavery*. Teachers exhorted us to be like him, to lift ourselves from poverty by our bootstraps. We were required to memorize passages from the book, including "The Atlanta Exposition Address."[5] For some reason, I never quite **4** liked the book. It had an unsettlingly familiar ring to it.

But that was not the case with Tsonga translations of Greek and Roman mythology. I was drawn to the stories of Atalanta, Philemon and Bacchus, Odysseus and the Trojan War, Jason and the quest for the Golden Fleece. Admittedly they resembled much of African folklore, but they had a freshness that appealed to my imagination. I regularly chose to read them as prose during exams. My animated orations consistently scored high marks. I soon became one of the best prose and poetry readers in school, and would often get picked to represent the school whenever white inspectors came to assess our progress.

Another thing that caused a stir among teachers and students was my peculiar way of writing: **5** I wrote upside down, literally. When I first learned how to write in Substandard A, I found it natural to write upside down, for it seemed that somehow my brain and left hand could only coordinate when I wrote upside down. To me, writing this way was the most normal thing; yet those who saw me do it shook their heads in disbelief and remarked that they had never seen anyone who wrote like me.

• • •

---

3. **Tsonga** [tsōn'gä]: Bantu language of southern Africa.
4. **Booker T. Washington** (1865–1915): American black leader and educator.
5. **"The Atlanta Exposition Address"** (Sept. 18, 1895): classic statement of Booker T. Washington's opinion of race relations.

---

## GUIDED READING

**LITERAL QUESTION**

**1a.** What is the narrator's feeling about Booker T. Washington's autobiography? (He does not like the book.)

**INFERENTIAL QUESTION**

**1b.** How do you explain his attitude? (Washington's striving is too much like his own. The narrator wants to escape from the grim challenges of his life when he reads. Also, Washington's message of patient acceptance is too much like what the narrator's teachers tell him.)

When Mrs. Smith gave me an old wood tennis racket one Saturday after I had done what she called "a splendid job" in cleaning her silver and brassware, and shining Mr. Smith's half a dozen pairs of shoes, I was already beginning to get bored with soccer.

"Practice hard," she said, "for one day I want to read about you in the papers, as our next Arthur Ashe."[6]

"I don't know if I can be like him, madam," I said apologetically. "He's good." I had been reading about Arthur Ashe's exploits in the old tennis magazines Mrs. Smith regularly gave me. I couldn't even begin to imagine how a black man could become so good in a sport dominated by whites. Besides, what kind of a black man was he to be allowed to mix with whites, compete against them, even beat them? What kind of society did he live in which allowed a black man to become rich and famous at the expense of whites, instead of the other way round?

How could I begin teaching myself tennis? I was almost fourteen years old, had never handled a tennis racket in my life and knew absolutely nothing about the rules of the game. What I had read in the tennis magazines simply confounded rather than enlightened me.

I began pounding the tennis wall at the Alexandra Stadium. The one thing I liked about tennis was that it was not a team sport like soccer. My success and improvement depended upon my own efforts.

•  •  •

Had I been able to find part-time jobs to fill my spare time, I probably wouldn't have continued playing tennis. As it turned out, part-time jobs were as scarce as money to pay for school. The more I read about the world of tennis, and Arthur Ashe's role in it, the more I began to dream of its possibilities. What if I too were

someday to attain the same fame and fortune as Arthur Ashe? Would whites respect me as they did him? Would I be as free as he? The dreams were tantalizing, but I knew they were only dreams. Nevertheless, I kept on dreaming; after all, what harm could that do me?

One weekday afternoon I was at the stadium practicing against the wall when a big Colored man, with a face full of freckles, approached the court. He leaned against its fence and watched me play.

Arthur Ashe, mid-1970s.

*Kaffir Boy*  **273**

---

6. **Arthur Ashe** (born 1943): first black male tennis player to win the U.S. Open and Wimbledon tournaments.

---

- Mathabane discusses the relationships among whites, Coloreds, and blacks in South Africa.
- Scaramouche says the author has potential and agrees to be his coach.

## 1 PURPOSE

Mathabane explains how apartheid separates Coloreds from blacks and whites, aggravating and compounding resentments among people.

## 2 BACKGROUND

Changing attitudes among Coloreds had created an atmosphere in which Scaramouche and Mathabane can work comfortably together.

Mark Mathabane with members of his family, reunited in Chicago in 1987.

"Hit that backhand! Hit that backhand!" he said insistently, "don't run around it."

I tried hitting one backhand; the stroke was horrible; I returned to only whacking my forehand, my best stroke.

"You fool," the Colored man said, "practice that backhand, or you might just as well forget about tennis. Have you no common sense! Don't you know you never work on your strength but your weakness! And your backhand is atrocious."

The man's name was Scaramouche.[7] He resented being called "Colored," but according to apartheid, that was his official designation as one of over two million people of mixed race who were more than a blemish to the white man's theory of racial purity. According to the govern-

1 ment Coloreds were neither black nor white, even though some of them were as black as the blackest black man, or as white as the whitest white man. Coloreds were allowed to live with blacks, though special areas had been set aside for them under the Group Areas Act.

The government generally treated Coloreds slightly better by giving them better jobs, better housing and better education than blacks. As a result most of the Coloreds were ashamed of their black blood, and often their prejudice against blacks was fiercer than the white man's.

2 But a new generation of young Coloreds, which saw itself as more black than white, was emerging, and it embraced the entire range of black aspirations.

Scaramouche, a self-employed painter, was one of the best tennis players among people of color in Johannesburg. An excellent coach, he

---

7. **Scaramouche** [skär'ə mōōsh']

**274** *Nonfiction*

---

## GUIDED READING

### LITERAL QUESTION

**1a.** How did many of the older Coloreds feel toward blacks? (Their prejudice against blacks was fiercer than that of the whites.)

### INFERENTIAL QUESTION

**1b.** Why do you think they felt this way? (Their own "blackness" prevented them from being treated as full-fledged citizens.)

was well connected in white and black tennis circles. He evaluated my game this way: I had potential to become a decent player provided I was prepared to work hard to unlearn the numerous bad habits I had taught myself. He agreed to be my coach.

   • • •

How did Arthur Ashe get to be so good in a white man's sport? What miracles did the environment in America provide that nurtured blacks into great athletes like Arthur Ashe? Were the blacks in America really like us? Or was there something mixed up in their blood, maybe in their brains too, which made them capable of accomplishing prodigious feats, which seemed beyond the capability of even the best among us?

I had read somewhere that there were, among blacks in America, singers, educators, politicians, mayors, inventors, scientists, actors, actresses, judges, army generals, pilots, writers and so on—people whose names weren't African, yet some of whom were as black as I was. W. E. B. Dubois, Frederick Douglass, Martin Luther King, Jr., Joe Louis, Muhammad Ali, Jesse Owens, Harry Belafonte, Marcus Garvey, Paul Robeson, Richard Wright, Sammy Davis, Jr., Nat "King" Cole, Lena Horne, Booker T. Washington, James Baldwin, Jesse Jackson, Sidney Poitier, Duke Ellington, George Washington Carver, Malcolm X, Marian Anderson, Ralph Bunche, Jackie Robinson, Thurgood Marshall, Ella Fitzgerald, Eldridge Cleaver, Langston Hughes, Louis Armstrong, and the list went on and on.

I came across these names in newspapers, magazines and books. On reading of their accomplishments, I found it beyond me to believe that they, whom history depicted as descendants of slaves, slaves taken from the *very* Africa in which I lived, could have achieved so much.

[*Mark Mathabane continues his struggle to develop as a student and as a tennis player. Friends, especially Stan and Marjory Smith, help him to realize his dream, and he wins a scholarship to an American college. After still another struggle to obtain a passport and an exit visa, the day comes when Mark must leave his family.*]

At four o'clock in the morning, September 16, 1978, everyone in the family was up—my mother, father, brother and five sisters—watching me as I packed my last bags. All was ready. After eighteen years of living life as a fourth-class citizen, a slave, in the land of apartheid, I was at last leaving for another world, a different way of life, a better existence, away from bondage.

In a few hours, I would be flying through clouds, across vast oceans, on my way to the Promised Land, where I hoped to find the freedom and opportunity to realize my dreams, my fullest potential as a human being. Little was I aware as I packed that last bag that I was soon to become the first black boy ever to leave South Africa on a tennis scholarship, one more vital link the oppressed of South Africa had with the outside world.

The bags packed, I cast my eyes about the crowded kitchen, dimly lit by a flickering, half-burned candle. I tried to avoid looking at the faces surrounding me; I could not bear the expression of fear and anguish written on them, as they realized that yes, I was leaving. Their faces told me that they thought my imminent departure a dream from which they would surely awaken, and find I was going nowhere. To many blacks in Alexandra, in Soweto[8] and in the whole of South Africa for that matter, the fact that I was leaving for America, to study and to play tennis, was unprecedented, beyond belief, a miracle. It simply didn't happen that way for black children in South Africa.

I glanced at my wristwatch; it read half-past five. It was time to say farewell to everybody. I kissed my mother, forty-four years old, a born

---

8. **Soweto** [sō wā'tō]: acronym for South-Western Townships; urban area designated for habitation by blacks.

*Kaffir Boy* **275**

## GUIDED READING

### LITERAL QUESTION

**1a.** How does the author refer to the other "world" he is leaving for? (He calls it a different way of life, a better existence, away from bondage.)

### INFERENTIAL QUESTION

**1b.** How do you think he actually feels about going? (He is probably conflicted—happy for the opportunity he has always dreamed of but sad to leave his family.)

AT A GLANCE

- He bids good-bye to his mother, promising not to waste his opportunity.
- His father breaks down and cries.
- He wonders how he and South Africa will have changed when he returns.

1 **VOCABULARY: WORD CHOICE**

The phrase *didn't resist the kiss* suggests that his father is unused to showing the affection he feels.

2 **PURPOSE**

Mathabane shows the insidious effect of apartheid. By constricting the lives of black South Africans, Mathabane suggests, apartheid constricts their feelings as well, hardening them against showing their feelings.

3 **THEME**

Accepting the hard-won opportunity to live in a different reality means giving up his life among loved ones.

REFLECTING ON THE SELECTION

As he leaves, why does Mathabane think about the coming changes in his own life and change in South Africa? (He knows that life in a freer country will make him a different man. He wonders if that man will fit into his family and country. He also hopes that South Africa might become a freer society in the future.)

survivor. Tears began forming in her big eyes, and slowly rolled down her cheeks, onto her nightgown. She made no effort to dry them.

"Don't cry, Mama," I said, fighting back my own tears. "Please don't cry. I'll be back soon. I'm only going away for four years."

"These are tears of joy, my child," she said. "I'm very happy that God has given you this opportunity to make something of yourself, of your life. Don't waste it, child."

"I won't, Mama," I said. "I promise I won't."

I then turned and kissed my brother, George, standing near my mother. He too began crying. I then kissed each of my five sisters, and they too began crying. I too started crying. My father emerged from the bedroom and stood by the wall, behind everybody. I went over and kissed his gaunt face; he didn't resist the kiss. He was getting old now. His hairline was receding rapidly; his face was beginning to resemble an ancient topographical map of Africa.

Impassively he stood there against the wall, in the shadow of the flickering candle, seemingly trying to awaken himself from some bad dream, some nightmare. I could tell from the look on his face that he found the fact that I was leaving hard to believe: I, his son, his firstborn, his own flesh and blood, the son he had watched grow, the son whom he had wanted so much to be like him, but who had grown up to be so much different, was about to leave him suffering, gaunt, aging, helpless, hopeless, fearful of the future.

As I kissed him again, and embraced his emaciated body, a tear and a twinkle came to his eyes: He understood that despite my fanatical opposition to his way of life, despite all the shocks of childhood he had subjected me to, I still loved him, dearly.

"Take care of yourself, son," he said softly.

"I will, Papa."

Tears began streaming down his hollow cheeks. My father was crying. After eighteen years of my knowing him, he was, for the first time, crying. He's human after all; he loves me.

Tears began streaming down my face too. I pitied him, myself, my family, the rest of black South Africa. Why does apartheid do this to us? Why does it refuse us the right to lead normal lives? Why had it created within my father's heart a granite wall, which had prevented him from expressing feelings of love, care, compassion and understanding? But the wall had been shattered. My leaving had broken down the barrier which for eighteen years had barred me from reaching into my father and sharing with him the love and understanding of fathers and sons.

"Write to us always," my father said. He couldn't control his feelings, so he went back to the bedroom to don his overalls and go face the whims of white folks.

"I will, Papa," my voice trailed after him, reminding him that I was still his son; and he, still my father.

My mother left where she was standing and came over to where I was stashing my passport and other documents into a totebag. She embraced me tightly and kissed me again, saying:

"Wherever you go in this world, child, always believe in yourself. Always have hope. Always have faith. Always believe in the power of God and never forsake Him. Trust in Him, always, with all your heart and all your strength, and He'll guide you in all your ways. He made it all happen."

I nodded. Dawn was starting to break outside. Soon the car that was to take me to Jans Smuts Airport would be here. I again embraced and kissed my brother and sisters. I was overcome with grief at the thought of leaving them behind. They had become so much a part of me. They had become me in a way. I embraced them more tightly this time, aware that, possibly, I wouldn't be seeing them in a long time, perhaps for many years. How much would I have changed? How much would they have changed? How much would South Africa have changed?

**276** *Nonfiction*

---

## GUIDED READING

### LITERAL QUESTION

**1a.** How does the author describe the condition in which he is about to leave his father? ("suffering, gaunt, aging, helpless, hopeless, fearful of the future")

### INFERENTIAL QUESTION

**1b.** Why might the author feel guilty toward his father? (for leaving him alone—so to speak—in a hostile land)

## STUDY QUESTIONS

### Recalling

1. How did the books Mark read in school differ from the ones Mrs. Smith gave him?
2. What did Mark's teachers think of him as a student? What obstacle might have prevented him from going beyond Standard Four?
3. What role did each of the following play in Mark's life: a wooden tennis racket, Arthur Ashe and other outstanding black Americans, Scaramouche, Stan and Marjory Smith, a tennis scholarship?

### Interpreting

4. What was the goal of Dr. Verwoerd's ideas about Bantu education?
5. What specific personality traits helped Mathabane to realize his dream?
6. As Mathabane was preparing to leave for America, he thought of himself as "one more vital link the oppressed of South Africa had with the outside world." What did he mean?

### Extending

7. Do you think Mark Mathabane became a valuable link between his people and the outside world? Why or why not?

## VIEWPOINT

Mathabane's "main goal in life" was to learn to express his thoughts and feelings effectively in English. Apparently he achieved his goal, for he wrote *Kaffir Boy* in English and, according to one critic, he

> writes with compelling energy, and the details of his struggle . . . grip readers with immediate intensity.
>
> —Diana C. Hirsch, *School Library Journal*

■ Find at least one instance in which Mathabane's details grip you with "immediate intensity"—that is, make you feel that you are an eyewitness to what is going on.

## LITERARY FOCUS

### Purpose in Autobiography

An **autobiography**, as you know, is the story of a person's life written by that person. Like every author of an autobiography, Mark Mathabane set down the facts of his life that he considered most important for readers to know. Yet Mathabane's purpose for writing his autobiography went beyond simply recording the facts and experiences of his life. The **purpose** of Mathabane's autobiography is the central idea—a general truth about life—that he wanted to convey to his readers.

### Thinking About the Purpose in Autobiography

■ State in a sentence or two Mathabane's chief purpose in writing *Kaffir Boy*, based on this excerpt. Begin your statement with an introduction similar to this: "Mark Mathabane's purpose for writing *Kaffir Boy* was to share the following general truth about life."

## COMPOSITION

### Writing About Autobiography

■ Recall Mathabane's purpose as you stated it in the Literary Focus, above. Write a composition in which you show that your statement of Mathabane's purpose is based upon evidence in his autobiography. Cite details, facts, and examples that, considered together, suggest the general truth about life Mathabane wanted to convey to the readers of *Kaffir Boy. For help with this assignment, refer to Lesson 10 in the Writing About Literature Handbook at the back of this book.*

### Writing an Autobiographical Incident

■ Recall an incident in your life that had a powerful impact upon you. Write an autobiographical account of this incident. Begin by describing it in detail. Then explain what you learned from the incident. Did you immediately realize its lesson, or did the realization come later? How might other people profit from a similar incident? If you would rather not write about yourself, write a fictitious autobiographical account.

*Kaffir Boy* **277**

## STUDY QUESTIONS

1. *schoolbooks*—in Tsonga, had tribal point of view; *Mrs. Smith's books*—in English, opened Mark to outside world
2. that he had great potential; lack of money
3. *tennis racket*—showed him way to realize his dream; *Arthur Ashe,* etc.—served as role models; *Scaramouche*—became tennis coach; *the Smiths*—made him realize that not all whites were hostile; *tennis scholarship*—helped him develop his potential outside of his oppressive country
4. to keep whites and people of color segregated
5. intelligence, determination, optimism
6. that he would let others in the world know what apartheid was doing to all South Africans
7. Yes—his autobiography paints a vivid picture of the effects of racism in South Africa.

### VIEWPOINT

Possible answers: the discussion between Mark and Mrs. Smith; Mark's first meeting with Scaramouche; Mark's parting with his family

### LITERARY FOCUS

Obstacles, even those as terrible as apartheid, can be overcome with spirit and determination.

---

## COMPOSITION: GUIDELINES FOR EVALUATION

### WRITING ABOUT AUTOBIOGRAPHY

**Objective**

To support a statement with evidence

**Guidelines for Evaluation**

- Suggested length: one to two paragraphs
- evidence to support statement may include the following:
- "I saw command of the English language. . . . "
- "My success and improvement. . . . "
- "Nevertheless, I kept on dreaming. . . . "
- "In a few hours . . . as a human being"

### WRITING AN AUTOBIOGRAPHICAL INCIDENT

**Objective**

To write a real or imagined autobiographical incident

**Guidelines for Evaluation**

- Suggested length: minimum of one paragraph
- should be detailed account of an incident from student's or fictitious person's life
- should be written in the first person
- should state what was learned

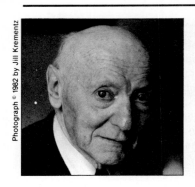

Photograph © 1982 by Jill Krementz

Isaac Bashevis Singer (born 1904) spent his childhood in the Jewish community around Krochmalna Street in Warsaw, Poland. As a rabbi, his father presided in their tenement apartment over *beth din*, a religious court. Here the young Singer, nicknamed Itchele, heard many stories dealing with domestic, religious, and business matters, subjects he would treat later on as a writer.

Singer has written in both English and Yiddish, a language spoken by Jews throughout the world. He received the Nobel Prize for Literature in 1978.

■ Imagine you are thirty years old. Whom among your childhood friends would you want to visit?

*Isaac Bashevis Singer*

# Shosha

1   In the days when we used to live at 10 Krochmalna Street, I mostly stayed home at night. Our courtyard was dark and the small kerosene lamps in the hallway gave more smoke than light. The stories my parents told about devils, demons, and werewolves made me afraid to go out, so I would remain indoors and read.

In those days, we had a neighbor called Basha, who had three daughters: Shosha, who was nine; Ippa, five; and Teibele, two. Basha owned a store that stayed open until late in the evening.

In the summertime the nights are short, but in winter they are very long. The only place I could go at night was Shosha's apartment, but to get there I had to pass through a dark corridor. It took only a minute, yet that minute was filled with terror. Luckily, Shosha would almost always hear me coming, running and breathing heavily, and would quickly open the door. At the sight of her, I lost all fear. Shosha, though she was a year older than I, was more childish. She was fair, with blond braids and blue eyes.

2   We were drawn to each other because we loved to tell each other stories, and we also loved to play together.

The moment I entered the apartment, Shosha took out "the things." Her toys consisted of articles discarded by grown-ups: buttons from old coats, a tea-kettle handle, a wooden spool with no thread left, tinfoil from a package of tea, and other such objects. With my colored pencils, I often drew people and animals for Shosha. Shosha and her sister Ippa admired my artwork.

3   There was a tile stove in Shosha's apartment behind which there lived a cricket. It chirped the nights through all winter long. I imagined that the cricket was telling a story that would never end. But who can understand the language of crickets? Shosha believed that a house imp[1] also made its home behind the stove. A house imp never does anyone any harm. Sometimes it even helps the household. Just the same, one is afraid of it.

---

1. **imp:** mischievous spirit.

Shosha's house imp liked to play little tricks. When Shosha took off her shoes and stockings before she went to sleep and placed them near her bed, she'd find them on the table in the morning. The house imp had put them there. Several times when Shosha went to bed with her hair unbraided, the house imp braided it while she was asleep. Once when Shosha was playing at casting goat shadows on the wall with her fingers, the shadow goat jumped off the wall and butted her on the forehead. This, too, was a trick of the house imp. Another time Shosha's mother sent her to the baker to buy fresh rolls and gave her a silver gulden[2] to pay for them. Shosha lost the gulden in the gutter and came home frightened and crying. Suddenly she felt a coin in her hand. The house imp tweaked her left braid and whispered into her ear: "Shlemiel."[3]

I had heard these stories many times, but they never failed to make me shiver with excitement. I myself liked to invent things. I told the girls that my father had a treasure that was hidden in a cave in the forest. I boasted that my grandfather was the King of Bilgoray.[4] I assured Shosha that I knew a magic word that could destroy the world if spoken. "Please, Itchele, please don't say it," she would beg me.

The trip home was even more frightening than getting to Shosha's. My fear grew with the stories we told each other. It seemed to me that the dark hall was full of evil spirits. I had once read a story about a boy who had been forced by the demons to marry one of their she-devils. I was afraid that it might happen to me. According to the story, the couple lived somewhere in the desert near Mount Seir. Their children were half human and half demon. As I ran through the dark corridor, I kept repeating words that would guard me against the creatures of the night:

"Thou shalt not permit a witch to live—
A witch to live thou shalt not permit."

When we moved to 12 Krochmalna Street, there was no question of visiting Shosha at night. Also, it was not fitting for a Hasidic[5] boy, a student of the Talmud,[6] to play with girls. I missed Shosha. I hoped we'd meet on the street sometime, but months and years passed and we did not see each other.

In time Shosha became for me an image of the past. I often thought about her during the day and dreamed about her at night. In my dreams Shosha was as beautiful as a princess. Several times I dreamed that she had married the house imp and lived with him in a dark cellar. He brought her food but never let her go out. I saw her sitting on a chair, to which she had been tied with rope, while the house imp fed her jam with a tiny spoon. He had the head of a dog and the wings of a bat.

After the First World War, I left my family in Bilgoray and returned to Warsaw. I began to write and my stories appeared in newspapers and magazines. I also wrote a novel called *Satan in Goray* in which I described the devils and demons of olden times. I was married and had a son. I applied for a passport and a visa to emigrate to the United States, and one day they arrived. I was about to leave Warsaw forever.

A few days before I left, my feet led me to Krochmalna Street. I hadn't been there for years and I wanted once again to see the street where I grew up.

Few changes had taken place, though the buildings were older and even shabbier. I peered into some courtyards: huge trash cans; barefoot, half-naked children. The boys played tag, hide-

---

2. **silver gulden** [goold'ən]: coin used widely in central Europe. It is more commonly known as a guilder and is now worth about 40 cents.
3. **Shlemiel** [shlə mēl']: Yiddish term for "unlucky fool."
4. **Bilgoray**: town in eastern Poland.

5. **Hasidic** [ha sēd'ik]: belonging or pertaining to a mystical sect of Judaism. Hasidism originated in Poland in the eighteenth century.
6. **Talmud** [tal'mood]: collection of Jewish laws, based on the Old Testament and other religious works.

*Shosha* 279

---

## GUIDED READING

**LITERAL QUESTIONS**

**1a.** Why did Itchele and Shosha's visits end? (Itchele moved up the street and it wasn't fitting for a Hasidic boy studying the Talmud to play with girls.)

**2a.** What prompted Itchele to return to Krochmalna Street? (Before leaving Warsaw, his "feet led" him there; he wanted to see the street where he grew up.)

**INFERENTIAL QUESTIONS**

**1b.** Besides the short distance and Itchele's studies, what might explain their complete separation? (Itchele was growing away from Shosha, "more childish" than he was.)

**2b.** What might the almost involuntary return to his former street suggest? (His past remained a vital part of his life.)

### 1 POINT OF VIEW

Singer tells us how he felt at the time: both hopeful and foolish, looking for the child Shosha in an environment that appears unchanged but is actually twenty years older.

### 2 THEME

Forgetting reality for a moment, Singer thinks he has stumbled back into his childhood when the familiar face appears before him.

### 3 STYLE: DIALOGUE

Basha's simple and natural response telescopes the distance between the past and the present.

### 4 THEME

Once again firmly rooted in the present, Singer, the adult, can no longer believe in the magic he once invented.

and-seek, cops-and-robbers, just as we had twenty-five years ago. The girls occupied themselves with hopscotch. Suddenly it occurred to me that I might be able to find Shosha. I made my way to the building where we used to live.

**1** God in heaven, everything was the same—the peeling walls, the refuse. I reached the corridor that led to Shosha's apartment, and it was just as dark as in the old days. I lit a match and found the door. As I did so, I realized how foolish I was being. Shosha would be over thirty now. It was most unlikely that the family would still be living in the same place. And even if her parents were still alive and living there, Shosha would surely have married and moved away. But some power I cannot explain forced me to knock on the door.

There was no reply. I drew the latch (as I had sometimes done in the old days) and the door opened. I entered a kitchen that looked exactly like Basha's kitchen of twenty-five years before. I recognized the mortar and pestle,[7] the table, the chairs. Was I dreaming? Could it be true?

**2** Then I noticed a girl of about eight or nine. My God, it was Shosha! The same fair face, the same blond hair braided with red ribbons, the same longish neck. The girl stared at me in surprise, but she didn't seem alarmed.

"Who are you looking for?" she asked, and it was Shosha's voice.

"What is your name?" I said.

"Me? Basha."

"And your mother's name?"

"Shosha," the girl replied.

"Where is your mother?"

"In the store."

**3** "I once lived here," I explained. "I used to play with your mother when she was a little girl."

Basha looked at me with large eyes and inquired, "Are you Itchele?"

---

7. **mortar and pestle:** bowl and blunt short rod used together for grinding substances.

"How do you know about Itchele?" I said. A lump stuck in my throat. I could barely speak.

"My mother told me about him."

"Yes, I am Itchele."

"My mother told me everything. Your father **4** had a cave in the forest full of gold and diamonds. You knew a word that could set the whole world on fire. Do you still know it?"

"No, not any more."

"What happened to the gold in the cave?"

"Somebody stole it," I said.

"And is your grandfather still a king?"

"No, Basha, he is not a king any more."

For a while we were both silent. Then I asked, "Did your mother tell you about the house imp?"

"Yes, we used to have a house imp, but he's gone."

"What happened to him?"

"I don't know."

"And the cricket?"

"The cricket is still here, but it chirps mostly at night."

I went down to the candy store—the one where Shosha and I used to buy candy—and bought cookies, chocolate, and halvah.[8] Then I went back upstairs and gave them to Basha.

"Would you like to hear a story?" I asked her.

"Yes, very much."

I told Basha a story about a beautiful blond girl whom a demon had carried away to the desert, to Mount Seir, and had forced to marry him, and about the children that were born of the marriage, who were half human, half demon.

Basha's eyes grew pensive. "And she stayed there?"

"No, Basha, a saintly man called Rabbi Leib learned about her misfortune. He traveled to the desert and rescued her."

"How?"

---

8. **halvah** [hal vä′]: candy made from sesame seeds and honey.

---

## GUIDED READING

### LITERAL QUESTIONS

**1a.** What did Itchele observe about the corridor leading to Shosha's apartment? (It was as dark as it had been in the old days.)

**2a.** What did Basha already know about Itchele before they met? (She knew his stories about the cave full of treasure, his "royal" grandfather, and his magic word.)

### INFERENTIAL QUESTIONS

**1b.** What formerly important quality of the corridor does Itchele not mention, and what might that omission signify? (He doesn't say that it is scary; though the corridor is the same, he has changed.)

**2b.** What do Basha's questions about Itchele's stories imply about the past and present? (The past and present come together in the old stories, still fresh to Basha.)

"An angel helped him."

"And what happened to her children?"

"The children became completely human and went with their mother. The angel carried them to safety on his wings."

"And the demon?"

"He remained in the desert."

"And he never married again?"

"Yes, Basha, he did. He married a she-demon, one of his own kind."

1   We were both silent again, and suddenly I heard the familiar chirping of a cricket. Could it be the cricket of my childhood? Certainly not. Perhaps her great-great-great-granddaughter. But she was telling the same story, as ancient as time, as puzzling as the world, and as long as the dark winter nights of Warsaw.

## STUDY QUESTIONS

### Recalling

1. What was Singer's childhood home like? What things frightened him there?

2. What games did Itchele and Shosha play together?

3. Explain how Singer loses contact with Shosha. What causes him to look for her again? Whom does he meet?

4. Find three things that have not changed in Shosha's apartment when the adult Singer returns. Name one or two things that have changed.

### Interpreting

5. How does the adult Singer feel when he finds Basha and learns that she has heard of him from her mother?

6. How is I. B. Singer, the writer, similar to the boy Itchele? How are they different? What do you think Singer means when he tells Basha that he no longer knows the "word that could set the whole world on fire"?

7. What cycles of life come full circle in "Shosha"? What do you think Singer is saying in this memoir about the relationship between the present and the past?

### Extending

8. Why does the idea of reentering the past appeal so much to people? Why do you think people take pleasure in finding things, like Singer's cricket, that do not change?

## VIEWPOINT

As he does in "Shosha," Singer often writes of the relationship between past and present. He explains:

I always wanted to say…that even though life looks to us chaotic, it is not as chaotic as we think. There is a scheme and a design behind it.

■ Explain how the journey into the past in "Shosha" reveals a "scheme and design" in Singer's life.

## COMPOSITION

### Writing About Autobiography

■ What picture of his past does Singer provide in "Shosha," and how does the adult writer interpret his childhood experiences? Note the memories that Singer emphasizes in "Shosha." Then explain why these memories have become important to Singer. Conclude by telling what insights about the past he has gained through time.

### Writing a Story for a Child

■ Imagine that you are entertaining a young child who has asked you to make up a story. Choose one of the stories that Itchele and Shosha tell, and make up one brief episode for it. Describe the characters, scenes, and events in more detail than Singer gives in "Shosha." Be sure to write the story as if you are telling it to a child.

*Shosha*   **281**

AT A GLANCE

- Singer answers Basha's questions.
- A cricket suddenly begins chirping.

1 SYMBOL

The cricket, bringing Singer's story and Itchele's experience full circle, represents both change and the unchanging.

REFLECTING ON THE SELECTION

What is the cricket's "same story, as ancient as time, as puzzling as the world"? (Possible answers: Nothing that we have ever felt is lost forever; life, despite change and upheaval, has a basic continuity that becomes apparent as time goes on.)

STUDY QUESTIONS

1. shabby apartment in Warsaw, dark hallways; evil spirits

2. They invented stories of magic, evil spirits, hidden treasure.

3. his family moves; revisits neighborhood; meets Shosha's daughter

4. ■ Unchanged: kitchen table and chairs, little girl, cricket
   ■ Changed: Shosha is adult; imp is gone.

5. surprised; speechless; joyful

6. similar: cares about Shosha, likes to tell stories; different: does not believe in magic or demons; no longer believes what he invents

7. Itchele/Shosha are grown and have children: The present repeats the past.

8. The past often seems better than the present. The endurance of things is reassuring.

VIEWPOINT

Singer and Shosha and their children reflect themselves and their parents. He witnesses a regeneration of the past.

## COMPOSITION: GUIDELINES FOR EVALUATION

### WRITING ABOUT AUTOBIOGRAPHY

**Objective**

To explain how Singer identifies relationship between past and present

**Guidelines for Evaluation**

- suggested length: three paragraphs
- should describe Singer's memories of childhood
- should explain how Singer feels about memories
- should explain what the adult understands about past that the child did not

### WRITING A STORY FOR A CHILD

**Objective**

To tell an entertaining story in a simple style

**Guidelines for Evaluation**

- suggested length: 300–500 words
- should be based on stories described in "Shosha"
- should elaborate on the story Singer describes, adding details
- should be written like a fairy tale or folk tale

AT A GLANCE

- All Thomas's Christmases roll into one holiday memory.
- Mrs. Prothero's cry "Fire!" interrupts young Thomas and her son Jim at play.

LITERARY OPTIONS

- figurative language
- style
- main idea

THEMATIC OPTIONS

- childhood memories
- ritual and tradition
- imagination and wonder

**1 SETTING**

The seaside town is enveloped in snow that establishes an atmosphere and shapes the entire memory.

**2 MAIN IDEA**

Thomas uses vivid imagery to draw out magically from the snow a particular childhood memory.

**3 STYLE: METAPHOR**

The boys' imaginations transform familiar things and surroundings into high adventures in a distant land.

Growing up in a seaport in Wales, a country on the western coast of Great Britain, Dylan Thomas (1914–1953) made up for his mediocre schoolwork with his enthusiasm for words. His early interest in amateur dramatics and mock radio broadcasts led to his later work in various media. Thomas wrote the play *Under Milk Wood* for the radio and also wrote several film scripts. His fame, however, rests primarily with his poetry, the first collection of which was published when he was only twenty.

Of his youth Dylan Thomas recalls that his "memories of childhood have no order, and no end." "A Child's Christmas in Wales" is a patchwork of memories from many of the author's boyhood Christmases, stitched together by Thomas' magical use of language.

■ Which holiday would *you* highlight in a childhood memoir? Why?

*Dylan Thomas*

# A Child's Christmas in Wales

1 One Christmas was so much like another, in those years around the sea-town corner now and out of all sound except the distant speaking of the voices I sometimes hear a moment before sleep, that I can never remember whether it snowed for six days and six nights when I was twelve or whether it snowed for twelve days and twelve nights when I was six. All the Christmases roll down toward the two-tongued sea, like a cold and headlong moon bundling down the sky that was our street; and they stop at the rim of the ice-edged, fish-freezing waves, 2 and I plunge my hands in the snow and bring out whatever I can find. In goes my hand into that wool-white bell-tongued ball of holidays resting at the rim of the carol-singing sea, and out come Mrs. Prothero and the firemen.

It was on the afternoon of the day of Christmas Eve, and I was in Mrs. Prothero's garden, waiting for cats, with her son Jim. It was snowing. It was always snowing at Christmas. December, in my memory, is white as Lapland, though there were no reindeer. But there were cats. Patient, cold, and callous, our hands wrapped in socks, we waited to snowball the cats. Sleek and long as jaguars and horrible-whiskered, spitting and snarling, they would slink and sidle over the 3 white back-garden walls, and the lynx-eyed hunters, Jim and I, fur-capped and moccasined trappers from Hudson Bay,[1] off Mumbles Road, would hurl our deadly snowballs at the green of their eyes. The wise cats never appeared. We were so still, Eskimo-footed arctic marksmen in the muffling silence of the eternal snows—eternal, ever since Wednesday—that we never heard Mrs. Prothero's first cry from her igloo at the bottom of the garden. Or, if we heard it at all, it was, to us, like the far-off challenge of our enemy and prey, the neighbor's polar cat. But soon the voice grew louder.

"Fire!" cried Mrs. Prothero, and she beat the dinner gong.

---

1. **Hudson Bay:** a large body of water in Canada.

## GUIDED READING

**LITERAL QUESTIONS**

**1a.** What is it that Thomas can never remember about the snow at Christmastime? (He forgets how long it snowed on any particular Christmas.)

**2a.** Where are the boys and Mrs. Prothero when she shouts, "Fire!" (The boys are in her garden; she is in her "igloo.")

**INFERENTIAL QUESTIONS**

**1b.** What do you think Thomas implies by admitting his blurred memory? (This story, containing some one-time events such as a fire, is a composite of many boyhood Christmases.)

**2b.** What do these locations tell you about the speaker and his story? (The factual and the imaginative coexist for the boy, and the adult recreates this state of mind in his recollection of the story.)

And we ran down the garden, with the snow-balls in our arms, toward the house; and smoke, indeed, was pouring out of the dining room, and the gong was bombilating[2] and Mrs. Prothero was announcing ruin like a town crier in Pompeii.[3] This was better than all the cats in Wales standing on the wall in a row. We bounded into the house, laden with snowballs, and stopped at the open door of the smoke-filled room. Something was burning all right; perhaps it was Mr. Prothero, who always slept there after midday dinner with a newspaper over his face. But he was standing in the middle of the room, saying, "A fine Christmas!" and smacking at the smoke with a slipper.

"Call the fire brigade," cried Mrs. Prothero as she beat the gong.

"They won't be there," said Mr. Prothero, "it's Christmas."

There was no fire to be seen, only clouds of smoke and Mr. Prothero standing in the middle of them, waving his slipper as though he were conducting.

"Do something," he said.

And we threw all our snowballs into the smoke—I think we missed Mr. Prothero—and ran out of the house to the telephone box.[4]

"Let's call the police as well," Jim said.

"And the ambulance."

"And Ernie Jenkins, he likes fires."

But we only called the fire brigade, and soon the fire engine came and three tall men in helmets brought a hose into the house and Mr. Prothero got out just in time before they turned it on. Nobody could have had a noisier Christmas Eve. And when the firemen turned off the hose and were standing in the wet, smoky room, Jim's aunt, Miss Prothero, came downstairs and peered in at them. Jim and I waited, very quietly,

to hear what she would say to them. She said the right thing, always. She looked at the three tall firemen in their shining helmets, standing among the smoke and cinders and dissolving snowballs, and she said: "Would you like anything to read?"

Years and years and years ago, when I was a boy, when there were wolves in Wales, and birds the color of red-flannel petticoats whisked past the harp-shaped hills, when we sang and wallowed all night and day in caves that smelt like Sunday afternoons in damp front farmhouse parlors, and we chased, with the jawbones of deacons, the English and the bears, before the motor car, before the wheel, before the duchess-faced horse, when we rode the daft and happy hills bareback, it snowed and it snowed. But here a small boy says: "It snowed last year, too. I made a snowman and my brother knocked it down and I knocked my brother down and then we had tea."

"But that was not the same snow," I say. "Our snow was not only shaken from whitewash buckets down the sky, it came shawling[5] out of the ground and swam and drifted out of the arms and hands and bodies of the trees; snow grew overnight on the roofs of the houses like a pure and grandfather moss, minutely white-ivied the walls and settled on the postman, opening the gate, like a dumb, numb thunderstorm of white, torn Christmas cards."

"Were there postmen then, too?"

"With sprinkling eyes and wind-cherried noses, on spread, frozen feet they crunched up to the doors and mittened on them manfully. But all that the children could hear was a ringing of bells."

"You mean that the postman went rat-a-tat-tat and the doors rang?"

"I mean that the bells that the children could hear were inside them."

"I only hear thunder sometimes, never bells."

---

2. **bombilating:** buzzing or droning; here, as loudly as if a bomb were going off.
3. **Pompeii** [pom pā′]: ancient city in Italy destroyed in A.D. 79 by the eruption of a volcano.
4. **telephone box:** public telephone booth.

---

5. **shawling:** covering the ground like a shawl.

*A Child's Christmas in Wales* 283

**AT A GLANCE**

■ The boys run to the fire, then call the fire brigade, which comes to put it out.
■ Thomas recalls the great snows of his Christmases via a conversation with "a small boy" who asks him questions.

**1 STYLE: ALLUSION**

The reference to Pompeii is an exaggeration that lends additional humor to an already funny situation.

**2 IRONY**

Mr. Prothero is scarcely more effective awake then he would be if he had been taking his customary nap.

**3 DIALOGUE**

The incongruous question seems to contrast humorously with the speaker's assertion that this aunt "said the right thing, always." However, in the context of Thomas's whimsical evocation of childhood, the lady's hospitable question may indeed have been "the right thing" to say, under the circumstances.

**4 STYLE: TONE**

Originality, exaggeration, and humor mark Thomas's affectionate recollections of old times.

**5 STYLE: FIGURATIVE LANGUAGE**

The snow, active and encompassing, serves as a dynamic image that molds and envelops his varied perceptions of a Christmastime.

## GUIDED READING

**LITERAL QUESTION**

**1a.** What does a second voice in the story ask Thomas? (The voice asks him if there were postmen in the old days and if doors rang.)

**INFERENTIAL QUESTION**

**1b.** What is the difference between the second speaker's questions and the first speaker's answers? (The one asking questions tries to find factual logic in the story; the answers suggest that the true story lies in feelings that a factual account would not convey.)

**1 STYLE: FIGURATIVE LANGUAGE**

These uncommon metaphors paint appealing pictures in familiar words for the literal-minded youngster asking questions.

**2 STYLE: IMAGERY**

The images convey the bone-deep cold in which the postman moves as well as a vision of a child sliding down a snowy hill on a tea tray.

**3 POINT OF VIEW**

Writing as an adult, Thomas convincingly expresses both the child's unenthusiastic toleration of "Useful Presents" and the adult's nostalgic fondness for them.

**4 RESPONSE JOURNAL**

Have students write about gifts they have received that were particularly special for one reason or another.

"There were church bells, too."

"Inside them?"

"No, no, no, in the bat-black, snow-white belfries,[6] tugged by bishops and storks. And they 1 rang their tidings over the bandaged town, over the frozen foam of the powder and ice-cream hills, over the crackling sea. It seemed that all the churches boomed for joy under my window; and the weathercocks[7] crew for Christmas, on our fence."

"Get back to the postmen."

"They were just ordinary postmen, fond of walking and dogs and Christmas and the snow. They knocked on the doors with blue knuckles. . . ."

"Ours has got a black knocker. . . ."

"And then they stood on the white Welcome mat in the little, drifted porches and huffed and puffed, making ghosts with their breath, and jogged from foot to foot like small boys wanting to go out."

---

6. **belfries:** towers in which bells are hung.
7. **weathercocks:** weather vanes shaped like roosters.

**284** *Nonfiction*

"And then the Presents?"

"And then the Presents, after the Christmas box. And the cold postman, with a rose on his 2 button nose, tingled down the tea-tray-slithered run of the chilly glinting hill. He went in his ice-bound boots like a man on fishmonger's slabs.[8] He wagged his bag like a frozen camel's hump, dizzily turned the corner on one foot, and was gone."

"Get back to the Presents."

"There were the Useful Presents: engulfing mufflers of the old coach days, and mittens made for giant sloths; zebra scarfs of a substance like silky gum that could be tug-o-warred down to the galoshes; blinding tam-o'-shanters[9] like patchwork tea cozies[10] and bunny-suited busbies and balaclavas[11] for victims of headshrinking tribes; from aunts who always wore wool next to the skin there were mustached and rasping vests that made you wonder why the aunts had 3 any skin left at all; and once I had a little crocheted nose bag from an aunt now, alas, no longer whinnying with us. And pictureless books in which small boys, though warned with quotations not to, *would* skate on Farmer Giles's pond and did and drowned; and books that told me everything about the wasp, except why."

"Go on to the Useless Presents."

"Bags of moist and many-colored jelly babies and a folded flag and a false nose and a tram conductor's cap and a machine that punched tickets 4 and rang a bell; never a catapult;[12] once, by mistake that no one could explain, a little hatchet; and a celluloid duck that made, when you pressed it, a most unducklike sound, a mewing moo that an ambitious cat might make who

---

8. **fishmonger's slabs:** cold surfaces on which sellers of fish display their goods.
9. **tam-o'-shanters:** soft, flat woolen caps of Scottish origin.
10. **tea cozies:** thick covers used to keep teapots warm.
11. **busbies and balaclavas** [bal'ə kla'vəz]: Busbies are tall fur hats worn by British soldiers; balaclavas are hoodlike knitted caps covering the head, neck, and shoulders.
12. **catapult:** slingshot.

---

## GUIDED READING

**LITERAL QUESTIONS**

**1a.** According to Thomas, what were postmen fond of? (walking, dogs, Christmas, and snow)

**2a.** What does Thomas say about the "Useful" tam-o'-shanters and balaclavas? (The tam-o'-shanters were blinding and the balaclavas would only fit shrunken heads.)

**INFERENTIAL QUESTIONS**

**1b.** What do you make of his answer and the fact that the child does not question it? (He's joking, but his literal-minded companion neither questions the statement nor sees the humor in it.)

**2b.** What can you infer about the child Thomas from the adult's description of these gifts? (He regarded the gifts as neither "Useful" nor desirable.)

wished to be a cow; and a painting book in which I could make the grass, the trees, the sea and the animals any color I pleased, and still the dazzling sky-blue sheep are grazing in the red field under the rainbow-billed and pea-green birds. Hardboileds, toffee, fudge and all-sorts, crunches, cracknels, humbugs, glaciers, marzipan, and butterwelsh[13] for the Welsh. And troops of bright tin soldiers who, if they could not fight, could always run. And Snakes-and-Families and Happy Ladders.[14] And Easy Hobbi-Games for Little Engineers, complete with instructions. Oh, easy for Leonardo![15] and a whistle to make the dogs bark to wake up the old man

---

13. **Hardboileds . . . butterwelsh:** different sorts of candy.
14. **Snakes . . . Happy Ladders:** Thomas humorously mixes up the names of two popular British games, Snakes-and-Ladders (a board game) and Happy Families (a card game).
15. **Leonardo** [lā′ə när′dō]: Leonardo da Vinci (1452–1519), ingenious Italian artist, architect, and engineer.

next door to make him beat on the wall with his stick to shake our picture off the wall. And a packet of cigarettes: you put one in your mouth and you stood at the corner of the street and you waited for hours, in vain, for an old lady to scold you for smoking a cigarette, and then with a smirk you ate it. And then it was breakfast under the balloons.''

''Were there uncles, like in our house?''

''There are always uncles at Christmas. The same uncles. And on Christmas mornings, with dog-disturbing whistle and sugar fags,[16] I would scour the swatched town for the news of the little world, and find always a dead bird by the white post office or by the deserted swings; perhaps a robin, all but one of his fires out. Men and women wading or scooping back from chapel, with taproom noses and wind-bussed cheeks, all albinos,[17] huddled their stiff black jarring feath-

---

16. **sugar fags:** candy cigarettes.
17. **albinos** [al bī′nōz]: persons with pale skin and almost white hair.

*A Child's Christmas in Wales*  **285**

AT A GLANCE

■ Thomas describes the presents he liked—a coloring book and candy.
■ After Christmas breakfast he would go exploring in town.

1 **STYLE: TONE**

Thomas makes good-humored fun of the predictable or complicated games considered perfect for children of a certain age.

2 **THEME**

The presence of the same uncles, the usual toys, and the perennial Christmas games reinforce the sense of ritual and the impression that Thomas is packing the memories of many Christmases into one glorious Christmas.

---

## GUIDED READING

**LITERAL QUESTION**

**1a.** Why did Thomas especially like a painting book? (He could make things any color he pleased.)

**INFERENTIAL QUESTION**

**1b.** What do you think his preference for a painting book implies? (He delighted in using his imagination; throughout his story, he portrays common things in uncommon and original ways.)

- Christmas always brought the same relatives together.
- The blast of a boy's whistle made people stop eating to look.

## 1 AUDIENCE

A cozy atmosphere, abundant food, mistletoe, and chestnuts speak to a universal feeling about the season with which most readers can identify.

## 2 THEME

The unwanted aunts, in sad contrast to the vitality and conviviality of the day, are ever present and unchanging; they, too, are traditional.

## 3 IMAGERY

This remarkable scene mingles the predictability of ritual with broad comedy.

---

1 ers against the irreligious snow. Mistletoe hung from the gas brackets[18] in all the front parlors; there was sherry and walnuts and bottled beer and crackers by the dessertspoons; and cats in their furabouts watched the fires; and the high-heaped fire spat, all ready for the chestnuts and the mulling pokers. Some few large men sat in the front parlors, without their collars, uncles almost certainly, trying their new cigars, holding them out judiciously at arms' length, returning them to their mouths, coughing, then holding them out 2 again as though waiting for the explosion; and some few small aunts, not wanted in the kitchen, nor anywhere else for that matter, sat on the very edges of their chairs, poised and brittle, afraid to break, like faded cups and saucers.''

Not many those mornings trod the piling streets: an old man always, fawn-bowlered,[19] yellow-gloved and, at this time of year, with spats of snow,[20] would take his constitutional to the white bowling green and back, as he would take it wet or fire on Christmas Day or Doomsday; sometimes two hale young men, with big pipes blazing, no overcoats and wind-blown scarfs, would trudge, unspeaking, down to the forlorn sea, to work up an appetite, to blow away the fumes, who knows, to walk into the waves until nothing of them was left but the two curling smoke clouds of their inextinguishable briars.[21] Then I would be slapdashing home, the gravy smell of the dinners of others, the bird smell, the brandy, the pudding and mince, coiling up to my nostrils, when out of a snow-clogged side lane would come a boy the spit of myself, with a pink-tipped cigarette and the violet past of a black eye, cocky as a bullfinch, leering all to himself. I hated him on sight and

---

18. **gas brackets:** wall fixtures holding the burners for gaslights, which provided illumination before electricity.
19. **fawn-bowlered:** wearing a light tan bowler, or derby hat.
20. **spats of snow:** Spats are cloth or leather coverings worn over the instep and ankle.
21. **briars:** pipes made from the root of a briar, which is a shrub.

**286** *Nonfiction*

---

3 sound, and would be about to put my dog whistle to my lips and blow him off the face of Christmas when suddenly he, with a violet wink, put *his* whistle to *his* lips and blew so stridently, so high, so exquisitely loud that gobbling faces, their cheeks bulged with goose, would press against their tinseled windows, the whole length of the white echoing street. For dinner we had turkey and blazing pudding, and after dinner the uncles sat in front of the fire, loosened all buttons, put their large moist hands over their watch chains, groaned a little, and slept. Mothers, aunts, and sisters scuttled to and fro, bearing tureens.[22] Auntie Bessie, who had already been frightened, twice, by a clockwork mouse, whimpered at the sideboard and had some elderberry wine. The dog was sick. Auntie Dosie had to have three aspirins, but Auntie Hannah, who liked port,[23] stood in the middle of

---

22. **tureens:** deep, covered serving bowls.
23. **port:** sweet red wine.

---

## GUIDED READING

### LITERAL QUESTION

**1a.** On what mornings would the fawn-bowlered man take his constitutional? (all mornings—Christmas or Doomsday, in wet or fire)

### INFERENTIAL QUESTION

**1b.** What does this detail suggest about life in this Welsh town? (A quality of timelessness—tradition and habit—characterized the people and their activities.)

the snowbound backyard, singing like a big-bosomed thrush. I would blow up balloons to see how big they would blow up to; and, when they burst, which they all did, the uncles jumped and rumbled. In the rich and heavy afternoon, the uncles breathing like dolphins and the snow descending, I would sit among festoons²⁴ and Chinese lanterns and nibble dates and try to make a model man-o'-war,²⁵ following the Instructions for Little Engineers, and produce what might be mistaken for a seagoing tramcar.²⁶ Or I would go out, my bright new boots squeaking, into the white world, onto the seaward hill, to call on Jim and Dan and Jack and to pad through the still streets, leaving huge deep footprints on the hidden pavements.

"I bet people will think there's been hippos."

"What would you do if you saw a hippo coming down our street?"

"I'd go like this, bang! I'd throw him over the railings and roll him down the hill and then I'd tickle him under the ear and he'd wag his tail."

"What would you do if you saw *two* hippos?"

Iron-flanked and bellowing he-hippos clanked and battered through the scudding snow toward us as we passed Mr. Daniel's house.

"Let's post Mr. Daniel a snowball through his letter box."

"Let's write things in the snow."

"Let's write, 'Mr. Daniel looks like a spaniel' all over his lawn."

Or we walked on the white shore. "Can the fishes see it's snowing?"

The silent one-clouded heavens drifted on to the sea. Now we were snow-blind travelers lost on the north hills, and vast dewlapped²⁷ dogs, with flasks round their necks, ambled and

shambled up to us, baying "Excelsior."²⁸ We returned home through the poor streets where only a few children fumbled with bare red fingers in the wheel-rutted snow and catcalled after us, their voices fading away, as we trudged uphill, into the cries of the dock birds and the hooting of ships out in the whirling bay. And then, at tea the recovered uncles would be jolly; and the ice cake loomed in the center of the table like a marble grave. Auntie Hannah laced her tea with rum, because it was only once a year.

Bring out the tall tales now that we told by the fire as the gaslight bubbled like a diver. Ghosts whooed like owls in the long nights when I dared not look over my shoulder; animals lurked in the cubbyhole under the stairs where the gas meter ticked. And I remember that we went singing carols once, when there wasn't

---

24. **festoons:** decorative chains.
25. **man-o'-war:** type of warship.
26. **tramcar:** streetcar or trolley car.
27. **dewlapped:** having fleshy folds around the throat.

---

28. **Excelsior** [ik sel′sē ər]: Latin word meaning "onward and upward." Thomas imagines that St. Bernard dogs are urging them forward.

*A Child's Christmas in Wales* **287**

## AT A GLANCE

- While uncles dozed, Thomas would play with friends outside.
- At afternoon tea the family had ice cake and told stories.

### 1 PURPOSE

Thomas mingles many scenes, textures, and feelings to distill for the reader the essence of a childhood Christmas.

### 2 MAIN IDEA

The magic of the holiday spirit and the children's imaginations could make all things possible, even bellowing hippos chasing them through the snow.

### 3 STYLE: SIMILE

This simile comparing the cake to a tombstone marks an abrupt shift in tone, in contrast with the "jolly" uncles. The impression created is that holiday experience is many-faceted and has its wistful, even melancholy, moments.

### 4 STYLE: FIGURATIVE LANGUAGE

Coexisting with the comfortable and familiar experience are disquieting and strange possibilities for the child: ghosts *whooing* like owls and animals lurking in the cubbyhole.

## GUIDED READING

### LITERAL QUESTION

**1a.** What was the boy's reaction when the "ghosts whooed"? (He dared not look over his shoulder.)

### INFERENTIAL QUESTION

**1b.** What might the presence of ghosts imply? (The imagination has its dark side, inventing some creatures that are not friendly, tail-wagging hippos. Childhood is a time of many contrasting feelings and fantasies.)

- The boys go caroling at a dark house and run home in fright after a strange voice joins them.
- On Christmas night the family plays music and sings.
- The speaker prays and goes to sleep.

**1 STYLE: IMAGERY**

"Smoke-colored snow," "music rising," and "falling night" create a sense of closure and repose.

REFLECTING ON THE SELECTION

What might "some words" said to the "holy darkness" mean? (Possible answer: He ends a well-lived Christmas with some prayers; the darkness where dangers might lurk also inspires spiritual feelings; to a child the presence of God is general and enveloping.)

STUDY QUESTIONS

1. much time has passed; all very much alike
2. Smoke pours from dining room; he and Jim call firemen; they put out fire.
3. "Were there postmen then, too?"; "Were the church bells actually inside the children?"; "Were there uncles, like in our house?" Imaginative answers confuse boy.
4. opening presents; caroling
5. ■ "fur-capped and moccasined trappers"—saw themselves as great hunters
   ■ "Eskimo-footed marksmen"—conveys coldness
6. insists snow is different now; remembers bells ringing when there was no doorbell
7. The Christmas celebration was exciting; life seemed magical. The final sentence suggests religion was comforting and that childhood is sacred.

---

the shaving of a moon to light the flying streets. At the end of a long road was a drive that led to a large house, and we stumbled up the darkness of the drive that night, each one of us afraid, each one holding a stone in his hand in case, and all of us too brave to say a word. The wind through the trees made noises as of old and unpleasant and maybe webfooted men wheezing in caves. We reached the black bulk of the house.

"What shall we give them? Hark the Herald?"

"No," Jack said, "Good King Wenceslas. I'll count three."

One, two, three, and we began to sing, our voices high and seemingly distant in the snow-felted darkness round the house that was occupied by nobody we knew. We stood close together, near the dark door.

> "Good King Wenceslas looked out
> On the Feast of Stephen . . ."

And then a small, dry voice, like the voice of someone who has not spoken for a long time, joined our singing: a small, dry, eggshell voice from the other side of the door: a small dry voice through the keyhole. And when we stopped running we were outside *our* house; the front room

was lovely; balloons floated under the hot-water-bottle-gulping gas; everything was good again and shone over the town.

"Perhaps it was a ghost," Jim said.

"Perhaps it was trolls,"[29] Dan said, who was always reading.

"Let's go in and see if there's any jelly left," Jack said. And we did that.

Always on Christmas night there was music. An uncle played the fiddle, a cousin sang "Cherry Ripe," and another uncle sang "Drake's Drum." It was very warm in the little house. Auntie Hannah, who had got on to the parsnip wine, sang a song about Bleeding Hearts and Death, and then another in which she said her heart was like a Bird's Nest; and then everybody laughed again; and then I went to bed. Looking through my bedroom window, out into the moon-light and the unending smoke-colored snow, I could see the lights in the windows of all the other houses on our hill and hear the music rising from them up the long, steadily falling night. I turned the gas down, I got into bed. I said some words to the close and holy darkness, and then I slept.

---

29. **trolls:** mythical dwarves or giants who live in caves.

**STUDY QUESTIONS**

**Recalling**

1. Why have Thomas' memories of individual Christmases become mixed together?
2. Briefly retell what Thomas remembers of the Protheros' fire.
3. What various questions does the small boy ask the adult Thomas about the author's memories of Christmas (pages 283–285)? How does Thomas answer him in each case?
4. Describe two highlights of the Thomas family's Christmas Day celebration.

**Interpreting**

5. Thomas often exaggerates in describing real people—for example, when Mrs. Prothero announces "ruin like a town crier in Pompeii." Find two other such descriptions of people, and explain the effect of each.
6. Explain how Thomas' conversation with the small boy shows that memory cannot always be trusted.
7. What do you think Dylan Thomas wanted us to understand about his childhood from reading "A Child's Christmas in Wales"? What does the very last sentence add to his picture of his childhood?

**Extending**

8. If you were writing a new version of "A Child's Christmas," what colorful winter and holiday images of your own would you use?

## VIEWPOINT

A review in the *Atlantic Monthly* pointed out the importance of sound in Dylan Thomas' writing:

> The poetry in Thomas' prose is the delight in sound, the determination to make every word do its utmost.

■ Choose a passage from "A Child's Christmas in Wales," and read it aloud. Which words in particular do you think Thomas chose for their sounds? What do you think the sounds of these words add to the effect of the passage?

## LITERARY FOCUS

### Figurative Language

**Figurative language** consists of expressions that are not literally true but express some truth *beyond* the literal level. Such language shakes ordinary speech from its usual patterns by combining words and images in an unusual way. Figurative language also shakes up our imaginations as we read and helps us see the world in a new way.

The most common types of figurative language connect seemingly unlike things. A **simile** connects two items by using the words *like* or *as*: For example, Thomas' "his bag like a frozen camel's hump" is a simile. A **metaphor**, on the other hand, equates the two items: For instance, "My love is a red, red rose" is a metaphor.

An **implied metaphor** hints at the connection rather than expressing it directly. Most of Thomas' metaphors are implied: For example, he describes the small dry voice that joins the carolers as an "eggshell voice," thus connecting two very dissimilar things in a striking way. Such expressions often startle us with their freshness and make us stop to think about the image the writer has created.

### Thinking About Figurative Language

■ Thomas' various memories are held together by images of snow. Find two similes and two metaphors that he uses to describe snow. Explain what effect is created by each comparison.

## VOCABULARY

### Hyphenated Adjectives

Dylan Thomas often uses hyphenated adjectives to make vivid descriptions with few words. For example, he describes letter carriers in winter as having "wind-cherried noses," meaning that their noses were made as red as cherries by the cold wind.

1. In Thomas' memoir find at least ten hyphenated adjectives that are short, vivid, and original, and write them down on a separate sheet.
2. Explain the meaning and effect of five of these adjectives.

## COMPOSITION

### Writing About Tone

■ The tone of a piece of literature expresses the author's attitude toward his or her subject and is conveyed in the language and details the author uses (see page 186). Describe the tone of "A Child's Christmas in Wales." What specific events, settings, details, and words convey Thomas' feeling for his childhood Christmases? You may consider in particular the effect of Thomas' use of figurative language and other unusual word choices. *For help with this assignment, see Lesson 6 in the Writing About Literature Handbook at the back of this book.*

### Writing a Memoir

■ Imagine that you are writing something that you will set aside and read twenty years from now. Describe your memory of a special occasion that is as important to you as Thomas' Christmases were to him. Identify the occasion itself, and describe in specific and vivid terms the setting and details you remember from it. Be sure to express your present feelings about the occasion. You might begin, "I remember when...."

## COMPARING AUTOBIOGRAPHIES

1. Compare the ways in which "Shosha" and "A Child's Christmas in Wales" capture the make-believe and magic of childhood.
2. How much factual information do Singer and Thomas give in their autobiographies? In addition to facts, what impressions about their lives do they share with the reader?

*A Child's Christmas in Wales*  **289**

8. Answers should include details describing the weather and images creating pictures of holiday celebrations, food, sounds, people.

**VIEWPOINT**

Students should select passages that contain

- alliterative phrases: *slink and sidle, wolves in Wales*
- onomatopoeic words: *mewing, moo, bombilating*
- rhyming phrases: *dumb / numb*

Students should explain that sounds create music, establish rhythm, and convey images.

**LITERARY FOCUS**

**Similes**

- "Like a thunderstorm of white, torn Christmas cards" creates a picture of large snowflakes.
- "Snow grew overnight on the roofs of the houses like a pure and grandfather moss" conveys the idea that snow appeared from nowhere.

**Metaphors**

- "Bandaged town" creates a picture of buildings wrapped in snow.
- "Powder and ice-cream hills" compares the landscape to dessert.

**VOCABULARY**

1. Possible answers: *two-tongued, fish-freezing, Eskimo-footed, bunny-suited, iron-flanked*
2. Answers should explain
   - what is being described
   - what quality is being remarked on
   - why description is apt

**COMPARING AUTOBIOGRAPHIES**

1. *Shosha* describes how children believe magic exists. "Christmas" reveals how children inject fantasy into everyday life.
2. Both provide descriptions of settings and people and information concerning the change from childhood to adulthood. Both convey idea that childhood is magical.

## COMPOSITION: GUIDELINES FOR EVALUATION

### WRITING ABOUT TONE

**Objective**

To analyze how tone of autobiography is created

**Guidelines for Evaluation**

- suggested length: three to five paragraphs
- should state Thomas' attitude toward childhood Christmases
- should cite details that convey this attitude
- should include examples of figurative language
- should explain how language shapes tone

### WRITING A MEMOIR

**Objective**

To create a vivid recollection of an event

**Guidelines for Evaluation**

- suggested length: 300–500 words
- should identify the occasion
- should include images and details of people, places, events
- should describe the occasion and express the writer's feelings

# LITERARY FOCUS: *Essay*

In French *essai* means "an attempt." Michel de Montaigne [mē shel′ də mon ten′ yə] (1533–1592) applied the term *essais* to his experiments with writing short, personal pieces of nonfiction on various topics. Montaigne pioneered the **essay,** a brief informal piece of prose nonfiction.

An author always has a purpose in writing an essay; he or she writes to communicate a particular idea or opinion on a particular topic. The essayist uses facts, details, incidents, and reasons to develop that idea or support that opinion. We can learn more about the purpose of any essay by looking at the essay's title, its topic, its language, and the particular facts, details, incidents, and reasons the author brings to the essay.

An author's purpose determines whether an essay will be formal or informal. **Formal essays** are serious and impersonal. **Informal essays** are more personal and entertaining. In fulfilling their various purposes, authors of essays use and often mix different kinds of writing: narration, description, persuasion, and exposition.

A **narrative essay** tells a true story, usually to express some larger idea about life. Writers of factual narratives often heighten reader interest by taking advantage of the storytelling techniques used by writers of fiction.

A **descriptive essay** makes its point by creating a verbal picture of a person, place, or object. The use of vivid sensory language and figures of speech helps the reader to form a mental image of the essay's subject.

A **persuasive essay** tries to convince the reader of the author's opinion and sometimes to move the reader to action. This type of essay demonstrates how a skillful author can arrange and interpret facts to influence the ideas of the reader.

An **expository essay** seeks to explain an idea. Anyone who has ever tried to explain a complicated issue will know that logical organization is an important skill for the author of expository essays.

Charles Lindbergh's life (1902–1974) is entwined with the history of aviation. After learning to fly, he performed daredevil stunts at fairs, flew for the U.S. Army, and delivered mail for the first airmail service. In 1927 Lindbergh flew the *Spirit of St. Louis,* a plane he helped design, in the first solo nonstop flight across the Atlantic Ocean. His feat made Lindbergh an international hero and demonstrated to the world the exciting future of aviation. Later his support helped gain acceptance for early rocket research.

The following selection is an excerpt from Lindbergh's Pulitzer Prize–winning book about his historic transatlantic flight.

■ Being alone can be scary. What do you miss most?

*Charles Lindbergh*

## from **The Spirit of St. Louis**

I'm flying along dreamily when it catches my eye, that black speck on the water two or three miles southeast. I realize it's there with the same jerk to awareness that comes when the altimeter[1] needle drops too low in flying blind. I squeeze my lids together and look again. A boat! A small boat! Several small boats, scattered over the surface of the ocean!

Seconds pass before my mind takes in the full importance of what my eyes are seeing. Then, all feeling of drowsiness departs. I bank the *Spirit of St. Louis* toward the nearest boat and nose down toward the water. I couldn't be wider awake or more keenly aware if the engine had stopped.

Fishing boats! *The coast, the European coast, can't be far away!* The ocean is behind, the flight completed. Those little vessels, those chips on the sea, are Europe. What nationality? Are they Irish, English, Scotch, or French? Can they be from Norway, or from Spain? What fishing bank are they anchored on? How far from the coast do fishing banks extend? It's too early to reach Europe unless a gale blew behind me through the night. Thoughts press forward in confused succession. After fifteen hours of solitude, here's human life and help and safety.

The ocean is no longer a dangerous wilderness. I feel as secure as though I were circling Lambert Field[2] back home. I could land alongside any one of those boats, and someone would throw me a rope and take me on board where there'd be a bunk I could sleep on, and warm food when I woke up.

The first boat is less than a mile ahead—I can see its masts and cabin. I can see it rocking on

1. **altimeter** [al tim′ə tər]: instrument for measuring altitude.

2. **Lambert Field:** airport in St. Louis, Missouri.

- Lindbergh has been flying along dreamily when the sight of fishing boats jolts him to awareness.
- With land seemingly near, the pilot feels more secure.

LITERARY OPTIONS

- narrative essay
- plot
- point of view

THEMATIC OPTIONS

- attempting the untried
- the hero as human being
- reality versus illusion

**1 BACKGROUND**

This is the homestretch of Charles Lindbergh's historic flight; he has been flying twenty-seven straight hours in an attempt to become the first solo pilot to cross the Atlantic.

**2 PLOT: NARRATIVE HOOK**

The presence of fishing boats indicates the pilot is near land and his long-awaited goal.

**3 POINT OF VIEW**

Lindbergh's personal comments enable the reader to recognize the significance of each event and detail he meticulously records. Here he intimately conveys the great sense of relief he felt on seeing the boats.

## GUIDED READING

**LITERAL QUESTION**

**1a.** What are Lindbergh's feelings about seeing human life after so many hours of solitude? (He feels secure and at home.)

**INFERENTIAL QUESTION**

**1b.** What might Lindbergh's restored sense of security imply about the previous hours of his flight? (Loneliness, risk, and doubt had all been part of his flight across the Atlantic Ocean.)

- Lindbergh buzzes the boats in an effort to evoke a response.
- Suddenly losing the "feel" of flight, he focuses on the plane.
- A head, visible on one of the boats, looks pale and lifeless.

**1 STYLE: WORD CHOICE**

Forceful verbs drive the narrative and create clear images. In addition, the percussive *d* sound in "dive down" is repeated in "dropping," "decks," and "dories."

**2 PLOT: RISING ACTION**

Lindbergh continues his vigorous efforts to provoke a response from the mysterious and uncooperative fishing boats.

**3 NARRATIVE ESSAY**

By sharing in this split-second sequence of events, the reader acquires a genuine sense of the emotions arising from Lindbergh's experience and participates in the suspenseful atmosphere.

**4 POINT OF VIEW**

The face that appears but registers nothing begins to seem unreal to the pilot, who has flown many hours over the sea.

---

**1** the water. I close the mixture control and dive down fifty feet above its bow,[3] dropping my wing to get a better view.

But where is the crew? There's no sign of life on deck. Can all the men be out in dories?[4] I climb higher as I circle. No, there aren't any dories. I can see for miles, and the ocean's not rough enough to hide one. Are the fishermen frightened by my plane, swooping down suddenly from the sky? Possibly they never saw a plane before. *Of course* they never saw one out so far over the ocean. Maybe they all hid below the decks when they heard the roar of my engine. Maybe they think I'm some demon from the sky, like those dragons that decorate ancient mariners' charts. But if the crews are so out of contact with the modern world that they hide from the sound of an airplane, they must come from some isolated coastal village above which airplanes never pass. And the boats look too small to have ventured far from home. I have visions of riding the top of a hurricane during the night, with a hundred-mile-an-hour wind drift. Possibly these vessels are anchored north of Ireland, or somewhere in the Bay of Biscay.[5] Then shall I keep on going straight, or turn north, or south?

I fly over to the next boat bobbing up and down on the swells. Its deck is empty too. But as I drop my wing to circle, a man's head appears, thrust out through a cabin porthole, motionless, staring up at me. In the excitement and joy of the moment, in the rush of ideas passing through my reawakened mind, I decide to make that head withdraw from the porthole, come out of the cabin, body and all, and to point toward the Irish coast. No sooner have I made the decision than I realize its futility. Probably that fisherman can't speak English. Even if he can, he'll be too star-

tled to understand my message, and reply. But I'm already turning into position to dive down past the boat. It won't do any harm to try. Why deprive myself of that easy satisfaction? Probably if I fly over it again, the entire crew will come on deck. I've talked to people before from a plane, flying low with throttled engine,[6] and received the answer through some simple gesture—a nod or an outstretched arm.

**2** I glide down within fifty feet of the cabin, close the throttle, and shout as loudly as I can: "WHICH WAY IS IRELAND?"

How extraordinary the silence is with the engine idling! I look back under the tail, watching the fisherman's face for some sign of understanding. **3** But an instant later, all my attention is concentrated on the plane. For I realize that I've lost the "feel" of flying. I shove the throttle open, and watch the air-speed indicator while I climb and circle. As long as I keep the needle above sixty miles an hour, there's no danger of stalling. Always before, I've known instinctively just what condition my plane was in—whether it had flying speed or whether it was stalling, and how close to the edge it was riding in between. I didn't have to look at the instruments. Now, the pressure of the stick no longer imparts its message clearly to my hand. I can't tell whether air is soft or solid.

When I pass over the boat a third time, the head is still at the porthole. It hasn't moved or **4** changed expression since it first appeared. It came as suddenly as the boats themselves. It seems as lifeless. I didn't notice before how pale it is—or am I now imagining its paleness? It looks like a severed head in that porthole, as though a guillotine[7] had dropped behind it. I feel baffled. After all, a man who dares to show his face would hardly fear to show his body. There's

---

3. **bow** [bou]: front of a boat.
4. **dories**: small fishing boats.
5. **Bay of Biscay**: that part of the Atlantic Ocean that lies between the western coast of France and the northern coast of Spain.

6. **with throttled engine**: with an engine that has been choked off.
7. **guillotine** [gil′ə tēn′]: machine consisting of a large wooden frame and a sharp blade, used for beheading prisoners condemned to death.

**292** *Nonfiction*

---

*GUIDED READING*

**LITERAL QUESTIONS**

**1a.** Where does Lindbergh suppose that the sailors might have come from? (some place above which airplanes never fly)

**2a.** What had Lindbergh always known instinctively before he lost the "feel" of flying? (his flying speed and whether or not his plane was stalling)

**INFERENTIAL QUESTIONS**

**1b.** What do you think is the serious implication if his guess is correct? (He fears that he is far off course—a serious error or accident, considering his unprecedented undertaking.)

**2b.** What could the absence of his usual instinctive knowledge indicate? (Confusion about his location and frustration at the unresponsive people have shaken his confidence.)

Charles Lindbergh and the
*Spirit of St. Louis.*

something unreal about these boats. They're as weird as the night's temples, as those misty islands of Atlantis,[8] as the fuselage's phantoms[9] that rode behind my back.

Why don't sailors gather on the decks to watch my plane? Why don't they pay attention to my circling and shouting? What's the matter with this strange flight, where dreams become reality, and reality returns to dreams? But these aren't vessels of cloud and mist. They're tangible, made of real substance like my plane—sails furled, ropes coiled neatly on the decks, masts swaying back and forth with each new swell. Yet the only sign of crew is that single head, hanging motionless through the cabin porthole. It's like ''The Rime of the Ancient Mariner''[10] my mother

---

8. **Atlantis:** legendary island continent that, according to ancient myth, sank into the Atlantic Ocean because of the wickedness of its people.
9. **fuselage's** [fū′sə lazh′əz] **phantoms:** smoke from the airplane's engines. The fuselage is the plane's body.
10. **''The Rime of the Ancient Mariner'':** long narrative poem by the English writer, Samuel Taylor Coleridge (1772–1834). The line quoted from the poem describes a ghost ship.

used to read aloud. These boats remind me of the ''painted ship upon a painted ocean.''

I want to stay, to circle again and again, until that head removes itself from the porthole and the crews come out on deck. I want to see them standing and waving like normal, living people. I've passed through worlds and ages since my last contact with other men. I've been away, far away, planets and heavens away, until only a thread was left to lead me back to earth and life. I've followed that thread with swinging compasses, through lonely canyons, over pitfalls of sleep, past the lure of enchanted islands, fearing that at any moment it would break. And now I've returned to earth, returned to these boats bobbing on the ocean. I want an earthly greeting. I deserve a warmer welcome back to the fellowship of men.

Shall I fly over to another boat and try again to raise the crew? No, I'm wasting minutes of daylight and miles of fuel. There's nothing but frustration to be had by staying longer. It's best to leave. There's something about this fleet that tries my mind and spirit, and lowers confidence with every circle I make. Islands that turn to fog, I understand. Ships without crews, I do not. And that motionless head at the porthole—it's no phantom, and yet it shows no sign of life. I straighten out the *Spirit of St. Louis* and fly on eastward.

Land *must* be somewhere near. Those boats were too small to be anchored far at sea—or were they? When I first saw them, navigating

*The Spirit of St. Louis*   **293**

AT A GLANCE

- The ghostlike boats challenge his sense of reality.
- Lindbergh decides to head on, turning his plane eastward.

**1 STYLE: SIMILE**

These three comparisons convey the powerful, unnerving effect of the strange boats on Lindbergh's sensibilities.

**2 STYLE: ALLUSION**

The reference to the ghost ship of Coleridge's poem reinforces and further illustrates the unearthly quality of the scene.

**3 POINT OF VIEW**

His desire for a warm welcome back to the fellowship of men emphasizes that he is a human being in need, not an invulnerable, conventional hero.

**4 MAIN IDEA**

The mysterious head epitomizes the strangeness of Lindbergh's situation and the confusion he feels between reality and illusion.

## GUIDED READING

### LITERAL QUESTION

**1a.** Where does Lindbergh say he has been since his last contact with living people? (''through worlds and ages, planets and heavens away'')

### INFERENTIAL QUESTION

**1b.** What can you infer from his description of his remarkable journey? (In attempting what no one else has done, Lindbergh feels as if he has been a pioneer on strange planets and through ''other'' times.)

- Lindbergh scans the horizon, uncertain again of his bearings.
- Scarcely able to trust his eyes, Lindbergh sights land.

### 1 MAIN IDEA

"There's no way to tell" sums up the strange uncertainty and enormity of being a pioneer in such a frontier as Lindbergh has challenged.

### 2 NARRATIVE ESSAY

Chronology and measurable facts provide the structure for this account of moving and eerie events.

### 3 THEME

The excitement of discovery and the doubts about what perceptions Lindbergh can trust recur in continuing contrast.

### 4 POINT OF VIEW

Lindbergh shares his unique experience—the questions, sensations, and triumphs; the confusion of illusion and reality.

---

problems seemed past, as though their bows pointed my direction like signposts, saying: "This way to Paris." But as I leave them behind, a few black dots on an endless waste of ocean—about to vanish, as birds vanish into distant air—reason argues that I know nothing more about my latitude than I did before. They might be north of Scotland; they might be south of Ireland. They might be anywhere along the coast. There's no way to tell. And it's dangerous to take for granted that land is very near; even small boats sometimes venture far to sea. The Grand Banks of Newfoundland[11] run hundreds of miles offshore. For all I know, similar shallows may extend from the European side. What can I do but continue on the course I set before, and follow the same plan of navigation?

Patches of blue sky above me are shrinking in size. To the north, heavier storm clouds gather.

---

THE TWENTY-EIGHTH HOUR

*Over the Atantic*

HOURS OF FUEL CONSUMED

NOSE TANK

¼ + ⊥⊥⊥⊤ 1 1

| LEFT WING | CENTER WING | RIGHT WING |
|---|---|---|
| ¼ + 1 1 1 | ¼ + | ¼ + 1 1 1 |

FUSELAGE

⊥⊥⊥⊤ ⊥⊥⊥⊤ 1 1 1

---

**2** Ten fifty-two A.M. Twenty-seven hours behind me. If I've covered sixty degrees of longitude since leaving New York, it's four

---

11. **Grand Banks of Newfoundland:** large shoal, or shallow area, in the North Atlantic southeast of Newfoundland, an island off the coast of Canada.

294  *Nonfiction*

---

hours later here—or about three o'clock in the afternoon. I reset my heading and bring the compass needle back to center.

I keep scanning the horizon through breaks between squalls. Any one of those rain curtains may hide a ship or another fishing fleet. The air is cool, fresh, and pleasantly turbulent. I fly a hundred feet or so above the ocean—now under open sky, now with rain streaming over wings and struts.[12]

**3** Is that a cloud on the northeastern horizon, or a strip of low fog—or—*can it possibly be land?* It looks like land, but I don't intend to be tricked by another mirage. Framed between two gray curtains of rain, not more than ten or fifteen miles away, a purplish blue band has hardened from the haze—flat below, like a waterline—curving on top, as though composed of hills or aged mountains.

I'm only sixteen hours out from Newfoundland. I allowed eighteen and a half hours to strike the Irish coast. If that's Ireland, I'm two and a half hours ahead of schedule. Can this be another, clearer image, like the islands of the morning? Is there something strange about it too, like the fishing fleet and that haunting head? **4** Is each new illusion to become more real until reality itself is meaningless? But my mind is clear. I'm no longer half asleep. I'm awake—alert—aware. The temptation is too great. I can't hold my course any longer. The *Spirit of St. Louis* banks over toward the nearest point of land.

I stare at it intently, not daring to believe my eyes, keeping hope in check to avoid another disappointment, watching the shades and contours unfold into a coast line—a coast line coming down from the north—a coast line bending toward the east—a coast line with rugged shores and rolling mountains. It's much too early to

---

12. **struts:** braces.

---

## GUIDED READING

**1a.** What besides human contact had Lindbergh hoped the "phantom" boats could offer him? (direction to Paris)

**2a.** With what words does he describe the air as he flies through squalls, scanning the horizon? ("cool, fresh, and pleasantly turbulent")

**1b.** What do you think were Lindbergh's emotions as he left the boats behind? (He must have had a period of intense disappointment, doubt, and fear as he groped for a recognizable landmark along hundreds of miles of coast.)

**2b.** What can you infer about Lindbergh from his reaction to flying in a violent storm? (He loves flying with all its challenge, adventure, and risk.)

strike England. France, or Scotland. It's early to be striking Ireland; but that's the nearest land.

A fjorded coast[13] stands out as I approach. Barren islands guard it. Inland, green fields slope up the sides of warted mountains. This *must* be Ireland. It can be no other place than Ireland. The fields are too green for Scotland; the mountains too high for Brittany or Cornwall.[14]

Now, I'm flying above the foam-lined coast, searching for prominent features to fit the chart on my knees. I've climbed to two thousand feet so I can see the contours of the country better. The mountains are old and rounded; the farms small and stony. Rain-glistened dirt roads wind narrowly through hills and fields. Below me lies a great tapering bay; a long, bouldered island; a village. Yes, there's a place on the chart where it all fits—line of ink on line of shore—Valentia and Dingle Bay, *on the southwestern coast of Ireland!*

I can hardly believe it's true. I'm almost exactly on my route, closer than I hoped to come in my wildest dreams back in San Diego. What happened to all those detours of the night around the thunderheads? Where has the swinging compass error gone? The wind above the storm clouds must have blown fiercely on my tail. In edging northward, intuition must have been more accurate than reasoned navigation.

The southern tip of Ireland! On course; over two hours ahead of schedule; the sun still well up in the sky; the weather clearing! I circle again, fearful that I'll wake to find this too a phantom, a mirage fading into mid-Atlantic mist. But there's no question about it; every detail on the chart has its counterpart below; each major feature on the ground has its symbol on the chart. The lines correspond exactly. Nothing in that world of dreams and phantoms was like this. I spiral lower, looking down on the little village. There are boats in the harbor, wagons on the stone-fenced roads. People are running out into the streets, looking up and waving. This is earth again, the earth where I've lived and now will live once more. Here are human beings. Here's a human welcome. Not a single detail is wrong. I've never seen such beauty before— fields so green, people so human, a village so attractive, mountains and rocks so mountainous and rocklike. . . .

Ireland, England, France, Paris! The night at Paris! *This* night at Paris—less than six hours from now—*France and Paris!* It's like a fairy tale. Yesterday I walked on Roosevelt Field; today I'll walk on Le Bourget.[15]

---

13. **fjorded** [fyôrd′əd] **coast:** coastline indented with long narrow bays.
14. **Brittany or Cornwall:** Brittany, which is a province in northwest France, and Cornwall, which is a county in southwest England, both jut out into the Atlantic Ocean.

15. **Roosevelt Field . . . Le Bourget** [lə boor zhā′]: Roosevelt Field is the airport in New York from which Lindbergh took off; Le Bourget is an airport near Paris.

## STUDY QUESTIONS

### Recalling

1. As the piece opens, how long has Lindbergh been in the air? What is the significance to Lindbergh of the "black speck" he sees on the water?

2. Why does Lindbergh want to communicate with the crews of the fishing boats? In what way is he disappointed?

3. Relate the sequence of events in which Lindbergh becomes sure that he is flying over the coast of Ireland. What is his reaction to this information?

4. How do the people on the ground react to the sight of Lindbergh? How does he respond to the sight of them?

*The Spirit of St. Louis* **295**

5. His dream of crossing the Atlantic has become a reality: Fatigue makes real events seem dreamlike.
6. ■ Like an eagle, Lindbergh is making a solitary, daring flight.
   ■ The nickname is not entirely consistent, for Lindbergh also craves the company of others.
7. freedom and adventure; gives running account of his thoughts and emotions
8. Achieving something no one else has done is thrilling and rewarding.

## VIEWPOINT

Lindbergh's descriptions of what he is seeing and his reactions (for example, his first sight of land and initial disbelief) give a sense of immediacy.

## LITERARY FOCUS

1. *exposition:* has been flying over water; *hook:* sees boats; *rising action:* buzzes boats; rechecks navigation plan; *climax:* realizes coastline is Ireland; *falling action:* confirms discovery; sights people; *resolution:* realizes he will soon be in Paris
2. ■ descriptions of the world as seen only from the air; details of flying plane
   ■ allow reader to share new experiences; perspective
3. ■ Personal comments: "How extraordinary the silence is. . . .; There's something unreal about these boats."
   ■ Purpose: to let reader share experience
   ■ Overall idea: Flight was dreamlike, challenging.

## VOCABULARY

1. (d) attached
2. (d) casually
3. (b) give
4. (b) dim
5. (c) usefulness

---

### Interpreting

5. What do you think Lindbergh means when he calls his trip "a strange flight, where dreams become reality, and reality returns to dreams"?
6. On the basis of this selection, explain why The Lone Eagle was an appropriate nickname for Lindbergh. Is his wish to contact the fishermen consistent with that nickname?
7. What do you think Lindbergh likes most about flying? How does this essay share that feeling?

### Extending

8. Why do you think people are driven to establish records, as Lindbergh was?

## VIEWPOINT

Almost thirty years after his historic flight, Charles Lindbergh again excited the world. He published a full-length account of his great exploit. The *New York Times* review of *The Spirit of St. Louis* said that the book

> sustains the tension of the flight and enables the reader to feel himself a stowaway aboard the plane, sharing the dangers, the uncertainties and the eventual triumph.

■ Which parts of the selection made you feel as if you were an eyewitness to Lindbergh's flight?

## LITERARY FOCUS

### The Narrative Essay

A **narrative essay** is a nonfiction work that tells a true story, presenting actual events in chronological order. The chronological organization of a narrative essay is similar to the plot line of a story. Writers of narrative essays thus build reader interest much as short story writers do. In addition, writers of narrative essays use skillfully chosen details to draw their readers into the experience being narrated.

Narrative essays relate facts, but they go beyond the objective reporting of these facts. Writers of narrative essays often offer their personal comments and reflections on the events they relate. Just as a short story has a theme, a narrative essay relates an experience for a particular purpose: to illustrate an idea or to find within the incident some truth about life in general.

**296**   *Nonfiction*

---

### Thinking About the Narrative Essay

1. Using the diagram on page 20 for plot structure in short stories, identify the exposition, narrative hook, rising action, climax, falling action, and resolution in Lindbergh's essay.
2. What details do you think are most effective in drawing us into the events Lindbergh narrates? Why are they so effective?
3. Find an example of a personal comment by Lindbergh on his flight. What is his purpose in writing about his flight? What overall idea does this narrative communicate?

## VOCABULARY

### Antonyms

**Antonyms** are words that have opposite or nearly opposite meanings. *Dangerous* and *secure* are antonyms. The words in capitals are from *The Spirit of St. Louis.* Write the letter of the word that is *most nearly the opposite* of each word in capitals, *as the word is used in the selection.*

1. SEVERED:  (a) lingered  (b) eased  (c) removed  (d) attached
2. INTENTLY:  (a) alertly  (b) angrily  (c) obviously  (d) casually
3. DEPRIVE:  (a) corrupt  (b) give  (c) hasten  (d) react
4. PROMINENT:  (a) distinct  (b) dim  (c) elevated  (d) rounded
5. FUTILITY:  (a) pride  (b) choice  (c) usefulness  (d) beginning

## COMPOSITION

### Writing About a Narrative Essay

■ The creation of suspense is an important part of the storyteller's art, whether the story is fictional or factual. Choose one incident in Lindbergh's essay, and explain how each event raises questions about what will follow.

### Writing a Narrative Essay

■ Write a brief narrative essay about an actual event in which you participated. Use chronological order to structure your account and build suspense. In addition, choose details that give readers an eyewitness view of the event.

---

## COMPOSITION: GUIDELINES FOR EVALUATION

### WRITING ABOUT A NARRATIVE ESSAY

**Objective**
To analyze how a writer creates suspense

**Guidelines for Evaluation**
■ suggested length: one to three paragraphs
■ should describe one incident from essay
■ should isolate several events constituting this incident
■ should show how each event leaves a question unanswered

### WRITING A NARRATIVE ESSAY

**Objective**
To describe an event in a suspenseful way

**Guidelines for Evaluation**
■ suggested length: 150–300 words
■ should relate an event in chronological order
■ should raise questions as to what will happen next
■ should include details that allow the reader to assume the writer's perspective

Hanson Baldwin (born 1903) began his career as a newspaper reporter for the *Baltimore Sun*. A graduate of the U.S. Naval Academy at Annapolis, Baldwin became the military/naval correspondent for the *New York Times* in 1937. His dispatches from Guadalcanal and the western Pacific during World War II earned Baldwin the Pulitzer Prize for Journalism in 1942.

Baldwin's naval background and his skill as a reporter make his account of the sinking of the Royal Mail Steamship *Titanic* read like an eyewitness report, even though Baldwin was only a boy when the disaster occurred. A magnificent luxury liner built by the White Star shipping lines, the *Titanic* was supposedly unsinkable.

■ Confidence enables us to do our best. What can over-confidence lead to?

*Hanson W. Baldwin*

# R.M.S. Titanic

## I

The White Star liner *Titanic*, largest ship the world had ever known, sailed from Southampton[1] on her maiden voyage to New York on April 10, 1912. The paint on her strakes[2] was fair and bright; she was fresh from Harland and Wolff's Belfast yards, strong in the strength of her forty-six thousand tons of steel, bent, hammered, shaped, and riveted through the three years of her slow birth.

There was little fuss and fanfare at her sailing; her sister-ship, the *Olympic*—slightly smaller than the *Titanic*—had been in service for some months and to her had gone the thunder of the cheers.

But the *Titanic* needed no whistling steamers or shouting crowds to call attention to her superlative qualities. Her bulk dwarfed the ships near her as longshoremen singled up her mooring lines and cast off the turns of heavy rope from the dock bollards.[3] She was not only the largest ship afloat, but was believed to be the safest. Carlisle, her builder, had given her double bottoms and had divided her hull[4] into sixteen water-tight compartments, which made her, men thought, unsinkable. She had been built to be and had been described as a gigantic lifeboat. Her designers' dreams of a triple-screw giant,[5] a luxurious, floating hotel, which could speed to New York at twenty-three knots,[6] had been carefully translated from blue prints and mold loft lines at the Belfast yards into a living reality.

---

1. **Southampton:** port on the southern coast of England.
2. **strakes:** protective plates on the body of a ship.

3. **bollards** [bal′ərds]: dock posts to which a ship's mooring lines are tied.
4. **hull:** body of a ship.
5. **triple-screw giant:** The *Titanic* had three propellers.
6. **twenty-three knots:** A knot is a nautical measure of speed equivalent to one nautical mile (6,076 feet) per hour.

*R.M.S. Titanic* **297**

---

---

## GUIDED READING

### LITERAL QUESTION

**1a.** What design features gave people reason to think the *Titanic* was unsinkable? (double bottoms and a hull divided into sixteen watertight compartments)

### INFERENTIAL QUESTION

**1b.** What do you think Baldwin's repeated emphasis on the *Titanic*'s supposed safety might suggest? (The *Titanic*'s reputation could contribute to a dangerous complacence on the part of passengers and crew.)

## AT A GLANCE

- Leaving the dock, the *Titanic* nearly collides with a steamer.
- A warning about icebergs ahead comes over the wireless.

### 1 FORESHADOWING

A ship so large that its slowest speed can be dangerous is off to an "ominous start."

### 2 NARRATIVE ESSAY

Newspaper facts and exact chronology combined with a poetic image of screaming, soaring gulls impart a storylike quality to the account of the sailing.

### 3 STYLE

Alliteration (*steamed smoothly*) and imagery (*faint streamers of brownish smoke*) create the feeling of serenity and leisure on a fair Sunday and enhance the atmosphere Baldwin creates.

### 4 PLOT: NARRATIVE HOOK

This first message of warning interrupts a cheerful scene, introducing conflict and alerting the reader to trouble ahead.

The *Titanic's* sailing from Southampton, though quiet, was not wholly uneventful. As the liner moved slowly toward the end of her dock that April day, the surge of her passing sucked away from the quay[7] the steamer *New York*, moored just to seaward of the *Titanic's* berth. There were sharp cracks as the manila mooring lines of the *New York* parted under the strain. The frayed ropes writhed and whistled through the air and snapped down among the waving crowd on the pier; the *New York* swung toward the *Titanic's* bow,[8] was checked and dragged back to the dock barely in time to avert a collision. Seamen muttered, thought it an ominous start.

Past Spithead and the Isle of Wight[9] the *Titanic* steamed. She called at Cherbourg[10] at dusk and then laid her course for Queenstown.[11]

At 1:30 P.M., on Thursday, April 11, she stood out of Queenstown harbor, screaming gulls soaring in her wake, with 2,201 persons—men, women and children—aboard.

Occupying the Empire bedroom and Georgian suites of the first-class accommodations were many well-known men and women—Colonel John Jacob Astor and his young bride; Major Archibald Butt, military aide to President Taft, and his friend, Frank D. Millet, the painter; John B. Thayer, vice-president of the Pennsylvania Railroad, and Charles M. Hays, president of the Grand Trunk Railway of Canada; W.T. Stead, the English journalist; Jacques Futrelle, French novelist; H. B. Harris, theatrical manager, and Mrs. Harris; Mr. and Mrs. Isidor Straus; and J. Bruce Ismay, chairman and managing director of the White Star line.

Down in the plain wooden cabins of the steerage class[12] were 706 immigrants to the land of promise,[13] and trimly stowed in the great holds was a cargo valued at $420,000: oak beams, sponges, wine, calabashes,[14] and an odd miscellany of the common and the rare.

The *Titanic* took her departure on Fastnet Light[15] and, heading into the night, laid her course for New York. She was due at Quarantine[16] the following Wednesday morning.

Sunday dawned fair and clear. The *Titanic* steamed smoothly toward the west, faint streamers of brownish smoke trailing from her funnels. The purser[17] held services in the saloon[18] in the morning; on the steerage deck aft[19] the immigrants were playing games and a Scotsman was puffing "The Campbells Are Coming" on his bagpipes in the midst of the uproar.

At 9 A.M. a message from the steamer *Caronia* sputtered into the wireless shack:[20]

> Captain, *Titanic*—Westbound steamers report bergs growlers and field ice[21] in 42 degrees N.[22] from 49 degrees to 51 degrees W.[23] 12th April.
>
> Compliments—
> Barr

It was cold in the afternoon; the sun was brilliant, but the *Titanic*, her screws turning

---

7. **quay** [kē]: wharf.
8. **bow** [bou]: ship's front.
9. **Spithead and the Isle of Wight:** Spithead is a sand peninsula off the southern coast of England; the Isle of Wight is an island in the English Channel between England and France.
10. **Cherbourg** [shär'boorg']: port in northwestern France on the English Channel.
11. **Queenstown:** port on the southern coast of Ireland.

12. **steerage class:** section of the ship with the poorest accommodations.
13. **land of promise:** America.
14. **calabashes** [kal'ə bash'əz]: dried fruit of a tropical tree, often used for bowls and water jugs.
15. **Fastnet Light:** lighthouse on the Irish coast.
16. **Quarantine** [kwor'ən tēn']: place in a port where an arriving ship is inspected for carriers of contagious diseases.
17. **purser:** ship's officer concerned with the comfort and welfare of the passengers.
18. **saloon:** large hall for social gatherings on the ship.
19. **aft:** toward the back of the ship.
20. **wireless shack:** cabin for the wireless radio and its operators.
21. **bergs growlers and field ice:** icebergs, smaller icebergs, and stray pieces of ice from an ice field.
22. **42 degrees N.:** 42 degrees north latitude.
23. **from 49 degrees to 51 degrees W.:** from 49 to 51 degrees west longitude.

## GUIDED READING

### LITERAL QUESTIONS

**1a.** What causes the near mishap between the *Titanic* and the *New York*? (The *Titanic's* passing sucked the *New York* away from the dock.)

**2a.** What sort of passengers occupy the first-class accommodations? (people of wealth and rank, many of them well known)

### INFERENTIAL QUESTIONS

**1b.** What might the incident at the dock indicate? (The *Titanic's* size does not preclude trouble, and may even cause it. The crew's inability to anticipate such trouble indicates inexperience that does not bode well.)

**2b.** What can you infer from this impressive passenger list? (The ship, its passengers, and the voyage are not ordinary; these people are unlikely to board a ship they do not trust.)

over at 75 revolutions per minute, was approaching the Banks.[24]

In the Marconi cabin[25] Second Operator Harold Bride, ear-phones clamped on his head, was figuring accounts; he did not stop to answer when he heard MWL, Continental Morse[26] for the nearby Leyland liner, *Californian,* calling the *Titanic.* The *Californian* had some message about the icebergs; he didn't bother then to take it down. About 1:42 P.M. the rasping spark of those days spoke again across the water. It was the *Baltic,* calling the *Titanic,* warning her of ice on the steamer track.[27] Bride took the message down and sent it up to the bridge.[28] The officer-of-the-deck glanced at it; sent it to the bearded master of the *Titanic,* Captain E. C. Smith, a veteran of the White Star service. It was lunch time then; the Captain, walking along the promenade deck, saw Mr. Ismay, stopped, and handed him the message without comment. Ismay read it, stuffed it in his pocket, told two ladies about the icebergs, and resumed his walk. Later, about 7:15 P.M., the Captain requested the return of the message in order to post it in the chart room for the information of officers.

Dinner that night in the Jacobean dining room was gay. It was bitter on deck, but the night was calm and fine; the sky was moonless but studded with stars twinkling coldly in the clear air.

After dinner some of the second-class passengers gathered in the saloon, where the Reverend Mr. Carter conducted a "hymn sing-song." It was almost ten o'clock and the stewards were waiting with biscuits and coffee as the group sang:

> *O, hear us when we cry to Thee*
> *For those in peril on the sea.*

On the bridge Second Officer Lightoller—short, stocky, efficient—was relieved at ten o'clock by First Officer Murdoch. Lightoller had talked with other officers about the proximity of ice; at least five wireless ice warnings had reached the ship; lookouts had been cautioned to be alert; captains and officers expected to reach the field at any time after 9:30 P.M. At 22 knots, its speed unslackened, the *Titanic* plowed on through the night.

Lightoller left the darkened bridge to his relief and turned in. Captain Smith went to his cabin. The steerage was long since quiet; in the first and second cabins[29] lights were going out; voices were growing still, people were asleep. Murdoch paced back and forth on the bridge, peering out over the dark water, glancing now and then at the compass in front of Quartermaster Hichens at the wheel.

In the crow's nest,[30] Lookout Frederick Fleet and his partner, Leigh, gazed down at the water, still and unruffled in the dim, starlit darkness. Behind and below them the ship, a white shadow with here and there a last winking light; ahead of them a dark and silent and cold ocean.

There was a sudden clang. "Dong-dong. Dong-dong. Dong-dong. Dong!" The metal clapper of the great ship's bell struck out 11:30. Mindful of the warnings, Fleet strained his eyes, searching the darkness for the dreaded ice. But there were only the stars and the sea.

In the wireless room, where Phillips, first operator, had relieved Bride, the buzz of the *Californian's* set again crackled into the ear-phones:

---

24. **the Banks:** the Grand Banks of Newfoundland, a large shallow area in the North Atlantic.
25. **Marconi** [mär kō′nē]: **cabin:** another name for the cabin housing the wireless radio. The cabin was named for Guglielmo Marconi (1874–1937), the Italian engineer who developed the wireless radio.
26. **Continental Morse:** international Morse Code, the signaling system used by telegraph operators.
27. **steamer track:** route used by steamships crossing the ocean.
28. **bridge:** platform above the ship's deck. The captain directs the ship from the bridge.

29. **first and second cabins:** accommodations for first- and second-class passengers.
30. **crow's nest:** lookout platform high up on the ship's mast.

*R.M.S. Titanic* **299**

AT A GLANCE

- Additional warnings about icebergs are received but handled casually.
- Lookouts are put on alert, yet the *Titanic*'s speed remains unslackened.

**1 NARRATIVE ESSAY**

This narrative essay juxtaposes precise, objective information such as the exact time with more subjective language *(didn't bother)* or sensory image *(rasping spark)* to create a striking mixture of fact and impression.

**2 PURPOSE**

Without directly commenting, Baldwin expresses his attitude toward the participants' inappropriate behavior by including significant details: Ismay's casual reaction and the time Captain Smith lets elapse.

**3 STYLE: IRONY**

The group unknowingly sings a song that is quite appropriate for the ordeal they will soon be facing.

**4 FORESHADOWING**

The words describing the ocean ahead—*dark, silent, cold*—are words indicative of danger and death.

---

## GUIDED READING

**LITERAL QUESTION**

**1a.** What precaution do the officers take in response to five warnings, and what remains unchanged? (They put lookouts on alert, but the *Titanic* plows on at the same high speed.)

**INFERENTIAL QUESTION**

**1b.** What might these facts taken together imply? (The alert is routine procedure in the face of a warning—five warnings in the case of an "unsinkable ship"—but the threat of icebergs is still not enough to slow down the *Titanic*.)

## 1 PURPOSE

The conversation illustrates one of Baldwin's major points: Disaster could have been averted because the crew had foreknowledge of the threat of icebergs.

## 2 STYLE: IMAGERY

The "monstrous" iceberg bears down on the *Titanic* almost like an active, malevolent force.

## 3 IRONY

This exchange shows the grim irony of the passengers' obliviousness of the impending disaster.

## 4 READING SKILLS: CONTRAST

What the passengers believe is in stark opposition to what the crew members know about the event, the "mortal" hurt to the *Titanic*.

---

**1**

*Californian:* "Say, old man, we are stuck here, surrounded by ice."
*Titanic:* "Shut up, shut up; keep out. I am talking to Cape Race;[31] you are jamming my signals."

Then, a few minutes later—about 11:40...

## II

**2** Out of the dark she came, a vast, dim, white, monstrous shape, directly in the *Titanic's* path. For a moment Fleet doubted his eyes. But she was a deadly reality, this ghastly *thing*. Frantically, Fleet struck three bells—*something dead ahead*. He snatched the telephone and called the bridge:

"Iceberg! Right ahead!"

The First Officer heard but did not stop to acknowledge the message.

"Hard-a-starboard!"[32]

Hichens strained at the wheel; the bow swung slowly to port.[33] The monster was almost upon them now.

Murdoch leaped to the engine-room telegraph. Bells clanged. Far below in the engine-room those bells struck the first warning. Danger! The indicators on the dial faces swung round to "Stop!" Then "Full speed astern!"[34] Frantically the engineers turned great valve wheels; answered the bridge bells. . . .

There was a slight shock, a brief scraping, a small list to port.[35] Shell ice—slabs and chunks of it—fell on the foredeck.[36] Slowly the *Titanic* stopped.

Captain Smith hurried out of his cabin.

"What has the ship struck?"

Murdoch answered, "An iceberg, sir. I hard-a-starboarded and reversed the engines, and I was going to hard-a-port around it, but she was

---

31. **Cape Race:** southeast part of Newfoundland.
32. **"Hard-a-starboard!":** an order for a sharp right turn. *Starboard* is the nautical term for "right."
33. **port:** nautical term for "left."
34. **astern:** in reverse, backward.
35. **list to port:** downward tilt to the left.
36. **foredeck:** front part of the deck.

---

too close. I could not do any more. I have closed the water-tight doors."

Fourth Officer Boxhall, other officers, the carpenter, came to the bridge. The Captain sent Boxhall and the carpenter below to ascertain the damage.

A few lights switched on in the first and second cabins; sleepy passengers peered through porthole glass; some casually asked the stewards:

**3** "Why have we stopped?"

"I don't know, sir, but I don't suppose it is anything much."

In the smoking room a quorum of gamblers and their prey were still sitting around a poker table; the usual crowd of kibitzers[37] looked on. They had felt the slight jar of the collision and had seen an eighty-foot ice mountain glide by the smoking room windows, but the night was **4** calm and clear, the *Titanic* was "unsinkable"; they hadn't bothered to go on deck.

But far below, in the warren[38] of passages on the starboard side forward, in the forward holds and boiler rooms, men could see that the *Titanic's* hurt was mortal. In No. 6 boiler room, where the red glow from the furnaces lighted up the naked, sweaty chests of coal-blackened firemen, water was pouring through a great gash about two feet above the floor plates. This was no slow leak; the ship was open to the sea; in ten minutes there were eight feet of water in No. 6. Long before then the stokers had raked the flaming fires out of the furnaces and had scrambled through the water-tight doors into No. 5 or had climbed up the long steel ladders to safety. When Boxhall looked at the mailroom in No. 3 hold, twenty-four feet above the keel,[39] the mailbags were already floating about in the slushing water. In No. 5 boiler room a stream of water

---

37. **kibitzers** [kib'it sərs]: informal term for spectators who give unwanted advice to players.
38. **warren:** densely populated place.
39. **keel:** the ship's chief support, which runs along its bottom edge.

---

## *GUIDED READING*

### LITERAL QUESTION

**1a.** Why don't people in the smoking room go on deck after they feel a slight jar and see an ice mountain glide by? (The night is calm and clear, and the *Titanic* is "unsinkable.")

### INFERENTIAL QUESTION

**1b.** What do you think this explanation suggests about the passengers' reaction to the accident? (Even after the collision has occurred, the people trust more in the reputation of the ship than in what they actually feel and see.)

spurted into an empty bunker.[40] All six compartments forward of No. 4 were open to the sea; in ten seconds the iceberg's jagged claw had ripped a three-hundred-foot slash in the bottom of the great *Titanic*.

Reports came to the bridge; Ismay in dressing gown ran out on deck in the cold, still, starlit night, climbed up the bridge ladder.

"What has happened?"

Captain Smith: "We have struck ice."

"Do you think she is seriously damaged?"

Captain Smith: "I'm afraid she is."

Ismay went below and passed Chief Engineer William Bell fresh from an inspection of the damaged compartments. Bell corroborated the Captain's statement; hurried back down the glistening steel ladders to his duty. Man after man followed him—Thomas Andrews, one of the ship's designers, Archie Frost, the builder's chief engineer, and his twenty assistants—men who had no posts of duty in the engine room but whose traditions called them there.

On deck, in corridor and stateroom, life flowed again. Men, women, and children awoke and questioned; orders were given to uncover the lifeboats; water rose into the firemen's quarters; half-dressed stokers streamed up on deck. But the passengers—most of them—did not know that the *Titanic* was sinking. The shock of the collision had been so slight that some were not awakened by it; the *Titanic* was so huge that she must be unsinkable; the night was too calm, too beautiful, to think of death at sea.

Captain Smith half ran to the door of the radio shack. Bride, partly dressed, eyes dulled with sleep, was standing behind Phillips, waiting.

"Send the call for assistance."

The blue spark danced: "CQD[41]—CQD— CQD— CQ—"

---

40. **bunker:** large fuel tank.
41. **CQD:** distress signal used during the early years of wireless telegraphy.

Miles away Marconi men heard. Cape Race heard it, and the steamships *La Provence* and *Mt. Temple*.

The sea was surging into the *Titanic's* hold. At 12:20 the water burst into the seamen's quarters through a collapsed fore and aft wooden bulkhead.[42] Pumps strained in the engine rooms—men and machinery making a futile fight against the sea. Steadily the water rose.

The boats were swung out—slowly; for the deckhands were late in reaching their stations, there had been no boat drill, and many of the crew did not know to what boats they were assigned. Orders were shouted; the safety valves had lifted, and steam was blowing off in a great rushing roar. In the chart house Fourth Officer Boxhall bent above a chart, working rapidly with pencil and dividers.

12:25 A.M. Boxhall's position is sent out to a fleet of vessels: "Come at once; we have struck a berg."

To the Cunarder[43] *Carpathia* (Arthur Henry Rostron, Master, New York to Liverpool, fifty-eight miles away): "It's a CQD, old man. Position 41—46 N.; 50—14 W."

The blue spark dancing: "Sinking; cannot hear for noise of steam."

12:30 A.M. The word is passed: "Women and children in the boats." Stewards finish waking their passengers below; life preservers are tied on; some men smile at the precaution. "The *Titanic* is unsinkable." The *Mt. Temple* starts for the *Titanic*; the *Carpathia*, with a double-watch in her stokeholds, radios, "Coming hard." The CQD changes the course of many ships—but not of one; the operator of the *Californian*, nearby, has just put down his ear-phones and turned in.

The CQD flashes over land and sea from

---

42. **bulkhead:** one of the partitions within the ship designed to contain leakage or fire.
43. **Cunarder:** ship owned by the Cunard Lines, a British fleet of ocean liners. The *Titanic* was part of another large shipping fleet, the White Star Line.

*R.M.S. Titanic* **301**

- Fourth Officer Boxhall radios to a fleet of vessels for help.
- Passengers are awakened and lifeboats are swung out.
- Many ships answer the *Titanic*'s distress signal, but the nearby *Californian* does not hear it.

### 1 NARRATIVE ESSAY

The ship continues to seem safe as its size masks the force of impact; nevertheless, it is sinking. Baldwin enters the minds of the passengers, allowing us to share their general feeling that "the night was too calm, too beautiful, to think of death at sea."

### 2 MAIN IDEA

Overconfidence results in lack of organization and preparation for the potential dangers at sea.

### 3 STYLE: SHIFT IN TENSE

Baldwin creates suspense and a sense of immediacy with the countdown that begins and continues in the present tense.

### 4 IRONY

The one ship that could offer immediate help—the ship that in fact sent the *Titanic* an early warning—is not listening now, even as the *Titanic* had failed to heed its warnings earlier.

---

## GUIDED READING

### LITERAL QUESTION

**1a.** What damage did the impact of the collision cause? (A three-hundred-foot slash in the bottom of the ship opened six consecutive watertight compartments.)

### INFERENTIAL QUESTION

**1b.** What do you think makes this harm so ironic? (The hull's double bottom and sixteen watertight compartments were the basis for believing the *Titanic* was unsinkable; both features proved useless in a matter of seconds.)

- Boxhall sends up rockets, and the band strikes up ragtime.
- Lifeboats are lowered, many of them loaded under capacity.

**1 PLOT: CONFLICT**

Engineers heroically battle the overwhelming force of rising water, but the ocean is winning the fight.

**2 PURPOSE**

Baldwin implies criticism of the haphazard evacuation procedure by juxtaposing these two images—the departure of a nearly empty lifeboat and the pathetic scramble of the steerage passengers for safety.

**3 SYMBOL**

All hope for rescue centers on the "dancing spark," but the water is rising and destined to obliterate this symbol of life.

Cape Race to New York; newspaper city rooms leap to life and presses whir.

On the *Titanic,* water creeps over the bulkhead between Nos. 5 and 6 firerooms. She is going down by the head; the engineers—fighting a losing battle—are forced back foot by foot by the rising water. Down the promenade deck, Happy Jock Hume, the bandsman, runs with his instrument.

12:45 A.M. Murdoch, in charge on the starboard side, eyes tragic, but calm and cool, orders boat No. 7 lowered. The women hang back; they want no boat-ride on an ice-strewn sea; the *Titanic* is unsinkable. The men encourage them, explain that this is just a precautionary measure: "We'll see you again at breakfast." There is little confusion; passengers stream slowly to the boat deck. In the steerage the immigrants chatter excitedly.

302   *Nonfiction*

The *Carpathia*'s wireless operator, who was one of the first people to intercept the *Titanic*'s distress signal.

A sudden sharp hiss—a streaked flare against the night; Boxhall sends a rocket toward the sky. It explodes, and a parachute of white stars lights up the icy sea. The band plays ragtime.

No. 8 is lowered, and No. 5. Ismay, still in dressing gown, calls for women and children, handles lines, stumbles in the way of an officer, is told to "get out of here." Third Officer Pitman takes charge of No. 5; as he swings into the boat Murdoch grasps his hand. "Good-by and good luck, old man."

No. 6 goes over the side. There are only twenty-eight people in a lifeboat with a capacity of sixty-five.

A light stabs from the bridge; Boxhall is calling in Morse flashes, again and again, to a strange ship stopped in the ice jam five to ten miles away. Another rocket drops its shower of sparks above the ice-strewn sea and the dying ship.

1:00 A.M. Slowly the water creeps higher; the fore ports of the *Titanic* are dipping into the sea. Rope squeaks through blocks: lifeboats drop jerkily seaward. Through the shouting on the deck comes the sound of the band playing ragtime.

The "Millionaires' Special" leaves the ship—boat No. 1, with a capacity of forty people, carries only Sir Cosmo and Lady Duff Gordon and ten others. Aft, the frightened immigrants mill and jostle and rush for a boat. An officer's fist flies out; three shots are fired in the air, and the panic is quelled.... Four Chinese sneak unseen into a boat and hide in its bottom.

1:20 A.M. Water is coming into No. 4 boiler room. Stokers slice and shovel as water laps about their ankles—steam for the dynamos, steam for the dancing spark! As the water rises, great ash hoes rake the flaming coals from the furnaces. Safety valves pop; the stokers retreat

---

**GUIDED READING**

**LITERAL QUESTIONS**

**1a.** What does the band do as the passengers scramble for safety? (plays ragtime)

**2a.** What is called the "Millionaires' Special"? (the lifeboat that left the *Titanic* with only twelve passengers on board)

**INFERENTIAL QUESTIONS**

**1b.** What does this detail add to the portrayal of the *Titanic*'s final hours? (irony; gallantry; poignancy)

**2b.** What do you think is Baldwin's view of this boat? (He probably views it as a shameful waste and a further indication of the crew's unpreparedness.)

aft, and the water-tight doors clang shut behind them.

The rockets fling their splendor toward the stars. The boats are more heavily loaded now, for the passengers know the *Titanic* is sinking. Women cling and sob. The great screws aft are rising clear of the sea. Half-filled boats are ordered to come alongside the cargo ports and take on more passengers, but the ports are never opened—and the boats are never filled. Others pull for the steamer's light miles away but never reach it; the lights disappear, the unknown ship steams off.

The water rises and the band plays ragtime.

1:30 A.M. Lightoller is getting the port boats off; Murdoch the starboard. As one boat is lowered into the sea a boat officer fires his gun along the ship's side to stop a rush from the lower decks. A woman tries to take her Great Dane into a boat with her; she is refused and steps out of the boat to die with her dog. Millet's "little smile which played on his lips all through the voyage" plays no more; his lips are grim, but he waves good-by and brings wraps for the women.

Benjamin Guggenheim, in evening clothes, smiles and says, "We've dressed up in our best and are prepared to go down like gentlemen."

1:40 A.M. Boat 14 is clear, and then 13, 16, 15 and C. The lights still shine, but the *Baltic* hears the blue spark say, "Engine-room getting flooded."

The *Olympic* signals, "Am lighting up all possible boilers as fast as can."

Major Butt helps women into the last boats and waves good-by to them. Mrs. Straus puts her foot on the gunwale[44] of a lifeboat, then she draws back and goes to her husband: "We have been together many years; where you go I will go." Colonel John Jacob Astor puts his young wife in a lifeboat, steps back, taps a cigarette on fingernail: "Good-by, dearie; I'll join you later."

---

44. **gunwale** [gun'əl]: upper edge of a ship.

---

**5**

1:45 A.M. The foredeck is under water, the fo'c'sle[45] head almost awash; the great stern is lifted high toward the bright stars; and still the band plays. Mr. and Mrs. Harris approach a lifeboat arm in arm.

Officer: "Ladies first, please."

Harris bows, smiles, steps back: "Of course, certainly; ladies first."

Boxhall fires the last rocket, then leaves in charge of boat No. 2.

2:00 A.M. She is dying now; her bow goes deeper, her stern higher. But there must be steam. Below in the stokeholds the sweaty firemen keep steam up for the flaring lights and the dancing spark. The blowing coals slide and tumble over the slanted grate bars; the sea pounds behind that yielding bulkhead. But the spark dances on.

The *Asian* hears Phillips try the new signal—SOS.[46]

Boat No. 4 has left now; boat D leaves ten minutes later. Jacques Futrelle clasps his wife: "Go! It's your last chance; go!" Madame Futrelle is half-forced into the boat. It clears the side.

There are about 660 people in the boats, and 1,500 still on the sinking *Titanic*.

On top of the officers' quarters men work frantically to get the two collapsibles stowed there over the side. Water is over the forward part of A deck now; it surges up the companionways[47] toward the boat deck. In the radio shack, Bride has slipped a coat and lifejacket about Phillips as the first operator sits hunched over his key, sending—still sending—"41—46 N.; 50—14 W. CQD—CQD—SOS—SOS—"

The captain's tired white face appears at the radio-room door: "Men, you have done your full duty. You can do no more. Now, it's every man

---

45. **fo'c'sle** [fōk'səl]: short for "forecastle," the forward upper deck of the ship.
46. **new signal—SOS:** The signal *SOS*—three dots, three dashes, and three dots—replaced *CQD* as a distress signal.
47. **companionways:** stairways leading to the ship's deck from the compartments below.

---

- The crew continues frantic efforts to evacuate the ship and get help.
- The band continues to play.
- Finally the captain dismisses the radio operators from duty.

**1 STYLE: DICTION**

The "splendor" of the desperate rockets suggests the former glory of the sinking *Titanic*.

**2 STYLE: IRONY**

Lifeboats that do not save lives mock the earlier description of the ship as a "gigantic lifeboat."

**3 ANECDOTE**

Anecdotes such as the story about the lady and her dog add an eccentric, almost fictionlike poignancy to this real-life account.

**4 RESPONSE JOURNAL**

Have students respond to these examples of grace in the face of adversity. How might they react in similar circumstances?

**5 REPETITION**

Baldwin's repeated mention of the band's playing makes that event take on special, haunting significance. The band's gallant but pathetic music symbolizes both the valor and the futility of the *Titanic*'s final hours.

---

## GUIDED READING

### LITERAL QUESTIONS

**1a.** For what purpose do the firemen keep the fires going in a doomed ship? (Steam is needed for the lights and the wireless—the "dancing spark.")

**2a.** What do Bride and Phillips do in the radio shack? (Bride slips a coat and a life jacket about Phillips, who continues transmitting the ship's position and SOS.)

### INFERENTIAL QUESTIONS

**1b.** What do you infer from the stokers' action? (They have not given up hope of rescue, and the lights and radio are their only chance.)

**2b.** What might these actions imply about the effect of crisis on people? (It can expose people's deepest values and nature—in the case of these men, friendship, humanity, and duty.)

- The band plays hymns rather than ragtime.
- The "blue spark" and the lights flicker out.
- People panic and jump into the sea.
- The *Titanic* goes under.

## 1 IRONY

Hartley's gesture offers a gentle and ironic contrast to the violence and enormity of the disaster.

## 2 STYLE: SIMILE

The comparison of the vanquished *Titanic* to a dying monster helps to recreate the horror of its last moments as viewed by those in the lifeboats.

## 3 STYLE: IMAGERY

Sparks, previously symbolizing the efforts and hope for rescue, now signify the death of the liner.

## 4 PLOT: CLIMAX

As the *Titanic* goes down, the tragedy is emphasized through the prolonged, agonized description, "one long continuous moan." Baldwin's quoting of this memorable phrase suggests that it comes from an eyewitness account.

for himself." The captain disappears—back to his sinking bridge, where Painter, his personal steward, stands quietly waiting for orders. The spark dances on. Bride turns his back and goes into the inner cabin. As he does so, a stoker, grimed with coal, mad with fear, steals into the shack and reaches for the lifejacket on Phillips' back. Bride wheels about and brains him with a wrench.

2:10 A.M. Below decks the steam is still holding, though the pressure is falling—rapidly. In the gymnasium on the boat deck the athletic instructor watches quietly as two gentlemen ride the bicycles and another swings casually at the punching bag. Mail clerks stagger up the boat-deck stairways, dragging soaked mail sacks. The spark still dances. The band still plays—but not ragtime:

> *Nearer my God to Thee,*
> *Nearer to Thee...*

A few men take up the refrain; others kneel on the slanting decks to pray. Many run and scramble aft, where hundreds are clinging above the silent screws on the great uptilted stern. The spark still dances and the lights still flare; the engineers are on the job. The hymn comes to its **1** close. Bandmaster Hartley, Yorkshireman violinist, taps his bow against a bulkhead, calls for "Autumn" as the water curls about his feet, and the eight musicians brace themselves against the ship's slant. People are leaping from the decks into the nearby water—the icy water. A woman cries, "Oh, save me, save me!" A man answers, "Good lady, save yourself. Only God can save you now." The band plays "Autumn":

> *God of Mercy and Compassion!*
> *Look with pity on my pain....*

The water creeps over the bridge where the *Titanic's* master stands; heavily he steps out to meet it.

2:17 A.M. "CQ—" The *Virginian* hears a ragged, blurred CQ, then an abrupt stop. The blue

spark dances no more. The lights flicker out; the engineers have lost their battle.

2:18 A.M. Men run about blackened decks; leap into the night; are swept into the sea by the curling wave which licks up the *Titanic's* length. Lightoller does not leave the ship; the ship leaves him; there are hundreds like him, but only a few who live to tell of it. The funnels still swim above the water, but the ship is climbing to the perpendicular; the bridge is under and most **2** of the foremast; the great stern rises like a squat leviathan.[48] Men swim away from the sinking ship; others drop from the stern.

The band plays in the darkness, the water lapping upwards:

> *Hold me up in mighty waters,*
> *Keep my eyes on things above,*
> *Righteousness, divine atonement,*
> *Peace and everlas...*

The forward funnel snaps and crashes into the sea: its steel tons hammer out of existence swimmers struggling in the freezing water. **3** Streams of sparks, of smoke and steam, burst from the after funnels. The ship upends to 50—to 60 degrees.

Down in the black abyss of the stokeholds, of the engine-rooms, where the dynamos have whirred at long last to a stop, the stokers and the engineers are reeling against hot metal, the rising water clutching at their knees. The boilers, the engine cylinders, rip from their bed plates; crash through bulkheads; rumble—steel against steel.

The *Titanic* stands on end, poised briefly for the plunge. Slowly she slides to her grave—slowly at first, and then more quickly—quickly—quickly.

**4** 2:20 A.M. The greatest ship in the world has sunk. From the calm, dark waters, where the floating lifeboats move, there goes up, in the white wake of her passing, "one long continuous moan."

---

48. **leviathan** [li vī'ə thən]: huge sea monster

## GUIDED READING

### LITERAL QUESTION

**1a.** What does the captain do when the water comes over the bridge where he stands? (He steps into the water.)

### INFERENTIAL QUESTION

**1b.** What do you think the captain's act implies? (He realizes fully that he can do no more and chooses to go as one in charge of his own fate.)

## III

The boats that the *Titanic* had launched pulled safely away from the slight suction of the sinking ship, pulled away from the screams that came from the lips of the freezing men and women in the water. The boats were poorly manned and badly equipped, and they had been unevenly loaded. Some carried so few seamen that women bent to the oars. Mrs. Astor tugged at an oar handle; the Countess of Rothes took a tiller. Shivering stokers in sweaty, coal-blackened singlets[49] and light trousers steered in some boats; stewards in white coats rowed in others. Ismay was in the last boat that left the ship from the starboard side; with Mr. Carter of Philadelphia and two seamen he tugged at the oars. In one of the lifeboats an Italian with a broken wrist—disguised in a woman's shawl and hat—huddled on the floor boards, ashamed now that fear had left him. In another rode the only baggage saved from the *Titanic*—the carry-all of Samuel L. Goldenberg, one of the rescued passengers.

There were only a few boats that were heavily loaded; most of those that were half empty made but perfunctory efforts to pick up the moaning swimmers, their officers and crew fearing they would endanger the living if they pulled back into the midst of the dying. Some boats beat off the freezing victims; fear-crazed men and women struck with oars at the heads of swimmers. One woman drove her fist into the face of a half-dead man as he tried feebly to climb over the gunwale. Two other women helped him in and stanched the flow of blood from the ring-cuts on his face.

One of the collapsible boats, which had floated off the top of the officers' quarters when the *Titanic* sank, was an icy haven for thirty or forty men. The boat had capsized as the ship

---

49. **singlets:** undershirts.

sank; men swam to it, clung to it, climbed upon its slippery bottom, stood knee-deep in water in the freezing air. Chunks of ice swirled about their legs; their soaked clothing clutched their bodies in icy folds. Colonel Archibald Gracie was cast up there, Gracie who had leaped from the stern as the *Titanic* sank; young Thayer who had seen his father die; Lightoller who had twice been sucked down with the ship and twice blown to the surface by a belch of air; Bride, the second operator, and Phillips, the first. There were many stokers, half-naked; it was a shivering company. They stood there in the icy sea, under the far stars, and sang and prayed—the Lord's Prayer. After a while a lifeboat came and picked them off, but Phillips was dead then or died soon afterward in the boat.

Only a few of the boats had lights; only one—No. 2—had a light that was of any use to the *Carpathia*, twisting through the ice-field to the rescue. Other ships were "coming hard" too; one, the *Californian*, was still dead to opportunity.

The blue sparks still danced, but not the *Titanic's*. *La Provence* to *Celtic*: "Nobody has heard the *Titanic* for about two hours."

It was 2:40 when the *Carpathia* first sighted the green light from No. 2 boat; it was 4:10 when she picked up the first boat and learned that the *Titanic* had foundered. The last of the moaning cries had just died away then.

Captain Rostron took the survivors aboard, boatload by boatload. He was ready for them, but only a small minority of them required much medical attention. Bride's feet were twisted and frozen; others were suffering from exposure; one died, and seven were dead when taken from the boats, and were buried at sea.

It was then that the fleet of racing ships learned they were too late; the *Parisian* heard the weak signals of *MPA*, the *Carpathia*, report the death of the *Titanic*. It was then—or soon afterward, when her radio operator put on his ear-phones—that the *Californian*, the ship that

**AT A GLANCE**

- Survivors in lifeboats leaving the ship fear to return or stop for swimmers.
- The *Carpathia* arrives and picks up lifeboats carrying survivors.

**1 STYLE: SHIFT IN TENSE**

The pace of the narrative slows as it shifts to past tense to tell about the aftermath of the *Titanic's* sinking—the progress of the lifeboats.

**2 READING SKILLS: CONTRAST**

Staggering contrasts in people's behavior and reactions characterize every phase of the *Titanic's* demise.

**3 STYLE: TONE**

The phrase *still dead to opportunity* conveys Baldwin's scorn for the *Californian*.

**4 PLOT: FALLING ACTION**

The *Carpathia* begins its rescue of the survivors of the *Titanic*, who are huddled aboard the lifeboats.

---

## GUIDED READING

**LITERAL QUESTION**

**1a.** Who rowed and steered the lifeboats? (Those who were able: Mrs. Astor, the Countess of Rothes, Mr. Ismay, stewards, stokers, etc.)

**INFERENTIAL QUESTION**

**1b.** What might Baldwin imply by citing such names? (The lines drawn by social class or gender no longer held; survival depended on the fittest pulling together.)

- Survivors get a glimpse of the iceberg.
- Newspapers had fed hopes that the *Titanic*'s company was safe.
- The *Carpathia* brings the 711 survivors to New York.

### 1 STYLE: IMAGERY

The iceberg, formerly a "dim, monstrous shape," now appears as majestic and luxuriously at leisure as the *Titanic* once seemed to be.

### 2 BACKGROUND

Students might need to be reminded that the *Titanic* sank in an age when communication took much more time than it does today. You might ask students how long it would take for such news to spread today.

Survivors of the *Titanic* being picked up by the *Carpathia*.

**306** *Nonfiction*

had been within sight as the *Titanic* was sinking, first learned of the disaster.

And it was then, in all its white-green majesty, that the *Titanic*'s survivors saw the iceberg, tinted with the sunrise, floating idly, pack-ice jammed about its base, other bergs heaving slowly nearby on the blue breast of the sea.

### IV

But it was not until later that the world knew, for wireless then was not what wireless is today, and garbled messages had nourished a hope that all of the *Titanic*'s company were safe. Not until Monday evening, when P. A. S. Franklin, Vice-President of the International Mercantile Marine Company, received relayed messages in New York that left little hope, did the full extent of the disaster begin to be known. Partial and garbled lists of the survivors; rumors of heroism and cowardice; stories spun out of newspaper imagination, based on a few bare facts and many false reports, misled the world, terrified and frightened it. It was not until Thursday night, when the *Carpathia* steamed into the North River,[50] that the full truth was pieced together.

Flashlights flared on the black river when the *Carpathia* stood up to her dock. Tugs nosed about her; shunted her toward Pier 54. Thirty thousand people jammed the streets; ambulances and stretchers stood on the pier; coroners and physicians waited.

In mid-stream the Cunarder dropped over the *Titanic*'s lifeboats; then she headed toward the dock. Beneath the customs letters on the pier stood relatives of the 711 survivors, relatives of the missing—hoping against hope. The *Carpathia* cast her lines ashore; stevedores looped them over bollards. The dense throngs stood quiet as the first survivor stepped down the gangway. The woman half-staggered—led by

---

50. **North River:** southernmost five miles of the Hudson River between New York and New Jersey.

## GUIDED READING

### LITERAL QUESTION

**1a.** How many people await the arrival of the *Carpathia*? (thirty thousand, plus medical attendants, coroners, etc.)

### INFERENTIAL QUESTION

**1b.** What can you infer from this great number of people present to meet 711 survivors? (Many relatives and friends, confused by conflicting newspaper reports, came hoping to find loved ones among the survivors.)

customs guards—beneath her letter. A "low wailing" moan came from the crowd; fell, grew in volume, and dropped again.

Thus ended the maiden voyage of the *Titanic*. The lifeboats brought to New York by the *Carpathia*, a few deck chairs and gratings awash in the ice-field off the Grand Banks 800 miles from shore, were all that was left of the world's greatest ship.

## V

The aftermath of weeping and regret, of recriminations and investigations, dragged on for weeks. Charges and countercharges were hurled about; the White Star line was bitterly criticized; Ismay was denounced on the floor of the Senate as a coward, but was defended by those who had been with him on the sinking *Titanic* and by the Board of Trade investigation in England.

It was not until weeks later, when the hastily convened Senate investigation in the United States and the Board of Trade report in England had been completed, that the whole story was told. The Senate investigating committee, under the chairmanship of Senator Smith, who was attacked in both the American and British press as a "backwoods politician," brought out numerous pertinent facts, though its proceedings verged at times on the farcical. Senator Smith was ridiculed for his lack of knowledge of the sea when he asked witnesses, "Of what is an iceberg composed?" and "Did any of the passengers take refuge in the water-tight compartments?" The Senator seemed particularly interested in the marital status of Fleet, the lookout, who was saved. Fleet, puzzled, growled aside, "Wot questions they're arskin' me!"

The report of Lord Mersey, Wreck Commissioner in the British Board of Trade's investigation, was tersely damning.

The *Titanic* had carried boats enough for 1,178 persons, only one-third of her capacity. Her sixteen boats and four collapsibles had saved but 711 persons; 400 people had needlessly lost their lives. The boats had been but partly loaded; officers in charge of launching them had been afraid the falls[51] would break or the boats buckle under their rated loads; boat crews had been

---

51. **falls:** tackle used to lower the lifeboats.

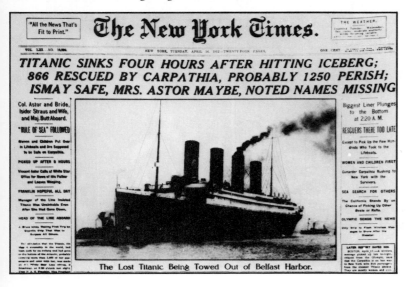

# The New York Times.

VOL. LXI. NO. 19,604.    NEW YORK, TUESDAY, APRIL 16, 1912.—TWENTY-FOUR PAGES.    ONE CENT

## TITANIC SINKS FOUR HOURS AFTER HITTING ICEBERG; 866 RESCUED BY CARPATHIA, PROBABLY 1250 PERISH; ISMAY SAFE, MRS. ASTOR MAYBE, NOTED NAMES MISSING

Col. Astor and Bride, Isidor Straus and Wife, and Maj. Butt Aboard.

"RULE OF SEA" FOLLOWED

Women and Children Put Over in Lifeboats and Are Supposed to be Safe on Carpathia.

PICKED UP AFTER 8 HOURS

Vincent Astor Calls at White Star Office for News of His Father and Leaves Weeping.

FRANKLIN HOPEFUL ALL DAY

Manager of the Line Insisted Titanic Was Unsinkable Even After She Had Gone Down.

HEAD OF THE LINE ABOARD

J. Bruce Ismay Making First Trip on Gigantic Ship That Was to Surpass All Others.

The Lost Titanic Being Towed Out of Belfast Harbor.

Biggest Liner Plunges to the Bottom at 2:20 A.M.

RESCUERS THERE TOO LATE

Except to Pick Up the Few Hundreds Who Took to the Lifeboats.

WOMEN AND CHILDREN FIRST

Cunarder Carpathia Rushing to New York with the Survivors.

SEA SEARCH FOR OTHERS

The California Stands By on Chance of Picking Up Other Boats or Rafts.

OLYMPIC SENDS THE NEWS

Only Ship to Flash Wireless Messages to Shore After the Disaster.

Front page of the April 16, 1912, edition of the *New York Times* headlining the news that the *Titanic* had sunk.

*R.M.S. Titanic* **307**

---

AT A GLANCE

- The U.S. Senate and the Board of Trade in England investigate the disaster.
- The investigations are damning: for example, 400 people had needlessly lost their lives because of unfilled lifeboat seats.

**1 STYLE: IMAGE PATTERN**

The moan from the crowd echoes the last sounds of drowning swimmers and the "one long continuous moan" of the *Titanic* as it sank.

**2 NARRATIVE ESSAY**

This essay has broad appeal as a gripping account of a tragic event.

**3 PURPOSE**

Baldwin's intention is to make it clear why so many lives were needlessly lost: The *Titanic*, having sped through ice fields despite warnings of danger, was pitifully unprepared for serious mishap, carrying too few lifeboats and failing to use those it had.

---

## GUIDED READING

**LITERAL QUESTION**

**1a.** For what proportion of its passengers did the *Titanic* carry lifeboats? How many passengers could have been carried by the lifeboats but were not? (only one-third; 400)

**INFERENTIAL QUESTION**

**1b.** What preparations *should* the *Titanic* have made? (The ship should have carried more lifeboats and should have had disaster drills so that more people could have used the lifeboats.)

- The Mersey report cites the captain's error in speed, but negates charges of negligence.
- The *Californian* is found most culpable in the loss of lives.

## 1 POINT OF VIEW

The final, unqualified quotation indicates where Baldwin places the heaviest blame for the loss of so many lives.

## REFLECTING ON THE SELECTION

What positive message might Baldwin's sad narrative convey? (Possible answers: People can prevent or at least reduce the scope of such disasters; higher standards should be set for professional navigation; correctable mistakes, not mysterious forces or malicious neglect, led to the tragedy.)

## STUDY QUESTIONS

1. double bottoms; hull's sixteen watertight compartments
2. sent radio signals, pumped water from engine rooms, tried to maintain electricity; sleeping radio operator
3. Lifeboats are lowered slowly; passengers awakened; lifeboats leave half-filled; boiler rooms flood; most passengers still aboard; ship sinks.
4. 2,201 aboard; 711 survived
5. *Titanic* should have carried more lifeboats; emergency procedures should have been rehearsed; more attention should have been paid to warnings; *Titanic* should have slowed its speed.
6. Possible answers: Woman chooses to die with dog; Mrs. Straus stays with husband; stoker tries to steal lifejacket; men continue to ride exercise bikes; captain stays on bridge.
7. Ship had been described as gigantic lifeboat; passengers believed ship to be unsinkable; band continued playing ragtime.

---

slow in reaching their stations; launching arrangements were confused because no boat drill had been held; passengers were loaded into the boats haphazardly because no boat assignments had been made.

But that was not all. Lord Mersey found that sufficient warnings of ice on the steamer track had reached the *Titanic*, that her speed of 22 knots was "excessive under the circumstances," that "in view of the high speed at which the vessel was running it is not considered that the lookout was sufficient," and that her master made "a very grievous mistake"—but should not be blamed for negligence. Captain Rostron of the *Carpathia* was highly praised. "He did the very best that could be done." The *Californian* was damned. The testimony of her master, officers, and crew showed that she was not, at the most, more than nineteen miles away from the sinking *Titanic* and probably no more than five to ten miles distant. She had seen the *Titanic*'s lights; she had seen the rockets; she had not received the CQD calls because her radio operator was asleep. She had attempted to get in communication with the ship she had sighted by flashing a light, but vainly.

"The night was clear," reported Lord Mersey, **1** "and the sea was smooth. When she first saw the rockets the *Californian* could have pushed through the ice to the open water without any serious risk and so have come to the assistance of the *Titanic*. Had she done so she might have saved many if not all of the lives that were lost.

"She made no attempt."

---

## STUDY QUESTIONS

### Recalling

1. Why was the *Titanic* considered the safest ship afloat?
2. Briefly summarize the efforts of the captain and crew to save the *Titanic* after it has struck the iceberg. Why did the *Californian* not answer the *Titanic*'s distress signal?
3. Describe the evacuation of the passengers and the sinking of the ship.
4. How many passengers were on the *Titanic*? How many survived?
5. According to the investigation of the disaster, in what ways might the loss of so many lives have been avoided?

### Interpreting

6. Mention five incidents from this account that show how a disaster such as the sinking of the *Titanic* brings out very different responses in different people.
7. Baldwin uses many details—like the reference to the "706 immigrants to the land of promise"—to emphasize the irony of the *Titanic*'s sinking. Find three additional examples of such irony.
8. Where does Baldwin place the blame for the tragedy of the *Titanic*? How does he make his attitude clear?

### Extending

9. According to Baldwin's essay, what is the danger of a false sense of security? Give another example of inappropriate confidence.

## VIEWPOINT

Days after the sinking of the *Titanic*, one magazine editor wrote:

The *Titanic*, in her way, was a [symbol] of current civilization: enormous, luxurious, the last triumph of mechanics, rushing headlong on her course, as though there were no ice in the sea and the touch of death was no longer cold.

- Is Baldwin's account of the disaster consistent with this view of the *Titanic*? Why or why not?

---

8. on *Californian;* by concluding statement *She made no attempt.*
9. prevents people from taking necessary precautions; should mention historical, personal, or fictional event

Yes—it explains why precautions were not taken.

# LITERARY FOCUS

## Techniques of Fiction in the Narrative Essay

Like a work of fiction, a narrative essay tells a story. Whereas writers of fiction invent their materials, writers of narrative essays tell stories that are true. However, in order to tell their stories more effectively, writers of narrative essays sometimes use inventive techniques associated with the writing of fiction.

For example, in "R.M.S. *Titanic*" Hanson Baldwin uses **dialogue**, or speech, to advance the narrative, much as a short story writer would. He also changes tenses in his account of the disaster and indicates the passage of time in an inventive way. In addition, he creates imaginative effects by repeating certain images—such as the "dancing spark" of the radio—throughout his essay.

### Thinking About the Narrative Essay

1. Choose one example of Baldwin's use of dialogue in "R.M.S. *Titanic*," and describe the effect of this technique in the passage that you choose.
2. Locate the point at which the essay shifts tenses. How else does Baldwin alter his presentation of time in this portion of the essay? What is the effect of this technique?
3. Find one image that Baldwin repeats at several points in the essay. What is the effect of this repetition?

# VOCABULARY

## Analogies

An **analogy** is a comparison. Analogy items appear on vocabulary tests as double comparisons between two pairs of words. You may be given the first pair of words and asked to find or complete a second pair of words that has the same relationship as the first pair. For example, you would complete the analogy FRONT : BACK : : _____ : _____ with the pair FORE : AFT, since both pairs of words are antonyms, or opposites.

Each of the following items begins with two related words in capital letters from "R.M.S. *Titanic*." First decide how the two words in capitals are related to each other. Then choose the letter of the pair that has the same relationship.

1. PORT : LEFT : :
   (a) awake : asleep
   (b) lost : found
   (c) list : sink
   (d) starboard : right
2. SUPERLATIVE : SUPERIOR : :
   (a) ashore : afloat
   (b) noble : common
   (c) best : better
   (d) rich : poor
3. ABYSS : DEPTH : :
   (a) hollow : filled
   (b) lake : river
   (c) mountain : valley
   (d) summit : height
4. KNOTS : SHIP : :
   (a) miles per hour : car
   (b) cable : rudder
   (c) force : energy
   (d) lights : signals
5. FOUNDERED : SANK : :
   (a) profit : loss
   (b) ran : walked
   (c) collided : wrecked
   (d) storm : calm

# COMPOSITION

## Writing About a Narrative Essay

■ What was Hanson Baldwin's purpose in writing "R.M.S. *Titanic*," and how did he achieve it? Give examples of specific facts, statistics, descriptive details, incidents, and opinions used by Baldwin to accomplish his purpose. *For help in this assignment, see Lesson 10 in the Writing About Literature Handbook at the back of this book.*

## Retelling a Narrative from Another Point of View

■ Imagine that you are a surviving passenger or crew member of the *Titanic*. Using the information in Baldwin's essay, write your own account of one of these episodes: (a) the time preceding the collision, (b) the time between the collision and the evacuation, (c) the evacuation, or (d) the investigation of the disaster.

# COMPARING ESSAYS

■ *The Spirit of St. Louis* was written by a man who had firsthand experience of the events he relates but who was not a professional writer. On the other hand, "R.M.S. *Titanic*" was written by a trained reporter who did not witness the events he relates. What do these two essays have in common? How are they different, and how might the differences between the two authors explain the difference between their essays?

## LITERARY FOCUS

1. Answers should
   - cite a passage containing dialogue
   - explain how dialogue advances the narrative
2. shifts from past to present tense: "12:25 A.M. Boxhall's position is sent out. . . ."; begins countdown; creates suspense; sense of immediacy
3. dancing spark: symbolizes hope; water rising: emphasizes inevitability of the sinking

## VOCABULARY

1. (d) starboard : right
2. (c) best : better
3. (d) summit : height
4. (a) miles per hour : car
5. (c) collided : wrecked

## COMPARING ESSAYS

- *Similar:* Both use present tense to convey a sense of immediacy; both are organized chronologically with the plot structure of a suspenseful short story; both are written in a direct style.
- *Different:* Lindbergh describes his own responses to events; Baldwin, a journalist, is more objective.

# COMPOSITION: GUIDELINES FOR EVALUATION

## WRITING ABOUT A NARRATIVE ESSAY

### Objective
To explain how the purpose of a narrative essay is achieved

### Guidelines for Evaluation
- suggested length: three to five paragraphs
- should state author's purpose
- cite facts, details, opinions from essay
- should show how these convey purpose

## RETELLING A NARRATIVE FROM ANOTHER POINT OF VIEW

### Objective
To give an imaginary *eyewitness* account of events described in essay

### Guidelines for Evaluation
- suggested length: 150–450 words
- should focus on one of the episodes listed
- should elaborate on the incidents described
- should use an informal, first-person point of view

Rudolfo Anaya (born 1937) is proud to be a Chicano, "a native son of the Mexican community of the United States," and equally proud of "that part of me that is a native American." His trilogy of novels as well as his many short stories and articles reflect his Mexican-Indian heritage. The narrative essay that follows records Anaya's impressions of a trip to China in 1984.

■ Read the title of Anaya's essay, and try to predict in a general way what the essay will be about. As you read, test your prediction. Is it accurate, or is Anaya writing about more than a trip to China?

*Rudolfo A. Anaya*

# A Chicano[1] in China

*May 20, 1984*
*The Great Wall of China*

When I was a child attending school in Santa Rosa, New Mexico, I remember we studied China. We read about the Great Wall of China.[2] We looked at the huge globe of the world Mr. Gold had in his room. We knew that China was on the other side of the world. Later, in the dusty playground of the school, I scooped out a small hole. Better watch out, somebody said, if you dig a hole and fall through, you'll fall into China. That became part of our childhood mythology: A hole dug through the Earth, even from the comfortable little town we came from in New Mexico, led to China. That rule of the round Earth stayed with me, became part of my dream.

Now the dream has become reality. I have fallen into that hole of time and history and travel, and I have arrived in China. What part of me remains in that small town which nurtured my early dreams? Why do I see the farming villages of my youth in the rural villages of China?

The commune. Each village is composed of units, communes. So was the village of Puerto de Luna,[3] my grandfather's home. In Puerto de Luna the farmers owned their land, they nourished their families from the earth, they sold their produce, but they led a communal life. At the heart of the village was the family, but at the heart of the commune was the Church. Other aspects of village life created the sense of community. Among these was the system of irrigation which the farmers used. A main irrigation ditch, *la acequia madre*,[4] brought water from the river, and the care of that ditch was the com-

---

1. **Chicano** [chi kä′nō]: American of Mexican descent.
2. **Great Wall of China**: 1,500-mile-long wall, built across northern China in the third century B.C. as a protection against invaders.

3. **Puerto de Luna** [pwer′tō dā lōō′nä]
4. **la acequia madre** [lä ä sā′kē ä mä′drā]

**310** *Nonfiction*

---

munal responsibility. The most friendly feelings of community and the most vociferous arguments took place around the delegation of cleaning crews, the choosing of the ditch rider, *el Mayordomo*.[5] The water for the fields created the communal sharing; all for one and one for all, assignment of labor, the equal sharing of the water. The Mayordomo was the cadre leader in the commune, a man on horseback who rode the ditch and saw to it that the source of life was kept clean. He assigned watering days. In the evenings or around the post office, the men of the village gathered and together as a group they made the rules to govern themselves and the men they gave power to; it was a commune. The

5. **el Mayordomo** [el mä yōr dō′mō]

2

cadre was in charge. Old village life in New Mexico. How simple it is for me to relate to these brown men and women I see bent over rice fields or vegetable gardens. I have seen them before, there where I began to dig my hole to China. Once as a child I stayed in Puerto de Luna for the summer. I stayed with my grandfather, a silent stern man who kept the Sabbath, prayed his rosary. But one evening he had one too many cups at the cantina. He came home speaking in tongues. I swear he's speaking Chinese, my grandmother said. She was his second wife. I don't remember her as well as I should. I do remember her admonition, "You're speaking Chinese."

3

Grandfather, I think, as I hear old men speak Chinese in the fields.

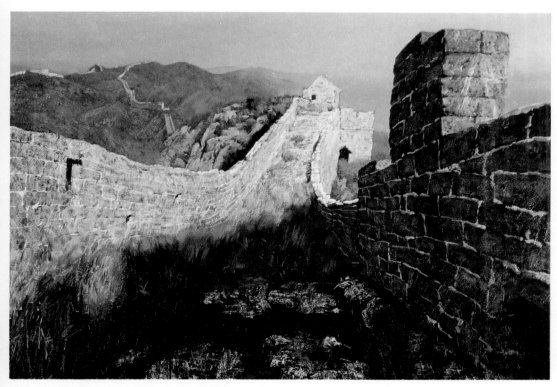

Detail, *Fossil of the Dragon,* Wang Huaiqing, 1987.

*A Chicano in China* **311**

### AT A GLANCE

- Anaya draws a comparison between the political structure of his New Mexico village and the Chinese villages.
- He thinks of his grandfather's speech when he hears old men speak Chinese in the field.

### 1 VOCABULARY: WORD CHOICE

A cadre literally refers to the key officials in a military unit; the cadre of Anaya's commune were the caretakers of their life source.

### 2 THEME

Anaya feels that he already knows the people he sees working the fields in China.

### 3 IRONY

Chinese was the strangest language his grandmother could imagine when she chided her husband; Anaya remarks later that the speech of the Chinese field workers actually does remind him of his grandfather.

## GUIDED READING

### LITERAL QUESTION

**1a.** What does Anaya think when he hears the old men speak Chinese in the fields? (He thinks about his grandfather.)

### INFERENTIAL QUESTION

**1b.** Why does Anaya make this connection? (The spoken Chinese reminds him of his grandmother's remark that her husband was speaking Chinese. In a broader sense these farmers remind him of the Chicano farmers he remembers.)

- Anaya passes through communes and thinks of the Mongols.
- He compares the Great Wall to an imaginary wall of culture in New Mexico that was "battered" by Anglo-Americans.
- He thinks philosophically about nuclear reactors.

**1 THEME**

The farmers, rather than the conquerors, are the builders and guardians of civilization.

**2 PURPOSE**

Anaya points out that even though the Great Wall failed to keep out invaders, it symbolizes the history and enrichment of Chinese culture.

**3 THEME**

Like the Great Wall of China, the wall protecting Hispanic culture has withstood assaults, but Anaya wonders about its durability.

**4 READING SKILLS: COMPARISON AND CONTRAST**

Anaya wonders if the wall of resistance merely represents a waning culture or, like the Great Wall of China, symbolizes a living force.

---

On the road north to the Great Wall today, we passed through farmland. Everywhere, there are the smaller ditches carrying the water of the main canal. Water pumps rush the water to the fields. Men and women stand by the pumps, working, talking. The Mayordomos of the water. The life spirit of the commune flows into the fields, fields of rice, wheat, peach orchards, vegetables; all around us as far as I can see in the haze, the farmers work the valley. To the north are the mountains. The Great Wall calls. I am falling through my time in history to complete my destiny.

("See, I told you you'd fall through to China," I imagine Ida, or June, or Rita, or Agnes calling to me.)

On a small Toyota bus we enter the pass of the mountains, the same pass the Mongols from Mongolia used to ride down from the north to sack and conquer China. They burned Beijing[6] because they didn't know what houses were for. Only the persistence of farmers rebuilt the city, taught the warrior, horseback nomads how to enter and live in houses. House equals civilization. Today on the bus, some of our group's voices are strident and irritating. Our leader asks too many questions. He had no Grampa to teach him about China, I guess.

About an hour and a half north of Beijing, we come to the Great Wall, the tourist part of the Great Wall. It is Sunday, the crowds are thick, and still one feels awed at the first sight of the massive wall. Built on the back of a mountain slope, it is like a serpent that crawls up and down the hog backs. In how many ways does the symbol of the snake repeat itself in China? The Great Wall was built by the Chinese to protect them from the Mongolians of the north. It was a Maginot Line:[7] It could not hold back the barbarians

---

6. **Beijing** [bā'zhing']: known at the time as Yenking; now the capital of the People's Republic of China.
7. **Maginot** [mazh'ə nō'] **Line:** line of heavy fortifications along France's eastern border, which failed to prevent a Nazi invasion in World War II.

---

from the north who swept southward to leave their mark on China.

I am reminded that when the Anglo-Americans first swept into New Mexico, the Great Wall of resistance was the Hispanic culture they found there. That wall of culture has been battered and bruised, but it's still in place. Will it disappear, or will it always be there like the Great Wall of China? The Chinese drove the Mongols back up north and so the battles of history moved north and south, and throughout that vast movement of clashing armies the Great Wall remained in place. I wonder how the culture of the Hispanics will fare; the culture built by the grandfathers of the communes of the small villages. How battered is the Wall? Is it now only a tourist attraction, the last remnants of a culture, or is our culture a force living in the soul of the people? A force connecting us to our history, a force as powerful as the Great Wall of China, that wall which is a symbol of Chinese resistance. No one knows except, perhaps, the winds of time, which have many things to reveal to us yet.

A month ago Reagan was here at the Great Wall, our guide says. He promised to build ten nuclear power plants. Will they become the new symbols of China? Dragon breath, dragon fire. Is the power of the dragon both good and bad? Does the new dragon feed on Uranium-232?

Along the Wall, Chinese families pause to eat their lunches: boiled eggs, bread, cakes, soft drinks, and beer. It is their Wall, their history. They feel comfortable pausing to eat their food. It is their day at the Great Wall. Let the tourists pass. In the future will Chinese families go to visit the nuclear reactors? Will they take their families on Sunday outings? Will they sit in the shade of the nuclear power plants to eat their picnic lunches of boiled eggs, bread, cakes, soft drinks, and beer?

Man creates dragons, but dragons, once given form and soul in the mind of men, create their own power. Who controls the dragons we set loose on the Earth? Somebody says Nixon looked

---

## GUIDED READING

**LITERAL QUESTION**

**1a.** Why does Anaya compare the Great Wall and the Maginot Line? (Both failed to keep out invaders.)

**INFERENTIAL QUESTION**

**1b.** In what sense did the Great Wall succeed in its purpose? (It became a symbol of Chinese culture, helping the Chinese to maintain their special identity in the face of change.)

at the Great Wall and said, ''That's a great wall, all right.'' Reagan now has looked at the Great Wall. Mao[8] exhorted all Chinese to visit the Great Wall because great men go to the Great Wall. Today I have come to the Great Wall of North-

ern China. I have fallen through that little hole I began to dig on the playground of my child- **1** hood. I am afraid now that all great men have died. I think of my grandfather and wonder if in his dreams he saw the Great Wall. I know he was a great man, a simple farmer from Puerto de Luna. Now even those farmers are all dead. They would have been able to speak to the Chinese who press around me now.

---

8. **Mao:** Mao Zedong (1893–1976), Chairman of the People's Republic of China (1949–1976).

## STUDY QUESTIONS

### Recalling

1. To what childhood myth does Anaya refer in the first paragraph of the essay? He unifies the essay by referring to this myth again and again. Find these references.
2. What do the communes in China bring to Anaya's mind? What does his grandfather have to do with China?
3. Why does Anaya refer to the Great Wall of China as ''a Maginot line''?

### Interpreting

4. Why do you think the author begins the essay with a reference to digging a hole to China?
5. What other ''wall'' does the Great Wall make Anaya think of?
6. What ''new symbols of China'' and ''new dragon'' is the author referring to on page 312?

### Extending

7. What advantages and disadvantages do you see where cultural groups in the United States keep alive the languages, customs, and other aspects of their cultures?

## LITERARY FOCUS

### Purpose of the Narrative Essay

''A Chicano in China'' is a **narrative essay,** which presents actual events in chronological order. The author's purpose in writing a narrative essay is not merely to relate real events, however. The more important purpose is to present events to illustrate an idea or to find within them some truth about life in general.

### Thinking About the Purpose of a Narrative Essay

■ Identify the idea or general truth about life that Anaya wishes to illustrate by describing the trip to China.

## COMPOSITION

### Using Comparison in a Narrative Essay

■ In his essay Anaya compares people, places, things, and activities he encounters in China with those in his or his people's—the Chicanos'—past. Write several paragraphs about these compari- sons. In the first paragraph explain your purpose for writing: to point out the comparisons Anaya makes. Next write a paragraph about each comparison: Cite what Anaya encounters in his travels; then explain what he compares it with and what similarities he sees between the two.

### Writing an Entry in a Traveler's Journal

■ Recall a trip you have made. Write about the trip in an entry for a traveler's journal. In at least one paragraph, describe the place and the incident or incidents that occurred there. In an additional paragraph or paragraphs explain what idea or truth about life the place or incident signifies for you.

*A Chicano in China* **313**

## COMPOSITION: GUIDELINES FOR EVALUATION

### USING COMPARISON IN NARRATIVE ESSAY
**Objective**
To identify and explain comparisons in an essay

**Guidelines for Evaluation**
■ Suggested length: three to six paragraphs
■ should pair events such as the trip to China and the childhood myth; the Chinese communes and similar social units in New Mexico; the Great Wall and the Hispanic culture of New Mexico

### WRITING AN ENTRY IN A TRAVELER'S JOURNAL
**Objective**
To write a journal entry about a trip

**Guidelines for Evaluation**
■ Suggested length: minimum of two paragraphs
■ entry should begin with date and place visited
■ should describe place visited and what took place
■ should explain truth illustrated

■ Anaya thinks about ''great men'' and about his grand- father and other simple farm- ers.
■ He thinks the farmers could have communicated with the Chinese.

**1** PURPOSE

Anaya pays tribute to all the farmers of the past, the simple people who built great cultures; the Great Wall is a monument to them.

REFLECTING ON THE SELECTION

Why could farmers of Puerto de Luna speak to the Chinese? (Both honor the cultural link to the past.)

STUDY QUESTIONS

1. falling through a hole in the ground to China; ''I am falling through my time''; ''I have fallen through''
2. village life in Puerto de Luna; the grandfather speaking ''Chinese''
3. Both the wall and the line failed to keep invaders out.
4. to capture readers' attention; to dramatize the connection he feels between his child- hood scenes and China
5. the ''wall'' of Hispanic culture that resisted the Anglo-Ameri- cans who first invaded New Mexico
6. nuclear power plants
7. Possible advantages: identity, self-respect, stability; possi- ble disadvantages: isolation, possible misunderstanding

LITERARY FOCUS

Some aspects of Chicano and Chinese life are similar; both have great value and have sur- vived a long history of assault.

- Hurricane Agnes turns Tinker Creek into a roaring river.
- Dillard hurries down to the bridge to see the flood.

LITERARY OPTIONS

- descriptive essay
- style

THEMATIC OPTIONS

- natural disasters
- transformations
- human cooperation

**1 STYLE: SHIFT IN TENSE**

The abrupt change to the present tense draws the reader into the immediacy of the experience.

**2 DESCRIPTIVE ESSAY**

Dillard wants to show how the flood changes the actual appearance of her surroundings as well as her subjective impression of them.

**3 MAIN IDEA**

The flood brings people together. This is typical human behavior in times of disaster—especially natural disaster.

Photograph © 1982 by Jill Krementz

Annie Dillard (born 1945) both writes and teaches writing. One of her principal subjects is the natural world. Dillard won the Pulitzer Prize for her first book, *Pilgrim at Tinker Creek,* from which the following selection has been taken. The book presents the author's experiences living in Tinker Creek, Virginia. In this excerpt Dillard watches the creek become a raging river during Hurricane Agnes, a storm that caused heavy flooding in the eastern United States in 1972.

■ What might make a person want to walk into a flood to record it?

*Annie Dillard*

# Flood

It was just this time last year that we had the flood. It was Hurricane Agnes, really, but by the time it got here, the weather bureau had demoted it to a tropical storm. I see by a clipping I saved that the date was June twenty-first, the solstice, midsummer's night, the longest daylight of the year; but I didn't notice it at the time. Everything was so exciting, and so very dark.

All it did was rain. It rained, and the creek started to rise. The creek, naturally, rises every time it rains; this didn't seem any different. But it kept raining, and, that morning of the twenty-first, the creek kept rising.

That morning I'm standing at my kitchen window. Tinker Creek is out of its four-foot banks, way out, and it's still coming. The high creek doesn't look like our creek. Our creek splashes transparently over a jumble of rocks; the high creek obliterates everything in flat opacity. It looks like somebody else's creek that has usurped or eaten our creek and is roving frantically to escape, big and ugly, like a black-snake caught in a kitchen drawer. The color is foul, a rusty cream. Water that has picked up clay soils looks worse than other muddy waters, because the particles of clay are so fine; they spread out and cloud the water so that you can't see light through even an inch of it in a drinking glass.

Everything looks different. Where my eye is used to depth, I see the flat water, near, too near. I see trees I never noticed before, the black verticals of their rain-soaked trunks standing out of the pale water like pilings for a rotted dock. The stillness of grassy banks and stony ledges is gone; I see rushing, a wild sweep and hurry in one direction, as swift and compelling as a waterfall. The Atkins kids are out in their tiny rain gear, staring at the monster creek. It's risen up to their gates; the neighbors are gathering; I go out.

I hear a roar, a high windy sound more like air than like water, like the run-together whaps of a helicopter's propeller after the engine is off, a high million rushings. The air smells damp and acrid, like fuel oil, or insecticide. It's raining.

I'm in no danger; my house is high. I hurry down the road to the bridge. Neighbors who have barely seen each other all winter are there, shaking their heads. Few have ever seen it before: the water is *over* the bridge. Even when I

## GUIDED READING

**LITERAL QUESTIONS**

**1a.** What are the Atkins kids wearing and what are they doing? (They are out in their tiny rain gear, staring at the monster creek.)

**2a.** Where does Dillard "hurry" after observing the roaring creek from her kitchen window? (down the road to the bridge)

**INFERENTIAL QUESTIONS**

**1b.** What might the children's clothing imply? (A flood like this is a great exception to the usual storms in Tinker Creek; their *tiny* rain gear indicates how much water they are accustomed to dealing with.)

**2b.** What does this behavior imply about her attitude toward the flood? (She finds the flood more interesting than terrifying.)

see the bridge now, which I do every day, I still can't believe it: the water was *over* the bridge, a foot or two over the bridge, which at normal times is eleven feet above the surface of the creek.

Now the water is receding slightly; someone has produced empty metal drums, which we roll to the bridge and set up in a square to keep cars from trying to cross. It takes a bit of nerve even to stand on the bridge; the flood has ripped away a wedge of concrete that buttressed the bridge on the bank. Now one corner of the bridge hangs apparently unsupported while water hurls in an arch just inches below.

It's hard to take it all in, it's all so new. I look at the creek at my feet. It smashes under the bridge like a fist, but there is no end to its force; it hurtles down as far as I can see till it lurches round the bend, filling the valley, flattening, mashing, pushed, wider and faster, till it fills my brain.

It's like a dragon. Maybe it's because the bridge we are on is chancy, but I notice that no one can help imagining himself washed overboard, and gauging his chances for survival. You couldn't live. Mark Spitz[1] couldn't live. The water arches where the bridge's supports at the banks prevent its enormous volume from going wide, forcing it to go high; that arch drives down like a diving whale, and would butt you on the bottom. "You'd never know what hit you," one of the men says. But if you survived that part and managed to surface...? How fast can you live? You'd need a windshield. You couldn't keep your head up; the water under the surface is fastest. You'd spin around like a sock in a clothes dryer. You couldn't grab onto a tree trunk without leaving that arm behind. No, you couldn't live. And if they ever found you, your gut would be solid red clay.

It's all I can do to stand. I feel dizzy, drawn,

___

1. **Mark Spitz:** American swimmer who won seven gold medals in the 1972 summer Olympics.

mauled. Below me the floodwater roils to a violent froth that looks like dirty lace, a lace that continuously explodes before my eyes. If I look away, the earth moves backwards, rises and swells, from the fixing of my eyes at one spot against the motion of the flood. All the familiar land looks as though it were not solid and real at all, but painted on a scroll like a backdrop, and that unrolled scroll has been shaken, so the earth sways and the air roars.

Everything imaginable is zipping by, almost too fast to see. If I stand on the bridge and look downstream, I get dizzy; but if I look upstream, I feel as though I am looking up the business end of an avalanche. There are dolls, split wood and kindling, dead fledgling songbirds, bottles, whole bushes and trees, rakes and garden gloves. Wooden, rough-hewn railroad ties charge by faster than any express. Lattice fencing bobs along, and a wooden picket gate. There are so many white plastic gallon milk jugs that when the flood ultimately recedes, they are left on the grassy banks looking from a distance like a flock of white geese.

I expect to see anything at all. In this one way, the creek is more like itself when it floods than at any other time: mediating, bringing things down. I wouldn't be at all surprised to see John Paul Jones[2] coming round the bend, standing on the deck of the *Bon Homme Richard,* or Amelia Earhart[3] waving gaily from the cockpit of her floating Lockheed. Why not a cello, a basket of breadfruit,[4] a casket of antique coins? Here comes the Franklin expedition[5] on snowshoes,

___

2. **John Paul Jones** (1747–1792): American naval hero during the Revolutionary War. His boat was named the *Bon Homme Richard.*
3. **Amelia Earhart** (1897–1937): American aviator who was the first woman to fly solo across the Atlantic Ocean. During her 1937 attempt to fly around the world, Earhart's Lockheed airplane disappeared over the Pacific Ocean and was never found.
4. **breadfruit:** large round tropical fruit.
5. **Franklin expedition:** doomed 1845 British naval expedition that tried to find a Northwest Passage between the Atlantic and Pacific Oceans. The expedition's ship disappeared, and no survivors were ever found.

*Flood* **315**

## GUIDED READING

**LITERAL QUESTIONS**

**1a.** What do Dillard and some others do to keep cars from trying to cross the bridge? (They set up a barrier of metal drums.)

**2a.** What are some things that Dillard "wouldn't be at all surprised to see" in the flood? (lost heroes as they were in their glory, a cello, a basket of breadfruit, old coins)

**INFERENTIAL QUESTIONS**

**1b.** What do you think this heroic effort suggests? (The flood is bringing people together who take personal risk on an endangered bridge to prevent harm to others.)

**2b.** What might you infer about the flood's power from this varied list? (The flood's astonishing force and transforming power seem to reach beyond the ordinary limits of time and distance.)

- The earth seems to slide like sand down a chute.
- Dillard wonders how animals survive and return.
- Some children find a huge snapping turtle.

**1 STYLE: IMAGERY**

The images of water streaming, dripping, coursing, pouring—making the *whole earth* slide—convey the flood's enormity.

**2 STYLE: SIMILE**

The homey comparison of the flood to a stew creates the sense that ordinary life still goes on.

**3 DESCRIPTIVE ESSAY**

Precise details (*the rediscovered log, the fence cable*) and strong verbs (*leaps, smashes*) describe the scene vividly for readers who have not witnessed a great flood.

**4 ANECDOTE**

Through anecdotes like the one about the turtle, Dillard shares her fascination with what the flood reveals of life near Tinker Creek.

and the three magi,[6] plus camels, afloat on a canopied barge!

The whole world is in flood, the land as well [1] as the water. Water streams down the trunks of trees, drips from hat-brims, courses across roads. The whole earth seems to slide like sand down a chute; water pouring over the least slope leaves the grass flattened, silver side up, pointing downstream. Everywhere windfall and flotsam twigs[7] and leafy boughs, wood from woodpiles, bottles, and saturated straw spatter the ground [2] or streak it in curving windrows. Tomatoes in flat gardens are literally floating in mud; they look as though they have been dropped whole into a boiling, brown-gravy stew. The level of the water table is at the top of the toe of my shoes. Pale muddy water lies on the flat so that it all but drowns the grass; it looks like a hideous parody of a light snow on the field, with only the dark tips of the grass blades visible.

When I look across the street, I can't believe my eyes. Right behind the road's shoulder are waves, waves whipped in rhythmically peaking scallops, racing downstream. The hill where I watched the praying mantis lay her eggs is a waterfall that splashes into a brown ocean. I can't even remember where the creek usually [3] runs—it is everywhere now. My log is gone for sure, I think—but in fact, I discover later, it holds, rammed between growing trees. Only the cable suspending the steers' fence is visible, and not the fence itself; the steers' pasture is entirely in flood, a brown river. The river leaps its banks and smashes into the woods where the motorbikes go, devastating all but the sturdiest trees. The water is so deep and wide it seems as though you could navigate the *Queen Mary*[8] in it, clear to Tinker Mountain.

What do animals do in these floods? I see a drowned muskrat go by like he's flying, but they all couldn't die; the water rises after every hard rain, and the creek is still full of muskrats. This flood is higher than their raised sleeping platforms in the banks; they must just race for high ground and hold on. Where do the fish go, and what do they do? Presumably their gills can filter oxygen out of this muck, but I don't know how. They must hide from the current behind any barriers they can find, and fast for a few days. They must: otherwise we'd have no fish; they'd all be in the Atlantic Ocean. What about herons and kingfishers,[9] say? They can't see to eat. It usually seems to me that when I see any animal, its business is urgent enough that it couldn't easily be suspended for forty-eight hours. Crayfish, frogs, snails, rotifers?[10] Most things must simply die. They couldn't live. Then I suppose that when the water goes down and clears, the survivors have a field day with no competition. But you'd think the bottom would be knocked out of the food chain—the whole pyramid would have no base plankton,[11] and it would crumble, or crash with a thud. Maybe enough spores and larvae and eggs are constantly being borne down from slower upstream waters to repopulate.... I don't know.

[4] Some little children have discovered a snapping turtle as big as a tray. It's hard to believe that this creek could support a predator that size: its shell is a foot and a half across, and its head extends a good seven inches beyond the shell. When the children—in the company of a shrunken terrier—approach it on the bank, the snapper rears up on its thick front legs and hisses very impressively. I had read earlier that since turtles' shells are rigid, they don't have bellows lungs; they have to gulp for air. And, also since their shells are rigid, there's only room for so

---

6. **three magi:** the three wise men who visited the infant Jesus in Bethlehem.
7. **flotsam** [flot′səm] **twigs:** bits of wreckage floating in water.
8. **Queen Mary:** large ocean liner.

9. **herons and kingfishers:** birds that live on fish.
10. **rotifers** [rō′tə fərz]: microscopic aquatic animals, often found in ponds or puddles.
11. **plankton:** tiny plants and animals that drift in water and serve as a major food source for larger animals.

## GUIDED READING

**LITERAL QUESTION**

**1a.** What does Dillard suppose keeps the food chain going after base plankton is destroyed? (Enough spores and larvae wash down from upstream to repopulate.)

**INFERENTIAL QUESTION**

**1b.** What can you infer about the persistence of life from her question and answer? (Despite what seems to be total destruction, life always goes on.)

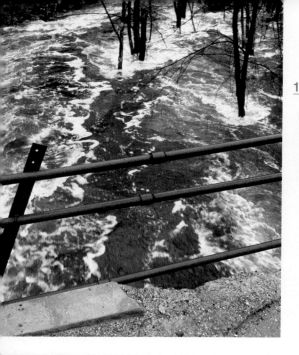

much inside, so when they are frightened and planning a retreat, they have to expel air from their lungs to make room for head and feet—hence the malevolent hiss.

1   The next time I look, I see that the children have somehow maneuvered the snapper into a washtub. They're waving a broom handle at it in hopes that it will snap the wood like a matchstick, but the creature will not deign to oblige. The kids are crushed; all their lives they've heard that this is the one thing you do with a snapping turtle—you shove a broom handle near it, and it "snaps it like a matchstick." It's nature's way; it's sure-fire. But the turtle is having none of it. It avoids the broom handle with an air of patiently repressed rage. They let it go, and it beelines down the bank, dives unhesitatingly into the swirling floodwater, and that's the last we see of it.

A cheer comes up from the crowd on the bridge. The truck is here with a pump for the

AT A GLANCE

■ Children play with the snapping turtle, then let it go.
■ A cheer comes up from the crowd on the bridge.

1 **DESCRIPTIVE ESSAY**

Dillard's comic scene and commentary suggest that children continue doing the things children do, with the flood simply providing a novel source of entertainment.

## GUIDED READING

### LITERAL QUESTION

**1a.** What is the children's feeling when the snapping turtle refuses to snap at the broom handle? (disappointment)

### INFERENTIAL QUESTION

**1b.** What do you think Dillard's mention of the turtle's unturtlelike behavior illustrates? (Nothing is predictable in Tinker Creek at the moment; hence, she sees a snapping turtle that refuses to snap.)

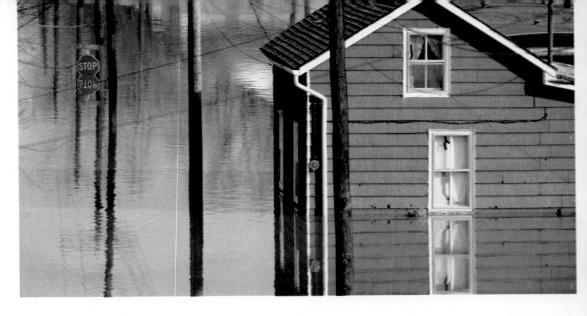

## AT A GLANCE

- A truck carrying a pump "makes it" over the bridge.
- A crowd tries to salvage property for the Bings, who are away.

### 1 MAIN IDEA

Hoorays and cheers express the feeling of team spirit in response to the flood.

### 2 READING SKILLS: CONTRAST

This rapid change of scene dramatizes the sudden transformation of a town into a *sea*.

### 3 TONE

Dillard views the children's attraction to the snake with mildly mocking humor: "now they all want . . . to get bitten by the snake." This generous amusement is characteristic of her tone throughout the essay.

1 Bowerys' basement, hooray! We roll away the metal drums, the truck makes it over the bridge, to my amazement—the crowd cheers again. State police cruise by; everything's fine here; downstream people are in trouble. The bridge over by the Bings' on Tinker Creek looks like it's about to go. There's a tree trunk wedged against its railing, and a section of concrete is out. The Bings are away, and a young couple is living there, "taking care of the house." What can they 2 do? The husband drove to work that morning as usual; a few hours later, his wife was evacuated from the front door in a *motorboat*.

I walk to the Bings'. Most of the people who are on our bridge eventually end up over there; it's just down the road. We straggle along in the rain, gathering a crowd. The men who work away from home are here, too; their wives have telephoned them at work this morning to say that the creek is rising fast, and they'd better get home while the gettin's good.

There's a big crowd already there; everybody knows that the Bings' is low. The creek is coming in the recreation-room windows; it's half-

**318** *Nonfiction*

way up the garage door. Later that day people will haul out everything salvageable and try to dry it: books, rugs, furniture—the lower level was filled from floor to ceiling. Now on this bridge a road crew is trying to chop away the wedged tree trunk with a long-handled ax. The handle isn't so long that they don't have to stand on the bridge, in Tinker Creek. I walk along a low brick wall that was built to retain the creek away from the house at high water. The wall holds just fine, but now that the creek's receding, it's retaining water around the house. On the wall I can walk right out into the flood and stand in the middle of it. Now on the return trip I meet a young man who's going in the opposite direction. The wall is one brick wide; we can't pass. So we clasp hands and lean out backwards over the turbulent water; our feet interlace like teeth on a zipper, we pull together, stand, and 3 continue on our ways. The kids have spotted a rattlesnake draping itself out of harm's way in a bush; now they all want to walk over the brick wall to the bush, to get bitten by the snake.

The little Atkins kids are here, and they are

---

## GUIDED READING

### LITERAL QUESTION

**1a.** How do Dillard and the man manage to pass on the narrow wall? (They clasp hands, lean back, and interlace their feet as they step around each other.)

### INFERENTIAL QUESTION

**1b.** What attitude might this scene suggest about people's response to the flood? (The graceful maneuver conveys a lightheartedness, which contrasts with the raging, haphazard torrent that has enveloped the day.)

hopping up and down. I wonder if I hopped up and down, would the bridge go? I could stand at the railing as at the railing of a steamboat, shouting deliriously, ''Mark three! Quarter-less-three! Half twain! Quarter twain!...''[12] as the current bore the broken bridge out of sight around the bend before she sank....

Everyone else is standing around. Some of the women are carrying curious plastic umbrellas that look like diving bells[13]—umbrellas they don't put up, but on; they don't get under, but in. They can see out dimly, like goldfish in

bowls. Their voices from within sound distant, but with an underlying cheerfulness that plainly acknowledges, ''Isn't this ridiculous?'' Some of the men are wearing their fishing hats. Others duck their heads under folded newspapers held not very high in an effort to compromise between keeping their heads dry and letting rain run up their sleeves. Following some form of courtesy, I guess, they lower these newspapers when they speak with you, and squint politely into the rain.

Women are bringing coffee in mugs to the road crew. They've barely made a dent in the tree trunk, and they're giving up. It's a job for power tools; the water's going down anyway, and the danger is past. Some kid starts doing tricks on a skateboard; I head home.

---

12. **Mark three! ... twain!:** terms used to indicate the depth of a body of water. ''Mark three'' means that the water is three fathoms, or eighteen feet, deep.
13. **diving bells:** bell-shaped, watertight compartments used for underwater work.

## STUDY QUESTIONS

### Recalling

1. In what ways does the creek look "different" to Dillard at the beginning of the essay?
2. Once Dillard has arrived at the bridge, what sights and sounds surprise her? What things rush by her in the flood?
3. Cite two incidents involving Dillard's neighbors during the flood.

### Interpreting

4. What effect does Dillard achieve by switching to present tense after the first two paragraphs?
5. Why does Dillard say that she expects to see John Paul Jones or the three magi floating down the creek? What is the effect of images like these?
6. Find three examples showing that the flood represents a clash between the forces of nature and the works of human beings.
7. The essay begins and ends in the author's house. What overall impression do you think she formed of the flood and her neighborhood during her walk?

### Extending

8. Why do you think a natural disaster like a flood brings people closer together as it does during the episode recorded in this essay?

## VIEWPOINT

Besides offering a detailed account of the flood's appearance and effects, Dillard's description is very personal. She does more than report facts. One critic observes that, in reading Dillard's work,

...we pass easily...from observation to reflection.

— J. B. Breslin, *America* magazine

■ Give two examples of reflections that interrupt the observation of the flood.

## LITERARY FOCUS

### The Descriptive Essay

A **descriptive essay** re-creates a person, an object, a place, or a scene in the reader's imagination. Good descriptive writing creates a strong impres-

*Flood* **319**

1. "color is foul, rusty cream; black verticals of rain soaked trunks standing out of pale water; violent froth that looks like dirty lace"
2. ■ *Sound:* "a roar, a high windy sound"; "snapper hisses"
   ■ *Smell:* "air smells damp and acrid, like fuel oil, or insecticide"
   ■ *Motion:* "roving frantically to escape: rushing, a wild sweep and hurry"
3. The flood changes the world's appearance and brings people closer together.

## VOCABULARY

1. *Buttressed* is contrasted with *unsupported;* means "supported."
2. *Violent* and *explodes* suggest that *roils* means "moves turbulently."
3. *Left* suggests that *recedes* means "moves backward."
4. *Rhythmically peaking* suggests that *scallops* means "series of curved projections."
5. *Interlace* means "to cross over and under," as suggested by *like teeth on a zipper.*

---

sion of its subject for a *purpose:* to illustrate vividly a general idea or observation about life.

A descriptive essay leads the reader to such observations by presenting specific details and concrete language that add up to an overall idea about life. **Concrete language** is another name for sensory language, or words that appeal to our senses of sight, hearing, taste, smell, touch, and motion. For example, in "A Child's Christmas in Wales" (page 286), Dylan Thomas remembers "the gravy smell . . . the brandy, the pudding and mince, coiling up to my nostrils. . . ." Because of his enticing appeal to the senses of sight, smell, and taste, Thomas draws the reader into the scene with him and vividly illustrates the idea that childhood memories are so intense that they never fade.

### Thinking About the Descriptive Essay

1. Find three examples in "Flood" of descriptions that appeal to the sense of sight.
2. To what senses besides sight does Dillard's sensory language appeal? Give examples of each.
3. What is the purpose of Dillard's essay? That is, to what observation about life do the concrete details of the flood add up?

## VOCABULARY

### Context Clues

**Context clues** help us determine the meaning of an unfamiliar word by examining the meanings of the words around it. As in the example below, the context often suggests a comparison or a contrast that clarifies the meaning of the unfamiliar word:

> The high creek doesn't look like our creek. Our creek splashes transparently over a jumble of rocks; the high creek obliterates everything in flat *opacity.*

Here the italicized word *opacity* is contrasted with the word *transparently. Opacity,* therefore, must mean something not transparent, a surface that cannot be seen through.

Sometimes the surrounding words are restatements or synonyms of the unknown word, as in the following example:

> . . .the date was June twenty-first, the *solstice,* midsummer's night, the longest daylight of the year. . . .

*Solstice* is actually defined by the phrases that precede and follow it.

The following excerpts are from "Flood." Decide the meaning of each italicized word by studying its context. Check your answers in the Glossary or in a dictionary. Then use the word in an original sentence.

1. It takes a bit of nerve even to stand on the bridge; the flood has ripped away a wedge of concrete that *buttressed* the bridge on the bank. Now one corner of the bridge hangs apparently unsupported. . . .
2. Below me the floodwater *roils* to a violent froth that looks like dirty lace, a lace that continually explodes before my eyes.
3. There are so many white plastic gallon milk jugs that when the flood ultimately *recedes,* they are left on the grassy banks looking from a distance like a flock of white geese.
4. Right behind the road's shoulder are waves, waves whipped in rhythmically peaking *scallops,* racing downstream.
5. The wall is one brick wide; we can't pass. So we clasp hands and lean out backwards over the turbulent water; our feet *interlace* like teeth on a zipper, we pull together, stand, and continue on our ways.

## COMPOSITION

### Evaluating a Descriptive Essay

■ A descriptive essay should create a single overall impression of its subject. What impression does Dillard create in "Flood," and how does she create it? First identify the overall impression of "Flood." Then find specific descriptive details that Dillard uses, and explain how they create the essay's overall impression.

### Writing a Description from a Moving Vantage Point

■ Because Dillard walks through the scene she describes, her vantage point changes as she goes. Take a short stroll—perhaps from your home to a place that looks quite different. Make notes on the changing scenery that you find as you walk. Then write an essay describing what you saw. Be sure to include specific images of people, buildings, the landscape, and the weather, and to use sensory language.

---

## COMPOSITION: GUIDELINES FOR EVALUATION

### EVALUATING A DESCRIPTIVE ESSAY

**Objective**

To determine the overall impression conveyed by a descriptive essay

**Guidelines for Evaluation**

- suggested length: three to five paragraphs
- should identify the overall impression
- should cite specific examples of description
- should show how these examples contribute to the overall impression

### WRITING DESCRIPTION FROM A MOVING VANTAGE POINT

**Objective**

To convey a vivid impression of the experience of taking a walk

**Guidelines for Evaluation**

- suggested length: 250–500 words
- should describe people, buildings, landscape, weather as experienced by the writer
- should use figurative language

Mark Twain (1835–1910), the pen name of Samuel Langhorne Clemens, grew up beside the Mississippi River. The river traffic awakened in him an urge to travel and provided him with a wealth of inspiration. It also provided him with his pen name, which was actually a term used by riverboat pilots to indicate the depth of the river. Twain's classic novels, *The Adventures of Tom Sawyer* and *The Adventures of Huckleberry Finn,* are set near and on the Mississippi.

*Life on the Mississippi* includes a history of the river and describes Twain's boyhood, his experiences as a riverboat pilot, and his impressions of the river after years of being away from it.

■ When you were a child riding in a car, you probably were entertained by the passing cars and scenery. How will becoming a driver yourself change the experience?

AT A GLANCE

- In mastering the language of the river, Twain lost its poetry.
- Twain recalls a glorious sunset when steamboating was still new.

LITERARY OPTIONS

- descriptive essay
- purpose
- figurative language

THEMATIC OPTIONS

- innocence vs. experience
- fact vs. imagination

**1 STYLE: IMAGERY**

The rich color imagery expresses Twain's initial point of view before he exchanged poetry for knowledge.

**2 STYLE: SIMILE**

Twain expresses his first fresh, untutored perception in vivid comparisons of the water to silver and the branch to a flame.

**3 RESPONSE JOURNAL**

Have students write about seeing something marvelous for the first time—something that they "had never seen . . . at home."

*Mark Twain*

# Two Views of the River

Now when I had mastered the language of this water and had come to know every trifling feature that bordered the great river as familiarly as I knew the letters of the alphabet, I had made a valuable acquisition. But I had lost something, too. I had lost something which could never be restored to me while I lived. All the grace, the beauty, the poetry had gone out of the majestic river! I still keep in mind a certain wonderful sunset which I witnessed when steamboating was new to me. A broad expanse of the river was turned to blood; in the middle distance the red hue brightened into gold, through which a solitary log came floating, black and conspicuous; in one place a long, slanting mark lay sparkling upon the water; in another the surface was broken by boiling, tumbling rings, that were as many-tinted as an opal; where the ruddy flush was faintest, was a smooth spot that was cov-ered with graceful circles and radiating lines, ever so delicately traced; the shore on our left was densely wooded, and the somber shadow that fell from this forest was broken in one place by a long, ruffled trail that shone like silver; and high above the forest wall a clean-stemmed dead tree waved a single leafy bough that glowed like a flame in the unobstructed splendor that was flowing from the sun. There were graceful curves, reflected images, woody heights, soft distances; and over the whole scene, far and near, the dissolving lights drifted steadily, enriching it, every passing moment, with new marvels of coloring.

I stood like one bewitched. I drank it in, in a speechless rapture. The world was new to me, and I had never seen anything like this at home. But as I have said, a day came when I began to cease from noting the glories and the charms

*Two Views of the River*  **321**

**LITERAL QUESTION**

**1a.** What vision did he keep in mind from the time when steamboating was new to him? (a certain wonderful sunset)

**INFERENTIAL QUESTION**

**1b.** Why do you think he treasured that memory? (Not only was it beautiful, it was also a unique, unchanging experience that he could never duplicate because he had changed.)

**1 PURPOSE**

Twain shows how the pilot's practical analysis does not take splendor into account and reduces a beautiful scene into a handful of useful clues about the river's condition.

*A Midnight Race on the Mississippi,* 1860 Currier and Ives lithograph.

which the moon and the sun and the twilight wrought upon the river's face; another day came when I ceased altogether to note them. Then, if that sunset scene had been repeated, I should have looked upon it without rapture, and should have commented upon it, inwardly, after this fashion: This sun means that we are going to have wind tomorrow; that floating log means that the river is rising, small thanks to it; that slanting mark on the water refers to a bluff reef[1] which is going to kill somebody's steamboat one of these nights, if it keeps on stretching out like that; those tumbling "boils" show a dissolving bar[2] and a changing channel there; the lines and circles in the slick water over yonder are a warn-

ing that that troublesome place is shoaling up[3] dangerously; that silver streak in the shadow of the forest is the "break" from a new snag, and he has located himself in the very best place he could have found to fish for steamboats; that tall dead tree, with a single living branch, is not going to last long, and then how is a body ever going to get through this blind place at night without the friendly old landmark?

No, the romance and the beauty were all gone from the river. All the value any feature of it had for me now was the amount of usefulness it could furnish toward compassing the safe piloting of a steamboat. Since those days, I have pitied doctors from my heart. What does the

---

1. **reef:** an underwater ridge of sand or rock.
2. **dissolving bar:** a sandbar gradually worn away by a change in the river's current.

3. **shoaling up:** becoming shallow. A shoal is a shallow area in a river or ocean.

---

## GUIDED READING

### LITERAL QUESTION

**1a.** What does Twain see in the slanting line that once "lay sparkling upon the water?" (a bluff reef that will kill a steamboat some night)

### INFERENTIAL QUESTION

**1b.** What does this prediction suggest about his ability to enjoy the present moment for itself? (With his knowledge he projects ahead into the future—a dangerous one—and is no longer able to enjoy the present.)

lovely flush in a beauty's cheek mean to a doctor but a "break" that ripples above some deadly disease? Are not all her visible charms sown thick with what are to him the signs and symbols of hidden decay? Does he ever see her beauty at all, or doesn't he simply view her professionally, and comment upon her unwholesome condition all to himself? And doesn't he sometimes wonder whether he has gained most or lost most by learning his trade?

## STUDY QUESTIONS

### Recalling

1. What does Twain say he has acquired over his years as a riverboat pilot? What does he say he has lost?
2. Find several details of color in Twain's description of his first view of sunset on the river.
3. What is the significance of the floating log to the inexperienced Twain? To the experienced Twain?

### Interpreting

4. Choose four details from Twain's first description of the sunset on the river, and explain how they reveal the poetry he once saw in it.
5. Explain how the experienced pilot's view of each of these four details contrasts with Twain's earlier view.
6. Which of the two views does Twain expect the reader to prefer? Explain how he makes that clear in the essay.

### Extending

7. What attitudes or stages of life do the two views of the river represent? What value can you find in each view that the other lacks?

## VIEWPOINT

Mark Twain once wrote a letter expressing an idea similar to the central idea in "Two Views of the River":

> . . . the romance of life is the only part of it that is overwhelmingly valuable, and romance dies with youth.

■ Do you agree with Twain that romance—the first "view of the river"—must "die with youth"? Or do you feel that it is possible to hold onto both views at the same time? Explain.

## COMPOSITION

### Writing About a Descriptive Essay

■ Explain how the change in Twain's view of the Mississippi is reflected in the language of this essay. First contrast the similes Twain uses in his first description of the river with the plainer language he uses in his second view of it. Then explain how this change reinforces his statement, "No, the romance and beauty were all gone from the river."

### Writing a Description from Two Perspectives

■ Write two descriptions of a place you loved as a child, showing your past and present feelings toward it. For example, you might write two descriptions of a zoo, a playground, or a favorite spot in your neighborhood or home. Describe the place as you used to see it, choosing details and language that reflect your earlier feelings. Then describe the way you see it and feel about it now. Do you hardly notice the details that were important to you before? Have other details become more important? Be sure that your two descriptions make the contrast in your views very clear.

## COMPARING ESSAYS

1. Both "Flood" and "Two Views of the River" use color to describe bodies of water. Compare the use of color in the two essays. What colors are used? Why are different colors used? What effect does each author's use of color have on the mood of the essay?
2. Twain takes two approaches to his description of the Mississippi, the poetic and the practical. Compare his two approaches with Dillard's approach in "Flood."

*Two Views of the River* **323**

## COMPOSITION: GUIDELINES FOR EVALUATION

### WRITING ABOUT A DESCRIPTIVE ESSAY

**Objective**

To analyze Twain's control of language

**Guidelines for Evaluation**

- suggested length: two to three paragraphs
- should mention Twain's contrasting views
- should describe three similes in first paragraph
- should show how language of second paragraph differs from first

### WRITING A DESCRIPTION FROM TWO PERSPECTIVES

**Objective**

To describe two different views of same place

**Guidelines for Evaluation**

- suggested length: two to three paragraphs
- should describe earlier view in first paragraph
- should use second paragraph to describe present view
- should contrast two views using details

The novelist John Dos Passos (1896–1970) was born in Chicago and was educated at Harvard University. His most famous work is the series of three novels known as the *U.S.A.* trilogy. Like all his novels, the trilogy is marked by social and political concerns and by Dos Passos' experimentation with style. Although they are works of fiction, these books include much factual material.

Dos Passos wrote the following powerfully persuasive essay in 1955, in response to a letter from a group of German students.

■ What do you admire about America?

*John Dos Passos*

# The American Cause

**1** Not long ago I received a letter from some German students asking me to explain to them in three hundred words why they should admire the United States. "Young people in Germany," they wrote "as in other places in the world are disillusioned, weary of pronouncements on the slogan level. They are not satisfied with negations, they have been told over and over again what to hate and what to fight.... They want to know what to be and what to do."

This is what I didn't tell them: I didn't tell them that they should admire the United States for the victories of our armed forces or because we had first developed the atomic bomb or the hydrogen bomb, or because we had shinier automobiles or more washing machines and deep freeze or more televisions or ran up more passenger miles of airplane travel a year than any other people in the world. I didn't tell them to admire us for getting more productive work done with less backbreaking than any other people in the world or for our high wages, or our social security system. I didn't tell them to admire us because our popular leaders had the sweetest smiles before the television cameras or because we lived on a magnificent continent that offered an unbelievable variety of climates, mountains, plains, rivers, estuaries,[1] seashores. Some of these are very good things but they are not things that would help them "to know what to be and what to do."

**2** This is what I told them: I told them they should admire the United States not for what we were but for what we might become. Selfgoverning democracy was not an established creed, but a program for growth. I reminded them that industrial society was a new thing in the world and

---

1. **estuaries** [es'choo er'ēs]: places where rivers feed into the ocean.

that although we Americans had gone further than any people in spreading out its material benefits we were just beginning, amid crimes, illusions, mistakes and false starts, to get to work on how to spread out what people needed much more: the sense of belonging, the faith in human dignity, the confidence of each man in the greatness of his own soul without which life is a meaningless servitude. I told them to admire our failures because they might contain the seeds of great victories to come, not of the victories that come through massacring men, women and children, but of the victories that come through overcoming the evil inherent in mankind through urgent and warmhearted use of our best brains. I told them to admire us for our foolish trust in other peoples, for our failure to create an empire when empire building was easy. I told them to admire us for our still unstratified[2] society, where every man has the chance, if he has the will and the wit, to invent his own thoughts and to make his own way. I told them to admire us for the hope we still have that there is enough goodness in man to use the omnipotence science has given him to ennoble his life on earth instead of degrading it. Selfgovernment, through dangers and distortions and failures, is the American cause. Faith in selfgovernment, when all is said and done, is faith in the eventual goodness of man.

---

2. **unstratified:** not structured into different social classes.

## STUDY QUESTIONS

### Recalling

1. For what reason did the German students write to Dos Passos?
2. Among the reasons Dos Passos mentions for admiring America, give two that he chooses not to tell the German students.
3. Give two of the reasons that Dos Passos does offer the students for admiring America.

### Interpreting

4. What do the students mean when they say they want "to know what to be and what to do"? Explain why Dos Passos' first set of reasons would not help the students learn this.
5. Explain the statement that faith in democracy is "faith in the eventual goodness of man."
6. "The American Cause" comes from a book entitled *The Theme Is Freedom.* Explain the message included in both of these titles.

### Extending

7. What is the basic difference between the reasons Dos Passos gives the students and those he does not give them? Which of his reasons for admiring America do you think is the most important? Why?

## LITERARY FOCUS

### Techniques of Persuasive Essays

In a **persuasive essay** the author expresses an opinion on a particular matter and tries to convince the reader of that opinion. By noting the opinion and the action called for, the reader can determine the author's purpose. In order to persuade their readers, writers of persuasive essays marshal objective evidence such as facts, incidents, and examples in support of their opinions. Persuasive writers also present ideas, reasons, and logical arguments showing why readers should agree with their opinions on the matter.

In addition, many writers make their essays especially persuasive by mentioning alternative opinions and explaining why they find these opinions unsatisfactory. By recognizing and disposing of alternative views, a persuasive writer can convince readers that the opinion stated in the essay has been formed only after careful and objective thought.

*The American Cause* **325**

- Our failures may contain the seeds of future victories.
- Self-government—faith in people's goodness—is the American cause.

Admitting to mistakes and failures clears the way for strong affirmations that support Dos Passos' case for self-government.

Dos Passos reiterates the controlling theme, stressing that self-government triumphs over the forces that threaten freedom.

### REFLECTING ON THE SELECTION

What is the connection between faith in self-government and faith in human goodness? (Those who are content to be ruled "by the people" thereby place their trust in basic human nature to make the right choices and rule well.)

### STUDY QUESTIONS

1. wanted him to explain why they should admire the United States
2. Possible answers: military victories; luxuries; wages and productivity
3. Possible answers: self-governing democracy; "foolish" trust in others; unstratified society
4. want to know what ideals and goals are important; material achievements, not priorities for freedom seekers
5. expresses belief that most people will choose what is right and fair
6. Freedom is the American cause.
7. ▪ *not given:* material concerns; *given:* ideals
   ▪ Answers should choose one of the qualities mentioned by Dos Passos and justify the choice.

## Thinking About the Persuasive Essay

1. ■ Democracy is what makes America great.
   ■ to persuade people to see America's greatness as residing in democratic spirit, not in material success
2. ■ by pointing out ways in which democracy makes people free, discussing its potential for improvising society, arguing that it attests to a faith in basic human values
   ■ listing them, offering more powerful, moving arguments to support his own opinion
3. Answers will vary but should clearly state whether the essay is convincing and offer reasons to support this opinion.

## VOCABULARY

1. (d) self-government
2. (d) negations
3. (d) inherent
4. (c) unstratified
5. (a) estuaries

### Thinking About the Persuasive Essay

1. In one sentence state the opinion that Dos Passos expresses in "The American Cause." What is his purpose in writing this essay?
2. How does Dos Passos support his opinion in this essay? How does he dispose of alternative opinions?
3. Do you find Dos Passos' essay convincing? Why or why not?

## VOCABULARY

### Sentence Completions

Each of the following sentences contains a blank to be filled by four possible word choices. Each of the four choices comes from "The American Cause." Write the letter of the word that completes each sentence correctly and that uses the word in the same sense as it is used in "The American Cause."

1. Democracy is another word for _____.
   (a) faith              (c) goodness
   (b) omnipotence        (d) self-government
2. The senator's speech contained several _____ of the false rumors spread by his political enemies.
   (a) pronouncements     (c) distortions
   (b) benefits           (d) negations
3. Freedom of speech is _____ in our democratic system.
   (a) young              (c) disillusioned
   (b) warmhearted        (d) inherent

4. While some countries have a rigid class system, others are largely _____.
   (a) failures           (c) unstratified
   (b) productive         (d) unbelievable
5. In _____ river water is made salty by the sea.
   (a) estuaries          (c) climates
   (b) mountains          (d) empire

## COMPOSITION

### Writing About a Persuasive Essay

■ What is Dos Passos' purpose in "The American Cause," and how does he accomplish this purpose? What persuasive techniques does Dos Passos use in this essay: What facts, examples, ideas, reasons, and arguments does he present? *For help with this assignment, see Lesson 10 in the Writing About Literature Handbook at the back of this book.*

### Writing a Persuasive Essay

■ Imagine that you are writing to a foreign friend who has asked what you think is the most positive aspect of American life. Write a letter answering your friend's question. You may consider some of the following aspects of American life: freedom of speech and of the press, democracy and free elections, natural resources and wealth, educational and job opportunities, technological advances. Be sure to support your opinion with relevant evidence and reasonable arguments.

## COMPOSITION: GUIDELINES FOR EVALUATION

### WRITING ABOUT A PERSUASIVE ESSAY

**Objective**

To identify essay's purpose and analyze the way it is achieved

**Guidelines for Evaluation**

■ suggested length: one to three paragraphs
■ should state author's purpose: to convince readers that democracy is what makes America great
■ should tell what persuasive techniques author uses
■ should cite specific examples from essay

### WRITING A PERSUASIVE ESSAY

**Objective**

To present an opinion in a convincing way

**Guidelines for Evaluation**

■ suggested length: 250–450 words
■ should clearly state what writer thinks is most positive aspect of American life
■ should present sufficient evidence and ample ideas, reasons, or arguments to support opinion
■ should use informal style of a personal letter

Martin Luther King, Jr. (1929–1968), was ordained a Baptist minister at the age of eighteen. He first came to national prominence eight years later when he organized a boycott of the bus system by the black citizens of Montgomery, Alabama. King's crusade of nonviolent resistance helped lead the way to the Civil Rights Act of 1964 and the Voting Rights Act of 1965. His work also earned him the Nobel Prize for Peace in 1964. Often the target of violence, King was assassinated at the age of thirty-nine.

One highlight of King's career occurred on August 28, 1963, when 200,000 civil rights marchers heard him make the following speech from the steps of the Lincoln Memorial in Washington, D.C.

■ Why can telling others your dreams be risky?

**AT A GLANCE**

King states that the gathering has come to the nation's capital to dramatize an appalling condition and to cash a "promissory note" that has not been honored.

**LITERARY OPTIONS**

■ persuasive speech
■ parallelism
■ metaphor

**THEMATIC OPTIONS**

■ freedom and justice
■ cooperation and fellowship
■ overcoming obstacles

*Martin Luther King, Jr.*

# I Have a Dream

1 Five score years ago, a great American, in whose symbolic shadow we stand, signed the Emancipation Proclamation.[1] This momentous decree came as a great beacon light of hope to millions of Negro slaves who had been seared in the flames of withering injustice. It came as a joyous daybreak to end the long night of captivity.

But one hundred years later, we must face the tragic fact that the Negro is still not free. One hundred years later, the life of the Negro is still sadly crippled by the manacles[2] of segregation and the chains of discrimination. One hundred years later, the Negro lives on a lonely island of poverty in the midst of a vast ocean of material prosperity. One hundred years later, the Negro is still languished in the corners of American society and finds himself an exile in his own land. So we have come here today to dramatize an appalling condition.

In a sense we have come to our nation's Capital to cash a check. When the architects of our republic wrote the magnificent words of the Constitution and the Declaration of Independence, they were signing a promissory note[3] to which every American was to fall heir. This note was a promise that all men would be guaranteed the unalienable rights of life, liberty, and the pursuit of happiness.

It is obvious today that America has defaulted on[4] this promissory note insofar as her citizens

---

1. **great American . . . Emancipation Proclamation:** Speaking in front of the Lincoln Memorial in Washington, D.C., King draws a connection between the civil rights movement of the 1960s and Abraham Lincoln's freeing of the slaves a century before. The Emancipation Proclamation was the law signed by Lincoln declaring that, on January 1, 1863, all slaves in the United States would become free.
2. **manacles:** chains.
3. **promissory note:** written promise to pay a sum of money at a future time.
4. **defaulted on:** failed to live up to.

*I Have a Dream* **327**

**1 SETTING**

The Lincoln Memorial is the stage chosen for a historic speech to inspire action against injustice.

**2 STYLE: METAPHOR**

King uses the metaphor *manacles of segregation* to dramatize his point that blacks—although no longer bound by the physical chains of slavery—are still not free.

**3 STYLE: EXTENDED METAPHOR**

*Check* and *promissory note* introduce the metaphor with which King develops the idea that injustice is a default that can still be corrected.

## GUIDED READING

**LITERAL QUESTION**

**1a.** What is King's opening statement? ("Five score years ago, a great American . . . signed the Emancipation Proclamation.")

**INFERENTIAL QUESTION**

**1b.** What other famous speech might these words recall, and what point might King be making with this reference? (These words recall Lincoln's Gettysburg Address. King is emphasizing the point that America's struggle for freedom is historic and unfinished, and that blacks are not yet truly emancipated.)

**1 STYLE: METAPHOR**

The metaphor *rock of brotherhood* creates a reassuring image of the solidity of human fellowship.

**2 PURPOSE**

King wants the nation to understand that the civil rights movement, only a few years old in 1963, is not a passing phenomenon, and that it will continue until it achieves all of its goals.

**3 AUDIENCE**

By acknowledging the presence of many whites in the gathering, King extends a hand to the millions of whites watching his speech on television. Having established that whites and blacks have begun to work together for racial justice, King can argue further that all people must join in the struggle for equality and justice.

**4 STYLE: PARALLELISM**

The rhetorical question and answers dramatize the principle that true justice must be universal.

of color are concerned. Instead of honoring this sacred obligation, America has given the Negro people a bad check; a check which has come back marked "insufficient funds." But we refuse to believe that the bank of justice is bankrupt. We refuse to believe that there are insufficient funds in the great vaults of opportunity of this nation. So we have come to cash this check—a check that will give us upon demand the riches of freedom and the security of justice. We have also come to this hallowed spot to remind America of the fierce urgency of *now*. This is no time to engage in the luxury of cooling off or to take the tranquilizing of gradualism.[5] *Now* is the time to make real the promises of Democracy. *Now* is the time to rise from the dark and desolate valley of segregation to the sunlit path of racial justice. *Now* is the time to open the doors of opportunity to all of God's children. *Now* is the time to lift our nation from the quicksands of racial injustice to the solid rock of brotherhood.

It would be fatal for the nation to overlook the urgency of the moment and to underestimate the determination of the Negro. This sweltering summer of the Negro's legitimate discontent will not pass until there is an invigorating autumn of freedom and equality. 1963 is not an end, but a beginning. Those who hope that the Negro needed to blow off steam and will now be content will have a rude awakening if the nation returns to business as usual. There will be neither rest nor tranquility in America until the Negro is granted his citizenship rights. The whirlwinds of revolt will continue to shake the foundation of our nation until the bright day of justice emerges.

But there is something that I must say to my people who stand on the warm threshold which leads into the palace of justice. In the process of gaining our rightful place we must not be guilty

___

5. **gradualism:** attitude favoring the slow evolution of social equality over the active promotion of it.

of wrongful deeds. Let us not seek to satisfy our thirst for freedom by drinking from the cup of bitterness and hatred. We must forever conduct our struggle on the high plane of dignity and discipline. We must not allow our creative protest to degenerate into physical violence. Again and again we must rise to the majestic heights of meeting physical force with soul force. The marvelous new militancy which has engulfed the Negro community must not lead us to a distrust of all white people, for many of our white brothers, as evidenced by their presence here today, have come to realize that their destiny is tied up with our destiny and their freedom is inextricably bound to our freedom. We cannot walk alone.

And as we walk, we must make the pledge that we shall march ahead. We cannot turn back. There are those who are asking the devotees of civil rights, "When will you be satisfied?" We can never be satisfied as long as the Negro is the victim of the unspeakable horrors of police brutality. We can never be satisfied as long as our bodies, heavy with the fatigue of travel, cannot gain lodging in the motels of the highways and the hotels of the cities. We cannot be satisfied as long as the Negro's basic mobility is from a smaller ghetto to a larger one. We can never be satisfied as long as a Negro in Mississippi cannot vote and a Negro in New York believes he has

*Above left,* Martin Luther King in 1967; *below right,* singing with several civil rights workers in Montgomery, Alabama. *Background,* the crowd of over 200,000 that heard King deliver his historic speech in Washington on August 28, 1963.

## GUIDED READING

**LITERAL QUESTION**

**1a.** What word does King use to describe the protest, and what does he tell his followers not to allow? (*creative;* physical violence)

**INFERENTIAL QUESTION**

**1b.** What do you think he means by the word *creative,* and how might *creative struggle* be opposed to physical violence? (The struggle he envisions is one that builds and grows; its aims are the opposite of physical violence, which destroys and inhibits.)

## 1 AUDIENCE

King speaks personally to the people present, giving them recognition and encouragement.

## 2 STYLE: PARALLELISM

The repetition of the now-historic phrase *I have a dream* sets forth King's goals in a series of powerful images and introduces a memorable refrain that unifies the climactic portion of his speech.

## 3 STYLE: METAPHOR

The transformation of the desert into an oasis depicts King's belief that we can overcome obstacles to create the world in which we want to live.

## 4 BACKGROUND

King refers here to Governor George Wallace, who opposed the attendance of black students in Alabama schools. Years after King's speech Wallace himself came to advocate many of the goals King describes in his speech.

---

nothing for which to vote. No, no, we are not satisfied, and we will not be satisfied until justice rolls down like waters and righteousness like a mighty stream.

I am not unmindful that some of you have come here out of great trials and tribulations. Some of you have come fresh from narrow jail cells. Some of you have come from areas where your quest for freedom left you battered by the storms of persecution and staggered by the winds of police brutality. You have been the veterans of creative suffering. Continue to work with the faith that unearned suffering is redemptive.

Go back to Mississippi, go back to Alabama, go back to South Carolina, go back to Georgia, go back to Louisiana, go back to the slums and ghettos of our northern cities, knowing that somehow this situation can and will be changed. Let us not wallow in the valley of despair.

I say to you today, my friends, that in spite of the difficulties and frustrations of the moment I still have a dream. It is a dream deeply rooted in the American dream.

I have a dream that one day this nation will rise up and live out the true meaning of its creed: "We hold these truths to be self-evident; that all men are created equal."[6]

I have a dream that one day on the red hills of Georgia the sons of former slaves and the sons of former slaveowners will be able to sit down together at the table of brotherhood.

I have a dream that one day even the state of Mississippi, a desert state sweltering with the heat of injustice and oppression, will be transformed into an oasis of freedom and justice.

I have a dream that my four little children will one day live in a nation where they will not be judged by the color of their skin but by the content of their character.

---

6. "We hold . . . equal.": King is quoting from the Declaration of Independence.

---

I have a dream today.

I have a dream that one day the state of Alabama, whose governor's lips are presently dripping with the words of interposition[7] and nullification,[8] will be transformed into a situation where little black boys and black girls will be able to join hands with little white boys and white girls and walk together as sisters and brothers.

I have a dream today.

I have a dream that one day every valley shall be exalted, every hill and mountain shall be made low, the rough places will be made plain, and the crooked places will be made straight, and the glory of the Lord shall be revealed, and all flesh shall see it together.

This is our hope. This is the faith with which I return to the South. With this faith we will be able to hew out of the mountain of despair a stone of hope. With this faith we will be able to transform the jangling discords of our nation into a beautiful symphony of brotherhood. With this faith we will be able to work together, to pray together, to struggle together, to go to jail together, to stand up for freedom together, knowing that we will be free one day.

This will be the day when all of God's children will be able to sing with new meaning

*My country, 'tis of thee,*
*Sweet land of liberty,*
*Of thee I sing:*
*Land where my fathers died,*
*Land of the pilgrims' pride,*
*From every mountain-side*
*Let freedom ring.*

And if America is to be a great nation this must become true. So let freedom ring from the

---

7. **interposition:** interference; here, the claim by some state governors that the federal government's promotion of integration interferes with the rights of the states.
8. **nullification:** the attempt by a state to prevent the enforcement of a federal law within its territory.

---

## GUIDED READING

### LITERAL QUESTIONS

**1a.** Where does King envision the sons of former slaves and the sons of former slaveowners sitting together? (at the table of brotherhood)

**2a.** What does King say *all* children will sing with a new meaning? ("My country, 'tis of thee . . . ")

### INFERENTIAL QUESTIONS

**1b.** What can you infer about King's visions of equality from this metaphor? (His visions include everyone and have no place for revenge or unforgiving bitterness.)

**2b.** Why will this song take on "new meaning"? (The liberty in the familiar song will finally be experienced by black children.)

prodigious hilltops of New Hampshire. Let freedom ring from the mighty mountains of New York. Let freedom ring from the heightening Alleghenies of Pennsylvania!

Let freedom ring from the snowcapped Rockies of Colorado!

Let freedom ring from the curvaceous peaks of California!

But not only that; let freedom ring from Stone Mountain of Georgia!

Let freedom ring from Lookout Mountain of Tennessee!

Let freedom ring from every hill and molehill of Mississippi. From every mountainside, let freedom ring.

**1** When we let freedom ring, when we let it ring from every village and every hamlet, from every state and every city, we will be able to speed up that day when all of God's children, black men and white men, Jews and Gentiles, Protestants and Catholics, will be able to join hands and sing in the words of the old Negro spiritual, "Free at last! free at last! thank God almighty, we are free at last!"

---

## STUDY QUESTIONS

### Recalling

1. What is the "promissory note" to which King refers? What did it guarantee?
2. While demanding their rights, what two things does King urge his listeners to do?
3. Name three specific elements of the dream King describes for his audience.
4. What does King argue must happen before America can be great?

### Interpreting

5. Explain how King uses comparisons to weather and to day and night in order to describe the position of blacks in America. What is that position, as King sees it?
6. In what ways does King show that his message is intended for people of all races?
7. Describe the effect of the final words of King's speech. Explain the irony in the fact that these words, quoted from a hymn, are engraved on King's tombstone.

### Extending

8. What do you think are the advantages and disadvantages of reading "I Have a Dream," as opposed to hearing it delivered as a speech?

## VIEWPOINT

The crowd that assembled at the Lincoln Memorial on that humid August day in 1963 heard many speakers, but, according to one newspaper:

Dr. King touched all the themes of the day, only better than anybody else. He was both militant and sad, and he sent the crowd away feeling that the long journey had been worthwhile.

■ Give examples from the speech to show that King was both "militant and sad." Why would the speech have made the crowd feel that their journey to Washington had been worthwhile?

## LITERARY FOCUS

### Parallelism in Persuasive Writing

**Parallelism** is the use of a series of words, phrases, or sentences that have similar grammatical form. The repetition creates a rhythm and a dramatic force that are effective in persuasive writing but especially so in oratory, or speeches. The use of parallelism in oratory helps the listener to follow the speaker's arguments and to remember the key points of the speech. For example, Abraham Lincoln ended his famous Gettysburg Address with

*I Have a Dream* **331**

King promises that freedom will ring from everywhere in America.

**1 STYLE: PARALLELISM**

As King repeats *Let freedom ring,* he builds momentum, intensifying the urgency and eloquence of his appeal.

REFLECTING ON THE SELECTION

Why might the words of the spiritual create an especially powerful ending to King's speech? (These words remind Americans that this promise of freedom is still unfulfilled on earth; it also projects the hope that the slaves' dream may finally come true.)

STUDY QUESTIONS

1. Constitution and Declaration of Independence; life, liberty, the pursuit of happiness
2. avoid distrust, violence; to fight until justice is won
3. Ideals stated in Declaration will be realized; fellowship will be achieved; racism will end.
4. must be freedom, justice for all
5. *darkness/sweltering head:*—metaphors for oppression; *whirlwind*—metaphor for revolt; *daybreak/sunshine/autumn*—metaphors for justice
6. refers to freedom for all God's children; says blacks and whites must work together
7. *effect:* powerful, inspirational; *irony:* words referred to freedom from oppression; assassination has "freed" him from lifelong struggle
8. *advantages:* can be reread to gain greater understanding; *disadvantages:* lacks emotional force

VIEWPOINT

■ *sadness*—conveyed in description of blacks' condition; *militancy:*—description of fight for justice
■ The occasion was historic.

## LITERARY FOCUS

### Parallelism

- Repeated phrase *go back to* highlights importance of the fight for civil rights.
- Repetition of *I have a dream* highlights King's long-term goals.
- Repetition of *free at last!* inspires, motivates listeners.

### Analogy

- *funds*—justice/opportunity
- *depositors*—American citizens
- *note*—Constitution/Declaration
- *defaulted*—denial of justice
- *not bankrupt*—justice still possible

## VOCABULARY

1. (c) profaned
2. (b) joys
3. (b) pacifism
4. (a) foes
5. (d) ordinary

## COMPARING ESSAYS

1. ■ "Cause": undramatic, objective; written to a group of foreign students
   ■ "Dream": dramatic, emotional; speech to inspire and motivate civil rights supporters
2. ■ *Similarities:* Both feel justice is attainable in America.
   ■ *Differences:* Dos Passos believes every person has equal opportunity; King believes many are denied equality and opportunity.
   ■ Students should state an opinion and support it with reasons.

---

the statement that "government *of the people, by the people, for the people*, shall not perish from the earth."

### Thinking About Parallelism

■ Find three examples of parallelism in "I Have a Dream." For each example explain what the parallelism highlights in King's message.

### Analogy

An **analogy** is an extended comparison between two objects, ideas, or situations. Analogies can serve many purposes. An analogy often helps to explain unfamiliar terms by comparing them to more familiar ones. An analogy can also persuade an audience to accept the truth of one idea by comparing it to something else that is obviously true. The American poet Emily Dickinson used an analogy to define fame by comparing it to a bee:

> Fame is a bee.
>     It has a song—
> It has a sting—
>     Ah, too, it has a wing.

By means of this comparison, Dickinson explains that fame brings pleasure and pain and that it often does not last.

### Thinking About Analogy

■ Explain the analogy that King develops between justice and a bank in the first part of his speech: Identify the "funds" of the bank of justice, the bank's "depositors," and its "promissory note." How has the bank "defaulted" on that note, according to King? Why is the bank not "bankrupt"?

### VOCABULARY

#### Antonyms

**Antonyms** are words with opposite or nearly opposite meanings. *End* and *beginning* are antonyms. The words in capitals are from "I Have a Dream." On a separate sheet write the letter of the word that is *most nearly the opposite* of the word in capitals *as the word is used in the selection.*

1. HALLOWED: (a) devoted  (b) scary  (c) profaned  (d) dedicated
2. TRIBULATIONS: (a) fears  (b) joys  (c) sorrows  (d) histories

---

3. MILITANCY: (a) fervor  (b) pacifism  (c) antagonism  (d) neutrality
4. DEVOTEES: (a) foes  (b) fans  (c) tribulations  (d) voters
5. PRODIGIOUS: (a) stupid  (b) amazing  (c) monstrous  (d) ordinary

## COMPOSITION

### Writing About a Persuasive Essay

■ King achieves powerful effects through several persuasive techniques: (a) He repeats certain key words and phrases; (b) he uses personal pronouns to speak directly to his audience; (c) he refers to the Bible, to past and present events in America, and, in particular, to experiences shared by black Americans. Find one example in King's speech of each of these techniques, and explain how each contributes to the force of his message.

### Writing a Speech

■ Write a brief persuasive speech to present to your class. You may try to sway your audience to accept your view of one of the following matters: (a) a free college education for all able students; (b) special consideration for the aged; or (c) an issue current in your school. Begin by stating your opinion on your subject. As you write, try to adapt several of King's persuasive techniques—for example, parallelism, repetition, analogy, historical references, and the use of personal pronouns.

### COMPARING ESSAYS

1. "The American Cause" was written originally for a small group of German students. "I Have a Dream" was written for a huge crowd of civil rights marchers and, in a larger sense, for an international audience via television and newspapers. Explain how the differences between the two selections result from the differences in their audiences.
2. Both Dos Passos and King express visions of America. What similarities can you find between these visions? In what ways are they different? Which vision do you find more appealing?

---

## COMPOSITION: GUIDELINES FOR EVALUATION

### WRITING ABOUT A PERSUASIVE ESSAY

#### Objective

To explain how persuasive techniques are used to convey a message

#### Guidelines for Evaluation

- suggested length: one to three paragraphs
- should relate impact of King's message to the techniques he uses
- should present one example each of repetition, use of personal pronouns, biblical references

### WRITING A SPEECH

#### Objective

To convince others to accept an opinion or take a course of action

#### Guidelines for Evaluation

- suggested length: 300–600 words
- should state opinion on proposed subject
- should contain instances of parallelism, repetition, analogy, historical reference
- should have overall effect of persuasiveness

Isaac Asimov (born 1920) came with his parents from the Soviet Union to the United States at the age of three. As a boy he read the science fiction magazines on sale in his father's candy store. Now Asimov writes science fiction as well as nonfiction. Sometimes called a "writing machine," Asimov has written an average of one book every six weeks for almost thirty years.

Much of Asimov's nonfiction explains science and technology for readers who are not experts.

■ Have you awakened in the night with the solution to a math problem you could not solve earlier? How does this happen?

*Isaac Asimov*

# The Eureka[1] Phenomenon

In the old days, when I was writing a great deal of fiction, there would come, once in a while, moments when I was stymied. Suddenly, I would find I had written myself into a hole and could see no way out. To take care of that, I developed a technique which invariably worked.

It was simply this—I went to the movies. Not just any movie. I had to pick a movie which was loaded with action but which made no demands on the intellect. As I watched, I did my best to avoid any conscious thinking concerning my problem, and when I came out of the movie I knew exactly what I would have to do to put the story back on the track.

It never failed.

In fact, when I was working on my doctoral dissertation,[2] too many years ago, I suddenly came across a flaw in my logic that I had not

---

1. **Eureka** [yoo rē′kə]
2. **doctoral dissertation:** book-length discussion of a single topic, written to fulfill the requirements for a Ph.D.

noticed before and that knocked out everything I had done. In utter panic, I made my way to a Bob Hope movie—and came out with the necessary change in point of view.

It is my belief, you see, that thinking is a double phenomenon like breathing.

You can control breathing by deliberate voluntary action: you can breathe deeply and quickly, or you can hold your breath altogether, regardless of the body's needs at the time. This, however, doesn't work well for very long. Your chest muscles grow tired, your body clamors for more oxygen, or less, and you relax. The automatic involuntary control of breathing takes over, adjusts it to the body's needs and unless you have some respiratory disorder, you can forget about the whole thing.

Well, you can think by deliberate voluntary action, too, and I don't think it is much more efficient on the whole than voluntary breath control is. You can deliberately force your mind through channels of deductions and associations

*The Eureka Phenomenon* 333

## GUIDED READING

**LITERAL QUESTION**

**1a.** What would Asimov avoid doing while watching a movie, and what would he know when he came out? (conscious thinking concerning a problem; the solution to the problem)

**INFERENTIAL QUESTION**

**1b.** What might his experience indicate about thinking? (The mind works on more than one level at the same time.)

## 1 THESIS

Involuntary thought makes associations that one cannot think of consciously.

## 2 EXPOSITION: CAUSE AND EFFECT

Asimov further develops his thesis by pointing out the effect of emotion on conscious thought.

## 3 ANECDOTE

Asimov introduces a story to provide a classic example of an involuntary discovery.

## 4 TONE

Asimov's account of the historic event conveys his humor as well as communicating his intention to educate the reader.

## 5 AUDIENCE

Asimov clearly explains scientific facts so that the lay reader can follow and appreciate the story.

---

in search of a solution to some problem and before long you have dug mental furrows for yourself and find yourself circling round and round the same limited pathways. If those pathways yield no solution, no amount of further conscious thought will help.

**1** On the other hand, if you let go, then the thinking process comes under automatic involuntary control and is more apt to take new pathways and make erratic associations you would not think of consciously. The solution will then come while you *think* you are *not* thinking.

The trouble is, though, that conscious thought involves no muscular action and so there is no sensation of physical weariness that **2** would force you to quit. What's more, the panic of necessity tends to force you to go on uselessly, with each added bit of useless effort adding to the panic in a vicious cycle.

It is my feeling that it helps to relax, deliberately, by subjecting your mind to material complicated enough to occupy the voluntary faculty of thought, but superficial enough not to engage the deeper involuntary one. In my case, it is an action movie; in your case, it might be something else.

I suspect it is the involuntary faculty of thought that gives rise to what we call "a flash of intuition," something that I imagine must be merely the result of unnoticed thinking.

**3** Perhaps the most famous flash of intuition in the history of science took place in the city of Syracuse in third-century B.C. Sicily. Bear with me and I will tell you the story—

About 250 B.C., the city of Syracuse was experiencing a kind of Golden Age. It was under the protection of the rising power of Rome, but it retained a king of its own and considerable self-government; it was prosperous; and it had a flourishing intellectual life.

The king was Hieron[3] II, and he had commis-

---

3. **Hieron** [hī′ə rän′]

---

**334** *Nonfiction*

---

sioned a new golden crown from a goldsmith, to whom he had given an ingot of gold as raw material. Hieron, being a practical man, had carefully weighed the ingot and then weighed the crown he received back. The two weights were precisely equal. Good deal!

But then he sat and thought for a while. Suppose the goldsmith had subtracted a little bit of the gold, not too much, and had substituted an equal weight of the considerably less valuable copper. The resulting alloy would still have the appearance of pure gold, but the goldsmith would be plus a quantity of gold over and above his fee. He would be buying gold with copper, so to speak, and Hieron would be neatly cheated.

Hieron didn't like the thought of being cheated any more than you or I would, but he didn't know how to find out for sure if he had been. He could scarcely punish the goldsmith on mere suspicion. What to do?

**4** Fortunately, Hieron had an advantage few rulers in the history of the world could boast. He had a relative of considerable talent. The relative was named Archimedes[4] and he probably had the greatest intellect the world was to see prior to the birth of Newton.[5]

Archimedes was called in and was posed the problem. He had to determine whether the crown Hieron showed him was pure gold, or was gold to which a small but significant quantity of copper had been added.

**5** If we were to reconstruct Archimedes' reasoning, it might go as follows. Gold was the densest known substance (at that time). Its density in modern terms is 19.3 grams per cubic centimeter. This means that a given weight of gold takes up less volume than the same weight of anything else! In fact, a given weight of pure

---

4. **Archimedes** [är′kə mē′dēz]: Greek mathematician, physicist, and inventor who lived from 287 to 212 B.C.
5. **Newton:** Sir Isaac Newton (1642–1727), the English mathematician and physicist who formulated the laws of gravity and motion and developed the system of differential calculus.

---

## GUIDED READING

### LITERAL QUESTION

**1a.** What is the difference between thinking and breathing? (Thought involves no muscular action— no physical sensation—that forces you to quit.)

### INFERENTIAL QUESTION

**1b.** What can you infer from that difference? (One needs to *learn* when and how to let involuntary thinking take control.)

gold takes up less volume than the same weight of *any* kind of impure gold.

The density of copper is 8.92 grams per cubic centimeter, just about half that of gold. If we consider 100 grams of pure gold, for instance, it is easy to calculate it to have a volume of 5.18 cubic centimeters.[6] But suppose that 100 grams of what looked like pure gold was really only 90 grams of gold and 10 grams of copper. The 90 grams of gold would have a volume of 4.66 cubic centimeters, while the 10 grams of copper would have a volume of 1.12 cubic centimeters; for a total value of 5.78 cubic centimeters.

The difference between 5.18 cubic centimeters and 5.78 cubic centimeters is quite a noticeable one, and would instantly tell if the crown were of pure gold, or if it contained 10 per cent copper (with the missing 10 per cent of gold tucked neatly in the goldsmith's strongbox).

All one had to do, then, was measure the volume of the crown and compare it with the volume of the same weight of pure gold.

The mathematics of the time made it easy to measure the volume of many simple shapes: a cube, a sphere, a cone, a cylinder, any flattened object of simple regular shape and known thickness, and so on.

We can imagine Archimedes saying, "All that is necessary, sire, is to pound that crown flat, shape it into a square of uniform thickness, and then I can have the answer for you in a moment."

Whereupon Hieron must certainly have snatched the crown away and said, "No such thing. I can do that much without you; I've studied the principles of mathematics, too. This crown is a highly satisfactory work of art and I won't have it damaged. Just calculate its volume without in any way altering it."

But Greek mathematics had no way of deter- mining the volume of anything with a shape as irregular as the crown, since integral calculus[7] had not yet been invented (and wouldn't be for two thousand years, almost). Archimedes would have had to say, "There is no known way, sire, to carry through a non-destructive determina- tion of volume."

"Then think of one," said Hieron testily.

And Archimedes must have set about think- ing of one, and gotten nowhere. Nobody knows how long he thought, or how hard, or what hypotheses[8] he considered and discarded, or any of the details.

What we do know is that, worn out with thinking, Archimedes decided to visit the public baths and relax. I think we are quite safe in say- ing that Archimedes had no intention of taking his problem to the baths with him. It would be ridiculous to imagine he would, for the public baths of a Greek metropolis weren't intended for that sort of thing.

The Greek baths were a place for relaxation. Half the social aristocracy of the town would be there and there was a great deal more to do than wash. One steamed one's self, got a massage, exercised, and engaged in general socializing. We can be sure that Archimedes intended to forget the stupid crown for a while.

One can envisage him engaging in light talk, discussing the latest news from Alexandria and Carthage, the latest scandals in town, the latest funny jokes at the expense of the country-squire Romans—and then he lowered himself into a nice hot bath which some bumbling attendant had filled too full.

The water in the bath slopped over as Arch- imedes got in. Did Archimedes notice that at once, or did he sigh, sink back, and paddle his feet awhile before noting the water-slop? I guess the latter. But, whether soon or late, he noticed,

---

6. **5.18 cubic centimeters:** Asimov obtained this figure by dividing 100 grams by gold's density, which is 19.3 grams per cubic centimeter. Density is the weight of a substance per unit of volume.

7. **integral calculus:** mathematical system used to deter- mine the volumes of irregularly curved areas.
8. **hypotheses** [hī poth'ə sēs']: theories to be tested through experimentation.

## GUIDED READING

**LITERAL QUESTIONS**

**1a.** What fact leads Asimov to conclude that Archime- des didn't intend to take his problem with him to the baths? (The public baths "weren't intended for that sort of thing.")

**2a.** What does Asimov guess Archimedes did in the bath before he noticed the water-slop? (sighed, sank back, and paddled his feet)

**INFERENTIAL QUESTIONS**

**1b.** What might you infer about the truth of Asimov's anecdote? (Archimedes' discovery, its time, and the place are facts; exactly how the discovery occurred is conjecture based on Asimov's knowl- edge of ancient Greek life.)

**2b.** Why might Asimov assume that Archimedes didn't immediately notice the spillover? (Asimov's own experience is that insight comes when the mind is not consciously searching.)

## 1 PLOT: CLIMAX

The solution to Archimedes' problem dawns in a blinding flash as Asimov's anecdote reaches its climax.

## 2 READING SKILLS: CAUSE AND EFFECT

Asimov explains, step by step, the cause-effect chain that Archimedes discovered as the solution to his problem.

and that one fact, added to all the chains of reasoning his brain had been working on during the period of relaxation when it was unhampered by the comparative stupidities (even in Archimedes) of voluntary thought, gave Archimedes his answer in one blinding flash of insight.

Jumping out of the bath, he proceeded to run home at top speed through the streets of Syracuse....

And as he ran, Archimedes shouted over and over, "I've got it! I've got it!" Of course, knowing no English, he was compelled to shout it in Greek, so it came out, "*Eureka! Eureka!*"

Archimedes' solution was so simple that anyone could understand it—once Archimedes explained it.

If an object that is not affected by water in any way, is immersed in water, it is bound to displace an amount of water equal to its own volume, since two objects cannot occupy the same space at the same time.

Suppose, then, you had a vessel large enough

to hold the crown and suppose it had a small overflow spout set into the middle of its side. And suppose further that the vessel was filled with water exactly to the spout, so that if the water level were raised a bit higher, however slightly, some would overflow.

Next, suppose that you carefully lower the crown into the water. The water level would rise by an amount equal to the volume of the crown, and that volume of water would pour out the overflow and be caught in a small vessel. Next, a lump of gold, known to be pure and exactly equal in weight to the crown, is also immersed in the water and again the level rises and the overflow is caught in a second vessel.

If the crown were pure gold, the overflow would be exactly the same in each case, and the volume of water caught in the two small vessels would be equal. If, however, the crown were of alloy, it would produce a larger overflow than the pure gold would and this would be easily noticeable.

What's more, the crown would in no way be

**336** *Nonfiction*

## GUIDED READING

### LITERAL QUESTION

**1a.** What did Archimedes discover, and how did this discovery help him solve the king's problem? (An object immersed in water displaces an amount of water equal to its own volume. Therefore, the king can learn the crown's volume by immersing it in water and measuring the spillover.)

### INFERENTIAL QUESTION

**1b.** Why was Archimedes able to discover this scientific principle while he was relaxing in the tub? (Even while he relaxed, Archimedes' mind had been working on the problem unconsciously; noticing the spillover probably gave his unconscious thinking the final push it needed.)

harmed, defaced, or even as much as scratched. More important, Archimedes had discovered the "principle of buoyancy."[9]

And was the crown pure gold? I've heard that it turned out to be alloy and that the goldsmith was executed, but I wouldn't swear to it.

How often does this "Eureka phenomenon" happen? How often is there this flash of deep insight during a moment of relaxation, this triumphant cry of "I've got it! I've got it!" which must surely be a moment of the purest ecstasy this sorry world can afford?

I wish there were some way we could tell. I suspect that in the history of science it happens *often*; I suspect that very few significant discoveries are made by the pure technique of voluntary thought; I suspect that voluntary thought may possibly prepare the ground (if even that),

9. **principle of buoyancy:** law stating that a submerged object displaces a volume of water equal to its own volume. The object will float if it is less dense than water.

but that the final touch, the real inspiration, comes when thinking is under involuntary control.

But the world is in a conspiracy to hide the fact. Scientists are wedded to reason, to the meticulous working out of consequences from assumptions to the careful organization of experiments designed to check those consequences. If a certain line of experiments ends nowhere, it is omitted from the final report. If an inspired guess turns out to be correct, it is *not* reported as an inspired guess. Instead, a solid line of voluntary thought is invented after the fact to lead up to the thought, and that is what is inserted in the final report.

3   The result is that anyone reading scientific papers would swear that *nothing* took place but voluntary thought maintaining a steady clumping stride from origin to destination, and that just can't be true.

It's such a shame. Not only does it deprive science of much of its glamour (how much of the dramatic story in Watson's *Double Helix* do you suppose got into the final reports announcing the great discovery of the structure of DNA?[10]), but it hands over the important process of "insight," "inspiration," "revelation" to the mystic.

The scientist actually becomes ashamed of having what we might call a revelation, as though to have one is to betray reason—when actually what we call revelation in a man who has devoted his life to reasoned thought, is after all merely reasoned thought that is not under voluntary control....

Other cases? Certainly.

10. **Watson's *Double Helix* ... DNA:** In his book, *Double Helix,* the American biochemist James Watson explains how he and his British colleague, Francis Crick, discovered the structure of deoxyribonucleic acid, or DNA. DNA is the complicated molecule that is present in and determines the nature of every living cell. The shape of DNA is that of two intertwined ladders that form a double helix, or spiral.

## GUIDED READING

### LITERAL QUESTION

**1a.** For what reasons does Asimov regard it a shame that scientific papers report only voluntary thought? (Science loses its glamor, and the process of "insight" is handed over to the mystic.)

### INFERENTIAL QUESTION

**1b.** What can you infer about Asimov's view about all the factors that enter into scientific inquiry? (Scientific inquiry is a human activity affected by all aspects of the human experience—emotion, intuition, reason, and hard work.)

Watt's steam engine, Hamilton's mathematical theory of "quaternions," and Loewi's discovery of the chemical processes of nerve action all resulted from involuntary thinking.

## 1 THESIS

The anecdote involving Loewi reinforces Asimov's thesis: Important ideas can result from unconscious thought, as long as the groundwork of prior reasoning has been laid.

## REFLECTING ON THE SELECTION

Asimov provides examples of flashes of insight in the fields of writing, engineering, chemistry, and mathematics. What does this variety of activities suggest about involuntary thinking? (that it can be applied to any kind of problem-solving—scientific, artistic, and so forth)

## STUDY QUESTIONS

1. goes to movies
2. We think either deliberately or automatically.
3. While bathing, he realized that an object immersed in water displaces an amount of water equal to its own volume.
4. Watt and Hamilton: taking walk; Loewi: waking in middle of the night
5. They do not acknowledge that the mind works to solve problems even when one is not consciously thinking.
6. He reasoned that conscious thought prepares the ground for unconscious inspiration.
7. Scientists might be encouraged to give a true account of methods of discovery. More could be learned about the workings of the mind.
8. Students should state an opinion, support it with personal experiences, and compare them to Asimov's observations.

---

In 1764, the Scottish engineer James Watt was working as an instrument maker for the University of Glasgow. The university gave him a model of a Newcomen steam engine, which didn't work well, and asked him to fix it. Watt fixed it without trouble, but even when it worked perfectly, it didn't work well. It was far too inefficient and consumed incredible quantities of fuel. Was there a way to improve that?

Thought didn't help; but a peaceful, relaxed walk on a Sunday afternoon did. Watt returned with the key notion in mind of using two separate chambers, one for steam only and one for cold water only, so that the same chamber did not have to be constantly cooled and reheated to the infinite waste of fuel.

The Irish mathematician William Rowan Hamilton worked up a theory of "quaternions" in 1843 but couldn't complete that theory until he grasped the fact that there were conditions under which $p \times q$ was *not* equal to $q \times p$. The necessary thought came to him in a flash one time when he was walking to town with his wife.

The German physiologist Otto Loewi was working on the mechanism of nerve action, in particular, on the chemicals produced by nerve endings. He awoke at 3 A.M. one night in 1921 with a perfectly clear notion of the type of experiment he would have to run to settle a key point that was puzzling him. He wrote it down and went back to sleep. When he woke in the morning, he found he couldn't remember what his inspiration had been. He remembered he had written it down, but he couldn't read his writing.

The next night, he woke again at 3 A.M. with the clear thought once more in mind. This time, he didn't fool around. He got up, dressed himself, went straight to the laboratory and began work. By 5 A.M. he had proved his point and the consequences of his findings became important enough in later years so that in 1936 he received a share in the Nobel prize in medicine and physiology.

How very often this sort of thing must happen, and what a shame that scientists are so devoted to their belief in conscious thought that they so consistently obscure the actual methods by which they obtain their results.

---

## STUDY QUESTIONS

### Recalling

1. What does Asimov do to break out of a thinking problem of his own?
2. In what sense is thinking a "double phenomenon" according to Asimov?
3. Explain how a bath helped Archimedes calculate the volume of the crown.
4. Name two other scientists whom Asimov uses as examples, and tell what each was doing when suddenly inspired.

### Interpreting

5. Why does Asimov believe that scientists do not want to admit the existence of the "Eureka phenomenon"?

**338** *Nonfiction*

6. Prove that, in spite of his belief in involuntary thinking, Asimov is not denying the importance of study and hard work.
7. Explain how wider understanding of the "Eureka phenomenon" could bring "glamour" to science. For what other reasons might knowing about the phenomenon be important?

### Extending

8. Use your own general experience to explain whether or not you agree with Asimov's theory.

## VIEWPOINT

The skills that Isaac Asimov employs in his nonfiction are those of the scientist, the teacher, and the writer. Asimov himself has said:

I'm on fire to explain, and happiest when it's something reasonably intricate which I can make clear step by step.

■ Show how Asimov uses a "step-by-step" approach to explain his idea about the Eureka phenomenon. What historical examples does he find of the phenomenon? What other kinds of information does he include?

## LITERARY FOCUS

### The Expository Essay and Thesis

An **expository essay** explains a term, process, or idea to the reader. The writer of an expository essay often indicates the essay's purpose by means of a **thesis statement,** which directly tells the reader what the essay will explain. This statement usually occurs toward the beginning of the essay; the body of the essay develops this statement with explanations and examples; the conclusion of the essay may restate the thesis in different words. Sometimes, however, the thesis is not directly stated but is implied in the essay. An **implied thesis** is one that readers infer from the author's arguments and examples.

An expository essay on winter sports might begin with a thesis statement such as "Skiing offers a combination of fun and exercise to a wide range of people." The remainder of the essay would support this statement. On the other hand, the essay might imply rather than directly state its thesis. By describing each winter sport and its relative popularity, the essay might clearly show the special benefits and wide appeal of skiing without including a specific, direct statement to that effect. Rather than announcing the author's purpose in a thesis statement, the essay with an implied thesis gives readers enough information to recognize that purpose on their own.

### Thinking About the Thesis

1. What is Asimov's thesis in "The Eureka Phenomenon"?
2. What facts, examples, and arguments imply this thesis?
3. Do you think the essay would have been better if Asimov had included a thesis statement? Why or why not?

## VOCABULARY

### Greek Roots

Thousands of English words in the areas of science and philosophy have been borrowed or formed from Greek. In fact, the word *philosophy* itself comes from the Greek words *philos,* meaning "love," and *sophos,* meaning "wisdom." In this essay Asimov explains that the Greek word *Eureka* means "I've got it!" He does not, however, explain the other Greek word in his title, *phenomenon.* It comes from the Greek verb *phainesthai,* which means "to appear." In English *phenomenon* has come to mean anything that is apparent to the senses.

The following words from "The Eureka Phenomenon" are formed from roots that come from Greek. Look up at least five of the words. On a separate sheet write down the history, or etymology, of each. Begin with the original Greek spelling and meaning, and show the progression to the word's present meaning in English.

| | |
|---|---|
| 1. technique | 6. hypotheses |
| 2. problem | 7. metropolis |
| 3. panic | 8. aristocracy |
| 4. cycle | 9. ecstasy |
| 5. mathematics | 10. helix |

## COMPOSITION

### Writing About an Expository Essay

■ In an expository essay the writer sets out to inform the reader of a generalization about life by presenting facts or explaining an idea. What does Isaac Asimov set out to explain in "The Eureka Phenomenon"? What specific facts, examples, details, incidents, and ideas does he use to achieve this purpose? *For help with this assignment, see Lesson 10 in the Writing About Literature Handbook at the back of this book.*

### Explaining a Process in an Expository Essay

■ Write an essay explaining how you solved a particular problem. You may want to explain, for example, how you solved a difficult math problem, figured out how to repair a broken object, or overcame some difficulty in sports. Describe the problem, and then explain, step by step, the process by which you solved it.

*The Eureka Phenomenon* **339**

- first describes own experience; explains theory; gives examples that illustrate it
- *historical:* Archimedes, Watt, Hamilton, Loewi
- *information:* uses analogies; discusses methods of discovery and explains why he disagrees

### LITERARY FOCUS

1. Important ideas often result from unconscious thought.
2. *fact:* Asimov's ability to solve problems by going to movies; *examples:* involuntary discoveries of Archimedes; Watt; Hamilton; Loewi; *arguments:* analogy between breathing/thinking; idea that thinking when stymied is unproductive
3. Answers should state a preference and cite reasons to support it.

### VOCABULARY

1. *technikos:* workings; *technique:* Fr.; Eng.: method
2. *problema:* something thrown forward; *probleme:* Mid. Fr./Eng.; Eng.: question put forward
3. *panikos:* of or from god Pan believed to cause crazed mental states; *panique:* Fr.; Eng.: unreasoning fear
4. *kyklos:* circle; wheel; *cyclus:* Lat.; *cycle:* Fr.; Eng.: recurring sequence of events
5. *mathematikos:* inclined to learn; *mathematicus:* Lat.; Eng.: branch of learning involving numbers
6. *hypotithenai:* to put under or suppose; Eng.: assumptions underlying arguments
7. *metropolis:* mother city; Eng.: large city
8. *aristokratia: aristos:* best; *kratia:* power; Eng.: government by privileged class
9. *ekstasis:* derangement; *ex:* out; *tanai:* to cause to stand; *ecstasis:* Lat.; *exstasie:* Mid. Fr./Eng.; state of overwhelming delight
10. *helix:* spiral

*The Eureka Phenomenon* **T-339**

- Appomattox symbolizes infinite tragedy and infinite promise.
- Lee and Grant sat down together in Appomattox Court House to sign the agreement ending the Civil War.

## LITERARY OPTIONS

- comparison and contrast
- thesis
- purpose

## THEMATIC OPTIONS

- old order vs. new order
- human relationships
- forces of change

## 1 THESIS

Metaphors of sunset and dawn convey Catton's thesis: Appomattox symbolizes the end of aristocracy and the rise of a new society.

## 2 STYLE: CONTRAST

The humble image of the war horse nibbling spring grass contrasts with the solemn mood and meaning of this historic meeting for Lee.

For Bruce Catton (1899–1978) the Civil War was a lifelong interest. A historian and journalist, Catton won the Pulitzer Prize and the National Book Award for *A Stillness at Appomattox* [ap'ə mat'əks], one of many books he wrote about the Civil War. In his research for these works, Catton studied original documents and interviewed veterans of the war.

The following selection demonstrates Catton's talent for making history more than facts, names, and dates. On April 9, 1865, Ulysses S. Grant, commander of the Union forces of the North, and Robert E. Lee, commander of the Confederate forces of the South, met in a farmhouse in Appomattox Court House, Virginia, to arrange the surrender of the South to the North.

■ Is there such a thing as a good loser or a bad winner? What are the characteristics of a good winner?

*Bruce Catton*

# Grant and Lee at Appomattox

Until this Palm Sunday[1] of 1865 the word Appomattox had no meaning. It was a harsh name left over from Indian days, it belonged to a river and to a country town, and it had no overtones. But after this day it would be one of the haunted possessions of the American people, a great and unique word that would echo in the national memory with infinite tragedy and infinite promise, recalling a moment in which sunset and sunrise came together in a streaked glow that was half twilight and half dawn.

The business might almost have been stage-managed for effect. No detail had been overlooked. There was even the case of Wilmer McLean, the Virginian who once owned a place by a stream named Bull Run and who found his farm overrun by soldiers in the first battle of the war. He sold out and moved to southern Virginia to get away from the war, and he bought a modest house in Appomattox Court House; and the war caught up with him finally, so that Lee and Grant chose his front parlor—of all the rooms in America—as the place where they would sit down together and bring the fighting to an end.

Lee had one staff officer with him, and in Mr. McLean's front yard a Confederate orderly stood by while the war horse Traveler nibbled at the spring grass. Grant came with half a dozen officers of his own, including the famous Sheridan,[2] and after he and Lee had shaken hands

---

1. **Palm Sunday:** The surrender of the Confederate forces to the Union took place on the Sunday before Easter Sunday in 1865.

2. **Sheridan:** General Philip Henry Sheridan (1831–1888), a Union general who won major victories over the Confederate forces in Virginia late in the Civil War.

**340** *Nonfiction*

---

## GUIDED READING

### LITERAL QUESTION

**1a.** Why did Mr. McLean sell his farm at Bull Run, move to southern Virginia, and buy Appomattox Court House? (to get away from the war)

### INFERENTIAL QUESTION

**1b.** What do you think the use of his house for Lee and Grant's meeting implies? (The coincidence implies that no American could escape the Civil War. Also, Mr. McLean's connection to Bull Run links the war's beginning to its end.)

and taken their seats these trooped into the room to look and to listen. Grant and Lee sat at two separate tables, the central figures in one of the greatest tableaus of American history.

It was a great tableau not merely because of what these two men did but also because of what they were. No two Americans could have been in greater contrast. (Again, the staging was perfect.) Lee was legend incarnate—tall, gray, one of the handsomest and most imposing men who ever lived, dressed today in his best uniform, with a sword belted at his waist. Grant was—well, he was U. S. Grant, rather scrubby and undersized, wearing his working clothes, with mud-spattered boots and trousers and a private's rumpled blue coat with his lieutenant general's stars tacked to the shoulders. He wore no sword. The men who were with them noticed the contrast and remembered it. Grant himself seems to have felt it; years afterward, when he wrote his memoirs, he mentioned it and went to some lengths to explain why he did not go to this meeting togged out[3] in dress uniform. (In effect, his explanation was that he was just too busy.)

Yet the contrast went far beyond the matter of personal appearance. Two separate versions of America met in this room, each perfectly embodied by its chosen representative.

There was an American aristocracy, and it had had a great day. It came from the past and it looked to the past; it seemed almost deliberately archaic, with an air of knee breeches and buckled shoes and powdered wigs, with a leisured dignity and a rigid code in which privilege and duty were closely joined. It had brought the country to its birth and it had provided many of its beliefs; it had given courage and leadership, a sense of order and learning, and if there had been any way by which the eighteenth century could possibly have been carried forward into the future, this class would have provided the perfect vehicle. But from the day of its beginning America had been fated to be a land of unending change. The country in which this leisured class had its place was in powerful ferment, and the class itself had changed. It had been diluted. In the struggle for survival it had laid hands on the curious combination of modern machinery and slave labor, the old standards had been altered, dignity had begun to look like arrogance, and pride of purse had begun to elbow out pride of breeding. The single lifetime of Robert E. Lee had seen the change, although Lee himself had not been touched by it.

Yet the old values were real, and the effort to preserve them had nobility. Of all the things that went to make up the war, none had more poignance than the desperate fight to preserve these disappearing values, eroded by change from within as much as by change from without. The fight had been made and it had been lost, and everything that had been dreamed and tried and fought for was personified in the gray man who sat at the little table in the parlor at Appomattox and waited for the other man to start writing out the terms of surrender.

The other man was wholly representative too. Behind him there was a new society, not dreamed of by the founding fathers: a society with the lid taken off, western man standing up to assert that what lay back of a person mattered nothing in comparison to what lay ahead of him. It was the land of the mudsills,[4] the temporarily dispossessed, the people who had nothing to lose but the future; behind it were hard times, humiliation and failure, and ahead of it was all the world and a chance to lift oneself by one's bootstraps. It had few standards beyond a basic unformulated belief in the irrepressibility and ultimate value of the human spirit, and it could

---

3. **togged out:** dressed up.

4. **mudsills:** people whose homes were built on an earthen foundation. In general, the term refers to poor people.

*Grant and Lee at Appomattox*  **341**

AT A GLANCE

- Even in their dress Grant and Lee represent separate ideas of America.
- Catton explains that, by the end of the Civil War, old values had succumbed to change: A more democratic society was replacing the country's original aristocracy.

**1 READING SKILLS: COMPARISON AND CONTRAST**

Catton contrasts Grant's and Lee's appearance, detail by detail. The strong visual image he produces of each man becomes the foundation of his thesis about change in America.

**2 THESIS**

Lee and Grant also symbolize the meeting of an archaic aristocratic order and an emerging pragmatic, socially mobile society.

**3 POINT OF VIEW**

Rather than judging the Confederacy's cause, Catton sympathetically concentrates on Lee the man, presenting him as the embodiment of courage and grace in defending his world and in accepting defeat.

---

## GUIDED READING

### LITERAL QUESTIONS

**1a.** What had the American aristocracy brought to this country at its birth? (many of its beliefs, courage, leadership, order, and learning)

**2a.** What does Catton say was eroding the values Lee represented? (change from *within* and *without*)

### INFERENTIAL QUESTIONS

**1b.** How might that legacy have contributed to the Civil War? (The new society also valued courage, leadership, and learning, from which it derived the strength to confront and change a rigid, closed social order.)

**2b.** What does the fact that change came from within and without suggest about the chances of preserving the old order? (The old order would have fallen in time.)

Ulysses S. Grant.

tramp with heavy boots down a ravaged Shenandoah Valley[5] or through the embers of a burned Columbia[6] without giving more than a casual thought to the things that were being destroyed. Yet it had its own nobility and its own standards; it had, in fact, the future of the race in its keeping, with all the immeasurable potential that might reside in a people who had decided that they would no longer be bound by the limitations of the past. It was rough and uncultivated and it came to important meetings wearing muddy boots and no sword, and it had to be listened to.

It could speak with a soft voice, and it could even be abashed by its own moment of triumph, as if that moment were not a thing to be savored and enjoyed. Grant seems to have been almost embarrassed when he and Lee came together in this parlor, yet it was definitely not the embarrassment of an underling ill at ease in a superior's presence. Rather it was simply the diffidence of a sensitive man who had another man in his

power and wished to hurt him as little as possible. So Grant made small talk and recalled the old days in the Mexican War,[7] when Lee had been the polished staff officer in the commanding general's tents and Grant had been an acting regimental quartermaster,[8] slouching about like the hired man who looked after the teams. Perhaps the oddest thing about this meeting at Appomattox was that it was Grant, the nobody from nowhere, who played the part of gracious host, trying to put the aristocrat at his ease and, as far as might be, to soften the weight of the blow that was about to come down. In the end it was Lee who, so to speak, had to call the meeting to order, remarking (and the remark must have wrenched him almost beyond endurance) that they both knew what they were there for and that perhaps they had better get down to business. So Grant opened his orderly book and got out his pencil. He confessed afterward that when he did so he had no idea what words he was going to write.

He knew perfectly well what he was going to say, however, and with a few pauses he said it in straightforward words. Lee's army was to be surrendered, from commanding general down to humblest private. All public property would be turned over to the United States Army—battle flags, guns, muskets, wagons, everything. Officers might keep their side arms (Grant wrote this after a speculative glance at the excellent sword Lee was wearing) and their horses, but the army and everything it owned was to go out of existence.

It was not, however, to go off to a prison camp. Throughout the war Lincoln had stressed one point: the people of the South might have peace whenever they chose just by laying down their arms and going home. Grant made this official. Officers and men, having disarmed them-

---

5. **Shenandoah Valley** [shen′ən dō′ə]: valley of the Shenandoah River, which flows through northern Virginia.
6. **Columbia:** capital of South Carolina, captured by Union troops in 1865.

7. **Mexican War:** war fought between Mexico and the United States from 1846 to 1848.
8. **quartermaster:** officer in charge of living quarters and supplies in an army camp.

**342**   *Nonfiction*

---

selves, would simply give their paroles.[9] Then they could go to their homes . . . and here Grant wrote one of the greatest sentences in American history, the sentence that, more than any other thing, would finally make it impossible for any vengeful government in Washington to proceed against Confederate veterans as traitors. Having gone home, he wrote, officers and men could stay there, "not to be disturbed by the United States authorities so long as they observe their paroles and the laws in force where they may reside." When the powerful signature, "U. S. Grant," was signed under that sentence, the chance that Confederate soldiers might be hanged or imprisoned for treason went out the window.

Having written all of this, Grant handed it over for Lee to read.

Lee's part was not easy. He made a business of getting out his glasses, polishing them carefully, crossing his legs, and adjusting himself. Once he borrowed a lead pencil to insert a word that Grant had omitted. When he had finished he raised a point. In the Confederate army, he said, horses for cavalry and artillery were not government issue; the soldiers themselves owned them. Did the terms as written permit these men to take their horses home with them? Grant shook his head. He had not realized that Confederate soldiers owned their steeds, and the terms he had written were explicit: all such animals must be turned in as captured property. Still—Grant went on to muse aloud; the last battle of the war was over, the war itself was over except for picking up the pieces, and what really mattered was for the men of the South to get back home and become civilians again. He would not change the written terms, but he supposed that most of Lee's men were small farmers anxious to return to their acres and get a crop in, and he would instruct the officers in charge of the surrender ceremonies to give a horse or a mule to

Robert E. Lee.

any Confederate soldier who claimed to own one, so that the men would have a chance "to work their little farms." And in those homely words the great drama of Appomattox came to a close.

The draft of the terms having been agreed on, one of Grant's staff officers took the document to make a fair copy.[10] The United States Army, it appeared, lacked ink, and to write the copy the officer had to borrow a bottle of ink from Lee's staff officer; a moment later, when the Confederate officer sat down to write Lee's formal acceptance, it developed that the Confederate army lacked paper, and he had to borrow from one of Grant's men. The business was finally signed and settled. Lee went out on the porch, looked off over the hills and smote his hands together absently while Traveler was being bridled, and then mounted and started to ride away. Grant and his officers saluted, Lee returned the salute, and there was a little silence while the man in gray rode off to join the pathetic remnant of an army that had just gone out of exis-

---

9. **paroles** [pə rōlz']: promises made by prisoners of war to fulfill the conditions of their release.

10. **fair copy**: neat copy that exactly reproduces the original.

*Grant and Lee at Appomattox* **343**

---

## GUIDED READING

**LITERAL QUESTIONS**

**1a.** What did Grant agree to do when Lee said that his men owned their own mounts? (Although he would not change the written terms, he would instruct his officers to give a horse or mule to any Confederate who claimed ownership.)

**2a.** What did Grant and his officers do while Lee rode away? (They remained silent.)

**INFERENTIAL QUESTIONS**

**1b.** What might that agreement imply about the value of Grant's word? (A spoken promise from a man of honor—a quality Lee and Grant had in common—would override written terms.)

**2b.** What can you infer from their silence? (They respected Lee and the dignity with which he faced defeat and surrender.)

## 1 RESPONSE JOURNAL

Have students record Mr. McLean's thoughts about the "piece of history" he was part of as he looks around his front parlor after the soldiers have left.

### REFLECTING ON THE SELECTION

Why might the meeting have been so subdued on *both* sides? (The Confederate soldiers were subdued by defeat; the Union soldiers were subdued by their respect for Lee.)

### STUDY QUESTIONS

1. Lee: aristocracy, past; Grant: uncultivated America, future
2. Lee's army was to surrender; officers could keep side arms; Confederate veterans were to return home.
3. regards surrendered army as fellow citizens
4. Lee: proud, defeated; Grant: folksy, unassuming, unvindictive
5. symbolizes idea that South and North need each other
6. observes aristocracy was fated to fall; Grant and Lee's reversed relationship during Mexican War
7. Sun sets on aristocracy and the Confederacy, rises on a new age.
8. to show that a new American age dawned at Appomattox; portrays Civil War as battle between old and new societies
9. Students should cite an American (such as Henry Ford or Thomas Edison) who exemplifies some aspect of America.

### VIEWPOINT

Both are concerned about well-being of soldiers; both are courteous, dignified, loyal to their causes.

---

tence—rode off into mist and legend, to take his place at last in the folklore and the cherished memories of the nation that had been too big for him.

Grant stayed in character. He heard a banging of guns; Union artillerists were firing salutes to celebrate the victory, and Grant sent word to have all that racket stopped—those men in gray were enemies no longer but simply fellow countrymen (which, as Grant saw it, was what the war had all been about), and nothing would be done to humiliate them. Instead, wagonloads of Federal hardtack[11] and bacon would start moving at once for the Confederate camp, so that Lee's hungry men might have a square meal. Grant himself would return to Washington by the next train, without waiting to observe the

---

11. **hardtack:** unleavened bread often used in military rations.

---

actual laying down of arms. He was commanding general of the nation's armies, the war was costing four million dollars a day, and it was high time to start cutting expenses. Back in the Federal camp, Grant sat down in front of his tent to wait for the moment of departure. He seemed relaxed and in a mood to talk, and his officers gathered around him to hear what he would say about the supreme moment he had just been through. Grant addressed one of them, who had served with him in the Mexican War . . . "Do you remember that white mule old so-and-so used to ride, down in Mexico?" The officer nodded, being just then, as he confessed later, in a mood to remember the exact number of hairs in the mule's tail if that was what Grant wanted. 1 So Grant chatted about the Mexican War, and if he had great thoughts about the piece of history he had just made he kept them to himself.

---

## STUDY QUESTIONS

### Recalling

1. What "version of America" does each general represent, according to Catton?
2. Cite three specific points of the treaty written by Grant.
3. Why does Grant order the Union soldiers to stop firing salutes in celebration?
4. After the signing of the surrender, what last picture does Catton give us of Lee? Of Grant?

### Interpreting

5. What is the significance of the fact that Union and Confederate officers must borrow ink and paper from each other to copy the treaty?
6. Catton notes that the farmer McLean tried to escape the war but that it "caught up with him finally." Where else in the essay does the author suggest this idea of fate or destiny?
7. Why does Catton call the meeting at Appomattox a moment of sunset and sunrise?
8. What is Catton's purpose in this essay? What

idea about the Civil War does he express by focusing on its two leading generals?

### Extending

9. Catton uses Grant and Lee to represent ideas — two different "versions of America." What other famous person might you use to represent some aspect of America?

## VIEWPOINT

One U.S. Army major general who has studied the lives and careers of the two Civil War leaders said of the two men:

Outwardly it would be impossible to discover men so different as Grant and Lee, yet inwardly they were very similar in type, endowed as they were with the same high principle of duty.

—J. F. C. Fuller, *Grant and Lee*

- What similarities do you find between Grant and Lee as presented by Catton?

# LITERARY FOCUS

## Comparison and Contrast

One effective technique in expository writing is the use of comparison and contrast. **Comparison** points out the similarities between two or more subjects; **contrast** examines the differences between them. Very often writers develop comparison and contrast by using parallel structure; they discuss the same points in the same order for each subject. As a result, the various similarities and differences between the subjects stand out more sharply.

A comparison and contrast that uses a parallel development can build from simple, obvious points to more subtle ones. For example, in his essay on Grant and Lee, Catton begins by describing the physical appearance of each general. He then moves on to the aspect of American history that each man represents.

## Thinking About Comparison and Contrast

1. Show how the details in the physical descriptions of Grant and Lee follow a parallel order.
2. How is the contrast between the different values of Grant and Lee related to the contrast between the physical appearances of the two men?
3. What contrasts can you find in the behavior of the two generals during and after the surrender ceremony? Is the behavior of each man consistent with what Catton has already said about him? Why or why not?

# VOCABULARY

## Synonyms

**Synonyms** are words that have the same or nearly the same meaning. *Rich* and *wealthy* are synonyms. The words in capitals are from "Grant and Lee at Appomattox." On a separate sheet write the letter of the word whose meaning is *most nearly the same* as that of the word in capitals *as the word is used in the selection.*

1. ARCHAIC: (a) extinct (b) old-fashioned
   (c) formal (d) worldly
2. PERSONIFIED: (a) animated (b) appeared
   (c) presented (d) embodied
3. ULTIMATE: (a) personal (b) necessary
   (c) absolute (d) final

4. SPECULATIVE: (a) abashed (b) considering
   (c) diffident (d) chancy
5. EXPLICIT: (a) formal (b) potential
   (c) changeable (d) definite

# COMPOSITION

## Writing About Symbols

▪ Like short story writers and poets, nonfiction writers use symbols to express general or abstract ideas in concrete terms (see page 114). Select a person or an object from "Grant and Lee at Appomattox." Write a brief essay in which you state what the person or object represents and what the person or object reveals about the author's purpose in writing the essay. *For help with this assignment, see Lesson 8 in the Writing About Literature Handbook at the back of this book.*

## Writing a Comparison/Contrast

▪ Compare and contrast two persons, places, or objects — for example, two athletes or vacation spots. Begin by pointing out the most important similarity and difference between the two items. For instance, you might say of two vacation spots, "Although their landscapes and climates are similar, Place X and Place Y attract two very different types of vacationers." Then discuss the items' various similarities in greater detail. Follow that discussion with more on the differences between the items. As you write, be sure to use transitions such as *similarly, in the same way, on the other hand,* and *in contrast.*

# COMPARING ESSAYS

1. Isaac Asimov is a scientist, and Bruce Catton was a historian. Compare "The Eureka Phenomenon" and "Grant and Lee at Appomattox." In what ways is each author's knowledge of his field apparent in the essay?
2. "The Eureka Phenomenon" and "Grant and Lee at Appomattox" both use real people to represent ideas. What ideas does Asimov use his people to represent? What ideas does Catton use his people to represent? What similarities, if any, can you find between these ideas?

*Grant and Lee at Appomattox* **345**

## LITERARY FOCUS

1. Catton first describes a general impression of each man, then his style of dress; he ends by stating whether or not each wears a sword.
2. Lee's elegant appearance suggests aristocratic breeding; Grant's informal appearance reflects his belief that tradition is unimportant.
3. ▪ During: Grant makes small talk, is relaxed; Lee wants to begin, fidgets.
   ▪ After: Grant is relaxed, talkative; Lee is silent, preoccupied.
   ▪ Each man's behavior is consistent with his beliefs and background.

## VOCABULARY

1. (b) old-fashioned
2. (d) embodied
3. (c) absolute
4. (d) chancy
5. (d) definite

## COMPARING ESSAYS

1. ▪ Asimov understands how scientists do research and make discoveries; cites many examples from history.
   ▪ Catton puts one incident into historical perspective; demonstrates understanding of past and future trends.
2. ▪ Asimov's scientists represent the idea that important discoveries often result from involuntary thought.
   ▪ Catton's generals contrast old and new values.
   ▪ Each author presents a contrast between a view that values rules and formal methods and another view in which results are more important than rules and methods.

---

# COMPOSITION: GUIDELINES FOR EVALUATION

## WRITING ABOUT SYMBOLS

### Objective

To explain how writer uses symbols to convey abstract ideas

### Guidelines for Evaluation

- suggested length: three to five paragraphs
- should cite person or object from essay and tell what idea is represented
- should explain which qualities suggest idea
- should show how symbol clarifies purpose

## WRITING A COMPARISON/CONTRAST

### Objective

To compare and contrast two persons, places, or things

### Guidelines for Evaluation

- suggested length: three paragraphs
- should cite two persons, places, or objects that are both similar and different
- should identify similarities and differences

Nonfiction, like anything else that you read, will give you more pleasure when you read it actively and attentively. In particular, an active reader will remember that a work of nonfiction, while factual in nature, represents one author's version of the truth. When you actively look for clues about the author's intentions in a work of nonfiction, you will be better able to weigh the particular version of the truth that the work presents. The following reminders will help you to make such judgments when you read nonfiction.

### Reminders for Active Reading of Nonfiction

1. The **title** often indicates the author's purpose, intended audience, and attitude.
2. The writer of **biography** emphasizes the facts of an individual's life or presents an impression of the individual, depending on the purpose of the biography.
3. The writer of **autobiography** presents recollections with the insights gained over time.
4. The writer of any form of nonfiction—**biography, autobiography,** or **essays**—uses various techniques, including the following:

   - anecdotes to illustrate character traits and portray key events
   - figurative language (similes and metaphors) and sensory language to communicate important ideas
   - details, incidents, and other evidence as well as analogies to support opinions or clarify explanations
   - a clear organization—such as chronological order, parallelism, or comparison and contrast—to help communicate a message
   - a clear thesis statement or clearly implied message

5. The writer of any piece of nonfiction has a **purpose** in mind. The reader should uncover that purpose.

### Model for Active Reading

On the following pages you will see how a careful reader considered the preceding reminders while reading "The Most Important Day" by Helen Keller. Marginal notations indicate the reader's observations about the work. Each notation includes a page reference for further information on the item in question. Read the selection first for your own enjoyment, and then read it along with the marginal notations. You can use the process illustrated in this model as you read any nonfiction work.

**346** *Nonfiction*

Helen Keller (1880–1968) overcame the handicaps of blindness and deafness to live a long and productive life. Born in Alabama, she was stricken in infancy by an illness that left her without sight and hearing. When Helen was nearly seven, her parents sought professional help for their "wild and unruly" daughter. They hired Anne Sullivan, a young teacher who had been trained at the Perkins Institute for the Blind in Boston.

Helen Keller devoted much of her life to the cause of handicapped people.

■ What attitude do you think a handicapped person would like you to have toward him or her?

AT A GLANCE

- On the most important day of her life, six-year-old Helen Keller meets teacher Anne Sullivan.
- Angry, bitter, and anxious, Helen waits on her porch for Anne's arrival.

LITERARY OPTIONS

- purpose
- audience
- anecdote

THEMATIC OPTIONS

- one person's influence
- communication and language
- growth and learning

*Helen Keller*

# The Most Important Day

The most important day I remember in all my life is the one on which my teacher, Anne Mansfield Sullivan, came to me. I am filled with wonder when I consider the immeasurable contrast between the two lives which it connects. It was the third of March, 1887, three months before I was seven years old.

On the afternoon of that eventful day, I stood on the porch, dumb, expectant. I guessed vaguely from my mother's signs and from the hurrying to and fro in the house that something unusual was about to happen, so I went to the door and waited on the steps. The afternoon sun penetrated the mass of honeysuckle that covered the porch and fell on my upturned face. My fingers lingered almost unconsciously on the familiar leaves and blossoms which had just come forth to greet the sweet southern spring. I did not know what the future held of marvel or surprise for me. Anger and bitterness had preyed upon me continually for weeks and a deep languor had succeeded this passionate struggle.

Have you ever been at sea in a dense fog, when it seemed as if a tangible white darkness shut you in, and the great ship, tense and anxious, groped her way toward the shore with plummet and sounding-line,[1] and you waited with beating heart for something to happen?

**Thesis statement** (p. 339): The author directly states her central idea in the first sentence.

**Narrative techniques** (p. 296): The author follows chronological order.

**Analogy** (p. 332): To communicate her emotions, the author compares herself to a ship in a fog.

---

1. **plummet and sounding-line:** device used to determine the depth of water. The plummet, a weight, is attached to the line and lowered into the water.

*The Most Important Day*  **347**

## GUIDED READING

**LITERAL QUESTIONS**

**1a.** What happens on Helen's "most important day"? (teacher Anne Sullivan arrives)

**2b.** To what does waiting Helen compare herself? (a ship in a fog)

**INFERENTIAL QUESTIONS**

**1b.** What "two lives" does this event connect? (lives with and without language)

**2b.** What emotional state does this comparison suggest? (Helen feels cut off, groping, confused.)

AT A GLANCE

- The blind and deaf child imitates but does not understand words traced in her hand.
- Impatiently she breaks a new doll. She goes with Anne to the well-house.

I was like that ship before my education began, only I was without compass or sounding-line, and had no way of knowing how near the harbor was. "Light! give me light!" was the wordless cry of my soul, and the light of love shone on me in that very hour.

I felt approaching footsteps. I stretched out my hand as I supposed to my mother. Someone took it, and I was caught up and held close in the arms of her who had come to reveal all things to me, and more than all things else, to love me.

The morning after my teacher came she led me into her room and gave me a doll. The little blind children at the Perkins Institution had sent it and Laura Bridgman had dressed it; but I did not know this until afterward. When I had played with it a little while, Miss Sullivan slowly spelled into my hand the word "d-o-l-l." I was at once interested in this finger play and tried to imitate it. When I finally succeeded in making the letters correctly I was flushed with childish pleasure and pride. Running downstairs to my mother I held up my hand and made the letters for doll. I did not know that I was spelling a word or even that words existed; I was simply making my fingers go in monkeylike imitation. In the days that followed I learned to spell in this uncomprehending way a great many words, among them *pin, hat, cup* and a few verbs like *sit, stand* and *walk*. But my teacher had been with me several weeks before I understood that everything has a name.

One day, while I was playing with my new doll, Miss Sullivan put my big rag doll into my lap also, spelled "d-o-l-l" and tried to make me understand that "d-o-l-l" applied to both. Earlier in the day we had had a tussle over the words "m-u-g" and "w-a-t-e-r." Miss Sullivan had tried to impress it upon me that "m-u-g" is *mug* and that "w-a-t-e-r" is *water*, but I persisted in confounding the two. In despair she had dropped the subject for the time, only to renew it at the first opportunity. I became impatient at her repeated attempts and, seizing the new doll, I dashed it upon the floor. I was keenly delighted when I felt the fragments of the broken doll at my feet. Neither sorrow nor regret followed my passionate outburst. I had not loved the doll. In the still, dark world in which I lived there was no strong sentiment or tenderness. I felt my teacher sweep the fragments to one side of the hearth, and I had a sense of satisfaction that the cause of my discomfort was removed. She brought me my hat, and I knew I was going out into the warm sunshine. This thought, if a wordless sensation can be called a thought, made me hop and skip with pleasure.

We walked down the path to the well-house, attracted by the smell of the honeysuckle with which it was covered. Some one was drawing water and my teacher placed my hand under the spout. As

348   *Nonfiction*

Autobiographer's insight (p. 264): The author reports the insights she gained later on.

Supporting details (p. 339): Several incidents support and develop the thesis—the importance of Helen's teacher in her life.

Anecdote (p. 270): The story of the doll offers an example of Helen's behavior before she learned to use words.

## GUIDED READING

### LITERAL QUESTIONS

**1a.** What does Helen do when Anne spells d-o-l-l in her hand? (copies the gesture)

**2a.** What does Helen feel when she breaks her new doll? (delight and satisfaction)

### INFERENTIAL QUESTIONS

**1b.** What does this action tell us about her learning progress? (She can imitate but does not yet make connections between the object and the word.)

**2b.** What does this reaction tell us about her emotional development? (She cannot yet feel love, loss, or regret. She is impulsive and violent.)

the cool stream gushed over one hand she spelled into the other the word *water,* first slowly, then rapidly. I stood still, my whole attention fixed upon the motions of her fingers. Suddenly I felt a misty consciousness as of something forgotten—a thrill of returning thought; and somehow the mystery of language was revealed to me. I knew then that ''w-a-t-e-r'' meant the wonderful cool something that was flowing over my hand. The living word awakened my soul, gave it light, hope, joy, set it free! There were barriers still, it is true, but barriers that could in time be swept away.

I left the well-house eager to learn. Everything had a name, and each name gave birth to a new thought. As we returned to the house every object which I touched seemed to quiver with life. That was because I saw everything with the strange new sight that had come to me. On entering the door I remembered the doll I had broken. I felt my way to the hearth and picked up the pieces. I tried vainly to put them together. Then my eyes filled with tears; for I realized what I had done, and for the first time I felt repentance and sorrow.

I learned a great many new words that day. I do not remember what they all were; but I do know that *mother, father, sister, teacher* were among them—words that were to make the world blossom for me, ''like Aaron's rod, with flowers.''[2] It would have been difficult to find a happier child than I was as I lay in my crib at the close of that eventful day and lived over the joys it had brought me, and for the first time longed for a new day to come.

> **Climax** (pp. 20, 296): Proceeding chronologically, the author here lets us know how her problem with language will work out.

> **Restatement of thesis** (p. 339): The author explains how important her teacher and discovery of language were.

———————
2. ''like Aaron's . . . flowers'': In the Old Testament God designated Moses' brother Aaron high priest of the Jews by making his staff blossom with flowers.

## STUDY QUESTIONS

### Recalling
1. What skill does Helen learn the day after her teacher arrives? Why does she call her behavior "uncomprehending"?
2. Retell the incident of the broken doll and the pump. What discovery about words does Helen finally make?

### Interpreting
3. Contrast Helen's behavior before and after she discovers language. What does she mean when she speaks of her "strange, new sight"?
4. Why is the arrival of Anne Sullivan the most important event in Helen Keller's life?

## COMPOSITION

### Evaluating Your Response to Nonfiction
■ Using examples, describe how Keller recreates the perspective of a child who cannot see, hear, or speak. End by explaining whether you think Keller successfully communicates the difference that her teacher made in her life.

### Writing an Autobiographical Essay
■ Write about a person and an event that changed your own life. Begin by describing the person who made a valuable contribution to your life. Then explain what that person did for you and why he or she made such a difference in your life.

*The Most Important Day* **349**

### AT A GLANCE
- Feeling both the water and the traced word, Helen suddenly makes the connection between the object and its name.
- Helen awakens to the world and her feelings. She is eager to learn.

### REFLECTING ON THE SELECTION
Why do you think Helen finally made the connection with the word *water* when she had just failed to make the connection with *doll*? (Answers will vary. Some students may suggest that water is a basic element in human life, one which even infants recognize. Helen may have had memories of the sight of water. Touching the water is also a powerful sensory experience that may have triggered the recognition.)

### STUDY QUESTIONS
1. to imitate manual spellings; does not understand that she is making words
2. Anne puts doll in Helen's lap and spells *doll;* Helen breaks doll in frustration. Anne places Helen's hand under water and spells *water;* Helen discovers that words stand for things.
3. *before:* impatient, self-absorbed, displays primitive emotions; *after:* happy, excited, eager to learn; refers to her new outlook
4. She teaches Helen language, which enables Helen to think in words.

## COMPOSITION: GUIDELINES FOR EVALUATION

### EVALUATING RESPONSE TO NONFICTION
**Objective**
To analyze and evaluate the way a nonfiction writer re-creates an experience

**Guidelines for Evaluation**
- suggested length: one to two paragraphs
- should relate examples from Keller's memoir that re-create her experience as child
- should state opinion as to whether or not Keller effectively conveys importance of Anne Sullivan

### WRITING AN AUTOBIOGRAPHICAL ESSAY
**Objective**
To explain the influence of a person and event

**Guidelines for Evaluation**
- suggested length: three to four paragraphs
- should describe person and state impact made
- should recount an event in which the subject affected writer's life in some way
- should explain how this event influenced the writer

# ACTIVE READING

## Making Inferences

In *The Spirit of St. Louis,* the account of the first lonely flight across the Atlantic Ocean, Charles Lindbergh shows us what he is thinking at each stage of his voyage. He thereby allows us to observe him making a series of inferences. An **inference** is a kind of reasonable or educated guess based on available evidence. Lindbergh was flying without the help of modern instruments; he had to make decisions by *inferring* where he was from what he could see. For example, he views several small boats, decides that they are fishing boats, and then infers that "The coast, the European coast, can't be far away!" He does not know for certain, but his inference is reasonable. Eventually he spots landmarks that tell him for sure that this inference is correct.

Making inferences is particularly important in reading nonfiction, since we need to look beyond the facts to the writer's interpretation of them. Writers often tell us directly what they mean. Yet at other times they expect us to be alert and to infer some of their meaning. In "The Eureka Phenomenon" Isaac Asimov says, ". . .when I was working on my doctoral dissertation, too many years ago. . . ." Inference: He feels himself growing old, realizing how long ago his days as a graduate student were.

In "A Child's Christmas in Wales" Dylan Thomas asks us to make a more complicated set of inferences. He describes his childhood memories of Christmas, memories that have been highly colored by time and imagination. However, he never tells us directly, "This is not exactly the way things were, but rather the way they seem now to me as a grown man who, like most adults, remembers his childhood in glowing terms." Instead he says, "All the Christmases roll down toward the two-tongued sea, . . . and I plunge my hands in the snow and bring out whatever I can find. In goes my hand into that wool-white, bell-tongued ball of holidays resting at the rim of the carol-singing sea. . . ." His fanciful language leads us to make several inferences: that Christmas was indeed a magical time for him as a child, that his memories make his childhood experiences glow even more brightly than they did in real life, and, most important, that the adult Thomas yearns for that past but knows that he can touch it only through memory and imagination.

350 *Nonfiction*

# REVIEW: NONFICTION

## Guide for Studying Nonfiction

The following guide will help you to understand and evaluate the methods a writer of nonfiction uses.

### Biography

1. For what **audience** does the author seem to have written this biography? What seems to be the author's **purpose**? That is, what general idea about the subject does the author communicate?
2. Is the author's opinion of the subject stated or implied?
3. What sources of information does the author seem to have used?
4. What details of appearance does the author use?
5. Does the biography convey the human qualities of the subject?
6. Is the life story told in **chronological order**? If not, what organization has the author used?

### Autobiography

1. For what **audience** does the author seem to have written this autobiography? What seems to have been the author's **purpose**?
2. With how much detail does the author recall the past?
3. What lessons does the author learn from experience?
4. What, if anything, does the author admit about himself or herself?

### Essay

1. For what **audience** does the essay seem to have been written? What seems to have been the author's **purpose**?
2. What is the author's attitude toward the essay's subject?
3. If the essay is **narrative**, how does it use details and chronological order to involve the reader?
4. If the essay is **descriptive**, what concrete language and figures of speech are used?
5. If the essay is **persuasive**, what techniques of persuasion are used? How persuasive is the essay?
6. If the essay is **expository**, is the main idea stated or implied? What facts, incidents, and other information are used to explain the main idea?

Refer to the unit review, the Guide for Studying Nonfiction. It suggests questions that can be used to review the unit section by section—biography, autobiography, essay—or to review the unit as a whole. These questions may also be used to focus students' attention as they read each selection. For example, you might use the six questions listed under the heading "Biography" to summarize class discussion of "My Friend, Albert Einstein" by Banesh Hoffmann.

The questions in the Guide for Reading Nonfiction appear with write-on lines, in blackline master form, among the materials for this unit in your *Teacher's Classroom Resources*.

# PREVIEW: DRAMA

*A dramatist is one who believes that the pure event, an action involving human beings, is more arresting than any comment that can be made upon it.*

—Thornton Wilder

**Drama** consists of a series of actions meant to be performed on a stage by live actors for an audience. More than any other literary form, drama resembles real life: It *shows* us action directly, rather than *telling* us about it as fiction does.

Like all other forms of literature, drama calls for the active participation of its audience. Whenever we attend a live performance or read a play, we are encouraged to add our own thoughts and feelings to the playwright's words. In the theater we actively respond to the actors on stage, and our response can in turn inspire them. As a result the play itself becomes more exciting. We also take an active role in *reading* a play, for our imaginations bring the playwright's words to life and make the play's people and events real. Because the audience always collaborates with the playwright, drama is the least solitary, the most communal of all forms of literature.

The communal nature of drama has been important ever since its origins over 2500 years ago in ancient Greece. Drama as an art form began as part of the public religious rituals honoring the god Dionysus. By 400 B.C. the theater had become a widely popular form of entertainment. The earliest known Greek dramas were **tragedies,** serious plays presenting the downfall of noble but flawed heroes. **Comedies**—plays that make fun of human problems—first appeared in Greece as light entertainments meant to amuse the audience after the performance of a tragedy.

*Drama* **353**

Drama has worn many faces throughout its history. The drama of the Greeks was **stylized:** That is, it presented life in terms that would strike us as unnatural. The actors wore masks and spoke or sang poetry, and a chorus of actors often spoke in unison to comment on the action. Greek drama was meant less to mirror everyday life than to illuminate the very heights and depths of human experience. By contrast, drama since the nineteenth century has largely been **naturalistic:** That is, it focuses on everyday life and attempts to recreate the illusion of that life on stage.

Plays can present a tremendous range of experiences and moods. They can be frivolous or deeply serious, showing us the broad smile of slapstick or the stark mask of tragedy. Today we may read and see dramas from all periods of history presenting widely varying pictures of human experience.

The following three plays offer some idea of the range possible in drama. *The Life and Adventures of Nicholas Nickleby* by David Edgar is a dramatization of a novel by Charles Dickens; it portrays the social problems of nineteenth-century England. *Cyrano de Bergerac* by Edmond Rostand takes us to the witty and colorful world of seventeenth-century France. Finally, *Julius Caesar* by William Shakespeare presents the tragic events surrounding the assassination of Julius Caesar in ancient Rome.

Since drama is meant to be performed, the reader of a play should understand the basic parts of any drama: the **script** that is written by the playwright and the **staging** that brings that script to life in the theater through scenery, lighting, costumes, and acting. The script of a play is made up of **dialogue,** which is the speech of the characters, and **stage directions,** which include descriptions of the characters, setting, and action, along with instructions for performing the play. In reading a play we should imagine how each character's words would sound when spoken by a real person. We should also try to envision what the play would look like when it is performed on stage. If we let our imaginations work in this way, we will collaborate with the playwright in the creation of the play.

354  *Drama*

# LITERARY FOCUS: The Life and Adventures of Nicholas Nickleby

## A Dramatization of a Novel

The original form of *The Life and Adventures of Nicholas Nickleby* is a novel. Its author is the great nineteenth-century English writer Charles Dickens (1812–1870). Nearly 150 years after it was written, Dickens' novel was **dramatized**, or turned into a play, by David Edgar, an English playwright associated with the Royal Shakespeare Company.

## The Life of Charles Dickens

Charles Dickens was born to a middle-class English family near Portsmouth, a seaport not far from London. Dickens lived during a time of startling change in England. He saw the rural simplicity of his early childhood give way to the bustling technology of the industrial age, ushered in with the noise and dirt of steam engines, railroads, and textile mills.

Like many others, Dickens' lovable but irresponsible father could not keep pace with the difficult times. When Dickens was only twelve years old, his parents and younger brothers and sisters were forced to enter debtors' prison. Dickens himself went to work for a manufacturer of boot polish and became so skilled that the factory owners placed him in a window so that passersby could pause at their leisure to watch the boy work. He returned to school when his family was released from prison but left his studies at the age of fifteen to work as a law clerk. Shortly afterward, he became a newspaper reporter and launched what was to become a triumphant writing career.

Dickens achieved success very early as a writer of fiction and soon established himself as the most popular writer of his day. At twenty-four he published his first novel, *The Pickwick Papers* (1836–1837), which became a bestseller. Writing in serial form for magazines, Dickens followed the success of *The Pickwick Papers* with *Oliver Twist* (1837) and *The Life and Adventures of Nicholas Nickleby* (1838–1839), both of which increased his popularity, as readers in England and America eagerly awaited the next installment of each work. Dickens eventually wrote a dozen more novels, including the autobiographical *David Copperfield* (1849–1850), *A Tale of Two Cities* (1859), and his masterpiece, *Great Expectations* (1860–1861).

Dickens' combination of powerful sentiment, dramatic flair, a keen social conscience, and a wonderful sense of comedy won him celebrity during his lifetime as well as a lasting place among the world's greatest writers. However, despite his dazzling success, Dickens' memories of

*The Life and Adventures of Nicholas Nickleby*　**355**

his own childhood never faded. They convinced him that no adult suffers as much as a child can suffer, and, perhaps more than any other message, his books have carried that conviction to readers all over the globe.

### *The Life and Adventures of Nicholas Nickleby:* The Novel

Dickens wrote *The Life and Adventures of Nicholas Nickleby* over a period of two years, eventually filling three volumes with the story of his hero, Nicholas, and his poor but honorable family. Nicholas begins as a trusting youth of nineteen, the sole support of his beautiful sister and scatterbrained mother. His rich uncle Ralph finds Nicholas a position at Dotheboys [do͞o′thə boyz] Hall, a boarding school in the region of Yorkshire in northern England. Shocked at the inhuman conditions at the school, Nicholas leaves Yorkshire and enters upon a series of tribulations and adventures, including a brief stint as an actor and playwright. Good eventually triumphs over evil, as Nicholas and his family find prosperity and happiness by the novel's end.

Like *Oliver Twist,* its predecessor, *Nicholas Nickleby* allowed Dickens to call widespread attention to the abuses of his society. The chief target of his eloquence in *Nicholas Nickleby* was the brutal mistreatment of children in a number of Yorkshire schools. In writing *Nicholas Nickleby,* Dickens visited several such schools. From this research he modeled one of his most memorable characters, Wackford Squeers, the proprietor of the fictional Dotheboys Hall. Dickens' graphic portrayal of Squeers and his establishment provoked a great outcry against the Yorkshire schools, many of which were forced to close.

### *The Life and Adventures of Nicholas Nickleby:* The Play

Like many of Dickens' other novels, *Nicholas Nickleby* has inspired a number of dramatic versions, including several stage productions and at least one film. It is not surprising that Dickens' works have lent themselves to such adaptations. Their author's highly developed sense of drama created characters, situations, and dialogue that are as vivid and theatrical as any material written directly for the stage. Dickens himself performed on stage, reading his own works on successful lecture tours as well as taking roles in theatrical productions throughout his life.

The first dramatic version of *Nicholas Nickleby* appeared before the novel itself was finished. Frederick Yates, a leading actor of Dickens' time, adapted several scenes from the highly popular work for the stage.

The most recent dramatization of *Nicholas Nickleby* is the work of David Edgar, a British playwright associated with the acclaimed Royal

**356** *Drama*

Shakespeare Company. The Royal Shakespeare Company's production dramatized the entire novel, lasted eight and one-half hours, and used 39 actors to play 150 different roles. This huge undertaking was hugely successful, running for several years in London and winning awards in both England and the United States.

The following excerpt from David Edgar's dramatization covers the first quarter of *Nicholas Nickleby,* the portion that depicts Nicholas' experiences at Dotheboys Hall.

■ What effect do poverty and cruelty have on people? Do they make people better or worse? How do their hardships affect the characters in *Nicholas Nickleby*?

Filming a scene for television from *The Life and Adventures of Nicholas Nickleby.*
*Next page:* members of the cast of the Royal Shakespeare Company production.

*The Life and Adventures of Nicholas Nickleby* **357**

358 *Drama*

# Adapting *The Life and Adventures of Nicholas Nickleby* to the Stage

The following foreword by David Edgar sets forth some of his reasons for adapting Charles Dickens' nineteenth-century novel to the contemporary stage.

When the Royal Shakespeare Company and I first sat down to figure out how to adapt Charles Dickens' huge novel *The Life and Adventures of Nicholas Nickleby* to the stage, we realized quickly that there was no point in undertaking the adaptation just because we liked the book (although we did), or because it has great characters and incidents (which indeed it has), or even because it would be a tremendous challenge to our energies and talents (which it certainly proved to be). The only legitimate reason for adapting a novel to the stage, we decided, was that a particular group of people (we) felt it important to tell a particular story to another particular group of people (the audience) on a particular night. In other words, in our case a group of people living in the 1980s had to decide why they needed to tell another group of people living in the 1980s a story written over 140 years ago.

Over the months that followed we discovered many such reasons. One was that Dickens himself was and is an important part of the British national culture—perhaps second only to Shakespeare—and by studying his work we were studying ourselves. But there was also something very specific about *Nicholas Nickleby,* which Dickens wrote at a time oddly comparable to our own. In the Britain of the 1830s, the advance of industrial technology was changing political, social, and economic life at bewildering speed. The old fixed certainties were breaking apart as thousands of people moved from the countryside to the mushrooming cities. For Dickens this process represented huge opportunities: He welcomed the collapse of the old aristocratic privileges that had allowed men and women to be judged by their rank rather than by their character. But there was a dark side to the picture too. The ancient feudal structures may have been rigid, but at least they were clear and often softened by kindness; now everything was uncertain, everything was changing, and the only thing that appeared to bind people together (although it more often split them apart) was the pursuit of money.

This conflict lies at the heart of Charles Dickens' personal life, as well as at the heart of his novel *Nicholas Nickleby.* Our first task was to make the adaptation a play *about* Charles Dickens himself, and so we used much of his own narrative comment. But we too live in a time of massive technological change, and we too share a desire to return to the old social certainties of "the good old days." So the play is about us as well, our feelings about the collapse of the old certainties—the good aspects as well as the bad.

The sequence of the play involving Nicholas' visit to Dotheboys Hall represents both sides of the picture. Nicholas' uncle Ralph and the evil schoolmaster Squeers represent the dark side of the new age. However, through Nicholas' growing relationship with the poor mistreated Smike, we also see the limitless human capacity for genuine friendship and love.

—*David Edgar*

*The Life and Adventures of Nicholas Nickleby* **359**

Nicholas Nickleby.

Kate Nickleby.

Wackford Squeers.

*A Dramatization by David Edgar*
*Based on the Novel by Charles Dickens*

## *from* **The Life and Adventures of Nicholas Nickleby**

## CHARACTERS

### The Nickleby Family

**NICHOLAS NICKLEBY:** impoverished gentleman of nineteen; the sole support of his sister and widowed mother

**KATE NICKLEBY:** his younger sister

**MRS. NICKLEBY:** mother of Nicholas and Kate; recently widowed

**RALPH NICKLEBY:** wealthy uncle of Nicholas and Kate (the brother of their late father)

### The Squeers Household

**WACKFORD SQUEERS:** proprietor of Dotheboys Hall, a boarding school for boys

**MRS. SQUEERS:** wife of Mr. Squeers

**WACKFORD:** son of Mr. and Mrs. Squeers

**SMIKE:** poor young man who works for the Squeerses

**PHIB:** maid in the Squeers household

### Students at Dotheboys Hall

| | |
|---|---|
| BELLING | BOLDER |
| YOUNGER SNAWLEY | PITCHER |
| OLDER SNAWLEY | JACKSON |
| TOMKINS | COBBEY |
| COATES | PETERS |
| GRAYMARSH | SPROUTER |
| JENNINGS | ROBERTS |
| MOBBS | BROOKS |

### Others

**WILLIAM:** waiter at the Saracen's Head Inn
**SNAWLEY:** stepfather of the Snawley boys

| | |
|---|---|
| COACHMAN | VENDORS |
| PASSENGERS | PORTERS |
| NEWSBOYS | |

NARRATOR. There once lived in a sequestered part of the county of Devonshire[1] one Mr. Godfrey Nickleby, who rather late in life took it into his head to get married. And in due course, when Mrs. Nickleby had presented her husband with two sons, he found himself in a situation of distinctly shortened means. This situation was relieved only when, one fine morning, there arrived a black-bordered letter informing him that his uncle was dead and had left him the bulk of his property, amounting in all to five thousand pounds.[2] With a portion of this property, Mr. Godfrey Nickleby purchased a small farm near Dawlish,[3] and on his death some fifteen years later he was able to leave to his eldest son some three thousand pounds in cash, and to his youngest, one thousand and the farm.

The younger boy was of a timid and retiring disposition, keen only to attach himself to the quiet routine of country life. The elder son, however, resolved to make use of his father's inheritance; for Ralph Nickleby had begun lending money on a limited scale even at school, putting out at interest a small capital of slate pencils and marbles. Now in adulthood, Ralph Nickleby resolved to live his life by the simple motto that there is nothing in the world as good as money.

While Ralph prospered in London, the young brother still lived on the farm, and took himself a wife, who gave birth to a boy and a girl. By the time this boy and girl were nearing twenty, he found his expenses much increased and his capital still more depleted.

"Speculate,"[4] his wife advised him. "Think of your brother, and speculate."

And Mr. Nickleby did speculate. But a bubble in the business world burst. Four stockbrokers

---

1. **Devonshire** [dev′ən shēr′]: rural county in southwest England.
2. **pounds**: the British pound was worth about five dollars in Dickens' time.
3. **Dawlish**: town in Devonshire.
4. **speculate**: buy and sell goods such as stocks and land in order to profit from the rise and fall of prices.

---

took villa residences far away in sunny Italy. Four hundred nobodies were ruined, and one of them was Mr. Nickleby.

And Mr. Nickleby took to his bed.

"Cheer up, sir!" said the apothecary.[5]

"You mustn't let yourself be cast down, sir," said the nurse.

"Such things happen every day," remarked the lawyer.

"It is very sinful to rebel against them," whispered the clergyman.

But Mr. Nickleby shook his head, and he motioned them all out of the room. Shortly afterwards his reason went astray, and he babbled about the goodness of his brother, Ralph, and about the merry times they had had together in school. Then one day he turned his face upon the wall, observing that he could fall asleep.

And so with no one in the world to help them but Ralph Nickleby, the widow and her children, Kate and Nicholas, journeyed forth to London.

*Scene i.*
*An entrance hall and adjoining room in nineteenth-century London.*

[MRS. NICKLEBY, KATE, *and* NICHOLAS *are on stage.* RALPH NICKLEBY *enters the hallway after giving the outer door a double knock. The* NICKLEBYS *stand.* RALPH *steps forward.*]

RALPH. Ah, young Nicholas, I suppose. Good morning, sir. And—Kate.

MRS. NICKLEBY. That is correct, sir. These are my —[*Bursts into tears.*]

RALPH. Well, ma'am, how are you? You must bear up against sorrow, ma'am, I always do. You didn't mention how he died. [RALPH *sits.*]

---

5. **apothecary** [ə poth′ə ker′ē]: pharmacist.

*The Life and Adventures of Nicholas Nickleby* **361**

AT A GLANCE

- The narrator explains the background of the Nicklebys' financial situation.
- Nicholas Nickleby, Sr., in need of extra income, speculated, lost everything, and died.
- *Scene i:* His penniless family goes to his brother, Ralph Nickleby, for help.

LITERARY OPTIONS

- dialogue
- staging and setting
- characterization

THEMATIC OPTIONS

- compassion vs. cruelty
- materialism vs. idealism
- a hero's growth

**1 NARRATOR**

This play introduces a narrator who comes directly from Dickens' novel, providing necessary exposition and also adding the flavor of Dickens' prose style. Here the narrator identifies a major preoccupation of the play: money.

**2 DIALOGUE**

This statement characterizes Ralph in a subtle, ironic way. Unlike the Nicklebys, he can "bear up against sorrow" because he is unfeeling. Note that he had not previously taken the trouble to learn how his brother died.

---

*GUIDED READING*

LITERAL QUESTIONS

**1a.** How does the Nickleby family come to be in its present financial circumstances? (Mr. Nickleby used his inheritance to speculate in the stock market. He lost all his money and he died.)

**2a.** What do the Nicklebys do about their financial situation? (They go to London to ask Ralph Nickleby for help.)

INFERENTIAL QUESTIONS

**1b.** What does their situation show about the economic situation of the period? (It suggests that it was a time of fraud and an unregulated market, when the economic system benefitted the rich and small investors were ruined.)

**2b.** Do you think this is a good plan? (They don't have much choice, but what we have learned about Ralph—he is rich, and money is most important to him—does not suggest that he will be generous.)

Nicholas, Kate, and Mrs. Nickleby.

Ralph Nickleby.

**MRS. NICKLEBY.** The doctors could attribute it to no particular disease. We have reason to fear that he died of a broken heart.

**RALPH.** Hm. What?

**MRS. NICKLEBY.** I beg your pardon?

**RALPH.** I don't understand. A broken leg or head, I know of them, but not a broken heart.

**NICHOLAS.** Some people, I believe, have none to break.

**RALPH.** What's that? How old is this boy, ma'am?

**MRS. NICKLEBY.** Nineteen.

**RALPH.** And what's he mean to do for bread?

**NICHOLAS.** To earn it, sir. And not look for anyone to keep my family, except myself.

**RALPH.** I see. Well, ma'am, the creditors have administered, you say, and you spent what little was left, coming all the way to London, to see me.

**MRS. NICKLEBY.** I hoped.... It was my husband's wish, I should appeal to you—

**RALPH.** I don't know why it is. But whenever a man dies with no property, he always thinks he has the right to dispose of other people's. If my brother had been acquainted with the world, and then applied himself to make his way in it, then you would not now be in this—in this situation. I must say it, Mrs. Nickleby: my brother was a thoughtless, inconsiderate man, and no one I am sure, can feel that fact more keenly than you do.

**MRS. NICKLEBY.** Well, well. That may be true. I've often thought, if he had listened to me.... Yes. It may well be true.

[NICHOLAS *and* KATE *give an uncertain glance at each other.* RALPH *clocks this.*]

**RALPH.** So, what's your daughter fit for, ma'am?

**MRS. NICKLEBY.** Oh, Kate has been well-educated, sir.

**KATE.** I'm willing to try anything that will give me home and bread.

**RALPH.** [*Slightly affected by* KATE.] Well. Well. [*To* NICHOLAS, *briskly.*] And you, sir? You're prepared to work?

**NICHOLAS.** Yes, certainly.

[RALPH *takes a newspaper cutting from his pocket.*]

**RALPH.** Then read that. Caught my eye this morning.

[NICHOLAS *takes the cutting and reads.*]

**NICHOLAS.** Education. The Master of the Academy, Dotheboys[6] Hall, near Greta Bridge in Yorkshire,[7] is in town, and attends at the Saracen's Head, Snow Hill. Able assistant wanted. Annual salary five pounds. A Master of Arts would be preferred.

**RALPH.** Well. There.

**MRS. NICKLEBY.** But he's not a Master of Arts.

**RALPH.** That I think can be got over.

**KATE.** And the salary is so small, uncle, and it is so far away—

**MRS. NICKLEBY.** Hush, Kate, your uncle must know best.

**RALPH.** And I'm convinced that he will have you, if I recommend it. [*Pause.*] Ma'am, if he can find another job, in London, now, which keeps him in shoe leather...he can have a thousand pounds.

[*Pause.*]

---

6. **Dotheboys** [doo′thə boyz]
7. **Yorkshire** [yôrk′shēr]: county in northeast England.

*The Life and Adventures of Nicholas Nickleby*   **363**

## AT A GLANCE

- *Scene i (continued):* The Nicklebys appeal to their uncle, who is reluctant to help.
- He suggests Nicholas take a job as an assistant at Dotheboys Hall, a boys school.

**1 MAIN IDEA**

Nickleby's death reveals the dark side of a society in which material values are supreme. Human lives are ruined, and someone dies "of a broken heart" because material goods are more important than human values.

**2 PLOT: FORESHADOWING**

Here Nicholas shows his pride and independence of spirit; he wishes to earn his own way. This flash of spirit foreshadows his later ability to assert himself in important ways.

**3 DIALOGUE**

Ralph is characterized by his peculiar ability to twist things so that the virtuous seem at fault and his own selfishness seems virtuous.

**4 CHARACTERIZATION**

The fact that Ralph is respected by a headmaster who will pay so little for a teacher further establishes Ralph's lack of humanity. It also prepares us to see the greed and inhumanity of the headmaster himself.

---

## GUIDED READING

### LITERAL QUESTIONS

**1a.** How does Ralph Nickleby describe his brother? (presumptuous to expect help from Ralph, worthy of blame for being unworldly and poor, inconsiderate for leaving his family in poverty)

**2a.** What solution does Uncle Ralph propose? (He urges Nicholas to accept a job as an assistant at a boy's school in Yorkshire at five pounds a year—a very small amount of money.)

### INFERENTIAL QUESTIONS

**1b.** What do his comments about his brother tell you about Ralph? (He has little concern for his relatives and does not value the qualities of simplicity and quiet living exemplified by his brother.)

**2b.** Why do you think he helps Nicholas get a job? (He wants to avoid supporting Nicholas himself and to get rid of him easily. He may also want to do the school's headmaster a favor.)

**1** KATE. We must be separated, then, so soon?

NICHOLAS. Sir, if I am appointed to this post, what will become of those I leave behind?

RALPH. If you're accepted, and you take it, they will be provided for. That will be my care.

[*Pause.*]

NICHOLAS. Then, uncle, I am ready to do anything you wish.

RALPH. That's good. And, come, who knows, you work well, and you'll rise to be a partner. And then, if he dies, your fortune's made.

NICHOLAS. Oh, yes? [RALPH *looks at* NICHOLAS.] Oh, yes, to be sure. Oh, Kate, and who knows, p'raps there will be some young nobleman or other, at the school, who takes a fancy to me, **2** and then I'll become his traveling tutor when he leaves. [KATE *is not quite convinced.*] And when we get back from the continent, his father might procure me some handsome appointment, in his household, or his business. Yes? [*To* RALPH.] Who knows, he might fall in love with Kate, and marry her.... Don't you think so, uncle?

[*Pause.* RALPH *doesn't know quite what to say.*]

RALPH. Yes. Of course. I—

KATE. Uncle. We're a simple family. We were born and bred in the country, we have never been apart, and we are unacquainted with the world.

RALPH. Well, then, my dear—

KATE. It will take time for us to understand it, to apply ourselves to make our way in it, and to bear that separation which necessity now forces on us. I am sure you understand.

[*Pause.*]

RALPH. Oh, yes. Indeed, I do. [*Slight pause. To* NICHOLAS.] I think, sir.... Shall we go?

NARRATOR. And so the uncle and his nephew took themselves with all convenient speed towards Snow Hill, and Mr. Wackford Squeers.

### Scene ii.
### The coffee house of the Saracen's Head Inn. Later that day.

[*In the coffee house are* WACKFORD SQUEERS, *dressed in an ill-fitting suit of scholastic black; also,* BELLING, *a small boy sitting on a small trunk.*]

**3** NARRATOR. In the Snow Hill section of London, near to the jail and to Smithfield, is the Saracen's Head, an inn on the stagecoach line. Outside the Saracen's Head are two stone heads of Saracens, both fearsome and quite hideously ugly. Inside, on this January afternoon, stood Mr. Squeers, whose appearance was not much more prepossessing.[8]

**4** He had only one eye, while popular prejudice runs in favor of two. And the side of his face was wrinkled, giving him a highly sinister appearance, especially when he smiled. And the eye that he had was a funny color—a kind of greenish gray, and in shape resembling the fanlight[9] of a streetdoor, through which Mr. Squeers was glaring at a tiny boy.

[*As* SQUEERS *and* BELLING *look at each other,* BELLING *sneezes.*]

SQUEERS. Hallo, sir! What's that, sir?

BELLING. Nothing, please, sir.

SQUEERS. Nothing, sir?

BELLING. Please, sir, I sneezed, sir.

SQUEERS. [*Taking the boy by the ear.*] Sneezed? You sneezed? Well, that's not nothing, is it?

---

8. **prepossessing** [prē′pə zes′ing]: pleasing.
9. **fanlight:** semicircular window over a door, with bars radiating like an open fan.

---

BELLING. No, sir.

SQUEERS. Wait till Yorkshire, my young gentleman. And then I'll give you something to remember.

[BELLING *is crying.* WILLIAM, *a waiter, enters.*]

WILLIAM. Mr. Squeers. There's a gentleman who's asking for you.

SQUEERS. Show him in, William, Show him in. [WILLIAM *goes out.* SQUEERS *looks at* BELLING, *who is still sniffling.* BELLING *cringes at this look, and is somewhat surprised when* SQUEERS *sits on the bench and puts his arm round the tiny boy.*] Now, dear child, why are you weeping? All people have their trials, but what is yours? You are losing your friends, that is true, but you will have a father in me, my dear, and a mother in Mrs. Squeers. [WILLIAM *admitting* SNAWLEY, *a sleek, flatnosed man in somber garments, and two little* SNAWLEY BOYS.] At the delightful village of Dotheboys, near Greta Bridge in Yorkshire, where youth are boarded, clothed, booked, furnished with pocket-money, provided with all necessaries... [SNAWLEY *checks* SQUEERS's *speech against a newspaper advertisement he carries. It is the same.*] ...instructed in all languages, living and dead, mathematics, orthography, geometry, astronomy, trigonometry, the use of the globes, algebra, single stick[10] (if required), writing, arithmetic, fortification,[11] and every other branch of classical literature. Terms, 20 guineas[12] per annum,[13] no extras, no vacations, and diet unparalleled, why good day, sir, I had no idea— [*And* SQUEERS *has turned to* SNAWLEY *and extended his hand.*]

SNAWLEY. Mr. Squeers?

---

10. **single stick:** fencing or fighting with a wooden stick.
11. **fortification:** review (literally, reinforcement of what students have already studied).
12. **20 guineas** [gin′ēz]: A guinea was an English coin, no longer in use, worth a little more than a pound.
13. **per annum:** per year.

SQUEERS. The same, sir.

SNAWLEY. My name is Snawley. I'm in the oil and color way.

SQUEERS. Well, how do you do, sir? [*To the little* SNAWLEYS.] And how do *you* do, young sirs?

SNAWLEY. Mr. Squeers, I have been thinking of placing my two boys at your school.

SQUEERS. Sir, I do not think you could do a better thing.

SNAWLEY. At—20 pounds per annum for two, perhaps? They're not great eaters.

SQUEERS. Then we will not be great feeders, sir. I am sure that we can reach accommodation.

SNAWLEY. And this is another boy, sir?

SQUEERS. Yes, sir, this is Belling, and his luggage that he's sitting on. Each boy requires two suits of clothes, six shirts, six pairs of stockings, two nightcaps, two pocket handkerchiefs, two pairs of shoes, two hats and a razor.

SNAWLEY. Razor? Sir, whatever for?

SQUEERS. To shave with. Off you go, Belling.

[*Pause.* SNAWLEY *takes* SQUEERS *aside. The little* BOYS *look at each other.*]

SNAWLEY. Sir, up to what age...?

SQUEERS. As long as payment's regularly made.

SNAWLEY. I see. [*Slight pause.*]

SQUEERS. Sir, let us understand each other. Are you the father of these boys?

SNAWLEY. No. I'm the husband of their mother. [*Slight pause.*] And as it's so expensive, keeping boys.... And as she has so little money of her own...which she will squander on them—which will be the ruination of them.... [*Slight pause.*] And hearing of a school, a great distance off, where there are none of those ill-judged

*The Life and Adventures of Nicholas Nickleby* **365**

- *Scene ii (continued):* Ralph Nickleby arrives, and Squeers remembers him for having paid the fees of a boy who died at the school.
- Nickleby asks him to take Nicholas as his assistant; Squeers agrees.
- *Scene iii:* Squeers eats; he allows the boys with him to eat nothing.

## 1 PLOT: FORESHADOWING

This line hints the boy died in mysterious circumstances and foreshadows the neglect and mistreatment at Dotheboys Hall.

## 2 CHARACTERIZATION

Squeers's reply again shows his hypocrisy. He speaks of the tender care of the boy given by Mrs. Squeers when the opposite is probably true. The fact that the dying boy was given a rock-hard dictionary for a pillow suggests what Dotheboys Hall is really like.

## 3 STYLE: WORD CHOICE

The humor is created by the clever repetition of the word *fermenting.* The word is a good one, since it suggests the bubbly, natural activity of a young mind and the flat condition of Nicholas' pocket.

## 4 DIALOGUE

Ralph's statement sets up a major internal conflict for Nicholas. He now knows he must keep at his job, no matter what he feels about it, or sacrifice the well-being of his mother and sister.

---

comings-home three times a year, that do unsettle the children so.... [*Pause.*]

SQUEERS. And payments regular, and then, no questions asked. [*Slight pause.*]

SNAWLEY. I should...I should want their morals particularly attended to.

[WILLIAM *brings in* RALPH *and* NICHOLAS.]

SQUEERS. Well, you've come to the right shop for morals, sir. I think we do, now, understand each other.

RALPH. Mr. Squeers. A matter of business, sir. My name is Ralph Nickleby. Perhaps you recollect me.

SQUEERS. Why, yes, sir.... Did you not pay me a small account for some years...on behalf of parents of a boy named Dorker who...

1 RALPH. That's right. Who died, unfortunately, in Yorkshire.

SQUEERS. Yes, sir, I remember well. [SNAWLEY *looks at* SQUEERS.] And I remember too, how Mrs.
2 Squeers nursed the boy...Dry toast and warm tea when he wouldn't swallow, and a candle in his bedroom on the night he died, a dictionary to lay his head upon....

RALPH. Yes, yes. So, shall we come to business? You have advertised for an able assistant, and here he is. [SQUEERS *looks at* NICHOLAS NICKLEBY.]
3 My nephew Nicholas, hot from school, with everything he learnt there fermenting in his head, and nothing fermenting in his pocket. [*Pause.*] His father lies dead, he is wholly ignorant of the world, he has no resources whatever, and he wants to make his fortune.

SQUEERS. Well...[*Pause.*]

NICHOLAS. I fear, sir, that you object to my youth, and my not being a Master of Arts?

SQUEERS. Well, the absence of a college degree *is* an objection....

---

4 RALPH. And if any caprice of temper should induce him to cast aside this golden opportunity I shall consider myself absolved from extending any assistance to his mother and sister. Now the question is, whether, for some time to come, he won't exactly serve your purpose.

[*Pause.* SQUEERS *makes a little gesture. He and* RALPH *withdraw a little.*]

SNAWLEY. [*To convince himself.*] A fine gentleman, sir. That Mr. Squeers, a gentleman of virtue and morality.

NICHOLAS. [*To convince himself.*] I'm sure of it.

[RALPH *and* SQUEERS *back.*]

RALPH. Nicholas, you are employed.

NICHOLAS. [*Delighted.*] Oh, sir—

SQUEERS. The coach leaves eight o'clock tomorrow morning, Mr. Nickleby—and you must be here a quarter before.

NICHOLAS. I shall be. Surely.

RALPH. And, your fare is paid.

[SQUEERS *takes* SNAWLEY *aside, taking money from him and inserting something in a ledger.*]

NICHOLAS. Well, thank you, uncle. I will not forget this kindness.

RALPH. See you don't. And I am late. You'd best go home and pack, sir. Early in the morning, you heard Mr. Squeers.

*Scene iii.*
*Again, the coffee shop of the Saracen's Head Inn, but now it is morning.*

[SQUEERS *sits at the head of a table eating a large plate of toast and beef.* BELLING *and the two* SNAWLEY BOYS *sit with nothing before them. Their luggage, including a trunk, is piled up*

---

## GUIDED READING

**LITERAL QUESTION**

**1a.** How do Squeers and Ralph Nickleby know each other? (Nickleby once paid the fees of a boy named Dorker who died at Squeers's school.)

**INFERENTIAL QUESTION**

**1b.** What can you infer about Ralph Nickleby from this? (He knows what kind of place Squeers's school is and even though the boy probably died from neglect, Ralph did not report the school to the authorities. Some students may note that the deal introduces a mystery concerning Ralph's character: Why did Ralph want to banish a boy to Yorkshire?)

*nearby.* SQUEERS *is presently looking into a large blue mug.* WILLIAM, *the waiter, is in attendance, with a jug of warm water and a piece of bread-and-butter on a plate.*]

SQUEERS. This is two penn'orth[14] of milk, is it, William?

WILLIAM. S'right, sir.

SQUEERS. What a rare article milk is in London, to be sure. Now fill it up with water, will you.

WILLIAM. To the top, sir?

SQUEERS. [*Starting to eat.*] That's correct.

WILLIAM. But, sir, you'll drown the milk.

SQUEERS. Well, serve it right for being so expensive. Now. Where's the bread-and-butter?

WILLIAM. Here, sir. [*He puts the bread-and-butter on the table. The little* BOYS *quickly reach for it.*]

SQUEERS. Wait! [*The* BOYS *freeze. Their hands go back.* WILLIAM *goes away.* SQUEERS *divides the slice of bread into three, as* NICHOLAS *approaches.*] Good morning, Nickleby. Sit down. We're breakfasting.

NICHOLAS. Good morning, sir.

SQUEERS. Now, boys, when I say "one," young Snawley takes a drink of milk and eats his bread. When I say "two," the older Snawley, and then "three" is Belling. Clear?

BOYS. Oh, yes, sir.

SQUEERS. [*Eating.*] Right. Now, wait. Subdue your appetites, my dears, you've conquered human nature. [*Pause.* SQUEERS *eats.*] One! [*The* YOUNGER SNAWLEY *eats and drinks.*] Say thank you.

YOUNGER SNAWLEY. [*Eating.*] 'ank 'ou.

_____
14. **penn'orth:** penny's worth.

[*Pause.* SQUEERS *eats.*]

SQUEERS. Two! [*The* OLDER SNAWLEY *eats and drinks.*] Well?

OLDER SNAWLEY. Thank you, sir.

[SQUEERS *finishes his food.*]

SQUEERS. And— [*He is interrupted by a horn. The coach guard,* DICK, *is blowing it.*] Oh, dear Belling, there's the horn. You've missed your turn. Come, my dears, let's bustle. William! Coat!

[*And bustle they do, while* DICK *is joined by the* COACHMAN *and* PASSENGERS, *and their* PORTERS *and* NEWSBOYS *and* VENDORS *and bits of crowd.* WILLIAM *brings in* SQUEERS's *case, the* BOYS *take their luggage out, the* PASSENGERS *pay their* PORTERS, *give their luggage to* DICK, *and pay their fare to the* COACHMAN. NICHOLAS *is following* SQUEERS *out of the inn into the street. At this point,* MRS. NICKLEBY *and* KATE *appear.*]

MRS. NICKLEBY. Nicholas!

NICHOLAS. Oh, mother, Kate—you shouldn't.

KATE. How could we just let you go?

MRS. NICKLEBY. So many kind words to be spoken....

KATE. So much bitter pain to be suppressed, and so little time to do it in.

NICHOLAS. These preparations for leaving are mournful indeed.

NARRATOR. As they grow nearer and nearer to the close of their preparations, Kate grows busier and busier and weeps more silently. Nicholas prepares his mind to say good-by and resolves that, come what may, he would bear whatever might be in store for him, for the sake of his mother and his sister, giving his uncle no excuse to desert them in their need.

*The Life and Adventures of Nicholas Nickleby*   367

## AT A GLANCE

- *Scene iii (continued):* Nicholas enters, and Squeers lets two of the three boys eat.
- The coach arrives, and Kate and Mrs. Nickleby come to see Nicholas off.

## 1 THEME

Dickens uses satiric humor to point up a serious situation: The boys are denied food to save Squeers money. Squeers's materialism will soon be brought into opposition with Nicholas' idealism.

## 2 DIALOGUE

Squeers's comment shows his casual cruelty. Belling will not get even the two penn'orth of milk or one-third of a slice of bread, but Squeers, having satisfied his own hunger and saved money by not feeding the boys, is perversely cheerful.

## 3 PLOT: CONFLICT

The narrator poses Nicholas' conflict: He must "bear whatever might be in store" or sacrifice his mother and sister. His growing knowledge suggests he might have to bear a good deal and that his uncle would need little excuse to desert his family.

## GUIDED READING

**LITERAL QUESTION**

**1a.** What does Squeers order for the boys to eat? (For three boys there is one glass of watered milk and one slice of bread and butter.)

**INFERENTIAL QUESTION**

**1b.** What does this scene hint about conditions at Dotheboys Hall? (Showing that Squeers is greedy and hypocritical, the scene hints that conditions at Dotheboys Hall, where Squeers reigns supreme, are probably like those in a prison.)

- *Scene iii (continued):* Nicholas, Squeers, and the boys board the coach, which rattles off.
- *Scene iv:* They arrive at the school, where Nicholas begins to feel grave doubts about Squeers and Dotheboys.
- Squeers goes into his house and chastises Smike, who has fallen asleep by the fire.

## 1 THEME

Squeers's reason for not wanting Belling to fall off is grimly humorous. Squeers's greed is so great that he equates the value of a human life only with the 20 pounds a year that it means for him.

## 2 CHARACTERIZATION

Nicholas tries to protect Kate from the harsh truth that is beginning to dawn on him. He will not admit that his job promises to be insupportable, yet, even for Kate, he cannot lie. He softens the truth: Squeers is only rough and uncultivated.

## 3 SETTING

The grimness of Dotheboys Hall crystallizes the doubts Nicholas has begun to feel. Note that the play uses the narrator here to reveal Nicholas' thoughts, thoughts that Nicholas cannot express aloud to Squeers.

## 4 BACKGROUND

Readers of the novel *Nicholas Nickleby* will recall that Smike is revealed at the novel's end to be the son of Ralph Nickleby. This revelation is not included in this excerpt, which concerns only the first part of *Nicholas Nickleby*, but you may want to share this information with students interested in exploring the work further.

---

[SQUEERS, *dragging* BELLING, *comes to* NICHOLAS.]

**1** SQUEERS. Now, Nickleby, I think you'd better ride behind. I'm feared of Belling falling off, and there goes 20 pounds a year.

NICHOLAS. Right, I, uh—

SQUEERS. [*Dragging* BELLING *back up to the coach.*] And, dear Belling, if you don't stop chattering your teeth and shaking, I'll warm you with a severe thrashing in about half a minute's time. Come, Nickleby!

**2** KATE. Oh, Nicholas, who is that man? What kind of place can it be that you're going to?

NICHOLAS. Well, I suppose—that Yorkshire folks are rather rough and uncultivated—

[*The coach is nearly ready to go.*]

SQUEERS. Nickleby, drat you!

NICHOLAS. Good-by, mother. To our meeting, one day, soon. And good-by, Kate.

KATE. You'll write?

NICHOLAS. Of course I will.

COACHMAN. Stage leaving! Stage leaving! Ev'one for the stage, up and sit fast!

[*Horn again.* SQUEERS, BELLING, *the* SNAWLEYS, *and the other* PASSENGERS *go out.* NICHOLAS *kisses* KATE *and runs to the coach.*]

NARRATOR. And a minute's bustle, and a banging of the coach doors, a swaying of the vehicle, a cry of "all right" and a few notes from the horn, and the coach was gone, and rattling over the stones of Smithfield.

 *Scene iv.*
*Outside Dotheboys Hall.*

[*Enter* NICHOLAS, *the three* BOYS, *and* SQUEERS. NICHOLAS *and the* BOYS *look at the building.*]

368 *Drama*

---

NICHOLAS. Dotheboys Hall.

SQUEERS. Oh, sir, you needn't call it a hall up here.

NICHOLAS. Why not?

SQUEERS. Cos the fact is, it ain't a hall.

**3** NARRATOR. A host of unpleasant misgivings, which had been crowding upon Nicholas during the whole journey, thronged into his mind. And he considered the dreary house and dark windows and the wild country round covered with snow, he felt a depression of heart and spirit which he had never experienced before.

SQUEERS. No, we call it a hall up in London, because it sounds better, but they don't know it by that name here. A man may call his house an island if he likes—there's no Act of Parliament against that, I believe? [SQUEERS *knocks on the door.*]

NICHOLAS. No, I think not, sir.

**4** SQUEERS. Well, then. Hey! Door! [*At which* SMIKE, *who has come to the door, opens it.*] Smike. Where have you been?

SMIKE. Please, sir, I fell asleep.

SQUEERS. You fell a-what?

SMIKE. Please, sir, I fell asleep over the fire.

[SQUEERS *goes into the house.*]

SQUEERS. Fire? What fire? Where's there a fire?

[SMIKE *trots in after* SQUEERS. NICHOLAS, *not sure what to do, comes in and stands just inside the door.*]

SMIKE. Please, sir, Missus said as I was sitting up, I might be by the fire for a warm...

SQUEERS. [*Turning and taking* SMIKE *by the collar.*] Your missus is a fool. You'd have been a deuced deal more wakeful in the cold.

[*He is interrupted by* MRS. SQUEERS, *who has*

---

## GUIDED READING

### LITERAL QUESTIONS

**1a.** What does Squeers tell Belling about his chattering teeth? (He tells him to stop or he'll thrash him.)

**2a.** How does the narrator describe Dotheboys Hall? (a *dreary house* with *dark windows* set in *wild country covered with snow*)

### INFERENTIAL QUESTIONS

**1b.** Why do you think Belling has chattering teeth and is shaking? (He is cold; he has had almost nothing to eat to maintain body heat. He is also frightened to death of Squeers and the whole situation.)

**2b.** How does the setting contribute to the mood of the play? (The dark, dreary house reflects the somber situation of the poor and unprotected children lodged there. The wild, frozen country mirrors the cold, uncultivated hearts that rule the place.)

The stagecoach leaving the Saracen's Head Inn.

Smike.

## 1 TONE

The tone of the author is revealed here: The exchange is sarcastically characterized as "affectionate," but the pair is made to look ridiculous by the content of their conversation.

## 2 CHARACTERIZATION AND THEME

Squeers inquires after the boys, but only after asking about the cows and pigs. These priorities show how little he values his charges.

## 3 DIALOGUE

Mrs. Squeers's comments show her irrationality and cruelty. Not wanting to care for sick boys, she assumes that they become ill on purpose to cause work for her. Her instinctively inhuman remedy is to "beat it out" of them.

## 4 THEME

Squeers goes through the mail and comments on who has sent money. Mrs. Squeers steals from the boys' luggage. These parallel actions show the casual rapacity that is part of everyday life at Dotheboys Hall.

---

appeared from the inside of the house, in a nightjacket and cap.]

MRS. SQUEERS. Squeers.

SQUEERS. [*Turning to her.*] My love. [*Turns quickly back to* SMIKE, *gesturing to the boys in the yard.*] There's boys. The boys, to bed.

MRS. SQUEERS. Oh, Squeers. How is my Squeery-dearie? [SQUEERS *embraces* MRS. SQUEERS.]

SQUEERS. Well, well, my love. How are the cows?

**1** [*The embrace continues during the following affectionate exchange. During it, a hungry-looking servant,* PHIB, *enters with a tray. She puts it on the table.*]

MRS. SQUEERS. All right, every one of 'em.

**2** SQUEERS. And the pigs?

MRS. SQUEERS. As well as they were when you went.

SQUEERS. Well, that's a great blessing. [*These sweet nothings over,* SQUEERS *leaves* MRS. SQUEERS *and takes letters and documents from his pocket. As an afterthought.*] The boys all as they were, I suppose?

[MRS. SQUEERS, *taking the letters from* SQUEERS *and placing them on the table, glancing at one or two.*]

MRS. SQUEERS. Oh, yes, they're well enough. But young Sprouter's had a fever.

SQUEERS. [*Taking off his greatcoat.*] No! Drat the boy, he's always at something of that sort.

[PHIB *takes* SQUEERS's *huge coat, and stands there, holding it.* SQUEERS *goes to the table and sits.*]

**3** MRS. SQUEERS. Never was such a boy, I do believe. Whatever he has is always catching, too. I say it's obstinacy, and nothing shall ever convince me that it isn't. I'd beat it out of him, and I told you that six months ago.

**370** *Drama*

---

SQUEERS. So you did, my love. We'll try what can be done. [*Slight pause.* MRS. SQUEERS *nods in the direction of* NICHOLAS, *who is still standing near the door, not knowing what to do.*] Ah, Nickleby. Come, sir, come in. [NICHOLAS *comes a little further into the room.*] This is our new young man, my dear.

MRS. SQUEERS. [*Suspiciously.*] Oh, is it?

SQUEERS. He can shake down here tonight, can't he?

MRS. SQUEERS. [*Looking round.*] Well, if he's not particular . . . .

NICHOLAS. [*Politely.*] Oh, no, indeed.

MRS. SQUEERS. That's lucky.

[*She looks at* SQUEERS *and laughs.* SQUEERS *laughs back. They laugh at each other. Meanwhile,* SMIKE *reappears outside the house, and drags the* BOYS' *luggage into the parlor.* MRS. SQUEERS *looks at* PHIB, *and snaps her head towards the door.* PHIB *goes out with the big coat.* SQUEERS *is looking through the letters.* SMIKE *has finished bringing in the luggage and stands, staring fixedly at the letters on the table.* MRS. SQUEERS *goes and picks up one of the* BOYS' *bags and takes it back to the table.*]

**4** SQUEERS. Bolder's father's short.

MRS. SQUEERS. Tt tt.

SQUEERS. But Cobbey's sister's sent something.

[MRS. SQUEERS *sits and goes through the* BOYS' *luggage, making a pile of bits and pieces she fancies.*]

MRS. SQUEERS. That's good.

SQUEERS. And Graymarsh's maternal aunt has written, with no money, but two pairs of stockings and a tract. [15]

---

15. **tract:** religious pamphlet.

---

## GUIDED READING

### LITERAL QUESTIONS

**1a.** What do the Squeerses do after Nicholas affirms he's not particular where he sleeps? (Mrs. Squeers says, "That's lucky," and they look at each other and laugh.)

**2a.** What comments does Squeers make as he goes through the boys' letters? (He comments only on the enclosures of money or goods.)

### INFERENTIAL QUESTIONS

**1b.** What does their laugh mean? (They callously acknowledge that the school will not offer Nicholas very plush accomodations or a very wholesome moral atmosphere. Dotheboys is not a place for particular people.)

**2b.** What does this tell you about his interest in the boys? (It is purely financial. He is only interested in them insofar as he can extract money from their parents or guardians.)

MRS. SQUEERS. Maternal aunt.

SQUEERS. My love?

MRS. SQUEERS. More likely, in my view, that she's Graymarsh's maternal mother.

[*The* SQUEERSES *look at each other. Then* SQUEERS *notices that* SMIKE *is very close, craning to see the letters.*]

SQUEERS. Yes? What's to do, boy?

SMIKE. Is there—

SQUEERS. What?

SMIKE. Is there. . . . There's nothing heard . . . ?

SQUEERS. No, not a word. And never will be.

MRS. SQUEERS. [*The very idea.*] Tt.

[*Pause.* SQUEERS *decides to rub it in.*]

SQUEERS. And it is a pretty sort of thing, that you should have been left here all these years and no money paid after the first six—nor no notice taken, nor no clue to who you belong to? It's a pretty sort of thing, is it not, that I should have to feed a great fellow like you, and never hope to get one penny for it, isn't it? [SQUEERS *looking at* SMIKE.]

NICHOLAS. [*Out front.*] The boy put his hand to his head as if he was making an effort to remember something, and then, looking vacantly at his questioner, gradually broke into a smile.

SQUEERS. That's right. Now, off with you, and send the girl.

[SMIKE *limps out.* MRS. SQUEERS, *having finished sifting the* BOY's *bag, stands and looks for something on the table.*]

MRS. SQUEERS. I tell you what, Squeers, I think that young chap's turning silly.

SQUEERS. [*Wiping his mouth.*] I hope not. For he's a handy fellow out of doors, and worth his

meat and drink anyway. [*He stands.*] But come, I'm tired, and want to go to bed.

**3** MRS. SQUEERS. Oh, drat the thing.

SQUEERS. What's wrong, my dear?

MRS. SQUEERS. The school spoon. I can't find it.

SQUEERS. Never mind, my love.

MRS. SQUEERS. What, never mind? It's brimstone[16] in the morning.

SQUEERS. Ah, I forgot. [*He helps the search.*] Yes, certainly, it is.

NICHOLAS. Uh . . . ?

SQUEERS. We purify the boys' bloods now and then, Nickleby.

MRS. SQUEERS. [*Crossly.*] Purify fiddlesticks. Don't think, young man, that we go to the expense of flour of brimstone and molasses just to purify them; because if you think we carry on the business in that way, you'll find yourself mistaken, and so I tell you plainly.

**4** [SQUEERS *is not sure this intelligence is quite discreet. Enter* PHIB, *who tidies round the table, putting things back on the tray.*]

SQUEERS. My dear . . . should you . . .

MRS. SQUEERS. Nonsense. If the young man comes to be a teacher, let him understand at once that we don't want any foolery about the boys. They have the brimstone and treacle, partly because if they hadn't something or other in the way of medicine they'd always be ailing and giving a world of trouble, and partly because it spoils their appetites and comes cheaper than breakfast and dinner. So it does them good and us good at the same time, and that's fair enough, I'm sure. [SQUEERS *looking embarrassed.* MRS. SQUEERS *shoots a glance at him.*] Now, where's the spoon?

---

16. **brimstone:** sulfur. In the nineteenth century brimstone was combined with molasses (also called *treacle*) to create a foul-tasting mixture used as a general medicine.

*The Life and Adventures of Nicholas Nickleby* **371**

**AT A GLANCE**

- Squeers provides background on Smike, who has been abandoned.
- Mrs. Squeers loses her spoon.
- She explains the policy of dosing the boys regularly with brimstone and treacle.

**1 READING SKILLS: INFERENCE**

From this comment we can infer that Mrs. Squeers thinks Graymarsh is the illegitimate child of the woman who claims to be his aunt. This is further evidence that Dotheboys is a dumping ground for unwanted children.

**2 CHARACTERIZATION**

Mrs. Squeers's comment establishes Smike as a slow-thinking, perhaps slightly retarded boy. His confusion may be caused by emotional deprivation and physical mistreatment by the Squeerses.

**3 DIALOGUE**

This fragment of dialogue reveals a great deal about Dotheboys. The fact that there is only one school spoon suggests how little is spent equipping the school and implies that most of the money brought in is taken as profit by the Squeerses.

**4 THEME**

Squeers—a hypocrite—protests the open avowal of greed and mistreatment by Mrs. Squeers. Both are equally cruel, but Squeers is slightly more concerned with appearances than his wife.

---

## GUIDED READING

**LITERAL QUESTIONS**

**1a.** What do you learn about Smike when he asks if there's a letter for him? (Squeers tells him there never will be one and recalls that Smike has been at the school a long time with no fees paid for him in the last years.)

**2a.** When Mrs. Squeers corrects her husband's statement about why they use brimstone, how does he react? (He says, "My dear . . . should you . . . .")

**INFERENTIAL QUESTIONS**

**1b.** Why do you think Squeers feels free to be particularly cruel to Smike? (Smike has apparently been abandoned, with no one to care about his welfare. Squeers may also justify himself by claiming that Smike has been a "burden.")

**2b.** What does this interchange tell you about the difference between Squeers and his wife? (Both are equally cruel, but he is more hypocritical about it.)

- *Scene iv (continued):* The school spoon is found around Mrs. Squeers's neck.
- *Scene v:* The next morning, the boys line up for brimstone and treacle.

## 1 STAGING

The stage directions underscore an important point about Mrs. Squeers. She doesn't distinguish between acts that are volitional and those that are not. Anything that annoys her she sees as done deliberately, and she acts accordingly.

## 2 IRONY

Squeers's comment is unintentionally ironic. He claims that Mrs. Squeers is better than most mothers, but irony results from the audience's realization that Mrs. Squeers is actually the most unmaternal of women.

## 3 SETTING

The physical setting for this scene is deliberately vague: Its major attribute is darkness. The general effect is one of gloom and disorientation, reflecting the psychological condition of the mistreated boys.

---

[PHIB *has picked up the tray.*]

1 PHIB. Uh. Ma'am.

MRS. SQUEERS. What is it?

PHIB. S'round your neck. [*And indeed the spoon is round* MRS. SQUEERS*'s neck. She cuffs* PHIB *lightly for telling her.*]

MRS. SQUEERS. Why did you not say *before?*

PHIB. M'sorry, ma'am. [PHIB *picks up the tray and goes out.*]

MRS. SQUEERS. [*Pleasantly.*] And so, dear Mr. Nickleby, good night. [MRS. SQUEERS *goes out. Pause.*]

SQUEERS. A most invaluable woman, Nickleby.

NICHOLAS. Indeed, sir.

SQUEERS. I do not know her equal. That woman, Nickleby, is always the same: always the same bustling, lively, active, saving creature that you see her now.

NICHOLAS. I'm sure of it.

2 SQUEERS. [*Warming further to his theme.*] It is my custom, when I am in London, to say that she is like a mother to those boys. But she is more, she's ten times more. She does things for those boys, Nickleby, that I don't believe half the mothers going would do for their own sons.

NICHOLAS. I'm certain of it, sir.

SQUEERS. And so, good night, then, Nickleby.

NICHOLAS. Good night, sir. [SQUEERS *exits and* NICHOLAS *lies down.*]

*Scene v.*
*The next morning.*

[*In the darkness.*]

SQUEERS. Past seven, Nickleby! It's morning come, and well iced already. Now, Nickleby, come, tumble up, will you?

---

[*Lights. The parlor has gone.* NICHOLAS *stands where he was, but looking upstage.*[17] SQUEERS, *in his gown with his canes, stands with* MRS. SQUEERS *and her spoon, her son,* WACKFORD, *and* SMIKE *with a basin of brimstone and treacle. They are looking into the empty gloom. Then through the darkness, we see, approaching us, the* BOYS *of Dotheboys Hall.*]

SQUEERS. This is our shop, Nickleby.

[*The* BOYS *line up for brimstone and treacle. They introduce themselves as* MRS. SQUEERS *spoons out their medicine from* SMIKE*'s bowl.*]

TOMKINS. First boy. Tomkins. Nine.

COATES. Second boy. Coates. Thirteen.

GRAYMARSH. Third boy. Graymarsh. Eleven.

JENNINGS. Fourth boy. Jennings. Thirteen.

MOBBS. Fifth boy. [*Pause.*] Mobbs. Uh—'leven.

BOLDER. Sixth. Bolder. Fourteen.

PITCHER. Seventh. Pitcher. Ten.

MRS. SQUEERS. Move on. Move *on.*

JACKSON. Eighth. Johnny.

MRS. SQUEERS. Johnny?

JACKSON. Jackson. Thirteen.

COBBEY. Ninth. Cobbey. Fifteen.

PETERS. Tenth. Uh—Peters. Seven.

SPROUTER. Eleventh. Sprouter. Seven.

ROBERTS. Twelfth. Roberts. Ten.

OLDER SNAWLEY. Robert Arthur Snawley.

MRS. SQUEERS. Number!

OLDER SNAWLEY. I'm eleven.

MRS. SQUEERS. [*Twisting the* OLDER SNAWLEY*'s ear.*] Number is Thirteen.

---

17. **upstage:** toward the rear of the stage.

---

## GUIDED READING

### LITERAL QUESTIONS

**1a.** What do the stage directions say Mrs. Squeers does when Phib tells her where the spoon is? *(She cuffs Phib lightly.)*

**2a.** How does Squeers characterize Mrs. Squeers to Nicholas? *(always the same bustling, lively, active, saving creature)*

### INFERENTIAL QUESTIONS

**1b.** What does this gesture reveal about the relationship between Mrs. Squeers and Phib? *(Mrs. Squeers is careful not to go too far in her bullying with someone who is not totally dependent on her.)*

**2b.** What negative interpretation should the audience place on this cheerful evaluation? *(that she is relentless and never softens or lets up in her cruelty; that her cruelty is appreciated by her husband)*

Mrs. Squeers.

Mrs. Squeers and Smike giving the boys their doses of brimstone and treacle.

## 1 THEME

A major preoccupation of this work is the fact that cruel actions are often disguised by hypocrisy and people are asked to bear pain because God supposedly wills it. Here the boys are forced not only to take the disgusting mixture, but to give thanks for it.

## 2 CHARACTERIZATION

A peculiar characteristic of both Squeers and his wife is their irrationality. Both continually blame innocent people for causing conditions over which these individuals have absolutely no control. Here Squeers threatens Bolder for having the temerity to develop warts.

## 3 THEME

One facet of Squeers's inhumanity to the boys is his casual revelation of various family tragedies. He attaches more importance to confiscating Cobbey's eighteen-pence than to the death of the boy's grandmother.

---

OLDER SNAWLEY. Thirteen.

YOUNGER SNAWLEY. Uh—fourteen-th. Snawley, H. Uh—seven.

BELLING. Fifteen. Anthony Belling. Seven years of age.

[MRS. SQUEERS *wipes her hands on* SMIKE. SQUEERS, *to his son* WACKFORD, *who has been pushing the new* BOYS *forward.*]

**1** SQUEERS. Thank you, young Wackford. Thank you, son. And what do you say? And what d'you say, to this? [*Pause.*]

BOYS. For what we have received, may the Lord make us truly thankful.

SQUEERS. Amen.

BOYS. Amen.

SQUEERS. That's better. Now, boys, I've been to London, and have returned to my family and you, as strong and well as ever.

[*Pause.* MRS. SQUEERS *kicks a boy.*]

COATES. [*Feebly.*] Hip hip.

BOYS. [*Equally feebly.*] Hooray.

COATES. Hip hip.

BOYS. Hooray.

COATES. Hip hip.

BOYS. Hooray.

[SQUEERS *takes various letters from his pockets and wanders around among the* BOYS *as he speaks. During this,* MRS. SQUEERS *and* SMIKE *continue brimstone-and-treacling.*]

SQUEERS. I have seen the parents of some boys, and they're so glad to hear how their sons are doing, that there's no prospect at all of their going home, which of course is a very pleasant thing to reflect upon for all parties. [*He con-*

374   *Drama*

*tinues to perambulate.*] But I have had disappointments to contend with. Bolder's father, for an instance, was two pound ten short. Where is Bolder? [*The* BOYS *around* BOLDER *kick him, and he puts up his hand.* SQUEERS *goes to* BOLDER.] Ah. Bolder. Bolder, if your father thinks that because— [SQUEERS *suddenly notices that* BOLDER *has a dirty cuff, and grabs his arm.*] What do you call this, sir?

BOLDER. Warts, sir.

SQUEERS. What, sir?

BOLDER. Warts, sir.

SQUEERS. Warts?

BOLDER. I can't help it, sir. They will come. . . . It's working in the garden does it sir, at least I don't know what it is, sir, but it's not my fault. . . .

**2** SQUEERS. Bolder. You are an incorrigible young scoundrel, and as the last thrashing did you no good, we must see what another will do towards beating it out of you. [BOLDER *looks terrified.*] La—ter. [*He lets* BOLDER *go and walks on, reading.*] Now, let's see. . . . A letter for Cobbey. Cobbey? [COBBEY *puts his hand up.* SQUEERS **3** *hardly acknowledges, but walks on.*] Oh. Cobbey's grandmother is dead, and his uncle John has took to drinking, which is all the news his sister sends, except eighteenpence, which will just pay for that broken square of glass. Mobbs! [MOBBS, *not sure whether this will be good or bad news, nervously puts up his hand. It is clear it is not good news when* SQUEERS *walks to him and stands near.*] Now, Mobbs' stepmother took to her bed on hearing that he would not eat fat, and has been very ill ever since. She wishes to know by an early post where he expects to go to, if he quarrels with his vittles; and with what feelings he could turn up his nose at the cow's liver broth, after his good master had asked a blessing on it. She is disconsolate to find he is

---

## GUIDED READING

### LITERAL QUESTIONS

**1a.** What does Mrs. Squeers do after Squeers announces his safe return? (She kicks a boy.)

**2a.** What news does Squeers give about Cobbey's family? (His grandmother is dead, his uncle John has taken to drink, and his sister has sent him eighteenpence.)

### INFERENTIAL QUESTIONS

**1b.** Why does she do this, and what does it tell you about the boys' feelings toward Squeers? (She is nudging them to welcome Squeers back. The fact that such prompting is necessary indicates that the boys do not like Squeers.)

**2b.** What can you infer about the families of the boys at Squeers's school from this news? (That they are mostly poor families with many problems.)

discentented, which is sinful and horrid, and hopes Mr. Squeers will flog him into a happier state of mind. [*Into* MOBBS's *ear.*] Which—he—will. [*Long pause to let this sink in to everyone. Then.*] Right, boys. I'd like you all to meet my new assistant, Mr. Nickleby. Good morning, Mr. Nickleby.

BOYS. Good morning, Mr. Nickleby.

NICHOLAS. Good morning.

SQUEERS. Now, this is the first class in English spelling and philosophy, Nickleby. We'll soon get up a Latin one and hand that over to you. [NICHOLAS *joins* SQUEERS.] Now, then, where's Smallpiece?

BOYS. Please, sir . . .

SQUEERS. Let any boy speak out of turn, and I'll have the skin off his back!

JENNINGS. Please, sir, he's cleaning the back parlor window.

SQUEERS. So he is, to be sure. We go on the practical mode of teaching, Nickleby; C–l–e–a–n, clean—

BOYS. *Clean.*

SQUEERS. —verb active, to make bright, to scour. W–i–n, *win,*—

BOYS. *Win*—

SQUEERS. —d–e–r, *der*—

BOYS. —*der, winder*—

SQUEERS. *Winder,* a casement. When a boy knows this out of a book, he goes and does it. It's just the same principle as the use of the globes. Where's Grinder?

COBBEY. Please, sir, he's weeding the garden.

SQUEERS. [*With the* BOYS *repeating.*] To be sure. So he is. B–o–t, *bot,* t–i–n, *tin, bottin,* n–e–y, *ney, Bottiney,* noun substantive, a knowledge of plants. When he has learned that *bottiney* means a knowledge of plants, he goes and he knows 'em. That's our system, Nickleby, what do you think of it?

NICHOLAS. It's a very useful one, at any rate.

SQUEERS. I believe you. Graymarsh, what's a horse?

GRAYMARSH. A beast, sir.

SQUEERS. So it is. A horse is a quadroped, and *quadroped*'s Latin for beast, as everybody that's gone through the grammar knows, or else where's the use of having grammars at all?

NICHOLAS. [*Abstractly.*] Where indeed.

SQUEERS. [*To* GRAYMARSH.] And as you're so perfect in that, go to *my* horse, and rub him down well, or I'll rub *you* down. The rest go and draw water up till somebody tells you to leave off, for it's washing day tomorrow, and they'll want the coppers filled. [*The* BOYS *get up to go out,* MOBBS *and* BOLDER *hurrying more than the others.*] Except for Mobbs and Bolder. [*Everyone stops. Some of the other* BOYS *push* MOBBS *and* BOLDER *towards* SQUEERS. *The others quickly go out.* MOBBS *and* BOLDER *stand there, terrified.* MRS. SQUEERS *goes out.* SMIKE *turns to go too.*] Stay there, Smike. They'll need taking to their beds. [SQUEERS *lifts his cane. Then he turns to* NICHOLAS.] This is the way we do it, Nickleby.

NARRATOR. And Nicholas sat down, so depressed and self-degraded that if death could have come upon him then he could have been happy to meet it. The cruelty of which he had been an unwilling witness, the coarse and ruffianly behavior of Squeers, the filthy place, the sights and sounds about him—all contributed to this feeling. But when he recollected that, being there as an assistant, he was the aider and abettor of a system which filled him with disgust and indignation, he loathed himself.

*The Life and Adventures of Nicholas Nickleby* **375**

2
3
4

---

**AT A GLANCE**

- Squeers gives a lesson to the boys and explains the school's "system" to Nicholas.
- Nicholas despairs.

**1 MAIN IDEA**

In this lesson, the deception of Squeers's educational claims for his school is clear. He displays his ignorance and lack of qualifications to teach. The casual attempt at lessons disguises a system of near slave labor.

**2 IRONY**

To Squeers's claim that his system is a good one, Nicholas ironically replies that it's a *useful* one. The careful answer allows Nicholas to preserve his integrity without openly antagonizing Squeers.

**3 CHARACTERIZATION**

The incident shows Squeers's extreme cruelty. He expects to beat both the boys so badly that they will not be able to walk.

**4 PLOT: CONFLICT**

Nicholas feels great inner conflict. He cannot condone Squeers's cruelty, nor can he escape partial responsibility for it as long as he is part of the system. But he cannot leave Squeers, since Ralph's continued care of the family depends on Nicholas' keeping his job.

---

## GUIDED READING

**LITERAL QUESTIONS**

**1a.** How does Squeers explain his educational system to Nicholas? (He says it's a practical system. The boys learn by doing.)

**2a.** How does Nicholas react to the thrashing? (He feels implicated in the cruelty, and it makes him hate himself.)

**INFERENTIAL QUESTIONS**

**1b.** What is the real purpose of Squeers's educational system? (To cause as little work and expense for him as possible and to get as much work out of the boys as possible.)

**2b.** What does this reveal about Nicholas' character? (He is acutely sensitive to cruelty and has an active conscience.)

- *Scene vi:* Squeers and his wife discuss Nicholas.
- Mrs. Squeers does not feel he is needed.
- *Scene vii:* Nicholas finds Smike in despair at his own isolation.

## 1 DIALOGUE

Squeers compares his own need for an assistant to that of a West Indian slave-driver. For him, this comparison is just a figure of speech, but it is closer to the reality of Dotheboys than he would admit.

## 2 CHARACTERIZATION

Young Wackford's promise that he will thrash the boys and Squeers's response characterize both father and son. It reveals Wackford's sadism and shows that Squeers approves of it.

## 3 CHARACTERIZATION

Smike's misery and despair are further revealed. His speeches are brief and seem disconnected. However, it is clear that he feels deeply both his abandonment and his mistreatment.

### Scene vi.
### The SQUEERSES' *parlor.*

[*Darker, it's evening.* SQUEERS *is drinking;* MRS. SQUEERS *is trying* BELLING'S *clothes on young* WACKFORD. PHIB *helps* MRS. SQUEERS, *throwing aside the clothes that obviously don't fit.*]

SQUEERS. Well, my dear, so what do you think of him?

MRS. SQUEERS. Think of who?

SQUEERS. The new man.

MRS. SQUEERS. Oh. Young Knuckleboy.

SQUEERS. Young Nickleby.

MRS. SQUEERS. Well, if you want to know, Squeers, I'll tell you that I think him quite the proudest, haughtiest, turned-up nosediest—

SQUEERS. He is quite cheap, my dear. In fact, he's very cheap.

MRS. SQUEERS. I don't see why we need another man at all.

SQUEERS. Because it says in the advertisement, quite clearly—

MRS. SQUEERS. Fiddlesticks it *says. You say,* in the advertisement, it's ''Education by Mr. Wackford Squeers and his able assistants,'' but that don't mean you have to have 'em, does it? Sometimes, Squeers, you try my patience.

SQUEERS. Sometimes, you try mine.

MRS. SQUEERS. What's that?

1 SQUEERS. Well, my love, any slave-driver in the West Indies is allowed a man under him, to see his slaves don't run away, or get up a rebellion, and I want a man under me, to do the same with the boys, till little Wackford is able to take charge.

WACKFORD. Oh, am I?

376 *Drama*

MRS. SQUEERS. [*Impatiently.*] Am you what?

WACKFORD. Oh, am I to take charge of the school when I grow up, father?

SQUEERS. Yes, of course you are.

2 WACKFORD. Oh. Oh. Oh, won't I give it to 'em. Won't I make 'em shriek and squeal and scream.

[*The* SQUEERSES *look at each other. This exemplary attitude on the part of their son has brought them back together.*]

SQUEERS. Of course you will, my boy, of course you will.

### Scene vii.
### Outside the hall.

[SMIKE *is seated on the ground;* NICHOLAS *stands there. He has a book.*]

NICHOLAS. Hallo. [SMIKE *looks up, scared, and flinches a little.*] Please, don't be frightened. [NICHOLAS *crouches down near* SMIKE. *He puts down his book.*] Are you cold? [SMIKE *shakes his head.*] You're shivering. [*Pause.* NICHOLAS *stands to go. He stops when* SMIKE *speaks.*]

SMIKE. Oh, dear. [NICHOLAS *turns back.*] Oh, dear, oh, dear. My heart. Will break. It will. [*Louder, more forceful.*] It *will.* I know it *will.*

NICHOLAS. [*Embarrassed, looking round.*] Shh, shh.

3 SMIKE. Remember Dorker, do you?

NICHOLAS. Dorker?

SMIKE. I was with him at the end, he asked for me. Who will I ask for? Who?

[*Pause.* NICHOLAS *doesn't know what* SMIKE *is talking about.*]

NICHOLAS. Who will you ask for when?

---

## GUIDED READING

### LITERAL QUESTIONS

**1a.** How does Mrs. Squeers feel about Nicholas? (She thinks that he is proud and that the school does not need him.)

**2a.** In Scene vii what question concerns Smike? (He wonders whom he will ask for at the end—that is, on his deathbed.)

### INFERENTIAL QUESTIONS

**1b.** What does her opinion of Nicholas tell you about Mrs. Squeers? (that on some level she feels and resents his superiority to Squeers and herself)

**2b.** What does this reveal about Smike's view of his life? (that he feels very isolated and abandoned, that nobody cares for him)

Wackford, Jr.

Mr. and Mrs. Squeers.

- *Scene vii (continued):* Smike characterizes himself as an outcast.
- *Scene viii:* Nicholas tries to comfort Smike.
- Nicholas says he plans to leave, and Smike wants to go, too.
- Nicholas attempts to write to Kate.
- *Scene ix:* The next morning, Squeers wakens Nicholas.

**1 MAIN IDEA**

Smike's plight reflects a major idea of the work: the cruel treatment of the outcasts of society. The pathos of Smike's statement is increased by his spelling it out as though it were one of Squeers's lessons—it is what *he* has learned.

**2 CHARACTERIZATION**

Nicholas is characterized by his compassionate treatment of Smike. His ability to be empathetic—"I cannot bear it"—distinguishes him clearly from the Squeers and reaffirms normal human feeling in a situation notable for its absence. His assumption of responsibility for Smike signals his movement from passive to active goodness.

**3 PLOT: RISING ACTION**

Nicholas divulges a future plan for escape. This decision speeds the rising action of the plot. It also indicates the extent of Nicholas' misery: Even his promise to Ralph can no longer hold him at Dotheboys.

**4 MAIN IDEA**

Nicholas' care not to worry Kate shows the lovingness of the Nicklebys, in contrast to the coldness of Squeers and Ralph Nickleby. Again, Nicholas phrases the uncomfortable truth in understatement: *The boys are not advanced.*

---

[SMIKE *back into himself again.*]

SMIKE. No One. No Hope. Hope Less. [*Slight pause.*]

NICHOLAS. There's always hope.

 SMIKE. Is there? O–U–T–C–A–S–T. A noun. Substantive. Person cast out or rejected. Abject. And forsaken. Homeless. Me. [NICHOLAS *doesn't know what to say.*]

**Scene viii.**
**The dormitory of Dotheboys Hall.**

[*The stage darkens. The* BOYS *of Dotheboys Hall enter and lie down. The* BOYS *are crushed together, several to a bed.* SMIKE *enters among the* BOYS, *and lies down at the front. Almost complete darkness.* NICHOLAS *enters with a candle. He hears a sound. It's* SMIKE, *crying.* NICHOLAS *tries to ignore it, but can't and goes and kneels by* SMIKE. SMIKE *still has* NICHOLAS's *book.*]

SMIKE. Can't do it. With the book. Can't do it with the book. At all.

 NICHOLAS. Oh. Please. Don't cry. [SMIKE *crying.*] Don't. I cannot bear it. [*Pause.* SMIKE *still whimpering.*] They are more hard on you, I know. [*Pause.* SMIKE *still whimpering.*] But, please . . .

[SMIKE *looks at* NICHOLAS. *He's stopped crying. Then, back into himself.*]

SMIKE. Except for you, I die. They kill me.

NICHOLAS. No, no. You'll be better off, I tell you, when I'm gone.

[*Pause.*]

SMIKE. You gone?

NICHOLAS. Shh. Yes.

SMIKE. You going?

**378** *Drama*

---

NICHOLAS. I was speaking to my thoughts.

SMIKE. *Tell* me. Will you? Will you go?

[*Pause.*]

NICHOLAS. I shall be driven to it. Yes. To go away.

[*Pause.*]

SMIKE. Please tell me. Is away as bad as here?

[*Pause.*]

NICHOLAS. Oh, no. Oh, no, there's nothing—

SMIKE. Can I meet you there? Away?

NICHOLAS. Well, yes . . . you can, of course . . .

SMIKE. Can meet you there? Away? And I will find you, in away?

NICHOLAS. You would. And, if you did, I'd try to help you. [*Pause.* NICHOLAS *moves away with the candle and sits. He takes out a paper and a pen. He is writing a letter to* KATE.] I miss you terribly, but at least I feel that if my work here prospers—I miss you terribly. [*Pause.*] I took a Latin class today. The boys are—they are not advanced and there is much to do. [*Pause.*] The countryside is— [*Pause. He puts away the letter. He blows out the candle.*]

**Scene ix.**
**The dormitory. The next morning.**

[*Darkness, then cold morning lights.* NICHOLAS *lies asleep.* SMIKE *has gone. The* BOYS *wake. Some sit up; a few crawl to their feet.* NICHOLAS *gets up.*]

SQUEERS. [*Offstage.*] Hey! Hey, you up there? Are you going to sleep all day?

NICHOLAS. We shall be down directly, sir. [*He gestures to the* BOYS, *who speed up.*]

SQUEERS. [*Offstage.*] Well, you'd better be, or I'll be down on some of you in less—Where's

---

## GUIDED READING

### LITERAL QUESTIONS

**1a.** What does Smike ask about "away"? (He asks if "away" is as bad as here.)

### INFERENTIAL QUESTIONS

**1b.** What can you guess from this about Smike's experiences outside Dotheboys? (That he has spent almost all his life in the school and that he does not remember anything about the world outside.)

Smike? [NICHOLAS *goes to* SMIKE's *place, but sees he isn't there. The* BOYS *are nearly fully up.*] I said—where's Smike? [NICHOLAS *turns and calls.*]

NICHOLAS. He isn't here, sir.

SQUEERS. [*Offstage.*] What? Not there? [*Pause.* SQUEERS *enters, rushes to* SMIKE's *place. He sees* SMIKE *is absent.*] What does this mean? Where have you hid him?

NICHOLAS. I have not seen him since last night.

SQUEERS. Oh, no? [*Turning to the* BOYS.] And you? You boys? Have any of you—

[JENNINGS, *who is obscured from* SQUEERS *by other* BOYS.]

JENNINGS. Please, sir . . .

SQUEERS. Yes? What's that?

JENNINGS. Please, sir, I think he's run away.

SQUEERS. Who said that?

SOME BOYS. Jennings, sir.

SQUEERS. And where is Jennings?

BOYS. Here, sir. [JENNINGS *is pushed forward by his fellows.*]

SQUEERS. So, you think he's run away, do you?

JENNINGS. Yes, sir. Please, sir.

SQUEERS. And what, sir, what reason have you to suppose that any boy would *want* to run away from this establishment? [SQUEERS *hits* JENNINGS.] Eh, sir? [JENNINGS *says nothing.* SQUEERS *looks to* NICHOLAS, *who is looking away.*] And you, Nickleby. I s'pose you think he's run away?

NICHOLAS. I think it's highly likely, yes.

SQUEERS. You do? Perhaps you *know* he's run away?

NICHOLAS. I do not know, sir. And I'm glad I did not, for it would then have been my duty to have warned you.

 SQUEERS. Which, no doubt, you would have been devilish sorry to do.

NICHOLAS. I should indeed, sir.

[MRS. SQUEERS *enters.*]

MRS. SQUEERS. What's going on? Where's Smike?

SQUEERS. He's gone.

MRS. SQUEERS. [*An order, to* SQUEERS.] Gone? Well, then, we'll find him, stupid. We must search the roads. He hasn't any money, any food. He must be on the public road.

SQUEERS. [*Going towards the exit.*] That's true.

MRS. SQUEERS. [*Following.*] And when we catch him, oh . . .

[SQUEERS *turns back to the* BOYS. *Slowly.*]

SQUEERS. And when we catch him, I will only stop just short of flaying him alive. So follow your leader, boys, and take your pattern by Smike, if you dare.

> ### Scene x.
> ### *The schoolroom. The next day.*

[*Two* BOYS *come on, pulling the thrashing-horse.*[18] *The* BOYS *pull the horse to the center and leave it. Then the other* BOYS *enter and line up on either side.* NICHOLAS *enters and surveys the scene. Pause. Then* SQUEERS *enters, with a new and fearsome cane. He taps it twice on the thrashing-horse.*]

SQUEERS. Is every boy here? [*Silence.* SQUEERS *looks round to check.*] Every boy keep his place. [*Pause.*] Nickleby. To your place, sir. Coates, Jackson.

[NICHOLAS *moves nearer the thrashing-horse.* MRS. SQUEERS, WACKFORD, *and* PHIB *enter.* WACKFORD *joins the line of* BOYS. *The women*

---

18. **thrashing-horse:** wooden structure used for restraining a person who is being whipped.

*The Life and Adventures of Nicholas Nickleby* 379

## AT A GLANCE

- *Scene x (continued):* Smike is brought in, and Squeers begins to thrash him.
- Nicholas interferes to save him, and Smike slips out.
- Nicholas strikes Squeers and leaves.
- *Scene xi:* Smike joins Nicholas, telling him "You are my home."

## 1 PLOT: CLIMAX

In this scene, the plot reaches its climax. All the preceding actions have led to this moment of high tension as Nicholas, driven too far, finally turns on Squeers.

## 2 IRONY

Squeers's family calls Nicholas *beast* and *madman* when in actuality these words perfectly describe their husband and father.

## 3 CHARACTERIZATION

Smike's life is summed up in the phrase *You are my home.* In it we see his history of deprivation and mistreatment; we also see that he has never lost belief in something better. His starved heart turns toward Nicholas: "You are my home."

## REFLECTING ON THE SELECTION

How would you contrast the Nickleby family, on the one hand, and their uncle and Squeers, on the other? (unworldly / worldly, honest / dishonest, generous/ greedy, kind / cruel, poor / rich, loving / cold)

---

stand to the side as if prepared to avert their eyes from the coming spectacle. COATES *and* JACKSON *enter, leading on* SMIKE, *who is bound and filthy, clearly having spent a night sleeping rough. He is brought down to the end of the thrashing-horse and stands there.*]

SQUEERS. Untie him, sirs. [*The two* BOYS *start to untie* SMIKE. BROOKS *and* COBBEY *hurry up. They stand to each side.* SQUEERS *to* SMIKE.] Now, sir, what do you have to say for yourself? [*Pause.*] Nothing, I suppose? [*Pause.* SMIKE *glances at* NICHOLAS, *who is looking away.*] Well, then. Let's begin.

SMIKE. Oh, spare me, sir.

SQUEERS. Oh, that's all, is it? Well, I'll flog you within an inch of your life, but I will spare you that. [*Pause.*] Coates, Jackson.

[COATES *and* JACKSON *push* SMIKE *down on the thrashing-horse.*]

SMIKE. I was driven to it, sir.

SQUEERS. Driven to it? Not your fault, but mine?

MRS. SQUEERS. Hm. That's a good one.

[SQUEERS *goes a little upstage, turns, runs, and delivers the first blow.* SMIKE *cries out,* SQUEERS *grunts. He goes upstage again, runs, and delivers the second blow. He is back upstage again, when* NICHOLAS *takes a slight step forward.*]

1 NICHOLAS. Uh. . . . This must stop.

[SQUEERS *looks round.*]

SQUEERS. Who said that? Who said *stop*?

NICHOLAS. I did. I said that it must stop, and stop it will. [*Pause.*] I have tried to intercede. I have begged forgiveness for the boy. You have not listened. You have brought this on yourself.

SQUEERS. [*Dismissively, preparing for his next stroke.*] Get out, get out.

380   *Drama*

---

[NICHOLAS *walks to stand between* SQUEERS *and* SMIKE.]

NICHOLAS. No, sir. I can't.

SQUEERS. Can't? You can't? We'll see. [SQUEERS *walks to* NICHOLAS *and strikes his face.* NICHOLAS *doesn't respond.*] Now leave, sir, and let me to my work.

[NICHOLAS *turns, as if to go, then suddenly turns back, grabs* SQUEERS, *pulls him round, and hits him.*]

NICHOLAS. You have— [SQUEERS *tries to hit* NICHOLAS *but* NICHOLAS *seizes the cane.* MRS. SQUEERS *and* WACKFORD *come, the* BOYS *crush round to see, and* SMIKE, *let go, slips away. There is much shouting.*]

2 MRS. SQUEERS. What do you think you're doing, you madman?

WACKFORD. Beastly! Beastly man! You beast!

[NICHOLAS, *finished, breaks through the* BOYS *and runs out.* MRS. SQUEERS, *holding her head, appears following him. She flails around at the* BOYS.]

**Scene xi.**
**The countryside. Morning.**

[NICHOLAS *starts to walk. Something he hears makes him stop. He turns back.* SMIKE *stands there.*]

NICHOLAS. Oh, Smike. Oh—Smike. [NICHOLAS *quickly to* SMIKE, *who falls to his knees.*] Why do you kneel to me?

3 SMIKE. To go. Go anywhere. Go everywhere. The world's end. To the churchyard grave. [*Pause.*] I can. You'll let me. Come away with you. [*Pause.*] You are my home.

[NICHOLAS *can't speak. He takes* SMIKE's *hand, and helps him up. The two of them go out together.*]

---

## GUIDED READING

### LITERAL QUESTIONS

**1a.** What does Nicholas say as Squeers prepares to beat Smike the third time? ("I said that it must stop, and stop it will.")

**2a.** What does Nicholas say when Squeers commands him to get out? (He says, "No, sir. I can't.")

### INFERENTIAL QUESTIONS

**1b.** Why do you think Nicholas waits so long to intervene? (His family's care depends on his staying at Dotheboys; he has lived a sheltered life and has not anticipated the full extent of Squeers's savagery.)

**2b.** Why is it that Nicholas cannot go? (As a moral, empathetic, kind human being, he is unable to walk out and allow Smike's suffering to continue. He *must* intervene.)

Nicholas and the boys with Mr. Squeers in the foreground.

Smike and Nicholas.

1. Mr. Nickleby has died leaving family destitute; Ralph, a London businessman, values money above everything, whereas his brother lived a quiet country life and valued his family.

2. that he take a low-paying job as headmaster's assistant; promises to take care of them; to do whatever his uncle wants

3. ■ implies he will keep them a long time
   ■ Tuition is twenty pounds, the boys must bring clothing, they can stay to any age.

4. The boys are treated very badly. They are practically starved, given no instruction, and beaten.

5. Nicholas loathed himself because he felt morally responsible for the cruelty inflicted on the boys.

6. young man with no family, left at the school as a child; as a servant whom they beat regularly

7. Smike runs away, is caught and flogged; Nicholas intervenes and hits Squeers; Nicholas runs away, and Smike follows him.

8. He is unfeeling; lectures Mrs. Nickleby, calls his brother thoughtless, inconsiderate; is quick to find Nicholas a job so he will not have to care for him.

9. All pretense is dropped as she explains that brimstone and treacle deaden the boys' appetites. He is interested only in profit.

10. They are unfeeling and interested only in money; Nicholas is kind, decent and appalled at cruelty.

11. ■ Scene i: naive country boy; Scene x: courageous young man
    ■ He has learned that the weak may be abused and must be protected.

12. wanted to draw public attention to a situation that needed to be remedied

## STUDY QUESTIONS

### Recalling

1. Summarize the circumstances that lead the Nickleby family to appeal to Ralph Nickleby in Scene i. According to the narrator, how is Ralph different from his late brother?

2. In Scene i what work does Ralph suggest to Nicholas? What does Ralph promise to do for Kate and her mother? What does Nicholas pledge in return?

3. In Scene ii why does Wackford Squeers ask each boy to bring a razor to Dotheboys Hall? What other information about the school does Squeers give Mr. Snawley?

4. Describe the Squeerses' actual treatment of the boys at Dotheboys Hall: How do they feed their pupils, instruct them, discipline them, and tend to their health?

5. What does the narrator reveal at the end of Scene v about Nicholas' opinion of himself?

6. Who is Smike? Why is he at the school, and how do the Squeerses treat him?

7. Relate the circumstances that lead to the clash between Nicholas and Squeers in Scene x. What happens to Nicholas and Smike?

### Interpreting

8. What impression of himself does Ralph create in Scene i when he says that he cannot understand a broken heart? What does he say and do to confirm this impression?

9. Explain how Mrs. Squeers's concern with the school spoon reveals her true attitude toward the boys and the school. What do Squeers's comments during the mail delivery in Scene v show about his real interest in the boys?

10. In what ways are Ralph Nickleby and the Squeerses alike? How is Nicholas different from them?

11. How is the Nicholas who stands up to Squeers in Scene x different from the Nicholas of Scene i? What has he learned about life?

### Extending

12. Dickens wrote that "Mr. Squeers and his school are faint and feeble pictures of an existing reality, purposely subdued...lest they should be deemed impossible." What do you think was

382    *Drama*

Dickens' purpose in depicting Dotheboys Hall and in stating that it was a pale version of actual institutions?

## VIEWPOINT

One critic writes of the portrayal of Wackford Squeers in *Nicholas Nickleby:*

> He and his school turn out to be quite as funny as they are horrific. . . . . [Dickens'] instinct was surely right. . . . Certainly, [the] Yorkshire schoolmasters would hardly have suffered such heavy professional damage if Dickens had not subjected them to such hilarious ridicule.
>
> —M. Slater, Introduction, *Nicholas Nickleby*

■ Give examples of both the funny and nightmarish aspects of Squeers and his school as they are presented in *Nicholas Nickleby*. Do you agree that Dickens was right to include comic touches in his portrayal of Squeers and his school? Why or why not?

## LITERARY FOCUS

### Dialogue

Dramatic **dialogue** is the conversation exchanged by the characters in a play. Because a play consists largely of people talking to one another, dialogue is a playwright's most important means of establishing a play's characters and advancing its action.

Even a play that includes a narrator, as *Nicholas Nickleby* does, relies primarily on dialogue to make its points. For example, in Scene ii of *Nicholas Nickleby*, Snawley asks Squeers if he can send his two boys to Dotheboys Hall at reduced tuition, explaining that "They're not great eaters." Mr. Squeers replies, "Then we will not be great feeders, sir." This brief exchange tells us a great deal about each man's priorities. Furthermore, this dialogue gives us an important clue about the Squeerses' treatment of their young charges at Dotheboys Hall.

### Thinking About Dialogue

Look at the dialogue in Scene v beginning with Squeers's line, "We go on the practical mode of teaching, Nickleby . . . ." and answer the following:

■ *funny:* rapid-drill breakfast; Mr. Squeers's nickname, *Squeerie dearie;* lesson in which he misspells words

■ *nightmarish:* Squeers's appearance; treatment of Smike; beatings

■ Some may argue that comedy weakens the serious impact; others, that ridicule is an effective weapon.

1. What do these exchanges show about the "education" the students at Dotheboys Hall can expect?
2. What do these exchanges reveal about Squeers's sincerity and qualifications as a teacher?
3. What do the boys' automatic responses reveal about their attitude toward Squeers?
4. What might Nicholas' polite answers imply about his opinions of Squeers's method?

## Staging and Setting

Reading the script of a play is a little like following the sheet music of a symphony: We can enjoy the written text, but we need to go beyond it to appreciate the full power of the work. Just as an orchestra makes music out of a composer's notes, **staging**—scenery, lighting, costumes, and acting—brings a playwright's words to vivid life for an audience. Therefore, as we read any play, we can add tremendously to our pleasure by imagining how it might come to life on stage.

**Setting** is an important part of the staging of a dramatic work. In deciding on the setting for a scene, the director and designers of a production would choose scenery and costumes appropriate to the historical period and social setting of the play; in addition, they would try to create a fitting mood for the scene. For example, the opening scene in a contemporary comedy might be set in a brightly lit living room full of elegant, modern furniture and warm colors, with the actors wearing stylish contemporary clothes. The appearance of the stage and actors would establish the play's overall setting and create a light, pleasant mood appropriate to a comedy.

## Thinking About Staging and Setting

During the classroom scene (Scene v) Mrs. Squeers and Smike dose the boys with brimstone and treacle while Mr. Squeers makes several announcements. Suggest ideas for staging this scene, concentrating on what the scene would *look like*. You may want to keep these questions in mind:

1. What is the play's general time period and social setting? What mood would be appropriate to the actions portrayed in the scene?
2. What furniture and other items would be on stage?
3. How dark or light would the stage be? What colors could the audience see?
4. How would the actors who play Nicholas, the Squeerses, Smike, and the boys be dressed?

## COMPOSITION

### Writing About Drama and Fiction

■ The following passage from the novel *Nicholas Nickleby* describes Nicholas' attempt to write to his family from Dotheboys Hall:

He had written to his mother and sister, announcing the safe conclusion of his journey, and saying as little about Dotheboys Hall, and saying that little as cheerfully, as he possibly could. He hoped that, by remaining where he was, he might do some good, even there. . . .

Reread the end of Scene viii in the play (page 378), which dramatizes this passage. Compare the two versions of this material in the novel and play. Begin by pointing out the similarities between the two versions. Then note the various differences between them. Conclude by indicating which version you prefer, explaining your choice.

### Writing Contrasting Descriptions

■ Write a pair of contrasting descriptions of Dotheboys Hall. First describe the school as it would be portrayed by Wackford Squeers in a full-blown advertisement meant to attract more students. Use sentences from his advertisement for the school in Scene ii, adding material about the accommodations and care provided at the hall. Then write a letter from Nicholas to a newspaper, and describe the actual conditions at the school. You might write your two descriptions to be read aloud, one alternating with the other, so that Nicholas' letter corrects Squeers's advertisement sentence for sentence or even phrase for phrase.

*The Life and Adventures of Nicholas Nickleby* **383**

# LITERARY FOCUS: *Cyrano de Bergerac*

## The Life of Edmond Rostand

Edmond Rostand (1869–1918) was the son of a distinguished French journalist, economist, and poet. He grew up in Marseilles [mär sā′], a city in southern France, and studied law in Paris but abandoned his legal career to write for the stage. The young playwright soon succeeded in the theater with a series of popular plays based on historical subjects. Several of these works starred the legendary French actress, Sarah Bernhardt.

Rostand's career was crowned by the triumphant *Cyrano de Bergerac* [sē′rə nō′ də bur′zhə rak′], a verse drama based on the life of a seventeenth-century French poet and playwright. First produced on December 28, 1897, this colorful and witty play became an overnight sensation in Paris, and its popularity spread rapidly throughout Europe and America.

Rostand's later works never matched the brilliance of *Cyrano de Bergerac*. However, that one triumph secured his literary reputation. Elected to the exclusive French Academy in 1902, Rostand spent the remainder of his life in southern France.

## *Cyrano de Bergerac*

Rostand scored a stunning success with *Cyrano de Bergerac* largely because the work departed strikingly from the plays of its time. Most of the plays written at the end of the nineteenth century were realistic dramas that focused on the social and domestic problems of modern characters. Rostand's play, in contrast, harked back to a distant historical period peopled by flamboyant characters caught up in exciting and colorful situations.

The play's continuing popularity rests largely on the many-faceted appeal of Rostand's hero, Cyrano de Bergerac. Rostand classified the play as a **heroic comedy**—that is, a comic play focusing on the exploits of a larger-than-life hero. Cyrano, the heart and soul of the play, is both heroic and comic. He is a dashing swordsman who fights bravely to defend his friends and his honor. He is also a poet who handles language as skillfully as he does his sword. Above all, Cyrano appeals to audiences because he is an ugly man who loves selflessly and hopelessly and eventually manages to triumph over his unhappy situation with style, grace, courage, and humor.

Rostand based his dashing hero upon an actual historical figure. The real Cyrano de Bergerac (1619–1655) was a poet and dramatist who wrote the first work of science fiction. The period in which the real Cyrano lived was a kind of golden age in France. The king's chief minister, Cardinal Richelieu [rēsh lyu′], expanded both the territories

**384** *Drama*

of France and the power of the crown. The gilded French court set the style for the rest of the country, and French intellectual life flourished. The true gentleman was expected, like Cyrano, to be both a man of action *and* a man of culture, to excel in both swordplay and wordplay, to fight bravely, compose music, and utter poetry with equal brilliance and ease.

As *Cyrano de Bergerac* begins, we enter that glittering but fiercely competitive world. Appropriately, this flamboyant play opens in a seventeenth-century Parisian theater just as a performance is about to start.

## Key Ideas in *Cyrano de Bergerac*

■ As you read *Cyrano de Bergerac,* look for references to each of the following. If you keep track of what the work says about these topics, you will begin to grasp its most important themes.

* Inner versus outer beauty
* Idealism
* Individualism
* The value of language and poetry
* Different attitudes toward love

Cyrano de Bergerac, 1619–1655.

*Cyrano de Bergerac*  **385**

Cyrano.

Roxane.

Christian.

*Edmond Rostand*

# Cyrano de Bergerac

translated by Lowell Bair

## CHARACTERS

CYRANO DE BERGERAC [sē′rə nō′ də bur′zhə rak′]: soldier, philosopher, and poet; famous for his wit, great courage, and large nose

CHRISTIAN DE NEUVILLETTE [krēs′tē an′ də nu′vē yet′]: handsome young soldier; inept at expressing himself

MAGDELEINE ROBIN [mad′lin rō ban′], known as ROXANE [roks an′]: beautiful, rich, and cultured cousin of Cyrano; loved by both Cyrano and Christian

### Friends of Cyrano

LIGNIÈRE [lē nyār′]: mischievous poet

RAGUENEAU [ra′gə nō′]: poet and pastrycook

LISE [lēz]: wife of Ragueneau

LE BRET [lə brā′]: officer in Cyrano's regiment

CARBON DE CASTEL-JALOUX [kär bon′ də kas tel′ zha lōō′]: captain of Cyrano's regiment

### Opponents of Cyrano

COUNT DE GUICHE [də gēsh′]: ambitious nobleman and military commander; in love with Roxane

VISCOUNT DE VALVERT [vĭ′kount də val vār′]: follower of de Guiche; wooer of Roxane

MONTFLEURY [mon′flu rē′]: fat, untalented actor

## Other named characters *(in order of their appearance)*

CUIGY [kwē zhē′]: officer in Cyrano's regiment
BRISSAILLE [brē sī′]: officer in Cyrano's regiment
BELLEROSE [bel rōz′]: theater manager
THE DUENNA [dwā′nə]: Roxane's chaperone, or companion
BERTRANDOU [bār′tron do͞o′]: fife-player
SISTER MARTHE [mär′tə]: nun of the Ladies of the Cross Convent
MOTHER MARGUERITE DE JESUS [mär′gə rēt′ də zhā′zo͞o]: Mother Superior of the Convent
SISTER CLAIRE: nun of the Convent

---

## Others *(in order of their appearance)*

| | | |
|---|---|---|
| A DOORKEEPER | A PICKPOCKET | THE CADETS OF GASCOYNE |
| SEVERAL CAVALIERS | A MEDDLER | TWO MUSICIANS |
| SEVERAL PAGES | ACTORS | A CAPUCHIN [kap′yə shin] PRIEST |
| AN ORANGE SELLER | ACTRESSES | A SPANISH OFFICER |
| SEVERAL MARQUIS [mär kē′] | PASTRYCOOKS | SEVERAL NUNS |
| A CROWD OF THEATER-GOERS | A MUSKETEER | |
| A LAMPLIGHTER | SEVERAL POETS | |

AT A GLANCE

- A play is about to begin.
- Two cavaliers and a band of pages arrive early, to the consternation of the doorkeeper.
- The chandelier lighter enters.

LITERARY OPTIONS

- dramatic irony
- staging
- characterization

THEMATIC OPTIONS

- inner beauty vs. outer beauty
- individual vs. society
- importance of language

**1** **SETTING**

The time and place of the play are established: an auditorium in a Paris hotel, mid-seventeenth century. The stylization of a more formal era is heightened by the artifice of a play within a play.

**2** **STYLE: HUMOR**

The pages' plan to hook the wigs of patrons during the performance sets the tone of the act: Humor is used to puncture pomposity.

**3** **DIALOGUE**

The marquis's jokes exemplify the common attitude of the upper classes, who believe that they have the right to inconvenience and injure the poor.

# ACT I

**1** *The auditorium of the Hôtel de Bourgogne* [ō tel′ də boor gō′nyə] *in Paris in 1640.*

[*It resembles an indoor tennis court, decorated and fitted out for theatrical performances. As the curtain rises, the auditorium is in semidarkness and still empty. The chandeliers have been lowered to the floor and are waiting to be lighted. A tumult of voices is heard from outside the door; then a* CAVALIER *enters abruptly, followed by an angry* DOORKEEPER.]

THE DOORKEEPER. [*Pursuing him.*] Stop! You haven't paid your fifteen sols.[1]

THE CAVALIER. I don't have to pay!

THE DOORKEEPER. Why not?

THE CAVALIER. I'm a light-horseman[2] of the King's Household.

THE DOORKEEPER. [*To another* CAVALIER *who has just entered.*] And you?

SECOND CAVALIER. I don't have to pay either.

THE DOORKEEPER. But . . .

SECOND CAVALIER. I'm a musketeer.[3]

FIRST CAVALIER. [*To the second.*] The play doesn't begin till two o'clock and the floor is empty. Let's have a little fencing practice. [*They fence with the foils they have brought.*]

[*A* BAND OF PAGES *enters.*]

THE DOORKEEPER. [*Sternly, to the* PAGES.] Behave yourselves, boys! No pranks!

FIRST PAGE. [*With wounded dignity.*] Oh, sir, how can you even suspect such a thing? [*With animation, to the* SECOND PAGE, *as soon as the*

**2** DOORKEEPER *has turned his back.*] Do you have your string?

SECOND PAGE. Yes, and my fishhook.

FIRST PAGE. Good. We'll fish for wigs when we're up there.

A VOICE FROM THE UPPER GALLERY. Light the chandeliers!

A PAGE. [*On the floor.*] Ah, here's the refreshment girl!

THE REFRESHMENT GIRL. [*Appearing behind the refreshment table.*] Oranges, milk, raspberry syrup, cider. . . .

[*Commotion at the door.*]

**3** A MARQUIS.[4] [*Seeing that the theater is half empty.*] What's this? We've arrived like tradesmen, without disturbing people, without stepping on their feet? What a shameful way to make an entrance! [*Finds himself in front of some other noblemen who have entered shortly before.*] Cuigy![5] Brissaille![6] [*They embrace enthusiastically.*]

CUIGY. Ah, the faithful are here! Yes, it's true: we've come before the candles. . . .

THE MARQUIS. No, don't talk about it! I'm so annoyed. . . .

ANOTHER MARQUIS. Cheer up, Marquis, here comes the lighter!

THE CROWD. [*Greeting the entrance of the* LIGHTER.] Ah! . . .

[LIGNIÈRE[7] *and* CHRISTIAN DE NEUVILLETTE[8] *enter,*

---

1. **sols:** The sol, or sou, is a French coin no longer in use. It was worth about one cent.
2. **light-horseman:** cavalry soldier who carries light arms.
3. **musketeer:** soldier armed with a musket.

---

4. **Marquis** [mär kē′]: nobleman who ranks below a duke and above a count.
5. **Cuigy** [kwē zhē′]
6. **Brissaille** [brē sī′]
7. **Lignière** [lē nyār′]
8. **Christian de Neuvillette** [krēs′tē an′ də nu′vē yet′]

---

## GUIDED READING

### LITERAL QUESTIONS

**1a.** What are the pages planning to do with their strings and hooks during the performance? (fish for people's wigs)

**2a.** How does the marquis feel about arriving before the candles are lit? (He is annoyed.)

### INFERENTIAL QUESTIONS

**1b.** What is the mood that this action creates? (one of humor and outrageousness)

**2b.** How does his irritation help characterize the nobility of the day? (He makes their concerns seem petulant, self-centered, and frivolous.)

*arm in arm.* LIGNIÈRE *is rather disheveled.* CHRISTIAN *is elegantly dressed, but in a somewhat outmoded style. He seems preoccupied, and looks up at the boxes.*]

CUIGY. Lignière!

LIGNIÈRE. [*To* CHRISTIAN.] Shall I introduce you? [CHRISTIAN *nods.*] Baron de Neuvillette. [*They bow.*]

THE CROWD. [*Acclaiming the raising of the first lighted chandelier.*] Ah!

CUIGY. [*To* BRISSAILLE, *looking at* CHRISTIAN.] He has a charming face!

LIGNIÈRE. [*Introducing them to* CHRISTIAN.] Messieurs[9] de Cuigy, de Brissaille. . . .

CHRISTIAN. [*Bowing.*] Delighted to meet you, gentlemen.

LIGNIÈRE. [*To* CUIGY.] Monsieur de Neuvillette has just arrived from Touraine.[10]

CHRISTIAN. Yes, I've been in Paris only three weeks. I'm entering the Guards tomorrow, as a Cadet.[11]

CUIGY. [*To* CHRISTIAN, *pointing to the auditorium, which is beginning to fill.*] People are arriving.

CHRISTIAN. Yes, in droves!

FIRST MARQUIS. All of fashionable society is here! Look, our lady intellectuals are taking their places.

**1** LIGNIÈRE. [*Taking* CHRISTIAN *aside.*] My friend, I came with you to help you, but since the lady isn't here—

CHRISTIAN. [*Imploringly.*] No, stay! You know

---

9. **Messieurs** [mā syu′]: sirs or gentlemen; plural for *Monsieur* [mə syu′], which means ''Mister.''
10. **Touraine** [tōō ren′]: region of central France.
11. **Cadet:** nobleman who served as a common soldier to gain experience and eventually earn a commission as an officer.

---

everyone at court and in the city: you'll be able to tell me the name of the lady for whom I'm dying of love. I'm afraid she may be coquettish and **2** refined. I don't dare to speak to her, because I have no wit. I don't know how to use the elegant language that's in style nowadays. I'm only a soldier, a shy soldier. . . . She always sits in that box—there, on the right. It's still empty. . . .

LIGNIÈRE. Aha! I'll stay a little longer, since you insist.

VOICES FROM THE CROWD. [*Greeting the entrance of a plump, jolly-looking little man.*] Ah, Ragueneau![12]

LIGNIÈRE. [*To* CHRISTIAN.] There's Ragueneau, the great baker.

RAGUENEAU. [*Dressed like a pastry cook in his Sunday best, hurrying toward* LIGNIÈRE.] Sir, have you seen Monsieur de Cyrano?

LIGNIÈRE. [*Introducing* RAGUENEAU *to* CHRISTIAN.] This is Ragueneau, the pastry cook of actors and poets!

RAGUENEAU. [*Embarrassed.*] You honor me too highly.

LIGNIÈRE. Not at all! You're a patron of the arts!

**3** RAGUENEAU. Poets do come to my shop . . .

LIGNIÈRE. To buy on credit. And you yourself are a talented poet.

RAGUENEAU. So I've been told.

LIGNIÈRE. You're madly in love with poetry!

RAGUENEAU. It's true that for an ode . . .

LIGNIÈRE. You give a tart.

RAGUENEAU. Only a little one, if it's a short ode.

LIGNIÈRE. You love the theater, too, don't you?

RAGUENEAU. I adore it.

---

12. **Ragueneau** [ra′gə nō′]

*Cyrano de Bergerac, Act I* **389**

AT A GLANCE

- Lignière and Christian meet some friends.
- Christian confesses he is in love with a lady expected at the play, but he is afraid to speak to her, since he is not witty.
- Ragueneau, the poetic pastry cook, proclaims his love for the arts.

**1** PLOT: RISING ACTION

The revelation that Christian and Lignière expect to see a lady at the play adds tension and interest.

**2** CHARACTERIZATION

Here Christian's self-evaluation gives hints of his character: He is a soldier, a man of action rather than words and does not trust his ability to speak eloquently.

**3** STYLE: HUMOR

An amusing concept is the idea of a poetic baker who pays for an ode with a pastry because of his love of art. This joke fits the humorous tone of this act, as well as foreshadowing the play's more serious concern with the relationship between body and spirit.

## GUIDED READING

**LITERAL QUESTIONS**

**1a.** Why has Lignière come to the play? (He has come to help his friend, Christian, identify the lady he is in love with.)

**2a.** How does Ragueneau help poets? (He lets them buy on credit at his pastry shop and trades them his pastries for their poetry.)

**INFERENTIAL QUESTIONS**

**1b.** What does the fact that Christian does not even know the name of this lady indicate about the conventions of love in his society? (Since he does not know her, the implication is that love affairs of the day were based only on appearances.)

**2b.** What can you infer about poets from this? (That poets were usually poor and needed help to survive.)

- Ragueneau expresses surprise that Cyrano is not there, as he knows Cyrano has taken a dislike to the lead actor, Montfleury.
- They discuss Cyrano, his uncommon character, and his nose.
- Roxane enters and is admired.

**1 PLOT: RISING ACTION**

Ragueneau prepares for later developments by divulging Cyrano's feelings for Montfleury and, specifically, his banishment of the actor from the stage for a month.

**2 CHARACTERIZATION**

Here the audience is prepared for an unconventional hero. Cyrano is characterized as a man of many talents and much charm.

**3 THEME**

One of the major ideas of the play is Cyrano's physical disfigurement. The conversation here portray's Cyrano's nose in outlandish, even comical terms. Physical ugliness is an unusual trait in a hero as dashing and accomplished as Cyrano.

**4 STYLE: FIGURATIVE LANGUAGE**

The "terrifyingly lovely" Roxane is described in simile and metaphor: *skin like a peach, strawberry lips*. This conventional poetic language prepares the audience for a conventional romantic heroine: beautiful and susceptible to handsome men.

---

LIGNIÈRE. You pay for your theater tickets with pastry! Tell me, just between ourselves, how much did you pay this time?

RAGUENEAU. Four custard tarts and fifteen cream puffs. [*Looks all around.*] Monsieur de Cyrano isn't here? I'm surprised.

LIGNIÈRE. Why?

RAGUENEAU. Montfleury[13] is in the play!

**1** LIGNIÈRE. Yes, that walking barrel will play the part of Phaedo[14] today. But what does it matter to Cyrano?

RAGUENEAU. Haven't you heard? He took a dislike to Montfleury and ordered him not to appear on the stage for a month.

LIGNIÈRE. Well, what of it?

RAGUENEAU. Ah, that's what I've come to see!

FIRST MARQUIS. Who is this Cyrano?

CUIGY. He's a Cadet in the Guards. [*Points to a gentleman who is walking back and forth as though looking for someone.*] But his friend Le Bret[15] can tell you. . . . [*Calls him.*] Le Bret! [LE BRET *comes over to them.*] You're looking for Bergerac?

LE BRET. Yes, and I'm worried. . . .

CUIGY. He's an extraordinary man, isn't he?

**2** LE BRET. [*Affectionately.*] The most delightful man under the sun!

RAGUENEAU. A poet!

CUIGY. A swordsman!

BRISSAILLE. A scientist!

LE BRET. A musician!

LIGNIÈRE. And what an uncommon appearance!

---

13. **Montfleury** [mon′flu rē′]: seventeenth-century French actor.
14. **Phaedo** [fā dō′]
15. **Le Bret** [lə brā′]

390 *Drama*

---

RAGUENEAU. Odd, impetuous, brash, and outlandish as he is, proudest of all the thin-skinned swaggerers lovingly spawned by Gascony,[16] I think he would have given the late Jacques Callot[17] a wild swashbuckler[18] to place among his portraits. With his triple-plumed hat, his billowing doublet,[19] and his cape majestically held out behind by a sword, he carries his nose above a punchinello ruff,[20] a nose that . . . Ah, **3** gentlemen, what a nose! Those who see it pass by can't help exclaiming, "No, it can't be true!" Then they smile and say, "He'll soon take it off." But Monsieur de Bergerac never takes it off.

LE BRET. [*Nodding.*] He keeps it on—and runs his sword through anyone who looks at it too closely.

FIRST MARQUIS. [*Shrugging.*] He won't come.

RAGUENEAU. He will! I'll bet you a chicken à la Ragueneau!

FIRST MARQUIS. [*Laughing.*] I'll take that bet!

[*Murmurs of admiration from the crowd:* ROXANE[21] *has just appeared in her box. She sits at the front of it, her* DUENNA[22] *sits at the rear.* CHRISTIAN, *occupied in paying the* REFRESHMENT GIRL, *has not yet seen her.*]

**4** SECOND MARQUIS. [*With little cries.*] Gentlemen, she's terrifyingly lovely!

FIRST MARQUIS. Skin like a peach, smiling with strawberry lips!

---

16. **Gascony:** a region of southwestern France; Gascons were famous for their boastfulness.
17. **Jacques Callot** [zhak ka lō′]: French artist (1592–1635) who was famous for his portraits of colorful figures, especially from the theater.
18. **swashbuckler:** flamboyant soldier or adventurer.
19. **doublet:** close-fitting, waist-length jacket.
20. **punchinello** [pun′chə nel′ō] **ruff:** A punchinello is a grotesque, humpbacked character in an Italian puppet show; his costume includes a ruff, or large frilled collar like those worn by clowns today.
21. **Roxane** [roks an′]
22. **Duenna** [dwā′nə]: older woman serving as a chaperone and companion to a young woman.

---

## GUIDED READING

### LITERAL QUESTIONS

**1a.** What talents do his friends say Cyrano has? (He is a poet, swordsman, scientist, and musician.)

**2a.** What does Le Bret say about how Cyrano reacts to anyone who looks at his nose too closely? (He says he runs his sword through them.)

### INFERENTIAL QUESTIONS

**1b.** What does this tell you about Cyrano? (He is a well-educated, cultured person with highly diverse abilities.)

**2b.** What can you assume from this about Cyrano's attitude toward his nose? (that he is sensitive about it and aggressive about defending himself from insults)

SECOND MARQUIS. And so fresh and cool that anyone coming near her might catch a cold in his heart!

CHRISTIAN. [*Looks up, sees* ROXANE, *and clutches* LIGNIÈRE's *arm.*] There she is!

LIGNIÈRE. [*Looking.*] Ah, so she's the one?

CHRISTIAN. Yes. Quickly, tell me who she is! I'm afraid.

**1** LIGNIÈRE. Magdeleine Robin,[23] known as Roxane. Sharp-witted, an intellectual. . .

CHRISTIAN. Alas!

LIGNIÈRE. . . . free, an orphan, a cousin of Cyrano, whom we were just discussing. . . .

[*At this point a very elegant gentleman, wearing the Cordon Bleu[24] around his neck, enters* ROXANE's *box and stands talking with her for a few moments.*]

CHRISTIAN. [*Starting.*] Who is that man?

**2** LIGNIÈRE. [*Winking.*] That, my friend, is Count de Guiche.[25] He's in love with her, but he's married to Cardinal Richelieu's[26] niece. He wants to arrange a marriage between Roxane and Viscount[27] de Valvert,[28] a sad specimen of a man whom he can count on to be obliging. She's opposed to it, but De Guiche is powerful: he can persecute an untitled girl like her. Incidentally, I've written a song exposing his crafty scheme. He must hate me for it! The ending is positively vicious. Listen, I'll sing it for you. . . . [*He rises to his feet ready to sing.*]

---

23. **Magdeleine Robin** [mad′lin rō ban′]
24. **Cordon Bleu** [kôr′don blu′]: blue ribbon worn as decoration by members of the order of the Holy Ghost, the highest order of French knighthood at the time.
25. **Count de Guiche** [də gēsh′]
26. **Cardinal Richelieu's** [rēsh lyuz′]: Cardinal Richelieu, born Armand Jean du Plessis (1585–1642), was a cardinal of the Roman Catholic Church, chief minister of King Louis XIII, and the most powerful man in France in the mid-1600s.
27. **Viscount** [vī′kount]: nobleman below the rank of count.
28. **de Valvert** [də val vār′]

CHRISTIAN. No. I'm leaving now.

LIGNIÈRE. Where are you going?

**3** CHRISTIAN. I'm going to pay a visit to Viscount de Valvert!

LIGNIÈRE. Don't do anything rash: there's a good chance he'd kill you. [*Discreetly calls his attention to* ROXANE.] Stay. You're being watched.

CHRISTIAN. It's true! [*He stands staring at her.*]

LIGNIÈRE. *I'm* the one who's leaving. I'm thirsty and I have an appointment. [*He leaves.*]

LE BRET. [*With relief, coming back to* RAGUENEAU *after having searched everywhere.*] No sign of Cyrano.

RAGUENEAU. [*Incredulously.*] It doesn't seem possible.

THE CROWD. Begin the play! Begin!

A MARQUIS. [*Watching* DE GUICHE *come down from* ROXANE's *box and walk across the floor, surrounded by obsequious noblemen, one of whom is* VISCOUNT DE VALVERT.] De Guiche has his own little court!

DE GUICHE. I'm going to sit on the stage. Are you coming with me? [*He walks toward the stage, followed by all the* MARQUIS *and other noblemen, then looks back and calls.*] Come, Valvert!

[CHRISTIAN *has been observing and listening to them. He starts when he hears* VALVERT's *name.*]

**4** CHRISTIAN. Valvert! I'll throw my glove in his face this instant! [*Reaches for his gloves and encounters the hand of a thief picking his pocket. Turns around.*] What . . .

THE THIEF. Oh, no!

CHRISTIAN. [*Holding him.*] I was reaching for a glove!

THE THIEF. [*With a pitiful smile.*] You found a

*Cyrano de Bergerac, Act I* **391**

**AT A GLANCE**

- Christian confesses that it is Roxane whom he loves. Lignière says she is Cyrano's cousin.
- Count de Guiche, who is also in love with Roxane is trying to marry her off to Valvert, who won't object if the count becomes her lover.

**1 PLOT: CONFLICT**

Christian experiences inner conflict over his inarticulateness. He fears he will never win the intelligent Roxane because he considers his own wits dull.

**2 PLOT: SUBPLOT**

De Guiche's love for Roxane is an important subplot in the play. His plans for Roxane indicate that he is unprincipled and manipulative; since he is also powerful, his unscrupulousness will have important effects on the other characters.

**3 CHARACTERIZATION**

Christian's immediate reaction to the information about Valvert reinforces his characterization as a man of action: brave, idealistic, and more than a bit heedless.

**4 BACKGROUND**

Christian reaches for his glove in order to challenge Valvert to a duel. In this swashbuckling era throwing down the gauntlet—or glove—was a challenge that had to be answered, lest one's honor be questioned.

---

## GUIDED READING

### LITERAL QUESTIONS

**1a.** What do you learn about Count de Guiche? (He is elegant, powerful, and married, is in love with Roxane, and wants to marry her off to his friend Valvert, who will "be obliging.")

**2a.** What does Lignière tell Christian right after he warns him not to be rash about Valvert? (He calls his attention to the fact that Roxane is watching him.)

### INFERENTIAL QUESTIONS

**1b.** What can you conclude about his character from this information? (that he is a typical aristocrat of the day and that he is not very scrupulous)

**2b.** What can you infer about her feelings for Christian from this? (that she is interested in him)

- Christian learns from a pick-pocket that one hundred men will attack Lignière.
- Christian goes off to warn Lignière.
- The play begins, and, as Montfleury recites his lines, Cyrano heckles him from the crowd.

## 1 PLOT: FORESHADOWING

This revelation underscores the methods of revenge De Guiche will use throughout the play. Cowardly and underhanded, he makes others fight his enemies and evades direct confrontation.

## 2 CHARACTERIZATION

Christian is shown as a loyal and devoted man, sacrificing his own desires for an innocent victim's safety.

## 3 STAGING

The stage directions tell how the play within a play is to be costumed, cast, and staged. The ridiculousness of the production parodies the pretentious theater of the day, which often featured highly artificial pastoral dramas.

## 4 THEME

Cyrano makes his first audacious appearance. Significantly, what he attacks is "acting"—specifically, acting that is artificial and pretentious. Thus, he is presented as a defender of truth and sincerity.

---

hand instead. [*Lowering his voice and speaking rapidly.*] Let me go and I'll tell you a secret.

CHRISTIAN. [*Still holding him.*] What is it?

THE THIEF. Lignière, who just left you...

CHRISTIAN. [*Without letting go of him.*] Yes? Go on.

1 THE THIEF. He's about to meet his death. He wrote a song that offended a certain very powerful person, and tonight a hundred men—I know, because I'm to join them soon—have been posted...

CHRISTIAN. A hundred! By whom?

THE THIEF. Sorry, I can't tell you that.

CHRISTIAN. [*Shrugging.*] Oh, come, come!

THE THIEF. [*With great dignity.*] It's a professional secret!

CHRISTIAN. Where are the men posted?

THE THIEF. At the Porte de Nesle,[29] on his way. Warn him!

2 CHRISTIAN. Yes, I'll go! Oh, the vile cowards! A hundred men against one! [*Looks at* ROXANE *with love.*] How can I bear to leave her? [*At* VALVERT *with fury.*] And him! But I must save Lignière!

[*He runs out.* DE GUICHE, VALVERT, *the* MARQUIS, *and the other noblemen have disappeared behind the curtain to take their places on the benches on the stage. The floor, the gallery, and the boxes are now completely filled.*]

THE CROWD. Begin the play!

A SPECTATOR. Silence!

[*Three more raps from the stage. The curtain opens. Tableau.*[30] *The* MARQUIS *are seated on either side of the stage in insolent poses. The*

---

29. **Porte de Nesle** [pôrt′ de nes′əl]
30. **Tableau** [tab lō′]: picturesque and motionless scene.

---

---

backdrop represents a bluish pastoral[31] scene. Four small crystal chandeliers light the stage. The violins are playing softly.*]

LE BRET. [*To* RAGUENEAU, *in a low voice.*] Will Montfleury soon be on the stage?

RAGUENEAU. [*Also in a low voice.*] He'll be the first to appear.

LE BRET. Cyrano isn't here.

3 [*A bagpipe melody is heard, then the enormously fat* MONTFLEURY *appears on the stage, wearing a shepherd's costume, a hat adorned with roses tilted over one ear, blowing into a beribboned bagpipe.*]

THE CROWD. [*Applauding.*] Montfleury!—Bravo! —Montfleury!

MONTFLEURY. [*After bowing, playing the part of Phaedo.*]

"Happy is he who shuns the pomp of courts
In solitary exile, self-imposed;
And who, when gentle breezes..."

4 A VOICE. [*From the middle of the floor.*] Haven't I ordered you off the stage for a month, you wretched scoundrel?

[*Astonishment in the audience. Everyone looks around. Murmurs.*]

VARIOUS VOICES. Oh!—What!—Who? [*Those in the boxes stand up to see.*]

CUIGY. He's here!

LE BRET. [*Terrified.*] Cyrano!

THE VOICE. Off the stage this instant, king of buffoons!

THE WHOLE AUDIENCE. [*Indignantly.*] Oh!

MONTFLEURY. But...

THE VOICE. You refuse?

---

31. **pastoral:** referring to shepherds and other rural subjects.

---

## GUIDED READING

### LITERAL QUESTION

**1a.** What do you learn about the plan against Lignière? (that a powerful person has plotted against him because he wrote an unflattering song; that one hundred men are to waylay him that evening at the Porte de Nesle)

### INFERENTIAL QUESTION

**1b.** What does this tell you about the aristocracy of the day? (It suggests that they had many petty quarrels and grudges, were quick to take offense, and were ruthless in settling scores. They were too arrogant to bother with even the appearance of a fair fight.)

AT A GLANCE

- Cyrano continues to heckle.
- Some members of the audience encourage him.
- Montfleury appeals to the audience for protection.

## 1 STYLE: IRONY

Montfleury's repetition of his first line—*Happy is he* . . . —makes a perfect ironic counterpoint to his actual unhappy situation.

## 2 STAGING

The stage directions describe Cyrano as a figure of perfect confidence, challenging but in control. This is the first time the audience actually sees him, and it is a fitting introduction.

---

**VARIOUS VOICES.** [*From the floor and the boxes.*] Sh!—Enough!—Go on, Montfleury!—Don't be afraid!

**MONTFLEURY.** [*In a faltering voice.*] "Happy is he who shuns the pomp of..."

**THE VOICE.** [*More threateningly.*] Well, prince of louts, must I give your shoulders a taste of wood?

[*An arm holding a cane rises above the heads of the audience.*]

**MONTFLEURY.** [*In an increasingly feeble voice.*] "Happy is he who..."

[*The arm waves the cane.*]

**THE VOICE.** Off the stage!

**THE CROWD.** Oh!

**MONTFLEURY.** [*Choking.*] "Happy is he who shuns..."

**2** **CYRANO.** [*Standing up on a chair with his arms folded, his hat cocked, his mustache bristling, and his nose pointing aggressively.*] I'm about to lose my temper! [*His appearance creates a sensation.*]

**MONTFLEURY.** [*To the* MARQUIS.] Protect me, gentlemen!

**A MARQUIS.** [*Nonchalantly.*] Go on with your acting.

*Cyrano de Bergerac, Act I* **393**

---

## GUIDED READING

### LITERAL QUESTION

**1a.** What kind of appeal does Montfleury make to the audience? (He says, "Protect me, gentlemen.")

### INFERENTIAL QUESTION

**1b.** What does this reveal about his character? (He is a cowardly, ineffectual person, who is unable to defend himself.)

- The crowd protests Cyrano's conduct.
- He asks them to challenge him individually, but no one steps forward.
- Montfleury leaves the stage.

**1 STYLE: FIGURATIVE LANGUAGE**

Cyrano threatens the noblemen, using a part, ribbons, to represent the whole—them.

**2 CHARACTERIZATION**

Cyrano shows his bravery by challenging the crowd to abandon the safety of numbers and step forward to fight him one by one.

**3 STYLE: HUMOR**

Cyrano does a mock magic trick: He makes Montfleury disappear by clapping his hands three times. The crowd is amused, and Montfleury is intimidated. This clever flourish reveals Cyrano's fertile imagination and humor.

**4 CHARACTERIZATION**

His critique of Montfleury's acting establishes Cyrano as a man of discrimination and intelligence who sees through sham.

---

CYRANO. If you do, you fat oaf, I'll tan your cheeks!

THE MARQUIS. Enough!

**1** CYRANO. [*To all the* MARQUIS.] I advise you all to sit quietly in your seats. Otherwise my cane will rumple your ribbons!

THE CROWD. [*Retreating.*] Make room!—Step back!

CYRANO. [*To* MONTFLEURY.] Off the stage! [*The crowd closes in with an angry murmur. He quickly turns around.*] Is there something you want to say to me? Speak up!

A LADY. [*In the boxes.*] This is incredible!

A NOBLEMAN. Scandalous!

A BURGHER. Exasperating!

A PAGE. Hilarious!

THE CROWD. Montfleury!—Cyrano!

CYRANO. Silence!

THE CROWD. [*Uproariously.*] Hee-haw!—Baa!—Woof, woof!—Cock-a-doodle-doo!

CYRANO. Quiet, or I'll...

A PAGE. Meow!

**2** CYRANO. I order you to be silent! And I issue a collective challenge! Come, I'll write down your names. Step forward, young heroes! You'll all have a turn, I'll give each of you a number. Now, who wants to be at the top of the list? You, sir? No? You? No? [*Silence.*] No names? No hands?... Then I'll get on with my business. [*He turns back toward the stage, where* MONTFLEURY *has been waiting in great anxiety.*] I want to see the theater cured of this boil. Otherwise... [*Puts his hand to his sword.*]...I'll lance it!

MONTFLEURY. I...

CYRANO. [*Descends from his chair, sits down in the middle of the circle that has formed around him, and settles himself as though at home.*] I'm

**394** *Drama*

---

going to clap my hands three times. By the third clap, you will be gone.

THE CROWD. [*Amused.*] Ah!

CYRANO. [*Clapping his hands.*] One!

MONTFLEURY. I...

A VOICE. [*From the boxes.*] Stay!

**3** THE CROWD. He'll stay—He'll go!

MONTFLEURY. Gentlemen, I believe...

CYRANO. Two!

MONTFLEURY. I'm sure it would be better...

CYRANO. Three!

[MONTFLEURY *suddenly disappears. Storm of laughter, hisses, and boos.*]

THE CROWD. Boo!—Boo!—Coward!—Come back!

CYRANO. [*Leans back in his chair, beaming, and crosses his legs.*] Let him come back if he dares!

A YOUNG MAN. [*To* CYRANO.] Tell me, sir, what reason do you have to hate Montfleury?

**4** CYRANO. [*Graciously, still seated.*] I have two reasons, my callow young friend, either of which would be sufficient. The first is that he's a deplorable actor who brays like an ass and wrestles ponderously with lines that ought to soar lightly from his lips. The second—is my secret.

BELLEROSE.[32] What about the money that will have to be refunded?

CYRANO. [*Turning his chair toward the stage.*] Now there's the first sensible thing that's yet been said! Far be it from me to impose hardship on practitioners of the Thespian[33] art. [*Stands*

---

32. **Bellerose** [bel rōz′]: seventeenth-century French actor.
33. **Thespian:** having to do with drama.

---

## GUIDED READING

**LITERAL QUESTIONS**

**1a.** What does Cyrano say to bring the crowd to order? (He orders them to be quiet, then challenges anyone who does not like his actions to step forward one by one and fight him.)

**2a.** What does Cyrano say about why he hates Montfleury? (He says it's because he's a bad actor and that he has a secret reason as well.)

**INFERENTIAL QUESTIONS**

**1b.** Why is this good psychology? (Most people can be brave in a mob, but it takes real courage to act individually.)

**2b.** What can we gather about Cyrano's character from this explanation? (He is a man of taste who knows bad acting when he sees it. He is also discreet, not readily divulging a personal motivation.)

*up and throws a bag onto the stage.*] Here, take this purse and be quiet.

THE CROWD. [*Astonished.*] Ah!—Oh!

AN ACTOR. [*Quickly picking up the purse and weighing it in his hand.*] At this price, sir, I'll be glad to have you come and stop our performance every day!

THE CROWD. Boo! Boo!

BELLEROSE. Please clear the hall!

[*The spectators begin leaving while* CYRANO *watches with satisfaction, but they soon stop when they hear the following scene. The ladies in the boxes, who have already stood up and put on their cloaks, stop to listen, and finally sit down again.*]

LE BRET. [*To* CYRANO.] This is madness!

A MEDDLER. [*Who has approached* CYRANO.] What a scandal! Montfleury, the great actor! Don't you know he's protected by the Duke de Candale?[34] Do you have a patron?[35]

CYRANO. No!

THE MEDDLER. What? You have no great lord whose name protects...

CYRANO. I don't rely on some remote patron for protection. [*Puts his hand to his sword.*] My protector is always near at hand.

THE MEDDLER. Are you going to leave the city?

CYRANO. That depends.

THE MEDDLER. But the Duke de Candale has a long arm!

CYRANO. Not as long as mine... [*Pointing to his sword.*] ...when I give it this extension!

THE MEDDLER. But surely you wouldn't dare...

---

34. **Duke of Candale** [kan dal′]
35. **patron:** wealthy person who supports an artist.

CYRANO. I would.

THE MEDDLER. But...

CYRANO. Go now.

THE MEDDLER. But...

3 CYRANO. Go! Or tell me why you're looking at my nose.

THE MEDDLER. [*Petrified.*] I...

CYRANO. [*Moving toward him.*] Do you find it surprising?

THE MEDDLER. [*Stepping back.*] You're mistaken, my lord...

CYRANO. Is it limp and dangling, like an elephant's trunk?

THE MEDDLER. [*Stepping back again.*] I didn't...

CYRANO. Or hooked like an owl's beak?

THE MEDDLER. I...

CYRANO. Do you see a wart at the end of it?

THE MEDDLER. I...

CYRANO. Or a fly walking on it? What's unusual about it?

THE MEDDLER. Nothing, I...

CYRANO. Then why that disdainful expression? Do you find it, perhaps, a little too large?

THE MEDDLER. [*Stammering.*] Oh, no, it's quite small...very small...diminutive....

CYRANO. What! How dare you accuse me of anything so ridiculous? A small nose? *My* nose? You've gone too far!

THE MEDDLER. Please, sir, I...

CYRANO. My nose is *enormous*, you snub-nosed, flat-faced wretch! I carry it with pride, because a big nose is a sign of affability, kindness, courtesy, wit, generosity, and courage. I have all those qualities, but you can never hope to have

*Cyrano de Bergerac, Act I* **395**

## AT A GLANCE

- Cyrano throws a bag of money on the stage to cover the refunds on the interrupted performance.
- A meddler stares at Cyrano's nose, and Cyrano challenges him.

### 1 CHARACTERIZATION

Cyrano makes a grand gesture—he repays the actors for the money they will have to refund for the interrupted performance. This act shows his sense of fairness: The actors should not have to suffer for his victory over Montfleury.

### 2 THEME

This exchange reflects a major theme of the play: Cyrano's individualism and independence of the conventions of his society.

### 3 DIALOGUE

Here Cyrano shows both his oversensitivity about his nose and his method of dealing with this disfigurement: Take the offensive and, if possible, turn the insult back to the other person.

---

## GUIDED READING

### LITERAL QUESTIONS

**1a.** What does the actor say when he picks up the purse Cyrano threw? ("At this price sir, I'll be glad to have you come and stop our performance every day!")

**2a.** What does the meddler tell Cyrano about Montfleury? (that he is protected by the Duke de Candale, who "has a long arm")

### INFERENTIAL QUESTIONS

**1b.** What can you gather about the amount of money Cyrano gave? (It is large, more than is needed to cover the refund. Cyrano made his gesture as grand and as extravagant as he could.)

**2b.** What does this information tell you about Cyrano's risk in interfering with Montfleury? (His risk becomes much greater—and his gesture becomes far braver and more defiant—when we know about Montfleury's powerful patron.)

AT A GLANCE

- Valvert tries to silence Cyrano with a tepid insult.
- Cyrano counters by composing a hymn to his huge nose, thereby turning the tables on Valvert.

**1 PLOT: CONFLICT**

De Guiche's hostility to Cyrano is a major source of the play's external conflict. This incident illustrates his method of dealing with Cyrano, always using someone else or manipulating events, never confronting Cyrano directly.

**2 STYLE: EXAGGERATION**

Cyrano's exuberant burst of language, which uses exaggeration to make his nose ridiculous rather than pitiable, shows his facility with language and his sense of humor.

**3 THEME**

Valvert's criticism of Cyrano's "uncouth" appearance reveals the values of the fashionable class of the time. Its members were more concerned with people's appearances than with their qualities of mind or heart.

**4 RESPONSE JOURNAL**

In their journals, have students write about the inner qualities they value most in the people they know.

---

any of them, since the ignoble face that my hand is about to meet above your collar has no more glory, nobility, poetry, quaintness, vivacity, or grandeur—no more *nose,* in short— [*Slaps him. The* MEDDLER *cries out in pain.*]

THE MEDDLER. [*Running away.*] Help! Guards!

**1** DE GUICHE. [*Who has come down from the seats on the stage, with the* MARQUIS.] He's beginning to be annoying!

VALVERT. [*Shrugging.*] He likes to bluster.

DE GUICHE. Isn't anyone going to silence him?

VALVERT. Yes, *I* will! Just watch his face when he hears what I have to say to him! [*Walks up to* CYRANO, *who observes him, and stands in front of him with a fatuous expression.*] You have a nose that . . . Your nose is . . . um . . . very big.

CYRANO. [*Gravely.*] Yes, very.

VALVERT. [*Laughing.*] Ha!

CYRANO. [*With perfect calm.*] Is that all?

VALVERT. Well . . .

**2** CYRANO. I'm afraid your speech was a little short, young man. You could have said . . . oh, all sorts of things, varying your tone to fit your words. Let me give you a few examples.

In an aggressive tone: "If I had a nose like that, I'd have it amputated!"

Friendly: "The end of it must get wet when you drink from a cup. Why don't you use a tankard?"

Descriptive: "It's a rock, a peak, a cape! No, more than a cape: a peninsula!"

Gracious: "What a kind man you are! You love birds so much that you've given them a perch to roost on."

Solicitous: "Be careful when you walk: with all that weight on your head, you could easily lose your balance and fall."

Thoughtful: "You ought to put an awning over it, to keep its color from fading in the sun."

Flippant: "That tusk must be convenient to hang your hat on."

396 *Drama*

Grandiloquent: "No wind but the mighty Arctic blast, majestic nose, could ever give you a cold from one end to the other!"

Dramatic: "When it bleeds, it must be like the Red Sea!"[36]

Admiring: "What a sign for a perfume shop!"

Rustic: "That don't look like no nose to me. It's either a big cucumber or a little watermelon."

Military: "The enemy is charging! Aim your cannon!"

There, now you have an inkling of what you might have said to me if you were witty and a man of letters. Unfortunately you're totally witless and a man of very few letters: only the four that spell the word "fool."

DE GUICHE. [*Trying to lead away the outraged* VALVERT.] Come, never mind.

**3** VALVERT. [*Choking with anger.*] Such arrogance from an uncouth barbarian who . . . who . . . isn't even wearing gloves! Who appears in public without ribbons, or tassels, or braid!

CYRANO. I have a different idea of elegance. I don't dress like a fop,[37] it's true, but my moral grooming is impeccable. I never appear in public with a soiled conscience, a tarnished honor, threadbare scruples, or an insult that I haven't washed away. I'm always immaculately clean, adorned with independence and frankness. I may not cut a stylish figure, but I hold my soul **4** erect. I wear my deeds as ribbons, my wit is sharper than the finest mustache, and when I walk among men I make truths ring like spurs.

VALVERT. [*Exasperated.*] Buffoon!

CYRANO. [*Crying out as if in pain.*] Oh! I have a cramp in my sword.

VALVERT. [*Drawing his own.*] So be it!

---

36. **Red Sea:** sea in the Near East that is colored by a reddish algae at certain periods of the year.

37. **fop:** man who is overly concerned with his appearance; a dandy.

---

## GUIDED READING

**LITERAL QUESTIONS**

**1a.** What does Valvert reply when De Guiche says Cyrano is annoying? *(He likes to bluster.)*

**2a.** What does Cyrano say when Valvert calls him a buffoon? *(I have a cramp in my sword.)*

**INFERENTIAL QUESTIONS**

**1b.** Do you think this is a true comment about Cyrano? *(Cyrano is not blustering—he backs up his extravagant talk with action.)*

**2b.** What does he mean by this? What does this fanciful way of expressing himself tell you about Cyrano? *(It means that he wants to fight in response to Valvert's insult. Cyrano's fanciful way of speaking suggests that he is imaginative and witty.)*

CYRANO. I'll give you a charming little thrust.

VALVERT. [Contemptuously.] Poet!

CYRANO. Yes, sir, I *am* a poet, as I'll demonstrate by composing an impromptu[38] ballade while I fence with you.

VALVERT. A ballade?

CYRANO. You don't know what that is? Allow me to explain.

VALVERT. But...

CYRANO. [As though reciting a lesson.] The ballade consists of three eight-line stanzas...

VALVERT. [Stamping his foot.] Oh!

CYRANO. [Continuing.] ...with a four-line refrain at the end.

VALVERT. You...

CYRANO. I'm going to compose one as I fight with you, and when I come to the last line, I'll draw blood.

VALVERT. No!

CYRANO. No? Wait and see.

THE CROWD. [Greatly excited.] Make room!— This will be worth seeing!—Step back!—Quiet!

CYRANO. [Closing his eyes for a moment.] Wait, I'm thinking of how to begin.... There, I have it. [His actions match his words throughout the ballade.]
I take off my hat and discard it,
I slowly abandon my cloak,
I draw my sword out of its scabbard,
Preparing to put it to use.
For the moment, I stand here before you,
Elegant, calm, and serene,
But I warn you, my impudent scoundrel,
When I end the refrain, I draw blood.

[They begin fencing.]

_____
38. **impromptu:** spontaneous, without preparation.

You should have avoided this battle.
Now, where shall I skewer you, goose?
In the side, 'neath the sleeve of your doublet?
In the heart, 'neath the ribbon you wear?
No, I've carefully thought and reflected,
And finally made up my mind;
The paunch: that's where I've decided,
When I end the refrain, to draw blood.

I see you give ground when I press you;
Your face is as white as a sheet;
Is "coward" a name that would suit you?
I dexterously parry the point[39]
That you hoped to thrust into my entrails;
Your efforts are doomed to be vain.
Prepare yourself now to be punctured:
When I end the refrain, I draw blood.

[Announces solemnly.]

Refrain:
Pray God to forgive your transgressions!
The close of our combat draws near;
A coupé,[40] then a feint,[41] then the finish!
[He lunges. VALVERT staggers. CYRANO bows.]
When I end the refrain, I draw blood.

[Cheers. Applause from the boxes. Flowers and handkerchiefs are thrown down. Officers surround and congratulate CYRANO. RAGUENEAU dances with delight. LE BRET is both happy and appalled. VALVERT's friends lead him away, holding him up.]

THE CROWD. [In a long cry.] Ah!...

A LIGHT-HORSEMAN. Magnificent!

A WOMAN. Charming!

RAGUENEAU. Phenomenal!

A MARQUIS. Unheard of!

LE BRET. Foolhardy!

_____
39. **parry the point:** prevent an opponent from striking with his sword.
40. **coupé** [kōō pā']: forceful stroke.
41. **feint** [fānt]: movement meant to deceive.

*Cyrano de Bergerac, Act I* **397**

## GUIDED READING

### LITERAL QUESTIONS

**1a.** What word does Valvert use to insult Cyrano before their fight? (He contemptuously calls him *Poet!*)

**2a.** What does Cyrano do while carrying on his fight with Valvert? (He spontaneously makes up a ballade.)

### INFERENTIAL QUESTIONS

**1b.** What do you gather about Cyrano's and Valvert's contrasting attitudes toward poets? (Valvert finds poets unattractive and despicable, whereas Cyrano believes that writing poetry is a delightful and worthy talent.)

**2b.** What is his motivation for doing this? (Cyrano wants to teach Valvert a lesson for insulting him and the art of poetry. He proves that being a poet does not make one a coward or a buffoon.)

### 1 READING SKILLS: CAUSE AND EFFECT

Because Cyrano is proud, he does not want the doorkeeper to know that he has no money. This motive explains Cyrano's shift of tone in this exchange.

### 2 CHARACTERIZATION

Cyrano reveals his love of the flamboyant. He will sacrifice a month of dinners in order to give a gesture more *panache*.

### 3 THEME

Cyrano's nobility of character is shown by his tact and consideration. He takes very little of the girl's food because she is poor, but he refuses so flatteringly that she goes away feeling appreciated.

---

THE CROWD. [*Swarming around* CYRANO.] Congratulations!—My compliments!—Bravo!

A WOMAN'S VOICE. He's a hero!

LE BRET. [*To* CYRANO, *taking his arm.*] I'd like to have a talk with you.

CYRANO. Wait till this crowd thins out a little. [*To* BELLEROSE.] May I stay?

BELLEROSE. [*Respectfully.*] Of course, sir! [*Changing his tone, to the* DOORKEEPER *and the man who is preparing to put out the candles.*] Sweep out the theater and lock the door, but leave the candles burning. We'll come back after dinner to rehearse the new farce we're going to present tomorrow. [*Goes out.*]

1 THE DOORKEEPER. [*To* CYRANO.] Aren't you going to dine, sir?

CYRANO. No. [*The* DOORKEEPER *withdraws.*]

LE BRET. [*To* CYRANO.] Why not?

CYRANO. [*Proudly.*] Because... [*Changing his tone, seeing that the* DOORKEEPER *is out of earshot.*] Because I have no money.

LE BRET. [*Making the gesture of throwing a bag.*] What! That bag of money...

2 CYRANO. Alas, my month's allotment lived only for a day!

LE BRET. And for the rest of the month...

CYRANO. I have nothing left.

LE BRET. What foolishness to throw it all away!

CYRANO. Yes, but what a gesture!

THE REFRESHMENT GIRL. [*Coughing from behind her little counter.*] Ahem!... [CYRANO *and* LE BRET *turn around. She comes forward timidly.*] Sir, I...I can't bear to think of you going hungry. [*Points to the refreshment table.*] I have plenty of food here... Take whatever you like!

3 CYRANO. [*Gallantly taking off his hat.*] My dear child, my Gascon pride forbids me to accept the slightest morsel from your fingers, but since I fear a refusal would offend you, I will accept... [*Goes to the refreshment table and chooses.*] Oh, very little! One of these grapes... [*She tries to give him the whole cluster; he picks off a single grape.*] Only one!...This glass of water... [*She tries to pour him a glass of wine; he stops her.*] And half a macaroon. [*Breaks one and gives her back the other half.*]

LE BRET. But that's ridiculous!

THE REFRESHMENT GIRL. Oh, please take something else!

CYRANO. I will. Your lovely hand. [*She holds out her hand to him and he kisses it as if she were a princess.*]

THE REFRESHMENT GIRL. Thank you, sir. [*Bows.*] Good-by. [*Leaves.*]

CYRANO. [*To* LE BRET.] You wanted to have a talk with me? I'm ready to listen. [*Sets the macaroon down on the refreshment table in front of him.*] My dinner!... [*Sets down the glass of water.*] My drink!... [*And finally the grape.*] My dessert! [*Sits down.*] There, I'm ready to begin. I have an excellent appetite this evening. [*Eating.*] What was it you wanted to tell me?

LE BRET. That you're going to have some badly distorted ideas if you listen only to those fools who like to give themselves such warlike airs. Talk with a few sensible people and you'll be better informed of the effect produced by your act of bravado.

CYRANO. [*Finishing his macaroon.*] It was enormous.

LE BRET. You've made too many enemies!

CYRANO. About how many would you say I made today?

---

## GUIDED READING

### LITERAL QUESTIONS

**1a.** What two things does Le Bret scold Cyrano about? (He tells him that it is foolish to throw a whole month's pay away and that he should be careful about making too many powerful enemies.)

**2a.** What does Cyrano take from the refreshment girl? (one grape, a glass of water, and half a macaroon)

### INFERENTIAL QUESTIONS

**1b.** Do you think Le Bret is right? (Some students may feel that Cyrano should have kept some of the money, and others, not. Some may feel that Cyrano should not make powerful enemies, because he cannot always avoid punishment.)

**2b.** Why do you think Cyrano takes such infinitesimal amounts of food? (He does not want to take the girl's livelihood away, but he does take a small amount of food to show his appreciation.)

LE BRET. There's Montfleury, then the burgher[42] you kicked, De Guiche, Valvert, of course, Baro,[43] the Academy[44]...

CYRANO. Stop! That's already enough to delight me!

LE BRET. I don't understand the way you live. Where will it lead you? What are you trying to accomplish?

CYRANO. I was once confused and bewildered by all the complicated courses of action that were open to me. Finally I chose...

LE BRET. What did you choose?

CYRANO. The simplest course of all. I decided to be admirable in everything!

LE BRET. If you say so....But let me ask you something else. What's the real reason for your hatred of Montfleury? You can tell *me* the truth.

CYRANO. [*Standing up.*] That bloated old sot, I've hated him since the day when I saw him look at...It was like watching a slimy slug crawling on a flower!

LE BRET. [*Astonished.*] What's this? Do I understand you rightly? Is it possible that...

CYRANO. [*With a bitter laugh.*] That I'm in love? [*Changing to a grave tone.*] Yes, it's true.

LE BRET. May I ask with whom? You've never told me...

CYRANO. With whom I'm in love? Come now, think a moment: this nose of mine, which precedes me by a quarter of an hour wherever I go, forbids me ever to dream of being loved by even an ugly woman. Whom else would I love but the most beautiful woman in the world?

LE BRET. The most beautiful...

CYRANO. Of course! The most beautiful of all women! The most captivating, the most intelligent...[*Dejectedly.*]...the blondest....

LE BRET. Tell me: who is she?

CYRANO. Anyone who has seen her smile has known perfection. She creates grace without movement, and makes all divinity fit into her slightest gesture. And neither Venus[45] in her shell, nor Diana[46] striding in the great, blossoming forest, can compare to her when she goes through the streets of Paris in her sedan chair![47]

LE BRET. Now I believe I know! It *is* becoming clear!

CYRANO. It's perfectly transparent.

LE BRET. Your cousin, Magdeleine Robin?

CYRANO. Yes—Roxane.

LE BRET. Then you ought to be overjoyed! You love her? Tell her so! You've covered yourself with glory in her eyes today!

CYRANO. Look at me and tell me what hope this protuberance might leave me! I have no illusions. Sometimes, in the blue shadows of evening, I give way to tender feelings. I go into a garden, smelling the fragrance of spring with my poor monstrous nose, and watch a man and a woman strolling together in the moonlight. I think how much I, too, would like to be walking arm in arm with a woman, under the moon. I let myself be carried away, I forget myself—and then I suddenly see the shadow of my profile on the garden wall.

LE BRET. [*Deeply moved.*] My friend...

---

42. **burgher:** person who lives in a town.
43. **Baro** [ba rō′]: Balthazar Baro (1600–1650), author of *La Clorise,* the play that Cyrano interrupted.
44. **Academy:** The French Academy, founded in 1635, is made up of France's forty most distinguished writers.

45. **Venus:** Roman goddess of love and beauty.
46. **Diana:** Roman goddess of the moon and hunting.
47. **sedan chair:** enclosed chair carried on poles.

*Cyrano de Bergerac, Act I* **399**

## GUIDED READING

### LITERAL QUESTIONS

**1a.** What does Cyrano tell Le Bret about a decision that ended his confusion? (He says he decided "to be admirable in everything.")

**2a.** What reason does Cyrano give for not telling Roxane of his love? (He says no woman could ever love him because of his big nose.)

### INFERENTIAL QUESTIONS

**1b.** Do you think he lives up to this motto? (Opinions will vary, but all students will have to admit that he has displayed a number of talents and an unusual integrity.)

**2b.** What does this tell you about Cyrano's self-image and his opinion of women? (In one area alone—romance—Cyrano is completely without self-confidence. He seems to think that women are incapable of appreciating deeper qualities.)

- Le Bret comforts and supports Cyrano.
- The duenna tells Cyrano that Roxane wants to see him; they arrange to meet at Ragueneau's bakery.
- Cyrano is deliriously happy about the forthcoming meeting.

## 1 THEME

Le Bret's speech emphasizes one of the major themes of the play: the relative values of inner and outer beauty.

## 2 CHARACTERIZATION

This revelation is a key to Cyrano's character. He is a proud man, one whose worst fear is being ridiculed.

## 3 DIALOGUE

The duenna's discreet wording here promotes ambiguity. Because he is in love, Cyrano thinks "things to tell you" means confessions of love. The duenna, however, leaves the nature of the "things" unclear.

## 4 STYLE: EXAGGERATION

Now that his moments of self-doubt are over, Cyrano resumes his extravagant use of language.

---

CYRANO. My friend, I have bad moments now and then, feeling myself so ugly, all alone....

LE BRET. [*With concern, taking his hand.*] Do you weep?

CYRANO. Oh, no, never! No, it would be grotesque if a tear ran down this nose! As long as it's in my power to prevent it, I'll never let the divine beauty of tears be sullied by such gross ugliness.

1 LE BRET. But you're overlooking your courage, your wit!...Take that girl who offered to give you dinner just now, for example: you could see for yourself that she was far from detesting you!

CYRANO. [*Struck by this realization.*] Yes, it's true!

LE BRET. Well, then? You see? And Roxane herself was pale as she watched your duel....

CYRANO. Pale?

2 LE BRET. You've already made a deep impression on her heart and her mind. Don't be timid: speak to her, tell her, so that...

CYRANO. So that she'll laugh in my face? No! That's the one thing in the world that I fear!

THE DOORKEEPER. [*Bringing in* ROXANE'S DUENNA.] Sir, this lady would like to speak to you.

CYRANO. [*Seeing the* DUENNA.] Her duenna!

THE DUENNA. [*With a deep bow.*] My lady wishes me to ask her valiant cousin where she can see him in private.

3 CYRANO. [*Thunderstruck.*] See me?

THE DUENNA. [*With another bow.*] Yes. She has things to tell you.

CYRANO. Things to...

THE DUENNA. [*Bowing again.*] To tell you.

CYRANO. [*Unsteady on his feet.*] My—

**400** *Drama*

---

THE DUENNA. She will go to early Mass at the Saint-Roch[48] church tomorrow morning.

CYRANO. [*Clutching* LE BRET *to steady himself.*] Ah—

THE DUENNA. When she leaves the church, where can she go to talk with you?

CYRANO. [*Agitated.*] Where?...I...Where...

THE DUENNA. Well?

CYRANO. I'm trying to think!

THE DUENNA. Tell me.

CYRANO. At...at Ragueneau's shop...Ragueneau, the pastry cook....

THE DUENNA. [*Withdrawing.*] Very well. At seven o'clock.

CYRANO. I'll be there.

[*The* DUENNA *leaves.*]

CYRANO. [*Falling into* LE BRET'S *arms.*] Me! She wants to see *me*!

LE BRET. I see your sadness has vanished!

CYRANO. Ah, for whatever reason, she knows I exist!

LE BRET. Please be calm.

4 CYRANO. No! I'm going to be frenzied and turbulent! I need a whole army to vanquish! I have ten hearts, twenty arms! It's no longer enough for me to cut down dwarfs...[*Shouts at the top of his lungs.*]...I need giants!

[*For some time now, the* ACTORS *and* ACTRESSES *have been moving on the stage: the rehearsal is beginning.*]

A VOICE. [*From the stage.*] Quiet! We're rehearsing!

---

48. **Saint-Roch** [san rōsh′]

---

## GUIDED READING

### LITERAL QUESTION

**1a.** Why does Le Bret encourage Cyrano to tell Roxane of his love despite his nose? (He says that Cyrano has other wonderful qualities to offer Roxane, such as his wit and courage, and that he has already made an impression on her.)

### INFERENTIAL QUESTION

**1b.** Do you think Le Bret is right? (Cyrano's many wonderful qualities are appreciated by his male friends. However, physical attractiveness often plays a large part in romance.)

AT A GLANCE

■ Cyrano learns that Lignière is being pursued by one hundred men.

■ Cyrano resolves to fight the men himself.

**1 CHARACTERIZATION**

Cyrano shows his bravery and heedlessness by this statement. In the ambush party of one hundred men, Cyrano has found the "giants" he just asked for.

CYRANO. [*Laughing.*] And we're leaving!

[*He goes upstage. Through the entrance of the theater come* CUIGY, BRISSAILLE, *and several* OFFICERS *holding up* LIGNIÈRE.]

CUIGY. Cyrano!

CYRANO. What is it?

CUIGY. We've brought a friend—

CYRANO. [*Recognizing him.*] Lignière!... What's happened to you?

CUIGY. He wants to see you.

BRISSAILLE. He can't go home.

CYRANO. Why not?

LIGNIÈRE. [*Holding up a rumpled piece of paper.*] This note warns me...hundred men against me...because of...of a song...great danger...Porte de Nesle...on my way home.... Will you let me...let me sleep under your roof tonight?

CYRANO. A hundred men, you say? You'll sleep at home tonight!

LIGNIÈRE. [*Alarmed.*] But...

1 CYRANO. [*In a thunderous voice.*] Take that lantern...[LIGNIÈRE *quickly obeys.*]...and walk! I'll cover you! [*To the* OFFICERS.] And you, follow at a distance: you'll be witnesses!

*Cyrano de Bergerac, Act I*  **401**

---

## GUIDED READING

**LITERAL QUESTION**

**1a.** What does Lignière ask Cyrano? (if he can stay the night at his house, since a hundred men are lying in wait for him)

**INFERENTIAL QUESTION**

**1b.** Why might Cyrano seem so excited at the prospect of defending Lignière? (The odds against him probably appeal to Cyrano's theatrical flair. He also despises injustice. And, exalted by the prospect of meeting Roxane, he had asked to have "giants" to battle; Lignière's one hundred opponents come close to being those giants.)

- Cyrano sets off for the confrontation.
- Cyrano says that Lignière's opponents find it necessary to dispatch one hundred men because they know that Lignière will have Cyrano on his side.

**1 STYLE: FIGURATIVE LANGUAGE**

The theatrical quality of Cyrano's bravado is underlined by the fact that he envisions all of Paris as a stage setting for his brave deeds.

**REFLECTING ON ACT I**

From what you have seen of Cyrano so far, what would you say is his most admirable quality? His least admirable quality? (Students may point to Cyrano's courage, charm, wit, generosity, or extravagant heroism as his *most* admirable quality. Students may see his pride, self-pity, or recklessness as his *least* admirable quality.)

**STUDY QUESTIONS**

1. to see Roxane; is afraid to speak to her, as he is not witty
2. He is odd, impetuous, brash, outlandish, and has a huge nose.
3. Cyrano orders him offstage; throws bag of money onstage to reimburse crowd for tickets.
4. Possible answers: *That tusk must be convenient to hang your hat on; When it bleeds, it must be like the Red Sea; What a sign for a perfume shop;* Cyrano composes a ballad and wounds him at last line
5. He loves Roxane. She tells him that Roxane wants to meet him, which overjoys him.
6. if he can spend the night at his house to hide from enemies; vows to fight enemies
7. his fairness, grandiosity, pride
8. wit, poetic ability, integrity, love of challenge

---

CUIGY. But a hundred men!...

CYRANO. I need at least that many this evening!

[*The* ACTORS *and* ACTRESSES, *in their various costumes, have come down from the stage and approached the group.*]

AN ACTRESS. [*To the others.*] But why should there be a hundred men against one poor poet?

CYRANO. Let's go! [*To the* OFFICERS.] Gentlemen, when you see me charge, don't come to my assistance, no matter how great the danger!

ANOTHER ACTRESS. [*Leaping down from the stage.*] I want to go and watch!

CYRANO. Bravo! Officers, ladies in costume, and twenty paces in front...[*He takes up the station he has described.*]...I will walk alone, under the plume that glory herself has placed on my hat, with twice the pride of Scipio,[49] and a nose three times as long!...Remember, now: no one is

---

49. **Scipio** [sip′ē ō] (234–183 B.C.): Roman general.

allowed to lift a finger to help me!...All ready? One, two, three! Doorkeeper, open the door! [*The* DOORKEEPER *opens both halves of the door, giving a glimpse of picturesque old Paris in the moonlight.*] Ah, Paris lies before us, dim and nebulous in the shadows, with moonlight flowing down the slopes of her roofs! An exquisite setting for the scene about to be performed! There, beneath the mist, the Seine[50] quivers like a mysterious magic mirror....And you will see what you will see!

ALL. To the Porte de Nesle!

CYRANO. [*Standing on the threshold.*] To the Porte de Nesle! [*Turns to the* ACTRESS.] You asked, mademoiselle, why a hundred men had been sent to attack one poet. [*Calmly, drawing his sword.*] I'll tell you: it's because that poet is known to be a friend of mine. [*He goes out. The procession moves forward into the night, to the sound of the violins, and in the dim glow of the candles.*]

---

50. **Seine** [sen]: river that flows through Paris.

---

**STUDY QUESTIONS**

**Recalling**

1. Why has Christian come to the play? What concern does he express to Lignière?
2. Prior to his entry on stage, what do we learn of Cyrano's appearance and personality from the descriptions of his friends?
3. Briefly retell what happens when Montfleury tries to begin the play. How does Cyrano appease the audience?
4. List three of the comments Cyrano makes up about his nose. Describe his duel with Valvert.
5. What does Cyrano confide to Le Bret after the crowd leaves? How does the duenna's visit change his mood?

**402** *Drama*

6. What favor does Lignière ask of Cyrano, and how does Cyrano respond?

**Interpreting**

7. What does the fact that Cyrano gives away his money to refund the tickets show about him?
8. In his verbal battles in Act I, what skills and qualities does Cyrano display?
9. What does Cyrano's eagerness to take on the enemies of Lignière reveal about him?
10. What does Cyrano mean when he says, "I may not cut a stylish figure, but I hold my soul erect"? List two actions that illustrate this statement.

**Extending**

11. Do you think pride like Cyrano's is foolish, or do you find it admirable? Why?

---

9. He is courageous, confident, exuberant about meeting Roxane.
10. He never compromises his ideals, honor, or integrity; keeps vow to banish actor; refunds money; volunteers to protect Lignière
11. *foolish:* makes enemies, gives away all his money; *admirable:* takes responsibility for his actions, has integrity, honor

# ACT II

*The large workroom of the pastry shop of* RAGUENEAU. *The next morning.*

[*The street, seen through the panes of the door in the background, is gray in the first glow of dawn. Copper pots and pans are gleaming. Spits are turning. The morning rush has begun. Fat* COOKS *and small* KITCHEN BOYS *are jostling one another. Some tables are covered with cakes and dishes. Others, surrounded by chairs, are awaiting eaters and drinkers. A smaller one in a corner is laden with papers.* RAGUENEAU *is seated at it, writing, as the curtain rises.*]

RAGUENEAU. The silver of dawn is already gleaming on the copper pots! Silence the god who sings within you, Ragueneau! The hour of the lute will come—it is now the hour of the oven! [*Stands up and speaks to a* COOK.] There's something lacking in this sauce.

THE COOK. What shall I do to it?

RAGUENEAU. Make it a little more lyrical.

AN APPRENTICE. [*Bringing a tray covered with a cloth.*] I've baked this in your honor, sir. I hope it will please you. [*He uncovers the tray, revealing a large pastry lyre.[1]*]

RAGUENEAU. [*Enraptured.*] A lyre!

THE APPRENTICE. Made of pastry dough.

RAGUENEAU. [*Deeply moved.*] With candied fruit!

THE APPRENTICE. And I made the strings of sugar.

RAGUENEAU. [*Giving him some money.*] Here, go and drink to my health! [*Sees* LISE[2] *coming in.*] My wife! Quickly, go about your business—and hide that money! [*To* LISE, *pointing to the lyre with embarrassment.*] Isn't it beautiful?

---

1. **lyre** [lῑr]: stringed musical instrument, used to accompany singing or poetry.
2. **Lise** [lēz]

LISE. It's ridiculous! [*She puts a pile of paper bags on the counter.*]

RAGUENEAU. You've brought some paper bags? Good, thank you. [*Looks at them more closely.*] Oh, no! My treasured books! My friends' poetry! Desecrated, dismembered, to make bags for pastry! How can you treat poetry with such disrespect?

LISE. I'll treat poetry however I please!

RAGUENEAU. I shudder to think of what you might do with prose!

[CYRANO *enters abruptly.*]

CYRANO. What time is it?

RAGUENEAU. [*Bowing to him.*] Six o'clock.

CYRANO. [*With great emotion.*] One more hour! [*He begins pacing the floor.*]

RAGUENEAU. [*Following him.*] Congratulations!

CYRANO. For what?

RAGUENEAU. I saw your duel!

CYRANO. Which one?

RAGUENEAU. At the Hôtel de Bourgogne!

CYRANO. [*Disdainfully.*] Oh, that one....

RAGUENEAU. [*Admiringly.*] A duel in verse!

LISE. He talks about nothing else!

CYRANO. I'm glad to hear it.

RAGUENEAU. [*Lunging with a spit that he has picked up.*] "When I end the refrain, I draw blood!"...Magnificent! [*With growing enthusiasm.*] "When I end the refrain..."

CYRANO. What time is it, Ragueneau?

RAGUENEAU. [*Looking at the clock while holding the position of the lunge he has just made.*] Five

*Cyrano de Bergerac, Act II* **403**

---

right sidebar

## AT A GLANCE

- It is a typical, busy morning at Ragueneau's pastry shop.
- Ragueneau's wife, Lise, reveals her contempt for poetry.
- Cyrano enters for his appointment with Roxane.

## LITERARY OPTIONS

- dramatic irony
- conflict
- dialogue

## THEMATIC OPTIONS

- appearance vs. reality
- personal integrity
- idealism vs. pragmatism

### 1 SETTING

The scene is set at Ragueneau's busy bakery. The prosaic workaday world of a busy pastry shop serves as a foil for the romanticism of Ragueneau.

### 2 CHARACTERIZATION

Ragueneau's poetic attitude carries over even into his cooking instructions: His reply adds humor and reveals his preoccupation with poetry.

### 3 PLOT: CONFLICT

Ragueneau's reaction to his wife's arrival as he rewards his apprentice, and his embarrassed reference to the lyre pastry, alerts the audience to conflict between them.

### 4 STYLE: HUMOR

Ragueneau's humorous reply to Lise reveals a difference in the values they place on the arts. Lise, practical and conventional, makes bags out of his poetry books, whereas Ragueneau has an almost excessive respect for the arts.

### 5 CHARACTERIZATION

This exchange tells a great deal about Cyrano's life. His duels are frequent: He is both brave and overeager to fight.

---

## GUIDED READING

### LITERAL QUESTIONS

**1a.** What does Ragueneau's apprentice make for him? (a pastry lyre)

**2a.** What question does Cyrano keep asking Ragueneau? (*What time is it?*)

### INFERENTIAL QUESTIONS

**1b.** Why does Ragueneau point the lyre out to Lise, with embarrassment? (The lyre is meant as a tribute to poetry, as it was an instrument used in ancient times to accompany verses. He is embarrassed because he knows Lise does not value poetry and mocks his own devotion to it.)

**2b.** What does this repeated question tell you about his state of mind? (He is anxious and excited about the coming meeting with Roxane.)

Cyrano . . . Act II  **T-403**

- Cyrano tells Ragueneau that he plans to meet someone and asks to be left alone during the meeting.
- Cyrano composes a love letter to Roxane.
- Ragueneau's poets arrive and discuss the previous night's exploits at the Porte de Nesle.

**1 STYLE: HUMOR**

Cyrano's joke refers to the folk belief that if you tell a lie, your nose twitches. His joke about this sensitive subject shows how at ease he feels, now that he believes that Roxane loves him.

**2 THEME**

Cyrano writes his letter by looking into his soul and copying the words inscribed in it. He believes in the correspondence between the inner self and poetry. This romantic attitude contrasts with the artifice and superficiality of the society of his day.

**3 STYLE: METAPHOR**

One of Ragueneau's poets compares him to an eagle among pastry cooks and his shop to a fragrant nest. This metaphor is amusing but also reveals that the main interest of his poet friends is in Ragueneau's cooking, not in his poetry.

**4 PLOT: DRAMATIC IRONY**

This incident is an example of dramatic irony: The audience is aware that Cyrano has routed the assassins, but the poets are not. This irony adds piquancy and humor to the scene, as Cyrano comments on the exaggerated story.

---

past six. "...I draw blood!" [*Stands up straight.*] Ah, what a ballade!

LISE. [*To* CYRANO, *who has absentmindedly shaken her hand while passing by her counter.*] Your hand is wounded!

CYRANO. It's nothing, just a small gash.

RAGUENEAU. Have you been doing something dangerous?

CYRANO. No, I've been in no danger.

1 LISE. [*Shaking her finger at him.*] I believe you're telling a lie!

CYRANO. Why? Was my nose twitching? If so, it must have been an enormous lie! [*Changing his tone.*] I'm waiting for someone here. If I don't wait in vain, I want you to leave us alone together.

RAGUENEAU. I can't do that: my poets will soon be here.

LISE. [*Sarcastically.*] For their first meal!

CYRANO. You will take them away when I give you a signal.... What time is it?

RAGUENEAU. Ten past six.

CYRANO. [*Nervously sitting down at* RAGUENEAU's *table and taking a sheet of paper.*] May I have a pen?

RAGUENEAU. [*Giving him the pen he has been carrying behind his ear.*] Here, take my swan's feather! [*A* MUSKETEER *with a superb mustache enters.*]

THE MUSKETEER. [*In a stentorian*[3] *voice.*] Greetings! [LISE *hurries toward him.*]

CYRANO. [*Looking around.*] Who's that?

RAGUENEAU. A friend of my wife's. A mighty warrior—according to what he says! He...

---

3. **stentorian** [sten tôr'ē ən]: loud. Stentor was a legendary Greek herald with a voice as loud as fifty men.

---

CYRANO. [*Taking his pen again and waving* RAGUENEAU *away.*] Never mind. [*To himself.*] Coward! You don't have the courage to say one word to her! [*To* RAGUENEAU.] What time is it?

RAGUENEAU. Quarter past six.

CYRANO. [*To himself.*] I'm afraid to speak a single one of all the words I have in here. [*Strikes his chest.*] But writing is a different matter.... 2 [*Takes his pen again.*] I'll now put down on paper the love letter that I've already written within myself a hundred times. I have only to look into my soul and copy the words inscribed in it. [*He begins writing. Through the glass of the door, thin figures are seen moving hesitantly.*]

LISE. [*Entering, to* RAGUENEAU.] Here come your mud-spattered poets!

FIRST POET. [*Entering, to* RAGUENEAU.] Colleague!

3 SECOND POET. Eagle of pastry cooks! [*Sniffs.*] What a fragrant nest you have!

THIRD POET. O culinary[4] god!

RAGUENEAU. [*Surrounded, embraced, shaken.*] They always make me feel at ease as soon as they come in!

4 FIRST POET. We were delayed by a crowd gathered at the Porte de Nesle.

SECOND POET. Eight bandits had been felled by swordplay and lay bleeding on the pavement!

CYRANO. [*Briefly looking up.*] Eight? I thought there were only seven. [*Resumes writing his letter.*] "I love you...." [*He is heard murmuring from time to time.*]

FIRST POET. We were told that one man had routed a whole band of assassins!

SECOND POET. There were pikes and clubs strewn all over the ground!

---

4. **culinary** [kū'lə ner'ē]: pertaining to cooking.

---

## GUIDED READING

**LITERAL QUESTIONS**

**1a.** What does Lise reply when Ragueneau says his poets will be there soon? (*For their first meal!*)

**2a.** How does Cyrano explain why it is easy for him to write a love letter to Roxane? (*He says that it is hard for him to speak of love but easy to write of it, since he has already composed the letter in his soul.*)

**INFERENTIAL QUESTIONS**

**1b.** How does this reveal Lise's understanding of why the poets are so friendly with Ragueneau? (*She thinks they are just using him to get a free meal.*)

**2b.** What does this explanation suggest about the nature and duration of his love for Roxane? (*He has loved her a long time and, though his love clamors strongly for expression, he has always been afraid to speak of it because he fears her reaction.*)

CYRANO. [Writing.] "Your eyes..."

FIRST POET. The man who could do a thing like that...

CYRANO. [Writing.] "Your lips..."

FIRST POET. ...must have been some sort of ferocious giant!

CYRANO. [Writing.] "...and I become faint with fear each time I see you."

SECOND POET. [Snatching a cake.] What have you been writing, Ragueneau?

CYRANO. [Writing.] "Your faithful worshiper..." [He stops as he is about to sign his name, stands up, and puts the letter in his doublet.] No need to sign it, since I'll give it to her myself.

RAGUENEAU. [To the SECOND POET.] I've written a recipe in verse.

THIRD POET. [Sitting down next to a tray of cream puffs.] Let's hear it!

RAGUENEAU. [Clears his throat, straightens his hat, strikes a pose, and prepares to recite.] A recipe in verse...

"How to Make Almond Tarts"
Beat some eggs till they are foamy;
Mix with tangy citron juice;
Then fold in sweet milk of almonds.
Line your pans with pastry dough,
Slowly pour your foam to fill them;
Let them bake till golden brown.
Now remove them from the oven:
Luscious, dainty almond tarts!

THE POETS. [With their mouths full.] Exquisite! Delightful!

CYRANO. [From the door in the background, motioning RAGUENEAU to take the POETS away.] Psst!...

RAGUENEAU. [Showing the POETS the door on the right.] Come this way, gentlemen, we'll be much more comfortable... [They all go out behind RAGUENEAU, in procession, after having snatched up several trays of pastry.]

CYRANO. I'll give her my letter if I feel that there's the slightest hope! [ROXANE appears behind the glass of the door, followed by the DUENNA. CYRANO throws open the door.] Come in! [Takes the DUENNA aside.] May I have a word with you?

THE DUENNA. Have several, if you like.

CYRANO. Are you fond of pastry?

THE DUENNA. I'm sinfully fond of it!

CYRANO. [Quickly taking some of the paper bags on the counter.] Good. Here are two sonnets by Monsieur Benserade[5]...

THE DUENNA. [Disappointed.] Oh....

CYRANO. ...which I will fill with custard tarts for you. [The DUENNA's face brightens.]

THE DUENNA. Ah!

CYRANO. Do you like cream puffs?

THE DUENNA. [With dignity.] I hold them in high regard.

CYRANO. Here are six of them for you, in a poem by Saint-Amant. And in this verse by Chapelain[6] I'll place a piece of butter cake. You really like pastry, do you?

THE DUENNA. I adore it!

CYRANO. [Loading her arms with filled bags.] Then I'm sure you'll enjoy going out and eating all this in the street.

THE DUENNA. But...

CYRANO. [Pushing her outside.] And please don't

---

5. Benserade [bon'sə rod']: Isaac de Benserade (1613–1691), French poet and playwright.

6. Saint-Amant [san'ta mon']...Chapelain [shap lan']: Marc-Antoine de Gerard, Sieur de Saint-Amant (1594–1661) and Jean Chapelain (1595–1674) were both French poets and original members of the Academy.

*Cyrano de Bergerac, Act II*  **405**

---

**1 PLOT: FORESHADOWING**

Cyrano's decision not to sign his love letter foreshadows the use of the letter later in the act.

**2 CHARACTERIZATION**

Even poets are not exempt from the hypocrisy and servility Cyrano so dislikes in the fashionable classes. They flatter Ragueneau where he is most susceptible—in his desire to be a poet—in order to eat his delicious pastries.

**3 THEME**

Humor reveals the practical values of the duenna: She prefers food for her stomach, not her mind. This pragmatism contrasts with Cyrano's idealistic, impractical attitudes—attitudes that frequently create trouble for him.

---

## GUIDED READING

**LITERAL QUESTION**

**1a.** What do the poets assume about the man who routed a whole band of assassins the night before? (He must have been some sort of ferocious giant.)

**INFERENTIAL QUESTION**

**1b.** In what way does this assumption make an ironic counterpoint to Cyrano's feelings as he writes the love letter? (He is at his most benign, writing soft words of love to Roxane and feeling frightened about giving the letter to her.)

- Roxane and Cyrano talk about their childhood together.
- She asks him about his exploits the night before.
- Roxane speaks of someone she loves who also loves her.

### 1 CHARACTERIZATION

Roxane skillfully begins the talk by flattering Cyrano, thanking him, and painting herself as vulnerable. This approach shows that she is intelligent and knows how to manipulate people.

### 2 IMAGERY AND MOOD

Cyrano and Roxane recall the naturalness of childhood in charming images of reed swords and corn-silk dolls. The gentle, carefree mood of this moment contrasts with the complexities and heartaches to come.

### 3 PLOT: DRAMATIC IRONY

Cyrano's building excitement at Roxane's declaration creates dramatic irony because the audience suspects that Roxane does not love Cyrano. We learned in Act I that Roxane had given Christian reason to believe that she was interested in *him*.

---

come back until you've finished. [*He closes the door and approaches* ROXANE.] May this day be blessed above all others: the day when you ceased to forget my existence and came here to tell me...to tell me?...

**1** ROXANE. First let me thank you for humbling that arrogant fop with your sword yesterday, because he's the man whom a certain great lord, infatuated with me...

CYRANO. De Guiche?

ROXANE. [*Lowering her eyes*.]...was trying to impose on me as...as a husband....

CYRANO. A husband only for the sake of form? [*Bows*.] I'm happy to know that I fought not for my ugly nose, but for your beautiful eyes.

ROXANE. And then, I wanted to tell you...But before I make my confession, give me time to see you again as I did in the past, when I thought of you almost as my brother. We used to play together in the park, beside the lake....

CYRANO. Yes....You came to Bergerac every summer.

**2** ROXANE. You used a reed for a sword in those days!

CYRANO. And you used corn silk to make hair for your dolls.

ROXANE. We played all sorts of games.

CYRANO. And ate blackberries before they were ripe.

ROXANE. You always did whatever I wanted! Was I pretty then?

CYRANO. You weren't ugly.

ROXANE. Sometimes you came to me with your hand bleeding from some accident and I acted as if I were your mother, trying to make my voice stern. [*Takes his hand*.] "What's this?" I'd say. "Have you hurt yourself again?" [*Looks at his

**406** *Drama*

hand*.] Oh! No! Let me see! You're still hurting yourself, at your age! How did you do it this time?

CYRANO. I was playing again—at the Porte de Nesle.

ROXANE. [*Sits down and wets her handkerchief in a glass of water*.] Give me that hand!

CYRANO. [*Also sits down*.] You still mother me!

ROXANE. While I wash away this blood, I want you to describe what happened. How many were there against you?

CYRANO. Oh, not quite a hundred.

ROXANE. Tell me about it!

CYRANO. No, never mind. Tell me what you couldn't bring yourself to say just now.

ROXANE. [*Without letting go of his hand*.] Yes, I can say it now that the past has returned to encourage me. Here it is. I'm in love with someone.

CYRANO. Ah!...

**3** ROXANE. Someone who doesn't know.

CYRANO. Ah!...

ROXANE. But he *will* know soon.

CYRANO. Ah!...

ROXANE. He's a poor man who till now has loved me timidly, from a distance, without daring to say anything.

CYRANO. Ah!...

ROXANE. Let me keep your hand, it feels feverish....But I've seen a confession of love trembling on his lips.

CYRANO. Ah!...

ROXANE. [*Bandaging his hand with her handkerchief*.] And it so happens, cousin, that he's a member of your regiment.

---

## GUIDED READING

### LITERAL QUESTIONS

**1a.** What does Roxane talk about before she begins her confession of love? (She thanks Cyrano for dealing with Valvert, she recalls their childhood together, she asks him to tell her how he received his wound.)

**2a.** Why does Roxane say she wants to continue holding Cyrano's hand? (She says it feels feverish.)

### INFERENTIAL QUESTIONS

**1b.** Why do you think she brings up these matters? (Undoubtedly to soften Cyrano for the favor she wants to ask and perhaps to delay the uncomfortable moment of confessing her love.)

**2b.** Why do you think his hand feels feverish? (He is growing very excited because her hints convince him that she loves him.)

AT A GLANCE
- Roxane confesses she loves Christian.
- Cyrano is heartbroken.

**1 CHARACTERIZATION**

Cyrano's self-evaluation is very clear: All the wonderful inner qualities Roxane attributes to Christian do not warn Cyrano that she is not talking about him. But when she says that her beloved is "handsome," he knows that she has been describing another man.

**2 STYLE: UNDERSTATEMENT**

With characteristic bravado, Cyrano belittles his considerable physical wound in order to mask his even greater spiritual wound. The "twinge" from a "scratch" is in reality a deep wound from a serious blow. His bravery in the face of his disappointment commands respect.

CYRANO. Ah!...

ROXANE. His face shines with wit and intelligence. He's proud, noble, young, fearless, handsome....

CYRANO. [*Standing up, with a stricken expression.*] Handsome!

ROXANE. What is it? What's the matter?

CYRANO. Nothing....It's...it's...[*Shows her his hand, with a smile.*] It's only a twinge of pain from this little scratch.

ROXANE. Well, I love him, even though I've never seen him anywhere but in the theater.

CYRANO. You've never spoken to each other?

ROXANE. Only with our eyes.

CYRANO. Then how do you know he loves you?

ROXANE. ...Talkative acquaintances have told me....

CYRANO. You say he's a Cadet?

ROXANE. Yes, in the Guards.

CYRANO. His name?

ROXANE. Baron Christian de Neuvillette.

CYRANO. Neuvillette? There's no Cadet by that name.

ROXANE. There is now. He began serving only this morning, under Captain Carbon de Castel-Jaloux.[7]

———————

7. **Carbon de Castel-Jaloux** [kär bon′ də kas tel′ zha loo′]

*Cyrano de Bergerac, Act II*   **407**

---

## GUIDED READING

### LITERAL QUESTION

**1a.** What word does Roxane say just before Cyrano realizes that she loves another man? *(handsome)*

### INFERENTIAL QUESTION

**1b.** What does his reaction to this word show about Cyrano's self-image? (He knows that he could never be considered handsome. He is quite realistic about his appearance but is nonetheless pained by it. The fact that the woman he adores loves a *handsome* man makes Cyrano's love seem hopeless to him—physical appearance is the one area in which he cannot compete with another man.)

- Roxane tells Cyrano that she's worried about Christian getting into duels and asks Cyrano to protect him.
- Cyrano agrees.
- Roxane leaves, and Rague- neau and his friends return.

## 1 THEME

Cyrano's observation points up one of the play's principal themes—the idea that a person's inner and outer qualities do not always correspond. Roxane, with less insight, insists that in Chris- tian's case external beauty must reflect a beautiful mind.

## 2 CHARACTERIZATION

Roxane is quick to anger when contradicted. This behavior sug- gests that she is perhaps slightly spoiled, a bit petulant—a woman used to having her own way.

## 3 PLOT: RISING ACTION

Roxane extracts a promise from Cyrano to protect Christian, thus setting in motion an unusual alli- ance.

## 4 DIALOGUE

Roxane's self-centeredness is apparent as she suddenly real- izes she has monopolized the talk and makes a gesture toward Cyrano. But unable to focus on any concerns but her own, she immediately says, *Tell him to write to me.*

## 5 IRONY

What Cyrano actually means here is this: "The courage I showed last night in fighting off a hundred men is nothing to what is required now, to hide my dis- appointment that you don't love me." He knows, of course, that Roxane will assume that he is re- ferring to yet another act of phys- ical courage.

---

CYRANO. You've lost your heart so quickly! But, my poor girl . . .

THE DUENNA. [*Opening the door in the background.*] I've eaten all the pastry, Monsieur de Bergerac!

CYRANO. Then read the poetry on the bags! [*The DUENNA disappears.*] My poor girl, you're so fond of fine words and gracious wit—what if he should prove to be an uncultured savage?

ROXANE. Impossible. He has the hair of one of d'Urfé's[8] heroes!

CYRANO. His speech may be as crude as his hair is elegant.

ROXANE. No, there's delicacy in everything he says. I feel it!

CYRANO. Yes, all words are delicate when they come from lips adorned with a shapely mustache. . . . But what if he's a fool?

ROXANE. [*Stamping her foot.*] Then I'll die! There, are you satisfied?

CYRANO. [*After a time.*] You brought me here to tell me this? I confess I don't quite understand why.

ROXANE. It's because someone terrified me yesterday by telling me that most of you in your company are Gascons, and . . .

CYRANO. And that we always provoke a duel with any newcomer who gains the favor of being admitted among us without being a Gascon? Is that what you were told?

ROXANE. Yes. You can imagine how I trembled for him when I heard it! But when I saw you yesterday, great and invincible, punishing that scoundrel and holding all those brutes at bay, I said to myself, "Everyone fears him. If he were willing to . . ."

---

8. **D'Urfé's** [dur fāz']: Honoré d'Urfé (1567–1625), French novelist whose heroes were models of chivalry.

---

CYRANO. Very well, I'll protect your little baron.

ROXANE. Oh, I knew you would! I've always had such tender affection for you. . . .

CYRANO. Yes, yes.

ROXANE. You'll be his friend?

CYRANO. I will.

ROXANE. And he'll never have a duel?

CYRANO. No. I promise.

ROXANE. I knew I was right to like you so much! And now I must go. But you haven't told me about your battle last night. It must have been in- credible! . . . Tell him to write to me. [*Throws him a kiss.*] Oh, I love you!

CYRANO. Yes, yes.

ROXANE. A hundred men against you? Well, good-by. You're my best friend!

CYRANO. Yes, yes.

ROXANE. Tell him to write! . . . A hundred men! You'll tell me about it some other time; I can't stay now. A hundred men! What courage!

CYRANO. [*Bowing to her.*] Oh, I've done better since then.

[*She leaves. He remains motionless, looking down at the floor. A silence, then the door opens and* RAGUENEAU *puts in his head.*]

RAGUENEAU. May we come back in?

CYRANO. [*Without moving.*] Yes.

[RAGUENEAU *signals to his friends and they come in. At the same time* CARBON DE CASTEL- JALOUX, *dressed as a Captain of the Guards, appears at the door in the background and makes broad gestures when he sees* CYRANO.]

CARBON. Here he is!

CYRANO. [*Looking up.*] Captain!

---

## GUIDED READING

### LITERAL QUESTION

**1a.** What words of affection does Roxane address to Cyrano after he has promised to protect Christian? *(I've always had such tender affection for you . . . ; I knew I was right to like you so much!; Oh, I love you!; You're my best friend!)*

### INFERENTIAL QUESTION

**1b.** How do you think these comments make him feel? *(They pain him: Although her words are exactly what he wants to hear, he sees that she means them in a very superficial way.)*

CARBON. [*Exultant.*] Our hero! We know all about it! Thirty of my Cadets are here!

CYRANO. [*Stepping back.*] But...

CARBON. [*Rubbing his hands together.*] Here they come!

A CADET. [*Entering.*] Bravo!

SEVERAL CADETS. [*Entering.*] Let's all embrace him!

LE BRET. [*Entering and hurrying to* CYRANO.] Everyone wants to see you! There's a wild crowd led by those who were with you last night....

A BURGHER. [*Entering, followed by a group.*] Sir, all the fashionable people in Paris are coming here!

[*Outside, the street is filled with people. Sedan chairs and carriages are stopping.*]

LE BRET. [*Softly, smiling at* CYRANO.] Have you seen Roxane?

CYRANO. [*Sharply.*] Quiet!

THE CROWD. [*Shouting from outside.*] Cyrano!

[*A throng bursts into the shop. Jostling. Cheers.*]

RAGUENEAU. [*Standing on a table.*] They're invading my shop! They're breaking everything! It's magnificent!

**1** PEOPLE. [*Around* CYRANO.] My friend!—My friend!

CYRANO. I didn't have so many friends yesterday!

LE BRET. [*Delighted.*] What a triumph!

MARQUIS. Sir, I'd like to introduce you to some ladies who are outside in my carriage.

CYRANO. [*Coldly.*] And who will introduce me to *you?*

**2** LE BRET. [*Surprised.*] What's the matter with you?

CYRANO. Quiet! Enough!

[*Movement, then the disorder of the crowd begins to subside.* DE GUICHE *enters, escorted by* OFFICERS, *then* CUIGY, BRISSAILLE, *and the* OFFICERS *who left with* CYRANO *at the end of Act I.* CUIGY *hurries to* CYRANO.]

CUIGY. [*To* CYRANO.] Monsieur de Guiche... [*Murmurs. Everyone stands aside.*]...has come with a message from Marshal de Gassion![9]

DE GUICHE. [*Bowing to* CYRANO.] The Marshal has just learned of your latest exploit and wishes me to express his admiration to you.

THE CROWD. Bravo!

LE BRET. [*Aside, to* CYRANO, *who appears to be distracted.*] Aren't you going to...

CYRANO. Quiet!

**3** LE BRET. You seem to be suffering!

CYRANO. [*Starting, then quickly drawing himself erect.*] In front of all these people? [*His mustache bristles; he throws out his chest.*] I, suffering? You'll see!

DE GUICHE. [*To whom* CUIGY *has been whispering.*] Your career is already rich in noble exploits. You serve with those wild Gascons, don't you?

CYRANO. Yes, I'm a Cadet in the Guards.

A CADET. [*With fierce pride.*] He's one of us!

DE GUICHE. [*Looking at the Gascons grouped behind* CYRANO.] Ah! Then all these haughty-looking gentlemen are the famous...

CARBON. Cyrano!

CYRANO. Yes, Captain?

---

9. **Marshal de Gassion** [mär shal′ də gas yōn′]

*Cyrano de Bergerac, Act II* **409**

- The Captain of the Guards and several Cadets arrive, praising Cyrano's exploit the night before.
- Le Bret enters and says a crowd is on its way to praise Cyrano.
- Le Bret notices Cyrano's pain, but Cyrano is too proud to let anyone else see his suffering.

**1 THEME**

Cyrano shows his innate integrity, refusing to be flattered by the adulation of the fashionable world, which he knows is fickle.

**2 PLOT: CONFLICT**

Although Le Bret is a loving and admiring friend to Cyrano, his personality provides an external conflict that Cyrano must deal with. His more tolerant, practical personality contrasts with Cyrano's uncompromising idealism.

**3 CHARACTERIZATION**

Le Bret is characterized as sensitive and caring: He notices Cyrano's pain. Cyrano's response shows his pride: He does not want anyone to know he is suffering. Rather than express his hurt, he masks his pain as anger and bitterness.

---

## GUIDED READING

### LITERAL QUESTIONS

**1a.** What does Le Bret say after Cyrano comments that he didn't have so many friends yesterday? (*What a triumph!*)

**2a.** What does Le Bret notice about Cyrano's feelings? (*Cyrano seems to be suffering.*)

### INFERENTIAL QUESTIONS

**1b.** Why is this triumph particularly ironic for Cyrano at this time? (He has just had the greatest defeat he can imagine: Roxane does not love him.)

**2b.** What does this observation tell you about Le Bret's relationship with Cyrano? (He is observant and knows Cyrano's moods well. He is able to see below the surface into Cyrano's real feelings.)

- De Guiche arrives and offers Cyrano his patronage; Cyrano refuses.
- De Guiche admits to having hired the men Cyrano defeated.
- Cyrano insults him, and he threatens Cyrano.

**1 BACKGROUND**

Cyrano's "introduction" of the Cadets is a spontaneous *Gasconade*, or formalized hyperboasting. He displays his wit and skill in a parody of the form, by boasting of their humble birth and ability to quarrel and lie.

**2 BACKGROUND**

At the time of the play, the French court was complex and competitive, with courtiers vying for the king's favor. Patrons used their influence at court to protect and advance their protégés in social, political, or cultural pursuits.

**3 THEME**

The importance of language, a major preoccupation of the play, is underscored here. It is significant that the one temptation Cyrano nearly succumbs to is De Guiche's offer to promote his writing.

**4 ALLUSION**

De Guiche's allusion to *Don Quixote* underlines Cyrano's idealism. Where Quixote was devoted to the chivalric code, Cyrano believes in his own integrity and independence.

---

CARBON. Since all the men of my company are here, please introduce them to the Count.

CYRANO. [*Taking two steps toward* DE GUICHE *and pointing to the* CADETS.]

1
These are the stouthearted Gascon Cadets
Of Carbon de Castel-Jaloux;
They fight over trifles and shamelessly lie;
These are the stouthearted Gascon Cadets!
Their knowledge of heraldry can't be
surpassed;
No plowman can claim nobler birth;
These are the stouthearted Gascon Cadets
Of Carbon de Castel-Jaloux.

DE GUICHE. [*Casually seated in an armchair that* RAGUENEAU *has quickly brought for him.*]
2 Poets are a fashionable luxury these days. Would you like to become one of my followers?

CYRANO. No, sir, I prefer to follow no one.

DE GUICHE. My uncle, Cardinal Richelieu, was amused by your dashing combat yesterday. I'm willing to help you with him, if you like.

LE BRET. [*Dazzled.*] Ah!

DE GUICHE. You've written a play, I believe....

LE BRET. [*Aside, to* CYRANO.] Your *Agrippine*[10] will soon be performed, my friend!

DE GUICHE. Take it to him.

3 CYRANO. [*Tempted and rather pleased.*] Really, I . . .

DE GUICHE. He knows a great deal about the theater. He'll rewrite a few lines....

CYRANO. [*Whose face has immediately darkened.*] Impossible, sir; my blood curdles at the thought of having a single comma changed.

DE GUICHE. But when a piece of writing pleases him, he pays very well for it.

---

10. *Agrippine* [a grə pēn']: *La Mort d'Agrippine* (*The Death of Agrippine*) was a play written by the real Cyrano.

**410**   *Drama*

---

CYRANO. He couldn't pay as well as I do. When I write something that I like, I reward the author by reciting it to myself.

DE GUICHE. You're a proud man.

CYRANO. Have you noticed that?

[*A* CADET *enters, holding his sword aloft to display the hats that are spitted on it. They are all shabby and misshapen, with bedraggled plumes.*]

THE CADET. Look, Cyrano, at the strange feathered game we took in the street this morning! The men you routed seem to have run away too fast for their hats to follow them!

CUIGY. The man who hired those cowardly brutes must be in a rage today!

BRISSAILLE. Do you know who did it?

DE GUICHE. I did. [*The laughter ceases.*] I hired them for a task that one doesn't do oneself: punishing a drunken rhymester.

[*Uncomfortable silence.* CYRANO *takes the sword on which the hats are spitted and lowers it in a gesture of homage to* DE GUICHE, *making them all slide off onto the floor at his feet.*]

CYRANO. Sir, would you like to take these back to your friends?

DE GUICHE. [*In a peremptory tone, standing up.*] Bring my sedan chair immediately. I'm leaving. [*With a smile, having regained his self-control.*]
4 Have you read *Don Quixote?*[11]

CYRANO. Yes, I have, and I take off my hat to you in the name of that scatterbrained hero.

DE GUICHE. You would do well to meditate on the chapter concerning windmills.

---

11. *Don Quixote* [don' kē hō'tā]: tragicomical novel by the Spanish writer Miguel de Cervantes (1547–1616). Don Quixote, an idealistic knight, mistakes windmills for giants and is knocked from his horse during a charge against them.

---

## GUIDED READING

**LITERAL QUESTION**

**1a.** Why does Cyrano decide not to show his play to Cardinal Richelieu after all? (De Guiche indicates that the Cardinal would rewrite it before helping Cyrano get it performed.)

**INFERENTIAL QUESTION**

**1b.** Why doesn't Cyrano want "a single comma changed?" (Part of his independence and belief in his own talent is the feeling that he wants his play, if ever performed, to be entirely his own work.)

CYRANO. [Bowing.] Chapter Thirteen.

DE GUICHE. When one attacks them, their great arms often hurl one down into the mud!

CYRANO. Or up into the stars!

[DE GUICHE leaves. The CROWD leaves.]

CYRANO. [Mockingly bowing to those who are leaving without daring to bid him good-by.] Gentlemen.... Gentlemen.... Gentlemen....

LE BRET. [Coming back from the door and throwing up his arms in despair.] This time you've outdone yourself! You shatter every opportunity that comes your way! You'll have to admit that you go too far!

CYRANO. Yes, I go too far.

LE BRET. [Triumphantly.] You do admit it!

CYRANO. But for the sake of principle, and to set an example, too, I feel that it's good to go too far in that direction.

LE BRET. If you would only soften your haughty spirit a little, fortune and glory would...

CYRANO. But what would I have to do? Cover myself with the protection of some powerful patron? Imitate the ivy that licks the bark of a tall tree while entwining itself around its trunk, and make my way upward by guile, rather than climbing by my own strength? No, thank you. Dedicate poems to financiers, as so many others do? Change myself into a buffoon in the hope of seeing a minister give me a condescending smile? No, thank you. Swallow insults every day? Crawl till the skin of my belly is rubbed raw? Dirty my knees and make my spine as limber as an eel's? No, thank you. Develop the art of sitting on both sides of a fence at once? Pay for an ounce of favor with a ton of flattery? No, thank you. Be always scheming and afraid of schemes? Like paying visits better than writing poetry? Make humble requests? Seek introductions to useful people? No, thank you! No! No! I prefer to lead a different kind of life. I sing, dream, laugh, and go where I please, alone and free. My eyes see clearly and my voice is strong. I'm quarrelsome or benign as it suits my pleasure, always ready to fight a duel or write a poem at the drop of a hat. I dream of flying to the moon but give no thought to fame or fortune. I write only what comes out of myself, and I make it my modest rule to be satisfied with whatever flowers, fruit, or even leaves I gather, as long as they're from my own garden. I scorn to be like parasitic ivy, even though I'm not an oak. I may not rise very high, but I'll climb alone!

LE BRET. Be alone if you like, but why have everyone against you? How did you acquire that appalling mania for making enemies wherever you go?

CYRANO. Let's call it my vice. It pleases me to displease. I love to be hated.

LE BRET. [After a silence, passing his arm under CYRANO's.] Proclaim your pride and bitterness loudly to the world, but to me speak softly and tell me simply that she doesn't love you.

CYRANO. [Sharply.] Stop! Enough!

[CHRISTIAN has entered some time earlier and mingled with the CADETS, who have not spoken to him. He has finally sat down alone at a small table where LISE is now serving him.]

A CADET. [Seated at a table upstage, with a glass in his hand.] Cyrano! [CYRANO looks around.] Will you tell us your story now?

CYRANO. Not now. A little later. [He and LE BRET walk upstage, arm in arm, talking quietly together.]

THE CADET. [Standing up and coming downstage.] The story of Cyrano's combat will be the best lesson [Stops at CHRISTIAN's table.]...for this timid apprentice.

*Cyrano de Bergerac, Act II* **411**

## AT A GLANCE

- Le Bret again scolds Cyrano for his inability to compromise.
- Le Bret guesses that Cyrano has been disappointed by Roxane.

### 1 DIALOGUE

Here Cyrano shows his intimate knowledge of *Don Quixote*, by citing the exact chapter of the windmill scene. It reveals Cyrano's erudition but, more important, implies his identification with Cervantes' hero. Once again, he bests De Guiche by turning an intended insult into a compliment.

### 2 THEME

Cyrano's burst of language eloquently formulates a major theme of the play: the price of seeking fame and fortune on the world's terms. For Cyrano, the price is too high.

### 3 STYLE: FIGURATIVE LANGUAGE

To contrast his life of idealism and independence with the life of compromise and flattery De Guiche represents, Cyrano uses metaphors from the natural world, describing what he feels is a more genuine way of life.

### 4 DIALOGUE

Le Bret is again the understanding friend. He sees that this unusual—even for Cyrano—display of intransigence results from a broken heart. He asks Cyrano to put aside his pride and show his hurt in private.

## GUIDED READING

### LITERAL QUESTION

**1a.** What does De Guiche tell Cyrano that windmills can do, and what does Cyrano answer? (He says they can hurl one down into the mud, and Cyrano rejoins: *Or up into the stars!*)

### INFERENTIAL QUESTION

**1b.** What do you think their comments mean? (De Guiche threatens Cyrano by indicating that if he sticks to his principles too strongly and insults people, he will be destroyed. Cyrano argues that adherence to principles can elevate one spiritually.)

- The Cadets tell Christian never to mention Cyrano's nose.
- Christian tries to prove his courage by provoking Cyrano.
- Cyrano tells of his exploits while Christian interrupts with comments about noses.

### 1 STYLE: HUMOR

In order to impress their lesson on Christian, the Cadets use exaggeration. To take out a handkerchief would be to take out his shroud: That object's unfortunate association with noses would cause Cyrano to kill. The Cadets' boisterous style reveals another side of Cyrano—his exuberant joy in excess.

### 2 PLOT: RISING ACTION

The Captain's advice to Christian on how to prove his courage provides important motivation.

### 3 CHARACTERIZATION

In a kind of verbal duel, Christian, who has denied his facility with words, very cleverly interrupts Cyrano, interjecting phrases using the word *nose*. Perhaps his estimation of his verbal abilities is too modest.

### 4 PLOT: CONFLICT

The dialogue and stage directions clearly show Cyrano's inner conflict. He allows no one to insult his nose, yet he can't fight with Christian because he promised Roxane to protect him.

---

CHRISTIAN. [*Looking up.*] Apprentice?

ANOTHER CADET. Yes, you sickly northerner.

CHRISTIAN. Sickly?

FIRST CADET. [*Banteringly.*] Monsieur de Neuvillette, it's time for you to learn something. There's a certain object that we all avoid naming as scrupulously as we would refrain from mentioning rope in the house of a man whose father had been hanged.

CHRISTIAN. What is it?

SECOND CADET. [*With majestic authority.*] Look at me! [*Puts his finger to his nose three times, mysteriously.*] Do you understand?

CHRISTIAN. I think so. You must mean...

THIRD CADET. Sh! You must never speak that word! [*Points to* CYRANO, *who is still talking upstage with* LE BRET.] If you do, you'll have *him* to deal with!

FOURTH CADET. [*In a hollow tone, standing up after having crawled under the table.*] The slightest allusion to that protuberance brings an untimely death!

1 FIFTH CADET. [*Putting his hand on* CHRISTIAN's *shoulder.*] One word is enough! Even a gesture! If you take out your handkerchief, you've taken out your shroud! [*Silence. The* CADETS *are all around* CHRISTIAN, *looking at him. He stands up and goes to* CARBON DE CASTEL-JALOUX.]

CHRISTIAN. Captain!

CARBON. [*Turning around and looking him up and down.*] Yes?

2 CHRISTIAN. What should one do when southerners become too boastful?

CARBON. Prove to them that a northerner can be courageous. [*Turns his back on* CHRISTIAN.]

CHRISTIAN. Thank you.

412   *Drama*

---

FIRST CADET. [*To* CYRANO.] Now tell us your story!

ALL. Your story!

CYRANO. [*Comes toward them.*] My story?... [*They all draw up their stools and group themselves around him, straining their necks forward.* CHRISTIAN *has straddled a chair.*] Well, I was walking alone to meet them. The moon was gleaming like a big silver watch in the sky when suddenly some heavenly hand slipped it into a 3 pocket of clouds. The sky was black as pitch and there were no lights in the street. I couldn't see...

CHRISTIAN. Beyond the end of your nose.

[*Silence. The* CADETS *all stand up slowly, looking at* CYRANO *in terror. He has stopped short, dumbfounded. Several moments of tense waiting go by before he finally speaks.*]

CYRANO. Who is this man?

A CADET. [*In a low voice.*] He came to us only this morning.

CYRANO. [*Taking a step toward* CHRISTIAN.] This morning?

CARBON. [*In a low voice.*] His name is Baron de Neuvil—

4 CYRANO. [*Quickly, stopping.*] Oh! [*His face takes on an expression of shock, then anger, and he makes a movement as though to attack* CHRISTIAN.] I...[*He controls himself and speaks dully.*] Very well....As I was saying...[*With a burst of rage in his voice.*] Mordious! [*Continues in a natural tone.*] It was so dark that I couldn't see anything. [*The* CADETS *are amazed. They sit down again, staring at him.*] I walked on, thinking that for the sake of a poor drunkard I was about to anger some powerful nobleman who would surely...

CHRISTIAN. Resent your nosiness. [*The* CADETS *all stand up again.* CHRISTIAN *tilts his chair.*]

---

## GUIDED READING

### LITERAL QUESTION

**1a.** How does Cyrano react when he inquires about the man who is insulting his nose and discovers that man is Christian? (He is angry but then remembers his promise to Roxane and gains control of himself.)

### INFERENTIAL QUESTION

**1b.** How do you think Cyrano would have reacted if it had not been Christian who insulted his nose? (Because he obviously has to exert control, it is clear he would have punished any other offender in some way.)

CYRANO. [*Choking.*]...who would surely bear a grudge against me, and that I was rashly putting...

CHRISTIAN. Your nose into...

CYRANO. ...myself into a bad situation, because that nobleman might...

CHRISTIAN. Look down his nose at you.

CYRANO. [*Wiping sweat from his forehead.*]... be able to make things a bit difficult for me. But I said to myself, "Come, Gascon, do what has to be done. Onward, Cyrano!" A moment later, someone...

CHRISTIAN. Nosed you out in the darkness.

CYRANO. ...lunged at me with his sword. I parried the thrust and suddenly found myself...

CHRISTIAN. Nose to nose...

CYRANO. [*Rushing toward him.*] No! By all the saints in heaven, I'll...[*The Gascons crowd forward to see better, but as soon as he is in front of* CHRISTIAN *he again controls himself and continues his story.*] I found myself facing a hundred shouting brutes, all smelling...

CHRISTIAN. With their noses, of course.

CYRANO. [*Smiling wanly.*]...of onions and cheap wine. I plunged into the midst of them...

CHRISTIAN. Nose first!

CYRANO. ...and immediately cut down two of them. As I was attacking a third, I saw a sword...

CHRISTIAN. Right under your nose!

CYRANO. [*Bellowing.*] Out! All of you! Get out!

[*The* CADETS *all hurry toward the doors.*]

FIRST CADET. The tiger has finally awakened!

CYRANO. Leave me alone with this man!

SECOND CADET. He'll soon be turned into mincemeat!

THIRD CADET. It makes me tremble just to think of what's going to happen to him!

FOURTH CADET. [*Closing the door on the right as he goes out.*] It will be something horrifying!

[CHRISTIAN *and* CYRANO *are left standing face to face. They look at each other for a moment.*]

CYRANO. Embrace me!

CHRISTIAN. Sir...

CYRANO. You're a brave man.

CHRISTIAN. Perhaps, but...

CYRANO. Very brave. I'm glad to know that.

CHRISTIAN. Would you mind telling me...

CYRANO. Embrace me. I'm her brother.

CHRISTIAN. Whose brother?

CYRANO. *Hers!*

CHRISTIAN. Hers?

CYRANO. Roxane's!

CHRISTIAN. [*Hurrying toward him.*] Oh! You? Her brother?

CYRANO. Yes, or almost. A brotherly cousin.

CHRISTIAN. And she's told you...

CYRANO. Everything!

CHRISTIAN. Does she love me?

CYRANO. Perhaps!

CHRISTIAN. [*Taking his hands.*] How happy I am to know you!

CYRANO. That's a rather sudden change of feeling.

CHRISTIAN. Forgive me....

*Cyrano de Bergerac, Act II*   **413**

## AT A GLANCE

- Cyrano's story continues, along with Christian's comments.
- Cyrano, furious, asks to be left alone with Christian.
- The Cadets await disaster.
- Cyrano confesses his relationship to Roxane, and they embrace.

### 1 STYLE: FIGURATIVE LANGUAGE

A metaphor comparing Cyrano to a sleeping tiger that has awakened is appropriate. The Cadets know Cyrano to be fierce with anyone who insults his nose, yet he does nothing. Finally, he asks to be left alone with the offender.

### 2 DRAMATIC IRONY

Outside the door, the Cadets await disaster. Dramatic irony results from the fact that the audience knows that Cyrano cannot duel with Christian because of his promise to Roxane.

### 3 CHARACTERIZATION

Cyrano's nobility of character is shown by this comment. Even toward his rival in love, he can be generous—he is glad that Christian is brave, because he would hate to think of Roxane in love with a coward.

## GUIDED READING

### LITERAL QUESTIONS

**1a.** What doubts does Cyrano express about becoming involved in the fight with De Guiche's assassins? (He says perhaps he is rash, and De Guiche could make things difficult for him.)

**2a.** How does Cyrano answer when Christian asks if Roxane loves him? (*Perhaps!*)

### INFERENTIAL QUESTIONS

**1b.** What do these doubts show you about Cyrano's practical judgment? (Perhaps it is keener than he sometimes lets on. Whenever Le Bret expresses similar concerns, Cyrano argues, but apparently he has the same doubts at times.)

**2b.** Why does he give this answer when Roxane has said she loves Christian? (He respects Roxane's confidences. Also, he is indulging himself by toying with Christian.)

- Christian and Cyrano admire each other's strong points.
- Christian despairs at Roxane's expectation of a letter from him.

### 1 CHARACTERIZATION

Christian and Cyrano admire each other. Again, this exchange shows Cyrano's noble nature: He can admire his rival and concede his handsomeness. And Christian proves himself big enough to apologize for his insults.

### 2 DIALOGUE

Cyrano makes the point that Christian's insults were clever, despite Christian's claims that he is a fool.

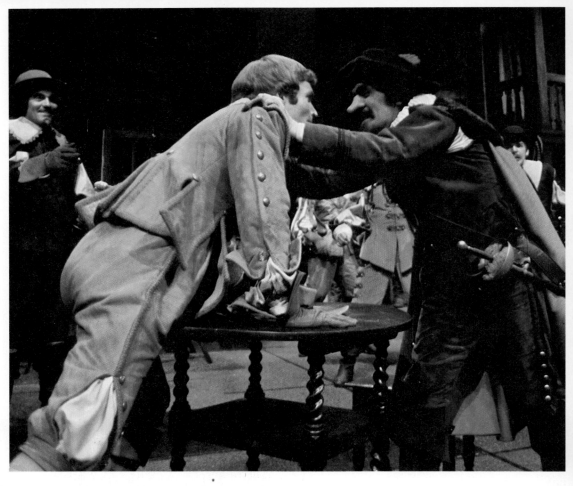

1 CYRANO. [*Looks at him and puts his hands on his shoulders.*] It's true: you *are* a handsome devil!

CHRISTIAN. If you only knew, sir, how much I admire you!

CYRANO. But all those ''noses'' you gave me....

CHRISTIAN. I take them all back!

CYRANO. Roxane expects to receive a letter from you this evening.

CHRISTIAN. Oh, no!

CYRANO. What?...

CHRISTIAN. If I write to her, she'll never want to see me again.

CYRANO. Why?

2 CHRISTIAN. Because I'm such a fool that I could die of shame!

CYRANO. No, you're not, since you've said it yourself. Besides, you didn't attack me like a fool.

CHRISTIAN. Words come easily to anyone when

**414** *Drama*

---

## *GUIDED READING*

### LITERAL QUESTION

**1a.** What does Cyrano reply when Christian claims he is a fool? *(No, you're not, since you've said it yourself.)*

### INFERENTIAL QUESTION

**1b.** What do you think he means by that? *(He means that those who are truly foolish never acknowledge it.)*

he wants to pick a quarrel. I may have a certain quick, soldierly wit, but with women I'm always at a loss for anything to say. Their eyes show interest when I pass by, but...

CYRANO. Aren't their hearts also interested when you stop?

CHRISTIAN. No! It's all too clear to me that I'm one of those men who don't know how to speak of love.

CYRANO. I have the feeling that if my features had been shaped more harmoniously, I would have been one of those men who *do* know how to speak of love.

1 CHRISTIAN. Ah, if only I could express myself gracefully!

CYRANO. If only I had a handsome face!

CHRISTIAN. Roxane is so elegant and refined—I'm sure to disillusion her!

CYRANO. [*Looking at* CHRISTIAN.] If I had such an interpreter to speak for my soul...

CHRISTIAN. [*Despairingly.*] I need eloquence, and I have none!

2 CYRANO. [*Abruptly.*] I'll lend you mine! Lend me your conquering physical charm, and together we'll form a romantic hero!

CHRISTIAN. What do you mean?

CYRANO. Do you feel capable of repeating what I tell you every day?

CHRISTIAN. Are you suggesting...

CYRANO. Roxane won't be disillusioned! Together, we can win her heart! Will you let my soul pass from my leather jerkin[12] and lodge beneath your embroidered doublet?

CHRISTIAN. But Cyrano...

---

12. **jerkin:** short, close-fitting coat or jacket, often sleeveless, worn in the 1500s and 1600s.

CYRANO. Are you willing?

3 CHRISTIAN. You frighten me! Your eyes are shining....

CYRANO. Will you do it?

CHRISTIAN. Would it please you so much?

CYRANO. [*Ardently.*] It would...[*Restrains himself and adopts a more detached tone.*] It would amuse me! It's an experiment that would tempt any poet. Shall we complete each other? We'll walk together: you in the light, I in the shadows. I'll make you eloquent, you'll make me handsome.

CHRISTIAN. But I must write her a letter without delay! I'll never be able to...

CYRANO. [*Taking out the letter he has written.*] Here's your letter!

CHRISTIAN. What...

CYRANO. It lacks only the name and address. You can send it as it is. Don't worry, it's well written.

CHRISTIAN. Had you already...

4 CYRANO. I always have a letter in my pocket, written to some imaginary lady, because I'm one of those men whose only sweethearts are dreams breathed into the bubble of a name. You can change my fantasy to reality. You'll see that in this letter my feelings are all the better expressed for being insincere! Here, take it.

CHRISTIAN. Won't some things in it have to be changed? How can it fit Roxane?

CYRANO. You can count on vanity to make her think it was written for her!

CHRISTIAN. Ah, my friend!...[*He throws himself into* CYRANO'*s arms. They stand embracing each other.*]

A CADET. [*Pushing the door ajar.*] Nothing....A deathly silence....I'm afraid to look....[*Puts his head through the doorway.*] What!

*Cyrano de Bergerac, Act II*  **415**

## AT A GLANCE

- Cyrano proposes that he and Christian combine forces—Christian's face, Cyrano's wit—to win Roxane.
- Cyrano gives Christian the letter he wrote to pass on as his own.

1 **PLOT: CONFLICT**

The exchange shows the internal conflicts of the men: Cyrano longs for a handsome face, whereas Christian laments his lack of eloquence. They share the same external conflict: how to win Roxane's love, given their inadequacies.

2 **PLOT: RISING ACTION**

Cyrano proposes an idea that becomes central to the play's plot. In addition, the fact that Cyrano's soul joins forces with Christian's face further develops the theme of inner vs. outer beauty.

3 **CHARACTERIZATION**

This alliance is more important to Cyrano than to Christian. This exchange evokes pathos, for it emphasizes Cyrano's desperation and ardent love: He cannot express his love without Christian's handsome exterior.

4 **STYLE: IRONY**

Cyrano paints himself as a lover of fantasy women rather than those he knows. He claims his love is not deep or sincere. The irony is that the opposite is true; in fact, the superficial infatuation he describes seems more like Christian's and Roxane's love.

---

## *GUIDED READING*

### LITERAL QUESTION

**1a.** What does Cyrano reply when Christian asks, "Would it please you so much?" (He says it would amuse him as an experiment.)

### INFERENTIAL QUESTION

**1b.** Why do you think he replies so carelessly when moments before he has been intensely interested? (He restrains himself so Christian will not guess his real reason for wanting a partnership: He wants to be able to express his love without being ridiculed.)

## AT A GLANCE

- The cadets return to find Cyrano embracing Christian and are amazed at his docility.
- Lise's musketeer insults Cyrano's nose. Cyrano slaps him.

## REFLECTING ON ACT II

How would you compare the love Christian has for Roxane to the love Cyrano has for her? (Cyrano's love is deeper, as it is based on real knowledge of her good and bad points and puts her happiness above his own.)

## STUDY QUESTIONS

1. She tells him she loves Christian; he promises he will protect Christian.
2. offers him patronage; no
3. taunts Cyrano with puns about his nose
4. Cyrano will provide the words; Christian will deliver them.
5. Disguising his disappointment that she loves Christian requires more courage.
6. She is manipulative; she charms him into getting what she wants; Roxane seems shallow; loves Christian for his handsomeness.
7. thinks everyone can be bought; values art and integrity above comfort, advancement
8. He loves Roxane, sees a chance to express his feelings to her, hopes she will love his eloquence
9. It is probably impractical: Both risk rejection if found out; neither will know if Roxane might have loved him for himself.

## LITERARY FOCUS

1. Cyrano loves Roxane and hopes for her love. We know that Cyrano thinks Roxane may love him, but she does not. We share Cyrano's hope and disappointment.
2. The audience knows that Cyrano has promised to protect Christian and therefore will not fight.

---

**ALL THE CADETS.** [*Entering and seeing* CYRANO *and* CHRISTIAN *embracing each other.*] Oh!—Ah!

**A CADET.** I can't believe my eyes! [*Consternation.*]

**THE MUSKETEER.** [*Jeeringly.*] Well, look at that!

**CARBON.** Our demon has become as gentle as a lamb! When he's struck on one nostril, he turns the other!

**THE MUSKETEER.** He lets people talk about his nose now? [*Calls out to* LISE, *with a triumphant expression.*] Lise! Watch this! [*Approaches* CYRANO *and insolently stares at his nose.*] What's that long thing on your face, sir? It reminds me of something, but I can't recall what it is.

**CYRANO.** Then let me help you by jarring your memory! [*Slaps him. The* CADETS *are delighted to see* CYRANO *behaving like himself again. They caper joyfully.*]

---

## STUDY QUESTIONS

### Recalling

1. Briefly relate Cyrano's conversation with Roxane in the beginning of Act II. What news does she give him, and what promise does he make to her?
2. Describe De Guiche's offer to Cyrano. What is Cyrano's response?
3. What does Christian do to prove himself to the Cadets?
4. Relate the terms of the private agreement between Cyrano and Christian concerning Roxane.

### Interpreting

5. In referring to his triumph over a hundred men, Cyrano tells Roxane, "Oh, I've done better since then." What does he mean?
6. What is your impression of Roxane from her conversation with Cyrano? How does she treat her cousin? Do you think she deserves his love? Explain.
7. What does his offer to Cyrano reveal about De Guiche's attitude toward other people? What does Cyrano's refusal reveal about *his* attitude toward himself and his art?
8. Why do you think Cyrano makes his agreement with Christian? What might he hope to gain?

### Extending

9. Do you think the agreement between Cyrano and Christian is practical? What problems do you foresee in it?

## LITERARY FOCUS

### Dramatic Irony

**Dramatic irony** is a form of irony that occurs when a character acts without knowing an important piece of information that the audience knows—for example, if the audience knows that a character is in danger, but the character does not know. Dramatic irony can occur in both fiction and drama, but it is an especially effective way of building tension in drama.

### Thinking About Dramatic Irony

1. Explain the dramatic irony in the scene between Cyrano and Roxane in the pastry shop. What piece of information does the audience know that a character on stage lacks? How does dramatic irony add to the tension in this scene?
2. In what way is Christian's attempt to provoke Cyrano in front of the Cadets another instance of dramatic irony?

# ACT III

*A little square in the Marais[1] quarter of Paris. A few weeks later.*

1 [ROXANE's *house and the wall of its garden are seen, overflowing with foliage. Above the door, a window and a balcony garlanded with quivering, drooping jasmine. As the curtain rises, the* DUENNA *is seated on the bench. Beside her stands* RAGUENEAU, *dressed in livery.[2] He is finishing a story and wiping his eyes.*]

RAGUENEAU. . . . and then she ran off with a musketeer! Alone and ruined, I felt I had nothing to live for, so I tried to hang myself, but Monsieur de Bergerac came in and cut me down. Then he offered me this position as his cousin's steward.

THE DUENNA. But how did you come to be ruined?

RAGUENEAU. Lise liked warriors and I liked poets. Mars ate everything that Apollo left.[3] At that rate, it didn't take long!

THE DUENNA. [*Standing up and calling toward the open window.*] Roxane, are you ready? We're late!

ROXANE'S VOICE. [*From the window.*] I'm just putting on my cloak!

THE DUENNA. [*To* RAGUENEAU, *pointing to the door opposite.*] That's where we're going, to Clomire's.[4] She holds regular discussion meetings in her house. A discourse on the Tender Passion[5] will be read today.

CYRANO'S VOICE. [*Singing offstage.*] La-la-la.

---

1. **Marais** [ma rā′]
2. **livery:** uniform.
3. **Mars...Apollo left:** The soldiers (represented by Mars, the god of war) ate all the pastries left by the poets (represented by Apollo, the god of poetry).
4. **Clomire's** [klō mērz′]
5. **Tender Passion:** that is, a lecture on love.

---

THE DUENNA. [*Surprised.*] Is someone coming to play for us?

CYRANO. [*Entering, followed by two* PAGES *carrying lutes.*] Those are thirty-second notes, you fool!

ROXANE. [*Appearing on the balcony.*] Ah, it's you!

CYRANO. [*Singing his words to the melody.*] I've come to salute your lilies, and pay my respects to your roses!

ROXANE. I'm coming down! [*Leaves the balcony.*]

THE DUENNA. [*Pointing to the* PAGES.] Where did these two virtuosi[6] come from?

2 CYRANO. I won them from d'Assoucy[7] on a bet. We were arguing about a point of grammar when suddenly he pointed to these lute-playing louts, who always accompany him wherever he goes, and said to me, "I'll bet you a day of music!" He lost, and therefore ordered them to follow me and bear harmonious witness to everything I do until tomorrow. It was charming at first, but it has already begun to pall. [*To the* PAGES.] Go and serenade Montfleury and tell him I sent you! [*The* PAGES *go upstage to leave.*

3 CYRANO *turns back to the* DUENNA.] I've come to ask Roxane, as I do every day . . . [*To the* PAGES, *as they are leaving.*] Play a long time—and off-key! [*To the* DUENNA.] . . . whether her soulmate is still a model of perfection.

ROXANE. [*Coming out of the house.*] Oh, he's so handsome! And such a brilliant mind! I can't tell you how much I love him!

---

6. **virtuosi** [vur′choō ō′sē]: those with great skill in a fine art, especially music.
7. **d'Assoucy** [da soō sē′]: probably a reference to Charles d'Assouci (1605–1677), who was a comic poet and contemporary of the real Cyrano de Bergerac.

*Cyrano de Bergerac, Act III* **417**

---

---

## GUIDED READING

**LITERAL QUESTIONS**

**1a.** What new information do you learn about Ragueneau here? (He is bankrupt, and Lise has run off with a musketeer. He tried to commit suicide. Cyrano got him a job as Roxane's steward.)

**2a.** What question does Cyrano come to ask Roxane every day? (". . . whether her soulmate is still a model of perfection." In other words, does she still love Christian?)

**INFERENTIAL QUESTIONS**

**1b.** What does this information reveal about Cyrano? (He's not just noble in speech but does practical things to help others.)

**2b.** What answer do you think he'd like to hear? (Naturally, he'd like to hear that she's disillusioned with Christian so that he might have a chance himself. Nevertheless, he is proud of making her love Christian by his own eloquence.)

■ Roxane affirms her love for Christian and praises his facility with language.

■ De Guiche arrives and Cyrano leaves. De Guiche announces that he is going away to war.

## 1 PLOT: RISING ACTION

Roxane's comment reveals that although Christian has been coached by Cyrano, he is not perfect.

## 2 IRONY

Roxane blunders into the truth and startles Cyrano with her comment. There is double irony here, since he is indeed jealous—but not of the writing, which is, in fact, his own.

## 3 DRAMATIC IRONY

Roxane does not know that the fluency she praises is Cyrano's, but the audience and Cyrano do, thus creating dramatic irony.

CYRANO. [*Smiling.*] You feel that Christian has a brilliant mind?

ROXANE. Even more brilliant than yours!

CYRANO. I won't contest that.

**1** ROXANE. I don't believe there's anyone in the world who can match him in saying those sweet nothings that mean everything. Sometimes he seems distracted and his inspiration falters, then all at once he says exquisite things to me!

CYRANO. [*Incredulously.*] Really?

ROXANE. Just like a man! Because he's handsome, you think he has to be dull-witted!

CYRANO. Does he speak well about matters of the heart?

ROXANE. Not well—superbly!

CYRANO. And how does he write?

ROXANE. Even better than he speaks! Just listen to this! [*Declaiming.*] "The more you take of my heart, the more I have!" [*Triumphantly.*] There, what do you think of that?

CYRANO. [*Unenthusiastically.*] Oh . . .

ROXANE. And this: "Since I need a heart with which to suffer, if you keep mine, send me yours!"

CYRANO. First he has too much heart, then not enough. He can't seem to make up his mind.

**2** ROXANE. [*Stamping her foot.*] You're exasperating! You only talk like that because you're jealous . . .

CYRANO. [*Starting.*] What?

ROXANE. . . . of the way he writes! Listen to this and tell me if you think anything could be more tender: "Believe me when I say that my heart cries out to you, and that if kisses could be sent in writing, you would read this letter with your lips."

418 *Drama*

CYRANO. [*Smiling with satisfaction in spite of himself.*] Well, those lines are . . . [*Catches himself and continues in a disdainful tone.*] . . . rather affected.

ROXANE. And listen to this. . . .

**3** CYRANO. [*Delighted.*] You know all his letters by heart?

ROXANE. Every one of them!

CYRANO. [*Twisting his mustache.*] That's quite flattering.

ROXANE. He's a master of eloquence!

CYRANO. [*Modestly.*] Let's not exaggerate. . . .

ROXANE. [*Peremptorily.*] A master!

CYRANO. [*Bowing.*] Very well, then, a master!

THE DUENNA. [*Hurrying downstage, after having gone upstage earlier.*] Monsieur de Guiche is coming! [*To* CYRANO, *pushing him toward the house.*] Go inside! It will be better for him not to find you here; it might put him on the scent. . . .

ROXANE. [*To* CYRANO.] Yes, on the scent of my precious secret! He's in love with me and he's powerful—he mustn't know! He might strike a cruel blow at my love for Christian!

CYRANO. [*Entering the house.*] I'll do as you wish.

[ DE GUICHE *appears.*]

ROXANE. [*To* DE GUICHE, *with a curtsey.*] We were about to leave. . . .

DE GUICHE. I've come to say good-by.

ROXANE. You're going away?

DE GUICHE. Yes. To war.

ROXANE. Ah!

DE GUICHE. I'm leaving tonight.

ROXANE. Ah!

## GUIDED READING

### LITERAL QUESTION

**1a.** What does Roxane tell Cyrano about Christian's delivery of "sweet nothings"? (that no one can match him but that sometimes he falters and then goes on to say exquisite things)

### INFERENTIAL QUESTION

**1b.** Why do you think Christian falters and then recovers? (He probably forgets the words Cyrano told him to use.)

DE GUICHE. I have my orders. We're besieging Arras.[8]

ROXANE. Ah! A siege?

DE GUICHE. Yes.... My departure seems to leave you cold.

ROXANE. [*Politely.*] Not at all.

DE GUICHE. For my part, I'm heartbroken. Will I ever see you again? If so, when?... Do you know that I've been made a colonel?

ROXANE. [*With indifference.*] Congratulations.

DE GUICHE. And I'm in command of the Guards.

ROXANE. [*Startled.*] The Guards?

DE GUICHE. Yes, the regiment in which your boastful cousin serves. I'll find a way to take revenge on him when we're at Arras.

ROXANE. [*Choking.*] What! The Guards are being sent there?

DE GUICHE. [*Laughing.*] Of course: that's my regiment!

ROXANE. [*Aside.*] Christian!...

DE GUICHE. What's the matter?

ROXANE. [*Overwhelmed with emotion.*] I'm in despair at...at what you've told me.... When a woman cares for a man and learns that he's going to war...

DE GUICHE. [*Surprised and delighted.*] Why did you wait for the day of my departure to say such a tender thing to me for the first time?

ROXANE. [*Changing her tone and fanning herself.*] So you're going to take revenge on my cousin?

DE GUICHE. Do you see him?

_____
8. **Arras** [a ra′]: city that was in the Spanish Netherlands and is now in France.

ROXANE. Very seldom.

DE GUICHE. He's seen everywhere with one of the Cadets...[*Tries to think of the name.*]...a young man named Neu...Neuvillen...Neuviller...

ROXANE. Tall?

DE GUICHE. Yes, with blond hair.

ROXANE. Reddish blond.

DE GUICHE. And handsome.

ROXANE. Not very.

DE GUICHE. But stupid.

ROXANE. He looks like it. [*Changing her tone.*] Are you planning to take revenge on Cyrano by exposing him to the fire of the enemy? If so, you'll get little satisfaction from it, because he loves danger! I know how you could really make him suffer!

DE GUICHE. How?

ROXANE. Leave him behind with his dear Cadets when the regiment goes off to fight. Make him sit idly in Paris through the whole war! He'll eat his heart out at not being in action, his friends will angrily chew their fingernails, and you'll be avenged.

DE GUICHE. [*Drawing closer.*] Then you do love me a little! [*She smiles.*] I like to think that your sharing my rancor is a sign of love, Roxane!

ROXANE. It is.

DE GUICHE. [*Showing her several sealed envelopes.*] I have orders that will be delivered to each company without delay, except...[*Separates one of them from the others.*]...for this one, addressed to the Cadets! [*Puts it in his pocket.*] I'll keep it. [*Laughing.*] Ha, ha, Cyrano! We'll see how your warlike temperament takes to this!... Tell me, Roxane, do you sometimes play tricks on people yourself?

*Cyrano de Bergerac, Act III* **419**

## GUIDED READING

### LITERAL QUESTIONS

**1a.** What feeling does Roxane pretend to have for De Guiche? (She lets him believe she loves him.)

**2a.** What trick does Roxane play on De Guiche? (She tells him that if he really wants to punish Cyrano, he should deny him the adventure of war and keep the Cadets home.)

### INFERENTIAL QUESTIONS

**1b.** Why do you think De Guiche is so eager to believe Roxane loves him? (It's what he wants to believe; and since he doesn't know about Christian, he doesn't know she is talking about someone else.)

**2b.** Do you think this will be a real punishment to Cyrano? (It certainly fits his character to want to be part of the action and to live dangerously.)

**1 CHARACTERIZATION**

Roxane's basic honesty comes across here. She doesn't lie but instead tells the truth in a way that reveals nothing.

**2 PLOT: DRAMATIC IRONY**

Roxane's answer is an honest one, but it creates dramatic irony because De Guiche is led to believe she's talking about him, even though she and the audience know that she means Christian.

---

1 ROXANE. [*Looking at him.*] Yes, sometimes.

DE GUICHE. [*Close to her.*] You drive me mad! I intended to leave tonight, but how can I part from you when you've just revealed such feelings to me? Listen.... Near here, on the Rue d'Orléans,[9] there's a monastery founded by the Capuchins.[10] Laymen aren't allowed to enter it, but I'll see to it that the good monks make an exception in my case. Everyone will believe I've left Paris. I'll then come to you, masked. Let me delay my departure one day!

ROXANE. [*Anxiously.*] But if it becomes known, your glory will be . . .

---

9. **Rue d'Orléans** [ro͞o′ dôr′lā ōn′]
10. **Capuchins** [kap′yə shinz]: monks who belong to a branch of the Franciscan order.

DE GUICHE. Never mind! Let me do it!

ROXANE. No!

DE GUICHE. Let me!

ROXANE. [*Tenderly.*] I must refuse.

DE GUICHE. Ah!

ROXANE. Go! [*Aside.*] And Christian will stay. [*To* DE GUICHE.] I want you to be heroic . . . Antoine!

2 DE GUICHE. What heavenly words! Do you love . . .

ROXANE. Yes, I love the man for whom I fear.

DE GUICHE. [*Overjoyed.*] I'm going now! [*Kisses her hand.*] Are you satisfied?

420    *Drama*

---

## GUIDED READING

### LITERAL QUESTION

**1a.** What do the stage directions say about how Roxane tells De Guiche that she refuses to accept a visit from him that evening? *(tenderly)*

### INFERENTIAL QUESTION

**1b.** Why do you suppose she suddenly speaks tenderly to De Guiche, a man she hates and fears? (She is grateful to him for keeping Christian safe, though he does not do it knowingly. She is thinking of Christian, and most of the tenderness is meant for him.)

ROXANE. Yes, Antoine. [*He leaves.*]

THE DUENNA. [*Bowing comically to him behind his back.*] Yes, Antoine!

ROXANE. [*To the* DUENNA.] Don't say a word about what I've done. Cyrano would never forgive me if he knew I'd robbed him of his war! [*Calls toward the house.*] Cousin! If Christian comes, as I presume he will, tell him to wait for me.

CYRANO. [*Quickly, as she is about to disappear.*] One moment! [*She turns back toward him.*] You always have a subject on which you question him; what will it be this time?

ROXANE. This time . . .

CYRANO. [*Eagerly.*] Yes?

ROXANE. You won't tell him?

CYRANO. I'll be as silent as a tomb.

ROXANE. Well, this time I'm not going to question him about anything! I'll say to him, "Give free rein to your mind! Improvise! Speak to me of love in your magnificent way!"

CYRANO. [*Smiling.*] Good.

ROXANE. Sh!

CYRANO. Sh!

ROXANE. Not a word! [*Goes inside and closes the door behind her.*]

CYRANO. [*Bowing to her, after the door is closed.*] I thank you.

[*The door opens again and* ROXANE'S *head appears.*]

ROXANE. If he knew, he might prepare a speech in advance!

BOTH TOGETHER. Sh! [*The door closes.*]

CYRANO. [*Calling.*] Christian! [CHRISTIAN *appears.*] I know what we need to know. Prepare your mem-

ory: here's a chance to cover yourself with glory! Why are you looking so unhappy? Come, there's no time to lose! We'll hurry to your house and I'll tell you . . .

CHRISTIAN. No!

CYRANO. What?

CHRISTIAN. No! I'm going to wait for Roxane here.

CYRANO. Have you lost your reason? Come with me, you must learn . . .

CHRISTIAN. No, I tell you! I'm tired of borrowing my letters and speeches, of always playing a part and trembling lest I forget my lines! It was necessary at the beginning and I'm grateful to you for your help, but now that I feel she really loves me, I'm no longer afraid. I'm going to speak for myself.

CYRANO. [*Ironically.*] Do you believe that's a good idea?

CHRISTIAN. What makes you think I can't do it? After all, I'm not so stupid! You'll see! Your lessons haven't been wasted on me, my friend: I'm sure I can speak without your guidance now. And in any case I'll certainly know how to take her in my arms! Here she comes! No, Cyrano, don't leave me!

CYRANO. [*Bowing to him.*] Speak for yourself, sir. [*Disappears behind the garden wall.*]

ROXANE. [*She sees* CHRISTIAN.] Ah, it's you! [*Goes to him.*] Dusk is gathering. Wait. . . . The air is pleasant and no one is passing by. Let's sit down. Talk to me. I'm listening.

[CHRISTIAN *sits down beside her on the bench. There is a silence.*]

CHRISTIAN. I love you.

ROXANE. [*Closing her eyes.*] Yes, speak to me of love.

*Cyrano de Bergerac, Act III*   **421**

AT A GLANCE

- Cyrano gets Roxane to reveal the evening's discussion topic.
- Christian dissolves the partnership with Cyrano.
- He appeals for Cyrano's help when he doubts himself again, but Cyrano refuses.

**1 DIALOGUE**

This exchange reveals how two men have worked out the practicalities of their partnership in wooing Roxane.

**2 CHARACTERIZATION**

Christian shows himself to be an essentially honest man. Assured of Roxane's love, he now wishes to appear before her without pretense.

**3 DIALOGUE**

Cyrano's refusal reveals his quick temper. He now can show Christian that Roxane is attracted to Christian's beautifully expressed deep feelings, not to his handsome face.

## GUIDED READING

**LITERAL QUESTIONS**

**1a.** What information does Cyrano find out from Roxane? (He finds out the topic on which she'll ask Christian to converse that evening.)

**2a.** What does Cyrano say when Christian tells him that he wants to speak for himself? ("Do you believe that's a good idea?")

**INFERENTIAL QUESTIONS**

**1b.** Why is this necessary information? (Since Cyrano can't be there to speak himself, he must learn the topic in advance in order to coach Christian.)

**2b.** Why do you think Cyrano says this? (By this time Cyrano has a good idea of Christian's limitations. Also, Cyrano is certain that no one else can match his eloquence.)

**1 THEME**

One of the play's themes—the value of self-expression—is underlined here. Christian cannot speak eloquently of his love, and as a result Roxane does not take his feelings seriously.

**2 STYLE: REPETITION**

Christian's repetition of the words *I love you* add humor to the scene and illustrate the idea that sincerity is not always enough to move people.

**3 CHARACTERIZATION**

Roxane is demanding. She has both physical beauty and wit and requires the same in her lover. She lacks tolerance for those less generously endowed.

**4 PLOT: CONFLICT**

Christian's rejection of Cyrano's help and his recent skepticism about its value pique Cyrano. However, Cyrano's love for Roxane prompts him to help Christian once more.

**5 READING SKILLS: INFERENCE**

From Christian's remark "I'll die!" we can infer his deep distress at Roxane's rejection.

---

CHRISTIAN. I love you.

ROXANE. That's the theme—now elaborate on it.

CHRISTIAN. I love . . .

ROXANE. Develop your theme!

CHRISTIAN. I love you so much!

ROXANE. Go on.

CHRISTIAN. I . . . I'd be so happy if you loved me! Tell me that you do, Roxane!

ROXANE. [*Pouting.*] You're giving me water when I expected cream! Tell me how you love me.

CHRISTIAN. I love you . . . very much!

1 ROXANE. Surely you can express your feelings better than that!

CHRISTIAN. [*Who has moved closer to her and is now devouring her neck with his eyes.*] Your neck! I'd like to kiss it . . . .

ROXANE. Christian!

2 CHRISTIAN. I love you!

ROXANE. [*Starting to stand up.*] Again!

CHRISTIAN. [*Quickly, holding her back.*] No, I don't love you!

ROXANE. [*Sitting down again.*] At least that's a change.

CHRISTIAN. I adore you!

ROXANE. [*Standing up and moving away.*] Oh!

CHRISTIAN. Yes. . . . I'm becoming foolish!

3 ROXANE. [*Curtly.*] And it displeases me! As it would displease me if you became ugly.

CHRISTIAN. But . . .

ROXANE. Try to bring back your vanished eloquence!

CHRISTIAN. I . . .

422    *Drama*

---

ROXANE. I know: you love me. Good-by. [*Goes toward the house.*]

CHRISTIAN. Wait! Let me tell you . . .

ROXANE. [*Opening the door.*] That you adore me? I already know that. No, no! Go away!

CHRISTIAN. But I . . . [*She closes the door in his face.*]

CYRANO. [*Who has returned a short time earlier without being seen.*] Congratulations on your success.

4 CHRISTIAN. Help me!

CYRANO. No.

CHRISTIAN. If I don't win her back immediately, I'll die!

CYRANO. How do you expect me to teach you immediately . . .

CHRISTIAN. [*Gripping his arm.*] Oh! Look! [*A light has appeared in the balcony window.*]

CYRANO. [*With deep emotion.*] Her window!

5 CHRISTIAN. [*Shouting.*] I'll die!

CYRANO. Lower your voice!

CHRISTIAN. [*Softly.*] I'll die. . . .

CYRANO. It's dark now.

CHRISTIAN. What of it?

CYRANO. The damage can be repaired. You don't deserve . . . Stand here, in front of the balcony, you wretched fool! I'll be under it, telling you what to say.

CHRISTIAN. But . . .

CYRANO. Quiet! [*The* PAGES *appear in the background.*] Sh! [*Signals them to speak softly.*]

FIRST PAGE. [*In an undertone.*] We've been serenading Montfleury!

CYRANO. [*Quickly, also in an undertone.*] I want

---

## GUIDED READING

### LITERAL QUESTIONS

**1a.** What happens when Christian tries to speak to Roxane on his own? (He keeps repeating "I love you"; she becomes annoyed at his uninspired speech and sends him away.)

**2a.** How does Cyrano react when Christian asks for help after his failure? (First he refuses; then he relents.)

### INFERENTIAL QUESTIONS

**1b.** Do you think his inability to speak in beautiful language means Christian doesn't love Roxane deeply? (His love seems sincere and deeply felt; he lacks the imagination to express it.)

**2b.** What do you think Cyrano feels about these events? (He's annoyed at Christian for thinking he can do without him; later, he is probably excited at the possibility of being more directly involved.)

you to stand watch, one at that corner, the other at that one. If you see anyone coming, begin playing your lutes.

SECOND PAGE. What shall we play?

CYRANO. A happy melody for a woman, a sad one for a man. [*The* PAGES *disappear, one toward each street corner.* CYRANO *speaks to* CHRISTIAN.] Call her!

CHRISTIAN. Roxane!

CYRANO. [*Picking up pebbles and throwing them against the window.*] Just a moment. First, a few pebbles. . . .

ROXANE. [*Partially opening her window.*] Who's there?

CHRISTIAN. It's I.

ROXANE. Who?

CHRISTIAN. Christian.

ROXANE. [*With disdain.*] Oh, it's you.

CHRISTIAN. I'd like to speak to you.

CYRANO. [*Under the balcony, to* CHRISTIAN.] That's good. Keep your voice down.

ROXANE. No! You speak too awkwardly. Go away.

CHRISTIAN. Please. . . .

ROXANE. No! You've stopped loving me!

CHRISTIAN. [*Repeating what* CYRANO *tells him.*] Impossible!. . . I could no more. . . stop loving you. . . than I could stop. . . the rising of the sun!

ROXANE. [*Pausing just as she was about to close the window.*] Ah! That's better!

CHRISTIAN. [*Still repeating* CYRANO's *words.*] My cruel love. . . has never ceased to grow. . . in my tormented soul. . . since the day. . . when it was born there.

ROXANE. [*Leaning forward with her elbows on the railing of the balcony.*] Very good!. . . But why do you speak so haltingly? Has your imagination gone lame?

CYRANO. [*Pulling* CHRISTIAN *under the balcony and taking his place.*] Sh! This is becoming too difficult!

ROXANE. Your words are hesitant tonight. Why?

CYRANO. [*Speaking softly, like* CHRISTIAN.] Because of the darkness, they must grope their way to your ears.

ROXANE. *My* words have no such difficulty.

CYRANO. They go straight to my heart, a goal too large to miss, whereas your ears are small. And your words travel swiftly because they fall, while mine must slowly climb.

ROXANE. But they seem to be climbing better now.

CYRANO. They've finally become accustomed to that exercise.

ROXANE. It's true that I'm speaking from high above you.

CYRANO. Yes, and it would kill me if you let a harsh word fall on my heart from that height!

ROXANE. [*Making a movement.*] I'll come down to you!

CYRANO. [*Urgently.*] No!

ROXANE. [*Pointing to the bench below the balcony.*] Then climb up on that bench.

CYRANO. [*Stepping back into the shadows.*] No!

ROXANE. Why not?

CYRANO. [*Increasingly overcome by emotion.*] I want to go on taking advantage of this opportunity. . . this chance for us to talk quietly. . . without seeing each other.

ROXANE. Why should we talk without seeing each other?

*Cyrano de Bergerac, Act III* **423**

AT A GLANCE

- Cyrano arranges a signal with the pages to warn him if anyone is coming.
- Christian and Cyrano stand under Roxane's balcony, with Cyrano whispering eloquent phrases that Christian repeats to Roxane.
- Frustrated with the awkwardness of this arrangement, Cyrano finally speaks in his own voice.

**1 PLOT: FORESHADOWING**

Cyrano sets up a musical signal with the pages and creates the expectation of an imminent arrival, a plot device that adds tension.

**2 STYLE: FIGURATIVE LANGUAGE**

Cyrano is driven to new inventiveness in order to explain these irregular happenings to Roxane. He uses metaphor to explain why her speeches are more successful than his.

**3 CHARACTERIZATION**

Cyrano believes that he must remain hidden if Roxane is to listen to his declaration of love. In the dark he need not be self-conscious about his appearance.

## GUIDED READING

### LITERAL QUESTIONS

**1a.** How does Roxane interpret Christian's sudden inability to speak fluently of his love? (She says he doesn't love her anymore.)

**2a.** What does Cyrano do when Roxane complains that his words are halting? (He pushes Christian out of the way, takes his place, and begins to speak to Roxane in his own voice.)

### INFERENTIAL QUESTIONS

**1b.** What does this show about Roxane's character? (She is frivolous. Unadorned feeling bores her.)

**2b.** Why is this an extremely important event for Cyrano? (It is the first time he speaks directly of his love without using Christian to deliver the lines.)

## 1 PLOT: RISING ACTION

Tension develops as Cyrano comes close to revealing that it is he, not Christian, who is speaking. But he is not ready to risk an open confession of love.

## 2 CHARACTERIZATION

A new side of Cyrano is revealed: a man who can be less than smooth and fluent in expressing his most deeply held feelings.

## 3 STYLE: FIGURATIVE LANGUAGE

Cyrano contrasts the "little flowers" of conventional eloquence with the utterance of true passion. Of course, Cyrano does not abandon eloquence for passion; his open passion makes him *more* eloquent.

## 4 THEME

Cyrano articulates a major theme: the hypocrisy to which society leads us.

## 5 STYLE

Cyrano's language, freed from the constraints of artifice and cleverness, soars. The playful verbal fencing of past encounters gives way to a sense of urgency.

---

CYRANO. I find it delightful. We're almost invisible to each other. You see the blackness of a long cloak, I see the whiteness of a summer dress. I'm only a shadow, you're only a spot of brightness. You can't know what these moments mean to me! I may sometimes have been eloquent in the past . . .

ROXANE. You have!

CYRANO. . . . but until now my words have never come from my true heart.

ROXANE. Why?

**1** CYRANO. Because . . . till now I always spoke through . . .

ROXANE. Through what?

CYRANO. The intoxication that seizes anyone who stands before your gaze! . . . But tonight it seems to me that I'm speaking to you for the first time.

ROXANE. Perhaps it's true—even your voice is different.

**2** CYRANO. [*Impetuously moving closer.*] Yes, quite different, because in the protecting darkness I dare at last to be myself, I dare . . . [*Pauses, then continues distractedly.*] What was I saying? I don't know . . . . All this . . . Excuse my agitation! All this is so enchanting . . . so new to me!

ROXANE. So new?

CYRANO. [*Deeply stirred, trying to cover up what he has admitted.*] Yes, it's new to me to be sincere . . . without fear of being laughed at. . . .

ROXANE. Laughed at for what?

**3** CYRANO. For . . . for an outburst of feeling! My heart always timidly hides itself behind my mind. I set out to bring down stars from the sky, then, for fear of ridicule, I stop and pick little flowers of eloquence.

ROXANE. Those little flowers have their charm.

424   *Drama*

---

CYRANO. Yes, but let's scorn them tonight!

ROXANE. You've never talked to me like this before.

CYRANO. One look at the starry sky above us is enough to make me want to throw off all artificiality. If the expression of feeling is refined too much, the feeling itself is lost.

ROXANE. But it seems to me that elegant language . . .

**4** CYRANO. It has no place in true love! It's only a game, and those who love will suffer if they play it too long. For most of them there comes a time—and I pity those for whom it doesn't come!—when they feel a noble love inside themselves that's saddened by every grandiloquent word they say.

ROXANE. Well, if that time has come for us, what words will you say to me?

**5** CYRANO. All those that enter my mind of their own accord. I'll give them to you as they come, without arranging them in bouquets: I love you, I'm overwhelmed, I love you to the point of madness! Your name is in my heart like a bell shaken by my constant trembling, ringing day and night: Roxane, Roxane, Roxane! Loving everything about you, I forget nothing. I remember the day last year, the twelfth of May, when you wore your hair in a different style. Just as a man who has looked at the sun too long sees red circles everywhere, when I've gazed on the bright glory of your hair my dazzled eyes see golden spots on everything!

ROXANE. [*In a tremulous voice.*] Yes, that's really love. . . .

CYRANO. The feeling that holds me in its merciless grip could be nothing else but love! It has all the terrible jealousy and somber violence of love, and all the unselfishness, too. How gladly I would give my happiness for the sake of yours, even without your knowledge, asking only to

---

## GUIDED READING

### LITERAL QUESTION

**1a.** What does Cyrano say is new about his speeches? (It is new for him to be sincere without fear of being laughed at.)

### INFERENTIAL QUESTION

**1b.** What does he mean by this? (He had not declared his love because he was afraid of her ridicule. Now he knows she won't laugh, because she thinks he's Christian.)

*Cyrano de Bergerac, Act III* **425**

- Roxane confesses herself much moved by Cyrano's language.
- Christian, Roxane, and Cyrano negotiate a kiss.
- A Capuchin enters looking for Roxane, and Cyrano misdirects him.

1 **PLOT: DRAMATIC IRONY**

Cyrano speaks his heart, and Roxane is moved to love. But there are several ironies here. Cyrano says you listen to "me," but she thinks that's how it's always been, and although his words move her, she doesn't know that the words are Cyrano's.

2 **PLOT: CONFLICT**

The conflict between the two men surfaces: They are rivals in love. Christian tries to get a kiss, and Cyrano tries to prevent it.

3 **PARAPHRASING**

I know it's inevitable that this love will be fulfilled with Christian, but at least I'll feel the love is offered partly to me if it's prompted by my eloquence.

---

hear from a distance, now and then, the laughter born of my sacrifice! Are you beginning to understand now? Do you feel my soul rising to you in the darkness? Ah, it's all too beautiful, too 1 sweet, this evening! I say all these things and you listen to me—*you* listen to *me*! It's more than my poor heart can bear! Even in my most daring dreams I never hoped for so much! I could die happily at this moment! It's because of my words that you're trembling—for you *are* trembling, like one of the leaves in the dark foliage above me: I've felt the beloved tremor of your hand descending along the jasmine branches! [*Fervently kisses the end of a drooping branch.*]

ROXANE. Yes, I'm trembling, and I'm weeping, and I love you, and I'm yours!

CYRANO. Then let death come, now that I've aroused such feelings in you! I ask only one thing . . .

CHRISTIAN. [*From under the balcony.*] A kiss!

ROXANE. [*Quickly drawing back.*] What?

CYRANO. Oh!

ROXANE. You ask . . .

2 CYRANO. Yes, I . . . [*To* CHRISTIAN, *in an undertone.*] You're going too fast!

CHRISTIAN. She's in a willing mood—I must take advantage of it!

CYRANO. [*To* ROXANE.] Yes, I . . . I asked for a kiss, but I now realize that I was much too bold.

ROXANE. [*A little disappointed.*] You don't insist?

CYRANO. Yes, I insist . . . but not insistently! I've offended your modesty. . . . Don't give me that kiss!

CHRISTIAN. [*To* CYRANO, *tugging at his cloak.*] Why do you say that?

CYRANO. Quiet, Christian!

426 *Drama*

---

ROXANE. [*Leaning forward.*] What are you saying?

CYRANO. I was scolding myself for having gone too far. I just said to myself, "Quiet, Christian!" [*The lutes begin playing.*] Wait! Someone's coming! [ ROXANE *closes the window.*] A sad tune and a happy one, both at the same time? What do they mean? Is it a man or a woman? . . . Ah! [*A* CAPUCHIN *enters; holding a lantern in his hand, he goes from house to house, looking at the doors.*]

CYRANO. [*To the* CAPUCHIN.] What are you doing?

THE CAPUCHIN. I'm looking for the house of Madame . . . Magdeleine Robin.

CYRANO. [*To the* CAPUCHIN, *showing him an uphill street.*] It's that way. Straight ahead.

THE CAPUCHIN. Thank you. [*He leaves.*]

CHRISTIAN. You must get that kiss for me!

CYRANO. No!

CHRISTIAN. Sooner or later . . .

3 CYRANO. Yes, it's true. Sooner or later there will be an ecstatic moment when your mouths are drawn together. [*To himself.*] I prefer it to be because of . . .

[*Sound of the window being opened again.* CHRISTIAN *hides under the balcony.*]

ROXANE. [*Coming out onto the balcony.*] Are you still there? We were talking about . . . about a . . .

CYRANO. A kiss. The word is so sweet! Why should you be afraid to say it? Don't be alarmed; you've already given up your bantering tone and gradually drifted from smiles to sighs, and then from sighs to tears! Let yourself drift a little further!

ROXANE. Stop!

CYRANO. After all, what is a kiss? A vow made at

---

## GUIDED READING

### LITERAL QUESTIONS

**1a.** What is Roxane's reaction to Cyrano when he speaks from the heart? (She is very moved; she trembles, weeps, and confesses her love.)

**2a.** How does Cyrano feel when his heartfelt speeches are over? (He is proud that his words have affected Roxane so deeply; it is a fulfilling moment.)

### INFERENTIAL QUESTIONS

**1b.** Why do you think this speech affects her differently from the ones he's been making through Christian? (It truly does express his love in a deeper, more genuine way, and the beauty and lyricism of the language is moving.)

**2b.** Why does Cyrano feel so fulfilled, even though it's still Christian Roxane thinks she loves? (He has moved her in his own voice with his truest feelings. And it is to this Cyrano that she responds.)

closer range, a more precise promise, a confession that contains its own proof, a seal placed on a pact that has already been signed; a fleeting moment filled with the hush of eternity, a communion that has the fragrance of a flower, a way of living by the beat of another heart.

ROXANE. Come to me! Come and give me that matchless flower...

CYRANO. [*Pushing* CHRISTIAN *toward the balcony.*] Climb up to her!

ROXANE. ...that communion...

CYRANO. Climb!

ROXANE. ...that hush of eternity...

CYRANO. Climb!

CHRISTIAN. [*Hesitating.*] But now it seems to me that it's wrong!

CYRANO. [*Pushing him.*] Climb, you fool!

[CHRISTIAN *stands on the bench, then climbs up onto the balcony.*]

CHRISTIAN. Ah, Roxane! [*Takes her in his arms and kisses her.*]

CYRANO. What a strange pang in my heart! I must content myself with very little, but I still have a few small crumbs. Yes, I feel something of that kiss in my heart, because Roxane is kissing not only Christian's lips, but also the words I spoke to her! [*The lutes begin playing again.*] A sad tune and a happy one: the Capuchin! [*Takes a few rapid steps, pretending to have just arrived, and calls out loudly.*] Roxane!

ROXANE. Who is it!

CYRANO. It's I. I was passing by.... Is Christian still here?

CHRISTIAN. [*Surprised.*] Cyrano!

ROXANE. Good evening, cousin.

CYRANO. Good evening, cousin.

ROXANE. I'm coming down! [*She disappears into the house. The* CAPUCHIN *enters in the background.*]

CHRISTIAN. [*Seeing him.*] No! Not again! [*Follows* ROXANE.]

THE CAPUCHIN. *This* is Magdeleine Robin's house!

CYRANO. You said "Rolin" before.

THE CAPUCHIN. No, I said "Robin!" R-O-B-I-N!

ROXANE. [*Appearing in the doorway of the house, followed by* RAGUENEAU, *who carries a lantern, and* CHRISTIAN.] Who's this?

THE CAPUCHIN. I have a letter for you.

CHRISTIAN. A letter?

THE CAPUCHIN. [*To* ROXANE.] It surely concerns some holy matter. It's from a worthy lord who...

ROXANE. [*To* CHRISTIAN.] It's from De Guiche!

CHRISTIAN. How dare he...

ROXANE. He won't bother me much longer! [*Opening the letter.*] I love you, and if... [*By the light of* RAGUENEAU's *lantern, she reads the letter to herself in a low voice.*] "The drums are beating and my regiment is preparing to leave. Everyone believes that I have already gone, but I am staying, in disobedience to your orders. I am in a monastery. This letter is to inform you that I will soon come to visit you. The monk who will deliver it to you is as simpleminded as a goat, so there is no danger of his guessing my plan. Your lips have smiled at me too much today; I must see them again. I hope that you have already forgiven my boldness, and I remain your..." And so on. [*To the* CAPUCHIN.] Father, you must hear what's in this letter. Listen. [*The others gather around her and she pretends to read aloud.*] "You must bow to the Cardinal's will, however difficult it may be for you. This letter will be delivered into your charming hands by a saintly,

*Cyrano de Bergerac, Act III* **427**

- Christian and Roxane kiss, and Cyrano feels conflict.
- Cyrano announces his presence to Roxane.
- The Capuchin enters again with a letter for Roxane from De Guiche.
- Roxane reads the letter to the Capuchin, altering the contents.

**1 CHARACTERIZATION**

Christian doubts the propriety of the kiss now that it's within his reach. This change of heart shows him to be a man eager to protect Roxane's honor.

**2 PLOT: CONFLICT**

Cyrano is proud of his words that bring about the kiss but feels "a strange pang" in his heart that another man is enjoying the kiss that he has earned.

**3 SUBPLOT**

De Guiche's love for Roxane is an important subplot throughout most of the play. Roxane's use of his letter now links the subplot directly to the main plot: the romance between Roxane and Christian.

## GUIDED READING

### LITERAL QUESTION

**1a.** When do Christian and Roxane kiss? (after Cyrano persuades Roxane and pushes Christian up the balcony)

### INFERENTIAL QUESTION

**1b.** Why does Cyrano arrange this kiss when he tried to stop them from kissing before? (He knows that the kiss is inevitable. If he arranges it, he proves the power of his words to move her.)

- Roxane pretends that the letter orders her to marry Christian.
- Cyrano schemes to intercept and delay De Guiche.

## 1 CHARACTERIZATION

Roxane's use of the letter shows her ability to think quickly and also to manipulate others to do what she wants.

## 2 DIALOGUE

This exchange adds humor. Roxane hastily adds a small bribe to help persuade the Capuchin when she sees that he has doubts. He quickly forgets his suspicions.

## 3 STAGING

That De Guiche is not supposed to recognize Cyrano because he is wrapped in a cloak and uses his Gascon accent shows the highly artificial quality of the play. The audience is expected to suspend its disbelief.

## 4 THEME

The play celebrates Cyrano's creativity and his facility with language. Here he uses both to try to delay De Guiche. His zany talk is typical of his unfettered imagination.

---

1 intelligent, and discreet Capuchin. You will inform him that we wish him to give you the blessing of holy matrimony . . ." [*Turns the page.*] ". . . in your house, and without delay. Christian must secretly become your husband. I have already sent him to you. I know that you dislike him, but you must accept the Cardinal's decision, and you may rest assured that heaven will bless you for your resignation. With the respect that I have always borne for you, I remain your humble and devoted . . ." And so on. [*Loudly, with despair.*] Oh! This is horrible!

THE CAPUCHIN. [*Turning the light of his lantern on* CYRANO.] Are you the . . .

CHRISTIAN. No, *I* am!

THE CAPUCHIN. [*Turns the light on* CHRISTIAN, *then, seeing how handsome he is, appears to become suspicious.*] But . . .

2 ROXANE. [*Quickly, pretending to read again.*] "P.S. You will make a gift of a thousand francs[11] to the monastery."

THE CAPUCHIN. A worthy, worthy lord! [*To* ROXANE.] Resign yourself!

ROXANE. [*In a tone of martyrdom.*] I am resigned. [*While* RAGUENEAU *opens the door for the* CAPUCHIN, *whom* CHRISTIAN *has invited to enter, she speaks softly to* CYRANO.] De Guiche will soon be here. Delay him, don't let him come in until . . .

CYRANO. I understand. [*To the* CAPUCHIN.] How long will you need for the wedding ceremony?

THE CAPUCHIN. About a quarter of an hour.

CYRANO. [*Pushing them all toward the house.*] Hurry! I'll stay here.

ROXANE. [*To* CHRISTIAN.] Come! [*They go inside.*]

---

11. **francs:** The franc is the French monetary unit; it is worth about twenty cents.

**428** *Drama*

---

CYRANO. How can I make De Guiche waste a quarter of an hour? [*Leaps onto the bench and climbs up the wall, toward the balcony.*] Up we go! . . . I have my plan! [*The lutes begin playing a mournful melody.*] Aha! A man is coming! [*The tremolo becomes sinister.*] No doubt of it this time! [*He is now on the balcony. He pushes his hat down over his eyes, takes off his sword, wraps his cloak around himself, leans forward, and looks down.*] No, it's not too high. . . . [*He sits on the railing, takes one of the long tree branches that overhang the garden wall, pulls it toward him, and holds it with both hands, ready to swing down.*] I am going to trouble this peaceful atmosphere a little!

DE GUICHE. [*Entering masked, groping in the darkness.*] What's happened to that Capuchin?

3 CYRANO. My voice! What if he recognizes it? [*Lets go of the branch with one hand and makes the motion of turning an invisible key.*] There! I've unlocked my Gascon accent!

DE GUICHE. [*Looking at the house.*] Yes, this is it. I can hardly see where I'm going. This mask is so annoying! [*He walks toward the door.* CYRANO *leaps from the balcony, holding the branch, which bends and sets him down between* DE GUICHE *and the door. He pretends to fall heavily, as if from a great height, and lies motionless on the ground, as though dazed.* DE GUICHE *jumps back.*] What! . . . What's this? . . . [*He looks up, but the branch has already sprung back into place. Seeing nothing but the sky, he is mystified.*] Where did this man fall from?

4 CYRANO. [*Sitting up, and speaking with a Gascon accent.*] From the moon!

DE GUICHE. Did you say . . .

CYRANO. [*Dreamily.*] What time is it?

DE GUICHE. He's lost his reason!

CYRANO. What time is it? What country is this? What day? What season?

---

**LITERAL QUESTION**

**1a.** What job is Cyrano given during the wedding ceremony? (He is asked to intercept De Guiche and keep him occupied until the ceremony is over.)

**INFERENTIAL QUESTION**

**1b.** How do you think he feels about this? (He seems comfortable with the job and certainly throws himself into it once De Guiche arrives. He seems to understand that his moment with Roxane is over.)

DE GUICHE. But . . .

CYRANO. I'm still dazed.

DE GUICHE. Sir . . .

CYRANO. I fell from the moon like a cannonball!

DE GUICHE. [*Impatiently.*] Look, sir . . .

CYRANO. [*Loudly and emphatically, standing up.*] I fell from the moon!

DE GUICHE. [*Stepping back.*] Very well, then, you fell from the moon! [*Aside.*] He may be a maniac!

CYRANO. A hundred years ago, or perhaps a minute ago—I have no idea how long my fall lasted—I was on that yellow sphere!

DE GUICHE. [*Shrugging.*] Yes, of course. Let me pass.

CYRANO. [*Stepping in front of him.*] Where am I? Be frank, don't hide anything from me! What is this place where I've just fallen like a meteorite?

DE GUICHE. Enough of this!

CYRANO. As I was falling, I wasn't able to choose my destination, and I don't know where I've landed. Has the weight of my posterior brought me back to earth, or to another moon?

DE GUICHE. [*Trying to get past him.*] A lady is expecting me. . . .

CYRANO. Ah, then I'm in Paris!

DE GUICHE. [*Smiling in spite of himself.*] This lunatic is rather amusing!

CYRANO. You're smiling?

DE GUICHE. Yes, but I still want you to let me pass!

CYRANO. [*Beaming.*] I've fallen back into Paris! [*Thoroughly at ease, smiling, brushing himself off, bowing.*] Excuse me; I've just come by the latest whirlwind and I have ether all over me. Such a journey! My eyes are full of stardust. I still

have a little planet fur on my spurs. [*Picks something off his sleeve.*] A comet hair on my doublet! [*Pretends to blow it away.*]

DE GUICHE. [*Beside himself with exasperation.*] Sir! . . . [*Just as* DE GUICHE *is about to pass,* CYRANO *stops him by putting out his leg, as though to show him something on it.*]

CYRANO. The Great Bear bit me as I passed. Look, you can see the tooth marks on my leg. Then, when I swerved to avoid Orion's Sword, I fell into the Scales.[12] The pointer still marks my weight. [*Prevents* DE GUICHE *from passing and takes hold of his doublet.*] If you were to squeeze my nose, sir, milk would spurt from it.

DE GUICHE. Milk?

CYRANO. From the Milky Way!

DE GUICHE. Sir, I've been very patient with you. Now will you please . . .

CYRANO. I understand. I'll be glad to oblige you.

DE GUICHE. At last!

CYRANO. You want me to tell you what the moon is like and whether anyone lives there, isn't that right?

DE GUICHE. No! No! I want to . . .

CYRANO. Yes, of course—you want to know how I got to the moon. I did it by a method that I invented myself.

DE GUICHE. [*Discouraged.*] He's raving mad!

CYRANO. I didn't imitate anything that had been done before! [DE GUICHE *succeeds in getting past him. He walks toward* ROXANE'S *door while* CYRANO *follows him, ready to take hold of him.*] I invented six ways.

DE GUICHE. [*Stopping and turning around.*] Six?

---

12. **Great Bear, Orion's Sword, Scales:** constellations in the zodiac.

*Cyrano de Bergerac, Act III* **429**

AT A GLANCE

Cyrano continues his stories about space travel; De Guiche tries to get away.

**1 HUMOR: EXAGGERATION**

Cyrano's reply to De Guiche's insistent remark, "A lady is expecting me," adds humor by using exaggeration. His reply implies that romantic assignations take place only in Paris.

**2 STYLE: FIGURATIVE LANGUAGE**

Cyrano uses metaphor—traveling by whirlwind, covered with ether, eyes filled with stardust—to describe his imaginary journey from the moon. These vivid details help make his story compelling despite its incredibility.

**3 DIALOGUE**

By the sheer power of his imagination and language Cyrano has finally managed to interest De Guiche, quite against his will.

---

## GUIDED READING

**LITERAL QUESTION**

**1a.** What does De Guiche think of the man from the moon? (He thinks he is crazy. At first he wants to get rid of him, but then he becomes intrigued.)

**INFERENTIAL QUESTION**

**1b.** How does Cyrano pretend to be crazy? (He pretends to be disoriented in space and time and makes up wild and unbelievable stories about space travel.)

**1 DIALOGUE**

De Guiche's reluctant interest testifies to the power of Cyrano's improvisational ability and the charm of his language.

**2 CHARACTERIZATION**

Cyrano shows his cleverness: He has said there were six methods of getting to the moon, but now, seeing the time is not yet up, he uses his last resource and comes up with a seventh.

**3 DIALOGUE**

Cyrano reveals his dislike for De Guiche by wasting no more time or imagination on him than is necessary. He abruptly switches from foolishness to the brutal truth as soon as it is safe to do so.

**4 PLOT: RISING ACTION**

Christian and Roxane are married. However, since theirs is not a traditional romance but a triangle, the marriage is not the climax of the play.

---

CYRANO. [*Volubly.*] I could have clothed my naked body with crystal bottles full of dew and exposed myself to the morning sun; then, as the sun drew up the dew, I would have been drawn up with it!

DE GUICHE. [*Surprised, and taking a step toward* CYRANO.] Yes, that's one way!

CYRANO. [*Stepping back to lead him away from the door.*] And I could have rarefied[13] the air in a cedar chest by means of twenty burning-mirrors[14] suitably arranged, thus producing a great rush of wind that would have sent me on my way!

DE GUICHE. [*Taking another step toward him.*] Two!

CYRANO. [*Still moving back.*] Or, with my mechanical skill and my knowledge of pyrotechnics,[15] I could have constructed a large steel grasshopper propelled by successive explosions of gunpowder.

DE GUICHE. [*Following him without realizing it, and counting on his fingers.*] Three!

CYRANO. Since smoke tends to rise, I could have blown enough of it into a globe to carry me away!

DE GUICHE. [*Increasingly surprised, and still following him.*] Four!

CYRANO. Since the new moon likes to suck up the marrow of cattle, I could have coated my body with it!

DE GUICHE. [*Fascinated.*] Five!

CYRANO. [*Who, while speaking, has led him to the other side of the square, near a bench.*]

---

13. **rarefied:** made thinner, like the hot air in a balloon. The real Cyrano de Bergerac wrote a work of science fiction proposing these various methods of space travel.
14. **burning-mirrors:** curved mirrors used for producing great heat by focusing the sun's rays.
15. **pyrotechnics** [pī′rə tek′niks]: art of making and using fireworks.

**430** *Drama*

---

Finally, I could have sat on a sheet of iron and thrown a magnet into the air. It's a very good method: the iron follows the magnet in its flight, then you quickly throw the magnet again, and keep repeating the process until you've reached the moon!

DE GUICHE. Six!. . .But which of those six excellent methods did you choose?

CYRANO. A seventh!

DE GUICHE. Amazing! Tell me about it.

CYRANO. Try to guess.

DE GUICHE. This rascal is becoming interesting!

CYRANO. [*Making a sound of waves, with broad, mysterious gestures.*] Hoo!. . .Hoo!. . .

DE GUICHE. What's that?

CYRANO. Can't you guess?

DE GUICHE. No!

CYRANO. The tide!. . .After taking a dip in the sea, I lay on the beach at the hour when the moon was exerting the pull that causes the tides, and I was lifted into the air—head first, of course, since it was my hair that held the most moisture. I was rising straight up, slowly and effortlessly, like an angel, when suddenly I felt a shock! Then. . .

DE GUICHE. [*Sitting down on the bench, seized with curiosity.*] Yes? Then what?

CYRANO. Then. . .[*Resumes his natural voice.*] The quarter of an hour has passed, so I won't keep you any longer. The wedding is over.

DE GUICHE. [*Leaping to his feet.*] I must be losing my mind! That voice!. . .And that nose!. . . Cyrano!

CYRANO. [*Bowing.*] At your service. They've just been married.

DE GUICHE. Who? [*He turns around. Tableau. ROXANE and CHRISTIAN are holding hands. The*

---

## GUIDED READING

### LITERAL QUESTION

**1a.** How does De Guiche finally recognize that the man from the moon is Cyrano? (Cyrano begins to use his real voice; De Guiche also recognizes Cyrano's nose.)

### INFERENTIAL QUESTION

**1b.** Does the unrealistic nature of the encounter with De Guiche add to or detract from the play? (Possible answers: The fanciful nature of the scene adds to the play's entertainment; the scene detracts by stretching belief too far and digressing from the romantic plot.)

CAPUCHIN *follows them, smiling.* RAGUENEAU *is also holding a candelabrum. The* DUENNA *brings up the rear. To* ROXANE.] You! [*With amazement, recognizing* CHRISTIAN.] And he?...[*Bowing to* ROXANE *with admiration.*] I congratulate you on your cleverness! [*To* CYRANO.] And to you, the great inventor, my compliments! Your story would have stopped a saint at the gates of heaven! Write down the details of it, because you really could use them in a book!

CYRANO. [*Bowing.*] I promise to follow your advice.

THE CAPUCHIN. [*Showing the couple to* DE GUICHE.] Here's the handsome couple you've united, my son!

DE GUICHE. [*Giving him an icy look.*] Yes. [*To* ROXANE.] And now you must tell your husband good-by, madame.

ROXANE. Why?

DE GUICHE. [*To* CHRISTIAN.] The regiment is about to leave. Join it!

ROXANE. To go to war?

DE GUICHE. Of course!

ROXANE. But the Cadets aren't going!

DE GUICHE. Yes, they are. [*Takes the envelope from his pocket.*] Here's the order. [*To* CHRISTIAN.] Deliver it at once, Baron.

ROXANE. [*Throwing herself in* CHRISTIAN'S *arms.*] Christian!

CHRISTIAN. It's hard to leave her.... You can't know....

CYRANO. [*Trying to lead him away.*] I do know....

[*Drums are heard beating in the distance.*]

DE GUICHE. [*Who has gone upstage.*] The regiment! It's leaving!

ROXANE. [*To* CYRANO, *clutching* CHRISTIAN, *whom he is still trying to lead away.*] I trust you to look after him! Promise me that nothing will endanger his life!

CYRANO. I'll do my best, but I can't promise anything.

ROXANE. [*Still holding* CHRISTIAN *back.*] Promise me that you'll make him be very careful!

CYRANO. I'll try, but...

ROXANE. [*Still holding* CHRISTIAN.] Promise me that he'll never be cold during that terrible siege!

CYRANO. I'll do whatever I can, but...

ROXANE. [*Still holding* CHRISTIAN.] Promise me that he'll write often!

CYRANO. [*Stopping.*] Ah! That's one thing I can promise you!

---

## STUDY QUESTIONS

### Recalling

1. In the beginning of Act III, what does Roxane tell Cyrano about Christian and his letters?
2. Explain the circumstances that lead to Cyrano's speech under the balcony to Roxane.
3. During the balcony speech what does Cyrano tell Roxane about his feelings for her? Describe Roxane's response to him.
4. Explain how Roxane arranges for her marriage to Christian.
5. What does Cyrano do to delay De Guiche, and what does De Guiche do to retaliate?

*Cyrano de Bergerac, Act III* **431**

- The happy newlyweds are introduced.
- De Guiche announces that the Cadets must go to war after all.
- Cyrano promises Roxane that he will look after Christian.

### 1 IRONY

Christian tells Cyrano he cannot know what the pain of leave-taking is like. Ironically, the audience and Cyrano both know that Cyrano suffers also.

### 2 PLOT: FORESHADOWING

Although Cyrano cannot guarantee Christian's safety in the siege, he is happy to have the opportunity to continue wooing Roxane from afar through the power of his words.

### REFLECTING ON ACT III

How would you compare Christian's love for Roxane to Cyrano's? (Opinions will vary. Some may feel that Christian's love is of shorter duration than Cyrano's and is therefore less intense. However, Christian does seem to love her sincerely.)

### STUDY QUESTIONS

1. His eloquence in speaking is matched only by his writing; she has memorized all of his letters.
2. Christian insists on speaking for himself; Roxane is angered by his awkwardness, dismisses him; he asks Cyrano for his help.
3. It is the first he has spoken truly from his heart; eloquence can mask true feelings. She admits the intensity of her love.
4. pretends she has been ordered to marry by Cardinal Richelieu
5. disguises himself; pretends to be a madman; orders Christian and Cyrano to return to the regiment

**6.** happy that Roxane is responding to his words but sad that she loves Christian for his beauty

**7.** The passion of Cyrano's spirit triumphs over his appearance; ingenious story captivates De Guiche.

**8.** Roxane represents idealized love; in his dealings with society, Cyrano insists on following his own course, often to his own detriment.

**9.** Their willingness to combine resources suggests they may love Roxane with equal intensity.

## LITERARY FOCUS

**1.** Sample answers: Cyrano would stand below balcony wearing cloak, plumed hat, looking up at Roxane. He would be able to see her back and part of her face. He may kneel with his hand on his chest holding his hat with the other hand.

**2.** His voice would be tremulous at first and would grow and become filled with conviction.

**3.** Cyrano would show profound joy, tinged with melancholy. He would watch Roxane to see how his words affected her. He would show the greatest emotion when repeating her name.

### Interpreting

**6.** Describe Cyrano's mixed feelings when he speaks to Roxane unseen. Why might he be both happy and sad?

**7.** Explain how Cyrano's speech to Roxane and his deception of De Guiche each represents a triumph of the imagination over physical reality.

**8.** An idealist is someone who follows his or her beliefs beyond the point of practicality and who acts as if the world were better than it really is. From what you have seen of Cyrano so far, show how he is an idealist.

### Extending

**9.** Do you think a love like Cyrano's is actually greater than a love like Christian's? Why or why not?

## LITERARY FOCUS

### Staging and Character

Because plays are written to be performed by actors for an audience, acting is a vital part of any dramatic work. Actors greatly increase the impact of a play by creating living, breathing people from the playwright's words. In addition, actors can emphasize certain aspects of the characters, presenting the audience with a particular interpretation not simply of their characters but of the play as a whole.

The role of Cyrano is a favorite one for actors because it is so colorful and lends itself to different interpretations. Some actors have played Cyrano as a big-voiced swashbuckler; others, as a soft-spoken poet. Some actors have emphasized Cyrano's wit; others, his pride; still others, his bittersweet love of Roxane. In order to appreciate the play fully, we should imagine what dimensions an actor's performance might add to Cyrano's words.

### Thinking About Staging and Character

Look again at the balcony scene in Act III of this play, and decide how you would direct the actor playing the role of Cyrano. You might want to keep the following questions in mind:

1. How far would Cyrano be from Roxane? Would he look at Roxane throughout his speech to her? Would he move or stand still?

2. Would Cyrano speak softly or in full voice? Would he grow louder or softer during his speech to Roxane?

3. What emotions would he show during the scene? Would he seem happy or sad? How would he show his love for Roxane? At what lines would he show the greatest emotion?

432  *Drama*

# ACT IV

*The post occupied by* CARBON DE CASTEL-JALOUX'S *company in the siege of Arras. About a month later.*

[*In the background, an embankment crosses the entire stage. Beyond is a plain covered with siegeworks. Far off in the distance, the walls and rooftops of Arras are silhouetted against the sky. Tents, scattered weapons, drums, etc. Daybreak is near. Yellowish glow in the east. Sentries at intervals. Campfires. Wrapped in their cloaks, the* GASCON CADETS *are asleep.* CARBON *and* LE BRET *are awake. They are both pale and gaunt.* CHRISTIAN, *sleeping like the others, is in the foreground, with the light of a campfire on his face. Silence.*]

LE BRET. It's horrible!

CARBON. Yes. Not one scrap of food left.

[*A few shots are heard in the distance.*]

CARBON. Those shots! They'll wake my children! [*To the* CADETS, *who have begun to raise their heads.*] Go back to sleep! [*The* CADETS *settle down again, then there are more shots, from closer range.*]

A CADET. [*Stirring.*] What, again?

CARBON. It's nothing, only Cyrano coming back. [*The heads that have been raised are lowered again.*]

THE SENTRY ON THE PARAPET. Halt! Who goes there?

CYRANO. [*Appearing on the parapet.*] Bergerac, you idiot! [*Comes down from the parapet.* LE BRET *anxiously goes forward to meet him.*]

LE BRET. Thank God you're back!

CYRANO. [*Motioning him not to awaken anyone.*] Sh!

LE BRET. Are you wounded?

**3** CYRANO. You know very well that they make it a habit to miss me every morning!

LE BRET. Don't you think it's going a little too far to risk your life every day to send a letter?

CYRANO. [*Stopping in front of* CHRISTIAN.] I promised he would write often! [*Looks at him.*] He's asleep. His face is pale. If poor Roxane knew he was dying of hunger . . . But he's still handsome!

LE BRET. You ought to bring us some food.

CYRANO. I have to travel light to get through! . . . But you can expect a change by this evening. If I saw what I think I saw, the French will soon either eat or die.

LE BRET. Tell me about it!

CYRANO. No, I'm not sure. . . . You'll see!

**4** CARBON. We're the besiegers, and yet we're starving! It's shameful!

LE BRET. Unfortunately, nothing could be more complicated than this siege. We're besieging Arras, we ourselves are caught in a trap, the Cardinal Prince of Spain is besieging us. . . .

LE BRET. Excuse me if I don't laugh.

CYRANO. You're excused.

LE BRET. To think that every day you risk a life like yours to carry . . . [*Sees* CYRANO *walking toward a tent.*] Where are you going?

CYRANO. I'm going to write another one. [*Lifts the flap of the tent and disappears. Reveille[1] is heard.*]

CARBON. [*With a sigh.*] Reveille, alas! [*The* CADETS *stir in their cloaks and stretch.*] Their de-

---

1. **reveille** [rev'ə lē]: signal on bugle or drum to waken soldiers.

*Cyrano de Bergerac, Act IV* **433**

## AT A GLANCE

- The Cadets are at war.
- Cyrano returns from sending a letter to Roxane.
- The army is besieged and starving.

## LITERARY OPTIONS

- setting
- conflict
- climax

## THEMATIC OPTIONS

- confronting obstacles
- sacrifice
- appearance and reality
- inner and outer beauty

## 1 SETTING

The grim military setting of Act IV reflects the shift in the play's mood: There is still humor but the mood is darkening.

## 2 CHARACTERIZATION

Carbon is shown as paternal and loving to his men. His feelings help the audience care about the fate of the Cadets.

## 3 THEME

The dialogue reveals the extent of the danger Cyrano risks to send letters to Roxane. Typically, he dismisses the danger with a joke.

## 4 PLOT: RISING ACTION

We learn how the Cadets' current situation came about: They are besieged and starving.

## GUIDED READING

### LITERAL QUESTION

**1a.** What thoughts does Cyrano express as he looks at the sleeping Christian? (He thinks how pale he is and how worried Roxane would be if she knew he was starving. He thinks, despite everything, that Christian is still handsome.)

### INFERENTIAL QUESTION

**1b.** What does this show about Cyrano? (His major interest and concern is still Roxane, but he has compassion for Christian. He is still envious of Christian's handsomeness.)

- The Cadets complain about their hunger.
- Cyrano tries to cheer them up.
- He distracts them with sorrow.

## 1 PLOT: CONFLICT

The cadet reveals the serious external conflict war has imposed: starvation.

## 2 CHARACTERIZATION

Cyrano takes a flippant attitude toward a situation that is essentially tragic.

## 3 THEME

Noble in character, Cyrano tries to preserve his idealism even under the harsh conditions of war.

## 4 STYLE: FIGURATIVE LANGUAGE

Cyrano turns to poetry to distract his countrymen. His approach shows both his understanding of the Gascons and his own love of lyrical language.

licious sleep has ended, and I know only too well what their first words will be!

A CADET. [*Sitting up.*] I'm hungry!

**1** ANOTHER. I'm starving!

ALL. Oh!...

CARBON. On your feet, all of you!

FIRST CADET. [*Looking at himself in a piece of polished armor.*] My tongue is yellow—living on air has given me indigestion!

SECOND CADET. We must have food!

CARBON. [*Calling softly into the tent where* CYRANO *has gone.*] Cyrano!

OTHER CADETS. We're dying!

CARBON. [*Still softly, standing at the doorway of the tent.*] I need your help! You always know how to answer them—come and cheer them up!

SECOND CADET. [*Hurrying to the* FIRST CADET, *who is chewing something.*] What are you eating?

FIRST CADET. Ammunition wadding cooked in axle grease, using a steel helmet as a pot. There's not much game in this country!

CYRANO. [*Calmly coming out of the tent with a quill pen behind his ear and a book in his hand.*] What's the trouble? [*Silence. He speaks to the* FIRST CADET.] Why are you standing so stiffly?

FIRST CADET. I have to.

CYRANO. Why?

FIRST CADET. My stomach is so empty that if I bend at the waist I'll break in half!

**2** CYRANO. Be glad you've lost weight: it may save your life.

FIRST CADET. How?

CYRANO. By making you a smaller target for the enemy!

**434** *Drama*

**3** THIRD CADET. Why is it that *you* never complain about your hunger?

CYRANO. Because there's one thing I'm not hungry enough to swallow: my pride.

FIRST CADET. [*Shrugging.*] You're never at a loss for a clever remark.

CYRANO. Yes, and I hope that when death comes to me it will find me fighting in a good cause and making a clever remark! I want to be struck down by the only noble weapon, the sword, wielded by an adversary worthy of me, and to die not in a sickbed but on the field of glory, with sharp steel in my heart and a flash of wit on my lips!

ALL THE CADETS. [*Shouting.*] I'm hungry!

CYRANO. [*Folding his arms.*] Can't you think of anything but food?...Come here, Bertrandou.[2] You're a fifer[3] now, but you were once a shepherd; take out your fife and play some of the old Gascon music for these gluttons! Let them hear those soft, haunting melodies in which each note is like a little sister, melodies that hold the sound of loved voices and have the slowness of smoke rising from the chimneys of our home villages, melodies that speak to us in our mother tongue! [BERTRANDOU *begins playing melodies from the south of France.*] Listen, Gascons.... He's no longer playing the martial fife: it's now the flute of our forests! It's not a call to battle, but the slow piping of our goatherds! Listen.... It's our valleys, our moors, our woodlands; it's a dark-haired little cowherd wearing a red beret; it's the sweetness of evenings on the banks of the Dordogne[4]....Listen, Gascons: it's all of Gascony!

[*The* CADETS *have all sat down and dreamily*

---

2. **Bertrandou** [bār'tron dōō']
3. **fifer:** one who plays a fife, an instrument like a flute, that often accompanies a military drum.
4. **Dordogne** [dôr dō'nyə]: region of southwestern France.

---

## GUIDED READING

### LITERAL QUESTION

**1a.** What kind of help does Carbon ask Cyrano for? (He asks him to answer the Cadets' complaints about their hunger and to cheer them up.)

### INFERENTIAL QUESTION

**1b.** What does this reveal about Cyrano's place in the regiment? (Although he is not the commander of the Cadets, he is their natural leader. He understands them and their problems and knows how to rally them. Carbon often depends on him.)

*bowed their heads. Now and then one of them furtively wipes away a tear with his sleeve or his cloak.*]

CARBON. [*Softly, to* CYRANO.] You're making them weep!

CYRANO. Yes, from homesickness! It's a nobler pain than hunger. I'm glad that their suffering has shifted from their bellies to their hearts.

CARBON. You'll weaken them by stirring up such feelings!

CYRANO. [*Motioning the drummer to approach.*] Not at all! The courage in their blood is easily awakened. It takes only . . . [*He makes a gesture and the drummer beats a roll.*]

ALL THE CADETS. [*Leaping to their feet and rushing for their weapons.*] What?—Where?—What is it?

CYRANO. [*Smiling.*] You see? It takes only a drumbeat! Farewell dreams, regrets . . .

A CADET. Oh! Here comes Monsieur de Guiche! [*The* CADETS *all murmur irritably.*]

CYRANO. [*Smiling.*] That's a flattering greeting!

THE CADET. He annoys us!

SECOND CADET. He's coming to strut in front of us with his big lace collar over his armor!

SECOND CADET. He's not a soldier, he's a courtier!

CARBON. He's still a Gascon.

LE BRET. He looks pale.

THIRD CADET. He's hungry, like the rest of us poor devils, but since his armor has gilded studs, his stomach cramps glitter in the sunlight!

CYRANO. [*Urgently.*] We mustn't let him see us looking miserable! Take out your cards, your pipes, your dice. . . . [*They all quickly begin*

*playing cards and dice on drums, stools, and their cloaks spread out on the ground, and they light their long pipes.*] As for me, I'm going to read Descartes.[5]

[*He walks slowly back and forth, reading from a small book that he has taken from his pocket. Tableau.* DE GUICHE *enters. The* CADETS *all seem happily absorbed in what they are doing.* DE GUICHE *is very pale. He walks toward* CARBON.]

DE GUICHE. [*To* CARBON.] Ah! Good morning! [*Aside, with satisfaction, after they have observed each other a moment.*] He looks green around the gills!

CARBON. [*Aside, also with satisfaction.*] His eyes are sunken, and big as saucers!

DE GUICHE. [*Looking at the* CADETS.] So here are the grumblers! . . . Yes, gentlemen, it's been reported to me from all sides that you jeer at me, that you rustic barons have nothing but contempt for your colonel. [*Silence. The* CADETS *continue their games and smoking.*] Am I going to have you punished by your captain? No.

CARBON. Let me point out to you that I'm free to do as I see fit, and I don't choose to punish my men. I've paid for my company; it's my own. I obey only battle orders.

DE GUICHE. That will do! [*To the* CADETS.] I can afford to despise your mockery, because my conduct under fire is well known. Only yesterday, at Bapaume, I furiously drove back Count de Bucquoi.[6] Bringing my men down upon his like an avalanche, I charged three times!

CYRANO. [*Without looking up from his book.*] And don't forget your white scarf.

---

5. **Descartes** [dā kärt′]: René Descartes (1596–1650), French philosopher and mathematician.
6. **Bapaume** [ba pōm′], **de Bucquoi** [də bū kwa′]

*Cyrano de Bergerac, Act IV* **435**

AT A GLANCE

- De Guiche arrives, to the disdain of the Cadets, who try not to let him see how miserable they are.
- De Guiche chastises them and brags, only to be challenged by Carbon and Cyrano.

1 **CHARACTERIZATION**

Up until now De Guiche has been seen only through the eyes of those who have a personal reason to dislike him, but now the more objective Cadets confirm his character as pretentious and vain.

2 **DIALOGUE**

De Guiche is a braggart, but Cyrano hints that once again he's lying. Despite the pretense of not caring about their opinion, De Guiche shows himself to be curiously defensive.

---

*GUIDED READING*

**LITERAL QUESTIONS**

**1a.** What does Cyrano tell the Cadets to do when they see De Guiche coming? (He doesn't want them to be caught looking miserable, so they begin gambling and smoking. Cyrano begins to read.)

**2a.** What comment does Cyrano make after De Guiche brags about his conduct under fire? (He says, "And don't forget your white scarf.")

**INFERENTIAL QUESTIONS**

**1b.** Why is it important to him that De Guiche not see the Cadets looking miserable? (De Guiche is an enemy who has contempt for the Cadets. Cyrano's pride forbids exposing vulnerability to him.)

**2b.** What does this comment tell you? (It suggests that Cyrano knows that De Guiche's behavior has been less than noble under fire.)

- De Guiche tells the story of the white scarf.
- Cyrano returns the scarf, and De Guiche signals with it.
- De Guiche reveals that the enemy is going to attack.

## 1 BACKGROUND

Military strategy dictates killing or capturing officers first in order to leave troops leaderless and ineffective. De Guiche realizes this and in a cowardly way disposes of his emblem of rank.

## 2 THEME

Cyrano articulates his own ideas of honor and courage: He will not save his skin at the expense of ideals. De Guiche serves throughout most of the play as a foil for Cyrano's idealism.

## 3 CHARACTERIZATION

Cyrano never avoids physical danger. His physical bravery contrasts with his inability to risk himself emotionally.

## 4 PLOT: RISING ACTION

De Guiche reveals two important pieces of information: (1) food is on the way; (2) the Cadets are vulnerable to attack because half the army has gone for supplies.

---

DE GUICHE. [*Surprised and pleased.*] Ah, you know about that?...Yes, as I was rallying my men for the third charge, I was caught in a rush of fugitives and swept along toward the enemy. I was in danger of being captured or shot when I had the good sense to take off the scarf that showed my rank and drop it on the ground. I was thus able to slip away from the Spaniards without attracting attention, then come back to them, followed by all my men, and beat them!... Well, what do you think of that?

[*The* CADETS *do not seem to have been listening, but they now stop puffing on their pipes and suspend the movements of their card and dice games; they are waiting.*]

CYRANO. I think that Henry the Fourth[7] would never have given up his white plume, even when surrounded by the enemy.

[*Silent joy among the* CADETS. *They resume laying down their cards, rolling their dice, and smoking their pipes.*]

DE GUICHE. But my trick succeeded! [*The* CADETS *again become motionless, waiting.*]

CYRANO. Perhaps, but I don't believe in declining the honor of being a target. [*The* CADETS *resume their activities with growing satisfaction.*] You and I, sir, have different ideas of courage. If I had been there when you dropped the scarf, I would have picked it up and put it on.

DE GUICHE. That's nothing but Gascon bragging!

CYRANO. Bragging? Lend me the scarf and accept my offer to wear it while I lead an assault today.

DE GUICHE. And that's a Gascon offer! You know very well that my scarf remained on the river bank, in a place that's now under heavy enemy

---

7. **Henry the Fourth** (1553–1610): king of France from 1589 to 1610, who often led his army in battle. Before a battle he told his soldiers, "If you lose your banners, rally around my white plume; you will always find it on the path of honor and glory."

436  *Drama*

---

fire, so that no one can go and bring it back.

CYRANO. [*Taking the white scarf from his pocket and holding it out to* DE GUICHE.] Here it is.

[*Silence. The* CADETS *stifle their laughter behind their cards and dice cups.* DE GUICHE *turns around and looks at them. They immediately take on serious expressions and resume their games. One of them casually whistles a melody played earlier by the fifer.*]

DE GUICHE. [*Taking the scarf.*] Thank you. Now that I have this piece of white cloth, I can use it for a signal that I was hesitating to make. [*Climbs to the top of the embankment and waves the scarf several times.*]

ALL THE CADETS. What!...

THE SENTINEL ON THE PARAPET. I see a man down there, running away!

DE GUICHE. [*Returning.*] He's a false Spanish spy. He's very useful to me. He reports to the enemy whatever I tell him, which makes it possible for us to influence their decisions. Now, what was I saying?...Ah, yes, I was about to tell you some news. Last night, in a supreme effort to get food for us, the Marshal quietly left for Dourlens,[8] where our supplies are. He'll arrive there by traveling across the fields, but in order to come back safely he took so many troops with him that we're now extremely vulnerable to an enemy attack: half the army is absent!

CARBON. If the Spaniards knew that...But they don't, do they?

DE GUICHE. Yes, they know. And they're going to attack.

CARBON. Ah!

DE GUICHE. My false spy came to warn me. He said, "I can make the attack come at any place you like, by reporting that it's your most weakly

---

8. **Dourlens** [dŏŏr lon']

---

**LITERAL QUESTION**

**1a.** What does De Guiche accuse Cyrano of when he offers to wear the white scarf in battle? (He says it's nothing but Gascon bragging.)

**INFERENTIAL QUESTION**

**1b.** How does Cyrano's return of the white scarf refute that charge? (In order to get it, he had to brave heavy enemy fire, thus proving he wouldn't be afraid to risk himself in battle.)

defended point. Just tell me where." I answered, "Very well, leave the camp and watch our lines. I'll signal to you from the place I've chosen."

CARBON. [*To the* CADETS.] Gentlemen, prepare yourselves. [*They all stand up. Sounds of swords and sword belts being buckled on.*]

DE GUICHE. The attack will begin in an hour.

FIRST CADET. Oh . . . . In that case . . . [*They all sit down again and resume their games.*]

DE GUICHE. [*To* CARBON.] The most important thing is to gain time. The Marshal will soon be on his way back.

CARBON. And how shall we gain time?

DE GUICHE. You will be so kind as to fight till the last of you is killed.

CYRANO. Ah, so that's your revenge?

DE GUICHE. I won't pretend that if I liked you I would have chosen you and your men, but since you're known to be incomparably brave, I'm serving my king by serving my rancor.

CYRANO. [*Bowing.*] Allow me to be grateful to you, sir.

DE GUICHE. [*Returning his bow.*] I know that you like to fight against odds of a hundred to one. I'm sure this is an opportunity you wouldn't have wanted to miss. [*Goes upstage with* CARBON. *Preparations to meet the attack are being made.* CYRANO *goes to* CHRISTIAN, *who is standing motionless, with his arms folded.*]

CYRANO. [*Putting his hand on* CHRISTIAN'S *shoulder.*] Christian?

CHRISTIAN. [*Shaking his head.*] Roxane. . . .

CYRANO. Yes, I know. . . .

CHRISTIAN. I wish I could at least pour out my heart to her in one last letter.

CYRANO. I thought something might happen to-

day, so . . . [*Takes a letter from his doublet.*] . . . I wrote your farewell.

CHRISTIAN. Let me see!

CYRANO. Do you want . . .

CHRISTIAN. [*Taking the letter.*] Of course! [*Opens it and begins reading it, then stops.*] What's this?

CYRANO. Where?

CHRISTIAN. Here—this little stain.

CYRANO. [*Quickly takes the letter back and looks at it with an innocent expression.*] A stain?

CHRISTIAN. It was made by a tear!

CYRANO. Yes. . . . A poet is sometimes caught up in his own game; that's what makes it so fascinating. This letter, you understand . . . It was so moving that I made myself weep while I was writing it.

CHRISTIAN. Weep?

CYRANO. Yes, because . . . Dying is no great matter. What's unbearable is the thought of never seeing her again. And it's true: I'll never see her . . . [CHRISTIAN *looks at him.*] . . . we'll never . . . [*Quickly.*] . . . you'll never . . .

CHRISTIAN. [*Snatching the letter from him.*] Give me that letter!

[*A distant clamor is heard from the edge of the camp.*]

CARBON. What is it?

THE SENTRY. [*Now on the parapet.*] A carriage! [*Everyone rushes to look.*]

VOICES. What!—It seems to have come from the direction of the enemy!—Shoot!—No! Didn't you hear what the driver shouted?—He said, "King's service!" [*Everyone is now on the parapet, looking down. The sound of jingling bells is coming closer.*]

*Cyrano de Bergerac, Act IV*   437

- De Guiche reveals that he has chosen Cyrano and the Cadets to receive the enemy's attack.
- Facing death, Christian wants to write Roxane, and Cyrano reveals that he has already written.
- A carriage arrives.

## 1 PLOT: CONFLICT

The conflict between De Guiche and Cyrano is acknowledged openly as De Guiche prepares to take his final revenge.

## 2 CHARACTERIZATION

Cyrano reveals the depth of his love and suffering by the tears on the letter to Roxane. Christian begins to make an important discovery about his partner.

## 3 PLOT: FORESHADOWING

In his grief Cyrano almost reveals that he, too, loves Roxane. This near-revelation foreshadows several discoveries that Christian makes in this act.

## GUIDED READING

### LITERAL QUESTION

**1a.** What plan has De Guiche devised with the false Spanish spy? (He will signal the spy from the place he wants the Spanish to attack.)

### INFERENTIAL QUESTION

**1b.** Why do you think he would want to choose the place of attack on his own troops? (He sends the enemy to the most strongly held part of the defense. He can also avenge himself on Cyrano.)

## 1 MAIN IDEA

Roxane styles herself as "in the service of the greatest of all kings: love." This comment shows her wit and touches on one of the play's themes: Genuine love can lead to character growth.

## 2 STAGING

The stage directions reveal a Cyrano uncharacteristically paralyzed by Roxane's arrival. His inability to speak or move tells, more than words could, how deeply affected he is.

## 3 CHARACTERIZATION

Roxane is conscious of her beauty and not above using it to get what she wants. She is also brave, playing down her risk.

---

DE GUICHE. [*Shouting into the wings.*] King's service!. . . Line up, you rabble! Don't you know how to receive a carriage in the king's service?

[*The carriage enters at a rapid trot. It is covered with mud and dust. The curtains are drawn. Two* FOOTMEN *behind. It stops abruptly.*]

CARBON. [*Shouting.*] Beat the general salute! [*Ruffle of drums. All the* CADETS *take off their hats.*]

DE GUICHE. Lower the step! [*Two men rush forward. The carriage door opens.*]

ROXANE. [*Alighting from the carriage.*] Good morning! [*The men have bowed low; hearing the sound of a woman's voice, they all straighten up at once. Stupefaction.*]

1 DE GUICHE. King's service? You?

ROXANE. I'm in the service of the greatest of all kings: love!

CYRANO. Oh!

CHRISTIAN. [*Hurrying to her.*] You! Why?

ROXANE. This siege had lasted too long!

CHRISTIAN. Why. . .

ROXANE. I'll tell you!

2 CYRANO. [*Who, at the sound of her voice, has remained rooted to the spot, not daring to turn his eyes toward her.*] I can't look at her. . . .

DE GUICHE. You can't stay here!

ROXANE. [*Gaily.*] Yes I can! [*Laughs.*] They shot at my carriage! [*Proudly.*] We met a patrol!. . .It looks as if it had been made from a pumpkin, like the carriage in the fairy tale, doesn't it? And my footmen look as if they had once been rats. [*Throws a kiss to* CHRISTIAN.] Good morning! [*Looks at everyone.*] You don't seem very cheerful!. . .[*Notices* CYRANO.] Cousin! Delighted to see you!

CYRANO. [*Approaching.*] And I'm amazed How. . .

ROXANE. How did I find the army? It was quite simple: I went where I saw that the countryside had been laid waste. Oh, such horrors! I would never have believed them if I hadn't seen them. Gentlemen, if that's how you serve your king, I much prefer to serve mine!

CYRANO. This is insane! How did you get here?

ROXANE. I went through the Spanish lines.

DE GUICHE. How were you able to pass?

3 ROXANE. I simply rolled along in my carriage. Whenever a Spanish officer gave me a suspicious look, I smiled at him sweetly from the window, and since, with all due deference to the French, Spaniards are the most gallant gentlemen in the world, I was always allowed to continue on my way.

CHRISTIAN. But. . .

ROXANE. What's the matter?

DE GUICHE. You must leave here!

ROXANE. Leave?

CYRANO. Yes, and quickly!

LE BRET. Immediately!

CHRISTIAN. Yes!

ROXANE. But why?

CHRISTIAN. [*Embarrassed.*] Because. . .

CYRANO. [*Embarrassed.*] In three-quarters of an hour. . .

DE GUICHE. [*Embarrassed.*] Or maybe an hour. . .

CARBON. [*Embarrassed.*] You'd better. . .

LE BRET. [*Embarrassed.*] You might. . .

ROXANE. I'm staying. There's going to be a battle, isn't there?

---

## GUIDED READING

### LITERAL QUESTIONS

**1a.** How does Roxane say she was able to find the army? (She says she followed the devastation of the countryside.)

**2a.** What do the Cadets tell Roxane she must do, and how do they tell her? (They say she must leave, but they are embarrassed about it.)

### INFERENTIAL QUESTIONS

**1b.** What does this tell you about the kind of war the Cadets are in? (It is a hard-fought, destructive war, with the countryside destroyed by both sides.)

**2b.** Why are they embarrassed about their request? (They are reluctant to refer to the danger they accept so casually.)

ALL. Oh, no!

ROXANE. He's my husband! [*Throws herself into* CHRISTIAN*'s arms.*] Let them kill me with you!

CHRISTIAN. Such a look in your eyes!

ROXANE. Do I have to tell you why?

DE GUICHE. [*Desperately.*] This is a terribly dangerous post!

ROXANE. [*Turning around.*] Dangerous?

CYRANO. He knows what he's saying: he gave it to us!

ROXANE. [*To* DE GUICHE.] Ah, so you wanted to make me a widow!

DE GUICHE. Oh! I swear to you that . . .

ROXANE. No! I don't care what happens to me now! I'm staying! Besides, it's amusing.

CYRANO. What? You're both an intellectual and a heroine?

ROXANE. I'm your cousin, Monsieur de Bergerac. [*Looks at* DE GUICHE.] Don't you think it's time for you to leave? The fighting may begin. . . .

DE GUICHE. This is too much! I'm going to inspect my cannons, and then I'll come back. . . . You still have time: change your mind!

ROXANE. Never! [DE GUICHE *leaves.*]

CHRISTIAN. [*Beseechingly.*] Roxane! . . .

ROXANE. No!

FIRST CADET. [*To the others.*] She's staying!

ALL. [*Jostling one another as they hurry to make themselves more presentable.*] A comb!— Soap!—Give me a needle, I have to sew up a hole!—A ribbon!—Your mirror!—My cuffs!— Your mustache curler!—A razor!

A CADET. [*To the others.*] Now that I've seen her face, I could die without regret if I only had a little food in my stomach!

CARBON. [*Indignantly, having overheard.*] Shame! Speaking of food when an exquisite lady . . .

ROXANE. But I'm hungry too! It must be the cool air. I'd like some pâté, cold chicken, and wine. Would you please bring it to me?

[*Consternation.*]

A CADET. Bring it to you?

ANOTHER. Where can we get it?

ROXANE. [*Calmly.*] In my carriage.

ALL. What!

ROXANE. But the food will have to be carved and served. Look at my coachman a little more closely, gentlemen, and you'll recognize a valuable man. If you like, each sauce will be reheated.

THE CADETS. [*Rushing toward the carriage.*] It's Ragueneau! [*Loud cheers.*]

ROXANE. [*Watching them.*] Poor men! . . .

THE CADETS. Bravo! Bravo!

RAGUENEAU. The Spaniards were so busy feasting their eyes that they didn't eye the feast! [*Applause.*]

CYRANO. [*Softly, to* CHRISTIAN.] Christian!

RAGUENEAU. Distracted by Beauty, they overlooked . . . [*Picks up a roast suckling pig on a tray and holds it aloft.*] the Beast! [*Applause. The tray is passed from hand to hand.*]

CYRANO. [*Softly, to* CHRISTIAN.] Please let me have a word with you.

RAGUENEAU. The sight they saw was so pleasant that they failed to notice . . . [*Picks up another tray.*] . . . this pheasant! [*More enthusiasm. The tray is seized by a dozen eager hands.*]

CYRANO. [*Softly, to* CHRISTIAN.] I want to talk to you! I must talk to you before you talk to her!

RAGUENEAU. [*More and more exuberant.*] The handle of my whip is a sausage!

*Cyrano de Bergerac, Act IV* 439

AT A GLANCE

- Roxane says she'll stay despite the danger.
- De Guiche leaves, giving Roxane more time to decide.
- Roxane reveals Ragueneau and a carriage full of food.
- Cyrano wants to speak to Christian before Christian and Roxane talk.

1 PLOT: CONFLICT

Roxane again recognizes De Guiche as an enemy who wants to get Christian killed so he can pursue her himself. De Guiche's behavior contrasts with that of Cyrano, who is Christian's protector.

2 PARAPHRASING THE LINES

"Of course I'm both intellectual and brave; you also have both qualities. I'm your cousin and it runs in the family." Roxane reveals her admiration of and appreciation for Cyrano.

3 DIALOGUE

Not wanting to tease starving men long, Roxane soon solves their problem. By joking she makes light of the service she has performed.

4 CHARACTERIZATION

Ragueneau is shown to be ever the poet, rhyming and punning his way through war and danger and starvation.

## GUIDED READING

### LITERAL QUESTIONS

**1a.** What do the Cadets begin to do as soon as it is clear Roxane is staying? (They begin to tidy themselves up and make themselves presentable.)

**2a.** How does Ragueneau explain their method of getting so much food past the Spaniards? (He says they were so dazzled by Roxane's beauty they didn't investigate.)

### INFERENTIAL QUESTIONS

**1b.** What do these actions tell you about the effect Roxane's presence has on the Cadets? (She is a morale booster, helping to restore their pride in themselves.)

**2b.** What does the fact that Roxane has succeeded tell you about her? (It underlines her intelligence. She's not as frivolous as she likes to pretend but is clever, brave, and resourceful.)

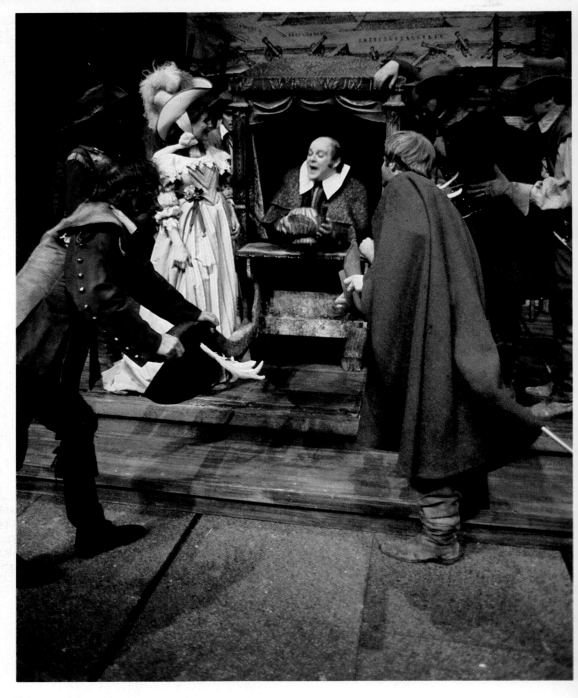

440 *Drama*

ROXANE. [*Pouring wine and handing out food.*] Since we're the ones who are going to be killed, we don't care about the rest of the army! Everything for the Gascons! And if De Guiche comes, he's not invited! [*Going from one to another.*] There's plenty of time. . . . Don't eat so fast! . . . Why are you weeping?

FIRST CADET. It's too good!

LE BRET. [*Who has gone upstage to pass a loaf of bread, at the end of a lance, to the* SENTRY *on the parapet.*] Here comes De Guiche!

CYRANO. Quickly! Hide the food, the bottles, the baskets, everything! And act as if nothing had happened! [*To* RAGUENEAU.] Hurry back to your driver's seat! . . . Is everything out of sight?

[*In the twinkling of an eye, everything is hidden in the tents or under cloaks and hats.* DE GUICHE *enters rapidly, then suddenly stops, sniffing. Silence.*]

DE GUICHE. Something smells good here.

A CADET. [*Casually singing.*] Tra-la-la . . .

DE GUICHE. [*Looking at him.*] What's the matter with you? Your face is red.

THE CADET. It's nothing. We'll soon be fighting, and the thought of it has made the blood rush to my head.

SECOND CADET. Poom-poom-poom . . .

DE GUICHE. [*Turning around.*] What's that?

SECOND CADET. Nothing. Just a song, a little song. . . .

DE GUICHE. You're in a gay mood!

SECOND CADET. It's because danger is approaching!

DE GUICHE. [*To* ROXANE.] Well, what have you decided?

ROXANE. I'm staying!

DE GUICHE. You must leave!

ROXANE. No!

DE GUICHE. In that case, I'll need a musket.

CARBON. What do you mean?

DE GUICHE. I'm staying too.

CYRANO. Sir, you've finally shown pure courage!

FIRST CADET. Are you really a Gascon, in spite of your lace?

ROXANE. What! . . .

DE GUICHE. I won't leave a woman in danger.

SECOND CADET. [*To the first.*] I think we can give him something to eat! [*The food reappears as though by magic.*]

DE GUICHE. [*His face lighting up.*] Food!

THIRD CADET. It's coming out from under every cloak!

DE GUICHE. [*Haughtily, controlling himself.*] Do you think I'm going to eat your leavings?

CYRANO. [*Bowing.*] You're making progress!

DE GUICHE. [*Proudly.*] An empty belly won't stop me from fighting!

FIRST CADET. [*Enthusiastically.*] Spoken like a Gascon!

DE GUICHE. [*Laughing.*] I *am* a Gascon!

FIRST CADET. It's true! He's really one of us!

CARBON. [*Reappearing on the parapet, after having disappeared behind the embankment a few moments earlier.*] I've stationed my pikemen.[9] They're ready to fight to the end! [*Points to a row of pikes showing above the parapet.*]

---

9. **pikemen:** soldiers armed with pikes, or long wooden shafts with pointed tips of iron or steel. Pikes were used in repelling attacks on forts and other walled structures.

*Cyrano de Bergerac, Act IV* **441**

**AT A GLANCE**

- The Cadets begin to eat but put the food away when De Guiche comes back.
- Roxane refuses to leave.
- De Guiche says he'll stay to protect her, and the Gascons approve.

**1 CHARACTERIZATION**

De Guiche puts aside personal safety to defend Roxane. His character begins to change in this scene.

**2 DIALOGUE**

De Guiche turns down—with a clever insult—food he badly wants, because he too is proud. Cyrano's response shows his generosity of spirit: he can compliment even an old enemy.

## GUIDED READING

### LITERAL QUESTION

**1a.** How does De Guiche behave toward Roxane and in relation to the food? (He refuses to leave the battle scene because he wants to protect Roxane; he refuses food out of pride, though starving.)

### INFERENTIAL QUESTION

**1b.** Why do these actions cause the Cadets and Cyrano to have more respect for De Guiche? (His sudden carelessness about his own well-being in order to protect Roxane and maintain his pride appeals to the brave, idealistic Gascon Cadets.)

- Roxane goes off with De Guiche.
- Cyrano confesses to Christian he has written Roxane more often than Christian knows.
- Roxane returns and reveals that she now loves Christian more deeply, because of his letters.

## 1 PLOT: CONFLICT

Cyrano's revelation shows one of his major conflicts: the need to conceal from Christian his own love for Roxane.

## 2 CHARACTERIZATION

Cyrano's devotion to Roxane and his need to tell her of his love is underscored. He is so compelled by love that he writes twice a day.

## 3 DIALOGUE

Christian expects to hear how she loves him and cannot stay away. He hardly considers the letters, since he had nothing to do with them.

## 4 STYLE: FIGURATIVE LANGUAGE

Roxane uses poetic language to describe the powerful effect of Cyrano's letters. Each page was a "petal fallen from your soul," each word a "flame." These images reflect both the tenderness and power of the love expressed.

---

DE GUICHE. [*To* ROXANE, *bowing.*] Will you accept my hand and go with me to inspect them?

[*She takes his hand and they go upstage toward the embankment. The others follow them, taking off their hats.*]

CHRISTIAN. [*Hurrying to* CYRANO.] Tell me what you have to say, quickly! What's your secret?

CYRANO. If Roxane should . . .

CHRISTIAN. Yes?

CYRANO. If she should speak to you about the letters . . .

CHRISTIAN. Go on!

1 CYRANO. Don't make the mistake of being surprised if . . .

CHRISTIAN. If what?

CYRANO. You've . . . you've written to her more often than you think.

CHRISTIAN. I have?

CYRANO. Yes. I made myself the interpreter of your passion. I sometimes wrote to her without telling you so.

CHRISTIAN. Oh?

CYRANO. It's quite simple!

CHRISTIAN. But we're blockaded! How did you send those letters?

CYRANO. I was able to get through the enemy lines before dawn.

2 CHRISTIAN. [*Folding his arms.*] And I suppose that was quite simple too? . . . How often have I been writing? Twice a week? Three times? Four?

CYRANO. More than that.

CHRISTIAN. Every day?

CYRANO. Yes, every day . . . twice.

CHRISTIAN. [*Violently.*] And you were carried

away by the letters you wrote! So much so that you defied death . . .

CYRANO. [*Seeing* ROXANE *returning.*] Quiet! Not in front of her! [*He quickly goes into his tent.*]

ROXANE. [*Hurrying to* CHRISTIAN.] And now, Christian! . . .

3 CHRISTIAN. [*Taking her hands.*] And now, Roxane, tell me why you traveled such appalling roads, infested with lawless soldiers, in order to join me here.

ROXANE. Because of your letters!

CHRISTIAN. What?

ROXANE. It's your fault if I'm in danger: your letters made me lose my reason! You've written so many of them in the last month, each more beautiful than the one before!

CHRISTIAN. Do you mean to say that because of a few love letters . . .

ROXANE. Yes! You can't know . . . . I've adored you since the evening when, under my window, you began to reveal your soul to me in a voice I'd never heard you use before, and when I read your letters it was like hearing that same voice.

CHRISTIAN. But . . .

4 ROXANE. I read your letters over and over, until I began to feel faint! I knew I belonged to you totally! Each page was like a petal fallen from your soul. In every word I felt the flame of a powerful, sincere love. . . .

CHRISTIAN. Powerful and sincere? Did you really feel that in my letters, Roxane?

ROXANE. Oh, yes!

CHRISTIAN. And so you came. . . .

ROXANE. I've come to ask you to forgive me—and now is the time to ask forgiveness, since we may be about to die!—for having insulted you, in my frivolity, by first loving you

---

## GUIDED READING

### LITERAL QUESTION

**1a.** What does Cyrano want to discuss with Christian before he sees Roxane? (He wants to warn him he's written to Roxane far more often than Christian is aware.)

**2a.** What does Roxane say about her new appreciation for Christian? (She says that reading the letters touched her in the same way his speech from the heart touched her and that she now loves him more deeply.)

### INFERENTIAL QUESTION

**1b.** Why do you suppose Cyrano kept this information from Christian in the first place? (He didn't want Christian to know he was so zealous, because then Christian might guess his love for Roxane.)

**2b.** How do you think the letters inspired such a change in her feelings? (The sincerity and depth of the feelings expressed inspired her to deepen her own feelings.)

only because you were handsome.

CHRISTIAN. [*In consternation.*] Oh, Roxane!

ROXANE. Later, when I became a little less frivolous, I was like a bird hopping before taking flight, held back by your handsome face and drawn forward by your soul. I then loved you for both of them together.

CHRISTIAN. And now?

**1** ROXANE. Your true self has prevailed over your outer appearance. I now love you for your soul alone.

CHRISTIAN. [*Stepping back.*] Oh, Roxane!

ROXANE. I know how painful it is for a noble heart to be loved because of an accident of nature that will soon pass away. But you can be happy now: your thoughts outshine your face. Your handsomeness was what first attracted me, but now that my eyes are open I no longer see it!

CHRISTIAN. Oh! . . .

**2** ROXANE. Do you still doubt your victory?

CHRISTIAN. I don't want it! I want to be loved simply for . . .

ROXANE. For what women have always loved in you till now? Let me love you in a better way!

CHRISTIAN. No! It was better before!

ROXANE. You don't know what you're saying! It's better now! I didn't really love you before. It's what makes you yourself that I now love. If you were less handsome . . .

CHRISTIAN. Enough!

ROXANE. I'd still love you. If you suddenly became ugly . . .

CHRISTIAN. Oh, don't say that!

ROXANE. I *will* say it!

CHRISTIAN. Even if I were ugly? . . .

ROXANE. Yes, even if you were ugly! I swear I'd still love you! Now are you happy?

CHRISTIAN. [*Choking.*] Yes . . . .

ROXANE. What's the matter?

CHRISTIAN. [*Gently pushing her away.*] Nothing. I must go and say a few words to someone. It will take only a minute.

ROXANE. But . . .

CHRISTIAN. [*Pointing to a group of* CADETS *in the background.*] My love has taken you away from those poor men. Go and smile at them a little, since they're about to die.

ROXANE. [*Deeply moved.*] Dear Christian! . . . [*She goes to the* CADETS, *who eagerly but respectfully crowd around her.*]

CHRISTIAN. [*Calling outside* CYRANO's *tent.*] Cyrano?

CYRANO. [*Coming out of the tent, armed for battle.*] Yes? Oh! How pale you are!

CHRISTIAN. She doesn't love me any more!

CYRANO. What!

**3** CHRISTIAN. It's you she loves!

CYRANO. No!

CHRISTIAN. She loves only my soul now!

CYRANO. No!

CHRISTIAN. Yes! That means it's you she loves—and you love her too!

CYRANO. I?

CHRISTIAN. I know it's true.

CYRANO. Yes, it's true.

CHRISTIAN. You love her with all your heart.

CYRANO. More than that.

CHRISTIAN. Tell her so!

*Cyrano de Bergerac, Act IV*  **443**

AT A GLANCE
- Roxane confesses her love has deepened: She now loves Christian for his inner qualities, not his looks.
- Christian, broken-hearted, tells Cyrano that it is Cyrano whom Roxane really loves.

**1 CHARACTERIZATION**

Roxane shows growth and development. She has changed from a silly, romantic girl able to love only a handsome face into a woman who recognizes the beauty in a man's soul.

**2 PLOT: CONFLICT**

Christian experiences an internal conflict as he realizes what these disclosures mean: If Roxane loves his inner self, not his handsome exterior, then she really loves Cyrano.

**3 THEME**

Christian shows that nobility of character requires self-sacrifice. He tells Cyrano Roxane loves him and urges his friend to confess his own love.

---

## GUIDED READING

### LITERAL QUESTIONS

**1a.** What does Christian say when Roxane asks him if he still doubts his victory? (He says, "I don't want it! I want to be loved simply for . . .")

**2a.** What does Cyrano say to Christian when he first enters the tent? ("How pale you are!")

### INFERENTIAL QUESTIONS

**1b.** Why does Christian not want such a victory in love? (He now sees that she doesn't really love him, with his inarticulate love, but Cyrano, who speaks and writes so well.)

**2b.** What does Christian's paleness tell you about his state of mind? (He is stunned and heartbroken.)

CYRANO. No!

CHRISTIAN. Why not?

CYRANO. Look at my face!

CHRISTIAN. She would still love me if I were ugly!

CYRANO. She told you that?

CHRISTIAN. Yes!

1 CYRANO. I'm glad she said it, but don't believe such nonsense! Yes, I'm very glad she had that thought.... But don't take her at her word! Don't become ugly—she would never forgive me!

CHRISTIAN. We'll see!

CYRANO. No, no!

CHRISTIAN. Let her choose! I want you to tell her everything!

CYRANO. No! I couldn't bear that torture!

CHRISTIAN. Do you expect me to kill your happiness because I'm handsome? That would be too unjust!

CYRANO. And do you expect me to kill yours because I happen to have been born with a gift for expressing . . . what you may feel?

CHRISTIAN. Tell her everything!

CYRANO. It's cruel of you to persist in tempting me!

CHRISTIAN. I'm tired of being my own rival!

CYRANO. Christian!

CHRISTIAN. Our wedding took place in secret, without witnesses. The marriage can be broken—if we survive!

CYRANO. You still persist! . . .

2 CHRISTIAN. I want to be loved for myself or not at all! We'll see what she decides. I'm going to walk to the end of the camp, then come back.

**444** *Drama*

Talk to her while I'm gone, and tell her she must choose one of us.

CYRANO. It will be you!

CHRISTIAN. I hope so! [*Calls.*] Roxane!

CYRANO. No! No!

ROXANE. [*Hurrying toward them.*] Yes?

CHRISTIAN. Cyrano has something important to tell you.

[CHRISTIAN *leaves.*]

ROXANE. Something important?

CYRANO. [*Frantically.*] He's leaving! . . . [*To* ROXANE.] No, it's really nothing. . . . You must know how he is: he often sees importance where none exists!

ROXANE. [*Anxiously.*] Does he doubt what I told him? Yes, he does! I could see he doubted it!

CYRANO. [*Taking her hand.*] But was it really the truth?

ROXANE. Yes. I'd love him even if he were . . . [*Hesitates.*]

CYRANO. [*Smiling sadly.*] The word embarrasses you in front of me?

ROXANE. No, I . . .

CYRANO. It won't hurt me! You'd love him even if he were ugly?

ROXANE. Yes! [*Several musket shots are heard offstage.*] The shooting seems to have begun.

3 CYRANO. [*Ardently.*] Even if he were hideous?

ROXANE. Yes!

CYRANO. Disfigured?

ROXANE. Yes!

CYRANO. Grotesque?

ROXANE. Nothing could make him seem grotesque to me!

---

## GUIDED READING

### LITERAL QUESTION

**1a.** What do Christian and Cyrano say about obstructing the other's chances? (Christian says he will not spoil Cyrano's happiness just because he is handsome; Cyrano says he will not spoil Christian's just because he can write well.)

### INFERENTIAL QUESTION

**1b.** What do these arguments tell you about the kind of love they value? (Each wants only a love that is won fairly and worthily. Each wants a love freely given and based on a true acceptance of who he is.)

CYRANO. You'd still love him?

ROXANE. Yes! Maybe even more!

1 CYRANO. [*Aside, losing his head.*] Perhaps it's true! Can it be that happiness is here, within my grasp? [*To* ROXANE.] I...Roxane...Listen to me....

LE BRET. [*Entering rapidly and calling softly.*] Cyrano!

CYRANO. [*Turning around.*] Yes?

LE BRET. Sh! [*Whispers something to* CYRANO, *who lets go of* ROXANE's *hand with a cry.*]

CYRANO. Oh!

ROXANE. What's the matter?

CYRANO. [*To himself, dazed.*] It's all over now. [*More shots are heard.*]

ROXANE. What is it? Those shots... [*Takes a few steps and looks offstage.*]

CYRANO. It's all over. Now I can never tell her!

ROXANE. What's happened?

CYRANO. [*Stopping her as she is about to rush forward.*] Nothing!

[*Some* CADETS *have entered, hiding the burden they are carrying. They group themselves to prevent* ROXANE *from approaching.*]

ROXANE. Those men...

CYRANO. [*Leading her away.*] Come away from them!

ROXANE. But what were you about to tell me?

2 CYRANO. Tell you? Oh, nothing....Nothing, I swear! [*Solemnly.*] I swear that Christian's mind and soul were...[*Catches himself in alarm.*]... are the greatest...

ROXANE. *Were?* [*She screams, runs to the group of* CADETS, *and pushes them aside.*]

CYRANO. It's all over.

ROXANE. [*Seeing* CHRISTIAN *lying wrapped in his cloak.*] Christian!

LE BRET. [*To* CYRANO.] The first shot fired by the enemy!

[ROXANE *throws herself onto* CHRISTIAN. *More shots. Clatter of weapons. Voices. Drums.*]

CARBON. [*Holding his drawn sword.*] Here comes the attack! Get ready! [*Followed by the* CADETS, *he climbs over the parapet.*]

ROXANE. Christian!

CARBON'S VOICE. [*From the other side of the embankment.*] Hurry!

ROXANE. Christian!

CARBON. Fall in!

ROXANE. Christian!

CHRISTIAN. [*In a dying voice.*] Roxane...

3 CYRANO. [*Speaking rapidly and softly in* CHRISTIAN's *ear while* ROXANE, *distraught, tears a strip of cloth from her dress and dips it in the water to wash his wound.*] I told her everything. It's still you she loves! [CHRISTIAN *closes his eyes.*]

ROXANE. Yes, my love? [*To* CYRANO.] He's not dead, is he?

CARBON. Bite open your charges!

ROXANE. I feel his cheek turning cold against mine!

CARBON. Ready! Aim!

ROXANE. Here's a letter he was carrying! [*Opens it.*] For me!

CYRANO. [*Aside.*] *My* letter!

CARBON. Fire! [*Shots. Cries. Sounds of battle.*]

CYRANO. [*Trying to draw his hand away from* ROXANE, *who clutches it, kneeling.*] Roxane! The attack has begun!

ROXANE. [*Holding him back.*] Stay a little longer.

*Cyrano de Bergerac, Act IV* **445**

## AT A GLANCE

- Cyrano begins to feel hope.
- Christian is mortally wounded.
- Cyrano vows never to tell Roxane the truth about the letters.
- Cyrano tells the dying Christian that Roxane's love remains unchanged.
- Roxane finds Christian's last letter, actually written by Cyrano.

**1 PLOT: CONFLICT**

Cyrano's greatest inner conflict is his belief that physical deformity has cut him off from Roxane's love forever. Haltingly, he begins to feel that happiness is within his reach.

**2 DIALOGUE**

Roxane first realizes that Christian is dead when Cyrano refers to him in the past tense. This past tense echoes with meaning, for the audience knows that now Cyrano's chance for happiness is also in the past.

**3 PLOT: CLIMAX**

The climax of the play occurs when Christian's death seals Cyrano's sacrifice.

## GUIDED READING

### LITERAL QUESTIONS

**1a.** What does Cyrano say after first hearing of Christian's death? ("It's all over. Now I can never tell her!")

**2a.** What does Cyrano tell Christian as he dies? (He lies and tells Christian that Roxane knows who wrote the letters but still loves Christian.)

### INFERENTIAL QUESTIONS

**1b.** Why does he feel that now he can never tell Roxane of his love and the part he played in the romance? (He cannot spoil her loving memories of Christian and feels it would be dishonorable to triumph over a dead man.)

**2b.** Why does Cyrano tell Christian a lie? (Out of compassion, Cyrano wants Christian to die happy.)

Roxane asks for reassurance about Christian's wonderful qualities, and Cyrano gives it to her.

### 1 STYLE: REPETITION

By repeating "Yes, Roxane," Cyrano spares Roxane the pain of disillusionment about Christian. The more he repeats it, the more the audience remembers that Christian was none of these things and that Cyrano is all of them.

He's dead. You were the only one who knew him. [*She weeps gently.*] He was a great and wonderful man, wasn't he?

CYRANO. [*Standing, bareheaded.*] Yes, Roxane.

1   ROXANE. A brilliant, captivating poet!

CYRANO. Yes, Roxane.

ROXANE. A magnificent mind!

CYRANO. Yes, Roxane.

**446** *Drama*

ROXANE. A vast heart whose depths remained hidden from the world! A noble and charming soul!

CYRANO. [*Firmly.*] Yes, Roxane!

ROXANE. [*Throwing herself onto* CHRISTIAN's *body.*] He's dead!

CYRANO. [*Aside, drawing his sword.*] And now I too must die, since, without knowing it, she's mourning for me in him!

## GUIDED READING

### LITERAL QUESTION

**1a.** What assessment of Christian does Roxane make? (She pays tribute to his powers of intellect, language, and feeling.)

### INFERENTIAL QUESTION

**1b.** Why does Cyrano assent to this evaluation when he knows it's not true? (He wants to reassure Roxane in her grief.)

[*Trumpets in the distance.* DE GUICHE *reappears on the parapet, bareheaded, with a wound on his forehead.*]

DE GUICHE. [*In a thunderous voice.*] That's the signal! A fanfare! The French are on their way back to camp with provisions! Hold fast a little longer!

ROXANE. There's blood on his letter, and tears!

A VOICE. [*Shouting from the other side of the embankment.*] Surrender!

CADETS' VOICES. No!

RAGUENEAU. [*Who has climbed up on his carriage to watch the battle beyond the embankment.*] They're coming closer!

CYRANO. [*To* DE GUICHE, *pointing to* ROXANE.] Take her away! I'm going to charge!

ROXANE. [*Feebly, kissing the letter.*] His blood! His tears!

RAGUENEAU. [*Leaping down from the carriage and running toward her.*] She's fainted!

DE GUICHE. [*On the parapet, shouting fiercely to the* CADETS.] Hold fast!

A VOICE. [*From beyond the embankment.*] Lay down your arms!

CADETS' VOICES. No!

CYRANO. [*To* DE GUICHE.] You've proved your valor, sir. [*Points to* ROXANE.] Flee now, and save her!

DE GUICHE. [*Hurrying to* ROXANE *and picking her up in his arms.*] I'll do it, for her sake. But we can win if you gain time!

CYRANO. We will! [*Watches* ROXANE, *unconscious, being carried away by* DE GUICHE *and* RAGUENEAU.] Good-by, Roxane!

[*Tumult. Shouts.* CADETS *reappear, wounded, and fall onstage.* CYRANO, *rushing toward the battle, is stopped on the parapet by* CARBON, *covered with blood.*]

CARBON. We're giving ground! I've been wounded twice!

CYRANO. [*Shouting to the* CADETS *in their native Gascon tongue. To* CARBON, *holding him up.*] Don't give up hope! I have two deaths to avenge: Christian's and that of my happiness! [*They go downstage.* CYRANO *brandishes the lance and fastens* ROXANE's *handkerchief to it.*] Float proudly, little lace banner bearing her monogram! [*Plants it on the parapet and again shouts. The fifer plays. Some of the wounded men stand up. Other* CADETS *come down the embankment and group themselves around* CYRANO *and the little flag. The carriage is filled and covered with men. Bristling with muskets, it is transformed. A* CADET *appears on the parapet, moving backward, still fighting.*]

THE CADET. [*Shouting.*] They're coming up the embankment! [*He falls dead.*]

CYRANO. We'll give them a salute! [*In an instant the parapet is crowned by a formidable line of enemy soldiers. Large Imperial banners are raised.*]

CYRANO. Fire! [*General volley.*]

A VOICE. [*Shouting from the enemy ranks.*] Fire! [*Murderous counterfire.* CADETS *fall on all sides.*]

A SPANISH OFFICER. Who are these men who have such scorn for death?

CYRANO. [*Reciting, facing the enemy fire.*]
These are the stouthearted Gascon Cadets
Of Carbon de Castel-Jaloux;
They fight over trifles and shamelessly lie . . . .

[*He rushes forward, followed by the few survivors.*]
These are the stouthearted Gascon . . .

[*The rest is lost in the tumult of battle.*]

*Cyrano de Bergerac, Act IV* **447**

3

1

2

AT A GLANCE

- The Spaniards attack.
- Cyrano sends De Guiche off with Roxane in order to save her.
- Many Cadets are killed and Cyrano leads a suicidal charge.

1 **CHARACTERIZATION**

The Cadets are characterized as proud, valorous, and unwilling to surrender, even with the odds overwhelmingly against them.

2 **DIALOGUE**

Cyrano again shows generosity. He reassures his old enemy about his bravery and respectfully calls him "sir."

3 **STAGING**

Cyrano uses Roxane's lace handkerchief to inspire him in battle. It is a symbol of what he's fighting for: the idealism of his love, unsullied by selfishness or compromise.

REFLECTING ON ACT IV

In Act IV several characters show growth. Which characters grow and in what ways? (Roxane becomes more mature, less frivolous; Christian gains understanding and confidence; De Guiche grows braver and more idealistic.)

## GUIDED READING

### LITERAL QUESTIONS

**1a.** Why does Cyrano tell the Cadets not to give up, that he'll fight extra hard? (He says he has two deaths to avenge: Christian's and that of his happiness.)

**2a.** How does Act IV end? (It ends with many Cadets dead and Cyrano advancing on the enemy with the few survivors, reciting his tribute to the Cadets.)

### INFERENTIAL QUESTIONS

**1b.** What does he mean by saying that he must avenge himself for the death of his happiness? (Cyrano's chance to declare his love to Roxane ended with Christian's death; and, as a result, his chance at happiness is also dead.)

**2b.** What effect does this ending create? (The act ends on a high pitch of uncertainty, with disaster at hand. These feelings reflect the status of Cyrano's love for Roxane.)

1. takes letter to Roxane through enemy lines
2. She was moved to come by his letters. At first she loved him for his beauty; after receiving letters she loves his soul.
3. is shattered; realizes she is in love with Cyrano; tell her the truth and let her choose
4. Christian's death; that she knows the truth and still loves Christian
5. bravery, depth of feeling; that Christian is disturbed
6. in love with each other; his depth, integrity
7. because Christian has been mortally wounded; wants him to die happy
8. Some may agree with Christian; others may feel she loves both.
9. She may have been able to overcome her shock and grief to respond; may not have believed Cyrano; may be in love with an ideal, neither Cyrano nor Christian.
10. No—his idealism will probably prevent him. He may prefer to love her from afar than to turn his dreams into mundane reality.

## LITERARY FOCUS

*Exposition:* Act I: introduces characters; conflicts
*Conflicts:* Christian's love for Roxane; fear she will not love him because of his lack of eloquence; Cyrano's love for her; fear she will not love him because of his ugliness
*Rising Action:* Act II: Roxane reveals she loves Christian; Cyrano / Christian decide to work together to create *romantic hero;* Act III: Cyrano woos Roxane; Christian marries her; both are sent to war
*Climax:* Act IV: Christian dies

## STUDY QUESTIONS

### Recalling

1. What mission does Cyrano undertake each morning at Arras?
2. How does Roxane explain the reason for her visit to the camp to Christian? According to her, how and why has her love for him changed?
3. How does Christian feel about Roxane's declaration? What does he ask Cyrano to do?
4. What event prevents Cyrano from fulfilling Christian's request? What does Cyrano tell Christian about Roxane's love?

### Interpreting

5. What new dimensions does Roxane reveal in her conversation with Christian? What does she fail to see?
6. What discoveries about Roxane and Cyrano does Christian make in this act? What new sides to his character do we see?
7. Why does Cyrano not tell Roxane the truth about the letters? Why does he not tell Christian the truth about Roxane?
8. Do you agree with Christian when he says that it is really Cyrano whom Roxane loves? Explain.

### Extending

9. How do you think Roxane would have responded if Cyrano had been able to tell her the truth about the letters and his feelings for her?

10. Do you think Cyrano will reveal his feelings to Roxane? Why or why not?

## LITERARY FOCUS

### Dramatic Plot

A play follows a **plot structure** that is similar in many ways to the plot structure of a story. In fact, since drama is an older form of literature than fiction, most of our ideas about plot originally come from ancient writers' observations about drama. The plot structure of a play, however, is usually defined more sharply than that of a story or novel. Because the audience at a play does not have the luxury of rereading what they have just seen, every speech and event must clearly advance the action and develop the characters.

In a well-made play, the exposition establishes the play's overall setting and introduces the main characters. Conflict appears very early in a drama; the rising action complicates this conflict, and the climax points toward the final outcome of this conflict. The falling action grows logically from the climax, and the resolution provides a satisfying conclusion to the play.

### Thinking About Dramatic Plot

■ In the first four acts of *Cyrano de Bergerac,* identify the exposition, the major conflicts, the rising action, and the climax.

# ACT V

*The park of the convent occupied by the Ladies of the Cross,[1] in Paris. Fifteen years later, in 1655.*

[*Magnificent shady foliage. To the left is the house, whose front steps lead up to a broad landing with several doors opening onto it. An enormous tree stands alone in the middle of the stage in a small oval-shaped open space. To the right is a semicircular stone bench among large box shrubs. It is autumn. The foliage above the green lawn has turned red. Dead leaves are falling and are strewn over the whole stage; they crackle underfoot along the lanes and half cover the bench. Between the bench on the right and the tree stands a large embroidery frame with a small chair in front of it. As the curtain rises,* NUNS *are coming and going in the park. Some are seated on the bench, around an older* NUN.]

SISTER MARTHE.[2] [*To* MOTHER MARGUERITE.[3]] Sister Claire has stopped in front of the mirror twice, to see how her headdress looks.

MOTHER MARGUERITE. [*Sternly.*] I'll tell Monsieur Cyrano this evening.

---

1. **Ladies of the Cross:** religious order.

2. **Marthe** [mär′tə]
3. **Marguerite** [mär′gə rēt′]

*Cyrano de Bergerac, Act V* **449**

AT A GLANCE

- The action jumps forward fifteen years, to a convent in autumn.
- Two nuns speak of Cyrano.

LITERARY OPTIONS

- dramatic irony
- symbolism
- mood

THEMATIC OPTIONS

- mortality
- love
- idealism

**1 SETTING**

Fifteen years have passed, suggesting changes in the characters and situations of the play.

**2 STYLE: MOOD**

The mood of Act V is suggested by its autumnal setting. The dying leaves reflect a somberness that permeates this act.

## GUIDED READING

### LITERAL QUESTION

**1a.** What place and season of the year does the setting specify? (the garden of a convent in the fall of the year)

### INFERENTIAL QUESTION

**1b.** What kind of mood does this setting create? (somber, with the black-and-white dress of the nuns and deep colors of fall; both time and place have serious associations: the season with death and the convent with life after death.)

## 1 DIALOGUE

The dialogue fills the audience in on the events that have occurred offstage and also demonstrates Cyrano's faithfulness to Roxane.

## 2 BACKGROUND

In the seventeenth century gentlewomen often retired to convents either in grief or in disgrace.

## 3 CHARACTERIZATION

The dialogue shows that Cyrano's idealism still keeps him poor, while his pride still prevents his asking for help.

## 4 PLOT: FORESHADOWING

Roxane's comment foreshadows her discovery that her lover is indeed still alive.

---

SISTER CLAIRE. [*Pious look.*] He'll make fun of us!

SISTER MARTHE. He'll say that nuns are very coquettish!

MOTHER MARGUERITE. [*Smiling.*] And very good.

**1** SISTER CLAIRE. He's been coming every Saturday for the past ten years, hasn't he, Mother Marguerite de Jésus?

MOTHER MARGUERITE. Longer than that! Ever since his cousin came to us fourteen years ago, mingling her black mourning veil with our linen hoods, like a raven among a flock of white doves.

**2** SISTER MARTHE. In all the time since she first took a room in this cloister, no one but Monsieur Cyrano has ever been able to distract her from the grief that afflicts her night and day.

ALL THE NUNS. He's so amusing!—His visits are delightful!—He teases us!—Such a nice man!—We all like him!—He always appreciates the pastry we make for him!

MOTHER MARGUERITE. Well, the last time he came, he hadn't eaten anything for two days.

SISTER MARTHE. Oh, Mother!

**3** MOTHER MARGUERITE. He's poor.

SISTER MARTHE. Who told you so?

MOTHER MARGUERITE. Monsieur Le Bret.

SISTER MARTHE. Doesn't anyone help him?

MOTHER MARGUERITE. No. It would only make him angry if anyone tried. [ROXANE *appears, walking slowly along a lane in the background. She is dressed in black, with a widow's cap and long veils.* DE GUICHE, *who has aged gracefully, walks beside her.* MOTHER MARGUERITE *stands up.*] Come, we must go inside. Madame Magdeleine is strolling in the park with a visitor.

SISTER MARTHE. This is the first time he's come to see her for months!

---

OTHER NUNS. He's very busy—The court—The army. . . .

SISTER CLAIRE. Worldly concerns!

[*The* NUNS *leave.* DE GUICHE *and* ROXANE *come downstage in silence and stop near the embroidery frame. Several moments pass.*]

THE DUKE. [*Formerly* DE GUICHE.] And so you remain here, letting your blond beauty go to waste, still in mourning?

ROXANE. Still in mourning.

THE DUKE. And still faithful?

ROXANE. Still faithful.

THE DUKE. [*After a moment of silence.*] Have you forgiven me?

ROXANE. [*Simply, looking at the cross of the convent.*] Of course, since I'm here. [*Another silence.*]

THE DUKE. Was he really such a . . .

ROXANE. He showed his true nature only to those who knew him well.

THE DUKE. His true nature? . . . Yes, perhaps I didn't know him well enough. . . . Do you still carry his last letter over your heart?

ROXANE. Yes, like a holy relic.

**4** THE DUKE. You love him even in death?

ROXANE. Sometimes it seems to me that he's not really dead. I feel that our hearts are together, and that his love floats around me, very much alive!

THE DUKE. [*After another silence.*] Does Cyrano come to see you?

ROXANE. Yes, often. My old friend gives me all the news; he replaces the gazettes⁴ for me. He

---

4. **gazettes:** newspapers.

---

## GUIDED READING

### LITERAL QUESTION

**1a.** What information do the nuns give about Cyrano? (He has visited Roxane weekly for fifteen years; all the nuns like him; he is very poor and allows no one to help him because of his pride.)

### INFERENTIAL QUESTION

**1b.** From what the nuns say what can you infer about the changes, or lack of them, in Cyrano's life? (Not much has changed: He loves Roxane, he's still witty, idealistic, poor, and very proud.)

visits me regularly. If the weather is good, his chair is always brought out and placed under this tree. I embroider while I wait for him. When the clock strikes the hour of his arrival, I don't even turn around to look for him, because I know I'll hear his cane coming down the steps immediately after the last stroke. He sits down and laughs at my eternal tapestry. Then he begins telling me about the week's happenings, and... [LE BRET *appears on the steps.*] Ah! Here's Le Bret! [LE BRET *comes down.*] How is our friend doing?

LE BRET. Badly.

THE DUKE. Oh!

ROXANE. [*To the* DUKE.] He's exaggerating!

LE BRET. Cyrano is living in isolation and poverty, just as I predicted! His writings constantly make new enemies for him! He attacks false noblemen, false saints, false heroes, plagiarists —everyone!

ROXANE. But his sword fills everyone with terror. No one will ever get the best of him.

THE DUKE. [*Shaking his head.*] Who knows?

LE BRET. I'm not afraid of his meeting a violent death. Loneliness, hunger, the cold of winter creeping into his dark room—those are the assassins that will end his life! He tightens his belt one more notch every day, his poor nose has turned as pale as ivory, he has only one threadbare black coat....

THE DUKE. It's certainly true that he hasn't scaled the heights of worldly success, but don't feel too sorry for him. He lives without compromise, free in both his thoughts and his acts.

LE BRET. [*Still smiling bitterly.*] Sir, you...

THE DUKE. [*Loftily.*] Yes, I know: I have everything and he has nothing. But I'd be honored to shake his hand. [*Bows to* ROXANE.] I must go. Good-by.

ROXANE. I'll accompany you to the door. [*The DUKE bows to* LE BRET *and walks toward the steps with* ROXANE.]

THE DUKE. [*Stopping as they are climbing the steps.*] Yes, sometimes I envy him. When a man has been too successful in life, even though he hasn't done anything really wrong, he still has all sorts of reasons for feeling a little disgusted with himself. Their combined weight isn't enough to form a burden of remorse, but he can never escape a kind of vague uneasiness. As he continues to climb toward even greater success, he hears dead illusions and old regrets rustling under his mantle, like the fallen leaves swept along by the train of your black dress when you mount these steps.

ROXANE. [*Ironically.*] You're in a thoughtful mood today.

THE DUKE. Yes, I'm afraid so. [*Abruptly, just as he is about to leave.*] Monsieur Le Bret! [*To* ROXANE.] Will you excuse me? I want to have a word with him. [*Goes to* LE BRET *and speaks in a low voice.*] It's true that no one would dare to attack our friend openly, but it's also true that he's hated by many people. Only yesterday, during a card game at court, someone said to me, "That Cyrano may have a fatal accident someday."

LE BRET. Oh?

THE DUKE. Yes. Tell him not to go out very often, and to be careful.

LE BRET. [*Throwing up his arms.*] Careful!... He'll soon be here; I'll warn him. But...

ROXANE. [*Who has remained on the steps, to a* NUN *coming toward her.*] What is it?

THE NUN. Ragueneau would like to see you, madame.

ROXANE. Bring him in. [*To the* DUKE *and* LE BRET.] He's come to complain about his poverty. Since the day when he set out to be a writer, he's been a singer...

LE BRET. A bathhouse attendant...

*Cyrano de Bergerac, Act V* **451**

## GUIDED READING

### LITERAL QUESTIONS

**1a.** According to Le Bret in what way does Cyrano get into trouble? (His writings attack hypocrisy and falsehood, thus keeping him poor and isolated.)

**2a.** What secret information does De Guiche give Le Bret about Cyrano? (He tells him that Cyrano has many enemies at court and should be careful because someone may try to kill him, making it look like an accident.)

### INFERENTIAL QUESTIONS

**1b.** What does this account tell you about Cyrano's idealism? (He still stands up for his ideals at the cost of worldly advancement.

**2b.** What does his warning tell you about De Guiche's attitude toward Cyrano? (He is no longer Cyrano's enemy.)

- Ragueneau tells Le Bret that Cyrano has been attacked and injured.
- Le Bret goes off with Ragueneau to Cyrano.
- Roxane prepares for Cyrano's visit.

## 1 PLOT

Ragueneau's eyewitness account serves as a way to get an important event of the plot before the audience.

## 2 STYLE: METAPHOR

Roxane uses metaphor to describe her state of mind: The melancholy of autumn suits her gentle grief for Christian.

## 3 CHARACTERIZATION

Roxane's monologue shows her confidence in Cyrano. His visits are important to her, but she is a bit smug and insensitive, accepting them as her due all these years and never wondering what he gets from them.

ROXANE. A hairdresser...

LE BRET. A lute teacher...

ROXANE. What can he have become now?

RAGUENEAU. [*Entering rapidly.*] Ah, madame! [*Sees* LE BRET.] Sir!

ROXANE. [*Smiling.*] Tell Le Bret your troubles. I'll be back soon.

RAGUENEAU. But madame... [ROXANE *ignores him and leaves with the* DUKE. RAGUENEAU *goes to* LE BRET.]

1 RAGUENEAU. Since you're here, I'd rather she didn't know....As I was approaching our friend's house this afternoon, on my way to visit him, I saw him come out. I hurried to catch up with him. I can't say for certain that it wasn't an accident, but when he was about to turn the corner a lackey dropped a piece of firewood on him from an upstairs window.

LE BRET. The cowards!...Cyrano!...

RAGUENEAU. I ran to him....

LE BRET. It's horrible!

RAGUENEAU. Our friend, sir, our poet, was lying on the ground with a big hole in his head!

LE BRET. Is he dead?

RAGUENEAU. No, but...I carried him back into his house, to his room, rather. Oh, that room! What a wretched little closet!

LE BRET. Is he in pain?

RAGUENEAU. No, sir, he's unconscious.

LE BRET. Did you bring a doctor?

RAGUENEAU. Yes, I found one who was willing to come out of charity.

LE BRET. Poor Cyrano!...We mustn't tell Roxane all at once....What did the doctor say?

RAGUENEAU. I don't remember very clearly,

**452** *Drama*

something about fever....Oh, if you'd seen him lying there, with his head wrapped in bandages!...Come with me quickly! There's no one with him now, and he may die if he tries to get up!

LE BRET. [*Leading him to the right.*] Let's go this way, through the chapel. It's shorter. [ROXANE *appears on the steps and sees* LE BRET *hurrying along the colonnade that leads to the side door of the chapel.*]

ROXANE. Monsieur Le Bret! [LE BRET *and* RAGUENEAU *leave without answering.*] Le Bret runs away when I call him? Poor Ragueneau must really be in trouble this time! [*She comes* 2 *down the steps.*] What a beautiful autumn day! Even my sorrow is smiling. It's offended by April, but gives in to the gentler charm of September. [*She sits down in front of her embroidery frame. Two* NUNS *come out of the house, carrying a large armchair, and set it down under a tree.*] Ah, here's the chair for my old friend! He'll soon be here. [*She begins working. The clock strikes.*] There, it's time. I'll take 3 out my skeins[5]....This is surprising: the clock has finished striking and he's not here yet. Is he going to be late for the first time? The Sister at the door must be—Where's my thimble? There, I see it—must be trying to persuade him to repent of his sins. [*Several moments pass.*] Still persuading him! He'll surely be here before long.... A dead leaf....[*She brushes aside the leaf that has fallen onto the embroidery frame.*] Nothing could—My scissors...in my bag!—prevent him from coming!

A NUN. [*Appearing on the steps.*] Monsieur de Bergerac is here.

ROXANE. [*Without turning around.*] I knew it! [*She continues her work.* CYRANO *appears. He is very pale, and his hat is pulled down over his eyes. The* NUN *who has accompanied him leaves.*]

---

5. **skeins** [skānz]: thread or yarn wound in a coil.

## GUIDED READING

**LITERAL QUESTION**

**1a.** What does Roxane say when she sees Ragueneau go off with Le Bret? ("Le Bret runs away when I call him? Poor Ragueneau must really be in trouble this time!")

**INFERENTIAL QUESTION**

**1b.** How does her comment create dramatic irony? (The audience knows, but Roxane does not, that it is Cyrano who is in trouble, not Ragueneau.)

*He slowly comes down the steps, leaning on his cane and making an obvious effort to stay on his feet.* ROXANE *is still working.*] Oh, these faded colors!...How will I ever match them? [*To* CYRANO, *in a tone of friendly rebuke.*] Late, for the first time in fourteen years!

[CYRANO *has succeeded in reaching his chair and sitting down in it. When he speaks, his cheerful voice contrasts with his face.*]

CYRANO. Yes, it's scandalous! I can't tell you how annoyed I am. I was delayed by . . .

ROXANE. By what?

CYRANO. By an untimely visit.

ROXANE. [*Distractedly, still working.*] A friend of yours?

1 CYRANO. An old acquaintance. We've met on the battlefield, among other places. I knew we'd meet again some day, but this wasn't the time for it.

ROXANE. You sent him away?

CYRANO. Yes, I said to him, "Excuse me, but this is Saturday, the day when I always keep a certain appointment. Nothing can make me miss it. Come back in an hour."

ROXANE. [*Lightly.*] Well, I'm afraid he'll have to wait for you, because I won't let you leave before nightfall.

CYRANO. [*Gently.*] I may have to leave a little sooner than that. [*He closes his eyes and remains silent.* SISTER MARTHE *walks across the park, from the chapel to the steps.* ROXANE *sees her and nods to her.*]

2 ROXANE. [*To* CYRANO.] Aren't you going to tease Sister Marthe today?

CYRANO. [*Quickly, opening his eyes.*] Yes, of course! [*In a comically gruff voice.*] Sister Marthe! Come here! [*She comes to him.*] When you have such lovely eyes, why do you keep them cast down?

SISTER MARTHE. [*Looking up with a smile.*] I . . . [*Sees his face and makes a gesture of astonishment.*] Oh!

CYRANO. [*In an undertone, pointing to* ROXANE.] Sh! It's nothing. . . .

ROXANE. [*Who has heard them whispering.*] She's trying to convert you!

SISTER MARTHE. I'm doing no such thing!

3 CYRANO. Now that I think of it, you never preach to me! It's amazing! [*With mock ferocity.*] I'll show you that you're not the only one who can be amazing! Just listen to this! I'm going to . . . [*Seems to be trying to think of a good way to tease her.*] Ah! I've got it! I'm going to allow you to pray for me tonight in the chapel!

ROXANE. Oh! Oh!

CYRANO. [*Laughing.*] Sister Marthe is dumbfounded!

SISTER MARTHE. [*Gently.*] I haven't waited for your permission. [*She goes into the house.*]

CYRANO. [*Turning back to* ROXANE, *who is leaning over her work.*] May the devil take me if I ever see that tapestry finished!

ROXANE. I was expecting some such remark. [*A breeze makes some leaves fall.*]

CYRANO. The leaves . . .

ROXANE. [*Raising her head and looking into the distance.*] They're Titian red[6]. . . . Look at them falling.

CYRANO. How well they fall! Such beauty in that short drop from branch to earth! They give their fall the grace of flight.

---

6. **Titian** [tē′shən] **red:** a particular shade of red used by Titian (1477–1576), an Italian painter.

*Cyrano de Bergerac, Act V* **453**

## GUIDED READING

### LITERAL QUESTIONS

**1a.** What does Cyrano say when Roxane tells him she won't let him leave before nightfall? ("I may have to leave a little sooner than that.")

**2a.** What does Cyrano admire about the autumn leaves? (He admires the way they fall so gracefully.)

### INFERENTIAL QUESTIONS

**1b.** Why might Cyrano really have to leave early? (He's afraid he'll die before then.)

**2b.** Why do you think Cyrano is suddenly so interested in the leaves? (He knows he's dying and is saying good-by to the beauty of the world; also, he identifies with the dying leaves.)

## AT A GLANCE

- Cyrano tells Roxane news of the fashionable world.
- He faints, then revives.
- He asks to see Christian's last letter and reads it aloud.

**1 DIALOGUE**

Cyrano effaces his feelings for the sake of Roxane and his secret love. He denies his physical pain and his sadness at leaving Roxane.

**2 HUMOR: EXAGGERATION**

Cyrano exaggerates the news for humorous effect. Exaggeration is appropriate as it reflects the court, which magnifies its petty concerns out of proportion.

**3 PLOT: FALLING ACTION**

Cyrano faints, showing the extent of his weakness and the closeness of death. The events of Cyrano's fatal injury and last interview with Roxane bring the plot closer to resolution.

**4 DRAMATIC IRONY**

Roxane draws a parallel between her grief and Cyrano's physical pain. The parallel is more exact than she knows: Cyrano also suffers grief for a love that could never be.

**5 STAGING**

Cyrano's reading the letter aloud creates pathos by its eerie appropriateness: It was Cyrano's last letter to Roxane, and this time he is actually dying.

---

ROXANE. Can it be that you're melancholy—you?

CYRANO. [*Catching himself.*] Not at all!

**1** ROXANE. Then forget about the falling leaves and tell me the latest news. Aren't you still my gazette?

CYRANO. I'll begin this very moment.

ROXANE. Good.

CYRANO. [*More and more pale, struggling*
**2** *against his pain.*] Last Saturday, the nineteenth, after eating eight helpings of preserved fruit, the King took to his bed with a fever; his illness was convicted of high treason and executed by his physician, and since then the royal pulse has returned to normal.

ROXANE. That will do, Monsieur de Bergerac!

CYRANO. [*Whose face is increasingly twisted by pain.*] On Tuesday, the whole court went to Fontainebleau.[7] On Wednesday, Madame Montglat[8] said no to Count de Fiesque.[9] On Thursday, Olympe[10] Mancini was the Queen of France—or almost! On Friday, the twenty-fifth, Madame Montglat said yes to Count de Fiesque. And today, Saturday the twenty-sixth . . . [*He closes his eyes and his head falls. Silence. Surprised at no longer hearing him speak,* ROXANE *turns and looks at him, then stands up in alarm.*]

**3** ROXANE. Has he fainted? [*Hurries to him with a cry.*] Cyrano!

CYRANO. [*Vaguely, opening his eyes.*] What is it? . . . What . . . [*Seeing her leaning over him, he quickly puts his hand to his hat to make sure it is still pulled down, and draws away from her in his chair.*] No! It's nothing, believe me! Go back to your chair.

---

7. **Fontainebleau** [fon'tən blō']: town near Paris and site of the royal palace.
8. **Madame Montglat** [mon gla']
9. **Count de Fiesque** [də fē esk']
10. **Olympe** [ō lēmp']

454 *Drama*

---

ROXANE. But you . . .

CYRANO. It's only my old wound from Arras. Sometimes it . . . You know. . . .

ROXANE. My poor friend!

CYRANO. It's really nothing. It will soon go away. [*Smiles with an effort.*] There, it's gone.

**4** ROXANE. [*Standing beside him.*] Each of us has his wound. Mine is old but still unhealed, here . . . [*Puts her hand to her bosom.*] . . . under the yellowed paper of a letter still stained with tears and blood! [*Twilight is beginning to fall.*]

CYRANO. His letter! . . . Didn't you once tell me that you might let me read it some day?

ROXANE. You want to read . . . his letter?

CYRANO. Yes, I do. Now.

ROXANE. [*Removing the little bag that hangs from around her neck.*] Here!

CYRANO. [*Taking it.*] May I open it?

ROXANE. Yes, read it. [*She goes back to the embroidery frame and begins putting away her thread.*]

CYRANO. [*Reading.*] "Farewell, Roxane! Death is near. . . ."

**5** ROXANE. [*Stopping in surprise.*] You're reading it aloud?

CYRANO. [*Reading.*] "I believe this will be my last day, my beloved. My soul is still heavy with unexpressed love, and I must die! Never again will my eyes delight . . ."

ROXANE. How well you read his letter!

CYRANO. [*Continuing.*] ". . . will my eyes delight in kissing each of your graceful gestures. I remember one of them, a way of putting your hand to your forehead, and I want to cry out . . ."

ROXANE. [*Troubled.*] How well you read . . . that letter! [*The twilight is turning to darkness.*]

---

## GUIDED READING

### LITERAL QUESTIONS

**1a.** As her "gazette" what kind of news does Cyrano bring Roxane? (He tells her about the happenings at court and in the fashionable world.)

**2a.** After Cyrano faints, what does he tell Roxane is the cause? (He says it's only his old wound from Arras.)

### INFERENTIAL QUESTIONS

**1b.** What attitude toward the fashionable world does he project in the way he tells the news? (He jokes, making the inconsequential nature of their concerns seem ridiculous. He shows his scorn through humor.)

**2b.** What does he really mean by this statement, and what does Roxane think he means? (He really means the wound in his heart from being unable to express his love for Roxane and ask for hers in return. She thinks he means a war wound.)

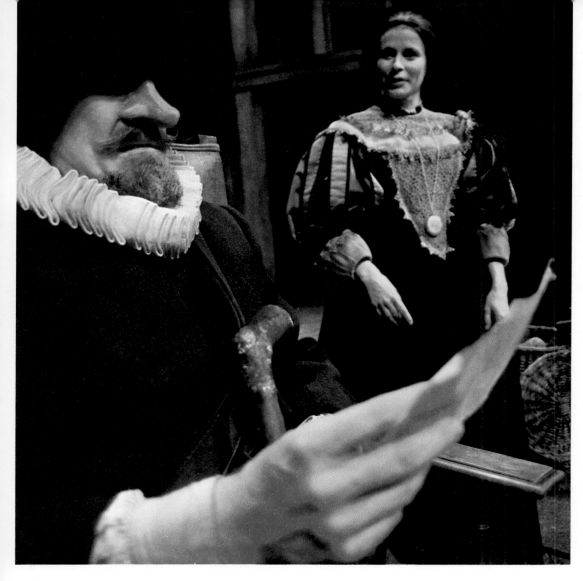

AT A GLANCE

As Cyrano reads the letter, Roxane recalls hearing Cyrano's voice speaking words of love once before.

**1 DIALOGUE**

Roxane's halting words show that she is slowly realizing that it was Cyrano all along who voiced his own love through words she accepted as Christian's.

CYRANO. "...to cry out, 'Good-by!'..."

ROXANE. You read it...

CYRANO. "...my dearest, my darling, my treasure..."

ROXANE. [*Thoughtfully.*]...in a voice that...

CYRANO. "...my love!"

**1** ROXANE. ...that...[*She starts.*] A voice that I'm not hearing for the first time! [*She slowly approaches him without his seeing her, stands behind his chair, silently bends down, and looks at the letter. The darkness is deepening.*]

*Cyrano de Bergerac,* Act V **455**

---

## GUIDED READING

### LITERAL QUESTION

**1a.** What does Roxane say about the way Cyrano reads the letter? (She says, "You read it . . . in a voice that . . . that . . . A voice that I'm not hearing for the first time!")

### INFERENTIAL QUESTION

**1b.** What do her words and actions show about what she is realizing? (It is slowly beginning to dawn on her that Cyrano spoke to her under the balcony the night she was so moved by sincere words of love and that he wrote the letters she loved so.)

- Roxane guesses Cyrano wrote the letters and was "the voice in the night."
- Le Bret and Ragueneau find Cyrano with Roxane.
- Cyrano announces his death, and Roxane realizes for the first time that he is mortally wounded.

### 1 READING SKILLS: CAUSE AND EFFECT

Because it is now dark, Roxane realizes Cyrano is unable to see well enough to read. She then realizes that he must be speaking the words of the letter from memory.

### 2 CHARACTERIZATION

Roxane's word choice sums up Cyrano's character: He has been selfless in love, always thinking of her happiness and well-being before his own interests.

### 3 STYLE: IRONY

After years of wanting to speak his love without disguise, Cyrano denies it.

### 4 CHARACTERIZATION

Cyrano dies as he lived: witty and brave. His ability to gain detachment and treat his own murder as a newspaper story, as though it happened to someone else, is typical of his lack of self-pity.

---

CYRANO. "My heart has never left you for a moment, and in the next world my love for you will still be as boundless, as . . ."

ROXANE. [*Putting her hand on his shoulder.*] How can you read now? It's dark. [*He starts, turns around, sees her standing close to him, makes a gesture of alarm, and bows his head. A long silence. Then, in the shadowy darkness, she clasps her hands and speaks slowly.*] And for fourteen years you played the part of an old friend who came to be amusing!

CYRANO. Roxane!

ROXANE. It was you.

CYRANO. No, Roxane, no!

ROXANE. I should have guessed it each time I heard you say my name!

CYRANO. No! It wasn't . . .

ROXANE. It *was* you!

CYRANO. I swear . . .

ROXANE. I see the whole selfless imposture now! The letters . . . It was you.

CYRANO. No!

ROXANE. The wild, endearing words . . . It was you.

CYRANO. No!

ROXANE. The voice in the night . . . It was you.

CYRANO. I swear it wasn't!

ROXANE. The soul . . . It was yours!

CYRANO. I didn't love you!

ROXANE. You did love me!

CYRANO. [*Desperately.*] It was Christian!

ROXANE. You loved me!

CYRANO. No, no, my love, I didn't love you!

456   *Drama*

---

ROXANE. Ah, how many things have died, and how many have now been born! Why were you silent for fourteen years, knowing that he hadn't written that letter, and that the tears on it were yours?

CYRANO. [*Handing her the letter.*] The blood was his.

ROXANE. And why have you let that sublime silence be broken this evening?

CYRANO. Why? . . .

[LE BRET *and* RAGUENEAU *enter, running.*]

LE BRET. What foolhardiness! I knew we'd find him here!

CYRANO. [*Smiling, and sitting more erect.*] You were right. Here I am.

LE BRET. [*To* ROXANE.] He's killed himself by leaving his bed!

ROXANE. [*To* CYRANO.] Your faintness a little while ago . . . Was it . . .

CYRANO. That reminds me: I didn't finish my gazette! Today, Saturday the twenty-sixth, an hour before dinner time, Monsieur de Bergerac was murdered. [*He takes off his hat, showing the bandages around his head.*]

ROXANE. What is he saying? . . . Cyrano! . . . Those bandages! . . . What have they done to you? Why?

CYRANO. "To be struck down by the only noble weapon, the sword, wielded by an adversary worthy of me . . ." Yes, I once said that. Fate is a great jester! I've been struck down, but from behind, in an ambush, by a lackey wielding a log! I've been consistent to the end. I've failed in everything, even in my death.

RAGUENEAU. Oh, sir! . . .

CYRANO. Don't weep so loudly, Ragueneau.

---

## GUIDED READING

### LITERAL QUESTION

**1a.** What does Cyrano say when Roxane confronts him with her knowledge that he wrote the letters? (He denies it all.)

### INFERENTIAL QUESTION

**1b.** Why does Cyrano reject his last chance to confess his love to Roxane? (He is still faithful to his original honorable intentions toward Roxane. He won't cause her pain by degrading her memories of her great love.)

[*Takes his hand.*] Tell me, brother poet, what are you doing these days?

RAGUENEAU. [*Through his tears.*] I'm the candle-snuffer in a theater . . . Molière's[11] company. . . .

CYRANO. Molière!

RAGUENEAU. Yes, but I'm leaving him tomorrow. I'm outraged! Yesterday they played his *Scapin*, and I saw that he'd taken a scene from you!

LE BRET. A whole scene!

CYRANO. Be calm. He was right to take it. [*To* RAGUENEAU.] How did the audience react to the scene?

RAGUENEAU. [*Sobbing.*] Oh, sir, they laughed and laughed!

CYRANO. Yes, my life has been that of a man who provides words and ideas for others, spurs them to action, and is then forgotten. [*To* ROXANE.] Do you remember the evening when Christian spoke to you below your balcony? Well, that evening was the essence of my life: while I remained below, in the shadows, others climbed up to receive the kiss of glory. But now, on the threshold of my grave, I acknowledge the justice of it all—Molière is a genius, and Christian was handsome! [*The chapel bell has begun ringing; the* NUNS *are now seen walking along the lane in the background, on their way to Vespers.*[12]] Let them go to their prayers, since their bell is ringing.

ROXANE. [*Looking up and calling.*] Sister! Sister!

CYRANO. [*Holding her back.*] No, no, don't go to bring anyone! You'd find me gone when you returned. [*The* NUNS *have entered the chapel, and the organ is heard.*] I needed a little harmony, and there it is.

---

11. **Molière's** [mō lyārz′]: Moliere (1622–1673) was a famous French dramatist, actor, and director.
12. **Vespers**: church service held in the evening.

ROXANE. I love you! You must live!

CYRANO. No. In the fairy tale, when Beauty said, "I love you" to the prince, his ugliness melted away like snow in the warmth of the sun, but as you can see, those words have no such magic effect on me.

ROXANE. Your life has been unhappy because of me! Me!

CYRANO. No, Roxane, quite the contrary. Feminine sweetness was unknown to me. My mother made it clear that she didn't find me pleasant to look at. I had no sister. Later, I dreaded the thought of seeing mockery in the eyes of a mistress. Thanks to you, I've at least had a woman's friendship, a gracious presence to soften the harsh loneliness of my life.

LE BRET. [*Pointing to the moonlight shining through the branches.*] Your other friend has come to visit you.

CYRANO. [*Smiling at the moon.*] Yes, I see her.

ROXANE. I've loved only one man, and I've lost him twice!

CYRANO. Le Bret, I'll soon be soaring up to the moon, this time without having to invent a machine. . . . "Philosopher, scientist, poet, swordsman, musician, aerial traveler, maker of sharp retorts, and lover (not to his advantage!), here lies Savinien[13] de Cyrano de Bergerac, who was everything, and who was nothing." [*Half raising himself from his chair.*] Excuse me, I must go now: a moonbeam has come to take me away, and I can't keep it waiting! [*He falls back into his chair.* ROXANE's *weeping recalls him to reality. He looks at her and strokes her veils.*] I don't want you to mourn any less for that good, charming, handsome Christian; my only hope is that when the great cold has seeped into my bones, you'll give a double meaning to those

---

13. **Savinien** [sa vē nyan′]: Cyrano's first name.

*Cyrano de Bergerac, Act V* **457**

## AT A GLANCE
- Cyrano reviews his life.
- Roxane confesses her love.

### 1 THEME
Cyrano reviews his life and finds that its essence consists of being in shadow while others collect the prizes. This recognition underscores one of the play's main themes: that sacrifice is necessary for idealism.

### 2 PLOT: RESOLUTION
The resolution of plot occurs when Roxane realizes that she loves Cyrano. This resolution is both satisfying and tragic, since it is too late for them to enjoy their love.

### 3 PLOT: CONFLICT
Cyrano confesses his vulnerability concerning his disfigurement. He reveals the origin of his major conflict: His ugliness was rejected even by his mother.

## GUIDED READING

### LITERAL QUESTION
**1a.** How does Cyrano compare Roxane and himself to Beauty and the Beast? (He says, in the story when Beauty said she loved the Beast, he turned into a handsome prince, but when Roxane says she loves him, he stays the same.)

### INFERENTIAL QUESTION
**1b.** What does his reference to this story tell you about his feelings about his appearance? (He still feels that his great ugliness is a barrier to love, and despite Roxane's confession of love, he still feels unlovable as he is.)

- Cyrano asks Roxane to mourn him along with Christian.
- As death comes closer, Cyrano wishes to die as he has lived, fighting all that is ignoble.

**1 RESPONSE JOURNAL**

Cyrano maintains that the noblest battles are fought with the knowledge that one cannot possibly win. Ask students to comment on his statement in their journals—do they agree or disagree?

black veils, and mourn for me a little when you mourn for him.

ROXANE. I swear to you that... [CYRANO *is shaken by a great tremor, and abruptly stands up.*]

CYRANO. No! Not there! Not in a chair! [*The others move toward him.*] Stand back! I want no support from anyone! [*Leans against the tree.*] Only from this tree! [*Silence.*] He's coming. I already feel stone boots...lead gloves.... [*Stiffens himself.*] Yes, he's coming, but I'll meet him on my feet... [*Draws his sword.*]...sword in hand!

**458** *Drama*

LE BRET. Cyrano!

ROXANE. [*Half fainting.*] Cyrano! [*They all draw back in terror.*]

CYRANO. I believe I see...yes, I see him, with his noseless face, daring to look at my nose! [*Raises his sword.*] What's that you say? It's useless? Of course, but I've never needed hope of victory to make me fight! The noblest battles are always fought in vain!...You there, all of you, who are you? Your numbers seem endless....Ah, I recognize you now: my old enemies! Lies! My greetings to you! [*Thrusts his sword into the empty air.*] And here's Com-

## GUIDED READING

**LITERAL QUESTION**

**1a.** What images does Cyrano use to tell how death feels? (He says the coming of death makes him feel as though he were wearing stone boots and lead gloves.)

**INFERENTIAL QUESTION**

**1b.** What sensations do you think Cyrano is describing by these images? (He may be referring to the loss of feeling due to the weakness of coming death.)

promise! And Prejudice! And Cowardice! [*Thrusts again.*] What's that? Come to terms with you? Never! Never!... Ah, there you are, Stupidity!... I know I can't defeat you all, I know that in the end you'll overwhelm me, but I'll still fight you as long as there's a breath in my body! [*Swings his sword in great arcs, then stops, panting.*] Yes, you've robbed me of everything: the laurels of glory, the roses of love! But there's one thing you can't take away from me. When I go to meet God this evening, and doff my hat before the holy gates, my salute will sweep the blue threshold of heaven, because I'll still have one thing intact, without a stain, something that I'll take with me in spite of you! [*Springs forward with his sword raised.*] You ask what it is? I'll tell you! It's... [*His sword drops from his hand; he staggers and falls into the arms of* LE BRET *and* RAGUENEAU.]

ROXANE. [*Bending down and kissing him on the forehead.*] What is it?

1 CYRANO. [*Opening his eyes and smiling at her.*] My white plume.

---

## STUDY QUESTIONS

### Recalling

1. According to the nuns, what has happened since Christian's death? What do they and Le Bret reveal about Cyrano's circumstances?
2. Describe Cyrano's condition when he arrives at the convent. How does he disguise it from Roxane?
3. How does Cyrano finally reveal his feelings to Roxane? How does she respond?
4. What "old enemies" does Cyrano see in his dying vision? What are his last words?

### Interpreting

5. Why do you think Cyrano finally reveals his love to Roxane?
6. What does Roxane mean when she says that she has lost the man she loved twice? Do you agree?
7. Show that Cyrano meets his death in a style that is consistent with his life. What do his very last words mean?
8. Cyrano says of himself that he "was everything and was nothing." Why would he make such a comment about his life? Do you agree with him?

### Extending

9. Cyrano is a very colorful character. Do you think that he is too flamboyant for real life, or do you believe that people like Cyrano actually exist?

## VIEWPOINT

The introduction to one of the first English translations of Rostand's play notes that Cyrano's idealism might serve as a model for all of us:

The brilliant author of *Cyrano* tells of things better than those we see around us, of things of beauty which [we might] bring somewhat nearer to our touch, if we will only have the courage to live up to them.

— A. Cohn

■ What ideals does Cyrano live up to in this play, and why might it take courage to live up to them? In what way does the play point to a better world than the one in which we live?

## LITERARY FOCUS

### The Total Effect

In staging a play, a director tries to present the audience with an integrated view of the entire work. *Cyrano de Bergerac* presents a fascinating challenge to any director, because it is full of contrasting emotions and effects that move audiences both to laughter and to tears. Anyone who directs this rich work must be aware of the impact of each of the various elements in the play — its plot, characters, setting, symbols, irony, and themes — on the work as a whole.

*Cyrano de Bergerac, Act V* **459**

1. Roxane's retreat into convent; Cyrano's decline into poverty. Ending is satisfying: Cyrano reveals his love; Roxane tells him she loves him; he dies as he lived, eloquently, fearlessly.

2. is dashing in duel; shows restraint with Roxane; is eloquent; unusual in his ugliness

3. *Act I*—theater establishes Cyrano's flamboyance; *Act II*—pastry shop creates comic counterpoint; *Act III*—night under Roxane's balcony is infused with romanticism; *Act IV*—battlefield represents struggle to survive; *Act V*—convent represents love transcending physical reality.

4. *battle:* personal courage, sense of honor; *end:* pride, commitment to ideals, love

5. mirrors the irony that his physical ugliness masks the beauty of his inner soul

6. Spiritual beauty endures; physical does not; spiritual beauty is more real, gives life meaning.

7. His virtue is uncompromised; suggests idealism cannot be defeated by apparent reality.

8. *good:* is courageous, colorful, inspiring; *bad:* unwillingness to compromise makes life difficult

9. It is the expression of the soul; some may feel that language is valued over feeling.

## VOCABULARY

1. *capdet:* Gascon dialect
2. *étage:* Mod. Fr.
3. *secret:* Old Fr.
4. *fol:* Old Fr.
5. *corage:* Old Fr.
6. *brillant:* Fr.
7. *danger:* Old Fr.
8. *trembler:* Old Fr.
9. *fleur:* Mod. Fr.
10. *plume:* Mid. Fr.

*panache:* a plume; elegance of style; Cyrano's white plume symbolizes his elegance

## Thinking About Plot, Character, and Setting

1. Explain how the falling action and resolution of the play follow logically from the play's major conflict and its climax. Did you find the ending a satisfying conclusion to the play? Why or why not?

2. Romantic heroes are colorful characters, more dashing and flamboyant than the people around them. In addition, they are usually attractive and inspire great love. Using examples from the play, explain why Cyrano could be regarded as a romantic hero. In what ways is he an *unusual* romantic hero?

3. Identify the setting of each act of *Cyrano de Bergerac*. Briefly explain how the action of each act is appropriate to the setting in which it occurs.

## Thinking About Symbol

4. The image of the white plume appears several times in the play: for example, in the exchange between Cyrano and De Guiche in Act IV (page 436). What might the white plume symbolize in this exchange? What does it come to symbolize at the end of the play?

## Thinking About Irony

5. Since irony often involves a gap between appearance and reality, why is it fitting that Cyrano's life should be so full of irony?

## Thinking About Theme

6. What does the play say about the relationship between physical and spiritual beauty? Is one more "real" than the other? Explain.

7. According to the play, why should we admire an idealist like Cyrano? Does the play suggest that idealists are ultimately defeated by the real world? Explain.

8. What are the good and bad sides to individualism like Cyrano's, according to the play?

9. What is the value of poetry and beautiful language, according to the play? Do you think the play places too high a value on language? Why or why not?

## VOCABULARY

### English Words Borrowed from French

William the Conqueror invaded England in 1066 from Normandy, a province on the northern coast of France. The Norman conquest made French the official language of the ruling class of England, and a tremendous number of French words came into the English language. The English word *language* itself comes from the French word *langage*, meaning "speech." In most cases, the spellings and pronunciations of the French loan-words gradually changed as they entered the English language.

All of the following words, taken from the English version of *Cyrano de Bergerac*, were originally French words and have since become part of our language. Using a dictionary, write the original French word and note any changes in spelling.

| | |
|---|---|
| 1. cadet | 6. brilliant |
| 2. stage | 7. danger |
| 3. secret | 8. tremble |
| 4. fool | 9. flower |
| 5. courage | 10. plume |

In English we also use many French words *without* changing their French spellings and pronunciations—for example, *tableau* and *gazette*. Another French word used by speakers of English is *panache* [pə nash′], which is actually the last word that Cyrano speaks in the original French text of *Cyrano de Bergerac*. Look up the various meanings of *panache*, and explain why the word is a fitting one for Cyrano.

## COMPOSITION

### Writing About Character

■ Of all of Cyrano's speeches, choose the one that you think best sums up his character. Identify the speech, noting where it occurs in the play, to whom it is addressed, and why Cyrano speaks it. Then explain what it reveals about Cyrano, and why you think it represents his character so well. You should take into account both what Cyrano says in the speech and the style in which he says it. Use quotations from the speech to support your opinion.

### Writing a Speech for a Character

■ Look again at Cyrano's "nose" speech to Valvert in Act I, and add new descriptions to it. Follow the form that Cyrano uses; for example, "Dramatic: When it bleeds, it must be like the Red Sea!" Try to match Cyrano's humor.

---

## COMPOSITION: GUIDELINES FOR EVALUATION

### WRITING ABOUT CHARACTER

**Objective**

To show how a character is revealed through his speeches

**Guidelines for Evaluation**

■ suggested length: three to four paragraphs
■ should cite one of Cyrano's speeches
■ should explain which characteristics are revealed in speech and why these represent Cyrano's personality

### WRITING A SPEECH FOR A CHARACTER

**Objective**

To write a humorous speech for a character

**Guidelines for Evaluation**

■ suggested length: fifty to one hundred words
■ should create new descriptions in established format
■ should be in humorous and witty style
■ should focus on Cyrano's nose as target of humor

# LITERARY FOCUS: *Julius Caesar*

*He was not of an age, but for all time.*
—Ben Jonson, "To the Memory of
My Beloved Master, William Shakespeare"

The words of Ben Jonson about his friend William Shakespeare (1564–1616) have proven to be prophetic. Shakespeare's works have continued to delight and move audiences for four hundred years. Today Shakespeare is regarded by many as the greatest writer in the English language, and his plays have been translated into many languages and performed on stages all over the world.

Shakespeare appeals to audiences so much because of the unequaled richness and abundance of his work. He wrote thirty-seven plays that range from wonderfully broad comedies to tormented and powerful tragedies. His works combine rich language with the realistic portrayal of human emotions. Above all, his plays are full of living, breathing characters, as real as people we know and yet more eloquent and memorable than anyone we will ever meet.

## Shakespeare's Life

While Shakespeare's plays, characters, and lines are familiar to millions, very little is known about the life of their creator. Even his birthdate is not certain; the date usually given for his birth is April 23, 1564. His father, John Shakespeare, was a prosperous merchant and town officer in Stratford-on-Avon, a small market town northwest of London. His mother, Mary Arden, was the daughter of a wealthy landowner. It is likely that Shakespeare attended the local grammar school, which taught Latin, rhetoric, logic, and classical literature. However, his father's fortunes declined, and Shakespeare probably left school in his midteens. At eighteen he married Anne Hathaway, a woman eight years his senior, and they had three children: Susanna, born in 1583, and Judith and Hamnet, twins born in 1585. The boy Hamnet died in 1596 at the age of eleven.

The period between the birth of the twins and Shakespeare's emergence as a playwright in the early 1590s has been called "the lost years." All that is known about this time is that at some point Shakespeare went to London while his family stayed in Stratford. By 1592 he was well established in London as an actor and dramatist. He must have enjoyed performing because he continued to act throughout his writing career.

Shakespeare wrote his first plays in the early 1590s; they were, for the most part, broad **comedies**, which are relatively light plays with

*Julius Caesar* 461

happy outcomes. He followed these with a series of history plays based on the lives of English kings. When the London theaters closed during a plague epidemic, Shakespeare published several poems. He returned to drama when the theaters reopened in 1594, writing *Romeo and Juliet,* his first **tragedy,** which is a serious play that ends unhappily. He also wrote several more history plays and a group of sparkling comedies, including *A Midsummer Night's Dream* and *As You Like It.* His work was crowned by a series of high tragedies, including *Julius Caesar* in 1599, *Hamlet* in 1601, *King Lear* in 1605, and *Macbeth* in 1606. He retired to Stratford in 1611 and died on or near his fifty-second birthday, on April 23, 1616.

## Shakespeare's Time

Shakespeare lived and wrote during a time different from ours in many ways. Europeans were just beginning to explore and settle the New World, physicians still bled their patients with leeches, and the majority of the people could not read. Yet Shakespeare's time also marked the beginning of our own modern age. Europe had just emerged from a long period of ignorance and superstition and entered a brilliant age known as the **Renaissance,** which takes its name from the French word meaning "rebirth." The Renaissance produced a great flowering of interest in science, philosophy, art, literature, history, and especially the classical learning of the ancient Greeks and Romans. Shakespeare himself wrote several plays with Greek and Roman subjects, including *Julius Caesar.* However, such works looked at ancient subjects with a new and modern eye. Unlike the Greeks and Romans, who believed that the world was governed by forces largely beyond human control, Shakespeare and his contemporaries lived during an age in which people were awakening to the ability of human beings to shape their own lives and the world around them.

The Renaissance came late to England. A long civil war known as the Wars of the Roses raged in the country during the 1400s. The coming of the Tudors to the throne in 1485 restored order, but then, after the death of King Henry VIII in 1547, the country was torn by several years of religious strife and uncertainty about the monarchy. Finally, the crowning in 1558 of Elizabeth I, Henry's daughter, ushered in a glorious golden age in England. The country enjoyed peace and prosperity under a strong and popular monarch, and music and literature flourished among people of all classes. In particular, drama became a prime source of entertainment for nobles, merchants, laborers—a cross-section of Elizabethan society. Theaters were usually full and playwrights prospered. The sun shone on the English theater, and it shone most brightly on William Shakespeare as that theater's supreme playwright.

A woodcut celebrating the Cotswold Games, a sporting event popular in Shakespeare's time.

462   *Drama*

## Shakespeare's Theater

The theater for which Shakespeare wrote was very different from our own. The very first permanent theater in London was not built until 1576, only a few years before Shakespeare began to write. Before that time, bands of actors traveled around the country, performing on portable wooden stages placed in the courtyards of inns.

The first permanent theaters copied the layout of the innyard productions. These theaters were wooden structures partly covered by thatched roofs, with central yards open to the air. The Globe—the theater for which Shakespeare wrote *Julius Caesar* and his later plays—was a three-story, eight-sided building with an open area in

Costumes from Shakespeare's time.

the center and a stage at one end. The Globe could hold about two thousand spectators. Almost two thirds of them sat in the three roofed galleries that surrounded the yard while the rest—called groundlings—paid only a penny and stood in the yard around the stage.

The major stage at the Globe was a rectangular platform, twenty-seven feet by forty-three feet, that jutted out into the yard. Several trapdoors in the stage floor allowed ghosts, bodies, and heavy scenery to be raised or lowered during a performance. At the back of the main stage was a smaller inner stage that could be either curtained off or used for scenes that took place indoors. A balcony above the inner stage added another level to the playing area and was used for scenes requiring little action. For example, Juliet stood on this balcony when she was courted by Romeo. The balcony could also represent a tower or hill, as the scene required. Since most plays used music in some form, a music gallery projected over the balcony.

In Shakespeare's time performances were held during the afternoon, when there was good natural light for the productions. The

*Julius Caesar*  463

Model of the Globe Theatre.

plays began at two o'clock and lasted about two hours without intermission. The pace of the performance was very swift. No curtains interrupted the action, and there was very little scenery to change.

Because the Elizabethan stage was almost bare, the principal attractions in the theater were the playwright's language and the actors who spoke it. The actors performed very close to their audiences, who crowded around them on three sides. These actors usually worked in companies similar to modern repertory companies, the same group of actors performing different plays over a short period of time. Shakespeare wrote for and acted in a company called the Lord Chamberlain's Men. After James I was crowned king in 1603, the group became known as the King's Men. The term *men* is literal since male actors played all of the roles—male and female. Young boys acted as the female characters in Shakespeare's time, continuing the practice until around 1660.

The lack of scenery, the closeness of the actors to the audience, and the use of male actors in female roles never struck Elizabethan audiences as unrealistic because these audiences never expected to see productions that were realistic in every detail. Their theater was a place where glorious poetry took the place of everyday prose, and where life took on a color and brilliance that everyday experience lacked.

Shakespeare knew what his audiences expected. He appealed to sophisticated viewers, who enjoyed his poetry, vibrant characters, and exciting situations. He also pleased less sophisticated playgoers, who cheered or booed frequently and expected to be entertained at the theater by clowns, wordplay, swordplay, music, and dancing.

In addition, Shakespeare understood the serious concerns of his audience. The Elizabethans believed in God and an orderly universe in which everything—including mankind—had its proper place. While they were fascinated with the possibility of growth and change, they looked for order and stability in the world. Having suffered through a long period of civil unrest, they were especially concerned with the need for stable government and strong leadership. Like other people during the Renaissance, they turned to the past—to the great civilizations of Greece and Rome—in the hope that they would learn how to build a civilization of their own.

## Historical Background to *Julius Caesar*

In *Julius Caesar* Shakespeare dramatized a series of exciting and tragic events in Roman history, events that ultimately led to the downfall of the 450-year-old Roman republic. Founded according to legend as a monarchy around 753 B.C., Rome became a republic in 509 B.C., when the Romans rebelled against the brutal Tarquin kings

*Julius Caesar* **465**

who had been ruling their city. As a result of the excesses of the Tarquins, the Romans became fierce opponents of monarchy, favoring instead a republican form of government in which the people elected their rulers.

By the time of *Julius Caesar,* the first century B.C., Rome was governed chiefly by two consuls, who were elected to preside over the republic for limited terms of office, and by the Senate, a legislative body whose members were appointed by the consuls. Both patricians, or nobles, and plebeians [pli bē'ənz], or commoners, could serve as senators and consuls, although for the most part the nobles dominated the government.

Julius Caesar, one of the most gifted politicians and military leaders in the history of the world, was born in 102 B.C. of a noble family. His life consisted of a series of brilliant and daring ploys that eventually made him the most powerful man of his time. Caesar entered politics during a period when the republic suffered from instability arising from conflict between factions in the Senate. He boldly sided with the common people's party against the nobles, wooing the commoners by spending his own wealth on public entertainments and tax relief.

In 60 B.C. Caesar joined forces with Pompey, a famous general, and Crassus, a wealthy noble, to form a triumvirate, or three-man governing body. Two years later Caesar led an army into Gaul

*Brutus and the Ghost of Caesar,* 1802, engraving by Edward Scriven from a painting by R. Westall. The Folger Shakespeare Library, Washington, D.C.

466   *Drama*

(southern France and northern Italy) and became governor of that region. His popularity grew as he sent the people of Rome money from his numerous conquests.

After Crassus' death, Pompey and his allies in Rome began to fear Caesar's growing popularity. He ordered Caesar to disband his army and return to Rome. Instead, Caesar crossed the Rubicon River and defeated Pompey's forces. Pompey fled to Greece and was killed in Egypt in 48 B.C., but his sons carried on his fight against Caesar. Caesar finally defeated Pompey's sons in the Battle of Munda in Spain in 45 B.C.

Caesar returned to Rome in triumph, more popular than ever. In the previous year he had been appointed dictator for life. Caesar was an ambitious man, and many people feared that he would not be satisfied until he had been crowned king, thus putting an end to the 450-year-old republic. The tyranny of the Tarquin kings had left many Romans violently opposed to the very idea of monarchy. Therefore, concern about Caesar's driving ambition made him the target of intrigue among supporters of the Roman republic.

It is at this point that Shakespeare begins his account of the assassination of Julius Caesar and the bloody aftermath of that event. Shakespeare used *The Lives of the Noble Greeks and Romans* by Plutarch, a first-century historian, as his main source of information about Julius Caesar, his friend Mark Antony, and the two leaders of

A scene from the British Broadcasting Company's television production of *Julius Caesar*.

*Julius Caesar* **467**

the conspiracy against Caesar, Marcus Brutus and Caius Cassius. However, Shakespeare interpreted Plutarch's history from the perspective of an Elizabethan writer. He wrote *Julius Caesar* toward the end of the reign of Elizabeth I, a ruler who had established stability after years of civil unrest in England. But Elizabeth had not named a successor, and as she grew older, many of her subjects feared the prospect of renewed turmoil after her death. The example of ancient Rome stood as a warning to Elizabethan England. For reasons of their own, Shakespeare and his audience were very concerned about the problems of leadership, political power, and civil order.

*Julius Caesar* shows that these problems do not lend themselves to easy solutions. The play presents leaders who abuse their power, and yet it also portrays the chaos that arises without a strong leader to maintain order in the state. Above all, the play shows that noble intentions often result in ignoble outcomes. The men who killed Caesar acted to preserve the Roman republic; ironically, their action led to great bloodshed and brought about the end of that republic. A civil war raged for years after Caesar's death. Even the men who joined forces to avenge his death fought with one another for power. Finally, seventeen years after the assassination, Caesar's great-nephew Octavius was crowned as Augustus, the sole ruler and first emperor of Rome. The Roman republic, for which Caesar had been killed, ceased to exist.

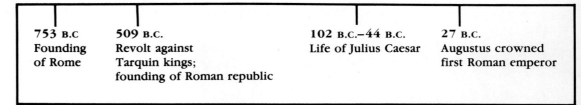

| **753** B.C | **509** B.C. | | **102** B.C.–**44** B.C. | **27** B.C. |
|---|---|---|---|---|
| Founding of Rome | Revolt against Tarquin kings; founding of Roman republic | | Life of Julius Caesar | Augustus crowned first Roman emperor |

**Key Ideas in** *Julius Caesar*

■ As you read *Julius Caesar*, look for references to each of the following topics. If you keep track of what the work says about these subjects, you will begin to grasp the most important themes of the play.

- Rebellion against tyranny
- Strong leadership and order in the state
- The world as it might be versus the world as it is
- The attempt of individuals to influence history
- Omens and dreams

**468** *Drama*

## Key Quotations from *Julius Caesar*

As you read *Julius Caesar,* you will come across some of the most famous lines in English drama. Here are a few familiar quotations from the play.

Beware the ides of March.

—SOOTHSAYER, Act I, Scene ii, line 18

The fault, dear Brutus, is not in our stars,
But in ourselves, that we are underlings.

—CASSIUS, Act I, Scene ii, lines 140–141

Yond Cassius has a lean and hungry look;
He thinks too much: such men are dangerous.

—CAESAR, Act I, Scene ii, lines 194–195

Cowards die many times before their deaths;
The valiant never taste of death but once.

—CAESAR, Act II, Scene ii, lines 32–33

*Et tu, Brutè?* Then fall Caesar.

—CAESAR, Act III, Scene i, line 77

Friends, Romans, countrymen, lend me your ears;
I come to bury Caesar, not to praise him.
The evil that men do lives after them,
The good is oft interrèd with their bones.

—MARK ANTONY, Act III, Scene ii, lines 71–74

This was the most unkindest cut of all.

—MARK ANTONY, Act III, Scene ii, line 180

There is a tide in the affairs of men
Which, taken at the flood, leads on to fortune.

—BRUTUS, Act IV, Scene iii, lines 217–218

O Julius Caesar, thou art mighty yet!
Thy spirit walks abroad, and turns our swords
In our own proper entrails.

—BRUTUS, Act V, Scene iii, lines 94–96

This was the noblest Roman of them all. . . .
His life was gentle, and the elements
So mixed in him that Nature might stand up
And say to all the world, "This was a man!"

—MARK ANTONY, Act V, Scene v, lines 68–75

Portia.                                        Mark Antony.

*William Shakespeare*

# Julius Caesar

## CHARACTERS

**JULIUS CAESAR:** ambitious military leader and politician; the most powerful man in Rome
**CALPURNIA:** wife of Caesar
**MARCUS BRUTUS:** friend of Caesar, appointed by him to high office in the Roman government; a believer in the republic and member of the conspiracy against Caesar
**PORTIA:** wife of Brutus and daughter of a Roman patriot
**CAIUS CASSIUS:** brother-in-law of Brutus and member of the conspiracy against Caesar
**MARK ANTONY:** friend of Caesar, senator, and eloquent orator; member of the triumvirate, the three-man governing body that ruled Rome after Caesar's death
**OCTAVIUS CAESAR:** Caesar's great-nephew and official heir; member of the triumvirate
**AEMILIUS LEPIDUS:** military leader and member of the triumvirate

## Conspirators Against Caesar

| | | |
|---|---|---|
| CASCA | METELLUS CIMBER | TREBONIUS |
| CINNA | DECIUS BRUTUS | |

## Senators

| | | |
|---|---|---|
| CICERO | PUBLIUS | POPILIUS LENA |

470   *Drama*

Brutus.

**Tribunes** *(Public Officials)*

FLAVIUS             MARULLUS

## Officers in the Armies of Brutus and Cassius

| LUCILIUS | MESSALA | VOLUMNIUS |
|----------|---------|-----------|
| TITINIUS | YOUNG CATO | |

## Servants of Brutus

| LUCIUS | CLITUS | STRATO |
|--------|--------|--------|
| VARRO | CLAUDIUS | DARDANIUS |

## Others

A SOOTHSAYER (one who predicts the future)

ARTEMIDORUS OF CNIDOS: teacher of rhetoric

CINNA: a poet

PINDARUS: servant of CASSIUS

ANOTHER POET

SERVANTS to CAESAR, ANTONY, and OCTAVIUS; CITIZENS, GUARDS, SOLDIERS.

*Julius Caesar*    471

- *Scene i:* Romans gather in the streets to celebrate a religious festival and Caesar's victory over Pompey's sons.
- Two Pompey loyalists, Marullus and Flavius, meet some commoners, celebrating Caesar's return.
- A cobbler angers the tribunes with his clever wordplay.

## ACT I: LITERARY OPTIONS

- conflict in drama
- foreshadowing
- characterization

## ACT I: THEMATIC OPTIONS

- idealism vs. realism
- personal loyalty vs. concern for the public good
- class conflict

### 1 PLOT: FORESHADOWING

Flavius' unconcealed anger and confrontational stance toward the commoners hint at trouble ahead for Caesar.

### 2 BLANK VERSE

By making the tribunes speak in "elevated" blank verse and the plebeians speak in "common" prose, Shakespeare highlights the class differences that separate them.

### 3 VOCABULARY: WORD CHOICE

The cobbler's pun *(bad soles)* shows his casual attitude toward upper-class authority figures.

### 4 PLOT: CONFLICT

The cobbler's provocative wordplay, implying that Flavius has a bad soul ("sir, I can mend you"), reveals the tension between the two classes.

---

SELECTION FOR PRACTICE
IN ACTIVE READING
(TCR 5, p. 67)

---

# ACT I

## Scene i. A street in Rome. 44 B.C.

*[It is the fifteenth of February, and Romans are gathering in the streets to celebrate two events: the religious festival of Lupercal and the recent victory of* JULIUS CAESAR *over Pompey's sons. Pompey had opposed* CAESAR *for control of the Roman republic and was later murdered. As the play begins,* MARULLUS *and* FLAVIUS, *two civic officials, meet a group of high-spirited* PLEBEIANS, *or commoners, dressed in their best clothes. The* PLEBEIANS, *who had once supported Pompey, are now celebrating* CAESAR'S *triumphant return; the tribunes, loyal to Pompey, become angry at them.]*

1  FLAVIUS. Hence! Home, you idle creatures, get you home!
   Is this a holiday? What, know you not,
   Being mechanical,[1] you ought not walk
   Upon a laboring day without the sign
5  Of your profession?[2] Speak, what trade art thou?

   CARPENTER. Why, sir, a carpenter.

2  MARULLUS. Where is thy leather apron and thy rule?
   What dost thou with thy best apparel on?
   You, sir, what trade are you?

10 COBBLER. Truly, sir, in respect of a fine workman, I am but, as
   you would say, a cobbler.[3]

   MARULLUS. But what trade art thou? Answer me directly.

   *[MARULLUS has taken the word* cobbler *to mean "bungler" and does not seem to understand the joke. The* COBBLER, *however, continues to make puns.]*

3  COBBLER. A trade, sir, that, I hope, I may use with a safe conscience, which is indeed, sir, a mender of bad soles.

   FLAVIUS. What trade, thou knave? Thou naughty knave, what
15    trade?

4  COBBLER. Nay, I beseech you, sir, be not out[4] with me: yet, if
   you be out,[5] sir, I can mend you.

   MARULLUS. What mean'st thou by that? Mend me, thou saucy
   fellow?

20 COBBLER. Why, sir, cobble you.

**472**  *Drama*

1 **Being mechanical:** being laborers.

2 **sign...profession:** Workers normally carried the tools of their trades and wore working clothes. These men are dressed in their best clothes.

3 **cobbler:** shoemaker; also, a clumsy worker. The plebeian is playing on the word's double meaning.

4 **out:** angry.
5 **out:** The cobbler refers here to worn-out shoes.

---

## GUIDED READING

### LITERAL QUESTIONS

**1a.** Why are the plebeians in their best clothes? (They are celebrating the religious festival of Lupercal and Caesar's recent victory over Pompey's sons.)

**2a.** What does Marullus think about the cobbler's behavior? (He thinks that the cobbler is being saucy.)

### INFERENTIAL QUESTIONS

**1b.** Contrast the attitudes of the tribunes with the high spirits of the plebeians. (Flavius and Marullus resent the plebeians' festive attitude; the tribunes probably resent this public jubilation over Caesar's victory.)

**2b.** What does the cobbler's behavior show about him? (It shows that he is quicker witted than Marullus and unafraid of—even perhaps disrespectful toward—those of a higher class.)

**FLAVIUS.** Thou art a cobbler, art thou?

**COBBLER.** Truly, sir, all that I live by is with the awl:[6] I meddle
with no tradesman's matters, nor women's matters; but
withal, I am indeed, sir, a surgeon to old shoes: when they
25   are in great danger, I recover them. As proper men as ever
trod upon neat's leather[7] have gone upon my handiwork.

**FLAVIUS.** But wherefore art not in thy shop today?
Why dost thou lead these men about the streets?

**COBBLER.** Truly, sir, to wear out their shoes, to get myself into
30   more work. But indeed, sir, we make holiday to see Caesar
and to rejoice in his triumph.

[*At this reference to* CAESAR'S *triumph,* MARULLUS *becomes
furious and ends the* COBBLER'S *wordplay.*]

**MARULLUS.** Wherefore rejoice? What conquest brings he home?
What tributaries[8] follow him to Rome,
To grace in captive bonds his chariot wheels?
35   You blocks, you stones, you worse than senseless things!
O you hard hearts, you cruel men of Rome,
Knew you not Pompey? Many a time and oft
Have you climbed up to walls and battlements,
To tow'rs and windows, yea, to chimney tops,
40   Your infants in your arms, and there have sat
The livelong day, with patient expectation,
To see great Pompey pass the streets of Rome.
And when you saw his chariot but appear,
Have you not made an universal shout,
45   That Tiber[9] trembled underneath her banks
To hear the replication[10] of your sounds
Made in her concave shores?
And do you now put on your best attire?
And do you now cull out[11] a holiday?
50   And do you now strew flowers in his way
That comes in triumph over Pompey's blood?[12]
Be gone!
Run to your houses, fall upon your knees,
Pray to the gods to intermit[13] the plague
55   That needs must light on this ingratitude.

**FLAVIUS.** Go, go, good countrymen, and, for this fault,
Assemble all the poor men of your sort;
Draw them to Tiber banks and weep your tears

---

6 **awl:** cobbler's tool. He is making a
triple pun on *with awl, with all,* and
*withal,* which means "nevertheless."

7 **neat's leather:** calfskin. The
cobbler is saying that as fine men as
ever walked in shoes have worn his
shoes.

8 **tributaries:** prisoners who pay
tribute, or ransom money, for their
release.

9 **Tiber:** river running through Rome.

10 **replication:** echo.

11 **cull out:** give yourselves.

12 **Pompey's blood:** Pompey's sons;
also, bloodshed. Caesar has just
defeated Pompey's sons in a battle in
Spain.

13 **intermit:** hold back.

*Julius Caesar, Act I, Scene i*   **473**

## AT A GLANCE

- *Scene i (continued):* When the
cobbler says that the plebeians are celebrating Caesar's
triumph, Marullus becomes
furious.
- Marullus orders the plebeians
to go home and pray to the
gods to avert the plague their
ingratitude will inevitably
cause.

**1 PLOT: CONFLICT**

Marullus' anger that Caesar has
enhanced his own glory but not
brought back money for the
Roman people ("What tributaries
follow him to Rome?") contains
the seeds of future conflict.

**2 STYLE: PERSONIFICATION**

Marullus' personification of the
Tiber ("trembled . . . / To hear
the replication of your sounds")
makes the great shift the plebeians have made in their alle-
giances seem like a breach in
the natural order.

**3 PLOT: FORESHADOWING**

Marullus sternly predicts a dire
misfortune ("the plague") as an
inevitable result of the plebeians'
fickleness and "ingratitude."
Rome will indeed be visited by
misfortune, but not because of
Caesar's triumph—rather, because of his downfall.

---

## GUIDED READING

### LITERAL QUESTIONS

**1a.** According to Marullus, what is wrong with Caesar's triumph? (Caesar has not returned with any
tributaries.)

**2a.** What does Marullus think of the plebeians? (He
thinks that they are hard-hearted, disloyal to Pompey's memory, and fickle in their affections.)

### INFERENTIAL QUESTIONS

**1b.** In what ways do Marullus' feelings about Caesar's
triumph portend trouble? (Those who share Marullus' views might someday oppose Caesar, either
peacefully or violently.)

**2b.** In what way does Marullus distinguish himself
from the plebeians? (He is steadfastly loyal to
Pompey's memory.)

- *Scene i (continued):* Subdued by Marullus' words, the plebeians leave; the two tribunes then go off to strip decorations from the statues.
- *Scene ii:* Caesar and his entourage prepare for a footrace.
- An old soothsayer tries to attract Caesar's attention.

**1 CHARACTERIZATION**

Marullus defers to Flavius, who seems to be unafraid of making strategic decisions.

**2 STYLE: METAPHOR**

That Caesar's feathers will be plucked hints not only that he may "fly an ordinary pitch" but that he may even fall.

**3 PLOT: FORESHADOWING**

That the soothsayer is "trying to attract Caesar's attention" suggests that he may have something important to predict about Caesar's future.

---

Into the channel, till the lowest stream

60 Do kiss the most exalted shores[14] of all.

[*The* PLEBEIANS *leave looking subdued.*]

See, whe'r their basest mettle be not moved;[15]
They vanish tongue-tied in their guiltiness.
Go you down that way towards the Capitol;
This way will I. Disrobe the images,

65 If you do find them decked with ceremonies.[16]

**1** MARULLUS. May we do so?
You know it is the feast of Lupercal.[17]

FLAVIUS. It is no matter; let no images
Be hung with Caesar's trophies. I'll about

70 And drive away the vulgar[18] from the streets;
So do you too, where you perceive them thick.

**2** These growing feathers plucked from Caesar's wing
Will make him fly an ordinary pitch,[19]
Who else would soar above the view of men

75 And keep us all in servile fearfulness.

[*They leave together to remove the decorations from the statues.*]

*Scene ii. A public square near the Roman Forum. Later the same day.*

[*Following a flourish of trumpets,* CAESAR, CALPURNIA *(his wife), his friend* MARK ANTONY *(also called* ANTONIUS*), and many followers enter the square to prepare for a footrace as part of the festivities of Lupercal. Lupercal was celebrated in honor of a fertility god, and according to tradition, a childless woman touched by a runner in the race would be able to bear children.* CAESAR *and his wife have no children, and* CAESAR *wants* ANTONY *to touch* CALPURNIA *as he races by her. Many leading Romans accompany* CAESAR, *including* CASSIUS, BRUTUS, PORTIA *(his wife),* CASCA, CICERO, *and* DECIUS. *In the crowd of* PLEBEIANS *gathered*

**3** *for the race, an old* SOOTHSAYER, *or person who predicts the future, waits, trying to attract* CAESAR'S *attention.*]

CAESAR. Calpurnia!

CASCA.                    Peace, ho! Caesar speaks.

[*All fall silent as* CAESAR *calls for his wife.*]

CAESAR.                                        Calpurnia!

474   *Drama*

14 **most exalted shores:** the river's highest bank. Flavius tells the commoners to weep into the Tiber until it overflows.

15 **whe'r...moved:** whether their basic nature has not been touched.

16 **Disrobe...ceremonies:** Strip the statues of their decorations.

17 **feast of Lupercal:** religious festival for a fertility god.

18 **vulgar:** common people.

19 **pitch:** height. If feathers are plucked from a bird's wing, it cannot soar very high.

---

## GUIDED READING

**LITERAL QUESTION**

**1a.** What does Flavius want to pluck from Caesar's wing, and why? (He speaks of feathers and says he wants Caesar to fly at a normal height.)

**INFERENTIAL QUESTION**

**1b.** Who are the "feathers" that Flavius refers to and how are they growing? (He is referring to the plebeians who support Caesar; he fears their increasing support for Caesar, as the decorations give witness.)

CALPURNIA. Here, my lord.

CAESAR. Stand you directly in Antonius' way
    When he doth run his course. Antonius!

5 ANTONY. Caesar, my lord?

**1**

CAESAR. Forget not in your speed, Antonius,
    To touch Calpurnia; for our elders say
    The barren, touchèd in this holy chase,
    Shake off their sterile curse.[1]

ANTONY.                              I shall remember:
10  When Caesar says "Do this," it is performed.

CAESAR. Set on, and leave no ceremony out.

[CAESAR *and his followers start to leave when the* SOOTHSAYER
*calls out to him.*]

SOOTHSAYER. Caesar!

CAESAR. Ha! Who calls?

CASCA. Bid every noise be still; peace yet again!

[*The crowd becomes silent.*]

**2** 15 CAESAR. Who is it in the press[2] that calls on me?
    I hear a tongue, shriller than all the music,
    Cry "Caesar." Speak; Caesar is turned to hear.

SOOTHSAYER. Beware the ides of March.[3]

CAESAR.                              What man is that?

BRUTUS. A soothsayer bids you beware the ides of March.

20 CAESAR. Set him before me; let me see his face.

CASSIUS. Fellow, come from the throng; look upon Caesar.

CAESAR. What say'st thou to me now? Speak once again.

SOOTHSAYER. Beware the ides of March.

**3** CAESAR. He is a dreamer, let us leave him. Pass.

[CAESAR *and the crowd depart, leaving* BRUTUS *and* CASSIUS,
*both prominent Romans, alone. Because* BRUTUS *is both close
to* CAESAR *and widely respected in Rome,* CASSIUS *takes the opportunity to learn how he feels about the recent growth of*
CAESAR's *power.*]

*Julius Caesar, Act I, Scene ii* **475**

---

1 **To touch...sterile curse:** Caesar is concerned because he has no child to continue his line.

2 **press:** crowd.

3 **ides of March:** March 15. In the Roman calendar, the middle of every month was called the ides.

---

- *Scene ii (continued):* Caesar asks Antony to touch Calpurnia as he runs so that she may become fertile.
- When the soothsayer urges Caesar to "beware the ides of March," Caesar dismisses the warning.

**1 CHARACTERIZATION**

Now that Caesar has consolidated his power by defeating Pompey's sons, he turns his attention to continuing his line.

**2 PLOT: FORESHADOWING**

The soothsayer's warning pierces the celebratory surface ("shriller than all the music"), striking its own ominous note.

**3 CHARACTERIZATION**

For Caesar the realist, the soothsayer is a "dreamer" and therefore can be dismissed along with his unpleasant portent. As he does later in the play, Caesar disregards such omens as the products of superstitious minds. Such "realism" is, in some senses, an aspect of Caesar's pride. He considers himself above the concerns of ordinary people.

---

## GUIDED READING

### LITERAL QUESTIONS

**1a.** How does Antony reply when Caesar reminds him to touch Calpurnia as he runs by? (Antony says, "I shall remember:/When Caesar says 'Do this,' it is performed.")

**2a.** What does Caesar say about the soothsayer? (According to Caesar, the soothsayer is a dreamer.)

### INFERENTIAL QUESTIONS

**1b.** What does this suggest about the relationship between Caesar and Antony? (Antony is a loyal disciple of Caesar, ready and willing to do his bidding.)

**2b.** What does Caesar's response to the soothsayer demonstrate about him? (Caesar is shown to be an unsuperstitious person, unaffected by dire predictions, and perhaps somewhat overconfident.)

Mervyn Blake as the Soothsayer. Jack Medley as Caesar. Photo courtesy of Stratford Festival, Canada, 1982.

476   *Drama*

25 CASSIUS. Will you go see the order of the course?[4]

BRUTUS. Not I.

CASSIUS. I pray you do.

BRUTUS. I am not gamesome:[5] I do lack some part
    Of that quick spirit that is in Antony.
30  Let me not hinder, Cassius, your desires;
    I'll leave you.

1  CASSIUS. Brutus, I do observe you now of late;
    I have not from your eyes that gentleness
    And show of love as I was wont to have;[6]
35  You bear too stubborn and too strange a hand
    Over your friend that loves you.

BRUTUS.                          Cassius,
    Be not deceived: if I have veiled my look,
    I turn the trouble of my countenance
2  Merely upon myself. Vexèd I am
40  Of late with passions of some difference,[7]
    Conceptions only proper to myself,
    Which give some soil,[8] perhaps, to my behaviors;
    But let not therefore my good friends be grieved
    (Among which number, Cassius, be you one)
45  Nor construe any further my neglect
    Than that poor Brutus, with himself at war,
    Forgets the shows of love to other men.

CASSIUS. Then, Brutus, I have much mistook your passion;[9]
    By means whereof[10] this breast of mine hath buried
50  Thoughts of great value, worthy cogitations.[11]
    Tell me, good Brutus, can you see your face?

BRUTUS. No, Cassius; for the eye sees not itself
    But by reflection, by some other things.

CASSIUS. 'Tis just:
55  And it is very much lamented, Brutus,
    That you have no such mirrors as will turn
    Your hidden worthiness into your eye,
    That you might see your shadow.[12] I have heard
3  Where many of the best respect in Rome
60  (Except immortal Caesar), speaking of Brutus,
    And groaning underneath this age's yoke,
    Have wished that noble Brutus had his eyes.[13]

BRUTUS. Into what dangers would you lead me, Cassius,

4 **order...course:** the race.

5 **gamesome:** fond of games and sports.

6 **was wont to have:** used to have.

7 **passions of some difference:** mixed emotions. Brutus explains that he has been upset with himself, not with Cassius.
8 **soil:** blemish.

9 **mistook your passion:** misunderstood your feelings.
10 **By means whereof:** because of this.
11 **cogitations:** musings.

12 **shadow:** reflection.

13 **many...eyes:** That is, many respected citizens of Rome, suffering under Caesar's tyranny, have wished that Brutus would recognize his own worth and challenge Caesar.

*Julius Caesar, Act I, Scene ii*   **477**

- *Scene ii (continued):* Cassius says that Brutus has been cool to him recently, and Brutus replies that he is upset with himself, not with Cassius.
- Cassius wishes aloud that Brutus would recognize his own worth and challenge Caesar.

1 **CHARACTERIZATION**

Cassius subtly uses his insight that Brutus is lately changed ("I have not from your eyes that gentleness") to delicately probe what he suspects are the reasons for it.

2 **CONFLICT**

Brutus' sense of honor has made him mask some of his conflicting emotions ("passions of some difference") about Caesar.

3 **PLOT: RISING ACTION**

Deftly, Cassius suggests that many Romans, unhappy ("groaning") under Caesar, want Brutus to act. Brutus clearly, despite his protests, has been mulling this very question.

## GUIDED READING

### LITERAL QUESTIONS

**1a.** What does Brutus say is wrong with him? (He says that some mixed emotions have upset him of late.)

**2a.** What does Cassius want Brutus to do? (He wants him to see his own worth.)

### INFERENTIAL QUESTIONS

**1b.** What do you think has been troubling Brutus? (Brutus is probably troubled about Caesar, since he seems reluctant to join wholeheartedly in the festivities that celebrate Caesar's latest victory.)

**2b.** What does Brutus' response to Cassius' indirect request show about him? (It shows that he is neither naïve nor incautious.)

- *Scene ii (continued):* Cassius says that he will be a trustworthy mirror to Brutus.
- Brutus admits that, though he loves Caesar, he opposes crowning Caesar king.
- Cassius discloses his envy of Caesar's increasing power.

**1 STYLE: METAPHOR**

Indeed, Cassius' "mirror" may bring to the surface not only Brutus' virtues but his discontent ("that of yourself which you yet know not of").

**2 CONFLICT**

Perhaps it is Cassius' flattering and confiding remarks that permit Brutus to express openly for the first time his conflicting feelings about Caesar ("I would not, Cassius, yet I love him well").

**3 DIALOGUE**

Already the reader may suspect that Cassius' concept of honor ("Well, honor is the subject of my story") may be less heroic than Brutus'. Cassius is a shrewd man and knows that a reference to "honor" will make his arguments more convincing to Brutus.

**4 CHARACTERIZATION**

After Brutus reveals his conflict, Cassius permits himself to show his own bitterness over what he perceives as Caesar's ascendancy over them ("I was born as free as Caesar").

---

That you would have me seek into myself
65    For that which is not in me?

**1**   CASSIUS. Therefore, good Brutus, be prepared to hear;
        And since you know you cannot see yourself
        So well as by reflection, I, your glass[14]
        Will modestly discover to yourself
70      That of yourself which you yet know not of.
        And be not jealous on me,[15] gentle Brutus:
        Were I a common laughter,[16] or did use
        To stale with ordinary oaths my love
        To every new protester;[17] if you know
75      That I do fawn on men and hug them hard,
        And after scandal them;[18] or if you know
        That I profess myself in banqueting
        To all the rout,[19] then hold me dangerous.

[*Trumpets sound in the distance, followed by a loud shout. Startled,* BRUTUS *and* CASSIUS *look toward the commotion.*]

**2**   BRUTUS. What means this shouting? I do fear the people
        Choose Caesar for their king.

80    CASSIUS.                              Ay, do you fear it?
        Then must I think you would not have it so.

        BRUTUS. I would not, Cassius, yet I love him well.
        But wherefore do you hold me here so long?
        What is it that you would impart to me?
85      If it be aught toward the general good,
**3**      Set honor in one eye and death i' th' other,
        And I will look on both indifferently;[20]
        For let the gods so speed me, as I love
        The name of honor more than I fear death.

90    CASSIUS. I know that virtue to be in you, Brutus,
        As well as I do know your outward favor.[21]
        Well, honor is the subject of my story.
        I cannot tell what you and other men
        Think of this life, but for my single self,
95      I had as lief not be,[22] as live to be
        In awe of such a thing as I myself.[23]
**4**      I was born free as Caesar; so were you:
        We both have fed as well, and we can both
        Endure the winter's cold as well as he:
100     For once, upon a raw and gusty day,
        The troubled Tiber chafing with her shores,

**478**   *Drama*

---

14 **glass:** mirror. Cassius offers to reveal Brutus' inner strengths and deepest feelings.

15 **jealous on me:** suspicious of me.

16 **laughter:** jester.

17 **To stale...protester:** to cheapen my affection by swearing friendship to everyone.
18 **after scandal them:** afterward slander them.

19 **rout:** common crowd.

20 **If it be aught...indifferently:** If a matter concerns the public welfare, I face honor and death impartially (without concern for my own safety).

21 **outward favor:** appearance.

22 **I had as lief not be:** I would rather not live.
23 **such a thing as I myself:** another human being.

---

## GUIDED READING

**LITERAL QUESTIONS**

**1a.** What does Brutus fear? (He does not want Caesar to be crowned king.)

**2a.** What kind of life would Cassius rather not live? (He would rather not live under Caesar's rule.)

**INFERENTIAL QUESTIONS**

**1b.** What problem does this fear cause for Brutus? (He does not know how to reconcile love for Caesar with opposition to his being crowned king.)

**2b.** What about Caesar's rule would gall Cassius most? (He regards himself as Caesar's equal, not his inferior.)

Caesar said to me "Dar'st thou, Cassius, now
Leap in with me into this angry flood,
And swim to yonder point?" Upon the word,
105 Accout'red[24] as I was, I plungèd in
And bade him follow: so indeed he did.
The torrent roared, and we did buffet it
With lusty sinews,[25] throwing it aside
And stemming it with hearts of controversy.[26]
110 But ere we could arrive the point proposed,
Caesar cried "Help me, Cassius, or I sink!"
I, as Aeneas,[27] our great ancestor,
Did from the flames of Troy upon his shoulder
The old Anchises bear, so from the waves of Tiber
115 Did I the tired Caesar. And this man
Is now become a god, and Cassius is
A wretched creature, and must bend his body
If Caesar carelessly but nod on him.
He had a fever when he was in Spain,
120 And when the fit was on him, I did mark
How he did shake; 'tis true, this god did shake.
His coward lips did from their color fly,
And that same eye whose bend[28] doth awe the world
Did lose his luster; I did hear him groan;
125 Ay, and that tongue of his, that bade the Romans
Mark him and write his speeches in their books,
Alas, it cried, "Give me some drink, Titinius,"
As a sick girl. Ye gods! It doth amaze me,
A man of such a feeble temper should
130 So get the start of[29] the majestic world,
And bear the palm[30] alone.

[*Another shout, followed by trumpets.* BRUTUS *is becoming concerned about the show of popular support for* CAESAR.]

BRUTUS. Another general shout?
I do believe that these applauses are
For some new honors that are heaped on Caesar.

135 CASSIUS. Why, man, he doth bestride the narrow world
Like a Colossus,[31] and we petty men
Walk under his huge legs and peep about
To find ourselves dishonorable graves.
Men at some time are masters of their fates:
140 The fault, dear Brutus, is not in our stars,[32]
But in ourselves, that we are underlings.
Brutus and Caesar: what should be in that "Caesar"?

24 **Accout'red:** dressed.

25 **sinews:** muscles.
26 **stemming...controversy:** conquering the torrent in our rivalry with each other.

27 **Aeneas** [i nē´əs]: the legendary founder of Rome. Carrying his father, Anchises [an kī´sēz], on his back, Aeneas fled the burning city of Troy after the Greeks defeated his fellow Trojans.

28 **bend:** glance, look.

29 **get the start of:** get ahead of.
30 **palm:** victor's prize.

31 **Colossus:** the gigantic statue of the Greek god Apollo in the harbor of Rhodes. The Colossus of Rhodes was said to be so tall that ships could sail through its legs.

32 **stars:** fate, as determined by the position of the stars and planets at someone's birth.

*Julius Caesar, Act I, Scene ii* **479**

AT A GLANCE

- *Scene ii (continued):* Cassius recounts how he rescued Caesar from drowning and how pathetic Caesar seemed when ill.
- Hearing the people shout, Brutus becomes concerned that Caesar is receiving new honors.

**1 STYLE: ALLUSION**

Cassius' comparison of himself to Aeneas and of Caesar to Anchises reveals that he feels superior in youth and strength to Caesar.

**2 STYLE: SIMILE**

Cassius makes his envious contempt of Caesar clear in referring to the great soldier as a "sick girl."

**3 CHARACTERIZATION**

Brutus now feels comfortable in expressing to Cassius his uneasiness at Caesar's growing power ("Another general shout?")

**4 CHARACTERIZATION**

To exhort Brutus to act against Caesar, Cassius urgently states that they themselves are responsible for their present "underling" status. Cassius confirms that his true motivation for opposing Caesar is personal ambition, not concern for the public good.

## GUIDED READING

### LITERAL QUESTIONS

**1a.** What happened to Caesar in the Tiber, and what did Cassius do at that time? (While swimming in the river, Caesar began to sink, and Cassius carried him to safety.)

**2a.** What is Brutus' reaction to the shout of acclaim for Caesar? (He is concerned by it.)

### INFERENTIAL QUESTIONS

**1b.** In what way does this incident fuel Cassius' antagonism toward Caesar? (Cassius feels that he, a stronger and younger man, saved the life of a tired old man who now lords it over him.)

**2b.** Why does Brutus feel this way? (He seems worried that Caesar is gaining too much power.)

- *Scene ii (continued):* Cassius reminds Brutus that his ancestor, Lucius Junius Brutus, overthrew a tyrant.
- Brutus tells Cassius he understands his hints; he is not ready to act but will listen to him further.
- An angry Caesar returns.

## 1 STYLE: ALLUSION

By alluding to Brutus' ancestor, Cassius appeals to his friend's patriotism and family pride.

## 2 CHARACTERIZATION

Although he is idealistic, Brutus is not completely naïve; he knows what Cassius has been trying to do and cagily delays disclosing his own thoughts.

## 3 PLOT: RISING ACTION

Cassius has assessed his prey well; although unready to act, Brutus is prepared to discuss matters further because of his patriotism during what he acknowledges to be hard times.

---

Why should that name be sounded more than yours?
Write them together, yours is as fair a name;
145    Sound them, it doth become the mouth as well;
Weigh them, it is as heavy; conjure³³ with 'em,
"Brutus" will start a spirit as soon as "Caesar."
Now, in the names of all the gods at once,
Upon what meat doth this our Caesar feed,
150    That he is grown so great? Age, thou art shamed!
Rome, thou hast lost the breed of noble bloods!
When went there by an age, since the great flood,³⁴
But it was famed with more than with one man?³⁵
When could they say (till now) that talked of Rome,
155    That her wide walks encompassed but one man?
Now is it Rome indeed, and room³⁶ enough,
When there is in it but one only man.
O, you and I have heard our fathers say,
There was a Brutus³⁷ once that would have brooked
160    Th' eternal devil to keep his state in Rome
As easily as a king.³⁸

[BRUTUS *understands* CASSIUS' *hints and shares many of his concerns about* CAESAR. *However, he is not yet ready to discuss his views fully with* CASSIUS.]

BRUTUS. That you do love me, I am nothing jealous;³⁹
What you would work me to, I have some aim;⁴⁰
How I have thought of this, and of these times,
165    I shall recount hereafter. For this present,
I would not so (with love I might entreat you)
Be any further moved. What you have said
I will consider; what you have to say
I will with patience hear, and find a time
170    Both meet⁴¹ to hear and answer such high things.
Till then, my noble friend, chew upon this:
Brutus had rather be a villager
Than to repute himself a son of Rome
Under these hard conditions as this time
175    Is like to lay upon us.

CASSIUS.            I am glad
That my weak words have struck but thus much show
Of fire from Brutus.

[CAESAR *and his followers return. All seem very upset, and* CAESAR *looks angry.*]

33 **conjure:** call up spirits.

34 **great flood:** In Roman mythology the god Zeus let loose a flood that drowned all but two people.
35 **But...man:** Every prior age in Rome's history had seen many heroes. Now Caesar dominates all.
36 **Rome...room:** *Rome* and *room* once sounded alike. Cassius says Rome is now Caesar's private room.
37 **a Brutus:** Lucius Junius Brutus, who expelled the Tarquin kings and made Rome a republic in 509 B.C. As Cassius knows, Brutus regards this hero as his ancestor.
38 **brooked...king:** The first Brutus found any king's rule as intolerable as the devil's.

39 **am nothing jealous:** have no doubt.
40 **have some aim:** can guess.

41 **meet:** suitable.

**480**   *Drama*

---

## GUIDED READING

**LITERAL QUESTIONS**

**1a.** According to Cassius, what is Brutus' worth compared to Caesar's? (Cassius says that they are of equal worth.)

**2a.** What is Brutus' response to Cassius' appeal? (Brutus says that he can guess what Cassius is talking about, has had similar thoughts, will consider what has been said, and will discuss the matter with Cassius later.)

**INFERENTIAL QUESTIONS**

**1b.** In mentioning Brutus' worth, what qualities in him is Cassius appealing to? (He is appealing to Brutus' self-esteem.)

**2b.** What does Brutus' response show about him? (It shows that he is cautious, somewhat secretive, worried about Caesar's growing power, and surprisingly susceptible to Cassius' flattery and designs.)

**BRUTUS.** The games are done, and Caesar is returning.

**CASSIUS.** As they pass by, pluck Casca by the sleeve,
180     And he will (after his sour fashion) tell you
    What hath proceeded worthy note today.

**BRUTUS.** I will do so. But look you, Cassius,
    The angry spot doth glow on Caesar's brow,
    And all the rest look like a chidden[42] train:
**1** 185     Calpurnia's cheek is pale, and Cicero[43]
    Looks with such ferret[44] and such fiery eyes
    As we have seen him in the Capitol,
    Being crossed in conference by some senators.

**CASSIUS.** Casca will tell us what the matter is.

[CAESAR *notices* CASSIUS *and turns to* ANTONY.]

190 **CAESAR.** Antonius.

**ANTONY.** Caesar?

**CAESAR.** Let me have men about me that are fat,
    Sleek-headed men, and such as sleep a-nights.
**2**     Yond Cassius has a lean and hungry look;
195     He thinks too much: such men are dangerous.

**ANTONY.** Fear him not, Caesar, he's not dangerous;
    He is a noble Roman, and well given.[45]

**CAESAR.** Would he were fatter! But I fear him not.
    Yet if my name were liable to fear,[46]
200     I do not know the man I should avoid
    So soon as that spare Cassius. He reads much,
    He is a great observer, and he looks
    Quite through the deeds of men.[47] He loves no plays,
    As thou dost, Antony; he hears no music,
**3** 205     Seldom he smiles, and smiles in such a sort
    As if he mocked himself, and scorned his spirit
    That could be moved to smile at anything.
    Such men as he be never at heart's ease
    Whiles they behold a greater than themselves,
210     And therefore are they very dangerous.
    I rather tell thee what is to be feared
    Than what I fear; for always I am Caesar.
    Come on my right hand, for this ear is deaf,
    And tell me truly what thou think'st of him.

[CAESAR *and his train leave.* BRUTUS, *eager to learn the*

*Julius Caesar, Act I, Scene ii* ·**481**

**42 chidden:** scolded.
**43 Cicero:** an eminent senator and orator.
**44 ferret:** weasellike animal with red eyes.

**45 well given:** favorably disposed toward Caesar.

**46 if my name...fear:** if it were possible for me to fear anyone.

**47 looks...men:** Caesar says that Cassius can see through people's actions to their true motives.

- *Scene ii (continued):* Brutus and Cassius wonder at the cause of Caesar's anger; Cassius says that Casca will tell them.
- Caesar discloses his mistrust of Cassius to Antony.

**1 STYLE: METAPHOR**

Brutus' comparison of Cicero to a ferret shows the depth of his cutting bitterness when so inspired.

**2 CHARACTERIZATION**

Caesar's description of Cassius suggests a wolfish rapaciousness and cunning with his "lean and hungry look."

**3 CHARACTERIZATION**

Like Cassius, Caesar is a keen psychologist, able to divine that a man who seldom smiles is envious and therefore dangerous.

## GUIDED READING

### LITERAL QUESTIONS

**1a.** What in Cassius' appearance makes Caesar decide that he is dangerous? (Cassius is lean and hungry looking.)

**2a.** What traits of Cassius' cause Caesar to conclude that he is envious? (Cassius sees into people's real motives, is uninterested in the arts, and seldom smiles.)

### INFERENTIAL QUESTIONS

**1b.** Do you think Caesar has judged Cassius' character correctly? (Caesar is right in noting that Cassius is driven, observant, and envious. Caesar's intimation that Cassius may be dangerous is also true.)

**2b.** What do Caesar's remarks about Cassius reveal about Caesar? (They reveal that, like Cassius, he is a shrewd observer of character and motive.)

R. H. Thomson. Jack Medley. Photo courtesy of Stratford Festival, Canada, 1982.

**482** *Drama*

[*reasons for the earlier shouting, stops* CASCA. *Unlike the other noble Romans,* CASCA *speaks here in blunt prose.*]

215 CASCA. You pulled me by the cloak; would you speak with me?

BRUTUS. Ay, Casca; tell us what hath chanced today,
That Caesar looks so sad.

CASCA. Why, you were with him, were you not?

BRUTUS. I should not then ask Casca what had chanced.

220 CASCA. Why, there was a crown offered him; and being offered him, he put it by[48] with the back of his hand, thus; and then the people fell a-shouting.

BRUTUS. What was the second noise for?

CASCA. Why, for that too.

225 CASSIUS. They shouted thrice; what was the last cry for?

CASCA. Why, for that too.

BRUTUS. Was the crown offered him thrice?

CASCA. Ay, marry, was't,[49] and he put it by thrice, every time gentler than other; and at every putting-by mine honest
230 neighbors shouted.

CASSIUS. Who offered him the crown?

CASCA. Why, Antony.

BRUTUS. Tell us the manner of it, gentle Casca.

CASCA. I can as well be hanged as tell the manner of it: it was
235 mere foolery; I did not mark it. I saw Mark Antony offer him a crown—yet 'twas not a crown neither, 'twas one of these coronets[50]—and, as I told you, he put it by once; but for all that, to my thinking, he would fain[51] have had it. Then he offered it to him again; then he put it by again; but
240 to my thinking, he was very loath to lay his fingers off it. And then he offered it the third time. He put it the third time by; and still as he refused it, the rabblement hooted, and clapped their chopt[52] hands, and threw up their sweaty nightcaps, and uttered such a deal of stinking breath be-
245 cause Caesar refused the crown, that it had, almost, choked Caesar; for he swounded[53] and fell down at it. And for mine own part, I durst not laugh, for fear of opening my lips and receiving the bad air.

48 **put it by:** pushed it aside.

49 **Ay, marry, was't:** Indeed it was.

50 **coronets:** smaller crowns than those worn by kings.
51 **fain:** rather.

52 **chopt:** chapped.

53 **swounded:** fainted.

*Julius Caesar, Act I, Scene ii* **483**

## AT A GLANCE

■ *Scene ii (continued):* Casca recounts how Caesar, when offered the crown three times by Mark Antony, refused it, although more reluctantly each time. Caesar fainted when the crowd cheered after his third refusal.

**1 DIALOGUE**

Brutus' insistent interrogation of Casca reveals his keen interest in Caesar's actions and popularity.

**2 CHARACTERIZATION**

Antony's closeness to Caesar is suggested by the fact that he is the one who offered Caesar the crown.

**3 STYLE: PROSE**

Although Casca is a nobleman, he does not speak in blank verse like Brutus and Cassius, perhaps because prose best suits his blunt cynicism.

## GUIDED READING

### LITERAL QUESTIONS

**1a.** What makes the people shout three times? (They shout each time Caesar refuses the crown.)

**2a.** What happens after Caesar refuses the crown a third time? (The crowd cheers, and Caesar faints.)

### INFERENTIAL QUESTIONS

**1b.** Why is Brutus so interested in discovering what caused the crowd to shout? (He is concerned that their shouts mean that something has happened affecting Caesar's power and/or popular support.)

**2b.** What do you think explains Caesar's response? (He may have fainted out of disappointment that the crowd did not want him to be king.)

### 1 VOCABULARY: PUN

Cassius' ironic play on words *(falling-sickness)* is directed at Brutus, Casca, and himself. This sarcasm exemplifies the kind of mocking humor Caesar attributed to Cassius in line 206.

### 2 MOOD

The common people's suggestibility ("and forgave him with all their hearts") arouses Casca's contempt, but also shows the volatile political atmosphere of the time.

### 3 PLOT: CONFLICT

Marullus' and Flavius' punishment marks the relatively rapid response of Caesar to his opponents. Such an action can only trouble Brutus more.

---

CASSIUS. But, soft, I pray you; what, did Caesar swound?

250 CASCA. He fell down in the market place, and foamed at mouth, and was speechless.

1     BRUTUS. 'Tis very like he hath the falling-sickness.[54]

        CASSIUS. No, Caesar hath it not; but you, and I,
And honest Casca, we have the falling-sickness.

255 CASCA. I know not what you mean by that, but I am sure Caesar fell down. If the tag-rag people did not clap him and hiss him, according as he pleased and displeased them, as they use to do the players in the theater, I am no true man.

        BRUTUS. What said he when he came unto himself?

260 CASCA. Marry, before he fell down, when he perceived the common herd was glad he refused the crown, he plucked me ope his doublet[55] and offered them his throat to cut. An I had been a man of any occupation,[56] if I would not have taken him at a word, I would I might go to hell among the
265    rogues. And so he fell. When he came to himself again, he said, if he had done or said anything amiss, he desired their worships to think it was his infirmity. Three or four wenches,[57] where I stood, cried "Alas, good soul!" and forgave him with all their hearts; but there's no heed to be taken of
270    them; if Caesar had stabbed their mothers, they would have done no less.

        BRUTUS. And after that, he came thus sad away?

        CASCA. Ay.

        CASSIUS. Did Cicero say anything?

275 CASCA. Ay, he spoke Greek.

        CASSIUS. To what effect?

        CASCA. Nay, an I tell you that, I'll ne'er look you i' th' face again. But those that understood him smiled at one another and shook their heads; but for mine own part, it was Greek to
280    me. I could tell you more news too: Marullus and Flavius, for pulling scarfs off Caesar's images, are put to silence.[58] Fare you well. There was more foolery yet, if I could remember it.

        CASSIUS. Will you sup with me tonight, Casca?

484   *Drama*

---

54 **falling-sickness:** epilepsy.

55 **doublet:** short jacket. Shakespeare's actors usually wore Elizabethan clothes, even in plays set in other periods of history.
56 **An I...occupation:** If I had been a laborer with cutting tools.

57 **wenches:** common women.

58 **put to silence:** barred from all public affairs.

---

## GUIDED READING

### LITERAL QUESTIONS

**1a.** According to Casca what was the crowd's response to Caesar before he fainted? (They clapped for him when he refused the crown and hissed at him when he displeased them.)

**2a.** What crime did Flavius and Marullus commit, and what was their punishment? (They removed decorative banners from statues of Caesar and for this were barred from all public affairs.)

### INFERENTIAL QUESTIONS

**1b.** Did the crowd act as if they were solidly behind Caesar? Explain your answer. (Their hissing and clapping indicates that they alternated between support and opposition.)

**2b.** What does Caesar's response to the actions of Marullus and Flavius show about him? (that he is concerned with consolidating his power)

285 CASCA. No, I am promised forth.

CASSIUS. Will you dine with me tomorrow?

CASCA. Ay, if I be alive, and your mind hold, and your dinner
worth the eating.

CASSIUS. Good; I will expect you.

290 CASCA. Do so. Farewell, both. [CASCA *leaves.*]

BRUTUS. What a blunt fellow is this grown to be!
He was quick mettle⁵⁹ when he went to school.

59 **quick mettle:** lively, clever.

**1**

CASSIUS. So is he now in execution
Of any bold or noble enterprise,
295 However he puts on this tardy form.⁶⁰
This rudeness is a sauce to his good wit,
Which gives men stomach to disgest⁶¹ his words
With better appetite.

60 **tardy form:** dull manner.

61 **disgest:** digest.

BRUTUS. And so it is. For this time I will leave you.
300 Tomorrow, if you please to speak with me,
I will come home to you; or if you will,
Come home to me, and I will wait for you.

CASSIUS. I will do so. Till then, think of the world.

[BRUTUS *leaves.* CASSIUS, *alone, notes with surprise the willingness of* BRUTUS, CAESAR's *trusted friend, to hear of talk against*
CAESAR.]

**2**

Well, Brutus, thou art noble; yet I see
305 Thy honorable mettle may be wrought
From that it is disposed;⁶² therefore it is meet
That noble minds keep ever with their likes;
For who so firm that cannot be seduced?
Caesar doth bear me hard,⁶³ but he loves Brutus.

62 **Thy honorable...disposed:**
Your honorable nature can be
manipulated to go against its normal
inclinations.

63 **doth bear me hard:** dislikes me.

**3**

310 If I were Brutus now, and he were Cassius,
He should not humor⁶⁴ me. I will this night,
In several hands,⁶⁵ in at his windows throw,
As if they came from several citizens,
Writings, all tending to the great opinion

64 **humor:** influence.

65 **several hands:** different
handwritings.

**4**

315 That Rome holds of his name; wherein obscurely
Caesar's ambition shall be glancèd at.⁶⁶
And after this, let Caesar seat him sure;
For we will shake him, or worse days endure. [CASSIUS exits.]

66 **wherein...glancèd at:** in which
Caesar's ambition shall be subtly
hinted at.

*Julius Caesar, Act I, Scene ii* **485**

**AT A GLANCE**

- *Scene ii (continued):* Cassius and Casca plan to dine.
- Brutus and Cassius agree to meet the next day.
- Alone, Cassius notes with surprise how easy it had been to manipulate Brutus.
- Cassius goes to distribute messages to Brutus about Caesar written in various handwritings.

**1 CHARACTERIZATION**

It is Cassius, not Brutus, who sees the method behind Casca's rudeness. Cassius is a shrewder judge of character than his friend.

**2 SOLILOQUY**

Now that he is alone, Cassius reveals his severe and honest judgment of Brutus' behavior: He had not fully anticipated the extent to which he can manipulate this honorable man.

**3 CHARACTERIZATION**

Cassius reveals his complex nature by stating that he would never be as influenced as Brutus if he were Caesar's friend.

**4 PLOT: RISING ACTION**

Cassius acts deviously to heighten the conflict in Brutus' mind by appealing to his fears about Caesar ("wherein obscurely Caesar's ambition shall be glanced at").

## GUIDED READING

### LITERAL QUESTIONS

**1a.** What does Brutus invite Cassius to do? (He invites Cassius to meet with him the next day.

**2a.** What adjectives does Cassius use to describe Brutus? (He uses the adjectives *noble* and *honorable* to describe Brutus.)

### INFERENTIAL QUESTIONS

**1b.** What does Brutus' invitation reveal about him? (It reveals a surprising readiness to continue to hear talk against Caesar.)

**2b.** Do you think Cassius may be using these adjectives somewhat ironically? Explain your answer. (He may be using them ironically because he feels that he, Cassius, would be more loyal to Caesar if they were friends.)

**1 SETTING**

This scene, like its two predecessors, takes place in the streets of Rome, a proper backdrop to the political conflicts at the heart of the play. However, in Scene iii the stormy physical scene becomes a kind of metaphor for the civil unrest developing in Rome.

**2 READING SKILLS: CONTRAST**

Cicero's calm ("Why are you breathless?"), so sharply contrasted to Casca's terror, only makes Casca's testimony more vividly compelling.

**3 PLOT: FORESHADOWING**

Casca's suggestion that the violent weather may be caused by "civil strife in heaven" invokes the possibility of civil strife in Rome as well.

**4 STYLE: IMAGERY**

The image of fire ("Men, all in fire, walk up and down the streets") conjures up visions of Romans aflame or bloodied during civil strife.

---

**1** *Scene iii. A Roman street. One month later.*

[*A violent storm rages, and thunder and lightning interrupt the scene. It is the night before the ides of March.* CASCA, *hurrying through the street, meets* CICERO, *a senator.* CASCA *is concerned about the violent weather and other unnatural happenings of this night. Like many, he believes that such events are bad omens, foretelling disaster of some kind to the state.* CICERO, *who does not believe in omens, is surprised to see the normally calm* CASCA *so upset.*]

**2**

CICERO. Good even, Casca; brought you Caesar home?
   Why are you breathless? And why stare you so?

CASCA. Are not you moved, when all the sway of earth[1]
   Shakes like a thing unfirm? O Cicero,
5  I have seen tempests, when the scolding winds
   Have rived[2] the knotty oaks, and I have seen
   Th' ambitious ocean swell and rage and foam,
   To be exalted with[3] the threat'ning clouds;

**3**
   But never till tonight, never till now,
10  Did I go through a tempest dropping fire.
   Either there is a civil strife in heaven,
   Or else the world, too saucy with the gods,
   Incenses[4] them to send destruction.

CICERO. Why, saw you anything more wonderful?

15 CASCA. A common slave—you know him well by sight—
   Held up his left hand, which did flame and burn
   Like twenty torches joined, and yet his hand,
   Not sensible of fire, remained unscorched.
   Besides—I ha' not since put up my sword—
20  Against the Capitol I met a lion,
   Who glazed[5] upon me and went surly by

**4**
   Without annoying me. And there were drawn
   Upon a heap[6] a hundred ghastly women,
   Transformèd with their fear, who swore they saw
25  Men, all in fire, walk up and down the streets.
   And yesterday the bird of night[7] did sit
   Even at noonday upon the market place,
   Hooting and shrieking. When these prodigies[8]
   Do so conjointly meet, let not men say,
30  "These are their reasons, they are natural,"
   For I believe they are portentous things
   Unto the climate that they point upon.[9]

**486** *Drama*

1 **sway of earth:** natural order.

2 **rived** [rīved]: split.

3 **exalted with:** raised as high as.

4 **incenses:** enrages.

5 **glazed:** stared.

6 **drawn...heap:** huddled together.

7 **bird of night:** screech owl.

8 **prodigies:** bizarre events.

9 **portentous...point upon:** bad omens for the place in which they occur.

---

## GUIDED READING

**LITERAL QUESTIONS**

**1a.** According to Casca, what is different about this night's storm? (The storm is "dropping fire.")

**2a.** What is unusual about the owl's behavior? (It screeches and hoots at noon, not night.)

**INFERENTIAL QUESTIONS**

**1b.** What dramatic purpose does the storm serve? (It foreshadows the violence to come.)

**2b.** In what way might future events parallel the owl's unnatural behavior? (Just as the owl's universe is turned upside down—with its night behavior transferred to day—so the order of life in Rome may be turned to chaos.)

CICERO. Indeed, it is a strange-disposèd time:
But men may construe things after their fashion,
35    Clean from the purpose of the things themselves.[10]
Comes Caesar to the Capitol tomorrow?

CASCA. He doth; for he did bid Antonius
Send word to you he would be there tomorrow.

CICERO. Good night then, Casca; this disturbèd sky
Is not to walk in.

40 CASCA.             Farewell, Cicero.

[CICERO *leaves. There is another clap of thunder and flash of lightning as* CASSIUS *enters. Since the feast of Lupercal,* CASSIUS *has been organizing a conspiracy against* CAESAR. *He attempts to learn if* CASCA *will join his group.*]

CASSIUS. Who's there?

CASCA.           A Roman.

CASSIUS.                  Casca, by your voice.

CASCA. Your ear is good. Cassius, what night is this?

CASSIUS. A very pleasing night to honest men.

CASCA. Who ever knew the heavens menace so?

45 CASSIUS. Those that have known the earth so full of faults.
For my part, I have walked about the streets,
Submitting me unto the perilous night,
And thus unbracèd,[11] Casca, as you see,
Have bared my bosom to the thunder-stone;[12]
50    And when the cross blue lightning seemed to open
The breast of heaven, I did present myself
Even in the aim and very flash of it.

CASCA. But wherefore did you so much tempt the heavens?
It is the part of men to fear and tremble
55    When the most mighty gods by tokens send
Such dreadful heralds to astonish us.

CASSIUS. You are dull, Casca, and those sparks of life
That should be in a Roman you do want,[13]
Or else you use not. You look pale, and gaze,
60    And put on fear, and cast yourself in wonder,
To see the strange impatience of the heavens;
But if you would consider the true cause
Why all these fires, why all these gliding ghosts,

*Julius Caesar, Act I, Scene iii*   **487**

---

**10 men may construe...themselves:** People always find their own meanings in such events, no matter what the actual cause of the events may be.

**11 unbracèd:** with open coat.

**12 thunder-stone:** People once believed that thunder hurled stones to the earth.

**13 want:** lack.

---

AT A GLANCE

- *Scene iii (continued):* Casca tells Cicero that Caesar will be at the Capitol tomorrow.
- After Cicero leaves, Cassius enters and tells Casca that he shows an un-Roman fear.

**1 PLOT: FORESHADOWING**

Because the reader knows the soothsayer's prediction and has heard about Casca's omens, Cicero's question ("Comes Caesar to the Capitol tomorrow?") and Casca's answer ("He doth") strike an ominous note.

**2 CHARACTERIZATION**

Cassius has a certain fearless bravado that makes him a natural leader.

**3 THEME**

Casca wonders if there is something wrong in not being afraid of the gods and trembling before their "tokens." Cassius' scornful reply indicates that, at this point in the play, he does not acknowledge any authority other than his own will.

---

## GUIDED READING

### LITERAL QUESTIONS

**1a.** What has Cassius been doing during the night? (He has been walking the streets with his coat unbuttoned.)

**2a.** What does Cassius accuse Casca of being? (He accuses Casca of not being a true Roman with a spark of life.)

### INFERENTIAL QUESTIONS

**1b.** What does Cassius' behavior during the night show about him? (It shows his reckless defiance of both heavenly and earthly authorities.)

**2b.** What is the purpose of Cassius' accusation? (He wants to make Casca feel like a coward if he refuses to join the conspiracy.)

■ *Scene iii (continued):* Cassius interprets the night's events as a warning to the Roman people.

■ Casca repeats the rumor that Caesar is to be crowned king tomorrow.

■ Cassius replies that he will kill himself rather than submit to Caesar.

## 1 PLOT: RISING ACTION

To make sure of Casca, Cassius compares the night's abnormal events to Caesar's abnormal power. Cassius is playing upon Casca's superstition, just as he had played upon Brutus' sense of honor in the previous scene.

## 2 CHARACTERIZATION

If Caesar is crowned, Cassius may indeed feel bitter and hopeless enough to kill himself. However, it seems more likely that he would continue to conspire. Given Cassius' skill and boldness in manipulating others, it is probable that the threat is meant to impress Casca and bind him to the murder plot. Cassius will use the dagger to free himself from bondage—by killing Caesar.

Why birds and beasts from quality and kind,
65  Why old men, fools, and children calculate,[14]
Why all these things change from their ordinance,
Their natures and preformèd faculties,[15]
To monstrous quality, why, you shall find
That heaven hath infused them with these spirits
70  To make them instruments of fear and warning
Unto some monstrous state.

[*Having distracted* CASCA *from his fear,* CASSIUS *now interprets the night's abnormal events as a warning to the people of Rome. According to* CASSIUS, *the Romans have been abnormally passive, and* CAESAR, *in his turn, has taken advantage of this passiveness to acquire an abnormal amount of power.*]

**1**  Now could I, Casca, name to thee a man
Most like this dreadful night,
That thunders, lightens, opens graves, and roars
75  As doth the lion in the Capitol;
A man no mightier than thyself, or me,
In personal action, yet prodigious grown[16]
And fearful, as these strange eruptions are.

CASCA. 'Tis Caesar that you mean, is it not, Cassius?

80  CASSIUS. Let it be who it is; for Romans now
Have thews[17] and limbs like to their ancestors;
But, woe the while![18] Our fathers' minds are dead,
And we are governed with our mothers' spirits;
Our yoke and sufferance show us womanish.

85  CASCA. Indeed, they say the senators tomorrow
Mean to establish Caesar as a king;
And he shall wear his crown by sea and land,
In every place save here in Italy.

**2**  CASSIUS. I know where I will wear this dagger then;
90  Cassius from bondage will deliver Cassius.[19]
Therein, ye gods, you make the weak most strong;
Therein, ye gods, you tyrants do defeat.
Nor stony tower, nor walls of beaten brass,
Nor airless dungeon, nor strong links of iron,
95  Can be retentive to the strength of spirit;
But life, being weary of these worldly bars,
Never lacks power to dismiss itself.
If I know this, know all the world besides.

14 **calculate:** make prophecies.

15 **ordinance . . . faculties:** the established behavior, nature, and instincts of their species.

16 **prodigious grown:** become huge and ominous.

17 **thews:** muscles.

18 **woe the while:** Alas for these times.

19 **Cassius . . . will deliver Cassius:** Cassius will kill himself rather than submit to Caesar.

**488**  *Drama*

## GUIDED READING

### LITERAL QUESTIONS

**1a.** According to Cassius, in what ways do the night's abnormal events resemble Caesar? (Like them, he seems huge, ominous, and frightening in his actions.)

**2a.** What is Cassius prepared to do if Caesar is crowned the next day? (He is prepared to kill himself.)

### INFERENTIAL QUESTIONS

**1b.** What is Cassius' motive in comparing the abnormal events to Caesar? (He wants to ensure Casca's support by appealing to his superstitions; he may also want to fortify his own courage.)

**2b.** Do you think that Cassius would make good his suicide threat? (Some students may note that Cassius is a passionate, obsessed man who might indeed kill himself; others may note that this threat might be another ploy.)

That part of tyranny that I do bear
I can shake off at pleasure.

[*Another clap of thunder.* CASCA *ignores it to answer* CASSIUS.]

100 CASCA.                          So can I;
         So every bondman in his own hand bears
         The power to cancel his captivity.

         CASSIUS. And why should Caesar be a tyrant then?
         Poor man, I know he would not be a wolf
105      But that he sees the Romans are but sheep;
         He were no lion, were not Romans hinds.[20]
         Those that with haste will make a mighty fire
         Begin it with weak straws. What trash is Rome,
         What rubbish and what offal,[21] when it serves
110      For the base matter to illuminate
         So vile a thing as Caesar! But, O grief,
         Where hast thou led me? I, perhaps, speak this
         Before a willing bondman;[22] then I know
         My answer must be made. But I am armed,
115      And dangers are to me indifferent.

         CASCA. You speak to Casca, and to such a man
         That is no fleering[23] tell-tale. Hold, my hand.
         Be factious[24] for redress of all these griefs,
         And I will set this foot of mine as far
         As who goes farthest.

[CASCA *shakes* CASSIUS' *hand to show that he is joining the conspiracy.*]

120 CASSIUS.                  There's a bargain made.
         Now know you, Casca, I have moved already
         Some certain of the noblest-minded Romans
         To undergo with me an enterprise
         Of honorable dangerous consequence;
125      And I do know, by this they stay for me
         In Pompey's porch;[25] for now, this fearful night,
         There is no stir or walking in the streets,
         And the complexion of the element
         In favor's like the work we have in hand,[26]
130      Most bloody, fiery, and most terrible.

[CASSIUS *and* CASCA *notice* CINNA, *a member of the conspiracy, hurrying toward them.*]

         CASCA. Stand close awhile, for here comes one in haste.

*Julius Caesar, Act I, Scene iii*  **489**

20 **hinds:** female deer.

21 **offal:** garbage.

22 **willing bondman:** Cassius suggests that Casca, unlike himself, accepts slavery under Caesar and might therefore inform on him.

23 **fleering:** sneering.

24 **Be factious:** form a faction, or group.

25 **Pompey's porch:** entrance to the theater built by Pompey.

26 **complexion...hand:** The appearance of the sky is like the work we are to do.

AT A GLANCE

- *Scene iii (continued):* Cassius suggests that Casca accepts slavery under Caesar and may therefore inform on him.
- Casca shakes Cassius' hand to show he is joining the conspiracy.
- Cinna, another conspirator, hurries toward them.

**1 STYLE: METAPHOR**

Cassius' scathing metaphors stress the Romans' weakness in allowing a rapacious Caesar to rule them.

**2 VOCABULARY: DICTION**

Cassius' repeated use of words denoting nobility (*noblest-minded*) and honor (*honorable*) to describe the conspirators serves to remove their guilt and perhaps his own.

**3 STYLE: SIMILE**

Cassius' comparison ironically raises the possibility that he refuses to acknowledge: that the conspiracy evokes the wrath of the gods.

## GUIDED READING

### LITERAL QUESTIONS

**1a.** What does Cassius say worries him about Casca? (He says that he is worried that Casca may inform on him.)

**2a.** What qualities does Cassius say describe his fellow conspirators? (He says they are noble-minded and honorable.)

### INFERENTIAL QUESTIONS

**1b.** What is Cassius' motive in expressing his worry aloud? (He wants to test Casca and tighten Casca's ties to the conspiracy.)

**2b.** What is Cassius' purpose in emphasizing these qualities? (He wants to justify the conspiracy to Casca and perhaps to himself as well.)

## 1 CHARACTERIZATION

Cassius' repeated question ("Am I not stayed for?") betrays his anxiety as the time for action draws near.

## 2 STYLE: SIMILE

By comparing Brutus' participation in the conspiracy to alchemy, Casca implies that the plotters themselves may not be entirely certain of the purity of their motives. Brutus' presence is expected to win public support; on another level, it may reassure the conspirators of the rightness of their actions.

### REFLECTING ON ACT I

From what you have seen so far, would you say that the conspirators are traitors or patriots? (Some students may argue that the conspirators are traitors because the chief motive of the leader, Cassius, appears to be envy; others may argue that, if Caesar shows himself to be tyrannical, the conspirators' plot is patriotic.)

---

CASSIUS. 'Tis Cinna; I do know him by his gait;
    He is a friend. Cinna, where haste you so?

CINNA. To find out you. Who's that? Metellus Cimber?

135 CASSIUS. No, it is Casca, one incorporate[27]
    To our attempts. Am I not stayed[28] for, Cinna?

CINNA. I am glad on't. What a fearful night is this!
    There's two or three of us have seen strange sights.

CASSIUS. Am I not stayed for? Tell me.

CINNA.                        Yes, you are.
140     O Cassius, if you could
    But win the noble Brutus to our party—

CASSIUS. Be you content. Good Cinna, take this paper,
    And look you lay it in the praetor's[29] chair,
    Where Brutus may but find it; and throw this
145     In at his window; set this up with wax
    Upon old Brutus' statue.[30] All this done,
    Repair to Pompey's porch, where you shall find us.
    Is Decius Brutus and Trebonius there?

CINNA. All but Metellus Cimber, and he's gone
150     To seek you at your house. Well, I will hie,[31]
    And so bestow these papers as you bade me.

CASSIUS. That done, repair to Pompey's Theater.

[CINNA *hurries off to carry out* CASSIUS' *directions.*]

    Come, Casca, you and I will yet ere day
    See Brutus at his house; three parts of him
155     Is ours already, and the man entire
    Upon the next encounter yields him ours.

CASCA. O, he sits high in all the people's hearts;
    And that which would appear offense in us,
    His countenance, like richest alchemy,[32]
160     Will change to virtue and to worthiness.

CASSIUS. Him, and his worth, and our great need of him,
    You have right well conceited.[33] Let us go,
    For it is after midnight, and ere day
    We will awake him and be sure of him.

[CASSIUS *and* CASCA *leave together to wake* BRUTUS.]

27 **incorporate:** joined.
28 **stayed:** waited.

29 **praetor's** [prē′tərz]: Brutus was a praetor, a high-ranking judge second in Rome only to Caesar.

30 **old Brutus' statue:** the statue of the hero Lucius Junius Brutus.

31 **hie:** hurry.

32 **alchemy:** Alchemists tried to turn baser metals into gold. Casca says that Brutus' noble reputation will make the public regard the plot as a worthy undertaking.

33 **conceited:** understood.

---

## GUIDED READING

### LITERAL QUESTIONS

**1a.** What does Cassius ask Cinna to do? (He asks Cinna to put the forged papers in various places where Brutus may find them.)

**2a.** What does Casca mean by comparing Brutus' reputation to the "richest alchemy"? (By his participation, Brutus will give the plot an appearance of virtue.)

### INFERENTIAL QUESTIONS

**1b.** What does Cinna's obedience to Cassius show about their respective roles in the conspiracy? (It shows that Cassius is the leader and Cinna is a follower.)

**2b.** By this comparison what is Casca implying about the plotters' real motives? (He is implying that the motives may not be as pure as the conspirators would like to believe.)

## STUDY QUESTIONS

### Recalling

1. Why are the tribunes Marullus and Flavius angry with the plebeians in Act I, Scene i? What do the tribunes hope to accomplish by sending the plebeians home and removing the decorations from the statues?
2. What warning does the soothsayer give to Caesar in Scene ii? What is Caesar's response?
3. How does Cassius feel about Caesar? What is Brutus' response in Scene ii, lines 162–175, to Cassius' arguments against Caesar?
4. What qualities in Cassius does Caesar describe to Antony in Scene ii?
5. What does Brutus promise Cassius as he leaves the square?
6. In Scene iii, what has Casca seen on the night of the storm, and why is he frightened? What explanation of the evening's strange sights does Cassius offer to Casca?
7. List three of the actions that Cassius undertakes in Scene iii to persuade Brutus to join the conspiracy. Why is it important to the conspirators that Brutus join them?

### Interpreting

8. What point is made about the plebeians in Scene i when Marullus recalls their once-loud support of Pompey?
9. What is your impression of Caesar from his actions and words in Scene ii?
10. From what you have seen of Cassius, are Caesar's remarks about him in Scene ii accurate? What do they reveal about Caesar himself?
11. To what extent does Brutus agree with Cassius' concerns in Scene ii? Why would he be reluctant to join the conspiracy against Caesar? What happens during the scene to make the problem of Caesar more urgent?

### Extending

12. Do you find Cassius' arguments in Scenes ii and iii convincing reasons for destroying Caesar? Why or why not? What arguments would you offer to oppose Cassius' arguments?

## LITERARY FOCUS

### Conflict in Drama

**Conflict** is the clash between opposing forces, individuals, or ideas. While conflict is important in fiction, it is the very essence of drama. Most plays present their action through a series of confrontations between characters, without a narrator to describe what is happening. Drama therefore depends entirely on conflict between and within characters to move the action forward. In addition, because no narrator comments on the action, a play may present the audience with conflicting views of its various characters and events, views that may differ from one speaker to the next.

From its opening scene, *Julius Caesar* involves us in many different types of conflict. It develops conflicts between and within individuals involved in an explosive situation. It presents conflicting views of its various characters and events. It also portrays conflicts between groups of people and between individuals and the political system. Finally, because it presents historical events, *Julius Caesar* is especially concerned with the conflict between the world as it might be and the world as it actually is.

### Thinking About Conflict in Drama

1. What various conflicts between the tribunes and the plebeians does Scene i present?
2. How many different kinds of conflict can you identify in Scene ii? List conflicts within characters, between characters, between characters and external forces, and conflicting views of characters.
3. In Scene iii what conflicting views of the night's events are expressed by Casca, Cicero, and Cassius? Explain how nature is shown in conflict with itself in this scene. What parallels can you draw between the conflicts within the natural world and other conflicts that are presented in Act I?

### Blank Verse

Like Shakespeare's other plays, most of *Julius Caesar* is written in blank verse. **Blank verse** is unrhymed **iambic pentameter** poetry, which is made up of lines that are ten syllables long with a strong

*Julius Caesar, Act I*  **491**

1. Plebeians are celebrating Caesar's return; to check his ascent to greater power.
2. beware the ides of March; calls soothsayer a dreamer
3. thinks he has too much power; has already considered them
4. thinks too much, ignores pleasures, never smiles; is dangerous
5. He will meet with him.
6. man whose hand was in flames; lion walking in streets; bird of night appearing in afternoon; fears events foreshadow things to come; compares unnatural night to Caesar's power
7. asks him to leave letter on his chair; throw another through his window; leave another on statue; to win support
8. They would support anyone in power.
9. is shrewd, vain, overconfident
10. sees through Caesar's motives, is envious; Caesar—shrewd judge of character
11. It would be bad for Rome if Caesar were crowned king. He loves Caesar. He refuses the crown with increasing reluctance.
12. No—Caesar has not yet committed any abuses, is strong, capable, popular; his death may cause more harm than good.

### Conflict in Drama

1. conflict between social classes; conflict regarding the meaning of words; conflict between plebeians favoring Caesar and tribunes' loyalty to Pompey
2. *external:* Caesar vs. fate; Brutus vs. Cassius; Cassius vs. Caesar; *internal:* Brutus' love for Caesar vs. his love for Rome; Caesar's desire for crown vs. his realization that kingship is unpopular; *conflicting views:* Cassius as seen by Antony and Caesar

3. *Casca:* omens of bad times
*Cicero:* disturbed sky
*Cassius:* parallels to Rome's political situation
They suggest unrest in the Roman state.

1. *verse:* Marullus, Flavius; *prose:* plebeians; stresses class differences; prose used as comic effect
2. Lines 136, 137, 139, 140 depart from blank verse, provide variety, emphasize meaning.
3. *Scene ii:* Speech is sarcastic; blunt; contrast to Brutus' elegance; mocks Caesar's crowd. *Scene iii:* Blank verse eliminates sarcasm, adds serious tone.

accent on every other syllable. The light accents are marked ⏑ and the heavy accents ´ in the following lines spoken by Cassius in Act I, Scene iii:

Poor man, I know he would not be a wolf
But that he sees the Romans are but sheep....

We can easily distinguish blank verse from prose as we read because each new line of blank verse begins with a capital letter. Blank verse also differs from prose in that it follows a definite rhythmical pattern. However, that pattern does not differ markedly from the normal rhythms of the English language. Therefore, when we read blank verse aloud, we do not need to emphasize the stresses. In most cases, our normal pronunciation of the words will bring out the rhythm of the lines naturally. For this reason, blank verse is very popular among writers of English.

In Shakespeare's time playwrights used blank verse a great deal. However, they often altered the verse pattern to emphasize certain words or to pre-vent a passage from becoming monotonous. Playwrights also mixed blank verse with prose in their plays. For example, Shakespeare substituted prose for blank verse to represent the speech of the lower classes; in contrast, his upper-class characters usually speak in blank verse. Shakespeare also used prose rather than blank verse in comic passages in his plays.

**Thinking About Blank Verse**

1. In Act I, Scene i, which characters speak in verse, and which speak in prose? What is the effect of this difference?
2. Copy lines 135–141 in Scene ii, and mark the accents in each line. Indicate which lines follow the blank verse pattern exactly, and which ones depart from it. What is the effect of the lines that change the pattern?
3. Casca speaks prose in Scene ii and verse in Scene iii. Read aloud one of his speeches from each scene. What is the effect in each case? Why might Shakespeare have used these two different styles of speech for the same character?

# ACT II

*Scene i.* BRUTUS' *garden. The ides of March.*

[*It is a few hours before daybreak. The night's storm has quieted.* BRUTUS, *unable to sleep, paces in his garden thinking. In the month since the feast of Lupercal, he has been weighing* CASSIUS' *warning about the threat posed by* CAESAR *to the republic.* BRUTUS *has also been influenced by many unsigned messages planted by the conspirators urging him to take action against* CAESAR'S *tyranny. He has now lost track of time and calls for his young servant* LUCIUS.]

BRUTUS. What, Lucius, ho!
  I cannot, by the progress of the stars,
  Give guess how near to day. Lucius, I say!
  I would it were my fault to sleep so soundly.
5  When, Lucius, when? Awake, I say! What, Lucius!

[LUCIUS *enters sleepily from the house.*]

LUCIUS. Called you, my lord?

BRUTUS. Get me a taper[1] in my study, Lucius.
  When it is lighted, come and call me here.

LUCIUS. I will, my lord.

[LUCIUS *returns to the house, and* BRUTUS, *left alone, reviews the reasons for killing* CAESAR.]

10  BRUTUS. It must be by his death;[2] and for my part,
  I know no personal cause to spurn at him,
  But for the general.[3] He would be crowned.
  How that might change his nature, there's the question.
  It is the bright day that brings forth the adder,[4]
15  And that craves[5] wary walking. Crown him that,
  And then I grant we put a sting in him
  That at his will he may do danger with.
  Th' abuse of greatness is when it disjoins
  Remorse[6] from power; and, to speak truth of Caesar,
20  I have not known when his affections[7] swayed
  More than his reason. But 'tis a common proof
  That lowliness[8] is young ambition's ladder,
  Whereto the climber upward turns his face;
  But when he once attains the upmost round,
25  He then unto the ladder turns his back,

1 **taper:** candle.

2 **his death:** Caesar's death.

3 **for the general:** for the public good.

4 **adder:** poisonous snake.

5 **craves:** demands.

6 **Remorse:** consideration for others.

7 **his affections:** his personal desires.

8 **lowliness:** humility.

*Julius Caesar, Act II, Scene i* **493**

---

## AT A GLANCE

- *Scene i:* Unable to sleep, Brutus paces his garden a few hours before daybreak on the ides of March.
- Confused about the time, he asks his servant Lucius to get a candle.
- Alone, Brutus reviews his reasons for killing Caesar; chiefly, he is afraid that when crowned Caesar may become tyrannical.

## LITERARY OPTIONS

- characterization
- soliloquy
- aside

## THEMATIC OPTIONS

- emotions vs. principles
- leadership
- conflict

## 1 SETTING

This setting—inside Brutus' garden—is the first intimate setting of the play and is appropriate, for the conflict waged here occurs in Brutus' mind: He is torn between personal friendship and concern for the public good.

## 2 SOLILOQUY

Brutus' first soliloquy shows that he has already decided to kill Caesar but needs to go over the reasons again in order to reassure himself.

## 3 CONFLICT

Brutus can find no evidence in Caesar's past to prove that he will act unreasonably, or tyrannically.

---

## GUIDED READING

### LITERAL QUESTIONS

**1a.** When does the scene begin? (before dawn on the ides of March)

**2a.** What does Brutus say might be put into Caesar if he is crowned? (a sting)

### INFERENTIAL QUESTIONS

**1b.** What might explain Brutus' sleeplessness? (Although he seems to have decided that Caesar must die, he is uneasy about his decision and keeps reviewing it.)

**2b.** What does he mean? (Caesar might become as dangerous as a poisonous snake when he gains absolute power.)

- *Scene i (continued):* Lucius brings a letter he has found.
- Brutus asks Lucius to see if the coming day is the ides of March.
- Brutus comments on the contents of the letter as he reads it, saying finally that he will redress Rome's grievances.

**1  STYLE: SIMILE**

Perhaps to work himself up, Brutus compares Caesar to a serpent's egg which, when hatched, would "grow mischievous." This simile echoes the implied comparison of Caesar to an adder in lines 14–16.

**2  PLOT: FORESHADOWING**

Brutus' question to Lucius ("Is not tomorrow, boy, the ides of March?") sustains the dramatic tension by reminding the reader that the conspirators plan to kill Caesar then.

**3  STYLE: SITUATIONAL IRONY**

In the light of Brutus' insomnia, the writer's accusation that he is sleeping ("Brutus, thou sleep'st; awake.") is unintentionally ironic.

**4  SOLILOQUY**

In his second soliloquy, Brutus shows the depth of his attachment to Rome by directly addressing it as if they have a personal relationship and he is responsible for its welfare ("O Rome, I make thee promise").

---

Looks in the clouds, scorning the base degrees
By which he did ascend. So Caesar may;
Then lest he may, prevent.⁹ And, since the quarrel
Will bear no color for the thing he is,
30   Fashion it thus:¹⁰ that what he is, augmented,
Would run to these and these extremities;
**1**   And therefore think him as a serpent's egg
Which hatched, would as his kind grow mischievous,
And kill him in the shell.

[LUCIUS *enters with a letter.*]

35   LUCIUS. The taper burneth in your closet,¹¹ sir.
Searching the window for a flint, I found
This paper thus sealed up, and I am sure
It did not lie there when I went to bed.

[LUCIUS *gives* BRUTUS *the letter.*]

**2**   BRUTUS. Get you to bed again; it is not day.
40   Is not tomorrow, boy, the ides of March?

LUCIUS. I know not, sir.

BRUTUS. Look in the calendar and bring me word.

LUCIUS. I will, sir.

[LUCIUS *returns to the house.*]

BRUTUS. The exhalations¹² whizzing in the air
45   Give so much light that I may read by them.

[BRUTUS *reads the letter aloud and then comments on the hints contained in it.*]

**3**   "Brutus, thou sleep'st; awake, and see thyself.
Shall Rome, etc. Speak, strike, redress.¹³
Brutus, thou sleep'st; awake."

Such instigations have been often dropped
50   Where I have took them up.
"Shall Rome, etc." Thus must I piece it out:¹⁴
**4**   Shall Rome stand under one man's awe? What, Rome?
My ancestors did from the streets of Rome
The Tarquin¹⁵ drive, when he was called a king.
55   "Speak, strike, redress." Am I entreated
To speak and strike? O Rome, I make thee promise,
If the redress will follow, thou receivest
Thy full petition at the hand of Brutus!

9  **prevent:** Let us stop him while we can.

10  **since the quarrel...thus:** Since our complaints are not clearly supported by Caesar's present behavior, we will have to put our case the following way.

11  **closet:** small private study.

12  **exhalations:** meteors.

13  **redress:** correct a wrong.

14  **piece it out:** Brutus must fill in the gaps the writer has deliberately left in the note.

15  **Tarquin:** the last king of Rome, driven out by Lucius Junius Brutus.

**494**   *Drama*

---

## GUIDED READING

### LITERAL QUESTIONS

**1a.** What reason does Brutus use to persuade himself that Caesar must be killed now? (If Caesar is not killed now, he will grow into a tyrant.)

**2a.** What does the letter accuse Brutus of? (It accuses him of sleeping while Rome is being wronged.)

### INFERENTIAL QUESTIONS

**1b.** What is the difference between Brutus' reason for killing Caesar and Cassius'? (Brutus wants to save Rome, whereas Cassius is personally envious of Caesar.)

**2b.** In what way is the accusation situationally ironic? (Brutus is actually *unable* to sleep because of his conflict between loyalty to Caesar and loyalty to Rome.)

[LUCIUS *returns, having checked the calendar.*]

LUCIUS. Sir, March is wasted fifteen days.

[*They hear a knock at the gate.*]

60 BRUTUS. 'Tis good. Go to the gate; somebody knocks.

[LUCIUS *goes to see who is knocking, leaving* BRUTUS *to reflect on his own troubled state of mind.*]

Since Cassius first did whet me against Caesar,
I have not slept.
Between the acting of a dreadful thing
And the first motion,[16] all the interim is
65 Like a phantasma, or a hideous dream.
The genius and the mortal instruments[17]
Are then in council, and the state of a man,
Like to a little kingdom, suffers then
The nature of an insurrection.[18]

[LUCIUS *returns.*]

70 LUCIUS. Sir, 'tis your brother[19] Cassius at the door,
Who doth desire to see you.

BRUTUS.                    Is he alone?

LUCIUS. No, sir, there are moe[20] with him.

BRUTUS.                    Do you know them?

LUCIUS. No, sir; their hats are plucked about their ears,
And half their faces buried in their cloaks,
75 That by no means I may discover them
By any mark of favor.[21]

BRUTUS.            Let 'em enter

[LUCIUS *leaves to admit the visitors.*]

They are the faction. O conspiracy,
Sham'st thou to show thy dang'rous brow by night,
When evils are most free? O, then by day
80 Where wilt thou find a cavern dark enough
To mask thy monstrous visage? Seek none, conspiracy;
Hide it in smiles and affability:
For if thou path, thy native semblance on,[22]
Not Erebus[23] itself were dim enough
85 To hide thee from prevention.[24]

16 **first motion:** first idea.

17 **The genius and the mortal instruments:** spirit and bodily powers; that is, the part of a person that makes decisions and the part that acts on them.
18 **in council...insurrection:** The internal debate goes on constantly, becoming like a civil war.

19 **brother:** brother-in-law. Cassius is married to Brutus' sister, Junia.

20 **moe:** more people.

21 **favor:** appearance.

22 **path...semblance on:** go about with your real feelings showing.
23 **Erebus** [er′ə bəs]: The dim entrance to hell.
24 **prevention:** discovery.

*Julius Caesar, Act II, Scene i*   **495**

AT A GLANCE
■ *Scene i (continued):* Lucius returns and tells Brutus that it is the ides of March.
■ Lucius announces that Cassius has come with others who are hiding their faces.
■ When Lucius leaves to admit the visitors, Brutus notes the furtive nature of conspiracy.

**1 SOLILOQUY**

In his third soliloquy, Brutus, for the first time, discloses the pain his conflict has caused him.

**2 STYLE: SIMILE**

That Brutus sees his internal conflict as similar to a "little kingdom" during an insurrection shows the political cast of his mind. This comparison is apt, since the action Brutus contemplates is literally an "insurrection" against the head of his own state.

**3 CHARACTERIZATION**

Brutus cannot "hide" from himself the "monstrous" nature of the conspiracy he has joined. All his reasoning cannot mask the shameful nature of the action he plans.

## GUIDED READING

### LITERAL QUESTIONS

**1a.** To what does Brutus compare the time between his first thoughts about killing Caesar and the murder itself? (He compares it to a hideous dream.)

**2a.** According to Brutus, why do the other conspirators hide their faces? (They hide them because they know they are doing something "monstrous.")

### INFERENTIAL QUESTIONS

**1b.** What does this comparison reveal about Brutus' state of mind? (He feels trapped inside a nightmare. In a way, finally taking action will be a relief.)

**2b.** What do Brutus' observations on the other conspirators reveal about his own state of mind? (They indicate that part of him still thinks it is wrong, even monstrously so, to kill Caesar.)

- *Scene i (continued):* Entering with Cassius and hiding their faces are the other conspirators who introduce themselves to Brutus.
- As Cassius and Brutus step aside to talk privately, the others make light conversation.

**1 STAGE DIRECTIONS**

After Brutus' remarks that the conspirators need to mask their hideous faces, the stage directions visually reinforce this point.

**2 CHARACTERIZATION**

Cassius is almost relentless in his flattery of Brutus.

**3 CHARACTERIZATION**

Brutus' innocent-seeming question shows that he is still cautiously hiding his real thoughts. He knows what "watchful cares" have brought the conspirators to his house.

**4 PLOT: FORESHADOWING**

The conspirators' disagreement about the location of the east may suggest that they have, metaphorically, lost their bearings. Their confusion may also foreshadow the confusion and disorder they will bring to Rome by killing Caesar.

**1** [CASSIUS *and the other conspirators enter. They include* CASCA, DECIUS, CINNA, METELLUS CIMBER, *and* TREBONIUS. *All wear their cloaks wrapped about their faces so that they cannot be easily recognized.*]

CASSIUS. I think we are too bold upon your rest.
Good morrow, Brutus; do we trouble you?

BRUTUS. I have been up this hour, awake all night.
Know I these men that come along with you?

**2** 90 CASSIUS. Yes, every man of them; and no man here
But honors you; and every one doth wish
You had but that opinion of yourself
Which every noble Roman bears of you.
This is Trebonius.

[*One by one the conspirators step forward to reveal themselves to* BRUTUS.]

95 BRUTUS.                He is welcome hither.

CASSIUS. This, Decius Brutus.

BRUTUS.                          He is welcome too.

CASSIUS. This, Casca; this, Cinna; and this, Metellus Cimber.

BRUTUS. They are all welcome.

**3** What watchful cares do interpose themselves
Betwixt your eyes and night?²⁵

25 **What watchful...night:** What cares keep you awake?

100 CASSIUS. Shall I entreat a word?

[BRUTUS *and* CASSIUS *step away from the conspirators and whisper. As they wait for these two to finish their private conversation, the conspirators make light conversation among themselves.*]

DECIUS. Here lies the east; doth not the day break here?

CASCA. No.

CINNA. O, pardon, sir, it doth; and yon gray lines
That fret²⁶ the clouds are messengers of day.

26 **fret:** interlace.

**4** 105 CASCA. You shall confess that you are both deceived.
Here, as I point my sword, the sun arises,
Which is a great way growing on the south,
Weighing the youthful season of the year.²⁷
Some two months hence, up higher toward the north

27 **Weighing...year:** keeping in mind that it is early spring. Casca argues that in early spring the sun rises south of the spot picked by Decius and Cinna.

**496** *Drama*

---

*GUIDED READING*

**LITERAL QUESTIONS**

**1a.** What does Cassius say the conspirators feel about Brutus? (He says they honor him and wish that he thought as well of himself as they do.)

**2a.** What does Cassius ask of Brutus? (He asks if they may speak together.)

**INFERENTIAL QUESTIONS**

**1b.** What motivates Cassius to describe the conspirators' feelings in this way? (Because Brutus still has not joined the conspiracy, Cassius continues to flatter him into becoming a part of it.)

**2b.** What do you think Brutus and Cassius are saying to each other? (Cassius is probably trying to convince Brutus to join the conspiracy, and Brutus may be telling him that he will.)

110 He first presents his fire;[28] and the high east
    Stands as the Capitol, directly here.

[BRUTUS *and* CASSIUS *join the others.* BRUTUS *now seems resolved to enter the conspiracy. He offers his hand to each man as he returns to the group.*]

BRUTUS. Give me your hands all over, one by one.

CASSIUS. And let us swear our resolution.

BRUTUS. No, not an oath. If not the face of men,
115 The sufferance of our souls, the time's abuse[29]—
    If these be motives weak, break off betimes,[30]
    And every man hence to his idle bed.
    So let high-sighted[31] tyranny range on
    Till each man drop by lottery.[32] But if these
120 (As I am sure they do) bear fire enough
    To kindle cowards and to steel with valor
    The melting spirits of women, then, countrymen,
    What need we any spur but our own cause
    To prick us to redress? What other bond
125 Than secret Romans that have spoke the word,
    And will not palter?[33] And what other oath
    Than honesty to honesty engaged[34]
    That this shall be, or we will fall for it?
    Swear priests and cowards and men cautelous,[35]
130 Old feeble carrions[36] and such suffering souls
    That welcome wrongs; unto bad causes swear
    Such creatures as men doubt; but do not stain
    The even virtue of our enterprise,
    Nor th' insuppressive mettle[37] of our spirits,
135 To think that or[38] our cause or our performance
    Did need an oath; when every drop of blood
    That every Roman bears, and nobly bears,
    Is guilty of a several bastardy[39]
    If he do break the smallest particle
140 Of any promise that hath passed from him.

CASSIUS. But what of Cicero? Shall we sound him?
    I think he will stand very strong with us.

CASCA. Let us not leave him out.

CINNA.                              No, by no means.

METELLUS. O, let us have him, for his silver hairs
145 Will purchase us a good opinion,

*Julius Caesar, Act II, Scene i*   **497**

---

28 **Some two months...fire:** Only later in the spring will the sun rise as far north as Decius and Cinna pointed.

29 **the face...abuse:** the sadness in people's faces, our own suffering, and the corruption of the time.
30 **betimes:** now.

31 **high-sighted:** arrogant.
32 **by lottery:** by chance.

33 **palter:** take lightly or betray.
34 **what other oath...engaged:** What other oath is needed than that of one honest man to another?
35 **cautelous:** overly cautious; also, crafty.
36 **carrions:** men no better than corpses.

37 **insuppressive mettle:** indomitable courage.
38 **or:** either.

39 **Is guilty of a several bastardy:** shows itself to be not Roman blood and therefore illegitimate.

---

**1 CHARACTERIZATION**

Cassius believes that an oath will firm up the conspirators' loyalty and resolve.

**2 CHARACTERIZATION**

In contrast to Cassius, Brutus shows that he relies more on people's inward virtue than on some external token of it.

**3 VERBAL IRONY**

Brutus' statement that only priests, cowards, and crafty ("cautelous") men need to swear an oath is unintentionally ironic, for the reader is by now well aware of Cassius' craftiness and doubtful of the enterprise's "virtue."

**4 CHARACTERIZATION**

Cassius' dropping of the matter of the oath after Brutus' opposition indicates how much he wants Brutus to join the conspiracy.

---

## GUIDED READING

### LITERAL QUESTIONS

**1a.** What reasons does Brutus give for opposing the oath? (He says that only priests, cowards, and weak or crafty men need an oath to bind them together; in short, no honorable Roman needs to swear to one.)

**2a.** Why do the conspirators want Cicero to join them? (If someone so old and well-respected joined, the Romans would back the conspirators.)

### INFERENTIAL QUESTIONS

**1b.** What does Brutus' opposition to the oath reveal about him? (It reveals that he is guided by internal standards of honor. It also suggests that he is incapable of imagining standards of behavior other than his own.)

**2b.** What does their need for Cicero show about the conspirators? (It shows that they are very worried about public support.)

- *Scene i (continued):* Brutus' opposition to Cicero sways the other conspirators.
- Worried by Mark Antony's shrewdness, Cassius urges that he be killed with Caesar.
- Brutus opposes Cassius, arguing that Antony is powerless without Caesar and that his death would make the conspiracy seem too bloodthirsty.

**1 PLOT: RISING ACTION**

The exchange involving Brutus, Cassius, and Casca regarding Cicero shows Brutus' ascendancy among the conspirators. Cassius' deference to Brutus is meant to placate him, but it also offers an interesting contrast to the impression of Cassius in Act I as a man who rebels against authority. Throughout the play Cassius accepts Brutus' authority, where he had chafed under Caesar's.

**2 CHARACTERIZATION**

Cassius' assessment of Mark Antony shows that one "shrewd contriver" certainly knows another.

**3 PLOT: CONFLICT**

Brutus' wish that the conspirators could murder Caesar's spirit but "not dismember" his body betrays that he still has conflicting feelings about the assassination plot.

**4 CHARACTERIZATION**

Less ruthless and less realistic than Cassius, Brutus opposes killing Mark Antony, whom he sees as powerless without Caesar's intelligence to direct him. This decision to spare Antony will haunt the conspirators.

---

And buy men's voices to commend our deeds.
It shall be said his judgment ruled our hands;
Our youths and wildness shall no whit appear,
But all be buried in his gravity.

**1** 150 BRUTUS. O, name him not! Let us not break with him;[40]
  For he will never follow anything
  That other men begin.

 CASSIUS.        Then leave him out.

 CASCA. Indeed, he is not fit.

 DECIUS. Shall no man else be touched but only Caesar?

155 CASSIUS. Decius, well urged. I think it is not meet
  Mark Antony, so well beloved of Caesar,
  Should outlive Caesar; we shall find of him

**2**   A shrewd contriver; and you know, his means;
  If he improve[41] them, may well stretch so far
160   As to annoy us all; which to prevent,
  Let Antony and Caesar fall together.

 BRUTUS. Our course will seem too bloody, Caius Cassius,
  To cut the head off and then hack the limbs,
  Like wrath in death and envy afterwards;
165   For Antony is but a limb of Caesar.
  Let's be sacrificers, but not butchers, Caius.

**3**   We all stand up against the spirit of Caesar,
  And in the spirit of men there is no blood.
  O, that we then could come by Caesar's spirit,
170   And not dismember Caesar! But, alas,
  Caesar must bleed for it. And, gentle friends,
  Let's kill him boldly, but not wrathfully;
  Let's carve him as a dish fit for the gods,
  Not hew him as a carcass fit for hounds.
175   And let our hearts, as subtle masters do,
  Stir up their servants[42] to an act of rage,
  And after seem to chide 'em. This shall make
  Our purpose necessary, and not envious;
  Which so appearing to the common eyes,
180   We shall be called purgers, not murderers.

**4**   And for Mark Antony, think not of him;
  For he can do no more than Caesar's arm
  When Caesar's head is off.

 CASSIUS.        Yet I fear him;
  For in the ingrafted[43] love he bears to Caesar—

40 **break with him:** reveal our plot to him.

41 **improve:** use fully.

42 **servants:** hands.

43 **ingrafted:** deep-rooted.

**498** *Drama*

---

## GUIDED READING

**LITERAL QUESTION**

**1a.** What reasons does Brutus give in opposing the murder of Mark Antony? (Without Caesar's leadership Antony cannot harm the conspirators; moreover, by killing Caesar only, they look like purgers, not butchers.)

**INFERENTIAL QUESTION**

**1b.** What does his opposition to murdering Mark Antony show about Brutus? (He is noble-minded, moderate, desirous of the people's support, and may be fatally naïve.)

Len Cariou. Raymond Hunt. Photo courtesy of Stratford Festival, Canada, 1982.

AT A GLANCE

- *Scene i (continued):* Brutus tells Cassius not to worry about Mark Antony.
- A clock strikes three and the plotters decide to part.
- Cassius wonders if Caesar will show up or heed the omens.

**1 PLOT: FORESHADOWING**

The debate between Cassius and Brutus about the threat Mark Antony poses shifts the reader's attention momentarily to what may happen after the murder.

**2 STAGE DIRECTIONS**

The clock's striking makes the reader identify with the plotters' tension; the decisive moment is drawing near.

**3 PLOT: RISING ACTION**

At this moment the reader, along with Cassius, does not know if Caesar will come to the Capitol.

**1**
185 BRUTUS. Alas, good Cassius, do not think of him.
    If he love Caesar, all that he can do
    Is to himself—take thought and die for Caesar.[44]
    And that were much he should,[45] for he is given
    To sports, to wildness, and much company.

190 TREBONIUS. There is no fear in him;[46] let him not die,
    For he will live and laugh at this hereafter.

**2**
    [*A clock strikes in the distance.*]

BRUTUS. Peace! Count the clock.

CASSIUS.                   The clock hath stricken three.

TREBONIUS. 'Tis time to part.

**3**
CASSIUS.                 But it is doubtful yet
    Whether Caesar will come forth today or no;
195     For he is superstitious grown of late,
    Quite from the main opinion he held once
    Of fantasy, of dreams, and ceremonies.[47]
    It may be these apparent prodigies,
    The unaccustomed terror of this night,

44 **die for Caesar:** die of grief.
45 **that were much he should:** It is unlikely that he would do such a thing.

46 **no fear in him:** nothing to fear from him.

47 **ceremonies:** omens. Cassius suggests that Caesar had once scorned omens but now takes them more seriously.

*Julius Caesar, Act II, Scene i* **499**

---

## GUIDED READING

**LITERAL QUESTION**

**1a.** What does Brutus think Mark Antony should do after Caesar is murdered? (He thinks Antony should commit suicide out of love for Caesar.)

**INFERENTIAL QUESTION**

**1b.** What is ironic about Brutus' comment regarding the behavior of a loyal friend? (Brutus thinks Antony should commit suicide out of love for Caesar, whereas Brutus, although he loves Caesar, is about to kill him.)

- *Scene i (continued):* Decius says that he will persuade Caesar to go to the Capitol through flattery.
- Metellus suggests asking Caius Ligarius, whom Caesar has rebuked, to join in the conspiracy.
- After the others leave, Portia enters, worried by Brutus' recent behavior.

### 1 CHARACTERIZATION

According to Decius, Caesar prides himself on his immunity to flattery but actually is highly susceptible to it. The conspirators may not know where the east is, but they do know Caesar.

### 2 CHARACTERIZATION

Note how Brutus has flung himself into the conspiracy; here he volunteers to persuade Caius Ligarius to join it and uses the language of manipulation earlier associated with Cassius.

---

200      And the persuasion of his augurers[48]
     May hold him from the Capitol today.

DECIUS. Never fear that. If he be so resolved,
     I can o'ersway him; for he loves to hear
     That unicorns may be betrayed with trees,[49]
205      And bears with glasses,[50] elephants with holes,[51]
     Lions with toils,[52] and men with flatterers;
     But when I tell him he hates flatterers,
     He says he does, being then most flatterèd.
     Let me work;
210      For I can give his humor the true bent,[53]
     And I will bring him to the Capitol.

CASSIUS. Nay, we will all of us be there to fetch him.

BRUTUS. By the eighth hour; is that the uttermost?

CINNA. Be that the uttermost, and fail not then.

215 METELLUS. Caius Ligarius doth bear Caesar hard,
     Who rated[54] him for speaking well of Pompey.
     I wonder none of you have thought of him.

BRUTUS. Now, good Metellus, go along by him.
     He loves me well, and I have given him reasons;
220      Send him but hither, and I'll fashion[55] him.

CASSIUS. The morning comes upon 's; we'll leave you, Brutus.
     And, friends, disperse yourselves; but all remember
     What you have said, and show yourselves true Romans.

BRUTUS. Good gentlemen, look fresh and merrily.
225      Let not our looks put on[56] our purposes,
     But bear it as our Roman actors do,
     With untired spirits and formal constancy.
     And so good morrow to you every one.

[*The conspirators leave. Alone,* BRUTUS *calls for* LUCIUS.]

     Boy, Lucius! Fast asleep? It is no matter;
230      Enjoy the honey-heavy dew of slumber.
     Thou hast no figures nor no fantasies
     Which busy care draws in the brains of men;
     Therefore thou sleep'st so sound.

[PORTIA, BRUTUS' *wife, comes into the garden from the house. She is upset by* BRUTUS' *recent behavior and appears very pale.*]

PORTIA.                 Brutus, my lord.

**500**   *Drama*

---

**48 augurers:** officials who foretell the future from omens.

**49 unicorns...trees:** It was believed that a unicorn could be tricked into charging a tree and getting its horn stuck.
**50 bears with glasses:** It was thought that bears could be lured with mirrors.
**51 holes:** pits hidden by underbrush.
**52 toils:** nets.

**53 I...bent:** I can put him in the right mood.

**54 rated:** rebuked.

**55 fashion:** persuade.

**56 put on:** reveal.

---

## GUIDED READING

### LITERAL QUESTIONS

**1a.** What will Decius do to bring Caesar to the Capitol? (He will flatter Caesar and so persuade him to disregard his superstitions.)

**2a.** What does Brutus offer to do with Caius Ligarius? (He offers to persuade him to join the conspiracy.)

### INFERENTIAL QUESTIONS

**1b.** Do you think Decius' judgment of Caesar is correct? (Caesar seems to be an egotistical man, as indicated by his behavior in Act I. Such a man may well be susceptible to flattery.)

**2b.** What does Brutus' offer indicate about a change in his attitude toward the plot? (Brutus now sees himself as an active, fully committed participant.)

**BRUTUS.** Portia, what mean you? Wherefore rise you now?
235    It is not for your health thus to commit
   Your weak condition to the raw cold morning.

**PORTIA.** Nor for yours neither. Y'have ungently, Brutus,
   Stole from my bed; and yesternight at supper
   You suddenly arose and walked about,
240    Musing and sighing, with your arms across;
   And when I asked you what the matter was,
   You stared upon me with ungentle looks.
   I urged you further; then you scratched your head,
   And too impatiently stamped with your foot.
245    Yet I insisted, yet you answered not,
   But with an angry wafter[57] of your hand
   Gave sign for me to leave you. So I did,
   Fearing to strengthen that impatience
   Which seemed too much enkindled, and withal
250    Hoping it was but an effect of humor,[58]
   Which sometime hath his hour with every man.
   It will not let you eat, nor talk, nor sleep,
   And could it work so much upon your shape
   As it hath much prevailed on your condition,
255    I should not know you Brutus. Dear my lord,
   Make me acquainted with your cause of grief.

**BRUTUS.** I am not well in health, and that is all.

**PORTIA.** Brutus is wise and, were he not in health,
   He would embrace the means to come by it.

260 **BRUTUS.** Why, so I do. Good Portia, go to bed.

**PORTIA.** Is Brutus sick, and is it physical[59]
   To walk unbracèd and suck up the humors
   Of the dank morning?[60] What, is Brutus sick,
   And will he steal out of his wholesome bed,
265    To dare the vile contagion of the night,[61]
   And tempt the rheumy and unpurgèd[62] air
   To add unto his sickness? No, my Brutus;
   You have some sick offense within your mind,
   Which by the right and virtue of my place
270    I ought to know of; and upon my knees [*She kneels.*]
   I charm you, by my once commended beauty,
   By all your vows of love, and that great vow
   Which did incorporate and make us one,
   That you unfold to me, your self, your half,
275    Why you are heavy, and what men tonight

57 **wafter:** gesture.

58 **humor:** a passing mood.

59 **physical:** healthy.

60 **humors...morning:** damp morning mist.

61 **vile...night:** It was believed that breathing night air was unhealthy.
62 **rheumy and unpurgèd:** damp and not yet purified by the sun.

*Julius Caesar, Act II, Scene i*   **501**

**AT A GLANCE**

- *Scene i (continued):* Portia asks Brutus to tell her why he has withdrawn.
- Brutus says he is physically unwell, but Portia says his problem is mental and again begs him to disclose the reason to her.

**1 CHARACTERIZATION**

Brutus shows a tender concern for his wife. He may also be disturbed that she has seen the conspirators. He does not wish to burden her with his troubles.

**2 PLOT: CONFLICT**

Portia's intimate knowledge of her husband makes her a reliable witness to his tormented state of mind.

**3 DIALOGUE**

Although Brutus wishes to hide the truth from Portia, she loves and knows him too well to believe him. She respects her husband, but she does not fear him.

**4 STAGE DIRECTION**

Portia kneels to Brutus to reinforce her insistent pleas. Their relationship is a loving, dignified one, so that her action of kneeling to him seems unusual and meant to show him how profoundly she is distressed.

## GUIDED READING

### LITERAL QUESTIONS

**1a.** What explanation does Brutus give for his recent odd behavior? (He says that he is physically unwell.)

**2a.** What reason does Portia give for rejecting Brutus' explanation? (She says that if he were physically sick he would not be walking around in the unhealthy night air.)

### INFERENTIAL QUESTIONS

**1b.** What reasons may Brutus have for hiding the truth from Portia? (He may want to protect her.)

**2b.** What does Portia's disbelief reveal about her and her relationship with Brutus? (It shows that she is wise and persistent, knows Brutus well and loves him, and is unafraid of any confrontation between them.)

- *Scene i (continued):* Portia reminds Brutus that she is stronger than other women.
- She shows him a self-inflicted wound.
- Hearing a knock at the door, Brutus asks Portia to leave but promises to tell her his secrets.

## 1 CHARACTERIZATION

Portia speaks to Brutus as an equal and as the partner of his spirit. She feels that they share an identity ("Am I your self . . ."). Although he loves her, Brutus' secretive behavior suggests that he does not share the same view of their marriage.

## 2 PLOT: FORESHADOWING

Portia's "voluntary wound" shows that she has courage and will even injure herself as proof of her loyalty. Brutus' stunned reaction suggests that he has underestimated his wife's courage and devotion.

## 3 PLOT: RISING ACTION

By agreeing to tell Portia about the plot ("And by and by thy bosom shall partake / The secrets of my heart."), Brutus must now consider her opinions and feelings in whatever he does.

Have had resort to you; for here have been
Some six or seven, who did hide their faces
Even from darkness.

BRUTUS.     Kneel not, gentle Portia. [*He helps her rise.*]

PORTIA. I should not need, if you were gentle Brutus.
280 Within the bond of marriage, tell me, Brutus,
Is it excepted I should know no secrets
That appertain to you? Am I your self
But, as it were, in sort or limitation,[63]
To keep with you at meals, comfort your bed,
285 And talk to you sometimes? Dwell I but in the suburbs
Of your good pleasure? If it be no more,
Portia is Brutus' harlot, not his wife.

BRUTUS. You are my true and honorable wife,
As dear to me as are the ruddy drops
290 That visit my sad heart.

PORTIA. If this were true, then should I know this secret.
I grant I am a woman; but withal
A woman that Lord Brutus took to wife.
I grant I am a woman; but withal
295 A woman well reputed, Cato's daughter.[64]
Think you I am no stronger than my sex,
Being so fathered and so husbanded?
Tell me your counsels, I will not disclose 'em.
I have made strong proof of my constancy,
300 Giving myself a voluntary wound
Here in the thigh; can I bear that with patience,
And not my husband's secrets?

BRUTUS.     O ye gods,
Render me worthy of this noble wife!

[*They hear a knock.*]

Hark, hark! One knocks. Portia, go in a while,
305 And by and by thy bosom shall partake
The secrets of my heart.
All my engagements I will construe[65] to thee,
All the charactery of my sad brows.[66]
Leave me with haste.

[PORTIA, *obeying, leaves. After* PORTIA *has gone,* LUCIUS *enters with* CAIUS LIGARIUS, *who wears a handkerchief around his head, indicating that he is ill.*]

**502** *Drama*

63 **But . . . limitation:** only in part.

64 **Cato's daughter:** Portia's father, Cato of Utica, killed himself rather than submit to Caesar's rule after Pompey was defeated.

65 **construe:** explain.

66 **charactery . . . brows:** what is written in my sad brows; that is, the reasons why I am sad.

## GUIDED READING

### LITERAL QUESTION

**1a.** What arguments does Portia use with Brutus? (She argues that if he thought of her as a real wife he would disclose his secrets. She says that she is stronger than other women and has proved her constancy by a self-inflicted wound.)

### INFERENTIAL QUESTION

**1b.** What do her arguments show about Portia's relationship with Brutus? (They show that she believes they are, or should be, equals.)

Len Cariou. Susan Wright. Photo courtesy of Stratford Festival, Canada, 1982.

*Julius Caesar, Act II, Scene i*   **503**

- *Scene i (continued):* At the door is Caius Ligarius, wearing a kerchief as a sign that he is ill.
- On hearing that Brutus has joined the conspiracy, Caius discards his kerchief.
- Without knowing Brutus' plan, Caius says that he will follow him.
- *Scene ii:* On the morning of the ides of March, Caesar is at home.

## 1 THEME

In their dialogue Brutus and Caius play on the ideas of personal and political illness. The idea of a correspondence between the individual and the state is developed throughout the play.

## 2 STYLE: VERBAL IRONY

Brutus' and Caius' verbal play is unintentionally ironic, in that it not only refers to murdering Caesar but suggests the possibility that Brutus' involvement in the plot has converted him from someone "whole" to someone "sick."

## 3 CHARACTERIZATION

Caius' loyalty to Brutus ("but it sufficeth / That Brutus leads me on.") is another illustration of the high regard in which Brutus is held throughout Rome.

---

Lucius, who's that knocks?

310 LUCIUS. Here is a sick man that would speak with you.

BRUTUS. Caius Ligarius, that Metellus spake of.
Boy, stand aside. Caius Ligarius! How?

CAIUS. Vouchsafe good morrow from a feeble tongue.

BRUTUS. O, what a time have you chose out, brave Caius,
315 To wear a kerchief! Would you were not sick!

CAIUS. I am not sick, if Brutus have in hand
Any exploit worthy the name of honor.

BRUTUS. Such an exploit have I in hand, Ligarius,
Had you a healthful ear to hear of it.

320 CAIUS. By all the gods that Romans bow before,
I here discard my sickness!

[*He takes off the handkerchief.*]

Soul of Rome,
Brave son, derived from honorable loins,
Thou, like an exorcist,[67] hast conjured up
My mortifièd[68] spirit. Now bid me run,
325 And I will strive with things impossible,
Yea, get the better of them. What's to do?

BRUTUS. A piece of work that will make sick men whole.

CAIUS. But are not some whole that we must make sick?

330 BRUTUS. That must we also. What it is, my Caius,
I shall unfold to thee, as we are going
To whom it must be done.[69]

CAIUS.                          Set on your foot,
And with a heart new-fired I follow you,
To do I know not what; but it sufficeth
335 That Brutus leads me on.

[*A clap of thunder.*]

BRUTUS.                       Follow me, then.

[*They leave together.*]

*Scene ii.* CAESAR'S *house. A few hours later.*

[*It is shortly before eight on the morning of the ides of March.*
CAESAR *appears in his dressing gown, intending to go to the*

**504** *Drama*

67 **exorcist:** one who summons up spirits.
68 **mortifièd:** deadened.

69 **To whom it must be done:** They are going to Caesar's house to escort him to the Capitol.

---

## GUIDED READING

### LITERAL QUESTIONS

**1a.** What causes Caius to remove his kerchief? (Brutus tells Caius that he needs to be healthy to hear about an honorable exploit.)

**2a.** What does Caius reply after Brutus says the work will "make sick men whole"? (He says, "But are not some whole that we must make sick?")

### INFERENTIAL QUESTIONS

**1b.** What does Caius' instant "cure" show about him? (He is wholly committed to Brutus.)

**2b.** What does Caius mean by this? (He means that they must kill at least one man—Caesar—and possibly more.)

*Capitol soon. Like many other Romans, he has spent a restless night. There are still flashes of lightning and rumbles of thunder from the recent storm.*]

**1** CAESAR. Nor heaven nor earth have been at peace tonight:
Thrice hath Calpurnia in her sleep cried out,
"Help, ho! They murder Caesar!" Who's within?

[*A* SERVANT *enters.*]

SERVANT. My lord?

**5** CAESAR. Go bid the priests do present sacrifice,
And bring me their opinions of success.[1]

SERVANT. I will, my lord.

[*The* SERVANT *leaves.* CALPURNIA, CAESAR's *wife, enters from her bedroom, alarmed at* CAESAR's *activity.*]

**2** CALPURNIA. What mean you, Caesar? Think you to walk forth?
You shall not stir out of your house today.

**10** CAESAR. Caesar shall forth. The things that threatened me
Ne'er looked but on my back; when they shall see
The face of Caesar, they are vanishèd.

CALPURNIA. Caesar, I never stood on ceremonies,[2]
Yet now they fright me. There is one within,
**15** Besides the things that we have heard and seen, .
Recounts most horrid sights seen by the watch.[3]
A lioness hath whelpèd[4] in the streets,
And graves have yawned, and yielded up their dead;
Fierce fiery warriors fought upon the clouds
**20** In ranks and squadrons and right form of war,
Which drizzled blood upon the Capitol;
The noise of battle hurtled in the air,
Horses did neigh and dying men did groan,
And ghosts did shriek and squeal about the streets.
**3 25** O Caesar, these things are beyond all use,[5]
And I do fear them.

CAESAR.                    What can be avoided
Whose end is purposed by the mighty gods?
Yet Caesar shall go forth; for these predictions
Are to the world in general as to Caesar.[6]

**30** CALPURNIA. When beggars die, there are no comets seen;
The heavens themselves blaze forth the death of princes.

*Julius Caesar,* Act II, Scene ii    **505**

**1 Go bid...of success:** Ask the priests to make a sacrifice immediately, and tell me their predictions regarding my success today.

**2 stood on ceremonies:** believed in omens.

**3 watch:** night watchman.

**4 whelpèd:** given birth.

**5 use:** normal experience.

**6 Are...Caesar:** apply to everyone else as much as they apply to me.

**AT A GLANCE**

- *Scene ii (continued):* Caesar says Calpurnia has cried out in her sleep.
- Calpurnia warns Caesar against leaving the house because of horrifying, unnatural events that may be bad omens.
- Caesar insists on going out, arguing that the omens are not necessarily directed at him.

**1 PLOT: FORESHADOWING**

Calpurnia's cries ("Help, ho! They murder Caesar!") hint once again at Caesar's imminent death.

**2 CHARACTERIZATION**

In contrast to Brutus, Caesar disregards his wife's pleas at this point ("Caesar shall forth.").

**3 CHARACTERIZATION**

Caesar shows an almost willful arrogance in disregarding the omens. This attitude is consistent with his treatment of the soothsayer in Act I ("He is a dreamer").

## GUIDED READING

### LITERAL QUESTIONS

**1a.** What causes Calpurnia to tell Caesar not to depart from home? (She has had a nightmare in which Caesar was murdered.)

**2a.** What argument does Caesar use to disregard the predictions? (He says that they apply to everyone else as much as to him.)

### INFERENTIAL QUESTIONS

**1b.** What does Caesar's response show about their relationship? (It shows that he treats Calpurnia as his inferior; he does not consider her advice.)

**2b.** What does Caesar's disregard of the predictions show about him? (It shows that he may believe himself invincible.)

- *Scene ii (continued):* Caesar even refuses to listen to the augurers.
- Calpurnia suggests that Caesar say that her fear keeps him home, and finally he agrees to stay.
- When Decius enters, Caesar orders him to tell the senators that he will not come to the Senate.

**1 RESPONSE JOURNAL**

Ask students to state in their journals whether they agree or disagree with Caesar, and why.

**2 PLOT: FORESHADOWING**

The augurers lend their voices to the growing chorus predicting trouble for Caesar if he sets forth.

**3 CHARACTERIZATION**

Caesar's appropriation of Calpurnia's excuse ("Mark Antony shall say I am not well") suggests that his previous posturing may have concealed real fear.

**4 CHARACTERIZATION**

Caesar reveals an autocratic streak in telling Decius not to give any explanation to the senators for his absence; it is actions like this that lead Brutus to fear Caesar's tyranny if crowned.

---

**1** CAESAR. Cowards die many times before their deaths;
The valiant never taste of death but once.
Of all the wonders that I yet have heard,
35 It seems to me most strange that men should fear,
Seeing that death, a necessary end,
Will come when it will come.

[*The* SERVANT *returns with news of the sacrifice.*]

**2**                                         What say the augurers?

SERVANT. They would not have you to stir forth today.
Plucking the entrails of an offering forth,
40 They could not find a heart within the beast.[7]

CAESAR. The gods do this in shame of cowardice:
Caesar should be a beast without a heart
If he should stay at home today for fear.
No, Caesar shall not; Danger knows full well
45 That Caesar is more dangerous than he.
We are two lions littered in one day,
And I the elder and more terrible,
And Caesar shall go forth.

CALPURNIA.                            Alas, my lord,
Your wisdom is consumed in confidence.
50 Do not go forth today. Call it my fear
That keeps you in the house and not your own.
**3** We'll send Mark Antony to the Senate House,
And he shall say you are not well today.
Let me, upon my knee, prevail in this. [*She kneels.*]

55 CAESAR. Mark Antony shall say I am not well,
And for thy humor,[8] I will stay at home.

[CAESAR *helps* CALPURNIA *rise as the conspirator* DECIUS *enters.*
*He has been sent to make certain that* CAESAR *goes to the*
*Capitol.*]

Here's Decius Brutus, he shall tell them so.

DECIUS. Caesar, all hail! Good morrow, worthy Caesar;
I come to fetch you to the Senate House.

**4** 60 CAESAR. And you are come in very happy time[9]
To bear my greeting to the senators,
And tell them that I will not come today.
Cannot, is false; and that I dare not, falser:
I will not come today. Tell them so, Decius.

**506** *Drama*

---

7 **Plucking...beast:** Augurers would examine the inner organs of the animal in order to predict the future. The absence of a heart, the most important organ, would be a very unusual and unfavorable omen.

8 **humor:** whim.

9 **in very happy time:** at the right moment.

---

## *GUIDED READING*

**LITERAL QUESTIONS**

**1a.** What reason does Caesar give for disregarding the augurers? (He says that he would be acting like a coward, and he is not a coward.)

**2a.** What way out does Calpurnia suggest to Caesar? (She suggests that Mark Antony explain to the senators that Caesar is unwell.)

**INFERENTIAL QUESTIONS**

**1b.** What other, unstated reasons may be motivating Caesar to disregard the augurers? (He may be afraid of seeming afraid, or he may be stubborn and willful.)

**2b.** What does his final acceptance of Calpurnia's suggestion reveal about Caesar? (It reveals that he is changeable in his decisions.)

65 CAESAR.          Shall Caesar send a lie?
    Have I in conquest stretched mine arm so far
    To be afeard to tell graybeards the truth?
    Decius, go tell them Caesar will not come.

    DECIUS. Most mighty Caesar, let me know some cause,
70     Lest I be laughed at when I tell them so.

**1**

    CAESAR. The cause is in my will: I will not come.
    That is enough to satisfy the Senate.
    But for your private satisfaction,
    Because I love you, I will let you know.
75     Calpurnia here, my wife, stays me at home.
    She dreamt tonight she saw my statue,
    Which, like a fountain with an hundred spouts,
    Did run pure blood, and many lusty Romans
    Came smiling and did bathe their hands in it.
80     And these does she apply for warnings and portents
    And evils imminent, and on her knee
    Hath begged that I will stay at home today.

    DECIUS. This dream is all amiss interpreted;
    It was a vision fair and fortunate:

**2** 85     Your statue spouting blood in many pipes,
    In which so many smiling Romans bathed,
    Signifies that from you great Rome shall suck
    Reviving blood, and that great men shall press
    For tinctures, stains, relics, and cognizance.[10]
90     This by Calpurnia's dream is signified.

    CAESAR. And this way have you well expounded it.

    DECIUS. I have, when you have heard what I can say;
    And know it now, the Senate have concluded
    To give this day a crown to mighty Caesar.
95     If you shall send them word you will not come,
    Their minds may change. Besides, it were a mock

**3**     Apt to be rendered,[11] for someone to say
    "Break up the Senate till another time,
    When Caesar's wife shall meet with better dreams."
100     If Caesar hide himself, shall they not whisper
    "Lo, Caesar is afraid"?
    Pardon me, Caesar, for my dear dear love
    To your proceeding bids me tell you this,
    And reason to my love is liable.[12]

105 CAESAR. How foolish do your fears seem now, Calpurnia!

10 **great men...cognizance:** To show their devotion to Caesar, great men shall come to him for souvenirs.

11 **Apt to be rendered:** likely to be made.

12 **liable:** subservient: Decius is saying that his love of Caesar makes him speak the truth, even if he is overstepping himself.

*Julius Caesar, Act II, Scene ii*   **507**

- *Scene ii (continued):* To Decius alone Caesar reveals his reason for not coming: Calpurnia's dream. He asks him to tell the Senate, however, that the reason is simply his will.
- Decius warns Caesar that the senators may attribute his absence to fear and may postpone crowning him.
- Caesar chides Calpurnia for her foolish fears.

**1 CHARACTERIZATION**

Although Caesar acts high-handedly toward the senators, he reveals his vulnerability to Decius, whom he trusts.

**2 STYLE: DIALOGUE**

The exchange between Decius and Caesar reveals the former's quick-wittedness ("from you great Rome shall suck/Reviving blood") and the latter's gullibility and fickleness ("And this way have you well expounded it.").

**3 CHARACTERIZATION**

Decius plays artfully on Caesar's desire to be crowned and on his fears of being ridiculed as a weakling under his wife's sway.

## GUIDED READING

### LITERAL QUESTIONS

**1a.** What explanation for his absence does Caesar tell Decius to give to the senators? (Caesar says simply to state that it is his will.)

**2a.** What is Caesar's reaction to Decius' reinterpretation? (He approves of it.)

### INFERENTIAL QUESTIONS

**1b.** What does Caesar's order to Decius reveal about how he feels toward the senators? (Caesar feels superior to the senators and so believes he owes them no explanation.)

**2b.** What does Caesar's acquiescence show about him? (It shows that he is easily flattered into changing his mind.)

- *Scene ii (continued):* Caesar changes his mind and decides to go to the senate house.
- Publius, accompanied by the conspirators, arrives to escort him.
- Caesar welcomes them.

**1 CHARACTERIZATION**

Caesar cannot admit that Calpurnia's fears are also his; he prefers to make it appear as if he had given in to them purely for her sake.

**2 PLOT: SUSPENSE**

The constant references to time—here, Caesar's question and Brutus' answer—remind the reader that the time of the assassination attempt is near.

**3 CHARACTERIZATION**

Caesar reinforces the image of Antony as a playboy, already referred to in Act I, Scene ii.

---

**1**
> I am ashamèd I did yield to them.
> Give me my robe, for I will go.

[PUBLIUS, *an elderly senator, enters accompanied by the conspirators* BRUTUS, LIGARIUS, METELLUS CIMBER, CASCA, TREBONIUS, *and* CINNA.]

And look where Publius is come to fetch me.

PUBLIUS. Good morrow, Caesar.

CAESAR.                              Welcome, Publius.
110 What, Brutus, are you stirred so early too?
Good morrow, Casca. Caius Ligarius,
Caesar was ne'er so much your enemy[13]
As that same ague[14] which hath made you lean.

**2**
What is't o'clock?

BRUTUS.          Caesar, 'tis strucken eight.

115 CAESAR. I thank you for your pains and courtesy.

[MARK ANTONY *enters, and* CAESAR *jokes with* CALPURNIA *about seeing* ANTONY *up so early.*]

**3**
> See! Antony, that revels long a-nights,
> Is notwithstanding up. Good morrow, Antony.

13 **your enemy:** Caesar had recently pardoned Ligarius for his support of Pompey during the civil war.
14 **ague** [ā′gū]: sickness.

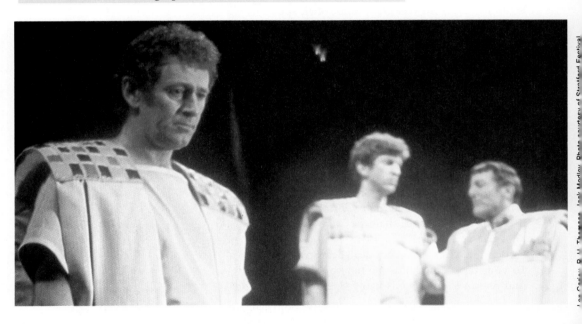

508   *Drama*

---

## GUIDED READING

**LITERAL QUESTION**

**1a.** What does Caesar tease Antony about? (He teases Antony about his late nights spent in revelry.)

**INFERENTIAL QUESTION**

**1b.** Does this comment support Brutus' or Cassius' view of Antony? (By portraying Antony as a playboy, Caesar supports the view of Brutus, who said Antony would be helpless without Caesar.)

ANTONY. So to most noble Caesar.

CAESAR.                              Bid them prepare within.
I am to blame to be thus waited for.
120  Now, Cinna; now, Metellus; what, Trebonius,
I have an hour's talk in store for you;
Remember that you call on me today;
Be near me, that I may remember you.

TREBONIUS. Caesar, I will [*Aside.*] and so near will I be,
125  That your best friends shall wish I had been further.

CAESAR. Good friends, go in and taste some wine with me,
And we (like friends) will straightway go together.

BRUTUS. [*Aside.*] That every like is not the same,[15] O Caesar,
The heart of Brutus earns[16] to think upon.

[*They all go into another part of the house for wine before
leaving for the Capitol.*]

15 **every...same:** every seeming friend is not necessarily a real friend.
16 **earns:** grieves.

*Scene iii. A street near the Capitol. Shortly afterward.*

[ARTEMIDORUS, *a rhetoric teacher who is loyal to* CAESAR, *enters
reading a message he hopes to give* CAESAR.]

ARTEMIDORUS. "Caesar, beware of Brutus; take heed of Cassius;
come not near Casca; have an eye to Cinna; trust not
Trebonius; mark well Metellus Cimber; Decius Brutus loves
thee not; thou hast wronged Caius Ligarius. There is but
5    one mind in all these men, and it is bent against Caesar. If
thou beest not immortal, look about you: security gives
way to conspiracy.[1] The mighty gods defend thee!
                    Thy lover,[2] ARTEMIDORUS."
Here will I stand till Caesar pass along,
10   And as a suitor[3] will I give him this.
My heart laments that virtue cannot live
Out of the teeth of emulation.[4]
If thou read this, O Caesar, thou mayest live;
If not, the Fates with traitors do contrive.[5] [*He leaves.*]

1 **security...conspiracy:** overconfidence opens the way for enemy plots.
2 **lover:** devoted friend.

3 **suitor:** person presenting a special request to a ruler.

4 **emulation:** envy.

5 **contrive:** conspire.

*Scene iv. Another Roman street. Immediately after.*

[PORTIA *hurries into the street near her house with her servant*
LUCIUS. *She appears very worried and nervous.* BRUTUS *has left
earlier to escort* CAESAR *to the Senate, and she wants to learn
what is happening at the Capitol.*]

*Julius Caesar, Act II, Scene iv*   **509**

## GUIDED READING

### LITERAL QUESTIONS

**1a.** What emotion does Brutus express in his aside? (He expresses sadness or guilt.)

**2a.** How does Portia behave? (She appears very worried.)

### INFERENTIAL QUESTIONS

**1b.** What does this emotional reaction show about Brutus? (It shows that he is still troubled over his decision to put aside his personal loyalty to Caesar.)

**2b.** What does Portia's nervousness imply about the extent of her knowledge? (It implies that Brutus has kept his word and has told her about the plot.)

**1 DIALOGUE**

Portia's question to Lucius and his reply reveal her agitated state of confusion.

**2 PLOT: RISING ACTION**

If Portia reveals the plot, she could cause ruin for all the conspirators.

**3 PLOT: FORESHADOWING**

Portia's question ("What is't o'clock?") and the soothsayer's reply ("About the ninth hour") add to the tension of the approaching events.

**4 CHARACTERIZATION**

Although agitated, Portia has not lost her caution, as shown by her "innocent" probing.

---

**PORTIA.** I prithee, boy, run to the Senate House;
Stay not to answer me, but get thee gone.
Why dost thou stay?

**LUCIUS.**                    To know my errand, madam.

**PORTIA.** I would have had thee there and here again
5 Ere I can tell thee what thou shouldst do there.
O constancy,[1] be strong upon my side;
Set a huge mountain 'tween my heart and tongue!
I have a man's mind, but a woman's might.
How hard it is for women to keep counsel![2]
Art thou here yet?

10 **LUCIUS.**                    Madam, what should I do?
Run to the Capitol, and nothing else?
And so return to you, and nothing else?

**PORTIA.** Yes, bring me word, boy, if thy lord look well,
For he went sickly forth; and take good note
15 What Caesar doth, what suitors press to him.
Hark, boy, what noise is that?

**LUCIUS.** I hear none, madam.

**PORTIA.**                    Prithee, listen well.
I heard a bustling rumor like a fray,[3]
And the wind brings it from the Capitol.

20 **LUCIUS.** Sooth,[4] madam, I hear nothing.

[*The* SOOTHSAYER *enters.*]

**PORTIA.** Come hither, fellow. Which way hast thou been?

**SOOTHSAYER.** At mine own house, good lady.

**PORTIA.** What is't o'clock?

**SOOTHSAYER.**                    About the ninth hour, lady.

**PORTIA.** Is Caesar yet gone to the Capitol?

25 **SOOTHSAYER.** Madam, not yet; I go to take my stand,
To see him pass on to the Capitol.

**PORTIA.** Thou hast some suit to Caesar, hast thou not?

**SOOTHSAYER.** That I have, lady; if it will please Caesar
To be so good to Caesar as to hear me,
30 I shall beseech him to befriend himself.

**PORTIA.** Why, know'st thou any harm's intended towards him?

1 **constancy:** firmness.

2 **counsel:** a secret.

3 **rumor...fray:** noise like a battle.

4 **Sooth:** truly.

**510** *Drama*

---

## GUIDED READING

**LITERAL QUESTION**

**1a.** What does only Portia hear? (a noise like a battle coming from the Capitol)

**INFERENTIAL QUESTION**

**1b.** What does this strange phenomenon suggest about the change in Portia? (Normally very calm and rational, she is so distressed that her imagination has run away with her. Shortly, however, the noise coming from the Capitol will be all too real.)

**SOOTHSAYER.** None that I know will be, much that I fear may
    chance

    Good morrow to you. Here the street is narrow;
    The throng that follows Caesar at the heels,
35  Of senators, of praetors, common suitors,
    Will crowd a feeble man almost to death.
    I'll get me to a place more void,[5] and there
    Speak to great Caesar as he comes along.

5 **void:** empty.

[*The* SOOTHSAYER *leaves to find* CAESAR.]

**PORTIA.** I must go in. Ay me, how weak a thing
40  The heart of woman is! O Brutus,
    The heavens speed thee in thine enterprise!
    [*Aside.*] Sure, the boy heard me—Brutus hath a suit
    That Caesar will not grant[6]—O, I grow faint.
    Run, Lucius, and commend me to my lord;[7]
45  Say I am merry;[8] come to me again,
    And bring me word what he doth say to thee.

6 **Brutus...grant:** Portia makes this statement so that Lucius will not be suspicious.
7 **commend...lord:** Wish my husband well for me.
8 **merry:** in good spirits.

[LUCIUS *leaves to find* BRUTUS. PORTIA *hurries home.*]

---

## STUDY QUESTIONS

### Recalling

1. What reasons does Brutus give in Act II, Scene i, lines 10–34, for killing Caesar?
2. Summarize the contents of the letter that Lucius finds on the windowsill in Scene i. What does Brutus add to the letter?
3. In Scene i what arguments regarding the treatment of Antony are presented by Cassius and by Brutus? What does the group decide to do about Antony?
4. In Scene i why is Portia disturbed about Brutus' recent behavior? What does she ask of Brutus, and what proof does she offer of her steadfastness? How does Brutus respond?
5. In Scene ii what request does Calpurnia make of Caesar? Retell her dream and Decius' interpretation of it in that scene.
6. Why does Artemidorus wish to see Caesar? Why does the soothsayer wish to see Caesar?

### Interpreting

7. Does Caesar give any signs in Act II that he might eventually become a tyrant, as Brutus fears? Explain.
8. Explain the conflict in Brutus' mind over joining the conspiracy. Why do you think Cassius lets Brutus have his way in Scene i?
9. Contrast Brutus' treatment of Portia in Scene i with Caesar's behavior toward Calpurnia in Scene ii. What does each man reveal about himself in his treatment of his wife?
10. Explain how the actions and speeches of the characters in Act II build up suspense over the coming assassination attempt.

### Extending

11. Rather than joining the conspiracy, what else might Brutus have done to save Rome from Caesar's potential tyranny? Do you agree with his decision to join the conspirators? Why or why not?

*Julius Caesar, Act II, Scene iv* **511**

---

## AT A GLANCE

- The soothsayer leaves to find a safe place to stand so he can speak to Caesar.
- Asking Lucius to bring her word from Brutus, Portia pretends that she is nervous about a trivial matter.

### 1 PLOT: RISING ACTION

We suppose that the soothsayer's answer reassures Portia: At least news of the plot has not leaked out.

### REFLECTING ON ACT II

Compare the personalities of Brutus and Caesar. (Brutus is cautious, idealistic, loving, and has conflicting loyalties; Caesar is vain, shrewd, fickle, autocratic, and generous.)

### STUDY QUESTIONS

1. fears he will abuse power if crowned king
2. urges Brutus to awake; should save Rome
3. *Cassius:* sees him as dangerous, thinks he should be killed; *Brutus:* thinks he poses no threat; to let him live
4. he has been sleepless, preoccupied; asks him to share his trouble; has wounded herself; is moved
5. that he stay home from the Capitol; Caesar's statue spouted blood and Romans washed in it; Caesar would save Rome
6. to tell him to beware of the conspirators; to warn him
7. yes; is autocratic, seems to believe he is godlike
8. love for Caesar in conflict with his love for Rome; does not want him to back out
9. Brutus considers Portia his equal; reveals decency; Caesar is paternalistic; reveals his arrogance.
10. Calpurnia's dream / Decius' interpretation; Caesar's pleasure at seeing conspirators; attempts to warn Caesar
11. could have spoken to Caesar; decision seems hasty

## Thinking About Shakespeare's Characters

*Brutus:* needs to consider all aspects of a situation; is an idealist; is conflicted about his love for Caesar and concern for Rome; *Caesar:* is good judge of character but does not want to reveal his weaknesses; is autocratic; is generous toward friends

## Thinking About Soliloquies and Asides

1. *lines 10–34:* thinks Caesar must be killed; *lines 61–69:* he has been in turmoil since talking to Cassius; *lines 77–85:* dislikes being involved in conspiracy
2. *Scene ii, lines 124–125:* Trebonius refers to his part in assassination; *Scene ii, lines 129–130:* Brutus reveals his ambivalence

## LITERARY FOCUS

### Shakespeare's Characters

Like characters in stories, characters in drama can be round or flat. Shakespeare is famous for the roundness and complexity of his characters.

Understanding one of Shakespeare's major characters is a little like putting together the pieces of a jigsaw puzzle or mosaic. Among the most important pieces are the character's speeches. Each speech can reveal very different, even contrasting, sides of the character.

For example, in Act I, Scene ii, as Cassius tries to persuade Brutus to join the opposition to Caesar, he reveals both his love of freedom and his personal envy of Caesar. Then, after Brutus leaves, Cassius shows us yet another side of his character. He explains that if he were Caesar's friend, he would not have been persuaded by his own arguments against Caesar. As we read the play, we need to be alert for such contrasts, conflicts, and shifts in a character —to continue fitting the new pieces of that character together.

### Thinking About Shakespeare's Characters

■ What different sides of Brutus and of Caesar are revealed in the following speeches?

*Brutus*
I am not gamesome: I do lack some part
Of that quick spirit that is in Antony.
Let me not hinder, Cassius, your desires;
I'll leave you.
— Act I, Scene ii, lines 28–31

Let's carve him as a dish fit for the gods.
— Act II, Scene i, line 173

That every like is not the same, O Caesar,
The heart of Brutus earns to think upon.
— Act II, Scene ii, lines 128–129

*Caesar*
Yond Cassius has a lean and hungry look;
He thinks too much: such men are dangerous....
Would he were fatter! But I fear him not.
— Act I, Scene ii, lines 194–195, 198

And you are come in very happy time
To bear my greeting to the senators,
And tell them that I will not come today.
Cannot, is false; and that I dare not, falser:
I will not come today.
— Act II, Scene ii, lines 60-64

Good friends, go in and taste some wine with me,
And we (like friends) will straightway go together.
— Act II, Scene ii, lines 126-127

### Soliloquies and Asides

A **soliloquy** is a dramatic speech that a character makes when he or she is alone on the stage. Since no other character is listening, we can assume that the character on stage is speaking the truth. For example, at the end of Act I, Scene ii, Cassius reveals his judgment of Brutus only after he is completely alone on the stage.

An **aside** is a brief remark that a character says out of the hearing of the other people on the stage. The speaker usually turns to one side, or "aside," so that the others cannot hear the remark. In some cases, two characters may speak in asides to each other in order to have a private conversation in the presence of others.

### Thinking About Soliloquies and Asides

1. Which of Brutus' speeches in Act II, Scene i, are soliloquies? What does he reveal in these speeches that he does not say to other people?
2. Find two asides in Act II. In each case, what circumstances make it necessary for the character to speak in this way? In each case, what feelings that are concealed from the others on stage does the character reveal to the audience?

512 *Drama*

# ACT III

### Scene i. *The Capitol in Rome. The ides of March.*

[*There is a flourish of trumpets as* CAESAR *and his train approach the steps of the Capitol, where the Roman Senate has been awaiting his arrival.* CAESAR *is accompanied by the conspirators* BRUTUS, CASSIUS, CASCA, DECIUS, METELLUS, TREBONIUS, *and* CINNA, *as well as other prominent citizens, including* MARK ANTONY, *the senators* PUBLIUS *and* POPILIUS, *and the general* LEPIDUS. *A crowd of people with petitions waits in front of the Senate chamber to catch* CAESAR'S *attention; among them are* ARTEMIDORUS *and the old* SOOTHSAYER. CAESAR *notices the* SOOTHSAYER *and stops to joke with him.*]

> CAESAR. The ides of March are come.
>
> SOOTHSAYER. Ay, Caesar, but not gone.
>
> [ARTEMIDORUS *approaches* CAESAR *with his warning.*]
>
> ARTEMIDORUS. Hail, Caesar! Read this schedule.[1]
>
> [DECIUS *pushes forward with a paper.*]
>
> DECIUS. Trebonius doth desire you to o'er-read,
> 5   At your best leisure, this his humble suit.
>
> ARTEMIDORUS. O Caesar, read mine first; for mine's a suit
> That touches Caesar nearer. Read it, great Caesar.
>
> CAESAR. What touches us ourself shall be last served.
>
> ARTEMIDORUS. Delay not, Caesar; read it instantly.
>
> CAESAR. What, is the fellow mad?
>
> [*The old senator* PUBLIUS, *offended at* ARTEMIDORUS' *boldness toward* CAESAR, *pushes him aside.*]
>
> 10  PUBLIUS.                  Sirrah,[2] give place.
>
> CASSIUS. What, urge you your petitions in the street?
> Come to the Capitol.
>
> [CAESAR *goes up to the Senate chamber, and the rest follow.* POPILIUS *remains a little to the side to speak with* CASSIUS.]
>
> POPILIUS. I wish your enterprise today may thrive.
>
> CASSIUS. What enterprise, Popilius?

1 **schedule:** document.

2 **Sirrah:** insulting form of address to an inferior.

*Julius Caesar, Act III, Scene i*   **513**

**1** 15 BRUTUS. What said Popilius Lena?

CASSIUS. He wished today our enterprise might thrive.
I fear our purpose is discoverèd.

BRUTUS. Look how he makes to Caesar; mark him.

CASSIUS. Casca, be sudden, for we fear prevention.
20 Brutus, what shall be done? If this be known,
Cassius or Caesar never shall turn back,
For I will slay myself.

**2** BRUTUS.                    Cassius, be constant.[3]
Popilius Lena speaks not of our purposes;
For look, he smiles, and Caesar doth not change.

**3** 25 CASSIUS. Trebonius knows his time; for look you, Brutus,
He draws Mark Antony out of the way.

[TREBONIUS *leaves with* ANTONY.]

DECIUS. Where is Metellus Cimber? Let him go
And presently prefer his suit to Caesar.

BRUTUS. He is addressed.[4] Press near and second him.

30 CINNA. Casca, you are the first that rears your hand.

CAESAR. Are we all ready? What is now amiss
That Caesar and his Senate must redress?

METELLUS. Most high, most mighty, and most puissant[5] Caesar,
Metellus Cimber throws before thy seat
An humble heart.

[*He kneels to make sure that* CAESAR *will pay attention to him
first, in accordance with the conspirators' plan.*]

35 CAESAR.                    I must prevent thee, Cimber.
These couchings and these lowly courtesies
Might fire the blood of ordinary men,
And turn preordinance and first decree[6]
Into the law of children.[7] Be not fond[8]
40 To think that Caesar bears such rebel blood
That will be thawed from the true quality
With that which melteth fools—I mean sweet words,
Low-crookèd curtsies, and base spaniel fawning.
Thy brother by decree is banishèd.

**514** *Drama*

---

3 **constant:** calm.

4 **addressed:** ready.

5 **puissant** [pwis′ənt]: powerful.

6 **preordinance...decree:** established laws and decisions.
7 **law of children:** laws that are changed at whim.
8 **fond:** foolish.

---

AT A GLANCE

- *Scene i (continued):* The plotters fear that Popilius will unmask them, but he does not.
- Trebonius draws Antony aside.
- Metellus kneels before Caesar to present a suit and thus distract his attention.
- Unswayed by Metellus' flattery, Caesar refuses to pardon Publius Cimber.

**1 PLOT: RISING ACTION**

Popilius' remarks alert the conspirators to the possibility that their plot may be thwarted at the last moment.

**2 CHARACTERIZATION**

In this crisis Brutus reveals himself as more observant than Cassius, calmer, and less ready to jump to an unjustified conclusion.

**3 PLOT: RISING ACTION**

It is essential that Antony not be at Caesar's side if the plotters are to prevail.

---

## GUIDED READING

### LITERAL QUESTIONS

**1a.** What arouses the conspirators' fear? (Popilius hints that he knows about their plot.)

**2a.** What is Metellus' role in the plot? (He is to divert Caesar's attention by presenting a suit.)

### INFERENTIAL QUESTIONS

**1b.** What do their different reactions to Popilius show about Cassius and Brutus? (Brutus is calmly analytical, whereas Cassius is emotional.)

**2b.** What does their use of Metellus in this way show about the plotters? (It shows that they have planned carefully.)

45    If thou dost bend and pray and fawn for him,
   I spurn thee like a cur out of my way.
   Know, Caesar doth not wrong, nor without cause
   Will he be satisfied.

METELLUS. Is there no voice more worthy than my own,
50    To sound more sweetly in great Caesar's ear
   For the repealing of my banished brother?

[*One by one, the other conspirators approach* CAESAR.]

**1**

BRUTUS. I kiss thy hand, but not in flattery, Caesar,
   Desiring thee that Publius Cimber may
   Have an immediate freedom of repeal.

CAESAR. [*Surprised.*] What, Brutus?

55 CASSIUS.                      Pardon, Caesar; Caesar,
    pardon!
   As low as to thy foot doth Cassius fall
   To beg enfranchisement[9] for Publius Cimber.

CAESAR. I could be well moved, if I were as you;
   If I could pray to move, prayers would move me;
60    But I am constant as the Northern Star,
   Of whose true-fixed and resting quality
   There is no fellow in the firmament.[10]
   The skies are painted with unnumb'red sparks,
   They are all fire and every one doth shine;
65    But there's but one in all doth hold his place.
   So in the world; 'tis furnished well with men,
   And men are flesh and blood, and apprehensive;[11]

**2**

   Yet in the number I do know but one
   That unassailable holds on his rank,
70    Unshaked of motion; and that I am he,
   Let me a little show it, even in this—
   That I was constant Cimber should be banished,
   And constant do remain to keep him so.

**3**

CINNA. O Caesar——

CAESAR.              Hence! Wilt thou lift up Olympus?[12]

DECIUS. Great Caesar——

75 CAESAR.            Doth not Brutus bootless[13] kneel?

CASCA. Speak hands for me!

**4**

[*The conspirators have been pressing closer and closer to* CAESAR. CASCA *draws his knife and stabs him, and the other conspirators follow his lead.* BRUTUS *stabs* CAESAR *last.*]

*Julius Caesar, Act III, Scene i*   **515**

---

9 **enfranchisement:** restoration of his rights as a citizen.

10 **no fellow...firmament:** no equal in the heavens. While other stars change their positions in the sky with the seasons, the North Star remains fixed above the North Pole.

11 **apprehensive:** subject to their feelings.

12 **Olympus:** mountain in Greece that was the legendary home of the gods. Caesar associates himself with both the immovability of the mountain and the aloofness of the gods.
13 **bootless:** in vain. If Brutus, his best friend, cannot sway Caesar, no one can.

---

AT A GLANCE

- *Scene i (continued):* After Metellus has appealed to them, the other conspirators approach Caesar, ostensibly to ask him to repeal Cimber's banishment.
- Caesar is surprised that Brutus is among them but refuses to change his mind.
- Casca and the other conspirators stab Caesar; Brutus goes last.

**1 CHARACTERIZATION**

Caesar knows Brutus well enough to perceive his action as uncharacteristic yet not well enough to guess the real reason behind it.

**2 IRONY**

Even in the moment before Caesar's death, he is unintentionally ironic in describing his own constancy.

**3 IRONY**

Unware that he is about to die, Caesar indirectly compares himself to the immortal gods, whose home was Mount Olympus.

**4 PLOT: CLIMAX**

Note how, for dramatic and symbolic purposes, Shakespeare has Brutus stab Caesar last.

---

## GUIDED READING

### LITERAL QUESTIONS

**1a.** What does Brutus do that surprises Caesar? (He asks for Publius Cimber's pardon.)

**2a.** Who stabs Caesar last? (Brutus)

### INFERENTIAL QUESTIONS

**1b.** What do Caesar's remarks about this vain action reveal about his feelings for Brutus? (They reveal that Caesar regards Brutus as his best and most loyal friend.)

**2b.** What might cause Brutus to be the last to stab Caesar? (He might be the most reluctant to kill Caesar.)

## 1 PLOT: RISING ACTION

Caesar instinctively connects his death to Brutus' betrayal.

## 2 CHARACTERIZATION

After the murder, Brutus is the first conspirator who thinks of calming the public.

## 3 STAGE DIRECTIONS

Stage directions show that Brutus has failed to calm the onlookers, since everyone but the conspirators flees.

## 4 STYLE: DIALOGUE

Trebonius' answer ("Fled to his house amazed.") to Cassius' question ("Where is Antony?") indicates that Antony is, at least momentarily, in shocked retreat.

---

**1** CAESAR. *Et tu, Brutè?*[14] Then fall Caesar. [*Recognizing his friend as one of his assassins,* CAESAR *dies.*]

[*Pandemonium breaks out as the bystanders realize what has happened.* BRUTUS *tries to calm the excited conspirators and frightened onlookers.*]

CINNA. Liberty! Freedom! Tyranny is dead!
Run hence, proclaim, cry it about the streets.

80 CASSIUS. Some to the common pulpits,[15] and cry out
"Liberty, freedom, and enfranchisement!"

**2** BRUTUS. People, and senators, be not affrighted.
Fly not; stand still; ambition's debt is paid.

CASCA. Go to the pulpit, Brutus.

DECIUS.                              And Cassius too.

85 BRUTUS. Where's Publius?

[CINNA *brings the stunned* PUBLIUS *forward through the crowd.*]

CINNA. Here, quite confounded[16] with this mutiny.

METELLUS. Stand fast together, lest some friend of Caesar's
Should chance——

BRUTUS. Talk not of standing. Publius, good cheer;
90    There is no harm intended to your person,
Nor to no Roman else. So tell them, Publius.

CASSIUS. And leave us, Publius, lest that the people
Rushing on us should do your age some mischief.

**3** BRUTUS. Do so; and let no man abide[17] this deed
95    But we the doers.

[*Everyone but the conspirators has fled from the scene.* TREBONIUS, *who had escorted* ANTONY *from the Capitol before the assassination, returns alone.*]

**4** CASSIUS. Where is Antony?

TREBONIUS.                              Fled to his house amazed.
Men, wives, and children stare, cry out and run,
As[18] it were doomsday.

BRUTUS.                              Fates, we will know your pleasures.
That we shall die, we know; 'tis but the time,
100   And drawing days out, that men stand upon.[19]

516   *Drama*

---

14 *Et tu, Brutè* [et tōō brōō′tā]: Latin for "And you as well, Brutus?"

15 **pulpits:** platforms for public speaking.

16 **confounded:** confused.

17 **abide:** suffer for.

18 **As:** as if.

19 **stand upon:** worry about.

---

## GUIDED READING

### LITERAL QUESTIONS

**1a.** Who is the last person Caesar speaks to before dying? (Brutus)

**2a.** What are the bystanders' reactions to Brutus' attempt to calm them? (They flee anyway.)

### INFERENTIAL QUESTIONS

**1b.** What do these words show about Caesar's feelings toward Brutus? (They show that he has loved Brutus and feels his betrayal both literally and figuratively as a "death blow.")

**2b.** Do the bystanders' reactions bode well for the conspirators? Explain your answer. (The bystanders' flight suggests that they mistrust the conspirators and therefore may not be counted on to support them.)

Len Cariou. Photo courtesy of Stratford Festival, Canada, 1982.

*Julius Caesar, Act III, Scene i* **517**

**1 CHARACTERIZATION**

Having just rationalized that they have done Caesar a favor by murdering him, Brutus now tries to paint the assassination as a glorious, almost sacrificial, act.

**2 DRAMATIC IRONY**

Brutus' unwitting words remind the audience that both Caesar and Brutus are characters in *this* play ("How many times shall Caesar bleed in sport").

**3 CHARACTERIZATION**

Cassius may not fully believe his own glowing description of the conspirators. He seems to be trying to follow Brutus' lead in building morale.

**4 VERBAL IRONY**

Antony's remark ("Say I love Brutus and I honor him") is the first of a series of ironic statements that disguise his true feelings.

---

CASCA. Why, he that cuts off twenty years of life
 Cuts off so many years of fearing death.

BRUTUS. Grant that, and then is death a benefit.
 So are we Caesar's friends, that have abridged
105 His time of fearing death. Stoop, Romans, stoop,
 And let us bathe our hands in Caesar's blood
 Up to the elbows, and besmear our swords.
 Then walk we forth, even to the market place,
 And waving our red weapons o'er our heads,
110 Let's all cry "Peace, freedom, and liberty!"

CASSIUS. Stoop then, and wash. How many ages hence
 Shall this our lofty scene be acted over
 In states unborn and accents yet unknown!

[*The conspirators all dip their hands in* CAESAR's *blood.*]

BRUTUS. How many times shall Caesar bleed in sport,[20]
115 That now on Pompey's basis lies along[21]
 No worthier than the dust!

CASSIUS.       So oft as that shall be,
 So often shall the knot of us be called
 The men that gave their country liberty.

DECIUS. What, shall we forth?

CASSIUS.      Ay, every man away.
120 Brutus shall lead, and we will grace his heels
 With the most boldest and best hearts of Rome.

[ANTONY's SERVANT *enters and kneels before* BRUTUS.]

BRUTUS. Soft, who comes here? A friend of Antony's.

SERVANT. Thus, Brutus, did my master bid me kneel;
 Thus did Mark Antony bid me fall down;
125 And, being prostrate, thus he bade me say:
 Brutus is noble, wise, valiant, and honest;
 Caesar was mighty, bold, royal, and loving.
 Say I love Brutus and I honor him;
 Say I feared Caesar, honored him, and loved him.
130 If Brutus will vouchsafe that Antony
 May safely come to him and be resolved[22]
 How Caesar hath deserved to lie in death,
 Mark Antony shall not love Caesar dead
 So well as Brutus living; but will follow
135 The fortunes and affairs of noble Brutus

20 **in sport:** in plays.

21 **on Pompey's...along:** lies at the foot of Pompey's statue.

22 **be resolved:** receive a satisfactory explanation.

---

## GUIDED READING

**LITERAL QUESTIONS**

**1a.** What does Brutus suggest the assassins do? (He suggests they bathe their hands and dip their swords in Caesar's blood and then walk to the market place crying, "Peace, freedom, and liberty!")

**2a.** What does Antony want Brutus to do? (He wants Brutus to explain why Caesar deserved to die.)

**INFERENTIAL QUESTIONS**

**1b.** What is Brutus' motive in making this suggestion? (He wants the public to see that the assassins acted for the benefit of all Romans. He may also be trying to justify the assassination to the other conspirators and to himself.)

**2b.** In making his request, what tone does Antony assume? (a complimentary and conciliatory tone.)

Thorough the hazards of this untrod state[23]
With all true faith. So says my master Antony.

23 **Thorough...state:** through all the dangers of this new, uncertain government.

BRUTUS. Thy master is a wise and valiant Roman;
I never thought him worse.
140 Tell him, so please him come unto this place,
He shall be satisfied and, by my honor,
Depart untouched.

SERVANT.                    I'll fetch him presently.[24] [*He leaves.*]

24 **presently:** immediately.

BRUTUS. I know that we shall have him well to friend.[25]

25 **well to friend:** as a good friend.

CASSIUS. I wish we may. But yet have I a mind
145 That fears him much; and my misgiving still
Falls shrewdly to the purpose.[26]

26 **my misgiving...purpose:** My instinct for danger is usually accurate.

**1** [ANTONY *enters. He ignores the conspirators and walks directly to the body of* CAESAR.]

BRUTUS. But here comes Antony. Welcome, Mark Antony.

ANTONY. O mighty Caesar! Dost thou lie so low?
Are all thy conquests, glories, triumphs, spoils,
150 Shrunk to this little measure? Fare thee well.

[*Turning to the conspirators.*]

**2** I know not, gentlemen, what you intend,
Who else must be let blood,[27] who else is rank.[28]
If I myself, there is no hour so fit
As Caesar's death's hour, nor no instrument
155 Of half that worth as those your swords, made rich
With the most noble blood of all this world.
I do beseech ye, if you bear me hard,
Now, whilst your purpled hands do reek and smoke,
Fulfill your pleasure. Live a thousand years,
160 I shall not find myself so apt[29] to die;
No place will please me so, no mean of death,
**3** As here by Caesar, and by you cut off,
The choice and master spirits of this age.

27 **let blood:** killed.
28 **rank:** diseased; also, grown too large. Antony is referring to the practice of drawing blood from diseased people (especially those whose diseases had made them swell).

29 **apt:** ready.

BRUTUS. O Antony, beg not your death of us!
165 Though now we must appear bloody and cruel,
As by our hands and this our present act
You see we do, yet see you but our hands
And this the bleeding business they have done.
Our hearts you see not; they are pitiful;[30]
170 And pity to the general wrong of Rome—

30 **pitiful:** full of pity.

*Julius Caesar, Act III, Scene i* **519**

AT A GLANCE

■ *Scene i (continued):* Brutus predicts that Antony will be a friend, but Cassius remains skeptical.
■ When Antony begs the assassins to kill him now, Brutus says they do not want his death.

**1 PLOT: FORESHADOWING**

Antony's behavior should cause the conspirators to worry about his threat to them.

**2 THEME**

Antony reveals his intense loyalty and devotion to Caesar by begging the assassins to kill him.

**3 STYLE: VERBAL IRONY**

The reader may already guess that Antony's description of the assassins is ironic.

## GUIDED READING

### LITERAL QUESTIONS

**1a.** About what do Brutus and Cassius disagree? (Brutus believes Antony will be the conspirators' friend, whereas Cassius still mistrusts him.)

**2a.** What is Brutus' response to Antony's plea? (He asks Antony not to request that the assassins kill him, too.)

### INFERENTIAL QUESTIONS

**1a.** Do you think future events will prove Brutus or Cassius correct? Explain your answer. (Antony's flattering words suggest Brutus may be right, but his initial behavior suggests that Cassius may be right.)

**2b.** What does Brutus' response show about him? (It shows that he may be naive in assuming that as soon as Antony understands why the conspirators murdered his friend, he will join them.)

**1 CONTRAST**

Whereas Brutus acts with high-minded generosity toward Antony, Cassius is more practical, offering him a say in the government.

**2 CHARACTERIZATION**

Antony skillfully voices what must be the assassins' own doubts about his behavior ("Either a coward or a flatterer").

**3 CONFLICT**

Having voiced his good will to the conspirators, Antony permits himself to express his more heartfelt, anguished, and conflicting feelings toward Caesar.

**4 STYLE: FIGURES OF SPEECH**

By comparing Caesar to a deer slain by hunters, Antony comes perilously close to revealing his real feelings about the assassination.

---

As fire drives out fire, so pity pity[31]—
Hath done this deed on Caesar. For your part,
To you our swords have leaden[32] points, Mark Antony:
Our arms in strength of malice,[33] and our hearts
175  Of brothers' temper, do receive you in
With all kind love, good thoughts, and reverence.

CASSIUS. Your voice shall be as strong as any man's
In the disposing of new dignities.[34]

BRUTUS. Only be patient till we have appeased
180  The multitude, beside themselves with fear,
And then we will deliver you the cause
Why I, that did love Caesar when I struck him,
Have thus proceeded.

ANTONY.                I doubt not of your wisdom.
Let each man render me his bloody hand.

[*As he speaks,* ANTONY *shakes the hand of each of the conspirators.*]

185  First, Marcus Brutus, will I shake with you;
Next, Caius Cassius, do I take your hand;
Now, Decius Brutus, yours; now yours, Metellus;
Yours, Cinna; and, my valiant Casca, yours;
Though last, not least in love, yours, good Trebonius.
190  Gentlemen all—alas, what shall I say?
My credit[35] now stands on such slippery ground
That one of two bad ways you must conceit[36] me,
Either a coward or a flatterer.

[*He turns back to* CAESAR*'s body and addresses it.*]

That I did love thee, Caesar, O, 'tis true!
195  If then thy spirit look upon us now,
Shall it not grieve thee dearer than thy death
To see thy Antony making his peace,
Shaking the bloody fingers of thy foes,
Most noble, in the presence of thy corse?[37]
200  Had I as many eyes as thou hast wounds,
Weeping as fast as they stream forth thy blood,
It would become me better than to close[38]
In terms of friendship with thine enemies.
Pardon me, Julius! Here wast thou bayed,[39] brave hart;[40]
205  Here didst thou fall, and here thy hunters stand,
Signed in thy spoil[41] and crimsoned in thy lethe.[42]
O world, thou wast the forest to this hart;

**520** *Drama*

---

31 **so pity pity:** Pity drives out pity. Brutus says that the conspirators' concern for Rome's misery has overcome their pity for Caesar.
32 **leaden:** blunt.
33 **Our arms...malice:** our arms, fresh from their bloody deed and seemingly full of malice.

34 **disposing...dignities:** deciding who will hold office.

35 **credit:** reputation.
36 **conceit:** judge.

37 **corse:** corpse.

38 **close:** make peace.
39 **bayed:** trapped like a hunted animal.
40 **hart:** a male deer.
41 **Signed...spoil:** marked with your slaughter.
42 **lethe:** death. Lethe was the legendary river that ran through Hades, the world of the dead. It also referred to the blood of a slain deer.

---

## GUIDED READING

**LITERAL QUESTIONS**

**1a.** What is the reason that Brutus gives for delaying the explanation of why Caesar had to be murdered? (He says that first the public has to be calmed.)

**2a.** For what does Antony apologize to Caesar? (for shaking the bloody fingers of Caesar's foes)

**INFERENTIAL QUESTIONS**

**1b.** Why does Brutus want to deal with the multitudes first? (He is aware that a fearful and overexcited public may not support the assassins.)

**2b.** What might cause Antony to act in a way that he knows would pain Caesar? (He might be trying to save his own life; he might also want to make the assassins let their guard down.)

And this indeed, O world, the heart of thee.
How like a deer, stroken by many princes,
210 Dost thou here lie!

CASSIUS. Mark Antony—

ANTONY.                    Pardon me, Caius Cassius.
The enemies of Caesar shall say this;
Then, in a friend, it is cold modesty.[43]

CASSIUS. I blame you not for praising Caesar so;
215 But what compact mean you to have with us?
Will you be pricked[44] in number of our friends,
Or shall we on, and not depend on you?

ANTONY. Therefore I took your hands, but was indeed
Swayed from the point by looking down on Caesar.
220 Friends am I with you all, and love you all,
Upon this hope, that you shall give me reasons
Why, and wherein, Caesar was dangerous.

BRUTUS. Or else were this a savage spectacle.
Our reasons are so full of good regard[45]
225 That were you, Antony, the son of Caesar,
You should be satisfied.

ANTONY.                    That's all I seek;
And am moreover suitor that I may
Produce his body to the market place,
And in the pulpit, as becomes a friend,
230 Speak in the order[46] of his funeral.

BRUTUS. You shall, Mark Antony.

CASSIUS.                    Brutus, a word with you.
[Aside to BRUTUS.] You know not what you do; do not
    consent
That Antony speak in his funeral.
Know you how much the people may be moved
By that which he will utter?

235 BRUTUS.                    By your pardon:
[Aside to CASSIUS.] I will myself into the pulpit first,
And show the reason of our Caesar's death.
What Antony shall speak, I will protest[47]
He speaks by leave and by permission,
240 And that we are contented Caesar shall
Have all true rites and lawful ceremonies.
It shall advantage[48] more than do us wrong.

43 **cold modesty:** restraint.

44 **pricked:** listed.

45 **full of good regard:** worthy,
convincing.

46 **order:** ceremony.

47 **protest:** declare.

48 **advantage:** help us.

*Julius Caesar, Act III, Scene i*   **521**

## AT A GLANCE

- *Scene i (continued):* His impassioned speech having aroused Cassius' fears, Antony reassures him of his loyalty.
- Brutus allows Antony to speak at Caesar's funeral.
- Cassius asks Brutus to reconsider, but Brutus overrules him.

### 1 CHARACTERIZATION

Antony's impassioned words cause the sharp-sighted Cassius to question his protestations of friendship.

### 2 PLOT: FORESHADOWING

Cassius senses the danger in permitting Antony to speak at Caesar's funeral. ("Know you how much the people may be moved / By that which he will utter?")

### 3 THEME

Brutus' consuming desire to show that the assassins are really fair-minded patriots prevents him from seeing the danger Antony poses.

## GUIDED READING

### LITERAL QUESTIONS

**1a.** What does Cassius question Antony about? (He questions whether the conspirators can count on him.)

**2a.** According to Brutus, what is the advantage of letting Antony speak at the funeral? (It will show the people that the assassins are treating Caesar fairly.)

### INFERENTIAL QUESTIONS

**1b.** What about Antony's behavior provokes Cassius' question? (Antony has just delivered a passionate, grief-stricken speech to Caesar's body.)

**2b.** What characteristics has Antony already shown that indicate Brutus' decision may be unwise? (Antony is loyal to Caesar, an impassioned speaker, and perhaps shrewd in hiding his real feelings.)

**1  CHARACTERIZATION**

Brutus has a stubborn streak; he continues to disregard Cassius' warnings about Antony.

**2  SOLILOQUY**

Immediately, Antony reveals that he has been hiding his real feelings about the murderers.

**3  PLOT: FORESHADOWING**

Antony's prediction sets the stage for a violent confrontation between the assassins and the forces loyal to Caesar.

---

CASSIUS. [*Aside to* BRUTUS.] I know not what may fall;[49] I like
    it not.

49 **fall:** happen.

**1**

BRUTUS. Mark Antony, here, take you Caesar's body.
245    You shall not in your funeral speech blame us,
    But speak all good you can devise of Caesar,
    And say you do't by our permission;
    Else shall you not have any hand at all
    About his funeral. And you shall speak
250    In the same pulpit whereto I am going,
    After my speech is ended.

ANTONY.                Be it so;
    I do desire no more.

BRUTUS. Prepare the body then, and follow us.

[*The conspirators go, leaving* ANTONY *alone with* CAESAR's
*body. He now speaks directly to his dead friend without
fear of being overheard.*]

**2**

ANTONY. O pardon me, thou bleeding piece of earth,
255    That I am meek and gentle with these butchers!
    Thou art the ruins of the noblest man
    That ever livèd in the tide of times.[50]
    Woe to the hand that shed this costly blood!
    Over thy wounds now do I prophesy
260    (Which like dumb mouths do ope their ruby lips
    To beg the voice and utterance of my tongue),

**3**

    A curse shall light upon the limbs of men;
    Domestic fury and fierce civil strife
    Shall cumber[51] all the parts of Italy;
265    Blood and destruction shall be so in use,[52]
    And dreadful objects so familiar,
    That mothers shall but smile when they behold
    Their infants quartered[53] with the hands of war,
    All pity choked with custom of fell deeds;[54]
270    And Caesar's spirit, ranging[55] for revenge,
    With Atè[56] by his side come hot from hell,
    Shall in these confines with a monarch's voice
    Cry "Havoc,"[57] and let slip the dogs of war,
    That this foul deed shall smell above the earth
275    With carrion[58] men, groaning for burial.

[*The* SERVANT *of* OCTAVIUS, CAESAR's *grandnephew and
adopted heir, enters.*]

    You serve Octavius Caesar, do you not?

50 **tide of times:** all history.

51 **cumber:** burden, oppress.

52 **so in use:** so habitual.

53 **quartered:** torn to pieces.
54 **custom...deeds:** the habit of evil deeds.
55 **ranging:** roving for prey.
56 **Atè** [a´tā]: goddess of vengeance and strife.

57 **"Havoc":** battle signal for mass slaughter.

58 **carrion:** rotting.

---

## GUIDED READING

### LITERAL QUESTIONS

**1a.** What does Antony reveal about his feelings when he is alone? (He reveals that he thinks the murderers are butchers.)

**2a.** What does Antony predict will happen as a result of the murder? (He predicts that Rome will be torn apart by civil war.)

### INFERENTIAL QUESTIONS

**1b.** What does Antony's revelation suggest about his present behavior toward the assassins? (It suggests that he is trying to keep them off guard with his seeming meekness.)

**2b.** What role do you think Antony will play in the civil strife he predicts? (Because of his loyalty to Caesar, Antony will probably lead the forces seeking to avenge Caesar's death.)

R. H. Thomson. Jack Medley. Photo courtesy of Stratford Festival, Canada, 1982.

*Julius Caesar, Act III, Scene i*   **523**

**1 PLOT: RISING ACTION**

With Octavius, Caesar's heir, waiting in the wings, the stage is set for a confrontation between the assassins and Caesar's supporters.

**2 SETTING**

In its present unsettled state, Rome is itself an actor in the unfolding drama.

**3 STAGE DIRECTIONS**

From the stage directions it is clear that the assassins have yet to appease the plebeians.

**4 CHARACTERIZATION**

Cleverly, Brutus tries to divide the unruly crowd in two.

---

SERVANT. I do, Mark Antony.

**1** ANTONY. Caesar did write for him to come to Rome.

SERVANT. He did receive his letters and is coming,
280   And bid me say to you by word of mouth—
  [*He notices* CAESAR*'s body and begins to weep.*] O Caesar!

ANTONY. Thy heart is big; get thee apart and weep.
  Passion, I see, is catching, for mine eyes,
  Seeing those beads of sorrow stand in thine,
285   Began to water. Is thy master coming?

SERVANT. He lies tonight within seven leagues[59] of Rome.

ANTONY. Post back with speed, and tell him what hath chanced.
**2**   Here is a mourning Rome, a dangerous Rome,
  No Rome of safety for Octavius yet.
290   Hie hence and tell him so. Yet stay awhile;
  Thou shalt not back till I have borne this corse
  Into the market place; there shall I try[60]
  In my oration how the people take
  The cruel issue[61] of these bloody men;
295   According to the which, thou shalt discourse
  To young Octavius of the state of things.
  Lend me your hand.

  [*They leave together, carrying* CAESAR*'s body.*]

**Scene ii.** *The Roman Forum, the city's great public square.
    A few days later.*

**3** [CAESAR*'s funeral is about to take place.* BRUTUS *and* CASSIUS *stand near a speaker's platform. They are surrounded by a large crowd of* PLEBEIANS *loudly protesting* CAESAR*'s death.* BRUTUS *goes to the platform and prepares to explain the conspirators' reasons for killing* CAESAR.]

PLEBEIANS. We will be satisfied![1] Let us be satisfied!

BRUTUS. Then follow me, and give me audience, friends.
**4**   Cassius, go you into the other street
  And part the numbers.[2]
5   Those that will hear me speak, let 'em stay here;
  Those that will follow Cassius, go with him;
  And public reasons shall be renderèd
  Of Caesar's death.

FIRST PLEBEIAN.     I will hear Brutus speak.

**524**  *Drama*

---

59 **seven leagues:** within twenty-one miles.

60 **try:** test.

61 **cruel issue:** outcome of their cruelty.

1 **satisfied:** The plebeians demand a full explanation of the assassination.

2 **part the numbers:** divide the crowd.

---

## GUIDED READING

**LITERAL QUESTIONS**

**1a.** What help has come for Antony? (Octavius, Caesar's nephew and heir.)

**2a.** What do the plebeians demand? (They want the assassins to explain why they had to kill Caesar.)

**INFERENTIAL QUESTIONS**

**1b.** What is important about the identity of this ally? (As Caesar's nephew and lawful heir, Octavius lends legitimacy to any attempt to vanquish the assassins.)

**2b.** What problems do the plebeians' demands pose for the assassins? (They need to explain themselves satisfactorily or else lose their power and, possibly, their lives.)

**SECOND PLEBEIAN.** I will hear Cassius, and compare their reasons,

10   When severally³ we hear them renderèd.

[CASSIUS *leaves with the* PLEBEIANS *who wish to hear him speak. The rest remain to hear* BRUTUS, *who goes into the pulpit.*]

**THIRD PLEBEIAN.** The noble Brutus is ascended. Silence!

**BRUTUS.** Be patient till the last.⁴

[*The crowd grows silent.*]

Romans, countrymen, and lovers,⁵ hear me for my cause, and be silent, that you may hear. Believe me for mine honor, and have respect to mine honor,⁶ that you may
15   believe. Censure⁷ me in your wisdom, and awake your senses,⁸ that you may the better judge. If there be any in this assembly, any dear friend of Caesar's, to him I say that Brutus' love to Caesar was no less than his. If then that friend demand why Brutus rose against Caesar, this is my
20   answer: Not that I loved Caesar less, but that I loved Rome more. Had you rather Caesar were living, and die all slaves, than that Caesar were dead, to live all free men? As Caesar loved me, I weep for him; as he was fortunate, I rejoice at it; as he was valiant, I honor him; but, as he was ambitious, I
25   slew him. There is tears, for his love; joy, for his fortune; honor, for his valor; and death, for his ambition. Who is here so base, that would be a bondman?⁹ if any, speak; for him have I offended. Who is here so rude,¹⁰ that would not be a Roman? If any, speak; for him have I offended. Who is
30   here so vile, that will not love his country? If any, speak; for him have I offended. I pause for a reply.

**ALL.** None, Brutus, none!

**BRUTUS.** Then none have I offended. I have done no more to
35   Caesar than you shall do to Brutus. The question of his death is enrolled in the Capitol;¹¹ his glory not extenuated,¹² wherein he was worthy, nor his offenses enforced,¹³ for which he suffered death.

[MARK ANTONY *enters with bearers carrying* CAESAR's *body in an open coffin. The body is covered with the mantle* CAESAR *was wearing when he was killed.*]

Here comes his body, mourned by Mark Antony, who,
40   though he had no hand in his death, shall receive the benefit

3 **severally:** separately.

4 **the last:** end of the speech.

5 **lovers:** friends.

6 **have...honor:** Remember that I am honorable.
7 **Censure:** judge.
8 **senses:** reason (as opposed to passion).

9 **bondman:** slave.

10 **rude:** barbaric.

11 **question...Capitol:** The reasons for his death are recorded in the public archives of the Capitol.
12 **extenuated:** belittled.
13 **enforced:** overemphasized.

*Julius Caesar, Act III, Scene ii*   **525**

**AT A GLANCE**

- *Scene ii (continued):* Brutus explains to the plebeians that he loved Rome more than Caesar.
- The crowd voices support for Brutus.
- Antony enters with Caesar's body.

**1 STYLE: PROSE**

In attempting to reach the plebeians, Brutus tries to address them in their own plain speech; thus, for the first time he substitutes prose for blank verse. The prose speech seems flatter, more cut and dried than blank verse would.

**2 RESPONSE JOURNAL**

Students may want to comment in their journals about what they might do if they had to choose between loyalty to a friend or loyalty to a "higher" principle or ideal.

**3 MONOLOGUE**

Brutus' genuine concern for all Romans permeates his speech. The speech is logical and rather eloquent but is too brief to have truly reached the listeners' minds and hearts.

## GUIDED READING

**LITERAL QUESTIONS**

**1a.** What is different about Brutus' mode of speech when he gives his funeral oration? (He is speaking in prose, not his usual blank verse.)

**2a.** What is Brutus' explanation for the assassination? (He says that he acted because he loved Rome more than Caesar, who would have made the people into slaves.)

**INFERENTIAL QUESTIONS**

**1b.** What reason might Brutus have for making this change? (He might want to appeal to the plebeians by speaking more like them.)

**2b.** What in Brutus' explanation causes the people to now support him? (He seems sincere when he says he acted not out of hatred or personal ambition but to prevent Romans from becoming slaves.)

**AT A GLANCE**

- *Scene ii (continued):* When Brutus offers to kill himself if the people desire it, they shout their support for him.
- When Brutus asks them to hear Antony, they agree to listen for Brutus' sake.

**1 PLOT: RISING ACTION**

Brutus' eloquence has quieted the people, who now see him as Caesar's heir.

**2 SITUATIONAL IRONY**

If Brutus knew Antony's intent, he might not implore the crowd to stay, nor would he himself leave.

**3 PLOT: RISING ACTION**

For the moment, the people are entirely behind Brutus, even stating the case against Caesar more strongly than he ("This Caesar was a tyrant.").

---

**1** of his dying, a place in the commonwealth, as which of you shall not? With this I depart, that, as I slew my best lover for the good of Rome, I have the same dagger for myself, when it shall please my country to need my death.

45 ALL. Live, Brutus! Live, live!

FIRST PLEBEIAN. Bring him with triumph home unto his house.

SECOND PLEBEIAN. Give him a statue with his ancestors.

THIRD PLEBEIAN. Let him be Caesar.

FOURTH PLEBEIAN.                    Caesar's better parts¹⁴
   Shall be crowned in Brutus.

FIRST PLEBEIAN. We'll bring him to his house with shouts and
50    clamors.

BRUTUS. My countrymen——

SECOND PLEBEIAN.               Peace! Silence! Brutus speaks.

FIRST PLEBEIAN. Peace, ho! [*They grow silent.*]

BRUTUS. Good countrymen, let me depart alone,
   And, for my sake, stay here with Antony.
55 Do grace to Caesar's corpse, and grace his speech¹⁵
   Tending to Caesar's glories, which Mark Antony
   By our permission, is allowed to make.
**2** I do entreat you, not a man depart,
   Save I alone, till Antony have spoke.

   [BRUTUS *comes down from the pulpit and leaves.*]

60 FIRST PLEBEIAN. Stay, ho! And let us hear Mark Antony.

THIRD PLEBEIAN. Let him go up into the public chair;¹⁶
   We'll hear him. Noble Antony, go up.

ANTONY. For Brutus' sake, I am beholding¹⁷ to you.

   [ANTONY *goes into the pulpit and faces the crowd, ready to deliver his funeral oration. The* PLEBEIANS *continue to voice their support of* BRUTUS.]

FOURTH PLEBEIAN. What does he say of Brutus?

THIRD PLEBEIAN.                    He says, for Brutus' sake,
65    He finds himself beholding to us all.

**3** FOURTH PLEBEIAN. 'Twere best he speak no harm of Brutus
   here!

FIRST PLEBEIAN. This Caesar was a tyrant.

14 **parts:** qualities.

15 **Do grace...speech:** Pay respect to Caesar's body and Antony's speech.

16 **public chair:** pulpit.

17 **beholding:** indebted.

**526** *Drama*

---

## GUIDED READING

**LITERAL QUESTIONS**

**1a.** What does Brutus offer to do? (He offers to kill himself if the people desire it.)

**2a.** What does Brutus request the people to do? (He requests that they stay for Antony's speech.)

**INFERENTIAL QUESTIONS**

**1b.** Why do the people reject Brutus' offer? (Brutus' eloquence has won them over, especially his protestations that he murdered Caesar for the good of Rome.)

**2b.** What is the mood of the crowd when Brutus makes his request? (They are wary of Antony and will listen to him only if he speaks no ill of Brutus, whom they now regard as a hero.)

THIRD PLEBEIAN.                                Nay, that's certain.
We are blest that Rome is rid of him.

SECOND PLEBEIAN. Peace! Let us hear what Antony can say.

ANTONY. You gentle Romans——

[*The noise continues.*]

70  ALL.                                  Peace, ho! Let us hear him.

[*They quiet enough for him to be heard. As* ANTONY *speaks,
the crowd gradually becomes more attentive.*]

ANTONY. Friends, Romans, countrymen, lend me your ears;
I come to bury Caesar, not to praise him.
The evil that men do lives after them,
The good is oft interrèd[18] with their bones;          18 **interrèd:** buried.
75  So let it be with Caesar. The noble Brutus
Hath told you Caesar was ambitious.
If it were so, it was a grievous fault,
And grievously hath Caesar answered it.
Here, under leave[19] of Brutus and the rest          19 **leave:** permission.
80  (For Brutus is an honorable man,
So are they all, all honorable men),
Come I to speak in Caesar's funeral.
He was my friend, faithful and just to me;
But Brutus says he was ambitious,
85  And Brutus is an honorable man.
He hath brought many captives home to Rome,
Whose ransoms did the general coffers[20] fill;          20 **general coffers:** public treasury.
Did this in Caesar seem ambitious?
When that the poor have cried, Caesar hath wept;
90  Ambition should be made of sterner stuff.
Yet Brutus says he was ambitious;
And Brutus is an honorable man.
You all did see that on the Lupercal[21]          21 **Lupercal:** See Act I, Scene ii.
I thrice presented him a kingly crown,
95  Which he did thrice refuse. Was this ambition?
Yet Brutus says he was ambitious;
And sure he is an honorable man.
I speak not to disprove what Brutus spoke,
But here I am to speak what I do know.
100  You all did love him once, not without cause;
What cause withholds you then to mourn for him?
O judgment, thou art fled to brutish beasts,
And men have lost their reason! Bear with me;

*Julius Caesar, Act III, Scene ii*    **527**

## GUIDED READING

**LITERAL QUESTIONS**

**1a.** Which conspirator does Antony focus on? (He focuses on Brutus.)

**2a.** What word does Antony repeatedly use to describe Brutus? (He uses the adjective *honorable*.)

**INFERENTIAL QUESTIONS**

**1b.** Why does Antony focus on him? (He recognizes that Brutus is the most popular and esteemed conspirator and that if he can discredit him, he will have discredited the entire plot.)

**2b.** What is Antony's motive in using this word? (He wants the crowd to think that Brutus is really dishonorable.)

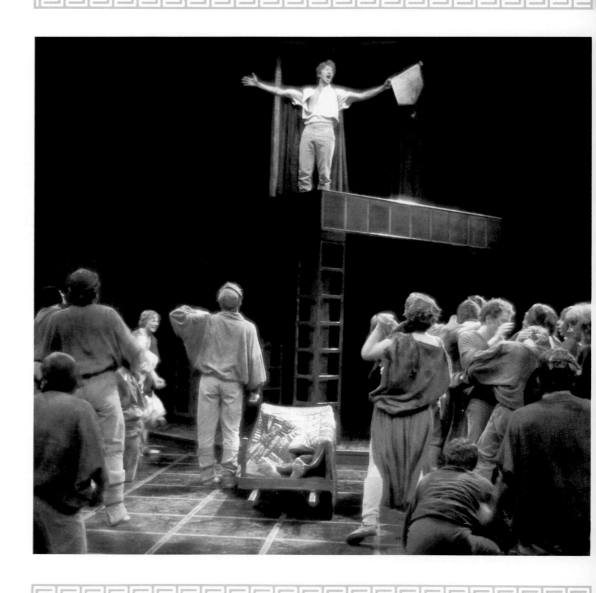

R. H. Thomson. Photo courtesy of Stratford Festival, Canada, 1982.

**528**   *Drama*

My heart is in the coffin there with Caesar,
105  And I must pause till it come back to me.

[ANTONY *seems to be overcome with emotion. Moved by his
speech, the* PLEBEIANS *begin to talk among themselves.*]

FIRST PLEBEIAN. Methinks there is much reason in his sayings.

SECOND PLEBEIAN. If thou consider rightly of the matter,
Caesar has had great wrong.

THIRD PLEBEIAN.                    Has he, masters?
I fear there will a worse come in his place.

110  FOURTH PLEBEIAN. Marked ye his words? He would not take
the crown,
Therefore 'tis certain he was not ambitious.

FIRST PLEBEIAN. If it be found so, some will dear abide it.[22]

1
SECOND PLEBEIAN. Poor soul, his eyes are red as fire with
weeping.

THIRD PLEBEIAN. There's not a nobler man in Rome than
Antony.

115  FOURTH PLEBEIAN. Now mark him, he begins again to speak.

[*All commotion stops as soon as* ANTONY *resumes.*]

ANTONY. But yesterday the word of Caesar might
Have stood against the world; now lies he there,
And none so poor to do him reverence.[23]
O masters! If I were disposed to stir
120  Your hearts and minds to mutiny and rage,
I should do Brutus wrong and Cassius wrong,
Who, you all know, are honorable men.
I will not do them wrong; I rather choose
To wrong the dead, to wrong myself and you,
125  Than I will wrong such honorable men.
But here's a parchment with the seal of Caesar;

[*He produces a document.*]

2
I found it in his closet, 'tis his will.
Let but the commons[24] hear this testament,
Which, pardon me, I do not mean to read,
130  And they would go and kiss dead Caesar's wounds,
And dip their napkins[25] in his sacred blood;
Yea, beg a hair of him for memory,

22 **dear abide it:** pay dearly for it.

23 **none...reverence:** No one will
stoop to honor Caesar now.

24 **commons:** public.

25 **napkins:** handkerchiefs. Antony
refers to the custom of dipping cloths
into the blood of martyrs.

*Julius Caesar, Act III, Scene ii*  **529**

---

AT A GLANCE

- Overcome with emotion, Antony stops speaking, but already the crowd has become sympathetic.
- When Antony resumes, he produces Caesar's will.

**1 MONOLOGUE**

The fickleness of the plebeians makes it easy for them to shift their sympathy to Antony, who, unlike Brutus, knows that they are swayed by their emotions.

**2 PLOT: RISING ACTION**

Antony hammers the final nail in the conspirator's coffin. ("I found it in his closet, 'tis his will.")

---

## GUIDED READING

**LITERAL QUESTIONS**

**1a.** What is the plebeians' reaction to Antony's speech? (They shift their support to him.)

**2a.** What does Antony produce, and what effect does he say it should have on the crowd? (He produces Caesar's will and says that after it is read, the crowd will revere Caesar.)

**INFERENTIAL QUESTIONS**

**1b.** What does their reaction show about the plebeians? (It shows once again that they are easily swayed because they are unstable in their opinions.)

**2b.** What do you think are the terms of the will? (It will probably leave some or all of Caesar's estate to the people.)

## 1 CHARACTERIZATION

Like a master actor, Antony piques the crowd's curiosity, doing exactly what he *says* he wants to avoid—that is, "inflaming" them.

## 2 STYLE: IRONY

The frenzied people, reversing their adulation after Brutus' speech, now hate the conspirators.

## 3 STAGE DIRECTIONS

Antony's descent into the crowd is a visual emblem of his success in moving them: they are now visually and emotionally at one with him.

And dying, mention it within their wills,
Bequeathing it as a rich legacy
135     Unto their issue.²⁶

26 **issue:** children.

FOURTH PLEBEIAN. We'll hear the will; read it, Mark Antony.

ALL. The will, the will! We will hear Caesar's will!

**1**

ANTONY. Have patience, gentle friends, I must not read it.
It is not meet²⁷ you know how Caesar loved you.
140     You are not wood, you are not stones, but men;
And being men, hearing the will of Caesar,
It will inflame you, it will make you mad.
'Tis good you know not that you are his heirs;
For if you should, O, what would come of it?

27 **meet:** proper.

145 FOURTH PLEBEIAN. Read the will! We'll hear it, Antony!
You shall read us the will, Caesar's will!

ANTONY. Will you be patient? Will you stay awhile?
I have o'ershot myself²⁸ to tell you of it.
I fear I wrong the honorable men
150     Whose daggers have stabbed Caesar; I do fear it.

28 **o'ershot myself:** gone too far.

**2**

FOURTH PLEBEIAN. They were traitors. Honorable men!

ALL. The will! The testament!

SECOND PLEBEIAN. They were villains, murderers! The will!
Read the will!

ANTONY. You will compel me then to read the will?
155     Then make a ring about the corpse of Caesar,
And let me show you him that made the will.

**3**

Shall I descend? And will you give me leave?

ALL. Come down.

SECOND PLEBEIAN. Descend.

[ANTONY *comes down from the platform and walks over to*
CAESAR's *body as the* PLEBEIANS *crowd around him in a
circle.*]

160 THIRD PLEBEIAN. You shall have leave.

FOURTH PLEBEIAN. A ring! Stand round.

FIRST PLEBEIAN. Stand from the hearse, stand from the body!

SECOND PLEBEIAN. Room for Antony, most noble Antony!

ANTONY. Nay, press not so upon me; stand far off.

**530** *Drama*

## GUIDED READING

### LITERAL QUESTIONS

**1a.** What reason does Antony give for refusing initially to read the will to the crowd? (He fears they will be inflamed by hearing it because Caesar has made the people his heirs.)

**2a.** What does Antony ask the crowd to permit him to do? (He asks that they permit him to descend.)

### INFERENTIAL QUESTIONS

**1b.** What is the real motive behind Antony's refusal? (He wants to stir the crowd up to fever pitch.)

**2b.** What does Antony's request and the crowd's assent symbolize? (They symbolize the merging of the people's will and desires with Antony's.)

165 **ALL.** Stand back! Room! Bear back.

[*The crowd clears a space around* ANTONY *and the coffin.*]

**ANTONY.** If you have tears, prepare to shed them now.
You all do know this mantle; I remember
The first time ever Caesar put it on:
'Twas on a summer's evening, in his tent,
170 That day he overcame the Nervii.²⁹
Look, in this place ran Cassius' dagger through;
See what a rent³⁰ the envious Casca made;
Through this the well-belovèd Brutus stabbed,
And as he plucked his cursèd steel away,
175 Mark how the blood of Caesar followed it,
As³¹ rushing out of doors, to be resolved³²
If Brutus so unkindly³³ knocked, or no;
For Brutus, as you know, was Caesar's angel.³⁴
Judge, O you gods, how dearly Caesar loved him!
180 This was the most unkindest cut of all;
For when the noble Caesar saw him stab,
Ingratitude, more strong than traitors' arms,
Quite vanquished him. Then burst his mighty heart;
And, in his mantle muffling up his face,
185 Even at the base of Pompey's statue
(Which all the while ran blood) great Caesar fell.
O, what a fall was there, my countrymen!
Then I, and you, and all of us fell down,
Whilst bloody treason flourished over us.
190 O, now you weep, and I perceive you feel
The dint³⁵ of pity; these are gracious drops.
Kind souls, what weep you when you but behold
Our Caesar's vesture³⁶ wounded? Look you here,
Here is himself, marred as you see with traitors.

[ANTONY *lifts the mantle and reveals* CAESAR'*s bloody body
to the crowd.*]

195 **FIRST PLEBEIAN.** O piteous spectacle!

**SECOND PLEBEIAN.** O noble Caesar!

**THIRD PLEBEIAN.** O woeful day!

**FOURTH PLEBEIAN.** O traitors, villains!

**FIRST PLEBEIAN.** O most bloody sight!

200 **SECOND PLEBEIAN.** We will be revenged.

*Julius Caesar, Act III, Scene ii* **531**

---

**29 Nervii** [nur'vē ĭ]: warlike Belgian tribe defeated by Caesar thirteen years before.
**30 rent:** rip.

**31 As:** as if.
**32 to be resolved:** to confirm.
**33 unkindly:** cruelly; also, unnaturally.
**34 angel:** favorite.

**35 dint:** force.

**36 vesture:** clothing.

---

**AT A GLANCE**

- *Scene ii (continued):* Antony shows the rents in Caesar's mantle made by the assassins' daggers.
- Antony says that because Caesar loved him, Brutus' betrayal "burst" his heart.
- After Antony shows the crowd Caesar's body, the plebeians vow revenge.

**1 CHARACTERIZATION**

In a master stroke Antony rouses the crowd's pity by identifying the tears in Caesar's mantle made by some of the assassins' daggers.

**2 VOCABULARY: WORD CHOICE**

By referring to Brutus as Caesar's "angel," Antony makes his betrayal seem crueler than was that of the other assassins.

**3 PLOT: CLIMAX**

Now the assassins have to worry about their lives because the crowd has become bloodthirsty. ("We will be revenged.")

---

## GUIDED READING

### LITERAL QUESTIONS

**1a.** What does Antony show the crowd? (He shows them the tears in Caesar's mantle made by the assassins' daggers.)

**2a.** What word does Antony use at the end of his speech for the first time to describe the conspirators? (He calls them "traitors.")

### INFERENTIAL QUESTIONS

**1b.** What is Antony's motive in showing these to the crowd? (He wants to arouse their pity for Caesar and their anger against the conspirators.)

**2b.** Why does Antony feel free to use this word now? (He feels that having won the crowd and turned the tide, he no longer has to fear the conspirators.)

## 1 VERBAL IRONY

By saying that he does not want to stir the people to mutiny, Antony plants the idea in their minds.

## 2 STYLE: SITUATIONAL IRONY

Antony's brilliant manipulation of the crowd belies his modest self-appraisal.

## 3 CHARACTERIZATION

Antony's "switching places" with Brutus perhaps goes deeper than intended: They are the most noble and charismatic characters in the play.

ALL. *[In great commotion.]* Revenge! About! Seek! Burn! Fire!
  Kill! Slay!
  Let not a traitor live!

ANTONY. Stay, countrymen.

FIRST PLEBEIAN. Peace there! Hear the noble Antony.

SECOND PLEBEIAN. We'll hear him, we'll follow him, we'll die
205   with him!

ANTONY. Good friends, sweet friends, let me not stir you up
  To such a sudden flood of mutiny.
  They that have done this deed are honorable.
  What private griefs[37] they have, alas, I know not,
210  That made them do it. They are wise and honorable,
  And will, no doubt, with reasons answer you.
  I come not, friends, to steal away your hearts;
  I am no orator, as Brutus is;
  But (as you know me all) a plain blunt man
215  That love my friend, and that they know full well
  That gave me public leave to speak of him.
  For I have neither writ, nor words, nor worth,[38]
  Action, nor utterance,[39] nor the power of speech
  To stir men's blood; I only speak right on.
220  I tell you that which you yourselves do know,
  Show you sweet Caesar's wounds, poor poor dumb mouths,
  And bid them speak for me. But were I Brutus,
  And Brutus Antony, there were an Antony
  Would ruffle up your spirits, and put a tongue
225  In every wound of Caesar that should move
  The stones of Rome to rise and mutiny.

[*The commotion increases as the crowd erupts into shouting.*]

ALL. We'll mutiny.

FIRST PLEBEIAN.   We'll burn the house of Brutus.

[*They begin to hurry in the direction* BRUTUS *took when he left.*]

THIRD PLEBEIAN. Away, then! Come, seek the conspirators.

ANTONY. Yet hear me, countrymen. Yet hear me speak.

ALL. Peace, ho! Hear Antony, most noble Antony!

230 ANTONY. Why, friends, you go to do you know not what:
  Wherein hath Caesar thus deserved your loves?

532   *Drama*

---

37 **private griefs:** personal grievances. Antony suggests that the conspirators killed Caesar not for the public reasons Brutus mentions in line 36 but rather for personal (and therefore less worthy) motives.

38 **worth:** high personal standing or reputation.
39 **Action, nor utterance:** neither the gestures nor the vocal delivery of a skilled orator.

---

## GUIDED READING

### LITERAL QUESTION

**1a.** To whom does Antony compare himself unfavorably? (He compares himself unfavorably to Brutus, who he says is a real orator.)

### INFERENTIAL QUESTION

**1b.** What motive does Antony have in making this comparison? (He wishes to make himself appear as an innocent man of the people, like someone in the crowd; he also wants to focus the crowd's anger on Brutus.)

You have forgot the will I told you of.

ALL. Most true, the will! Let's stay and hear the will.

[*The crowd quiets once again, but a constant murmur grows under* ANTONY's *speech as he reads the terms of the will.*]

235 ANTONY. Here is the will, and under Caesar's seal.
To every Roman citizen he gives,
To every several[40] man, seventy-five drachmas.[41]

SECOND PLEBEIAN. Most noble Caesar! We'll revenge his death!

THIRD PLEBEIAN. O royal[42] Caesar!

240 ANTONY. Hear me with patience.

ALL. Peace, ho!

ANTONY. Moreover, he hath left you all his walks,
His private arbors, and new-planted orchards,[43]
On this side Tiber; he hath left them you,
245 And to your heirs forever: common pleasures,[44]
To walk abroad and recreate yourselves.
Here was a Caesar! When comes such another?

[*With a great roar, the crowd rages out of control.*]

FIRST PLEBEIAN. Never, never! Come, away, away!
We'll burn his body in the holy place,[45]
250 And with the brands fire the traitors' houses.
Take up the body.

SECOND PLEBEIAN. Go fetch fire.

THIRD PLEBEIAN. Pluck down benches.

FOURTH PLEBEIAN. Pluck down forms, windows,[46] anything!

[*Several* PLEBEIANS *take up* CAESAR's *body from the coffin. The rest run in different directions from the Forum, leaving* ANTONY *alone.*]

255 ANTONY. Now let it work: Mischief, thou art afoot,
Take thou what course thou wilt.

[*The* SERVANT *of* OCTAVIUS *enters.* ANTONY *hails him.*]

How now, fellow?

SERVANT. Sir, Octavius is already come to Rome.

ANTONY. Where is he?

---

40 **several:** individual.
41 **drachmas** [drak′məz]: Greek silver coins valued at about nineteen cents each in Shakespeare's time. The legacy would have been impressive in Elizabethan times.

42 **royal:** most generous.

43 **orchards:** gardens.

44 **common pleasures:** public recreation areas.

45 **holy place:** where the most sacred Roman temples stood.

46 **forms, windows:** benches and shutters.

*Julius Caesar, Act III, Scene ii* **533**

AT A GLANCE

- *Scene ii (continued):* Antony reads aloud Caesar's will, which gives each Roman seventy-five drachmas as well as the use of his walks, arbors, and orchards.
- When the plebeians run off to burn Caesar's body and set fire to the traitors' houses, they leave behind a satisfied Antony.

**1 CHARACTERIZATION**

With an impeccable sense of drama, Antony leaves the best for last: the reading of Caesar's will.

**2 SETTING**

The crowd has moved from threats of mutiny to actual acts.

**3 PLOT: SUSPENSE**

The net around the conspirators tightens as Octavius moves toward the center of the action.

---

## GUIDED READING

### LITERAL QUESTIONS

**1a.** What does Caesar leave the people in his will? (He leaves them each seventy-five drachmas and the use of his walks, arbors, and orchards.)

**2a.** What do the people run off to do? (They run off to burn Caesar's body and torch the conspirators' houses.)

### INFERENTIAL QUESTIONS

**1b.** What does his will show about Caesar? (It shows that he was generous toward the people and perhaps not the villain the conspirators claimed him to be.)

**2b.** What might the conspirators do now that the tide has turned against them? (They might flee or attempt to win back the crowd.)

- *Scene ii (continued):* Before Antony goes to greet Octavius, he hears that Brutus and Cassius have fled Rome.
- *Scene iii:* On his way to Caesar's funeral, Cinna the poet is stopped and questioned by rioting plebeians.

**1 PLOT: CLIMAX**

Everything is going Antony's way: Brutus and Cassius have fled "like madmen."

**2 FORESHADOWING**

In the context of Caesar's death, Cinna's dream that he did "feast" with Caesar hints at Cinna's own fate.

**3 CHARACTERIZATION**

The plebeians seem to enjoy ruling the streets, questioning and bullying anyone walking abroad.

**4 COMEDY**

To ease the tension, Shakespeare injects some comic relief.

---

SERVANT. He and Lepidus⁴⁷ are at Caesar's house.

260 ANTONY. And thither will I straight to visit him;
   He comes upon a wish.⁴⁸ Fortune is merry,
   And in this mood will give us anything.

**1** SERVANT. I heard him say, Brutus and Cassius
   Are rid⁴⁹ like madmen through the gates of Rome.

265 ANTONY. Belike⁵⁰ they had some notice of the people,
   How I had moved them. Bring me to Octavius.

   [*They leave to join* OCTAVIUS.]

*Scene iii. Shortly afterward. A street near the Forum.*

[CINNA *the poet—a different man from* CINNA *the conspirator— is on his way to* CAESAR's *funeral.*]

**2** CINNA. I dreamt tonight¹ that I did feast with Caesar,
   And things unluckily charge my fantasy.²
   I have no will to wander forth of doors,
   Yet something leads me forth.

   [*A group of* PLEBEIANS, *rioting since* ANTONY's *oration, sur- round* CINNA *and begin to question him.*]

**3** 5 FIRST PLEBEIAN. What is your name?

   SECOND PLEBEIAN. Whither are you going?

   THIRD PLEBEIAN. Where do you dwell?

   FOURTH PLEBEIAN. Are you a married man or a bachelor?

   SECOND PLEBEIAN. Answer every man directly.

10 FIRST PLEBEIAN. Ay, and briefly.

   FOURTH PLEBEIAN. Ay, and wisely.

   THIRD PLEBEIAN. Ay, and truly, you were best.

   CINNA. What is my name? Whither am I going? Where do I
      dwell? Am I a married man or a bachelor? Then, to answer
   15   every man directly and briefly, wisely and truly: wisely I
      say, I am a bachelor.

**4** SECOND PLEBEIAN. That's as much as to say, they are fools that
      marry; you'll bear me a bang³ for that, I fear. Proceed
      directly.

20 CINNA. Directly, I am going to Caesar's funeral.

**534** *Drama*

**Side notes:**

47 **Lepidus:** one of Caesar's generals.

48 **upon a wish:** just when he is wanted.

49 **are rid:** have ridden.

50 **Belike:** probably.

1 **tonight:** last night.

2 **unluckily . . . fantasy:** ominously weigh on my imagination.

3 **bear me a bang:** get a thrashing from me.

---

*GUIDED READING*

**LITERAL QUESTIONS**

**1a.** What news does Antony receive? (He hears that Brutus and Cassius have fled like madmen from Rome.)

**2a.** What kinds of questions do the plebeians ask Cinna? (They ask him whom he is, where he is going, and whether he is married.)

**INFERENTIAL QUESTIONS**

**1b.** What is the significance of this news? (It means that for now, at least, the conspiracy seems broken.)

**2b.** What do the plebeians' behavior suggest about conditions in Rome at that moment? (Mob rule seems to prevail.)

FIRST PLEBEIAN. As a friend or an enemy?

CINNA. As a friend.

SECOND PLEBEIAN. That matter is answered directly.

FOURTH PLEBEIAN. For your dwelling, briefly.

25 CINNA. Briefly, I dwell by the Capitol.

THIRD PLEBEIAN. Your name, sir, truly.

CINNA. Truly, my name is Cinna.

FIRST PLEBEIAN. Tear him to pieces! He's a conspirator.

CINNA. I am Cinna the poet! I am Cinna the poet!

30 FOURTH PLEBEIAN. Tear him for his bad verses! Tear him for his bad verses.

CINNA. I am not Cinna the conspirator.

FOURTH PLEBEIAN. It is no matter, his name's Cinna; pluck but his name out of his heart, and turn him going.

35 THIRD PLEBEIAN. Tear him, tear him!

[The PLEBEIANS attack CINNA in a frenzy.]

Come, brands, ho! Firebrands! To Brutus', to Cassius'! Burn all! Some to Decius' house, and some to Casca's; some to Ligarius'! Away, go!

[The PLEBEIANS drag CINNA off with them.]

## STUDY QUESTIONS

### Recalling

1. What excuse do the conspirators use to approach Caesar at the Capitol in Act III, Scene i? How does Caesar react to them?

2. Who stabs Caesar first? Who stabs him last? What does Caesar say as he dies?

3. Why is Cassius reluctant to allow Antony to speak at Caesar's funeral? How does Brutus answer Cassius?

4. At Caesar's funeral in Scene ii, what reasons does Brutus offer for the assassination?

5. What does the crowd say it will do for Brutus?

What does the crowd say about Caesar? Why does the crowd let Antony speak at all?

6. To which qualities and actions of Caesar's does Antony refer in Scene ii, lines 83–95? What does Antony say about the assassins in lines 171–194? Relate the terms of Caesar's will, and describe the crowd's behavior as Antony ends his speech.

### Interpreting

7. Why does Caesar say what he does when Brutus stabs him? Does Caesar's reaction to Brutus' attack make you question Brutus' decision to join the conspiracy? Explain.

*Julius Caesar, Act III, Scene iii*   **535**

- *Scene iii (continued):* Mistaking Cinna for the conspirator of the same name, the plebeians decide to tear him apart.
- When their mistake is disclosed, they attack him anyway because he is a bad poet.
- Then, dragging him along, they set off to burn the plotters' houses.

## 1 COMEDY

At first, the audience thinks that Shakespeare is merely poking fun at bad poets by using the plebeians to suggest that they should be punished for their "sins" against poetry.

## 2 PLOT

The stage directions indicate that the plebeians' mood is ugly; therefore, they may be earnest in their threats against Cinna. The civil strife foreseen by Antony has come to Rome with a vengeance.

## REFLECTING ON ACT III

What technique does Antony use to turn the crowd against the conspirators? (He uses irony, contrasting the conspirators' version of Caesar as a tyrant with the generous Caesar who, in his will, left money to every Roman citizen.)

## STUDY QUESTIONS

1. ask that banished brother of Metellus Cimber be pardoned; he refuses

2. Casca; Brutus; *Et tu, Brute? Then fall Caesar.*

3. fears he will move crowd against them; plans to speak first

4. Caesar was ambitious; his tyranny would make the Romans slaves

5. crown him; calls him a tyrant; promises Brutus to hear him out

6. sympathy for poor, refusal of crown; calls them traitors; has left each man seventy-five drachmas; left public recreation areas; wants to avenge Caesar's death

7. his betrayal shocks Caesar; yes—makes Brutus seem heartless

8. is politically naive; Cassius
9. as true Romans; as traitors; seems at first sincere, later is sarcastic, discredits Brutus
10. *Brutus:* reason; *Antony:* emotion; Antony—knows people are moved more by emotion than reason
11. Antony; lost a capable leader in Caesar without gaining freedom from tyranny
12. Plebeians are easily manipulated, given to mindless violence; giving them power—i.e., democracy—is dangerous. Opinions will vary.

## LITERARY FOCUS

### Monologue
- *lines 71–105:* begins by paying respect to Brutus; ends by discrediting him; incites crowd
- *lines 116–135:* begins reminding Romans of their abandonment of Caesar; ends alluding to his generosity; inspires loyalty
- *lines 166–194:* focuses on details of assassination; builds anger
- *lines 206–226:* pretends he is a less skillful orator than Brutus; builds sympathy; shorter speeches reveal terms of will; playing on grief and arousing anger

### Staging and Theme
1. Stage would be empty except for podium and coffin; Caesar's body would be covered with shroud and accented by lighting.
2. acts humbly; fearful at first; shifts to controlled indignation; grief; feels sincere grief and anger; begins speech at podium; later stands or kneels next to Caesar's body
3. begin by showing some hostility; grudging attention; later peaked interest; some weeping, then stillness; reactions only when called for; near end, building tension; at end, uncontrolled frenzy
4. Caesar's death has brought chaos and horror; littered with trash; Caesar's mantle cast aside; empty coffin askew

8. In Scene i why do you think Brutus brushes aside Cassius' concern about allowing Antony to speak at the funeral? Which man—Brutus or Cassius—proves the better judge of Antony?
9. How should the people view the conspirators and Caesar, according to Brutus' funeral speech? According to Antony's? How does the meaning of the line "Brutus is an honorable man" change during Antony's speech?
10. To what different aspects of human nature do Brutus and Antony appeal? Which man is a better judge of people? Explain.
11. Who has replaced Caesar as the most powerful man in Rome by the end of Act III? Has Rome gained or lost from this change of power?

### Extending
12. On the basis of the plebeians' behavior in Scenes ii and iii, describe Shakespeare's attitude toward democracy. How valid is this attitude? Explain.

## LITERARY FOCUS

### Monologue

A **monologue** is a long speech by a character in a play. Monologues can be spoken to other characters, or they can be **soliloquies**, spoken while the speaker is alone (see page 512). Shakespeare often uses monologues in his plays, since they allow characters to express complicated thoughts or build lengthy arguments.

A monologue is especially satisfying when it builds in excitement and power. For example, Antony's soliloquy at the end of Act III, Scene i, builds in power from his grief-stricken apology to the murdered Caesar. Antony becomes more and more angry in his description of the various horrors that will come to Rome as a result of the assassination. Finally, he reaches the emotional high point of the monologue in his thundering demand for revenge: "Cry 'Havoc,' and let slip the dogs of war...."

### Thinking About Monologue
■ Look again at Antony's funeral oration (Act III, Scene ii), which takes the form of several monologues because it is interrupted several times. Choose one of these monologues and show how it builds in power from beginning to end. With

what ideas and feelings does it begin? With what ideas and feelings does it end? What is its effect on the plebeians?

### Staging and Theme

In Shakespeare's time people seldom read plays; in fact, until relatively recently, most people knew dramas only from seeing them performed live on a stage. Today we have the luxury of reading Shakespeare's plays and reflecting on the richness of their language, feelings, and ideas. However, we can add to our understanding of a Shakespearean play by considering how staging might highlight the play's important developments and themes.

For example, the director of a production of *Julius Caesar* might play up the violent storm in Act I, Scene iii. The director might choose to let the storm flare up occasionally during the first two scenes in Act II in order to draw the audience's attention to the parallels between the night's disturbances, Brutus' inner turmoil, and the coming disruption in the Roman state.

### Thinking About Staging and Theme

Imagine that you are directing a production of *Julius Caesar* and are about to stage Antony's funeral oration. You want the audience to recognize that Caesar's importance to Rome continues after his death. You also want the audience to recognize the signficance of the change in power that takes place during Antony's speech. Suggest ideas for staging the scene, keeping the following questions in mind.
1. In what ways might the placement, lighting, and appearance of Caesar's coffin underline the importance of Caesar even in death?
2. In what ways would Antony speak and move at the beginning of his speech? What emotions would he show throughout the speech? Would he seem sincere? How would he act at the end of the speech?
3. In directing the crowd, how would you emphasize Antony's growing power over his listeners? What physical and vocal reactions would they make to the various parts of Antony's speech?
4. What opinion do you want the audience to have about the future of Rome at the end of the scene? What would the stage look like?

# ACT IV

**Scene i.** ANTONY'*s house in Rome. A year and a half after* CAESAR'*s death.*

[*Rome is now ruled by a triumvirate, a committee of three men, consisting of* MARK ANTONY, OCTAVIUS CAESAR, *and* LEPIDUS. BRUTUS *and* CASSIUS *have fled to Asia Minor and are waging war against the new rulers of Rome. In* ANTONY'*s house* ANTONY, OCTAVIUS, *and* LEPIDUS *meet to make up a list of possible enemies to be killed.*]

ANTONY. These many then shall die; their names are pricked.[1]

OCTAVIUS. Your brother too must die; consent you, Lepidus?

LEPIDUS. I do consent—

OCTAVIUS.           Prick him down, Antony.

LEPIDUS. Upon condition Publius shall not live,
5    Who is your sister's son, Mark Antony.

ANTONY. He shall not live; look, with a spot I damn him.
    But, Lepidus, go you to Caesar's house;
    Fetch the will hither, and we shall determine
    How to cut off some charge in legacies.[2]

10  LEPIDUS. What, shall I find you here?

OCTAVIUS. Or here or at the Capitol.

    [LEPIDUS *leaves.*]

ANTONY. This is a slight unmeritable man,
    Meet to be sent on errands; is it fit,
    The threefold world[3] divided, he should stand
    One of the three to share it?

15  OCTAVIUS.               So you thought him,
    And took his voice who should be pricked to die
    In our black sentence and proscription.[4]

ANTONY. Octavius, I have seen more days than you;
    And though we lay these honors on this man,
20  To ease ourselves of divers sland'rous loads,[5]
    He shall but bear them as the ass bears gold,
    To groan and sweat under the business,
    Either led or driven, as we point the way;
    And having brought our treasure where we will,

1 **pricked:** marked down on a list.

2 **cut...legacies:** reduce the grants made to the people in Caesar's will.

3 **threefold world:** Europe, Africa, and Asia. The triumvirs had divided up among themselves the lands conquered by Rome on these continents.

4 **proscription:** accusation of treason.

5 **divers sland'rous loads:** various deeds likely to bring blame on us.

*Julius Caesar, Act IV, Scene i* **537**

## AT A GLANCE

- *Scene i:* The triumvirate of Antony, Octavius, and Lepidus draws up a list of enemies to be killed.
- Antony suggests that they reduce Caesar's grants to the people.
- Antony belittles Lepidus.

## LITERARY OPTIONS

- characterization
- theme
- comparison and contrast

## THEMATIC OPTIONS

- power as a corrupting influence
- civil order and disorder

## 1 SETTING

The shift in setting from the streets of Rome to Antony's house mirrors the shift in power to Antony.

## 2 CHARACTERIZATION

Antony had incited the crowd by describing these bequests. His plan to reduce them shows that he is opportunistic.

## 3 THEME

This scene demonstrates the corrupting effect of power. Already Antony dislikes sharing power with Lepidus.

## GUIDED READING

### LITERAL QUESTIONS

**1a.** What change does Antony want to make in Caesar's will? (He wants to reduce the grants Caesar made to the people.)

**2a.** What does Octavius say when Antony criticizes Lepidus? (He reminds Antony that he accepted Lepidus as a partner.)

### INFERENTIAL QUESTIONS

**1b.** What does his desire to make this change show about Antony? (It shows that his reading of the will at Caesar's funeral was simply a ploy to gain control.)

**2b.** What seems to be the relationship among the members of the triumvirate? (Antony is the most powerful, but he seems to be in conflict with the other two leaders.)

- *Scene i (continued):* When Antony suggests dropping Lepidus, Octavius objects but says Antony can do as he wishes.
- Antony tells Octavius they must assemble an army immediately.
- *Scene ii:* Brutus and Cassius arrange to meet after a long separation.

**1 CHARACTERIZATION**

Unlike Antony, Octavius does not demean Lepidus but recognizes his value as a human being and as an ally.

**2 STYLE: METAPHOR**

Antony's unflattering comparisons of Lepidus to animals show his contempt for people and his tendency to discard them when they are no longer useful.

**3 TONE**

In speaking with Octavius, Antony assumes a condescending tone. Octavius seems to be biding his time, allowing Antony to have his way for now.

**4 BACKGROUND**

Stage directions indicating conflict between Brutus and Cassius alert the audience to look for signs of tension.

25   Then take we down his load, and turn him off,
     (Like to the empty ass) to shake his ears
     And graze in commons.[6]

**OCTAVIUS.**                    You may do your will;
     But he's a tried and valiant soldier.

ANTONY. So is my horse, Octavius, and for that
30   I do appoint him store of provender.[7]
     It is a creature that I teach to fight,
     To wind,[8] to stop, to run directly on,
     His corporal[9] motion governed by my spirit.
     And, in some taste,[10] is Lepidus but so.
35   He must be taught, and trained, and bid go forth.
     A barren-spirited fellow; one that feeds
     On objects, arts, and imitations,[11]
     Which, out of use and staled by other men,
     Begin his fashion.[12] Do not talk of him
40   But as a property. And now, Octavius,
     Listen great things. Brutus and Cassius
     Are levying powers; we must straight make head.[13]
     Therefore let our alliance be combined,
     Our best friends made, our means stretched;
45   And let us presently go sit in council
     How covert matters may be best disclosed,
     And open perils surest answerèd.

OCTAVIUS. Let us do so; for we are at the stake,[14]
     And bayed about with many enemies;
50   And some that smile have in their hearts, I fear,
     Millions of mischiefs. [*They leave.*]

*Scene ii. A military camp near Sardis in Asia Minor. Several months later.*

[BRUTUS *and* CASSIUS *have been traveling separately with their armies and have not seen each other for some time; a number of differences have sprung up between them. They are joining forces at Sardis. Drums beat as* BRUTUS *stands in front of his tent with his servant* LUCIUS, LUCILIUS *(who is one of his lieutenants), and several other* SOLDIERS. *They are met by* TITINIUS, *a messenger from* CASSIUS, *and* PINDARUS, CASSIUS' *servant, who bring word that* CASSIUS *is on his way to join them.*]

BRUTUS. Stand ho!

LUCILIUS. Give the word, ho! and stand.

**538** *Drama*

6 **commons:** public pasture.

7 **store of provender:** plenty of food.

8 **wind** [wĭnd]: turn.

9 **corporal:** bodily.

10 **taste:** degree.

11 **feeds...imitations:** is most interested in gadgets, artifices, and copies. In other words, he has no substantial or original ideas.
12 **out of use...fashion:** Not only are his interests unworthy, but he also takes them up when they are outmoded.
13 **straight make head:** gather our army right away.

14 **we are at the stake:** We are in the position of a bear tied to a stake and surrounded by snarling dogs. Bearbaiting was a popular sport in Shakespeare's time.

## *GUIDED READING*

**LITERAL QUESTION**

**1a.** What is Octavius' response to Antony's suggestion that they dismiss Lepidus? (He objects but leaves the matter to Antony.)

**INFERENTIAL QUESTION**

**1b.** What does Octavius' response reveal about him? (It reveals that he has his own mind and does not discard people; moderate in both word and deed, he avoids a showdown with Antony over Lepidus.)

BRUTUS. What now, Lucilius, is Cassius near?

LUCILIUS. He is at hand, and Pindarus is come
5   To do you salutation from his master.

**1**

BRUTUS. He greets me well. Your master, Pindarus,
In his own change, or by ill officers,[1]
Hath given me some worthy cause to wish
Things done undone;[2] but if he be at hand,
I shall be satisfied.[3]

10 PINDARUS.          I do not doubt
But that my noble master will appear
Such as he is, full of regard and honor.

BRUTUS. He is not doubted. [*He draws* LUCILIUS *aside.*] A word,
  Lucilius,
How he received you; let me be resolved.

**2** 15 LUCILIUS. With courtesy and with respect enough,
But not with such familiar instances,[4]
Nor with such free and friendly conference
As he hath used of old.

BRUTUS.            Thou hast described
A hot friend cooling. Ever note, Lucilius,
20 When love begins to sicken and decay
It useth an enforced ceremony.

**3** There are no tricks in plain and simple faith;
But hollow[5] men, like horses hot at hand,[6]
Make gallant show and promise of their mettle;
25 But when they should endure the bloody spur,
They fall their crests,[7] and like deceitful jades[8]
Sink in the trial.[9]

[*Faint marching music is heard in the distance.*]

          Comes his army on?

LUCILIUS. They mean this night in Sardis to be quartered;
The greater part, the horse in general,[10]
Are come with Cassius.

[CASSIUS *and some of his* SOLDIERS *enter.*]

30 BRUTUS.           Hark! He is arrived.
March gently on to meet him.

CASSIUS. Stand, ho!

BRUTUS. Stand, ho! Speak the word along.

---

1 **In...officers:** because of some change in his own feelings or through the behavior of unworthy officers.
2 **Things...undone:** that I could undo what I have done.
3 **I...satisfied:** I shall see for myself.

4 **familiar instances:** signs of friendship.

5 **hollow:** insincere.
6 **hot at hand:** spirited at the start.

7 **fall their crests:** droop their proud necks.
8 **jades:** nags.
9 **Sink...trial:** fail when put to the test.

10 **horse in general:** the entire cavalry.

*Julius Caesar, Act IV, Scene ii* **539**

---

AT A GLANCE

- *Scene ii (continued):* Brutus tells Pindarus that Cassius' changed behavior makes him regret what he has done.
- Pindarus reassures Brutus that Cassius will resolve his doubts.
- Cassius arrives.

**1 CHARACTERIZATION**

Perceiving a difference in Cassius' behavior makes Brutus again question the rightness of killing Caesar.

**2 POINT OF VIEW**

Lucilius' independent observation confirms Brutus' own perception that Cassius has cooled his friendship.

**3 STYLE: IMAGE PATTERN**

Like Antony, Brutus contemptuously compares a man to a horse; the point of this comparison is that under stress Cassius has revealed his "hollow" and "deceitful" self.

---

## GUIDED READING

**LITERAL QUESTION**

**1a.** What has caused Brutus to regret his part in the conspiracy? (He has noted some change in Cassius' behavior.)

**INFERENTIAL QUESTION**

**1b.** What does this regret indicate about Brutus? (His conflict about killing Caesar is still unresolved; also, his feelings toward Cassius strongly influenced his decision to join the conspiracy.)

## 1 CHARACTERIZATION

Brutus displays his impetuosity by publicly defending himself against Cassius' accusations.

## 2 READING SKILLS: CONTRAST

In contrast to Cassius, Brutus is cautious and reserved, warning his co-conspirator against any public displays of conflict.

## 3 PLOT: CONFLICT

Cassius and Brutus' differing views of Lucius Pella's conduct indicate the rift between them.

## 4 READING SKILLS: CONTRAST

Whereas Octavius disagreed with Antony but did not criticize him in their meeting, Brutus attacks Cassius for his defense of Lucius.

FIRST SOLDIER. Stand!

35    SECOND SOLDIER. Stand!

THIRD SOLDIER. Stand!

**1**

CASSIUS. Most noble brother, you have done me wrong.

BRUTUS. Judge me, you gods! Wrong I mine enemies?
   And if not so, how should I wrong a brother.

40    CASSIUS. Brutus, this sober form[11] of yours hides wrongs;
   And when you do them—

**2**

BRUTUS. [*Drawing* CASSIUS *aside.*] Cassius, be content.
   Speak your griefs softly; I do know you well.
   Before the eyes of both our armies here
   (Which should perceive nothing but love from us)
45    Let us not wrangle. Bid them move away;
   Then in my tent, Cassius, enlarge your griefs,
   And I will give you audience.[12]

CASSIUS.                  Pindarus,
   Bid our commanders lead their charges off
   A little from this ground.

50    BRUTUS. Lucius, do you the like, and let no man
   Come to our tent till we have done our conference.
   Let Lucilius and Titinius guard our door.

[BRUTUS *and* CASSIUS *go into* BRUTUS' *tent. Everyone else leaves.*]

*Scene iii.* BRUTUS' *tent. A few minutes later.*

[BRUTUS *and* CASSIUS *are meeting privately to air their differences.* CASSIUS *is very angry and wants to discuss accusations that have been made against him.*]

**3**

CASSIUS. That you wronged me doth appear in this:
   You have condemned and noted[1] Lucius Pella
   For taking bribes here of the Sardians;
   Wherein my letters, praying on his side,
5    Because I knew the man, was slighted off.

**4**

BRUTUS. You wronged yourself to write in such a case.

CASSIUS. In such a time as this it is not meet
   That every nice offense should bear his comment.[2]

BRUTUS. Let me tell you, Cassius, you yourself

11   **sober form:** calm manner.

12   **enlarge...audience:** Explain your grievances, and I will listen.

1   **noted:** publicly disgraced.

2   **That...comment:** that each minor breach should be criticized.

**540**   *Drama*

---

## GUIDED READING

### LITERAL QUESTIONS

**1a.** What does Cassius do on his arrival? (He immediately defends himself to Brutus before the soldiers.)

**2a.** About what do Cassius and Brutus disagree? (They disagree about the way to assess Lucius Pella's conduct.)

### INFERENTIAL QUESTIONS

**1b.** What new aspect of Cassius' character does his action reveal? (He is impetuous and indiscreet.)

**2b.** In what way does Cassius' and Brutus' disagreement over Lucius indicate their changed relationship? (Before, they respected each other and were united; now, Brutus has lost respect for Cassius, and they are fighting.)

To sell and mart[3] your offices for gold
To undeservers.

CASSIUS.                    I an itching palm?
You know that you are Brutus that speaks this,
Or, by the gods, this speech were else your last.

15  BRUTUS. The name of Cassius honors this corruption,
And chastisement doth therefore hide his head.[4]

CASSIUS. Chastisement!

BRUTUS. Remember March, the ides of March remember.
Did not great Julius bleed for justice' sake?
20  What villain touched his body, that did stab,
And not for justice? What, shall one of us,
That struck the foremost man of all this world
But for supporting robbers,[5] shall we now
Contaminate our fingers with base bribes,
25  And sell the mighty space of our large honors
For so much trash as may be graspèd thus?
I had rather be a dog, and bay the moon,
Than such a Roman.

CASSIUS.                    Brutus, bait[6] not me;
I'll not endure it. You forget yourself
30  To hedge me in.[7] I am a soldier, I,
Older in practice, abler than yourself
To make conditions.[8]

BRUTUS.                    Go to! You are not, Cassius.

CASSIUS. I am.

BRUTUS. I say you are not.

35  CASSIUS. Urge me no more, I shall forget myself;
Have mind upon your health; tempt me no farther.

BRUTUS. Away, slight man!

CASSIUS. Is't possible?

BRUTUS.                    Hear me, for I will speak.
Must I give way and room to your rash choler?[9]
40  Shall I be frighted when a madman stares?

CASSIUS. O ye gods, ye gods! Must I endure all this?

BRUTUS. All this? Ay, more: fret till your proud heart break.
Go show your slaves how choleric you are,

3  **mart:** peddle.

4  **honors...head:** Because Cassius is linked with this corruption, no one dares punish lesser men who commit these crimes.

5  **robbers:** Brutus now suggests that one of Caesar's offenses was protecting those who robbed under his authority.

6  **bait:** provoke.

7  **hedge me in:** give me orders.

8  **conditions:** regulations

9  **rash choler:** quick temper.

*Julius Caesar, Act IV, Scene iii*  **541**

AT A GLANCE

- *Scene iii (continued):* When Brutus accuses him of being corrupt, Cassius is extremely upset.
- Cassius argues that his greater experience entitles him to set the rules, but Brutus is unimpressed.

**1 THEME**

Brutus' accusation echoes the theme that power inevitably corrupts those who hold it.

**2 SITUATIONAL IRONY**

Brutus ironically contrasts the conspirators' original just intent with their present moral decay.

**3 READING SKILLS: COMPARISON**

Like Antony earlier, Cassius tries to convert his main ally by reminding him of his superior experience.

**4 READING SKILLS: CONTRAST**

Brutus' calm contrasts pointedly with Cassius' rashness and quick temper.

**5 CHARACTERIZATION**

Brutus is openly contemptuous of Cassius now, treating him as if he were a child having a tantrum.

## GUIDED READING

### LITERAL QUESTIONS

**1a.** What does Brutus accuse Cassius of? (He accuses him of being corrupt and selling his offices for money.)

**2a.** What does Cassius warn Brutus that he will do? (He warns Brutus that he will attack him physically.)

### INFERENTIAL QUESTIONS

**1b.** What does Cassius' defense indicate about the truth of the charges? (Because Cassius does not deny them but insists that he can set the rules, Brutus' accusations seem to be based on truth.)

**2b.** What does Cassius' warning show about him? (It shows that he is rash, violent, and childish.)

**1 STYLE: VERBAL IRONY**

Taking a leaf from Antony's book, Brutus ironically refers to Cassius as "noble."

**2 CHARACTERIZATION**

Brutus seems to have discovered that Cassius' brave words disguise a cowardly streak.

**3 STYLE: SITUATIONAL IRONY**

In view of Cassius' past behavior, it might be unwise for anyone to "presume too much" on his "love."

**4 STYLE: FIGURE OF SPEECH**

Brutus' play on words ("I had rather coin my heart") vividly show how much his honesty means to him.

**5 THEME**

Not only has Cassius been corrupt in selling his offices, but he has kept back money from Brutus.

And make your bondmen tremble. Must I budge?

45　Must I observe[10] you? Must I stand and crouch
Under your testy humor?[11] By the gods,
You shall digest the venom of your spleen,[12]
Though it do split you; for, from this day forth,
I'll use you for my mirth, yea, for my laughter,
When you are waspish.

50　CASSIUS.　　　　　　　Is it come to this?

BRUTUS. You say you are a better soldier:
Let it appear so; make your vaunting[13] true,
And it shall please me well: For mine own part,
I shall be glad to learn of noble men.

55　CASSIUS. You wrong me every way; you wrong me, Brutus;
I said, an elder soldier, not a better.
Did I say, better?

BRUTUS.　　　　　If you did, I care not.

CASSIUS. When Caesar lived, he durst[14] not thus have moved[15]
me.

BRUTUS. Peace, peace, you durst not so have tempted him.

60　CASSIUS. I durst not?

BRUTUS. No.

CASSIUS. What? Durst not tempt him?

BRUTUS.　　　　　　　　　　For your life you durst
not.

CASSIUS. Do not presume too much upon my love;
I may do that I shall be sorry for.

65　BRUTUS. You have done that you should be sorry for.
There is no terror, Cassius, in your threats;
For I am armed so strong in honesty
That they pass by me as the idle wind,
Which I respect not. I did send to you

70　For certain sums of gold, which you denied me;
For I can raise no money by vile means.
By heaven, I had rather coin my heart
And drop my blood for drachmas than to wring
From the hard hands of peasants their vile trash[16]

75　By any indirection.[17] I did send
To you for gold to pay my legions,
Which you denied me. Was that done like Cassius?

10 **observe:** defer to.

11 **testy humor:** irritable mood.

12 **digest...spleen:** swallow the poison of your own anger. Anger was thought to be located in the spleen.

13 **vaunting:** boasting. Brutus tells Cassius to act like the seasoned leader he claims to be.

14 **durst:** dared.
15 **moved:** provoked.

16 **vile trash:** pathetic sums of money.
17 **indirection:** dishonest means.

---

## GUIDED READING

**LITERAL QUESTIONS**

**1a.** What does Cassius' say in citing Caesar? (He says that Caesar would not have dared to treat him the way Brutus is now.)

**2a.** What has Cassius refused to do? (He has refused to send Brutus any money to pay his legions.)

**INFERENTIAL QUESTIONS**

**1b.** In his reply, what is Brutus really accusing Cassius of? (He is accusing Cassius of being a coward.)

**2b.** What is the difference between Brutus and Cassius in regard to money? (Brutus is honest, whereas Cassius is corrupt.)

Should I have answered Caius Cassius so?
When Marcus Brutus grows so covetous
80  To lock such rascal counters[18] from his friends,      18  **rascal counters:** grubby coins.
Be ready, gods, with all your thunderbolts,
Dash him to pieces!

CASSIUS.                    I denied you not.

BRUTUS. You did.

CASSIUS.            I did not. He was but a fool
That brought my answer back. Brutus hath rived[19] my heart.      19  **rived:** broken.
85  A friend should bear his friend's infirmities;
But Brutus makes mine greater than they are.

BRUTUS. I do not, till you practice them on me.

CASSIUS. You love me not.

BRUTUS.                    I do not like your faults.

CASSIUS. A friendly eye could never see such faults.

90  BRUTUS. A flatterer's would not, though they do appear
As huge as high Olympus.

CASSIUS. Come, Antony, and young Octavius, come,
Revenge yourselves alone on Cassius,
For Cassius is aweary of the world:
95  Hated by one he loves; braved[20] by his brother;      20  **braved:** taunted.
Checked like a bondman;[21] all his faults observed,      21  **Checked...bondman:** scolded like a slave.
Set in a notebook, learned and conned by rote[22]      22  **conned by rote:** memorized.
To cast into my teeth. O, I could weep
My spirit from mine eyes!

[CASSIUS *takes out his dagger.*]

                    There is my dagger,
100  And here my naked breast; within, a heart
Dearer than Pluto's mine,[23] richer than gold;      23  **Pluto's mine:** Pluto was the Greek god of the underworld and ruled all the riches of the earth's mines.
If that thou be'st a Roman, take it forth.
I, that denied thee gold, will give my heart.
Strike as thou didst at Caesar; for I know,
105  When thou didst hate him worst, thou lovedst him better
Than ever thou lovedst Cassius.

BRUTUS.                    Sheathe your dagger.
Be angry when you will, it shall have scope.[24]      24  **scope:** free play.
Do what you will, dishonor shall be humor.[25]      25  **dishonor...humor:** Your insults shall be taken as arising from a bad mood.
O Cassius, you are yokèd with a lamb
110  That carries anger as the flint bears fire,

*Julius Caesar, Act IV, Scene iii*  **543**

AT A GLANCE

- *Scene iii (continued):* Cassius says that his messenger misinformed Brutus about the money.
- Cassius says Brutus does not love him.
- When Cassius asks Brutus to kill him, Brutus refuses.

**1 PLOT: CONFLICT**

Cassius' weak excuse gets the reception it deserves from Brutus: frank disbelief.

**2 READING SKILLS: CONTRAST**

Brutus and Cassius have differing ideas about the nature of friendship: Cassius sees it as uncritical, whereas Brutus says that flattery is hardly love.

**3 CONFLICT**

Cassius' melodramatic threat seems to have eased the tension between the two men.

## GUIDED READING

### LITERAL QUESTIONS

**1a.** What explanation does Cassius give about the money for Brutus' legions? (He says that the messenger misinformed Brutus; in other words, Cassius did not refuse Brutus' request.)

**2a.** What does Cassius ask Brutus to do? (He asks Brutus to take his dagger and stab him in the heart.)

### INFERENTIAL QUESTIONS

**1b.** What does this explanation reveal about Cassius? (He is probably desperate enough to lie in order to regain Brutus' good opinion.)

**2b.** What does his request reveal about Cassius? (It reveals him to be self-dramatizing, desperate for Brutus' friendship, daring, impetuous, and perhaps hysterical.)

AT A GLANCE

- *Scene iii (continued):* Cassius and Brutus end their dispute and shake hands.
- A poet, having gotten past the guards, entreats Brutus and Cassius to be loving friends.
- Brutus and Cassius mock him.

**1 CONFLICT**

On the surface, Brutus and Cassius seem to have completely resolved their conflict.

**2 CHARACTERIZATION**

His abject apology suggests that Brutus' good opinion may be more important to Cassius than Cassius' good opinion is to Brutus.

**3 READING SKILL: COMPARISON**

In this play poets have a hard time; first, the plebeians physically attack Cinna the poet, and now Brutus and Cassius mock another poet.

Who, much enforcèd,[26] shows a hasty spark,
And straight[27] is cold again.

**1** CASSIUS. [*Putting his dagger back into its sheath.*] Hath Cassius lived
To be but mirth and laughter to his Brutus
When grief and blood ill-tempered vexeth him?

115 BRUTUS. When I spoke that, I was ill-tempered too.

CASSIUS. Do you confess so much? Give me your hand.

BRUTUS. And my heart too. [*They clasp hands.*]

CASSIUS.                          O Brutus!

BRUTUS.                                   What's the matter?

**2** CASSIUS. Have not you love enough to bear with me
When that rash humor which my mother gave me
Makes me forgetful?

120 BRUTUS.                      Yes, Cassius, and from henceforth,
When you are over-earnest with your Brutus,
He'll think your mother chides,[28] and leave you so.

[*A* POET *struggles to get into the tent past the guards. He is followed closely by* LUCILIUS, TITINIUS, *and* LUCIUS.]

POET. Let me go in to see the generals;
There is some grudge between 'em; 'tis not meet
125   They be alone.

LUCILIUS. You shall not come to them.

POET. Nothing but death shall stay me.

CASSIUS. How now. What's the matter?

POET. For shame, you generals! What do you mean?
130   Love, and be friends, as two such men should be;
For I have seen more years, I'm sure, than ye.

**3** CASSIUS. Ha, ha! How vilely doth this cynic[29] rhyme!

BRUTUS. Get you hence, sirrah! Saucy fellow, hence!

CASSIUS. Bear with him, Brutus, 'tis his fashion.

135 BRUTUS. I'll know his humor when he knows his time.[30]
What should the wars do with these jigging fools?
Companion,[31] hence!

CASSIUS.                     Away, away, be gone! [*The* POET *leaves.*]

**544**   *Drama*

26 **enforcèd:** irritated.
27 **straight:** right away.

28 **your mother chides:** Your inherited bad temper shows itself.

29 **cynic:** rude fellow.

30 **I'll...time:** I'll laugh at his quirks when he learns the right time to give vent to them.
31 **Companion:** fellow, meant contemptuously.

## GUIDED READING

**LITERAL QUESTION**

**1a.** For what does Cassius apologize to Brutus? (He apologizes for his bad temper and rashness.)

**INFERENTIAL QUESTION**

**1b.** What does Cassius' way of apologizing show about him? (It shows that he has insight into his own weaknesses and that he wants Brutus' approval—perhaps more than Brutus wants his.)

BRUTUS. Lucilius and Titinius, bid the commanders
Prepare to lodge their companies tonight.

140 CASSIUS. And come yourselves, and bring Messala with you
Immediately to us.

[LUCILIUS *and* TITINIUS *leave*.]

BRUTUS.                     Lucius, a bowl of wine.

[LUCIUS *goes to another part of the tent*.]

CASSIUS. I did not think you could have been so angry.

BRUTUS. O Cassius, I am sick of many griefs.

**1** CASSIUS. Of your philosophy[32] you make no use,
145   If you give place to accidental evils.

BRUTUS. No man bears sorrow better. Portia is dead.

CASSIUS. Ha? Portia?

BRUTUS. She is dead.

**2** CASSIUS. How scaped I killing when I crossed you so?
150   O insupportable and touching loss!
Upon what sickness?

BRUTUS.                     Impatient of my absence,
And grief that young Octavius with Mark Antony
Have made themselves so strong—for with her death
That tidings came[33]—with this she fell distract,
155   And (her attendants absent) swallowed fire.[34]

CASSIUS. And died so?

BRUTUS.                     Even so.

CASSIUS.                     O ye immortal gods!

[LUCIUS *returns with wine and candles*.]

**3** BRUTUS. Speak no more of her. Give me a bowl of wine.
In this I bury all unkindness, Cassius. [BRUTUS *drinks*.]

CASSIUS. My heart is thirsty for that noble pledge.
160   Fill, Lucius, till the wine o'erswell the cup;
I cannot drink too much of Brutus' love.

[CASSIUS *drinks*. LUCIUS *leaves them as* TITINIUS *and* MESSALA
*enter the tent*.]

BRUTUS. Come in, Titinius! Welcome, good Messala.
Now sit we close about this taper here,
And call in question our necessities.[35]

32 **your philosophy:** Brutus is a Stoic, one who restrains his feelings and resigns himself to the inevitable.

33 **with...came:** Brutus learned of the strength of his enemies at the same time that he learned of Portia's death.
34 **fire:** hot coals.

35 **call...necessities:** discuss what we must do.

*Julius Caesar, Act IV, Scene iii*   **545**

AT A GLANCE

- *Scene iii (continued):* When Brutus confesses to Cassius that he is sick with grief, Cassius tells him to make better use of his Stoic philosophy.
- Brutus reveals that Portia has committed suicide.

**1 CHARACTERIZATION**

The relative calm that has characterized Brutus throughout the play is not only a matter of temperament but of philosophy as well.

**2 CONTRAST**

Cassius' reaction to Portia's death, genuine and more emotional than Brutus', shows an appealing warmth in his character.

**3 CHARACTERIZATION**

Nowhere is Brutus' restraint more apparent than in the one succinct sentence wherein he "disposes" of the wife he has loved.

## GUIDED READING

### LITERAL QUESTIONS

**1a.** What explanation for his mood does Brutus give Cassius? (He reveals that Portia has committed suicide.)

**2a.** What is Brutus' motive in drinking the wine? (He drinks it as a pledge to bury all his unkind thoughts about Cassius.)

### INFERENTIAL QUESTIONS

**1b.** What does Brutus' way of revealing this information show about him? (It shows his Stoic acceptance of fate and his self-control.)

**2b.** What does Cassius' response to Brutus' gesture with the wine reveal about him? (It reveals his warmth, particularly his affection for Brutus.)

Nicholas Pennell as Cassius. Simon Bradbury as Lucius. Len Cariou. Photo courtesy of Stratford Festival, Canada, 1982.

**546** *Drama*

**1**

**CASSIUS.** Portia, art thou gone?

165  **BRUTUS.**                    No more, I pray you.
Messala, I have here receivèd letters
That young Octavius and Mark Antony
Come down upon us with a mighty power,
Bending their expedition toward Philippi.[36]

36 **Philippi** [fə lip ′ī]: city in northern Greece.
37 **tenure:** basic meaning.

170  **MESSALA.** Myself have letters of the selfsame tenure.[37]

**BRUTUS.** With what addition?

**MESSALA.** That by proscription and bills of outlawry
Octavius, Antony, and Lepidus
Have put to death an hundred senators.

**2**  175  **BRUTUS.** Therein our letters do not well agree.
Mine speak of seventy senators that died
By their proscriptions, Cicero being one.

**CASSIUS.** Cicero one?

**MESSALA.**              Cicero is dead,
And by that order of proscription.
180  Had you your letters from your wife, my lord?

**BRUTUS.** No, Messala.

**MESSALA.** Nor nothing in your letters writ of her?

**BRUTUS.** Nothing, Messala.

**MESSALA.**                    That methinks is strange.

**BRUTUS.** Why ask you? Hear you aught of her in yours?

185  **MESSALA.** No, my lord.

**3**  **BRUTUS.** Now as you are a Roman, tell me true.

**MESSALA.** Then like a Roman bear the truth I tell,
For certain she is dead, and by strange manner.

**BRUTUS.** Why, farewell, Portia. We must die, Messala.
190  With meditating that she must die once,[38]
I have the patience to endure it now.

38 **once:** at some time.

**MESSALA.** Even so great men great losses should endure.

**CASSIUS.** I have as much of this in art[39] as you,
But yet my nature could not bear it so.

39 **in art:** in theory. Cassius also believes in Stoicism, but he cannot practice it as Brutus does.

195  **BRUTUS.** Well, to our work alive.[40] What do you think
Of marching to Philippi presently?

40 **alive:** at hand; also, of the living.

*Julius Caesar, Act IV, Scene iii* **547**

---

**AT A GLANCE**

■ *Scene iii (continued):* Brutus and Messala have heard that many senators, including Cicero, have been executed and that the enemy army moves toward Philippi.

■ Unaware that he already knows about Portia, Messala informs Brutus of her death.

**1** **READING SKILLS: CONTRAST**

Whereas Cassius is still upset about Portia, Brutus is determined to get on with other urgent matters.

**2** **THEME**

Here Shakespeare reminds us of the extent of the civil strife in Rome. Even the renowned Cicero—the great orator who mocked Caesar's superstitions in Act I—has been executed.

**3** **CHARACTERIZATION**

Perhaps Brutus' motive for hiding his prior knowledge of Portia's death from Messala is to maintain control in front of the officers.

---

## GUIDED READING

### LITERAL QUESTION

**1a.** What news have Messala and Brutus received? (They have heard that Antony and Octavius' legions are heading toward Philippi and that the triumvirs have executed many senators, including Cicero.)

### INFERENTIAL QUESTION

**1b.** What does the news concerning the senators suggest about the triumvirs? (It suggests that they have not hesitated to shed blood in cementing or expanding their power.)

- *Scene iii (continued):* Brutus and Cassius disagree about military strategy.
- Cassius counsels waiting for the triumvirs' forces to come to them.
- Brutus says they should go forward and wage battle at Philippi.
- Cassius defers to Brutus.

**1 CONFLICT**

Initially, Brutus and Cassius' disagreement over tactics seems to be based on differing strategies only.

**2 CHARACTERIZATION**

When Brutus cuts off his response, Cassius submits once again to Brutus. Even after his earlier mistakes, Brutus has not yet learned that Cassius is the better strategist.

**3 RESPONSE JOURNAL**

Ask students to state in their journals whether or not they agree with Brutus, and have them explain why.

CASSIUS. I do not think it good.

BRUTUS.                Your reason?

CASSIUS.                This it is:

    'Tis better that the enemy seek us;
    So shall he waste his means, weary his soldiers,   200
    Doing himself offense, whilst we, lying still,
    Are full of rest, defense, and nimbleness.

BRUTUS. Good reasons must of force give place to better.
    The people 'twixt Philippi and this ground
    Do stand but in a forced affection;[41]
    For they have grudged us contribution.   205
    The enemy, marching along by them,
    By them shall make a fuller number up,
    Come on refreshed, new-added and encouraged;
    From which advantage shall we cut him off
    If at Philippi we do face him there,   210
    These people at our back.

CASSIUS.              Hear me, good brother.

BRUTUS. Under your pardon.[42] You must note beside
    That we have tried the utmost of our friends,
    Our legions are brimful, our cause is ripe.
    The enemy increaseth every day;   215
    We, at the height, are ready to decline.
    There is a tide in the affairs of men
    Which, taken at the flood, leads on to fortune;
    Omitted, all the voyage of their life
    Is bound in shallows and in miseries.   220
    On such a full sea are we now afloat,
    And we must take the current when it serves,
    Or lose our ventures.

CASSIUS.         Then, with your will,[43] go on;
    We'll along ourselves and meet them at Philippi.

BRUTUS. The deep of night is crept upon our talk,   225
    And nature must obey necessity,
    Which we will niggard[44] with a little rest.
    There is no more to say?

CASSIUS.           No more. Good night.
    Early tomorrow will we rise and hence.

    [LUCIUS *returns.*]

**41 Do...affection:** are not our true friends.

**42 Under your pardon:** By your leave, let me continue.

**43 with your will:** since it is your will to do this.

**44 niggard:** satisfy only reluctantly.

**548**  *Drama*

---

## GUIDED READING

**LITERAL QUESTIONS**

**1a.** What different tactics do Brutus and Cassius suggest to defeat the enemy? (Brutus wants to meet the enemy at Philippi, whereas Cassius wants to stay put and have the enemy seek them out.)

**2a.** What argument convinces Cassius to follow Brutus' plan? (He is persuaded by Brutus' argument that there is a tide in the affairs of men which, if taken, leads to fortune.)

**INFERENTIAL QUESTIONS**

**1b.** What do the differences in strategy suggest about the differences between Brutus and Cassius? (It suggests that Cassius is the more cautious and less aggressive tactician.)

**2b.** What does Cassius' decision to follow Brutus' plan suggest about their relationship? (Brutus is the leader and Cassius the follower.)

BRUTUS. Lucius, my gown. [LUCIUS *leaves*.]

230                             Farewell, good Messala.
Good night, Titinius. Noble, noble Cassius,
Good night, and good repose.

CASSIUS.                             O my dear brother,
This was an ill beginning of the night.
Never come such division 'tween our souls!
Let it not, Brutus.

[LUCIUS *returns with the dressing gown*.]

235  BRUTUS.                   Everything is well.

CASSIUS. Good night, my lord.

BRUTUS.                         Good night, good brother.

TITINIUS AND MESSALA. Good night, Lord Brutus.

BRUTUS.                                 Farewell,
every one.

[CASSIUS, TITINIUS, *and* MESSALA *leave*.]

Give me the gown. Where is thy instrument?

LUCIUS. Here in the tent.

BRUTUS.                   What, thou speak'st drowsily?
240   Poor knave,[45] I blame thee not; thou art o'erwatched.[46]
Call Claudius and some other of my men;
I'll have them sleep on cushions in my tent.

LUCIUS. Varro and Claudius!

[*The soldiers* VARRO *and* CLAUDIUS *enter the tent*.]

VARRO. Calls my lord?

245  BRUTUS. I pray you, sirs, lie in my tent and sleep.
It may be I shall raise[47] you by and by
On business to my brother Cassius.

VARRO. So please you, we will stand and watch your pleasure.[48]

BRUTUS. I will not have it so; lie down, good sirs;
250   It may be I shall otherwise bethink me.

[VARRO *and* CLAUDIUS *lie down*.]

Look, Lucius, here's the book I sought for so;
I put it in the pocket of my gown.

LUCIUS. I was sure your lordship did not give it me.

---

45 **knave:** lad.
46 **o'erwatched:** tired with waiting up.

47 **raise:** rouse.

48 **watch your pleasure:** wait your command.

*Julius Caesar, Act IV, Scene iii*   **549**

---

AT A GLANCE

- *Scene iii (continued):* Brutus and Cassius bid each other good night.
- Brutus asks some of his men to sleep in his tent.

**1 READING SKILLS: CONTRAST**

Cassius is unable to let go of his concern over their previous disagreement, whereas Brutus says nothing about it.

**2 CHARACTERIZATION**

Brutus' consideration of his servant shows the gentle side of his nature.

**3 CONFLICT**

Brutus' instructions to his men hint at the possibility that his smooth words to Cassius earlier may have hidden some mistrust.

---

## GUIDED READING

### LITERAL QUESTION

**1a.** What is Cassius still disturbed about? (He is still disturbed by his previous disagreement with Brutus.)

### INFERENTIAL QUESTION

**1b.** What does his continuing concern about these matters reveal about Cassius? (It reveals that he may feel guilty.)

- *Scene iii (continued):* While he is playing and singing for Brutus, Lucius falls asleep.
- As Brutus sits down to read, Caesar's ghost appears before him.
- The ghost warns Brutus that they will meet at Philippi.

**1 CHARACTERIZATION**

Thinking about the possibility of his own death kindles Brutus' tenderness toward his servant.

**2 STYLE: FIGURE OF SPEECH**

Brutus' allusion to "murd'rous slumber" makes the audience aware of the sleep of death that may await him at Philippi.

**3 PLOT: FORESHADOWING**

Caesar's ghost foretells Brutus' death in the battle he has just persuaded Cassius to undertake.

---

BRUTUS. Bear with me, good boy, I am much forgetful.
255    Canst thou hold up thy heavy eyes awhile,
   And touch thy instrument a strain or two?

LUCIUS. Ay, my lord, an't[49] please you.         49 **an't:** if it.

BRUTUS.                         It does, my boy.
   I trouble thee too much, but thou are willing.

LUCIUS. It is my duty, sir.

260 BRUTUS. I should not urge thy duty past thy might;
   I know young bloods look for a time of rest.

LUCIUS. I have slept, my lord, already.

**1** BRUTUS. It was well done, and thou shalt sleep again;
   I will not hold thee long. If I do live,
265    I will be good to thee.

[*Only half-awake,* LUCIUS *begins to play and sing. He drifts off to sleep in the middle of his song.*]

**2** This is a sleepy tune. O murd'rous slumber!
   Layest thou thy leaden mace[50] upon my boy,      50 **mace:** club.
   That plays thee music? Gentle knave, good night;
   I will not do thee so much wrong to wake thee.
270    If thou dost nod, thou break'st thy instrument;
   I'll take it from thee; and, good boy, good night.

[BRUTUS *removes the lute without waking* LUCIUS.]

Let me see, let me see; is not the leaf turned down
Where I left reading? Here it is, I think.

[*As* BRUTUS *sits down to read, the* GHOST OF CAESAR *appears near the flickering candle.*]

How ill this taper burns.[51] Ha! Who comes here?    51 **ill...burns:** It was believed that
275    I think it is the weakness of mine eyes       a candle flickered when a ghost
   That shapes this monstrous apparition.         appeared.
   It comes upon me. Art thou anything?
   Art thou some god, some angel, or some devil,
   That mak'st my blood cold, and my hair to stare?[52]    52 **stare:** stand on end.

**3** 280 Speak to me what thou art.

GHOST. Thy evil spirit, Brutus.

BRUTUS.                  Why com'st thou?

GHOST. To tell thee thou shalt see me at Philippi.

**550** *Drama*

---

## GUIDED READING

### LITERAL QUESTIONS

**1a.** What happens to Lucius as he is playing and singing to Brutus? (Lucius falls asleep.)

**2a.** Who does the ghost say he is? (He says that he is Brutus' evil spirit.)

### INFERENTIAL QUESTIONS

**1b.** What does Brutus' response to Lucius show about him? (It shows that he can be tender to the young and the inferior.)

**2b.** In what way is the ghost what he says he is? (He might represent the "evil" part of Brutus, the part that killed Caesar. He might also represent Brutus' own fears or foreboding.)

BRUTUS. Well; then I shall see thee again?

GHOST. Ay, at Philippi.

285 BRUTUS. Why, I will see thee at Philippi then.

[*The* GHOST *disappears.*]

Now I have taken heart thou vanishest.
Ill spirit, I would hold more talk with thee.
Boy! Lucius! Varro! Claudius! Sirs, awake!
Claudius!

[*Only* LUCIUS *wakes, as the* SOLDIERS *continue to sleep.*]

290 LUCIUS. The strings, my lord, are false.[53]

53 **false:** out of tune.

BRUTUS. He thinks he still is at his instrument.
Lucius, awake!

LUCIUS. My lord?

BRUTUS. Didst thou dream, Lucius, that thou so criedst out?

295 LUCIUS. My lord, I do not know that I did cry.

BRUTUS. Yes, that thou didst. Didst thou see anything?

LUCIUS. Nothing, my lord.

BRUTUS. Sleep again, Lucius. Sirrah Claudius!

[*Shaking* CLAUDIUS *and then* VARRO.] Fellow thou, awake!

300 VARRO. My lord?

CLAUDIUS. My lord?

BRUTUS. Why did you so cry out, sirs, in your sleep?

BOTH. Did we, my lord?

BRUTUS.                    Ay. Saw you anything?

VARRO. No, my lord, I saw nothing.

CLAUDIUS.                    Nor I, my lord.

305 BRUTUS. Go and commend me to my brother Cassius;
Bid him set on his pow'rs betimes before,[54]
And we will follow.

54 **set...before:** start his troops moving early, ahead of ours.

BOTH.                    It shall be done, my lord.

[*The two* SOLDIERS *leave, and* BRUTUS *retires.*]

*Julius Caesar, Act IV, Scene iii*   **551**

**1 PLOT: FORESHADOWING**

Brutus takes up the challenge issued by Caesar's ghost, saying, in effect, that he is ready to meet him at Philippi.

**2 STYLE: SYMBOLISM**

When Lucius comments that the lute strings are out of tune, the audience may recognize that the whole night has been warped, from the quarrel between Brutus and Cassius to the appearance of the ghost.

**3 CHARACTERIZATION**

Brutus' repeated questioning, first of Lucius, then of his officers, suggests that he is agitated. He does not voice his concerns directly, however.

**REFLECTING ON ACT IV**

In what ways do Antony and Cassius show that power has corrupted them? (Antony has removed Lepidus from the triumvirate and executed many senators, including Cicero; Cassius has sold offices and has refused Brutus money to pay his soldiers.)

## GUIDED READING

**LITERAL QUESTIONS**

**1a.** What is Brutus' response to the ghost? (He accepts the ghost's challenge and says that they will meet at Philippi.)

**2a.** What does Brutus do after the ghost disappears? (He asks Lucius and his officers if they have heard anything.)

**INFERENTIAL QUESTIONS**

**1b.** What does Brutus' response to the ghost show about him? (It shows that he is brave and accepts his destiny, whatever it may be.)

**2b.** What do his actions after the ghost disappears reveal about Brutus? (They reveal that he is probably more frightened or agitated by the ghost's appearance than he initially showed.)

**1.** He wants to reduce grants. Antony says he is incompetent; Octavius says he is a valiant soldier. He is older, more experienced.

**2.** thinks he has wronged him; is accused of taking bribes; denies

**3.** has been a soldier longer; Cassius refused him gold to pay his troops; says message delivered incorrectly

**4.** She has committed suicide. He is upset; reacts emotionally. Brutus does not show his feelings; Cassius does.

**5.** Cassius wants to wait for enemy, let them deplete their supplies; Brutus fears erosion of support, wants to march to Philippi; march to Philippi

**6.** He will see him at Philippi. He is startled.

**7.** Antony seems infatuated with power. Antony uses people and discards them. Octavius is more decent. Antony dominates; Octavius may be more able.

**8.** They are opposite in nature. Brutus: idealistic; placid; Cassius: pragmatic; emotional. *Cassius:* seems corrupt; melodramatic; childish; his being hurt by Brutus' rejection makes him appealing; *Brutus:* seems self-righteous; childish; ability to lose temper makes him appealing

**9.** eerie quality; sense of doom

**10.** After disagreeing, Cassius concedes to Brutus. Antony and Octavius will probably win.

**11.** *Similarities:* Both discuss strategy; participants wrangle; corruption on both sides.
*Differences:* Triumvirs list who is to be killed; Brutus and Cassius quarrel about friendship; neither seems fit to rule.

**12.** State becomes unstable. New leaders may become tyrannical. Power is a corrupting force.

## STUDY QUESTIONS

### Recalling

1. As Act IV begins, what does Antony want to do about Caesar's will? What difference in opinion develops between Antony and Octavius over Lepidus? Why does Antony say he is a better judge than Octavius?

2. Why is Cassius angry with Brutus in Scene ii? In Scene iii, what specific charges does Brutus say have been raised against Cassius? What does Cassius say in his own defense?

3. According to Cassius, why is he better suited than Brutus to govern the conduct of his men? What grievance does Brutus bring up in Scene iii, lines 69–83? What is Cassius' answer?

4. What news has Brutus received about Portia? How does Cassius respond to this information? What contrast does he draw between himself and Brutus regarding Stoicism?

5. Explain the differing strategies of Brutus and Cassius for the coming battle against Octavius and Antony. What do they decide to do?

6. What does Caesar's ghost tell Brutus? Describe Brutus' reaction to the ghost.

### Interpreting

7. What new qualities does Antony reveal in Scene i? In what ways do Antony and Octavius differ as persons? Which dominates the triumvirate? Which seems the abler leader?

8. Based on what we have seen of their natures in the play, why is it not surprising that Brutus and Cassius are quarreling with each other? What appealing and unappealing qualities in each man are revealed in Scene iii? Whom do you find more sympathetic, and why?

9. What does the appearance of Caesar's ghost add to the mood of Scene iii?

10. In what way is the decision to go to Philippi similar to decisions made by the conspirators in Act II, Scene i, and Act III, Scene i? Given the outcomes of those other decisions, as well as the words of Caesar's ghost, which side do you think will win at Philippi?

11. In Act IV Shakespeare presents two parallel meetings, one among the triumvirs and the other between Brutus and Cassius. What similarities and differences can you find between these two meetings? Do you think either group seems more capable of ruling Rome than Caesar was? Explain.

### Extending

12. Brutus killed Caesar in order to protect Rome from one man's tyranny. What do the activities of the triumvirs show about the negative consequences of removing a strong leader like Caesar? In the portrayal of Mark Antony in Act IV, Scene i, what point does Shakespeare make about the effect of political power on those who hold it?

# ACT V

**Scene i.** *The Plains of Philippi in Greece. A few weeks later.*

[OCTAVIUS, ANTONY, *and their* ARMY *await the advancing* ARMY *of* BRUTUS *and* CASSIUS. *The triumvirs are surprised and pleased that the enemy has left the advantage of the high ground to come to them.*]

OCTAVIUS. Now, Antony, our hopes are answerèd;
  You said the enemy would not come down,
  But keep the hills and upper regions.
  It proves not so; their battles[1] are at hand;
5  They mean to warn[2] us at Philippi here,
  Answering before we do demand of them.

ANTONY. Tut, I am in their bosoms,[3] and I know
  Wherefore they do it. They could be content
  To visit other places, and come down
10  With fearful[4] bravery, thinking by this face[5]
  To fasten in our thoughts that they have courage;
  But 'tis not so.

[*A* MESSENGER *hurries from the camp of* BRUTUS *and* CASSIUS.]

MESSENGER.     Prepare you, generals,
  The enemy comes on in gallant show;
  Their bloody sign[6] of battle is hung out,
15  And something to be done immediately.

ANTONY. Octavius, lead your battle softly[7] on
  Upon the left hand of the even field.

OCTAVIUS. Upon the right hand I; keep thou the left.

ANTONY. Why do you cross me in this exigent?[8]

20 OCTAVIUS. I do not cross you; but I will do so.

[*Marching music and a drum announce the appearance of* BRUTUS *and* CASSIUS *with their* ARMY, *including* LUCILIUS, TITINIUS, *and* MESSALA, *among others. The two* ARMIES *stand opposite each other.*]

BRUTUS. They stand, and would have parley.

CASSIUS. Stand fast, Titinius, we must out and talk.

[CASSIUS *halts the men. He and* BRUTUS *walk toward* ANTONY *and* OCTAVIUS.]

*Julius Caesar, Act V, Scene i* **553**

---

1 **battles:** armies.

2 **warn:** challenge.

3 **am in their bosoms:** can read their thoughts.

4 **fearful:** both terrifying and timid. Antony dismisses the enemy's brave appearance as a front.
5 **face:** show.

6 **bloody sign:** A red flag was flown from the tent of a Roman general to signal the start of battle.

7 **softly:** slowly.

8 **exigent:** moment of crisis.

---

## AT A GLANCE

- *Scene i:* On the plains of Philippi, Octavius and Antony see Brutus and Cassius advancing.
- Antony and Octavius devise their battle plan.

## LITERARY OPTIONS

- tragedy
- plot: structure
- conflict

## THEMATIC OPTIONS

- instability of human nature
- restoring order
- idealism vs. pragmatism

## 1 SETTING

The stage directions indicate that Brutus and Cassius may have already made a strategic blunder by ceding the high ground to their enemies.

## 2 CHARACTERIZATION

Antony's dismissal of enemy tactics illustrates his supreme self-confidence.

## 3 CONFLICT

Evidently, tension exists between Antony and Octavius, and even here it manifests itself.

---

## GUIDED READING

### LITERAL QUESTIONS

**1a.** What does the enemy do that Antony dismisses as a "show" of bravery? (They cede the advantage of the high ground to Antony and Octavius.)

**2a.** About what do Antony and Octavius disagree? (Antony tells Octavius to lead his troops on the left side of the field, but Octavius says he will lead them on the right.)

### INFERENTIAL QUESTIONS

**1b.** What does Antony's reaction indicate about his state of mind? (It indicates that he is extremely self-confident.)

**2b.** What does the disagreement suggest about their relationship? (It suggests that they might be fighting each other over who dominates.)

**1 CHARACTERIZATION**

However Antony has changed, his passionate anger at the conspirators' murder of Caesar remains unchecked; here he compares them to wild and "low" animals.

**2 PLOT: FORESHADOWING**

Octavius' reminder that he is "another Caesar" raises the possibility that in the future he may also achieve Caesar's dominance.

---

OCTAVIUS. Mark Antony, shall we give sign of battle?

ANTONY. No, Caesar, we will answer on their charge.
25   Make forth; the generals would have some words.

OCTAVIUS. Stir not until the signal.

BRUTUS. Words before blows; is it so, countrymen?

OCTAVIUS. Not that we love words better, as you do.

BRUTUS. Good words are better than bad strokes, Octavius.

30 ANTONY. In your bad strokes, Brutus, you give good words;
     Witness the hole you made in Caesar's heart,
     Crying "Long live! Hail, Caesar!"

CASSIUS.                                    Antony,
     The posture of your blows are yet unknown;
     But for your words, they rob the Hybla[9] bees,
     And leave them honeyless.

35 ANTONY.                             Not stingless too.

BRUTUS. O, yes, and soundless too;
     For you have stol'n their buzzing, Antony,
     And very wisely threat before you sting.

ANTONY. Villains! You did not so, when your vile daggers
40   Hacked one another in the sides of Caesar.
     You showed your teeth like apes, and fawned like hounds,
     And bowed like bondmen, kissing Caesar's feet;
     Whilst damnèd Casca, like a cur, behind
     Struck Caesar on the neck. O you flatterers!

45 CASSIUS. Flatterers! Now, Brutus, thank yourself;
     This tongue had not offended so today,
     If Cassius might have ruled.[10]

OCTAVIUS. Come, come, the cause, If arguing make us sweat,
     The proof of it will turn to redder drops.
50   Look,
     I draw a sword against conspirators.
     When think you that the sword goes up again?[11]
     Never, till Caesar's three and thirty wounds
     Be well avenged; or till another Caesar[12]
55   Have added slaughter to the sword of traitors.[13]

BRUTUS. Caesar, thou canst not die by traitors' hands,
     Unless thou bring'st them with thee.[14]

**554** *Drama*

---

9 **Hybla:** area in Sicily noted for its honey. Cassius is reminding Antony of his false words of friendship to the conspirators after the assassination.

10 **If Cassius...ruled:** if Cassius had won out when he argued for Antony's death.

11 **goes up again:** goes back into its sheath.

12 **another Caesar:** Octavius.
13 **Have...traitors:** has been killed by the weapons of the conspirators.
14 **canst...with thee:** Brutus protests that there are no traitors on his side, but rather on the side of Octavius and Antony.

---

## GUIDED READING

### LITERAL QUESTIONS

**1a.** Of what do Antony and Brutus accuse each other? (They accuse each other of using false words of friendship to hide hostile intentions.)

**2a.** About what does Octavius remind everyone? (He reminds them that their verbal sparring is only a preliminary to a bloody battle.)

### INFERENTIAL QUESTIONS

**1b.** What do these mutual accusations reveal about their feelings concerning each other? (They reveal that each sees the other as his principal foe.)

**2b.** What do Octavius' remarks reveal about him? (He seems to have, at least initially, a calmer temperament than the others and to possess a secure view of himself as Caesar's heir.)

Len Cariou. Nicholas Pennell. Ian Deakin as Octavius. Photo courtesy of Stratford Festival, Canada, 1982.

*Julius Caesar, Act V, Scene i* **555**

- *Scene i (continued):* Octavius insults Brutus' honor, which Cassius defends by attacking Octavius.
- Octavius and Antony angrily depart to begin the battle.
- Cassius tells Messala that he has seen omens of death and is beginning to believe in them.

**1 CHARACTERIZATION**

With his usual sharp tongue Cassius jabs at Octavius; his comments, as usual, are equal parts venom and acute insight.

**2 READING SKILLS: CONTRAST**

In contrast to his behavior in Act I, Scene iii, Cassius no longer ridicules belief in omens. Perhaps the tribulations of the last few years account for his change of attitude.

**3 STYLE: SIMILE**

Cassius' comparison shows his overwhelming feelings of physical weakness and perhaps spiritual sickness.

---

OCTAVIUS.                                      So I hope.
  I was not born to die on Brutus' sword.

BRUTUS. O, if thou wert the noblest of thy strain,
60    Young man, thou couldst not die more honorable.

**1**  CASSIUS. A peevish schoolboy,[15] worthless of such honor,
  Joined with a masker and a reveler.[16]

ANTONY. Old Cassius still!

OCTAVIUS.                          Come, Antony; away!
  Defiance, traitors, hurl we in your teeth.
65    If you dare fight today, come to the field;
  If not, when you have stomachs.[17]

  [OCTAVIUS, ANTONY, *and their* ARMY *march away to assume
their positions for the battle*.]

CASSIUS. Why, now blow wind, swell billow, and swim bark!
  The storm is up, and all is on the hazard.[18]

BRUTUS. Ho, Lucilius, hark, a word with you.

LUCILIUS.                                      My lord?

  [BRUTUS *and* LUCILIUS *talk quietly apart from the rest. While
they are conversing,* CASSIUS *confides in* MESSALA.]

CASSIUS. Messala.

MESSALA.          What says my general?

70  CASSIUS.                                      Messala,
  This is my birthday; as this very day
  Was Cassius born. Give me thy hand, Messala:
  Be thou my witness that against my will
  (As Pompey was[19]) am I compelled to set
75    Upon one battle all our liberties.
**2**  You know that I held Epicurus[20] strong,
  And his opinion; now I change my mind,
  And partly credit things that do presage.[21]
  Coming from Sardis, on our former ensign[22]
80    Two mighty eagles fell, and there they perched,
  Gorging and feeding from our soldiers' hands,
  Who to Philippi here consorted[23] us.
  This morning are they fled away and gone,
  And in their steads do ravens, crows, and kites[24]
**3** 85  Fly o'er our heads and downward look on us
  As we were sickly prey; their shadows seem

15 **schoolboy:** Octavius was twenty-one at the time of the battle.
16 **masker and a reveler:** actor and playboy.

17 **stomachs:** appetites.

18 **all...hazard:** Everything is at stake.

19 **As Pompey was:** Pompey was persuaded against his will to risk everything in one battle at Pharsalia, where he was defeated by Caesar.
20 **Epicurus:** Greek philosopher whose followers do not believe in omens.
21 **presage:** foretell the future.
22 **former ensign:** foremost flag.

23 **consorted:** accompanied.

24 **kites:** hawks. All three birds are omens of death.

**556** *Drama*

---

## GUIDED READING

**LITERAL QUESTIONS**

**1a.** What does Cassius think of Octavius? (He thinks he's a bad-tempered child, unworthy of the honor of dying by Brutus' sword.)

**2a.** About what has Cassius changed his mind? (He now believes in omens.)

**INFERENTIAL QUESTIONS**

**1b.** What does Octavius' response to Cassius' comments ("Come, Antony; away!") reveal about him? (They reveal that Octavius has both a temper and pride but that he prefers acts to words.)

**2b.** What dramatic purpose does Cassius' change of mind serve? (It makes the audience anticipate the conspirators' eventual defeat and death.)

A canopy most fatal, under which
Our army lies, ready to give up the ghost.

**MESSALA.** Believe not so.

**CASSIUS.**                            I but believe it partly,
90   For I am fresh of spirit and resolved
To meet all perils very constantly.

**BRUTUS.** Even so, Lucilius.

[BRUTUS *ends his conversation with* LUCILIUS *and rejoins*
CASSIUS.]

**CASSIUS.**                          Now, most noble Brutus,
The gods today stand friendly, that we may,
Lovers in peace, lead on our days to age!
95   But since the affairs of men rests still incertain,
Let's reason with the worst that may befall.[25]
If we do lose this battle, then is this
The very last time we shall speak together.
What are you then determinèd to do?

100  **BRUTUS.** Even by the rule of that philosophy
By which I did blame Cato for the death
Which he did give himself;[26] I know not how,
But I do find it cowardly and vile,
For fear of what might fall, so to prevent[27]
105  The time of life, arming myself with patience
To stay the providence of some high powers[28]
That govern us below.

**CASSIUS.**                          Then, if we lose this battle,
You are contented to be led in triumph
Thorough the streets of Rome?

110  **BRUTUS.** No, Cassius, no; think not, thou noble Roman,
That ever Brutus will go bound to Rome;
He bears too great a mind. But this same day
Must end that work the ides of March begun;
And whether we shall meet again I know not.
115  Therefore our everlasting farewell take.
Forever, and forever, farewell, Cassius!
If we do meet again, why, we shall smile;
If not, why then this parting was well made.

**CASSIUS.** Forever, and forever, farewell, Brutus!
120  If we do meet again, we'll smile indeed;

25 **Let's reason...befall:** Let's
consider the worst that can happen.

26 **Cato...himself:** Brutus refers to
the suicide of his father-in-law, Cato,
when Caesar defeated Pompey.
Brutus' philosophy of Stoicism
considered suicide cowardly.
27 **prevent:** cut off early.

28 **To stay...powers:** to await my
fate.

*Julius Caesar*, Act V, Scene i   **557**

**AT A GLANCE**

- *Scene i (continued):* Cassius says to Messala that he only partly believes in the omens.
- When asked by Cassius what he will do if they are defeated, Brutus answers that although he despises suicide, he will never go to Rome as a prisoner.
- Cassius and Brutus say farewell.

**1  CHARACTERIZATION**

Either Messala's words revive him or Cassius decides to hide his depression, even from himself.

**2  PLOT: FALLING ACTION**

Brutus' and Cassius' discussion of suicide confirms the pessimistic feelings the audience has concerning any favorable outcome for the two conspirators.

**3  READING SKILLS: CONTRAST**

Brutus and Cassius remain as distinct as ever. Cassius has already decided what he will do if defeated. Brutus is torn between conflicting principles—his belief in his own preeminence and his disapproval of suicide.

**4  DIALOGUE**

The exchange between Cassius and Brutus is both tender and surprisingly realistic, as if their illusions have been stripped away and the prospect of death has been permitted to surface.

## GUIDED READING

### LITERAL QUESTIONS

**1a.** What does Cassius say might happen to Brutus and himself? (He says that they may lose the battle.)

**2a.** What does Brutus find offensive about suicide? (He thinks it is cowardly and vile.)

### INFERENTIAL QUESTIONS

**1b.** What do Cassius' remarks indicate about his state of mind? (They indicate that he is pessimistic about the battle's outcome.)

**2b.** What do Brutus' reflections on suicide as an alternative to captivity reveal about his state of mind? (They indicate that he too is probably pessimistic about the battle.)

- Scene i (continued): Brutus
  and Cassius withdraw to begin
  the battle.
- Scene ii: Believing that he has
  spotted a weakness in Octavius' ranks, Brutus sends Messala to Cassius with an order
  to attack.
- Scene iii: Cassius feels that his
  situation is growing desperate.

**1 CHARACTERIZATION**

Even in defeat, Cassius has
some notion about how soldiers
should act.

**2 PLOT: FALLING ACTION**

According to Titinius, Brutus'
poor judgment may be responsible for Cassius' desperate predicament.

If not 'tis true this parting was well made.

BRUTUS. Why then, lead on. O, that a man might know
The end of this day's business ere it come!
But it sufficeth that the day will end,
125    And then the end is known. Come, ho! Away!

[BRUTUS, CASSIUS, *and their* ARMY *withdraw to begin the battle.*]

**Scene ii.** *The field of battle. Shortly afterward.*

[*Drums and trumpets sound the alarum, or call to arms, as* BRUTUS *and* MESSALA *appear, ready for battle.* BRUTUS, *believing that he has spotted a weakness in* OCTAVIUS' *ranks, sends* MESSALA *to* CASSIUS *with an order to attack.*]

BRUTUS.  Ride, ride, Messala, ride, and give these bills[1]
Unto the legions on the other side.

1 **bills:** written orders.

[*The alarum sounds again.*]

Let them set on at once; for I perceive
But cold demeanor[2] in Octavius' wing,
5    And sudden push gives them the overthrow.
Ride, ride, Messala! Let them all come down.

2 **cold demeanor:** lack of spirit.

[*They hurry off.*]

**Scene iii.** *Another part of the battlefield. Several hours later.*

[*The fighting has been going against* CASSIUS, *who enters with his lieutenant* TITINIUS *and angrily watches some of his men retreating.* CASSIUS *feels that his own situation is growing desperate, but he does not know how* BRUTUS' *forces are faring.*]

CASSIUS.  O, look, Titinius, look, the villains[1] fly!
Myself have to mine own turned enemy.[2]
This ensign[3] here of mine was turning back;
I slew the coward, and did take it from him.

1 **villains:** his own retreating troops.

2 **Myself...enemy:** I have turned to fighting my own men.
3 **ensign:** flag bearer.

5    TITINIUS.  O Cassius, Brutus gave the word too early,
Who, having some advantage on Octavius,
Took it too eagerly; his soldiers fell to spoil,[4]
Whilst we by Antony are all enclosed.

4 **spoil:** looting.

[PINDARUS *rushes in.*]

PINDARUS.  Fly further off, my lord, fly further off!

**558**  *Drama*

## GUIDED READING

**LITERAL QUESTIONS**

**1a.** What does Brutus want to know? (He wants to
know how the day will end.)

**2a.** According to Titinius what is the consequence of
Brutus' mistake? (Too busy looting, his men have
allowed Cassius to be surrounded by Antony's
soldiers.)

**INFERENTIAL QUESTIONS**

**1b.** What does this desire reveal about Brutus' state of
mind? (It reveals that he is extremely anxious and
doubtful.)

**2b.** What flaw in his character does Brutus' mistake
reveal? (It reveals that he is overeager and lacks
judgment.)

10 Mark Antony is in your tents, my lord.
Fly, therefore, noble Cassius, fly far off!

CASSIUS. This hill is far enough. Look, look, Titinius!
Are those my tents where I perceive the fire?

TITINIUS. They are, my lord.

CASSIUS.                          Titinius, if thou lovest me,
15 Mount thou my horse and hide thy spurs in him
Till he have brought thee up to yonder troops
And here again, that I may rest assured
Whether yond troops are friend or enemy.

TITINIUS. I will be here again even with a thought.[5]
[TITINIUS *leaves*.]

CASSIUS. Go, Pindarus, get higher on that hill;
20 My sight was ever thick.[6] Regard Titinius,
And tell me what thou not'st about the field.

[PINDARUS *climbs the hill to watch* TITINIUS.]

This day I breathèd first. Time is come round,
And where I did begin, there shall I end.
25 My life is run his compass.[7] Sirrah, what news?

PINDARUS. [*From his vantage point on the hill*.] O my lord!

CASSIUS. What news?

PINDARUS. Titinius is enclosèd round about
With horsemen that make to him on the spur;[8]
30 Yet he spurs on. Now they are almost on him.
Now, Titinius! Now some light.[9] O, he lights too!
He's ta'en![10] [*A shout is heard in the distance*.] And, hark!
They shout for joy.

CASSIUS. Come down; behold no more.
O, coward that I am, to live so long,
35 To see my best friend ta'en before my face!

[PINDARUS *rejoins* CASSIUS.]

Come hither, sirrah.
In Parthia did I take thee prisoner;
And then I swore thee, saving of thy life,
That whatsoever I did bid thee do,
40 Thou shouldst attempt it. Come now, keep thine oath.
Now be a freeman, and with this good sword,

5 **even with a thought:** as quick as a thought.

6 **thick:** dim.

7 **is run his compass:** has come full circle.

8 **make...spur:** ride toward him quickly.

9 **some light:** Some of them dismount.
10 **ta'en:** taken. Pindarus misunderstands what has happened. Rather than being captured by enemy soldiers, Titinius has actually met soldiers on his side with good news.

*Julius Caesar, Act V, Scene iii* **559**

- *Scene iii (continued):* Thinking the enemy has set his tents afire, Cassius sends Titinius to see if the nearby troops are friend or foe.
- Pindarus mistakenly reports that the enemy has captured Titinius.
- Cassius is in despair over his best friend's "capture."

**1 SYMBOLISM**

Cassius' dim sight symbolizes his own dimming prospects—more specifically, the dimming of his own life.

**2 CHARACTERIZATION**

Ever the realist, Cassius recognizes that his life has come full circle and will shortly end.

**3 SITUATIONAL IRONY**

Thinking his own eyesight is poor, Cassius has sent Pindarus to see for him, but Pindarus sees dimly or incorrectly too.

## GUIDED READING

**LITERAL QUESTIONS**

**1a.** What does Cassius say about his life? (He says that his life has come full circle today.)

**2a.** What is Cassius' reaction to Titinius' supposed capture? (He cannot bear to see his best friend captured.)

**INFERENTIAL QUESTIONS**

**1b.** What causes Cassius to make this remark? (He believes that he has been defeated and will either be killed or have to commit suicide on this day.)

**2b.** After seeing Titinius "captured," what might Cassius ask Pindarus to do? (He will probably ask Pindarus to kill him.)

**1 PLOT: FALLING ACTION**

Cassius commits suicide with the same sword that killed Caesar and with Caesar's name on his lips.

**2 TRAGEDY**

Titinius links Cassius' personal tragedy to the public tragedy of Rome itself.

**3 CHARACTERIZATION**

Messala dissects for Titinius, and the audience as well, Cassius' tragic flaw: He possessed a melancholy nature that always imagined the worst.

---

That ran through Caesar's bowels, search[11] this bosom.
Stand not to answer. Here, take thou the hilts,

[PINDARUS *takes the sword*.]

And when my face is covered, as 'tis now,

**1  45** Guide thou the sword—[PINDARUS *stabs* CASSIUS.] Caesar, thou art revenged,
Even with the sword that killed thee. [CASSIUS *dies*.]

PINDARUS. So, I am free; yet would not so have been,
Durst I have done my will. O Cassius!
Far from this country Pindarus shall run,
**50** Where never Roman shall take note of him.

[PINDARUS *leaves. After he goes,* TITINIUS (*whom* PINDARUS *had mistakenly reported captured*) *returns with* MESSALA. TITINIUS *brings a victor's garland from* BRUTUS *to* CASSIUS.]

MESSALA. It is but change,[12] Titinius; for Octavius
Is overthrown by noble Brutus' power,
As Cassius' legions are by Antony.

TITINIUS. These tidings will well comfort Cassius.

MESSALA. Where did you leave him?

**55** TITINIUS.                                 All disconsolate,
With Pindarus his bondman, on this hill.

MESSALA. Is not that he that lies upon the ground?

TITINIUS. He lies not like the living. O my heart!

MESSALA. Is not that he?

TITINIUS.                          No, this was he, Messala,
**60** But Cassius is no more. O setting sun,
As in thy red rays thou dost sink to night,
**2** So in his red blood Cassius' day is set.
The sun of Rome is set. Our day is gone;
Clouds, dews,[13] and dangers come; our deeds are done!
**65** Mistrust of my success hath done this deed.

**3** MESSALA. Mistrust of good success hath done this deed.
O hateful Error, Melancholy's child,[14]
Why dost thou show to the apt[15] thoughts of men
The things that are not? O Error, soon conceived,
**70** Thou never com'st unto a happy birth,
But kill'st the mother that engend'red thee![16]

**560** *Drama*

11 **search:** penetrate.

12 **but change:** even exchange.

13 **dews:** Dews were considered poisonous.

14 **Melancholy's child:** Melancholy people like Cassius are likely to err by imagining the worst.
15 **apt:** easily deceived.

16 **mother...thee:** the mind that conceived the error.

---

## GUIDED READING

**LITERAL QUESTION**

**1a.** What are Cassius' last thoughts? (He thinks that Caesar is revenged.)

**INFERENTIAL QUESTION**

**1b.** What do these thoughts suggest about Cassius' attitude toward the assassination? (He may feel some guilt about Caesar and therefore some sense that his own defeat is just.)

**TITINIUS.** What, Pindarus! Where art thou, Pindarus?

**MESSALA.** Seek him, Titinius, whilst I go to meet
The noble Brutus, thrusting this report
75 Into his ears. I may say ''thrusting'' it;
For piercing steel and darts envenomed
Shall be as welcome to the ears of Brutus
As tidings of this sight.

**TITINIUS.**                    Hie you, Messala,
And I will seek for Pindarus the while.

[MESSALA *leaves to find* BRUTUS. TITINIUS *looks at* CASSIUS.]

80 Why didst thou send me forth, brave Cassius?
Did I not meet thy friends, and did not they
Put on my brows this wreath of victory,
And bid me give it thee? Didst thou not hear their shouts?

**1** Alas, thou hast misconstrued everything!
85 But hold thee, take this garland on thy brow;

[*Places the victor's garland on* CASSIUS' *brow*.]

Thy Brutus bid me give it thee, and I
Will do his bidding. Brutus, come apace,[17]
And see how I regarded[18] Caius Cassius.
**2** By your leave, gods.[19] This is a Roman's part:[20]
90 Come, Cassius' sword, and find Titinius' heart.

[*He stabs himself and dies. After* TITINIUS *dies, the noise of
battle is heard again.* BRUTUS, *told of* CASSIUS' *death by*
MESSALA, *arrives with him,* LUCILIUS, *and two other soldiers:*
VOLUMNIUS *and* YOUNG CATO, *who is* BRUTUS' *brother-in-law.*]

**BRUTUS.** Where, where, Messala, doth his body lie?

**MESSALA.** Lo, yonder, and Titinius mourning it.

**BRUTUS.** Titinius' face is upward.

**CATO.**                    He is slain.

**3** **BRUTUS.** O Julius Caesar, thou art mighty yet!
95 Thy spirit walks abroad, and turns our swords
In our own proper[21] entrails.

[*Alarums are heard in the distance.*]

**CATO.**                    Brave Titinius!
Look, whe'r[22] he have not crowned dead Cassius.

17 **apace:** soon.
18 **regarded:** honored.
19 **By . . . gods:** Titinius asks pardon of the gods, because he is cutting his life short.
20 **part:** duty.

21 **proper:** own.

22 **whe'r:** whether.

*Julius Caesar, Act V, Scene iii*    **561**

---

- *Scene iii (continued):* Messala leaves to tell Brutus of Cassius' death.
- Titinius places the victor's garland on Cassius' brow and then kills himself.
- Arriving at Cassius' side, Brutus discovers Titinius' body as well.

**1** **CHARACTERIZATION**

Titinius' remark to his dead friend may cause the audience to wonder (not for the first time) if Cassius has really ''misconstrued everything,'' including the views that led to Caesar's death.

**2** **PLOT: FALLING ACTION**

Not only the first conspirator but his best friend have killed themselves; Caesar's blood is indeed drowning the conspiracy.

**3** **CHARACTERIZATION**

Brutus implicitly acknowledges that Caesar's spirit ''haunts'' him too; also, Brutus' reference reminds the audience that he and the ghost have already met.

---

## GUIDED READING

### LITERAL QUESTION

**1a.** What does Brutus say on finding both Titinius and Cassius dead? (He says that Caesar is still mighty.)

### INFERENTIAL QUESTION

**1b.** In what sense is he right? (Those Romans avenging Caesar's death have triumphed over Caesar's assassins.)

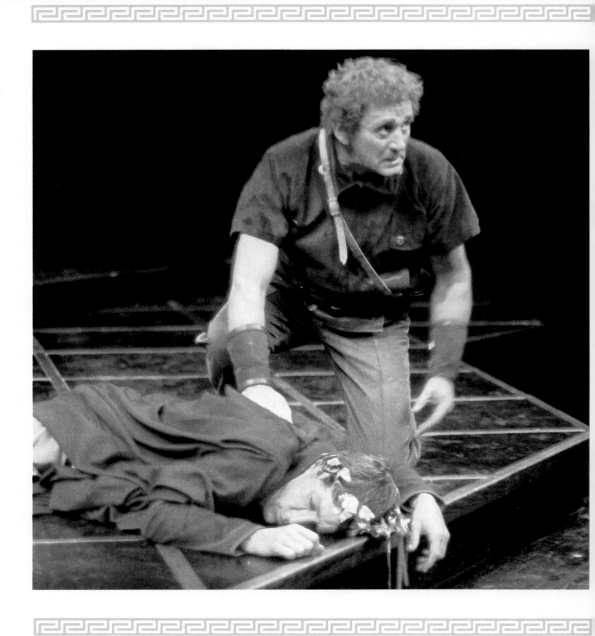

Len Cariou. Nicholas Pennell. Photo courtesy of Stratford Festival, Canada, 1982.

**562** *Drama*

BRUTUS. Are yet two Romans living such as these?
        The last of all the Romans, fare thee well!
100     It is impossible that ever Rome
        Should breed thy fellow. Friends, I owe moe[23] tears
        To this dead man than you shall see me pay.
        I shall find time, Cassius; I shall find time.
        Come, therefore, and to Thasos[24] send his body;
105     His funerals shall not be in our camp,
        Lest it discomfort[25] us. Lucilius, come,
        And come, young Cato; let us to the field.
        Labeo and Flavius set our battles on.
        'Tis three o'clock; and, Romans, yet ere night
110     We shall try fortune in a second fight.

        [*They leave to resume fighting.*]

23 **moe:** more.

24 **Thasos** [tha′sōs]: island near Philippi.

25 **discomfort:** dishearten.

*Scene iv. Another part of the battlefield. Shortly later.*

[*The tide is now turning against* BRUTUS, *who leads several of his men—including his brother-in-law,* YOUNG CATO, LUCILIUS, MESSALA, *and* FLAVIUS—*in last-ditch, sporadic fighting against several enemy* SOLDIERS.]

BRUTUS. Yet, countrymen, O, yet hold up your heads!

        [BRUTUS, MESSALA, FLAVIUS, *and several other* SOLDIERS *exit fighting, while* YOUNG CATO *and* LUCILIUS *remain, calling out to enemy* SOLDIERS *in the distance.* LUCILIUS *pretends to be* BRUTUS *in order to protect him*.]

CATO. What fellow doth not? Who will go with me?
        I will proclaim my name about the field.
        I am the son of Marcus Cato,[1] ho!
5       A foe to tyrants, and my country's friend.
        I am the son of Marcus Cato, ho!

        [*Enemy* SOLDIERS *enter and begin to fight with* YOUNG CATO *and* LUCILIUS.]

1 **Marcus Cato:** Portia's father.

LUCILIUS. And I am Brutus, Marcus Brutus, I;
        Brutus, my country's friend; know me for Brutus!

        [YOUNG CATO *falls during the fight and dies*.]

        O young and noble Cato, art thou down?
10      Why, now thou diest as bravely as Titinius,
        And mayst be honored, being Cato's son.

        [LUCILIUS *tries to fight on alone but is surrounded*.]

*Julius Caesar, Act V, Scene iv*   **563**

## AT A GLANCE

- *Scene iii (continued):* Brutus mourns Cassius and Titinius.
- *Scene iv:* The tide now against him, Brutus leads a last-ditch fight against several enemy soldiers.

### 1 CHARACTERIZATION

Cassius' death seems to move Brutus more than that of his own wife. Ironically, Brutus never does "find time" to mourn Cassius, since time is running out for him as well.

### 2 CHARACTERIZATION

Proclaiming himself to be Brutus, Lucilius proves his loyalty by risking his own life.

## GUIDED READING

### LITERAL QUESTIONS

**1a.** What does Brutus say about Cassius? (He says that Cassius is the last of all Romans, that Rome will never breed another like him, and that he, Brutus, owes him more tears than he will ever show.)

**2a.** What lie does Lucilius tell? (He pretends that he is Brutus.)

### INFERENTIAL QUESTIONS

**1b.** What do Brutus' remarks about Cassius show about his feelings toward him? (It shows that he has loved Cassius.)

**2b.** What is the purpose of this lie? (Lucilius hopes to protect Brutus with his own life.)

- *Scene iv (continued):* Antony arrives and says that the prisoner is Lucilius.
- Lucilius tells Antony that Brutus is safe and will never be taken alive.
- *Scene v:* Losing the battle, Brutus faces the choice of being captured or of committing suicide.

1 **PLOT: FALLING ACTION**

Lucilius' statement that Brutus will not permit himself to be taken alive prepares the audience for the possibility of his suicide.

2 **CHARACTERIZATION**

Antony's directives to his soldiers about how to treat Lucilius show the generous and shrewd side of his character.

3 **PLOT: FALLING ACTION**

As the day draws to a close, we see that the battle is nearly over. The conspirators' years of struggle are about to end in defeat.

---

**FIRST SOLDIER.** Yield, or thou diest.

**LUCILIUS.**                               Only I yield to die.
  There is so much that thou wilt kill me straight;
  Kill Brutus, and be honored in his death.

15 **FIRST SOLDIER.** We must not. A noble prisoner!

  [*The SOLDIERS crowd around LUCILIUS eagerly, believing that
  they have captured the enemy leader. ANTONY enters, unnoticed by most of his men.*]

**SECOND SOLDIER.** Room, ho! Tell Antony, Brutus is ta'en.

**FIRST SOLDIER.** I'll tell thee news. Here comes the general.
  Brutus is ta'en, Brutus is ta'en, my lord.

**ANTONY.** Where is he?

  [*The SOLDIERS draw back to reveal LUCILIUS to ANTONY.*]

20 **LUCILIUS.** Safe, Antony; Brutus is safe enough.
  I dare assure thee that no enemy
  Shall ever take alive the noble Brutus.
  The gods defend him from so great a shame!
  When you do find him, or alive or dead,
25 He will be found like Brutus, like himself.

**ANTONY.** This is not Brutus, friend, but, I assure you,
  A prize no less in worth. Keep this man safe;
  Give him all kindness. I had rather have
  Such men my friends than enemies. Go on,
30 And see whe'r Brutus be alive or dead,
  And bring us word unto Octavius' tent
  How everything is chanced.

  [*ANTONY leaves to join OCTAVIUS. Some SOLDIERS follow with
  LUCILIUS, and others hurry off in a different direction to
  report on the battle's progress.*]

**Scene v.** *Another part of the field. Late in the day.*

  [*BRUTUS and a few of his remaining friends, including CLITUS,
  DARDANIUS, VOLUMNIUS, and STRATO, straggle on and rest on a
  rock, exhausted and discouraged. They are losing the battle,
  and BRUTUS faces the choice of being captured by the enemy or
  dying by his own hand.*]

**BRUTUS.** Come, poor remains of friends, rest on this rock.

---

**LITERAL QUESTIONS**

**1a.** What orders does Antony give his soldiers concerning Lucilius? (He orders them to treat Lucilius kindly.)

**2a.** What choice does Brutus face? (He has to decide between suicide or capture.)

**INFERENTIAL QUESTIONS**

**1b.** What do the orders he gives his soldiers show about Antony? (They show that he can be both generous and politically shrewd.)

**2b.** What choice do you think Brutus will make? Explain your answer. (Brutus has said that he cannot bear the idea of being marched through the streets of Rome as a prisoner; thus, he will probably commit suicide.)

**CLITUS.** Statilius showed the torchlight,[1] but, my lord,
He came not back; he is or ta'en or slain.

**BRUTUS.** Sit thee down, Clitus. Slaying is the word;
5   It is a deed in fashion. Hark thee, Clitus.

[BRUTUS *whispers to* CLITUS, *who seems shocked by his request*.]

**CLITUS.** What, I, my lord? No, not for all the world!

**BRUTUS.** Peace then, no words.

**CLITUS.**                    I'll rather kill myself.

**BRUTUS.** Hark thee, Dardanius. [*He whispers to* DARDANIUS.]

**DARDANIUS.**                    Shall I do such a deed?

[*After* DARDANIUS' *reply*, BRUTUS *sits apart from the rest*.]

**CLITUS.** O Dardanius!

10  **DARDANIUS.** O Clitus!

**CLITUS.** What ill request did Brutus make to thee?

**DARDANIUS.** To kill him, Clitus. Look, he meditates.

**CLITUS.** Now is that noble vessel full of grief,
That it runs over even at his eyes.

15  **BRUTUS.** Come hither, good Volumnius; list[2] a word.

**VOLUMNIUS.** What says my lord?

**BRUTUS.**                    Why, this, Volumnius:
The ghost of Caesar hath appeared to me
Two several[3] times by night; at Sardis once,
And this last night here in Philippi fields.
I know my hour is come.

20  **VOLUMNIUS.**                    Not so, my lord.

**BRUTUS.** Nay, I am sure it is, Volumnius.
Thou seest the world, Volumnius, how it goes;
Our enemies have beat us to the pit.[4]

[*Fighting is heard in the distance*.]

It is more worthy to leap in ourselves
25  Than tarry till they push us. Good Volumnius,
Thou know'st that we two went to school together;

---

1 **showed the torchlight:** signaled with a torch. Statilius went to scout Cassius' camp and signaled that he found all well there.

2 **list:** listen to.

3 **several:** separate.

4 **pit:** hole into which hunted animals are driven; also, a grave.

*Julius Caesar, Act V, Scene v*   **565**

## AT A GLANCE

- Brutus asks his servant Clitus to kill him but is refused.
- Brutus then makes the same request of Dardanius, another servant.
- Brutus tells Volumnius, an officer and a friend, that they have been beaten, and it is better to commit suicide than to wait to be killed.

### 1 PLOT: FALLING ACTION

Brutus' request of Clitus indicates that he has made his choice: suicide.

### 2 POINT OF VIEW

Clitus observes Brutus sympathetically, thus enabling the audience to mourn him even before his death.

### 3 CHARACTERIZATION

Brutus' Stoicism is apparent in his resigned acceptance of the fate that awaits him. The second appearance of Caesar's ghost may have fatally undermined Brutus' hopes for success.

### 4 PLOT: FALLING ACTION

Brutus is prepared to die because, for once, he accepts the world as it is: He is defeated and either he must kill himself or be dishonored.

## GUIDED READING

### LITERAL QUESTIONS

**1a.** What does Brutus ask Clitus to do? (He asks Clitus to help him kill himself.)

**2a.** What estimate does Brutus give Volumnius of how the battle has gone? (He says that they have lost.)

### INFERENTIAL QUESTIONS

**1b.** What causes Clitus to refuse Brutus' request? (He loves Brutus and so cannot bear to help him kill himself.)

**2b.** What does Brutus' estimate show about him? (It shows that Brutus is realistic enough to accept defeat.)

- Volumnius also refuses Brutus' request that he kill him.
- Brutus bids farewell to his men, saying he is joyful that everyone has always been loyal to him.
- As Brutus' servant Strato holds his master's sword, Brutus runs on it and dies.

**1 CHARACTERIZATION**

That a third person refuses Brutus' request to kill him testifies to the love and loyalty he inspires.

**2 TRAGEDY**

Brutus' downplaying of the "glory" his enemies will attain may rouse the audience's own doubts about the possible tragic destiny awaiting a Rome ruled by an arrogant Antony and his possible rival: Octavius.

**3 PLOT: RESOLUTION**

Brutus finally finds peace, killing himself more easily than he killed Caesar.

**1** Even for that our love of old, I prithee
Hold thou my sword-hilts whilst I run on it.

VOLUMNIUS. That's not an office for a friend, my lord.

[*The sounds of battle grow closer. An alarum sounds*.]

30 CLITUS. Fly, fly, my lord, there is no tarrying here.

BRUTUS. Farewell to you; and you; and you, Volumnius.
Strato, thou hast been all this while asleep;
Farewell to thee too, Strato. Countrymen,
My heart doth joy that yet in all my life
35 I found no man but he was true to me.

**2** I shall have glory by this losing day
More than Octavius and Mark Antony
By this vile conquest shall attain unto.
So fare you well at once, for Brutus' tongue
40 Hath almost ended his life's history.
Night hangs upon mine eyes; my bones would rest,
That have but labored to attain this hour.

[*An alarum and cries of "Fly, fly, fly!" are heard. The enemy is very near*.]

CLITUS. Fly, my lord, fly!

BRUTUS.                          Hence! I will follow.

[CLITUS, DARDANIUS, *and* VOLUMNIUS *leave*.]

I prithee, Strato, stay thou by thy lord,
45 Thou art a fellow of a good respect
Thy life hath had some smatch⁵ of honor in it;
Hold then my sword, and turn away thy face,
**3** While I do run upon it. Wilt thou, Strato?

STRATO. Give me your hand first. Fare you well, my lord.

50 BRUTUS. Farewell, good Strato— [*He runs on his sword*.] Caesar, now be still;
I killed not thee with half so good a will.

[BRUTUS *dies*.]

[*An alarum signals the entrance of* ANTONY, OCTAVIUS, *and the rest of their* ARMY. MESSALA *and* LUCILIUS *are with them*.]

OCTAVIUS. What man is that?

MESSALA. My master's man. Strato, where is thy master?

5 **smatch:** taste.

---

## GUIDED READING

**LITERAL QUESTIONS**

**1a.** What makes Brutus feel joyful in the moments before his death? (He says that he is joyful because no friend was ever untrue to him.)

**2a.** What does Strato do? (He holds Brutus' sword and thus allows him to run into it and die.)

**INFERENTIAL QUESTIONS**

**1b.** What is ironic about this feeling, in the context of Brutus' own behavior? (Brutus was not true to his friend Caesar.)

**2b.** What does Brutus' death signify for Rome? (It signifies the total defeat of the conspiracy and, as a result, the unchallenged supremacy of Octavius and Antony.)

STRATO. Free from the bondage you are in, Messala;
55  The conquerors can but make a fire of him.
    For Brutus only overcame himself,[6]
    And no man else hath honor by his death.

LUCILIUS. So Brutus should be found. I thank thee, Brutus,
    That thou hast proved Lucilius' saying true.

60  OCTAVIUS. All that served Brutus, I will entertain them.[7]
    Fellow, wilt thou bestow thy time with me?

STRATO. Ay, if Messala will prefer[8] me to you.

OCTAVIUS. Do so, good Messala.

MESSALA. How died my master, Strato?

65  STRATO. I held the sword, and he did run on it.

MESSALA. Octavius, then take him to follow thee,
    That did the latest service to my master.

ANTONY. This was the noblest Roman of them all.
    All the conspirators save only he
70  Did that they did in envy of great Caesar;
    He, only in a general honest thought
    And common good to all,[9] made one of them.
    His life was gentle, and the elements
    So mixed in him that Nature might stand up
75  And say to all the world, "This was a man!"

OCTAVIUS. According to his virtue, let us use[10] him
    With all respect and rites of burial.
    Within my tent his bones tonight shall lie,
    Most like a soldier ordered honorably.[11]
80  So call the field to rest, and let's away
    To part[12] the glories of this happy day.

[*They all leave, several* SOLDIERS *carrying the body of* BRUTUS.]

**6 Brutus only...himself:** Only Brutus overcame Brutus.

**7 entertain them:** let them serve me.

**8 prefer:** recommend.

**9 in a general...to all:** with an honorable and unselfish concern for the good of all Rome.

**10 use:** treat.

**11 ordered honorably:** with all due honor.

**12 part:** divide.

*Julius Caesar, Act V, Scene v*   **567**

AT A GLANCE

- Brutus' men agree to serve with Octavius.
- Antony says Brutus was the noblest Roman among the conspirators, the only one motivated by concern for the good of all Rome.

**1 TRAGEDY**

Strato suggests Brutus' greatest strength and tragic flaw: Guided by his own noble principles, he removed himself from the real world of shrewd men with baser motives than his own.

**2 PLOT: RESOLUTION**

Like Antony, Octavius is gracious to Brutus' officers, asking them to serve with him.

**3 CHARACTERIZATION**

Because Antony formerly reserved his greatest bitterness for Brutus, his tribute seems heartfelt and perhaps reflects the way Shakespeare wants the audience to finally perceive Brutus.

**4 PLOT: RESOLUTION**

With Brutus' death the play fittingly ends, for the two major conspirators are dead. Yet the differences between Antony and Octavius are unresolved, so the restored order may be fragile.

**REFLECTING ON THE PLAY**

Who are the hero and villain of *Julius Caesar*? (Answers will vary. Most students will probably see either Brutus (for his ideals) or Antony (for his loyalty and intelligence) as the hero. Most students will nominate envious Cassius as the villain, though a few may choose Brutus (for his disloyalty and blindness) or Antony (for his corruption).

## GUIDED READING

**LITERAL QUESTION**

**1a.** What words of praise does Antony lavish on Brutus? (He says that Brutus was the noblest Roman, for he was the only one to act out of concern for the public good.)

**INFERENTIAL QUESTION**

**1b.** In what way do Antony's words show that order has been restored? (Because the civil war is ended, Antony now seeks to heal the wounds by generously giving Brutus his due.)

## STUDY QUESTIONS

1. Antony predicted Brutus and Cassius would stay on high ground; Octavius disagreed.
2. They quarrel.
3. Brutus is defeating Octavius; that he has been captured; is surrounded by own troops.
4. sign that he will die; slave stabs him with own sword
5. turns against Brutus; to protect him from being captured
6. battle is lost and more noble to kill himself than be captured; runs on Strato's sword; *I killed not thee with half so good a will.*
7. say he was the noblest Roman; the only conspirator who acted in the public interest
8. how Rome will be governed; neither side; one is disorganized and the other is corrupt
9. He has been haunted by Caesar's death; feels guilty; has lost desire to live.
10. He was the only conspirator who acted selflessly; he could be regarded as an ideal man; some may agree; others may note Brutus' naiveté, poor judgment. Antony's sincere respect for Brutus adds depth to his character.
11. *part* means both share and divide; suggests future conflicts; hints at Octavius' victory
12. Students should consider
   - portrayal of Caesar
   - motives of conspirators
   - effect of assassination

## VIEWPOINT

Common people are shown to be fickle and unstable; Caesar's vanity and ambition overrule his judgment; Cassius acts out of envy; Antony is hungry for power, corrupt, impetuous; Brutus' judgment is wavering and unstable.

## LITERARY FOCUS

### Thinking About Tragedy

1. *Caesar:* arrogance; ambition; vanity; *Brutus:* naiveté; pride; Brutus; has nobler intentions

## STUDY QUESTIONS

### Recalling

1. Explain the disagreement in Act V, Scene i, between Octavius and Antony.
2. What happens during the parley among the four leaders before the battle?
3. In Scene iii, how is the battle going for Brutus and Cassius? What does Cassius think has happened to Titinius? What has actually happened to him?
4. What significance does Cassius see in the fact that the battle of Philippi occurs on his birthday? Describe his death.
5. How does the course of the battle change later in the day? Why does Lucilius impersonate Brutus in Scene iv?
6. What reasons does Brutus give in Scene v for killing himself, and how does he do it? What does he say as he dies?
7. Describe the reactions of Antony and Octavius to Brutus' death. What does Antony say about Brutus?

### Interpreting

8. What is being decided at the battle of Philippi? Does Shakespeare portray one side as more deserving of victory than the other? Explain.
9. What is the meaning of the words that Brutus addresses to Caesar as he kills himself? What do these words indicate about Brutus' attitude toward Caesar and the assassination? Toward his own life?
10. What does Antony mean in his final comments about Brutus? Do you agree with Antony's description of Brutus? Why or why not? What is your final impression of Antony?
11. Octavius says that the triumvirs will "part the glories of this happy day." In light of the future conflict between Antony and Octavius, why might this line be ironic? Why do you think Octavius, rather than Antony, has the last word in the play?

### Extending

12. From all you have seen in the play, do you think Shakespeare is saying that the conspirators were unquestionably wrong? Explain.

## VIEWPOINT

One well-known Shakespearean scholar has suggested that the death of Brutus, besides being a private misfortune, also represents the death of an ideal:

[Brutus'] death is but a symbol of a greater disaster, the death of liberty, and the defeat is brought about, not at Philippi, but through the corruption and instability of human nature.

— John Dover Wilson, Introduction, *Julius Caesar*

■ What evidence do you see in the play of the "corruption and instability of human nature"? How do these aspects of human nature contribute to the grim outcome in *Julius Caesar*?

## LITERARY FOCUS

### Tragedy

A **tragedy** is a play that presents the eventual downfall of a great and worthy figure. In Greek and Elizabethan tragedy, the **tragic hero**, or central character in the tragedy, is a person who holds high rank and has many admirable qualities. However, the character of the tragic hero also includes a fatal **tragic flaw**, a weakness—such as pride or short-sightedness—that eventually brings about his or her downfall. The tragic hero usually dies in a tragedy; however, many tragedies end with a hint that order will be restored.

### Thinking About Tragedy

1. Many people have differing views about the identity of the tragic hero in *Julius Caesar*. Some argue that the tragic hero is Caesar, while others say that it is Brutus. What is the tragic flaw of each of these characters? Which do you think is the hero of this tragedy?
2. To what extent is *Julius Caesar* the tragedy not of a single character but of Rome itself? From what "tragic flaw" might Rome's tragedy have come?
3. Can you find a hint of restored order at the end of *Julius Caesar*? Why or why not?

2. Assassination causes civil war; Rome plagued by violence; ruled by dictatorship.
3. Caesar's death is avenged and the two sides make peace; on the other hand, Octavius' and Antony's relationship hints at future conflict.

## The Total Effect

A director staging a play aims to present a coherent vision of the work to the audience. Therefore, a director must think about the overall effect created by the various elements originally brought together by the playwright: the plot, characters, setting, imagery, symbols, irony, and themes of the work.

### Thinking About Plot, Character, and Setting

1. What tactical errors do the conspirators make during the course of the play? What causes each of these errors? How do these errors bring about the failure of the conspiracy?
2. What are the major conflicts in the play? How is each of these conflicts resolved? Are any left unresolved by the end of the play? Explain.
3. List the prophecies, dreams, and omens that foreshadow later events in the play. What do these unrealistic elements add to the play?
4. Some people believe that Brutus is one of the noblest and most selfless of Shakespeare's heroes. Others feel that he is a fool and an egotist. What is your opinion of his strengths and limitations?
5. Antony says that, aside from Brutus, all the conspirators killed Caesar out of envy, not out of concern for Rome. Do you think that this is true of Cassius? What are his strengths and weaknesses?
6. Describe the various changes Mark Antony undergoes in the play, from Act I through Act V. What do you think causes these changes?
7. What are Julius Caesar's various strengths and weaknesses as a ruler? From the funeral scene on, give examples of the ways in which Caesar's presence lingers in the play after his death.
8. The play begins on a Roman street decked with flowers for a happy occasion. It ends on a bloody battlefield far from Rome. Explain how this change in setting parallels what happens in the play.

### Thinking About Imagery and Symbol

9. Shakespeare uses certain images many times in Julius Caesar. For example, the play includes many references to animals, especially to animals of prey and their victims. Find two references to animals in the play (you might look especially at Act III, Scene i, and Act V, Scene i). What might these animal images be doing in a play about politics and human affairs?
10. What might be symbolized by the storm and the other disturbances on the eve of Caesar's death? What might the apparition of Caesar's ghost in Act IV, Scene iii, symbolize?

### Thinking About Irony

11. How is Caesar's behavior toward Decius and the other conspirators in Act II, Scene ii, an example of dramatic irony? What does the audience know that Caesar does not know?
12. Find two examples of verbal irony in Antony's funeral oration in Act III, Scene ii.
13. What is ironic about the outcome of the assassination, given the expressed goals of the conspirators?

### Thinking About Theme

14. Explain how Julius Caesar is in part the story of the conflict between Brutus' ideals and the real world. Does Shakespeare suggest that the world needs idealists like Brutus? Explain.
15. As a political play, Julius Caesar revolves around two dangers: the danger of instability in the state and the danger of tyranny in a strong ruler. How are these ideas shown to be in conflict in the play? Does Shakespeare show one danger to be greater than the other? Explain.
16. What view of an individual's ability to influence history is presented in Julius Caesar?

## VOCABULARY

### Puns

**Puns** are jokes based on words with several meanings, or on words that sound alike but have different meanings. Shakespeare's audience loved puns, and it is likely that Shakespeare was very fond of them himself, since he wrote hundreds of them into his plays.

Puns were so popular during Shakespeare's time partly because the English language was changing constantly. New words were constantly entering the

---

1. *errors:* allow Antony to address crowd; cause conspirators to be driven out of Rome; march to Philippi; *cause:* Brutus' bad judgment; *results:* gives enemy advantage; lose battle
2. Brutus' internal conflict; conspirators vs. Caesar; republic vs. dictatorship; Brutus' vision vs. reality; the conflicts within and between the characters are resolved by compromises; the form of government resolved in dictatorship; conflict between Antony and Octavius left unresolved
3. soothsayer's warning; Casca's visions; Calpurnia's dream; appearance of Caesar's ghost; create mysterious, ominous mood; suggest forces at work that are beyond human control
4. Answers will vary. Students should consider strengths and weaknesses.
5. Cassius envied Caesar but also valued republic; is pragmatic; shrewd, loyal friend; petty, impetuous, corruptible, prone to melancholy and anger
6. begins as shallow character; after murder reveals depth, intelligence; is manipulative; becomes corrupt, hard; changes to suit circumstances or they bring to light unseen aspects of him
7. is practical; good judge of people; generous; inspires loyalty; vain, arrogant, autocratic; in funeral scene; appearance of ghost; verbal references to him; dying remarks of Brutus / Cassius
8. Change from city to bloody battlefield parallels violence, turmoil that plague Rome.
9. Antony's references to Caesar as a hart, conspirators as hounds suggest that human affairs can be irrational, violent, bestial.
10. chaos following Caesar's death; Brutus' conscience
11. irony lies in Caesar's hospitality to conspirators; assassination plans

---

12. Antony says he has come to bury Caesar not praise him; refers to conspirators as "honorable men."
13. Caesar is killed to save the republic; his death brought about what the conspirators hoped to prevent—a dictatorship.
14. Brutus believed in an ideal of freedom; did not consider the political climate or the inability of the people to handle freedom; his sense of honor is admirable; his adherence to ideals results in tragedy.
15. State becomes unstable when a strong leader is overthrown; Caesar's death imposes greater tyranny; suggests instability as the greater danger.
16. Attempts to change the course of history will most likely fail.

**1.** *bad soles:* the sole of a shoe; the corrupt human soul

**2.** *falling-sickness:* epilepsy; have fallen under Caesar's rule

**3.** *hart / heart:* refers to Caesar as deer; center, spirit of the world

## COMPARING PLAYS

**1.** Answers will vary. Students should discuss incidents, characters, problems that seem realistic.

**2.** Answers will vary. Students should state specific qualities they would want to see in a theatrical performance.

---

language, and the rules of spelling and grammar were less fixed than they are today. Words acquired several different meanings, and these different meanings lent themselves to puns.

Shakespeare used puns largely to win easy laughs from his audiences. However, although Shakespeare's puns are usually meant to be humorous, they also make a serious point: that things are not always what they seem.

Identify the puns in the following lines from *Julius Caesar*. You may need to refer to the marginal notes in the text, but explain the puns in your own words.

1. COBBLER. A trade, sir, that, I hope, I may use with a safe conscience, which is indeed, sir, a mender of bad soles.
   — Act I, Scene i, lines 13–14

2. CASCA. He fell down in the market place, and foamed at mouth and was speechless.
   BRUTUS. 'Tis very like he hath the falling-sickness.
   CASSIUS. No, Caesar hath it not; but you, and I, And honest Casca, we have the falling-sickness.
   — Act I, Scene ii, lines 250–254

3. ANTONY. O world, thou wast the forest to this hart; And this indeed, O world, the heart of thee.
   — Act III, Scene i, lines 207–208

## COMPOSITION

### Writing About the Total Effect

◼ Discuss the total effect of *Julius Caesar*. That is, describe the play's overall impact on you after you finished reading it. Support your statement by explaining how Shakespeare uses the following literary elements to achieve this effect: plot, character, setting, imagery and symbol, irony,

and theme. *For help with this assignment, see Lesson 12 in the Writing About Literature Handbook at the back of this book.*

### Writing About Character

◼ Compare and contrast any two of the four major characters in *Julius Caesar*: Brutus, Cassius, Antony, and Caesar. Discuss the principal similarities and differences between these characters. You might want to consider both men as politicians and leaders, as judges of other people, as patriotic Romans, and as private individuals. End by telling which character you prefer, and why. *For help with this assignment, see Lesson 3 in the Writing About Literature Handbook at the back of this book.*

### Writing Dialogue

◼ In Act II, Scene i, Brutus and Cassius have a private conversation, after which Brutus indicates that he will join the conspiracy against Caesar. Write some dialogue revealing what you think Brutus and Cassius said to each other during this conversation. Keep in mind what you know about each character: their different goals and personalities, their attitudes toward Caesar and toward each other. Write the dialogue in prose.

## COMPARING PLAYS

1. *Nicholas Nickleby*, *Cyrano de Bergerac*, and *Julius Caesar* all portray societies that actually existed. Which of these plays do you think offers the most realistic picture of human life? Which of these plays seems the least realistic? Explain your answer in each case.

2. Which of the three plays would you most like to see performed in a theater? Why?

---

## COMPOSITION: GUIDELINES FOR EVALUATION

### WRITING ABOUT THE TOTAL EFFECT

**Objective**
To use components of drama to describe total effect

**Guidelines for Evaluation**
- suggested length: six to eight paragraphs
- should include all components mentioned
- should cite specific examples from text
- should show an understanding of elements involved

### WRITING ABOUT CHARACTER

**Objective**
To compare and contrast two characters

**Guidelines for Evaluation**
- suggested length: six to eight paragraphs
- should compare any two characters
- should bring out each character's major traits
- should end with a subjective statement of preference and support it with reasons

# ACTIVE READING

## Dramatic Voices

When we read a play, our minds become theaters. We see the sets and costumes; we visualize the action. Most of all, we create the voices of the characters.

As we play out the various roles, we should remember that drama intensifies life, brings out its hidden lines and colors. All the plays in this unit take place on a heroic scale; that is, they are emphatically larger than life. Therefore, when we play the various characters in each drama, we should give them the voices they cry out for. Let Nicholas Nickleby be the noble gentleman; let Squeers be the oily villain; let Cyrano be the proud, romantic swashbuckler. When Mark Antony begins his speech to the Roman crowd, give him the ringing tones of a great orator who feels the power that his words have over the people. Truth in drama is seen at its best in bold colors and strong contrasts.

Look, for example, at the climactic scene from *Nicholas Nickleby* in which Nicholas finally opposes Squeers. This is high drama in which the clash of personalities stands for a great deal. It is an extraordinary thing for a well-bred young man like Nicholas, who needs his job so badly, to turn against authority. Nicholas' words remain clipped, plain, and polite, yet they must suggest the molten anger that burns beneath the polite surface. In contrast, Squeers, who is not used to being crossed, roars out of control. The contrast between the two men is extreme, and this final confrontation between what each represents seethes with tension. Justice is pitted against injustice, humanity against brutality; the lines between right and wrong are clearly drawn. It is a wonderful, thrilling moment in which the play of dramatic voices allows truths too often muffled in real life to ring out loud and clear.

*Julius Caesar* also revolves to a large extent around the contrast between the personalities of two men, Brutus and Mark Antony. Brutus is subdued, a man of reason; Antony is flamboyant, a man of emotion. Brutus tries to remain true to his ideals through many difficult situations; Antony changes from one situation to the next. Antony is a theatrical personality who relishes the idea of playing roles. Which voice do you think he uses in his final speech over the

Point out to the students that, in reading the plays in this unit, they have heard many different dramatic voices speak in their imaginations. After reading this essay, go back and reread the particular speeches used as examples. For example, have students read aloud the confrontation between Nicholas Nickleby and Squeers in Scene x of *The Life and Adventures of Nicholas Nickleby*. In preparation, point out portions of earlier scenes that show Nicholas as a restrained, polite young man, someone who naturally respects his elders and those in authority. For example, you might remind the students of Nicholas' tactful answers in Scene v when Squeers reveals his ignorance by misspelling *botany*. The reading of the confrontation in Scene x should contrast sharply with this earlier scene. Encourage those reading the scene to play up Nicholas' sincerity, restraint, and virtue, on the one hand, and Squeers's temper and villainy, on the other. Ask students to give examples from the scene of the ways in which drama intensifies life (for example, in life we seldom have the opportunity to oppose the sort of pure evil that Squeers represents).

You will find among the materials for this unit in your *Teacher's Classroom Resources* the related blackline masters Dramatic Voices.

## WRITING DIALOGUE

### Objective
To use knowledge of characters to write appropriate dialogue

### Guidelines for Evaluation
- suggested length: one page
- should create dialogue for suggested scene
- should end dialogue with Brutus' decision to join conspiracy
- should write dialogue in prose

body of Brutus? Is he sincerely moved? Or is he playing the part of a man who would like us to *believe* that he is moved?

Like Antony, Cyrano de Bergerac is at heart a player of many roles. He is a poet and a fighter, a lover and a clown, an idealistic dreamer and a sarcastic truth-teller. In playing the part of Cyrano in the theater of the mind, we must find many voices for this man because he never speaks as simply "himself." He is usually playing a role, disguising his true feelings. Cyrano uses words to compensate for the lack of love he feels in his life. When he mocks himself in his famous "nose speech," he becomes a whole chorus of rapidly changing voices, quickly and ingeniously making fun of himself before the rest of the world can beat him to it. Each voice that we give Cyrano in reading this speech must be definite, theatrical, full of self-mockery and even greater mockery for his less-clever adversaries. Even when he is about to die, Cyrano cannot prevent himself from putting on a great show. He imagines all of his enemies coming at him, and he slashes wildly at each one with his faltering sword and his never-faltering words. He even imagines his own death in the form of a little dramatic scene:

> When I go to meet God this evening, and doff my hat before the holy gates, my salute will sweep the blue threshold of heaven.

In the theater of your mind, play Cyrano to the hilt; play him as the true actor that he is. Cyrano's theatricality speaks to us of things we too often forget in real life: It reminds us of the many possibilities of the human spirit and the great capacity of the imagination to transform ugliness into beauty, pain into laughter, and death into heroically soaring life.

572 *Drama*

# REVIEW: DRAMA

## Guide for Studying Drama

Like other forms of literature, drama requires the active involvement of its audience. When we read a play, we actively imagine how the playwright's words might come to life on stage. When we see a play in the theater, we add our own thoughts and feelings to what we see on the stage. Review the following questions when you read or see a play. In helping you to understand how drama creates its impact, this guide will increase your enjoyment of any play.

1. What important **conflicts** does the play present? What events of the **plot** develop these conflicts? What event is the play's **climax**, and how does it resolve the play's conflicts?
2. Who are the major **characters** in the play? What personality traits do they reveal in their **dialogue** with each other? In their **soliloquies** and **asides**? What do we learn about them from the comments of other characters?
3. What is the **setting** of the play? What is the play's historical and social background? How is the setting appropriate to the play's action?
4. What are the **themes** of the play? How are these themes revealed through the play's plot, setting, and characters?
5. In what ways could **staging**—scenery, lighting, costumes, and acting—establish the play's atmosphere, bring its characters to life, and highlight its major developments and themes?
6. Is the play a **comedy** or **tragedy**? If it is a tragedy, what is the **tragic flaw** of its hero?

*Drama* **573**

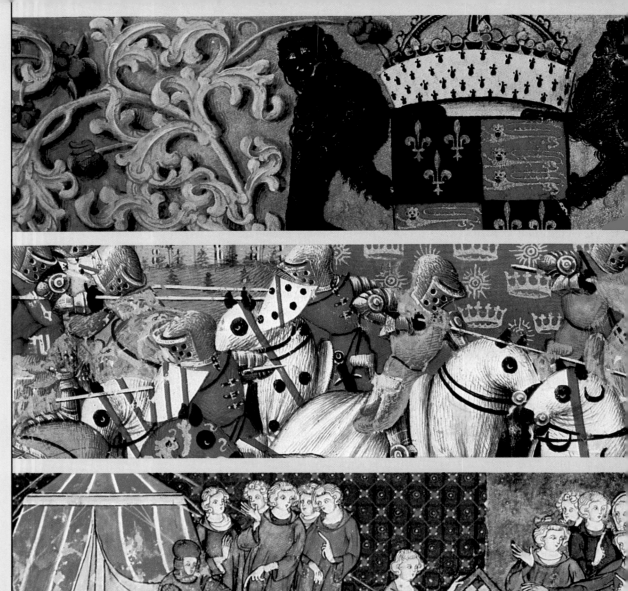

574    *The King Arthur Legend*

# PREVIEW:
# THE KING ARTHUR LEGEND

*All that evening I sat by my fire . . . steeped in a dream of olden time. . . . I dipped into old Sir Thomas Malory's enchanting book and fed at its rich feast of prodigies and adventures, breathed in the fragrance of its obsolete names, and dreamed again.*

—Mark Twain, *A Connecticut Yankee in King Arthur's Court*

Flags flap in the breeze, trumpets blare, and warriors gallop on armored horses, their lances poised for combat. Sorcerers work their spells, and knights in coats of mail rescue maidens in distress. King Arthur takes his rightful place on the throne, driving back the forces of evil and bringing peace, prosperity, and virtue to the land. Then Arthur's noble order falls apart, and the king vanishes into the mist. Some say that he has died; others say he sleeps and will awaken in his country's hour of greatest need.

Such are the events that make up the legend of King Arthur and the knights of the Round Table, a legend that has haunted the imaginations of people all over the world for over a thousand years. A **legend** is a tale that is handed down for generations among the people of a certain region. The tale usually magnifies the achievements of a real-life individual, turning this figure into a larger-than-life hero. A legend often gives a people a proud image of their history, a way of expressing their values in heroic and exciting terms. Some legends circulate beyond the regions where they begin and become identified with a whole nation or civilization: Examples include the Greek legend of the Trojan War, the French legend of Roland, and the British legend of King Arthur.

The legend of King Arthur began in early Britain as a number of

*The King Arthur Legend* **575**

Before the students read the Preview, ask them to provide definitions of a superhero, and list the qualities they mention. Discuss why ordinary people need to believe in such extraordinary heroes (for example, because they allow us to forget such limitations as our own physical and moral weaknesses, the dullness or banality of our surroundings, and our own inevitable mortality).

As the students read the historical information in the Preview, help them by suggesting that the King Arthur legend is like a small seed that eventually developed into a large and many-branched tree. Emphasize the idea that the "real" Arthur was probably a local warrior who filled people's need for a hero. This local warrior gradually grew into a superhero as more stories were absorbed into his legend over time. The Celtic sagas added superhuman traits to the legend; the works of Nennius and Geoffrey rooted the legend in British history; and, as the legend spread to Europe, the romances added colorful and entertaining stories of love and chivalry.

Remind the students that *Le Morte d'Arthur* concerns a time centuries ago when life was very difficult and most people were poor, uneducated, and did not live long. Ask them to imagine life without such conveniences as electricity, plumbing, and penicillin, in a society in which most people had to obey someone else, could not read, and had no legal rights. Ask them to imagine the sort of hero and the kinds of stories that would appeal to people living in such a world.

folk stories. As the legend spread, it gave rise to a rich collection of art and literature in many different countries. From the Dark Ages to the present, poets, historians, novelists, composers, and filmmakers have found something in the King Arthur story to suit their own times and audiences. However, although the story of King Arthur has been interpreted in many different ways, the basic source of its appeal has never changed. The story of King Arthur remains a tale of high adventure and romance, of glorious achievement and tragic failure, of the rise and fall of a great hero and his noble ideal.

## The Historical Basis of the King Arthur Legend

One fascinating part of the King Arthur story is the possibility that Arthur may have actually existed. A sixth-century account of the invasion of Britain by Saxon warriors from Germany mentions a heroic British cavalry general named Arturius. In 517 he led the Britons to a decisive victory over the Saxons at Mount Badon, near present-day London. Eventually, however, his people were defeated, and Arturius was believed to have been killed and buried at Glastonbury, in southwest England.

Six centuries later, in 1190, excavators working for King Henry II reportedly found a tomb near the Abbey of Glastonbury. From the tomb was drawn a huge coffin bearing an inscription that read in translation, ''Here lies buried the renowned King Arthur in the Isle of Avalon.'' The coffin contained the skeleton of a tall man, whose skull was damaged, and some smaller bones, thought to be the remains of his queen.

## The Growth of the King Arthur Legend

The real Arthur—whoever he was—was eventually transformed by legend into a gloriously heroic king of the Britons. Arthur figured in several epic poems in which the British people celebrated their history before the Saxon conquest. An **epic** is a long verse narrative that tells the story of a hero who represents the values of a particular group of people. In the early British epics Arthur became such a hero, performing great deeds and taking on mythic, almost superhuman, powers. Some of the stories that sprang up around him even made him immortal. According to one Welsh version, Arthur sleeps in a cave and will awaken only to rescue his land from oppression.

These tales eventually found their way into scholarly writing. Around 800 a Welsh monk named Nennius wrote a Latin account of Arthur in the *History of the Britons,* blending historical information about Arturius with some of the more fanciful tales circulating among Welsh storytellers. In 1136 Geoffrey of Monmouth, another monk, wrote the *History of the Kings of Britain,* using Nennius' account

Combat between Sir Tristram and Sir Palomides, two of Arthur's knights. Detail from
a medieval manuscript.

*The King Arthur Legend*  **577**

and other chronicles as his sources. Also writing in Latin, Geoffrey attempted to glorify the Norman rulers of his own time, who had conquered Britain in 1066. He introduced the order of knighthood to the story and claimed that Arthur was a descendant of Aeneas [i nē′əs], the founder of Ancient Rome.

King Arthur and the Round Table. Fourteenth-century wooden disk hanging in the Great Hall of Winchester Castle.

578    *The King Arthur Legend*

## The King Arthur Legend as a Medieval Romance

Eventually, the legend of King Arthur spread to the European continent, where it grew in substance and detail. Writing about twenty years after Geoffrey of Monmouth, the French writer Wace produced a version of the King Arthur story for his queen and her court. Wace introduced the idea of the Round Table, and another Frenchman, Chrétien de Troyes [krā tyan′ də trwa′], enriched the legend further with several appealing love stories. After the priest Layamon wrote the first widely read English account in 1205, other versions of Arthur's story appeared in Germany, Italy, and Spain. Many of these stories took the form of the most popular type of literature of the Middle Ages, the medieval romance.

The **medieval romance** was one of the forerunners of modern fiction. Most romances consisted of loose collections of incidents concerning a noble hero, his exciting adventures, and, especially, his pursuit of love. Many romances focused on the practice of **chivalry**, a knightly code of brave and courteous behavior. Like the legend and epic, the romance often began as oral literature. Minstrels—poets who sang their verses—wandered from court to court in medieval Europe performing well-known stories for noble audiences. The minstrels would usually embroider these tales, reworking them to please their listeners. When the romances were eventually written down by such authors as Chrétien de Troyes, they added to the Arthurian legend a series of sophisticated stories of brave knights and their devotion to beautiful ladies.

In the late fifteenth century Thomas Malory took these loosely linked romances and turned them into the first unified English version of the legend of King Arthur.

## Thomas Malory and the King Arthur Legend

Sir Thomas Malory was an English knight who lived in England during a time of great civil unrest known as the Wars of the Roses. Two noble families battled violently for the crown, and many people died on both sides. Like many other nobles of his time, Malory led a turbulent life, spending his last few years in prison. There he produced his great version of the King Arthur legend, *Le Morte d'Arthur* (*The Death of Arthur*).

Published in 1485 by the first English printer, William Caxton, Malory's work is important for a number of reasons. By Malory's time there were many conflicting versions of the story of King Arthur in several different languages. *Le Morte d'Arthur* became the first unified version of the legend to appear in print in the English language. Malory used French sources and kept many of the adven-

The Bodleian Library, Oxford, Ms. Douce 383 folio 16

*The King Arthur Legend* **579**

tures and love stories that had delighted the European courtly audiences. However, he gave new emphasis to the chivalric sense of duty and honor, to Arthur's moral mission, and to his importance as an English national hero. This last contribution was especially important at a time when the crown itself was threatened by civil war.

### Modern Versions of the King Arthur Legend

Malory's *Morte d'Arthur* became the main source for most subsequent versions of the King Arthur legend. The nineteenth-century British poet Alfred, Lord Tennyson reinterpreted many of Malory's incidents in his own *Idylls of the King*. Tennyson's poems focus on Arthur's creation of an ideal society and the failure of flawed human beings to live up to that ideal.

Writing nearly at the same time as Tennyson, Mark Twain also used Malory as a source for *A Connecticut Yankee in King Arthur's Court* (included in this book, beginning on page 666). Twain approached the legend quite differently, however. Instead of idealizing Arthur's society, Twain's novel poked fun at it by sending a down-to-earth American back in time to Arthur's Britain.

The nineteenth-century German composer Richard Wagner wrote several majestic operas based on the Arthurian legend. British author T. H. White reworked Malory's material into a trilogy of novels published in 1958 under the title *The Once and Future King*. Alan Lerner and Frederick Loewe turned White's trilogy into a popular stage musical, *Camelot,* which was also made into a film. Numerous other films have brought the legendary Arthur and his knights to vivid life for millions of people around the world.

### Timeline for The King Arthur Legend

## Le Morte d'Arthur

The Arthurian legend as it comes down to us through Thomas Malory traces the unusual circumstances of Arthur's birth and youth, his drawing of a sword from a stone to prove his kingship, and his coronation. Arthur's early achievements are described, including his victories in battle under the guidance of Merlin the magician, his marriage to Gwynevere [gwin'ə vēr], the creation of the Round Table, and his establishment of the high code by which he expected his knights to live. Central to the legend are the adventures of the various knights—Launcelot, Gawain, Bedivere, Galahad—and their pursuit of the Holy Grail, the cup used by Jesus and the Apostles at the Last Supper. The story of Arthur comes to a tragic close in the conflict between Arthur and Sir Launcelot over Launcelot's relationship with Queen Gwynevere. This conflict ultimately leads to the attempt of the evil Sir Modred to abduct Gwynevere and to seize Arthur's throne, the final clash between Modred and Arthur, and Arthur's own disappearance.

Because Thomas Malory wrote in a version of English quite different from our language today, the selections presented here have been modernized. Malory's work differs in a number of other ways from modern narratives. He often tells of fairy-tale-like events, in which giants are slain and prophecies come true. Most of Malory's descriptions seem sparser than those of modern narratives, since Malory could evoke a whole world of associations for his readers with just a few important details. Malory emphasizes psychological development less than modern writers. *Le Morte d'Arthur* focuses more on what characters do than on what they think or feel, and their personalities include only a few dominant traits. Finally, Malory's narrative often uses **episodic** organization: Rather than following a conventional plot structure, some of the tales string together a loosely related series of incidents. Each incident is entertaining in itself, but even more important is the total effect Malory produces by piling incident upon incident.

### Key Ideas in *Le Morte d'Arthur*

■ As you read *Le Morte d'Arthur,* look for references to each of the following. If you keep track of what the work says about these subjects, you will begin to grasp its most important themes.

- Heroic adventures and glory
- Nobility
- Chivalry and the order of the Round Table
- Magic, prophecy, and mystery
- Loyalty to the king

The Bodleian Library, Oxford, Ms. Douce 383 folio 16

*The King Arthur Legend* **581**

*Thomas Malory*

# Le Morte d'Arthur

Modern Idiom by Keith Baines

Arthur being crowned king. Detail from a medieval manuscript. *Opposite*, King
Arthur enthroned. Detail from a medieval manuscript.

**582**   *The King Arthur Legend*

## ARTHUR BECOMES KING

*Uther Pendragon* [ū'thər pen drag'ən], *the king of all Britain, has recently married the beautiful Igraine* [ē grān'], *widow of the Duke of Cornwall. In return for arranging Uther's marriage to Igraine, Merlin the sorcerer asks Uther to allow him to oversee the rearing of the couple's first child. Merlin, who can foretell the future, knows that this child will be Arthur, who is destined to become Britain's greatest king. Shortly before the child is born, Merlin approaches Uther to arrange for his upbringing.*

Merlin appeared before the king. "Sire," he said, "you know that you must provide for the upbringing of your child?"

"I will do as you advise," the king replied.

"That is good," said Merlin. "Your child is destined for glory, and I want him brought to me for his baptism.[1] I shall then give him into the care of foster parents who can be trusted not to reveal his identity before the proper time. Sir Ector would be suitable: he is extremely loyal, owns good estates, and his wife has just borne him a child. She could give her child into the care of another woman, and herself look after yours."

Sir Ector was summoned, and gladly agreed to the king's request, who then rewarded him handsomely. When the child was born he was at once wrapped in a gold cloth and taken by two knights and two ladies to Merlin, who stood waiting at the rear entrance to the castle in his beggar's disguise. Merlin took the child to a priest, who baptized him with the name of Arthur, and thence to Sir Ector, whose wife fed him at her breast.

Two years later King Uther fell sick, and his enemies once more overran his kingdom, inflicting heavy losses on him as they advanced. Merlin prophesied that they could be checked only by the presence of the king himself on the battlefield, and suggested that he should be conveyed there on a horse litter. King Uther's army met the invader on the plain at St. Albans, and the king duly appeared on the horse litter. Inspired by his presence, and by the lively leadership of Sir Brastius and Sir Jordanus, his army quickly defeated the enemy and the battle finished in a rout. The king returned to London to celebrate the victory.

But his sickness grew worse, and after he had lain speechless for three days and three nights Merlin summoned the nobles to attend the king in his chamber on the following morning. "By the grace of God," he said, "I hope to make him speak."

In the morning, when all the nobles were assembled, Merlin addressed the king: "Sire, is it your will that Arthur shall succeed to the throne, together with all its prerogatives?"[2]

The king stirred in his bed, and then spoke so that all could hear: "I bestow on Arthur God's blessing and my own, and Arthur shall succeed to the throne on pain of forfeiting my blessing." Then King Uther gave up the ghost. He was buried and mourned the next day, as befitted his rank, by Igraine and the nobility of Britain.

During the years that followed the death of

---

1. **baptism:** religious ceremony in which a person, usually an infant, is sprinkled with water and becomes a Christian.

2. **prerogatives** [pri rog'ə tivz]: rights and privileges associated with a particular rank.

*Arthur Becomes King* **583**

### AT A GLANCE

- Merlin advises Uther Pendragon on how to raise his heir.
- Arthur goes to foster parents.
- King Uther bestows the throne on Arthur and dies.

### LITERARY OPTIONS

- epic hero
- character

### THEMATIC OPTIONS

- nobility/chivalric code
- magic and prophecy
- heroic deeds

### 1 THEME

Prophecy and magic play an important part in Malory's work. Merlin prophesies that Arthur is "destined for glory" even before his birth.

### 2 STYLE: IMAGERY

The use of concrete detail to create sensory images underscores the preciousness of the child: He's wrapped in cloth of gold.

### 3 CHARACTERIZATION

Merlin is characterized not only as magical and mysterious but also as practical and concerned with the legitimacy of the succession.

## GUIDED READING

### LITERAL QUESTION

**1a.** What advice does Merlin give King Uther when his enemies are about to win the battle? (He says that only the king's presence on the battlefield can save the day.)

### INFERENTIAL QUESTION

**1b.** What does this advice tell you about the importance of the throne? (It is very important as a symbol of unity and a focus for patriotism.)

- The nobles fight for the throne.
- The Archbishop announces that the succession will be decided by a test.
- Arthur passes the test by pulling a sword from a stone.
- Sir Kay claims he did it but then admits it was Arthur.

**1 THEME**

The idea of magic is emphasized: The king will be chosen by miraculous, not political, means.

**2 BACKGROUND**

In a society that has not yet separated church and state, the Archbishop of Canterbury, the head of the English church, has great political power.

**3 PLOT: RISING ACTION**

By his request Sir Kay sets in motion a major plot action. It also provides the motivation for Arthur's act and establishes his feat as unselfish, demonstrating that heroic deeds often result from pure and unselfish motives.

**4 CHARACTERIZATION**

Sir Kay is established as both selfish and ambitious. He provides the perfect foil for Arthur, who is neither.

King Uther, while Arthur was still a child, the ambitious barons fought one another for the throne, and the whole of Britain stood in jeopardy. Finally the day came when the Archbishop of Canterbury,[3] on the advice of Merlin, summoned the nobility to London for Christmas morning.

**1** In his message the Archbishop promised that the true succession to the British throne would be miraculously revealed. Many of the nobles purified themselves during their journey, in the hope that it would be to them that the succession would fall.

The Archbishop held his service in the city's greatest church (St. Paul's), and when matins[4] were done the congregation filed out to the yard. They were confronted by a marble block into which had been thrust a beautiful sword. The block was four feet square, and the sword passed through a steel anvil which had been struck in the stone, and which projected a foot from it. The anvil had been inscribed with letters of gold:

WHOSO PULLETH OUTE THIS SWERD OF THIS STONE AND ANVYLD IS RIGHTWYS KYNGE BORNE OF ALL BRYTAYGNE[5]

**2** The congregation was awed by this miraculous sight, but the Archbishop forbade anyone to touch the sword before mass had been heard. After mass, many of the nobles tried to pull the sword out of the stone, but none was able to, so a watch of ten knights was set over the sword, and a tournament proclaimed for New Year's Day, to provide men of noble blood with the opportunity of proving their right to the succession.

---

3. **Archbishop of Canterbury:** head of the church in England.
4. **matins** [mat′inz]: morning church service.
5. **Whoso...Brytaygne:** "Whoever pulls out this sword from this stone and anvil is by right of birth king of all Britain."

Sir Ector, who had been living on an estate near London, rode to the tournament with Arthur and his own son Sir Kay, who had been **3** recently knighted. When they arrived at the tournament, Sir Kay found to his annoyance that his sword was missing from its sheath, so he begged Arthur to ride back and fetch it from their lodging.

Arthur found the door of the lodging locked and bolted, the landlord and his wife having left for the tournament. In order not to disappoint his brother, he rode on to St. Paul's, determined to get for him the sword which was lodged in the stone. The yard was empty, the guard also having slipped off to see the tournament, so Arthur strode up to the sword, and, without troubling to read the inscription, tugged it free. He then rode straight back to Sir Kay and presented him with it.

Sir Kay recognized the sword, and taking it **4** to Sir Ector, said, "Father, the succession falls to me, for I have here the sword that was lodged in the stone." But Sir Ector insisted that they should all ride to the churchyard, and once there bound Sir Kay by oath to tell how he had come by the sword. Sir Kay then admitted that Arthur had given it to him. Sir Ector turned to Arthur and said, "Was the sword not guarded?"

"It was not," Arthur replied.

"Would you please thrust it into the stone again?" said Sir Ector. Arthur did so, and first Sir Ector and then Sir Kay tried to remove it, but both were unable to. Then Arthur, for the second time, pulled it out. Sir Ector and Sir Kay both knelt before him.

"Why," said Arthur, "do you both kneel before me?"

"My lord," Sir Ector replied, "there is only one man living who can draw the sword from the stone, and he is the true-born King of Britain." Sir Ector then told Arthur the story of his birth and upbringing.

"My dear father," said Arthur, "for so I shall

**584** *The King Arthur Legend*

---

## GUIDED READING

### LITERAL QUESTIONS

**1a.** How is the sword described? (It is beautiful and is stuck through a stone and steel anvil four feet thick.)

**2a.** What does Arthur neglect to do before pulling out the sword? (He does not read the inscription.)

### INFERENTIAL QUESTIONS

**1b.** What symbolic value could the sword have? (Removing it is a task that's difficult to do. All three of the elements involved—sword, stone, anvil—suggest strength and steadfastness, qualities needed for leadership.)

**2b.** Why is it important that Arthur not read the inscription? (Arthur's motivation for pulling out the sword is thus pure—free from ambition or thoughts of personal gain.)

always think of you—if, as you say, I am to be king, please know that any request you have to make is already granted.''

Sir Ector asked that Sir Kay should be made Royal Seneschal,[6] and Arthur declared that while they both lived it should be so. Then the three of them visited the Archbishop and told him what had taken place.

All those dukes and barons with ambitions to rule were present at the tournament on New Year's Day. But when all of them had failed, and Arthur alone had succeeded in drawing the sword from the stone, they protested against one so young, and of ignoble blood, succeeding to the throne.

The secret of Arthur's birth was known only to a few of the nobles surviving from the days of King Uther. The Archbishop urged them to make Arthur's cause their own; but their support proved ineffective. The tournament was

---

6. **Royal Seneschal** [sen′ə shəl]: person in charge of a royal household in medieval times. The Royal Seneschal held a position of considerable power and responsibility.

repeated at Candlemas[7] and at Easter, and with the same outcome as before.

Finally at Pentecost,[8] when once more Arthur alone had been able to remove the sword, the commoners arose with a tumultuous cry and demanded that Arthur should at once be made king. The nobles, knowing in their hearts that the commoners were right, all knelt before Arthur and begged forgiveness for having delayed his succession for so long. Arthur forgave them, and then, offering his sword at the high altar, was dubbed first knight of the realm. The coronation took place a few days later, when Arthur swore to rule justly, and the nobles swore him their allegiance.

King Arthur's first task was to re-establish those nobles who had been robbed of their lands during the troubled years since the reign of King Uther. Next, to establish peace and order in the counties near London.

---

7. **Candlemas:** Christian feast observed on February 2.
8. **Pentecost:** Christian feast observed on the seventh Sunday after Easter.

---

## STUDY QUESTIONS

### Recalling

1. Summarize Merlin's plan for raising young Arthur.
2. Describe what happens in Britain in the years after Uther's death.
3. What test does Merlin devise to reveal the true succession?
4. How does young Arthur first prove that he is Uther's rightful heir? What does he say to Sir Ector and Sir Kay when his identity is revealed?
5. Explain the nobles' first reaction to Arthur's succession to the throne. What makes them change their opinion? How does Arthur treat them?

### Interpreting

6. What is the main disadvantage of keeping Arthur's identity hidden from the nobles?
7. Why might the sword test be a more convincing proof of Arthur's identity than a statement by Merlin?
8. What does Arthur's treatment of Sir Ector, Sir Kay, and the nobles who had opposed him reveal about his character?
9. What effect do Merlin's various prophecies create in the story?

### Extending

10. Given his behavior in this tale, describe the kind of ruler you think Arthur will be.

*Arthur Becomes King* **585**

---

The presentation of Sir Galahad to King Arthur and the Knights of the Round Table. Detail from a medieval manuscript. *Opposite*, Sir Launcelot. Detail from a medieval manuscript.

**586** *The King Arthur Legend*

# THE TALE OF SIR LAUNCELOT

*After his coronation Arthur fights a number of battles with local rulers to prove that he is the rightful king of all Britain. The sorcerer Merlin guides him in these campaigns and arranges for Arthur to receive the magic sword, Excalibur, from the Lady of the Lake.*

*Settled at Camelot, Arthur falls in love with and marries Gwynevere, despite Merlin's warning that she is destined to love Sir Launcelot. As a wedding present, Arthur receives the Round Table. He dubs a number of young men knights of the Round Table and binds them by oath to a high code of ethics. These knights pursue a number of adventures of their own.*

*Meanwhile, Merlin has been trapped in a cave by a sorceress, and Arthur learns to rule without the magician's advice. The peace and stability that Arthur has established are endangered by the ruler of the Holy Roman Empire. Arthur sails to Europe with his knights and defeats the emperor's armies in France and Italy. Crowned in Rome by the Pope, Arthur distributes the emperor's wealth among his own knights and returns to Camelot in triumph.*

When King Arthur returned from Rome he settled his court at Camelot, and there gathered about him his knights of the Round Table, who diverted themselves with jousting and tournaments. Of all his knights one was supreme, both in prowess at arms and in nobility of bearing, and this was Sir Launcelot, who was also the favorite of Queen Gwynevere, to whom he had sworn oaths of fidelity.

One day Sir Launcelot, feeling weary of his life at the court, and of only playing at arms, decided to set forth in search of adventure. He asked his nephew Sir Lyonel to accompany him, and when both were suitably armed and mounted, they rode off together through the forest.

At noon they started across a plain, but the intensity of the sun made Sir Launcelot feel sleepy, so Sir Lyonel suggested that they should rest beneath the shade of an apple tree that grew by a hedge not far from the road. They dismounted, tethered their horses, and settled down.

"Not for seven years have I felt so sleepy," said Sir Launcelot, and with that fell fast asleep, while Sir Lyonel watched over him.

Soon three knights came galloping past, and Sir Lyonel noticed that they were being pursued by a fourth knight, who was one of the most powerful he had yet seen. The pursuing knight overtook each of the others in turn, and as he did so, knocked each off his horse with a thrust of his spear. When all three lay stunned he dismounted, bound them securely to their horses with the reins, and led them away.

Without waking Sir Launcelot, Sir Lyonel mounted his horse and rode after the knight, and as soon as he had drawn close enough, shouted his challenge. The knight turned about and they charged at each other, with the result that Sir Lyonel was likewise flung from his horse, bound, and led away a prisoner.

The victorious knight, whose name was Sir Tarquine, led his prisoners to his castle, and there threw them on the ground, stripped them

*The Tale of Sir Launcelot* **587**

## AT A GLANCE

- Launcelot wearies of court life and goes in search of adventure, taking Lyonel with him.
- They rest by a tree and Launcelot sleeps.
- Lyonel pursues a fierce knight, Sir Tarquine.

## LITERARY OPTIONS

- episodic narrative
- conflict

## THEMATIC OPTIONS

- chivalric code
- heroic deeds

## 1 SETTING

The scene is Camelot, where jousting and tournaments are often held. The fact that the knights spend their time only playing at arms shows that Arthur has established peace.

## GUIDED READING

**LITERAL QUESTION**

**1a.** Why did Launcelot go off in search of adventure? (Life at court was not exciting enough for him.)

**INFERENTIAL QUESTION**

**1b.** What does this decision tell you about Launcelot's values? (He prefers danger and action to security and passivity.)

- Lyonel is imprisoned by Sir Tarquine.
- Sir Ector de Marys follows Launcelot on his adventures.
- He fights with Tarquine, refuses to promise parole, and is also imprisoned.
- Launcelot is enchanted by four queens and imprisoned.

## 1 CHARACTERIZATION

Sir Ector shows his noble character, refusing to promise not to escape in return for more lenient treatment. He refuses to accept his status as a prisoner because the chivalric code requires death before surrender.

## 2 MOOD

The atmosphere changes from the clash of battle to a softer, more romantic mood.

---

naked, and beat them with thorn twigs. After that he locked them in a dungeon where many other prisoners, who had received like treatment, were complaining dismally.

Meanwhile, Sir Ector de Marys,[1] who liked to accompany Sir Launcelot on his adventures, and finding him gone, decided to ride after him. Before long he came upon a forester.

"My good fellow, if you know the forest hereabouts, could you tell me in which direction I am most likely to meet with adventure?"

"Sir, I can tell you: Less than a mile from here stands a well-moated castle. On the left of the entrance you will find a ford where you can water your horse, and across from the ford a large tree from which hang the shields of many famous knights. Below the shields hangs a caldron,[2] of copper and brass: strike it three times with your spear, and then surely you will meet with adventure—such, indeed, that if you survive it, you will prove yourself the foremost knight in these parts for many years."

"May God reward you!" Sir Ector replied.

The castle was exactly as the forester had described it, and among the shields Sir Ector recognized several as belonging to knights of the Round Table. After watering his horse, he knocked on the caldron and Sir Tarquine, whose castle it was, appeared.

They jousted, and at the first encounter Sir Ector sent his opponent's horse spinning twice about before he could recover.

"That was a fine stroke; now let us try again," said Sir Tarquine.

This time Sir Tarquine caught Sir Ector just below the right arm and, having impaled him on his spear, lifted him clean out of the saddle, and rode with him into the castle, where he threw him on the ground.

"Sir," said Sir Tarquine, "you have fought

---

1. **Sir Ector de Marys:** Sir Launcelot's younger brother; a different person from Sir Ector, Arthur's foster father.
2. **caldron** [kôl′drən]: large cooking pot.

better than any knight I have encountered in the last twelve years; therefore, if you wish, I will demand no more of you than your parole[3] as my prisoner."

"Sir, that I will never give."

"Then I am sorry for you," said Sir Tarquine, and with that he stripped and beat him and locked him in the dungeon with the other prisoners. There Sir Ector saw Sir Lyonel.

"Alas, Sir Lyonel, we are in a sorry plight. But tell me, what has happened to Sir Launcelot? for he surely is the one knight who could save us."

"I left him sleeping beneath an apple tree, and what has befallen him since I do not know," Sir Lyonel replied; and then all the unhappy prisoners once more bewailed their lot.

While Sir Launcelot still slept beneath the apple tree, four queens started across the plain. They were riding white mules and accompanied by four knights who held above them, at the tips of their spears, a green silk canopy, to protect them from the sun. The party was startled by the neighing of Sir Launcelot's horse and, changing direction, rode up to the apple tree, where they discovered the sleeping knight. And as each of the queens gazed at the handsome Sir Launcelot, so each wanted him for her own.

"Let us not quarrel," said Morgan le Fay.[4] "Instead, I will cast a spell over him so that he remains asleep while we take him to my castle and make him our prisoner. We can then oblige him to choose one of us."

Sir Launcelot was laid on his shield and borne by two of the knights to the Castle Charyot, which was Morgan le Fay's stronghold. He awoke to find himself in a cold cell, where a young noblewoman was serving him supper.

"What cheer?" she asked.

---

3. **parole** [pə rōl′]: word of honor, especially the pledge of a prisoner of war not to escape.
4. **Morgan le Fay:** an enchantress. In some works she is identified as Arthur's half-sister.

---

## GUIDED READING

### LITERAL QUESTIONS

**1a.** What does Sir Ector see when he knocks on the cauldron? (He sees shields that belong to some of the knights of the Round Table.)

**2a.** What offer does Tarquine make to Sir Ector after their battle? (If Ector swears parole—promises not to try to escape—Tarquine will not lock him in the dungeon.)

### INFERENTIAL QUESTIONS

**1b.** How do you think this sight affects his resolve to fight? (He is even more determined, because the fight is no longer just an adventure but a chance for revenge.)

**2b.** Why do you think Sir Ector refuses this lenient treatment? (It means accepting his status as a prisoner, and the chivalric code dictates that defeat must never be accepted.)

"My lady, I hardly know, except that I must have been brought here by means of an enchantment."

"Sir, if you are the knight you appear to be, you will learn your fate at dawn tomorrow." And with that the young noblewoman left him. Sir Launcelot spent an uncomfortable night but at dawn the four queens presented themselves and Morgan le Fay spoke to him:

"Now you are my prisoner, and you will have to choose: either to take one of us for your paramour, or to die miserably in this cell—just as you please. Now I will tell you who we are: I am Morgan le Fay, Queen of Gore; my companions are the Queens of North Galys, of Estelonde, and of the Outer Isles. So make your choice."

"A hard choice! Understand that I choose none of you, sorceresses that you are; rather will I die in this cell. But were I free, I would take pleasure in proving it against any who would champion you that Queen Gwynevere is the finest lady of this land."

"So, you refuse us?" asked Morgan le Fay.

"On my life, I do," Sir Launcelot said finally, and so the queens departed.

Sometime later, the young noblewoman who had served Sir Launcelot's supper reappeared.

"What news?" she asked.

"It is the end," Sir Launcelot replied.

"Sir Launcelot, I know that you have refused the four queens, and that they wish to kill you out of spite. But if you will be ruled by me, I can save you. I ask that you will champion my father at a tournament next Tuesday, when he has to combat the King of North Galys, and three knights of the Round Table, who last Tuesday defeated him ignominiously."

"My lady, pray tell me, what is your father's name?"

"King Bagdemagus."

"Excellent, my lady, I know him for a good king and a true knight, so I shall be happy to serve him."

"May God reward you! And tomorow at dawn I will release you, and direct you to an abbey which is ten miles from here, and where the good monks will care for you while I fetch my father."

"I am at your service, my lady."

As promised, the young noblewoman released Sir Launcelot at dawn. When she had led him through the twelve doors to the castle entrance, she gave him his horse and armor, and directions for finding the abbey.

"God bless you, my lady; and when the time comes I promise I shall not fail you."

Sir Launcelot rode through the forest in search of the abbey, but at dusk had still failed to find it, and coming upon a red silk pavilion,[5] apparently unoccupied, decided to rest there overnight, and continue his search in the morning. . . .

As soon as it was daylight, Sir Launcelot armed, mounted, and rode away in search of the abbey, which he found in less than two hours. King Bagdemagus' daughter was waiting for him, and as soon as she heard his horse's footsteps in the yard, ran to the window, and, seeing that it was Sir Launcelot, herself ordered the servants to stable his horse. She then led him to her chamber, disarmed him, and gave him a long gown to wear, welcoming him warmly as she did so.

King Bagdemagus' castle was twelve miles away, and his daughter sent for him as soon as she had settled Sir Launcelot. The king arrived with his retinue[6] and embraced Sir Launcelot, who then described his recent enchantment, and the great obligation he was under to his daughter for releasing him.

"Sir, you will fight for me on Tuesday next?"

"Sire, I shall not fail you; but please tell me

---

5. **pavilion:** tent.
6. **retinue** [ret′ə no͞o′]: servants and others accompanying a wealthy or important person.

*The Tale of Sir Launcelot*  **589**

AT A GLANCE
- Launcelot must choose one of the queens as a paramour or die.
- His jail keeper offers to help him escape if he will help her father, King Bagdemagus.
- Launcelot escapes and meets King Bagdemagus.

## 1 PLOT: CONFLICT

Launcelot experiences a conflict between the chivalric code and the request of the queens. The code of courtly love prescribes that he must be faithful to Gwynevere. He shows his nobility by choosing death rather than infidelity.

## 2 THEME

Launcelot often utters the pledge *I shall not fail you.* The chivalric code requires fidelity and reliability.

## 3 POINT OF VIEW

Throughout the work Malory uses the omniscient point of view. Here he shows Launcelot's arrival through the eyes of the noblewoman, emphasizing her anxiety about his safe arrival.

---

## GUIDED READING

### LITERAL QUESTION

**1a.** What does Launcelot tell King Bagdemagus when they first meet? (He tells him about the debt he owes his daughter and the events that led to incurring the debt.)

### INFERENTIAL QUESTION

**1b.** Why do you think he tells Bagdemagus this? (Launcelot wants to forestall Bagdemagus' thanks by making it clear that he is paying a debt.)

AT A GLANCE

- Launcelot promises to help the king in a tournament.
- He defeats the king's enemies.
- Launcelot rides off and meets a lady.

1 EPIC HERO

Launcelot is presented as the epic hero, larger than life, able to outfight and outmaneuver the best.

2 EPISODIC NARRATIVE

One adventure over, Launcelot searches for another. This kind of loose connection between many of the incidents holds the episodic plot together.

the names of the three Round Table knights whom I shall be fighting.''

''Sir Modred, Sir Madore de la Porte, and Sir Gahalantyne. I must admit that last Tuesday they defeated me and my knights completely.''

''Sire, I hear that the tournament is to be fought within three miles of the abbey. Could you send me three of your most trustworthy knights, clad in plain armor, and with no device, and a fourth suit of armor which I myself shall wear? We will take up our position just outside the tournament field and watch while you and the King of North Galys enter into combat with your followers; and then, as soon as you are in difficulties, we will come to your rescue, and show your opponents what kind of knights you command.''

This was arranged on Sunday, and on the following Tuesday Sir Launcelot and the three knights of King Bagdemagus waited in a copse,[7] not far from the pavilion which had been erected for the lords and ladies who were to judge the tournament and award the prizes.

The King of North Galys was the first on the field, with a company of ninescore[8] knights; he was followed by King Bagdemagus with fourscore knights, and then by the three knights of the Round Table, who remained apart from both companies. At the first encounter King Bagdemagus lost twelve knights, all killed, and the King of North Galys six.

1 With that, Sir Launcelot galloped onto the field, and with his first spear unhorsed five of the King of North Galys' knights, breaking the backs of four of them. With his next spear he charged the king, and wounded him deeply in the thigh.

''That was a shrewd blow,'' commented Sir Madore, and galloped onto the field to challenge Sir Launcelot. But he too was tumbled from his horse, and with such violence that his shoulder was broken.

Sir Modred was the next to challenge Sir Launcelot, and he was sent spinning over his horse's tail. He landed head first, his helmet became buried in the soil, and he nearly broke his neck, and for a long time lay stunned.

Finally Sir Gahalantyne tried; at the first encounter both he and Sir Launcelot broke their spears, so both drew their swords and hacked vehemently at each other. But Sir Launcelot, with mounting wrath, soon struck his opponent a blow on the helmet which brought the blood streaming from eyes, ears, and mouth. Sir Gahalantyne slumped forward in the saddle, his horse panicked, and he was thrown to the ground, useless for further combat.

Sir Launcelot took another spear, and unhorsed sixteen more of the King of North Galys' knights, and with his next, unhorsed another twelve; and in each case with such violence that none of the knights ever fully recovered. The King of North Galys was forced to admit defeat, and the prize was awarded to King Bagdemagus.

That night Sir Launcelot was entertained as the guest of honor by King Bagdemagus and his daughter at their castle, and before leaving was loaded with gifts.

''My lady, please, if ever again you should need my services, remember that I shall not fail you.''

2 The next day Sir Launcelot rode once more through the forest, and by chance came to the apple tree where he had previously slept. This time he met a young noblewoman riding a white palfrey.

''My lady, I am riding in search of adventure; pray tell me if you know of any I might find hereabouts.''

''Sir, there are adventures hereabouts if you believe that you are equal to them; but please tell me, what is your name?''

''Sir Launcelot du Lake.''

---

7. **copse** [kŏps]: grove of trees.
8. **ninescore**: one hundred eighty.

**590** *The King Arthur Legend*

---

## GUIDED READING

### LITERAL QUESTION

**1a.** What does Launcelot ask for after he promises to help King Bagdemagus? (He asks for three trustworthy knights and a suit of unmarked armor for himself.)

### INFERENTIAL QUESTION

**1b.** Why do you think he asks for unmarked armor? (His own would be readily identifiable, and he wants to go unrecognized. If the opposition underestimates him, he will have a better chance of winning.)

"Very well, Sir Launcelot, you appear to be a sturdy enough knight, so I will tell you. Not far away stands the castle of Sir Tarquine, a knight who in fair combat has overcome more than sixty opponents whom he now holds prisoner. Many are from the court of King Arthur, and if you can rescue them, I will then ask you to deliver me and my companions from a knight who distresses us daily, either by robbery or by other kinds of outrage."

"My lady, please first lead me to Sir Tarquine, then I will most happily challenge this miscreant knight of yours."

When they arrived at the castle, Sir Launcelot watered his horse at the ford, and then beat the caldron until the bottom fell out. However, none came to answer the challenge, so they waited by the castle gate for half an hour or so. Then Sir Tarquine appeared, riding toward the castle with a wounded prisoner slung over his horse, whom Sir Launcelot recognized as Sir Gaheris, Sir Gawain's brother and a knight of the Round Table.

"Good knight," said Sir Launcelot, "it is known to me that you have put to shame many of the knights of the Round Table. Pray allow your prisoner, who I see is wounded, to recover, while I vindicate the honor of the knights whom you have defeated."

"I defy you, and all your fellowship of the Round Table," Sir Tarquine replied.

"You boast!" said Sir Launcelot.

At the first charge the backs of the horses were broken and both knights stunned. But they

Two knights in a tournament. Detail from a fifteenth-century manuscript.

*The Tale of Sir Launcelot* **591**

AT A GLANCE

- The lady directs him to Tarquine and asks Launcelot to rid her of an importunate knight.
- He promises to help her, and she takes him to Tarquine.
- Launcelot and Tarquine fight.

**1 CHARACTERIZATION**

The other knights who signal Tarquine give the cauldron only a few knocks, but Launcelot beats it until the bottom falls out, suggesting his fierce intentions toward Tarquine.

**2 DIALOGUE**

Launcelot follows the chivalric code by seeking vindication for his fellow knights.

## GUIDED READING

### LITERAL QUESTION

**1a.** What does Launcelot see slung over the horse when he meets Tarquine? (He sees a wounded knight whom he recognizes as one of the knights of the Round Table.)

### INFERENTIAL QUESTION

**1b.** How do you think this affects his attitude toward Tarquine? (He wants to fight more than ever, in order to avenge his fellow knight.)

- Launcelot defeats Tarquine.
- He gives orders that the prisoners be released and goes off to help the lady.
- Sir Kay, Ector, and Lyonel decide to follow Launcelot in search of adventure.

## 1 THEME

This passage illustrates the generosity, even toward opponents, that is part of the chivalric code. Because Tarquine respects Launcelot's ability, he is willing to let him go and swear eternal friendship.

## 2 PLOT: CONFLICT

Tarquine sets up a situation that creates conflict for Launcelot: The chivalric code prescribes honesty, but personal safety dictates a lie. A true hero, Launcelot adheres to the code and tells the truth, thus endangering his life.

## 3 STYLE: SIMILE

In a rare simile the fighting knights are compared to wild bulls.

---

soon recovered and set to with their swords, and both struck so lustily that neither shield nor armor could resist. Finally they paused for a moment, resting on their shields.

"Worthy knight," said Sir Tarquine, "pray hold your hand for a while, and if you will, answer my question."

"Sir, speak on."

**1** "You are the most powerful knight I have fought yet, but I fear you may be the one whom in the whole world I most hate. If you are not, for the love of you I will release all my prisoners and swear eternal friendship."

"What is the name of the knight you hate above all others?"

"Sir Launcelot du Lake; for it was he who slew my brother, Sir Carados of the Dolorous Tower, and it is because of him that I have killed a hundred knights, and maimed as many more, apart from the sixty-four I still hold prisoner. And so, if you are Sir Launcelot, speak up, for we must then fight to the death."

**2** "Sir, I see now that I might go in peace and good fellowship, or otherwise fight to the death; but being the knight I am, I must tell you: I am Sir Launcelot du Lake, son of King Ban of Benwick, of Arthur's court, and a knight of the Round Table. So defend yourself!"

"Ah! this is most welcome."

**3** Now the two knights hurled themselves at each other like two wild bulls; swords and shields clashed together, and often their swords drove into the flesh. Then sometimes one, sometimes the other, would stagger and fall, only to recover immediately and resume the contest. At last, however, Sir Tarquine grew faint, and unwittingly lowered his shield. Sir Launcelot was swift to follow up his advantage, and dragging the other down to his knees, unlaced his helmet and beheaded him.

Sir Launcelot then strode over to the young noblewoman: "My lady, now I am at your service, but first I must find a horse."

Then the wounded Sir Gaheris spoke up: "Sir, please take my horse. Today you have overcome the most formidable knight, excepting only yourself, and by so doing have saved us all. But before leaving, please tell me your name."

"Sir Launcelot du Lake. Today I have fought to vindicate the honor of the knights of the Round Table, and I know that among Sir Tarquine's prisoners are two of my brethren, Sir Lyonel and Sir Ector, also your own brother, Sir Gawain. According to the shields there are also Sir Brandiles, Sir Galyhuddis, Sir Kay, Sir Alydukis, Sir Marhaus, and many others. Please release the prisoners and ask them to help themselves to the castle treasure. Give them all my greetings and say I will see them at the next Pentecost. And please request Sir Ector and Sir Lyonel to go straight to the court and await me there."

When Sir Launcelot had ridden away with the young noblewoman, Sir Gaheris entered the castle, and finding the porter in the hall, threw him on the ground and took the castle keys. He then released the prisoners, who, seeing his wounds, thanked him for their deliverance.

"Do not thank me for this work, but Sir Launcelot. He sends his greetings to you all, and asks you to help yourselves to the castle treasure. He has ridden away on another quest, but said that he will see you at the next Pentecost. Meanwhile, he requests Sir Lyonel and Sir Ector to return to the court and await him there."

"Certainly we shall not ride back to the court, but rather we shall follow Sir Launcelot wherever he goes," said Sir Ector.

"And I too shall follow him," said Sir Kay.

The prisoners searched the castle for their armor and horses and the castle treasure; and then a forester arrived with supplies of venison, so they feasted merrily and settled down for the night in the castle chambers—all but Sir Ector, Sir Lyonel, and Sir Kay, who set off immediately after supper in search of Sir Launcelot.

**592** *The King Arthur Legend*

---

## GUIDED READING

### LITERAL QUESTIONS

**1a.** How does the fight between Launcelot and Tarquine end? (Launcelot beheads Tarquine.)

**2a.** What do Sir Lyonel, Ector, and Kay decide to do after they are released from the dungeon? (They follow Launcelot in search of adventure.)

### INFERENTIAL QUESTIONS

**1b.** Why does Launcelot kill Tarquine, rather than simply defeat him? (Tarquine hates him for killing his brother; if Launcelot does not kill him, he will surely kill Launcelot.)

**2b.** Why do you think they decide to do this? (The chivalric code requires them to seek adventure, but they are also grateful to Launcelot for freeing them.)

Sir Launcelot and the young noblewoman were riding down a broad highway when the young noblewoman said they were within sight of the spot where the knight generally attacked her.

"For shame that a knight should so degrade his high calling," Sir Launcelot replied. "Certainly we will teach him a much-needed lesson. Now, my lady, I suggest that you ride on ahead, and as soon as he molests you, I will come to the rescue."

Sir Launcelot halted and the young noblewoman rode gently forward. Soon the knight appeared with his page, and seized the young noblewoman from her horse; she cried out at once, and Sir Launcelot galloped up to them.

"Scoundrel! what sort of knight do you think you are, to attack defenseless women?"

In answer the other knight drew his sword. Sir Launcelot did likewise, and they rushed together. With his first stroke Sir Launcelot split open the knight's head.

"Let that be your payment, though long overdue," said Sir Launcelot.

"Even so; he certainly deserved to die. His name was Sir Percy of the Forest Sauvage."

"My lady, do you require anything more of me?"

"No, good Sir Launcelot; and may the sweet Lord Jesu protect you, for certainly you are the bravest and gentlest knight I have known. But pray tell me one thing: why is it you do not take to yourself a wife? Many good ladies, both high born and low born, grieve that so fine a knight as yourself should remain single. It is whispered, of course, that Queen Gwynevere has cast a spell over you so that you shall love no other."

"As for that, people must believe what they will about Queen Gwynevere and me. But married I will not be, for then I should have to attend my lady instead of entering for tournaments and wars, or riding in search of adventure. And I will not take a paramour, both for the fear of God and in the belief that those who do so are always unfortunate when they meet a knight who is purer of heart; for whether they are defeated or victorious in such an encounter, either result must be equally distressing and shameful. I believe that a true knight is neither adulterous nor lecherous."

Sir Launcelot then took his leave of the young noblewoman, and for two days wandered alone through the forest, resting at night at the most meager of lodgings. On the third day, as he was crossing a bridge, he was accosted by a churlish porter,[9] who, after striking his horse on the nose so that it turned about, demanded to know by what right Sir Launcelot was riding that way.

"And what right do I need to cross this bridge? Surely, I cannot ride beside it," said Sir Launcelot.

"That is not for you to decide," said the porter, and with that he lashed at Sir Launcelot with his club. Sir Launcelot drew his sword, and after deflecting the blow, struck the porter on the head.

At the end of the bridge was a prosperous-looking village, overtopped by a fine castle. As Sir Launcelot advanced he heard someone cry: "Good knight, beware! You have done yourself no good by killing the chief porter of the castle."

Sir Launcelot rode on regardless, through the village and into the castle court, which was richly grassed. Thinking to himself that this would be a good place for combat, Sir Launcelot tied his horse to a ring in the wall and started across the lawn. Meanwhile people were peering at him from every door and window, and again he heard the warning: "Good knight, you come here at your peril!"

Before long two giants appeared, fully armed except for their heads, and brandishing huge

---

9. **churlish porter:** ill-mannered gatekeeper.

*The Tale of Sir Launcelot* **593**

## GUIDED READING

- Launcelot kills the giants and rescues threescore ladies.
- Sir Kay joins him, set upon by three knights whom Launcelot vanquishes.
- He makes the knights yield to Sir Kay.

## 1 CHARACTERIZATION

Here Launcelot is portrayed as the epic hero, larger than life: He can overcome even giants.

## 2 THEME

Launcelot's comment shows his sense of fairness: Three against one isn't a fair fight. The chivalric code believes in fighting often and fighting hard—but fighting fairly.

## 3 CHARACTERIZATION

Launcelot makes the knights yield to Sir Kay, even though Kay did not defeat them. This request typifies his modesty and tact.

clubs. Together they rushed at Sir Launcelot, who raised his shield to defend himself, and then struck at one of the giants and beheaded him. Thereupon the second giant roared with dismay and fled into the forest, where Sir Launcelot pursued him. In a few minutes, Sir Launcelot drew abreast of the giant and struck him on the shoulder, and the giant dropped dead.

When Sir Launcelot returned to the castle, he was greeted by threescore ladies, who all knelt before him.

"Brave knight! we thank you for delivering us. Many of us have been prisoners for seven years now, and although we are all high born, we have had to work like servants for our keep, doing silk embroidery. Pray tell us your name, so that our friends can know who has saved us."

"My ladies, I am called Sir Launcelot du Lake."

1 "Welcome, Sir Launcelot! It was you alone whom the giants feared, and you alone who could have overcome them. How often have we prayed for your coming!"

"My ladies, please greet your friends for me; and when I pass through this country again, grant me what hospitality you may feel is my due. Please recompense yourselves from the castle treasure, and then insure that the castle is restored to the rightful owner."

"Sir Launcelot, this is the castle of Tintagil, and belonged formerly to the duke of that name. But after his death, Igraine, who had been his wife, was made queen by King Uther Pendragon, to whom she bore Arthur, our present king."

"And so, after all, I know the owner of this castle. My ladies, I bless you, and farewell."

Always in quest of adventure, Sir Launcelot rode through many different countries, through wild valleys and forests, and across strange rivers; and at night he slept where he could, often in the roughest of lodgings. Then one day he came to a well-kept house where the lady of-

fered him the best of hospitality. After supper he was taken to his chamber, which overlooked the front door, and there Sir Launcelot disarmed and fell comfortably asleep.

He was awakened a short time later by a tremendous knocking at the door below, and looking through the window recognized Sir Kay in the moonlight, and three knights galloping toward him with drawn swords. The moment they got to the house, they dismounted and set upon Sir Kay, who turned about and drew his sword 2 to defend himself. Sir Launcelot hastily armed, saying to himself: "If they kill Sir Kay I shall be a party to his death, for three against one is unjust."

He let himself down from the window by means of his sheet, and then challenged the three attackers, whispering to Sir Kay to stand by while he dealt with them. Sir Kay did as he was advised, and then Sir Launcelot, with seven tremendous blows, brought all three knights to their knees and begging for mercy.

3 "Your lives will be spared if you yield to Sir Kay," said Sir Launcelot.

"Sir, it is surely you to whom we should yield, since we could easily have overcome Sir Kay."

"If you wish to be spared, you will go as prisoners of Sir Kay, and yield to Queen Gwynevere."

Each of the knights then swore on his sword to abide by the conditions of his surrender, and Sir Launcelot knocked once more at the door of the house.

"Why, I thought you were safely in bed," said the landlady, recognizing Sir Launcelot as she opened the door.

"Madam, I was, but then I had to jump out of the window and rescue this comrade of mine."

As they came into the light, Sir Kay recognized Sir Launcelot and thanked him humbly for twice saving his life.

"It was no more than I should have done, but

## GUIDED READING

**LITERAL QUESTION**

**1a.** How does Launcelot save Sir Kay from his pursuers? (He climbs out the window, using his sheet, and challenges them, whispering to Sir Kay to let him deal with them. He then quickly brings them to their knees with heavy blows.)

**INFERENTIAL QUESTION**

**1b.** What does this series of actions show about Launcelot's ability to deal with a crisis? (He can think and act quickly; he is capable of clever strategy as well as physical strength.)

come up to my chamber; you must be tired and hungry."

When Sir Kay had eaten, he lay on Sir Launcelot's bed, and they slept until dawn. Sir Launcelot woke first, and rising quietly, clad himself in Sir Kay's armor, and then, mounting Sir Kay's horse, rode away from the house.

When Sir Kay awoke, he was astonished to find that Sir Launcelot had exchanged armor with him, but then he realized he had done it so that he should ride home unmolested, while Sir Launcelot encountered his opponents. And when Sir Kay had taken his leave of the landlady he rode back to the court without further incident.

For several days Sir Launcelot rode through the forest, and then he came to a countryside of low meadows and broad streams. At the foot of a bridge he saw three pavilions, and a knight standing at the entrance to each, with a white

AT A GLANCE

- Launcelot wears Sir Kay's armor and rides off on Sir Kay's horse.
- Sir Kay realizes Launcelot has exchanged armor to protect him.
- Launcelot comes upon three pavilions and three knights.

### 1 CHARACTERIZATION

Launcelot again shows his protective attitude toward Sir Kay. In order to guarantee Sir Kay a safe trip home, Launcelot leaves his armor for Kay to wear. Everyone will think Sir Kay is Launcelot, fear him, and leave him alone.

Scenes from the life of Sir Launcelot. *Above left*, his birth; *above right*, his boyhood; *below left*, jousting; *below right*, the quest for the Holy Grail. Detail from a medieval manuscript.

*The Tale of Sir Launcelot* **595**

## GUIDED READING

### LITERAL QUESTION

**1a.** What surprises Sir Kay when he wakes up in Launcelot's room? (He sees Launcelot has exchanged armor with him in order to give him protection on the way home.)

### INFERENTIAL QUESTION

**1b.** What does this tell you about Launcelot's estimation of Sir Kay's abilities as a knight? (He obviously does not think Kay can take care of himself.)

- Twice, Launcelot is challenged by knights who think he is Sir Kay.
- Each time, Launcelot defeats the knights—who discover that he is not Sir Kay—and requires that they yield to Gwynevere in the name of Sir Kay.
- Launcelot returns to Camelot.

## 1 CHARACTERIZATION

Malory characterizes Sir Kay indirectly by reporting this conversation about him. He is described as arrogant: Despite his mediocre skills as a knight, he thinks too well of himself.

## 2 THEME

The chivalric code relies heavily on oaths, which are taken seriously. Knights must be honorable and keep their word. Here the knights are required to swear an oath to yield to Gwynevere.

## 3 EPIC HERO

The comments confirm Launcelot's status as an epic hero. The other knights guess that the mysterious knight must be Launcelot because he is so strong.

shield hanging above, and a spear thrust into the ground at one side. Sir Launcelot recognized the three knights, who were from Arthur's court, as Sir Gawtere, Sir Raynolde, and Sir Gylmere. However, he rode straight past them, looking neither to right nor to left, and without saluting them.

**1** "Why, there rides Sir Kay, the most overbearing knight of all, in spite of his many defeats. I think I will challenge him and see if I cannot shake his pride a little," said Sir Gawtere.

He then galloped up to Sir Launcelot and challenged him. They jousted, and Sir Gawtere was flung violently from the saddle.

"That is certainly not Sir Kay," said Sir Raynolde. "For one thing, he is very much bigger."

"Probably it is some knight who has killed Sir Kay and is riding in his armor," Sir Gylmere replied.

"Well, since he has overcome our brother we shall have to challenge him. But I think it must be either Sir Launcelot, Sir Tristram, or Sir Pelleas;[10] and we may not come well out of this."

Sir Gylmere challenged Sir Launcelot next, and was also overthrown. Then Sir Raynolde rode up to him.

"Sir, I would prefer not to challenge a knight so powerful as you, but since you have probably killed my brothers, I am obliged to; so defend yourself!"

They jousted; both broke their spears and they continued the combat with swords. Sir Gawtere and Sir Gylmere recovered, and attempted to rescue their brother, but Sir Launcelot saw them in time, and using more strength than hitherto, struck each off his horse again. At this, Sir Raynolde, badly wounded as he was, and with blood streaming from his head,

---

10. **Sir Tristram, or Sir Pelleas:** Tristram and Pelleas were two of the most famous knights of the Round Table and were among the strongest in the field.

**596**  *The King Arthur Legend*

picked himself up and once more rushed at Sir Launcelot.

"Sir, I should let things be," said Sir Launcelot. "I was not far away when you were knighted, and I know you to be worthy: therefore do not oblige me to kill you."

"May God reward you!" Sir Raynolde replied. "But speaking both for myself and my brothers, I would prefer to know your name before yielding to you, because we know very well that you are not Sir Kay, whom any one of us could have overcome."

**2** "That is as may be; but I still require that you yield to Queen Gwynevere at the next Pentecost, and say that Sir Kay sent you."

The three brothers took their oath, and Sir Launcelot left them. He had not ridden much further when, coming to a glade, he found four more knights of the Round Table: Sir Gawain, Sir Ector, Sir Uwayne, and Sir Sagramour le Desyrus.

"Look!" said Sir Sagramour, "there rides Sir Kay. I will challenge him."

Sir Sagramour first, then each of the other knights in turn, challenged Sir Launcelot, and was flung from his horse. Sir Launcelot left them gasping on the ground, and said to himself as he rode away: "Blessed be the maker of this spear; with it I have tumbled four knights off their horses." Meanwhile the four knights were picking themselves up and consoling each other.

**3** "To the devil with him! He is indeed powerful," said one.

"I believe that it must be Sir Launcelot," said another.

"Anyhow, let him go now; we shall discover when we return to Camelot," said a third, and so on....

Sir Launcelot returned to Camelot two days before the feast of Pentecost, and at the court was acclaimed by many of the knights he had met on his adventures.

Sir Gawain, Sir Uwayne, Sir Ector, and Sir

---

## GUIDED READING

### LITERAL QUESTIONS

**1a.** Why is Raynolde reluctant to challenge Launcelot, and why does he then do so? (He realizes Launcelot is very powerful but feels he has to avenge Sir Kay's death.)

**2a.** What does Launcelot say to Sir Raynolde as he rushes to attack? (He warns Raynolde not to attack again, or he will be forced to kill him.)

### INFERENTIAL QUESTIONS

**1b.** What can you assume about the chivalric code from this incident? (It requires revenge for the death of fellow knight, despite personal risk.)

**2b.** Why does Launcelot feel compelled to kill one of his own colleagues? (The chivalric code requires that a knight kill, or force to yield, anyone who challenges him, no matter who issues the challenge.)

Sagramour all laughed when they saw him in Sir Kay's armor, but without the helmet, and readily forgave his joke at their expense.

Sir Gaheris described to the court the terrible battle Sir Launcelot had fought with Sir Tarquine, and how sixty-four prisoners had been freed as a result of his victory.

Sir Kay related how Sir Launcelot had twice saved his life and then exchanged armor with him, so that he should ride unchallenged.

Sir Gawtere, Sir Gylmere, and Sir Raynolde described how he had defeated them at the bridge, and forced them to yield as prisoners of Sir Kay; and they were overjoyed to discover that it had been Sir Launcelot nevertheless.

Sir Modred, Sir Madore, and Sir Gahalantyne described his tremendous feats in the battle against the King of North Galys; and Sir Launcelot himself described his enchantment by the four queens, and his rescue at the hands of the daughter of King Bagdemagus.

And thus it was, at this time, that Sir Launcelot became the most famous knight at King Arthur's court.

---

## STUDY QUESTIONS

### Recalling

1. In what ways is Sir Launcelot "supreme" among the knights, according to Malory? Why does he leave Camelot?
2. How does Sir Ector end up at Sir Tarquine's castle? What does Sir Ector see there? What happens to him?
3. How is Launcelot helped by the daughter of King Bagdemagus? What does Launcelot do to repay the favor?
4. Describe what transpires between Launcelot and Sir Tarquine. What does Launcelot tell the knights whom he frees from the dungeon?
5. What does Launcelot do for the young woman who guides him to Tarquine? What reasons does Launcelot give her for remaining unmarried?
6. Describe Launcelot's adventure at the castle of Tintagil.

7. How does Launcelot save Sir Kay's life and see to it that no one will attack him again? What further adventures does this action lead to?

### Interpreting

8. Why, despite his loyalty to the Round Table, does Launcelot fight against his fellow knights several times? What higher good does Launcelot serve in each case?
9. What noble traits other than bravery does Launcelot reveal in this tale?
10. Arthur's code of chivalry demanded that a knight fight only in just causes, that he be merciful, and that he assist ladies. Choose three incidents that show how Launcelot lives by this code. How well do the other knights uphold this standard?

### Extending

11. Does any aspect of chivalry as practiced by Launcelot strike you as less than ideal? Explain.

*The Tale of Sir Launcelot* **597**

Arthur meets Modred on the battlefield. Detail from a medieval manuscript. *Opposite*,
Modred besieging the Tower of London. Detail from a medieval manuscript.

**598**   *The King Arthur Legend*

# THE DEATH OF ARTHUR

*The close bond between King Arthur and Sir Launcelot is marred and finally broken by their rivalry over Queen Gwynevere. Modred and Aggravayne, brothers of Sir Gawain—one of Arthur's chief knights—force the king into open conflict with Launcelot by exposing the mutual love between Launcelot and Gwynevere. Gwynevere is sentenced to death, but she is rescued by Launcelot, who unknowingly kills two innocent brothers of Gawain.*

*To avenge his slain brothers, Gawain urges Arthur to wage war against Launcelot, who has gone home to France. After a long siege the Pope commands Arthur to make peace, and an uneasy truce is established. However, at Gawain's urging Arthur attacks Launcelot's castle once again; Launcelot wounds Gawain but refuses to kill him. Shortly after, Arthur learns that Modred has been plotting to take over the throne in his absence.*

## AT A GLANCE

- Modred usurps the throne through deceit and trickery.
- He makes overtures to Gwynevere.
- She pretends to accept his marriage proposal but hides in a tower.

## LITERARY OPTIONS

- theme
- plot
- epic hero

## THEMATIC OPTIONS

- nobility
- betrayal and loss
- magic and prophecy

## 1 CHARACTERIZATION

Modred is ambitious, underhanded, and manipulative. His behavior is contrary to the chivalric code, and thus he makes both Arthur and Launcelot seem more noble by contrast.

## 2 THEME

Modred does not attain the nobility fostered by the chivalric code. Not only does he not protect women, but he tries to bully and deceive them.

## 3 BACKGROUND

The chivalric code evolved from the Christian tradition, so powerful in the Middle Ages. It required allegiance to God, then king. The Archbishop invokes the higher authority of God and church, since Modred has repudiated his king.

During the absence of King Arthur from Britain, Sir Modred, already vested with sovereign powers, had decided to usurp the throne. Accordingly, he had false letters written—announcing the death of King Arthur in battle—and delivered to himself. Then, calling a parliament, he ordered the letters to be read and persuaded the nobility to elect him king. The coronation took place at Canterbury and was celebrated with a fifteen-day feast.

Sir Modred then settled in Camelot and made overtures to Queen Gwynevere to marry him. The queen seemingly acquiesced,[1] but as soon as she had won his confidence, begged leave to make a journey to London in order to prepare her trousseau.[2] Sir Modred consented, and the queen rode straight to the Tower[3] which, with the aid of her loyal nobles, she manned and provisioned for her defense.

Sir Modred, outraged, at once marched against her, and laid siege to the Tower, but despite his large army, siege engines, and guns, was unable to effect a breach.[4] He then tried to entice the queen from the Tower, first by guile and then by threats, but she would listen to neither. Finally the Archbishop of Canterbury came forward to protest:

"Sir Modred, do you not fear God's displeasure? If you do not revoke your evil deeds I shall curse you with bell, book, and candle."[5]

"Fie on you![6] Do your worst!" Sir Modred replied.

"Sir Modred, I warn you take heed! or the wrath of the Lord will descend upon you."

"Away, false priest, or I shall behead you!"

The Archbishop withdrew, and after excommunicating[7] Sir Modred, abandoned his office and fled to Glastonbury. There he took up his

---

1. **acquiesced** [ak´wē est´]: agreed.
2. **trousseau** [troo´sō]: clothes and household items brought by a bride to her new home.
3. **Tower:** the Tower of London, a fortress.

4. **effect a breach:** break the system of defenses.
5. **bell, book, and candle:** items used in the ceremony that expels a person from the Catholic Church.
6. **"Fie on you!":** "For shame!"
7. **excommunicating:** expelling a person from membership in the Catholic Church.

*The Death of Arthur* **599**

---

## GUIDED READING

### LITERAL QUESTION

**1a.** What phrase in the first sentence tells what position of power Modred held before usurping the throne? (The phrase *already vested with sovereign powers* shows he has been acting as king while Arthur is away.)

### INFERENTIAL QUESTION

**1b.** What does Modred's position show about Arthur's attitude toward Modred? How does Arthur's attitude make Modred's treachery worse? (It shows Arthur trusted him. This compounds his treachery; he not only usurps the throne but betrays Arthur's trust.)

- Many nobles support Modred.
- Arthur returns from France.
- Arthur wins the first battle.
- Gawain is mortally wounded.
- He seeks reconciliation with Launcelot on his deathbed and asks him to help Arthur.

## 1 PLOT: RISING ACTION

News of Arthur's return reaches Modred and foreshadows the clash of armies to come. Arthur's return complicates the plot by making it clear that Modred's plan will not succeed without opposition.

## 2 POINT OF VIEW

Malory editorializes, expounding on Arthur's virtues and the faithlessness of the British people.

## 3 EPIC HERO

Gawain's deathbed repentance reinforces the image of both Launcelot and Arthur as epic heroes. Because Gawain accepts blame for what happened between them, the reader thinks better of these heroes after the previous disillusioning events.

abode as a simple hermit, and by fasting and prayer sought divine intercession in the troubled affairs of his country.

1 Sir Modred tried to assassinate the Archbishop, but was too late. He continued to assail the queen with entreaties and threats, both of which failed, and then the news reached him that King Arthur was returning with his army from France in order to seek revenge.

Sir Modred now appealed to the barony[8] to support him, and it has to be told that they came forward in large numbers to do so. Why? it will be asked. Was not King Arthur, the noblest sovereign Christendom had seen, now leading 2 his armies in a righteous cause? The answer lies in the people of Britain, who, then as now, were fickle. Those who so readily transferred their allegiance to Sir Modred did so with the excuse that whereas King Arthur's reign had led them into war and strife, Sir Modred promised them peace and festivity.

Hence it was with an army of a hundred thousand that Sir Modred marched to Dover.

As King Arthur with his fleet drew into the harbor, Sir Modred and his army launched forth in every available craft, and a bloody battle ensued in the ships and on the beach. If King Arthur's army were the smaller, their courage was the higher, confident as they were of the righteousness of their cause. Once ashore they put Sir Modred's entire army to flight.

The battle over, King Arthur began a search for his casualties, and on peering into one of the ships found Sir Gawain, mortally wounded. Sir Gawain fainted when King Arthur lifted him in his arms; and when he came to, the king spoke:

"Alas! dear nephew, that you lie here thus, mortally wounded! What joy is now left to me on this earth? You must know it was you and Sir Launcelot I loved above all others, and it seems that I have lost you both."

"My good uncle, it was my pride and my stub-

---

8. **barony:** nobles of the lowest rank.

**600**  *The King Arthur Legend*

bornness that brought all this about, for had not urged you to war with Sir Launcelot you subjects would not now be in revolt. Alas, tha Sir Launcelot is not here, for he would soor drive them out! And it is at Sir Launcelot's hand that I suffer my own death: the wound which h dealt me has reopened. I would not wish i otherwise, because is he not the greatest and gentlest of knights?

"I know that by noon I shall be dead, and repent bitterly that I may not be reconciled to Si Launcelot; therefore I pray you, good uncle, giv me pen, paper, and ink so that I may write t him."

A priest was summoned and Sir Gawain confessed;[9] then a clerk brought ink, pen, and paper and Sir Gawain wrote to Sir Launcelot as fol lows:

"Sir Launcelot, flower of the knighthood: I Sir Gawain, son of King Lot of Orkney and o King Arthur's sister, send you my greetings!

3 "I am about to die; the cause of my death i the wound I received from you outside the city of Benwick; and I would make it known that my death was of my own seeking, that I was moved by the spirit of revenge and spite to provoke you to battle.

"Therefore, Sir Launcelot, I beseech you to visit my tomb and offer what prayers you will on my behalf; and for myself, I am content to die at the hands of the noblest knight living.

"One more request: that you hasten with your armies across the sea and give succor[10] to our noble king. Sir Modred has usurped the throne and now holds against him with an army of a hundred thousand. He would have won the queen, too, but she fled to the Tower of London and there charged her loyal supporters with her defense.

"Today is the tenth of May, and at noon

---

9. **confessed:** made his last confession and repented his sins in preparation for his death.
10. **succor** [suk′ər]: assistance.

---

# GUIDED READING

## LITERAL QUESTION

**1a.** What reasons does Malory give for the nobles' shift of allegiance to Modred? (The nobles are fickle, and Modred promised them peace and festivity, whereas Arthur led them into wars and strife.)

## INFERENTIAL QUESTION

**1b.** What does this explanation suggest about Malory's attitude toward the king's subjects? (He feels they are self-indulgent and easily seduced.)

shall give up the ghost; this letter is written part-ly with my blood. This morning we fought our way ashore, against the armies of Sir Modred, and that is how my wound came to be reopened. We won the day, but my lord King Arthur needs you, and I too, that on my tomb you may bestow your blessing."

Sir Gawain fainted when he had finished, and the king wept. When he came to he was given extreme unction,[11] and died, as he had an-ticipated, at the hour of noon. The king buried him in the chapel at Dover Castle, and there many came to see him, and all noticed the wound on his head which he had received from Sir Launcelot.

Then the news reached Arthur that Sir Modred offered him battle on the field at Baron Down. Arthur hastened there with his army, they fought, and Sir Modred fled once more, this time to Canterbury.

When King Arthur had begun the search for his wounded and dead, many volunteers from all parts of the country came to fight under his flag, convinced now of the rightness of his cause. Ar-thur marched westward, and Sir Modred once more offered him battle. It was assigned for the Monday following Trinity Sunday,[12] on Salis-bury Down.

Sir Modred levied fresh troops from East An-glia and the places about London, and fresh volunteers came forward to help Arthur. Then, on the night of Trinity Sunday, Arthur was vouchsafed a strange dream:

He was appareled in gold cloth and seated in a chair which stood on a pivoted scaffold. Below him, many fathoms[13] deep, was a dark well, and in the water swam serpents, dragons, and wild beasts. Suddenly the scaffold tilted, and Arthur was flung into the water, where all the creatures

_____
11. **extreme unction:** sacrament of the Catholic Church given to dying persons to absolve them of their sins.
12. **Trinity Sunday:** eighth Sunday after Easter.
13. **fathoms** [fath'əmz]: A fathom is a unit of measurement equal to a depth of six feet of water.

struggled toward him and began tearing him limb from limb.

Arthur cried out in his sleep and his squires hastened to waken him. Later, as he lay between waking and sleeping, he thought he saw Sir Ga-wain, and with him a host of beautiful noble-women. Arthur spoke:

"My sister's son! I thought you had died; but now I see you live, and I thank the lord Jesu! I pray you, tell me, who are these ladies?"

"My lord, these are the ladies I championed in righteous quarrels when I was on earth. Our lord God has vouchsafed that we visit you and plead with you not to give battle to Sir Modred tomorrow, for if you do, not only will you your-self be killed, but all your noble followers too. We beg you to be warned, and to make a treaty with Sir Modred, calling a truce for a month, and granting him whatever terms he may demand. In a month Sir Launcelot will be here, and he will defeat Sir Modred."

Thereupon Sir Gawain and the ladies vanished, and King Arthur once more summoned his squires and his counselors and told them his vi-sion. Sir Lucas and Sir Bedivere were commis-sioned to make a treaty with Sir Modred. They were to be accompanied by two bishops and to grant, within reason, whatever terms he de-manded.

The ambassadors found Sir Modred in com-mand of an army of a hundred thousand and un-willing to listen to overtures of peace. However, the ambassadors eventually prevailed on him, and in return for the truce granted him suzerain-ty[14] of Cornwall and Kent,[15] and succession to the British throne when King Arthur died. The treaty was to be signed by King Arthur and Sir Modred the next day. They were to meet be-tween the two armies, and each was to be ac-companied by no more than fourteen knights.

_____
14. **suzerainty** [soo'zər in tē]: position of authority in the Middle Ages.
15. **Cornwall and Kent:** Cornwall is an area in south-western England; Kent is an area in southeastern England.

*The Death of Arthur* **601**

AT A GLANCE

- Gawain dies after writing Launcelot.
- Many volunteers join Arthur's forces; Modred enlists fresh troops.
- The night before battle, Arthur has a prophetic dream.
- As a result of the dream, Ar-thur negotiates a treaty with Modred.

**1 STYLE: IMAGERY**

The dream images are both hor-rifying enough to stem from the dark regions of the subconscious and symbolic of Arthur's actual situation.

**2 FORESHADOWING**

Arthur's dream foreshadows events to come and proves ac-curate in many details.

**3 THEME**

The importance of magic and prophecy in Malory's narrative is shown by Arthur's dream. The dream is interpreted as a proph-ecy of things to come, and it in-fluences the actions of Arthur.

**4 PLOT: RISING ACTION**

The meeting of the two leaders to sign the treaty brings the work close to its climax. What is meant to be a well-planned and con-trolled situation turns in a differ-ent direction.

## GUIDED READING

**LITERAL QUESTION**

**1a.** What does Arthur's vision tell him to do? (It tells him to make a truce with Modred, granting him whatever he asks, and then wait for Launcelot to arrive before fighting.)

**INFERENTIAL QUESTION**

**1b.** How do you think Malory feels about dreams as prophetic visions? (He takes dreams seriously and treats the event with respect. He expresses no reservations or skepticism.)

- The truce fails when a knight, bitten by a snake, draws his sword.
- Fighting begins, and Arthur kills Modred, despite the warning of Sir Lucas.
- Before he dies, Modred deals Arthur a fatal blow.

**1 PLOT: CLIMAX**

The final battle is a mistake: A soldier draws his sword to strike at a snake and thus sets the battle in motion. This chance beginning makes the battle's waste seem even more tragic.

**2 POINT OF VIEW**

The third-person narrator praises Arthur, thus enhancing his status as an epic hero. His prowess is further emphasized by the narrator's praise of Modred's skill in battle.

**3 DIALOGUE**

Arthur again shows the forgiveness that has made his bravery all the more noble.

---

Both King Arthur and Sir Modred suspected the other of treachery, and gave orders for their armies to attack at the sight of a naked sword. When they met at the appointed place the treaty was signed and both drank a glass of wine.

**1** Then, by chance, one of the soldiers was bitten in the foot by an adder[16] which had lain concealed in the brush. The soldier unthinkingly drew his sword to kill it, and at once, as the sword flashed in the light, the alarums were given, trumpets sounded, and both armies galloped into the attack.

"Alas for this fateful day!" exclaimed King Arthur, as both he and Sir Modred hastily mounted and galloped back to their armies. There followed one of those rare and heartless **2** battles in which both armies fought until they were destroyed. King Arthur, with his customary valor, led squadron after squadron of cavalry into the attack, and Sir Modred encountered him unflinchingly. As the number of dead and wounded mounted on both sides, the active combatants continued dauntless until nightfall, when four men alone survived.

King Arthur wept with dismay to see his beloved followers fallen; then, struggling toward him, unhorsed and badly wounded, he saw Sir Lucas the Butler and his brother, Sir Bedivere.

"Alas!" said the king, "that the day should come when I see all my noble knights destroyed! I would prefer that I myself had fallen. But what has become of the traitor Sir Modred, whose evil ambition was responsible for this carnage?"

Looking about him King Arthur then noticed Sir Modred leaning with his sword on a heap of the dead.

"Sir Lucas, I pray you give me my spear, for I have seen Sir Modred."

"Sire, I entreat you, remember your vision—how Sir Gawain appeared with a heaven-sent message to dissuade you from fighting Sir Mo-

---

16. **adder:** small poisonous snake very common throughout Britain and Europe.

**602** *The King Arthur Legend*

---

dred. Allow this fateful day to pass; it is ours, for we three hold the field, while the enemy is broken."

"My lords, I care nothing for my life now! And while Sir Modred is at large I must kill him: there may not be another chance."

"God speed you, then!" said Sir Bedivere.

When Sir Modred saw King Arthur advance with his spear, he rushed to meet him with drawn sword. Arthur caught Sir Modred below the shield and drove his spear through his body; Sir Modred, knowing that the wound was mortal, thrust himself up to the handle of the spear, and then, brandishing his sword in both hands, struck Arthur on the side of the helmet, cutting through it and into the skull beneath; then he crashed to the ground, gruesome and dead.

King Arthur fainted many times as Sir Lucas and Sir Bedivere struggled with him to a small chapel nearby, where they managed to ease his wounds a little. When Arthur came to, he thought he heard cries coming from the battlefield.

"Sir Lucas, I pray you, find out who cries on the battlefield," he said.

Wounded as he was, Sir Lucas hobbled painfully to the field, and there in the moonlight saw the camp followers stealing gold and jewels from the dead, and murdering the wounded. He returned to the king and reported to him what he had seen, and then added:

"My lord, it surely would be better to move you to the nearest town?"

**3** "My wounds forbid it. But alas for the good Sir Launcelot! How sadly I have missed him today! And now I must die—as Sir Gawain warned me I would—repenting our quarrel with my last breath."

Sir Lucas and Sir Bedivere made one further attempt to lift the king. He fainted as they did so. Then Sir Lucas fainted. When the king came to, he saw Sir Lucas lying dead with foam at his mouth.

"Sweet Jesu, give him succor!" he said.

---

## GUIDED READING

### LITERAL QUESTIONS

**1a.** What does Sir Lucas tell Arthur when he asks for his sword to kill Modred? (He reminds Arthur that his dream warned him not to fight Modred and asks that, since they have already won the battle, he forget about killing Modred.)

**2a.** When Arthur sends Sir Lucas to investigate the cries on the battlefield, what does he find? (He finds the camp followers stealing gold and jewels from the dead and wounded.)

### INFERENTIAL QUESTIONS

**1b.** What does the fact that Arthur ignores this warning tell you about his state of mind? (He is demoralized by the death of all his knights.)

**2b.** What does this grisly incident suggest about the survival of the chivalric code? (It shows the complete collapse of the ideals of chivalry.)

Sir Bedivere returns Excalibur to the Lady of the Lake; the wounded King Arthur sits in the foreground. Detail from a medieval manuscript.

AT A GLANCE

- Arthur asks Sir Bedivere to throw Excalibur into the lake.
- Bedivere tries twice but cannot bring himself to do it.

1 PLOT: RESOLUTION

The resolution of the plot begins with Arthur's realization that death is near and his rule is over.

2 SYMBOL

Bedivere's difficulty with throwing the sword in the water has to do with Excalibur's symbolic value. The sword represents Arthur's kingship, and it is this that Bedivere cannot bear to throw away.

3 READING SKILLS: SEQUENCE

The sequence of events here is parallel. Arthur asks Bedivere to throw Excalibur in the lake, but twice Bedivere cannot do so. Both times, Arthur asks Bedivere what he saw and then receives an answer that tells him that Bedivere did not do his bidding.

"This noble knight has died trying to save my life—alas that this was so!"

Sir Bedivere wept for his brother.

1 "Sir Bedivere, weep no more," said King Arthur, "for you can save neither your brother nor me; and I would ask you to take my sword Excalibur[17] to the shore of the lake and throw it in the water. Then return to me and tell me what you have seen."

"My lord, as you command, it shall be done."

Sir Bedivere took the sword, but when he came to the water's edge, it appeared so beautiful that he could not bring himself to throw it in, so instead he hid it by a tree, and then returned to the king.

—————

17. **Excalibur** [eks kal'ə bər]: magical sword that Merlin obtained for Arthur from the Lady of the Lake many years earlier.

"Sir Bedivere, what did you see?"

"My lord, I saw nothing but the wind upon the waves."

"Then you did not obey me; I pray you, go swiftly again, and this time fulfill my command."

2 Sir Bedivere went and returned again, but this time too he had failed to fulfill the king's command.

"Sir Bedivere, what did you see?"

"My lord, nothing but the lapping of the waves."

3 "Sir Bedivere, twice you have betrayed me! And for the sake only of my sword: it is unworthy of you! Now I pray you, do as I command, for I have not long to live."

This time Sir Bedivere wrapped the girdle[18]

—————

18. **girdle** [gurd'əl]: belt or waistband.

*The Death of Arthur* **603**

## GUIDED READING

**LITERAL QUESTION**

**1a.** Does Bedivere carry out the task Arthur gives him? (He tries twice but is unable to do so.)

**INFERENTIAL QUESTION**

**1b.** How do you think Arthur knows that Bedivere disobeyed him? (Arthur expects something to happen when the sword is returned to the lake. All Bedivere reports seeing is "the wind upon the waves.")

## AT A GLANCE

- Bedivere throws the sword in the lake, and a hand takes it.
- Arthur sails off to Avalon.
- Bedivere and the Archbishop live as hermits by a tomb believed to be Arthur's.
- Legend says Arthur is not dead but will return to rule.

## 1 THEME

Supernatural events glimmer around Arthur's final moments. The implication is that Arthur's earthly reign has been ordained by God.

## 2 ATMOSPHERE

Our last glimpse of Arthur—on a barge, surrounded by mourning women—creates a solemn and affecting mood, appropriate to the death of a hero.

## 3 PLOT: RESOLUTION

Bedivere is faithful to the end, spending the rest of his life near Arthur's tomb, in fasting and prayer. Thus he reaffirms the values of the chivalric code and of religion.

## 4 POINT OF VIEW

Malory takes the view that the legend of Arthur's return is not true, but he reports it as popular belief. Thus he adds to Arthur's heroic aura without making any claims for the legend's truth.

## REFLECTING ON THE SELECTION

In what sense does Arthur, the "once and future king," speak to the future that is our own age? (Some students may argue that Arthur's nobility and ideals make his relevance eternal. Others may suggest that Arthur's failures may offer a warning to our own age.)

---

1 around the sheath and hurled it as far as he could into the water. A hand appeared from below the surface, took the sword, waved it thrice, and disappeared again. Sir Bedivere returned to the king and told him what he had seen.

"Sir Bedivere, I pray you now help me hence, or I fear it will be too late."

2 Sir Bedivere carried the king to the water's edge, and there found a barge in which sat many beautiful ladies with their queen. All were wearing black hoods, and when they saw the king, they raised their voices in a piteous lament.

"I pray you, set me in the barge," said the king.

Sir Bedivere did so, and one of the ladies laid the king's head in her lap; then the queen spoke to him:

"My dear brother, you have stayed too long: I fear that the wound on your head is already cold."

Thereupon they rowed away from the land and Sir Bedivere wept to see them go.

"My lord King Arthur, you have deserted me! I am alone now, and among enemies."

"Sir Bedivere, take what comfort you may, for my time is passed, and now I must be taken to Avalon[19] for my wound to be healed. If you hear of me no more, I beg you pray for my soul."

The barge slowly crossed the water and out of sight while the ladies wept. Sir Bedivere walked alone into the forest and there remained for the night.

In the morning he saw beyond the trees of a copse a small hermitage. He entered and found a hermit kneeling down by a fresh tomb. The hermit was weeping as he prayed, and then Sir Bedivere recognized him as the Archbishop of Canterbury, who had been banished by Sir Modred.

"Father, I pray you, tell me, whose tomb is this?"

"My son, I do not know. At midnight the

---

19. **Avalon:** mythical island; in ancient British legends Avalon was the blissful underworld of the dead.

---

body was brought here by a company of ladies. We buried it, they lit a hundred candles for the service, and rewarded me with a thousand bezants."[20]

"Father, King Arthur lies buried in this tomb."

3 Sir Bedivere fainted when he had spoken, and when he came to he begged the Archbishop to allow him to remain at the hermitage and end his days in fasting and prayer.

"Father, I wish only to be near to my true liege."[21]

"My son, you are welcome; and do I not recognize you as Sir Bedivere the Bold, brother to Sir Lucas the Butler?"

Thus the Archbishop and Sir Bedivere remained at the hermitage, wearing the habits of hermits and devoting themselves to the tomb with fasting and prayers of contrition.[22]

Such was the death of King Arthur as written down by Sir Bedivere. By some it is told that there were three queens on the barge: Queen Morgan le Fay, the Queen of North Galys, and the Queen of the Waste Lands; and others include the name of Nyneve, the Lady of the Lake who had served King Arthur well in the past, and had married the good knight Sir Pelleas.

4 In many parts of Britain it is believed that King Arthur did not die and that he will return to us and win fresh glory and the Holy Cross of our Lord Jesu Christ; but for myself I do not believe this, and would leave him buried peacefully in his tomb at Glastonbury, where the Archbishop of Canterbury and Sir Bedivere humbled themselves, and with prayers and fasting honored his memory. And inscribed on his tomb, men say, is this legend:

HIC IACET ARTHURUS, REX QUONDAM REXQUE FUTURUS.[23]

---

20. **bezants** [bez'əntz]: gold coins.
21. **liege** [lēj]: lord.
22. **contrition** [kən trish'ən]: remorse for one's sins.
23. **Hic . . . Futurus:** Latin for "Here lies Arthur, the once and future king."

---

## GUIDED READING

### LITERAL QUESTION

**1a.** What does Malory tell you about the activities of the Archbishop and Bedivere? (They wear the habits of hermits and devote themselves to fasting and prayers of contrition.)

### INFERENTIAL QUESTION

**1b.** What did they have to be contrite for? (It is not so much their personal acts for which they show contrition, but the selfishness and infidelity of their society.)

## STUDY QUESTIONS

### Recalling

1. Why do the nobles accept Sir Modred as king and support him against Arthur?
2. Briefly retell the events of Arthur's campaign against Sir Modred before the final battle.
3. Describe the two dreams Arthur has on the eve of his last battle.
4. How does the last battle begin, and how does it end?
5. Briefly describe the return of Excalibur to the Lady of the Lake.
6. Relate the events of Arthur's departure and describe what Sir Bedivere does and sees after Arthur leaves.

### Interpreting

7. Contrast the characters of Arthur and Sir Modred.
8. In his request that Excalibur be returned to the lake, what is Arthur indicating about his reign?
9. Why do you think Malory left the question of Arthur's death open? What is the significance of the inscription he quotes?

### Extending

10. Do you think that actual people and societies can put high ideals like those of Arthur into practice? Why or why not?

## VIEWPOINT

The American novelist John Steinbeck was so fascinated with Malory's story that he wrote a modern version of it. Steinbeck was struck by the way Malory's own turbulent time may have shaped his *Morte d'Arthur:*

> Out of this...welter of change...he tried to create a world of order, a world of virtue governed by forces familiar to him.
>
> — John Steinbeck, Introduction,
> *The Acts of King Arthur
> and his Noble Knights*

■ Show how Malory tries to create a world of order and virtue in *Le Morte d'Arthur*. What aspects, if any, of Arthur's world would benefit today's society?

## LITERARY FOCUS

### The Total Effect

Any work of literature meshes a number of separate elements into a unified whole. *Le Morte d'Arthur* weaves its version of the King Arthur legend from the strands that make up most fictional narratives: plot, character, setting, point of view, tone, symbol, irony, and theme.

### Thinking About Plot, Character, and Setting

1. Which of the three selections presented here would you describe as the most clearly episodic? Why? What would you say are the main advantages and problems of this approach to telling a story?
2. Did you find the ending of *Le Morte d'Arthur* a satisfying and logical outcome of the events and tales that preceded it? Why or why not?
3. What different traits do Arthur and Launcelot display? How are these two figures contrasted with the other characters?
4. How does Arthur change during the course of these tales? What other characters change in these selections?
5. Describe the social setting of these tales: the living conditions, clothing, government, the roles of men and women. How does Arthur's Britain differ in these respects from modern life?

### Thinking About Point of View and Tone

6. Identify the point of view from which each tale is told. Would you have preferred to read Launcelot's and Arthur's own accounts of their stories? Why or why not?
7. What is Malory's tone, or attitude, in his presentation of the events in these tales? Is he serious about them or amused by them?

### Thinking About Symbol

8. What might Arthur's dream on the eve of his last battle symbolize? What might the battle between Arthur and Sir Modred symbolize?
9. What ideas and qualities might Arthur himself symbolize?

### Thinking About Irony

10. What ironic contrast can you see between the code of chivalry and the behavior of Arthur's knights?

*The Death of Arthur* 605

**STUDY QUESTIONS**

1. believe Arthur is dead; believe Modred brings peace
2. defeats Modred at sea and on beach; fight again; Modred flees to Canterbury
3. falls into well full of attacking serpents; dead Gawain tells him not to fight Modred
4. Soldier draws sword to kill snake; armies attack; four survive; Arthur kills Modred; is mortally wounded.
5. Arthur asks Bedivere to throw Excalibur into lake; twice he fails; third time he throws it into water; hand waves it three times; disappears
6. carries Arthur to water; places him on barge that women row out of sight; finds hermit weeping at Arthur's grave; remains at hermitage
7. *Arthur:* noble; chivalrous; *Modred:* scheming; disloyal
8. It is over.
9. to keep his legendary aspects alive; will return to rule Britain
10. Some may note weaknesses in human nature; others may believe in living by ideals

**VIEWPOINT**

He allies Arthur's virtue with Launcelot's power; shows good can triumph over evil. Some may feel that justice, protection of the weak are values inherent in our society. Others may feel these have never been fully realized.

**LITERARY FOCUS**

1. second section; describes the adventures of Launcelot; can introduce many characters; lessen dramatic effect
2. Yes—Arthur is seen at the beginning and end of life; the nobles' fickleness prepares for switch of allegiance.
3. *Arthur:* selfless; generous; forgiving; majestic; *Launcelot:* brave; strong; loyal; courteous. Others are of lesser stature; some are bullies; Modred is evil.

4. Arthur gains confidence; allows rivalry to come between him and Launcelot; later spirit is defeated. Launcelot abandons loyalty to king for love of queen. Bedivere becomes a hermit.

5. portrays upper stratum of society; landscape full of dangers; *government:* hierarchical; king at top, nobles beneath; *knights:* profess loyalty to king, spend time upholding order; *women:* were sorceresses or helpless maidens; modern life more civilized; people dress for comfort; women have more power

6. omniscient narrator; provides wider perspective
7. respectful; serious
8. end of his reign; battle between good and evil
9. best of humanity, selflessness, nobility
10. Knights attack over trivial matters; Tarquine does not behave in exemplary manner; Modred is treacherous.
11. Arthur battles for peace; most nobles are killed; disorder rules once again.
12. ■ loyalty to God and king, courage, truthfulness, vow to help those in distress
    ■ Possible answer: Chivalry does not exist as a system of manners, but ethics of chivalry remains.
13. strong, good leader who can inspire trust, not power-hungry
14. He is beyond reproach; dedicated to his country. Hero raises ideas of our capabilities, goals.
15. Possible answers: World is portrayed in terms of good vs. evil; heroes are male; fight for justice. Cowboys observe no formal code of behavior; Malory includes supernatural events missing from westerns.

## VOCABULARY
1. advantage
2. knight
3. queens
4. about
5. castle
6. promise
7. prisoners
8. beside
9. enchantment
10. sleeping

---

11. What is ironic about the relationship between Arthur's aims and the outcome of the Battle of Salisbury Down?

### Thinking About Theme
12. What virtues and values make up the code of chivalry as it is presented in these tales? Is chivalry still alive today? Explain.
13. According to Malory, what kind of ruler is necessary for maintaining order in the state?
14. In what ways might Arthur's legend help build British national pride? Why do you think people need to believe in heroes like King Arthur?
15. The novelist John Steinbeck compared the story of King Arthur and his knights to tales of the American West. What do you think Malory's work has in common with westerns, and how does it differ from them?

## VOCABULARY

### Middle English

The English language has changed greatly during the course of its history. The language we speak today began as a Germanic dialect that was brought to England by Saxon invaders in the sixth century. This language formed the basis of what is now referred to as **Old English.**

Then in 1066 William the Conqueror invaded England from France, and during the Middle Ages French became the language of the upper classes in England. The lower classes continued to speak English, but their language absorbed a number of French words. We call the English spoken and written during this period **Middle English.**

Middle English included a number of different dialects. The speech of people in London was called the **Midland dialect**, and it was in this dialect that Malory wrote *Le Morte d'Arthur.* When Caxton printed Malory's work in 1485, this dialect emerged

as the dominant national language in England and eventually formed the basis of the English that we speak today.

The following words are taken from Malory's original *Morte d'Arthur.* Write the modern English spelling of these words. Then list at least two of the major differences you see between the Middle English and modern English versions of these words.

| | |
|---|---|
| 1. advauntage | 6. promyse |
| 2. knyght | 7. presoneres |
| 3. queenys | 8. besyde |
| 4. aboute | 9. inchauntement |
| 5. castell | 10. slepynge |

## COMPOSITION

### Writing About the Epic Hero
■ An **epic hero** is a character who (a) performs great deeds and (b) represents the values of a particular society. King Arthur can be regarded as an epic hero. Using evidence from the selections, first show how Arthur meets the definition of an epic hero. Then choose a modern hero — either actual or fictional — and explain how Arthur's character and actions differ from those of this figure.

### Writing a Newspaper Article
■ Imagine that you are a modern journalist and that Launcelot's victory over the two giants at Tintagil is a big news story. Write an account of that battle for your newspaper. Be sure to explain the background of the battle and to include full descriptions of Launcelot, the castle, the giants, the battle itself, and the reactions of the rescued noblewomen. You may want to include a brief interview with Launcelot or with one of the ladies. Remember to write in the style of a modern newspaper.

---

## COMPOSITION: GUIDELINES FOR EVALUATION

### WRITING ABOUT THE EPIC HERO
**Objective**
To show how King Arthur meets the definition of an epic hero and to contrast him with a modern hero

**Guidelines for Evaluation**
■ suggested length: five to eight paragraphs
■ should describe Arthur's heroism
■ should describe a modern hero
■ should cite differences between the two

### WRITING A NEWSPAPER ARTICLE
**Objective**
To describe a feat of one of Arthur's knights from a twentieth-century point of view

**Guidelines for Evaluation**
■ suggested length: ten to fifteen short paragraphs
■ should begin with answers to questions: who? what? where? when? how? why?
■ should include invented interviews
■ should be written in modern journalistic style

# ACTIVE READING

## Recognizing Patterns

Down through the centuries the King Arthur legend has stimulated the imaginations of writers, who have shaped and reshaped the story of King Arthur and his knights. Writing over five hundred years ago, Sir Thomas Malory added his version of the legend to what was already a great wealth of literature. Taken together, all of these versions of the legend form a body of writing known as Arthurian Romance. Each retelling of the legend of Arthur is different, and yet there are common motifs, or repeated patterns, that run through all of them.

Repetition is always a clue to meaning in literature. Authors repeat words that are central to their visions, and they repeat story elements that show the inner structure of their fictional worlds. For example, a story might include such parallel events as the coming of spring, the birth of a child, and a reawakened interest in life on the part of a character. All of these events create a pattern of renewal in the story. The more we observe such patterns or repetitions, the more we will see in a work of literature.

Sir Thomas Malory used many patterns in his version of the King Arthur legend. On the first page, Merlin says to Arthur's father, "Your child is destined for glory." The concept of *glory* or *fame* runs through the entire Arthurian Romance and is central to Malory's *Morte d'Arthur*. At the end of the story, when Malory speaks of the legend of Arthur's return, he describes it as a time when Arthur will "win fresh glory." Fame and glory clearly were positive values in Malory's time, just as they had been thousands of years before in Greece to the audience of Homer's epics.

The concepts of fame and glory are closely connected with another word that Malory repeats: *nobility*. The importance of nobility is established early in the King Arthur story. The contest to pull the magical sword from the stone is meant "to provide men of noble blood" with the opportunity to discover who should be the next king. The nobles object to the young Arthur's kingship because they think he is of ignoble (that is, low or common) blood. When we read later that Sir Launcelot is supreme among all the knights in nobility of bearing, we take this description as a signal of Launcelot's great worth as a character.

*The King Arthur Legend*  **607**

Nobility goes hand in hand with such admirable activities as fighting for *justice* and seeking *adventure*. Adventure is in fact the word most frequently repeated in Malory's story. King Arthur's knights do not sit around waiting for things to happen. Rather, they go out actively seeking adventures in order to prove themselves noble and increase their own glory and that of the Round Table. They may not always succeed in these efforts, but they know very well the standard that they should live up to.

Malory frequently praises the value of *loyalty* and opposes to it such negative concepts as *treachery, deception,* and *lies.* The tension between loyalty and treachery appears often in Malory's work. For example, the last section of the work contrasts the loyal behavior of Sir Bedivere with the treacherous behavior of Sir Modred. Out of loyalty to Arthur, Sir Bedivere returns Excalibur to the lake. He later enters a hermitage in order to spend the rest of his life near the tomb of King Arthur, his "true liege." In contrast, Sir Modred is the arch-traitor in Malory's work. Modred is worse than an enemy; like Bedivere he has sworn an oath of loyalty to Arthur, but in his ambition he betrays this sacred trust. When Arthur returns to face Modred in battle, each man suspects the other of treachery. We see that the precious, civilizing bond of trust has broken down and that the noble system that Arthur built on that bond is about to collapse.

All of these concepts are important in Malory's version of the King Arthur legend. They reveal the central structure of the Arthurian legend—the heroic vision of the world that this legend expresses. Arthur is known as Britain's first great king because of his heroic effort (portrayed in the code of the Round Table) to raise people above the barbaric values of brute force, meaningless violence, and blind ambition for power. In contrast, Arthur stands for civilization and the civilizing values of nobility, trust, and loyalty. Without these values there can be no social order, no constructive effort, no truly human life. When we see the patterns that Malory repeats in describing many different characters and events, we recognize that the glory that surrounds Arthur and his knights is not merely that of individual men and deeds; it is the glory that surrounds an ideal. And it is this noble vision of life that has drawn writers to the King Arthur legend for over a thousand years.

# REVIEW:
# THE KING ARTHUR LEGEND

The King Arthur story began as a legend and evolved into a large body of writings that included many different literary forms. The most popular of these was the romance. Review the following guide before you read more about King Arthur or other romances. It will help you to see the similarities between the King Arthur story and other legends and romances. It will also help you to recognize the main elements of the King Arthur story.

## Legends and Romances

1. When and where did the legend or romance originate?
2. Who is the hero? If that person really existed, what were his or her actual accomplishments?
3. What qualities and deeds are attributed to the hero? Which of these might be regarded as superhuman?
4. Does the hero succeed or fail? What forces work for and against the hero?
5. If the story is a legend, in what way does the hero represent the values of a particular group of people?

## The King Arthur Legend

1. What specific qualities are associated with King Arthur? Is he presented entirely as a real person, or is he given superhuman traits?
2. Which knights appear in the work, and what adventures are presented?
3. What specific qualities are associated with these knights? In what ways do the knights differ from Arthur?
4. Is Arthur's world presented as an actual time and place or as a mythical time and place?
5. What instances of magic and prophecy are included?
6. What values are represented in the society created by Arthur? To what extent is that society admirable?
7. What reasons are given or implied for Arthur's failure? What account is given of his end?
8. Was the author's purpose primarily to entertain the reader? What serious purpose guided the author?

*The King Arthur Legend* **609**

REVIEW

Discuss the traits of legends and romances as these traits are listed in the Review. Ask for other examples of legendary figures (for example, Paul Bunyan, Davy Crockett, George Washington), and discuss the aspects of these heroes that make them legendary (size, strength, bravery, historical circumstances). Finally, discuss the ways in which the selections from *Le Morte d'Arthur* resemble both a legend and a romance.

The questions in the Guide for Reading Legends and Romances appear with write-on lines, in blackline master form, among the materials for this unit in your *Teacher's Classroom Resources*.

610    *The Novel*

# PREVIEW:
# THE NOVEL

*I should say that the main object of the novel is to represent life. . . . The success of a work of art, to my mind, may be measured by the degree to which it produces a certain illusion; that illusion makes it appear to us for the time that we have lived another life—that we have had a miraculous enlargement of experience.*

—Henry James

A **novel** is an extended fictional prose narrative. Like a short story writer, a novelist creates an imaginary world in order to present readers with a particular vision of life. However, the greater length of the novel gives a writer greater freedom and scope in representing life than the short story does. An author writes a novel rather than a short story in order to present a larger vision of life, one that develops over time. For where a short story recreates an individual experience, a novel can recreate the fullness, complexity, and ongoing flow of life itself.

The novel is actually one of the most recent forms of literature; in fact, the word *novel* comes from a Latin word meaning "new." People began to read novels only two hundred years ago, in the middle of the eighteenth century. During this time education began to reach beyond the wealthy classes, and the spread of democratic ideas led to a new awareness of the worth of all individuals regardless of their social position. In addition, machines began to revolutionize the production of goods and increase people's leisure time. A huge reading public arose, wanting to be entertained with stories about people like themselves. In response, the novel sprang into being as the first literary form to be written for and about ordinary people.

*The Novel* **611**

The novel is a very versatile literary form and offers writers unlimited freedom in their choice of form and subject. Some novels unfold slowly as months, years, even decades roll by, and generations of characters are born, live, and die. Other novels invite us to peer intently at the doings of a few people over a relatively short time. However, every novel regardless of its content molds and combines the same elements that come together in the short story: plot, character, setting, point of view, tone, symbol, irony, and theme. In the case of the novel, greater length allows each of these elements much more range than we usually find in short stories.

The plot of a novel may develop in a greater variety of ways than is generally possible for a short story. Some novels follow a traditional plot structure, with a narrative hook, rising action, climax, falling action, and resolution. Other novels may include **subplots,** or minor plots that branch off from the main plot. Still other novels use an even looser structure, presenting a series of related **episodes,** or incidents, somewhat like a series of short stories. Furthermore, conflicts arise in a novel in greater number and with more complications than are possible in a short story.

A novel usually introduces us to a greater variety of characters than a story and may include several major characters as well as a number of minor ones. A novel often includes several settings in order to accommodate all its characters and all the twists and turns of its plot. The narrator must beckon us into the novel's world and sustain our interest in it over the long run. Some novels even use more than one point of view in order to give us different perspectives on the events of the narrative. Symbols can change and develop over the course of a novel; similarly, irony can be used with great subtlety in a novel, emerging gradually as the narrative unfolds. Finally these elements come together in one or more themes, or ideas about life.

The following two novels present very different visions of life. John Steinbeck's *Pearl* is a **novella,** or a very short novel; it focuses on a few significant days in the life of a young Mexican fisherman who finds a beautiful pearl that changes his life in unexpected and tragic ways. Mark Twain's *Connecticut Yankee in King Arthur's Court,* on the other hand, is an episodic novel that narrates the adventures—both humorous and otherwise—of a nineteenth-century Connecticut man who travels back in time to the Britain of King Arthur. Like all good novels, both works invite us to forget our own surroundings for a time, immerse ourselves in other worlds, and inhabit other lives.

### The Life of John Steinbeck

John Steinbeck (1902–1968) is best known for making his readers remember those whom the world has forgotten. In work after work, Steinbeck dramatizes the plight of poor, uneducated, and powerless individuals—men and women who are caught up in circumstances beyond their understanding or control. More important, he also portrays the ability of such people to preserve their humanity in the face of dehumanizing forces.

Steinbeck's own background and varied experiences gave him ample material for his writing. As a youth in Salinas, California, he read avidly, especially in the Greek and Roman classics and the Bible. He later attended Stanford University, where he studied marine biology. The young Steinbeck held a number of jobs, working as a fruit picker, road laborer, laboratory assistant, and newspaper reporter before finally committing himself in his late twenties to a full-time writing career.

Steinbeck first achieved recognition for *Tortilla Flat* (1935), a humorous, episodic novel about the adventures of a group of people living in a poor area near Monterey, California. His popularity soared in 1937 with *Of Mice and Men,* a short novel about the tragic friendship of two migrant workers. Shortly after its publication, Steinbeck turned his novel into a highly successful play. Then in 1939 Steinbeck established himself as one of the country's major authors with his Pulitzer Prize–winning masterpiece, *The Grapes of Wrath.* This novel, set in the Great Depression of the 1930s, traces the long journey of a group of farmers from the Dust Bowl of Oklahoma to what they hoped would be a better life in California. In 1962, after publishing his last novel, *The Winter of Our Discontent,* Steinbeck was awarded the Nobel Prize for Literature.

### The Pearl

*The Pearl* was published in 1947, about midway through Steinbeck's literary career. A few years before, while sailing along the Gulf of California in search of marine specimens, Steinbeck heard a story that had interested him enough to record it in *The Sea of Cortez* (1941), his nonfiction account of this expedition. The story concerned a young Indian who found a beautiful and valuable pearl that brought him nothing but misery. Steinbeck transformed this simple folk tale into *The Pearl.*

In his opening lines he calls the story a **parable,** which is a brief narrative intended to teach a moral, or universal lesson. For example, the biblical parable of the Good Samaritan teaches the universal lesson

*The Pearl* **613**

that all people must care for one another. The story makes the lesson convincing and memorable, while the lesson makes the story's characters and events radiate a meaning larger than themselves. Steinbeck found in the young Indian's story a universal truth about people's eternal search for happiness in things outside of themselves. In *The Pearl* he creates characters and events that radiate that truth and make it memorable.

## Key Ideas in *The Pearl*

■ As you read *The Pearl*, look for references to each of the following topics. If you keep track of what the work says about these subjects, you will begin to grasp the most important themes of *The Pearl*.

- Harmony between human beings and nature
- Love and the family
- Worldly goods and greed
- The poor villagers versus the wealthy townspeople
- Acceptance versus defiance of one's fate
- Instinctive wisdom versus worldly knowledge
- Natural innocence versus worldy corruption

*John Steinbeck*

# The Pearl

"In the town they tell the story of the great pearl—how it was found and how it was lost again. They tell of Kino, the fisherman, and of his wife, Juana, and of the baby, Coyotito.[1] And because the story has been told so often, it has taken root in every man's mind. And, as with all retold tales that are in people's hearts, there are only good and bad things and black and white things and good and evil things and no in-between anywhere.

"If this story is a parable, perhaps everyone takes his own meaning from it and reads his own life into it. In any case, they say in the town that ..."

## I

Kino awakened in the near dark. The stars still shone and the day had drawn only a pale wash of light in the lower sky to the east. The roosters had been crowing for some time, and the early pigs were already beginning their ceaseless turning of twigs and bits of wood to see whether anything to eat had been over-

2 looked. Outside the brush house in the tuna[2] clump, a covey of little birds chittered and flurried with their wings.

Kino's eyes opened, and he looked first at the lightening square which was the door and then he looked at the hanging box where Coyotito slept. And last he turned his head to Juana, his wife, who lay beside him on the mat, her blue head shawl over her nose and over her breasts and around the small of her back. Juana's eyes were open too. Kino could never remember seeing them closed when he awakened. Her dark eyes made little reflected stars. She was looking at him as she was always looking at him when he awakened.

3 Kino heard the little splash of morning waves on the beach. It was very good—Kino closed his eyes again to listen to his music. Perhaps he alone did this and perhaps all of his people did it. His people had once been great makers of songs so that everything they saw or thought or did or heard became a song. That was very long ago. The songs remained; Kino knew them, but no new songs were added. That does not mean that

---

1. **Kino** [kē′nō] . . . **Juana** [hwä′nä] . . . **Coyotito** [kō′yō tē′tō]

2. **tuna:** prickly-pear cactus.

*The Pearl* **615**

## AT A GLANCE

- A story is told of a splendid pearl once found and then lost.
- Kino awakens at dawn and sees his son, Coyotito, and his wife, Juana.

## LITERARY OPTIONS

- plot
- characterization
- point of view

## THEMATIC OPTIONS

- the meaning of happiness
- love and family
- the value of money

## 1 BACKGROUND

A folktale or parable in which one may find a moral lesson is the basis of *The Pearl*.

## 2 SETTING

Details of the seaside village—brush houses, roving pigs, wild birds, open sky—appear throughout the narration.

## 3 CHARACTERIZATION

Kino responds to the rhythms of nature and the songs of his ancestors but also has his *own* music.

## GUIDED READING

### LITERAL QUESTION

**1a.** What does Kino always remember about Juana's eyes in the morning? (They are open, making reflected stars, and looking at him when he awakens.)

### INFERENTIAL QUESTION

**1b.** What can you infer about Kino and Juana's relationship? (They love each other.)

**1 POINT OF VIEW**

As the omniscient observer, Steinbeck reveals the thoughts that Kino himself is unable to speak.

**2 MOOD**

The blending rhythms of the Song of the Family and Juana's work create an atmosphere of harmony and contentment.

**3 PLOT: FORESHADOWING**

A deadly trap and a mortal struggle on this tranquil morning reveal another side of nature and life.

**4 THEME**

Kino and Juana's lives are centered on their love for each other and for Coyotito.

**5 CHARACTERIZATION**

Kino is a distinct individual; at the same time, he is seen as a member of the community.

---

**1** there were no personal songs. In Kino's head there was a song now, clear and soft, and if he had been able to speak it, he would have called it the Song of the Family.

His blanket was over his nose to protect him from the dank air. His eyes flicked to a rustle beside him. It was Juana arising, almost soundlessly. On her hard bare feet she went to the hanging box where Coyotito slept, and she leaned over and said a little reassuring word. Coyotito looked up for a moment and closed his eyes and slept again.

Juana went to the fire pit and uncovered a coal and fanned it alive while she broke little pieces of brush over it.

Now Kino got up and wrapped his blanket about his head and nose and shoulders. He slipped his feet into his sandals and went outside to watch the dawn.

Outside the door he squatted down and gathered the blanket ends about his knees. He saw the specks of Gulf[3] clouds flame high in the air. And a goat came near and sniffed at him and stared with its cold yellow eyes. Behind him Juana's fire leaped into flame and threw spears of light through the chinks of the brush-house wall and threw a wavering square of light out the door. A late moth blustered in to find the **2** fire. The Song of the Family came now from behind Kino. And the rhythm of the family song was the grinding stone where Juana worked the corn for the morning cakes.

The dawn came quickly now, a wash, a glow, a lightness, and then an explosion of fire as the sun arose out of the Gulf. Kino looked down to cover his eyes from the glare. He could hear the pat of the corncakes in the house and the rich smell of them on the cooking plate. The ants were busy on the ground, big black ones with shiny bodies, and little dusty quick ants. Kino

**3** watched with the detachment of God while a dusty ant frantically tried to escape the sand trap an ant lion[4] had dug for him. A thin, timid dog came close and, at a soft word from Kino, curled up, arranged its tail neatly over its feet, and laid its chin delicately on the pile. It was a black dog with yellow-gold spots where its eyebrows should have been. It was a morning like other mornings and yet perfect among mornings.

**4** Kino heard the creak of the rope when Juana took Coyotito out of his hanging box and cleaned him and hammocked him in her shawl in a loop that placed him close to her breast. Kino could see these things without looking at them. Juana sang softly an ancient song that had only three notes and yet endless variety of interval. And this was part of the family song too. It was all part. Sometimes it rose to an aching chord that caught the throat, saying this is safety, this is warmth, this is the *Whole*.

**5** Across the brush fence were other brush houses, and the smoke came from them too, and the sound of breakfast, but those were other songs, their pigs were other pigs, their wives were not Juana. Kino was young and strong and his black hair hung over his brown forehead. His eyes were warm and fierce and bright and his mustache was thin and coarse. He lowered his blanket from his nose now, for the dark poisonous air was gone and the yellow sunlight fell on the house. Near the brush fence two roosters bowed and feinted at each other with squared wings and neck feathers ruffed out. It would be a clumsy fight. They were not game chickens. Kino watched them for a moment, and then his eyes went up to a flight of wild doves twinkling inland to the hills. The world was awake now, and Kino arose and went into his brush house.

As he came through the door Juana stood up from the glowing fire pit. She put Coyotito back

---

3. **Gulf:** the Gulf of California, which is a body of water between Baja California (a peninsula in Mexico) and the main portion of Mexico.

4. **ant lion:** insect whose larvae dig conical pits in sand in order to trap other insects, usually ants.

---

## GUIDED READING

**LITERAL QUESTIONS**

**1a.** What does Kino go outside to do while Juana tends Coyotito and makes breakfast? (He goes out to watch the dawn.)

**2a.** What characterizes Juana's song of only three notes? (endless variety of interval)

**INFERENTIAL QUESTIONS**

**1b.** What can you infer about Kino from his morning habit? (He lives close to nature, appreciating its beauty and enjoying simple pleasures.)

**2b.** What might her song and its variety of rhythms tell about Juana's life? (She has few possessions and she lives simply, but her life is richly satisfying.)

in his hanging box and then she combed her black hair and braided it in two braids and tied the ends with thin green ribbon. Kino squatted by the fire pit and rolled a hot corncake and dipped it in sauce and ate it. And he drank a little pulque[5] and that was breakfast. That was the only breakfast he had ever known outside of feast days and one incredible fiesta on cookies that had nearly killed him. When Kino had finished, Juana came back to the fire and ate her breakfast. They had spoken once, but there is not need for speech if it is only a habit anyway. Kino sighed with satisfaction—and that was conversation.

The sun was warming the brush house, breaking through its crevices in long streaks. And one of the streaks fell on the hanging box where Coyotito lay, and on the ropes that held it.

It was a tiny movement that drew their eyes to the hanging box. Kino and Juana froze in their positions. Down the rope that hung the baby's box from the roof support a scorpion moved slowly. His stinging tail was straight out behind him, but he could whip it up in a flash of time.

Kino's breath whistled in his nostrils and he opened his mouth to stop it. And then the startled look was gone from him and the rigidity from his body. In his mind a new song had come, the Song of Evil, the music of the enemy, of any foe of the family, a savage, secret, dangerous melody, and underneath, the Song of the Family cried plaintively.

The scorpion moved delicately down the rope toward the box. Under her breath Juana repeated an ancient magic to guard against such evil, and on top of that she muttered a Hail Mary[6] between clenched teeth. But Kino was in motion. His body glided quietly across the room, noiselessly and smoothly. His hands were in front of him, palms down, and his eyes were on

---

5. **pulque** [pōol'kā]: fermented drink made from the juice of a desert plant in Mexico.
6. **Hail Mary:** traditional Catholic prayer to the Virgin Mary.

---

the scorpion. Beneath it in the hanging box Coyotito laughed and reached up his hand toward it. It sensed danger when Kino was almost within reach of it. It stopped, and its tail rose up over its back in little jerks and the curved thorn on the tail's end glistened.

Kino stood perfectly still. He could hear Juana whispering the old magic again, and he could hear the evil music of the enemy. He could not move until the scorpion moved, and it felt for the source of the death that was coming to it. Kino's hand went forward very slowly, very smoothly. The thorned tail jerked upright. And at that movement the laughing Coyotito shook the rope and the scorpion fell.

Kino's hand leaped to catch it, but it fell past his fingers, fell on the baby's shoulder, landed and struck. Then, snarling, Kino had it, had it in his fingers, rubbing it to a paste in his hands. He threw it down and beat it into the earth floor with his fist, and Coyotito screamed with pain in his box. But Kino beat and stamped the enemy until it was only a fragment and a moist place in the dirt. His teeth were bared and fury flared in his eyes and the Song of the Enemy roared in his ears.

But Juana had the baby in her arms now. She found the puncture with redness starting from it already. She put her lips down over the puncture and sucked hard and spat and sucked again while Coyotito screamed.

Kino hovered; he was helpless, he was in the way.

The screams of the baby brought the neighbors. Out of their brush houses they poured—Kino's brother Juan Tomás and his fat wife Apolonia and their four children crowded in the door and blocked the entrance, while behind them others tried to look in, and one small boy crawled among legs to have a look. And those in front passed the word back to those behind—"Scorpion. The baby has been stung."

Juana stopped sucking the puncture for a moment. The little hole was slightly enlarged and

*The Pearl* **617**

## AT A GLANCE

- A scorpion stings Coyotito.
- Kino kills the scorpion, and Juana sucks venom from the wound.

## 1 PLOT

The Song of Evil changes the Song of the Family to fear as the scorpion creeps toward Coyotito.

## 2 PLOT: NARRATIVE HOOK

The scorpion succeeds in stinging Coyotito, despite Kino's efforts to protect the child.

## 3 CHARACTERIZATION

Juana instinctively takes prudent, practical actions to help Coyotito.

## 4 THEME

Family feeling characterizes the community, as Coyotito's screams bring relatives and neighbors.

## GUIDED READING

### LITERAL QUESTION

**1a.** What do Kino and Juana each do after the scorpion strikes? (He rubs the scorpion into paste, then beats and stamps it into the dirt; she sucks the poison from the wound.)

### INFERENTIAL QUESTION

**1b.** What might their different reactions imply about them? (Kino acts out of rage, going beyond killing the scorpion as though to destroy death; Juana acts out of practical wisdom.)

- Juana demands that they take Coyotito to the doctor.
- Neighbors and family follow Juana and Kino to the city.

### 1 CHARACTERIZATION

Kino admires Juana's inner strength.

### 2 STYLE: SIMILE

Eyes as cold as those of a lioness reveal Juana's intensity.

### 3 PLOT: RISING ACTION

Kino and Juana, followed by their community, take Coyotito to the doctor.

---

its edges whitened from the sucking, but the red swelling extended farther around it in a hard lymphatic mound.[7] And all of these people knew about the scorpion. An adult might be very ill from the sting, but a baby could easily die from the poison. First, they knew, would come swelling and fever and tightened throat, and then cramps in the stomach, and then Coyotito might die if enough of the poison had gone in. But the stinging pain of the bite was going away. Coyotito's screams turned to moans.

1 Kino had wondered often at the iron in his patient, fragile wife. She, who was obedient and respectful and cheerful and patient, she could arch her back in child pain with hardly a cry. She could stand fatigue and hunger almost better than Kino himself. In the canoe she was like a strong man. And now she did a most surprising thing.

"The doctor," she said. "Go to get the doctor."

The word was passed out among the neighbors where they stood close packed in the little yard behind the brush fence. And they repeated among themselves, "Juana wants the doctor." A wonderful thing, a memorable thing, to want the doctor. To get him would be a remarkable thing. The doctor never came to the cluster of brush houses. Why should he, when he had more than he could do to take care of the rich people who lived in the stone and plaster houses of the town.

"He would not come," the people in the yard said.

"He would not come," the people in the door said, and the thought got into Kino.

"The doctor would not come," Kino said to Juana.

2 She looked up at him, her eyes as cold as the eyes of a lioness. This was Juana's first baby—this was nearly everything there was in Juana's world. And Kino saw her determination and the

---

7. **lymphatic mound:** swelling caused by poison or some other infection.

music of the family sounded in his head with a steely tone.

"Then we will go to him," Juana said, and with one hand she arranged her dark blue shawl over her head and made of one end of it a sling to hold the moaning baby and made of the other end of it a shade over his eyes to protect him from the light. The people in the door pushed against those behind to let her through. Kino followed her. They went out of the gate to the rutted path and the neighbors followed them.

The thing had become a neighborhood affair. They made a quick soft-footed procession into the center of the town, first Juana and Kino, and behind them Juan Tomás and Apolonia, her big stomach jiggling with the strenuous pace, then all the neighbors with the children trotting on the flanks. And the yellow sun threw their black shadows ahead of them so that they walked on their own shadows.

They came to the place where the brush houses stopped and the city of stone and plaster

---

## GUIDED READING

### LITERAL QUESTION

**1a.** What do the people gathered there say when Juana requests a doctor? (They say that he won't come.)

### INFERENTIAL QUESTION

**1b.** What can you infer from their reaction? (They have never known the doctor to visit poor people; he is a doctor *only* for the rich.)

began, the city of harsh outer walls and inner cool gardens where a little water played and the bougainvillea[8] crusted the walls with purple and brick-red and white. They heard from the secret gardens the singing of caged birds and heard the splash of cooling water on hot flagstones. The procession crossed the blinding plaza and passed in front of the church. It had grown now, and on the outskirts the hurrying newcomers were being softly informed how the baby had been stung by a scorpion, how the father and mother were taking it to the doctor.

And the newcomers, particularly the beggars from the front of the church who were great experts in financial analysis, looked quickly at Juana's old blue skirt, saw the tears in her shawl, appraised the green ribbon on her braids, read the age of Kino's blanket and the thousand washings of his clothes, and set them down as pov-

---

8. **bougainvillea** [bōō′gən vil′ē ə]: tropical vine with bright flowers.

erty people and went along to see what kind of drama might develop. The four beggars in front of the church knew everything in the town. They were students of the expressions of young women as they went into confession, and they saw them as they came out and read the nature of the sin. They knew every little scandal and some very big crimes. They slept at their posts in the shadow of the church so that no one crept in for consolation without their knowledge. And they knew the doctor. They knew his ignorance, his cruelty, his avarice, his appetites, his sins. They knew his clumsy operations and the little brown pennies he gave sparingly for alms. They had seen his corpses go into the church. And, since early Mass was over and business was slow, they followed the procession, these endless searchers after perfect knowledge of their fellow men, to see what the fat lazy doctor would do about an indigent baby with a scorpion bite.

The scurrying procession came at last to the big gate in the wall of the doctor's house. They

## GUIDED READING

### LITERAL QUESTION

**1a.** What happens to the size of the procession as it moves along into the city? (It grows.)

### INFERENTIAL QUESTION

**1b.** What might you infer from the fact that more and more people join the procession? (The poor—both in and out of town—form a community. Poor people going to a doctor is a notable event.)

## 1 STYLE: IMAGERY

The sounds and smells that reach the procession create a picture of opulence the poor people can scarcely imagine.

## 2 BACKGROUND

Kino's "race" is native to America, whereas the doctor's background is European.

## 3 THEME

Out of overriding love for his family, Kino stands with hat in hand, raging.

## 4 STYLE: CONTRAST

The doctor has overgrown his trappings of refinement and self-indulgence..

## 5 DIALOGUE

The doctor's comments show his contempt for the poor as well as the value he places on money.

---

1 could hear the splashing water and the singing of caged birds and the sweep of the long brooms on the flagstones. And they could smell the frying of good bacon from the doctor's house.

Kino hesitated a moment. The doctor was not of his people. This doctor was of a race which for nearly four hundred years had beaten and starved and robbed and despised Kino's 2 race, and frightened it too, so that the indigene[9] came humbly to the door. And as always when he came near to one of this race, Kino felt weak and afraid and angry at the same time. Rage and terror went together. He could kill the doctor more easily than he could talk to him, for all of the doctor's race spoke to all of Kino's race as though they were simple animals. And as Kino 3 raised his right hand to the iron ring knocker in the gate, rage swelled in him, and the pounding music of the enemy beat in his ears, and his lips drew tight against his teeth—but with his left hand he reached to take off his hat. The iron ring pounded against the gate. Kino took off his hat and stood waiting. Coyotito moaned a little in Juana's arms and she spoke softly to him. The procession crowded close the better to see and hear.

After a moment the big gate opened a few inches. Kino could see the green coolness of the garden and little splashing fountain through the opening. The man who looked out at him was one of his own race. Kino spoke to him in the old language.[10] "The little one—the firstborn—has been poisoned by the scorpion," Kino said. "He requires the skill of the healer."

The gate closed a little, and the servant refused to speak in the old language. "A little moment," he said. "I go to inform myself," and he closed the gate and slid the bolt home. The glaring sun threw the bunched shadows of the people blackly on the white wall.

---

9. **indigene** [in'di jēn']: native to an area.
10. **the old language:** the Indian language of the original inhabitants. The doctor and other members of the upper class speak Spanish.

---

4 In his chamber the doctor sat up in his high bed. He had on his dressing gown of red watered silk that had come from Paris, a little tight over the chest now if it was buttoned. On his lap was a silver tray with a silver chocolate pot and a tiny cup of eggshell china, so delicate that it looked silly when he lifted it with his big hand, lifted it with the tips of thumb and forefinger and spread the other three fingers wide to get them out of the way. His eyes rested in puffy little hammocks of flesh and his mouth drooped with discontent. He was growing very stout, and his voice was hoarse with the fat that pressed on his throat. Beside him on a table was a small Oriental gong and a bowl of cigarettes. The furnishings of the room were heavy and dark and gloomy. The pictures were religious, even the large tinted photograph of his dead wife, who, if Masses willed and paid for out of her own estate could do it, was in Heaven. The doctor had once for a short time been a part of the great world and his whole subsequent life was memory and longing for France. "That," he said, "was civilized living"—by which he meant that on a small income he had been able to keep a mistress and eat in restaurants. He poured his second cup of chocolate and crumbled a sweet biscuit in his fingers. The servant from the gate came to the open door and stood waiting to be noticed.

"Yes?" the doctor asked.

"It is a little Indian with a baby. He says a scorpion stung it."

The doctor put his cup down gently before he let his anger rise.

5 "Have I nothing better to do than cure insect bites for 'little Indians'? I am a doctor, not a veterinary."

"Yes, *Patron*,"[11] said the servant.

"Has he any money?" the doctor demanded. "No, they never have any money. I, I alone in the world am supposed to work for nothing—and I am tired of it. See if he has any money!"

---

11. *Patron* [pä trōn']: Spanish for "boss," "master."

---

## GUIDED READING

### LITERAL QUESTIONS

**1a.** What language does the servant—one of Kino's race—refuse to speak? (the old language that Kino uses and that both understand)

**2a.** What is the doctor's word for the kind of living he did in Paris? ("civilized")

### INFERENTIAL QUESTIONS

**1b.** What do you think the servant's refusal indicates? (He has disowned his background; he now belongs to the doctor's world, and he wants Kino to know it.)

**2b.** What can you infer about the doctor's view of the life he leads? (Although he lives in luxury and is surrounded by lavish possessions, he is not satisfied—he wants more.)

At the gate the servant opened the door a trifle and looked out at the waiting people. And this time he spoke in the old language.

"Have you money to pay for the treatment?"

Now Kino reached into a secret place somewhere under his blanket. He brought out a paper folded many times. Crease by crease he unfolded it, until at last there came to view eight small misshapen seed pearls,[12] as ugly and gray as little ulcers, flattened and almost valueless. The servant took the paper and closed the gate again, but this time he was not gone long. He opened the gate just wide enough to pass the paper back.

"The doctor has gone out," he said. "He was called to a serious case." And he shut the gate quickly out of shame.

And now a wave of shame went over the whole procession. They melted away. The beggars went back to the church steps, the stragglers moved off, and the neighbors departed so that the public shaming of Kino would not be in their eyes.

For a long time Kino stood in front of the gate with Juana beside him. Slowly he put his suppliant hat on his head. Then, without warning, he struck the gate a crushing blow with his fist. He looked down in wonder at his split knuckles and at the blood that flowed down between his fingers.

## II

The town lay on a broad estuary,[13] its old yellow plastered buildings hugging the beach. And on the beach the white and blue canoes that came from Nayarit[14] were drawn up, canoes preserved for generations by a hard shell-like waterproof plaster whose making was a secret of the fishing people. They were high and graceful canoes with curving bow and stern and a braced section midships where a mast could be stepped to carry a small lateen sail.[15]

The beach was yellow sand, but at the water's edge a rubble of shell and algae took its place. Fiddler crabs bubbled and sputtered in their holes in the sand, and in the shallows little lobsters popped in and out of their tiny homes in the rubble and sand. The sea bottom was rich with crawling and swimming and growing things. The brown algae waved in the gentle currents and the green eel grass swayed and little sea horses clung to its stems. Spotted botete,[16] the poison fish, lay on the bottom in the eelgrass beds, and the bright-colored swimming crabs scampered over them.

On the beach the hungry dogs and the hungry pigs of the town searched endlessly for any dead fish or sea bird that might have floated in on a rising tide.

Although the morning was young, the hazy mirage was up. The uncertain air that magnified some things and blotted out others hung over the whole Gulf so that all sights were unreal and vision could not be trusted; so that sea and land had the sharp clarities and the vagueness of a dream. Thus it might be that the people of the Gulf trust things of the spirit and things of the imagination, but they do not trust their eyes to show them distance or clear outline or any optical exactness. Across the estuary from the town one section of mangroves stood clear and telescopically defined, while another mangrove clump was a hazy black-green blob. Part of the far shore disappeared into a shimmer that looked like water. There was no certainty in seeing, no proof that what you saw was there or was not there. And the people of the Gulf expected all places were that way, and it was not strange to

---

12. **seed pearls:** tiny pearls of little value.
13. **estuary** [es'chōō er'ē]: bay formed where a river meets the ocean.
14. **Nayarit** [nä'yä rēt']: state of Mexico across the Gulf of California from Baja California.

15. **stepped . . . lateen** [la tēn'] **sail:** raised and set into position to carry a triangular sail. This triangular sail is attached to a long arm that hangs from the mast at an oblique angle.
16. **botete** [bō tä'tä]

*The Pearl* **621**

AT A GLANCE

- Kino offers tiny, flawed pearls as payment for treatment, and the doctor sends word that he's out.
- Kino strikes the gate with a blow that splits his knuckles.

## 1 PLOT: RISING ACTION

Kino's pearls can't buy help for a "little Indian."

## 2 CHARACTERIZATION

Kino acts out his rage with a suddenness and a force that move faster and truer than thoughts do.

## 3 STYLE: CONTRAST

Busy crabs scrambling around poison fish typify the many contrasts in nature that surround and affect the lives of Kino and Juana.

## 4 STYLE: IMAGERY

The changing appearance of mangrove clusters and the shimmering water illustrate the illusory quality of life on the Gulf.

## GUIDED READING

### LITERAL QUESTION

**1a.** What does the procession sense and do when the servant tells Kino the doctor is out? (They sense the shame and melt away.)

### INFERENTIAL QUESTION

**1b.** Why do they disappear? (As one body they feel Kino's humiliation, but they turn away so he won't have to see his shame in their eyes.)

## AT A GLANCE

- Juana applies a poultice of seaweed to the baby's shoulder.
- Kino and Juana, with Coyotito, canoe out to the oyster bed.

### 1 STYLE: METAPHOR

A "bulwark against starvation" connotes the solidity of the canoe's value and promise.

### 2 THEME

Even the sensible Juana has more confidence in a doctor's "official" treatment that costs money.

### 3 POINT OF VIEW

The omniscient observer expresses his own views about the characters in his tale.

### 4 STYLE: IMAGE PATTERN

Steinbeck's use of light throughout the novel focuses the reader's attention and heightens the drama and visual impact of a scene.

them. A copper haze hung over the water, and the hot morning sun beat on it and made it vibrate blindingly.

The brush houses of the fishing people were back from the beach on the right-hand side of the town, and the canoes were drawn up in front of this area.

Kino and Juana came slowly down to the beach and to Kino's canoe, which was the one thing of value he owned in the world. It was very old. Kino's grandfather had brought it from Nayarit, and he had given it to Kino's father, and so it had come to Kino. It was at once property and source of food, for a man with a boat can guarantee a woman that she will eat something. It is the bulwark against starvation. And every year Kino refinished his canoe with the hard shell-like plaster by the secret method that had also come to him from his father. Now he came to the canoe and touched the bow tenderly as he always did. He laid his diving rock and his basket and the two ropes in the sand by the canoe. And he folded his blanket and laid it in the bow.

Juana laid Coyotito on the blanket, and she placed her shawl over him so that the hot sun could not shine on him. He was quiet now, but the swelling on his shoulder had continued up his neck and under his ear and his face was puffed and feverish. Juana went to the water and waded in. She gathered some brown seaweed and made a flat damp poultice¹⁷ of it, and this she applied to the baby's swollen shoulder, which was as good a remedy as any and probably better than the doctor could have done. But the remedy lacked his authority because it was simple and didn't cost anything. The stomach cramps had not come to Coyotito. Perhaps Juana had sucked out the poison in time, but she had not sucked out her worry over her firstborn. She had not prayed directly for the recovery of the baby—she had prayed that they might find a pearl with which to hire the doctor to cure the baby, for the minds of people are as unsubstantial as the mirage of the Gulf.

Now Kino and Juana slid the canoe down the beach to the water, and when the bow floated, Juana climbed in, while Kino pushed the stern in and waded beside it until it floated lightly and trembled on the little breaking waves. Then in coordination Juana and Kino drove their double-bladed paddles into the sea, and the canoe creased the water and hissed with speed. The other pearlers were gone out long since. In a few moments Kino could see them clustered in the haze, riding over the oyster bed.

Light filtered down through the water to the bed where the frilly pearl oysters lay fastened to the rubbly bottom, a bottom strewn with shells of broken, opened oysters. This was the bed that had raised the King of Spain to be a great power in Europe in past years, had helped to pay for his wars, and had decorated the churches for his soul's sake. The gray oysters with ruffles like skirts on the shells, the barnacle-crusted oysters with little bits of weed clinging to the skirts and small crabs climbing over them. An accident could happen to these oysters, a grain of sand could lie in the folds of muscle and irritate the flesh until in self-protection the flesh coated the

---

17. **poultice** [pōl′tis]: absorbent material applied to the body as a medicine for inflammation or soreness.

**622** *The Novel*

---

## GUIDED READING

### LITERAL QUESTIONS

**1a.** What word describes the way Kino always touches the bow of his canoe? ("tenderly")

**2a.** What had the oyster bed done for the King of Spain? (It raised him to power, paid for his wars, and decorated the churches.)

### INFERENTIAL QUESTIONS

**1b.** What might the gesture suggest about Kino's values? (He shows respect and love for his family, past and present; the boat once belonged to his grandfather, and it now means he can provide for Juana and Coyotito.)

**2b.** What does the allusion to the King of Spain imply? (The oyster bed still holds the promise of riches.)

grain with a layer of smooth cement. But once started, the flesh continued to coat the foreign body until it fell free in some tidal flurry or until the oyster was destroyed. For centuries men had dived down and torn the oysters from the beds and ripped them open, looking for the coated grains of sand. Swarms of fish lived near the bed to live near the oysters thrown back by the searching men and to nibble at the shining inner shells. But the pearls were accidents, and the finding of one was luck, a little pat on the back by God or the gods or both.

Kino had two ropes, one tied to a heavy stone and one to a basket. He stripped off his shirt and trousers and laid his hat in the bottom of the canoe. The water was oily smooth. He took his rock in one hand and his basket in the other, and he slipped feet first over the side and the rock carried him to the bottom. The bubbles rose behind him until the water cleared and he could see. Above, the surface of the water was an undulating mirror of brightness, and he could see the bottoms of the canoes sticking through it.

Kino moved cautiously so that the water would not be obscured with mud or sand. He hooked his foot in the loop on his rock and his hands worked quickly, tearing the oysters loose, some singly, others in clusters. He laid them in his basket. In some places the oysters clung to one another so that they came free in lumps.

Now, Kino's people had sung of everything that happened or existed. They had made songs to the fishes, to the sea in anger and to the sea in calm, to the light and the dark and the sun and the moon, and the songs were all in Kino and in his people—every song that had ever been made, even the ones forgotten. And as he filled his **3** basket the song was in Kino, and the beat of the song was his pounding heart as it ate the oxygen from his held breath, and the melody of the song was the gray-green water and the little scuttling animals and the clouds of fish that flitted by and were gone. But in the song there was a secret little inner song, hardly perceptible, but always there, sweet and secret and clinging, almost **4** hiding in the countermelody, and this was the Song of the Pearl That Might Be, for every shell thrown in the basket might contain a pearl. Chance was against it, but luck and the gods might be for it. And in the canoe above him Kino knew that Juana was making the magic of prayer, her face set rigid and her muscles hard to force the luck, to tear the luck out of the god's hands, for she needed the luck for the swollen shoulder of Coyotito. And because the need was great and the desire was great, the little secret melody of

AT A GLANCE

- Kino dives down to the oyster bed.
- In the boat Juana prays for luck.

**1 BACKGROUND**

The description of nature and the history of pearl diving make the scene seem both real and timeless.

**2 STYLE: DETAIL**

The importance of seeing and being able to trust what one sees are recurring motifs in the novel.

**3 STYLE: IMAGERY**

Kino's heart, "pounding" and "eating" oxygen, conveys his intensity and the life-and-death urgency of this day's work.

**4 VOCABULARY: PREFIX**

The prefix *counter-* means "opposition"; the Song of the Pearl counters the melody of surrounding animals and water—i.e., "nature."

## GUIDED READING

### LITERAL QUESTIONS

**1a.** What were the songs of Kino's people about? (everything that happened or existed: fishes, the moods of the sea, the sun and moon, light and dark)

**2a.** What did Kino know Juana was making in the canoe above? (the "magic of prayer")

### INFERENTIAL QUESTIONS

**1b.** What do you think the subjects of their songs indicate? (They have always lived in tune with nature and its changes.)

**2b.** What might the combination of "magic" and "prayer" suggest about Juana and Kino's religion? (The "primitive" views of their ancestors blend with the "civilized" concept of newcomers.)

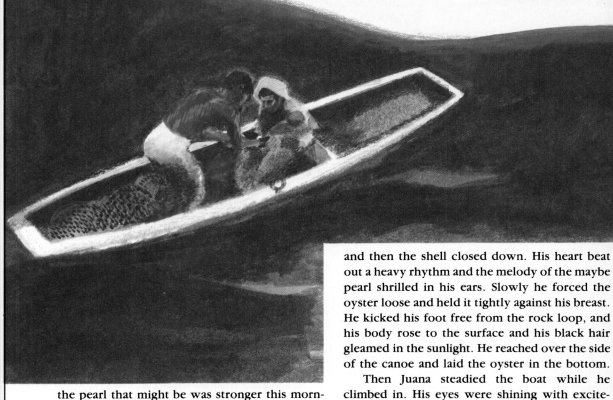

AT A GLANCE

- Kino harvests an old, solitary oyster from which a gleam comes.
- Kino surfaces and begins opening the smaller oysters.

## 1 CHARACTERIZATION

Kino's actions here—deliberate, skillful, and practiced—show the ease with which he moves in his own world, in contrast to his awkwardness in the city.

## 2 STYLE: WORD CHOICE

The word *ghostly* connotes an eeriness as well as a doubt about whether or not the "gleam" is real or bodes well.

## 3 RESPONSE JOURNAL

Have students comment on Kino's unspoken thoughts, or have them relate a similar experience of their own.

the pearl that might be was stronger this morning. Whole phrases of it came clearly and softly into the Song of the Undersea.

**1** Kino, in his pride and youth and strength, could remain down over two minutes without strain, so that he worked deliberately, selecting the largest shells. Because they were disturbed, the oyster shells were tightly closed. A little to his right a hummock[18] of rubbly rock stuck up, covered with young oysters not ready to take. Kino moved next to the hummock, and then, beside it, under a little overhang, he saw a very large oyster lying by itself, not covered with its clinging brothers. The shell was partly open, for the overhang protected this ancient oyster, and **2** in the liplike muscle Kino saw a ghostly gleam,

---

18. **hummock:** mound or hill.

**624** *The Novel*

and then the shell closed down. His heart beat out a heavy rhythm and the melody of the maybe pearl shrilled in his ears. Slowly he forced the oyster loose and held it tightly against his breast. He kicked his foot free from the rock loop, and his body rose to the surface and his black hair gleamed in the sunlight. He reached over the side of the canoe and laid the oyster in the bottom.

Then Juana steadied the boat while he climbed in. His eyes were shining with excitement, but in decency he pulled up his rock, and then he pulled up his basket of oysters and lifted them in. Juana sensed his excitement, and she pretended to look away. It is not good to want a thing too much. It sometimes drives the luck away. You must want it just enough, and you must be very tactful with God or the gods. But Juana stopped breathing. Very deliberately Kino **3** opened his short strong knife. He looked speculatively at the basket. Perhaps it would be better to open *the* oyster last. He took a small oyster from the basket, cut the muscle, searched the folds of flesh, and threw it in the water. Then he seemed to see the great oyster for the first time. He squatted in the bottom of the canoe, picked up the shell and examined it. The flutes were shining black to brown, and only a few small

## GUIDED READING

**LITERAL QUESTIONS**

**1a.** What distinguishes the ancient oyster from the others when Kino first notices it? (It's lying by itself and is still partly open.)

**2a.** What does Juana do even though she pretends not to want a thing too much by looking away from the basket? (She stops breathing.)

**INFERENTIAL QUESTIONS**

**1b.** What might you infer from its position? (This oyster, set apart from others that cling and shut according to their nature, is not ordinary.)

**2b.** What might Juana's action imply about her true feelings? (Her hope, almost involuntary, overpowers superstition, respect, and fear of God or the gods.)

barnacles adhered to the shell. Now Kino was reluctant to open it. What he had seen, he knew, might be a reflection, a piece of flat shell accidentally drifted in or a complete illusion. In this Gulf of uncertain light there were more illusions than realities.

But Juana's eyes were on him and she could not wait. She put her hand on Coyotito's covered head. "Open it," she said softly.

Kino deftly slipped his knife into the edge of the shell. Through the knife he could feel the muscle tighten hard. He worked the blade leverwise and the closing muscle parted and the shell fell apart. The liplike flesh writhed up and then subsided. Kino lifted the flesh, and there it lay, the great pearl, perfect as the moon. It captured the light and refined it and gave it back in silver incandescence. It was as large as a sea gull's egg. It was the greatest pearl in the world.

Juana caught her breath and moaned a little. And to Kino the secret melody of the maybe pearl broke clear and beautiful, rich and warm and lovely, glowing and gloating and triumphant. In the surface of the great pearl he could see dream forms. He picked the pearl from the dying flesh and held it in his palm, and he turned it over and saw that its curve was perfect. Juana came near to stare at it in his hand, and it was the hand he had smashed against the doctor's gate, and the torn flesh of the knuckles was turned grayish white by the sea water.

Instinctively Juana went to Coyotito where he lay on his father's blanket. She lifted the poultice of seaweed and looked at the shoulder. "Kino," she cried shrilly.

He looked past the pearl, and he saw that the swelling was going out of the baby's shoulder, the poison was receding from its body. Then Kino's fist closed over the pearl and his emotion broke over him. He put back his head and howled. His eyes rolled up and he screamed and his body was rigid. The men in the other canoes looked up, startled, and then they dug their paddles into the sea and raced toward Kino's canoe.

## STUDY QUESTIONS

### Recalling

1. What does Kino see when he wakes up? What "music" does he hear?
2. Soon after the story begins, what danger arises to disrupt Kino's morning? What "song" does Kino hear when he first becomes aware of this danger?
3. What action does Kino take in response to the danger? What does Juana do? Describe what happens to Coyotito.
4. What does the doctor think about Kino and his people? How does he respond to Kino's request for help?
5. Why do Kino and Juana go pearl fishing? Describe what Kino finds. What other piece of good fortune occurs to Kino and Juana?

### Interpreting

6. In spite of their poverty, what do Kino and Juana seem to think about life at the very beginning of the novel? How do you know?
7. Contrast the doctor and his house with Kino and his. Which man has a better life, according to Steinbeck, and how do you know?
8. What does the Song of the Family express for Kino? What do such songs show about the way Kino and his people view the world?
9. What kind of meaning might Kino see in events like the scorpion bite, the discovery of the pearl, and Coyotito's recovery?

### Extending

10. All of Kino's, Juana's, and Coyotito's problems seem to be solved by the end of this section. What do you think could happen to them next?

*The Pearl* **625**

## AT A GLANCE

- News of the pearl spreads immediately to the city.
- People everywhere see their dreams in Kino's pearl.

## LITERARY OPTIONS

- folk tale
- symbol
- round and flat characters

## THEMATIC OPTIONS

- greed
- basic human dignity
- exploitation of the poor

### 1 STYLE: SIMILE

Comparing the town to a colonial animal explains the speed with which news spreads and illustrates the importance of the pearl.

### 2 STYLE: DIALOGUE

The doctor's lie emphasizes his depraved character; his tone changes, but his craving remains the same.

### 3 STYLE: REPETITION

Repetition of "the news came" gives the novel a timeless, poetic quality.

### 4 THEME

One powerful buyer controls the pearl market, creating a semblance of competition to exploit the poor.

### 5 STYLE: METAPHOR

The "dark residue" foreshadows danger; the promise of great riches mixed with human nature produces something that seems to be evil.

## III

**1** A town is a thing like a colonial animal. A town has a nervous system and a head and shoulders and feet. A town is a thing separate from all other towns, so that there are no two towns alike. And a town has a whole emotion. How news travels through a town is a mystery not easily to be solved. News seems to move faster than small boys can scramble and dart to tell it, faster than women can call it over the fences.

Before Kino and Juana and the other fishers had come to Kino's brush house, the nerves of the town were pulsing and vibrating with the news—Kino had found the Pearl of the World. Before panting little boys could strangle out the words, their mothers knew it. The news swept on past the brush houses, and it washed in a foaming wave into the town of stone and plaster. It came to the priest walking in his garden, and it put a thoughtful look in his eyes and a memory of certain repairs necessary to the church. He wondered what the pearl would be worth. And he wondered whether he had baptized Kino's baby, or married him for that matter. The news came to the shopkeepers, and they looked at men's clothes that had not sold so well.

The news came to the doctor where he sat with a woman whose illness was age, though neither she nor the doctor would admit it. And when it was made plain who Kino was, the doctor grew stern and judicious at the same time. **2** "He is a client of mine," the doctor said. "I'm treating his child for a scorpion sting." And the doctor's eyes rolled up a little in their fat hammocks and he thought of Paris. He remembered the room he had lived in there as a great and luxurious place, and he remembered the hard-faced woman who had lived with him as a beautiful and kind girl, although she had been none of

**626** *The Novel*

these three. The doctor looked past his aged patient and saw himself sitting in a restaurant in Paris and a waiter was just opening a bottle of wine.

**3** The news came early to the beggars in front of the church, and it made them giggle a little with pleasure, for they knew that there is no almsgiver in the world like a poor man who is suddenly lucky.

Kino has found the Pearl of the World. In the town, in little offices, sat the men who bought pearls from the fishers. They waited in their chairs until the pearls came in, and then they cackled and fought and shouted and threatened until they reached the lowest price the fisherman would stand. But there was a price below which they dared not go, for it had happened that a fisherman in despair had given his pearls to the church. And when the buying was over, these buyers sat alone and their fingers played restlessly with the pearls, and they wished they owned **4** the pearls. For there were not many buyers really—there was only one, and he kept these agents in separate offices to give a semblance of competition. The news came to these men, and their eyes squinted and their fingertips burned a little, and each one thought how the patron could not live forever and someone had to take his place. And each one thought how with some capital he could get a new start.

All manner of people grew interested in Kino—people with things to sell and people with favors to ask. Kino had found the Pearl of the World. **5** The essence of pearl mixed with essence of men and a curious dark residue was precipitated. Every man suddenly became related to Kino's pearl, and Kino's pearl went into the dreams, the speculations, the schemes, the plans, the futures, the wishes, the needs, the

## GUIDED READING

**LITERAL QUESTION**

**1a.** What does the priest wonder? (He wonders what the pearl is worth, or if he has baptized Coyotito, or even if he has married Kino and Juana.)

**INFERENTIAL QUESTION**

**1b.** What do you think the priest's questions suggest? (The poor are as inconsequential and forgettable to the cleric as they are to the doctor; the pearl's worth is what matters to him.)

lusts, the hungers, of everyone, and only one person stood in the way and that was Kino, so that he became curiously every man's enemy. The news stirred up something infinitely black and evil in the town; the black distillate was like the scorpion, or like hunger in the smell of food, or like loneliness when love is withheld. The poison sacs of the town began to manufacture venom, and the town swelled and puffed with the pressure of it.

But Kino and Juana did not know these things. Because they were happy and excited they thought everyone shared their joy. Juan Tomás and Apolonia did, and they were the world too. In the afternoon, when the sun had gone over the mountains of the Peninsula to sink in the outward sea, Kino squatted in his house with Juana beside him. And the brush house was crowded with neighbors. Kino held the great pearl in his hand, and it was warm and alive in his hand. And the music of the pearl had merged with the music of the family so that one beautified the other. The neighbors looked at the pearl in Kino's hand and they wondered how such luck could come to any man.

And Juan Tomás, who squatted on Kino's right hand because he was his brother, asked, "What will you do now that you have become a rich man?"

Kino looked into his pearl, and Juana cast her eyelashes down and arranged her shawl to cover her face so that her excitement could not be seen. And in the incandescence of the pearl the pictures formed of the things Kino's mind had considered in the past and had given up as impossible. In the pearl he saw Juana and Coyotito and himself standing and kneeling at the high altar, and they were being married now that they could pay. He spoke softly, "We will be married—in the church."

In the pearl he saw how they were dressed— Juana in a shawl stiff with newness and a new skirt, and from under the long skirt Kino could see that she wore shoes. It was in the pearl—the

picture glowing there. He himself was dressed in new white clothes, and he carried a new hat— not of straw but of fine black felt—and he too wore shoes—not sandals but shoes that laced. But Coyotito—he was the one—he wore a blue sailor suit from the United States and a little yachting cap such as Kino had seen once when a pleasure boat put into the estuary. All of these things Kino saw in the lucent[1] pearl and he said, "We will have new clothes."

And the music of the pearl rose like a chorus of trumpets in his ears.

Then to the lovely gray surface of the pearl came the little things Kino wanted: a harpoon to take the place of one lost a year ago, a new harpoon of iron with a ring in the end of the shaft; and—his mind could hardly make the leap—a rifle—but why not, since he was so rich. And Kino saw Kino in the pearl, Kino holding a Winchester carbine. It was the wildest daydreaming and very pleasant. His lips moved hesitantly over this—"A rifle," he said. "Perhaps a rifle."

It was the rifle that broke down the barriers. This was an impossibility, and if he could think of having a rifle whole horizons were burst and he could rush on. For it is said that humans are never satisfied, that you give them one thing and they want something more. And this is said in disparagement, whereas it is one of the greatest talents the species has and one that has made it superior to animals that are satisfied with what they have.

The neighbors, close pressed and silent in the house, nodded their heads at his wild imaginings. And a man in the rear murmured, "A rifle. He will have a rifle."

But the music of the pearl was shrilling with triumph in Kino. Juana looked up, and her eyes were wide at Kino's courage and at his imagination. And electric strength had come to him now the horizons were kicked out. In the pearl he saw Coyotito sitting at a little desk in a school,

---

1. **lucent** [lōō'sənt]: shining; luminous.

*The Pearl* **627**

AT A GLANCE

- The pearl arouses unsuspected greed and envy in others.
- Kino envisions a church marriage, new clothes, a harpoon, and a rifle.

## 1 THEME

Greed transforms the town into an animal like a scorpion, manufacturing poison for its victim.

## 2 PLOT: CONFLICT

The difference between the envious world, on the one hand, and Kino and Juana's naive view, on the other, establishes the central conflict in the novel.

## 3 SYMBOL

For Kino the pearl represents a future of respectability and pleasure for his family.

## 4 RESPONSE JOURNAL

Have students respond to the implied question: Is dissatisfaction a virtue or a fault?

## GUIDED READING

### LITERAL QUESTIONS

**1a.** What has Kino become to every man by virtue of finding the pearl? (an enemy)

**2a.** What is the first vision Kino sees in the pearl? (Juana, Coyotito, and himself; he is being married before the high altar)

### INFERENTIAL QUESTIONS

**1b.** What can you infer from that transformation? (Greed changes the way people see each other; Kino, once just another poor Indian, becomes everyone's enemy.)

**2b.** What do you think Kino's dream says about his values? (First he values his family, but he also wants the respectability of a church marriage and the prestige afforded by a ceremony at the "high altar.")

AT A GLANCE

- Kino says that Coyotito will learn to read and write.
- The priest comes to Kino and Juana's house.

**1 THEME**

Kino views knowledge as the means to freedom from exploitation.

**2 POINT OF VIEW**

The omniscient observer sees into the future and presents his view of human nature—the need to be proved right.

**3 ATMOSPHERE**

Darkness, shadows, and whispers create a sinister atmosphere for the arrival of the priest.

**4 CHARACTERIZATION**

The priest, a flat character, condescends and flatters with his reference to a "namesake" in a book that Kino cannot read.

just as Kino had once seen it through an open door. And Coyotito was dressed in a jacket, and he had on a white collar and a broad silken tie. Moreover, Coyotito was writing on a big piece of paper. Kino looked at his neighbors fiercely. "My son will go to school," he said, and the neighbors were hushed. Juana caught her breath sharply. Her eyes were bright as she watched him, and she looked quickly down at Coyotito in her arms to see whether this might be possible.

**1** But Kino's face shone with prophecy. "My son will read and open the books, and my son will write and will know writing. And my son will make numbers, and these things will make us free because he will know—he will know and through him we will know." And in the pearl Kino saw himself and Juana squatting by the little fire in the brush hut while Coyotito read from a great book. "This is what the pearl will do," said Kino. And he had never said so many words together in his life. And suddenly he was afraid of his talking. His hand closed down over the pearl and cut the light away from it. Kino was afraid as a man is afraid who says, "I will,"[2] without knowing.

Now the neighbors knew they had witnessed a great marvel. They knew that time would now date from Kino's pearl, and that they would discuss this moment for many years to come. If these things came to pass, they would recount how Kino looked and what he said and how his eyes shone, and they would say, "He was a man transfigured. Some power was given to him, and there it started. You see what a great man he has become, starting from that moment. And I myself saw it."

**2** And if Kino's planning came to nothing, those same neighbors would say, "There it started. A foolish madness came over him so that he spoke foolish words. God keep us from such things. Yes, God punished Kino because he rebelled against the way things are. You see

---

2. **"I will":** the marriage vow.

what has become of him. And I myself saw the moment when his reason left him."

Kino looked down at his closed hand and the knuckles were scabbed over and tight where he had struck the gate.

Now the dusk was coming. And Juana looped her shawl under the baby so that he hung against her hip, and she went to the fire hole and dug a coal from the ashes and broke a few twigs over it and fanned a flame alive. The little flames danced on the faces of the neighbors. They knew they should go to their own dinners, but they were reluctant to leave.

**3** The dark was almost in, and Juana's fire threw shadows on the brush walls when the whisper came in, passed from mouth to mouth. "The Father is coming—the priest is coming." The men uncovered their heads and stepped back from the door, and the women gathered their shawls about their faces and cast down their eyes. Kino and Juan Tomás, his brother, stood up. The priest came in—a graying, aging man with an old skin and a young sharp eye. Children, he considered these people, and he treated them like children.

**4** "Kino," he said softly, "thou art named after a great man—and a great Father of the Church."[3] He made it sound like a benediction. "Thy namesake tamed the desert and sweetened the minds of thy people, didst thou know that? It is in the books."

Kino looked quickly down at Coyotito's head, where he hung on Juana's hip. Some day, his mind said, that boy would know what things were in the books and what things were not. The music had gone out of Kino's head, but now, thinly, slowly, the melody of the morning, the music of evil, of the enemy sounded, but it was faint and weak. And Kino looked at his neighbors to see who might have brought this song in.

But the priest was speaking again. "It has

---

3. **Father of the Church:** Eusebius Kino, a seventeenth-century Spanish missionary and explorer.

---

## GUIDED READING

### LITERAL QUESTIONS

**1a.** What are the reactions of Juana and the neighbors to Kino's declaration that his son will go to school? (Juana catches her breath; a hush falls over the neighbors.)

**2a.** What words describe the aging priest's eye? (young and sharp)

### INFERENTIAL QUESTIONS

**1b.** What might their reactions indicate? (Education, for one of their people, is scarcely believable; it goes beyond what they imagine.)

**2b.** What do you think his eye might suggest? (Like other inhabitants of the town, he is untiring and practiced in watching for fortune and sizing up opportunity.)

come to me that thou hast found a great fortune, a great pearl."

Kino opened his hand and held it out, and the priest gasped a little at the size and beauty of the pearl. And then he said, "I hope thou wilt remember to give thanks, my son, to Him who has given thee this treasure, and to pray for guidance in the future."

Kino nodded dumbly, and it was Juana who spoke softly. "We will, Father. And we will be married now. Kino has said so." She looked at the neighbors for confirmation, and they nodded their heads solemnly.

The priest said, "It is pleasant to see that your first thoughts are good thoughts. God bless you, my children." He turned and left quietly, and the people let him through.

But Kino's hand had closed tightly on the pearl again, and he was glancing about suspiciously, for the evil song was in his ears, shrilling against the music of the pearl.

The neighbors slipped away to go to their houses, and Juana squatted by the fire and set her clay pot of boiled beans over the little flame. Kino stepped to the doorway and looked out. As always, he could smell the smoke from many fires, and he could see the hazy stars and feel the damp of the night air so that he covered his nose from it. The thin dog came to him and threshed itself in greeting like a windblown flag, and Kino looked down at it and didn't see it. He had broken through the horizons into a cold and lonely outside. He felt alone and unprotected, and scraping crickets and shrilling tree frogs and croaking toads seemed to be carrying the melody of evil. Kino shivered a little and drew his blanket more tightly against his nose. He carried the pearl still in his hand, tightly closed in his palm, and it was warm and smooth against his skin.

Behind him he heard Juana patting the cakes before she put them down on the clay cooking sheet. Kino felt all the warmth and security of his family behind him, and the Song of the Fam-

ily came from behind him like the purring of a kitten. But now, by saying what his future was going to be like, he had created it. A plan is a real thing, and things projected are experienced. A plan once made and visualized becomes a reality along with other realities—never to be destroyed but easily to be attacked. This Kino's future was real, but having set it up, other forces were set up to destroy it, and this he knew, so that he had to prepare to meet the attack. And this Kino knew also—that the gods do not love men's plans, and the gods do not love success unless it comes by accident. He knew that the gods take their revenge on a man if he be successful through his own efforts. Consequently Kino was afraid of plans, but having made one, he could never destroy it. And to meet the attack, Kino was already making a hard skin for himself against the world. His eyes and his mind probed for danger before it appeared.

Standing in the door, he saw two men approach; and one of them carried a lantern which lighted the ground and the legs of the men. They turned in through the opening of Kino's brush fence and came to his door. And Kino saw that one was the doctor and the other the servant who had opened the gate in the morning. The split knuckles on Kino's right hand burned when he saw who they were.

The doctor said, "I was not in when you came this morning. But now, at the first chance, I have come to see the baby."

Kino stood in the door, filling it, and hatred raged and flamed in back of his eyes, and fear too, for the hundreds of years of subjugation were cut deep in him.

"The baby is nearly well now," he said curtly.

The doctor smiled, but his eyes in their little lymph-lined hammocks did not smile.

He said, "Sometimes, my friend, the scorpion sting has a curious effect. There will be apparent improvement, and then without warning—pouf!" He pursed his lips and made a little explosion to show how quick it could be, and he

*The Pearl* **629**

## 1 READING SKILLS: CONTRAST

Juana shows her first uncertainty as she looks to others for confirmation.

## 2 STYLE

Throughout the novel music comments, summarizes, and foreshadows; here the creatures in nature project a warning of evil that echoes Kino's suspicion and vulnerability.

## 3 PLOT: CONFLICT

Kino now knows that the world does not take pleasure in his advancement; he must fight to keep his pearl and realize his dreams.

## GUIDED READING

### LITERAL QUESTION

**1a.** What sensation does Kino feel in his hand when he sees the doctor approaching? (His split knuckles burn.)

### INFERENTIAL QUESTION

**1b.** What might the burning feeling mean? (It signifies an unforgotten humiliation when the doctor refused to treat Coyotito.)

**1 ATMOSPHERE**

The doctor sets the stage for his act, making use of the light and his props to exploit Kino's ignorance.

**2 PLOT: CONFLICT**

Kino, caught in the conflict between hatred for the doctor and love for his son, fears risking possible harm to Coyotito.

**3 THEME**

This obvious and inhumane trick illustrates the dehumanizing effect of greed.

---

**1** shifted his small black doctor's bag about so that the light of the lamp fell upon it, for he knew that Kino's race love the tools of any craft and trust them. "Sometimes," the doctor went on in a liquid tone, "sometimes there will be a withered leg or a blind eye or a crumpled back. Oh, I know a sting of the scorpion, my friend, and I can cure it."

**2** Kino felt the rage and hatred melting toward fear. He did not know, and perhaps this doctor did. And he could not take the chance of putting his certain ignorance against this man's possible knowledge. He was trapped as his people were always trapped, and would be until, as he had said, they could be sure that the things in the books were really in the books. He could not take a chance—not with the life or with the straightness of Coyotito. He stood aside and let the doctor and his man enter the brush hut.

Juana stood up from the fire and backed away as he entered, and she covered the baby's face with the fringe of her shawl. And when the doctor went to her and held out his hand, she clutched the baby tight and looked at Kino where he stood with the fire shadows leaping on his face.

Kino nodded, and only then did she let the doctor take the baby.

"Hold the light," the doctor said, and when the servant held the lantern high, the doctor looked for a moment at the wound on the baby's shoulder. He was thoughtful for a moment and then he rolled back the baby's eyelid and looked at the eyeball. He nodded his head while Coyotito struggled against him.

"It is as I thought," he said. "The poison has gone inward and it will strike soon. Come look!" He held the eyelid down. "See—it is blue." And Kino, looking anxiously, saw that indeed it was a little blue. And he didn't know whether or not it was always a little blue. But the trap was set. He couldn't take the chance.

The doctor's eyes watered in their little hammocks. "I will give him something to try to turn the poison aside," he said. And he handed the baby to Kino.

Then from his bag he took a little bottle of white powder and a capsule of gelatine. He filled the capsule with the powder and closed it, and then around the first capsule he fitted a second capsule and closed it. Then he worked very deftly. He took the baby and pinched its lower lip until it opened its mouth. His fat fingers placed the capsule far back on the baby's tongue, back of the point where he could spit it out, and then from the floor he picked up the little pitcher of pulque and gave Coyotito a drink, and it was done. He looked again at the baby's eyeball and he pursed his lips and seemed to think.

At last he handed the baby back to Juana, and **3** he turned to Kino. "I think the poison will attack within the hour," he said. "The medicine may save the baby from hurt, but I will come back in an hour. Perhaps I am in time to save him." He took a deep breath and went out of the hut, and his servant followed him with the lantern.

Now Juana had the baby under her shawl, and she stared at it with anxiety and fear. Kino came to her, and he lifted the shawl and stared at the baby. He moved his hand to look under the eyelid, and only then saw that the pearl was still in his hand. Then he went to a box by the wall, and from it he brought a piece of rag. He wrapped the pearl in the rag, then went to the corner of the brush house and dug a little hole with his fingers in the dirt floor, and he put the pearl in the hole and covered it up and concealed the place. And then he went to the fire where Juana was squatting, watching the baby's face.

The doctor, back in his house, settled into his chair and looked at his watch. His people brought him a little supper of chocolate and sweet cakes and fruit, and he stared at the food discontentedly.

In the houses of the neighbors the subject that would lead all conversations for a long time to come was aired for the first time to see how it

---

## GUIDED READING

**LITERAL QUESTIONS**

**1a.** What does Juana do when the doctor holds out his hand for Coyotito? (She tightens her clutch on the baby and looks at Kino.)

**2a.** What had Kino forgotten until he moved his hand to re-examine Coyotito's eyelid? (the pearl, still in his hand)

**INFERENTIAL QUESTIONS**

**1b.** What can you infer from Juana's reaction? (She doesn't trust the doctor and acts first according to her intuition, but she also fears that he may be right.)

**2b.** What might you infer from this incident? (Coyotito's safety and the ancient hatred for people like the doctor matter more to Kino than the pearl does.)

AT A GLANCE

- The neighbors wonder if riches will change Kino and Juana.
- Coyotito becomes very sick with severe stomach spasms.

## 1 STYLE: IMAGERY

Animal behavior parallels and foreshadows activities in the human domain.

## 2 READING SKILLS: CONTRAST

While the doctor stares in discontent at a supper of sweets, Kino eats simple food with a natural appetite.

## 3 PLOT: RISING ACTION

Shortly after Coyotito is given the doctor's "medicine," he becomes very sick, just as the doctor had predicted.

would go. The neighbors showed one another with their thumbs how big the pearl was, and they made little caressing gestures to show how lovely it was. From now on they would watch Kino and Juana very closely to see whether riches turned their heads, as riches turn all people's heads. Everyone knew why the doctor had come. He was not good at dissembling and he was very well understood.

Out in the estuary a tight-woven school of small fishes glittered and broke water to escape a school of great fishes that drove in to eat them. And in the houses the people could hear the swish of the small ones and the bouncing splash of the great ones as the slaughter went on. The dampness arose out of the Gulf and was deposited on bushes and cacti and on little trees in salty drops. And the night mice crept about on the ground and the little night hawks hunted them silently.

The skinny black puppy with flame spots over his eyes came to Kino's door and looked in.

He nearly shook his hind quarters loose when Kino glanced up at him, and he subsided when Kino looked away. The puppy did not enter the house, but he watched with frantic interest 2 while Kino ate his beans from the little pottery dish and wiped it clean with a corncake and ate the cake and washed the whole down with a drink of pulque.

Kino was finished and was rolling a cigarette when Juana spoke sharply. "Kino." He glanced at her and then got up and went quickly to her for he saw fright in her eyes. He stood over her, looking down, but the light was very dim. He kicked a pile of twigs into the fire hole to make a blaze, and then he could see the face of Coyotito. The baby's face was flushed and his throat was working and a little thick drool of saliva 3 issued from his lips. The spasm of the stomach muscles began, and the baby was very sick.

Kino knelt beside his wife. "So the doctor knew," he said, but he said it for himself as well

*The Pearl* **631**

## GUIDED READING

### LITERAL QUESTION

**1a.** What is the school of great fish in the estuary doing? (eating the small fish)

### INFERENTIAL QUESTION

**1b.** What do you think Steinbeck is implying with this observation? (This occurrence in the animal world is a metaphor for what the powerful, dehumanized by greed, do to the powerless.)

## 1 IRONY

The doctor's lie is the truth, for his poison has worked: His words worked on Kino and Juana, and the powder has worked on Coyotito.

## 2 PLOT: FORESHADOWING

Like the nighthawks hunting mice, the doctor watches Kino's eyes to discover where the pearl is hidden.

## 3 CHARACTERIZATION

These characters are instinctively wary, even in sleep.

as for his wife, for his mind was hard and suspicious and he was remembering the white powder. Juana rocked from side to side and moaned out the little Song of the Family as though it could ward off the danger, and the baby vomited and writhed in her arms. Now uncertainty was in Kino, and the music of evil throbbed in his head and nearly drove out Juana's song.

The doctor finished his chocolate and nibbled the little fallen pieces of sweet cake. He brushed his fingers on a napkin, looked at his watch, arose, and took up his little bag.

The news of the baby's illness traveled quickly among the brush houses, for sickness is second only to hunger as the enemy of poor people. And some said softly, "Luck, you see, brings bitter friends." And they nodded and got up to go to Kino's house. The neighbors scuttled with covered noses through the dark until they crowded into Kino's house again. They stood and gazed, and they made little comments on the sadness that this should happen at a time of joy, and they said, "All things are in God's hands." The old women squatted down beside Juana to try to give her aid if they could and comfort if they could not.

Then the doctor hurried in, followed by his man. He scattered the old women like chickens. He took the baby and examined it and felt its head. **1** "The poison it has worked," he said. "I think I can defeat it. I will try my best." He asked for water, and in the cup of it he put three drops of ammonia, and he pried open the baby's mouth and poured it down. The baby spluttered and screeched under the treatment, and Juana watched him with haunted eyes. The doctor spoke a little as he worked. "It is lucky that I know about the poison of the scorpion, otherwise—" and he shrugged to show what could have happened.

But Kino was suspicious, and he could not take his eyes from the doctor's open bag, and from the bottle of white powder there. Gradually the spasms subsided and the baby relaxed under the doctor's hands. And then Coyotito

sighed deeply and went to sleep, for he was very tired with vomiting.

The doctor put the baby in Juana's arms. "He will get well now," he said. "I have won the fight." And Juana looked at him with adoration.

The doctor was closing his bag now. He said, "When do you think you can pay this bill?" He said it even kindly.

"When I have sold my pearl I will pay you," Kino said.

"You have a pearl? A good pearl?" the doctor asked with interest.

And then the chorus of the neighbors broke in. "He has found the Pearl of the World," they cried, and they joined forefinger with thumb to show how great the pearl was.

"Kino will be a rich man," they clamored. "It is a pearl such as one has never seen."

The doctor looked surprised. "I had not heard of it. Do you keep this pearl in a safe place? Perhaps you would like me to put it in my safe?"

Kino's eyes were hooded now, his cheeks were drawn taut. "I have it secure," he said. "Tomorrow I will sell it and then I will pay you."

The doctor shrugged, and his wet eyes never left Kino's eyes. He knew the pearl would be buried in the house, and he thought Kino might look toward the place where it was buried. **2** "It would be a shame to have it stolen before you could sell it," the doctor said, and he saw Kino's eyes flick involuntarily to the floor near the side post of the brush house.

When the doctor had gone and all the neighbors had reluctantly returned to their houses, Kino squatted beside the little glowing coals in the fire hole and listened to the night sound, the soft sweep of the little waves on the shore and the distant barking of dogs, the creeping of the breeze through the brush house roof **3** and the soft speech of his neighbors in their houses in the village. For these people do not sleep soundly all night; they awaken at intervals and talk a little and then go to sleep again. And

## GUIDED READING

### LITERAL QUESTION

**1a.** What do Juana's eyes express toward the doctor after he cures Coyotito? (adoration)

### INFERENTIAL QUESTION

**1b.** Why might Juana, whose instincts are usually correct, be fooled? (When Coyotito is made well, relief and gratitude are all she feels; the cause of his suffering is overshadowed by the "miracle" of the cure.)

after a while Kino got up and went to the door of his house.

He smelled the breeze and he listened for any foreign sound of secrecy or creeping, and his eyes searched the darkness, for the music of evil was sounding in his head and he was fierce and afraid. After he had probed the night with his senses he went to the place by the side post where the pearl was buried, and he dug it up and brought it to his sleeping mat, and under his sleeping mat he dug another little hole in the dirt floor and buried his pearl and covered it up again.

And Juana, sitting by the fire hole, watched him with questioning eyes, and when he had buried his pearl she asked, "Who do you fear?"

Kino searched for a true answer, and at last he said, "Everyone." And he could feel a shell of hardness drawing over him.

After a while they lay down together on the sleeping mat, and Juana did not put the baby in his box tonight, but cradled him on her arms and covered his face with her head shawl. And the last light went out of the embers in the fire hole.

But Kino's brain burned, even during his sleep, and he dreamed that Coyotito could read, that one of his own people could tell him the truth of things. And in his dream, Coyotito was reading from a book as large as a house, with letters as big as dogs, and the words galloped and played on the book. And then darkness spread over the page, and with the darkness came the music of evil again, and Kino stirred in his sleep; and when he stirred, Juana's eyes opened in the darkness. And then Kino awakened, with the evil music pulsing in him, and he lay in the darkness with his ears alert.

Then from the corner of the house came a sound so soft that it might have been simply a thought, a little furtive movement, a touch of a foot on earth, the almost inaudible purr of controlled breathing. Kino held his breath to listen, and he knew that whatever dark thing was in his house was holding its breath too, to listen. For a

time no sound at all came from the corner of the brush house. Then Kino might have thought he had imagined the sound. But Juana's hand came creeping over to him in warning, and then the sound came again! the whisper of a foot on dry earth and the scratch of fingers in the soil.

And now a wild fear surged in Kino's breast, and on the fear came rage, as it always did. Kino's hand crept into his breast where his knife hung on a string, and then he sprang like an angry cat, leaped striking and spitting for the dark thing he knew was in the corner of the house. He felt cloth, struck at it with his knife and missed, and struck again and felt his knife go through cloth, and then his head crashed with lightning and exploded with pain. There was a soft scurry in the doorway, and running steps for a moment, and then silence.

Kino could feel warm blood running down from his forehead, and he could hear Juana calling to him. "Kino! Kino!" And there was terror in her voice. Then coldness came over him as quickly as the rage had, and he said, "I am all right. The thing has gone."

He groped his way back to the sleeping mat. Already Juana was working at the fire. She uncovered an ember from the ashes and shredded little pieces of cornhusk over it and blew a little flame into the cornhusks so that a tiny light danced through the hut. And then from a secret place Juana brought a little piece of consecrated candle and lighted it at the flame and set it upright on a fireplace stone. She worked quickly, crooning as she moved about. She dipped the end of her shawl in water and swabbed the blood from Kino's bruised forehead. "It is nothing," Kino said, but his eyes and his voice were hard and cold and a brooding hate was growing in him.

Now the tension which has been growing in Juana boiled up to the surface and her lips were thin. "This thing is evil," she cried harshly. "This pearl is like a sin! It will destroy us," and her voice rose shrilly. "Throw it away, Kino. Let

*The Pearl* **633**

AT A GLANCE

- Kino attacks an intruder with his knife.
- Juana implores Kino to throw the pearl away.

**1 CHARACTERIZATION**

Watching and preparing for enemies, Kino grows increasingly wary and animallike in his actions.

**2 STYLE: SIMILE**

The comparison between the movements of Kino and those of a cat illustrates the defensive and spontaneous nature of his violence.

**3 READING SKILLS: CONTRAST**

Juana's ministering actions following the attack show that love is her motivation, while Kino focuses on his hatred for their enemies.

**4 SYMBOL**

The pearl that once seemed to hold the promise of a better life for her family now represents ruin to Juana.

---

## GUIDED READING

**LITERAL QUESTIONS**

**1a.** What spreads over the page that Coyotito reads in Kino's dream? (darkness)

**2a.** What does Juana bring from hiding to place on a fireplace stone? (a piece of consecrated candle that she has lighted)

**INFERENTIAL QUESTIONS**

**1b.** What do you think the darkness might suggest? (Something evil threatens Kino's dream for Coyotito.)

**2b.** What can you infer from Juana's gesture? (The lighted candle, which has been blessed, represents her prayer against encroaching evil.)

- Kino won't throw away the pearl; they will sell it the next day.
- The image reflected by the pearl deceives and reassures Kino.

## 1 READING SKILLS: COMPARISON AND CONTRAST

Both Juana and Kino want the best opportunity for their family, but Kino struggles for advancement while Juana fights for survival.

## 2 CHARACTERIZATION

Kino's apparent surprise that he holds a bloody knife shows that his reaction to danger is an immediate, unplanned reflex.

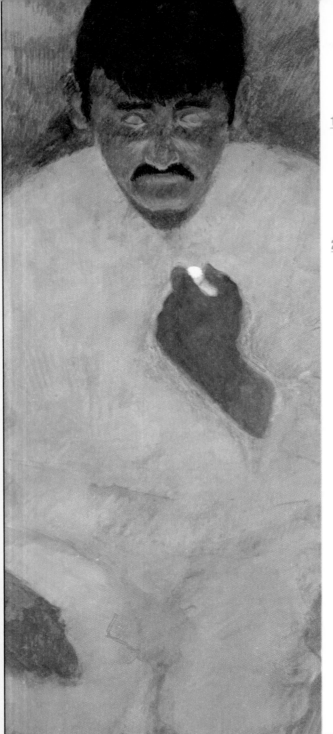

us break it between stones. Let us bury it and forget the place. Let us throw it back into the sea. It has brought evil. Kino, my husband, it will destroy us.'' And in the firelight her lips and her eyes were alive with her fear.

But Kino's face was set, and his mind and his will were set. ''This is our one chance,'' he said. **1** ''Our son must go to school. He must break out of the pot that holds us in.''

''It will destroy us all,'' Juana cried. ''Even our son.''

''Hush,'' said Kino. ''Do not speak any more. In the morning we will sell the pearl, and then the evil will be gone, and only the good remain. Now hush, my wife.'' His dark eyes scowled into **2** the little fire, and for the first time he knew that his knife was still in his hands, and he raised the blade and looked at it and saw a little line of blood on the steel. For a moment he seemed about to wipe the blade on his trousers but then he plunged the knife into the earth and so cleansed it.

The distant roosters began to crow and the air changed and the dawn was coming. The wind of the morning ruffled the water of the estuary and whispered through the mangroves, and the little waves beat on the rubbly beach with an increased tempo. Kino raised the sleeping mat and dug up his pearl and put it in front of him and stared at it.

And the beauty of the pearl, winking and glimmering in the light of the little candle, cozened[4] his brain with its beauty. So lovely it was, so soft, and its own music came from it—its music of promise and delight, its guarantee of the future, of comfort, of security. Its warm lucence promised a poultice against illness and a wall against insult. It closed a door on hunger. And as he stared at it Kino's eyes softened and his face relaxed. He could see the little image of the consecrated candle reflected in the soft surface of the pearl, and he heard again in his ears

---

4. **cozened** [kuz′ənd]: deceived.

## GUIDED READING

### LITERAL QUESTIONS

**1a.** What is Juana's plea and warning to Kino about the pearl? (She wants to throw the pearl back into the sea; she believes that it will destroy them.)

**2a.** What does the music of the pearl seem to guarantee to Kino? (future, comfort, and security)

### INFERENTIAL QUESTIONS

**1b.** What can you infer about Juana's values? (Anything that threatens the integrity of her family is of no worth.)

**2b.** What might this view of the pearl say about Kino, who once revered his canoe as the ''bulwark against starvation''? (The opportunity to work for subsistence as his ancestors did pales before this new ''opportunity.'')

the lovely music of the undersea, the tone of the diffused green light of the sea bottom. Juana, glancing secretly at him, saw him smile. And because they were in some way one thing and one purpose, she smiled with him.

And they began this day with hope.

## IV

It is wonderful the way a little town keeps track of itself and of all its units. If every single man and woman, child and baby, acts and conducts itself in a known pattern and breaks no walls and differs with no one and experiments in no way and is not sick and does not endanger the ease and peace of mind or steady unbroken flow of the town, then that unit can disappear and never be heard of. But let one man step out of the regular thought or the known and trusted pattern, and the nerves of the townspeople ring with nervousness and communication travels over the nerve lines of the town. Then every unit communicates to the whole.

Thus, in La Paz,[5] it was known in the early morning through the whole town that Kino was going to sell his pearl that day. It was known among the neighbors in the brush huts, among the pearl fishermen; it was known among the Chinese grocery-store owners; it was known in the church, for the altar boys whispered about it. Word of it crept in among the nuns; the beggars in front of the church spoke of it, for they would be there to take the tithe[6] of the first fruits of the luck. The little boys knew about it with excitement, but most of all the pearl buyers knew about it, and when the day had come, in the offices of the pearl buyers, each man sat alone with his little black velvet tray, and each man rolled the pearls about with his fingertips and considered his part in the picture.

It was supposed that the pearl buyers were

---
5. **La Paz:** city in southern Baja California.
6. **tithe** [tīth]: one tenth of one's income; in this case a small amount given to charity.

individuals acting alone, bidding against one another for the pearls the fishermen brought in. And once it had been so. But this was a wasteful method, for often, in the excitement of bidding for a fine pearl, too great a price had been paid to the fishermen. This was extravagant and not to be countenanced. Now there was only one pearl buyer with many hands, and the men who sat in their offices and waited for Kino knew what price they would offer, how high they would bid, and what method each one would use. And although these men would not profit beyond their salaries, there was excitement among the pearl buyers, for there was excitement in the hunt, and if it be a man's function to break down a price, then he must take joy and satisfaction in breaking it as far down as possible. For every man in the world functions to the best of his ability, and no one does less than his best, no matter what he may think about it. Quite apart from any reward they might get, from any word of praise, from any promotion, a pearl buyer was a pearl buyer, and the best and happiest pearl buyer was he who bought for the lowest prices.

The sun was hot yellow that morning, and it drew the moisture from the estuary and from the Gulf and hung it in shimmering scarves in the air so that the air vibrated and vision was insubstantial. A vision hung in the air to the north of the city—the vision of a mountain that was over two hundred miles away, and the high slopes of this mountain were swaddled with pines and a great stone peak arose above the timber line.

And the morning of this day the canoes lay lined up on the beach; the fishermen did not go out to dive for pearls, for there would be too much happening, too many things to see when Kino went to sell the great pearl.

In the brush houses by the shore Kino's neighbors sat long over their breakfasts, and they spoke of what they would do if they had found the pearl. And one man said that he would give it as a present to the Holy Father in Rome.

*The Pearl* **635**

### AT A GLANCE
- All La Paz knows that Kino is coming to sell his pearl.
- Buyers, having agreed on the price they will offer, wait for Kino.

### 1 POINT OF VIEW
The observer explains how the temperament of a small town is affected when someone breaks the unwritten rules of conformity.

### 2 STYLE: REPETITION
The repeated passive form *it was known* creates an impression that such news permeates the town almost without the help of messengers.

### 3 THEME
The economic structure of the community perpetuates injustice to the poor.

### 4 RESPONSE JOURNAL
Have students respond to the idea that all people strive for excellence. They should cite examples from personal observations.

### 5 STYLE: IMAGERY
The "shimmering scarves" and vibrating air that obscure perception mirror the trickery planned for Kino.

## GUIDED READING

### LITERAL QUESTIONS

**1a.** What provides excitement and satisfaction for the pearl buyers, whose only profit is their salaries? (the "hunt" and bringing the price down as far as possible)

**2a.** Where are the fishermen's canoes on the day Kino plans to sell his pearl? (They lie lined up on the beach.)

### INFERENTIAL QUESTIONS

**1b.** What might the pearl buyers' attitude imply about their business? (For them it's a game in which their bargaining skills are more important than the pearls.)

**2b.** What can you infer from the idle canoes? (The selling of the Pearl of the World constitutes a holiday for the fishermen.)

- Juana, Kino, and Coyotito are dressed in their best clothes.
- The family, with neighbors following, takes the pearl to town.

## 1 IRONY

The neighbors' ideas for spending riches express piety and compassion, in marked contrast to the pictures that formed instantly in the minds of the priest and doctor.

## 2 FOLK TALE

The involvement and behavior of the community, a collective personality, provide a context in which Kino and Juana's aspirations have universal significance.

## 3 STYLE: REPETITION

The way Kino wears and handles his hat, a recurring motif, shows how he assesses his position.

## 4 THEME

Despite their poverty Kino and Juana march to town in confidence and dignity.

---

Another said that he would buy Masses for the souls of his family for a thousand years. Another **1** thought he might take the money and distribute it among the poor of La Paz; and a fourth thought of all the good things one could do with the money from the pearl, of all the charities, benefits, of all the rescues one could perform if one had money. All of the neighbors hoped that sudden wealth would not turn Kino's head, would not make a rich man of him, would not graft onto him the evil limbs of greed and hatred and coldness. For Kino was a well-liked man; it would be a shame if the pearl destroyed him. "That good wife Juana," they said, "and the beautiful baby Coyotito, and the others to come. What a pity it would be if the pearl should destroy them all."

For Kino and Juana this was the morning of mornings of their lives, comparable only to the day when the baby was born. This was to be the day from which all other days would take their arrangement. Thus they would say, "It was two years before we sold the pearl," or, "It was six weeks after we sold the pearl." Juana, considering the matter, threw caution to the winds, and she dressed Coyotito in the clothes she had prepared for his baptism, when there would be money for his baptism. And Juana combed and braided her hair and tied the ends with two little bows of red ribbon, and she put on her marriage skirt and waist.[7] The sun was quarter high when they were ready. Kino's ragged white clothes were clean at least, and this was the last day of his raggedness. For tomorrow, or even this afternoon, he would have new clothes.

**2** The neighbors, watching Kino's door through the crevices in their brush houses, were dressed and ready too. There was no self-consciousness about their joining Kino and Juana to go pearl selling. It was expected, it was an historic moment, they would be crazy if they

---

7. **waist:** shirtwaist; blouse.

**636** *The Novel*

---

didn't go. It would be almost a sign of unfriendship.

Juana put on her head shawl carefully, and she draped one end under her right elbow and gathered it with her right hand so that a hammock hung under her arm, and in this little hammock she placed Coyotito, propped up against the head shawl so that he could see everything and perhaps remember. Kino put on his large **3** straw hat and felt it with his hand to see that it was properly placed, not on the back or side of his head, like a rash, unmarried, irresponsible man, and not flat as an elder would wear it, but tilted a little forward to show aggressiveness and seriousness and vigor. There is a great deal to be seen in the tilt of a hat on a man. Kino slipped his feet into his sandals and pulled the thongs up over his heels. The great pearl was wrapped in an old soft piece of deerskin and placed in a little leather bag, and the leather bag was in a pocket in Kino's shirt. He folded his blanket carefully and draped it in a narrow strip over his left shoulder, and now they were ready.

**4** Kino stepped with dignity out of the house, and Juana followed him, carrying Coyotito. And as they marched up the freshet-washed alley toward the town, the neighbors joined them. The houses belched people; the doorways spewed out children. But because of the seriousness of the occasion, only one man walked with Kino, and that was his brother, Juan Tomás.

Juan Tomás cautioned his brother. "You must be careful to see they do not cheat you," he said.

And, "Very careful," Kino agreed.

"We do not know what prices are paid in other places," said Juan Tomás. "How can we know what is a fair price, if we do not know what the pearl buyer gets for the pearl in another place?"

"That is true," said Kino, "but how can we know? We are here, we are not there."

As they walked up toward the city, the

---

## GUIDED READING

### LITERAL QUESTION

**1a.** What does Kino reply to Juan Tomás' caution to see that they don't cheat him? (Kino agrees that he must be very careful.)

### INFERENTIAL QUESTION

**1b.** What does his reply reveal about his understanding of pearl buyers? (He knows they are shrewd and apt to cheat, but he does not realize that being careful will not help him get a fair price.)

crowd grew behind them, and Juan Tomás, in pure nervousness, went on speaking.

"Before you were born, Kino," he said, "the old ones thought of a way to get more money for their pearls. They thought it would be better if they had an agent who took all the pearls to the capital and sold them there and kept only his share of the profit."

Kino nodded his head. "I know," he said. "It was a good thought."

"And so they got such a man," said Juan Tomás, "and they pooled the pearls, and they started him off. And he was never heard of again and the pearls were lost. Then they got another man, and they started him off, and he was never heard of again. And so they gave the whole thing up and went back to the old way."

"I know," said Kino. "I have heard our father tell of it. It was a good idea, but it was against religion, and the Father made that very clear. The loss of the pearl was a punishment visited on those who tried to leave their station. And the Father made it clear that each man and woman is like a soldier sent by God to guard some part of the castle of the Universe. And some are in the ramparts and some far deep in the darkness of the walls. But each one must remain faithful to his post and must not go running about, else the castle is in danger from the assaults of Hell."

"I have heard him make that sermon," said Juan Tomás. "He makes it every year."

The brothers, as they walked along, squinted their eyes a little, as they and their grandfathers and their great-grandfathers had done for four hundred years, since first the strangers came with arguments and authority and gunpowder to back up both. And in the four hundred years Kino's people had learned only one defense—a slight slitting of the eyes and a slight tightening of the lips and a retirement. Nothing could break down this wall, and they could remain whole within the wall.

The gathering procession was solemn, for they sensed the importance of this day, and any children who showed a tendency to scuffle, to scream, to cry out, to steal hats and rumple hair, were hissed to silence by their elders. So important was this day that an old man came to see, riding on the stalwart shoulders of his nephew. The procession left the brush huts and entered the stone and plaster city where the streets were a little wider and there were narrow pavements beside the buildings. And as before, the beggars joined them as they passed the church; the grocers looked out at them as they went by; the little saloons lost their customers and the owners closed up shop and went along. And the sun beat down on the streets of the city and even tiny stones threw shadows on the ground.

The news of the approach of the procession ran ahead of it, and in their little dark offices the pearl buyers stiffened and grew alert. They got out papers so that they could be at work when Kino appeared, and they put their pearls in the desks, for it is not good to let an inferior pearl be seen beside a beauty. And word of the loveliness of Kino's pearl had come to them. The pearl buyers' offices were clustered together in one narrow street, and they were barred at the windows, and wooden slats cut out the light so that only a soft gloom entered the offices.

A stout slow man sat in an office waiting. His face was fatherly and benign, and his eyes twinkled with friendship. He was a caller of good mornings, a ceremonious shaker of hands, a jolly man who knew all jokes and yet who hovered close to sadness, for in the midst of a laugh he could remember the death of your aunt, and his eyes could become wet with sorrow for your loss. This morning he had placed a flower in a vase on his desk, a single scarlet hibiscus, and the vase sat beside the black velvet-lined pearl tray in front of him. He was shaved close to the blue roots of his beard, and his hands were clean and his nails polished. His door stood open

*The Pearl* **637**

## AT A GLANCE

- Kino and Juan Tomás discuss pearls and the Father's sermon.
- One buyer, shaved and polished, sits waiting in his office.

### 1 PLOT: FORESHADOWING

In telling the history of the pearl trade in La Paz, Juan Tomás also points out the risks in trying to change the system.

### 2 STYLE: METAPHOR

The image of soldiers ordained to guard the castle against Hell cajoles and threatens the poor; town people conspire to keep the money and power in their own hands.

### 3 THEME

Behind slitted eyes and tight lips Kino's people maintain dignity in the face of subjugation.

### 4 MOOD

The solemnity of the day sets a standard of decorum that governs everyone's thoughts and actions.

### 5 STYLE: IMAGERY

The description of the buyers, "stiffened" and "alert" in little dark offices, suggests nocturnal animals poised for prey.

## GUIDED READING

### LITERAL QUESTIONS

**1a.** What point does the Father make clear in his sermon about the lost pearls? (People who try to leave their station are punished.)

**2a.** What could the jolly pearl buyer do in the midst of a joke? (He could "remember the death of your aunt" and make his eyes "wet with sorrow.")

### INFERENTIAL QUESTIONS

**1b.** How might the Father's sermon affect the fishermen's transactions with pearl buyers? (Out of fear of punishment and desire for divine approval, they accept less than their due without protest.)

**2b.** What can you infer about this buyer? (He is practiced in feigning friendship in order to drive down the price of pearls.)

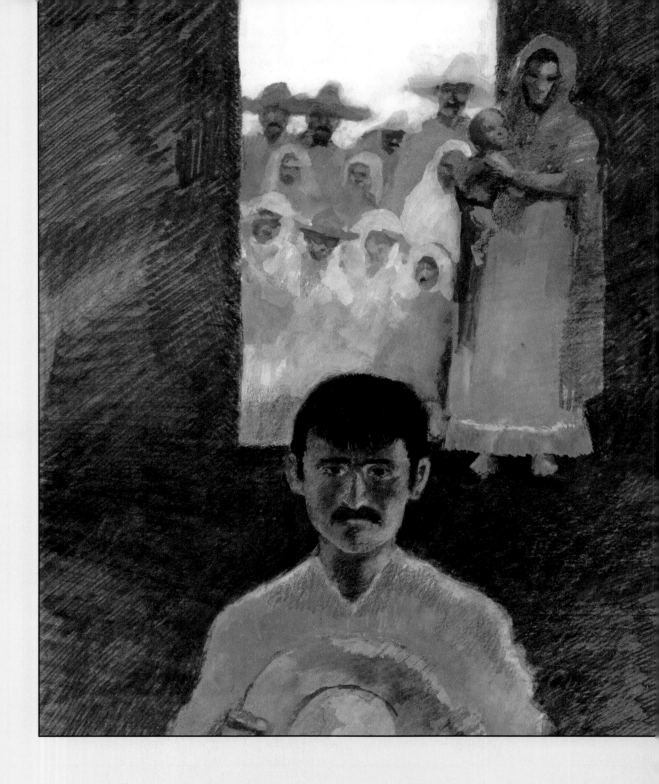

to the morning, and he hummed under his breath while his right hand practiced legerdemain.[8] He rolled a coin back and forth over his knuckles and made it appear and disappear, made it spin and sparkle. The coin winked into sight and as quickly slipped out of sight, and the man did not even watch his own performance. The fingers did it all mechanically, precisely, while the man hummed to himself and peered out the door. Then he heard the tramp of feet of the approaching crowd, and the fingers of his right hand worked faster and faster until, as the figure of Kino filled the doorway, the coin flashed and disappeared.

"Good morning, my friend," the stout man said. "What can I do for you?"

Kino stared into the dimness of the little office, for his eyes were squeezed from the outside glare. But the buyer's eyes had become as steady and cruel and unwinking as a hawk's eyes, while the rest of his face smiled in greeting. And secretly, behind his desk, his right hand practiced with the coin.

"I have a pearl," said Kino. And Juan Tomás stood beside him and snorted a little at the understatement. The neighbors peered around the doorway, and a line of little boys clambered on the window bars and looked through. Several little boys, on their hands and knees, watched the scene around Kino's legs.

"You have a pearl," the dealer said. "Sometimes a man brings in a dozen. Well, let us see your pearl. We will value it and give you the best price." And his fingers worked furiously with the coin.

Now Kino instinctively knew his own dramatic effects. Slowly he brought out the leather bag, slowly took from it the soft and dirty piece of deerskin, and then he let the great pearl roll into the black velvet tray, and instantly his eyes went to the buyer's face. But there was no sign, no movement, the face did not change, but the secret hand behind the desk missed in its precision. The coin stumbled over the knuckle and slipped silently into the dealer's lap. And the fingers behind the desk curled into a fist. When the right hand came out of hiding, the forefinger touched the great pearl, rolled it on the black velvet; thumb and forefinger picked it up and brought it near to the dealer's eyes and twirled it in the air.

Kino held his breath, and the neighbors held their breath, and the whispering went back through the crowd. "He is inspecting it—No price has been mentioned yet—They have not come to a price."

Now the dealer's hand had become a personality. The hand tossed the great pearl back to the tray, the forefinger poked and insulted it, and on the dealer's face there came a sad and contemptuous smile.

"I am sorry, my friend," he said, and his shoulders rose a little to indicate that the misfortune was no fault of his.

"It is a pearl of great value," Kino said.

The dealer's fingers spurned the pearl so that it bounced and rebounded softly from the sides of the velvet tray.

"You have heard of fool's gold," the dealer said. "This pearl is like fool's gold. It is too large. Who would buy it? There is no market for such things. It is a curiosity only. I am sorry. You thought it was a thing of value, and it is only a curiosity."

Now Kino's face was perplexed and worried. "It is the Pearl of the World," he cried. "No one has ever seen such a pearl."

"On the contrary," said the dealer, "it is large and clumsy. As a curiosity it has interest; some museum might perhaps take it to place in a collection of seashells. I can give you, say, a thousand pesos."[9]

---

8. **legerdemain** [lej′ər də mān′]: artful trickery, deceptions with the hand.

9. **a thousand pesos:** eighty dollars at the time of the story.

*The Pearl* 639

AT A GLANCE

- Kino presents the pearl to the buyer.
- The buyer belittles the pearl and offers a low price.

**1 VOCABULARY: WORD CHOICE**

The hand that is practiced in "legerdemain," or skillful deception, ironically reveals the buyer's one truth: He wants Kino's pearl.

**2 STYLE: SIMILE**

The buyer's eyes, cruel as a hawk's, convey the predatory, dehumanizing nature of his business.

**3 IRONY**

The buyer mouths a promise to offer Kino the "best price," but the fury of his hands betrays for whom the price is best.

**4 STYLE: IMAGERY**

The coin, stumbling and slipping through the man's fingers, indicates that the dexterous buyer is not in complete control.

**5 CHARACTERIZATION**

The buyer, a minor character who can simultaneously posture contempt and sympathy, represents the organized deception Kino faces.

## GUIDED READING

### LITERAL QUESTIONS

**1a.** What change occurs in the buyer's right hand as the crowd approaches? (The hand works faster and faster.)

**2a.** What makes Juan Tomás snort when Kino tells the buyer he has a pearl? (the understatement of Kino's announcement)

### INFERENTIAL QUESTIONS

**1b.** What might the buyer's hand indicate? (His excitement is growing at the prospect of possessing Kino's pearl.)

**2b.** Why might Kino have understated his introduction to the Pearl of the World? (Looking forward to the grand impression the pearl will make on the buyer, Kino plays down his presentation.)

**1 POINT OF VIEW**

The observer shows the circumstances surrounding Kino's lonely stand; his people, distrusting their own eyes and wanting to be right, believe the buyers' lies.

**2 TONE**

Steinbeck conveys a sympathetic regard for Kino, who perceives the evil and his own powerlessness against it.

**3 ATMOSPHERE**

Tension builds with the hushed and keen interest of the crowd, making way for the other "appraisers."

**4 STYLE: DIALOGUE**

The dealer signals to the arriving buyers where the game stands and how to play their parts.

Kino's face grew dark and dangerous. "It is worth fifty thousand," he said. "You know it. You want to cheat me."

And the dealer heard a little grumble go through the crowd as they heard his price. And the dealer felt a little tremor of fear.

"Do not blame me," he said quickly. "I am only an appraiser. Ask the others. Go to their offices and show your pearl—or better let them come here, so that you can see there is no collusion.[10] Boy," he called. And when his servant looked through the rear door, "Boy, go to such a one, and such another one and such a third one. Ask them to step in here and do not tell them why. Just say that I will be pleased to see them." And his right hand went behind the desk and pulled another coin from his pocket, and the coin rolled back and forth over his knuckles.

**1** Kino's neighbors whispered together. They had been afraid of something like this. The pearl was large, but it had a strange color. They had been suspicious of it from the first. And after all, a thousand pesos was not to be thrown away. It was comparative wealth to a man who was not wealthy. And suppose Kino took a thousand pesos. Only yesterday he had nothing.

**2** But Kino had grown tight and hard. He felt the creeping of fate, the circling of wolves, the hover of vultures. He felt the evil coagulating about him, and he was helpless to protect himself. He heard in his ears the evil music. And on the black velvet the great pearl glistened, so that the dealer could not keep his eyes from it.

The crowd in the doorway wavered and broke and let the three pearl dealers through. **3** The crowd was silent now, fearing to miss a word, to fail to see a gesture or an expression. Kino was silent and watchful. He felt a little tugging at his back, and he turned and looked in Juana's eyes, and when he looked away he had renewed strength.

---

10. **collusion:** secret agreement among people for a dishonest purpose.

The dealers did not glance at one another nor at the pearl. The man behind the desk said, "I have put a value on this pearl. The owner here does not think it fair. I will ask you to examine **4** this—this thing and make an offer. Notice," he said to Kino, "I have not mentioned what I have offered."

The first dealer, dry and stringy, seemed now to see the pearl for the first time. He took it up, rolled it quickly between thumb and forefinger, and then cast it contemptuously back into the tray.

"Do not include me in the discussion," he said dryly. "I will make no offer at all. I do not want it. This is not a pearl—it is a monstrosity." His thin lips curled.

Now the second dealer, a little man with a shy soft voice, took up the pearl, and he examined it carefully. He took a glass from his pocket and inspected it under magnification. Then he laughed softly.

"Better pearls are made of paste," he said. "I know these things. This is soft and chalky, it will lose its color and die in a few months. Look—." He offered the glass to Kino, showed him how to use it, and Kino, who had never seen a pearl's surface magnified, was shocked at the strange-looking surface.

The third dealer took the pearl from Kino's hands. "One of my clients likes such things," he said. "I will offer five hundred pesos, and perhaps I can sell it to my client for six hundred."

Kino reached quickly and snatched the pearl from his hand. He wrapped it in the deerskin and thrust it inside his shirt.

The man behind the desk said, "I'm a fool, I know, but my first offer stands. I still offer one thousand. What are you doing?" he asked, as Kino thrust the pearl out of sight.

"I am cheated," Kino cried fiercely. "My pearl is not for sale here. I will go, perhaps even to the capital."

Now the dealers glanced quickly at one

---

## GUIDED READING

**LITERAL QUESTION**

**1a.** What emotion does the dealer feel when he hears the crowd grumble? (fear)

**INFERENTIAL QUESTION**

**1b.** What might his fear indicate? (Sensing Kino's rage and realizing that he is outnumbered, he fears that he may lose control over the situation.)

another. They knew they had played too hard; they knew they would be disciplined for their failure, and the man at the desk said quickly, "I might go to fifteen hundred."

**1** But Kino was pushing his way through the crowd. The hum of talk came to him dimly, his rage blood pounded in his ears, and he burst through and strode away. Juana followed, trotting after him.

When the evening came, the neighbors in the brush houses sat eating their corncakes and beans, and they discussed the great theme of the morning. They did not know, it seemed a fine pearl to them, but they had never seen such a pearl before, and surely the dealers knew more about the value of pearls than they. "And mark this," they said. "Those dealers did not discuss these things. Each of the three knew the pearl was valueless."

"But suppose they had arranged it before?"

"If that is so, then all of us have been cheated all of our lives."

Perhaps, some argued, perhaps it would have been better if Kino took the one thousand five hundred pesos. That is a great deal of money, more than he has ever seen. Maybe Kino is being a pigheaded fool. Suppose he should really go to the capital and find no buyer for his pearl. He would never live that down.

And now, said other fearful ones, now that he had defied them, those buyers will not want **2** to deal with him at all. Maybe Kino has cut off his own head and destroyed himself.

And others said, Kino is a brave man, and a fierce man; he is right. From his courage we may all profit. These were proud of Kino.

In his house Kino squatted on his sleeping mat, brooding. He had buried his pearl under a stone of the fire hole in his house, and he stared at the woven tules[11] of his sleeping mat until the crossed design danced in his head. He had lost one world and had not gained another. And Kino

---

11. **tules** [tōō'les]: bulrushes or reeds.

was afraid. Never in his life had he been far from home. He was afraid of strangers and of strange places. He was terrified of that monster of strangeness they called the capital. It lay over the water and through the mountains, over a thousand miles, and every strange terrible mile **3** was frightening. But Kino had lost his old world and he must clamber on to a new one. For his dream of the future was real and never to be destroyed, and he had said "I will go," and that made a real thing too. To determine to go and to say it was to be halfway there.

Juana watched him while he buried his pearl, and she watched him while she cleaned Coyotito and nursed him, and Juana made the corncakes for supper.

Juan Tomás came in and squatted down beside Kino and remained silent for a long time, until at last Kino demanded, "What else could I do? They are cheats."

Juan Tomás nodded gravely. He was the elder, and Kino looked to him for wisdom. "It is **4** hard to know," he said. "We do know that we are cheated from birth to the overcharge on our coffins. But we survive. You have defied not the pearl buyers, but the whole structure, the whole way of life, and I am afraid for you."

"What have I to fear but starvation?" Kino asked.

But Juan Tomás shook his head slowly. "That we must all fear. But suppose you are correct—suppose your pearl is of great value—do you think then the game is over?"

"What do you mean?"

"I don't know," said Juan Tomás, "but I am afraid for you. It is new ground you are walking on, you do not know the way."

"I will go. I will go soon," said Kino.

"Yes," Juan Tomás agreed. "That you must do. But I wonder if you will find it any different in the capital. Here, you have friends and me, your brother. There, you will have no one."

**5** "What can I do?" Kino cried. "Some deep outrage is here. My son must have a chance. That

*The Pearl* **641**

- The first buyer raises his offer, but Kino leaves.
- Juan Tomás warns Kino of the danger in defying the system.

**1 PLOT: RISING ACTION**

Enraged, Kino refuses the second offer and leaves, hardly aware of the murmured reactions around him.

**2 MOOD**

The neighbors reflect the uncertainty of Kino's predicament, wondering if he is a hero or a fool.

**3 VOCABULARY: WORD CHOICE**

The word *clamber* suggests Kino's desperation: He feels he cannot fulfill his dream in the world he knows, and so he is driven to an unfamiliar one.

**4 THEME**

Juan Tomás acknowledges the exploitative conditions ruling their lives but warns that Kino's survival depends on acceptance.

**5 RESPONSE JOURNAL**

Have students respond to Kino's question either from another character's point of view or from their own.

---

## GUIDED READING

### LITERAL QUESTION

**1a.** What do the people say would be true if the pearl buyers had conspired against Kino? (that they had been cheated by the pearl buyers all their lives)

### INFERENTIAL QUESTION

**1b.** Why might the cheating be difficult for the people to recognize? (If they see it, they must face Kino's choice: to fight it at great risk or to live without self-respect.)

## AT A GLANCE

- Worried, Juana watches Kino and sings the song of family.
- Kino, sensing something outside, steps to the doorway.

### 1 STYLE: IMAGERY

The sounds and smells Kino receives convey his intimate knowledge of nature and his ability to determine if anything is out of place.

### 2 CHARACTERIZATION

Juana, in her unwavering concern for the preservation of her family, is the foil for Kino, who is driven by hatred for his enemies and ambition for a better life.

### 3 PLOT: FORESHADOWING

With his hand on his knife, Kino instinctively prepares for some danger that waits outside.

is what they are striking at. My friends will protect me."

"Only so long as they are not in danger or discomfort from it," said Juan Tomás. He arose, saying, "Go with God."

And Kino said, "Go with God," and did not even look up, for the words had a strange chill in them.

Long after Juan Tomás had gone Kino sat brooding on his sleeping mat. A lethargy had settled on him, and a little gray hopelessness. Every road seemed blocked against him. In his head he heard only the dark music of the enemy. His senses were burningly alive, but his mind went back to the deep participation with all things, 1 the gift he had from his people. He heard every little sound of the gathering night, the sleepy complaint of settling birds, the love agony of cats, the strike and withdrawal of little waves on the beach, and the simple hiss of distance. And he could smell the sharp odor of exposed kelp from the receding tide. The little flare of the twig fire made the design on his sleeping mat jump before his entranced eyes.

Juana watched him with worry, but she knew him and she knew she could help him best 2 by being silent and by being near. And as though she too could hear the Song of Evil, she fought it, singing softly the melody of the family, of the safety and warmth and wholeness of the family. She held Coyotito in her arms and sang the song to him, to keep the evil out, and her voice was brave against the threat of the dark music.

Kino did not move nor ask for his supper. She knew he would ask when he wanted it. His eyes were entranced, and he could sense the wary, watchful evil outside the brush house; he could feel the dark creeping things waiting for him to go out into the night. It was shadowy and dreadful, and yet it called to him and threatened 3 him and challenged him. His right hand went into his shirt and felt his knife; his eyes were wide; he stood up and walked to the doorway.

Juana willed to stop him; she raised her hand

642   *The Novel*

## GUIDED READING

### LITERAL QUESTIONS

**1a.** What is Juan Tomás' response to Kino's statement that his friends will protect him? ("Only so long as they are not in danger or discomfort from it.")

**2a.** What does Kino feel from the shadowy evil outside that calls him? (a threat and a challenge)

### INFERENTIAL QUESTIONS

**1b.** What do you think Juan Tomás is saying about the neighbors? (They will not risk losing what little they have to help Kino or to fight the system; Kino is alone in this struggle.)

**2b.** What might you infer about the effect of danger on Kino? (While he fears it, he feels compelled to meet and defeat it.)

to stop him, and her mouth opened with terror. For a long moment Kino looked out into the darkness and then he stepped outside. Juana heard the little rush, the grunting struggle, the blow. She froze with terror for a moment, and then her lips drew back from her teeth like a cat's lips. She set Coyotito down on the ground. She seized a stone from the fireplace and rushed outside, but it was over by then. Kino lay on the ground, struggling to rise, and there was no one **1** near him. **Only the shadows and the strike and rush of waves and the hiss of distance. But the evil was all about, hidden behind the brush fence, crouched beside the house in the shadow, hovering in the air.**

Juana dropped her stone, and she put her arms around Kino and helped him to his feet and supported him into the house. Blood oozed down from his scalp and there was a long deep cut in his cheek from ear to chin, a deep, bleeding slash. And Kino was only half conscious. He shook his head from side to side. His shirt was torn open and his clothes half pulled off. Juana sat him down on his sleeping mat and she wiped the thickening blood from his face with her skirt. She brought him pulque to drink in a little pitcher, and still he shook his head to clear out the darkness.

"Who?" Juana asked.

"I don't know," Kino said. "I didn't see."

Now Juana brought her clay pot of water and she washed the cut on his face while he stared dazed ahead of him.

"Kino, my husband," she cried, and his eyes stared past her. "Kino, can you hear me?"

"I hear you," he said dully.

"Kino, this pearl is evil. Let us destroy it before it destroys us. Let us crush it between two stones. Let us—let us throw it back in the sea where it belongs. Kino, it is evil, it is evil!"

And as she spoke the light came back in Kino's eyes so that they glowed fiercely and his muscles hardened and his will hardened.

"No," he said. "I will fight this thing. I will win over it. We will have our chance." His fist **2** pounded the sleeping mat. **"No one shall take our good fortune from us,"** he said. His eyes softened then and he raised a gentle hand to Juana's shoulder. "Believe me," he said. "I am a man." And his face grew crafty.

"In the morning we will take our canoe and we will go over the sea and over the mountains **3** to the capital, you and I. **We will not be cheated. I am a man."**

"Kino," she said huskily, "I am afraid. A man can be killed. Let us throw the pearl back into the sea."

"Hush," he said fiercely. "I am a man. Hush." And she was silent, for his voice was command. "Let us sleep a little," he said. "In the first light we will start. You are not afraid to go with me?"

"No, my husband."

His eyes were soft and warm on her then, his hand touched her cheek. "Let us sleep a little," he said.

*The Pearl* **643**

## AT A GLANCE

- Juana hears a struggle, then finds Kino lying on the ground.
- She argues that they should throw the pearl into the sea.
- Kino says he is a man and he will win; they will go to the capital.

## 1 ATMOSPHERE

Ominous shadows and an evil presence envelop the night, shaping thoughts, actions, and emotions.

## 2 DIALOGUE

Kino's determination to protect their "good fortune" shows ironic bravery, given their experience since finding the pearl.

## 3 PLOT: CONFLICT

Kino still sees the pearl as their only chance at a better life, while Juana sees it as their destruction.

## REFLECTING ON CHAPTERS 3–4

What motivates Kino to fight on? (Possible answers: He wants opportunities for Coyotito, his family, and his people; he must distinguish himself as a man or lose his dignity; he strikes back at a "deep outrage" to all his people.)

## GUIDED READING

### LITERAL QUESTIONS

**1a.** What does Juana do when she hears the struggle outside? (She sets Coyotito down, grabs a stone, and rushes outside.)

**2a.** What expression comes over Kino's face as he says he is a man? (His face grows crafty.)

### INFERENTIAL QUESTIONS

**1b.** What can you infer about Juana from her action? (She is ready to defend Kino, whatever the danger might be to herself.)

**2b.** What might his expression indicate? (He will be as cunning and evil as his enemies to defeat them.)

## STUDY QUESTIONS

1. *Townspeople:* spread news, become interested; *priest:* thinks of repairs; *doctor:* claims Kino as patient, thinks of Paris; *buyers:* think of business advantage; all think pearl could satisfy their desires.
2. being married in church; new clothes; harpoon; rifle; education for son; disappears; music of the pearl
3. He examines him; gives white powder. Juana is anxious, trusting; Kino is suspicious but does not want to risk son's life.
4. Pearl is evil, will destroy them unless they throw it away. It is their only chance to improve lives; evil will be gone when they sell pearl.
5. not offered fair price; take it to city to sell it
6. need to sell pearls; have been cheated in the past attempting to be own agents
7. Kino is determined that pearl will better their lives; Juana believes it to be evil; wants to get rid of it. They had been in harmony, contented.
8. has lost peace of mind; believes selling pearl will improve situation
9. Some may feel story contradicts statement; others may cite gains made by striving.

## LITERARY FOCUS

1. *repetitions: he would not come; It was known; I am a man;* timelessness: descriptions of the beach and canoes; idea that time would date from Kino's pearl
2. doctor, priest, pearl buyers—all negative; round; have conflicting desires and emotions
3. Couple reflects belief in family, fear of the powerful, the hope for luck, close connection to nature.

## STUDY QUESTIONS

### Recalling

1. Describe the reactions of the townspeople, priest, doctor, and pearl buyers to Kino's discovery of the pearl. According to the narrator, why has Kino become every man's enemy?
2. List four of the items Kino envisions the pearl bringing to him and his family. What happens to the music of the family during Kino's vision? What other music does he hear then?
3. When the doctor visits Juana and Kino, what does he do to Coyotito? How do Juana and Kino interpret his actions?
4. What warning does Juana give Kino after the first intruder leaves their house? What answer does Kino give her?
5. Why does Kino refuse to sell his pearl to the buyers? What does he decide to do with it?

### Interpreting

6. Why do the pearl fishers submit to the practices of the pearl buyers?
7. What differences do you perceive developing between Kino and Juana? How are these two characters different from the way they were in the very beginning of the novel?
8. Why does Kino feel that he has lost his old world and "must clamber on to a new one"?

### Extending

9. The narrator says that it is a "talent" and not a "disparagement" of human beings never to be satisfied with their lot. Do you agree or disagree? Why?

## LITERARY FOCUS

### The Folk Tale

John Steinbeck said of *The Pearl* that he wanted to "write it as folklore, to give it that set-aside, raised-up quality that all folk stories have." **Folk tales,** like the one on which *The Pearl* is based, are usually passed down by word of mouth from generation to generation in societies where the most important communications are oral rather than written. Folk tales reconstruct the most important events in a people's history and express the attitudes, values, and hopes around which their lives are built.

The "set-aside, raised-up quality" of such stories comes from their role as communicators of basic truths. So that these truths can shine through unmistakably, folk tales are simple and often repetitious in style and are not complicated with many realistic details or round characters (see page 44). Their characters are either good or bad, and their events seem to take place in a timeless world set apart from everyday reality.

### Thinking About the Folk Tale

1. Find three examples of repetitions in the first four chapters of *The Pearl*. Find three examples in which Steinbeck's description of the setting creates a sense of timelessness.
2. Find three examples of characters in *The Pearl* who are flat. Are these characters primarily good or bad? Are Kino and Juana flat or round characters? Explain.
3. Explain how *The Pearl* expresses the attitudes, values, and hopes of Kino's people.

# V

The late moon arose before the first rooster crowed. Kino opened his eyes in the darkness, for he sensed movement near him, but he did not move. Only his eyes searched the darkness, and in the pale light of the moon that crept through the holes in the brush house Kino saw Juana arise silently from beside him. He saw her move toward the fireplace. So carefully did she work that he heard only the lightest sound when she moved the fireplace stone. And then like a shadow she glided toward the door. She paused for a moment beside the hanging box where Coyotito lay, then for a second she was back in the doorway, and then she was gone.

And rage surged in Kino. He rolled up to his feet and followed her as silently as she had gone, and he could hear her quick footsteps going toward the shore. Quietly he tracked her, and his brain was red with anger. She burst clear of the brush line and stumbled over the little boulders toward the water, and then she heard **1** him coming and she broke into a run. Her arm was up to throw when he leaped at her and caught her arm and wrenched the pearl from her. He struck her in the face with his clenched fist and she fell among the boulders, and he kicked her in the side. In the pale light he could see the little waves break over her, and her skirt floated about and clung to her legs as the water receded.

Kino looked down at her and his teeth were **2** bared. He hissed at her like a snake, and Juana stared at him with wide unfrightened eyes, like a sheep before the butcher. She knew there was murder in him, and it was all right; she had accepted it, and she would not resist or even protest. And then the rage left him and a sick disgust took its place. He turned away from her and walked up the beach and through the brush line. His senses were dulled by his emotion.

He heard the rush, got his knife out and **3** lunged at one dark figure and felt his knife go home, and then he was swept to his knees and swept again to the ground. Greedy fingers went through his clothes, frantic fingers searched him, and the pearl, knocked from his hand, lay winking behind a little stone in the pathway. It glinted in the soft moonlight.

Juana dragged herself up from the rocks on the edge of the water. Her face was a dull pain and her side ached. She steadied herself on her knees for a while and her wet skirt clung to her. There was no anger in her for Kino. He had said, "I am a man," and that meant certain things to Juana. It meant that he was half insane and half god. It meant that Kino would drive his strength against a mountain and plunge his strength against the sea. Juana, in her woman's soul, knew that the mountain would stand while the man broke himself; that the sea would surge **4** while the man drowned in it. And yet it was this thing that made him a man, half insane and half god, and Juana had need of a man; she could not live without a man. Although she might be puzzled by these differences between man and woman, she knew them and accepted them and needed them. Of course she would follow him, **5** there was no question of that. Sometimes the quality of woman, the reason, the caution, the sense of preservation, could cut through Kino's manness and save them all. She climbed painfully to her feet, and she dipped her cupped palms in the little waves and washed her bruised face with the stinging salt water, and then she went creeping up the beach after Kino.

*The Pearl* **645**

AT A GLANCE

- Juana attempts to throw away the pearl, and Kino hits her.
- Kino attacks a dark figure with his knife and drops the pearl.

LITERARY OPTIONS

- total effect
- conflict
- tone

THEMATIC OPTIONS

- the importance of loved ones
- inner happiness vs. external gain
- taking risks

**1 PLOT: CONFLICT**

Juana and Kino's conflict over the pearl erupts into her bold defiance. Juana's uncharacteristic act provokes his violent punishment. The pearl has made Kino turn against his own wife.

**2 CHARACTERIZATION**

Kino hisses like one fending off attack while Juana receives her blows with the certainty that led her to throw away the pearl.

**3 PLOT: CONFLICT**

Kino must protect himself and the pearl from sinister, faceless enemies who will kill for riches.

**4 STYLE: FOLK TALE**

These myths about manhood and womanhood make Kino and Juana into human prototypes.

**5 TONE**

Steinbeck expresses the view that Juana's prudence can save the family.

---

## GUIDED READING

### LITERAL QUESTIONS

**1a.** Where does Juana pause a moment before she leaves their house with the pearl? (beside the hanging box where Coyotito lies)

**2a.** What emotion does Kino feel as his rage against Juana leaves him? (sick disgust)

### INFERENTIAL QUESTIONS

**1b.** What might that hesitation imply? (She pauses near Coyotito to strengthen her will to defy Kino and save her family.)

**2b.** What might be the object of his disgust? (It might be several things together: himself for harming Juana; Juana for provoking him to violence; the exposure of his meanness; the realization that he is out of control.)

- Juana picks up the pearl, then sees that Kino has killed a man.
- Kino discovers that his canoe has been destroyed.

### 1 STYLE: SIMILE

Comparing Kino with a crushed bug suggests how small he is in relation to his enemy—and hints that Kino is already defeated.

### 2 CHARACTERIZATION

Juana's change in outlook ends her conflict with Kino and signals a turning point in their struggle.

### 3 SYMBOL

Having seen the destruction she tried to prevent, Juana hands Kino the pearl as if it were a toy that can no longer inspire fear or hope.

### 4 DIALOGUE

The dialogue shows Juana's acuity and strength in a situation that Kino doesn't yet fully understand.

A flight of herring clouds had moved over the sky from the south. The pale moon dipped in and out of the strands of clouds so that Juana walked in darkness for a moment and in light the next. Her back was bent with pain and her head was low. She went through the line of brush when the moon was covered, and when it looked through she saw the glimmer of the great pearl in the path behind the rock. She sank to her knees and picked it up, and the moon went into the darkness of the clouds again. Juana remained on her knees while she considered whether to go back to the sea and finish her job, and as she considered, the light came again, and she saw two dark figures lying in the path ahead of her. She leaped forward and saw that one was Kino and the other a stranger with dark shiny fluid leaking from his throat.

**1** Kino moved sluggishly, arms and legs stirred like those of a crushed bug, and a thick muttering came from his mouth. Now, in an instant, Juana knew that the old life was gone forever. A dead man in the path and Kino's knife, dark bladed beside him, convinced her. All the time Juana **2** had been trying to rescue something of the old peace, of the time before the pearl. But now it was gone, and there was no retrieving it. And knowing this, she abandoned the past instantly. There was nothing to do but to save themselves.

Her pain was gone now, her slowness. Quickly she dragged the dead man from the pathway into the shelter of the brush. She went to Kino and sponged his face with her wet skirt. His senses were coming back and he moaned.

"They have taken the pearl. I have lost it. **3** Now it is over," he said. "The pearl is gone."

Juana quieted him as she would quiet a sick child. "Hush," she said. "Here is your pearl. I found it in the path. Can you hear me now? Here is your pearl. Can you understand? You have killed a man. We must go away. They will come for us, can you understand? We must be gone before the daylight comes."

**646** *The Novel*

**4** "I was attacked," Kino said uneasily. "I struck to save my life."

"Do you remember yesterday?" Juana asked. "Do you think that will matter? Do you remember the men of the city? Do you think your explanation will help?"

Kino drew a great breath and fought off his weakness. "No," he said. "You are right." And his will hardened and he was a man again.

"Go to our house and bring Coyotito," he said, "and bring all the corn we have. I will drag the canoe into the water and we will go."

He took his knife and left her. He stumbled toward the beach and he came to his canoe. And when the light broke through again he saw that a great hole had been knocked in the bottom. And a searing rage came to him and gave him strength. Now the darkness was closing in on his family; now the evil music filled the night, hung over the mangroves, skirled[1] in the wave beat.

---

1. **skirled:** made a high, shrill sound.

## GUIDED READING

### LITERAL QUESTIONS

**1a.** What does Juana consider doing after she finds the pearl? (going back to the sea and finishing her job)

**2a.** What does Kino derive from his rage at finding his canoe destroyed? (strength)

### INFERENTIAL QUESTIONS

**1b.** Why might Juana consider such an action after being beaten? (She regards protecting her family from the pearl's evil as her mission.)

**2b.** How might this strength change him? (It only intensifies his resolve to fight back despite his fears and regardless of consequences.)

The canoe of his grandfather, plastered over and over, and a splintered hole broken in it. This was an evil beyond thinking. The killing of a man was not so evil as the killing of a boat. For a boat does not have sons, and a boat cannot protect itself, and a wounded boat does not heal. There was sorrow in Kino's rage, but this last thing had tightened him beyond breaking. He was an animal now, for hiding, for attacking, and he lived only to preserve himself and his family. He was not conscious of the pain in his head. He leaped up the beach, through the brush line toward his brush house, and it did not occur to him to take one of the canoes of his neighbors. Never once did the thought enter his head, any more than he could have conceived breaking a boat.

The roosters were crowing and the dawn was not far off. Smoke of the first fires seeped out through the walls of the brush houses, and the first smell of cooking corncakes was in the air. Already the dawn birds were scampering in the bushes. The weak moon was losing its light and the clouds thickened and curdled to the southward. The wind blew freshly into the estuary, a nervous, restless wind with the smell of storm on its breath, and there was change and uneasiness in the air.

Kino, hurrying toward his house, felt a surge of exhilaration. Now he was not confused, for there was only one thing to do, and Kino's hand went first to the great pearl in his shirt and then to his knife hanging under his shirt.

He saw a little glow ahead of him, and then without interval a tall flame leaped up in the dark with a crackling roar, and a tall edifice of fire lighted the pathway. Kino broke into a run; it was his brush house, he knew. And he knew that these houses could burn down in a very few moments. And as he ran a scuttling figure ran toward him—Juana, with Coyotito in her arms and Kino's shoulder blanket clutched in her hand. The baby moaned with fright, and Juana's eyes were wide and terrrified. Kino could see the house was gone, and he did not question Juana. He knew, but she said, "It was torn up and the floor dug—even the baby's box turned out, and as I looked they put the fire to the outside."

The fierce light of the burning house lighted Kino's face strongly. "Who?" he demanded.

"I don't know," she said. "The dark ones."

The neighbors were tumbling from their houses now, and they watched the falling sparks and stamped them out to save their own houses. Suddenly Kino was afraid. The light made him afraid. He remembered the man lying dead in the brush beside the path, and he took Juana by the arm and drew her into the shadow of a house away from the light, for light was danger to him. For a moment he considered and then he worked among the shadows until he came to the house of Juan Tomás, his brother, and he slipped into the doorway and drew Juana after him. Outside, he could hear the squeal of children and the

*The Pearl* **647**

- Thieves search Kino and Juana's house and set it on fire.
- Kino and Juana, with Coyotito, slip into Juan Tomás' house.

## 1 THEME

Kino must become like an animal to protect himself from his enemies, who are themselves dehumanized by greed.

## 2 CONTRAST

As evil closes in on Kino, another day begins—much like mornings he once watched in contentment.

## 3 CHARACTERIZATION

Kino has lost his trusted means for a living as well as his best means of escape; yet, spurred by fury, he is ready to fight against the odds with a pearl and a knife.

## GUIDED READING

### LITERAL QUESTION

**1a.** What do the neighbors do when they see Kino and Juana's house on fire? (They watch the falling sparks and stamp them out to save their own houses.)

### INFERENTIAL QUESTION

**1b.** What might you infer from their actions? (They wisely put out live sparks near their houses, which are built of dry brush, but as Juan Tomás predicted, they do not endanger themselves to help Kino and Juana.)

## 1 PLOT: CONFLICT

Apolonia's demanding tone and helpless gesture show that she was prepared for his death but not his life, which attracts danger.

## 2 SYMBOL

For Juan Tomás the pearl represents the devil and the cause of the darkness that surrounds Kino.

## 3 DIALOGUE

Kino summarizes his desperate situation, which forces Juan Tomás to choose between risking danger or sending his brother into peril.

## 4 THEME

Juan Tomás, valuing family more than personal safety, agrees to protect Kino and Juana until dark.

## 5 STYLE: IMAGERY

A rising wind, beating, tearing, and crying, further stresses the peril surrounding the escape.

---

shouts of the neighbors, for his friends thought he might be inside the burning house.

The house of Juan Tomás was almost exactly like Kino's house; nearly all the brush houses were alike, and all leaked light and air, so that Juana and Kino, sitting in the corner of the brother's house, could see the leaping flames through the wall. They saw the flames tall and furious, they saw the roof fall and watched the fire die down as quickly as a twig fire dies. They heard the cries of warning of their friends, and the shrill, keening[2] cry of Apolonia, wife of Juan Tomás. She, being the nearest woman relative, raised a formal lament for the dead of the family.

Apolonia realized that she was wearing her second-best head shawl and she rushed to her house to get her fine new one. As she rummaged in a box by the wall, Kino's voice said quietly, **1** "Apolonia, do not cry out. We are not hurt."

"How do you come here?" she demanded.

"Do not question," he said. "Go now to Juan Tomás and bring him here and tell no one else. This is important to us, Apolonia."

She paused, her hands helpless in front of her, and then, "Yes, my brother-in-law," she said.

In a few moments Juan Tomás came back with her. He lighted a candle and came to them where they crouched in a corner and he said, "Apolonia, see to the door, and do not let anyone enter." He was older, Juan Tomás, and he assumed the authority. "Now, my brother," he said.

"I was attacked in the dark," said Kino. "And in the fight I have killed a man."

"Who?" asked Juan Tomás quickly.

"I do not know. It is all darkness—all darkness and shape of darkness."

**2** "It is the pearl," said Juan Tomás. "There is a devil in this pearl. You should have sold it and passed on the devil. Perhaps you can still sell it and buy peace for yourself."

---

2. **keening:** wailing because of someone's death.

---

And Kino said, "Oh, my brother, an insult has been put on me that is deeper than my life. **3** For on the beach my canoe is broken, my house is burned, and in the brush a dead man lies. Every escape is cut off. You must hide us, my brother."

And Kino, looking closely, saw deep worry come into his brother's eyes and he forestalled him in a possible refusal. "Not for long," he said quickly. "Only until a day has passed and the new night has come. Then we will go."

**4** "I will hide you," said Juan Tomás.

"I do not want to bring danger to you," Kino said. "I know I am like a leprosy. I will go tonight and then you will be safe."

"I will protect you," said Juan Tomás, and he called, "Apolonia, close up the door. Do not even whisper that Kino is here."

They sat silently all day in the darkness of the house, and they could hear the neighbors speaking of them. Through the walls of the house they could watch their neighbors raking the ashes to find the bones. Crouching in the house of Juan Tomás, they heard the shock go into their neighbors' minds at the news of the broken boat. Juan Tomás went out among the neighbors to divert their suspicions, and he gave them theories and ideas of what had happened to Kino and to Juana and to the baby. To one he said, "I think they have gone south along the coast to escape the evil that was on them." And to another, "Kino would never leave the sea. Perhaps he found another boat." And he said, "Apolonia is ill with grief."

**5** And in that day the wind rose up to beat the Gulf and tore the kelps and weeds that lined the shore, and the wind cried through the brush houses and no boat was safe on the water. Then Juan Tomás told among the neighbors, "Kino is gone. If he went to the sea, he is drowned by now." And after each trip among the neighbors Juan Tomás came back with something borrowed. He brought a little woven straw bag of red beans and a gourd full of rice. He borrowed a

---

## GUIDED READING

### LITERAL QUESTION

**1a.** What do Kino and Juana see and hear as they crouch in Juan Tomás' house? (They see neighbors raking through ashes for their bones and hear the shock caused by news of the broken boat.)

### INFERENTIAL QUESTION

**1b.** What might the neighbors' reaction imply? (They accept the mortality of a person, but a boat, passed on from one generation to the next, connects them to their ancestors and ensures the future of their people.)

cup of dried peppers and a block of salt, and he brought in a long working knife, eighteen inches long and heavy, as a small ax, a tool and a weapon. And when Kino saw this knife his eyes lighted up, and he fondled the blade and his thumb tested the edge.

The wind screamed over the Gulf and turned the water white, and the mangroves plunged like frightened cattle, and a fine sandy dust arose from the land and hung in a stifling cloud over the sea. The wind drove off the clouds and skimmed the sky clean and drifted the sand of the country like snow.

Then Juan Tomás, when the evening approached, talked long with his brother. "Where will you go?"

"To the north," said Kino. "I have heard that there are cities in the north."

"Avoid the shore," said Juan Tomás. "They are making a party to search the shore. The men in the city will look for you. Do you still have the pearl?"

"I have it," said Kino. "And I will keep it. I might have given it as a gift, but now it is my misfortune and my life and I will keep it." His eyes were hard and cruel and bitter.

Coyotito whimpered and Juana muttered little magics over him to make him silent.

"The wind is good," said Juan Tomás. "There will be no tracks."

They left quietly in the dark before the moon had risen. The family stood formally in the house of Juan Tomás. Juana carried Coyotito on her back, covered and held in by her head shawl,

and the baby slept, cheek turned sideways against her shoulder. The head shawl covered the baby, and one end of it came across Juana's nose to protect her from the evil night air. Juan Tomás embraced his brother with the double embrace and kissed him on both cheeks. "Go with God," he said, and it was like a death. "You will not give up the pearl?"

"This pearl has become my soul," said Kino. "If I give it up I shall lose my soul. Go thou also with God."

## VI

The wind blew fierce and strong, and it pelted them with bits of sticks, sand, and little rocks. Juana and Kino gathered their clothing tighter about them and covered their noses and went out into the world. The sky was brushed clean by the wind and the stars were cold in a black sky. The two walked carefully, and they avoided the center of town where some sleeper in a doorway might see them pass. For the town closed itself in against the night, and anyone who moved about in the darkness would be noticeable. Kino threaded his way around the edge of the city and turned north, north by the stars, and found the rutted sandy road that led through the brushy country toward Loreto where the miraculous Virgin has her station.[3]

Kino could feel the blown sand against his

---

3. **station:** religious shrine.

**AT A GLANCE**

- Juan Tomás tells Kino a search party is forming to find them.
- Kino and Juana edge around the town and head toward Loreto.

**1 DIALOGUE**

The conversation advances the plot and heightens the drama; from the outset Kino is hunted and watched for.

**2 SYMBOLISM**

Kino's metaphor, equating the pearl with misfortune, is in ironic contrast to our initial view of the pearl as a miraculous stroke of good luck.

**3 FORESHADOWING**

The farewell embrace and parting words "like a death" portend the gravity of what lies ahead. Kino's statement, "This pearl has become my soul," also shows how profound his entanglement has become.

**4 MOOD**

A fierce and punishing wind and a cold, black sky mirror the harsh loneliness of the family's plight.

## GUIDED READING

**LITERAL QUESTIONS**

**1a.** What two purposes are served by the work knife that Kino fondles and tests? (It's a tool and a weapon.)

**2a.** What does Kino tell Juan Tomás he will lose if he gives up the pearl? (his soul)

**INFERENTIAL QUESTIONS**

**1b.** What might the knife and Kino's reaction to it imply? (Kino's life, once a simple struggle to survive in nature, is now also a war against enemies; he reveres the knife as he once did his fishing boat.)

**2b.** What might you infer from his view? (To keep the pearl he has defied everyone, lost his home and canoe, and killed a man; to give it up would mean his dream, struggle, and life have been futile.)

**1 MOOD**

The animals' noises, threatening and eerie, increase the sense of danger surrounding Kino and Juana.

**2 READING SKILLS: COMPARISON AND CONTRAST**

The triumphant music and underlying melody, in vivid contrast to the harsh night sounds, suggest renewed hope and sustaining family love.

**3 READING SKILLS: DETAILS**

These details show the constant foresight and care required for them to make the journey unharmed.

---

ankles and he was glad, for he knew there would be no tracks. The little light from the stars made out for him the narrow road through the brushy country. And Kino could hear the pad of Juana's feet behind him. He went quickly and quietly, and Juana trotted behind him to keep up.

Some ancient thing stirred in Kino. Through his fear of dark and the devils that haunt the night, there came a rush of exhilaration; some animal thing was moving in him so that he was cautious and wary and dangerous; some ancient thing out of the past of his people was alive in him. The wind was at his back and the stars guided him. The wind cried and whisked in the brush, and the family went on monotonously, hour after hour. They passed no one and saw no one. At last, to their right, the waning moon arose, and when it came up the wind died down, and the land was still.

Now they could see the little road ahead of them, deep cut with sand-drifted wheel tracks. With the wind gone there would be footprints, but they were a good distance from the town and perhaps their tracks might not be noticed. Kino walked carefully in a wheel rut, and Juana followed in his path. One big cart, going to the town in the morning, could wipe out every trace of their passage.

All night they walked and never changed their pace. Once Coyotito awakened, and Juana shifted him in front of her and soothed him until he went to sleep again. And the evils of the night were about them. The coyotes cried and laughed in the brush, and the owls screeched and hissed over their heads. And once some large animal lumbered away, crackling the undergrowth as it went. And Kino gripped the handle of the big working knife and took a sense of protection from it.

The music of the pearl was triumphant in Kino's head, and the quiet melody of the family underlay it, and they wove themselves into the soft padding of sandaled feet in the dusk. All night they walked, and in the first dawn Kino

**650** *The Novel*

searched the roadside for a covert to lie in during the day. He found his place near to the road, a little clearing where deer might have lain, and it was curtained thickly with the dry brittle trees that lined the road. And when Juana had seated herself and had settled to nurse the baby, Kino went back to the road. He broke a branch and carefully swept the footprints where they had turned from the roadway. And then, in the first light, he heard the creak of a wagon, and he crouched beside the road and watched a heavy two-wheeled cart go by, drawn by slouching oxen. And when it had passed out of sight, he went back to the roadway and looked at the rut and found that the footprints were gone. And again he swept out his traces and went back to Juana.

She gave him the soft corncakes Apolonia had packed for them, and after a while she slept a little. But Kino sat on the ground and stared at the earth in front of him. He watched the ants moving, a little column of them near to his foot, and he put his foot in their path. Then the column climbed over his instep and continued on its way, and Kino left his foot there and watched them move over it.

The sun arose hotly. They were not near the Gulf now, and the air was dry and hot so that the brush cricked[4] with heat and a good resinous smell came from it. And when Juana awakened, when the sun was high, Kino told her things she knew already.

"Beware of that kind of tree there," he said, pointing. "Do not touch it, for if you do and then touch your eyes, it will blind you. And beware of the tree that bleeds. See, that one over there. For if you break it the red blood will flow from it, and it is evil luck." And she nodded and smiled at him, for she knew these things.

"Will they follow us?" she asked. "Do you think they will try to find us?"

"They will try," said Kino. "Whoever finds us will take the pearl. Oh, they will try."

---

4. **cricked:** twisted.

---

## *GUIDED READING*

**LITERAL QUESTIONS**

**1a.** What does Kino feel despite his fear of the devils and dark of the night? (exhilaration)

**2a.** What does Kino see the ants doing when he puts his foot in their path? (They climb over his foot and continue on their way.)

**INFERENTIAL QUESTIONS**

**1b.** What might his surge of joy imply? (Kino feels challenged by danger and takes his fate into his own hands, regaining a sense of personal power.)

**2b.** What do you think the ants' progress suggests? (Kino's foot, a mountain to the ants, does not stop them; a mountain as well as unknown dangers stands between Kino and the capital, which he intends to reach.)

ing, and the music of the pearl had become sinister in his ears and it was interwoven with the music of evil.

The hot sun beat on the earth so that Kino and Juana moved into the lacy shade of the brush, and small gray birds scampered on the **2** ground in the shade. In the heat of the day Kino relaxed and covered his eyes with his hat and wrapped his blanket about his face to keep the flies off, and he slept.

But Juana did not sleep. She sat quiet as a stone and her face was quiet. Her mouth was still swollen where Kino had struck her, and big flies buzzed around the cut on her chin. But she sat as still as a sentinel, and when Coyotito awakened she placed him on the ground in front of her and watched him wave his arms and kick his feet, **3** and he smiled and gurgled at her until she smiled too. She picked up a little twig from the ground and tickled him, and she gave him water from the gourd she carried in her bundle.

Kino stirred in a dream, and he cried out in a guttural voice, and his hand moved in symbolic fighting. And then he moaned and sat up suddenly, his eyes wide and his nostrils flaring. He listened and heard only the cricking heat and the hiss of distance.

"What is it?" Juana asked.

"Hush," he said.

"You were dreaming."

"Perhaps." But he was restless, and when she gave him a corncake from her store he paused in his chewing to listen. He was uneasy and nervous; he glanced over his shoulder; he lifted the big knife and felt its edge. When Coyotito gurgled on the ground Kino said, "Keep him quiet."

"What is the matter?" Juana asked.

"I don't know."

**4** He listened again, an animal light in his eyes. He stood up then, silently; and crouched low, he threaded his way through the brush toward the road. But he did not step into the road; he crept into the cover of a thorny tree and peered out along the way he had come.

And Juana said, "Perhaps the dealers were right and the pearl has no value. Perhaps this has all been an illusion."

Kino reached into his clothes and brought out the pearl. He let the sun play on it until it burned in his eyes. "No," he said, "they would not have tried to steal it if it had been valueless."

"Do you know who attacked you? Was it the dealers?"

"I do not know," he said. "I didn't see them."

He looked into his pearl to find his vision. "When we sell it at last, I will have a rifle," he said, and he looked into the shining surface for his rifle, but he saw only a huddled dark body on the ground with shining blood dripping from its throat. And he said quickly, "We will be married in a great church." And in the pearl he saw Juana with her beaten face crawling home through the night. "Our son must learn to read," he said frantically. And there in the pearl Coyotito's face, thick and feverish from the medicine.

And Kino thrust the pearl back into his cloth-

*The Pearl* **651**

## GUIDED READING

### LITERAL QUESTIONS

**1a.** What is Kino's reaction to Juana's comment that the dealers may have been right? (He studies the pearl in the burning sun, then says that they would not try to steal it if it had no value.)

**2a.** What does Kino tell Juana after he says he doesn't know who attacked him? (When he sells the pearl he will have a rifle.)

### INFERENTIAL QUESTIONS

**1b.** What might you infer from Kino's carefully considered response? (By slowly examining the pearl and then basing his opinion on the fact that others want it, he betrays doubts of his own.)

**2b.** What might make his interest in a rifle different from his first extravagant daydream of owning one? (A rifle had been a luxury before; now it has become a necessity.)

- Kino sees the trackers moving along the road toward them.
- In hopelessness Kino considers letting them take him.

## 1 PLOT: RISING ACTION

The trackers, heretofore an ominous but unseen threat, become a chilling reality, closing in on Kino.

## 2 BACKGROUND

The explanation of the trackers' cunning and knowledge heightens the intensity of this deadly chase.

## 3 THEME

Seeing his options narrowed to one chance, Kino prepares to risk all on a desperate possibility.

## 4 MOOD

Kino's reckless disregard for his trail of telling signs builds the tension as the hunters make slow, relentless progress toward him.

## 5 PLOT: CONFLICT

Kino, succumbing to despair, weighs the odds against their escape and considers giving up the fight.

---

1 And then he saw them moving along. His body stiffened and he drew down his head and peeked out from under a fallen branch. In the distance he could see three figures, two on foot and one on horseback. But he knew what they were, and a chill of fear went through him. Even in the distance he could see the two on foot moving slowly along, bent low to the ground. Here, one would pause and look at the earth, while the other joined him. They were the trackers, they could follow the trail of a bighorn sheep in the stone mountains. They were as sensitive as hounds. Here, he and Juana might have stepped out of the wheel rut, and these people from the inland, these hunters, could follow, could read a broken straw or a little tumbled pile of dust. Behind them, on a horse, was a dark man, his nose covered with a blanket, and across his saddle a rifle gleamed in the sun.

Kino lay as rigid as the tree limb. He barely breathed, and his eyes went to the place where he had swept out the track. Even the sweeping 2 might be a message to the trackers. He knew these inland hunters. In a country where there is little game they managed to live because of their ability to hunt, and they were hunting him. They scuttled over the ground like animals and found a sign and crouched over it while the horseman waited.

The trackers whined a little, like excited 3 dogs on a warming trail. Kino slowly drew his big knife to his hand and made it ready. He knew what he must do. If the trackers found the swept place, he must leap for the horseman, kill him quickly and take the rifle. That was his only chance in the world. And as the three drew nearer on the road, Kino dug little pits with his sandaled toes so that he could leap without warning, so that his feet would not slip. He had only a little vision under the fallen limb.

Now Juana, back in her hidden place, heard the pad of the horse's hoofs, and Coyotito gurgled. She took him up quickly and put him under her shawl and gave him her breast and he was silent.

When the trackers came near, Kino could see only their legs and only the legs of the horse from under the fallen branch. He saw the dark horny feet of the men and their ragged white clothes, and he heard the creak of leather of the saddle and the clink of spurs. The trackers stopped at the swept place and studied it, and the horseman stopped. The horse flung his head up against the bit and the bit-roller clicked under his tongue and the horse snorted. Then the dark trackers turned and studied the horse and watched his ears.

Kino was not breathing, but his back arched a little and the muscles of his arms and legs stood out with tension and a line of sweat formed on his upper lip. For a long moment the trackers bent over the road, and they moved on slowly, studying the ground ahead of them, and the horseman moved after them. The trackers scuttled along, stopping, looking, and hurrying on. They would be back, Kino knew. They would be circling and searching, peeping, stooping, and they would come back sooner or later to his covered track.

4 He slid backward and did not bother to cover his tracks. He could not; too many little signs were there, too many broken twigs and scuffed places and displaced stones. And there was a panic in Kino now, a panic of flight. The trackers would find his trail, he knew it. There was no escape, except in flight. He edged away from the road and went quickly and silently to the hidden place where Juana was. She looked up at him in question.

"Trackers," he said. "Come!"

5 And then a helplessness and a hopelessness swept over him, and his face went black and his eyes were sad. "Perhaps I should let them take me."

Instantly Juana was on her feet and her hand lay on his arm. "You have the pearl," she cried

---

## GUIDED READING

### LITERAL QUESTION

**1a.** What do the trackers do when they crouch over a sign? (whine like excited dogs)

### INFERENTIAL QUESTION

**1b.** What do you think their excitement might indicate? (Tracking is a game in which they prove their skills; their prize is the thrill of the hunt and personal victory, as was the case with the pearl dealers.)

hoarsely. "Do you think they would take you back alive to say they had stolen it?"

His hand strayed limply to the place where the pearl was hidden under his clothes. "They will find it," he said weakly.

"Come," she said. "Come!"

And when he did not respond, "Do you think they would let me live? Do you think they would let the little one here live?"

Her goading struck into his brain; his lips snarled and his eyes were fierce again. "Come," he said. "We will go into the mountains. Maybe we can lose them in the mountains."

Frantically he gathered the gourds and the little bags that were their property. Kino carried a bundle in his left hand, but the big knife swung free in his right hand. He parted the brush for Juana and they hurried to the west, toward the high stone mountains. They trotted quickly through the tangle of the undergrowth. This was panic flight. Kino did not try to conceal his passages; he trotted, kicking the stones, knocking the telltale leaves from the little trees. The high sun streamed down on the dry creaking earth so that even vegetation ticked in protest. But ahead were the naked granite mountains, rising out of erosion rubble and standing monolithic against the sky. And Kino ran for the high place, as nearly all animals do when they are pursued.

This land was waterless, furred with the cacti which could store water and with the great-rooted brush which could reach deep into the earth for a little moisture and get along on very little. And underfoot was not soil but broken rock, split into small cubes, great slabs, but none of it water-rounded. Little tufts of sad dry grass grew between the stones, grass that had sprouted with one single rain and headed,[5] dropped its seed, and died. Horned toads watched the family go by and turned their little pivoting dragon heads. And now and then a great jackrabbit,

---

5. **headed:** grew to maturity.

disturbed in his shade, bumped away and hid behind the nearest rock. The singing heat lay over this desert country, and ahead the stone mountains looked cool and welcoming.

And Kino fled. He knew what would happen. A little way along the road the trackers would become aware that they had missed the path, and they would come back, searching and judging, and in a little while they would find the place where Kino and Juana had rested. From there it would be easy for them—these little stones, the fallen leaves and the whipped branches, the scuffed places where a foot had slipped. Kino could see them in his mind, slipping along the track, whining a little with eagerness, and behind them, dark and half disinterested, the horseman with the rifle. His work would come last, for he would not take them back. Oh, the music of evil sang loud in Kino's head now, it sang with the whine of heat and with the dry ringing of snake rattles. It was not large and overwhelming now, but secret and poisonous, and the pounding of his heart gave it undertone and rhythm.

The way began to rise, and as it did the rocks grew larger. But now Kino had put a little distance between his family and the trackers. Now, on the first rise, he rested. He climbed a great boulder and looked back over the shimmering country, but he could not see his enemies, not even the tall horseman riding through the brush. Juana had squatted in the shade of the boulder. She raised her bottle of water to Coyotito's lips; his little dried tongue sucked greedily at it. She looked up at Kino when he came back; she saw him examine her ankles, cut and scratched from the stones and brush, and she covered them quickly with her skirt. Then she handed the bottle to him, but he shook his head. Her eyes were bright in her tired face. Kino moistened his cracked lips with his tongue.

"Juana," he said, "I will go on and you will

*The Pearl* 653

---

## GUIDED READING

**LITERAL QUESTION**

**1a.** What does Juana do when she sees Kino examine her cut and scratched ankles? (She covers them with her skirt.)

**INFERENTIAL QUESTION**

**1b.** What do you think her concealment might indicate? (She wants Kino to see her strength, not her injuries, so that he doesn't lose courage or lack confidence in her ability to keep up.)

## 1 CHARACTERIZATION

Juana, Kino's proven equal in judgment and determination, is not intimidated by his harsh tone or arguments that, by not obeying, she hinders him and endangers Coyotito.

## 2 PLOT: CONFLICT

Kino and Juana struggle against the relentless heat and dryness of nature as well as the deadly hunters.

## 3 STYLE: SOUND DEVICES

The repetition of hard "c" (cold and clean) and the phrases gushed out and crashing down suggest strength and abundance despite the area's apparent desolation.

---

hide. I will lead them into the mountains, and when they have gone past, you will go north to Loreto or to Santa Rosalia.[6] Then, if I can escape them, I will come to you. It is the only safe way."

**1** She looked full into his eyes for a moment. "No," she said. "We go with you."

"I can go faster alone," he said harshly. "You will put the little one in more danger if you go with me."

"No," said Juana.

"You must. It is the wise thing and it is my wish," he said.

"No," said Juana.

He looked then for weakness in her face, for fear or irresolution, and there was none. Her eyes were very bright. He shrugged his shoulders helplessly then, but he had taken strength from her. When they moved on it was no longer panic flight.

The country, as it rose toward the mountains, changed rapidly. Now there were long outcroppings of granite with deep crevices between, and Kino walked on bare unmarkable stone when he could and leaped from ledge to ledge. He knew that wherever the trackers lost his patch they must circle and lose time before they found it again. And so he did not go straight for the mountains any more; he moved in zigzags, and sometimes he cut back to the south and left a sign and then went toward the mountains over bare stone again. And the path rose steeply now, so that he panted a little as he went.

The sun moved downward toward the bare stone teeth of the mountains, and Kino set his direction for a dark and shadowing cleft in the range. If there were any water at all, it would be there where he could see, even in the distance, a hint of foliage. And if there were any passage through the smooth stone range, it would be by this same deep cleft. It had its danger, for the

---

6. **Loreto** [lō rā′tō] . . . **Santa Rosalia** [san′tə rō za′lē ə]: towns on the western coast of Baja California.

**2** trackers would think of it too, but the empty water bottle did not let that consideration enter. And as the sun lowered, Kino and Juana struggled wearily up the steep slope toward the cleft.

High in the gray stone mountains, under a frowning peak, a little spring bubbled out of a rupture in the stone. It was fed by shade-preserved snow in the summer, and now and then it died completely and bare rocks and dry **3** algae were on its bottom. But nearly always it gushed out, cold and clean and lovely. In the times when the quick rains fell, it might become a freshet and send its column of white water crashing down the mountain cleft, but nearly always it was a lean little spring. It bubbled out into a pool and then fell a hundred feet to another pool, and this one, overflowing, dropped again, so that it continued, down and down, until it came to the rubble of the upland, and there it disappeared altogether. There wasn't much left of it then anyway, for every time it fell over an escarpment the thirsty air drank it, and it

---

## GUIDED READING

### LITERAL QUESTIONS

**1a.** What does Kino do when he cannot persuade Juana to go north without him? (He shrugs helplessly and takes strength from her.)

**2a.** What does Kino do to throw the trackers off and make them lose time? (He zigzags, cuts back south to leave a sign, and then goes back toward the bare stone.)

### INFERENTIAL QUESTIONS

**1b.** What can you infer about Kino's relationship to Juana? (They have become more equal as Kino recognizes Juana's strength and certainty and trusts her wisdom.)

**2b.** What can you infer about Kino from his movements? (He has regained control of his thoughts and actions.)

splashed from the pools to the dry vegetation. The animals from miles around came to drink from the little pools, and the wild sheep and the deer, the pumas and raccoons, and the mice—all came to drink. And the birds which spent the day in the brushland came at night to the little pools that were like steps in the mountain cleft. Beside this tiny stream, wherever enough earth collected for root-hold, colonies of plants grew, wild grape and little palms, maidenhair fern, hibiscus, and tall pampas grass with feathery rods raised above the spike leaves. And in the pool lived frogs and waterskaters, and waterworms crawled on the bottom of the pool. Everything that loved water came to these few shallow places. The cats took their prey there, and strewed feathers and lapped water through their bloody teeth. **The little pools were places of life because of the water, and places of killing because of the water, too.**

The lowest step, where the stream collected before it tumbled down a hundred feet and dis-

appeared into the rubbly desert, was a little platform of stone and sand. Only a pencil of water fell into the pool, but it was enough to keep the pool full and to keep the ferns green in the underhang of the cliff, and wild grape climbed the stone mountain and all manner of little plants found comfort here. The freshets had made a small sandy beach through which the pool flowed, and bright green watercress grew in the damp sand. The beach was cut and scarred and padded by the feet of animals that had come to drink and to hunt.

The sun had passed over the stone mountains when Kino and Juana struggled up the steep broken slope and came at last to the water. From this step they could look out over the sunbeaten desert to the blue Gulf in the distance. They came utterly weary to the pool, and Juana slumped to her knees and first washed Coyotito's face and then filled her bottle and gave him a drink. And the baby was weary and petulant, and he cried softly until Juana gave him her breast, and then he gurgled and clucked against her. Kino drank long and thirstily at the pool. For a moment, then, he stretched out beside the water and relaxed all his muscles and watched Juana feeding the baby, and then he got to his feet and went to the edge of the step where the water slipped over, and he searched the distance carefully. His eyes set on a point and he became rigid. Far down the slope he could see the two trackers; they were little more than dots or scurrying ants and behind them a larger ant.

Juana had turned to look at him and she saw his back stiffen.

"How far?" she asked quietly.

"They will be here by evening," said Kino. He looked up the long steep chimney of the cleft where the water came down. "We must go west," he said, and his eyes searched the stone shoulder behind the cleft. And thirty feet up on the gray shoulder he saw a series of little erosion caves. He slipped off his sandals and clambered up to them, gripping the bare stone with his

*The Pearl* **655**

AT A GLANCE

- They come to a small beach, where they rest and drink.
- In the distance Kino spots the hunters scurrying after them.

**1 FORESHADOWING**

The pools, where both the hunted and the hunters must come, are the inevitable site for confrontation.

**2 STYLE: REPETITION**

The trackers, scurrying behind an "ant lion," undeterred by a mountain, evoke the recurring motif of Kino watching the behavior of ants.

## GUIDED READING

**LITERAL QUESTIONS**

**1a.** What do the animals that leave cuts and scars on the beach come to do? (drink and hunt)

**2a.** What does Kino do after he drinks? (He relaxes completely for a moment and watches Juana nurse Coyotito.)

**INFERENTIAL QUESTIONS**

**1b.** What might the animals' traffic have to do with Kino and Juana's plight? (The animals' behavior is a metaphor for Kino and Juana's situation; they seek water, and the trackers, seeking them, know where to hunt.)

**2b.** What do you think that brief scene might suggest? (Although his situation grows increasingly dire, Kino shows the first sign of contentment since finding the pearl; he still has what he values most.)

## 1 DIALOGUE

Kino lays out the plan for their escape, stressing his fear that Coyotito might make noise.

## 2 PLOT: CONFLICT

The trackers, thirsting more for blood than for water, check the beach for signs before they drink.

## 3 VOCABULARY: WORD CHOICE

"Murmur," describing the trackers' audible voices and Juana's whispers, stresses the proximity of the men and the importance of silence.

## 4 TONE

Steinbeck's respect for Kino shows in his portrayal of him as a man who, lacking soft words, expresses his devotion with personal sacrifice and dreadful instructions.

---

toes, and he looked into the shallow caves. They were only a few feet deep, wind-hollowed scoops, but they sloped slightly downward and back. Kino crawled into the largest one and lay down and knew that he could not be seen from the outside. Quickly he went back to Juana.

"You must go up there. Perhaps they will not find us there," he said.

Without question she filled her water bottle to the top, and then Kino helped her up to the shallow cave and brought up the packages of food and passed them to her. And Juana sat in the cave entrance and watched him. She saw that he did not try to erase their tracks in the sand. Instead, he climbed up the brush cliff beside the water, clawing and tearing at the ferns and wild grape as he went. And when he had climbed a hundred feet to the next bench, he came down again. He looked carefully at the smooth rock shoulder toward the cave to see that there was no trace of passage, and last he climbed up and crept into the cave beside Juana.

1 "When they go up," he said, "we will slip away, down to the lowlands again. I am afraid only that the baby may cry. You must see that he does not cry."

"He will not cry," she said, and she raised the baby's face to her own and looked into his eyes and he stared solemnly back at her.

"He knows," said Juana.

Now Kino lay in the cave entrance, his chin braced on his crossed arms, and he watched the blue shadow of the mountain move out across the brushy desert below until it reached the Gulf, and the long twilight of the shadow was over the land.

The trackers were long in coming, as though they had trouble with the trail Kino had left. It was dusk when they came at last to the little pool. And all three were on foot now, for a horse could not climb the last steep slope. From above 4 they were thin figures in the evening. The two 2 trackers scurried about on the little beach, and they saw Kino's progress up the cliff before they

drank. The man with the rifle sat down and rested himself, and the trackers squatted near him, and in the evening the points of their cigarettes glowed and receded. And then Kino could see that they were eating, and the soft murmur of their voices came to him.

Then darkness fell, deep and black in the mountain cleft. The animals that used the pool came near and smelled men there and drifted away again into the darkness.

3 He heard a murmur behind him. Juana was whispering, "Coyotito." She was begging him to be quiet. Kino heard the baby whimper, and he knew from the muffled sounds that Juana had covered his head with her shawl.

Down on the beach a match flared, and in its momentary light Kino saw that two of the men were sleeping, curled up like dogs, while the third watched, and he saw the glint of the rifle in the match light. And then the match died, but it left a picture on Kino's eyes. He could see it, just how each man was, two sleeping curled and the third squatting in the sand with the rifle between his knees.

Kino moved silently back into the cave. Juana's eyes were two sparks reflecting a low star. Kino crawled quietly close to her and he put his lips near to her cheek.

"There is a way," he said.

"But they will kill you."

"If I get first to the one with the rifle," Kino said, "I must get to him first, then I will be all right. Two are sleeping."

Her hand crept out from under her shawl and gripped his arm. "They will see your white clothes in the starlight."

"No," he said. "And I must go before moon-rise."

4 He searched for a soft word and then gave it up. "If they kill me," he said, "lie quietly. And when they are gone away, go to Loreto."

Her hand shook a little, holding his wrist.

"There is no choice," he said. "It is the only way. They will find us in the morning."

---

## GUIDED READING

### LITERAL QUESTIONS

**1a.** What does Kino do as he climbs up the brush cliff beside the water? (claws and tears at the ferns and wild grapes)

**2a.** What picture could Kino still see after the man's match goes out? (He could see how each man was, two sleeping and a third squatting with the rifle between his knees.)

### INFERENTIAL QUESTIONS

**1b.** Why might he have stopped trying to cover their trail? (He leaves desperate signs to throw the trackers off and delay them so that he and Juana can leave the cave and head back to the lowlands.)

**2b.** What do you think is the importance of that lingering image? (In that moment Kino sees his opportunity for an attack and memorizes the exact position of each man.)

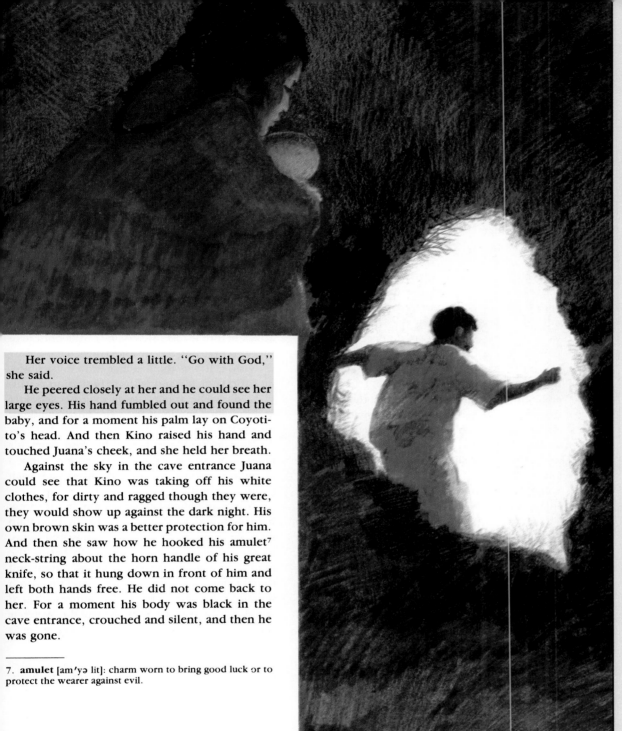

AT A GLANCE

- Trembling, Juana tells Kino to "Go with God."
- Kino prepares to climb down the cleft, then leaves the cave.

**1 DESCRIPTION**

Juana's voice, words, and eyes convey her fear and love for Kino, as well as her trust that his plan is their best chance for escape.

Her voice trembled a little. "Go with God," she said.

He peered closely at her and he could see her large eyes. His hand fumbled out and found the baby, and for a moment his palm lay on Coyotito's head. And then Kino raised his hand and touched Juana's cheek, and she held her breath.

Against the sky in the cave entrance Juana could see that Kino was taking off his white clothes, for dirty and ragged though they were, they would show up against the dark night. His own brown skin was a better protection for him. And then she saw how he hooked his amulet[7] neck-string about the horn handle of his great knife, so that it hung down in front of him and left both hands free. He did not come back to her. For a moment his body was black in the cave entrance, crouched and silent, and then he was gone.

---

7. **amulet** [am′yə lit]: charm worn to bring good luck or to protect the wearer against evil.

## GUIDED READING

### LITERAL QUESTION

**1a.** What does Kino do to prepare for his climb down the cleft? (He removes his white clothing and secures his knife to his amulet neck-string to free his hands.)

### INFERENTIAL QUESTION

**1b.** How does Kino's preparation make this attack unlike his previous encounters with enemies? (This time, Kino plans the attack; he can be the calculating strategist rather than the reacting victim.)

- Kino edges his way slowly down the smooth rock.
- The moon casts light on the mountain, and Kino knows he must leap.

## 1 DETAIL

Concrete detail, describing how Kino moves without noise and without error, imbues the scene with a feeling of flesh-and-blood reality.

## 2 STYLE: SIMILE

Comparing Kino's descent to a shadow, in his silent race with the moon, implies his paradoxical unity with and struggle against the forces of nature.

## 3 MOOD

Suspense builds as Kino's only camouflage remains his imperceptible movement and utter silence.

## 4 PLOT: CONFLICT

Kino struggles against the obstacles of his stalkers, his own cramping muscles, and the relentless progress of the moon.

## 5 PLOT: RISING ACTION

Just as Kino is positioned to attack, Coyotito's little cry draws the watcher to attention.

---

Juana moved to the entrance and looked out. She peered like an owl from the hole in the mountain, and the baby slept under the blanket on her back, his face turned sideways against her neck and shoulder. She could feel his warm breath against her skin, and Juana whispered her combination of prayer and magic, her Hail Marys and her ancient intercession, against the black unhuman things.

The night seemed a little less dark when she looked out, and to the east there was a lightning in the sky, down near the horizon where the moon would show. And, looking down, she could see the cigarette of the man on watch.

1 Kino edged like a slow lizard down the smooth rock shoulder. He had turned his neck-string so that the great knife hung down from his back and could not clash against the stone. His spread fingers gripped the mountain, and his bare toes found support through contact, and even his chest lay against the stone so that he would not slip. For any sound, a rolling pebble or a sign, a little slip of flesh on rock, would rouse the watchers below. Any sound that was not germane[8] to the night would make them alert. But the night was not silent; the little tree frogs that lived near the stream twittered like birds, and the high metallic ringing of the cicadas filled the mountain cleft. And Kino's own music was in his head, the music of the enemy, low and pulsing, nearly asleep. But the Song of the Family had become as fierce and sharp and feline as the snarl of a female puma. The family song was alive now and driving him down on the dark enemy. The harsh cicada seemed to take up its melody, and the twittering tree frogs called little phrases of it.

2 And Kino crept silently as a shadow down the smooth mountain face. One bare foot moved a few inches and the toes touched the stone and gripped, and the other foot a few inches, and then the palm of one hand a little downward,

---

8. **germane** [jər mān′]: directly related.

---

3 and then the other hand, until the whole body, without seeming to move, had moved. Kino's mouth was open so that even his breath would make no sound, for he knew that he was not invisible. If the watcher, sensing movement, looked at the dark place against the stone which was his body, he would see him. Kino must move so slowly he could not draw the watcher's eyes. It took him a long time to reach the bottom and to crouch behind a little dwarf palm. His heart thundered in his chest and his hands and face were wet with sweat. He crouched and took slow long breaths to calm himself.

4 Only twenty feet separated him from the enemy now, and he tried to remember the ground between. Was there any stone which might trip him in his rush? He kneaded his legs against cramp and found that his muscles were jerking after their long tension. And then he looked apprehensively to the east. The moon would rise in a few moments now, and he must attack before it rose. He could see the outline of the watcher, but the sleeping men were below his vision. It was the watcher Kino must find—must find quickly and without hesitation. Silently he drew the amulet string over his shoulder and loosened the loop from the horn handle of his great knife.

He was too late, for as he rose from his crouch the silver edge of the moon slipped above the eastern horizon, and Kino sank back behind his bush.

It was an old and ragged moon, but it threw hard light and hard shadow into the mountain cleft, and now Kino could see the seated figure of the watcher on the little beach beside the pool. The watcher gazed full at the moon, and then he lighted another cigarette, and the match
5 illumined his dark face for a moment. There could be no waiting now; when the watcher turned his head, Kino must leap. His legs were as tight as wound springs.

And then from above came a little murmuring cry. The watcher turned his head to listen

---

## GUIDED READING

### LITERAL QUESTIONS

**1a.** What does Juana see when she looks down from the cave toward the trackers? (the cigarette of the man on watch)

**2a.** What makes the music of the enemy different from that of the family as Kino moves down the cleft? (The music of the enemy is nearly asleep; the Song of the Family, like a female puma, is fierce, alive, and driving.)

### INFERENTIAL QUESTIONS

**1b.** What can you infer about Juana's position relative to the trackers? (She sits directly above them where only a short distance and darkness separate her from the man with the rifle.)

**2b.** What might the contrasting songs suggest? (Kino is becoming a vengeful force protecting his family as he makes deadly progress toward his enemies, who are momentarily lulled.)

and then he stood up, and one of the sleepers stirred on the ground and awakened and asked quietly, "What is it?"

"I don't know," said the watcher. "It sounded like a cry, almost like a human—like a baby."

The man who had been sleeping said, "You can't tell. Some coyote bitch with a litter. I've heard a coyote pup cry like a baby."

The sweat rolled in drops down Kino's forehead and fell into his eyes and burned them. The little cry came again and the watcher looked up the side of the hill to the dark cave.

"Coyote maybe," he said, and Kino heard the harsh click as he cocked the rifle.

"If it's a coyote, this will stop it," the watcher said as he raised the gun.

Kino was in midleap when the gun crashed and the barrel-flash made a picture on his eyes. The great knife swung and crunched hollowly. It bit through neck and deep into chest, and Kino was a terrible machine now. He grasped the rifle even as he wrenched free his knife. His strength and his movement and his speed were a machine. He whirled and struck the head of the seated man like a melon. The third man scrabbled away like a crab, slipped into the pool, and then he began to climb frantically, to climb up the cliff where the water penciled down. His hands and feet threshed in the tangle of the wild grapevine, and he whimpered and gibbered as he tried to get up. But Kino had become as cold and deadly as steel. Deliberately he threw the lever of the rifle, and then he raised the gun and aimed deliberately and fired. He saw his enemy tumble backward into the pool, and Kino strode to the water. In the moonlight he could see the frantic frightened eyes, and Kino aimed and fired between the eyes.

And then Kino stood uncertainly. Something was wrong, some signal was trying to get through to his brain. Tree frogs and cicadas were silent now. And then Kino's brain cleared from its red concentration and he knew the sound—the keening, moaning, rising hysterical cry from the little cave in the side of the stone mountain, the cry of death.

4 Everyone in La Paz remembers the return of the family; there may be some old ones who saw it, but those whose fathers and whose grandfathers told it to them remember it nevertheless. It is an event that happened to everyone.

It was late in the golden afternoon when the first little boys ran hysterically in the town and spread the word that Kino and Juana were coming back. And everyone hurried to see them. The sun was settling toward the western mountains and the shadows on the ground were long. And perhaps that was what left the deep impression on those who saw them.

The two came from the rutted country road into the city, and they were not walking in single file, Kino ahead and Juana behind, as usual, but side by side. The sun was behind them and their long shadows stalked ahead, and they seemed to 5 carry two towers of darkness with them. Kino had a rifle across his arm and Juana carried her shawl like a sack over her shoulder. And in it was a small limp heavy bundle. The shawl was crusted with dried blood, and the bundle swayed a little as she walked. Her face was hard and lined and leathery with fatigue and with the tightness with which she fought fatigue. And her wide eyes stared inward on herself. She was as remote and as removed as Heaven. Kino's lips were thin and his jaws tight, and the people say that he carried fear with him, that he was as dangerous as a rising storm. The people say that the two seemed to be removed from human experience; that they had gone through pain and had come out on the other side; that there was almost a magical protection about them. And those people who had rushed to see them crowded back and let them pass and did not speak to them.

Kino and Juana walked through the city as though it were not there. Their eyes glanced neither right nor left nor up nor down, but stared only straight ahead. Their legs moved a

*The Pearl* **659**

- As the rifle explodes, Kino attacks, then hears Juana's cry.
- Kino and Juana return home with Coyotito's body and a rifle.

## 1 VOCABULARY: WORD CHOICE

*Coyotito*, a variation of *coyote*, emphasizes the parallel between human and animal behavior, whether innocent or evil, as seen throughout the story.

## 2 PLOT: CLIMAX

A blind shot directed at a baby's cry coincides with the instant of Kino's fatal, judicious attack.

## 3 READING SKILLS: CONTRAST

Kino, previously on the defense against furtive attacks, has become cold, thorough, and deliberate in the destruction of his enemies.

## 4 FOLK TALE

The story, remembered and retold by generations, resumes a tone of universality and timelessness.

## 5 IRONY

Kino now owns a rifle, the one that killed Coyotito, whose body Juana carries in her shawl.

## GUIDED READING

**LITERAL QUESTION**

**1a.** Where does Juana walk when she and Kino return to La Paz? (at Kino's side rather than behind him)

**INFERENTIAL QUESTION**

**1b.** What might you infer from the change in her position? (Their experience has proven them to be equals in loss, endurance, and dignity.)

## AT A GLANCE

- In the pearl's surface Kino sees ugliness, destruction, and loss.
- Kino flings the pearl back into the sea.

### 1 TONE

The narrator's empathy shows in his description of Kino and Juana's indifference to the losses they had endured before losing Coyotito.

### 2 SYMBOL

The pearl, once the promise of every success, represents only loss and destruction to Kino.

## REFLECTING ON THE NOVEL

How might Kino's story be relevant today? (Possible answers: Love, hope, and greed are timeless; parents always want a better life for their children.)

little jerkily, like well-made wooden dolls, and they carried pillars of black fear about them. And as they walked through the stone and plaster city brokers peered at them from barred windows and servants put one eye to a slitted gate and mothers turned the faces of their youngest children inward against their skirts. Kino and Juana strode side by side through the stone and plaster city and down among the brush houses, and the neighbors stood back and let them pass. Juan Tomás raised his hand in greeting and did not say the greeting and left his hand in the air for a moment uncertainly.

In Kino's ears the Song of the Family was as fierce as a cry. He was immune and terrible, and **his song had become a battle cry. They trudged past the burned square where their house had been without even looking at it. They cleared the brush that edged the beach and picked their way down the shore toward the water. And they did not look toward Kino's broken canoe.**

And when they came to the water's edge they stopped and stared out over the Gulf. And then Kino laid the rifle down, and he dug among his clothes, and then he held the great pearl in his hand. He looked into its surface and it was gray and ulcerous. Evil faces peered from it into his eyes, and he saw the light of burning. And in the surface of the pearl he saw the frantic eyes of the man in the pool. And in the surface of the pearl he saw Coyotito lying in the little cave with the **top of his head shot away. And the pearl was ugly; it was gray, like a malignant growth. And Kino heard the music of the pearl, distorted and insane.** Kino's hand shook a little, and he turned slowly to Juana and held the pearl out to her. She stood beside him, still holding her dead bundle over her shoulder. She looked at the pearl in his hand for a moment and then she looked into Kino's eyes and said softly, "No, you."

And Kino drew back his arm and flung the pearl with all his might. Kino and Juana watched it go, winking and glimmering under the setting sun. They saw the little splash in the distance, and they stood side by side watching the place for a long time.

And the pearl settled into the lovely green water and dropped toward the bottom. The waving branches of the algae called to it and beckoned to it. The lights on its surface were green and lovely. It settled down to the sand bottom among the fernlike plants. Above, the surface of the water was a green mirror. And the pearl lay on the floor of the sea. A crab scampering over the bottom raised a little cloud of sand, and when it settled the pearl was gone.

And the music of the pearl drifted to a whisper and disappeared.

## GUIDED READING

**LITERAL QUESTION**

**1a.** What does Juana say when Kino holds out the pearl to her? ("No, you.")

**INFERENTIAL QUESTION**

**1b.** Why does she say this? (The struggle with the pearl has been primarily Kino's, and he must be the one to finally reject it.)

## STUDY QUESTIONS

### Recalling

1. What does Kino do when Juana tries to throw the pearl away at the beginning of Chapter V?
2. List the events that force Kino and Juana to leave La Paz on foot.
3. As Kino and Juana try to escape and hide from the trackers, describe what happens to the music of the family and the music of the pearl.
4. Why does the family flee to the mountains? What happens to them in the mountains?
5. In what terms does the narrator describe Kino and Juana on their return to La Paz? What do they do when they get there?

### Interpreting

6. What does Kino mean at the end of Chapter V by the statement, "This pearl has become my soul....If I give it up I shall lose my soul"? What does it show about him at this point in the novel?
7. At what point do we know that something terrible will happen to Kino and Juana? What event is the climax of the novel?
8. When Kino looks at the pearl for the last time, how has it changed? Why has it changed?
9. Why does Juana make Kino take the novel's final action by himself? What does the action reveal about Kino's values?
10. What meaning do you find in the final statements (on page 660) about the Song of the Family and the music of the pearl?

### Extending

11. The narrator begins the story by saying: "If this story is a parable, perhaps everyone takes his own meaning from it and reads his own life into it." What meaning did *you* take from it?

## VIEWPOINT

Two literary critics have offered differing opinions of Steinbeck's ability to create characters in *The Pearl.* One praised him for:

his ability in shaping up the stuff of human lives in forms that delight the mind and imagination.

— J. W. Beach, *American Fiction 1920–1940*

Another reviewer was less admiring:

Steinbeck's people are always on the verge of becoming human, but never do.

— A. Kazin, *On Native Grounds*

■ Are the characters in *The Pearl* believable human beings with real feelings, hopes, and fears? Or are they more like puppets that are manipulated by the author? Explain your answer with examples from the text.

## LITERARY FOCUS

### The Total Effect

Like any work of art, *The Pearl* is more than the sum of its parts. Steinbeck meshes these parts — plot, character, setting, point of view, tone, symbol, irony, and theme — to create a unified effect on the reader. The events of the plot clearly lead Kino and Juana step by step from happiness into tragedy. The characters change under the impact of these events and so does the setting, as Kino and Juana are uprooted from their home. The omniscient narrator's comments emphasize the effect of the pearl on the characters' lives, and symbols and irony reveal the larger meaning of their experience.

### Thinking About Plot, Character, and Setting

1. What different kinds of conflicts does Kino undergo in *The Pearl*? How is each of these conflicts resolved?
2. Which characters are dynamic, and what brings about the changes in them? Who changes most? Explain.
3. Describe each of the novel's different settings. Explain how each is appropriate to the action that takes place within it.

### Thinking About Point of View and Tone

4. How would the novel have been different if Kino had been the narrator?
5. What details reveal Steinbeck's attitude toward the doctor and the pearl buyer? Toward Kino and Juana in the beginning of the novel? At the end of the novel?
6. Imagery is another aspect of a writer's tone. Find two or three examples of disease images in the novel. To what does each image refer? What attitude does each express?

*The Pearl* **661**

### STUDY QUESTIONS

1. grabs pearl; hits her in face; kicks her
2. Kino kills man; someone destroys canoe; house is burned.
3. Music of pearl is louder, becomes sinister; music of family becomes warlike.
4. They have better chance of losing trackers; Kino kills a tracker; Coyotito is killed.
5. had come out on the other side of pain; throw pearl into sea
6. Pearl symbolizes all his hopes. He values dream of betterment over peace.
7. when Kino sees bad things in pearl; fight between Kino and trackers
8. Surface is gray and ulcerous. It has led to evil acts and death.
9. wants to make sure it has lost its grip on his soul; values family more than wealth
10. *family:* described as battle cry, represents protective instinct; *pearl:* has become distorted, symbolizes destructiveness
11. Possible answers: Wealth does not bring happiness; ambition can be dangerous; loved ones are most important.

### VIEWPOINT

Some may feel that couple have real feelings, hopes, fears; others may argue they are too general to be believable individuals.

### LITERARY FOCUS

1. *internal:* desire for gain vs. evil of pearl—realizes pearl is not worth unhappiness; *external:* Kino's desire to keep pearl vs. Juana's wish to get rid of it—he throws it away; Kino vs. doctor, buyers, thieves—murders to keep pearl; Kino vs. trackers—he kills them, but they kill son
2. Kino/Juana; pearl raises their expectations; Kino; becomes attached to his hopes, then must relinquish them

3. village of brush huts—simplicity; city—alien, unwelcome world; gulf—hope of wealth; inland—fear; mountains—haven
4. thoughts and actions of others would not have been revealed
5. *doctor*—looked silly holding tiny cup, *buyer*—played with coin mechanically; steady, cruel eyes; *beginning:* Kino— young, strong, bright eyes; Juana—cheerful, patient; *end:* both dark, remote, removed
6. *the little hole was slightly enlarged*—scorpion bite; *poison sacs of the town*—greed, envy; *pearl was . . . like a malignant growth*—danger of sudden wealth

**7.** *finding:* hope, good luck; *envisions:* chance for betterment; *flight:* misfortune; *end:* nothing—is simply a pearl

**8.** *Kino:* protection, ambition, masculinity; *Juana:* prudence, loyalty, femininity; *Coyotito:* future, vulnerability

**9.** *doctor and buyers:* forces of oppression, greed; *hunters:* retribution for greed, murder

**10.** It ultimately caused his death.

**11.** The first reveals his dreams; the second, only evil—Kino and Juana have lost what was most precious.

**12.** Desire for worldly possessions leads to misery.

**13.** The powerless become victims.

**14.** *gained:* new strength, understanding of true values; *lost:* canoe, house, hopes, innocence, contentment

## VOCABULARY

**1.** (b) merciful : kindness
**2.** (a) sentence : book
**3.** (b) sand : beach
**4.** (d) despair : hope
**5.** (b) stiffness : rigidity

---

### Thinking About Symbol

7. What does the pearl symbolize (a) when Kino finds it; (b) when he envisions what he will buy with it; (c) during the flight; (d) at the end of the novel?

8. What might Kino, Juana, and Coyotito each symbolize?

9. What larger force might the doctor and the pearl buyers symbolize? The men who hunt Kino and Juana?

### Thinking About Irony

10. Explain the irony in the fact that the pearl was originally intended to buy medical care for Coyotito.

11. Compare the visions Kino has as he looks at the pearl on pages 627 and 651. What irony do we come to see in the first vision?

### Thinking About Theme

12. What relationship between happiness and worldly possessions does Kino's experience with the pearl express?

13. What ideas about the relationships between the powerful and the powerless do Kino's scenes with the doctor and pearl buyers express?

14. What do you think Kino and Juana have gained from their tragic experience? What besides Coyotito have they lost?

## VOCABULARY

### Analogies

**Analogies** are comparisons that point out relationships between items. In vocabulary tests analogies are usually written as two pairs of words; the words in the first pair are always related to each other in the *same* way as those in the second pair. For example, in the analogy COVEY : BIRD : : SCHOOL : FISH, the first word of each pair names a group, and the second word names a member of that group.

The capitalized words in the following analogies appear in *The Pearl*. Complete the following analogies by choosing the pair of words that are related in the same way as the pair in capital letters.

1. INDIGENT : POVERTY : :
  (a) ulcer : sac      (c) venom : snake
  (b) merciful : kindness  (d) rhyme : rhythm

---

2. CHORD : SONG : :
  (a) sentence : book   (c) mirage : illusion
  (b) wail : keen       (d) vagueness : clarity

3. ALGAE : SEA : :
  (a) germs : health   (c) hard : soft
  (b) sand : beach    (d) land : water

4. LETHARGY : EXCITEMENT : :
  (a) lazy : happy     (c) death : grief
  (b) appraise : property (d) despair : hope

5. LUCENCE : INCANDESCENCE : :
  (a) sun : light     (c) writhe : sleep
  (b) stiffness : rigidity (d) mocking : reassuring

## COMPOSITION

### Comparing and Contrasting Characters

◼ Compare and contrast the characters of Kino and Juana in *The Pearl*. Devote one paragraph to answering each of the following questions. Be sure to cite examples from the novel:

  a. Are both characters equally developed?
  b. Is one more admirable than the other?
  c. Does one grow more than the other?

Then decide what explains the differences in their behavior. For example, does Juana warn Kino against the pearl because she is wiser than he, or because her imagination is more limited than his? *For help with this assignment, see Lesson 3 in the Writing About Literature Handbook at the back of this book.*

### Writing for a Camera

◼ Choose one *brief* descriptive passage from *The Pearl,* and rewrite it as a filmmaker might prepare instructions for a camera operator. Decide on the effect you want to create: Do you want to show a wide view or a narrow one? What do you want your audience to see in the scene and feel about it? What objects do you want to show and how close do you want to be to them? For example, if you selected the scene on page 616 in which Kino looks at the ant lion, you might first want to show the ants and Kino from each other's perspective. Then you might pull back and show Kino from a vantage point that makes him as small as the ants, to dramatize his vulnerability in the novel.

---

## COMPOSITION: GUIDELINES FOR EVALUATION

### COMPARING AND CONTRASTING CHARACTERS

**Objective**

To analyze the differences and similarities between two main characters

**Guidelines for Evaluation**

- suggested length: 5–7 paragraphs
- should compare and contrast traits of the two
- should compare and contrast the growth of each
- should explain differences in their behavior

### WRITING FOR A CAMERA

**Objective**

To use physical description of a place to convey atmosphere

**Guidelines for Evaluation**

- suggested length: 250–300 words
- should cite one brief descriptive passage
- should describe location in which scene should be shot
- should make clear desired audience response

# LITERARY FOCUS: *A Connecticut Yankee in King Arthur's Court*

### The Life of Mark Twain

The first major American author to be born west of the Mississippi River, Mark Twain (1835–1910) established a new frontier in American literature. He brought a refreshing realism to fiction by portraying his society with unsparing honesty, humor, and the down-to-earth language of the American West. Nearly a century after they were written, his works continue to tickle the funny bone, touch the heart, and prod the conscience of readers all over the world.

Mark Twain was actually the pen name of Samuel Langhorne Clemens, who grew up in Hannibal, Missouri, a sleepy town on the Mississippi River. Family hardships forced him to leave school at the age of twelve to work as an apprentice printer. Always interested in traveling, the young printer later became a riverboat pilot on the Mississippi River. This experience introduced him to the term *mark twain,* which was used by pilots to indicate the depth of the water. Twain's apprenticeship on the river was very important to him, and, as he later commented, it gave him more than a new name: "In that brief, sharp schooling I got . . . familiarly acquainted with all the different types of human nature that are to be found in fiction, biography, or history."

When the Civil War closed the Mississippi River to traffic, Twain took a stagecoach across the plains to Nevada, where he worked as a prospector, printer, and journalist. Trekking through the river towns and mining camps, he spent hours listening to frontier tales and folklore and soon mastered the art of storytelling. Twain combined that skill with a natural comic gift and gradually built a reputation as a western humorist with stories like "The Celebrated Jumping Frog of Calaveras County" (1865).

Mark Twain's first novel, *The Gilded Age* (1873), established him as a satirist. **Satire** is a form of writing that ridicules abuses for the sake of remedying them. Twain's skill in satirizing the frailties of people and institutions became an important factor in his growing fame as a writer.

Twain's career received a tremendous boost when he published the very popular *Adventures of Tom Sawyer* (1876), a novel that drew on his boyhood experiences near the Mississippi. He followed this classic with *The Prince and the Pauper* (1882), a novel intended as a children's story but one nevertheless heavily laced with satire. In this work an English prince disguised as a poor boy gets a close look at the flaws of his society. Twain turned again to English history for his sub-

*A Connecticut Yankee in King Arthur's Court* **663**

ject matter a few years later in *A Connecticut Yankee in King Arthur's Court* (1889). Between these two novels, Twain produced the autobiographical *Life on the Mississippi* (1883). This journey back into his youth sparked him to complete another book he had begun years before, his masterpiece, *The Adventures of Huckleberry Finn* (1884). *Huckleberry Finn* satirizes the shortcomings Twain saw in the people and institutions of his day, but the novel also celebrates the deep kinship people feel for one another and for nature.

Mark Twain's later works were darkened by his personal losses: his business failures and the early deaths of his wife and daughters. However, he never ceased to speak out against evil and for freedom and justice. Because of Twain's democratic spirit and defense of the underdog, one critic has referred to him as the "Lincoln of literature." Just as he invented his identity as Mark Twain, he helped to invent a uniquely American kind of writing. As a result, for millions of people throughout the world the name of Mark Twain has come, above all others, to stand for American literature.

### A Connecticut Yankee in King Arthur's Court

*Dream of being a knight errant in armor in the middle ages.*
*Have the notions & habit of thought of the present day. . . . No*
*pockets in the armor. . . . Can't scratch. . . . See Morte D'Arthur.*

Mark Twain made these notes shortly after he read *Le Morte d'Arthur,* Sir Thomas Malory's account of the adventures of King Arthur and the knights of the Round Table (selections from Malory's work appear in this book). Twain was fascinated with the idea of mixing a nineteenth-century American perspective with that of Malory's medieval British view. Twain favored the modern perspective; rather than treating the legend of King Arthur reverently, he set out to expose the flaws in the medieval social system and chivalric code. However, as his notes suggest, he intended to have fun in doing it.

*A Connecticut Yankee in King Arthur's Court* begins and ends in the nineteenth century. In this frame to the novel, Twain encounters a "Connecticut Yankee" who claims to have visited King Arthur's Britain. For the remainder of the novel both Twain and the reader are transported to sixth-century Britain as we read the Yankee's own story of his exploits. The Yankee's transplantation to sixth-century Britain provides a rich source of humor. The modern Yankee struggles to get his ancient clanking armor on and off, astounds the Britons with "miracles" of nineteenth-century technology, and pokes fun at the code of chivalry and other sacred institutions.

The novel also satirizes the backwardness, corruption, and superstition of the Middle Ages. Twain lived during a time of rapid industrial progress when many people longed for an earlier, simpler age. Although Twain sympathized with that view in some of his other works, *A Connecticut Yankee in King Arthur's Court* dampens that longing for the past by reminding nineteenth-century readers how difficult life would be without such modern conveniences as plumbing and soap. More important, like *The Prince and the Pauper* and *Huckleberry Finn, A Connecticut Yankee in King Arthur's Court* depicts the misery of life under an unjust system. The novel shows that the common person in the Middle Ages had few rights and led a meager and usually brief existence.

In addition, Twain recognized the shortcomings of his own time, and the novel satirizes them as well. Many of the abuses Twain sets in Arthur's Britain still existed in the nineteenth century. Furthermore, the Yankee's up-to-date technological wizardry ultimately leads to catastrophe on a scale of which Malory could never have dreamed.

*A Connecticut Yankee in King Arthur's Court,* then, can be read on a number of levels. It is an entertaining satire of the King Arthur legend. It is also a serious examination of two societies thirteen hundred years apart. Finally, the novel exposes flaws in the human character that seem to persist throughout the ages.

## Key Ideas in *A Connecticut Yankee in King Arthur's Court*

■ As you read *A Connecticut Yankee in King Arthur's Court*, look for references to each of the following topics. If you keep track of what the work says about these subjects, you will begin to grasp the most important themes of the novel.

- Magic, mystery, and superstition
- Fact and fancy
- Living conditions in Arthur's Britain
- Democracy and social justice
- Technological progress
- Attitudes toward change
- Time and history
- The limitations of human nature

*A Connecticut Yankee in King Arthur's Court* **665**

- The narrator talks to a stranger while touring an English castle.
- The stranger says he has been "transposed" into another epoch.
- The narrator returns to his hotel and reads about King Arthur.

LITERARY OPTIONS

- episodic narrative
- satire
- setting

THEMATIC OPTIONS

- the limitations of human nature
- democracy and social justice
- superstition vs. science

## 1 POINT OF VIEW

The story is begun by a first-person narrator. The narrator creates a frame for the tales of King Arthur's court that follow.

## 2 FORESHADOWING

The tour guide's speech points to a puzzle combining elements from the sixth century and a much later era. We may sense that the puzzle will somehow be solved in the tale that follows.

## 3 MOOD

A snug fireside mood is created. The rain and darkness outside make it cozier within, as the narrator loses himself in the romance and adventure of old times, creating an atmosphere ripe for a story.

**SELECTION FOR PRACTICE IN ACTIVE READING**

(TCR 5, p. 71)

---

*Mark Twain*

# A Connecticut Yankee in King Arthur's Court

## 1. A Word of Explanation

1    It was in Warwick Castle[1] that I came across the curious stranger whom I am going to talk about. We fell together, as modest people will, in the tail of the herd that was being shown through, and he at once began to say things which interested me. As he talked along, softly, pleasantly, flowingly, he seemed to drift away imperceptibly out of this world and time, and into some remote era and old forgotten country; and so he gradually wove such a spell about me that I seemed to move among the specters and shadows and dust and mold of a gray antiquity, holding speech with a relic of it! Exactly as I would speak of my nearest personal friends or enemies, or my most familiar neighbors, he spoke of Sir Bedivere, Sir Bors de Ganis, Sir Launcelot of the Lake, Sir Galahad,[2] and all the other great names of the Table Round—and how old, old, unspeakably old and faded and dry and musty and ancient he came to look as he went on! Presently he turned to me and said, just as one might speak of the weather or any other common matter—

"You know about transmigration of souls;[3] do you know about transposition of epochs—and bodies?"[4]

I said I had not heard of it. There was half a moment of silence, immediately interrupted by the droning voice of the salaried cicerone:[5]

"Ancient hauberk,[6] date of the sixth century, time of King Arthur and the Round Table; said to have belonged to the knight Sir Sagramore le Desirous; observe the round hole through the chain-mail[7] in the left breast; can't be accounted for; supposed to have been done with a bullet since invention of firearms—perhaps maliciously by Cromwell's[8] soldiers."

My acquaintance smiled—not a modern smile, but one that must have gone out of general use many, many centuries ago—and muttered apparently to himself:

"Wit ye well, *I saw it done.*" Then, after a pause, added: "I did it myself."

By the time I had recovered from the electric surprise of this remark, he was gone.

3    All that evening I sat by my fire at the Warwick Arms, steeped in a dream of the olden time, while the rain beat upon the windows, and the wind roared about the eaves and corners. From time to time I dipped into old Sir Thomas Malory's enchanting book[9] and fed at its rich feast of prodigies and adventures, breathed in the fragrance of its obsolete names, and dreamed again. Midnight being come at length, I read another tale, for a nightcap—this which here follows, to wit:

---

1. **Warwick** [wôr′ik] **Castle:** castle located in the county of Warwick, in central England.
2. **Sir Bedivere . . . Sir Galahad:** knights of King Arthur's Round Table.
3. **transmigration of souls:** Hindu belief that the soul passes at death into another body.
4. **transposition . . . bodies:** idea that a person can be moved bodily to a different historical era.

5. **cicerone** [sis′ə rō′nē]: guide who explains the history and chief features of a place to sightseers.
6. **hauberk** [hô′burk]: medieval coat of arms.
7. **chain-mail:** flexible armor made of joined metal links.
8. **Cromwell's:** referring to Oliver Cromwell (1599–1658), an English revolutionary leader.
9. **Sir Thomas Malory's . . . book:** *Le Morte d'Arthur* (see page 551 in this book).

---

## GUIDED READING

### LITERAL QUESTION

**1a.** How does the narrator rate the stranger as a storyteller? (He indicates that the stranger made the old days seem real, as though he knew them personally.)

### INFERENTIAL QUESTION

**1b.** What purpose does the narrator's evaluation serve? (It establishes the stranger as a believable storyteller and suggests he got his material firsthand. It makes the reader ready to believe his future tales.)

### HOW SIR LAUNCELOT SLEW TWO GIANTS, AND MADE A CASTLE FREE.[10]

**1** Anon withal[11] came there upon him two great giants, well armed, all save the heads, with two horrible clubs in their hands. Sir Launcelot put his shield afore him, and put the stroke away of the one giant, and with his sword he clave[12] his head asunder. When his fellow saw that, he ran away as he were wood,[13] for fear of the horrible strokes, and Sir Launcelot after him with all his might, and smote him on the shoulder, and clave him to the middle. Then Sir Launcelot went into the hall, and there came afore him three score[14] ladies and damsels, and all kneeled unto him, and thanked God and him of their deliverance. For, sir, said they, the most part of us have been here this seven year their prisoners, and we have worked all manner of silk works for our meat, and we are all great gentlewomen born, and blessed be the time, knight, that ever thou wert born; for thou hast done the most worship that ever did knight in the world, that will we bear record, and we all pray you to tell us your name, that we may tell our friends who delivered us out of prison. Fair damsels, he said, my name is Sir Launcelot du Lake. And so he departed from them and betaught them unto God. And then he mounted upon his horse, and rode into many strange and wild countries, and through many waters and valleys, and evil[15] was he lodged.

---

10. This passage and the story that follows contain many words that are no longer in common use.
11. **Anon withal** [ə non′ with ôl′]: soon after that.
12. **clave**: split.
13. **wood**: insane.
14. **threescore**: sixty.
15. **evil**: poorly.

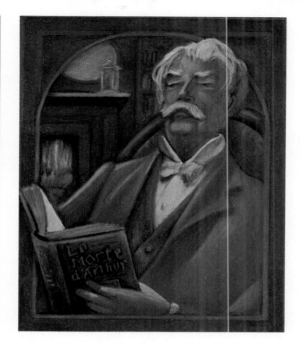

**2** As I laid the book down there was a knock at the door, and my stranger came in. I gave him a pipe and a chair and made him welcome, hoping always for his story. He drifted into it himself, in a quite simple and natural way:

### THE STRANGER'S HISTORY.

I am an American. I was born and reared in Hartford, in the State of Connecticut—anyway, **3** just over the river, in the country. So I am a Yankee of the Yankees—and practical; yes, and nearly barren of sentiment, I suppose—or poetry, in other words. My father was a blacksmith, my uncle was a horse doctor, and I was both, along at first. Then I went over to the great arms factory and learned my real trade; learned all there was to it; learned to make everything; guns, revolvers, cannon, boilers, engines, all sorts of labor-saving machinery. Why, I could make anything a body wanted—anything in the world, it didn't make

*A Connecticut Yankee in King Arthur's Court* **667**

---

## GUIDED READING

### LITERAL QUESTIONS

**1a.** What qualities are indirectly praised in the story about Sir Launcelot? (superhuman bravery and strength, protectiveness toward ladies, a spirit of adventure)

**2a.** How does the narrator reveal he is anxious to hear the Yankee's story? (He makes him welcome and says that he was "hoping always for his story.")

### INFERENTIAL QUESTIONS

**1b.** Why is it important to have this authentic version of an Arthurian tale at the beginning? (It introduces us to the values of King Arthur's England.)

**2b.** How does the narrator's attitude add interest to the story? (His interest makes the reader remember the reason for this interest: that the Yankee claims to have been transposed into an ancient epoch.)

- The Yankee tells how he was knocked out by a crowbar.
- Upon awakening he meets a knight, and they ride to Camelot.
- The Yankee gives the narrator a manuscript.

**1 VOCABULARY: DICTION**

The Yankee's diction contains many down-to-earth, colloquial expressions. Besides adding humor to his narrative, this language establishes him as an ordinary, plain-spoken man.

**2 SATIRE**

Twain satirizes the rough-and-ready nineteenth century by his description of the Yankee's fight with Hercules. This fight parallels the jousting of the knights and suggests that the romantic attitude toward aggression lives, although knights have vanished.

**3 PLOT: EXPOSITION**

The Yankee explains how he melted from his own time into the days of King Arthur. The dream-like landscape eases the reader into Arthur's world.

**4 DIALOGUE**

The exchange creates humor and characterizes both the Yankee and the knight: The Yankee speaks in the racy, informal style of his day, while the knight uses the highly formal language of an earlier age.

**5 PLOT: EXPOSITION**

The introduction of the ancient manuscript allows the Yankee's tale to be told in the first person and establishes its authenticity.

---

1 any difference what; and if there wasn't any quick new-fangled way to make a thing, I could invent one—and do it as easy as rolling off a log. I became head superintendent; had a couple of thousand men under me.

2 Well, a man like that is a man that is full of fight—that goes without saying. With a couple of thousand rough men under one, one has plenty of that sort of amusement. I had, anyway. At last I met my match, and I got my dose. It was during a misunderstanding conducted with crowbars with a fellow we used to call Hercules.[16] He laid me out with a crusher alongside the head that made everything crack, and seemed to spring every joint in my skull and make it overlap its neighbor. Then the world went out in darkness, and I didn't feel anything more, and didn't know anything at all—at least for a while.

3 When I came to again, I was sitting under an oak tree, on the grass, with a whole beautiful and broad country landscape all to myself—nearly. Not entirely; for there was a fellow on a horse, looking down at me—a fellow fresh out of a picture book. He was in old-time iron armor from head to heel, with a helmet on his head the shape of a nail keg with slits in it; and he had a shield, and a sword, and a prodigious spear; and his horse had armor on, too, and a steel horn projecting from his forehead, and gorgeous red and green silk trappings that hung down all around him like a bed quilt, nearly to the ground.

4 "Fair sir, will ye just?" said this fellow.

"Will I which?"

"Will ye try a passage of arms for land or lady or for—"

"What are you giving me?" I said. "Get along back to your circus, or I'll report you."

Now what does this man do but fall back a couple of hundred yards and then come rushing at me as hard as he could tear, with his nail keg bent down nearly to his horse's neck and his long spear pointed straight ahead. I saw he meant business, so I was up the tree when he arrived.

He allowed that I was his property, the captive of his spear, so I judged it best to humor him. We fixed up an agreement whereby I was to go with him and he was not to hurt me. We marched comfortably along, through glades and over brooks which I could not remember to have seen before—which puzzled me and made me wonder—and yet we did not come to any circus or sign of a circus. So I gave up the idea of a circus, and concluded he was from an asylum. But we never came to any asylum—so I was up a stump, as you may say. I asked him how far we were from Hartford. He said he had never heard of the place; which I took to be a lie, but allowed it to go at that. At the end of an hour we saw a faraway town sleeping in a valley by a winding river; and beyond it on a hill, a vast gray fortress, with towers and turrets, the first I had ever seen out of a picture.

"Bridgeport?"[17] said I, pointing.

"Camelot,"[18] said he.

5 My stranger had been showing signs of sleepiness. He caught himself nodding, now, and smiled one of those pathetic, obsolete smiles of his, and said:

"I find I can't go on; but come with me, I've got it all written out, and you can read it if you like."

In his chamber, he said: "First, I kept a journal; then by and by, after years, I took the journal and turned it into a book. How long ago that was!"

He handed me his manuscript, and pointed out the place where I should begin:

"Begin here—I've already told you what goes before." He was steeped in drowsiness by

---

16. **Hercules** [hur′kyə lēz′]: In Greek and Roman mythology, a hero celebrated for his great strength.

17. **Bridgeport:** city in Connecticut.
18. **Camelot:** legendary site of King Arthur's Court.

---

## GUIDED READING

**LITERAL QUESTIONS**

**1a.** How does the Yankee act when the knight charges him? (He quickly climbs a tree.)

**2a.** What explanation does the Yankee give himself as to why the knight behaves in such a strange manner? (First he thinks that the knight belongs to a circus; then he decides that the knight has escaped from an insane asylum.)

**INFERENTIAL QUESTIONS**

**1b.** Why is this action satiric? (The chivalric code values bravery; by doing the expedient rather than the brave thing, the Yankee satirizes these values.)

**2b.** How do these explanations add ironic humor? (The Yankee thinks the knight is in costume and acting strange. Actually, the knight fits into his surroundings, while the Yankee is strangely dressed and "crazy," given the time and place.)

AT A GLANCE

- The narrator examines the book and begins to read.
- The book describes Camelot and records the startled reaction of a young girl to the Yankee.

this time. As I went out at his door I heard him murmur sleepily: "Give you good den,[19] fair sir."

I sat down by my fire and examined my treasure. The first part of it—the great bulk of it—was parchment, and yellow with age. I scanned a leaf particularly and saw that it was a palimpsest.[20] Under the old dim writing of the Yankee historian appeared traces of a penmanship which was older and dimmer still—Latin words and sentences. I turned to the place indicated by my stranger and began to read—as follows.

## 2. Camelot

"Camelot—Camelot," said I to myself. "I don't seem to remember hearing of it before. Name of the asylum, likely."

---

19. **Give . . . den:** archaic expression for "fare well."
20. **palimpsest** [pal′imp sest′]: parchment written over several times, with the previous texts still partly visible.

**3** It was a soft, reposeful summer landscape, as lovely as a dream, and as lonesome as Sunday. The air was full of the smell of flowers, and the buzzing of insects, and the twittering of birds, and there were no people, no wagons, there was no stir of life, nothing going on. The road was mainly a winding path with hoofprints in it, and now and then a faint trace of wheels on either side in the grass—wheels that apparently had a tire as broad as one's hand.

Presently a fair slip of a girl, about ten years old, with a cataract of golden hair streaming down over her shoulders, came along. Around her head she wore a hoop of flame-red poppies. It was as sweet an outfit as ever I saw. The circus man paid no attention to her; didn't even seem to see her. And she—she was no more startled at his fantastic makeup than if she was used to his like every day of her life. But when she happened to notice me, *then* there was a change! Up went her hands, and she was turned to stone. And there she stood gazing, in a sort of stupefied

*A Connecticut Yankee in King Arthur's Court* **669**

**1 VOCABULARY: WORD CHOICE**

The technical word *palimpsest* and the description of the document—parchment, yellow with age, faded writing, Latin—suggests its antiquity and authenticity.

**2 TONE**

By mistaking Camelot for an insane asylum, the Yankee prepares us for Twain's satiric view of Arthur's court, a perspective that will question the values of a much-idealized age. Of course, the Yankee is also showing his own ignorance of history by not recognizing Camelot.

**3 SETTING**

The setting re-creates the rural peace of an earlier day. Many readers in the bustling nineteenth century would see this landscape as idyllic, but the Yankee points out the price of peace: boredom—*nothing going on.*

## GUIDED READING

### LITERAL QUESTION

**1a.** Who are the two first-person narrators of this section of the novel? (The narrator who begins the story describes the Yankee's document; the novel reproduces the contents of the document, narrated in the first person by the Yankee.)

### INFERENTIAL QUESTION

**1b.** Why do you think Twain uses two first-person narrators? (He creates a frame for the Yankee's outlandish adventures by beginning in a more realistic situation, with the first narrator. Shifting over to the Yankee's narration allows us to have his "modern" perspective on Arthur's world.)

- They pass through Camelot, and the Yankee observes the people and customs of the place.
- The Yankee, confused about where he is, talks to some people he meets.
- He meets a page.

**1 MAIN IDEA**

The Yankee reveals his attitude toward a hierarchical social system in which the aristocracy haughtily take the homage of the common people for granted.

**2 MOOD**

The music, dress, and setting create a mood of richness and color. The contrast with the description of the common people furthers the satire of the aristocracy.

**3 STYLE: HUMOR**

The joke plays on the Yankee's fear he's fallen into a lunatic asylum. He makes fun of the archaic language of the Arthurian legends and adds humor to the novel with his own slangy idiom and plain speaking.

**4 STYLE: FIGURATIVE LANGUAGE**

A simile describing the page in orange tights as a "forked carrot" suggests the form-fitting costume of the day. The originality of the simile makes for humor as well as an accurate image.

**5 STYLE: HUMOR**

Twain uses a pun to create humor, playing on the double meaning of page as a position at court and a part of a book. The pun suggests the youth and slightness of the boy.

---

fascination, till we turned a corner of the wood and were lost to her view.

As we approached the town, signs of life began to appear. At intervals we passed a wretched cabin, with a thatched roof, and about it small fields and garden patches in an indifferent state of cultivation. There were people, too; brawny men, with long, coarse, uncombed hair that hung down over their faces and made them look like animals. They and the women, as a rule, wore a coarse tow-linen robe that came well below the knee, and a rude sort of sandals, and many wore an iron collar. All of these people stared at me, talked about me, ran into the huts and fetched out their families to gape at me; but **1** nobody ever noticed that other fellow, except to make him humble salutation and get no response for their pains.

In the town were some substantial windowless houses of stone scattered among a wilderness of thatched cabins; the streets were mere crooked alleys, and unpaved; troops of dogs and children played in the sun and made life and noise; hogs roamed and rooted contentedly about, and one of them lay in a reeking wallow in the middle of the main thoroughfare and **2** suckled her family. Presently there was a distant blare of military music; it came nearer, still nearer, and soon a noble cavalcade wound into view, glorious with plumed helmets and flashing mail and flaunting banners and rich doublets[21] and horsecloths and gilded spearheads; and through the muck and swine, and joyous dogs, and shabby huts it took its gallant way, and in its wake we followed. Followed through one winding alley and then another—and climbing, always climbing—till at last we gained the breezy height where the huge castle stood. There was an exchange of bugle blasts; then a parley from the walls, and then the great gates were flung open, the drawbridge was lowered,

---

21. **doublets:** close-fitting, waist-length jackets, worn in the Middle Ages.

and the head of the cavalcade swept forward under the frowning arches; and we, following, soon found ourselves in a great paved court, with towers and turrets stretching up into the blue air on all the four sides; and all about us the dismount was going on, and much greeting and ceremony, and running to-and-fro, and a gay display of moving and intermingling colors, and an altogether pleasant stir and noise and confusion.

### 3. King Arthur's Court

The moment I got a chance I slipped aside privately and touched an ancient common looking man on the shoulder and said, in an insinuating, confidential way—

**3** "Friend, do me a kindness. Do you belong to the asylum, or are you just here on a visit or something like that?"

He looked me over stupidly, and said—

"Marry, fair, sir, me seemeth—"

"That will do," I said; "I reckon you are a patient."

I moved away, cogitating,[22] and at the same time keeping an eye out for any chance passenger in his right mind that might come along and give me some light. I judged I had found **4** one, presently. This was an airy slim boy in shrimp-colored tights that made him look like a forked carrot; the rest of his gear was blue silk and dainty laces and ruffles; and he had long yellow curls, and wore a plumed pink satin cap **5** tilted complacently over his ear. By his look, he was good-natured; he said he had come for me, and informed me that he was a page.

"Go 'long," I said; "you ain't more than a paragraph."

It was pretty severe, but I was nettled. However, it never phazed him. He began to talk and laugh, in happy, thoughtless, boyish fashion, as we walked along, and made himself old

---

22. **cogitating:** thinking seriously and deeply.

---

## *GUIDED READING*

**LITERAL QUESTIONS**

**1a.** What does the Yankee observe about the common people of Arthur's time? (Their living conditions are poor, their dress is coarse, their manners are crude, and they are subservient to the upper classes.)

**2a.** With whom does the Yankee check his impressions as soon as he gets the chance? (*an ancient common looking man*)

**INFERENTIAL QUESTIONS**

**1b.** Why do you think Twain is careful to include these descriptions and observations? (He makes the point that Malory deals only with the upper classes. He wants to show what life was like for the less privileged of the day.)

**2b.** What does it show about the Yankee's attitudes that he chooses such a person? (He trusts the common sense and truthfulness of a common man above the knights.)

friends with me at once; asked me all sorts of questions about myself and about my clothes, but never waited for an answer—always chattered straight ahead, as if he didn't know he had asked a question and wasn't expecting any reply, until at last he happened to mention that he was born in the beginning of the year 513.

It made the cold chills creep over me! I stopped, and said, a little faintly:

1 "Maybe I didn't hear you just right. Say it again—and say it slow. What year was it?"

"Five thirteen."

"Five thirteen! You don't look it! Come, my boy, I am a stranger and friendless: be honest and honorable with me. Are you in your right mind?"

He said he was.

"Are these other people in their right minds?"

He said they were.

"And this isn't an asylum? I mean, it isn't a place where they cure crazy people?"

He said it wasn't.

"Well, then," I said, "either I am a lunatic, or something just as awful has happened. Now tell me, honest and true, where am I?"

"IN KING ARTHUR'S COURT."

I waited a minute, to let that idea shudder its way home, and then said:

"And according to your notions, what year is it now?"

"Five twenty-eight—nineteenth of June."

I felt a mournful sinking at the heart, and muttered: "I shall never see my friends again—never, never again. They will not be born for more than thirteen hundred years yet." *Something* in me seemed to believe him—my consciousness, as you may say; but my reason didn't. My reason straightway began to clamor; that was natural. I didn't know how to go about satisfying it. But all of a sudden I stumbled on the very thing, just by luck. I knew that the only total eclipse of the sun in the first half of the sixth century occurred on the twenty-first of

2 June, A.D. 528, and began at three minutes after twelve noon. I also knew that no total eclipse of the sun was due in what to *me* was the present year—*i.e.,* 1879. So, if I could keep my anxiety and curiosity from eating the heart out of me for forty-eight hours, I should then find out for certain whether this boy was telling me the truth or not.

Wherefore, being a practical Connecticut man, I now shoved this whole problem clear out of my mind. One thing at a time, is my motto—and just play that thing for all it is worth. I made up my mind to two things; if it was still the nineteenth century and I was among lunatics and couldn't get away, I would presently boss that 3 asylum or know the reason why; and if on the other hand it was really the sixth century, all right, I would boss the whole country inside of three months; for I judged I would have the start of the best-educated man in the kingdom by a matter of thirteen hundred years and upwards. I'm not a man to waste time after my mind's made up and there's work on hand; so I said to the page—

"Now, Clarence, my boy—if that might happen to be your name—What is the name of that apparition that brought me here?"

"My master and thine? That is the good knight and great lord Sir Kay the Seneschal,[23] foster brother to our liege the king."

"Very good; go on, tell me everything."

He made a long story of it; but the part that 4 had immediate interest for me was this. He said I was Sir Kay's prisoner, and that in the due course of custom I would be flung into a dungeon and left there on scant commons[24] until my friends ransomed me—unless I chanced to rot, first. The page said, further, that dinner was about ended in the great hall by this time, and that as soon as the sociability should begin, Sir

---

23. **Seneschal** [sen′ə shəl]: official in charge of a royal or noble household.
24. **commons**: food rations.

*A Connecticut Yankee in King Arthur's Court* 671

AT A GLANCE
- The page claims it's the year A.D. 528.
- The Yankee doubts and believes at the same time.
- The Yankee makes up his mind that whatever his predicament, he'll be the boss.
- The page tells him he'll be thrown in the dungeon.

1 **STYLE: DIALOGUE**

The page claims he was born in A.D. 513; the Yankee's reply creates humor by taking a common social phrase and applying it to an exaggerated situation. The dialogue also provides information about the exact date of the Yankee's visit.

2 **FORESHADOWING**

The Yankee hits upon the dates of eclipses as a way to be sure which century he's really in. His information about eclipses also serves to foreshadow the important use to which he puts it later in the novel.

3 **VIEWPOINT**

The Yankee assumes his educational and scientific superiority will make him a leader. This attitude shows the limitations of his nineteenth-century view of progress.

4 **MAIN IDEA**

Twain points out the cruelty of the Middle Ages. The Yankee is innocent of anything but self-preservation, yet he is to be thrown in the dungeon forever. This penalty illustrates the lack of social justice.

---

*GUIDED READING*

**LITERAL QUESTIONS**

**1a.** How does the Yankee decide he'll be able to tell whether he's in the nineteenth century or the sixth? (He knows the dates of eclipses in each century, and if an eclipse occurs tomorrow, he will know it's the sixth century.)

**2a.** What two things does the Yankee make up his mind to? (If he's in an asylum and can't escape, he'll be the boss of it; if he's in the sixth century, he'll be boss of the country in three months.)

**INFERENTIAL QUESTIONS**

**1b.** Why is this method appropriate to the Yankee? (He is drawn as having technical, scientific knowledge, and it is possible he'd have such information at his command.)

**2b.** What does this decision reveal about his character? (that he's aggressive, ambitious, and confident of his own superiority)

- The Yankee is taken before the knights.
- He observes the manners and customs of the Round Table.

## 1 CHARACTERIZATION

Beneath the bravery and nobility of Arthur's knights, Twain shows the boasting, authoritarianism, and cruelty. His satire reveals the dark side of what looks so noble and picturesque in Malory.

## 2 SETTING

Despite his criticism of Arthur's England, Twain recognizes the color and grace of the aristocracy. But this veneer of gracious living only makes the reality of an often crude age more glaring.

## 3 STYLE: SATIRE

Twain contrasts their crudity and coarseness with the highly polished manners traditionally attributed to Arthur's court.

## 4 CHARACTERIZATION

Twain's satire is often biting but subtle. Here he ironically comments on the attractive, lovable qualities of the knights, right after he has revealed them as braggarts and cruel thugs.

---

Kay would have me in and exhibit me before King Arthur and his illustrious knights seated at
**1** the Table Round, and would brag about his exploit in capturing me, and would probably exaggerate the facts a little, but it wouldn't be good form for me to correct him, and not over safe, either; and when I was done being exhibited, then ho for the dungeon; but he, Clarence, would find a way to come and see me every now and then, and cheer me up, and help me get word to my friends.

Get word to my friends! I thanked him; I couldn't do less; and about this time a lackey came to say I was wanted; so Clarence led me in and took me off to one side and sat down by me.

Well, it was a curious kind of spectacle, and interesting. It was an immense place, and full of loud contrasts. It was very, very lofty; so lofty that the banners depending from the arched beams and girders away up there floated in a sort of twilight; there was a stone-railed gallery at each end, high up, with musicians in the one, and women, clothed in stunning colors, in the other. The floor was of big stone flags laid in black and white squares, rather battered by age and use, and needing repair. As to ornament, there wasn't any, strictly speaking; though on the walls hung some huge tapestries; battle pieces, they were, with horses shaped like those which children cut out of paper or create in gingerbread. There was a fireplace big enough to camp in. Along the walls stood men-at-arms, in breastplate, rigid as statues; and that is what they looked like.

**2** In the middle of this groined and vaulted[25] public square was an oaken table which they called the Table Round. It was as large as a circus ring; and around it sat a great company of men dressed in such various and splendid colors that it hurt one's eyes to look at them. They wore their plumed hats, right along, except that

---

25. **groined and vaulted:** having a ceiling formed by intersecting arches.

---

whenever one addressed himself directly to the king, he lifted his hat a trifle just as he was begin-
**3** ning his remark. There was about an average of two dogs to one man; and these sat in expectant attitudes till a spent bone was flung to them, and then they went for it by brigades and divisions, with a rush, and there ensued a fight which filled the prospect with a tumultuous chaos of plunging heads and bodies and flashing tails. The men rose, sometimes, to observe it the better and bet on it, and the ladies and the musicians stretched themselves out over their balusters[26] with the same object.

As a rule the speech and behavior of these people were gracious and courtly; and I noticed that they were good and serious listeners when anybody was telling anything—I mean in a dogfightless interval.

## 4. Knights of the Table Round

**4** Mainly the Round Table talk was monologues —narrative accounts of the adventures in which these prisoners were captured and their friends and backers killed and stripped of their steeds and armor. Yet there was something very engaging about these great simplehearted creatures, something attractive and lovable.

There was a fine manliness observable in

---

26. **balusters** [bal'əs tərz]: upright supports for the railing of a balcony or staircase.

---

## GUIDED READING

### LITERAL QUESTIONS

**1a.** What does Clarence promise to do for the Yankee? (He promises to come see him in the dungeon and help him get word to his friends.)

**2a.** How does the Yankee characterize the conversation at the Round Table? (He says it's mostly monologues—knights telling about their exploits.)

### INFERENTIAL QUESTIONS

**1b.** What does this deed show about real nobility at Arthur's court? (A lowly page, not the noble knights of the Round Table, has compassion and takes risks to help another. Nobility exists, but not in the expected places.)

**2b.** What light does this description throw on the character of the knights? (They are braggarts and bullies; the deeds of which they brag are cruel and destructive.)

almost every face; and in some a certain loftiness and sweetness that rebuked your belittling criticisms and stilled them. A most noble benignity and purity reposed in the countenance of him they called Sir Galahad, and likewise in the king's also; and there was majesty and greatness in the giant frame and high bearing of Sir Launcelot of the Lake.

A very old and white-bearded man, clothed in a flowing black gown, was standing at the table, swaying his ancient head and surveying the company with his watery and wandering eye.

"Marry,[27] we shall have it again," sighed the boy; "that same old weary tale that he hath told a thousand times in the same words."

"Who is it?"

"Merlin, the mighty liar and magician, perdition singe him for the weariness he worketh with his one tale! But that men fear him for that he hath the storms and the lightnings at his beck and call, they would have dug his entrails out these many years ago to get at that tale and squelch it."

The old man began his tale; and presently the lad was asleep; so also were the dogs, and the court, the lackeys, and the files of men-at-arms. The droning voice droned on; a soft snoring arose on all sides. Some heads were bowed upon folded arms, some lay back with open mouths

---

27. **Marry:** exclamation of agreement, surprise, or anger.

---

that issued unconscious music; it was a tranquil scene, and restful to the weary eye and the jaded spirit.

Sir Dinadan was the first to awake, and he soon roused the rest with a practical joke of a sufficiently poor quality. He tied some metal mugs to a dog's tail and turned him loose, and he tore around and around the place in a frenzy of fright, with all the other dogs bellowing after him and battering and crashing against everything that came in their way, at which every man and woman of the multitude laughed till the tears flowed, and some fell out of their chairs and wallowed on the floor in ecstasy.

Sir Kay arose and began to fire up on his history-mill, with me for fuel. It was time for me to feel serious, and I did. Sir Kay told how he had encountered me in a far land of barbarians, who all wore the same ridiculous garb that I did—a garb that was a work of enchantment, and intended to make the wearer secure from hurt by human hands. However, he had nullified the force of the enchantment by prayer, and had killed my thirteen knights in a three-hours' battle, and taken me prisoner, sparing my life in order that so strange a curiosity as I was might be exhibited to the wonder and admiration of the king and the court. He spoke of me all the time, in the blandest way, as "this prodigious giant," and "this horrible sky-towering monster," and "this tusked and taloned man-devouring ogre"; and everybody took in all this

*A Connecticut Yankee in King Arthur's Court*  **673**

---

## GUIDED READING

### LITERAL QUESTIONS

**1a.** How is Merlin described? (He wears a flowing black gown, is very old with a white beard and watery eyes; he tells the same story over and over.)

**2a.** What kind of exaggerations does Sir Kay use in his tale? (He suggests that he has overcome a magic spell, not just a person, and that the Yankee is some superhuman monster instead of an ordinary man who ran up a tree to escape him.)

### INFERENTIAL QUESTIONS

**1b.** What does this description imply about Merlin? (It suggests he has become senile and boring.)

**2b.** What is the purpose of these exaggerations? (Sir Kay makes himself look better by exaggerating his feat; Twain uses them to suggest that many of the noble deeds passed down to us are probably just as exaggerated.)

AT A GLANCE

- Sir Kay finishes his story.
- The Yankee is imprisoned.
- Clarence visits the dungeon and tells him he is to be burned.

## 1 SETTING

The dungeon is a "dark and narrow cell" with rats, and moldy straw to sleep on. There is little food. These conditions underscore the cruelty and lack of social justice typical of that era.

## 2 PLOT: EPISODE

With the Yankee's capture and imprisonment, a new episode begins: the Yankee's scheme to escape death. Twain's episodic narrative parodies the episodic form used by Malory.

## 3 FLAT CHARACTER

The Yankee says Clarence is "nothing but a work of the imagination." Twain's people are flat—cartoon characters; he manipulates them easily for satiric effect.

bosh in the naïvest way, and never smiled or seemed to notice that there was any discrepancy between these watered statistics and me. He said that in trying to escape from him I sprang into the top of a tree two hundred cubits high at a single bound, but he dislodged me with a stone the size of a cow, which "all-to brast"[28] the most of my bones, and then swore me to appear at Arthur's court for sentence. He ended by condemning me to die at noon on the twenty-first; and was so little concerned about it that he stopped to yawn before he named the date.

1 Finally I was carried off. I was shoved into a dark and narrow cell in a dungeon, with some scant remnants for dinner, some moldy straw for a bed, and no end of rats for company.

---

28. **brast:** burst.

**674** *The Novel*

### 5. An Inspiration

I was so tired that even my fears were not able to keep me awake long.

When I next came to myself, I seemed to have been asleep a very long time. My first thought was, "Well, what an astonishing dream I've had!"

2 But just then I heard the harsh music of rusty chains and bolts, a light flashed in my eyes, and that butterfly, Clarence, stood before me! I gasped with surprise; my breath almost got away from me.

"What!" I said, "you here yet? Go along with the rest of the dream! scatter!"

But he only laughed, in his lighthearted way, and fell to making fun of my sorry plight.

3 "All right," I said resignedly, "let the dream go on; I'm in no hurry."

"Prithee[29] what dream?"

"What dream? Why, the dream that I am in Arthur's court—a person who never existed; and that I am talking to you, who are nothing but a work of the imagination."

"Oh, la, indeed! And is it a dream that you're to be burned tomorrow? Ho-ho—answer me that!"

The shock that went through me was distressing. I now began to reason that my situation was in the last degree serious, dream or no dream. So I said beseechingly:

"Ah, Clarence, good boy, only friend I've got—for you *are* my friend, aren't you—don't fail me; help me to devise some way of escaping from this place!"

"Now do but hear thyself! Escape? Why, man, the corridors are in guard and keep of men-at-arms."

"No doubt, no doubt. But how many, Clarence? Not many, I hope?"

"Full a score. One may not hope to escape." After a pause—hesitatingly: "and there be other reasons—and weightier."

---

29. **Prithee:** I pray thee; please.

---

## GUIDED READING

### LITERAL QUESTIONS

**1a.** What does Sir Kay do before he names the date of the Yankee's death? (yawns)

**2a.** What is the Yankee's first thought when he wakes up in the dungeon? (He thinks his experiences have all been an astonishing dream.)

### INFERENTIAL QUESTIONS

**1b.** How does this detail satirize Arthur's court? (It reveals a casual attitude toward killing.)

**2b.** How does this thought add to the realism of the novel? (It contrasts sharply with the fantasy and shows the Yankee as a rational, skeptical person who assumes that these fantastic events cannot really be happening to him.)

"Other ones? What are they?"

He hesitated, pulled one way by desire, the other way by fear; then he stole to the door and peeped out, listening; and finally crept close to me and put his mouth to my ear and told me his fearful news in a whisper.

"Merlin, in his malice, has woven a spell about this dungeon, and there bides not the man in these kingdoms that would be desperate enough to essay to cross its lines with you! Now God pity me, I have told it!"

I laughed the only really refreshing laugh I had had for some time; and shouted—

"Merlin has wrought a spell! *Merlin,* for-sooth![30] That cheap old humbug. Bosh, pure bosh, the silliest bosh in the world!"

But Clarence had slumped to his knees, and he was like to go out of his mind with fright.

"Oh, beware! These are awful words! Any moment these walls may crumble upon us if you say such things. Oh call them back before it is too late!"

Now this strange exhibition gave me a good idea and set me to thinking. If everybody about here was so honestly and sincerely afraid of Merlin's pretended magic as Clarence was, certainly a superior man like me ought to be shrewd enough to contrive some way to take advantage of such a state of things. I went on thinking, and worked out a plan. Then I said:

"Get up. Pull yourself together; look me in the eye. Do you know why I laughed?"

"No—but for our blessed Lady's sake, do it no more."

"Well, I'll tell you why I laughed. Because I'm a magician myself."

"Thou!" The boy recoiled a step, and caught his breath, for the thing hit him rather sudden; but the aspect which he took on was very, very respectful. I resumed:

"I've known Merlin seven hundred years, and he—"

30. **forsooth:** indeed; in truth.

"Seven hun—"

"Don't interrupt me. He has died and come alive again thirteen times, and traveled under a new name every time: Smith, Jones, Robinson, Jackson, Peters, Haskins, Merlin. He is always blethering around in my way, everywhere I go; he makes me tired. He don't amount to shucks, as a magician; knows some of the old common tricks, but has never got beyond the rudiments, and never will. Now look here, Clarence, I want you to get word to the king that I am a magician myself—and the Supreme Grand High-yu-Muckamuck and head of the tribe, at that; and I want him to be made to understand that I am just quietly arranging a little calamity here that will make the fur fly in these realms if Sir Kay's project is carried out and any harm comes to me. Will you get that to the king for me?"

The poor boy was in such a state that he could hardly answer me. But he promised everything; and on my side he made me promise over and over again that I would remain his friend, and never turn against him or cast any enchantments upon him. Then he worked his way out, staying himself with his hand along the wall, like a sick person.

It occurred to me that I had made a blunder: I had sent the boy off to alarm his betters with a threat—intending to invent a calamity at my leisure. Suppose I should be asked to name my calamity? Yes, I had made a blunder; I ought to have invented my calamity first. "What shall I do? what can I say, to gain a little time? There's a footstep—they're coming! If I had only just a moment to think. . . . Good, I've got it. I'm all right."

You see, it was the eclipse. It came into my mind, in the nick of time, how Columbus, or Cortez,[31] or one of those people, played an eclipse as a saving trump[32] once, on some

31. **Cortez** [kôr tez′]: Hernando Cortez (1485–1547), Spanish conqueror of Mexico.
32. **trump:** advantage held in reserve until needed.

*A Connecticut Yankee in King Arthur's Court* **675**

AT A GLANCE

- Merlin says he has put a spell on the Yankee.
- The Yankee pretends to be a magician; he sends Clarence off to threaten a "calamity" if he's not released.
- He realizes he has to name the calamity.

**1 PLOT: CONFLICT**

Clarence shows internal conflict—he wants to help the Yankee but is afraid of Merlin's magic. His terror indicates the destructive hold of superstition during the Middle Ages.

**2 THEME**

The Yankee's comments reveal Twain's negative attitude toward magic and superstition. He shares the Yankee's nineteenth-century belief in science and rationality.

**3 PLOT: RISING ACTION**

The Yankee's plan increases the pace and tension of the story. This major shift in plot mirrors a shift of ideas: The satire now focuses on the superstition of Arthur's time.

**4 STYLE: DICTION**

The Yankee uses the slangy vernacular of the nineteenth century to speak of the deepest mystery of the Middle Ages. This language reveals his debunking attitude toward magic and makes the reader laugh at what is treated with high seriousness in Arthurian legend.

## GUIDED READING

### LITERAL QUESTIONS

**1a.** When the Yankee asks him to take a message to the king, what does Clarence promise and what does he ask in return? (The boy promises to help in every way and asks the Yankee to be his friend and never work magic on him.)

**2a.** What sort of "blunder" does the Yankee make? (He threatens a calamity but doesn't know exactly what kind of "magic" to work.)

### INFERENTIAL QUESTIONS

**1b.** What does this show about the power of magic in Arthur's time? (Magic had great power to compel fear and respect and influence behavior.)

**2b.** Why is this threat a blunder? (The knights will insist on some sort of demonstration of magic power and the Yankee has not yet thought of anything to do.)

- Merlin challenges the Yankee to name the calamity.
- The Yankee says he will "blot out the sun."
- Then he discovers that he is to be burnt a day early.

## 1 STYLE: POETIC LANGUAGE

Using repetition, parallel structure, and archaic word choice, the Yankee invents a medieval-sounding style of speaking.

## 2 CHARACTERIZATION

The Yankee likes to be admired and enjoys tricking people. Twain seems to admire the Yankee's canny ingenuity, while satirizing his egotism and ambition.

## 3 PLOT: CONFLICT

The change creates conflict for the Yankee: He can't work "magic" until the eclipse, and yet magic is the only way out of his predicament.

savages, and I saw my chance. I could play it myself, now.

Clarence came in, subdued, distressed, and said:

"I hasted the message to our liege the king, and straightway he had me to his presence. He was frighted even to the marrow, but in the end, Merlin, scoffing, said, 'Wherefore hath he not *named* his brave calamity? Verily it is because he cannot.' This thrust did in a most sudden sort close the king's mouth, and he could offer naught to turn the argument. He prayeth you to consider his perplexed case, and name the calamity—if so be you have determined the nature of it and the time of its coming. Prithee delay not; oh, be thou wise—name the calamity!"

I allowed silence to accumulate while I got my impressiveness together, and then said:

"How long have I been shut up in this hole?"

"Ye were shut up when yesterday was well spent. It is nine of the morning now."

"No! Then I have slept well, sure enough. Nine in the morning now! And yet it is the very complexion of midnight, to a shade. This is the 20th, then?"

"The 20th—yes."

"And I am to be burned alive tomorrow." The boy shuddered.

"At what hour?"

"At high noon."

"Now then, I will tell you what to say." I paused, and stood over that cowering lad a whole minute in awful silence; then in a voice deep, measured, charged with doom, I began:

"Go back and tell the king that at that hour I will smother the whole world in the dead blackness of midnight; I will blot out the sun, and he shall never shine again; the fruits of the earth shall rot for lack of light and warmth, and the peoples of the earth shall famish and die, to the last man!"

I had to carry the boy out myself, he sunk into such a collapse. I handed him over to the soldiers, and went back.

### 6. The Eclipse

I said to myself that my eclipse would be sure to save me, and make me the greatest man in the kingdom besides. I was as happy a man as there was in the world. I was even impatient for tomorrow to come, I so wanted to gather in that great triumph and be the center of all the nation's wonder and reverence.

Meantime there was one thing which had got pushed into the background of my mind. That was the half conviction that when the nature of my proposed calamity should be reported to those superstitious people, they would want to compromise. So, by and by when I heard footsteps coming, I said to myself, "As sure as anything, it's the compromise. Well, if it is good, all right, I will accept; but if it isn't, I mean to stand my ground and play my hand for all it is worth."

The door opened, and some men-at-arms appeared. The leader said—

"The stake is ready. Come!"

The stake! The strength went out of me, and I almost fell down.

"But this is a mistake—the execution is tomorrow."

"Order changed; been set forward a day. Haste thee!"

I was lost. There was no help for me. I was dazed, stupefied; the soldiers took hold of me, and pulled me along with them, out of the cell and along the maze of underground corridors, and finally into the fierce glare of daylight and the upper world. As we stepped into the vast inclosed court of the castle I got a shock; for the first thing I saw was the stake, standing in the center, and near it the piled fagots and a monk. On all four sides of the court the seated multitudes rose rank above rank, forming sloping terraces that were rich with color. The king and the queen sat in their thrones, the most conspicuous figures there, of course.

Clarence slipped from some place of concealment and was pouring news into my ear, his eyes

---

## GUIDED READING

### LITERAL QUESTIONS

**1a.** What did the Yankee ask Clarence when told to name the "calamity"? *(How long have I been shut up in this hole?)*

**2a.** What happens to make the Yankee say "I was lost"? *(The date of his burning at the stake is moved a day earlier.)*

### INFERENTIAL QUESTIONS

**1b.** Why does he ask this particular question? (He needs to know the date so that he can figure out when the eclipse will take place.)

**2b.** Why is this change such a catastrophe for him? (He needs the eclipse in order to prove himself as a magician, but moving his execution back prevents him from using the eclipse.)

beaming with triumph and gladness. He said:

"'Tis through *me* the change was wrought! When I revealed to them the calamity in store, and saw how mighty was the terror it did engender, then saw I also that this was the time to strike! Wherefore I diligently pretended that your power against the sun could not reach its full until the morrow; and so if any would save the sun and the world, you must be slain today, whilst your enchantments are but in the weaving and lack potency. Odsbodikins, it was but a dull lie, but you should have seen them seize it and swallow it. You will not need to do the sun a *real* hurt—only make a little darkness—only the littlest little darkness, mind, and cease with that. It will be sufficient. With the falling of the first shadow of that darkness you shall see them go mad with fear; and they will set you free and make you great! Go to thy triumph, now! But remember—ah, good friend, I implore thee remember my supplication, and do the blessed sun no hurt. For *my* sake, thy true friend."

I choked out some words through my grief and misery; as much as to say I would spare the sun; I had not the heart to tell him his good-hearted foolishness had ruined me and sent me to my death.

As the soldiers assisted me across the court the stillness was so profound that if I had been blindfold I should have supposed I was in a solitude instead of walled in by four thousand people. There was not a movement perceptible in those masses of humanity; they were as rigid as stone images, and as pale; and dread sat upon every countenance. This hush continued while I was being chained to the stake; it still continued while the fagots were carefully and tediously piled about my ankles, my knees, my thighs, my body. Then there was a pause, and a deeper hush, if possible, and a man knelt down at my feet with a blazing torch; the multitude strained forward, gazing, and parting slightly from their seats without knowing it; the monk raised his hands above my head, and his eyes toward the blue sky, and began some words in Latin; in this attitude he droned on and on, a little while, and then stopped. I waited two or three moments; then looked up; he was standing there petrified. With a common impulse the multitude rose slowly up and stared into the sky. I followed their eyes; as sure as guns, there was my eclipse beginning! The life went boiling through my veins; I was a new man! The rim of black spread slowly into the sun's disk, my heart beat higher and higher, and still the assemblage and the priest stared into the sky, motionless. I knew that this gaze would be turned upon me, next. When it was, I was ready. I was in one of the most grand attitudes I ever struck, with my arm stretched up pointing to the sun. It was a noble effect. You could *see* the shudder sweep the mass like a wave. Two shouts rang out, one close upon the heels of the other:

"Apply the torch!"

"I forbid it!"

The one was from Merlin, the other from the king. I said:

"If any man moves—even the king—before I give him leave, I will blast him with thunder. I will consume him with lightnings!"

The multitude sank meekly into their seats. I knew I was master of the situation now. The king said:

"Be merciful, fair sir, and essay no further in this perilous matter, lest disaster follow. It was reported to us that your powers could not attain unto their full strength until the morrow; but—"

"Your Majesty thinks the report may have been a lie? It *was* a lie."

That made an immense effect; up went appealing hands everywhere, and the king was assailed with a storm of supplications that I might be bought off at any price, and the calamity stayed. The king was eager to comply. He said:

"Name any terms, reverend sir, even to the halving of my kingdom; but banish this calamity, spare the sun!"

*A Connecticut Yankee in King Arthur's Court*   **677**

AT A GLANCE

- Clarence confesses that he has had the date of execution moved up.
- The Yankee is about to be burned; the eclipse begins.

**1 READING SKILLS: CAUSE AND EFFECT**

The Yankee's scheduled burning is moved up by Clarence. He says the Yankee's magic will not be in full force until the next day and urges that the Yankee be killed immediately. He lies to save both the sun and the Yankee.

**2 MOOD**

Twain creates a mood of tension by describing the quiet and stillness of the crowd.

**3 PLOT: SUSPENSE**

The Yankee is chained to the stake, with the fire about to be lit and the crowd breathless. Twain's depiction of the stake satirizes the cruelty of medieval justice.

**4 PLOT: CLIMAX**

This episode reaches its high point when the eclipse unexpectedly begins. We know now that the Yankee will be saved.

## GUIDED READING

### LITERAL QUESTIONS

**1a.** What lie does Clarence tell, and what suggestion does he make about the Yankee? (He says that the Yankee's power will not reach full strength until the next day. He suggests the Yankee be killed before his power over the sun increases.)

**2a.** What does Merlin say, as the sun darkens? (*Apply the torch!*)

### INFERENTIAL QUESTIONS

**1b.** Why does he tell this lie? (He is terrified of the Yankee's magic power and wants to prevent a full blotting out of the sun. By his lie, he thinks he has arranged "only a little darkness" and made it easier for the Yankee.)

**2b.** What do you think Merlin feels towards the Yankee? (Merlin is jealous and does not want the Yankee to establish himself as a greater magician.)

- The eclipse proceeds; the people are frightened.
- The Yankee tells Arthur he must make him minister and share the revenues, or he will blot out the sun forever.

## 1 THEME

A major focus of Twain's satire is superstition. Here he humorously portrays the fear and sense of helplessness that superstition engenders.

## 2 PLOT: RESOLUTION

The Yankee is out of danger, begins to realize he has the upper hand, and demands power and money. His triumph shows the power of knowledge over ignorance.

My fortune was made. I would have taken him up in a minute, but *I* couldn't stop an eclipse. So I asked time to consider. The king said—

1  "How long—ah, how long, good sir? Be merciful; look, it groweth darker, moment by moment. Prithee how long?"

"Not long. Half an hour—maybe an hour."

There were a thousand pathetic protests, but I couldn't shorten up any, for I couldn't remember how long a total eclipse lasts. I was in a puzzled condition, anyway, and wanted to think. Something was wrong about that eclipse, and the fact was very unsettling. If this wasn't the one I was after, how was I to tell whether this was the sixth century, or nothing but a dream? Dear me, if I could only prove it was the latter! Here was a glad new hope. If the boy was right about the date, and this was surely the twentieth, it *wasn't* the sixth century. I reached for the monk's sleeve, in considerable excitement, and asked him what day of the month it was.

Hang him, he said it was the *twenty-first!* It made me turn cold to hear him. I begged him not to make any mistake about it; but he was sure; he knew it was the twenty-first. Yes, I *was* in King Arthur's court, and I might as well make the most out of it I could.

The darkness was steadily growing, the people becoming more and more distressed. I now said:

"I have reflected, Sir King. For a lesson, I will let this darkness proceed, and spread night in the world; but whether I blot out the sun for good, or restore it, shall rest with you. These are the terms, to wit: You shall remain king over all your dominions, and receive all the glories and honors that belong to the kingship; but you shall

2  appoint me your perpetual minister and executive, and give me for my services one per cent of such actual increase of revenue over and above its present amount as I may succeed in creating for the state. Is it satisfactory?"

There was a prodigious roar of applause, and out of the midst of it the king's voice rose, saying:

"Away with his bonds, and set him free! and do him homage, high and low, rich and poor, for

## GUIDED READING

### LITERAL QUESTION

**1a.** What does the Yankee tell Arthur he plans to do about the sun? (He will let the darkness continue until it is complete; then if Arthur agrees to his demands, he will lift it.)

### INFERENTIAL QUESTION

**1b.** Why does he make this plan? (He cannot stop the eclipse and needs an explanation for why he does not.)

AT A GLANCE

- Arthur gives in to the Yankee's demands.
- The Yankee pretends to prolong the eclipse.
- When the eclipse is total, the Yankee calls for it to end.
- Everyone is relieved, and the Yankee is rewarded.

1 **MOOD**

Twain creates a solemn mood: total darkness, cold wind, groans of horror. This mood reflects both the eeriness of a total eclipse and the utter ignorance of Arthur's people.

2 **PLOT: EPISODE**

One episode ends; another begins. Twain's episodic structure is true to Arthurian tales and allows him the freedom to contrast many aspects of medieval and modern life.

3 **THEME**

One of the novel's themes is the difficulty of life in Arthurian England. Twain shows life in this often idealized society as crude and unpleasant, contrasting it with his own more civilized—if less picturesque—century.

---

he is become the king's right hand, is clothed with power and authority, and his seat is upon the highest step of the throne! Now sweep away this creeping night, and bring the light and cheer again, that all the world may bless thee.''

I wanted to keep things as they were till the eclipse was total, otherwise they would be trying to get me to dismiss the darkness, and of course I couldn't do it. So I had to make another excuse. I said it would be but natural if the king should change his mind and repent to some extent of what he had done under excitement; therefore I would let the darkness grow a while, and if at the end of a reasonable time the king had kept his mind the same, the darkness should be dismissed. Neither the king nor anybody else was satisfied with that arrangement, but I had to stick to my point.

It grew darker and darker and blacker and blacker. It got to be pitch dark, at last, and the multitude groaned with horror to feel the cold uncanny night breezes fan through the place and see the stars come out and twinkle in the sky. At last the eclipse was total, and I was very glad of it, but everybody else was in misery; which was quite natural. I said:

"The king, by his silence, still stands to the terms." Then I lifted up my hands—stood just so a moment—then I said, with the most awful solemnity: "Let the enchantment dissolve and pass harmless away!"

There was no response, for a moment, in that deep darkness and that graveyard hush. But when the silver rim of the sun pushed itself out a moment or two later, the assemblage broke loose with a vast shout and came pouring down like a deluge to smother me with blessings and gratitude; and Clarence was not the last of the wash, be sure.

## 7. Merlin's Tower

Inasmuch as I was now the second personage in the Kingdom, as far as political power and authority were concerned, much was made of me. My raiment was of silks and velvets and cloth of gold, and by consequence was very showy, also uncomfortable. I was given the choicest suite of apartments in the castle, after

*A Connecticut Yankee in King Arthur's Court* **679**

---

## GUIDED READING

**LITERAL QUESTIONS**

**1a.** What excuse does the Yankee give for allowing the eclipse to proceed? (He says he wants to test whether or not Arthur will keep his word.)

**2a.** What does the Yankee do when the eclipse becomes total? (He declares himself satisfied that Arthur will keep his agreement, strikes a pose, and bids the enchantment dissolve.)

**INFERENTIAL QUESTIONS**

**1b.** What does this excuse tell you about the Yankee? (It shows his ability to turn even circumstances beyond his control to his advantage.)

**2b.** Why does he strike a pose and recite a pretended magic formula? (He knows that the superstition of the people will make them accept what he does if he uses the trappings of magic.)

- The Yankee complains about conditions at court.
- He inspires curiosity and respect in the people.
- Merlin is jealous and spreads discontent.
- The people demand another miracle.

## 1 SATIRE

Now Twain turns his satire on nineteenth-century popular taste in art—the love of mass-produced prints and pious slogans.

## 2 THEME

The Yankee reflects his century's enthusiasm for progress and improvement. Twain satirizes this preoccupation as well as the backwardness of the Middle Ages.

## 3 VOCABULARY: DIALECT

The use of Southern dialect adds humor, because it is so unexpected in this context. The folksy term *Brer* reduces Merlin's dignity and makes his claim to magic powers seem silly.

the king's. They were aglow with loud-colored silken hangings, but the stone floors had nothing but rushes on them for a carpet. As for conveniences, properly speaking, there weren't any. I mean *little* conveniences; it is the little conveniences that make the real comfort of life. The big oaken chairs, graced with rude carvings, were well enough, but that was the stopping place. There was no soap, no matches, no looking glass—except a metal one, about as powerful as a pail of water. And not a chromo.[33] It made me homesick to look around over this proud and gaudy but heartless barrenness and remember that in our house in East Hartford, all unpretending as it was, you couldn't go into a room but you would find at least a three-color God-Bless-Our-Home over the door; and in the parlor we had nine. But here, even in my grand room of state, there wasn't anything in the nature of a picture except a thing the size of a bed quilt, which was either woven or knitted (it had darned places in it), and nothing in it was the right color or the right shape; and as for proportions, even Raphael[34] himself couldn't have botched them more formidably. Raphael was a bird. We had several of his chromos; one was his "Miraculous Draught of Fishes," where he puts in a miracle of his own—puts three men into a canoe which wouldn't have held a dog without upsetting. I always admired to study R.'s art, it was so fresh and unconventional.

There wasn't even a bell or a speaking tube in the castle. There was no gas, there were no candles; a bronze dish half full of boarding-house butter[35] with a blazing rag floating in it was the thing that produced what was regarded as light. A lot of these hung along the walls and modified the dark, just toned it down enough to make it

dismal. If you went out at night, your servants carried torches. There were no books, pens, paper, or ink, and no glass in the openings they believed to be windows. It is a little thing—glass is—until it is absent, then it becomes a big thing. But perhaps the worst of all was, that there wasn't any sugar, coffee, tea, or tobacco. I saw that I was just another Robinson Crusoe[36] cast away on an uninhabited island, with no society but some more or less tame animals, and if I wanted to make life bearable I must do as he did—invent, contrive, create, reorganize things; set brain and hand to work, and keep them busy. Well, that was in my line.

One thing troubled me along at first—the immense interest which people took in me. Apparently the whole nation wanted a look at me. It soon transpired that the eclipse had scared the British world almost to death. Of course I was all the talk—all other subjects were dropped; even the king became suddenly a person of minor interest and notoriety. Within twenty-four hours the delegations began to arrive, and from that time onward for a fortnight they kept coming. I had to go out a dozen times a day and show myself to these reverent and awestricken multitudes. It turned Brer[37] Merlin green with envy and spite, which was a great satisfaction to me.

There was another thing that troubled me a little. Those multitudes presently began to agitate for another miracle. The pressure got to be pretty strong. There was going to be an eclipse of the moon, and I knew the date and hour, but it was too far away. Two years. I would have given a good deal for license to hurry it up and use it now when there was a big market for it. It seemed a great pity to have it wasted so, and come lagging along at a time when a body wouldn't have any use for it as like as not.

---

33. **chromo:** colored picture printed from a flat stone to which grease and inks have been applied to form the design.
34. **Raphael:** Raffaello Santi (1483–1520), an Italian painter.
35. **boarding-house butter:** oil used as a cheaper substitute for butter in boarding-houses.

36. **Robinson Crusoe:** shipwrecked hero of the novel *Robinson Crusoe* by Daniel Defoe.
37. **Brer:** southern American dialect for "brother."

## GUIDED READING

### LITERAL QUESTION

**1a.** What art does the Yankee criticize? (He criticizes the tapestries in his room and the art of Raphael.)

### INFERENTIAL QUESTION

**1b.** What does the Yankee appear to value? (newness, convenience, realism)

Next, Clarence found that old Merlin was making himself busy on the sly among those people. He was spreading a report that I was a humbug, and that the reason I didn't accommodate the people with a miracle was because I couldn't. I saw that I must do something. I presently thought out a plan.

By my authority as executive I threw Merlin into prison—the same cell I had occupied myself. Then I gave public notice by herald and trumpet that I should be busy with affairs of state for a fortnight, but about the end of that time I would take a moment's leisure and blow up Merlin's stone tower by fires from heaven; in the meantime, whoso listened to evil reports about me, let him beware. Furthermore, I would perform but this one miracle at this time, and no more; if it failed to satisfy and any murmured, I would turn the murmurers into horses, and make them useful. Quiet ensued.

I took Clarence into my confidence, to a certain degree, and we went to work privately. I told him that this was a sort of miracle that required a trifle of preparation; and that it would be sudden death to ever talk about these preparations to anybody. That made his mouth safe enough. Clandestinely we made a few bushels of first-rate blasting powder, and I superintended my armorers while they constructed a lightning rod and some wires. This old stone tower was very massive—and rather ruinous, too, for it was Roman, and four hundred years old. It stood on a lonely eminence, in good view from the castle, and about half a mile away.

Working by night, we stowed the powder in the tower—dug stones out, on the inside, and buried the powder in the walls themselves, which were fifteen feet thick at the base. We could have blown up the Tower of London[38] with these charges. When the thirteenth night

---

38. **Tower of London:** massive stone fortress in London consisting of two fortified walls and several buildings and turrets. It has served as a prison and a palace.

was come we put up our lightning rod, bedded it in one of the batches of powder, and ran wires from it to the other batches. Everybody had shunned that locality from the day of my proclamation, but on the morning of the fourteenth I thought best to warn the people, through the heralds, to keep clear away—a quarter of a mile away. Then added, by command, that at some time during the twenty-four hours I would consummate the miracle, but would first give a brief notice.

Thundershowers had been tolerably frequent, of late, and I was not much afraid of a failure; still, I shouldn't have cared for a delay of a day or two; I should have explained that I was busy with affairs of state, yet, and the people must wait.

Of course we had a blazing sunny day—almost the first one without a cloud for three weeks; things always happen so. I kept secluded, and watched the weather. Clarence dropped in from time to time and said the public excitement was growing and growing all the time, and the whole country filling up with human masses as far as one could see from the battlements. At last the wind sprang up and a cloud appeared—in the right quarter, too, and just at nightfall. For a little while I watched that distant cloud spread and blacken, then I judged it was time for me to appear. I ordered the torch baskets to be lit, and Merlin liberated and sent to me. A quarter of an hour later I ascended the parapet and there found the king and the court assembled and gazing off in the darkness toward Merlin's tower.

Merlin arrived in a gloomy mood. I said:

**3** "You wanted to burn me alive when I had not done you any harm, and latterly you have been trying to injure my professional reputation. Therefore I am going to call down fire and blow up your tower, but it is only fair to give you a chance; now if you think you can break my enchantments and ward off the fires, step to the bat, it's your innings."

"I can, fair sir, and I will. Doubt it not."

*A Connecticut Yankee in King Arthur's Court*   **681**

AT A GLANCE

- Merlin spreads a rumor that the Yankee does not have magical powers.
- The Yankee imprisons Merlin and threatens "fire from heaven."
- The Yankee and Clarence set up lightning rods and make blasting powder.
- The Yankee challenges Merlin to ward off his magic powers.

**1 PLOT: CONFLICT**

Throughout the novel the Yankee becomes involved in open conflict with Merlin. These confrontations symbolize one of the novel's central conflicts: the Yankee's rationalism vs. Merlin's superstition.

**2 CHARACTERIZATION**

The Yankee demonstrates technical know-how by manufacturing blasting powder, proving he is as practical as he claims.

**3 THEME**

The Yankee makes a case against the cruelty of the Middle Ages. It is significant that he plans only to blow up Merlin's tower, not Merlin, indicating Twain's belief that in the modern world humanity and kindness have increased.

---

## GUIDED READING

**LITERAL QUESTION**

**1a.** What causes the delay in destroying Merlin's tower? (The Yankee needs to wait for a storm so that lightning will ignite the powder.)

**INFERENTIAL QUESTION**

**1b.** Why doesn't he simply blow the tower up by lighting the blasting powder? (He wants to make the explosion look as much like traditional magic as possible.)

The Yankee calls himself practical; how does he show his practicality? (He manages to maneuver his way out of a death sentence and triumph over his rival by his practical knowledge of science and human psychology.)

## STUDY QUESTIONS

1. on tour of Warwick castle; tells his story at hotel
2. practical; unsentimental; clever at building; inventing; full of fight; knows how to manufacture firearms; invents devices
3. blow to the head during fight; under an oak in strange country sees man in armor on a horse
4. in an asylum; page tells him the date/year; *advantage:* he is better educated; *disadvantage:* he is prisoner
5. pretends to cause eclipse; claims to be magician; says he will blacken sun if he is not released; eclipse occurs; he is freed; made minister of court
6. is second in power to King; uncomfortable—clothes, no soap, matches, mirrors, coffee, sugar
7. blows up stone tower; to squelch rumors he is a fraud; fills tower with blasting power, hooks wires to lightning rod, storm breaks, tower explodes
8. are superstitious; many are oppressed, lack knowledge; belief in magic, lack of technical knowledge
9. saves himself with eclipse; manufactures blasting powder; has sense of humor; remains calm in crisis; is practical, observant, self-confident
10. is narrow-minded; fails to see beauty of surroundings; is vindictive, condescending, power-hungry
11. "Miracle" might fail; he may be asked to do something he cannot do; Merlin may plot against him.

---

He drew an imaginary circle on the stones of the roof. Then he began to mutter and make passes in the air with his hands. He worked himself up slowly and gradually into a sort of frenzy, and got to thrashing around with his arms like the sails of a windmill. By this time the storm had about reached us; the gusts of wind were flaring the torches and making the shadows swash about, the first heavy drops of rain were falling, the world abroad was black as pitch, the lightning began to wink fitfully. Of course my rod would be loading itself now. In fact, things were imminent. So I said:

"You have had time enough. I have given you every advantage, and not interfered. It is plain your magic is weak. It is only fair that I begin now."

I made about three passes in the air, and then there was an awful crash and that old tower leaped into the sky in chunks, along with a vast volcanic fountain of fire that turned night to noonday, and showed a thousand acres of human beings groveling on the ground in a general collapse of consternation. Well, it rained mortar and masonry the rest of the week. This was the report; but probably the facts would have modified it.

It was an effective miracle. The great bothersome temporary population vanished. There were a good many thousand tracks in the mud the next morning, but they were all outward bound. If I had advertised another miracle I couldn't have raised an audience with a sheriff.

Merlin's stock was flat. The king wanted to stop his wages; he even wanted to banish him, but I interfered. I said he would be useful to work the weather, and attend to small matters like that, and I would give him a lift now and then when his poor little parlor magic soured on him.

---

## STUDY QUESTIONS

### Recalling
1. Explain how the narrator meets "the stranger" and learns his story.
2. List three or four personality traits with which the Yankee describes himself in the beginning of his "history." What special skills and knowledge does he claim to have?
3. What incident sends the Yankee back in time to the sixth century? Describe the strange person and scene he sees when he first opens his eyes.
4. Where does the Yankee think he is at first, and how does he discover the truth? What advantages and disadvantages does he see in his peculiar situation?
5. With what "miracle" does the Yankee save himself from burning at the stake? Relate the details of this incident.

6. Describe the Yankee's position in the kingdom as the result of his first "miracle." List three of his complaints about his living conditions.
7. What second "miracle" does the Yankee perform? Why and how does he do it?

### Interpreting
8. In what ways are the Britons backward? What qualities in the Britons enable the Yankee to gain power?
9. Find examples of the Yankee's resourcefulness. What other positive qualities does he display?
10. The Yankee says that he is barren of poetry. Explain how his complaints about Arthur's Britain might illustrate this side of his character. What other shortcomings can you see in his character?

### Extending
11. What problems do you foresee for the Yankee?

682    *The Novel*

## 8. The Boss and the Beginnings of Civilization

To be vested with enormous authority is a fine thing; but to have the onlooking world consent to it is a finer. The tower episode solidified my power, and made it impregnable. If any were perchance disposed to be jealous and critical before that, they experienced a change of heart, now. There was not anyone in the kingdom who would have considered it good judgment to meddle with my matters.

I was fast getting adjusted to my situation and circumstances. For a time, I used to wake up, mornings, and smile at my "dream," and listen for the Colt's factory whistle; but that sort of thing played itself out, gradually, and at last I was fully able to realize that I was actually living in the sixth century, and in Arthur's court, not a lunatic asylum. After that, I was just as much at home in that century as I could have been in any other; and as for preference, I wouldn't have traded it for the twentieth. Look at the opportunities here for a man of knowledge, brains, pluck, and enterprise to sail in and grow up with

the country. The grandest field that ever was; and all my own; not a competitor; not a man who wasn't a baby to me in acquirements and capacities; whereas, what would I amount to in the twentieth century? I should be foreman of a factory, that is about all; and could drag a seine[1] downstreet any day and catch a hundred better men than myself.

What a jump I had made! I couldn't keep from thinking about it, and contemplating it, just as one does who has struck oil.

I was no shadow of a king; I was the substance; the king himself was the shadow. My power was colossal; and it was not a mere name, as such things have generally been, it was the genuine article.

It was a curious country, and full of interest. And the people! They were the quaintest and simplest and trustingest race; why, they were nothing but rabbits. It was pitiful for a person born in a wholesome free atmosphere to listen to their humble and hearty outpourings of loyalty toward their king and nobility.

Here I was, a giant among pigmies,[2] a man among children, a master intelligence among intellectual moles: by all rational measurement the one and only actually great man in that whole British world; and yet there and then, just as in the remote England of my birth time, any sheep-witted earl was a better man than I was. Such a personage was fawned upon in Arthur's realm. There were times when *he* could sit down in the king's presence, but I couldn't. I could have got a title easily enough, and that would have raised me a large step in everybody's eyes; even in the king's, the giver of it. But I didn't ask for it; and I declined it when it was offered. I couldn't have enjoyed such a thing with my notions. I couldn't have felt really and satisfactorily fine and proud and set up over any title except one that should come from the nation itself, the only legitimate

----
1. **seine** [sān]: large fishing net.
2. **pigmies:** here, insignificant persons.

*A Connecticut Yankee in King Arthur's Court*   **683**

## AT A GLANCE

- The Yankee muses on how powerful he is as a modern man in a backward age.
- He disdains inherited titles.

### LITERARY OPTIONS

- characterization
- plot
- satire

### THEMATIC OPTIONS

- the quest for power
- justice and democracy
- conflict between cultures

### 1  CHARACTERIZATION

The Yankee reveals his vanity and love of power. His pleasure in absolute power is ironic, because he often criticizes Arthur's court for being undemocratic.

### 2  POINT OF VIEW

First-person narrative allows the Yankee to share his inner dialogue, revealing how he adapted to the sixth century. By using such informal phrases as *played itself out,* he adds the flavor of his own colloquial speech to the narration.

### 3  PLOT: CONFLICT

The Yankee shows internal conflict: He loves having power but wants to earn it rather than enjoy the automatic respect accorded a title.

---

## GUIDED READING

### LITERAL QUESTIONS

**1a.** Which century does the Yankee prefer? (the sixth)

**2a.** How does the Yankee characterize the people of Arthur's time? (They are "rabbits": simple, trusting, and subservient.)

### INFERENTIAL QUESTIONS

**1b.** At first, the Yankee is negative about Arthur's court; why has he become so positive? (He is not powerless anymore; he sees that opportunities for him to advance are far greater in Arthur's time than in his own.)

**2b.** How does his estimation of the people as "rabbits" contradict his professed belief in democracy? (Democracy requires a belief in the wisdom of the people and their ability to choose rulers.)

- The Yankee earns the title of "The Boss."
- The Yankee plans to develop Arthur's England a little at a time.
- Four years pass, and the Yankee's secret modernizations begin to take hold.

## 1 THEME

The Yankee's observations about the scarcity of *THE'S* is humorous but also shows that he shares the age-old lust for power. This passage suggests one of the novel's themes: Basic human nature does not change.

## 2 RESPONSE JOURNAL

Have students comment in their journals about the Yankee's adage: "Unlimited power is the ideal thing when it is in safe hands." Do they agree or disagree?

## 3 STYLE: FIGURATIVE LANGUAGE

A volcano metaphor describes industrial growth. The volcano's fire and smoke suggest the Yankee's factories; the volcano's explosion suggests the social change the Yankee aims to produce.

---

source; and such an one I hoped to win; and in the course of years of honest and honorable endeavor, I did win it and did wear it with a high and clean pride. This title fell casually from the lips of a blacksmith, one day, in a village, was caught up as a happy thought and tossed from mouth to mouth with a laugh and an affirmative vote; in ten days it had swept the kingdom, and was become as familiar as the king's name. I was never known by any other designation afterward. This title, translated into modern speech, would be THE BOSS. Elected by the nation. That **1** suited me. And it was a pretty high title. There were very few THE'S, and I was one of them. If you spoke of the duke, or the earl, or the bishop, how could anybody tell which one you meant? But if you spoke of The King or The Queen or The Boss, it was different.

I was pretty well satisfied with what I had already accomplished. In various quiet nooks and corners I had the beginnings of all sorts of industries under way— nuclei of future vast factories, the iron and steel missionaries of my future civilization. In these were gathered together the brightest young minds I could find, and I kept agents out raking the country for

**684** *The Novel*

more, all the time. I was training a crowd of ignorant folk into experts—experts in every sort of handiwork and scientific calling. These nurseries of mine went smoothly and privately along undisturbed in their obscure country retreats, for nobody was allowed to come into their precincts without a special permit. I had started a teacher factory, and, as a result, I now had an admirable system of graded schools in full blast.

**2** Four years rolled by—and then! Well, you would never imagine it in the world. Unlimited power *is* the ideal thing when it is in safe hands.

My works showed what a despot could do with the resources of a kingdom at his command. Unsuspected by this dark land, I had the civilization of the nineteenth century booming under its very nose! It was fenced away from the public view, but there it was, a gigantic and unassailable fact—and to be heard from, yet, if I **3** lived and had luck. There it was, as sure a fact, and as substantial a fact as any serene volcano, standing innocent with its smokeless summit in the blue sky and giving no sign of the rising hell in its bowels. My schools were children four years before; they were grown-up, now; my shops of that day were vast factories, now; where I had a dozen trained men then, I had a thousand, now; where I had one brilliant expert then, I had fifty now. I stood ready to flood the midnight world with light at any moment. But I was not going to do the thing in that sudden way. It was not my policy. The people could not have stood it.

No, I had been going cautiously all the while. I had had confidential agents trickling through the country some time, whose office was to undermine knighthood by imperceptible degrees, and to gnaw a little at this and that and the other superstition, and so prepare the way gradually for a better order of things. I was turning on my light one candlepower at a time, and meant to continue to do so.

---

## GUIDED READING

### LITERAL QUESTIONS

**1a.** Where does the Yankee locate his industries to begin with? (in "quiet nooks and corners" and "obscure country retreats")

**2a.** What "policy" does the Yankee have about modernizing the sixth century? (to act gradually)

### INFERENTIAL QUESTION

**1b.** Why does he locate them there? (He wants to keep them secret because he fears opposition to his plans and ideas if they are known.)

**2b.** He holds this policy because "the people could not have stood it" otherwise. What does he mean? (He knows that industrial growth causes great upheaval if it comes too rapidly.)

I had scattered some branch schools secretly about the kingdom, and they were doing very well. I meant to work this racket more and more, as time wore on, if nothing occurred to frighten me. One of my deepest secrets was my West Point—my military academy. I kept that most jealously out of sight; and I did the same with my naval academy which I had established at a remote seaport. Both were prospering to my satisfaction.

Clarence was my head executive, my right hand. He was equal to anything; there wasn't anything he couldn't turn his hand to. Of late I had been training him for journalism, for the time seemed about right for a start in the newspaper line; nothing big, but just a small weekly for experimental circulation in my civilization-nurseries. He took to it like a duck; there was an editor concealed in him, sure. Already he had doubled himself in one way; he talked sixth century and wrote nineteenth.

We had another large departure on hand, too. This was a telegraph and a telephone; our first venture in this line. These wires were for private service only, as yet, and must be kept private until a riper day should come. We had a gang of men on the road, working mainly by night. They were stringing ground wires; we were afraid to put up poles, for they would attract too much inquiry.

As for the general condition of the country, it was as it had been when I arrived in it, to all intents and purposes. I had made changes, but they were necessarily slight, and they were not noticeable. Thus far, I had not even meddled with taxation, outside of the taxes which provided the royal revenues. I had systematized those, and put the service on an effective and righteous basis. As a result, these revenues were already quadrupled, and yet the burden was so much more equably distributed than before, that all the kingdom felt a sense of relief, and the praises of my administration were hearty and general.

## 9. The Yankee in Search of Adventures

There never was such a country for wandering liars; and they were of both sexes. Hardly a month went by without one of these tramps arriving; and generally loaded with a tale about some princess or other wanting help to get her out of some faraway castle where she was held in captivity by a lawless scoundrel, usually a giant. Now you would think that the first thing the king would do after listening to such a novelette from an entire stranger, would be to ask for credentials—yes, and a pointer or two as to locality of castle, best route to it, and so on. But nobody ever thought of so simple and commonsense a thing as that. No, everybody swallowed these people's lies whole, and never asked a question of any sort or about anything. Well, one day when I was not around, one of these people came along—it was a she one, this time—and told a tale of the usual pattern. Her mistress was a captive in a vast and gloomy castle, along with forty-four other young and beautiful girls; the masters of the castle were three stupendous brothers, each with four arms and one eye—the eye in the center of the forehead, and as big as a fruit. Sort of fruit not mentioned; their usual slovenliness in statistics.

Would you believe it? The king and the whole Round Table were in raptures over this preposterous opportunity for adventure. Every knight of the Table jumped for the chance, and begged for it; but to their vexation and chagrin the king conferred it upon me, who had not asked for it at all.

I could have cursed the kindness that conferred upon me this benefaction, but I kept my vexation under the surface for policy's sake, and did what I could to let on to be glad. Indeed, I *said* I was glad. And in a way it was true; I was as glad as a person is when he is scalped.

Well, one must make the best of things, and not waste time with useless fretting, but get down to business and see what can be done. In

*A Connecticut Yankee in King Arthur's Court*  **685**

**1 CHARACTERIZATION**

Clarence reveals his intelligence and versatility. His positive qualities are important, balancing the satire Twain levels at the people of the time.

**2 THEME**

The lack of social justice in Arthur's England is a major idea in the novel. The Yankee reforms the royal revenues to make them more equitable, thus promoting social justice and demonstrating his organizational ability.

**3 CHARACTERIZATION**

His comments prove that the Yankee is indeed "barren of poetry," as he claims. His imagination is not stirred by romance and adventure.

**4 SATIRE**

A major focus of Twain's satire is the chivalric code. The practical Yankee is reluctant to rescue a damsel in distress, unlike chivalric knights eager to rush off on such missions.

## GUIDED READING

### LITERAL QUESTION

**1a.** What kind of story does the "wandering liar" tell? (Her mistress is held captive, along with forty-four other maidens, by three large and monstrous brothers.)

### INFERENTIAL QUESTION

**1b.** What aspects of chivalry might this story satirize? (the heedless rush to adventure and the portrayal of foes as superhuman beings)

- The Yankee questions the girl.
- She cannot give him any specific or verifiable information.

### 1 PLOT: CONFLICT

For all his adjustment to the sixth century, the Yankee cannot escape "the way I've been raised."

### 2 DIALOGUE

This exchange contrasts the English language of the nineteenth and sixth centuries. The values, as well as the words, are very different: The nineteenth century values logic, facts, and proof; the sixth, romance, poetry, and magic.

### 3 CHARACTERIZATION

The Yankee shows his practical streak and his skepticism about the girl's story. The exchange satirizes both the Yankee's insistence on hard facts and Alisande's disregard for them.

all lies there is wheat among the chaff; I must get at the wheat in this case: so I sent for the girl and she came. She was a comely enough creature, and soft and modest, but if signs went for anything, she didn't know as much as a lady's watch. I said—

"My dear, have you been questioned as to particulars?"

She said she hadn't.

**1** "Well, I didn't expect you had, but I thought I would ask to make sure; it's the way I've been raised. I'm obliged to ask you a few questions; just answer up fair and square, and don't be afraid. Where do you live, when you are at home?"

**686** *The Novel*

"In the land of Moder, fair sir."

"Land of Moder. I don't remember hearing of it before. Parents living?"

"As to that, I know not if they be yet on live, sith[3] it is many years that I have lain shut up in the castle."

"Your name, please?"

"I hight[4] the Demoiselle Alisande la Carteloise, an it please you."

"Do you know anybody here who can identify you?"

"That were not likely, fair lord, I being come hither now for the first time."

**2** "Have you brought any letters—any documents—any proofs that you are trustworthy and truthful?"

"Of a surety, no; and wherefore should I? Have I not a tongue, and cannot I say all that myself?"

"But *your* saying it, you know, and somebody else's saying it, is different."

"Different? How might that be? I fear me I do not understand."

"Don't *understand?* Land of—why, you see—Let us change the subject. Now as to this castle, with forty-five princesses in it, and three ogres at the head of it, tell me—where is this harem?"

"Harem?"

**3** "The *castle,* you understand; where is the castle?"

"Oh, as to that, it is great, and strong, and well beseen, and lieth in a far country. Yes, it is many leagues."

"*How* many?"

"Ah, fair sir, it were woundily hard to tell, they are so many, and do so lap the one upon the other, and being made all in the same image and tincted with the same color, one may not know the one league from its fellow, nor how to count them except they be taken apart, and ye wit well

---

3. **sith:** since.
4. **hight** [hīt]: am called.

## GUIDED READING

### LITERAL QUESTION

**1a.** What kind of information does the Yankee want from the girl? (He wants to know where she lives, who she is, if anyone can verify this information, where the castle with the captive maids is, and how far away it is.)

### INFERENTIAL QUESTION

**1b.** Why do you think the girl cannot give him exact answers? (Medieval custom had not prepared her to relate precise, logical, factual information.)

it were God's work to do that, being not within man's capacity; for ye will note—"

Oh, well, it was reasonably plain, now, why these donkeys didn't prospect these liars for details. It may be that this girl had a fact in her somewhere, but I don't believe you could have sluiced it out with a hydraulic;[5] nor got it with the earlier forms of blasting, even; it was a case for dynamite and yet the king and his knights had listened to her as if she had been a leaf out of the gospel. It kind of sizes up the whole party. And think of the simple ways of this court: this wandering wench hadn't any more trouble to get access to the king in his palace than she would have had to get into the poorhouse in my day and country. In fact he was glad to see her, glad to hear her tale; with that adventure of hers to offer, she was as welcome as a corpse is to a coroner.

My expedition was all the talk that day and that night. I was to have an early breakfast, and start at dawn, for that was the usual way; but I had the demon's own time with my armor, and this delayed me a little. It is troublesome to get into, and there is so much detail. First you wrap a layer or two of blanket around your body, for a sort of cushion and to keep off the cold iron; then you put on your sleeves and shirt of chain mail—these are made of small steel links woven together, and they form a fabric so flexible that if you toss your shirt onto the floor, it slumps into a pile like a peck of wet fishnet. Then you put on your shoes—flatboats roofed over with interleaving bands of steel—and screw your clumsy spurs into the heels. Next you buckle your greaves[6] on your legs, and your cuisses[7] on your thighs; then come your backplate and your breastplate, and you begin to feel crowded; then you hitch onto the breastplate and the half-petticoat of broad overlapping bands of steel which

---

5. **sluiced . . . hydraulic:** forced it out using water pressure.
6. **greaves:** armor for the leg below the knee.
7. **cuisses** [kwis'əz]: armor for protecting the thigh.

hangs down in front but is scalloped out behind so you can sit down, and isn't any real improvement on an inverted coal scuttle, either for looks or for wear, or to wipe your hands on; next you belt on your sword; then you put your stovepipe joints onto your arms, your iron gauntlets onto your hands, your iron rattrap onto your head, with a rag of steel web hitched onto it to hang over the back of your neck—and there you are, snug as a candle in a candle mold. This is no time to dance. Well, a man that is packed away like that is a nut that isn't worth the cracking, there is so little of the meat, when you get down to it, by comparison with the shell.

The boys helped me, or I never could have got in. The sun was just up, the king and the court were all on hand to see me off and wish me luck; so it wouldn't be etiquette for me to tarry. You don't get on your horse yourself; no, if you tried it you would get disappointed. They carry you out, just as they carry a sunstruck man to the drug store, and put you on, and help get you to rights, and fix your feet in the stirrups; and all the while you do feel so strange and stuffy. Then they stood up the mast they called a spear, in its socket by my left foot, and I gripped it with my hand; lastly they hung my shield around my neck, and I was all complete and ready to up anchor and get to sea. Everybody was as good to me as they could be, and a maid of honor gave me the stirrup cup her own self. There was nothing more to do, now, but for that damsel to get up behind me on a pillion,[8] which she did, and put an arm or so around me to hold on.

And so we started; and everybody gave us a good-bye and waved their handkerchiefs or helmets. And everybody we met, going down the hill and through the village was respectful to us, except some shabby little boys on the outskirts. They said—

"Oh, what a guy!" And hove clods at us.

---

8. **pillion** [pil'yən]: pad attached behind the saddle of a horse.

*A Connecticut Yankee in King Arthur's Court* **687**

AT A GLANCE

- The Yankee prepares for his rescue mission.
- He has a difficult time donning his armor.
- He sets off, with the girl riding on horseback behind him.

## 1 THEME

His struggle with the armor reflects one of the novel's main ideas: the discomfort and inconvenience of the medieval age. Twain makes armor a symbol for all he finds cumbersome and ridiculous about Arthurian times.

## 2 STYLE: METAPHOR

Twain compares a knight in armor to a nutmeat in a shell. The metaphor humorously demonstrates the bulk of the armor and the vulnerability of the "meat" inside.

## 3 IRONY

Twain comments ironically on a system intended to protect but fostering immobility and helplessness.

---

## GUIDED READING

### LITERAL QUESTIONS

**1a.** What does the Yankee find incredible about the girl's access to the king? (It was so easy; no one stopped her, questioned her, or denied her access to the highest authority of the land.)

**2a.** What does the Yankee need help with when he's all dressed and ready to go? (He needs help getting on his horse.)

### INFERENTIAL QUESTIONS

**1b.** What does this suggest about his own time? (It is considerably harder to meet and talk with important, powerful people.)

**2b.** How does this incident satirize the use of armor? (It points out that armor, which is supposed to protect knights, actually makes them vulnerable by restricting movement.)

**1 SETTING**

The idyllic setting creates a sense of peace and well-being and contrasts with the difficulties the Yankee is about to experience.

**2 SATIRE**

The Yankee's realistic and very human need for a handkerchief satirizes the lofty aspirations of knights in armor.

**3 STYLE: METAPHOR**

Twain sums up the Yankee's uncomfortable and vulnerable state with a metaphor: In the sun the metal armor becomes a stove, and the Yankee is being fried.

## 10. Slow Torture

Straight off, we were in the country. It was most lovely and pleasant in those sylvan[9] solitudes in the early cool morning in the first freshness of autumn. From hilltops we saw fair green valleys lying spread out below, with streams winding through them, and island groves of trees here and there; and beyond the valleys we saw the ranges of hills, blue with haze, stretching away in billowy perspective to the horizon, with at wide intervals a dim fleck of white or gray which we knew was a castle. At times we left the world behind and entered into the solemn great deeps and rich gloom of the forest, where furtive wild things whisked and scurried by and were gone before you could even get your eye on the place where the noise was. And by and by out we would swing again into the glare.

About the third or fourth or fifth time that we swung out into the glare—it was along there somewhere, a couple of hours or so after sun-up—it wasn't as pleasant as it had been. It was beginning to get hot. This was quite noticeable. Now it is curious how progressively little frets grow and multiply after they once get a start. Things which I didn't mind at all, at first, I began to mind now—and more and more, too, all the time. The first ten or fifteen times I wanted my handkerchief I didn't seem to care; I got along, and said never mind, it isn't any matter, and dropped it out of my mind. But now it was different; I wanted it all the time; it was nag, nag, nag, right along, and no rest; I couldn't get it out of my mind; and so at last I lost my temper and said hang a man that would make a suit of armor without any pockets in it. You see I had my handkerchief in my helmet; and some other things; but it was that kind of a helmet that you can't take off by yourself. That hadn't occurred to me when I put it there. And so now, the thought of its being there, so handy and close by, and yet not get-at-able, made it all the worse and

the harder to bear. Well, it took my mind off from everything else; took it clear off, and centered it in my helmet; and mile after mile, there it stayed, imagining the handkerchief, picturing the handkerchief; and it was bitter and aggravating to have the salt sweat keep trickling down into my eyes, and I couldn't get at it. It seems like a little thing, on paper, but it was not a little thing at all; it was the most real kind of misery.

We couldn't seem to meet anybody in this lonesome Britain, not even an ogre; and in the mood I was in then, it was well for the ogre; that is, an ogre with a handkerchief. Most knights would have thought of nothing but getting his armor; but so I got his bandanna, he could keep his hardware.

Meantime it was getting hotter and hotter in there. You see, the sun was beating down and warming up the iron more and more all the time. Well, when you are hot, that way, every little thing irritates you. When I trotted, I rattled like a crate of dishes, and that annoyed me; and moreover I couldn't seem to stand that shield slatting and banging, now about my breast, now around my back; and if I dropped into a walk my joints creaked and screeched in that wearisome way that a wheelbarrow does, and as we didn't create any breeze at that gait, I was like to get fried in that stove.

Well, you know, when you perspire that way, in rivers, there comes a time when you—when you—well, when you itch. You are inside, your hands are outside; so there you are; nothing but iron between. First it is one place; then another; then some more; and it goes on spreading and spreading, and at last the territory is all occupied, and nobody can imagine what you feel like, nor how unpleasant it is. And when it had got to the worst, and it seemed to me that I could not stand anything more, a fly got in through the bars and settled on my nose, and I couldn't get the visor up; and I could only shake my head, which was baking hot by this time, and

---

9. **sylvan** [sil'vən]: relating to woods, rustic.

## GUIDED READING

### LITERAL QUESTION

**1a.** Where is the Yankee's handkerchief, and why can't he get it? (It is in his helmet, and he cannot remove the helmet by himself.)

### INFERENTIAL QUESTION

**1b.** What does this problem tell you about the armor of the Middle Ages? (It was extremely heavy and cumbersome and not very convenient.)

AT A GLANCE

- The Yankee is bedeviled by flies.
- He cannot remount his horse without help.

**1 WORD CHOICE**

In his breezy American way the Yankee calls Alisande *Sandy*. Thus, Twain contrasts the Yankee's informality with the customs of a more formal time.

the fly—well, you know how a fly acts when he has got a certainty—he only minded the shaking long enough to change from nose to lip, and lip to ear, and buzz and buzz all around in there, and keep on lighting and biting. I gave in, and got Alisande to unship the helmet and relieve me of it. Then she fetched it full of water, and I drank and then stood up and she poured the rest down inside the armor. One cannot think how refreshing it was. She continued to fetch and pour until I was well soaked and thoroughly comfortable.

Gradually, as the time wore along, one annoying fact was borne in upon my understanding. An armed novice cannot mount his horse without help and plenty of it. Sandy was not enough; not enough for me, anyway. We had to

*A Connecticut Yankee in King Arthur's Court*   **689**

## GUIDED READING

**LITERAL QUESTION**

**1a.** How does the Yankee finally get rid of the fly? (He gets Alisande to take off his helmet.)

**INFERENTIAL QUESTION**

**1b.** What do the Yankee's difficulties with his armor suggest about the knights who regularly wore such armor? (They were probably less accustomed to comfort and therefore were more forebearing than the Yankee.)

- The Yankee complains that Alisande is too talkative.
- He suffers additional tortures from his armor.
- Morning comes; they set off again, the Yankee on foot and Alisande riding.

**1 CHARACTERIZATION**

Twain satirizes the puritanism of his own century: The Yankee refuses to remove his armor because it would be "like undressing before folk."

**2 HUMOR**

Twain uses humor in personifying the insects: they *behave well, snuggle up,* are *quiet,* or are *restless and uncomfortable.*

**3 SATIRE**

Twain mocks the sixth century for its lack of cleanliness at the same time that he satirizes the American obsession with plumbing.

wait until somebody should come along. Waiting, in silence, would have been agreeable enough, for I was full of matter for reflection, and wanted to give it a chance to work. I wanted to try and think out how it was that rational or even half-rational men could ever have learned to wear armor, considering its inconveniences; but thinking was out of the question in the circumstances. You couldn't think, where Sandy was. She was a quite biddable[10] creature and good-hearted, but she had a flow of talk that was as steady as a mill, and made your head sore like the drays and wagons in a city. Her clack was going all day, and she never had to slack up for words. She could grind, and pump, and churn and buzz by the week, and never stop to oil up or blow out. And yet the result was just nothing but wind. She never had any ideas, any more than a fog has. She was a perfect blatherskite; I mean for jaw, jaw, jaw, talk, talk, talk, jabber, jabber, jabber; but just as good as she could be. I hadn't minded her mill that morning, on account of having that hornet's nest of other troubles; but more than once in the afternoon I had to say—

"Take a rest, child; the way you are using up all the domestic air, the kingdom will have to go to importing it by tomorrow, and it's a low enough treasury without that."

**11. Freemen and Prisoners**

Night approached, and with it a storm. The darkness came on fast. We must camp, of course. I found a good shelter for the demoiselle under a rock, and went off and found another for myself. But I was obliged to remain in my armor, because I could not get it off by myself and yet could not allow Alisande to help, because it would have seemed so like undressing before folk. It would not have amounted to that in reality, because I had clothes on underneath; but the

_____
10. **biddable:** obedient.

prejudices of one's breeding are not gotten rid of just at a jump, and I knew that when it came to stripping off that bobtailed iron petticoat I should be embarrassed.

With the storm came a change of weather; and the stronger the wind blew, and the wilder the rain lashed around, the colder and colder it got. Pretty soon, various kinds of bugs and ants and worms and things began to flock in out of the wet and crawl down inside my armor to get warm; and while some of them behaved well enough, and snuggled up among my clothes and got quiet, the majority were of a restless, uncomfortable sort, and never stayed still, but went on prowling and hunting for they did not know what; especially the ants, which went tickling along in wearisome procession from one end of me to the other by the hour. It would be my advice to persons situated in this way, to not roll or thrash around, because this excites the interest of all the different sorts of animals and makes every last one of them want to turn out and see what is going on, and this makes things worse than they were before.

When the morning came at last, I was in a bad enough plight: seedy, drowsy from want of sleep; weary from thrashing around, famished from long fasting; pining for a bath, and to get rid of the animals; and crippled with rheumatism. And how had it fared with the nobly born, the titled aristocrat, the Demoiselle Alisande la Carteloise? Why, she was as fresh as a squirrel; she had slept like the dead; and as for a bath, probably neither she nor any other noble in the land had ever had one, and so she was not missing it.

We were off before sunrise, Sandy riding and I limping along behind. In half an hour we came upon a group of ragged poor creatures who had assembled to mend the thing which was regarded as a road. They were as humble as animals to me; and when I proposed to breakfast with them, they were so flattered, so overwhelmed by this

**LITERAL QUESTION**

**1a.** What contrast does the Yankee draw between himself and Alisande in the morning? (She sleeps well; he does not—he wakes drowsy, hungry, feeling dirty and unkempt, full of bugs, and stiff with rheumatism.)

**INFERENTIAL QUESTION**

**1b.** Why do you think Alisande slept so much better than the Yankee? (She wasn't wearing armor, and she was used to the conditions under which they slept.)

extraordinary condescension of mine that at first they were not able to believe that I was in earnest. My lady put up her scornful lip and withdrew to one side; she said in their hearing that she would as soon think of eating with the other cattle. And yet they were not slaves, not chattels. By a sarcasm of law and phrase they were freemen. Seven-tenths of the free population of the country were of just their class and degree: small "independent" farmers, artisans, etc.

To talk of these meek people had a strange enough sound in a formerly American ear. They were freemen, but they could not leave the estates of their lord without his permission; they could not sell a piece of their own property without paying him a handsome percentage of the proceeds, nor buy a piece of somebody else's without remembering him in cash for the privilege.

These poor ostensible freemen who were sharing their breakfast and their talk with me, were as full of humble reverence for their king and nobility as their worst enemy could desire. There was something pitifully ludicrous about it. I asked them if they supposed a nation of people ever existed, who, with a free vote in every man's hand, would elect that a single family and its descendants should reign over it forever.

They all looked unhit, and said they didn't know; that they had never thought about it before, and it hadn't ever occurred to them that a nation could be so situated that every man *could* have a say in the government. I said I had seen one. Again they were all unhit—at first. But presently one man looked up and asked me to state that proposition again; and state it slowly, so it could soak into his understanding. I did it; and after a little he had the idea, and he brought his fist down and said *he* didn't believe a nation where every man had a vote would voluntarily get down in the mud and dirt in any such way; and that to steal from a nation its will and

preference must be a crime and the first of all crimes.

I said to myself:

"This one's a man. If I were backed by enough of his sort, I would make a strike for the welfare of this country, and try to prove myself its loyalest citizen by making a wholesome change in its system of government."

I did not talk blood and insurrection to that man there who sat munching black bread with that abused and mistaught herd of human sheep, but took him aside and talked matter of another sort to him. After I had finished, I got him to lend me a little ink from his veins; and with this and a sliver I wrote on a piece of bark—

*Put him in the Man Factory—*

and gave it to him, and said—

"Take it to the palace at Camelot and give it into the hands of Amyas le Poulet, whom I call Clarence, and he will understand."

I paid three pennies for my breakfast, and a most extravagant price it was, too, seeing that one could have breakfasted a dozen persons for that money; but I was feeling good by this time, and I had always been a kind of spendthrift any way.

The farmers were bound to throw in something, to sort of offset my liberality, whether I would or no; so I let them give me a flint and steel; and as soon as they had comfortably bestowed Sandy and me on our horse, I lit my pipe. When the first blast of smoke shot out through the bars of my helmet, all those people broke for the woods, and Sandy went over backwards and struck the ground with a dull thud. They thought I was one of those fire-belching dragons they had heard so much about from knights and other professional liars. I had infinite trouble to persuade those people to venture back within explaining distance. Then I told them that this was only a bit of enchantment

*A Connecticut Yankee in King Arthur's Court* **691**

## AT A GLANCE

- The Yankee shares breakfast with road workers and discusses democracy.
- He sends one potential free man to Clarence.
- The Yankee frightens the Britons when he smokes his pipe.

### 1 MAIN IDEA

In this episode Twain begins to develop a new theme—the lack of democracy in Arthur's England. Alisande's refusal to associate with commoners illustrates the rigidity of the medieval class system.

### 2 IRONY

Twain points out the irony of applying the term *freemen* to people who have no freedom of movement or control over their property.

### 3 THEME

The Yankee's criticism of monarchy and inherited power underscores his democratic values.

## GUIDED READING

### LITERAL QUESTION

**1a.** Where does Twain send the one man who shows interest in his political ideas? (He sends him to Camelot to the "Man Factory.")

### INFERENTIAL QUESTION

**1b.** What do you think the Man Factory is, and what is the Yankee's definition of a man? (It's probably a place for political education. The Yankee wants men to think for themselves and have the courage to oppose restrictions on freedom.)

692    *The Novel*

which would work harm to none but my enemies. And I promised, with my hand on my heart, that if all who felt no enmity toward me would come forward and pass before me they should see that only those who remained behind would be struck dead. The procession moved with a good deal of promptness. There were no casualties to report, for nobody had curiosity enough to remain behind to see what would happen. I had learned something. I was ready for any giant or any ogre that might come along, now.

We tarried with a holy hermit, that night, and my opportunity came about the middle of the next afternoon. We were crossing a vast meadow by way of shortcut, and I was musing absently, hearing nothing, seeing nothing, when Sandy suddenly interrupted a remark which she had begun that morning, with the cry—

"Defend thee, lord—peril of life is toward!"

And she slipped down from the horse and ran a little way and stood. I looked up and saw, far off in the shade of a tree, half a dozen armed knights and their squires. My pipe was ready and would have been lit, if I had not been lost in thinking about how to banish oppression from this land and restore to all its people their stolen rights and manhood without disobliging anybody. I lit up at once, and by the time I had got a good head of reserved steam on, here they came. All together, too; they came in a body, they came with a whirr and a rush, they came like a volley from a battery; came with heads low down, plumes streaming out behind, lances advanced at a level. It was a handsome sight, a beautiful sight—for a man up a tree. I laid my lance in rest and waited, with my heart beating, till the iron wave was just ready to break over me, then spouted a column of white smoke through the bars of my helmet. You should have seen the wave go to pieces and scatter! This was a finer sight than the other one.

But these people stopped, two or three hundred yards away, and this troubled me. My satisfaction collapsed, and fear came; I judged I was a

## GUIDED READING

### LITERAL QUESTION

**1a.** What does the Yankee tell the frightened farmers about how to save themselves from the "dragon"? (He says his magic works only against enemies.)

### INFERENTIAL QUESTION

**1b.** What did the Yankee learn from this experience? (He learned a simple way to control people by their superstitious fear of dragons. He could meet his enemies and defeat them by fear without even having to fight.)

lost man. But Sandy was radiant; and was going to be eloquent, but I stopped her, and told her my magic had miscarried, somehow or other, and she must mount, with all dispatch, and we must ride for life. No, she wouldn't. She said that my enchantment had disabled those knights; they were not riding on, because they couldn't; wait, they would drop out of their saddles presently, and we would get their horses and harness.

"Well, then, what are they waiting for? Why don't they leave? Nobody's hindering. Good land, I'm willing to let bygones be bygones, I'm sure."

"Leave, is it? Oh, give thyself easement as to that. They dream not of it, no, not they. They wait to yield them."

"Come—really, is that 'sooth'[11]—as you people say? If they want to, why don't they?"

"It would like them much; but an ye wot how dragons are esteemed, ye would not hold them blamable. They fear to come."

"Well, then, suppose I go to them instead, and—"

"Ah, wit ye well they would not abide your coming. I will go."

And she did. She was a handy person to have along on a raid. I would have considered this a doubtful errand, myself. I presently saw the knights riding away, and Sandy coming back. She said that when she told those people I was The Boss, it hit them where they lived: "smote them sore with fear and dread" was her word; and then they were ready to put up with anything she might require. So she swore them to appear at Arthur's court within two days and yield them, with horse and harness, and be my knights henceforth, and subject to my command. How much better she managed that thing than I should have done it myself! She was a daisy.

"And so I'm proprietor of some knights," said I, as we rode off. "Who would ever have

supposed that I should live to list up assets of that sort. I shan't know what to do with them; unless I raffle them off. How many of them are there, Sandy?"

"Seven, please you, sir, and their squires."

"It is a good haul. Who are they? Where do they hang out?"

"Where do they hang out?"

"Yes, where do they live?"

"Ah, I understood thee not. That will I tell thee eftsoons."[12] Then she said musingly, and softly, turning the words daintily over her tongue: "Hang they out—hang they out—where hang—where do they hang out; eh, right so; where do they hang out. Of a truth the phrase hath a fair and winsome grace, and is prettily worded withal. I will repeat it anon and anon in mine idlesse, whereby I may peradventure learn it. Where do they hang out. Even so! Already it falleth trippingly from my tongue, and forasmuch as—"

"Don't forget the cowboys, Sandy."

"Cowboys?"

"Yes; the knights, you know: You were going to tell me about them. A while back, you remember."

"I will well, and lightly will begin. So they two departed and rode into a great forest. And—"

"Great Scott!"

You see, I recognized my mistake at once. I had set her works agoing; it was my own fault; she would be thirty days getting down to those facts. And she generally began without a preface and finished without a result. If you interrupted her she would either go right along without noticing, or answer with a couple of words, and go back and say the sentence over again. So, interruptions only did harm; and yet I had to interrupt, and interrupt pretty frequently, too, in order to save my life; a person would die if he let her monotony drip on him right along all day.

---

11. **sooth:** the truth.

12. **eftsoons** [eft soōnz′]: immediately, without delay; it also can mean "often."

*A Connecticut Yankee in King Arthur's Court* **693**

## AT A GLANCE

- Sandy says the knights are frightened, and she approaches them.
- They surrender to the Yankee.
- Sandy tries out nineteenth-century slang.

### 1 CHARACTERIZATION

Sandy functions as a translator for the Yankee, helping him to understand medieval customs. Far from disparaging her as a "liar," he is coming to depend on her.

### 2 DIALOGUE

Humor results from the contrast between the slangy, informal speech of the nineteenth century and the formal, flowery language of the sixth century.

## GUIDED READING

### LITERAL QUESTION

**1a.** What does Sandy tell the knights to do to signify their surrender to the Yankee? (She asks them to appear at Arthur's court in two days and surrender their horses, harness, and themselves to the Yankee.)

### INFERENTIAL QUESTION

**1b.** What does Sandy's assumption that they will keep their word tell you about the chivalric code? (The knights are bound merely by their word. For all practical purposes, they could go away and never surrender, but their honor binds them to carry out their promise.)

- Sandy continues her story.
- They meet one of the Yankee's missionaries of cleanliness.
- The Yankee discusses his plan to promote soap and its use.

## 1 SETTING

The castle and setting conform to the best Romantic traditions—huge, gray, draped with ivy, seen at sunset. The episode that takes place in this seemingly idyllic setting will add to the satire leveled at the Arthurian tradition.

## 2 THEME

The Yankee's concern with cleanliness reflects the preoccupations of his century and nation. This view of hygiene represents more conflict between his society and Arthur's.

## 3 THEME

One of the novel's major themes is superstition—the fear it causes and its role in obstructing progress. In convincing the nobility to use soap, the Yankee must overcome their superstitious fear.

---

"Great Scott!" I said in my distress. She went right back and began over again:

"So they two departed and rode into a great forest. And—"

The sun was now setting. It was about three in the afternoon when Alisande had begun to tell me who the cowboys were; so she had made pretty good progress with it—for her. She would arrive some time or other, no doubt, but she was not a person who could be hurried.

## 12. Morgan le Fay

We were approaching a castle which stood on high ground: a huge, strong venerable structure, whose gray towers and battlements were charmingly draped with ivy, and whose whole majestic mass was drenched with splendors flung from the sinking sun. It was the largest castle we had seen, and so I thought it might be the one we were after, but Sandy said no. She did not know who owned it; she said she had passed it without calling, when she went down to Camelot.

If knights-errant[13] were to be believed, not all castles were desirable places to seek hospitality in; if I could find out something about a castle before ringing the doorbell—I mean hailing the warders—it was the sensible thing to do. So I was pleased when I saw in the distance a horseman making the bottom turn of the road that wound down from this castle.

As we approached each other, I saw that he wore a plumed helmet, and seemed to be otherwise clothed in steel, but bore a curious addition also—a stiff square garment like a herald's tabard.[14] However, I had to smile at my own forgetfulness when I got nearer and read this sign on his tabard:

---

13. **knights-errant:** medieval knights who traveled in search of adventure.
14. **herald's tabard** [tab´ərd]: royal or noble messenger's official coat, decorated with his king's or lord's coat-of-arms.

---

> "Persimmon's Soap—
> All the Prime-Donne[15]
> Use It."

That was a little idea of my own, and had several wholesome purposes in view toward the civilizing and uplifting of this nation. In the first place, it was a furtive, underhand blow at this nonsense of knight errantry, though nobody suspected that but me. I had started a number of these people out—the bravest knights I could get—each sandwiched between bulletin boards bearing one device or another, and I judged that by and by when they got to be numerous enough they would begin to look ridiculous.

Secondly, these missionaries would gradually, and without creating suspicion or exciting alarm, introduce a rudimentary cleanliness among the nobility, and from them it would work down to the people. My missionaries were taught to spell out the gilt signs on their tabards—the showy gilding was a neat idea, I could have got the king to wear a bulletin board for the sake of that barbaric splendor—they were to spell out these signs and then explain to the lords and ladies what soap was; and if the lords and ladies were afraid of it, get them to try it on a dog. The missionary's next move was to get the family together and try it on himself; he was to stop at no experiment, however desperate, that could convince the nobility that soap was harmless; if any final doubt remained, he must catch a hermit—the woods were full of them; saints they called themselves, and saints they were believed to be. They were unspeakably holy, and worked miracles, and everybody stood in awe of them. If a

---

15. *Prime-Donne* [prē´mā dôn´ā]: Italian for "first ladies."

---

## GUIDED READING

### LITERAL QUESTIONS

**1a.** Why is the Yankee happy to see a horseman near the castle? (He wants to find out something about the castle before entering.)

**2a.** What steps does the Yankee take to interest the people in cleanliness? (He sends knights around with sandwich boards advertising soap and then demonstrating the harmlessness of soap.)

### INFERENTIAL QUESTIONS

**1b.** Why do you think Twain shows the Yankee taking a "sensible" precaution before entering this castle? (It may be Twain's way of alerting the reader to be suspicious about the castle.)

**2b.** Why does the Yankee need such elaborate plans to introduce soap and its uses? (Soap is a totally new concept to the Britons, who are so superstitious that they fear and resist everything new.)

hermit could survive a wash, and that failed to convince a duke, give him up, let him alone.

Whenever my missionaries overcame a knight errant on the road they washed him, and when he got well they swore him to go and get a bulletin board and disseminate soap and civilization the rest of his days. As a consequence the workers in the field were increasing by degrees, and the reform was steadily spreading.

This missionary knight's name was La Cote Male Taile, and he said that this castle was the abode of Morgan le Fay, sister of King Arthur, and wife of King Uriens.

In due time we were challenged by the warders, from the castle walls, and after a parley admitted. I have nothing pleasant to tell about that visit. But it was not a disappointment, for I knew Mrs. le Fay by reputation, and was not expecting anything pleasant. She was held in awe by the whole realm, for she had made everybody believe she was a great sorceress. All her ways were wicked, all her instincts devilish. She was loaded to the eyelids with cold malice. All her history was black with crime; and among her crimes murder was common. I was most curious to see her; as curious as I could have been to see Satan. To my surprise she was beautiful; black thoughts had failed to make her expression repulsive, age had failed to wrinkle her satin skin or mar its bloomy freshness.

As soon as we were fairly within the castle gates we were ordered into her presence. King Uriens was there, a kind-faced old man with a subdued look. But Morgan was the main attraction, the conspicuous personality here; she was head chief of this household, that was plain. She caused us to be seated, and then she began, with all manner of pretty graces and graciousnesses, to ask me questions. Dear me, it was like a bird or a flute, or something, talking. I felt persuaded that this woman must have been misrepresented, lied about. She trilled along, and trilled along, and presently a handsome young page, clothed like the rainbow, and as easy and undulatory of

*A Connecticut Yankee in King Arthur's Court* **695**

- Morgan le Fay casually stabs a page.
- She threatens to send the Yankee to the dungeon for complimenting Arthur.
- Sandy tells Morgan that the Yankee is "The Boss," and Morgan is impressed.
- The Yankee inspects the prisons and remarks on the cruel practices of the day.

**1 CHARACTERIZATION**

Morgan le Fay stabs the page for a petty mistake, revealing herself as hasty and tyrannical. The off-handedness of this murder is especially chilling.

**2 HUMOR**

The guards are naturally terrified at the thought of being burnt to ashes by occult power. The humor helps satirize a time in which a lady claims to be "childishly curious to see" such a spectacle.

**3 CHARACTERIZATION**

The Yankee reveals himself as a man of conscience who cares about the rights of others.

**4 THEME**

This encounter satirizes one more feature that made medieval society unjust: a prison system that operated arbitrarily at the whim of the powerful.

---

movement as a wave, came with something on a golden salver, and kneeling to present it to her, overdid his graces and lost his balance, and so **1** fell lightly against her knee. She slipped a dirk[16] into him in as matter-of-course a way as another person would have harpooned a rat!

Morgan le Fay rippled along as musically as ever. Marvelous woman. And what a glance she had: when it fell in reproof upon those servants, they shrunk and quailed as timid people do when the lightning flashes out of a cloud. I could have got the habit myself. It was the same with the poor old Brer Uriens; he was always on the ragged edge of apprehension; she could not even turn towards him but he winced.

In the midst of the talk I let drop a complimentary word about King Arthur, forgetting for the moment how this woman hated her brother. That one little compliment was enough. She clouded up like a storm; she called for her guards, and said—

"Hale me these varlets[17] to the dungeons!"

That struck cold on my ears, for her dungeons had a reputation. Nothing occurred to me to say—or do. But not so with Sandy. As the guard laid a hand upon me, she piped up with the tranquilest confidence, and said—

"Dost thou covet destruction, thou maniac? It is The Boss!"

Now what a happy idea that was—and so simple; yet it would never have occurred to me. I was born modest, not all over, but in spots; and this was one of the spots.

The effect upon madame was electrical. It cleared her countenance and brought back her smiles and all her persuasive graces and blandishments; but nevertheless she was not able to entirely cover up with them the fact that she was in a ghastly fright. She said:

"La, but do list to thine handmaid! As if one gifted with powers like to mine might say the

---

16. **dirk:** dagger.
17. **varlets:** scoundrels.

---

thing which I have said unto one who has vanquished Merlin, and not be jesting. By mine enchantments I foresaw your coming, and by them I knew you when you entered here. I did but play this little jest with hope to surprise you into some display of your art, as not doubting you would blast the guards with occult fires, consuming them to ashes on the spot, a marvel much beyond mine own ability, yet one which I have long been childishly curious to see."

**2** The guards were less curious, and got out as soon as they got permission.

I had had enough of this grisly place by this time, and wanted to leave, but I couldn't, **3** because I had something on my mind that my conscience kept prodding me about, and wouldn't let me forget.

So I braced up and placed my matter before her royal Highness. I said I had been having a general jail delivery at Camelot and among neighboring castles, and with her permission I would like to examine her collection, her bric-a-brac—that is to say, her prisoners. She resisted; but she finally consented. She called her guards and torches, and we went down into the dungeons. These were down under the castle's foundations, and mainly were small cells hollowed out of the living rock. Some of these cells had no light at all.

**4** I set forty-seven prisoners loose out of those awful ratholes. Dear me, for what trifling offenses the most of those forty-seven men and women were shut up there! Indeed some were there for no distinct offense at all, but only to gratify somebody's spite; and not always the queen's by any means, but a friend's.

Consider it: among these forty-seven captives, there were five whose names, offenses and dates of incarceration were no longer known! The king and the queen knew nothing about these poor creatures, except that they were heirlooms, assets inherited, along with the throne, from the former firm. Nothing of their history had been transmitted with their persons, and so

---

## GUIDED READING

**LITERAL QUESTION**

**1a.** How does Sandy save the Yankee from Morgan le Fay's dungeon? (She informs Morgan that he is The Boss and thus more powerful than she.)

**INFERENTIAL QUESTION**

**1b.** What does Morgan's deference to the Yankee show about what is important in Arthur's England? (Power—especially magical power—is most important. The Yankee is a more powerful "sorcerer" than Morgan le Fay, and so she defers to him.)

the inheriting owners had considered them of no value, and had felt no interest in them. I said to the queen—

"Then why in the world didn't you set them free?"

The question was a puzzler. She didn't know *why* she hadn't; the thing had never come up in her mind.

When I brought my procession of human bats up into the open world and the glare of the afternoon sun—previously blind-folding them, in charity for eyes so long untortured by light—they were a spectacle to look at. Skeletons, scarecrows, goblins, pathetic frights, every one. I muttered absently—

"I *wish* I could photograph them!"

You have seen that kind of people who will never let on that they don't know the meaning of a new big word. The more ignorant they are, the more pitifully certain they are to pretend you haven't shot over their heads. The queen was just one of that sort, and was always making the stupidest blunders by reason of it. She hesitated a moment; then her face brightened up with sudden comprehension, and she said she would do it for me.

I thought to myself: She? why what can she know about photography? But it was a poor time to be thinking. When I looked around, she was moving on the procession with an ax!

Well, she certainly was a curious one, was Morgan le Fay. I have seen a good many kinds of women in my time, but she laid over them all, for variety. And how sharply characteristic of her this episode was. She had no more idea than a horse of how to photograph a procession; but being in doubt, it was just like her to try to do it with an ax.

## 13. The Ogre's Castle

Sandy and I were on the road again, next morning, bright and early. Two days later, toward noon, Sandy began to show signs of excitement and feverish expectancy. She said we were approaching the ogre's castle.

The object of our quest had gradually dropped out of my mind; this sudden resurrection of it made it seem quite a real and startling thing, for a moment, and roused up in me a smart interest. Sandy's excitement increased every moment; and so did mine, for that sort of thing is catching. My heart got to thumping. Presently, when Sandy slid from the horse, motioned me to stop, and went creeping stealthily, with her head bent nearly to her knees, toward a row of bushes that bordered a declivity, the thumpings grew stronger and quicker. And they kept it up while she was gaining her ambush and getting her glimpse over the declivity and also while I was creeping to her side on my knees. Her eyes were burning, now, as she pointed with her finger, and said in a panting whisper—

"The castle! The castle! Lo, where it looms!"

What a welcome disappointment I experienced! I said—

"Castle? It is nothing but a pigsty; a pigsty with a wattled fence around it."

She looked surprised and distressed. The animation faded out of her face, and during many moments she was lost in thought and silent. Then—

"It was not enchanted aforetime," she said in a musing fashion, as if to herself. "And how strange is this marvel, and how awful—that to the one perception it is enchanted and dight[18] in a base and shameful aspect; yet to the perception of the other it is not enchanted, hath suffered no change, but stands firm and stately still, girt with its moat and waving its banners in the blue air from its towers. And God shield us, how it pricks the heart to see again these gracious captives, and the sorrow deepened in their sweet faces! We have tarried long, and are to blame."

I saw my cue. The castle was enchanted to *me*, not to her. It would be wasted time to try

_____
18. **dight** [dīt]: adorned.

*A Connecticut Yankee in King Arthur's Court*  **697**

AT A GLANCE

- The prisoners are brought out.
- Morgan le Fay tries to "photograph" them with an axe.
- Sandy and the Yankee approach the ogre's castle, which seems to be a mere pigsty to the Yankee.

1 **CHARACTERIZATION**

Morgan le Fay is vain, unable to admit ignorance of anything. It is also typical of her to assume that the Yankee's impulse to photograph the prisoners must involve mayhem.

2 **PLOT: EPISODE**

The Yankee and Sandy move on to further adventure. After many episodes, they near the completion of their "quest"—the rescue of maidens imprisoned by ogres.

3 **THEME**

Sandy sees a castle where the Yankee sees a pigsty. This humorous discrepancy represents another gibe at medieval superstition.

## GUIDED READING

### LITERAL QUESTION

**1a.** What explanation does Sandy offer about why she sees a castle and the Yankee sees a pigsty? (She says that the place is enchanted to his sight but that she sees it as it really is.)

### INFERENTIAL QUESTION

**1b.** How does this incident reveal Sandy's beliefs about magic and romance? (Convinced that there is a romantic adventure at hand, she deludes herself into seeing a castle.)

- The Yankee buys ("rescues") the hogs ("maidens") from the swineherds ("ogres").
- Sandy and the Yankee drive the rescued pigs home, Sandy insisting that they be treated as noblewomen.

## 1 HUMOR

In a charmingly nonsensical exchange Sandy wonders how the Yankee will be able to aim properly at the ogres when they have shrunk to the size of swineherds.

## 2 PLOT: RESOLUTION

The quest is accomplished, not through great bravery but through the Yankee's common sense and commerce. Twain's modern skepticism continually debunks the myths of the chivalric age.

## 3 THEME

Twain creates some psychological realism behind the belief in magic and enchantment: People see what they expect.

## 4 SATIRE

Twain's satire on the relative worthlessness of the aristocracy reaches its height in this passage.

---

to argue her out of her delusion, it couldn't be done; I must just humor it. So I said—

"This is a common case—the enchanting of a thing to one eye and leaving it in its proper form to another. But no harm is done. In fact it is lucky the way it is. If these ladies were hogs to everybody and to themselves, it would be necessary to break the enchantment, and that might be impossible if one failed to find out the particular process of the enchantment. But here, by good luck, no one's eyes but mine are under the enchantment, and so it is of no consequence to dissolve it. These ladies remain ladies to you, and to themselves, and to everybody else; and at the same time they will suffer in no way from my delusion, for when I know that an ostensible hog is a lady, that is enough for me, I know how to treat her."

"Thanks, oh sweet my lord, thou talkest like an angel. And I know that thou wilt deliver them, for that thou art minded to great deeds and art as strong a knight of your hands and as brave to will and to do, as any that is on live."

"I will not leave a princess in the sty, Sandy. Are those three yonder that to my disordered eyes are starveling swineherds"—

1 "The ogres? Are *they* changed also? It is most wonderful. Now am I fearful; for how canst thou strike with sure aim when five of their nine cubits of stature are to thee invisible? Ah, go warily, fair sir; this is a mightier emprise[19] than I wend."

"You be easy, Sandy. All I need to know is, how *much* of an ogre is invisible; then I know how to locate his vitals. Don't you be afraid, I will make short work of these bunco steerers. Stay where you are."

2 I left Sandy kneeling there, corpse-faced but plucky and hopeful, and rode down to the pigsty, and struck up a trade with the swineherds. I won their gratitude by buying out all the hogs at the lump sum of sixteen pennies. I was just in

---

19. **emprise:** adventure.

time; for the tax gatherers would have been along next day and swept off pretty much all the stock, leaving the swineherds very short of hogs and Sandy out of princesses. But now the tax people could be paid in cash, and there would be a stake left besides.

I sent the three men away, and then opened the sty gate and beckoned Sandy to come—which she did; and not leisurely, but with the 3 rush of a prairie fire. And when I saw her fling herself upon those hogs, with tears of joy running down her cheeks, and strain them to her heart, and kiss them, and caress them, and call them reverently by grand princely names, I was ashamed of her, ashamed of the human race.

We had to drive those hogs home—ten miles; and no ladies were ever more fickle-minded or contrary. They would stay in no road, no path; they broke out through the brush on all sides, and flowed away in all directions, over rocks, and hills, and the roughest places they could find. And they must not be struck, or roughly accosted; Sandy could not bear to see them treated in ways unbecoming their rank. The troublesomest old sow of the lot had to be called my Lady, and your Highness, like the rest. It is annoying and difficult to scour around after hogs, 4 in armor. There was one small countess, with an iron ring in her snout and hardly any hair on her back, that was the devil for perversity. She gave me a race of an hour, over all sorts of country, and then we were right where we had started from, having made not a rod of real progress. I seized her at last by the tail, and brought her along, squealing. When I overtook Sandy, she was horrified, and said it was in the last degree indelicate to drag a countess by her train.

We got the hogs home just at dark—most of them. The princess Nerovens de Morganore was missing, and two of her ladies in waiting: namely, Miss Angela Bohun, and the Demoiselle Elaine Courtemains. Also among the missing were several mere baronesses—and I wanted them to stay missing; but no, all that sausage meat had to be

---

## GUIDED READING

### LITERAL QUESTION

**1a.** Does the Yankee try to convince Sandy she is wrong about the castle? (No, he lets her continue in her delusion.)

### INFERENTIAL QUESTION

**1b.** Why does the Yankee abet her in her delusion? (In his practical way, he realizes that he will never be able to convince her to see the world as he does.)

*A Connecticut Yankee in King Arthur's Court* **699**

- The Yankee and Sandy go on a religious pilgrimage.
- Sir Ozana le Cure Hardy brings news: A miraculous fountain has ceased to flow.
- He reports that because the Boss could not be found Merlin is already trying to restore the fountain.

## 1  BACKGROUND

Pilgrimages to holy places were important in the religious life of the time. The major English literary work of the later Middle Ages, Chaucer's *Canterbury Tales,* concerns such a pilgrimage.

## 2  READING SKILLS: PREDICTING OUTCOMES

Merlin reenters the narrative in this episode. From their previous confrontations, we can predict that the Yankee will take up the challenge of the fountain and manage to defeat Merlin once again.

found; so, servants were sent out with torches to scour the woods and hills to that end.

Of course the whole drove was housed in the house, and great guns—well, I never saw anything like it! Nor ever heard anything like it. And never smelt anything like it. It was an insurrection in a gasometer.[20]

### 14. The Holy Fountain

The next morning Sandy assembled the swine in the dining room and gave them their breakfast, waiting upon them personally and manifesting in every way deep reverence. Then I spoke up and said:

"All right; let us make a start."

While she was gone to cry her farewells over the pork, I gave that whole peerage[21] away to the servants.

The first thing we struck that day was a procession of pilgrims. It was not going our way, but we joined it nevertheless; for it was hourly being borne in upon me, now, that if I would govern this country wisely, I must be posted in the details of its life, and not at second hand but by personal observation and scrutiny.

1  Sandy knew the goal and purpose of this pilgrimage and she posted me. She said:

"They journey to the Valley of Holiness, for to drink of the miraculous waters."

"Where is this watering place?"

"It lieth a two day journey hence, by the borders of the land that hight the Cuckoo Kingdom."

We put up at the inn in a village just at nightfall, and when I rose next morning and looked abroad, I was ware where a knight came riding in the golden glory of the new day, and recognized him for knight of mine—Sir Ozana le Cure Hardy. He was in the gentlemen's furnish-

ing line, clothed all in steel, in the beautifulest armor of the time—up to where his helmet ought to have been; but he hadn't any helmet, he wore a shiny stovepipe hat, and was as ridiculous a spectacle as one might want to see. It was another of my surreptitious schemes for extinguishing knighthood by making it grotesque and absurd.

I dressed and ran down to welcome Sir Ozana and get his news.

"Where have you been foraging of late?"

"I am but now come from the Valley of Holiness, please you sir."

"I am pointed for that place myself. Is there anything stirring?"

"Sir, it is parlous[22] news I bring, and—be these pilgrims? Then ye may not do better, good folk, than gather and hear the tale I have to tell, sith it concerneth you, forasmuch as ye go to find that ye will not find, my life being hostage for my word, and my word and message being these, namely: That a hap has happened whereof the like has not been seen no more but once this two hundred years, which was the first and last time that that said misfortune strake the holy valley—"

"The miraculous fount hath ceased to flow!" This shout burst from twenty pilgrim mouths at once.

"Ye say well, good people. I was verging to it, even when ye spake."

"How are they feeling about the calamity?"

2  "None may describe it in words. The fount is these nine days dry. At last they sent for thee, Sir Boss, to try magic and enchantment; and if you could not come, then was the messenger to fetch Merlin, and he is there these three days, now, and saith he will fetch that water though he burst the globe and wreck its kingdoms to accomplish it; and right bravely doth he work his magic, but not a whiff of moisture hath he

_____
20. **gasometer** [gas om′ə tər]: tank or reservoir for storing gas.
21. **peerage:** members of the nobility; here, the hogs.

_____
22. **parlous:** perilous.

## GUIDED READING

### LITERAL QUESTIONS

**1a.** Why does the Yankee join the pilgrimage? (He feels that if he wants to govern the country wisely, he should personally observe all important aspects of the country's life.)

**2a.** What has been done so far about the fountain? (First the monks sent for the Yankee; not finding him, they called in Merlin.)

### INFERENTIAL QUESTIONS

**1b.** What does this tell you about the kind of ruler the Yankee is? (He takes his responsibilities seriously and realizes he must temper his reforms to medieval realities.)

**2b.** How does this sequence make clear the relative standings of Merlin and the Yankee as magicians? (They call the Yankee first, thus confirming him as the more powerful of the two.)

started yet, even so much as might qualify as mist upon a copper mirror an ye count not the barrel of sweat he sweateth betwixt sun and sun over the dire labors of his task; and if ye—"

Breakfast was ready. As soon as it was over I showed to Sir Ozana these words which I had written on the inside of his hat: *"Chemical Department, Laboratory extension, Section G. Pxxp. Send two of the first size, two of No. 3 and six of No. 4, together with the proper complementary details—and two of my trained assistants."* And I said:

"Now get you to Camelot as fast as you can fly, brave knight, and show the writing to Clarence, and tell him to have these required matters in the Valley of Holiness with all possible dispatch."

"I will well, Sir Boss," and he was off.

## 15. The Restoration of the Holy Fountain

We made good time, and a couple of hours before sunset we stood upon the high confines of the Valley of Holiness and our eyes swept it from end to end and noted its features.

We reached the monastery before dark. The old abbot's joy to see me was pathetic. He said:

"Delay not, son, but get to thy saving work. An we bring not the water back again, and soon, we are ruined, and the good work of two hundred years must end. And see thou do it with enchantments that be holy."

"When I work, Father, be sure there will be no devil's work connected with it. I shall use no arts that come of the devil, and no elements not created by the hand of God. But is Merlin working strictly on pious lines?"

"Ah, he said he would, my son, he said he would, and took oath to make his promise good."

"Well, in that case, let him proceed."

"But surely you will not sit idle by, but help?"

"It will not answer to mix methods, Father; neither would it be professional courtesy. Merlin is a very good magician in a small way, and has quite a neat provincial reputation. He is struggling along, doing the best he can, and it would not be etiquette for me to take his job until he himself abandons it."

I was at the well next day betimes.[23] Merlin was there, enchanting away but not raising the moisture. He was not in a pleasant humor; and every time I hinted that perhaps this contract

—————
23. **betimes:** in good time; early.

*A Connecticut Yankee in King Arthur's Court* **701**

## AT A GLANCE

- The Yankee sends a note to Clarence requesting chemicals and assistants to help with the fountain.
- They reach the fountain and the Yankee determines to let Merlin finish, before he himself begins work.

### 1 PLOT: RISING ACTION

The Yankee makes plans to work his "magic." We suspect that his solution to the problem of the fountain will involve explosive or mechanical devices.

### 2 IRONY

The abbot asks the Yankee to use only good magic. The Yankee's reply is ironic: He can say that he uses no "arts of the devil," nothing not "created by the hands of God," because he uses no magic at all—only technology.

### 3 CHARACTERIZATION

The wily Yankee pretends to be polite, whereas, in reality, he wishes only to give Merlin enough time to prove his utter powerlessness.

## GUIDED READING

### LITERAL QUESTION

**1a.** What reason does the Yankee give the abbott for not helping Merlin? (He says it is not good to mix methods of magic and that it would not be professional courtesy for him to take the job until Merlin gives up on it.)

### INFERENTIAL QUESTION

**1b.** What are his real reasons for not helping? (He wants it to be clear that Merlin is helpless, in order to make his own success even more spectacular.)

- The Yankee discovers that the fountain is an ordinary well with a leak.
- Merlin says the well is enchanted and that no one can break the spell.
- The Yankee demands the area be cleared overnight so that he can work.
- His experts arrive.

**1 CHARACTERIZATION**

The Yankee's impulse to use a person "of no especial value" as a detonator for dynamite suggests that he may not be above a bit of casual mayhem, if it will enhance his reputation. This impulse also hints at the darker side to the technology the Yankee has found so useful.

**2 CHARACTERIZATION**

Merlin covers his failure by the claim that no one can break the enchantment, showing himself as hypocritical and arrogant.

**3 THEME**

Twain suggests that superstition thrives on secrecy and lack of scientific knowledge. In order to present his repair as magic rather than technology, the Yankee needs to work in secret.

---

was a shade too hefty for a novice he unlimbered his tongue and cursed.

Matters were about as I expected to find them. The "fountain" was an ordinary well, it had been dug in the ordinary way, and stoned up in the ordinary way. I had an idea that the well had sprung a leak; that some of the wall stones near the bottom had fallen and exposed fissures that allowed the water to escape. I called in a couple of monks, locked the door, took a candle, and made them lower me in the bucket. When the chain was all paid out, the candle confirmed my suspicion; a considerable section of the wall was gone, exposing a good big fissure.

I almost regretted that my theory about the well's trouble was correct, because I had another one that had a showy point or two about it for a miracle. I remembered that in America, many centuries later, when an oil well ceased to flow, they used to blast it out with a dynamite torpedo. If I should find this well dry, and no explanation of it, I could astonish these people most nobly by having a person of no especial value drop a dynamite bomb into it.

Saturday noon I went to the well and looked on a while. Merlin was still burning smoke powders, and pawing the air, and muttering gibberish as hard as ever, but looking pretty downhearted, for of course he had not started even a perspiration in that well yet. Finally I said:

"How does the thing promise by this time, partner?"

"Behold, I am even now busied with trial of the powerfulest enchantment known to the princes of the occult arts in the lands of the East; an it fail me, naught can avail. Peace, until I finish."

He raised a smoke this time that darkened all the region. Now arrived the abbot and several hundred monks and nuns, and behind them a multitude of pilgrims and a couple of acres of foundlings, all drawn by the prodigious smoke, and all in a grand state of excitement. The abbot inquired anxiously for results. Merlin said:

"The most potent spirit known to the magicians of the East, and whose name none may utter and live, has laid his spell upon this well. The mortal does not breathe, nor ever will, who can penetrate the secret of that spell, and without that secret none can break it. The water will flow no more forever, good Father. I have done what man could. Suffer me to go."

Of course this threw the abbot into a good deal of consternation. He turned to me with the signs of it in his face, and said:

"Ye have heard him. Is it true?"

"Part of it is. There are conditions under which an effort to break it may have some chance—that is, some small, some trifling chance—of success."

"The conditions—"

"Oh, they are nothing difficult. Only these: I want the well and the surroundings for the space of half a mile, entirely to myself from sunset today until I remove the ban—and nobody allowed to cross the ground but by my authority."

"Are these all?"

"Yes."

"Wait," said Merlin, with an evil smile. "Ye wit that he that would break this spell must know that spirit's name?"

"Yes, I know his name."

"Art a fool? Are ye minded to utter that name and die?"

"Utter it? Why certainly. I would utter it if it was Welsh."

"Ye are even a dead man, then; and I go to tell Arthur."

"That's all right. Take your gripsack and get along. The thing for *you* to do is to go home and work the weather, John W. Merlin."

My two experts arrived in the evening. They had pack mules along, and had brought everything I needed—tools, pump, lead pipe, Greek fire,[24] sheaves of big rockets, roman candles,

---

24. **Greek fire:** incendiary material used as a weapon in ancient warfare; said to be able to burn in water.

---

---

## *GUIDED READING*

**LITERAL QUESTIONS**

**1a.** Why does the Yankee regret what his analysis of the well shows? (He had another theory that would lend itself to a more spectacular cure.)

**2a.** What conditions does the Yankee request in order to fix the well? (He asks for the area to be cleared for a half mile around from sunset to sunup.)

**INFERENTIAL QUESTIONS**

**1b.** What does this regret reveal about the Yankee's character? (He enjoys using bogus magic to amaze the people and put them in awe of him.)

**2b.** Why does he ask for these conditions? (He wants secrecy in order to conceal the very unmagical way in which he will actually fix the fountain and set up his magical effects.)

colored-fire sprays, electric apparatus, and a lot of sundries—everything necessary for the stateliest kind of a miracle. They got their supper and a nap, and about midnight we sallied out through a solitude so wholly vacant and complete that it quite overpassed the required conditions. We took possession of the well and its surroundings. My boys were experts in all sorts of things, from the stoning up of a well to the constructing of a mathematical instrument. An hour before sunrise we had that leak mended in shipshape fashion, and the water began to rise. Then we knocked the head out of an empty hogshead, poured in gunpowder till it lay loosely an inch deep on the bottom. Then we stood up rockets in the hogshead as thick as they could loosely stand, all the different breeds of rockets there are; and they made a portly and imposing sheaf, I can tell you. We grounded the wire of a pocket electrical battery in that powder, we placed a whole magazine of Greek fire on each corner of the roof—blue on one corner, green on another, red on another, and purple on the last, and grounded a wire in each.

About two hundred yards off, in the flat, we built a pen of scantlings, about four feet high, and laid planks on it, and so made a platform. We covered it with swell tapestries borrowed for the occasion, and topped it off with the abbot's own throne. I know the value of these things, for I know human nature. You can't throw too much style into a miracle. It costs trouble, and work, but it pays in the end. I instructed my boys to be ready to man the pumps at the proper time, and make the fur fly. Then we went home.

The news of the disaster to the well had traveled far, by this time; and now for two or three days a steady avalanche of people had been pouring into the valley. We should have a good house, no question about that. Criers went the rounds early in the evening and announced the coming attempt.

I was at the platform and all ready to do the honors. It was a starless black night and no

*A Connecticut Yankee in King Arthur's Court* **703**

AT A GLANCE

- The Yankee and his helpers mend the leak in the fountain and set up their "magic."
- They build a reviewing stand for watching the "miracle."

**1 THEME**

Twain shows how easily a little scientific know-how can create "magic"—illustrating one of his main themes: that superstition depends on ignorance. Twain also shows how much the Yankee's sense of his *own* power depends on technology.

**2 CHARACTERIZATION**

The Yankee is a showman—cynical about human nature—knowing that people are convinced more by flash than by substance. This incident shows the Yankee's shrewd side, which assesses the faults of human nature and uses them.

## GUIDED READING

### LITERAL QUESTION

**1a.** In what ways is the Yankee's miracle treated like a public spectacle? (Stands are built for reviewing it; many people from afar are coming to see it; criers announce the attempt.)

### INFERENTIAL QUESTION

**1b.** What value does this publicity have for the Yankee? (It will make his success all the more spectacular and enhance his already great reputation.)

**1 POINT OF VIEW**

The first-person narration reveals the Yankee's thoughts while he works his "miracle." He shows himself to be cynical and manipulative, a view of him possible only if we share his inner thoughts as well as witness his actions.

**2 VOCABULARY: WORD CHOICE**

Twain creates humor by having the Yankee utter long, bogus magic incantations as he works. Twain's creation of these unpronounceable words satirizes the conventions of magic.

**3 PLOT: CONFLICT**

The Yankee's nature contains significant internal conflicts: love of power vs. love of democracy and faith in the people vs. cynicism about them. We recognize these conflicts, but the Yankee does not.

REFLECTING ON CHAPTERS 8–15

The satire on Arthur's England is often easy to see; what aspects of the Yankee and nineteenth-century civilization are satirized? (love of power, his belief in progress and science to solve all human problems, manipulation, vanity, arrogance)

torches permitted. Merlin took a front seat on the platform. One could not see the multitudes banked together, but they were there, just the same.

1     We had a solemn stage wait, now, for about twenty minutes—a thing I had counted on for effect; it is always good to let your audience have a chance to work up its expectancy. I stood up on the platform and extended my hands abroad, for two minutes, with my face uplifted—that always produces a dead hush—and then slowly pronounced this ghastly word with a kind of awfulness which caused hundreds to tremble, and many women to faint:

"Constantinopolitanischerdudelsackspfeifenmachersgesellschafft!"

Just as I was moaning out the closing hunks of that word, I touched off one of my electric connections, and all that murky world of people stood revealed in a hideous blue glare! It was immense—that effect! Lots of people shrieked; Merlin held his grip, but he was astonished clear down to his corns; he had never seen anything to begin with that, before. Now was the time to pile in the effects. I lifted my hands and groaned out this word—as it were in agony—

"Nihilistendynamittheaterkaestchenssprengungsattentaetsbersuchungen!"

—and turned on the red fire! You should have heard that Atlantic of people moan and howl when that crimson joined the blue! After sixty seconds I shouted—

"Transbaaltruppentropentransporttrampelthiertreibertrauungsthraenentragoedie!"

—and lit up the green fire! After waiting only 2 forty seconds, this time, I spread my arms abroad and thundered out the devastating syllables of this word of words—

"Mekkamuselmannenmassenmenchenmoerdermohrenmuttermarmormonumentenmacher!"

—and whirled on the purple glare! There they were, all going at once, red, blue, green, purple! Four furious volcanoes pouring vast clouds of radiant smoke aloft, and spreading a blinding rainbowed noonday to the furthest confines of that valley.

I knew the boys were at the pump, now, and ready. So I said to the abbot:

"The time is come, Father. I am about to pronounce the dread name and command the spell to dissolve. You want to brace up and take hold of something." Then I made a grand exhibition of extra posturing and gesturing, and shouted:

"Lo, I command the fell spirit that possesses the holy fountain to now disgorge into the skies all the infernal fires that still remain in him, and straightway dissolve his spell and flee hence to the pit, there to lie bound a thousand years. By his own dread name I command it—

"BGWJJILLIGKKK!"

Then I touched off the hogshead of rockets, and a vast fountain of dazzling lances of fire burst in mid-sky into a storm of flashing jewels! One mighty groan of terror started up from the massed people—then suddenly broke into a wild hosannah of joy—for there, fair and plain in the uncanny glare, they saw the freed water leaping forth! The old abbot could not speak a word, for tears and the chokings in his throat; without utterance of any sort, he folded me in his arms and mashed me.

You should have seen those acres of people throw themselves down in that water and kiss it.

I sent Merlin home on a shutter. He had caved in and gone down like a landslide when I pronounced that fearful name.

3     When I started to the chapel, the populace uncovered and fell back reverently to make a wide way for me, as if I had been some kind of a superior being—and I was. I was aware of that. It was a great night, an immense night. There was reputation in it. I could hardly get to sleep for glorying over it.

---

*GUIDED READING*

**LITERAL QUESTIONS**

**1a.** What does the Yankee say as he performs his "miracle"? (He speaks gibberish in an impressive way.)

**2a.** What is the effect of the Yankee's miracle? (The fountain is repaired, the audience is impressed, and Merlin goes home "on a shutter.")

**INFERENTIAL QUESTIONS**

**1b.** Why does the Yankee speak in this way? (He knows that the people will be more impressed if they hear something they do not understand.)

**2b.** What conflict can you see between the Yankee's sense of his superiority and his belief in democracy? (He seems to believe that most people are created equal, but that he is superior to the rest.)

## STUDY QUESTIONS

### Recalling

1. List four of the social and technological innovations that the Yankee introduces during his first few years in Britain. Why does he act slowly and secretly?

2. How does the Yankee contrast his own power with that of the king? How does he contrast his mental abilities with those of the Britons? What title does he win?

3. Describe the Yankee's difficulties with his armor.

4. What ideas about government does the Yankee try to convey to the freemen, and how do they respond? Why does the Yankee regard the term *freemen* as ironic?

5. How does the Yankee encourage the use of soap in Britain?

6. In what way does Sandy's perception of the damsels and ogres differ from the Yankee's? How does the Yankee explain these differences? How does he rescue the damsels?

7. Explain how the Yankee repairs the Holy Fountain. What effect does his performance have on his own reputation and on Merlin's reputation?

### Interpreting

8. Relate two incidents in which Twain presents knighthood in a humorous and unflattering light.

9. What contrasting attitudes toward authority does the Yankee's interview with the freemen reveal? Find four other illustrations of the differences between the Yankee's way of looking at the world and that of the Britons.

10. What different personality traits does the Yankee reveal in the following actions at the monastery: his analysis of the leaky well, his treatment of Merlin, and the fanfare with which he unveils his achievement?

11. Explain two or three of the Yankee's motives— both humanitarian and otherwise—for introducing nineteenth-century inventions and ideas to sixth-century Britain.

### Extending

12. Do you think the Yankee's desire to bring sixth-century Britain into the nineteenth century is a realizable goal? Why or why not?

## LITERARY FOCUS

### Episodic Narrative

Some novels do not follow a conventional plot line; instead they are episodic in their organization. An **episodic narrative** strings together a series of loosely related incidents. Each incident, or episode, resembles a short story in that it is more or less independent of the other incidents and has its own beginning, middle, and end. Taken together, however, the episodes create a single effect or develop a single overall idea. Writers often use episodic narratives when they want to include a wider range of characters, incidents, places, and issues than might easily fit within a conventional plot structure.

### Thinking About the Episodic Narrative

1. List the separate episodes in the section from page 683 to page 704. Choose three of them, and explain what each adds to Twain's picture of Arthur's Britain. What does each add to the picture of the Yankee?

2. What idea ties these separate episodes together?

■ discussion with freemen: shows acceptance of authority; Yankee's belief in democracy

■ use of smoke to stop attack: shows knights' fearfulness; Yankee's resourcefulness

■ visit to Morgan le Fay: cruelty of nobles; Yankee's compassion

■ freeing enchanted ladies: Sandy's delusions; Yankee's pragmatism

■ repair of Holy Fountain: Britons' superstitions; Yankee's resourcefulness

2. All contrast Yankee's common sense, initiative, belief in democracy with the Britons' credulity, ignorance, submissiveness.

1. iron/steel factories, telephones, telegraphs, schools, military/naval academies; great shock if he introduced all these at once

2. He has real power; king is a figurehead. He has intelligence; Britons are ignorant. *The Boss*

3. has difficulty putting it on, moving in it, cannot scratch, is hot, cannot mount his horse, is plagued by bugs

4. democracy; are confused; not free at all

5. Wandering knights wear sandwich boards advertising soap, teach people how to use it.

6. Sandy sees damsels and ogres; he sees hogs and swineherds; thinks Sandy is deluded; pays swineherds sixteen pennies for hogs.

7. sends for experts, mends leak, sets off fireworks; enhances his reputation while hurting Merlin's

8. difficulties with armor; sandwich boards

9. He does not accept arbitrary authority; freemen do. He dislikes deferring to titles, is skeptical about Alisande's tale, is uncomfortable sleeping on ground and going without bath, questions why Morgan le Fay holds prisoners.

10. *well*—logic, practicality, resourcefulness; *Merlin*—vindictiveness; *fanfare*—vanity, showmanship, craftiness

11. to improve Britons' lives; to be powerful, important

12. Possible answer: Britons are too superstitious to accept his ideas.

### LITERARY FOCUS

1. ■ interrogation of Alisande: shows Britons' casual attitude toward facts; Yankee values

■ difficulties with armor: show inconvenience of knighthood; Yankee's regard for convenience

- The Yankee decides to travel disguised as a freeman.
- The king insists on joining him but first has to "heal the sick."
- The Yankee reads the first newspaper published at Camelot.

LITERARY OPTIONS

- theme
- characterization

THEMATIC OPTIONS

- capability for change
- human suffering
- justice

**1** PLOT: EPISODE

The Yankee's plan to travel in disguise ties the next few episodes together.

**2** SATIRE

Twain affectionately satirizes the modern world's addiction to newspapers. His choice of newspaper name lampoons the sensationalist journalism of his own time.

## 16. The First Newspaper

*King Arthur and his court travel from Camelot to see the restored fountain, and the Yankee greets them with much pomp and circumstance. He then conceives a new project.*

It was a good campaign that we made in that Valley of Holiness, and I was very well satisfied, and ready to move on. I made up my mind to turn out and go a cruise alone. My idea was to disguise myself as a freeman of peasant degree and wander through the country a week or two on foot. This would give me a chance to eat and lodge with the lowliest and poorest class of free citizens on equal terms. There was no other way to inform myself perfectly of their everyday life and the operation of the laws upon it. If I went among them as a gentleman, there would be restraints and conventionalities which would shut me out from their private joys and troubles, and I should get no further than the outside shell.

When I told the king I was going out disguised as a petty freeman to scour the country and familiarize myself with the humbler life of the people, he was all afire with the novelty of the thing in a minute, and was bound to take a

**706** *The Novel*

chance in the adventure himself—nothing should stop him—he would drop everything and go along—it was the prettiest idea he had run across for many a day. He wanted to glide out the back way and start at once; but I showed him that that wouldn't answer. You see, he was billed for the king's-evil[1]—to touch for it, I mean—and it wouldn't be right to disappoint the house.

There was a very good layout for the king's-evil business—very tidy and creditable. The king sat under a canopy of state, about him were clustered a large body of the clergy in full canonicals. There were eight hundred sick people present. The work was slow; it lacked the interest of novelty for me, because I had seen the ceremonies before; the thing soon became tedious, but the proprieties required me to stick it out.

Well, when the priest had been droning for three hours, and the sick were still pressing forward as plenty as ever, I got to feeling intolerably bored. I was sitting by an open window not far from the canopy of state, when outside there rang clear as a clarion a note that enchanted my soul and tumbled thirteen worthless centuries about my ears: "Camelot *Weekly Hosannah and Literary Volcano*—latest irruption—only two cents—" One greater than kings had arrived—the newsboy. But I was the only person in all that throng who knew the meaning of this mighty birth and what this imperial magician was come into the world to do.

I dropped a nickel out of the window and got my paper; the Adam-newsboy of the world went around the corner to get my change; is around the corner yet. It was delicious to see a newspaper again, yet I was conscious of a secret shock when my eye fell upon the first batch of display headlines. I had lived in a clammy atmosphere of reverence, respect, deference, so long, that they sent a quivery little cold wave through me:

---

1. **king's-evil:** It was believed that misfortune, suffering, and injury could be cured by a king's touch.

---

**LITERAL QUESTION**

**1a.** What does the Yankee realize the moment he sees the irreverent headlines of the newspaper? (He realizes just how much he has been changed by the respectful deference in which he has been living.)

**INFERENTIAL QUESTION**

**1b.** Why do you think the Yankee calls this reverence "clammy"? (He probably feels that it stifles fresh, independent thought and promotes a kind of spiritual decay.)

**HIGH TIMES IN THE VALLEY OF HOLINESS!**

**THE WATER-ᴍORKSCORKED!**

**BRER MERLIN WORKS HIS ARTS, BUT GETS LEFT!**

**But t he Boss scores on his first Innings!**

*The Miraculous Well Uncorked amid awful outbursts of*

**INFERNAL FIRE AND SMOKE ANDTHUNDER!**

**UNPARALLELED REJOIBINGS!**

—and so on and so on. Yes, it was too loud. Once I could have enjoyed it and seen nothing out of the way about it, but now its note was discordant. It was plain I had undergone a considerable change without noticing it. I found myself unpleasantly affected by pert little irreverencies which would have seemed but proper and airy graces of speech at an earlier period of my life. There was an abundance of the following breed of items, and they discomforted me:

*Local Smoke and Cinders.*

Sir Launceʟoʇ met up with old King' Vgrivance of Ireland unexpectedly last weok over on the moor south of Sir Balmoral le Merveilleuse's hog dasture. The widow has been notified.

Expedition No. 3 will start adout the first of next mgnth on a search f8r Sir Sagramour le Desirous. It is in comand of the renowned Knight of the Red Lawns, assissted by Sir Persant of Inde, who is competeqt. intelligent, courteous, and in every wav a brick, and furᴛʜer assisted by Sir Palamides the Saracen, who is no huckleberry himself. This is no pic-nic, these boys *m*ean busine&s.

The readers of the Hosannah will regret to learn that the hadndsome and popular Sir Charolais of Gaul, who during his four weeks' stay at the Bull and Halibut, this city, has won every heart by his polished manners and elegant c¶nversation, will pull out to-day for home. Give us another call, Charley !

The bdsiness end of the funeral of the late Sir Dalliance the duke's son of Cornwall, killed in an encounter with the Giant of the Knotted Bludgeon last ʇuesday on the borders of the Plain of Enchantment was in the hands of the ever affable and eʏʏcient Mumble, prince of unƷertakers, than whom there exists none by whom it were a more satisfying pleasure to have the last sad offices performed. Give him a trial.

*A Connecticut Yankee in King Arthur's Court* **707**

## GUIDED READING

**LITERAL QUESTION**

**1a.** What sort of items does the "Local Smoke and Cinders" column contain? (notes about death, fights and feuds, social visits, and funerals)

**INFERENTIAL QUESTION**

**1b.** Why do you think Twain includes this column? (to satirize both medieval romances of knightly adventures and columns in the newspapers of his day)

## 1 CHARACTERIZATION

Twain characterizes the people of Arthur's England as curious and eager about this strange new thing—a newspaper. This balances the satire which shows them as afraid of the new and unknown.

## 2 HUMOR

The Yankee's factual explanation of the newspaper contains so many undefined terms that it is meaningless to the Britons. The fact that journals, paper, and printing are utterly unknown to the Britons suggests how far they remain from the Yankee's former world.

## 3 STYLE: FIGURATIVE LANGUAGE

The Yankee compares himself to a proud new mother to show pride in an idea of his that has come to fruition.

Of course it was good enough journalism for a beginning. I was hungry enough for literature to want to take down the whole paper at this one meal, but I got only a few bites, and then had to postpone, because the monks around me besieged me so with eager questions: What is this curious thing? What is it for? Is it a handkerchief—saddle blanket—part of a shirt? What is it made of? How thin it is, and how dainty and frail, and how it rattles. Will it wear, do you think, and won't the rain injure it? Is it writing that appears on it, or is it only ornamentation? They suspected it was writing, because those among them who knew how to read Latin and had a smattering of Greek, recognized some of the letters, but they could make nothing out of the result as a whole. I put my information in the simplest form I could:

"It is a public journal; I will explain what that is, another time. It is not cloth, it is made of paper; sometime I will explain what paper is. The lines on it are reading matter; and not written by hand, but printed; by and by I will explain what printing is. A thousand of these sheets have been made, all exactly like this, in every minute detail—they can't be told apart." Then they all broke out with exclamations of surprise and admiration:

"A thousand! Verily a mighty work—a year's work for many men."

"No—merely a day's work for a man and a boy."

"Ah-h—a miracle, a wonder! Dark work of enchantment."

I let it go at that. They took it, handling it as cautiously and devoutly as if it had been some holy thing come from some supernatural region; and gently felt of its texture, caressed its pleasant smooth surface with lingering touch, and scanned the mysterious characters with fascinated eyes. These grouped bent heads, these charmed faces, these speaking eyes—how beautiful to me! For was not this my darling, and was not all this mute wonder and interest and homage a most eloquent tribute and unforced compliment to it? I knew, then, how a mother feels when women, whether strangers or friends, take her new baby, and close themselves about it with one eager impulse, and bend their heads over it in a tranced adoration that makes all the rest of the universe vanish out of their consciousness. Yes, this was heaven; I was tasting it once, if I might never taste it more.

## 17. The Yankee and the King Travel Incognito

About bedtime I took the king to my private quarters to cut his hair and help him get the hang of the lowly raiment he was to wear. I also trimmed his whiskers and moustache until they were only about a half inch long; and tried to do it inartistically, and succeeded. It was a villainous disfigurement. When he got his lubberly sandals on, and his long robe of coarse brown linen cloth, which hung straight from his neck to his anklebones, he was no longer the comeliest man in the kingdom, but one of the unhandsomest and most commonplace and unattractive. We were dressed and barbered alike, and could pass for small farmers, or farm bailiffs, or shepherds, or carters; yes, or for village artisans, if we chose, our costume being in effect universal among the poor, because of its strength and cheapness.

We slipped away an hour before dawn, and by broad sunup had made eight or ten miles, and were in the midst of a sparsely settled country.

I found a comfortable seat for the king by the roadside, and then gave him a morsel or two to stay his stomach with. Then I said I would find some water for him, and strolled away.

I found the water, some three hundred yards away, when I heard voices. The next moment these comers jingled into sight around a turn of the road—smartly clad people of quality, with luggage-mules and servants in their train! I

**708**   *The Novel*

---

## GUIDED READING

### LITERAL QUESTIONS

**1a.** What reaction do the people have when the Yankee tells them there are a thousand copies of the newspaper? (They're amazed and think it must be some kind of magic.)

**2a.** How does Arthur look, after the Yankee helps him with his disguise? (He's no longer "the comeliest man in the kingdom" but looks quite common and ordinary.)

### INFERENTIAL QUESTIONS

**1b.** What can you infer about the Britons' belief in magic from this incident? (The people explain whatever they do not understand as "enchantment.")

**2b.** What does this transformation suggest about the role clothes and grooming play among the nobility? (It suggests clothes make the person; without his royal outfit, Arthur looks ordinary—even *worse* than ordinary.)

was off like a shot, through the bushes, by the shortest cut.

"Pardon, my king, but it's no time for ceremony—jump! Jump to your feet—some quality are coming!"

"Is that a marvel? Let them come."

"But my liege! You must not be seen sitting. Rise—and stand in humble posture while they pass! You are a peasant, you know."

"True—I had forgot it, so lost was I in planning of a huge war with Gaul"—he was up by this time, but a farm could have got up quicker, if there was any kind of a boom in real estate— "and right-so a thought came randoming overthwart this majestic dream the which—"

"A humbler attitude, my lord the king—and quick! Duck your head—more—still more— droop it!"

He did his honest best, but lord it was not great things. He looked as humble as the leaning tower at Pisa.

If I could have foreseen what the thing was going to be like, I should have said, No, if anybody wants to make his living exhibiting a king as a peasant, let him take the layout; I can do better with a menagerie, and last longer.

On the morning of the fourth day, I came to a resolution: the king *must* be drilled; things could not go on so, he must be taken in hand and deliberately and conscientiously drilled, or we couldn't ever venture to enter a dwelling; the very cats would know this masquerader for a humbug and no peasant. So I called a halt and said:

"Sire, as between clothes and countenance, you are all right, but as between your clothes and your bearing, you are all wrong, there is a most noticeable discrepancy. You stand too straight, your looks are too high, too confident. The cares of a kingdom do not stoop the shoulders, they do not droop the chin, they do not depress the high level of the eye glance, they do not put doubt and fear in the heart and hang out

the signs of them in slouching body and unsure step. It is the sordid cares of the lowly born that do these things. You must learn the trick; you must imitate the trademarks of poverty, misery, oppression, insult, and the other several and common inhumanities that sap the manliness out of a man and make him a loyal and proper and approved subject and a satisfaction to his masters, or the very infants will know you for better than your disguise, and we shall go to pieces at the first hut we stop at. Pray try to walk like this."

The king took careful note, and then tried an imitation.

"Pretty fair—pretty fair. Chin a litle lower, please—there, very good. Eyes too high; pray don't look at the horizon, look at the ground, ten steps in front of you. Ah—that is better, that is very good. Wait, please; you betray too much vigor, too much decision; you want more of a shamble. Look at me, please—this is what I mean. ...Now you are getting it; that is the idea—at least, it sort of approaches it....Yes, that is pretty fair. *But!* There is a great big something wanting. I don't quite know what it is. Do it again, please ...*now* I think I begin to see what it is. Yes, I've struck it. You see, the genuine spiritlessness is wanting; that's what's the trouble. It's all *amateur*—mechanical details all right, almost to a hair; everything about the delusion perfect, except that it don't delude."

"What, then, must one do to prevail?"

"Let me think...I can't seem to quite get at it. In fact there isn't anything that can right the matter but practice. It will be well to move a little off the road and put in the whole day drilling you, sire."

After the drill had gone on a little while, I said:

"Now, sire, imagine that we are at the door of the hut yonder, and the family are before us. Proceed, please—accost the head of the house."

The king unconsciously straightened up like

*A Connecticut Yankee in King Arthur's Court*  **709**

AT A GLANCE

- The Yankee struggles to teach Arthur to act like a commoner.
- Arthur has difficulty learning to be humble and spiritless.

1 DIALOGUE

The exchange points out how difficult the king's ingrained habits of privilege are to break.

2 CHARACTERIZATION

The Yankee discovers that the king's rank has given him a confident spirit inappropriate to the average commoner. Twain uses this passage to comment on the dire effects of social injustice.

3 THEME

Twain points out that the real tragedy of the poor is not so much the lack of material goods but impoverishment of the spirit.

## GUIDED READING

### LITERAL QUESTION

**1a.** What sort of qualities does Arthur particularly lack to make a convincing common man? (He is not sufficiently humble and spiritless.)

### INFERENTIAL QUESTION

**1b.** What does Twain imply about the effects of poverty and social inequality? (He implies that they deeply affect the personality and that they diminish people far beyond the deprivation of material goods.)

## 1 THEME

Equality comes hard to Arthur, who has been trained in privilege. His difficulty in even imagining poor people as his *brothers* shows how far the Yankee has to go in developing democracy in Britain.

## 2 SETTING

The hut—lifeless with a look of ruin and poverty and next to denuded, skinned fields—is a perfect setting for the tragedy within and a perfect symbol for the desolation of poverty.

---

a monument and said, with frozen austerity:

"Varlet, bring a seat; and serve to me what cheer ye have."

"Ah, your grace, that is not well done."

"In what lacketh it?"

"These people do not call *each other* varlets. Only those above them call them so."

1 "Ah—so. Then peradventure I should call him goodman."

"That would answer, your grace, but it would be still better if you said friend, or brother."

"Brother! To dirt like that?"

"Ah, but *we* are pretending to be dirt like that, too."

"It is even true. I will say it. Brother, bring a seat, and thereto what cheer ye have, withal. *Now* 'tis right."

"Not quite, not wholly right. You have asked for one, not *us*—for one, not both; food for one, a seat for one."

The king looked puzzled—he wasn't a very heavy weight, intellectually. His head was an hourglass; it could stow an idea, but it had to do it a grain at a time, not the whole idea at once.

"Would *you* have a seat also—and sit?"

"If I did not sit, the man would perceive that we were only pretending to be equals—and playing the deception pretty poorly, too."

"It is well and truly said! How wonderful is truth, come it in whatsoever unexpected form it may! Yes, he must bring out seats and food for both."

"And there is even yet a detail that needs correcting. He must bring nothing outside—we will go in—in among the dirt, and possibly other repulsive things—and take the food with the household, and after the fashion of the house, and all on equal terms. Now, make believe you are in debt, and eaten up by relentless creditors; you are out of work—which is horseshoeing, let us say—and can get none; and your wife is sick, your children are crying because they are hungry—"

And so on, and so on. I drilled him as representing in turn, all sorts of people out of luck and suffering dire privations and misfortunes. But it was only just words, words—they meant nothing in the world to him. I might just as well have whistled. Words realize nothing, vivify nothing to you, unless you have suffered in your own person the thing which the words try to describe.

## 18. The Smallpox Hut

2 When we arrived at that hut at midafternoon, we saw no signs of life about it. The field near by had been denuded of its crop some time before, and had a skinned look, so exhaustively had it been harvested and gleaned. Fences, sheds, everything had a ruined look, and were eloquent of poverty. No animal was around anywhere, no living thing in sight. The stillness was awful, it was like the stillness of death. The cabin

---

## GUIDED READING

### LITERAL QUESTION

**1a.** What does the Yankee conclude after drilling Arthur in the misfortunes of the poor? (He says it is just "words, words"; he believes Arthur would have to actually suffer to understand the plight of the poor and lowly.)

### INFERENTIAL QUESTION

**1b.** What might the heading of the next chapter—"The Smallpox Hut"—suggest is going to happen to Arthur's image of poverty? (It is going to be deepened by exposure to real suffering.)

was a one-story one, whose thatch was black with age, and ragged from lack of repair.

The door stood a trifle ajar. We approached it stealthily—on tiptoe and at half breath. The king knocked. We waited. No answer. Knocked again. No answer. I pushed the door softly open and looked in. I made out some dim forms, and a woman started up from the ground and stared at me, as one does who is wakened from sleep. Presently she found her voice—

"Have mercy!" she pleaded. "All is taken, nothing is left."

**1** I was better used to the dim light, now. I could see her hollow eyes fixed upon me. I could see how emaciated she was. I picked up a wooden bowl and was rushing past the king on my way to the brook. It was ten yards away. When I got back and entered, the king was within, and was opening the shutter that closed the window hole, to let in air and light. The

place was full of a foul stench. I put the bowl to the woman's lips, and as she gripped it with her eager talons the shutter came open and a strong light flooded her face. Smallpox!

I sprang to the king, and said in his ear:

"Out of the door on the instant, sire! the woman is dying of that disease that wasted the skirts of Camelot two years ago."

He did not budge.

"Of a truth I shall remain—and likewise help."

I whispered again:

**2** "King, it must not be. You must go."

"Ye mean well, and ye speak not unwisely. But it were shame that a king should know fear, and shame that belted knight should withhold his hand where be such as need succor. Peace. I will not go. It is you who must go."

It was a desperate place for him to be in, and might cost him his life, but it was no use to argue with him. If he considered his knightly honor at stake here, that was the end of argument; he would stay, and nothing could prevent it; I was aware of that. And so I dropped the subject. The woman spoke:

**3** "Fair sir, of your kindness will ye climb the ladder there, and bring me news of what ye find? Be not afraid to report, for times can come when even a mother's heart is past breaking—being already broke."

"Abide," said the king, "and give the woman to eat. I will go." I turned to start but the king had already started.

There was a slight noise from the direction of the dim corner where the ladder was. It was the king, descending. I could see that he was bearing something in one arm, and assisting himself with the other. He came forward into the light; upon his breast lay a slender girl of fifteen. She was but half conscious; she was dying of smallpox.

**4** Here was heroism at its last and loftiest possibility, its utmost summit; this was challenging death in the open field unarmed, with all the odds against the challenger, no reward set upon the

*A Connecticut Yankee in King Arthur's Court* **711**

AT A GLANCE

- In the hut are a woman and her daughter, both dying of smallpox.
- The Yankee and Arthur give aid, and the king risks his life by exposing himself to the disease.

**1 CHARACTERIZATION**

The Yankee lays aside his egotism, showing that his practicality and quick thinking can be used for compassionate ends as well as selfish ones.

**2 CHARACTERIZATION**

Arthur's insistence on staying, despite the risk, shows that his nobility goes beyond grand gestures and extends to the very spirit of the chivalric code—protecting the weak.

**3 TONE**

Twain often uses humor to protest the condition of the poor in Arthur's England, but this incident is treated tragically.

**4 TONE AND THEME**

Twain shifts into a heartfelt, unqualified expression of one of the novel's central concerns—the true nature of heroism.

## GUIDED READING

### LITERAL QUESTION

**1a.** Why does the Yankee stop arguing with Arthur once he refuses to leave the hut? (He knows Arthur feels deeply bound by the chivalric code.)

### INFERENTIAL QUESTION

**1b.** What does Arthur's action show about the worth of the chivalric code? (At its best, the chivalric code makes knights behave according to the ideals of kindness and bravery.)

**1 THEME**

Here Twain expounds the code he proposes instead of the chivalric code: simple humanity for all and succor for the poor.

**2 PLOT: EPISODE**

A new episode with new characters begins but is loosely connected by theme to the rest of the section. All episodes in this section of the novel show the misery of the lowly in Arthur's England.

**3 DESCRIPTION**

By his choice of descriptive words and simile, Twain satirizes both high life and low life. The marks of gentlemen are costly clothes, a hard face, and a look of command. But the peasants are servile and fall back like "spaniels."

---

contest, and no admiring world in silks and cloth of gold to gaze and applaud; and yet the king's bearing was as serenely brave as it had always been in those cheaper contests where knight meets knight in equal fight and clothed in protecting steel. He was great, now; sublimely great. The rude statues of his ancestors in his palace should have an addition—I would see to that; and it would not be a mailed king killing a giant or a dragon, like the rest, it would be a king in commoner's garb bearing death in his arms that a peasant mother might look her last upon her child and be comforted.

He laid the girl down by her mother, who poured out endearments and caresses from an overflowing heart, and one could detect a flickering faint light of response in the child's eyes, but that was all.

At midnight all was over, and we sat in the presence of corpses. We covered them with such rags as we could find, and started away, fastening the door behind us.

We ventured out, and hurried cautiously away; and although we were worn out and sleepy, we kept on until we had put this place some miles behind us.

## 19. The Yankee and the King Sold as Slaves

*The Yankee and King Arthur travel to a village and impress a number of the villagers. At a dinner in their honor, the Yankee starts a political argument, and the king delivers a nonsensical lecture on agriculture. Because they are convinced that the Yankee is a spy and the king is a madman, the peasants attack them.*

I told the king to give his heels wings, and I would explain later. We made good time across the open ground, and as we darted into the shelter of the wood I glanced back and saw a mob of excited peasants swarm into view. They

were making a world of noise, but that couldn't hurt anybody; the wood was dense, and as soon as we were well into its depths we would take to a tree and let them whistle. Ah, but then came another sound—dogs!

We tore along at a good gait, and soon left the sounds far behind and modified to a murmur. We struck a stream and darted into it. We waded swiftly down it, in the dim forest light, for as much as three hundred yards, and then came across an oak with a great bough sticking out over the water. We climbed up on this bough, and began to work our way along it to the body of the tree; now we began to hear those sounds more plainly; so the mob had struck our trail.

Presently we heard it coming—and coming on the jump, too; yes, and down both sides of the stream. Louder—louder—next minute it swelled swiftly up into a roar of shoutings, barkings, tramplings, and swept by like a cyclone.

Suddenly some horsemen tore into the midst of the crowd, and a voice shouted:

"Hold—or ye are dead men!"

How good it sounded! The owner of the voice bore all the marks of a gentleman: picturesque and costly raiment, the aspect of command, a hard countenance. The mob fell humbly back, like so many spaniels. The gentleman inspected us critically, then said sharply to the peasants:

"What are ye doing to these people?"

"They be madmen, worshipful sir, that have come wandering we know not whence, and—"

"Peace! Ye know not what ye say. They are not mad. Who are ye? And whence are ye? Explain."

"We are but peaceful strangers, sir," I said, "and traveling upon our own concerns. We are from a far country, and unacquainted here. We have purposed no harm; and yet but for your brave interference and protection these people would have killed us. As you have divined, sir, we are not mad; neither are we violent or bloodthirsty."

---

## GUIDED READING

**LITERAL QUESTION**

**1a.** Who is chasing the Yankee and Arthur, and who rescues them? (A gang of peasants chase them; they are rescued by a group of "gentlemen" on horseback.)

**INFERENTIAL QUESTION**

**1b.** What kind of satire does this incident provide on both classes? (The peasants are ignorant and suspicious, violent but servile. The upper classes are arrogant and cruel.)

The gentleman turned to his retinue and said calmly:

"Lash me these animals to their kennels!"

The mob vanished in an instant; and after them plunged the horsemen, laying about them with their whips and pitilessly riding down such as were witless enough to keep the road instead of taking to the bush. The shrieks and supplications presently died away in the distance, and soon the horsemen began to straggle back. Meantime the gentleman had been questioning us more closely, but we revealed nothing more than that we were friendless strangers from a far country. When the escort were all returned, the gentlemen said to one of his servants:

"Bring the led horses and mount these people."

"Yes, my lord."

We were placed toward the rear, among the servants. We traveled pretty fast, and finally drew rein some time after dark at a roadside inn some ten or twelve miles from the scene of our troubles. My lord went immediately to his room, after ordering his supper, and we saw no more of him. At dawn in the morning we breakfasted and made ready to start.

My lord's chief attendant sauntered forward at that moment with indolent grace, and said:

"Ye have said ye should continue upon this road, which is our direction likewise; wherefore my lord, the earl Grip, hath given commandment that ye retain the horses and ride, and that certain of us ride with ye a twenty mile to a fair town that hight Cambenet, whenso ye shall be out of peril."

We could do nothing less than express our thanks and accept the offer. We jogged along, six in the party, at a moderate and comfortable gait, and in conversation learned that my lord Grip was a very great personage in his own region, which lay a day's journey beyond Cambenet. We loitered to such a degree that it was near the middle of the forenoon when we entered the market square of the town. We dismounted, and

left our thanks once more for my lord, and then approached a crowd assembled in the center of the square, to see what might be the object of interest. It was slaves!

The king was not interested, and wanted to move along, but I was absorbed, and full of pity. I could not take my eyes away from these worn and wasted wrecks of humanity. There they sat, grouped upon the ground, silent, uncomplaining, with bowed heads, a pathetic sight. And by hideous contrast, a redundant orator was making a speech to another gathering not thirty steps away, in fulsome laudation of "our glorious British liberties!"

I was boiling. I had forgotten I was a plebeian, I was remembering I was a man. Cost what it might, I would mount that rostrum and—

Click! the king and I were handcuffed together! Our companions, those servants, had done it; my lord Grip stood looking on. The king burst out in a fury, and said:

"What meaneth this ill-mannered jest?"

My lord merely said coolly: "Put up the slaves and sell them!"

*Slaves!* The word had a new sound—and how unspeakably awful! The king lifted his manacles and brought them down with a deadly force; but my lord was out of the way when they arrived. A dozen of the rascal's servants sprang forward, and in a moment we were helpless, with our hands bound behind us. We so loudly and so earnestly proclaimed ourselves freemen, that we got the interested attention of that liberty-mouthing orator and his patriotic crowd, and they gathered about us and assumed a very determined attitude. The orator said:

"If indeed ye are freemen, ye have nought to fear—the God-given liberties of Britain are about ye for your shield and shelter! (Applause.) Ye shall soon see. Bring forth your proofs."

"What proofs?"

"Proof that ye are freemen."

The king stormed out:

"Thou'rt insane, man. It were better, and

*A Connecticut Yankee in King Arthur's Court*   **713**

---

**AT A GLANCE**

- The gentlemen drive the peasants off and give the Yankee and Arthur horses.
- They visit a slave market and are betrayed by their "rescuer" and manacled as slaves.

**1 IRONY**

The Yankee points out the irony of an orator who speaks of "glorious British liberties" within sight of slaves.

**2 PLOT: RISING ACTION**

This incident provides the major tension for the following episodes, which concern the experiences of the king and Yankee as slaves and Arthur's education in suffering.

- The Yankee and Arthur are sold as slaves.
- They are chained to a slave convoy and marched off.

## 1 CHARACTERIZATION

The Yankee reveals his vanity by valuing himself above the king. His comments satirize slavery, which sets a price on human beings; his wry discussion of the sale in exclusively commercial terms adds irony as well as humor.

## 2 THEME

Twain expands on a major idea: the unchangeable quality of human nature. Not only does it endure across centuries but across class lines: Arthur is no different from anyone else when the trappings of kingship are removed.

more in reason, that this thief and scoundrel here prove that we are *not* freemen.''

The orator said—and this time in the tones of business, not of sentiment:

''An ye do not know your country's laws, it were time ye learned them. Ye are strangers to us; ye will not deny that. Ye may be freemen, we do not deny that; but also ye may be slaves. The law is clear: it doth not require the claimant to prove ye are slaves, it requireth you to prove ye are *not*.''

There is no use in stringing out the details. The earl put us up and sold us at auction. In a big town and an active market we should have brought **1** a good price; but this place was utterly stagnant so we sold at a figure which makes me ashamed, every time I think of it. The King of England brought seven dollars, and his prime minister nine; whereas the king was easily worth twelve dollars and I as easily worth fifteen. But that is the way things always go; if you force a sale on a

dull market, I don't care what the property is, you are going to make a poor business of it, and you can make up your mind to it.

The slave dealer bought us both, and hitched us onto that long chain of his, and we constituted the rear of his procession. We took up our line of march and passed out of Cambenet at noon; and it seemed to me unaccountably strange and odd that the King of England and his chief minister, marching manacled and fettered and yoked, in a slave convoy, could move by all manner of idle men and women, and under windows where sat the sweet and the lovely, and yet never attract a curious eye, never provoke a **2** single remark. Dear, dear, it only shows that there is nothing diviner about a king than there is about a tramp, after all. He is just a cheap and hollow artificiality when you don't know he is a king. But reveal his quality, and dear me it takes your very breath away to look at him. I reckon we are all fools. Born so, no doubt.

**714** *The Novel*

## GUIDED READING

### LITERAL QUESTION

**1a.** Why do their captors not let the Yankee and Arthur go when they claim they are freemen? (They have no proof, and the burden of proof is on the accused.)

### INFERENTIAL QUESTION

**1b.** How is Twain contrasting medieval English law to contemporary American law? (In medieval times, one was presumed guilty until proven innocent, instead of being presumed innocent until proven guilty.)

# 20. An Encounter in the Dark

London—to a slave—was a sufficiently interesting place. It was merely a great big village; and mainly mud and thatch. The streets were muddy, crooked, unpaved. The populace was an ever flocking and drifting swarm of rags and splendors, of nodding plumes and shining armor. The king had a palace there; he saw the outside of it. It made him sigh; yes, and swear a little, in a poor juvenile sixth-century way. We saw knights and grandees whom we knew, but they didn't know us in our rags and dirt and raw welts and bruises, and wouldn't have recognized us if we had hailed them, nor stopped to answer, either, it being unlawful to speak with slaves on a chain. Sandy passed within ten yards of me on a mule—hunting for me, I imagined. But the thing which clean broke my heart was something which happened in front of our old barrack in a square. It was the sight of a newsboy—and I couldn't get at him! Still, I had one comfort; here was proof that Clarence was still alive and banging away. I meant to be with him before long; the thought was full of cheer.

I had one little glimpse of another thing, one day, which gave me a great uplift. It was a wire stretching from housetop to housetop. Telegraph or telephone, sure. I did very much wish I had a little piece of it. It was just what I needed, in order to carry out my project of escape. My idea was, to get loose some night, along with the king, then gag and bind our master, change clothes with him, batter him into the aspect of a stranger, hitch him to the slave chain, assume possession of the property, march to Camelot, and—

But you get my idea; you see what a stunning dramatic surprise I would wind up with at the palace. It was all feasible, if I could only get hold of a slender piece of iron which I could shape into a lockpick. I could then undo the lumbering padlocks with which our chains were fastened, whenever I might choose. But I never had any luck; no such thing ever happened to fall in my way. However, my chance came at last. A gentleman who had come twice before to dicker for me, without result, or indeed any approach to a result, came again. I was not expecting to ever belong to this gentleman, but he had something which I expected would belong to me eventually, if he would but visit us often enough. It was a steel thing with a long pin to it, with which his long cloth outside garment was fastened together in front. There were three of them. He had disappointed me twice, because he did not come quite close enough to me to make my project entirely safe; but this time I succeeded; I captured the lower clasp of the three.

That evening we waited patiently for our fellow slaves to get to sleep and signify it by the usual sign, for you must not take many chances on those poor fellows if you can avoid it. It is best to keep your own secrets. No doubt they fidgeted only about as usual, but it didn't seem so to me. It seemed to me that they were going to be forever getting down to their regular snoring. As the time dragged on I got nervously afraid we shouldn't have enough of it left for our needs; so I made several premature attempts, and merely delayed things by it; for I couldn't seem to touch a padlock, there in the dark, without starting a rattle out of it which interrupted somebody's sleep and made him turn over and wake some more of the gang.

But finally I did get my last iron off, and was a free man once more. I took a good breath of relief, and reached for the king's irons. Too late! in comes the master, with a light in one hand and his heavy walking staff in the other. I snuggled close among the wallow of snorers, to conceal as nearly as possible that I was naked of irons; and I kept a sharp lookout and prepared to spring for my man the moment he should bend over me.

But he didn't approach. He stopped, gazed absently toward our dusky mass a minute, evidently thinking about something else; then set down his light, moved musingly toward the door, and before a body could imagine what he

*A Connecticut Yankee in King Arthur's Court* **715**

---

**1 THEME**

Signs of the Yankee's modernization of Britain are juxtaposed with descriptions of barbaric social customs.

**2 CHARACTERIZATION**

The Yankee shows his practicality and ability to turn his hand to almost anything mechanical—even picking locks.

**3 THEME**

Although the Yankee criticizes the lack of social justice in Arthur's England and favors social reform, he does not romanticize the poor. He pragmatically says one "must not take many chances on those poor fellows."

---

## GUIDED READING

### LITERAL QUESTIONS

**1a.** What sights cheer the Yankee on the walk through London? (a newsboy and wires stretching from housetop to housetop)

**2a.** What does the Yankee steal and why does he steal it? (He steals a pin fastening a gentleman's clothes, so that he can use it to pick the locks of their manacles.)

### INFERENTIAL QUESTIONS

**1b.** Why do these things cheer him? (The newsboy reminds him of continuing "reforms"; the wires tell him of the proximity of a telephone or telegraph, and he sees a chance to call for help.)

**2b.** What does this action show about the Yankee? (He is clever and resourceful.)

**1 CHARACTERIZATION**

The Yankee is shrewd. He is not above using the class prejudice of the time to his advantage.

**2 POINT OF VIEW**

Because the Yankee is the narrator, the important events must either happen in his presence or be included as exposition. The slave uprising took place during his absence, and so dialogue fills in the details.

was going to do, he was out of the door and had closed it behind him.

"Quick!" said the king. "Fetch him back!"

Of course it was the thing to do, and I was up and out in a moment. But dear me, there were no lamps in those days, and it was a dark night. But I glimpsed a dim figure a few steps away. I darted for it, threw myself upon it, and then there was a state of things and lively! Lanterns began to swing in all directions; it was the watch, gathering from far and near. Presently a halberd² fell across my back, as a reminder, and I knew what it meant. I was in custody. So was my adversary. We were marched off toward prison, one on each side of the watchman. Here was disaster, here was a fine scheme gone to sudden destruction! I tried to imagine what would happen when the master should discover that it was I who had been fighting him; and what would happen if they jailed us together in the general apartment for brawlers and petty law breakers, **1** as was the custom; and what might—

Just then my antagonist turned his face around in my direction, the freckled light from the watchman's tin lantern fell on it, and by George he was the wrong man!

## 21. An Awful Predicament

Sleep? It was impossible. It would naturally have been impossible in that noisome cavern of a jail, with its mangy crowd of drunken, quarrelsome and song-singing rapscallions. But the thing that made sleep all the more a thing not to be dreamed of, was my racking impatience to get out of this place and find out the whole size of what might have happened yonder in the slave quarters in consequence of that intolerable miscarriage of mine.

It was long night but the morning got around **2** at last. I made a full and frank explanation to the court. I said I was a slave, the property of the

---

2. **halberd** [hal′bərd]: battle-ax with a long spear and hook-shaped blade.

great Earl Grip, who had arrived just after dark at the Tabard inn in the village on the other side of the water, and had stopped there over night, by compulsion, he being taken deadly sick with a strange and sudden disorder. I had been ordered to cross to the city in all haste and bring the best physician; I was doing my best; naturally I was running with all my might; the night was dark, I ran against this common person here, who seized me by the throat and began to pummel me, although I told him my errand, and implored him, for the sake of the great earl my master's mortal peril—

The common person interrupted and said it was a lie; and was going to explain how I rushed upon him and attacked him without a word—

"Silence, sirrah!" from the court. "Take him hence and give him a few stripes whereby to teach him how to treat the servant of a nobleman after a different fashion another time. Go!"

Then the court begged my pardon, and hoped I would not fail to tell his lordship it was in no wise the court's fault that this high-handed thing had happened. I said I would make it all right, and so took my leave.

I didn't wait for breakfast. No grass grew under my feet. I was soon at the slave quarters. Empty—everybody gone! That is, everybody except one body—the slave master's. It lay there all battered to pulp; and all about were the evidences of a terrific fight. There was a rude board coffin on a cart at the door, and workmen, assisted by the police, were thinning a road through the gaping crowd in order that they might bring it in.

I picked out a man humble enough in life to condescend to talk with one so shabby as I, and got his account of the matter.

"There were sixteen slaves here. They rose against their master in the night, and thou seest how it ended."

"Yes. How did it begin?"

"There was no witness but the slaves. They said the slave that was most valuable got free of

---

## GUIDED READING

**LITERAL QUESTION**

**1a.** How does the Yankee's escape plan miscarry? (He runs after the master in the dark but grabs the wrong man and is taken to jail.)

**INFERENTIAL QUESTION**

**1b.** How is this incident uncharacteristic of the Yankee's adventures? (He fails—is not his usual competent, lucky self.)

his bonds and escaped in some strange way—by magic arts 'twas thought, by reason that he had no key, and the locks were neither broke nor in any wise injured. When the master discovered his loss, he was mad with despair, and threw himself upon his people with his heavy stick, who resisted and did give him hurts that brought him swiftly to his end."

"This is dreadful. It will go hard with the slaves, no doubt, upon the trial."

"Marry, the trial is over. They condemned them in a body. Wit ye not the law—which men say the Romans left behind them here when they went—that if one slave killeth his master all the slaves of that man must die for it."

"True. I had forgotten. And when will these die?"

"Belike within a four and twenty hours; albeit some say they will wait a pair of days more, if peradventure they may find the missing one meantime."

The missing one! It made me feel uncomfortable.

"Is it likely they will find him?"

"Before the day is spent—yes. They seek him everywhere."

At the first secondhand clothing shop I came to, up a back street, I got a rough rig suitable for a common seaman who might be going on a cold voyage, and bound up my face with a liberal bandage, saying I had a toothache. This concealed my worst bruises. It was a transformation. I no longer resembled my former self. Then I struck out for that wire, found it and followed it to its den. It was a little room over a butcher's shop—which meant that business wasn't very brisk in the telegraphic line. The young chap in charge was drowsing at his table. I locked the door and put the vast key in my bosom. This alarmed the young fellow, and he was going to make a noise; but I said:

"Save your wind; if you open your mouth you are dead, sure. Tackle your instrument. Lively, now! Call Camelot."

"This doth amaze me! How should such as you know aught of such matters as—"

"Call Camelot! I am a desperate man. Call Camelot, or get away from the instrument and I will do it myself."

"What—you?"

"Yes—certainly. Stop gabbling. Call the palace." He made the call.

"Now then, call Clarence."

"Clarence who?"

"Never mind Clarence who. Say you want Clarence; you'll get an answer."

He did so. We waited five nerve-straining minutes—ten minutes—how long it did seem!—and then came a click that was as familiar to me as a human voice; for Clarence had been my own pupil.

"Now, my lad, vacate! They wouldn't have known *my* touch, maybe, and so your call was surest; but I'm all right, now."

He vacated the place and cocked his ear to listen—but it didn't win. I used a cipher. I didn't waste any time in sociabilities with Clarence, but squared away for business, straight off—thus:

"The king is here and in danger. We were captured and brought here as slaves."

The instrument began to talk to the youth and I hurried away. I fell to ciphering. In half an hour it would be nine o'clock. Knights and horses in heavy armor couldn't travel very fast. These would make the best time they could, and now that the ground was in good condition, and no snow or mud, they would probably make a seven-mile gait; they would have to change horses a couple of times; they would arrive about six, or a little after; it would still be plenty light enough; they would see the white cloth which I should tie around my right arm, and I would take command. We would surround that prison and have the king out in no time. It would be showy and picturesque enough, all things considered, though I would have preferred noonday, on account of the more theatrical aspect the thing would have.

*A Connecticut Yankee in King Arthur's Court* **717**

AT A GLANCE

- The Yankee hears the tale of the slave uprising and learns that all the slaves are to be executed.
- He sends a telegram to Clarence asking for assistance.

**1 PLOT: RISING ACTION**

The Yankee manages to get a message to Clarence, thus setting up the machinery for the resolution of the episode.

**2 PLOT: CONFLICT**

The Yankee copes with external conflicts—Arthur in danger, the limitations time and space impose on his rescue plan. Practical as ever, the Yankee calculates the probable time of the rescuers' arrival and arranges a signal.

## GUIDED READING

**LITERAL QUESTION**

**1a.** What signal does the Yankee decide to give Clarence and the arriving knights? (He will tie a white cloth around his right arm.)

**INFERENTIAL QUESTION**

**1b.** Why is a signal necessary; why would they not simply recognize him? (He is much changed from his hardships and in disguise. Also, it is necessary to have a signal recognizable from some distance.)

## 1 CHARACTERIZATION

When one plan leads to a dead end, the Yankee makes an escape plan on the spot, once again showing his quick thinking.

But the scheme fell through like scat! The first corner I turned, I came plump upon one of our slaves, snooping around with a watchman. I coughed, at the moment, and he gave me a sudden look that bit right into my marrow. I turned immediately into a shop and worked along down the counter, pricing things and watching out of the corner of my eye. Those people had stopped, and were talking together and looking in at the door. I made up my mind to get out the back way, if there was a back way, and I asked the shopwoman if I could step out there and look for the escaped slave, who was believed to be in hiding back there somewhere, and said I was an officer in disguise, and my pard was yonder at the door with one of the murderers in charge, and would she be good enough to step there and tell him he needn't wait, but had better go at once to the further end of the back alley and be ready to head him off when I rousted him out.

She was blazing with eagerness to see one

**718** *The Novel*

## GUIDED READING

**LITERAL QUESTION**

**1a.** What does the Yankee ask the woman in the store to do? (To let him go out the back way after the escaped slave. He asks her to tell his "partner" outside that he need not wait but should go to the back alley.)

**INFERENTIAL QUESTION**

**1b.** How does he think this plan will help him escape? (He thinks he can run out the back way while the watchman is occupied with the woman in the store.)

of those already celebrated murderers, and she started on the errand at once. I slipped out the back way, locked the door behind me, put the key in my pocket and started off, chuckling to myself and comfortable.

Well, I had gone and spoiled it again, made another mistake. A double one, in fact. There were plenty of ways to get rid of that officer by some simple and plausible device, but no, I must pick out a picturesque one; it is the crying defect of my character. And then, I had ordered my procedure upon what the officer, being human, would *naturally* do; whereas when you are least expecting it, a man will now and then go and do the very thing which it's *not* natural for him to do. The natural thing for the officer to do, in this case, was to follow straight on my heels; he would find a stout oaken door, securely locked, between him and me. But instead of doing the natural thing, the officer took me at my word, and followed my instructions. And so, as I came trotting out of that cul-de-sac,[3] full of satisfaction with my own cleverness, he turned the corner and I walked right into his handcuffs.

Of course I was indignant, and swore I had just come ashore from a long voyage, and all that sort of thing—just to see, you know, if it would deceive that slave. But it didn't. He knew me. Then I reproached him for betraying me. He was more surprised than hurt. He stretched his eyes wide, and said:

"What, wouldst have me let thee, of all men, escape and not hang with us, when thou'rt the very *cause* of our hanging? Go to!"

Well, there was a sort of justice in his view of the case, and so I dropped the matter. When you can't cure a disaster by argument, what is the use to argue? It isn't my way. So I only said:

"You're not going to be hanged. None of us are."

Both men laughed, and the slave said:

---
3. **cul-de-sac** [kul′də sak′]: blind alley or a problem from which there is no way out.

"Ye have not ranked as a fool—before. You might better keep your reputation, seeing the strain would not be for long."

I kept my temper, and said, indifferently:

"Now I suppose you really think we are going to hang within a day or two."

"I thought it not many minutes ago, for so the thing was decided and proclaimed."

"Ah, then you've changed your mind, is that it?"

"Even that. I only *thought*, then; I *know*, now."

I felt sarcastical, so I said:

"Oh, sapient servant of the law, condescend to tell us, then, what you *know*."

"That ye will all be hanged *today*, at midafternoon! Oho! that shot hit home! Lean upon me."

The fact is I did need to lean upon somebody. My knights couldn't arrive in time. They would be as much as three hours too late. Nothing in the world could save the King of England; nor me, which was more important. More important, not merely to me, but to the nation— the only nation on earth standing ready to blossom into civilization. I was sick. I said no more, there wasn't anything to say. I knew what the man meant; that if the missing slave was found, the postponement would be revoked, the execution take place today. Well, the missing slave was found.

## 22. Sir Launcelot and Knights to the Rescue

Nearing four in the afternoon. The scene was just outside the walls of London. A cool, comfortable, superb day, with a brilliant sun; the kind of day to make one want to live, not die. The multitude was prodigious and far-reaching; and yet we fifteen poor devils hadn't a friend in it. There was something painful in that thought, look at it how you might. There we sat, on our tall scaffold, the butt of the hate and mockery of

*A Connecticut Yankee in King Arthur's Court* **719**

- Arthur declares that he is the king.
- The crowd mocks the king and The Boss.
- The hangings begin.

## 1 MOOD

Twain sketches the mood of the hanging: rowdiness, jeers, catcalls, no compassion for the victims. He satirizes a society that is so accustomed to cruelty that public hangings are enjoyable spectacles, not solemn occasions of death.

## 2 CHARACTERIZATION

Arthur shows nobility in silently suffering the crowd's contempt. His great dignity reveals his nobility as real, not merely an illusion.

all those enemies. We were being made a holiday spectacle. They had built a sort of grandstand for the nobility and gentry, and these were there in full force, with their ladies. We recognized a good many of them.

The crowd got a brief and unexpected dash of diversion out of the king. The moment we were freed of our bonds he sprang up, in his fantastic rags, with face bruised out of all recognition, and proclaimed himself Arthur, King of Britain, and denounced the awful penalties of treason upon every soul there present if hair of his sacred head were touched. It startled and surprised him to hear them break into a vast roar of laughter. It wounded his dignity, and he locked himself up in silence, then, although the crowd begged him to go on, and tried to provoke him to it by catcalls, jeers, and shouts of:

"Let him speak! The king! The king! his humble subjects hunger and thirst for words of wisdom out of the mouth of their master his Serene and Sacred Raggedness!"

But it went for nothing. He put on all his majesty and sat under this rain of contempt and insult unmoved. He certainly was great in his way. Absently, I had taken off my white bandage and wound it about my right arm. When the crowd noticed this, they began upon me. They said:

"Doubtless this sailorman is his minister—observe his costly badge of office!"

I let them go on until they got tired, and then I said:

"Yes, I am his minister, The Boss; and tomorrow you will hear that from Camelot which—"

I got no further. They drowned me out with joyous derision. But presently there was silence; for the sheriffs of London, in their official robes, with their subordinates, began to make a stir which indicated that business was about to begin. In the hush which followed, our crime was recited, the death warrant read, then everybody uncovered while a priest uttered a prayer.

Then a slave was blindfolded; the hangman unslung his rope. There lay the smooth road below us, we upon one side of it, the banked multitude walling its other side—a good clear road, and kept free by the police—how good it

**720** *The Novel*

## GUIDED READING

### LITERAL QUESTION

**1a.** What does the Yankee do that makes the crowd jeer even more at him? (He takes off his white bandage and winds it around his right arm.)

### INFERENTIAL QUESTION

**1b.** What purpose does this serve in the narrative, besides the immediate one of arousing the crowd? (It reminds the reader of the signal the Yankee had planned to use so that the knights can find him and Arthur in the crowd.)

AT A GLANCE

- One slave is hanged, and Arthur is to be next.
- The knights arrive on bicycles.
- The Yankee and Arthur are rescued and Arthur restored to the throne.

**1 PLOT: CLIMAX**

The plot reaches its highest point of tension: The noose is around Arthur's neck. The tension of the climax heightens the comic relief of the humorous resolution.

**2 RESPONSE JOURNAL**

Ask students to comment in their response journals about the Yankee's statement. Does he deserve to take credit for this "effect"? Why or why not?

<u>REFLECTING ON CHAPTERS 16–22</u>

When they first started on their adventures, the Yankee despaired of Arthur ever understanding the poor. What experiences does Arthur have to help him understand and what does he learn? (He cares for a dying family, becomes a slave, and is mistreated, imprisoned, sentenced to hang, and ridiculed. He learns that most of the people in his kingdom lead miserable lives.)

would be to see my five hundred horsemen come tearing down it! But, no, it was out of the possibilities. I followed its receding thread out into the distance—not a horseman on it, or sign of one.

There was a jerk, and the slave hung dangling; it was dreadful. I turned away my head a moment, and when I turned back I missed the king! They were blindfolding him! I was paralyzed; I couldn't move, I was choking, my tongue was petrified. They finished blindfolding him, they led him under the rope. When I saw them put the noose around his neck, then everything let go in me and I made a spring to the rescue—and as I made it I shot one more glance abroad—by George, here they came, atilting[4]—five hundred mailed and belted knights on bicycles!

The grandest sight that ever was seen. How the plumes streamed, how the sun flamed and flashed from the endless procession of webby wheels!

I waved my right arm as Launcelot swept

---
4. **atilting:** on the attack, armed with lances.

in—he recognized my rag—I tore away noose and bandage, and shouted:

"On your knees, every rascal of you, and salute the king! Who fails shall sup in hell tonight!"

I always use that high style when I'm climaxing an effect. Well, it was noble to see Launcelot and the boys swarm up onto that scaffold and heave sheriffs and such overboard. And it was fine to see that astonished multitude go down on their knees and beg their lives of the king they had just been deriding and insulting. And as he stood apart, there, receiving this homage in his rags, I thought to myself, well really there *is* something peculiarly grand about the gait and bearing of a king, after all.

I was immensely satisfied. Take the whole situation all around, it was one of the gaudiest effects I ever instigated.

And presently up comes Clarence, his own self! And winks, and says, very modernly:

"Good deal of a surprise, wasn't it? I knew you'd like it. I've had the boys practicing, this long time, privately; and just hungry for a chance to show off."

*A Connecticut Yankee in King Arthur's Court*  **721**

<u>*GUIDED READING*</u>

**LITERAL QUESTION**

**1a.** What is the Yankee about to do just before he sees the knights arriving? (He sees the noose around Arthur's neck and is about to spring forward to try to rescue the king.)

**INFERENTIAL QUESTION**

**1b.** What does this impulse show about how the Yankee's attitude toward Arthur has changed? (It shows true loyalty and genuine regard for Arthur, a change from his former attitude, in which he tolerated and manipulated the king.)

1. welcomes it; is disturbed by its irreverence; are curious
2. to find out more about freemen
3. He will not pass for a peasant; he cannot acquire spiritlessness.
4. women dying of smallpox; tends to them; thinks king shows true heroism
5. are rescued by earl Grip; sold at auction; require people to prove they are not slaves
6. He unlocks irons, follows master outside, mistakenly jumps stranger and is arrested but persuades court to release him. They have killed master and will be hanged.
7. telegraphs Clarence to send knights to rescue them; knights arrive on bicycles
8. lack of medical care; unsanitary conditions; poverty, slavery, crime, unjust legal system; grim, rough, oppressive place
9. displays bravery, compassion, awareness of justice; although dressed as commoner, shows true nobility for first time
10. Arthur becomes aware of the plight of the commoner through his own experience.
11. crime, unsanitary conditions, inadequate medical care, poverty, oppression

## LITERARY FOCUS

- ridicules idea that a human life's value can be measured in money
- by pretending to take it seriously

# STUDY QUESTIONS

### Recalling

1. What are the Yankee's two conflicting reactions to his newspaper? How do the monks react to the paper?
2. Why do the Yankee and King Arthur travel through the kingdom in disguise?
3. Why does the Yankee have to drill the king? Explain why this drill is only partly successful.
4. Describe what the Yankee and the king see in the hut. What does the king do, and what is the Yankee's response to his action?
5. Explain how the Yankee and king end up in the gang of slaves. What does the king learn about his own slavery laws?
6. Relate the events leading to the Yankee's departure from the slave quarters. What does he learn about the other slaves?
7. Briefly retell the Yankee's scheme for rescuing the king and the other slaves. How are the Yankee and the king finally saved from being hanged?

### Interpreting

8. As the king and the Yankee travel disguised as peasants, what serious social problems do they encounter? What picture do these problems create of Arthur's Britain?
9. Explain how the king's character changes in this section of the novel. Given his disguise, how might this change be ironic?
10. How do the various events in this section bear out the Yankee's statement, "Words realize nothing. . . to you, unless you have suffered in your own person the thing which the words try to describe"?

### Extending

11. Which of the problems seen by the Yankee and the king on their journey still exist in the world today?

## LITERARY FOCUS

### Satire

**Satire** is a form of writing that ridicules a weakness in individuals or society for the purpose of altering it. Satire usually makes its point through humor, either gentle or biting.

A satirist may make a subject look ridiculous by exaggerating it or by placing it in circumstances that cast a new light on it. For example, Twain makes King Arthur look ridiculous by placing him in new circumstances: showing his struggle to imitate the behavior of a poor man. The king's attempts to grasp the Yankee's instructions are funny, but the target of Twain's satire is a much more serious failure: the inability of the highborn to recognize the humanity and to understand the suffering of the poor.

### Thinking About Satire

■ Look again at the passage in which the Yankee complains about the price that he and the king bring at the slave auction. What might be the target of Twain's satire in this passage? How does he make that target look ridiculous?

722   *The Novel*

## 23. Three Years Later

Consider three years sped. Now look around on England. A happy and prosperous country, and strangely altered. Schools everywhere, and several colleges; a number of pretty good newspapers.

Slavery was dead and gone; all men were equal before the law; taxation had been equalized. The telegraph, the telephone, the phonograph, the typewriter, the sewing machine, and all the thousand willing and handy servants of steam and electricity were working their way into favor. We had a steamboat or two on the Thames, we had steam warships, and the beginnings of a steam commercial marine; I was getting ready to send out an expedition to discover America.

We were building several lines of railway, and our line from Camelot to London was already finished and in operation.

There was hardly a knight in all the land who wasn't in some useful employment. They were going from end to end of the country in all manner of useful missionary capacities; their pen-

chant for wandering, and their experience in it, made them altogether the most effective spreaders of civilization we had. They went clothed in steel and equipped with sword and lance and battle-ax, and if they couldn't persuade a person to try a sewing machine on the installment plan, or a melodeon,[1] or a barbed wire fence, or a prohibition journal, or any of the other thousand and one things they canvassed for, they removed him and passed on.

I was very happy.

*The Yankee has also married Sandy during this time, and they have had a baby girl. The child becomes ill, and the Yankee and Sandy are advised to leave Britain for France.*

The doctors said we must take the child away, if we would coax her back to health and strength again. And she must have sea air. So we took a man-of-war, and a suite of two hundred and sixty persons, and went cruising about, and after a fortnight of this we stepped ashore on the French coast, and the doctors thought it would be a good idea to make something of a stay there. The little king of that region offered us his hospitalities, and we were glad to accept. If he had had as many conveniences as he lacked, we should have been plenty comfortable enough; even as it was, we made out very well, in his queer old castle, by the help of comforts and luxuries from the ship.

At the end of a month I sent the vessel home for fresh supplies and for news. We expected her back in three or four days.

Our child began to lose ground again, and we had to go to sitting up with her, her case became so serious. We couldn't bear to allow anybody to help, in this service, so we two stood watch and watch, day in and day out. Ah, Sandy, what a right heart she had, how simple, and genuine, and good she was! She was a flawless wife and

_____
1. **melodeon:** small reed organ.

*A Connecticut Yankee in King Arthur's Court* **723**

### AT A GLANCE

- Three years later, England is progressing.
- The Yankee and Sandy, now married, take their child to France to restore her health.
- Their ship returns home for fresh supplies; the child takes a turn for the worse.

### LITERARY OPTIONS

- plot
- irony
- symbol

### THEMATIC OPTIONS

- war
- human frailty
- failure of technology

### 1 MOOD

This episode opens with a description of England after the Yankee's reforms. The content and tone of the Yankee's comments create an optimistic mood—a shortlived one.

### 2 THEME

The Yankee's recruitment of the knights as traveling salesmen satirizes the commercialism of the nineteenth century.

## GUIDED READING

**LITERAL QUESTION**

**1a.** What occupies the knights these days? (They travel around the country peddling various machines and ideas.)

**INFERENTIAL QUESTION**

**1b.** How does this development change the country? (It lowers the status of the knights and spreads new ideas and products.)

- The Yankee tells why he married Sandy and how happy he has been.
- They watch over the child, who recovers, and realize that their ship should have returned.
- The Yankee returns to England and finds the devastation of war.
- Clarence explains that the relationship between Queen Guenever and Sir Launcelot caused the war.

## 1 SYMBOL

The Yankee's domestic bliss symbolizes the happy union of his century and Sandy's. Unfortunately, in the society at large, this union breaks down with tragic consequences.

## 2 MOOD

The Yankee finds the castle at Camelot unguarded, its courts vacant and silent, echoing only with the sepulchral sound of his own footsteps. The mood mirrors recent events and foreshadows those to come.

## 3 DIALOGUE

Twain uses dialogue to relate the cause of the war: Launcelot's affair with the queen. It also serves to show Clarence's transformation into a nineteenth-century man—he now talks like the Yankee.

---

mother; and yet I had married her for no particular reason, except that by the customs of chivalry she was my property until some knight should win her from me in the field. She had hunted Britain over for me; had found me at the hanging-bout outside of London, and had straightway resumed her old place at my side in the placidest way and as of right. I was a New Englander, and in my opinion this sort of partnership would compromise her, sooner or later. She couldn't see how, but I cut argument short and we had a wedding.

1 Now I didn't know I was drawing a prize, yet that was what I did draw. Within the twelvemonth I became her worshiper; and ours was the dearest and perfectest comradeship that ever was.

During two weeks and a half we watched by the crib, and in our deep solicitude we were unconscious of any world outside of that sickroom. Then our reward came: the center of the universe turned the corner and began to mend. Grateful? It isn't the term. Then we looked the same startled thought into each other's eyes at the same moment: more than two weeks gone, and that ship not back yet!

In another minute I appeared in the presence of my train. They had been steeped in troubled bodings all this time—their faces showed it. I called an escort and we galloped five miles to a hilltop overlooking the sea. Where was my great commerce that so lately had made these glistering expanses populous and beautiful with its white-winged flocks? Vanished, every one! Not a sail, from verge to verge, not a smoke bank—just a dead and empty solitude, in place of all that brisk and breezy life.

I went swiftly back, saying not a word to anybody. I told Sandy this ghastly news. We could imagine no explanation that would begin to explain. Had there been an invasion? An earthquake? A pestilence? Had the nation been swept out of existence? But guessing was profitless. I must go—at once. I borrowed the king's navy—a

**724** *The Novel*

---

"ship" no bigger than a steam launch—and was soon ready.

A miserable journey. A desolate silence everywhere. Even in London itself. The Tower showed recent war scars. Verily, much had been happening.

2 Of course I meant to take the train for Camelot. Train! Why, the station was as vacant as a cavern. I moved on. The journey to Camelot was a repetition of what I had already seen. The drawbridge was down, the great gate stood wide, I entered without challenge, my own heels making the only sound I heard—and it was sepulchral enough, in those huge vacant courts.

### 24. War!

I found Clarence, alone in his quarters, drowned in melancholy; and in place of the electric light, he had reinstituted the ancient raglamp, and sat there in a grisly twilight with all curtains drawn tight. He sprang up and rushed for me eagerly, saying:

"Oh, it's worth a billion milrays to look upon a live person again!"

"Quick, now, tell me the meaning of this fearful disaster," I said. "How did it come about?"

"Well, if there hadn't been any Queen Guenever, it wouldn't have come so early; but it would have come, anyway. It would have come on your own account, by and by; by luck, it happened to come on the queen's."

"*And* Sir Launcelot's?"

"Just so."

3 "Give me the details."

"I reckon you will grant that during some years there has been only one pair of eyes in these kingdoms that has not been looking steadily askance at the queen and Sir Launcelot—"

"Yes, King Arthur's."

"Well, the king might have gone on, still happy and unsuspecting, to the end of his days, but for one of your modern improvements—the

---

## GUIDED READING

### LITERAL QUESTIONS

**1a.** What does the Yankee see from the top of the hill when he looks out for his ship? (He sees nothing at all—the sea is empty.)

**2a.** What is the first thing Clarence says when the Yankee asks him how the war came about? (He says it came earlier because of the queen, but it would have come anyway, "on your own account.")

### INFERENTIAL QUESTIONS

**1b.** What do his comments imply about the development of shipping in England? (His surprise at seeing no ships implies there has been much development of shipping traffic.)

**2b.** What do you think he means by saying war would have come anyway "on your own account"? (Perhaps the conflict between the Yankee's changes and the values of the sixth century would have inevitably caused war.)

stock board. When you left, three miles of the London, Canterbury and Dover were ready for the rails, and also ready and ripe for manipulation in the stock market. It was wildcat, and everybody knew it. The stock was for sale at a giveaway. What does Sir Launcelot do, but—"

"Yes, I know; he quietly picked up nearly all of it, for a song; then he bought about twice as much more, deliverable upon call; and he was about to call when I left."

"Very well, he did call. The boys couldn't deliver. Oh, he had them—and he just settled his grip and squeezed them. He skinned them alive, and they deserved it—anyway, the whole kingdom rejoiced. Well, among the flayed were Sir Agravaine and Sir Mordred, nephews to the king. Mordred and Agravaine propose to call the guileless Arthur's attention to Guenever and Sir Launcelot. A trap is laid for Launcelot, by the king's command, and Sir Launcelot walks into it. He made it sufficiently uncomfortable for the ambushed witnesses, for he killed every one of them but Mordred; but of course that couldn't straighten matters between Launcelot and the king, and didn't."

"Oh, dear, only one thing could result—I see that. War, and the knights of the realm divided into a king's party and a Sir Launcelot's party."

"Yes—that was the way of it. The king sent the queen to the stake, proposing to purify her with fire. Launcelot and his knights rescued her, and in doing it slew certain good old friends of yours and mine. Sir Launcelot smote down whoever came in the way of his blind fury, and he killed these without noticing who they were. Here is an instantaneous photograph one of our boys got of the battle; it's for sale on every newsstand. There—the figures nearest the queen are Sir Launcelot with his sword up, and Sir Gareth gasping his latest breath. You can catch the agony in the queen's face through the curling smoke. It's a rattling battle picture."

"Indeed it is. We must take good care of it; its historical value is incalculable. Go on."

"Well, the rest of the tale is just war, pure and simple. Launcelot retreated to his town and castle of Joyous Gard, and gathered there a great following of knights. The king, with a great host, went there, and there was desperate fighting during several days. Launcelot sailed to his Duchy of Guienne,[2] with his following. Arthur left the kingdom in Sir Mordred's hands until you should return—"

"Ah—a king's customary wisdom!"

"Yes. Sir Mordred set himself at once to work to make his kingship permanent. He was going to marry Guenever, as a first move; but she fled and shut herself up in the Tower of London. Mordred attacked. The king returned; Mordred fought him at Dover, at Canterbury, and again at Barham Down. Then there was talk of peace and a composition. Terms, Mordred to have Cornwall and Kent during Arthur's life, and the whole kingdom afterward. The two armies lay near Salisbury. Gawaine appeared to Arthur in a dream, and warned him to refrain from conflict for a month, let the delay cost what it might. But battle was precipitated by an accident. Arthur had given order that if a sword was raised during the consultation over the proposed treaty with Mordred, sound the trumpet and fall on! for he had no confidence in Mordred. Mordred had given a similar order to *his* people. Well, by and by an adder[3] bit a knight's heel; the knight forgot all about the order, and made a slash at the adder with his sword. Inside of half a minute those two prodigious hosts came together with a crash! They butchered away all day. Then the king—however, we have started something fresh since you left—our paper has."

"No? What is that?"

"War correspondence!"

"Why, that's good."

"Yes, the paper was booming right along,

---

2. **Duchy** [dūch′ē] **of Guienne** [gē yen′]: formerly a province of southwest France.
3. **adder:** poisonous snake.

*A Connecticut Yankee in King Arthur's Court*  **725**

## AT A GLANCE

- Clarence reads a report by one of his "war correspondents."
- Arthur is dead.
- Clarence says all but a handful of their knights will desert them.
- He relates his plans to save the Yankee and his supporters.

### 1 BACKGROUND

This account actually comes from Thomas Malory. You will find one rendering of Malory's description of this incident on page 602 of this textbook.

### 2 PLOT: SUBPLOT

The main plot, which deals with the Yankee's adventures, treats the story of Arthur as a subplot; the news of Arthur's death brings this subplot to an end.

### 3 THEME

The Yankee believes in progress and education but does not take into consideration two enduring aspects of human nature: fear and superstition. This failure shows the Yankee's naiveté about the kinds of change possible in people and societies.

### 4 PLOT: RISING ACTION

Because the Yankee and Clarence are outnumbered, they prepare to be besieged. This strategy illustrates their psychological position, too: As they represent the forces of progress and reform, they are under siege in a backward society.

---

while the war lasted. I had war correspondents with both armies. I will finish that battle by reading you what one of the boys says:

**1**

> Then the king looked about him, and then was he ware of all his host and of all his good knights were left no more on live but two knights, that was Sir Lucan de Butlere, and his brother Sir Bedivere: and they were full sore wounded. Mercy, said the king, where are all my noble knights becomen? Alas that ever I should see this doleful day. For now, said Arthur, I am come to mine end. Then the king gat his spear in both his hands, and ran toward Sir Mordred, crying, Traitor, now is thy death day come. And when Sir Mordred heard Sir Arthur, he ran until him with his sword drawn in his hand. And then King Arthur smote Sir Mordred under the shield, with a foin⁴ of his spear. And when Sir Mordred felt that he had his death's wound, he thrust himself, with the might that he had, up to the butt of King Arthur's spear. And right so he smote Arthur with his sword holden in both his hands, on the side of the head, that the sword pierced the helmet and therewithal Sir Mordred fell stark dead to the earth. And the noble Arthur fell in a swoon to the earth, and there he swooned ofttimes.

"That is a good piece of war correspondence, Clarence; you are a first-rate newspaper **2** man. Well—is the king all right? Did he get well?"

"Poor soul, no. He is dead."

I was utterly stunned; it had not seemed to me that any wound could be mortal to him.

---

4. **foin:** thrust.

"What changes! and in such a short while. It is inconceivable. What next, I wonder?"

"I can tell you what next."

"Well?"

"The clans are gathering. As soon as you are discovered we shall have business on our hands."

"Stuff! With our deadly scientific war material; with our hosts of trained—"

**3** "Save your breath—we haven't sixty faithful left!"

"What are you saying? Our schools, our colleges, our vast workshops, our—"

"When those knights come, those establishments will empty themselves and go over to the enemy. Did you think you had educated the superstition out of those people?"

"I certainly did think it."

"Well, then, you may unthink it. Make up your mind to it—when the armies come, the mask will fall."

"It's hard news. We are lost. They will turn our own science against us."

"No they won't."

"Why?"

"Because I and a handful of the faithful have blocked that game. From our various works I selected all the men—boys I mean—whose faithfulness under whatsoever pressure I could swear to, and I called them together secretly and gave them their instructions. There are fifty-two of them; none younger than fourteen, and none above seventeen years old. As a next move, I paid a private visit to that old cave of Merlin's—the big one—"

"Yes, the one where we secretly established our first great electric plant."

**4** "Just so. I thought it might be a good idea to utilize the plant now. I've provisioned the cave for a siege—"

"A good idea, a first-rate idea."

"Then I went out into the hills and uncovered and cut the secret wires which connected your bedroom with the wires that go to the

---

## GUIDED READING

**LITERAL QUESTION**

**1a.** Why does the Yankee not feel worried at first when Clarence tells him they will be attacked by those opposing Arthur? (He thinks all his knights and scientific weapons will defeat the enemy easily.)

**INFERENTIAL QUESTION**

**1b.** What does this assumption show about the Yankee's estimate of the depth of change in Arthur's society? (He overestimates how genuine any psychological change has been for most people, because the material changes have been so great.)

dynamite deposits under all our vast factories, hills, workshops, magazines, etc., and about midnight I and my boys turned out and connected that wire with the cave, and nobody but you and I suspects where the other end of it goes to. We laid it under ground, of course, and it was all finished in a couple of hours or so. We shan't have to leave our fortress, now, when we want to blow up our civilization."

"It was the right move—and the natural one; military necessity, in the changed condition of things. Well, what changes *have* come! We expected to be besieged in the palace some time or other, but—however, go on."

"Next, we built a wire fence. The wires go out from the cave and fence in a circle of level ground a hundred yards in diameter; they make twelve independent fences, ten feet apart—that is to say, twelve circles within circles—and their ends come into the cave again."

"Right; go on."

"In the center of the inner circle, on a spacious platform six feet high, I've grouped a battery of thirteen gatling guns, and provided plenty of ammunition."

"That's it. They command every approach, and when the knights arrive, there's going to be music. And the glass-cylinder dynamite torpedoes?"

"That's attended to. It's the prettiest garden

*A Connecticut Yankee in King Arthur's Court*  **727**

AT A GLANCE

- Clarence explains how he has connected the wires so that the Yankee's "civilization" can be blown up.
- He describes his fence: twelve circles within circles, defended by Gatling guns.

## 1 IRONY

Clarence and the Yankee contemplate destroying the civilization they worked so hard to build. Twain uses this irony to emphasize the destructive potential of technology and the inevitable tensions of a society experiencing rapid change.

## 2 VOCABULARY: DICTION

The Yankee phrases his threats in slang—*there's going to be music.* This breezy expression shows that the Yankee perhaps does not yet realize the full seriousness of the situation.

## GUIDED READING

### LITERAL QUESTION

**1a.** In the absence of troops, how do the Yankee and Clarence intend to defend themselves? (They will retreat to their cave and use their superior technology to defend themselves.)

### INFERENTIAL QUESTION

**1b.** What does this decision show about where they put their trust? (They have no doubts at all about the power of technology.)

**1 STYLE: FIGURATIVE LANGUAGE**

A metaphor compares the torpedo field to a garden. The metaphor is ironic: comparing a thing of natural beauty to man-made destructive technology.

**2 CHARACTERIZATION**

Deciding to strike first, the Yankee shows his aggressiveness and his confidence in scientific weaponry.

---

that was ever planted. It's a belt forty feet wide, and goes around the outer fence—distance between it and the fence one hundred yards—kind of neutral ground, that space is. There isn't a single square yard of that whole belt but is **1** equipped with a torpedo. We laid them on the surface of the ground, and sprinkled a layer of sand over them. It's an innocent looking garden, but you let a man start in to hoe it once, and you'll see."

"Clarence, you've done a world of work, and done it perfectly."

"We had plenty of time for it; there wasn't any occasion for hurry."

We sat silent awhile, thinking. Then my mind was made up, and I said:

"Yes, everything is ready; everything is ship-shape, no detail is wanting. I know what to do, now."

"So do I: sit down and wait."

"No, *sir!* rise up and *strike!*"

"Do you mean it?"

**2** "Yes, indeed! The *defensive* isn't in my line and the *offensive* is. That is, when I hold a fa[i]r hand—two-thirds as good a hand as the enemy['s]. Oh, yes, we'll rise up and strike; that's ou[r] game."

"A hundred to one, you are right. When do[es] the performance begin?"

"*Now!* We'll proclaim a Republic."

"Well, that *will* precipitate things, sur[e] enough!"

"It will make them buzz, *I* tell you! Englan[d] will be a hornet's nest before noon tomorrow[!] Now you write and I'll dictate—thus:

"PROCLAMATION."

"BE IT KNOWN UNTO ALL. Whereas the king having died and left no heir, it becomes my duty to continue the executive authority vested in me, until a government shall have been created and set in motion. The monarchy has lapsed, it no longer exists. By consequence, all political power has reverted to its original source, the people of the nation. *A Republic is hereby proclaimed*, as being the natural estate of a nation when other authority has ceased. It is the duty of the British people to meet together immediately, and by their votes elect representatives and deliver into their hands the government."

---

## GUIDED READING

### LITERAL QUESTION

**1a.** What metaphor does the Yankee use to describe how the people will react to his proclamation of a republic? (*England will be a hornet's nest. . . .*)

### INFERENTIAL QUESTION

**1b.** What does this metaphor show about the political reform the Yankee has accomplished? (It has failed, and the Yankee knows it. The people, not yet ready for political reform, will rise up in reaction against the imposition of a republic.)

Merlin's Cave. Clarence said:

"Why, that tells where we are, and invites them to call right away."

"That is the idea. We *strike*—by the Proclamation—then it's their innings. Now have the thing set up and printed and posted, right off; that is, give the order; then, if you've got a couple of bicycles handy at the foot of the hill, ho for Merlin's Cave!"

"I shall be ready in ten minutes. What a cyclone there is going to be tomorrow when this piece of paper gets to work!...It's a pleasant old palace, this is; I wonder if we shall ever again—but never mind about that."

## 25. The Battle of the Sand Belt

In Merlin's Cave—Clarence and I and fifty-two fresh, bright, well-educated, clean-minded young British boys. At dawn I sent an order to the factories and to all our great works to stop operations and remove all life to a safe distance, as everything was going to be blown up by secret mines *"and no telling at what moment—therefore, vacate at once."*

We had a week of waiting. I had spies out, every night, of course, to get news. Every report made things look more and more impressive. The hosts were gathering, gathering; down all the roads and paths of England the knights were riding. It was "Death to the Republic!" everywhere—not a dissenting voice. All England was marching against us! I was ready for the enemy. Let the approaching big day come along—it would find us on deck.

The big day arrived on time. At dawn the sentry on watch in the corral came into the cave and reported a moving black mass under the horizon, and a faint sound which he thought to be military music. I made the boys a little speech, and then sent out a detail to man the battery, with Clarence in command of it.

The sun rose presently and sent its unob-structed splendors over the land, and we saw a prodigious host moving slowly toward us, with the steady drift and aligned front of a wave of the sea. Nearer and nearer it came, and more and more sublimely imposing became its aspect; yes, all England was there, apparently.

At last we could make out details. All the front ranks, no telling how many acres deep, were horsemen—plumed knights in armor. Suddenly we heard the blare of trumpets; the slow walk burst into a gallop, and then—well, it was wonderful to see! Down swept that vast horseshoe wave—it approached the sand belt—my breath stood still; nearer, nearer—the strip of green turf beyond the yellow belt grew narrow—narrower still—became a mere ribbon in front of the horses—then disappeared under their hoofs. Great Scott! Why, the whole front of that host shot into the sky with a thundercrash, and became a whirling tempest of rags and fragments; and along the ground lay a thick wall of smoke that hid what was left of the multitude from our sight.

Time for the second step in the plan of campaign! I touched a button, and shook the bones of England loose from her spine!

In that explosion all our noble civilization-factories went up in the air and disappeared from the earth. It was a pity, but it was necessary. We could not afford to let the enemy turn our own weapons against us.

Now ensued one of the dullest quarter hours I had ever endured. We waited in a silent solitude enclosed by our circles of wire, and by a circle of heavy smoke outside of these. We couldn't see over the wall of smoke, and we couldn't see through it. But at last it began to shred away lazily, and by the end of another quarter hour the land was clear and our curiosity was enabled to satisfy itself. No living creature was in sight! The dynamite had dug a ditch more than a hundred feet wide, all around us, and cast up an embankment some twenty-five feet high on both borders of it. As to destruction of life, it was amazing.

*A Connecticut Yankee in King Arthur's Court*   **729**

## GUIDED READING

### LITERAL QUESTIONS

**1a.** What order does the Yankee send to his factories and institutions? (to stop working and get everybody out)

**2a.** What do the Yankee and his supporters see when the smoke clears away? (total devastation—a big ditch and an embankment caused by the dynamite)

### INFERENTIAL QUESTIONS

**1b.** Why does he give this order? (He intends to blow them all up shortly and he does not want to kill everyone.)

**2b.** What aspect of technology does this incident dramatize? (its great potential for destruction)

- The Yankee diverts a brook, checks his lines, and waits for the next attack.
- They see signs of a coming attack.
- They find a knight electrocuted on their fence.

## 1 THEME

The dialogue shows the dehumanizing effect of war—especially war waged with technology, which delivers death impersonally and at a remove.

## 2 THEME

In the novel's closing chapters Twain's depiction of knights in armor is less satiric than it is pathetic. Vulnerable in his armor, the knight comes to represent the hopelessness of the individual warrior pitted against superior technology.

I picketed the great embankments thrown up around our lines by the dynamite explosion—merely a lookout of a couple of boys to announce the enemy when he should appear again.

Next, I sent an engineer and forty men to a point just beyond our lines on the south, to turn a mountain brook that was there, and bring it within our lines and under our command, arranging it in such a way that I could make instant use of it in an emergency.

It was nightfall, now, and I withdrew my pickets. The one who had had the northern outlook reported a camp in sight, but visible with the glass only. He also reported that a few knights had been feeling their way toward us, and had driven some cattle across our lines, but that the knights themselves had not come very near. That was what I had been expecting. They were feeling us, you see; they wanted to know if we were going to play that red terror on them again. They would grow bolder in the night, perhaps.

Then, to business. I tested the electric signals from the gatling platform to the cave, and made sure that they were all right; I tested and retested those which commanded the fences—these were signals whereby I could break and renew the electric current in each fence independently of the others, at will.

As soon as it was good and dark, I shut off the current from all of the fences, and then groped my way out to the embankment bordering our side of the great dynamite ditch. I crept to the top of it and lay there on the slant of the muck to watch. It was too dark to see anything. I kept my ears strained to catch the least suspicious sound, for I judged I had only to wait and I shouldn't be disappointed.

At last I caught what you may call indistinct glimpses of sound—dulled metallic sound. This sound thickened, and approached a hundred feet or more away. Then I seemed to see a row of black dots appear along that ridge—human heads? I couldn't tell; it mightn't be anything at all. However, the question was soon settled. I heard that metallic noise descending into the great ditch. It augmented fast, it spread all along, and it unmistakably furnished me this fact: an armed host was taking up its quarters in the ditch. Yes, these people were arranging a little surprise party for us. We could expect entertainment about dawn, possibly earlier.

I groped my way back to the corral, now; I had seen enough. I went to the platform and signaled to turn the current onto the two inner fences. I woke Clarence and told him the great ditch was filling up with men, and that I believed all the knights were coming for us in a body. It was my notion that as soon as dawn approached we could expect the ditch's ambuscaded thousands to swarm up over the embankment and make an assault, and be followed immediately by the rest of their army.

We started a whispered conversation, but suddenly Clarence broke off and said:

1 "What is that?"

"What is what?"

"That thing yonder?"

"What thing—where?"

"There beyond you a little piece—a dark something—a dull shape of some kind—against the second fence."

I gazed and he gazed. I said:

"Could it be a man, Clarence?"

"No, I think not. If you notice, it looks a lit—why, it *is* a man—leaning on the fence!"

"I certainly believe it is; let's go and see."

We crept along on our hands and knees until 2 we were pretty close, and then looked up. Yes, it was a man—a dim great figure in armor, standing erect, with both hands on the upper wire. Poor fellow, dead as a doornail, and never knew what hurt him. He stood there like a statue—no motion about him, except that his plumes swished about a little in the night wind.

We heard muffled sounds approaching, and we sank down to the ground where we were. We made out another knight vaguely; he was

## GUIDED READING

### LITERAL QUESTION

**1a.** What does the Yankee have his men do to the brook? (He has them divert its flow inside their lines so that he can use it later if he wants to.)

### INFERENTIAL QUESTION

**1b.** What does this plan suggest about the Yankee's approach to problems? (Even in war, he remains practical and interested in technological solutions to problems.)

vicinity. We would now and then see a blue spark when the knight that caused it was so far away as to be invisible to us; but we knew what had happened, all the same, poor fellow; he had touched a charged wire with his sword and been elected.[5]

Pretty soon we detected a muffled and heavy sound, and next moment we guessed what it was. It was a surprise in force coming!

I sent a current through the third fence, now; and almost immediately through the fourth and fifth, so quickly were the gaps filled up. I believed the time was come, now, for my climax; I believed that that whole army was in our trap. Anyway, it was high time to find out. So I touched a button and set fifty electric suns aflame on the top of our precipice.

Land, what a sight! I shot the current through all the fences and struck the whole host dead in their tracks!

A glance showed that the rest of the enemy—perhaps ten thousand strong—were between us and the encircling ditch, and pressing forward to the assault. Consequently we had them *all!* and had them past help. Time for the last act of the tragedy. I fired three revolver shots—which meant:

"Turn on the water!"

There was a sudden rush and roar, and in a minute the mountain brook was raging through the big ditch and creating a river a hundred feet wide and twenty-five deep.

"Stand to your guns, men! Open fire!"

Within ten short minutes after we had opened fire, armed resistance was totally annihilated, the campaign was ended, we fifty-four were masters of England! Twenty-five thousand men lay dead around us.

But how treacherous is fortune! In a little while—say an hour—happened a thing, by my own fault, which—but I have no heart to write that. Let the record end here.

---

5. **elected:** here, electrocuted.

*A Connecticut Yankee in King Arthur's Court*   **731**

coming very stealthily, and feeling his way. Now he arrived at the first knight—and started slightly when he discovered him. He stood a moment—no doubt wondering why the other one didn't move on; then he said, in a low voice, "Why dreamest thou here, good Sir Mar—" then he laid his hand on the corpse's shoulder—and just uttered a little soft moan and sunk down dead. Killed by a dead man, you see—killed by a dead friend, in fact. There was something awful about it.

These early birds came scattering along after each other, about one every five minutes in our

- Clarence tells how the Yankee is wounded.
- Merlin, disguised as an old woman, enters the Yankee's camp.
- He puts a spell on the Yankee to make him go to sleep.
- Merlin is electrocuted.
- All of the Yankee's troops are dying, poisoned by the foul atmosphere of the enemy's corpses.

### 1 POINT OF VIEW

Clarence now becomes the first-person narrator, as the Yankee is asleep and can no longer record events. Clarence is also able to shed light on the Yankee's transposition of epochs—the mystery mentioned at the beginning of this work.

### 2 IRONY

The Yankee and his supporters are trapped: They risk death, whether they stay or leave.

### 3 PLOT: CONFLICT

The conflict between Merlin and the Yankee has run through the novel. Their personal animosity is caused by Merlin's jealousy of the Yankee's power. In a larger sense, their conflict represents that between superstition and science.

## 26. A Postscript by Clarence

I, Clarence, must write it for him. He proposed that we two go out and see if any help could be afforded the wounded. So we shut off the electric current from the fences, took an escort along, climbed over the enclosing ramparts of dead knights, and moved out upon the field. The first wounded man who appealed for help was sitting with his back against a dead comrade. When the Boss bent over him and spoke to him, the man recognized him and stabbed him.

We carried the Boss to the cave and gave his wound, which was not very serious, the best care we could. In this service we had the help of Merlin, though we did not know it. He was disguised as a woman, and appeared to be a simple old peasant goodwife. In this disguise, and smooth-shaven, he had appeared a few days after the Boss was hurt, and offered to cook for us. The Boss had been getting along very well, and had amused himself with finishing up his record.

We were glad to have this woman, for we

732   *The Novel*

were shorthanded. We were in a trap, you see—a trap of our own making. If we stayed where we were, our dead would kill us; if we moved out of our defenses, we should no longer be invincible. We had conquered; in turn we were conquered. The Boss recognized this; we all recognized it. If we could go and patch up some kind of terms with the enemy—yes, but the Boss could not go, and neither could I, for I was among the first that were made sick by the poisonous air bred by those dead thousands. Others were taken down, and still others. Tomorrow—

*Tomorrow.* It is here. And with it the end. About midnight I awoke, and saw that hag making curious passes in the air about the Boss's head and face, and wondered what it meant. I called out—

"What have you been doing?"

She halted, and said with an accent of malicious satisfaction:

"Ye were conquerors; ye are conquered! These others are perishing—you also. Ye shall all die in this place—every one—except *him*. He sleepeth, now—and shall sleep thirteen centuries. I am Merlin!"

Then such a delirium of silly laughter overtook him that he reeled about like a drunken man, and presently fetched up against one of our wires. His mouth is spread open yet; apparently he is still laughing.

The Boss has never stirred—sleeps like a stone. If he does not wake today we shall understand what kind of a sleep it is, and his body will then be borne to a place in one of the remote recesses of the cave where none will ever find it to desecrate it. As for the rest of us—well, it is agreed that if any one of us ever escapes alive from this place, he will write the fact here, and loyally hide this Manuscript with the Boss, our dear good chief, whose property it is, be he alive or dead.

### END OF THE MANUSCRIPT

## 27. Final P.S. by M.T.

The dawn was come when I laid the manuscript aside. The rain had almost ceased, the world was gray and sad, the exhausted storm was sighing and sobbing itself to rest. I went to the stranger's room, and listened at his door, which was slightly ajar. I could hear his voice, and so I knocked. There was no answer, but I still heard the voice. I peeped in. The man lay on his back, in bed, talking brokenly but with spirit, and punctuating with his arms, which he thrashed about, restlessly, as sick people do in delirium. I slipped in softly and bent over him. His mutterings went on. I spoke—merely a word, to call his attention. His glassy eyes and his ashy face were alight in an instant with pleasure, gratitude, gladness, welcome:

"O, Sandy, you are come at last—how I have longed for you! Sit by me—do not leave me—never leave me again, Sandy, never again. Now all is well, all is peace, and I am happy again—we are happy again, isn't it so, Sandy?...Have I been sick long? It must be so; it seems months to me. And such dreams! Such strange and awful dreams, Sandy! Dreams that were as real as reality—so real! Why, I thought the king was dead, I thought there was a revolution; I thought that Clarence and I and a handful of my cadets fought and exterminated the whole chivalry of England!

But even that was not the strangest. I seemed to be a creature out of a remote unborn age, centuries hence, and even *that* was as real as the rest! Yes, I seemed to have flown back out of that age into this of ours, and then forward to it again, and was set down, a stranger and forlorn in that strange England, with an abyss of thirteen centuries yawning between me and you! between me and my home and my friends! between me and all that is dear to me. It was awful—awfuler than you can ever imagine, Sandy. Ah, watch by me, Sandy—stay by me every moment—*don't* let me go out of my mind again; death is nothing, let it come, but not with those dreams—I cannot endure *that* again.... Sandy?..."

He lay muttering incoherently some little time; then for a time he lay silent, and apparently sinking away toward death. Presently his fingers began to pick busily at the coverlet, and by that sign I knew that his end was at hand. With the first suggestion of the death rattle in his throat he started up slightly, and seemed to listen; then he said:

"A bugle?...It is the king! The drawbridge, there! Man the battlements—turn out the—"

He was getting up his last "effect"; but he never finished it.

---

## STUDY QUESTIONS

### Recalling

1. List four or five of the technological advances reported by the Yankee in his account of the three years since his rescue from slavery. What social changes does he describe?
2. Why does the Yankee marry Sandy? Why do they go to France?
3. Relate the changes the Yankee sees when he returns to Britain. According to Clarence, what events have brought about the war between Arthur and Launcelot? What led to the war between the king and Mordred?
4. Outline the plan of defense Clarence describes to the Yankee.
5. Describe the Yankee's victory over the knights. What is the cost of this victory to the civilization he has built? To his own forces? To himself?
6. What is our last picture of the Yankee? What does he say about his travels through time?

*A Connecticut Yankee in King Arthur's Court* 733

### AT A GLANCE

- M. T. finishes the Yankee's manuscript.
- He visits the Yankee's room, finds him delirious.
- The Yankee dies.

### 1 POINT OF VIEW

Now it is "M. T." (Twain) who picks up the narration, completing the frame begun with his meeting of the Yankee on a castle tour.

### 2 PLOT: CONFLICT

On his deathbed, the Yankee reveals his conflict as a nineteenth-century man in the Middle Ages. Ironically, he has come to identify more with Arthur's time than with his own.

### REFLECTING ON THE NOVEL

Merlin and the Yankee personalize the conflict between science and superstition. In their final confrontation, which man does Twain show as the victor? (It is hard to say: Merlin puts a spell on the Yankee, but the Yankee's technology kills Merlin.)

### STUDY QUESTIONS

1. *advances:* telephone, telegraph, sewing machine, railroads, steel; *changes:* schools, newspapers, equal rights, end to slavery
2. She is his property. Daughter is sick; doctors advise sea air.
3. evidence of war; romance between Launcelot and Guinevere; Mordred left in charge while Arthur fights: tries to usurp throne
4. takes over Merlin's cave; wires explosives to blow up factories; protects cave with electric barbed wire and explosives
5. Knights marching on cave are blown up by explosives, electrocuted by fence. Civilization is destroyed. Troops are trapped by own barricades. He is stabbed by Merlin, who casts spell that makes him sleep for 300 years.
6. dying in nineteenth-century England while dreaming about sixth century; journey to nineteenth century is a dream

7. due to corruption, greed of knights; level of destruction—due to innovations

8. His insistence on winning, penchant for special effects, ingenuity, impulsiveness, belief in progress, all prevent him from predicting the consequences.

9. has divided his life between two centuries; has nineteenth-century temperament; sixth-century attitudes

10. His heart is in the sixth century.

11. He introduced valuable social reforms but also unnecessary technology and destructive weaponry.

## VIEWPOINT

Students should

- cite humorous incidents
- explain humor; mention devices
- give examples of opposition to injustice, love of equality

## LITERARY FOCUS

1. Yankee starts out succeeding with funny tricks and inventions; he ends by destroying civilization. Tragedy is foreshadowed by the smallpox hut, slavery. The climax is the final battle.

2. *between individuals:* Yankee vs. Merlin, slave dealer, sheriffs; Mordred's feud with Launcelot; *against nature:* struggle against elements, disease; *against society:* Yankee vs. injustice, superstition; *against fate:* attempt to rush history; *internal conflicts:* Yankee's love of progress vs. acceptance of sixth century; love of democracy vs. love of power

3. The Yankee becomes accustomed to Arthurian England, falls in love with Sandy; king learns about injustice

4. Nineteenth-century England and Connecticut, sixth-century England and France; Arthur's Britain ends where it began—a primitive society.

5. The frame allows reader to travel through time; anchors

### Interpreting

7. To what extent is the collapse of Camelot the result of social problems and human conflicts within Arthur's Britain? To what extent is this collapse the result of the Yankee's nineteenth-century innovations?

8. What traits in his character lead the Yankee to devise his plan against his opponents? How do you explain the Yankee's inability to foresee the logical consequences of his plan?

9. Why might the dying Yankee be confused about his place in history?

### Extending

10. In which century do *you* think the Yankee belongs?

11. One critic argues that our judgment of the Yankee should be based not on the final outcome of his efforts but rather on the relative merit of the changes he offered. Do you think he offered the Britons something better than what they had? Why or why not?

## VIEWPOINT

The range of Twain's talent and ambition makes *A Connecticut Yankee in King Arthur's Court* readable on a number of different levels. As a critic noted at the time of the novel's publication:

Here he is to the full the humorist, as we know him; but he is very much more, and his strong, indignant...hate of injustice, and his love of equality, burn hot through the manifold adventures and experiences of the tale.

— W. D. Howells, *Harper's* magazine

■ Discuss incidents from the novel that illustrate Twain's ability to make you laugh. Where in the novel do you see evidence of his opposition to injustice and his love of equality?

## LITERARY FOCUS

### The Total Effect

*A Connecticut Yankee in King Arthur's Court* draws together the elements that make up most works of fiction: plot, character, setting, point of view, tone, symbol, irony, and theme. The novel presents its ambitious plot in episodic style,

734    *The Novel*

loosely tying together numerous incidents involving a single character, the Yankee, who is caught in a strange web of circumstances. Twain's setting provides many illustrations of these circumstances, as the nineteenth-century Yankee explores sixth-century Britain and introduces bits of his own world into it. As our first-person narrator, the Yankee never hesitates to offer his nineteenth-century opinions of his sixth-century environment. This dreamlike story of a character traveling through time takes us beyond literal meaning to the levels of symbol and irony. All of these elements combine to present ideas about human nature, progress, and history.

### Thinking About Plot, Character, and Setting

1. Show how the plot of *A Connecticut Yankee* moves from a very humorous beginning to a tragic ending. What events in the third section of the novel foreshadow the sadness of the ending? What event is the novel's climax?

2. Identify the most important external conflicts in the novel, classifying them as follows: between individuals, between individuals and nature, between individuals and society, and between individuals and fate. In addition, what conflicts occur within individuals?

3. In what ways does the Yankee change in the novel? Do any other characters change during the course of the novel? Explain.

4. What various settings are presented throughout the novel? Explain how Arthur's Britain changes from the beginning to the end of the novel.

### Thinking About Point of View and Tone

5. The novel begins and ends with a frame story in which Twain is a nineteenth-century narrator who learns the Yankee's story. What does this frame add to the novel? Would you have preferred the novel if it had begun and ended in the sixth rather than the nineteenth century? Explain.

6. In what ways might the Yankee's practical-minded nature limit his view of Arthur's Britain?

7. The Yankee's tone changes throughout the novel. At times he is whimsical, serious, tender, sad, boastful, or complaining. Locate passages illustrating two or three of these differences in tone.

fantasy in realism. Preferences will vary.

6. fails to appreciate simplicity, beauty, poetry

7. *whimsical*—first impressions; *serious*—conversations with freemen; *tender*—king's care for dying women; *boastful*—brags of his skills; *complaining*—relates problems with armor

8. is gracious, superstitious, illogical

9. destroys civilization he was trying to establish

10. *sixth:* ridicules knighthood, social customs, ignorance; *nineteenth:* ridicules obsession with technology, materialism

11. cruelty, dishonesty, ignorance, ambition, compassion, resourcefulness, love, heroism; negative view

12. can be both helpful and dangerous

### Thinking About Symbol

8. In what ways might Sandy symbolize both the good qualities and the limitations of sixth-century Britain?

### Thinking About Irony

9. What irony do you see in the outcome of the Yankee's final battle?

### Thinking About Theme

10. Explain how *A Connecticut Yankee* satirizes both the sixth and the nineteenth centuries. What failings in each period does it point out?
11. What aspects of human nature that are universal does Twain portray? What overall image of human nature does he present?
12. What mixed view does the novel present of technological progress?

## VOCABULARY

### Slang

Slang is a highly informal type of speech usually associated with a particular group of people. It changes constantly, quickly going out of style as people look for newer and livelier ways of speaking.

In *A Connecticut Yankee in King Arthur's Court*, the Yankee, like many of Mark Twain's other characters, speaks in a colloquial, or informal, style that draws much of its appeal from slang expressions. Slang serves two additional purposes in the novel: It characterizes the Yankee as a down-to-earth person of his time, and it clashes sharply with the quaint speech of the sixth-century Britons.

The sentences below come from *A Connecticut Yankee in King Arthur's Court*. Identify the slang in each sentence. Then explain the meaning of each slang expression, and indicate whether or not it is still in use today.

1. . . . if there wasn't any quick new-fangled way to make a thing, I could invent one. . . .
2. I would presently boss that asylum or know the reason why.
3. Raphael was a bird.
4. Where do they hang out?
5. Brer Merlin works his arts but gets left.

Find five other slang expressions from *A Connecticut Yankee in King Arthur's Court*. Tell what they mean and whether they are still in use.

## COMPOSITION

### Writing About the Total Effect

■ Discuss the total effect of *A Connecticut Yankee in King Arthur's Court*. First describe the novel's overall impact on you. Then discuss how Twain uses plot, character, setting, point of view, tone, symbol, irony, and theme to create that impact. *For help with this assignment, see Lesson 12 in the Writing About Literature Handbook at the back of this book.*

### Writing a New Incident in the Yankee's History

■ Imagine that the Yankee has taken another jump in time, from the nineteenth century to the present day. Write a monologue in which he speaks about what he sees in today's world. Be sure to keep him in character, remembering his interests, limitations, and style of speaking. The monologue may be comic or serious, but it should end with some message to today's people based on his past experiences.

## COMPARING TWAIN AND MALORY

■ Compare the portrayals of King Arthur's Britain in Twain's *Connecticut Yankee in King Arthur's Court* and Malory's *Morte d'Arthur*. Concentrate on the way each work presents the following: (a) living conditions, (b) chivalry, (c) knightly adventures, and (d) magic and mystery.

## COMPARING NOVELS

1. Compare Steinbeck's and Twain's treatment of social issues in *The Pearl* and *A Connecticut Yankee in King Arthur's Court*. In particular, discuss the way each author portrays the difference between the powerful and the powerless. How important is the concern about social justice in each novel?
2. Show how both *The Pearl* and *A Connecticut Yankee in King Arthur's Court* concern characters who are uprooted from their normal lives and lose the sense of where they belong in the world. Where do Kino and the Yankee each belong, and what has cut each off from this world? How does each respond to his experiences? What might each novel be saying about the importance of knowing where you belong?

*A Connecticut Yankee in King Arthur's Court*  735

**Reading as Participation**

Help the students to recognize and appreciate the immersion we experience in reading a good novel by comparing this experience to similar ones—for example, the way watching a vivid movie can make our surroundings seem a little different for a while. Ask for examples (students might mention such films as *Star Wars, E.T., Raiders of the Lost Ark,* or *Chariots of Fire*). You could help students to characterize the different "feel" of *The Pearl* and *A Connecticut Yankee in King Arthur's Court* by asking them to read aloud contrasting passages from each novel and describe the effect of each.

# ACTIVE READING

## Reading as Participation

A book comes to life only when it has a reader, someone to re-create the author's original meaning and emotion. In a poem about a man reading, Wallace Stevens wrote, "The reader became the book." There are times when we read with such absorption that we forget ourselves and allow the language of the book to take over our minds, transporting us into the world of a novel, story, poem, play, or essay.

When you respond to a book in this way, you actually participate in the creative process. It is you who are allowing the author's words to have a sound, creating a space in which the characters can breathe and think and feel. When you become part of a book in this way, the book becomes part of you. Think of what happened to you when you read John Steinbeck's *Pearl* or Mark Twain's *Connecticut Yankee in King Arthur's Court*. You were able to open these books and find yourself rapidly transported to the world of Mexican peasants or to the world of a nineteenth-century American who travels back to sixth-century England.

How different the worlds of these two novels are—different in time, in place, in language. Steinbeck has written a kind of fable, and his Mexican peasants are very simple people. His language is solemn, poetic, plain, slow in its rhythms:

> Her back was bent with pain and her head was low. She went through the line of brush when the moon was covered, and when it looked through she saw the glimmer of the great pearl in the path behind the rock.

Now listen to a typical passage from *A Connecticut Yankee*:

> . . . next you belt on your sword; then you put your stovepipe joints onto your arms . . . and there you are, snug as a candle in candle mold. This is no time to dance.

If you feel and hear any difference between Steinbeck's poetic fable and Twain's boisterous satire, it is *your response* that makes the difference. In the end it is *you* who brings Kino and Juana, the Yankee and Merlin to life. And how much larger, how much richer your own world becomes when you bring these people and their worlds into it.

# REVIEW: THE NOVEL

## Guide for Studying the Novel

As you read novels, review the following guide in order to appreciate how a novelist creates a fictional world.

### Plot, Character, and Setting

1. If the novel follows the traditional plot structure, identify its **narrative hook, rising action, climax, falling action,** and **resolution.**
2. If the novel is structured more loosely, what does each episode add to the story, and how does each build on the preceding ones?
3. What kinds of **conflict** does the novel present?
4. Who are the major **characters**?
5. Are the characters **round** or **flat**? **Static** or **dynamic**? If round, what contradictions do the characters reveal? If dynamic, what makes the characters change?
6. Why do you sympathize or not sympathize with each character?
7. When and where does the novel take place? Which **settings** does the novel include?

### Point of View and Tone

1. What is the effect of the **point of view** that the author uses: **first-person, limited third-person,** or **omniscient**? Does the point of view ever change?
2. What attitude toward the novel's events and characters does the **tone** of the author express?

### Symbol

- What objects, persons, places, or events in the novel are given **symbolic** meaning? What do they symbolize? Does the meaning of any symbol change?

### Irony

- If the novel uses **irony**, what is its effect, and why is it used?

### Theme

1. Identify the novel's major **theme** or themes.
2. How do the **plot, characters, setting, point of view, symbols,** and **irony** express the novel's theme or themes?

*The Novel* 737

A major goal of this literature series is to help students become active, independent learners. Resources on the following pages are designed to help students develop and refine the skills that mature learners use constantly as they interact with literature. Such learners know how to *manage* their assignments by applying these skills:

- speaking and listening skills
- thinking skills
- reading and writing skills
- study skills

Students will be able to refer to these pages throughout the term — not just in connection with a single literary selection. In other words, students can use this *easy-to-find reference-and-practice guide* continually, as they experience all the literature they read. With outstanding literature, on the one hand, and a comprehensive resource guide, on the other, this literature series provides the means for you and your students to deal with both *ideas* and *skills*.

In addition, these pages also include the following elements, designed for successful teaching and learning:

- Literary Terms Handbook
- Glossary
- Vocabulary Review
- Index of Titles by Theme
- Index of Skills
- Index of Authors and Titles

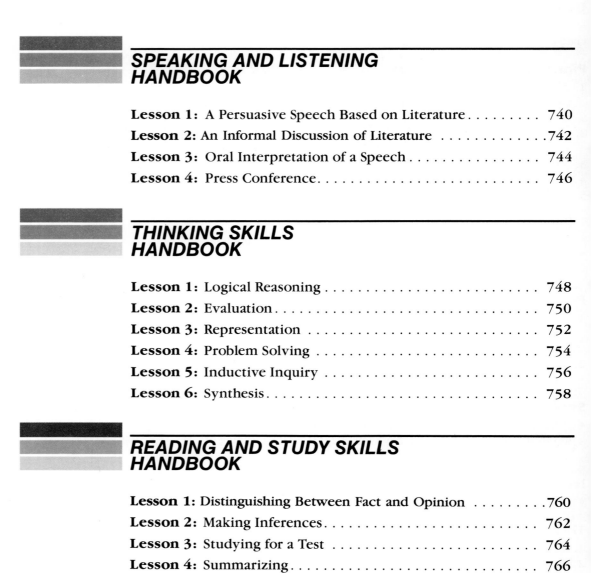

# STUDENT'S RESOURCES
## LESSONS IN ACTIVE LEARNING

### SPEAKING AND LISTENING HANDBOOK

### THINKING SKILLS HANDBOOK

### READING AND STUDY SKILLS HANDBOOK

# WRITING ABOUT LITERATURE HANDBOOK

# LITERARY TERMS HANDBOOK

This handbook enables students to practice and improve their speaking and listening skills while studying literature. The four lessons in the handbook cover a wide range of interrelated speaking and listening skills:

- public speaking
- listening/discussion
- oral interpretation of literature
- collaborative learning

Each literature-based lesson is set up in a step-by-step format so that students can easily work on the skill on their own. The final step in each lesson is a transfer activity in which the student is directed to apply the skill to a variety of selections in the anthology. In other words, the lessons are designed to be used or referred to many times—as often as you wish your students to work with a particular speaking or listening skill.

In addition to this handbook, speaking and listening skills are practiced in the Challenge strand of this textbook and in the Additional Projects in the unit booklets in your *Teacher's Classroom Resources*. The blackline masters Outline for Organizing a Speech About Literature and Questions for Planning an Oral Interpretation of a Speech (TCR 5, pages 33–34) and Overhead Transparency 27 will prove helpful as your students work with the lessons in this handbook.

## Lesson 1

The first lesson gives students an opportunity to work with public speaking—perhaps the activity they most often associate with speaking and listening. Here students practice techniques of preparing and delivering a speech and, at the same time, examine literature from new perspectives.

# SPEAKING AND LISTENING HANDBOOK

## LESSON 1: *A Persuasive Speech Based on Literature*

### ▮▮ OVERVIEW

You will present a speech about what literature teaches us, and—by citing evidence from two or more pieces of literature—you will persuade your audience to agree with you. Early in your speech you will state a **proposition**, which is a very specific statement of your belief or point of view—in this case, about the power of literature.

Generally, you should come up with a proposition that can truly be argued. If you come up with a statement that is so broad that it is bland, your audience will not be interested in your speech.

> *Example:* If your proposition is "I believe that literature helps us," you will not hold your audience's attention. If, however, you come up with a more focused proposition such as, "I believe that literature helps us understand why people act one way when they really want to act another way," you will have a more interesting time.

### ▮▮ PREPARING THE SPEECH

1. **Generate a proposition.**
   As you think about the literature you have read or are reading, ask yourself two questions:

   a. What does this piece of literature remind me about what literature can teach me?
   b. How do I feel about that lesson? Do I care?

   It is important that you believe strongly in the proposition.

2. **State your proposition clearly.**
   Make sure you know exactly what you want to say about the lessons of literature.

3. **Gather support for your proposition.**
   a. Make sure that you are totally familiar with the literature so that you do not distort its meaning. (You want your audience to have confidence in you and not think you are misinterpreting the story, poem, etc.)
   b. Think about each of the elements that make up a piece of literature, and collect your ideas on how the different elements may or may not support your proposition: How do the plot, characters, setting, point of view, tone, symbolism, irony, theme, poetic devices, and so on support your propositions?

### ▮▮ A SAMPLE SPEECH

Let us assume that as you read "To James" (page 234) you are very aware of an important message: keeping one's eye on a goal. Let us further assume that the message sounds familiar to you; you think you heard it somewhere else recently. Then you remember that the idea of finding and holding onto a goal is at least in part what the story "Through the Tunnel" (page 91) is also about. Struck by the message because you have noticed it twice recently, you decide to use it as the basis of your speech. You try various wordings and finally come up with the following proposition:

> I believe that one of the most important lessons of literature is to make us see that we can succeed if we try.

Then you will probably want to reread both "To James" and "Through the Tunnel," making sure you understand them as well as possible and gathering specific evidence to support your proposition. As a result of your rereading, you will come up with an outline such as the following one.

**I. Opening**
  **A.** Statement of proposition
  **B.** Explanation of why proposition is important to me

**II. Body**
  **A.** How "To James" touches on "success from dedication" theme
    **1.** What the poem is about on the surface
    **2.** What the other meanings of the poem are
  **B.** How "Through the Tunnel" also reflects the theme
    **1.** Coincidence in subject matter: physical endurance also
    **2.** Extra layer of meaning: importance of endurance for maturity and independence

**III. Conclusion**
  How identification of this theme can help us even if we are not engaged in athletic contests

### DELIVERING THE SPEECH

In actually presenting a persuasive speech to your audience, you will need to bear in mind the following three points:

**1. Speak with conviction.**
Mean what you say. Believe in your proposition. Be sincere. If you are not—if you really do not believe in the power of literature to help people shape their own lives—the audience will be able to tell, and they will not accept your proposition.

**2. Speak extemporaneously.**
Be prepared, and refer to your outline, but choose the exact words as you speak—spontaneously. Be sure to achieve direct eye contact with members of your audience.

**3. Speak dynamically.**
Use a variety of voice inflections, pitch variations, and rates of speaking. That is, speed up and slow down as the material demands. Speak with a certain intensity, and know your ideas well enough so that you can achieve a smooth presentation.

All three of these pointers work together to help you persuade your audience to agree with your proposition and to appreciate the support you cite for it. It does no good to have conviction without dynamism, and it may be even more damaging to appear dynamic without really believing in what you have to say.

### ASSIGNMENT

Use the Index of Titles by Theme at the back of this book to help remind yourself about selections you have already read. You should then be able to start forming a proposition about literature—a proposition that you will want to prove to an audience. Here are a couple of examples based on that index:

- Using "The Red-Headed League" and "The Sentimentality of William Tavener" to prove that literature encourages us to look beyond the surface of people
- Using "Chee's Daughter" and "Shaving" to prove that literature reminds us of the blessings of familial love

*Speaking and Listening Handbook*  **741**

# LESSON 2: *An Informal Discussion of Literature*

### ▉ OVERVIEW

The class as a whole will discuss one of the literary works in this anthology. A key characteristic of an informal discussion is that everyone participates, as follows:

- There is a discussion leader.
- The rest of the class are discussants, or discussion members.
- One member of the class may serve as a secretary or recorder to take notes in case you want to refer to what was said.

During a discussion the speaking is spontaneous; there are no set speeches. However, to give the discussion focus and structure, there is a discussion question and an agenda.

### ▉ SELECTING A LITERARY WORK FOR DISCUSSION

The best pieces of literature to work with in an informal discussion are those that are most open to interpretation, those that have multiple layers of meaning. If a selection is too straightforward, the class will not have enough to discuss. For the purpose of this lesson, we will assume a class is discussing the poem "Mirror" by Sylvia Plath (page 182).

### ▉ DISCUSSION QUESTION AND AGENDA

The discussion question is generally broad in scope. Coming up with an appropriate question requires much reading and thinking about the selection by the leader. Here are some suggested wordings:

- What is the most important idea in this work?
- Why does this work remain popular?
- What does this work have to say about love [or challenges or nature, etc.]?

*Example:* For Plath's poem "Mirror" the discussion question might be "What does the poem suggest about relationships?"

The agenda is the list of subordinate questions that the discussion leader will ask to help the class answer the discussion question. A good agenda contains at least two categories of subordinate questions:

1. **Questions about facts in the work**

   *Example:* For "Mirror" some questions might be
   - Who is speaking?
   - What or whom is the speaker talking about?
   - What happens in the poem?

2. **Questions about interpretations of the facts**

   *Example:* For "Mirror" some questions might be
   - What is the significance of the mirror's speaking?
   - Is the mirror as objective as it claims?
   - What might the mirror represent?

### ▉ GUIDELINES FOR DISCUSSION LEADER

1. After becoming familiar with the work, the leader develops the discussion question and agenda.

2. The discussion leader arranges the space to aid the discussion. The discussion leader may sit in the center of the space, and the discussants will form a semicircle around the leader.

3. The leader announces the discussion question, explains why it is important, and identifies the agenda in broad terms.

   *Example:* "Today we are going to discuss the poem 'Mirror' by Sylvia Plath. This discussion is important because Plath's works often contain layers and layers of meaning.

**742** *Speaking and Listening Handbook*

The basic question we will address is, 'What does this poem suggest about relationships?' First we will look at the basic facts of the poem; then we will discuss interpretations.''

4. The leader poses the questions, recognizes members of the group, and calls on people.

*Examples*

- ''We will begin by asking, 'Who is speaking in this poem?' ''
- ''Pamela, I see your hand is raised.''
- ''Dick, I wonder if you would suggest an answer to this question.''

5. The discussion leader summarizes as necessary, interprets answers, seeks consensus, makes transitions to keep the discussion moving forward, and summarizes the entire discussion.

*Examples*

- ''So far we have established that the speaker is a mirror, the mirror hangs on a wall, and the woman at times turns her back on the mirror.''
- ''You seem to be saying that the mirror plays a unique role in the woman's life.''
- ''Can we agree that the mirror uses emotional language?''
- ''We should now move on to figure out if the mirror stands for something more than a mirror.''
- ''Beginning with a statement of the facts of the poem, we have gone on to interpret the poem and to make observations about the nature of relationships.''

NOTE: One alternative is to have three leaders working together, jointly developing the discussion question and agenda. They can then divide the agenda into three parts, with each leader responsible for one part.

Or one person can be the main leader and can have two assistants, who will see that each member of the class is recognized or called upon and that the main leader sticks to the agenda.

## GUIDELINES FOR DISCUSSANTS

1. The discussants should read the work of literature before the discussion begins. They should read the work, think about it, and make notes about impressions of the work.

2. Each participant should speak up clearly and should address the *whole* group.

3. Each participant must back up an opinion with evidence, quoting from the literature itself.

4. No one should interrupt anyone else or should monopolize the discussion.

5. Discussants should enter the discussion with an open mind. The purpose of the discussion is not to force one's ideas on the group but rather to find a variety of points of view on or answers to the discussion question.

## ASSIGNMENT

You may apply these discussion guidelines to many pieces of literature in this anthology. Selections that will work particularly well because of their complexity and open-endedness are

- ''An Occurrence at Owl Creek Bridge'' by Ambrose Bierce (page 142)
- ''The Laugher'' by Heinrich Böll (page 151)
- ''A Blessing'' by James Wright (page 185)
- ''Boy at the Window'' by Richard Wilbur (page 254)
- ''A Child's Christmas in Wales'' by Dylan Thomas (page 282)

Oral interpretation—the performance of literature—is gaining increased attention as another avenue to the understanding and appreciation of literature. As students work on their oral presentations of poems, short stories, and so forth, they find themselves reading more closely and thinking about literature more critically than ever before.

# LESSON 3: Oral Interpretation of a Speech

## ▇▇ OVERVIEW

You will select a speech from this book and present a reading of it to the class. The speech may be an actual speech that a real person gave or a speech by a fictional character in one of the plays represented in this book.

This anthology contains several outstanding speeches: Martin Luther King's "I Have a Dream" speech, Cyrano de Bergerac's "nose" speech, Mark Antony's "Friends, Romans, countrymen" speech from *Julius Caesar*, speeches by Portia and Calpurnia from *Julius Caesar,* and a speech by Roxane in *Cyrano de Bergerac.*

## ▇▇ PLANNING AN ORAL INTERPRETATION

1. **Think about the speech.**

   Answer the following questions about the speech you will perform:

   a. Who is speaking the speech and to whom? (Martin Luther King, Jr., was speaking to civil-rights marchers gathered in Washington, D.C. Cyrano delivers his famous "nose" speech to the courtiers and high society gathered at a theater.)

   b. What is the occasion for the speech? What is the purpose of the speech? What is its intended effect upon its audience?

   c. What arguments does the speaker offer? What emotional appeals? How does the speaker depend on his or her own character and reputation to sway the audience?

   d. What is the organization, or pattern, of the speech? How does the speaker organize arguments and appeals for maximum effect? Where is the climax of the speech? Where are the major changes, or transitions?

2. **Adapt the speech for performance.**

   Some speeches are very long, such as the address by Martin Luther King, Jr. Decide if you want to read only a portion of the speech. You should perform for four to six minutes. With the King speech you may want to give only the final part, beginning with "I say to you today, my friends, that in spite of the difficulties and frustrations of the moment I still have a dream" (page 330).

3. **Create a script.**

   Type or print the script double-spaced. This way you can mark it for delivery—e.g., underline words that you want to stand out, indicate breath pauses, remind yourself of the meaning and pronunciation of all words, etc.

4. **Practice reading the speech out loud.**

   The structure of the speech is most important. First comes phrasing. Group together the words that make sense. Establish a rhythm to make sense of the words and ideas and engage your audience.

   Second, concentrate on the major contrasts. Where are the major changes in the speech? Be sure you realize these with corresponding (and appropriate) changes in voice. (E.g., you may change from a loud, declamatory tone to a more conversational, down-to-earth tone.)

   Third, consider the overall structure of the speech, and build emotionally to its climax.

5. **Design an introduction for your oral performance of the speech.**

   Explain to your present audience—classmates—who the speaker is, to whom he or she is speaking, and what the context of the speech is. Arouse their interest in it. Tell them why you think they might be

**744** *Speaking and Listening Handbook*

interested in the speech. What are they going to gain by listening to it?

## PRESENTATION OF THE SPEECH

1. Present your introduction to the speech in a conversational manner. Just talk to the audience extemporaneously. You may even stand in front of the lectern.

2. Before presenting the speech itself, pause. Assume the stance and character of the speaker of the speech. Have your script open on the lectern or reading stand.

3. Decide if you want to treat the audience in front of you as if they were the original audience hearing this speech. If you do, then look directly at them as you deliver the speech. Otherwise, create an image of the audience to whom the speech was originally addressed, and focus your eyes on them. For example, as King you might focus on the literally hundreds of thousands of people who were before him as he gave his "I Have a Dream" speech; as Cyrano you might look around the vast, large theater in which the original audience was seated.

4. Use a strong voice. Project well. Because speeches are often given to very large audiences, you do not want to deliver the speech in a timid manner.

5. Speeches also have a formality about them. There are moments of informality, even conversational ("plain folks") moments, but the main part of the speech will be formal.

6. Stand up straight, and use broad gestures. Do not be afraid to sweep your arm upward in a large gesture, but make sure the gesture is tied to the idea in the speech and has meaning.

## A SAMPLE ORAL INTERPRETATION

Let us work up an oral interpretation of Antony's speech in Act III, Scene ii, of *Julius Caesar* (lines 166– 194). This analysis of the speech contains suggestions for its presentation.

Here Antony talks to the citizens of Rome. Their ruler, Caesar, has just been murdered in a coup. The other rulers, Brutus and Cassius, felt that Caesar had been abusing his power. They have given his best friend, Antony, permission to speak at his funeral if he does not blame them for the murder.

Antony's persuasive task is to stir up the citizens in rebellion against Brutus and Cassius but to do it in a way that does not at first appear to call for rebellion. In this particular speech he holds up the garment worn by Caesar when he was killed and shows it to his audience. He—perhaps gently—recalls a time long ago when Caesar first wore the garment, thereby establishing a sentimental image of Caesar and, of course, his own closeness to Caesar. This technique establishes the speaker's credibility.

He also uses the strong imperative mood: "Look," "See," "Mark," "Judge," etc. He uses emotional words and even the exclamation "O" quite often. He re-creates the stabbing vividly for his audience. His main point is that Caesar was betrayed by those whom he loved most and that Caesar died not so much from the actual wounds but more from a broken heart.

At the end Antony builds up to actually showing the citizens Caesar's body itself. He moves from the bloody cloak to the body itself. Pulling the garment off the body is a dramatic final gesture.

## ASSIGNMENTS

1. Based on the preceding paragraphs about Antony's speech beginning on line 166, rehearse and present an oral interpretation. Alternatively, prepare an oral interpretation of another speech by Antony or other character in *Julius Caesar*.

2. Work on an oral presentation of a speech from another play in this book or of part of the speech by Martin Luther King, Jr.

*Speaking and Listening Handbook* **745**

# LESSON 4: *Press Conference*

## ▬▬ OVERVIEW

Working with five to nine other students, you will participate in planning and conducting a press conference with an author (dead or alive) represented in this book. Your group will divide itself into the following roles:

- author
- moderator
- members of the news media (who will ask questions of the author)
- assistants to the author (who will prepare the author for the press conference)

## ▬▬ PREPARING FOR THE PRESS CONFERENCE

### 1. Select an author.

Select an author whom all of you like and who will be interesting as the subject of a press conference. You may select an author who is well known to most of the class already, such as Mark Twain, or you may select an author who is perhaps less well known, such as William Carlos Williams.

### 2. Research the author's life and works.

As a group find out as much about the author as possible.

*Suggestions for research*

- The biographical sketch and the selection by the author in this book are starting points.
- An encyclopedia can provide basic facts.
- One or two books that include criticism of the author can probably be found in the library.
- Readings about the historical period in which the author lived may also help you.

The group may divide the responsibilities for conducting research on the author, assigning certain members to read specific books. Then the group as a whole can discuss what each person found in their individual research.

### 3. Decide who will play the various roles in the press conference.

- Choose as the author a student who is very knowledgeable about the author and who is a good speaker.
- Choose as the moderator a student who is a good administrator.
- Divide the remaining students into two groups— "journalists," who will pose questions to the author; "assistants," who will try to prepare the author for the questions.

NOTE: From this point until the press conference proper, the journalists and the assistants should work independently.

### 4. Formulate questions.

Those who will play journalists must plan their questions. The questions may relate to the literary works and to the author's life as well as to current events. You should ask the sorts of questions that you think your audience will want to know the answers to.

*Examples*

- You may ask Thomas Malory (author of the King Arthur material in this book) what it was like to live in the fifteenth century; you may also ask him what he thinks of modern warfare.
- You may ask Edgar Allan Poe if he personally identified with the narrator of "The Cask of Amontillado"; you may also ask him which current horror films he has enjoyed—and why.

### 5. Prepare the author.

Those who are playing the author's assistants must help the author anticipate what the journalists will ask and prepare effective answers. The assistants

**746** *Speaking and Listening Handbook*

might even conduct a mock press conference with the author.

## CONDUCTING THE PRESS CONFERENCE

1. **Classroom setup**
   - The author may stand at a lectern.
   - The panel of journalists may sit at a table.
   - The moderator may stand or sit at a separate small desk.
   - The assistants may sit behind the author—to consult with him or her as necessary.

2. **Role of the moderator**
   During the press conference the moderator must introduce the author and the panel of journalists to the audience. The moderator must recognize each individual, give that individual the floor, and allow him or her to ask a question. The moderator will need to monitor the questions and may decide to hold certain questions back. Toward the end of the press conference, the moderator may recognize questions from the audience. Lastly, the moderator will summarize the proceedings, thank the participants, and formally end the press conference.

3. **Guidelines for the journalists**
   The journalists should keep their questions short and phrase them so that the main point of the question is exceptionally clear. They should avoid long, rambling questions. They should also avoid leading questions—those questions to which they already know the answer and which they are asking just to trip up the author.

4. **Guidelines for the author**
   The author may initially want to make an opening statement. In answering a question the author may want to repeat or rephrase it to make sure that he or she understood it. The author should keep answers brief and should always stick to the topic.

   The author should maintain eye contact with the questioner while the question is being asked. Then during the answer the author can try to make eye contact with the entire audience.

5. **Role of the assistants**
   During the press conference the assistants should take notes on the author's performance—to discuss with the author during the debriefing after the conference. The assistants should also be prepared to help the author if he or she turns to them for facts or other details during the conference itself.

6. **Time limits**
   The press conference may have strict time limits. It is up to everyone, especially the moderator, to stay within those limits.

## ASSIGNMENT
Follow the guidelines listed here to conduct a press conference with an author of your choice.

Each of the six lessons in this handbook serves to integrate a particular thinking skill with the experience of literature. Each lesson is literature-based and demonstrates to the student that the active reader is a thinking reader, that the results of thinking are both understanding and enjoyment. The step-by-step format of each lesson allows for either teacher involvement or student independence. Gradually, as students continue to use the procedures shown in the lessons, they can grow more and more independent as thinkers about literature and as confident, thinking young adults. Each lesson is structured in the following way:

- DEFINITION—A clear, jargon-free definition that expresses the thinking skill in a student's own terms
- EXAMPLE—A model of the thinking skill being applied in a literature-based situation. Each example emphasizes the students' own experience in using the skill.
- EXPLANATION—A detailed "walk-through" of the example, demonstrating and discussing each individual step in the application of the thinking skill.
- PROCEDURES—A list and summary of the individual steps used in the example and the explanation. Identifying procedures is an essential step in thinking about thinking and developing independence.

# THINKING SKILLS HANDBOOK

## LESSON 1: Logical Reasoning

### ▓ DEFINITION

**Logical reasoning** is a way of explaining exactly why you believe that something is true. When you reason logically, you state the *necessary conditions* for the explanation to be true. Then you show that these necessary conditions do exist. When you reason logically, however, you must be sure that both you and your audience agree on the same set of assumptions. This means that you agree about what is important in the particular situation you are considering.

### ▓ EXAMPLE

Writers of short stories sometimes express their attitudes in the characterizations, settings, and plots of their stories. If you wanted to convince someone of the importance of a writer's sense of independence, resourcefulness, trust, risk taking, luck, integrity, or imagination, you would have to begin by determining the conditions necessary for a particular value to be evident. You would then have to show that there are sufficient details or implications to be drawn from the selection to support your opinion regarding the values of the author. Your audience would have to agree with your assumptions that the evidence you present does indeed reflect that value system.

### ▓ EXPLANATION

When you want to put together a logical, reasoned position to convince someone of an author's values, you must start by listing the conditions that are necessary for a particular value to be evident. If a character in a story is resourceful, solves problems with ingenuity, and performs heroic deeds, you could reason that the author values resourcefulness.

### ▓ PROCEDURES

When you intend to use logical reasoning to convince an audience that something is true or important, you will find the following steps helpful:

1. **State what you believe** to be true.

2. **Identify all of the conditions that are necessary** for the situation to be true.

3. Show how the necessary conditions have been met. **Give specific illustrations that constitute sufficient evidence** to support your position.

4. **Identify the important assumptions** your audience must share with you in order for your position to be convincing.

### ▓ ACTIVITY I. REASONING LOGICALLY ABOUT A SHORT STORY

The effectiveness of surprise in short stories relies heavily on the reader's assumption that the sequence of events and the behavior of the characters will continue in a predictable sequence or with predictable consequences. The necessary conditions for a character's behavior are usually established in the setting and plot. Your own prior experience leads you to expect certain outcomes from particular events.

1. **Select one short story** from the Short Story unit (pages 1–175) in which there is a surprise for the reader. **Describe the surprise.**

2. **Indicate whether anything in the story would have led you to expect another outcome.** Was this in the setting? In the characterization, or in the events of the plot?

3. **Describe how the author set up the cause-and-effect situation or the relationship that led to the surprise.** What other cause-and-effect relationship would have taken the story in another direction?

## ◼ ACTIVITY II. REASONING LOGICALLY ABOUT CHANGE IN A SHORT STORY

Change plays an important part in a number of stories in this book. Identify a story in which a specific change occurs.

1. **Identify the conditions prior to the change.** Then describe the new conditions.

2. **State an outcome that might have been possible under the first set of conditions but is no longer logical under the new conditions.** Explain why.

## ◼ ACTIVITY III. REASONING LOGICALLY ABOUT A CHARACTER

A well-developed character displays a plausible response to a given situation. As a reader, you may be able to anticipate that response if you have developed a sense of the character.

1. **Choose a story** you have read in which a character behaves in a logical, predictable fashion.

2. **Identify the necessary conditions** that lead you to expect a particular outcome. Some of these conditions may be explicitly stated by the author; others may be implied.

3. **Decide whether the conditions are sufficient** to support the outcome.

◾ ACTIVITIES—All activities are literature-based. Those activities keyed to specific literary selections give the student an opportunity to follow the correct procedures in thinking about some aspect of the selection. Those activities not keyed to specific literary selections provide the opportunity to transfer the thinking skill to a new literary situation.

The detailed lessons in this handbook are not the only application of thinking skills in this literature series. Throughout each book students also practice and reinforce thinking skills through the following features:

- Purpose-setting questions
- Study Questions divided into Recalling, Interpreting, and Extending categories
- Thinking About . . . questions within Reading and Literary Focuses
- Models for Active Reading
- Thinking Skills blackline masters, TCR 5, pages 35–38
- Thinking Skills Overhead Transparency 28

*Thinking Skills Handbook* **749**

# LESSON 2: *Evaluation*

### DEFINITION

When you determine the value, excellence, beauty, effectiveness, truthfulness, or reliability of something or someone, you are making an **evaluation.** Proper evaluation requires thoughtful application of an appropriate set of criteria. **Criteria** are the standards, rules, or tests you use to make judgments. The use of appropriate criteria determines whether an evaluation is valid.

### EXAMPLE

Tom, stage manager of the school play, rejects the sofa and chairs sent to the school by the theater rental agency. The manager of the agency wants to know why.

### EXPLANATION

Tom explains that the stage directions call for a Victorian stage setting—that is, a setting in nineteenth-century England. The agency sent to the school a set of mid-1940s overstuffed furniture. Tom is using pictures of Victorian furniture as criteria for evaluating the validity and beauty of the stage setting, following the stage directions of the playwright. Tom insists the agency replace the stage furniture with a set more suitable for the production.

### PROCEDURES

1. **Determine the reason or purpose** for evaluation.

2. **Identify the criteria**—the rules, tests, or standards you will apply in judging.

3. **Apply the criteria.**

4. **Draw a conclusion.** The evaluation is your conclusion based on the application of criteria.

### ACTIVITY I. EVALUATING THREE WAYS OF EXPERIENCING POETRY

The purpose of this activity is to make judgments about three methods of experiencing poems. Work in groups of three students.

1. **Each member of the group selects a poem** from the Poetry unit of this book (pages 177–261). Each person must select a different poem.

2. **Each poem will be experienced** in three ways: (1) Each person will read it silently; (2) the selector will read it orally; and (3) the group will read it aloud in unison.

3. **The group establishes a list of criteria** for evaluating the ways of experiencing a poem. For example, the experience of a poem should help the reader or listener to understand the literal meaning or the theme, or it may help him or her enjoy the rhythm or the language.

4. After each poem is experienced in the three ways, each group member determines the method that is most satisfying. **Making a chart** that lists the criteria **may be useful in applying the criteria.**

5. After all the presentations of the poems are complete, **compare ratings** of the methods among the group members.

6. If there is a preferred method, **decide which criterion the group considers the most important one.**

### ACTIVITY II. EVALUATING POEMS ON A SIMILAR SUBJECT

The purpose of this activity is to develop a set of criteria to judge the relative effectiveness of poems on a similar subject.

1. **Identify any two poems** on a similar subject.

2. **Brainstorm the subject** in your group, making sure to elicit as many associations with the subject as possible. Consider sensory associations (sights, sounds, smells, sensation of cold, heat, and so on), emotional associations, personal experiences, and observations.

3. **Organize the material** from the brainstorming session. Perhaps the material can be shown in outline form.

4. For each main component of the diagram or outline, **state a criterion.** For example, if the subject is "snow," one of the observations might be that "snow covers or blankets things." A criterion might be that poems on the subject of snow should tell how snow changes the scenery.

5. After the criteria are stated, **apply the criteria** to another poem sharing the appropriate subject.

6. **Decide how the criteria fit** the new poem. Are they too broad, too narrow, irrelevant, or unimportant?

# LESSON 3: *Representation*

### ■ DEFINITION

**Representation** involves changing the way that you perceive or understand information. A representation can be *internal*—a network of ideas or a series of images. Or a representation can be *external*—a drawing, picture, or graphic organizer. Both internal and external representations are developed by asking yourself what the important elements are and how they are related.

### ■ EXAMPLE

Lenore paused after reading portions of the selections to ask herself questions. Below is a description of her thoughts as she read "Two Views of the River" (page 321).

1. After reading the title and a few lines, she paused to ask herself: *What is this paragraph about?* She hypothesized that it was essentially a very colorful, poetic description of the objects in and around a river, recalled from Mark Twain's memory.

2. Then she asked herself: *What are the specific objects or elements described?* The "blcody" red river; a solitary log; a slanting mark (probably a branch under water); the boiling, tumbling rings like opals (probably a small whirlpool); the smooth spot with graceful circles (probably a very shallow area); the long, ruffled trail that shone like silver (I can't imagine what that is); and the dead tree that gleamed like a flame (probably the sun on some smooth object).

3. As she thought about these objects, she wondered why it was not clear what some of them were. She had these ideas or hypotheses:

   a. They could be symbols of some sort. They could represent some idea about life or death.
   b. They could be real objects whose true identity was obscured by the intense color of the sunset.

   c. The lack of clarity could be due to Twain's vague memory.
   d. It could be that Twain was trying to create interest and suspense about their meaning to spur the reader on to find out what they were.

4. As she finished reading paragraph 1, she asked herself again: *What are the key ideas?* This is only one view of the river—the poetic view recalled from Twain's memory, she realized. Probably this view will be contrasted with Twain's view as a riverboat captain.

### ■ EXPLANATION

These are Lenore's internal representations for paragraph 1. She does all this thinking more or less automatically, with very short pauses and little effort. If you are not in the habit of making networks of ideas and images, you may need to have many pauses and even take notes on your ideas.

### ■ PROCEDURES

1. After reading a given segment of text, pause and ask yourself any or all of these questions:

   a. What is this paragraph or section of the selection about?
   b. How does it relate to the title? To the previous section?
   c. What are the *important* details, elements, or objects?
   d. Are all the ideas clear? Do they contain implied meanings? Is there anything that I do not understand? Am I likely to find out more if I read further, or do I need to look back or get additional information?

2. Formulate tentative responses to your questions.

3. Predict what will come next (what reasons, point of view, ideas, etc.).

4. Continue reading in this start-stop fashion until you have completed a whole section (a whole description, argument, point of view, concept, and so on).

5. When you have finished this start-stop process, ask yourself:

   a. What are the most important main ideas or general ideas?
   b. How do the ideas or elements fit together?

### ACTIVITY I

With your teacher construct a network of images and ideas for a section from any of the following selections:

1. "A Child's Christmas in Wales" (page 282) or "Shosha" (page 278)

2. "R.M.S. Titanic" (page 297) or "Flood" (page 314)

3. "My Friend, Albert Einstein" (page 265)

### DEFINITION EXPANDED

The activities above focused on representing ideas internally. It is also possible to represent your feelings externally by finding or drawing pictures.

### EXAMPLE

Stuart was reading some nonfiction literature selections, and he wanted to find out what the author did to make a given part more or less interesting. First, he read the selection through for meaning and overall organization, jotting down a note or two to mark places that were more or less interesting to him. Then he constructed a graph to show his degree of interest over five paragraphs. The graph appears in the next column.

After Stuart completed the graph, he reread the selection to analyze what it was that might have made his interest increase or decrease. To represent the results of his thinking, he constructed two lists, which appear below the chart.

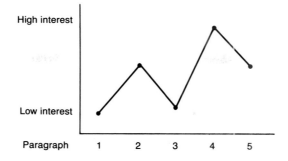

*Reasons for High Interest*
vivid language (metaphors, similes)
choice of topic that people care about
details that make you feel you're there

*Reasons for Low Interest*
too many unfamiliar words
not enough action

### PROCEDURES

1. Read the selection for meaning, but note places that are particularly interesting or uninteresting (e.g., paragraph 1 = + +).

2. Chart your degree of interest for the selection on a graph like the one above.

3. Reread the selection to analyze specifically what it was that captured your interest (or not).

4. Construct a list like the one above, giving specific examples from the selection.

### ACTIVITY II

1. Working by yourself, chart your feelings, and analyze the paragraphs for any *one* of the selections in the Nonfiction unit.

2. Select one of the less interesting paragraphs and rewrite it, trying to make it more interesting.

*Thinking Skills Handbook* **753**

# LESSON 4: *Problem Solving*

### DEFINITION

**Problem solving** is a way of thinking that involves a group of skills. Problem solving requires two different kinds of knowledge—information about the problem in its context (*what* the problem is) and steps to take in reaching a solution (*how* to solve it).

The first kind of knowledge (what the problem is) is the basic information about the problem, specific facts about the subject. After all, problems are solved in specific contexts, not in general ones. The problem solver must know about the particular situation, the context, of the problem.

The second kind of knowledge (how to solve it) consists of the procedures, the orderly progression of steps in problem solving—defining a problem, identifying the givens and the obstacles, planning a solution, carrying out the plan, and checking the results.

### EXAMPLE

John must deliver a monologue as an audition for membership in his school's dramatic society. If his performance is well received and he is accepted into the society, the problem will be solved.

### EXPLANATION

John knows the context of the problem. He knows the high standards of the dramatic society; he knows the kinds of auditions that have succeeded previously; he knows the competition this year will be intense. In order to define the problem, John considers the **givens**: He must deliver a ten-minute memorized monologue or oral interpretation of a dramatic role. He considers the **obstacles**: He must choose an impressive dramatic selection; he must deliver it well; he must conquer his "stage fright."

John decides upon a **plan,** a series of steps to overcome each of the obstacles. He does the necessary research to find a particularly powerful dramatic selection. He memorizes the selection perfectly and rehearses until he is fully prepared. He consults a drama coach and some friends who are actors for methods of conquering stage fright. He **carries out the plan** and performs the audition. He is happy to **check the results** of the plan: He is invited to join the dramatic society. The problem is solved.

### PROCEDURES

1. **State a goal.**
   Identify what you want to do or to achieve.

2. **List the givens.**
   What information is availabe to you as you start to think about reaching the goal?

3. **List the obstacles.**
   What will prevent you from reaching the goal? Obstacles may be easy to see and clearly stated. They may also be unstated or hidden. You may have to think very carefully to identify them.

4. **Identify the methods.**
   What will you do to reach a solution? What is your plan of attack? What specific steps will you follow to eliminate each obstacle?

5. **Carry out the plan.**

6. **Check the results.**
   Have you solved the problem? How will you be sure? Did you follow the best plan? Was there a better way to solve the problem?

### ACTIVITY I. IDENTIFYING A PROBLEM-SOLVING STRATEGY IN DRAMA

The purpose of this activity is to identify and describe the way a problem is solved in a particular work of drama.

Read Shakespeare's *Julius Caesar* (page 470). Identify each step of the problem-solving process as it is used by the conspirators in this play.

1. What is the **goal** of the conspirators?

2. What are the **givens** of the situation? What basic information and experience do the conspirators have? What is the context, the particular situation in which the problem exists?

3. What are the **obstacles**? Are all the obstacles obvious? Are some hidden?

4. What are the **methods** used to reach the goal? In the plan what steps are to be followed, and in what order?

5. Do the conspirators **carry out the plan**? Do they revise or change the plan in order to carry it out?

6. What are the **results**? Does the plan solve the problem? If not, why not? Did the conspirators make an error in the obstacles they considered? Did they choose the wrong methods? Did they have the correct methods but not carry out the plan properly?

## ▓▓▓ ACTIVITY II. DESCRIBING PROBLEM SOLVING IN ANY WORK OF DRAMA

The purpose of this activity is to identify and describe the steps of the problem-solving process in any work of drama in this book or any work of drama you have seen or read.

1. Select a work of drama—*The Life and Adventures of Nicholas Nickleby* (page 360), *Cyrano de Bergerac* (page 386), or any other play—and identify the **goal,** the problem to be solved in the main action of the plot.

2. State the **givens** in the situation.

3. State the **obstacles** to solving the problem.

4. Identify the **methods,** or the **plan,** used to solve the problem.

5. Tell whether the **plan is carried out.**

6. Check the **results** by telling whether or not the problem is solved. If the problem is not solved, tell what change in the methods or plan you would make in order to solve it.

# LESSON 5: *Inductive Inquiry*

### DEFINITION

**Inductive inquiry** is a way to *discover* meaning by observation. As you examine several examples of an idea, you discover what characteristics or features the examples share—that is, what they have in common. Once you have discovered what is special, or characteristic, about this idea, you can also tell how it differs from similar ideas.

### EXAMPLE

The legend of King Arthur, like other legends, offers many examples of heroic characters. What makes a character a genuine hero? To answer this question, you need to **inquire** into the idea of an Arthurian hero.

### EXPLANATION

In order to deliberately **inquire** into the idea of an Arthurian hero, you first need to **find some examples** of heroes. Using the characters in the King Arthur legend you know, you might list three examples of heroes—say, Arthur, Bedivere, and Lancelot. Your next step is to **identify the general characteristics** of each of the heroes. Then, after you have identified those characteristics, you **identify which characteristics are common** to all of the heroes.

Making a chart to **display** all of the characteristics is a practical and efficient way to reveal the pattern you are looking for. A chart that displays the general characteristics of Arthurian heroes might look like this one:

| Characteristics | Hero 1 | Hero 2 | Hero 3 |
|---|---|---|---|
| Strength | + | + | + |
| Beauty | – | – | + |
| Bravery | + | + | + |
| Wisdom | + | – | – |
| Loyalty | – | + | – |
| Humility | – | – | – |
| Generosity | + | – | – |
| Patriotism | + | + | + |

The plus and minus signs indicate whether or not a hero has ( + ) or does not have ( – ) that characteristic. Observing the chart, you see that three characteristics—strength, bravery, and patriotism—are common to all the examples you examined. Therefore, someone with those characteristics would be most likely to be an Arthurian hero.

It is also useful to **test your findings** against examples that are not likely to share the characteristics. In this case, you might test your findings about heroes against an example of a villain. Add one more column to your chart for a non-example (a villain).

| Characteristics | Hero 1 | Hero 2 | Hero 3 | Villain |
|---|---|---|---|---|
| Strength | + | + | + | + |
| Beauty | – | – | + | – |
| Bravery | + | + | + | – |
| Wisdom | + | – | – | – |
| Loyalty | – | + | – | – |
| Humility | – | – | – | – |
| Generosity | + | – | – | – |
| Patriotism | + | + | + | – |

Observing this chart, you see that the non-example does share one characteristic of heroes—strength. But the chart shows that one characteristic is not enough to make the villain a hero—at least based on these examples. This non-example still does not share any of the other characteristics. You will want to expand your list of characteristics and add more examples and non-examples to make the basis of your inquiry stronger.

### PROCEDURES

1. In order to inquire into a particular idea, first **examine several familiar examples** of the idea.

2. **List all the general characteristics** you can think of that are true of each of the examples.

3. **Display the list** in a way that helps you see the pattern of common characteristics.

4. **Identify the pattern** of common characteristics.

5. **Test your findings** by comparing what you found to be true of the idea with the characteristics of a closely related non-example. When you do this, you will find some combination of characteristics that is special to your idea and does not occur in the non-example.

## ▓ ACTIVITY I. INQUIRING INTO THE IDEA OF CHIVALRY IN THE KING ARTHUR LEGEND

The purpose of this activity is to apply the steps of inductive inquiry to discover the characteristics of chivalry in Malory's *Le Morte d'Arthur* (page 583).

1. **Identify five examples** of events in *Le Morte d'Arthur*.

2. Look at each example separately, and **list all the general characteristics** of each event. You may want to include such characteristics as setting, social ranks and relationships of the characters, ideals of the characters, and virtues demonstrated.

3. **Display the list** in a way that helps you see the pattern of common characteristics. Use a chart, or invent another kind of display.

4. **Identify the pattern** of common characteristics.

5. **Test your findings** by comparing what you found to be true of the examples with the characteristics of a closely related non-example. (Consider events in a novel or a play you have read.)

6. **Write a brief summary** of the characteristics of chivalry as you find it in *Le Morte d'Arthur*. Support your findings with the specific examples you used as the basis for your inquiry.

## ▓ ACTIVITY II. INQUIRING INTO AN IDEA IN WORKS OF LITERATURE

The purpose of this activity is to apply the steps of inductive inquiry to discover the common characteristics of ambition in *Le Morte d'Arthur* or in any work of literature.

Many characters in literature act out of ambition. Characters may have different goals and use different methods. Nevertheless, ambition in any person has some characteristics that are shared by other ambitious persons.

1. **Identify at least five examples** of characters in *Le Morte d'Arthur* or in any other work of literature who seem to be ambitious. (You may want to consider *Julius Caesar* and *Cyrano de Bergerac* as sources.)

2. **List all the general characteristics** of each example of ambition. For example, what is the object of the ambition? What are the obstacles? What methods are followed to reach the goal? Is violence involved? What or who is sacrificed to ambition? Does anyone profit from the ambition?

3. **Display the list** in a way that helps you see the pattern of common characteristics.

4. **Identify the pattern** of common characteristics.

5. **Test your findings** by comparing what you found to be true of the examples with the characteristics of a closely related non-example. (Consider a non-ambitious character.)

6. **Write a brief summary** of the characteristics of ambition as you find it in literature. Support your findings with the specific examples you used as the basis for your inquiry.

*Thinking Skills Handbook* **757**

# LESSON 6: Synthesis

## ■ DEFINITION

**Synthesis** involves the creation of something new, a pattern or perspective that was not present before. Synthesis requires a complex combination of skills to organize ideas from different sources. This new pattern may be stated in various forms: an essay, a definition, a speech, a play or poem, a work of art.

Note: An essay involving only one perspective is not a synthesis because it represents only one point of view. A synthesis must contain elements from more than one source or point of view.

## ■ EXAMPLE

Some selections in *Appreciating Literature* are about greed and its cruel effects on people. A group of students was asked to review the literary selections that relate to the topic of greed and develop a statement about the causes of greed. This assignment is an example of synthesis because the group had to organize ideas about greed from many different sources and discover patterns of behavior that were not previously apparent to them.

## ■ EXPLANATION

The task is to combine information from several different sources and organize it into a new statement. In other words, it is a task of synthesis. The **purpose** is clear—to examine a topic or a situation and clarify it for an audience by presenting a conclusion. The thinker must **identify the elements** that contribute to the situation. The thinker must **state a relationship** between the elements—tell how they are related or opposed or associated in some way. The thinker must **construct an original product**—a conclusion that expresses the relationship. The conclusion is a synthesis, a combining of information into something new that did not exist before. The most helpful synthesis will act as a jumping-off point for further thought.

## ■ PROCEDURES

1. **Establish a purpose** for the product. This step is given in the activities below.

2. **Identify the elements** to be considered together.

3. **State a relationship** among the elements, and represent the statement in a graphic form if possible.

4. **Construct an original product** that expresses the relationship.

## ■ ACTIVITY I. PLANNING A LITERARY WORK

The purpose of this activity is to identify the characteristics of a particular genre and then consider how to apply them to create a plan to write a new literary work in that genre.

1. The genres studied in *Appreciating Literature* are the short story, poetry, nonfiction, drama, legend, and the novel. Each group should **select** one genre.

2. **Develop a plan** to produce a work of literature in that genre. By asking the following questions, you may establish categories of information to be included in the plan.

   a. What elements (e.g., characters, setting) might be considered?
   b. What type of planning or thinking might the author do before beginning writing?
   c. What kind of work place would be best for writing? State reasons for your choice.
   d. What research would need to be conducted and where would the research take place?
   e. How would you describe the revising stage for this product?
   f. What kinds of problems would you anticipate in developing this product?
   g. How would you organize your time?

3. **Develop a representation** of the plan (such as a chart) to show the procedures you would follow.

4. **Construct a statement** of the plan, and present it in oral or written form.

## ░░░ ACTIVITY II. DEVELOPING A STATEMENT OF CAUSE-AND-EFFECT RELATIONSHIPS IN LITERATURE

The purpose of this analysis is to identify the various causes of problems as they are presented in literature and to consider which solutions are most effective and why.

1. Working as a group, **brainstorm** to identify works of literature that focus on problems.

2. **Divide the class** into small groups. Each group should work with two selections.

3. Each group should **construct a chart,** such as the one below, *for each selection.*

| The problem | The causes | The effects/ New problems | Solutions |
|---|---|---|---|
|  |  |  |  |

4. **Identify two or three specific problems** per selection if possible. Fill in the chart problem by problem. For example, in "Chee's Daughter" one problem is the death of Chee's wife. The causes are physical (tuberculosis) but also social (living conditions that lead to poor health). One effect is that there is no one to take care of the daughter. This is a new problem. The immediate solution is for the wife's parents to take the daughter to live with them. Mark the solution with a + if the solution was effective (if it solved the problem). Mark the solution with a − if it leads to other problems.

5. **Examine the chart** for patterns by answering these questions:

a. Could most of the problems have been avoided? If so, state which ones and why you think they could have been avoided.

b. Do most of the problems seem to be from similar or common sources such as social conditions?

c. Do the solutions work? Explain.

d. What types of solutions seem most effective?

6. **Develop some general statements** that show your understanding of the nature of problems and the effectiveness of solutions as presented in literature.

## ░░░ ACTIVITY III. DESCRIBING A SPECIFIC CULTURE AS SEEN IN LITERATURE

The purpose of this activity is to identify and organize knowledge of different cultures represented in the literature.

1. **Develop a series of questions** about culture and society such as the ones below.

a. What does the author say about this culture or society?

b. What kind of people are described? (e.g., courageous, greedy, superstitious)

c. How do they relate to each other? (e.g., warring, cooperative, competitive)

d. What values do they reflect? (e.g., hard work, equality, the desire to get ahead)

e. What social rules govern behavior? (customs, manners)

2. Working in small groups, **construct a chart** on which to answer the questions in step 1.

3. **Select a specific culture** as the focus of your study, and **identify works of literature** that describe that culture.

4. **Reread the selections** looking for information about that culture in relation to the questions above. Take notes using your chart.

5. **Reflect on your notes** looking for patterns.

6. **Construct a description or essay** describing the culture you studied.

Each of the four lessons in this handbook provides students with a direct instructional model of a reading skill or a study skill important for the active reading and study of literature. Each lesson is literature-based and emphasizes the application of a particular skill so that the student may more fully understand the ideas of a literary selection.

Each lesson is structured in the following way:

- EXPLANATION AND EXAMPLES—a definition of the reading or study skill, with clear examples drawn from students' own experiences. Each example is explained as the student is walked through each step in the application of the skill.
- PRACTICE—literature-based activities for using the reading or study skill and examining how it is used
- FURTHER ASSIGNMENTS—All assignments are literature-based. Those assignments keyed to specific literary selections give the students the opportunity to apply the skill. Those assignments not keyed to specific literary selections provide the opportunity to transfer the reading or study skill to any literary situation.

The detailed lessons in this handbook are not the only application of reading and study skills in this literature series. Throughout each book students also practice and reinforce reading and study skills through the following features:

- Purpose-setting questions
- Study Questions divided into Recalling, Interpreting, and Extending categories
- Reading and Literary Focuses
- Models for Active Reading
- Active Reading end-of-unit pages
- Reading and Study Skills blackline masters, TCR 5, pages 39–40
- Reading and Study Skills Overhead Transparency 29

## LESSON 1: *Distinguishing Between Fact and Opinion*

### ▬ EXPLANATION AND EXAMPLES

As you read, it is important to distinguish between factual statements and opinions. A **fact** is something that can be proved by first-hand observation or by consulting a reliable source of information (such as an encyclopedia) or by a consensus of experts. An **opinion** is a thought, a judgment, or a feeling. Sometimes opinions are false; they can be disproved by facts. More often, however, opinions can be neither proved nor disproved.

Sometimes writers signal the reader that they are expressing an opinion with specific words and phrases such as *think, feel, probably, perhaps, apparently, in my judgment, if you ask me, as I see it*. Authors also suggest their opinions through the careful use of words that have strong positive or negative connotations. Look at Bruce Catton's description of U. S. Grant in "Grant and Lee at Appomattox" (page 342):

> Grant seems to have been almost embarrassed when he and Lee came together in this parlor, yet it was definitely not the embarrassment of an underling ill at ease in a superior's presence. Rather it was simply the diffidence of a sensitive man who had another man in his power and wished to hurt him as little as possible.

Catton expresses a very positive opinion of Grant by his careful choice of words ("a *sensitive* man") and his interpretation of the situation ("wished to hurt him as little as possible").

The ability to distinguish fact from opinion is probably most important when reading newspaper editorials or in analyzing propaganda. Many times, writers will mix facts and opinions to emphasize a particular point.

Look at the editorial below:

> Kyle Scott has been mayor of this city for three terms and is now seeking a fourth. *Never in its long history has this metropolis been so plagued with corruption and vice.* Scott's brother, Jeffrey, was appointed police commissioner only to resign six months later, accused of receiving kickbacks.... Scott's uncle, Joseph Tallant, was also implicated in the same scheme. *Scott, however, remained oblivious to all of this scandal and...*

Here, the writer is mixing facts with opinions to try to convince you that Kyle Scott is a somewhat disreputable public official. The italicized sentences express *opinions*. All of the sentences that are not italicized are facts that can probably be verified by consulting newspapers and police records.

In literature, fact and opinion are also intertwined—particularly in nonfiction works.

> *Example:* When Banesh Hoffman writes about Albert Einstein (page 265), he carefully mixes fact and opinion to give you his impression of Einstein.

> I first met Albert Einstein in 1935, at the famous Institute for Advanced Study in Princeton, N.J.... His utter naturalness at once set me at ease.... There was something elusively whimsical about Einstein.

Which of these sentences expresses fact? Which express opinion? Obviously, the first sentence is fact, and the last two are opinion.

## PRACTICE

Read the third and fourth paragraphs of Bruce Catton's description of Grant and Lee at Appomattox (pages 340 and 341). Classify the following sentences from the selection as either fact (*F*) or opinion (*O*). If a sentence is both fact and opinion, label it as such (*F & O*), and identify the part that is opinion.

1. Lee had one staff officer with him.

2. Grant came with half a dozen officers of his own.

3. Grant and Lee sat at two separate tables, the central figures in one of the greatest tableaus of American history.

4. No two Americans could have been in greater contrast.

5. Lee was legend incarnate—tall, gray, one of the handsomest and most imposing men who ever lived.

6. He (Grant) wore no sword.

Which paragraph (three or four) is more factual?

## ASSIGNMENTS

1. Read the factual description of a news event below. Then convert the story to more of an editorial by inserting words, phrases, and sentences that express opinions.

Tomorrow, Mayville's City Council will vote on pay raises for city officials. Under the proposed bill the annual salary of cabinet officers would increase from $60,000 to $95,000. Heads of major departments such as police, fire, water, streets, human services, and health would receive increases up to $65,000 annually. The current cap is $55,000.

Council member Gray has spoken for this bill. On the other hand, Council member White has indicated that she will vote against the bill.

This proposal originally came before the legislature last year, but it was tabled.

There are many places where opinion could be inserted in this paragraph:

a. Why was the proposed pay raise postponed?
b. Are the proposed salaries exorbitant or modest?
c. What is the motivation for certain council members speaking for the bill and certain members against the bill?

2. Read Mark Twain's "Two Views of the River" (page 321). Most of what Twain has written is his opinions of the river at two times in his life. His opinions, however, are based on facts—actual natural phenomena on the river. See if you can list five *facts* about the river described by Twain. *Example*: There are floating logs in the river.

# LESSON 2: Making Inferences

### ▮▮ EXPLANATION AND EXAMPLES

To make an *inference* is to derive an idea or a judgment that is not directly stated by the author. All writers expect their readers to make some inferences as they are reading. In fact, better writers usually require their readers to make many inferences.

Authors carefully select words and situations that will elicit the desired inferences in their readers. Poetry requires the reader to make the most inferences; the poet generally uses very few words, and the reader is required to fill in many ideas and images. In many ways, making inferences is like completing a painting. The author provides a sketch of the painting and fills in some of the color and details, but the author expects the reader to make inferences and complete the rest of the painting, filling in some of the colors and details.

How do you make inferences? Usually, you rely on three interrelated cues: (1) the author's words; (2) your own reasoning; (3) your own personal experiences.

### 1. The *words* the author uses

The English language is filled with many synonyms, but generally no two words have exactly the same connotation. If any author says, "He was England's most famous king," you would probably produce an image of a well-known English monarch, perhaps someone like King Arthur or King George. If, however, the author says, "He was England's most notorious king," another image comes to mind, perhaps a monarch who was evil or did "dire deeds" to his subjects.

Certain common words also signal the reader to make inferences. The word *but* is a good example: Essentially *but* tells readers to change their thinking. For example, when Dorothy Canfield Fisher speaks of the Elwells' relationship to their Aunt Mehetabel in "The Bedquilt," she says:

They were even in a vague way fond of her; *but* she was so utterly insignificant a figure in their lives that they bestowed no thought whatever on her.

The word *but* tells the reader to change direction: Don't think of the family's fondness for Aunt Mehetabel; instead think of their thoughtlessness with regard to her.

### 2. Your own *reasoning*

The author gives you evidence and then you must reason it out. In the sentence "Sam is shorter than Carl, but he is taller than Mary," who is the shortest of the three? The author expects you to *reason* that Mary is the shortest and Carl is the tallest. Similarly, by the time you complete the story "The Open Window," the author wants you to infer that Mrs. Sappleton's niece Vera has just played an elaborate practical joke on Framton Nuttel. Furthermore, you are to infer through the story that Vera is an extremely clever and creative young lady, although perhaps she is a bit unscrupulous.

### 3. Your own *personal experience*

Writers assume that their readers have had certain personal experiences. These personal experiences include knowledge about the way stories, poems, and essays are constructed as well as knowledge of some common everyday experiences and feelings. For instance, look at the paragraph below:

Tommy Carlson buried his head under the pillow and tried to forget! Monday morning again! He could hear the bustle down below and knew that his mother's voice would soon pierce the relative stillness of his room.

The author of this passage expects readers will make inferences about the sequence of events that is to follow, about the character and setting of the story, and about the type of story that is to follow.

Now look at these statements. Consider which of these inferences is *most likely* to be true.

1. Tommy Carlson does not like to get up in the morning.

2. Tommy Carlson will have to go to school.

3. Tommy Carlson is twenty-five years old.

4. Tommy Carlson's mother is going to attempt to get him out of bed.

5. This story will not have a tragic ending.

Probably, you feel from your own experiences that items 1, 2, 4, and 5 are legitimate inferences. Some of these inferences most likely are based on your own personal experiences with getting up in the morning (1, 2, 4). And some of them will be based on your knowledge of the basic structure of stories.

> WARNING: *ALL INFERENCES SHOULD BE TENTATIVE.* Despite the fact that authors expect us to make inferences, sometimes our inferences are proved incorrect as we read further in a passage. We must always be prepared to revise our inferences.

### ■ PRACTICE

Turn to the Dorothy Canfield Fisher story "The Bedquilt." On page 22 in the first sentence of the first complete paragraph, there is a description of Sophia Elwell, Aunt Mehetabel's sister-in-law. Read the description and then look at the statements below; select the best inference about Sophia based on your reading. Explain why it is best.

1. How did Sophia Elwell probably treat her children?
   a. She bossed them around.
   b. She abused them.
   c. She catered to their every whim.
   d. She listened to them and counseled them when they had problems.

2. How did Sophia Elwell probably spend her days?
   a. working in the home
   b. sitting around reading her books
   c. helping her husband farm
   d. teaching school

3. How did Sophia Elwell most often respond to her sister-in-law Mehetabel?
   a. She mocked her.
   b. She ignored her.
   c. She talked to her about household concerns.
   d. She treated her with respect.

4. Which of the following adjectives best describes Sophia Elwell?
   a. wiry and energetic    c. large and bossy
   b. tall and skinny       d. slender and frail

### ■ ASSIGNMENTS

1. Read the poem "By Morning" on page 258. What inferences can you make about the author's attitude toward snow? Are the pictures sketched by the words pleasant or unpleasant? What are the words or phrases that support your inferences? Explain.

2. Write a one-paragraph description of a person you know or have seen. Write it in such a way that the reader will be forced to make inferences about the character's physical description as well as his or her personality. On the back of the paper, list the inferences you hope the reader will make. Does the reader make those inferences?

*Reading and Study Skills Handbook* **763**

# LESSON 3:  *Studying for a Test*

### ▰▰▰ EXPLANATION AND EXAMPLES

Studying for tests is important in order to do well in high school. Everyone wants to do well on a test, but good students realize that in order to do well they must study.

Look at the questions below. How would you answer them?

1. Do you try to study in the same place every day?

2. In the morning do you develop a plan for your day, knowing exactly how you intend to spend your time?

3. Do you prepare graphic organizers or outlines of the selections you have read?

4. Do you keep all your notes for English together in one notebook?

5. Do you try to summarize selections you have read in a sentence or a paragraph?

6. Do you avoid staying up late and trying to cram the night before a test?

7. Do you try to think of facts from other courses that may help you as you review literature selections?

Some studies in the past have suggested that good students are usually able to answer "yes" to all these questions. Here then, are some simple rules to follow when studying:

1. **Find a good place to study.**
   The best place to study is an uncluttered table or desk facing a wall. Ideally, there should be no pictures, trophies, or other distractions on the desk—only the material to be studied. A straight chair and good lighting are other assets for the study area. Needless to say, a quiet atmosphere also helps. You may not be able to find all these desirable features, but you should try for as many as possible.

2. **Schedule time for study.**
   As soon as a test is assigned, you should schedule specific times for study. Actually write these times down.

3. **Review your notes and the selections in the literature book.**
   As you study, you do not have to reread the selections. Rather, you should focus on your notes, any summaries you have made of the selections (see Lesson 4 of the "Reading and Study Skills Handbook"), and the previews that begin a unit. You also will want to skim the selections that are to be included in the test. Try to remember the content of the selections and why your teacher said a given selection was important. As you skim, make sure you look at the Study Questions at the end of each selection, and see if you can answer them. Also look at the "Literary Focus" strand for the selection, glancing at the boldface type. See if you can define each of the boldface terms without looking at the explanation in the book.

4. **Try to predict questions that will be asked.**
   As you skim the selections, try to predict the questions that are going to be asked on the test. Try to remember what your teacher stressed when the selection was discussed. For example, an essay question for the Short Story unit might be, "Select two of the stories in the unit, and describe an internal conflict that occurs in one and an external conflict in the other."

5. **Make graphic organizers of the major points studied.**
   Many times it is helpful to develop a graphic organizer for the important material in a unit. For example, a graphic organizer of the Poetry unit might look like the one on the next page.

# GRAPHIC ORGANIZER

```
                    ┌─────────────┐
                    │   POETRY    │
                    └─────────────┘
        ┌──────┬───────┼───────┬──────────┐
┌──────────────┐ ┌──────┐ ┌──────────┐ ┌───────┐ ┌──────────┐
│ Speaker/Tone │ │Sound │ │ Imagery/ │ │ Types │ │ Patterns │
└──────────────┘ └──────┘ │Figurative│ └───────┘ └──────────┘
                          │ Language │
                          └──────────┘
```

**After you make your graphic organizer, you should try to explain
each of the terms and provide examples from the selections.**

## ■ ASSIGNMENTS

1. Prepare a graphic organizer for the subunit on the essay (pages 291–344). Then see if you can note some of the characteristics of each type of essay in the subunit.

2. Think of your own home or a friend's. List six possible things in there that could distract you from studying. Then state a plan for eliminating the distractions.

3. Make a daily schedule for yourself from the time you wake up until the time you go to sleep. Make one schedule for each day of the week. A sample schedule follows:

| TIME | ACTIVITY |
|------|----------|
| 6:30–7:30 | Prepare for school |
| 7:30–8:00 | Bus |
| 8:00–2:15 | School |
| 2:15–2:45 | Bus |
| 2:45–5:00 | Homework |
| 5:00–6:00 | Chores |
| 6:00–7:00 | Dinner |
| 7:00–9:00 | Study for test |
| 9:00–10:00 | Television |

4. Look over the Drama unit; write two essay questions that your teacher might develop for a test on this unit. Consider the notes you took in class, the literary terms covered, and the selections.

*Reading and Study Skills Handbook* **765**

# LESSON 4: *Summarizing*

## ▖▖▖ EXPLANATION AND EXAMPLES

To **summarize** is to briefly retell an event or literary work, extracting the most important ideas or situations. Summaries are often important for writing book reports, for answering essay questions, and for compiling information for a research paper. Summaries also help you understand what you read because when you write summaries, you have to make decisions about what is important and what is not. When you summarize, remember these five rules:

1. **Delete information that is less important.**

   In good literature all the information given by the author helps to better understand the selection. Nevertheless, some information is less important than other information. For instance, in writing a summary of Dorothy Canfield Fisher's story "The Bedquilt," you may eliminate descriptions of characters other than Aunt Mehetabel.

2. **Delete any material that is redundant.**

   If any idea is particularly important, writers of nonfiction will often repeat it in a slightly different way to better clarify the concept for all readers. Similarily, an author of fiction might relate several incidents, all of which lead you to the same conclusion about a character or setting. For instance, Dorothy Canfield Fisher in the short story "The Bedquilt" gives several examples of Aunt Mehetabel's solitary life of drudgery (e.g., her sitting in the corner while the family gathered around the fire; her ironing monotonous successions of dish cloths, towels, and sheets). Not *all* these examples need be in a summary.

3. **Substitute more encompassing terms for lists of items or descriptions of action.**

   For instance, you might substitute the term *household goods* for a list that would include *chair, table,* *curtains, glassware,* etc. Similarly, you might condense a series of actions into one overall description. Thus, *He went to Paris* would substitute for descriptions of his leaving home, taking a train, a boat, and a carriage, and eventually getting to Paris.

4. **Select a topic sentence or generalization.**

   If the authors provide you with a topic sentence, use a condensed version of it in your summary. Generally, news articles from a newspaper will provide such a topic sentence—usually the first sentence of the story. (Unfortunately, writers other than journalists rarely provide a topic sentence. Less than one third of all paragraphs in exposition have topic sentences, and fiction writers rarely include topic sentences. Although you may find topic sentences for individual paragraphs, you are less likely to find them for complete selections.)

5. **Invent your own topic sentence or generalization.**

   Since most works of literature do not have topic sentences or overt generalizations, you will have to invent them to help your own summary. For instance, a generalization about the Hanson Baldwin selection "R.M.S. *Titanic*" might be "This account describes the 1912 sinking of the *Titanic,* as well as its aftermath."

   Depending on the purpose of your summary, a generalization might also include important information discussed in class or reviewed after reading. Thus, a generalization for a summary of Doris Lessing's "Through the Tunnel" would probably include a reference to the implied theme of the work: "This story describes an eleven-year-old boy's attempt to swim through an underwater tunnel, symbolic of the training and risk taking needed to grow and to mature."

## PRACTICE

1. Read the third paragraph of "Preview: The King Arthur Legend" (pages 575–576). What topic sentence from or about this paragraph might you use in your summary?

2. Look at the list of ideas and events taken from the Poe story "The Cask of Amontillado." Summarize these events in a three-sentence paragraph. Remember to

    a. invent a topic sentence or generalization
    b. delete unnecessary material
    c. delete redundancies
    d. substitute more encompassing terms

- Montresor, narrator of the story, was incensed that an acquaintance of his, Fortunato, had insulted him; he vowed revenge.
- One evening during the Italian carnival season he encounters a drunken Fortunato, dressed in a clown costume.
- Montresor told Fortunato that he had received a cask of amontillado wine and was looking for an expert to authenticate this acquisition.
- Fortunato was tricked into going to the wine cellar in Montresor's home.
- The wine cellar was dark and damp, and had been an underground cemetery (catacomb).
- Montresor carefully led Fortunato deeper and deeper into the catacombs, providing him with many tastes of wine along the way.
- Finally, at the most remote end of the crypt, Fortunato was enticed into a small recess once used as a burial place.

- Montresor then chained the totally drunken Fortunato to the back wall of the niche.
- Despite the moans and cries of Fortunato, Montresor began to wall up the niche in which his unfortunate captive was chained.
- For a moment, Fortunato thought this must be some elaborate practical joke, but then he realized it was not.
- Montresor completed the plastering of the crypt and then piled a stack of old bones in front of the newly plastered wall.
- Montresor ends his story by saying that "For the half of a century no mortal has disturbed them. *In pace requiescat!* (Rest in peace)."

## ASSIGNMENT

1. Read pages 611 and 612, "Preview: The Novel." Ignoring the Henry James quote, take each of the six paragraphs and write a summary sentence for each paragraph, applying as many summary-writing rules as are applicable.

2. Look at Hanson W. Baldwin's account of the sinking of the *Titanic* (pages 297–308). Write a six-sentence summary of the selection. First, write a generalization that summarizes the entire selection (you may use the one suggested in this lesson). Then write a summary sentence for each of the five sections of the narrative.

3. Write a summary for any other piece of nonfiction in this book. Your summary should be five to ten sentences long.

## WRITING ABOUT LITERATURE HANDBOOK

The Writing About Literature Handbook guides students through the types of writing assignments that they are most likely to encounter in literature classes. Twelve lessons show students how to write analyses of literary works, each lesson focusing on a different aspect of literary criticism. The handbook follows a writing-process approach to the various assignments, beginning with prewriting and continuing through writing and revising. Clearly sequenced instructions with specific examples reinforce students' familiarity with the writing process. Each lesson is cross-referenced to appropriate assignments throughout *Appreciating Literature*. In addition, to help students complete their assignments, your *Teacher's Classroom Resources* contains Writing About Literature blackline masters corresponding to each lesson in this handbook.

## WRITING LITERARY ANALYSIS

Focusing on the task of responding to an essay question on a literary work, this first lesson introduces students to a writing-process approach to writing about literature. You may want to teach this lesson in conjunction with your first writing assignment on the material in the Short Story unit. Since the lesson uses examples from the story "The Red-Headed League," you may want to assign that story before you teach this lesson. Under "Assignments" on the following page, you will find cross-references to appropriate Composition assignments throughout this textbook. In addition, in your *Teacher's Classroom Resources* you will find the Chart for Writing Literary Analysis (TCR 5, page 41; Overhead Transparency 30) and Checklist for Revising a Paper About a Literary Work (TCR 5, page 53).

## LESSON 1: *Writing Literary Analysis*

This first lesson will deal with the most general points you should observe in writing literary analysis. The following lessons will deal with writing specific kinds of literary analysis in response to common essay questions.

### PREWRITING

Before you begin to write apply these hints.

1. Read the question or assignment. Then reread it. As you reread the assignment, underline or copy the key words, which tell you specifically what is expected of you in your written answer.

   *Example:* Write an evaluation of a short story. First decide whether or not you like the story. Then explain your response, considering the following questions: Does the story arouse your interest at the beginning? What questions does it raise that you want to see answered? Does it sustain your interest and lead toward a logical solution? Support your opinions with specific examples.

2. Paraphrase the assignment to assure yourself that you know exactly what is expected of you.

   *Example:* Tell what you thought about a short story. Begin by saying whether or not you liked the story. Then give reasons for your opinion. Concentrate on whether the story grabbed your interest, held your interest, and ultimately satisfied you. Give examples to back up your generalizations.

3. Sketch diagrams or charts, or prepare an outline that will help you organize your thoughts as you reread the literature with the essay question in mind. For example, the following chart will help you think about the preceding assignment.

**768** *Writing About Literature Handbook*

| EVALUATION OF A STORY | | |
|---|---|---|
| SELECTION: _____ | | |
| LIKED _____ DID NOT LIKE _____ | | |
| **QUESTION** | **ANSWER** | **EXAMPLE** |
| DID THE STORY AROUSE YOUR INTEREST? | | |
| WHAT QUESTIONS DID THE STORY RAISE? | | |
| DID THE STORY SUSTAIN YOUR INTEREST? | | |
| DID THE ENDING SEEM LOGICAL? | | |

### WRITING AN ESSAY PARAGRAPH BY PARAGRAPH

1. Begin with an introductory paragraph that contains a thesis statement. A **thesis statement** addresses itself to the question that is directly asked or implied in the assignment. It suggests an answer to the question—an answer that the rest of your essay will discuss. The thesis statement is, in effect, an exact summary of the topic sentences that the reader will find in the body of the essay.

   *Example:* "The Red-Headed League" by A. Conan Doyle offers enjoyment and a satisfying reading experience from the beginning, when it arouses readers' interest and raises questions that cry out for answers, through its rising action, when the complications continue to intrigue readers, and to its conclusion, when the readers cannot help but be impressed with the logical wrap-up.

The thesis statement may at times be longer than a single sentence. The introductory paragraph can be made up of the thesis statement and any other sentences that you might need to clarify it.

2. Write the body of your essay, perhaps two to three paragraphs. In each paragraph develop further one of the ideas from your thesis statement. Each of these paragraphs should provide proof that your thesis statement is valid. Each of these paragraphs should have its own **topic sentence**, which will state the main idea of that particular paragraph. For example, the paragraph that comes after the introductory paragraph with the thesis statement about "The Red-Headed League" might begin with the following topic sentence:

*Example:* The story arouses readers' interest from the very beginning.

Each subsequent sentence in the paragraph must support the topic sentence of that paragraph. The supporting sentences should be examples, quotations, or incidents that come from the literature you are writing about.

3. Tie or hook your paragraphs together with transitions such as *however, in addition, similarly, next,* and *because.* For example, the paragraph that might follow the paragraph begun in the previous step could begin as follows:

*Example:* After readers find that they are hooked on the story, they realize they have questions about the plot and the characters.

4. Conclude your essay with a summary paragraph. Restate—in different words—the thesis statement from your introductory paragraph.

*Example:* From beginning to end, "The Red-Headed League" offers readers a thoroughly involving vicarious experience.

### WRITING A ONE-PARAGRAPH ANSWER

All the preceding advice on structure applies as well to answers that are only one paragraph long. If you are limited to one paragraph, begin with a strong topic sentence. Each of your following sentences should develop and provide evidence for one aspect of the topic sentence.

### REVISING AND EDITING

Once you have finished the first draft, you must take time to polish it into an improved second draft.

1. Read your writing aloud.
2. Use the following checklist to revise your writing. If you can answer "yes" to each question on the list, you will submit an essay that your audience will find interesting and logical.

  I. Organization
    a. Does your thesis statement relate directly to the assignment?
    b. Are the ideas mentioned in the thesis statement then taken up in the following paragraphs with a topic sentence for each?
    c. Is there effective, clear movement from paragraph to paragraph by means of transitions?
    d. Does the final paragraph offer a restatement of the thesis statement along with additional insights?
  II. Content
    a. Does the essay adequately answer the question posed in the assignment?
    b. Is each idea adequately developed with supporting details from the literature?
  III. Grammar, Usage, Mechanics
    a. Is each sentence complete (no fragments, no run-ons)?
    b. Have you avoided errors in the use of verbs, pronouns, and modifiers?
    c. Have you correctly capitalized and punctuated all sentences?
    d. Are all words spelled correctly?
  IV. Word Choice, Style
    a. Have you used words that are appropriate for your audience and your purpose?
    b. Have you avoided slang and clichés?
    c. Have you eliminated wordiness?
    d. Have you varied sentence length and structure while checking for parallelism?

### ASSIGNMENTS

1. Use the preceding checklist to evaluate and revise an essay that you have written.
2. Use the advice in this lesson to complete the assignment called "Evaluating a Response to a Story" on page 20.

*Writing About Literature Handbook* **769**

This lesson guides students through the process of writing about the plot of a story. The lesson reinforces the textbook's teaching about plot structure and conflict. You may want to teach this lesson in conjunction with the first subunit in the Short Story unit in this textbook. Since the lesson uses examples from the story "The Red-Headed League," you may want to assign that story before you teach this lesson. Under "Assignments" on the following page, you will find a cross-reference to a Composition assignment in this textbook that focuses on plot elements. In addition, in your *Teacher's Classroom Resources* you will find the Chart for Writing About Plot (TCR 5, page 42; Overhead Transparency 31) and Checklist for Revising a Paper About a Literary Work (TCR 5, page 53).

# LESSON 2: *Writing About Plot*

When you write about **plot** (the sequence of events or actions in a story), you may have to evaluate the story line by explaining how the problems and the conflicts lead up to the climax and resolution of the story. You have to demonstrate how the ending makes sense in light of what has come before, and you have to give one or more specific examples to prove your point.

### ■ CONCEPTS TO REMEMBER

In order to think clearly about a story's ending, you must know how all the parts of a story work together. Here are statements about each part:

*Exposition* — "Background" information that may tell you how and why the characters arrived at this particular place and time. Many stories have very brief or no exposition.

*Narrative hook* — The point at which the author snares your attention. This may be the point at which the reader begins to say, "I want to know what's going to happen next — and why!"

*Rising action* — The buildup of events and the presentation of the problems and conflicts faced by the characters.

*Climax* — The turning point of the story; the point of greatest emotional involvement. This is the point when you know whether the main character will be successful or not.

*Falling action* — The point at which the reader learns of the character's reaction to the climax. This section of the story may be very short.

*Resolution* — The end of the falling action; the final tying together of the story.

### ■ TYPICAL ESSAY QUESTION

When you are asked to write about the plot of a story, you are often answering an essay question such as the following:

Show how the events and conflicts prepare the reader for the climax and the resolution of the selection. Indicate if you are satisfied with the climax and the resolution or why you would have preferred different developments.

### ■ PREWRITING

Think of the overall structure of the work. "Map" the plot of the selection. For "The Red-Headed League" (page 2) your map might look like this:

## PLOT STRUCTURE

**SELECTION:** "The Red-Headed League"

**CLIMAX:** Holmes stops the robbery.

**PROBLEM:** Will they stop the robbers?

**PROBLEM:** What does Holmes see at the pawnshop?

**PROBLEM:** Why was the league dissolved?

*RISING ACTION*

**FALLING ACTION:** Holmes explains to Watson how he solved the mystery.

**EXPOSITION:** Reader learns who Watson, Holmes, and Wilson are.

**NARRATIVE HOOK:** Reader learns about the Red-Headed League.

**RESOLUTION:** Holmes remarks that man is nothing and work is everything.

**770** *Writing About Literature Handbook*

## WRITING PARAGRAPH BY PARAGRAPH

1. In your first paragraph write a thesis statement of one or two sentences in which you paraphrase the main idea of the essay question.

   *Example:* All the events and conflicts in "The Red-Headed League" prepare the reader for the suspense-filled climax and the resolution, the point at which the reader understands and appreciates how Sherlock Holmes solved the mystery.

2. In the next paragraph discuss the exposition and the narrative hook. What does the author tell you in the exposition that helps you understand the way a character acts later in the plot? What happens at the narrative hook that sets the stage for what comes later?

3. In the next paragraph discuss the conflicts in the rising action and the climax, explaining how the climax follows logically from preceding events.

4. In the next paragraph explain why the falling action and the resolution are necessary. What remaining questions about the character are answered during the falling action? How does the main character feel after the climax? Explain whether the resolution makes sense.

5. In your concluding paragraph reemphasize your thesis statement from the introductory paragraph, but use different words to state it. Are you satisfied with the climax and the resolution? If not, why do you think they should have been different?

## REVISING AND EDITING

See Lesson 1 for detailed reminders about improving your writing.

## ASSIGNMENTS

1. Use the "map" of "The Red-Headed League" to write about its plot and its ending. Show how the events and conflicts in the rising action prepare the reader for the climax and the resolution. Indicate if you are satisfied with them or why you would have preferred different developments.

2. Do the assignment called "Writing About Plot" for "The Bedquilt" (page 28), or select another story you have read in this book, and answer the following: Show how the events and conflicts prepare the reader for the climax and resolution. Indicate whether you are satisfied with the climax and resolution or why you would have preferred different developments.

*Writing About Literature Handbook*  **771**

This lesson guides students through the process of comparing two fictional characters. The lesson reinforces the textbook's teaching about character traits, motivation, and change. You may want to teach this lesson in conjunction with the first subunit in the Short Story unit in this textbook. Since the lesson uses examples from "The Bedquilt" and "Chee's Daughter," you may want to assign those stories before you teach this lesson. Under "Assignments" on the following page, you will find cross-references to Composition assignments in this textbook that focus on characterization. In addition, in your *Teacher's Classroom Resources* you will find the Chart for Writing About Character (TCR 5, page 43; Overhead Transparency 32) and Checklist for Revising a Paper About a Literary Work (TCR 5, page 53).

# LESSON 3: *Writing About Character*

We can gain insight into a character by looking at him or her in relation to another character. Sometimes we look at two characters from the same work of literature in order to learn more about each. Sometimes, though, a character in one work will remind us of a character in another selection. In either case — whether we are working with one selection or two — we can compare and contrast characters, examining the similarities and differences in the ways they act and react to conflicts, in how they think, in what they value and prize, in how they change, and so on.

## ▬ CONCEPTS TO REMEMBER

1. **To compare** in this lesson means "to examine two or more things, ideas, people, and so on, for the purpose of noting similarities." **To contrast** means "to examine two or more items for the purpose of noting differences."
2. A character may be **flat** or **round**. A flat character's personality is dominated by a single trait; a round character possesses many different traits, some of which may even seem to be contradictory.
3. A character may be **static** or **dynamic**. A static character does not change from the beginning of the work of literature to the end. A dynamic character changes in some way during the course of the work. This change may be a positive one (for example, toward maturity) or a negative one (for example, the worsening of a flaw).

## ▬ TYPICAL ESSAY QUESTION

When you are asked to compare and contrast characters in a story, you will often have to answer an essay assignment such as the following one:

Compare and contrast two characters within a piece of literature or in two different pieces of literature. Identify a number of points of comparison and contrast, and for each point explain how the characters are similar or different.

## ▬ PREWRITING

1. Select two characters, and ask yourself questions about them as a brainstorming technique for

**772** *Writing About Literature Handbook*

developing points of comparison and contrast. Here are just a few suggestions regarding the kinds of questions you can ask about each of the two characters.

a. What are each character's key traits? (Examining the character's actions, comments, thoughts, and feelings will help you determine key traits.)
b. What is each character's underlying motivation (the basic reason that he or she acts in a particular way) or goal?
c. Does each character remain the same from the beginning to the end, or does he or she change? In what way?

2. Prepare a chart on which to record your answers to the questions in Prewriting Step 1. The chart on the opposite page details the similarities and the differences between Mehetabel in "The Bedquilt" (page 21) and Chee from "Chee's Daughter" (page 29). The plus or minus indicates whether the two characters are similar (+) or different (−) in respect to the particular characteristic under discussion.

## ▬ WRITING PARAGRAPH BY PARAGRAPH

1. Begin your introductory paragraph with a thesis statement. The thesis statement (which, at times, may be longer than one sentence) should address the main points of the essay question and should clearly indicate whether you intend to compare and contrast two characters from the same work or two characters from different works. Be sure to state in a general way how the characters are alike and how they are different.

*Example:* Chee in "Chee's Daughter" and Mehetabel in "The Bedquilt" are two determined individuals who are driven to achieve difficult, if different, goals. Their efforts to realize their dreams change them, but each character is changed in a different way.

2. Use one of the following options for organizing the body of the essay:

## SIMILARITIES AND DIFFERENCES IN CHARACTERS

**SELECTIONS:** "The Bedquilt" and "Chee's Daughter"

| | 1ST CHARACTER (Mehetabel) | 2ND CHARACTER (Chee) | |
|---|---|---|---|
| KEY TRAITS | *Determination:*<br>Once she has her idea for the quilt, she never wavers in executing it.<br><br>*Patience:*<br>She devotes five years of painstaking work to her quilt. | *Determination:*<br>Chee always knows what he wants—to bring his daughter home.<br><br>*Patience:*<br>Chee quietly carries out his plan, waiting for nature to repay him. | ⊕ −<br><br><br>⊕ − |
| GOALS | *Dream:*<br>Her dream is that of an artist; it does not involve people.<br><br>*Result:*<br>She wins first prize and self-respect. | *Dream:*<br>He wants his daughter and to regain his closeness with nature.<br><br>*Result:*<br>Chee regains both his daughter and his feeling of oneness with nature. | + ⊖<br><br><br>⊕ − |
| CHANGES | *Major change:*<br>She gains pride for the first time in her life. | *Subtle change:*<br>He returns to his former self. | + ⊖ |

## Option A

*Introductory paragraph*
*Next paragraph:* Describe one character.
*Next paragraph:* Describe the other character.
*Next paragraph:* Discuss similarities and differences based on two preceding paragraphs.
*Concluding paragraph*

## Option B

*Introductory paragraph*
*Next paragraph:* Note the similarities between the two characters.
*Next paragraph:* Note the differences between the two characters.
*Concluding paragraph*

## Option C

*Introductory paragraph*
*Next paragraph:* Note similarities and differences in the characters' key traits.
*Next paragraph:* Note similarities and differences in the characters' goals.
*Next paragraph:* Note similarities and differences in the characters' tendencies to change.
*Concluding paragraph*

3. In the concluding paragraph use different words to remind readers of your thesis. Focus on whether the two characters are more alike or more different. You might end by noting whether one character seemed more admirable or appealing on the basis of the traits and experiences you have already discussed.

### ▦ REVISING AND EDITING

See Lesson 1 for detailed reminders about improving your writing.

### ▦ ASSIGNMENTS

1. Use the chart for "The Bedquilt" and "Chee's Daughter" to compare and contrast Mehetabel and Chee.

2. Do the assignment called "Writing About Character" for "The Sentimentality of William Tavener" (page 44), for *Julius Caesar* (page 570), or for *The Pearl* (page 662). Or select two other stories that you have read in this book, and answer the following: Compare and contrast two characters from the stories you have selected by showing how they are alike and how they are different with respect to their key traits, their motivation or goal, and the ways they change.

*Writing About Literature Handbook* **773**

This lesson guides students through the process of writing about the setting of a short story. The lesson reinforces the textbook's teaching about setting and atmosphere, as well as about the relationship between setting and plot, character, and theme. You may want to teach this lesson in conjunction with the first subunit in the Short Story unit in this textbook. Since the lesson uses examples from "Why Don't You Look Where You're Going?" you may want to assign that story before you teach this lesson. Under "Assignments" on the final page of this lesson, you will find a cross-reference to a Composition assignment in this textbook that focuses on setting. In addition, in your *Teacher's Classroom Resources* you will find the Chart for Writing About Setting (TCR 5, page 44; Overhead Transparency 33) and Checklist for Revising a Paper About a Literary Work (TCR 5, page 53).

# LESSON 4: *Writing About Setting*

As you read a story and note its setting, you should ask yourself why the author chose to create or use that setting and why he or she dropped characters and events into that time and place. Keep in mind that **setting** includes time, place, weather, seasons, physical props, and the characters' clothing, as well as the wider culture in which the conflicts and action occur. If setting is effective, it is impossible to consider these particular characters and these particular events existing elsewhere. That is to say, the theme of a story may be universal, but its time and place may still be very specific and precisely suitable.

Setting may become clear in the beginning of a story, or it may emerge as the story unfolds. Sometimes, if the author wants to focus on character or plot, setting serves only as a backdrop for action. It will simply be the place or situation in which events occur. At other times setting may take on much more importance, representing something abstract or symbolic.

### CONCEPTS TO REMEMBER

1. An author always has a purpose in telling a story. The **purpose** is the theme, or general idea about life, that the author wants to communicate.
2. The author's choice of setting can reveal that purpose by

   a. creating a mood or atmosphere
   b. illuminating the characters
   c. unifying or organizing the plot
   d. pointing beyond itself to a deeper symbolic meaning

   Sometimes the author uses the setting in only one of the preceding ways; sometimes the author uses the setting in all four ways.

### TYPICAL ESSAY QUESTION

When you are asked to write about the setting of a piece of literature, you are often answering a question such as the following:

Select a piece of literature that you have read. How does the choice of setting reveal the author's purpose?

**774** *Writing About Literature Handbook*

### PREWRITING

1. Fill in a chart on which you can record your thoughts about the ways in which setting reveals the author's purpose. The recommended chart has a left column that contains questions to help you think about what the setting adds to the story. In the middle column you should write your answers to those questions, and in the right column you should provide details to support your answers. For the short story "Why Don't You Look Where You're Going?" (page 53) the chart might look like the one on the opposite page.

2. The chart should help you learn more about the mood, characters, plot, and theme of the story. With these insights you should now be able to state the author's overall purpose in writing.

   *Example:* The author's purpose in "Why Don't You Look Where You're Going?" seems to be to applaud the lone individual who challenges giants.

### WRITING PARAGRAPH BY PARAGRAPH

1. Begin your introductory paragraph with a thesis statement that addresses the main ideas of the essay question. In this case, your thesis statement should note the author's purpose and indicate the ways in which the setting makes that purpose clear.

   *Example:* Walter Van Tilburg Clark selects a vast, darkening sea as his setting to contrast conventional, everyday living (the choice of the average person) with an individualistic, unique life style (the choice of the maverick, or "loner"). The author accomplishes his purpose with the ocean setting because it enables him to create a certain mood, illuminate the characters in the story, unify the plot, and underline the theme.

2. In each of the following paragraphs, write about one of the ways in which the setting reveals the author's purpose. That is, use the Prewriting chart to show how the setting affects the mood, characters, plot, and meaning of the story.

## SETTING REVEALS PURPOSE

SELECTION: "Why Don't You Look Where You're Going?"

| QUESTION | ANSWER | SUPPORTING DETAIL |
|---|---|---|
| **SETTING AND MOOD** WHAT IS THE PERVASIVE MOOD OF THE STORY? | humorous but nervous, with an undercurrent of mystery | "More like a white Utopian city than any the earth will ever bear, she parted the subservient waters and proceeded." |
| **SETTING AND PLOT** IS THE SETTING SIGNIFICANT AT EACH POINT IN THE PLOT? | The story's events all take place on the ocean, which is the only setting in which they could have taken place. | The exposition describes the attitude of the passengers toward the ocean and liner. At the narrative hook, when the man notices the object on the horizon, the passengers begin to gather on deck. Through the rising action more passengers gather, all staring at the ocean and the distant object, realizing that it is a sailboat. At the climax the sailor swerves his small boat through the water, almost capsizing. In the falling action and resolution, his boat pulls away and the passengers watch. |
| **SETTING AND CHARACTERS** WHAT PHYSICAL OR PSYCHOLOGICAL STRENGTHS OR WEAKNESSES ARE REVEALED AS CHARACTERS INTERACT WITH SETTING? | The passengers are passive. The sailor is energetic, frightened, yet in control—a fighter. | "There was nothing an ordinary mortal could do about a ship like this...." "The passengers knew he was frightened....The man, energetic as a jumping jack, worked at the rail for an instant, then threw himself aft...." |
| **SETTING AND THEME** WHAT DOES THE SETTING SAY ABOUT LIFE? | The defiance of the small boat going its own perilous way represents one choice that humans have—that of being independent and self-reliant. | The name of the small boat, *Flying Dutchman,* suggests the independent wanderer. |

3. In the concluding paragraph restate your thesis statement in different words.

### REVISING AND EDITING

See Lesson 1 for detailed reminders about improving your writing.

### ASSIGNMENTS

1. Use the chart for "Why Don't You Look Where You're Going?" to write about setting.

2. Do the assignment called "Writing About Setting" for "By the Waters of Babylon" (page 68), or select another story you have read in this book, and answer the following: What is the author's purpose in telling this story? How does the choice of setting reveal the author's purpose? In answering, consider how the setting creates mood, illuminates characters, unifies or organizes the plot, and has a more significant meaning than its literal meaning.

*Writing About Literature Handbook* **775**

This lesson guides students through the process of writing about the point of view of a short story. The lesson reinforces the textbook's teaching about first-person, limited third-person, and omniscient narration. You may want to teach this lesson in conjunction with the second subunit in the Short Story unit in this textbook. Since the lesson uses examples from "The Red-Headed League," you may want to assign that story before you teach this lesson. Under "Assignments" on the following page, you will find a cross-reference to a Composition assignment in this textbook that focuses on point of view. In addition, in your *Teacher's Classroom Resources* you will find the Chart for Writing About Point of View (TCR 5, page 45; Overhead Transparency 34) and Checklist for Revising a Paper About a Literary Work (TCR 5, page 53).

**Point of view** is the relationship between the narrator, or storyteller, and the story. One point of view is not inherently better or worse than another, but for any given work of literature one particular point of view may be a more effective choice. Every aspect of a story is affected by the author's choice of the point of view from which the story is told. Most obviously, the decision about point of view determines what information the reader receives and how that information is presented.

After you ask yourself, "Who is telling the story?" and "What does this narrator tell me, and not tell me, about the characters and events?" your next question should be "Why did the author select this particular point of view?"

### ▬▬ CONCEPTS TO REMEMBER

1. The narrator of a story may know everything about the characters and events in a story — or may not. It is important for you not only to determine what the narrator tells you but also to think about what the narrator does *not* tell you.
2. The author may choose to tell the story with a narrator who uses a **first-person point of view.** This narrator uses "I" and other first-person pronouns. The important thing about a first-person narrator is that he or she cannot directly know what is going on in anyone else's mind or what is happening anywhere else.

   *Strengths of first-person narrator:* The narrator's comments are immediate, vivid, personal.
   *Limitations of first-person narrator:* (1) The narrator may not be aware of the significance of events and implications of actions. (2) The narrator may be untrustworthy.
   *Effect of first-person narrator on reader:* The reader becomes very involved and must constantly question the narrator's truthfulness.

3. The author may choose to tell the story from the **limited third-person point of view.** In this case the narrator focuses on a particular character and tells us about events as they relate to this character. This narrator will report the *actions and words* of

all characters but will reveal the *thoughts and feelings* of only the focal character.

   *Strengths of limited third-person narrator:* The reader has fewer unanswered questions than with a first-person narrator.
   *Limitations of limited third-person narrator:* The narrator cannot tell us everything we may want to know.
   *Effect of limited third-person narrator on reader:* The reader will feel more secure than with a first-person narrator but will still have questions — especially about characters whose thoughts are not revealed by the narrator.

4. The author may choose to tell the story from an **omniscient point of view.** In this case the narrator knows about everything that is happening and knows what all the characters are thinking and feeling.

   *Strengths of omniscient narrator:* The narrator can tell us everything that is happening everywhere and can answer all our questions.
   *Limitations of omniscient narrator:* (1) Narration is not as intimate as with a first-person or limited third-person narrator. (2) There is less chance for suspense when the narrator seems to know everything that is happening.
   *Effect of omniscient narrator on reader:* The reader may trust the narrator.

### ▬▬ TYPICAL ESSAY QUESTION

When you are asked to write about the point of view of a story, you are often answering a question like this one:

Select a piece of literature that you have read. Why is the point of view chosen by the author effective? What are the strengths and limitations of the point of view? How does the point of view affect the reader's response?

### ▬▬ PREWRITING

1. Determine the point of view by asking the following questions:

**776** *Writing About Literature Handbook*

a. Does the narrator use first-person pronouns (e.g., *I, me, mine*) or third-person pronouns (e.g., *she, her, hers*)?

b. Does the narrator know about only the events that he or she witnesses, or does the narrator seem to know about everything?

2. Prepare a chart that focuses on the strengths and limitations of the particular point of view represented in the story you have selected (see Concepts to Remember). Consider also how this point of view in this story affects your response to the story. For "The Red-Headed League" (page 2), a story told from the first-person point of view, your chart might look like the one below.

## WRITING PARAGRAPH BY PARAGRAPH

1. Begin the introductory paragraph with a thesis statement. The thesis statement should restate the main ideas of the essay question. Identify the type of narrator, state whether the choice of narrator has advantages or limitations, and indicate whether the selection of the point of view and narrator is a key to the story's impact on the reader.

*Example:* A. Conan Doyle's choice of a first-person narrator, Dr. Watson, has several advantages. Specifically, the first-person narrator helps with the characterization of Sherlock Holmes, provides opportunities for foreshadowing, and heightens suspense.

2. In each of the following paragraphs select one of the characteristics (strengths and limitations) of this point of view, and give examples of it from the story.

3. In the concluding paragraph explain how the point of view affected your response to the story.

## REVISING AND EDITING

See Lesson 1 for detailed reminders about improving your writing.

## ASSIGNMENTS

1. Use the chart for "The Red-Headed League" to write about point of view. Why is the point of view effective? That is, what are the strengths and limitations of the first-person point of view in this story? How does the point of view affect your response to the story?

2. Do the assignment called "Writing About Point of View" for the story "The Cask of Amontillado" (page 75), or select another story you have read in this book, and answer the following questions: What is the point of view of this selection, and why is it effective? What are the strengths and limitations of this point of view? How does the point of view affect the reader's response?

---

### POINT OF VIEW: STRENGTHS, LIMITATIONS, EFFECT ON READER
**SELECTION:** "The Red-Headed League"
**POINT OF VIEW:** First person

| STRENGTHS | LIMITATIONS | EFFECT ON READER |
|---|---|---|
| *Intimacy:* We see Holmes through a good friend's eyes. *Suspense:* We gain insights only as the narrator does; Watson can drop hints (foreshadowing) without realizing he is doing so. *Vividness:* We learn many details about all the events as remembered by Watson, who was there with Holmes most of the time. | The first-person narrator cannot see into Holmes's mind, but this "limitation" actually builds suspense. Watson is not the most observant person, but again this "limitation" helps to build suspense and make Holmes even more fascinating. | We trust the narrator (Watson) and feel comfortable with him. Overall, we are influenced positively by his admiration for Holmes. |

*Writing About Literature Handbook* 777

This lesson guides students through the process of writing about the tone of a literary work. The lesson reinforces the textbook's teaching about connotation, denotation, imagery, and sound devices. You may want to teach this lesson in conjunction with the second subunit in the "Short Story" unit in this textbook. Since the lesson uses examples from "The Sentimentality of William Tavener," you may want to assign that story before you teach this lesson. Under "Assignments" on the following page, you will find cross-references to Composition assignments in this textbook that focus on tone. In addition, in your *Teacher's Classroom Resources* you will find the Chart for Writing About Tone (TCR 5, page 46; Overhead Transparency 35) and Checklist for Revising a Paper About a Literary Work (TCR 5, page 53).

# LESSON 6: *Writing About Tone*

When you listen to someone speak, you can usually tell how that individual feels about the subject by noticing pauses, inflections, emphasis, and speed—all of which contribute to "tone of voice." Similarly, when you read, you should be on the lookout for clues to the author's **tone**, or attitude, in the work. Determining tone in written literature is more difficult than determining tone in speech because you really have to read between the lines and infer what the author thought.

## CONCEPTS TO REMEMBER

1. There are as many tones in literature as there are in speaking. A writer's tone may be sarcastic, wry, sympathetic, objective, bantering, serious, ironic, saᵈ ', bitter, comic, or something else altogether. Usually, a particular tone is dominant, although undercurrents of other tones may occasionally surface.

2. Do not confuse mood with tone. The mood is the emotional climate or atmosphere that an author creates in the story and within which the action occurs; the tone is the attitude the author takes toward the characters and events in presenting the story to the reader. The mood of a story may be chilling, but the tone may be warm and sympathetic.

3. Here, as a reminder, is a list of language devices that an author may use to create tone:

   *Connotation*—The unspoken or unwritten meanings associated with a word beyond its dictionary definition.
   *Denotation*—The literal or dictionary definition.
   *Imagery*—The collection of sense images in a piece of literature.
   *Syntax*—Sentence patterns or structure.
   *Sound devices*—Alliteration, assonance, consonance, onomatopoeia.

## TYPICAL ESSAY QUESTION

When you are asked to write about the tone of a work, you are often answering a question such as the following:

Select a piece of literature that you have read. What is the tone of the work? How does the author's selection of details reveal his or her attitude, or tone, toward the subject? In your discussion consider characters, events, setting, and language.

## PREWRITING

1. Identify the tone of the literary work.
2. Answer the following questions to determine how the author communicates the tone of the work. Organize your answers on a chart including both general answers and specific examples.

   a. How does the author treat the characters? For example, does the author sympathize with or ridicule the characters?
   b. What does the author seem to think about the situation in which the characters find themselves? For example, does the author make the events seem somber or comic?
   c. What does the setting tell us about the author's attitude?
   d. How do word choice and sentence structure communicate the author's attitude?

The chart on the opposite page includes answers based on the story "The Sentimentality of William Tavener," page 40.

## WRITING PARAGRAPH BY PARAGRAPH

1. Begin the introductory paragraph with a thesis statement. The thesis statement should address the main points of the essay question by indicating the tone and the general means by which the author achieves this tone.

*Example:* A tone of wistful sadness pervades "The Sentimentality of William Tavener," a story in which details of character, events, setting, and word choice underline Hester's realization that she has lost something precious: sharing love with her silent, yet caring, husband.

## ANALYSIS OF TONE

**SELECTION:** "The Sentimentality of William Tavener"
**TONE:** wistful and sad

| MEANS OF CREATING TONE | EXAMPLES |
|---|---|
| CHARACTERS<br>Although the author is somewhat critical of Hester, she shows sympathy for her. | *Critical:* "an imperatrix," "incessantly denounced," "sniffed contemptuously"<br>*Sympathetic:* Hester's "painful sense of having missed something" |
| The author first pictures William as passive and disinterested but then shows him in a kinder light as a more decisive and complex character. | *Passive:* "Silence, indeed, was William's refuge and strength."<br>*Decisive:* He gives money to Hester so that their sons can go to the circus. |
| EVENTS OR SITUATION<br>The author seems saddened by the husband-wife relationship as it has developed. | "The strategic contest had gone on so long that it had almost crowded out the memory of a closer relationship."<br><br>"Hester had been a very happy bride." |
| SETTING<br>The spring setting suggests the possibility for romance and a kind of magic. | "The little locust trees. . .were white with blossoms. Their heavy odor floated in to her. . . ." |
| LANGUAGE<br>Similes underscore what the author sees as the problems in the relationship between Hester and William. | "No debtor ever haggled with his usurer more doggedly than did Hester with her husband." |
| Strong sensory images underscore the rekindled romance between Hester and William. | "first whippoorwill of the spring"<br><br>"laughing and struggling under the locust trees" |

2. In each of the following paragraphs, write about one of the ways the author achieves the dominant tone. Be sure to include specific examples.
3. In the final paragraph restate in other words the thesis statement from the first paragraph. Emphasize how all the details mentioned contribute to the same pervasive tone.

### ▨ REVISING AND EDITING

See Lesson 1 for detailed reminders about improving your writing.

### ▨ ASSIGNMENTS

1. Use the chart for "The Sentimentality of William Tavener" to write about tone. How does the author's selection of details reveal her attitude? In your discussion of details, consider the characters, events, setting, and choice of language.
2. Do the assignment called "Writing About Tone" for "The Woman Who Had No Prejudices" (page 86) or for "A Child's Christmas in Wales" (page 289).

*Writing About Literature Handbook* **779**

This lesson guides students through the process of writing about the theme of a fictional work. The lesson reinforces the textbook's teaching about stated and implied theme and about the way other fictional elements—plot, character, setting, point of view, and tone—all help to illuminate the work's theme. You may want to teach this lesson in conjunction with the third subunit in the Short Story unit in this textbook. Since the lesson uses examples from "Through the Tunnel," you may want to assign that story before you teach this lesson. Under "Assignments" on the following page, you will find cross-references to Composition assignments in this textbook that focus on theme. In addition, in your *Teacher's Classroom Resources* you will find the Chart for Writing About Theme (TCR 5, page 47; Overhead Transparency 36) and Checklist for Revising a Paper About a Literary Work (TCR 5, page 53).

# LESSON 7: *Writing About Theme*

The **theme** of a literary work is its underlying central idea or the generalization it communicates about life. The theme expresses the author's opinion or raises a question about human nature or the meaning of human experience. At times the author's theme may not confirm or agree with your own beliefs. Even then, if skillfully written, the story will have a theme that illuminates some aspect of true human experience.

## CONCEPTS TO REMEMBER

1. A piece of literature may have both a subject and a theme. The subject is the specific topic of the selection. The theme is the generalization about life at large that the specific selection leads you to see. For example, "baseball" may be the subject of a short story, but the theme goes beyond a one-word label such as "baseball." The theme of a story about baseball may be "Teamwork is particularly important when pressure builds."
2. A long work—for example, a novel—may contain not just one theme but several.
3. Sometimes the theme may be clearly stated. More often, the theme is implied or suggested through other elements. In fact, you can determine the theme by looking closely at characterization, setting, events, point of view, and tone.

## TYPICAL ESSAY QUESTION

When you are asked to write about the theme of a selection, you are often answering an essay assignment such as the following:

Some common themes in literature are

- Growth is achieved only through taking risks.
- Faithfulness to oneself is the ultimate law.
- Petty concerns may blind one to life's riches.

Select a piece of literature that presents one of these themes, or think of a work that reveals another truth about life. Write an essay in which you identify a piece of literature, state its theme, and then show how the author illuminates the theme through characterization, setting, events, point of view, and tone.

## PREWRITING

1. Identify the subject of a selection that you have read. The selection may have more than one subject, but select only one. For example, the subject of "Through the Tunnel" (page 91) is "a young boy's trials and success at swimming through an underwater passage."
2. Keeping the subject in mind, ask yourself the following questions so that you can get beyond the subject of the selection to its theme.

   a. What do various characters think, say, and do regarding the subject?
   b. What are the main character's key traits? Does the character change at all during the course of the selection?
   c. How do the time, place, clothing, and other details of setting serve as a suitable background for the work's subject, or topic?
   d. What do the particular conflicts of the selection have to do with the selection's subject matter?
   e. What do the work's climax and resolution have to say about the subject matter of the selection?
   f. What does the point of view make us realize about the subject matter?
   g. What is the author's tone, or attitude, toward the subject as revealed by the author's word choice and other details?

3. Prepare a chart on which to record your answers to the questions in Prewriting Step 2. The chart on the opposite page is a sample prepared for "Through the Tunnel."
4. Examine the completed chart, and try to formulate a statement of the selection's theme. For example, for "Through the Tunnel" you might state the theme as follows: A young person must take risks and develop courage in order to achieve independence and adulthood.

## WRITING PARAGRAPH BY PARAGRAPH

1. Begin your introductory paragraph with a thesis statement, which restates the main ideas of the

## ELEMENTS ILLUMINATING THEME

**SELECTION:** "Through the Tunnel"

**SUBJECT OF STORY:** a young boy's trials and success

| CHARACTERIZATION | SETTING | EVENTS |
|---|---|---|
| *Lonely, fatherless boy:* Jerry wants independence to confirm his adulthood; is chivalrous toward his mother. | *Big beach* (safe, crowded) *vs. wild bay* ("rough sharp rocks") | *Conflict with mother:* Jerry wants to obey but needs to be free. |
| *Urgency stressed in details:* He begs for goggles; practices breathing "as if everything, the whole of his life, all that he would become, depended upon it." | *Underwater:* magical place of white sand, like swimming in "flaked silver" | *Conflict with older boys:* Jerry wants acceptance. |
| *Change in boy:* Initially, he needs to see his mother on the beach; later takes risk. | *Tunnel:* "sharp rock," seemingly endless  *Midway through tunnel:* crack opening to sunlight | *Conflict with self:* Is he able physically and mentally to risk swimming the tunnel? |
| *Mother:* widow, trying hard to find balance in attitude toward son | | *Climax:* Jerry swims through the tunnel. |
| | | *Falling action and resolution:* Jerry does not share his success with his mother and does not need to rejoin the older boys. |

| POINT OF VIEW | TONE |
|---|---|
| *Omniscient:* The story includes some presentation of the mother's thoughts; however, the main focus is on Jerry's actions, fears, and thoughts, emphasizing his aloneness. | *Sympathy and empathy:* Author is appealing to reader to recall that the quest for independence and adulthood is solitary and painful. |

assignment. Indicate what the theme of the selection is, being certain to state the theme in terms of a generalization about human nature or experience. Then indicate that the theme is illuminated through the other elements of the selection.

*Example:* The theme of "Through the Tunnel" is that the achievement of independence and adulthood may require taking risks and developing courage. All the elements of the story—characterization, setting, events, point of view, and tone—heighten the tension within a young boy as the painful, risk-filled rites of passage to maturity begin.

2. In the next paragraph focus on how the characters, the settings, and the events reveal the generalization about life.

3. In the next paragraph focus on how the point of view and tone illustrate the theme.

4. In the concluding paragraph restate your thesis statement. You might explain whether the selection led you to understand a theme new to you or to renew a prior awareness.

### ▓▓ REVISING AND EDITING
See Lesson 1 for detailed reminders about improving your writing.

### ▓▓ ASSIGNMENTS
1. Use the chart for "Through the Tunnel" to write about theme. How do characterization, setting, events, point of view, and tone all illuminate the theme that the achievement of independence and adulthood is often painful, solitary, and full of risks?

2. Do the assignment called "Writing About Theme" for "The Shepherd's Daughter" (page 90) or for "Luck" (page 108).

*Writing About Literature Handbook* **781**

This lesson guides students through the process of writing about a symbol in a literary work. The lesson reinforces the textbook's teaching about symbolism and its relationship to character and theme. You may want to teach this lesson in conjunction with the fourth subunit in the Short Story unit in this textbook. Since the lesson uses examples from "By the Waters of Babylon," you may want to assign that story before you teach this lesson. Under "Assignments" on the following page, you will find cross-references to Composition assignments in this textbook that focus on symbol. In addition, in your *Teacher's Classroom Resources* you will find the Checklist for Revising a Paper About a Literary Work (TCR 5, page 53).

# LESSON 8: *Writing About a Symbol*

The first chore in writing about a symbol is proper identification of a person, object, or event as symbolic. Too often, readers who have learned about symbolism try to label anything and everything as a symbol. This lesson will review the characteristics of symbols and demonstrate how to write a coherent composition about symbolism.

## CONCEPTS TO REMEMBER

1. A **symbol** is something that stands for itself but also for something larger than itself. It may be a person, an animal, an inanimate object, or an action. A writer often uses a concrete object to express an abstract idea, a quality, or a belief. A symbol may also appeal to a reader's emotions and can provide a dramatic way to express an idea, communicate a message, or clarify meaning.
2. There are conventional symbols and private symbols. A conventional symbol is one that is widely accepted and used by many writers; for example, a nightingale is a symbol for melancholy, a dove for peace, a rose for beauty, red for danger, and autumn for death. A private symbol is one that an individual writer creates for a particular work of literature.
3. An object is a symbol only if it seems to be representative of something *of another kind*. For example, you would not say that the Hope diamond is symbolic of all magnificent diamonds; it is merely representative of all magnificent diamonds. You might, however, say that the Hope diamond is symbolic of wealth; a diamond is a concrete mineral, whereas wealth is something *of a different kind*—an abstract term.

## TYPICAL ESSAY QUESTION

When you are asked to write about the symbol in a work, you are often answering an essay question like the following:

Select a central symbol from a work of literature. State what the symbol reveals about the characters and the theme.

**782** *Writing About Literature Handbook*

## PREWRITING

1. To identify a symbol, ask yourself the following questions:

a. Is some person, place, animal, object, or action emphasized in this work and repeatedly mentioned to the extent that it seems to mean more than itself?
b. If so, what else could it stand for besides itself?

*Example:* In "By the Waters of Babylon" (page 59) the river is mentioned many times. It could stand for a forbidden boundary, for a dangerous being, for a means of testing oneself, for a mystery. Furthermore, the action of crossing the river may have symbolic meaning, such as crossing into a new mental or emotional state (for example, wisdom or adulthood).

2. Trace your candidate for a symbol throughout the work to see if it symbolizes something consistently or if it gathers new meaning from beginning to end.

*Example:* In "By the Waters of Babylon" the river's symbolic value seems to shift subtly in the course of the story, as follows:

- *page 59, paragraph 1:*
  The river seems to be a boundary that is not to be crossed.
- *page 61, paragraph 2:*
  The river is personified as a giant whose thirst is unquenchable, and so the river seems to symbolize a threat.
- *page 62, paragraph 3:*
  The crossing of the river symbolizes John's crossing into adulthood.
- *page 67, paragraph 4:*
  The river symbolizes a boundary that *should* be crossed in order for John to develop. It leads to a better future for John and for his people.

3. Analyze what the symbol reveals about the *character*. Identify the character's key traits and underlying motivation.

*Example:*

John is aware of his role in life as a
  priest's son and then as priest himself.
John is brave, although he admits his fears.
John is curious; he has a thirst for
  knowledge.
John is forward-looking because he wants to
  rebuild.

Explain how the symbol reveals the character's key traits, which you have listed.

*Example:* In "By the Waters of Babylon" the river and its symbolic value throw light on John. First we see him as a fearful but determined young man confronting the river, a symbol of a boundary not to be crossed, a symbol of danger, and a symbol of challenge. Then we see John as a maturer person, who has conquered the river and who will return again to cross the river, which has become a symbol of the means to a better future.

4. Analyze what the symbol reveals about *theme*. Identify the theme of the selection.

*Example:* The quest for knowledge is good, but we must absorb knowledge slowly and carefully or it may do more harm than good.

Then determine how the symbol summarizes or illustrates the theme.

*Example:* In "By the Waters of Babylon" John performs a symbolic act by journeying across the river to fulfill his own fate; he uses the power he has as a priest's son to seek the knowledge he craves. By the end of the story, as a result of his symbolic act, he has learned a great deal and determines to use his increased knowledge and power for the good of his people. His pledge to do good may be a direct result of his realization that his ancestors in the Place of the Gods used their knowledge for ill.

## ▬ WRITING PARAGRAPH BY PARAGRAPH

1. Begin the introductory paragraph with a thesis statement that addresses the major points in the essay question.

*Example:* The river in "By the Waters of Babylon" by Stephen Vincent Benét is a central symbol, which reveals a great deal about the development of the main character and, at the same time, illustrates the theme.

Finish the introductory paragraph by stating in general terms what the symbol tells you about the character and perhaps by actually stating the theme of the story.

2. In the next paragraph explain in more detail how the symbol and the character connect. Use your thoughts from Prewriting Step 3 here.
3. In the next paragraph explain in more detail how the symbol and the theme connect. Use your thoughts from Prewriting Step 4 here.
4. In the final paragraph restate in other words the thesis statement from the introductory paragraph. You might conclude by discussing the suitability of the symbol. For example, what is there in the nature of a river that suits it for symbolizing all that it does in "By the Waters of Babylon"?

## ▬ REVISING AND EDITING

See Lesson 1 for detailed reminders for improving your writing.

## ▬ ASSIGNMENTS

1. Use the examples from the Prewriting steps to prepare a brief composition that explains what the river in "By the Waters of Babylon" reveals about the main character and about the theme of the story.
2. Do the assignment called "Writing About Symbol" on page 114 for "Quality" or on page 117 for "Abalone, Abalone, Abalone" or on page 345 for "Grant and Lee at Appomattox," or consider another selection that you have read in this book. Choose a central symbol from the work. State what the symbol reveals about the characters and the theme of the work.

*Writing About Literature Handbook*  **783**

This lesson guides students through the process of writing about irony in a literary work. The lesson reinforces the textbook's teaching about situational, verbal, and dramatic irony, as well as the relationship between irony and theme. You may want to teach this lesson in conjunction with the fifth subunit in the Short Story unit in this textbook. Since the lesson uses examples from "April Showers," you may want to assign that story before you teach this lesson. Under "Assignments" on the following page, you will find a cross-reference to a Composition assignment in this textbook that focuses on irony. In addition, in your *Teacher's Classroom Resources* you will find the Chart for Writing About Irony (TCR 5, page 48; Overhead Transparency 37) and Checklist for Revising a Paper About a Literary Work (TCR 5, page 53).

The term **irony** refers to a discrepancy, or disagreement, of some sort. The discrepancy can be between what someone says and what he or she really means (**verbal irony**). The discrepancy can be between a situation that one would logically anticipate or that would seem appropriate and the situation that actually develops (**situational irony**). The discrepancy can be between the facts known to a character and the facts known to us, the readers or audience (**dramatic irony**).

### TYPICAL ESSAY QUESTION

When you are asked to write about irony in a work of literature, you are often answering an essay question worded as follows:

Select a piece of literature that you have read. In what ways does the author use irony in this selection? How does the irony support the theme of the selection?

### PREWRITING

Ask yourself the following questions, and note your answers. Include direct quotations from the story as you answer. You will be able to use these direct quotations as evidence for your generalizations when you begin to write the essay answer. The sample answers given here are based on "April Showers," page 76, by Edith Wharton.

1. *Verbal irony:* What, if anything, does the character say that is the opposite of what is really meant?

   *Example:* Knowing that she in fact stayed up all night to write, Dr. Dace says, "I suppose you didn't get home from the ball till midnight?"

2. *Situational irony:* What, if anything, happens that we would not expect or that seems inappropriate in this situation? In particular, does the ending introduce a twist or surprise of any kind?

   *Example:* Theodora's publishing efforts take a turn we do not expect based on the opening mood. Then things change once more at the

end in yet another surprise, as the following chart shows.

| CHARACTER'S EARLY OPINIONS, ASPIRATIONS, PLANS |
|---|
| Theodora wants the success of Kathleen Kyd, popular novelist. She is full of hope that her manuscript will bring her fame and fortune. She has grandiose ideas and justifies shirking her daily duties. |
| "It was a beautiful ending." (page 76) |
| "She was almost sure that 'April Showers' was a remarkable book." (page 77) |
| "Theodora was only seventeen; and she remembered . . . that George Eliot had not become famous till she was nearly forty." (page 77) |
| "Unfortunately, the writing of a great novel leaves little time or memory for the lesser obligations of life." (page 78) |

| CHARACTER'S LATER OPINIONS, ASPIRATIONS, PLANS |
|---|
| Theodora begins to worry that her novel will not be accepted, but when it is, she feels immense joy and becomes a celebrity among those she knows. Then she discovers her book has indeed NOT been published. |
| " . . . Theodora, locking herself in her room, resolved with tears that she would never write another novel." (page 79) |
| "Everything was crowding toward the light and in her own heart hundreds of germinating hopes had burst into sudden leaf." (page 79) |
| "Oh, cruel misprint! Oh, dastardly typographers!" (page 80) |
| "She clutched her manuscript, carrying it tenderly through the crowd, like a live thing that had been hurt." (page 81) |

| CHARACTER'S FINAL OPINIONS, ASPIRATIONS, PLANS |
|---|
| She is devastated by her publishing fiasco and certain she will have upset her parents and be mocked for her false successes. |
| " . . . and she shrank back involuntarily from his impending mirth." (page 81) |
| " . . . and she figured his mute hilarity." (page 81) |
| The final twist comes when her father is kind and comforting and admits, "I wrote a novel once. . . . I wanted to be a genius, so I wrote a novel." (page 82) |

**784** *Writing About Literature Handbook*

3. *Dramatic irony:* What knowledge, if any, do we the readers have that the character does not?

*Example:* Throughout "April Showers" Theodora seems very naive to think she will achieve easy celebrity and fortune as a seventeen-year-old writer. The reader suspects she is headed for disappointment. This is the basic irony of the piece, but there are others, such as the following.

---

**INCIDENT:** Theodora is late delivering her mother's breakfast tray. (page 78)

*Character's perception:* Mrs. Dace assumes Theodora is late because she has been doing a necessary chore. ("I suppose Johnny's buttons kept you.")

*Reader's understanding:* Theodora was late and did not sew the buttons. She forgot because she was too engrossed in her writing project.

**INCIDENT:** When she sees "April Showers" in print, Theodora sees Kathleen Kyd's name on it instead of hers. (page 80)

*Character's perception:* Theodora assumes the name is a mistake, an accident without malice, that will be fixed.

*Reader's understanding:* Reader suspects that for whatever reason the error has occurred—accident or malice—Theodora's publishing situation will not be fixed.

---

4. State the theme of the selection.

*Example:* The theme of "April Showers" is that young people who are naive and impressionable—especially, regarding first experiences and goals—cannot fully see the folly of their grandiose plans.

5. Determine how the irony noted in Prewriting Steps 1–3 supports, or highlights, the theme of the selection. For example, in the case of "April Showers," ask yourself the following questions:

   a. Do any of the instances of irony illustrate how young people can be "naive" and "very impressionable"?
   b. What do the instances of irony say about "first experiences and first life goals"?
   c. How do the instances of irony show that it is difficult to believe that one will not necessarily achieve those goals?

## ▨ WRITING PARAGRAPH BY PARAGRAPH

1. Begin the introductory paragraph with a thesis statement that addresses the main points of the essay question:

*Example:* With verbal, situational, and dramatic irony, "April Showers" by Edith Wharton presents the experiences of a young, naive girl to illustrate the idea that young people cannot fully appreciate the grandiosity or unrealistic nature of their life goals.

Fill out the rest of the introductory paragraph by giving details related to the thesis statement. For example, you could provide more details about Theodora's certainty that her book will succeed.

2. In each of the following paragraphs, identify and supply examples of the kind or kinds of irony the author uses. You might dedicate one paragraph to each of the kinds of irony if it is appropriate to do so.

3. In another paragraph show how the author's use of irony helps you recognize the selection's theme and, in fact, supports the theme.

4. In the concluding paragraph restate in other words the thesis statement from the introductory paragraph. Here you might briefly offer an opinion on the effectiveness of the irony.

## ▨ REVISING AND EDITING

See Lesson 1 for detailed reminders about improving your writing.

## ▨ ASSIGNMENTS

1. Use the charts for "April Showers" to write about the irony in that story. Indicate the various ways that the author uses irony in the story. How does the irony support the theme?

2. Do the assignment called "Writing About Irony" for "Mammon and the Archer" (page 129), or choose another selection that you have read in this book, and answer the following: In what ways does the author use irony in this selection? How does the use of irony support the theme of the selection?

*Writing About Literature Handbook* **785**

# LESSON 10: *Writing About Nonfiction*

A piece of nonfiction may be only a few paragraphs long or book length. It may be a biography, an autobiography, or an essay. When you write about any kind of nonfiction, however, you can use the same approach. Specifically, you can comment on the author's purpose in writing the piece and then show how the author achieved that purpose.

### CONCEPTS TO REMEMBER

1. The **purpose** of a piece of nonfiction is the central idea, or general statement about life, that the author wants to express.

2. To communicate the purpose, the author uses various techniques such as sensory details, facts, statistics, examples, and opinions.

### TYPICAL ESSAY QUESTION

When you are asked to write about a piece of nonfiction, you are often answering an assignment such as the following:

Select a piece of nonfiction that you have read. An author always has a purpose for writing nonfiction. To accomplish this purpose the author may use various techniques such as sensory details, facts, statistics, examples, and opinions.

What is the purpose of the piece of nonfiction that you have read? Cite with examples the particular techniques that the author uses to accomplish the purpose of the piece.

### PREWRITING

1. To determine the author's purpose in writing a work of nonfiction, ask yourself the following questions:

a. What, if anything, does the title suggest about the author's opinion of the subject of the biography, autobiography, or essay?
b. What opinion about the subject of the work or about life in general is suggested by the experiences that the author relates?
c. What opinion about the subject of the biography or autobiography or about people in general is suggested by details of behavior?
d. What ideas about the world in general are suggested by details of setting?
e. What tone, or attitude, toward the subject is revealed by the author's style?

2. Based on your answers to the preceding questions, prepare a statement of the author's purpose, and, on a chart like the one on the opposite page, record the techniques that the author uses to achieve that purpose. The filled-in chart represents an analysis of the autobiographical excerpt from *Kaffir Boy* by Mark Mathabane (page 271).

### WRITING PARAGRAPH BY PARAGRAPH

1. Begin the introductory paragraph with a thesis statement, which should specify the author's purpose and the techniques used to achieve it.

*Example:* In the excerpt from *Kaffir Boy*, the author's use of sensory details, facts, statistics, examples, and opinions communicates the speaker's struggles, achievements, and doubts as a young black person in South Africa.

2. In each of the following paragraphs, show how the author uses one technique to make the purpose clear.

3. In the concluding paragraph restate the thesis in other words.

### REVISING AND EDITING

See Lesson 1 for detailed reminders about improving your writing.

### ASSIGNMENTS

1. Use the chart for Mark Mathabane's autobiographical excerpt from *Kaffir Boy* (Prewriting Step 2) to write an essay about the author's purpose.

**786** *Writing About Literature Handbook*

## PURPOSE AND TECHNIQUES OF NONFICTION
### SELECTION: excerpt from *Kaffir Boy*

**PURPOSE:** To communicate the struggles, achievements, and doubts of a young black in South Africa.

| SENSORY DETAILS | EXAMPLES | FACTS |
|---|---|---|
| "...I cast my eyes about the crowded kitchen, dimly lit by a flickering, half-burnt candle."<br><br>"I went over and kissed his gaunt face...."<br><br>"His hairline was receding rapidly; his face was beginning to resemble an ancient topographical map of Africa."<br><br>"Tears began streaming down his hollow cheeks." | *Of struggles:* He works hard to learn English (rereading books and dictionaries, memorizing, studying), become a top student, and play tennis professionally.<br><br>*Of achievements:* He achieves the highest marks in his class, learns to play tennis, becomes youngest black boy in South Africa ever to leave that country on a tennis scholarship.<br><br>*Of doubts:* He doubts if money will hold out, if African blacks have same abilities as American blacks, and he questions if he, his family, or South Africa will change during his stay in America. | His grandmother borrowed classic European books for him to read, books not available to children under the Bantu education policy.<br><br>Mathabane wrote upside-down.<br><br>His teachers predicted great things for him—that he would be a good teacher or doctor.<br><br>He read in a tennis magazine about American tennis star Arthur Ashe.<br><br>Scaramouche became his coach.<br><br>Stan and Marjory Smith helped him to win a tennis scholarship to a four-year American college.<br><br>He leaves behind his mother, father, and siblings when he goes to America. |

| OPINIONS | STATISTICS | |
|---|---|---|
| "My pronunciation was appalling."<br><br>"My success and improvement depended upon my own efforts."<br><br>"Don't you know you never work on your strength but your weakness! And your backhand is atrocious."<br><br>"In a few hours, I would be flying ... on my way to the Promised Land...." | There are over 2,000,000 people of mixed race in South Africa.<br><br>At 4 a.m., on September 16, 1978, Mathabane got up to leave for the United States. | |

2. Do the assignment called "Writing About Biography" for "My Friend, Albert Einstein" (page 270), "Writing About a Narrative Essay" for "R.M.S. *Titanic*" (page 309), "Writing About a Persuasive Essay" for "The American Cause" (page 326), or "Writing About an Expository Essay" for "The Eureka Phenomenon" (page 339). These assignments all involve writing about nonfiction.

This lesson guides students through the process of writing about a poem. The lesson reinforces the textbook's teaching about speaker, sound devices, imagery, and figurative language. You may want to teach this lesson in conjunction with the final subunit in the Poetry unit in this textbook. Since the lesson uses examples from the poem "Solitaire," you may want to assign that poem before you teach this lesson. Under "Assignments" on the following page, you will find cross-references to Composition assignments in this textbook that focus on writing about poetry. In addition, in your *Teacher's Classroom Resources* you will find the Chart for Writing About Poetry (TCR 5, page 50; Overhead Transparency 39), Questions to Explore a Literary Work (TCR 5, page 52) and Checklist for Revising a Paper About a Literary Work (TCR 5, page 53).

# LESSON 11: *Writing About Poetry*

The pleasure experienced in listening to or reading poetry comes from the interrelationship of all the literary techniques that the poet uses to present the sense, or meaning, of the poem: choice of speaker, sound, imagery, and figurative language. When you write an essay about a poem, you will do well to show the connection between the techniques of the poem and its meaning.

## CONCEPTS TO REMEMBER

1. The **speaker** of the poem is the voice of the poem. Sometimes the speaker is the poet himself or herself; sometimes the speaker is a character or thing created by the poet.
2. Among the sound devices that a poet may use are **onomatopoeia** (a word or phrase that actually imitates or suggests the sound of what it describes); **alliteration** (the repetition of initial consonant sounds); **consonance** (the repetition of similar consonant sounds preceded by different accented vowels), and **assonance** (the repetition of vowel sounds).
3. Other aspects of sound in poetry are **rhyme** (the repetition at regular intervals of similar or identical sounds) and **rhythm** (the pattern created by arranging stressed and unstressed syllables).
4. A poem's **images** appeal to one or more senses.
5. The most common kinds of **figurative language** available to a poet are metaphor, simile, and personification. (**Metaphor** is a figure of speech in which two unlike things are compared without the use of *like* or *as*; **simile** is a comparison using *like* or *as*; **personification** is a figure of speech in which an animal, object, or idea is described as having human form or characteristics.)

## TYPICAL ESSAY QUESTION

When you are asked to write about poetry, you are often answering an assignment like this one:

Select a poem that you have read. What is the meaning of the poem? What techniques does the poet use to reveal this meaning? Techniques include the selection of speaker, sound, imagery, and figurative language.

**788** *Writing About Literature Handbook*

## PREWRITING

1. Use the following questions to help you determine the meaning of the poem.

   a. Does the poem focus on the actions of a character?
   b. Does the poem describe a person, place, or thing?
   c. Does the poem focus on an idea? A feeling?
   d. What emotional response does the poem seem to call up in you?
   e. After your immediate emotional response to the poem, on what does the poem cause you to reflect?

2. Prepare a chart on which to record your statement of the meaning of the poem and your observations about the techniques of the poem. The chart on the opposite page represents an analysis of "Solitaire" (page 208). Each column deals with one of the poetic techniques.

## WRITING PARAGRAPH BY PARAGRAPH

1. Begin your introductory paragraph with a thesis statement, which should restate the main points of the assignment. Indicate that the various techniques used by the poet all serve to enhance and present effectively the underlying meaning of the poem.

   *Example:* In "Solitaire" Amy Lowell uses the speaker, sound devices, imagery, and figurative language to present the playful, joyous vision of a mind that explores far-off places while ordinary people sleep.

2. In each of the following paragraphs discuss one or two of the techniques that the poet uses to underscore the poem's meaning. Show how each technique enhances the poem's overall meaning.
3. In the next paragraph develop your interpretation of the poem's meaning.
4. In the concluding paragraph restate your thesis in other words. You might discuss further your interpretation of the poem and describe in a bit more detail the poem's emotional impact on you.

## THE MEANING AND TECHNIQUES OF A POEM
### SELECTION: "Solitaire"

**MEANING:** While ordinary people sleep, the mind of the speaker, in a playful mood, ventures to explore far-off places and communicates the enjoyment of being alone and of being able to imagine such pictures.

| SPEAKER | SOUND | IMAGERY | FIGURATIVE LANGUAGE |
|---|---|---|---|
| *First-person speaker:* confidential, sharing; presumes the reader will understand | *Rhythm:* irregular, 4–5 feet per line; the last line is markedly short<br><br>*Onomatopoeia:* frequent, as in "drifts" and "flutter"; suggests quiet, gentle motion<br><br>*Alliteration:* "peek and peer," "light and laughing"<br><br>*Rhyme:* "drifts" and "sifts"<br><br>*Slant rhyme:* "shine" and "mind"<br><br>Generally subtle but fanciful sound effects | Contrasts *images of city* (poem's "frame") with *exotic places* in which the mind of the speaker plays: "old, blue Chinese gardens," "Pagan temples," "flutings of white pillars"<br><br>*Extensive color images:* "blue...gardens," "white pillars," "purple and yellow crocuses" | *Personification of night:* "drifts," "sifts down"<br><br>*Personification of mind:* seen as playing ball, dancing in grass with flowers in its hair and its feet shining with dew |

### ■ ASSIGNMENTS

1. Use the chart for "Solitaire" to write an essay about poetry. What is the meaning of the poem? What techniques does the poet use to reveal this meaning?

2. Do one of the assignments called "Writing About Poetry" that follow "A Hillside Thaw" (page 217), "The Destruction of Sennacherib" (page 227), "Shall I Compare Thee to a Summer's Day?" (page 239), and "Boy at the Window" (page 255). Or select another poem that you have read in this book and answer the following: What is the meaning of the poem? What techniques does the author use to reveal this meaning? Techniques include selection of speaker, sound devices, imagery, and figurative language.

This lesson guides students through the process of writing about the total effect of a fictional work. The lesson reinforces the textbook's teaching about how various literary elements interact in producing a particular impact on the reader. You may want to teach this lesson in conjunction with the final subunit in the Short Story unit in this textbook. Since the lesson uses examples from "An Occurrence at Owl Creek Bridge," you may want to assign that story before you teach this lesson. Under "Assignments" on the following page, you will find cross-references to Composition assignments in this textbook that focus on the total effect. In addition, in your *Teacher's Classroom Resources* you will find the Chart for Writing About the Total Effect (TCR 5, page 51; Overhead Transparency 40), Questions to Explore a Literary Work (TCR 5, page 52), and Checklist for Revising a Paper About a Literary Work (TCR 5, page 53).

# LESSON 12: *Writing About the Total Effect*

Like the conductor of an orchestra calling in each of the instruments on cue to create a magnificent symphony, the author of a skillfully crafted piece of literature orchestrates all the key literary elements — plot, character, setting, point of view, tone, theme, symbol, and irony — to achieve a specific emotional response on the part of the readers. Although we, the readers, immediately sense the impact of the literary work, we often have to analyze just *how* this effect is achieved.

### CONCEPTS TO REMEMBER

1. When discussing total effect, we often use the term *impact*. A selection makes an impact on a reader because of its theme and the skill with which all the other elements support this theme.
2. Consult the lessons dealing with writing about the various literary elements individually, and review the definitions and important concepts in each lesson.

### TYPICAL ESSAY QUESTION

When you are asked to write about the total effect of a selection, you are often answering an essay question such as the following:

What is the total effect of the selection? That is, what is its impact on the reader? How does the author use each of the following elements to achieve this effect: plot, character, setting, point of view, tone, theme, symbol, and irony?

### PREWRITING

1. Ask yourself the following questions as you reflect on the piece of literature:

   a. What is the impact of the work? Specifically, does the work delight you, irritate you, sadden you? Does the work surprise you, or does it verify an opinion or impression you already have?
   b. Which literary element dominates?
   c. How do the other literary elements support or relate to the dominant element?

2. Prepare a chart on which to record your answers to the questions in Prewriting Step 1. For "An Oc-

currence at Owl Creek Bridge" on page 142, a chart might look like the one on the opposite page.

### WRITING PARAGRAPH BY PARAGRAPH

1. Begin the first paragraph with a thesis statement. The thesis statement should indicate the total effect of the work on the reader and note that all the key literary elements work together to create this impact.

   *Example:* The dominant literary element of "An Occurrence at Owl Creek Bridge" is the plot, but all the elements work together to create the total effect of the piece — suspense about the fate of Peyton Farquhar, whose "escape" proves to be a mere illusion.

2. In the next paragraph focus on the dominant literary element, and show by the inclusion of details how it contributes to the total effect mentioned in the thesis statement.
3. In the subsequent paragraphs discuss additional literary elements, and show by the inclusion of details how each element supports or relates to the dominant element.
4. In the concluding paragraph remind your audience that the elements mentioned in the preceding paragraphs work together to produce the total impact on the reader.

### REVISING AND EDITING

See Lesson 1 for detailed reminders about improving your writing.

### ASSIGNMENTS

1. Use the chart for "An Occurrence at Owl Creek Bridge" to write about the total effect of the work. How does the author use the key elements of plot, character, setting, point of view, tone, theme, symbol, and irony to achieve this effect?
2. Do the assignment called "Writing About the Total Effect" for "Shaving" (page 141), "The Hiltons' Holiday" (page 167), *Julius Caesar* (page 570), or *A Connecticut Yankee in King Arthur's Court* (page 735). Or choose another selection in this book, and describe its overall impact.

## ANALYSIS OF THE TOTAL EFFECT

**SELECTION:** "An Occurrence at Owl Creek Bridge"

| QUESTION | ANSWER | DETAILS |
|---|---|---|
| A. WHAT IS THE IMPACT OF THE WORK? | The reader is kept in suspense, hoping for Peyton's escape from death. When that hope is ultimately crushed, the reader reflects on how fragile life is. | *Details creating suspense:* Suspense is created by inconclusiveness at the end of Part I and the vivid details of Part III, which suggest Peyton is still alive: "He watched them [his hands] . . . as first one and then the other pounced upon the noose at his neck." |
| B. WHAT IS THE DOMINANT LITERARY ELEMENT? | *Plot:* The dream sequence is "framed" by the real-life hanging at the beginning of the story and in the concluding paragraph. | The speed of the "framed" section is contrasted with the "slow-motion" dream sequence. |
| C. HOW DO THE OTHER LITERARY ELEMENTS SUPPORT THE DOMINANT ELEMENT? | *Character:* The reader feels sympathy for Peyton, a dedicated man dying for a lost cause. | Peyton is a gentleman; possesses deep patriotism and family values. |
|  | *Setting:* The dramatic, sensuous landscape underscores the value of life. The reader wants Peyton to live to appreciate it. | "brilliant-bodied flies"; "the prismatic colors in all the dewdrops upon a million blades of grass" |
|  | *Point of view:* Omniscient in beginning and end, but the point of view shifts to limited third person in the dream sequence, as the reader becomes involved with Peyton's hopes and dreams. | No details of thoughts or feelings of the Federal troops are given; the reader sympathizes with Peyton's agonies: "To die of hanging at the bottom of a river! the idea seemed to him ludicrous." "'God help me, I cannot dodge them all.'" |
|  | *Tone:* sympathy for Peyton and horror at his fate | Strong sense images portray the beauty of the world Peyton loses (see above). |
|  | *Theme:* "The imminence of death can heighten our perceptions": This theme is what the reader comes to realize once the suspense ends. | The emphasis on light and sound images underlines the heightened quality of Peyton's perceptions as death approaches. |
|  | *Symbol:* Owl Creek bridge is suspended between life and death; it leads inevitably to death. | Peyton sets out to destroy the bridge, but it destroys him. |
|  | *Irony:* Situational irony at the end shocks the reader and ends the suspense. | The reader maintains hope until the end, even though there have been clues that Peyton's perceptions may be distorted: the guards are "unarmed"; Peyton spends a long time underwater; the captain does not fire. |

In this handbook you will find all of the reading and literary terms taught in this book. Each entry defines a term and then briefly discusses it, elaborating with examples from the selections. Each entry ends with a cross-reference to the pages that teach the literary term and, in some cases, to related entries in this handbook.

# LITERARY TERMS HANDBOOK

**ALLITERATION** *The repetition of sounds, most often consonant sounds, at the beginnings of words.* This line from "The Bean Eaters" contains an example of alliteration:

Remembering with *tw*inklings and *tw*inges

See page 200.

**ALLUSION** *A reference in a work of literature to a well-known character, place, or situation from another work of literature, music, or art or from history.* For example, "Constantly risking absurdity" refers to a poet as "a little charleychaplin man." Readers know that Charlie Chaplin was a famous film comedian who often appeared as a tramp.

See page 200.

**ANALOGY** *A comparison made between two things to show how one is like the other.* In "The Eureka Phenomenon" Asimov draws an analogy between breathing and thinking.

See page 332.

**ANECDOTE** *A brief account of an event, usually intended to entertain, to explain an idea, and to reveal personality through a person's actions,* In "The Sentimentality of William Tavener," for example, Hester's strong personality is revealed through the anecdote of the hog corral.

See page 270.

**ANTAGONIST** *A person or force that opposes the* **protagonist,** *or central character in a story or drama.* For example, Old Man Fat in "Chee's Daughter" is the antagonist, opposing Chee.

See also CONFLICT.

**ARGUMENT** *That kind of writing in which reason is used to influence people's ideas or actions.*

See page 325.
See also PERSUASION.

**ASIDE** *In a play a comment made by a character who is heard by the audience but not by the other characters on stage.* Because other characters are on stage at the time, the speaker turns to one side, or "aside." Asides reveal what a character is thinking and feeling. For example Act II, Scene ii, of *Julius Caesar* includes the following exchange:

CAESAR: Be near me, that I may remember you.
TREBONIUS: Caesar, I will [*Aside.*] and so near
 will I be,
That your best friends shall wish I had been
 further.

See page 512.

**ASSONANCE** *The repetition of vowel sounds, especially in a line of poetry.* For example, the *i* sound is repeated in this line from "Shall I Compare Thee to a Summer's Day?":

So long l*i*ves th*i*s, and th*i*s g*i*ves life to thee.

See page 192.
See also ALLITERATION.

**ATMOSPHERE** *The emotional quality, or mood, of a story.* The elegant but ominous atmosphere of the garden adds to the unease that the children feel in "The Enchanted Garden."

See page 58.
See also SETTING.

**AUTOBIOGRAPHY** *The story of a person's life written by that person.* "Shosha" by Isaac Bashevis Singer is an autobiography.

See page 264.

**BALLAD** *A short, musical narrative poem.* **Folk ballads,** or popular ballads, were passed on by word of mouth of generations before being written down. **Literary ballads** are written in imitation of folk ballads. "The Destruction of Sennacherib" is a literary ballad.

See page 225.

**BIOGRAPHY** *The account of a person's life written by someone other than the subject.* Biographies can be short or can be book-length. "My Friend, Albert Einstein" is a short biography.

See pages 264, 265, 270.

**BLANK VERSE** *Poetry written in unrhymed* **iambic pentameter**, *which is a meter made up of five iambic feet to a line of verse, each foot containing one unstressed (◡) and one stressed (ˊ) syllable.* Shakespeare wrote his plays in blank verse. The following line, spoken by Mark Antony in Act III, Scene i, of *Julius Caesar*, is an example of blank verse. The stressed and unstressed syllables are marked, as are the five feet in the meter:

MARK ANTONY: Ŏ párˌdŏn me, / thŏu bleedˌĭng pieceˊ / of eaˊrth

> See pages 196, 491.
> See also FOOT, METER, RHYTHM.

**CHARACTER** *A person in a literary work.* Characters who reveal only one personality trait are called **flat**. The pearl buyer in Steinbeck's *Pearl*, for instance, is a flat character because we know only one aspect of his personality, his duplicity. Characters who show varied and sometimes contradictory traits are called **round**. Kino in *The Pearl* is a round character because he displays a variety of personality traits such as pride and self-doubt, shrewdness and naiveté.

A **static character** remains primarily the same throughout the story, as the pearl buyer does in *The Pearl*. A **dynamic character** changes during the story. Kino is a dynamic character because of the changes he undergoes as a result of his discovery of the pearl.

> See page 44.
> See also CHARACTERIZATION.

**CHARACTERIZATION** *The methods a writer uses to develop the personality of a character.* In **direct characterization** the writer makes direct statements about a character's personality, as in this statement in "The Bedquilt": "Of all the Elwell family Aunt Mehetabel was certainly the most unimportant member." In **indirect characterization** the writer reveals a character's personality through the character's words and actions and through what other characters say and think about the character. For example, Vera's behavior in "The Open Window" reveals her as a cool, clever, and rather cruel young lady. Indirect characterization requires readers to interpret the character's words and actions.

> See page 39.
> See also CHARACTER.

**CLIMAX** *The point of greatest emotional intensity, interest, or suspense in a narrative.* Usually the climax comes at the turning point in a story or drama, the point at which the resolution of the conflict becomes clear. In "Through the Tunnel" the climax occurs when Jerry finally goes through the tunnel.

> See page 20.

**COMEDY** *A type of drama that is humorous and has a happy ending.* A **heroic comedy** focuses on the exploits of a larger-than-life hero. *Cyrano de Bergerac* is a heroic comedy.

> See page 353.
> See also TRAGEDY.

**CONCRETE POEM** *A poem that stresses the visual appearance of the words and lines on the page.* For example, "400-Meter Freestyle" is a concrete poem.

> See page 244.

**CONFLICT** *The struggle between two opposing forces that lies at the center of a plot in a story or drama.* An **external conflict** exists when a character struggles against some outside force, such as another person, nature, society, or fate. In "Through the Tunnel," for example, when Jerry tries to swim through the tunnel, he is involved in an external conflict against nature. An **internal conflict** exists within the mind of a character who is torn between opposing feelings or goals. Jerry wrestles with an internal conflict when he tries to overcome his own fear in order to swim through the tunnel.

> See pages 28, 491.
> See also PLOT.

**CONNOTATION** *The unspoken or unwritten meanings associated with a word beyond its dictionary definition, or* **denotation**. In "Fifteen," for example, the poet speaks of the motorcycle's "pulsing gleam." Because readers generally associate life and heart beats with the word *pulsing*, they apply those associations to the poem and perceive the motorcycle as having lifelike qualities.

> See page 200.
> See also FIGURATIVE LANGUAGE

**COUPLET** *Two consecutive lines of poetry that rhyme.* For example, these two lines from Pope's "Sound and Sense" form a couplet:

'Tis not enough no harshness gives offense,
The sound must seem an echo to the sense.

> See also RHYME, SONNET.

*Literary Terms Handbook* **793**

**DENOTATION** *The literal or dictionary meaning of a word.* **Literal language** seeks to convey denotation, or exact meaning.

> See page 200.
> See also CONNOTATION.

**DESCRIPTION** *Any carefully detailed portrayal of a person, place, thing, or event.* While description is the writer's primary aim in the descriptive essay, this kind of writing is also used in stories, biography, and other forms of essays.

> See page 319.
> See also EXPOSITION,
> NARRATION, PERSUASION.

**DIALECT** *A variation of language spoken by a particular group, often within a particular region.* Dialects differ from standard language because they contain different sounds, forms, and meanings. The conversational language in "The Sentimentality of William Tavener" represents the dialect of midwestern farmers in the early twentieth century. For example: "Nobody was ever hurt by goin' to a circus. Why, law me!"

**DIALOGUE** *Conversation between characters in a literary work.*

> See page 382.

**DRAMA** *A play performed before an audience by actors and actresses on a stage.* Most drama before the modern period can be divided into two basic types: **tragedy**, such as Shakespeare's *Julius Caesar*, and **comedy**, such as *Cyrano de Bergerac*. The two basic parts of a drama are its script, which includes **dialogue** and **stage directions**, and the staging, which prepares the play to be performed.

> See page 353.
> See also COMEDY,
> TRAGEDY.

**DRAMATIC CONVENTON** *A device that a playwright uses to present a story on stage and that the audience accepts as realistic.* Shakespeare's audience, for example, accepted the convention of boys playing the roles of women.

**DRAMATIC MONOLOGUE** *A form of dramatic poetry that presents only one speaker, who addresses a silent listener.* "First Lesson," in which a father speaks to a silent daughter, is a dramatic monologue.

> See page 235.
> See also DRAMATIC POETRY.

**DRAMATIC POETRY** *Poetry in which one or more characters speak to other characters, themselves, or the reader.* In "Mirror," for example, a mirror speaks to the reader.

> See page 235.
> See also DRAMATIC
> MONOLOGUE, SPEAKER.

**EPIC** *A long narrative poem that traces the adventures of a hero.* Epics intertwine myths, legends, and history, reflecting the values of the societies in which they originate. In epics gods and goddesses often intervene in the affairs of humans. Homer's *Iliad* and *Odyssey*, two of the most famous epics, were first recited or sung before they were collected and written down.

> See page 576.
> See also EPIC HERO.

**EPIC HERO** *A legendary, larger-than-life figure whose adventures form the core of the epic poem.* The hero embodies the goals and virtues of an entire nation or culture. For example, King Arthur in Malory's *Morte d'Arthur* functions as an epic hero because he personifies his society's ideals of courage, nobility, and justice.

> See page 606.

**ESSAY** *A short piece of nonfiction writing on any topic.* The purpose of the essay is to communicate an idea or opinion. The **formal essay** is serious and impersonal, such as Hanson Baldwin's "R.M.S. *Titanic.*" The **informal essay** entertains while it informs; it usually takes a light approach to its subject and uses a conversational style. The personality of the author often shines through the informal essay. "The Eureka Phenomenon" by Isaac Asimov is an informal essay.

**Narrative essays**, such as Charles Lindbergh's account in *The Spirit of St. Louis*, relate true events, usually in chronological order. **Descriptive essays**, such as Mark Twain's "Two Views of the River," describe actual people, places, or things. **Persuasive essays**, such as John Dos Passos' "American Cause," aim to convince the reader of an opinion. **Expository essays**, such as Bruce Catton's "Grant and Lee at Appomattox," present information and explain ideas.

> See page 290.

**EXPOSITION** *An author's introduction to the characters, setting, and situation at the beginning of a story, novel, or play.* For example, in "The Cask of Amontillado," the exposition quickly reveals the speaker's thirst for revenge.

**794** *Literary Terms Handbook*

The term *exposition* also refers to the **expository essay**, in which the writer's purpose is to present facts or explain ideas. "The Eureka Phenomenon" by Isaac Asimov consists largely of exposition.

See pages 20, 339.
See also PLOT.

FABLE  *A very brief story told to teach a lesson.* Themes are usually stated explicitly, as in Aesop's fables. The story told by the grandmother in "The Shepherd's Daughter" is a fable that teaches the value of learning an honest trade.

See page 90.
See also MORAL, PARABLE, THEME.

FALLING ACTION  *In a play or story the action that follows the climax.* In *A Connecticut Yankee in King Arthur's Court,* for instance, the falling action consists of the narrator's description of the dying Yankee. In "Through the Tunnel" Jerry's return to the villa after successfully swimming the tunnel is the falling action.

See page 20.
See also PLOT.

FICTION  *A prose narrative in which situations and characters are invented by the writer.* Some aspects of a fictional work may be based on fact or experience, such as Mark Twain's knowledge of science in *A Connecticut Yankee in King Arthur's Court.* Fiction includes both short stories, such as "By the Waters of Babylon," and novels, such as *The Pearl.*

See also NOVEL, SHORT STORY.

FIGURATIVE LANGUAGE  *Language used for descriptive effect, often to imply ideas indirectly.* Expressions of figurative language are not literally true but express some truth beyond the literal level. For example, in his account of his flight in *The Spirit of St. Louis,* Charles Lindbergh uses the figurative phrase "fuselage's phantoms" to refer to the engine vapor that trails after his airplane. Lindbergh's use of figurative language reinforces the dreamlike aspects of his flight. Although it appears in all kinds of writing, figurative language is especially prominent in poetry.

See pages 177, 201, 289.
See also FIGURE OF SPEECH, LITERAL LANGUAGE, METAPHOR, PERSONIFICATION, SIMILE, SYMBOL.

FIGURE OF SPEECH  *A specific device or kind of figurative language such as* **metaphor, personification, simile,** *or* **symbol.**

See pages 177, 201, 209, 211, 213, 215, 217, 219, 289.
See also METAPHOR, PERSONIFICATION, SIMILE, SYMBOL.

FOIL  *A character who is used to contrast with another character.* In *The Pearl,* for instance, Juana, who is content with and resigned to her state in life, is a foil for Kino, who is restless and ambitious. In *Cyrano de Bergerac* Christian, who is handsome but inarticulate, serves as a foil for Cyrano, who is ugly and eloquent.

FOOT  *The basic unit in the measurement of rhythm.* A foot usually contains one accented syllable (ˊ) and one or more unaccented syllables (˘).

The sound/must seem/an e/cho to/the sense.
—"Sound and Sense"

The Assyr/ian came down/like the wolf/on the fold.
—"The Destruction of Sennacherib"

See also METER, RHYTHM.

FORESHADOWING  *The use of clues by the author to prepare readers for events that will happen in a story.* In "The Cask of Amontillado," for example, Fortunato says "I shall not die of a cough." The narrator responds, "True–true." Readers remember these words when the murder plot unfolds.

See page 20.
See also PLOT.

FRAME STORY  *A plot structure that includes the telling of a story within a story.* The frame is the outer story, which usually precedes and follows the inner and more important story. For example, in *A Connecticut Yankee in King Arthur's Court,* the narration by "M. T." introduces and concludes the Yankee's own narrative.

See page 90.

FREE VERSE  *Poetry that has no fixed pattern of meter, rhyme, line length, or stanza arrangement.* May Swenson uses free verse in "By Morning":

Some for everyone
plenty
and more coming

See pages 198, 246.
See also RHYTHM.

*Literary Terms Handbook*  **795**

**IAMBIC PENTAMETER** *A specific meter in a line of poetry comprised of five feet (pentameter) most of which are iambs.* The iamb consists of one unstressed syllable (◡) followed by a stressed syllable (◌́). This line from "Puritan Sonnet" exemplifies iambic pentameter:

◡    ◌́    ◡     ◌́    ◡    ◌́   ◡   ◌́   ◡   ◌́
I love/those skies,/thin blue/or snow/y gray.

> See pages 196, 491.
> See also BLANK VERSE, FOOT, METER.

**IMAGE** *A reference to something that can be experienced through one of the five senses of sight, sound, smell, taste, or touch.* Note the images of sight and touch in these lines from "A Blessing":

> And the light breeze moves me to caress her long ear
> That is delicate as the skin over a girl's wrist.

> See pages 75, 205.
> See also FIGURATIVE LANGUAGE, IMAGERY.

**IMAGERY** *The collection of sense images that helps the reader of a literary work to visualize scenes, hear sounds, feel textures, smell aromas, and taste foods that are described in the work.*

> See pages 75, 205.
> See also FIGURATIVE LANGUAGE, IMAGE.

**IRONY** *A contrast between reality and what seems to be real.* **Situational irony** exists when the actual outcome of a situation is the opposite of someone's expectations. In "The Sentimentality of William Tavener," for example, Hester expects the discussion of the circus to lead to an argument with her husband. Instead, it brings the couple closer together.

**Verbal irony** exists when a person says one thing and means another. For example, in "Mammon and the Archer" the narrator's description of Anthony Rockwall as "the champion of the root of evil" is an instance of verbal irony because Anthony is actually a good, kindly man.

**Dramatic irony** occurs when the audience has important information that characters in a literary work do not have. In *Julius Caesar*, for example, when Caesar's wife warns him not to go to the Senate, the audience knows of the murder plot, although those two characters do not.

> See pages 129, 133, 416.

**LITERAL LANGUAGE** *Language that means nothing more than exactly what it says.*

> See FIGURATIVE LANGUAGE.

**LOCAL COLOR** *A technique of writing that uses specific details to evoke a particular region.* Local color re-creates the language, customs, geography, and habits of the area. Steinbeck, for example, includes local color in writing about the fishing village in *The Pearl*.

> See page 167.

**LYRIC POETRY** *Poetry that expresses a speaker's personal thoughts and feelings.* Lyric poems are usually short and musical. For example, Robert Burns expresses his longing for his home in "My Heart's in the Highlands."

> See page 231.

**METAPHOR** *A type of figurative language used to compare or equate seemingly unlike things.* In these lines from "Tomorrow, and Tomorrow, and Tomorrow," for instance, life is equated with three different things:

> Life's but a walking shadow, a poor player
> That struts and frets his hour upon the stage
> And then is heard no more. It is a tale
> Told by an idiot, full of sound and fury
> Signifying nothing.

> See pages 213, 215, 217.
> See also FIGURATIVE LANGUAGE, SIMILE.

**METER** *A regular pattern of stressed and unstressed syllables that gives a line of poetry a predictable rhythm.* Note the pattern of stressed and unstressed syllables in these lines from "An Indian Summer Day on the Prairie":

◡   ◌́   ◡   ◡   ◌́   ◡   ◌̆
Atop of the spirit-cliffs
◡   ◌́    ◡   ◡   ◌́   ◡   ◌́
He builds him a crimson nest.

> See page 192.
> See also FOOT, RHYTHM.

**MONOLOGUE** *A long speech by a character in a play.* The burial speeches of Brutus and Antony in Act III, Scene ii, of *Julius Caesar* are monologues, as is Cyrano's "nose speech" in Act I of *Cyrano de Bergerac*.

> See page 536.
> See also SOLILOQUY.

**796** *Literary Terms Handbook*

**MOOD** *The emotional quality or atmosphere of a story.*

See page 58.
See also ATMOSPHERE, SETTING.

**MORAL** *A practical lesson about right and wrong conduct, often in an instructive story such as a fable or parable.*

See page 90.

**NARRATION** *The kind of writing or speech that tells a story.* Narration is used in novels, short stories, and narrative poetry. Narration can also be an important element in biographies, autobiographies, and essays.

See pages 225, 296.
See also DESCRIPTION, EXPOSITION, PERSUASION.

**NARRATIVE HOOK** *The point in a story or novel at which the author catches the reader's attention by presenting an interesting problem or situation.* In *The Pearl* Coyotito's scorpion bite is the narrative hook. In "Why Don't You Look Where You're Going?" the narrative hook is the first sighting of the distant object, which turns out to be the sailboat.

See page 20.
See also PLOT.

**NARRATIVE POETRY** *Verse that tells a story.* The narrative poem is generally more selective and concentrated than the prose story. "Eldorado" is a narrative poem.

See page 225.
See also BALLAD.

**NARRATOR** *The person who tells a story in a work of fiction.* In some cases the narrator is a character in the story—for example, Dr. Watson in "The Red-Headed League" or John in "By the Waters of Babylon." Sometimes the narrator stands outside the story, as in "Mammon and the Archer" and "Shaving."

See pages 75, 82, 86.
See also POINT OF VIEW.

**NONFICTION** *Factual prose writing.* Nonfiction deals with real people and experiences. Among the categories of nonfiction are **biographies, autobiographies,** and **essays.** "My Friend, Albert Einstein" by Banesh Hoffman is a biography. "Shosha" by Isaac Bashevis Singer is an autobiographical selec-

tion. "The American Cause" by John Dos Passos is an essay.

See page 263.
See also AUTOBIOGRAPHY, BIOGRAPHY, ESSAY, FICTION

**NOVEL** *An extended fictional prose narrative.* The novel has more scope than a short story in its presentation of plot, character, setting, and theme. Because novels are not subject to any limits in their presentation of these elements, they encompass a wide range of narratives. For example, John Steinbeck's *Pearl* is a novel set in a Mexican village, covering a few days, and portraying a fisherman's fight against poverty, injustice, and fate. Mark Twain's *Connecticut Yankee in King Arthur's Court*, on the other hand, is a novel that is set in the sixth and nineteenth centuries and blends fantasy, humor, social commentary, and tragedy.

See page 611.
See also SHORT STORY, FICTION

**ONOMATOPOEIA** *The use of a word or phrase that actually imitates or suggests the sound of what it describes.* For example, the following lines from Richard Wilbur's "Boy at the Window" imitate the sound of a windstorm:

The small boy weeps to hear the wind prepare
A night of gnashings and enormous moan.

See page 200.
See also SENSORY LANGUAGE.

**PARABLE** *A simple story from which a lesson should be drawn.* The biblical story of "The Prodigal Son," for example, is a parable.

See page 613.
See also FABLE, MORAL.

**PARALLELISM** *The use of a series of words, phrases, or sentences that have similar grammatical form.* Parallelism emphasizes the items that are arranged in the similar structures. Notice the parallel form, for example, of the clauses in this sentence from "Grant and Lee at Appomattox": "It came from the past and it looked to the past...." The subject of each clause is *it*, followed by a verb and prepositional phrase ending in the word *past*. Parallelism adds to the sense of unity in a piece of writing.

See pages 194, 331.
See also REPETITION.

*Literary Terms Handbook* **797**

**PERSONIFICATION** *A figure of speech in which an animal, object, or idea is given human form or characteristics.* In the following lines from "Fifteen," the motorcycle is given human features:

I led it gently
to the road, and stood with that
companion, ready and friendly.

> See page 209.
> See also FIGURATIVE
> LANGUAGE.

**PERSUASION** *The type of writing that aims to make the audience accept an opinion.*

> See page 326.
> See also ARGUMENT,
> DESCRIPTION, EXPOSITION,
> NARRATION.

**PLOT** *The sequence of events in a story, novel, or play, each event causing or leading to the next.* The plot begins with **exposition**, which introduces the story's characters, setting, and situation. The plot catches the reader's attention with the **narrative hook**. The **rising action** adds complications to the story's **conflicts**, or problems, leading to the **climax**, or point of highest emotional pitch. The **falling action** is the logical result of the climax, and the **resolution** presents the final outcome.

> See pages 20, 448.

**POETRY** *A concentrated kind of writing in which imagery, figurative language, rhythm, and often rhyme combine to create a special emotional effect.* Poetry is usually arranged in lines and groups of lines known as **stanzas**. Types of poetry include **narrative poetry**, which tells a story, **lyric poetry**, which expresses emotion, and **dramatic poetry**, which presents a character.

> See page 177.

**POINT OF VIEW** *The relationship of the narrator, or storyteller, to the story.* In a story with **first-person point of view**, the story is told by one of the characters, referred to as "I." The reader generally sees everything through that character's eyes. "Quality," for instance, has a first-person narrator.

In a story with a **limited third-person point of view**, the narrator reveals the thoughts of only one character but refers to that character as "he" or "she." "Chee's Daughter," told from Chee's perspective by a third-person narrator, is an example of limited third-person narration.

In a story with an **omniscient point of view**, the narrator reveals the thoughts of several charac-ters. "Why Don't You Look Where You're Going?" is told from an omniscient point of view.

> See pages 75, 82, 86.
> See also NARRATOR, TONE.

**PROTAGONIST** *The central character in a story or drama.* Generally the audience is meant to sympathize with the protagonist. For example, the reader of Ambrose Bierce's "Occurrence at Owl Creek Bridge" sympathizes with its protagonist, Peyton Farquhar, in his struggle against death. In *The Life and Adventures of Nicholas Nickleby*, Nicholas is the title character and the protagonist, and the audience sympathizes with him in his conflict with Squeers.

> See ANTAGONIST,
> CONFLICT.

**PUN** *A play on words, or a joke based on words with several meanings or words that sound alike but have different meanings.* Shakespeare uses puns frequently. For example, in *Julius Caesar*, Act I, Scene i, the citizen who is a cobbler makes puns on the words *awl* (a cobbler's tool) and *all*:

Truly, sir, *all* that I live by is with the *awl*. I meddle with no tradesman's matters nor women's matters, but with *awl*.

> See page 569.

**REPETITION** *The recurrence of sounds, words, phrases, lines, or stanzas in a speech or piece of writing.* Repetition increases the feeling of unity in a work. When a line or stanza is repeated in a poem, it is called a refrain. For example, each stanza of William Stafford's poem "Fifteen" concludes with the word *fifteen*.

> See page 194.
> See also PARALLELISM.

**RESOLUTION** *The part of a plot that concludes the falling action by revealing or suggesting the outcome of the conflict.* The resolution in "The Sentimentality of William Tavener," for example, comes when the boys recognize the change in their mother.

> See page 20.

**RHYME** *The repetition of sounds in words that appear close to each other in a poem.* **End rhymes** occur at the ends of lines. The following lines from "The Bean Eaters" exemplify end rhyme.

They eat beans mostly, this old yellow *pair*,
Dinner is a casual *affair*.

**798** *Literary Terms Handbook*

occur when words include sounds that are similar but not identical. Slant rhyme usually involves some variation of **consonance** (the repetition of consonant sounds) or **assonance** (the repetition of vowel sounds). For example, the following line from Alexander Pope's "Sound and Sense" contains an example of slant rhyme:

The *hoarse*, rough *verse* should like the torrent roar.

*Hoarse* and *verse* form a slant rhyme because they include the same final consonants but different vowel sounds.

See page 192.
See also REPETITION, RHYME SCHEME.

**RHYME SCHEME**   *The pattern of rhymes formed by the end rhyme in a poem.* Rhyme scheme is designated by the assignment of a different letter of the alphabet to each new rhyme. For instance, the rhyme scheme in the first part of "Puritan Sonnet" is *abba:*

| | |
|---|---|
| Down to the Puritan marrow of my *bones* | a |
| There's something in this richness that I *hate* | b |
| I love the look, austere, *immaculate* | b |
| Of landscapes drawn in pearly *monotones* | a |

See also SONNET.

**RHYTHM**   *The pattern of beats created by the arrangement of stressed and unstressed syllables, particularly in poetry.* Rhythm gives poetry a musical quality that helps convey its meaning. Rhythm can be regular, with a predictable pattern or meter, or irregular. Note the regular rhythm in these lines from "The Tuft of Flowers":

The dew was gone that made his blade so keen

Before I came to view the leveled scene

See page 192.

**RISING ACTION**   *The part of a plot that adds complications to the plot's problems and increases reader interest.* For example, in "Why Don't You Look Where You're Going?" the rising action occurs as more and more passengers speculate about the object in the distance.

**ROMANCE**   *A story concerning a knightly hero, his exciting adventures, and pursuit of love.* The King Arthur Legend includes many romances composed by medieval poets.

See page 579.

**SATIRE**   *A form of writing that ridicules abuses for the sake of remedying them.* Mark Twain's *Connecticut Yankee in King Arthur's Court*, for example, ridicules the injustice and inequality of life in King Arthur's time so that people in Twain's time could remedy the same evils in their own world.

See page 663.

**SCANSION**   *The analysis of the rhythm of a line of verse.* To scan a line of poetry means to note stressed and unstressed syllables and to divide the line into its feet, or rhythmical units.

See also FOOT, RHYTHM.

**SETTING**   *The time and place in which the events of a story, novel, or play occur.* The setting often helps create an atmosphere, or mood. For example, most of "Shaving" takes place in the sickroom where Barry's father lies dying. The close atmosphere of that room, with its smell of illness and medication, adds impact to the subdued action.

See page 58.
See also ATMOSPHERE, MOOD.

**SHORT STORY**   *A brief fictional narrative in prose.* Elements of the short story include plot, character, setting, point of view, theme, and sometimes symbol and irony.

See pages 1, 175.

**SIMILE**   *A figure of speech using* like *or as to compare seemingly unlike things.* For example, in "Flood" Annie Dillard describes the creek as roving "like a black snake caught in a kitchen drawer."

See pages 211, 289.
See also FIGURATIVE LANGUAGE, METAPHOR.

**SOLILOQUY**   *A long speech spoken by a character who is alone on stage.* This speech usually reveals the private thoughts and emotions of the character. For example, Antony vows his revenge of Caesar's murder in a soliloquy in *Julius Caesar*, Act III, Scene i.

See page 512.

**SONNET**   *A lyric poem of fourteen lines, almost always written in iambic pentameter and usually following strict patterns of stanza divisions and rhymes.*

*Literary Terms Handbook*   **799**

The **Shakespearean**, or **English, sonnet** consists of three **quatrains**, or four-line stanzas, followed by a **couplet**, or pair of rhyming lines. The rhyme scheme is usually *abab, cdcd, efef, gg*. The rhyming couplet often presents a conclusion to the issues or questions presented in the three quatrains. "Shall I Compare Thee to a Summer's Day?" is a Shakespearean sonnet.

In the **Petrarchan**, or **Italian, sonnet** fourteen lines are divided into two stanzas. The first eight lines, called an **octave**, usually present a situation, idea, or question. The remaining six lines, or **sestet**, provide a resolution, comment, or answer. The rhyme scheme for the octave is usually *abbaabba;* for the sestet the rhyme scheme is usually *cdecde.* "Puritan Sonnet" is a Petrarchan sonnet.

> See page 239.
> See also COUPLET, RHYME SCHEME, STANZA.

**SPEAKER** *The voice of a poem, sometimes that of the poet, sometimes that of a fictional person or even a thing.* The speaker's words communicate a particular *tone,* or attitude toward the subject of the poem. For example, the speaker in "First Lesson" is a father whose tone is tender and reassuring.

> See pages 178, 181.
> See also TONE.

**STAGE DIRECTIONS** *Instructions written by the dramatist to describe the appearance and actions of characters, as well as sets, costumes, and lighting.*

> See page 354.

**STANZA** *A group of lines forming a unit in a poem.* "The Bean Eaters" has three stanzas.

> See page 177.

**STYLE** *The author's choice and arrangement of words in a literary work.* Style can reveal an author's purpose in writing and attitude toward his or her subject and audience. For example, in "The Shepherd's Daughter" Saroyan uses a simple style that makes the story resemble a fairy tale.

> See page 263.

**SYMBOL** *Any object, person, place, or experience that means more than what it is.* Swimming through the tunnel, for example, is a symbolic experience for Jerry in Doris Lessing's "Through the Tunnel." The act means that he is growing up.

> See pages 114, 219.

**THEME** *The main idea of a story, poem, novel, or play, usually expressed as a general statement.* Some works have a **stated theme**, which is expressed directly and explicitly. More frequently works have an **implied theme**, which is revealed gradually through such other elements as plot, character, setting, point of view, symbol, and irony. For example, in "Quality" the implied theme is that devotion to an ideal can make a small life heroic.

> See pages 90, 99.

**THESIS** *The central idea or purpose in a work of nonfiction.* Often the thesis is expressed in a thesis statement. For example, in the opening sentence of "The American Cause," John Dos Passos states his thesis: "...to explain...why they should admire the United States." Sometimes the thesis is not stated but is rather implied in the work. For example, Charles Lindbergh's account of his transatlantic flight in *The Spirit of St. Louis* has an implied thesis: Lindbergh wants readers to feel the joy, wonder, and great sense of accomplishment he experienced on his flight.

> See page 339.

**TONE** *The attitude taken by the author or speaker toward the subject of a work.* The tone conveys an emotion or several emotions. For example, in John Galsworthy's "Quality" the tone is somber, almost reverential, while the tone of Edna St. Vincent Millay's "Fawn" is one of breathless wonder.

> See page 82.
> See also NARRATOR,
> POINT OF VIEW, SPEAKER.

**TRAGEDY** *A play in which a main character suffers a downfall.* That character often is a person of dignified or heroic stature. The downfall may result from outside forces or from a weakness within the character, which is known as a **tragic flaw**. *Julius Caesar* is a tragedy, dramatizing the deaths of a ruler and of the idealist who opposed him.

> See page 568.
> See also COMEDY, DRAMA.

**WORD CHOICE** *The selection of words in a piece of literature to convey meaning, suggest attitude, and create images.* In "Constantly risking absurdity," for example, the poet chooses words that convey both a playfulness and a love of poetry, as well as create images that compare a poet to an acrobat in a circus.

> See pages 200, 246.
> See also CONNOTATION.

The following Glossary lists words that are from the selections but may be unfamiliar to you. Although many of the words have several different meanings, they are defined only as they are used in the selections. Some words may be familiar to you in other contexts but may have unusual meanings in the text.

Each Glossary entry contains a pronunciation, a part of speech, and a definition. Some words are used in more than one way in the textbook and therefore have more than one definition and occasionally more than one part of speech. Related words are often combined in one entry: The main form (for example, the verb *abet*) is defined, and another form (for example, the noun *abettor*) is run on after the main definition. Adverbs ending in *-ly* are usually run on after the definition of the adjective form.

Some unusual words or meanings of words are labeled ARCHAIC (old-fashioned), OBSOLETE (no longer in use), RARE, or POETIC. Other special usage labels include COLLOQUIAL, SLANG, CHIEFLY BRITISH, MILITARY, and so on. Occasionally an unfamiliar idiomatic expression is used within a selection; in such cases the main word of the expression is listed, followed by a definition of the idiom.

The following abbreviations are used in this Glossary:

| | | | |
|---|---|---|---|
| *n.* | noun | *conj.* | conjunction |
| *v.* | verb | *prep.* | preposition |
| *adj.* | adjective | *interj.* | interjection |
| *adv.* | adverb | *pl.* | plural |
| *pron.* | pronoun | *n.pl.* | plural noun |

A key to pronunciations may be found in the lower right-hand corner of each right-hand page of the Glossary.

## A

**abash** [ə bash'] *v.* to make embarrassed and ashamed.
**abet** [ə bet'] *v.* to approve of, encourage, or help. — **abettor**, *n.*
**abject** [ab'jekt, ab jekt'] *adj.* having lost one's spirit and self-respect; wretched.
**abortive** [ə bôr'tiv] *adj.* unsuccessful. — **abortively**, *adv.*
**abrasion** [ə brā'zhən] *n.* a scraping.
**abscond** [ab skond'] *v.* to run off quickly and secretly.
**absolve** [ab zolv', -solv'] *v.* to set free from responsibility or blame.
**abut** [ə but'] *v.* to be next to; border on.
**abyss** [ə bis'] *n.* a bottomless depth.
**acclaim** [ə klām'] *v.* to praise, welcome, or approve.
**accommodations** [ə kom'ə dā'shəns] *n.pl.* a place to sleep and eat; lodgings.
**accord** [ə kôrd'] *v.* to give; present.
**accost** [ə kôst'] *v.* to approach and speak to.
**acquisition** [ak'wə zish'ən] *n.* something gotten or gained.
**acrid** [ak'rid] *adj.* bitter.
**adhere** [ad hēr'] *v.* to stick; hold on.
**administer** [ad min'is tər] *v.* to conduct one's business.
**adulation** [aj'ə lā'shən] *n.* lavish praise or flattery.
**adulterous** [ə dul'tər əs] *adj.* having an intimate relationship with a person other than one's husband or wife.
**adversary** [ad'vər ser'ē] *n.* enemy; opponent.

**affable** [af'ə bəl] *adj.* pleasant; friendly.
**aftermath** [af'tər math'] *n.* the result.
**aggressive** [ə gres'iv] *adj.* bold; forceful. — **aggressiveness**, *n.*
**agile** [aj'əl] *adj.* moving with ease and speed.
**agitate** [aj'ə tāt'] *v.* to move rapidly or violently.
**agitation** [aj'ə tā'shən] *n.* the state of being anxious.
**algae** [al'jē] *n.pl.* rootless plants that usually grow in water.
**alien** [āl'yən, ā'lē ən] *n.* a foreigner or outsider.
**allegiance** [ə lē'jəns] *n.* loyalty; devotion.
**allot** [ə lot'] *v.* to assign.
**alloy** [al'oi, ə loi'] *n.* a mixture of metals.
**allusion** [ə lōō'zhən] *n.* a casual or indirect reference.
**alms** [ämz] *n.pl.* money or other items given to the poor.
**amputate** [am'pyə tāt'] *v.* to cut off (a limb, etc.).
**annihilate** [ə nī'ə lāt'] *v.* to destroy; wipe out.
**anthem** [an'thəm] *n.* a song of praise or devotion.
**antiquity** [an tik'wə tē] *n.* ancient times.
**aperture** [ap'ər chər] *n.* an opening.
**appraise** [ə prāz'] *v.* to judge the value of. — **appraiser**, *n.*
**apprehension** [ap'ri hen'shən] *n.* fear or worry about what might happen.
**apprise** [ə prīz'] *v.* to tell; notify.
**archaic** [är kā'ik] *adj.* of an earlier time; old-fashioned.
**aria** [är'ē ə, ar'ē ə] *n.* a song from an opera for solo voice.
**aristocracy** [ar'is tok'rə sē] *n.* the upper class.
**armorer** [är'mər ər] *n.* a person who makes armor.
**aromatic** [ar'ə mat'ik] *adj.* having a strong, pleasant smell.
**arrest** [ə rest'] *n.* a stopping.
**artery** [är'tər ē] *n.* a road; highway.
**artisan** [är'tə zən] *n.* a person skilled in a craft.
**ascertain** [as'ər tān'] *v.* to find out; determine.
**askance** [ə skans'] *adv.* with distrust or disapproval.
**aspect** [as'pekt] *n.* appearance.
**aspirated** [as'pə rā'tid] *adj.* preceded or followed by the sound *h*.
**assail** [ə sāl'] *v.* to attack.
**astute** [əs tōōt', -tūt'] *adj.* clever; shrewd. — **astuteness**, *n.*
**augment** [ôg ment'] *v.* to increase.
**autocratic** [ô'tə krat'ik] *adj.* having absolute power; domineering.
**avarice** [av'ər is] *n.* greed.
**avowal** [ə vou'əl] *n.* an open declaration or admission.
**awry** [ə rī'] *adj.* twisted to one side; not straight.

## B

**bailiff** [bā'lif] *n.* CHIEFLY BRITISH. a manager of a farm.
**bank** [bangk] *v.* to tip (an airplane) sideways when turning.

---

at; āpe; cär; end; mē; it; īce; hot; ōld; fôrk; wood; fōōl; oil; out; up; ūse; turn; ə in ago, taken, pencil, lemon, circus; bat; chin; dear; five; game; hit; hw in white; joke; kit; lid; man; not; singer; pail; ride; sat; shoe; tag; thin; this; very; wet; yes; zoo; zh in treasure; KH in loch, German ach; N in French bon; œ in French feu, German schön

---

---

In the Glossary you will find the more difficult words in the selections, along with pronunciations and definitions of the words as they are used in the selections. In addition, you will find the Glossary words for each selection listed in the teacher's materials for that selection in your *Teacher's Resource Book*.

**banter** [ban′tər] *v.* to tease; joke. — **banteringly**, *adv.*

**barnacle** [băr′nə kəl] *n.* a kind of shellfish that attaches itself to underwater objects.

**bass** [bās] *n.* the lowest male singing voice.

**beleaguer** [bi lē′gər] *v.* to annoy; torment.

**belfry** [bel′frē] *n.* a tower for a bell.

**belie** [bi lī′] *v.* to disguise; give a false impression of.

**benediction** [ben′ə dik′shən] *n.* a blessing or prayer.

**benign** [bi nīn′] *adj.* kindly; gracious.

**berth** [burth] *n.* a place; position; job.

**beseech** [bi sēch′] *v.* to ask; beg.

**bizarre** [bi zăr′] *adj.* very unusual or strange; fantastic.

**blatherskite** [blath′ər skīt′] *n.* a silly, boastful, talkative person.

**block** [blok] *n.* a frame holding a wheel on which a rope runs.

**bodice** [bod′is] *n.* the top part of a dress.

**bolster** [bōl′stər] *n.* a narrow pad or cushion.

**botch** [boch] *v.* to make or do badly or clumsily.

**bowl** [bōl] *v.* to move smoothly and rapidly.

**brandish** [bran′dish] *v.* to wave threateningly.

**bravado** [brə vä′dō] *n.* pretended or boastful bravery.

**buoyant** [boi′ənt, boō′yənt] *adj.* able to keep something afloat.

**buttress** [but′ris] *v.* to support.

## C

**cadent** [kād′ənt] *adj.* moving rhythmically.

**calculus** [kal′kyə ləs] *n.* a kind of advanced mathematics.

**callous** [kal′əs] *adj.* unfeeling.

**callow** [kal′ō] *adj.* immature; inexperienced.

**candelabrum** [kand′əl ă′brəm, -ä′brəm] *n.* a large candlestick with holders for several candles.

**canonicals** [kə non′i kəlz] *n.pl.* the clothes worn by a clergyman during church services.

**canopy** [kan′ə pē] *n.* a rooflike covering, often of cloth; awning.

**caprice** [kə prēs′] *n.* a sudden change; whim.

**carbine** [kär′bīn, -bēn] *n.* a kind of rifle.

**carriage** [kar′ij] *n.* posture; bearing.

**cataract** [kat′ə rakt′] *n.* a waterfall.

**cavalier** [kav′ə lēr′] *n.* a gallant man; knight.

**chafe** [chāf] *v.* to be annoyed or impatient.

**chagrin** [shə grin′] *n.* distress due to failure, disappointment, or humiliation.

**chandelier** [shand′əl ēr′] *n.* a lamp that has holders for a number of candles or lightbulbs and hangs from the ceiling.

**chaperone** [shap′ə rōn′] *n.* an older person who supervises gatherings of young, unmarried people.

**chattel** [chat′əl] *n.* a possession.

**chivalry** [shiv′əl rē] *n.* the qualities of a knight; courtesy, bravery, helpfulness, etc.

**chronicle** [kron′i kəl] *v.* to record the events of; write the history of.

**cicada** [si kā′də, -kä′-] *n.* a large insect with transparent wings.

**circumambulation** [sur′kəm am′byə lā′shən] *n.* the act of walking around or in a circle.

**circumscribe** [sur′kəm skrīb′] *v.* to encircle; surround.

**citation** [sī tā′shən] *n.* a reference to a law.

**clairvoyant** [klār voi′ənt] *n.* a person who can perceive things that cannot be detected by the senses.

**clamber** [klam′bər, klam′ər] *v.* to climb clumsily.

**clamor** [klam′ər] *v.* to make a loud demand or complaint.

**clandestine** [klan des′tin] *adj.* secret; hidden; sneaky. — **clandestinely**, *adv.*

**clarion** [klar′ē ən] *n.* a trumpet.

**clarity** [klar′ə tē] *n.* clearness.

**cleft** [kleft] *n.* an opening; crack.

**clinical** [klin′i kəl] *adj.* free of germs; sterile. — **clinically**, *adv.*

**coagulate** [kō ag′yə lāt′] *v.* to form into a mass; thicken.

**collaborate** [kə lab′ə rāt′] *v.* to work together.

**colonnade** [kol′ə nād′] *n.* a row of columns.

**comely** [kum′lē] *adj.* attractive; handsome.

**commingle** [kə ming′gəl] *v.* to mix together; blend.

**commission** [kə mish′ən] *v.* to order something made.

**compass** [kum′pəs, kom′-] *v.* to gain; accomplish.

**compassion** [kəm pash′ən] *n.* sorrow for and a desire to help another person.

**complacent** [kəm plā′sənt] *adj.* self-satisfied. — **complacently**, *adv.*

**complementary** [kom plə men′tər ē, -trē] *adj.* completing.

**compound** [kom′pound] *n.* an enclosed area.

**compulsion** [kəm pul′shən] *n.* the act of forcing or being forced.

**compunction** [kəm pungk′shən] *n.* guilt; regret.

**confirmation** [kon′fər mā′shən] *n.* proof; support.

**confiscate** [kon′fis kāt′] *v.* to seize by authority or for public use.

**congest** [kən jest′] *v.* **1.** to cause too much blood, mucus, etc. to collect in (a part of the body). **2.** to fill too full; clog. — **congestion**, *n.*

**conical** [kon′i kəl] *adj.* cone-shaped; pointed.

**consecrate** [kon′sə krāt′] *v.* to make sacred or holy.

**consternation** [kon′stər nā′shən] *n.* shock or dismay that leads to confusion.

**constitutional** [kon′stə tōō′shən əl, -tū′-] *n.* a walk taken for one's health.

**constrained** [kən strānd′] *adj.* forced; obligated.

**consummate** [kon′sə māt′] *v.* to complete.

**contemplation** [kon′təm plā′shən] *n.* the act of planning, intending, or expecting.

**contemplative** [kon′təm plā′tiv, kən tem′plə-] *adj.* thoughtful; reflective.

**contract** [kən trakt′] *v.* to get smaller; shrink.

**contradictory** [kon′trə dik′tər ē] *adj.* not in agreement; opposite; contrary.

**contrive** [kən trīv′] *v.* to plan; scheme.

**controversial** [kon′trə vur′shəl] *adj.* causing argument; stirring up opposing opinions.

**contumelious** [kon′too mē′lē əs, -tyoo-] *adj.* insulting; contemptuous.

**convene** [kən vēn′] *v.* to call together; cause to assemble.

**converge** [kən vurj′] *v.* to meet; come together.

**convulsive** [kən vul′siv] *adj.* marked by violent motion.

**coordination** [kō ôr′də nā′shən] *n.* a working or acting together; harmony.

**coquettish** [kō ket′ish] *adj.* flirtatious.

**coroner** [kôr′ə nər, kor′-] *n.* an official who determines causes of deaths.

**corroborate** [kə rob′ə rāt′] *v.* to support or strengthen.

**corrugate** [kôr′ə gāt′, kor′-] *v.* to shape into a series of ridges and grooves.

**cosmic** [koz′mik] *adj.* relating to the universe.

**802** *Glossary*

**countenance** [koun′tə nəns] *n.* a person's face. — *v.* to approve or tolerate.

**countermelody** [koun′tər mel′ə dē] *n.* a melody that is played along with another melody.

**covet** [kuv′it] *v.* to want; long for.

**covey** [kuv′ē] *n.* a small flock.

**cower** [kou′ər] *v.* to hunch oneself up and tremble in fear.

**crane** [krān] *v.* to stretch one's neck.

**creditable** [kred′i tə bəl] *adj.* worthy of praise.

**creditor** [kred′i tər] *n.* someone to whom a person owes money.

**credo** [krē′dō, krā′-] *n.* a statement of belief.

**creed** [krēd] *n.* a set of basic beliefs.

**crescendo** [kri shen′dō] *n.* an increase in sound.

**crypt** [kript] *n.* an underground room or enclosed space.

**cryptic** [krip′tik] *adj.* written in code.

**cubit** [kū′bit] *n.* an ancient unit of length equaling 18 to 22 inches.

**curdle** [kurd′əl] *v.* to thicken into a soft or lumpy mass.

**curio** [kyoor′ē ō] *n.* an unusual object.

**curt** [kurt] *adj.* brief.


## D

**daft** [daft] *adj.* crazy; wildly merry.

**dauntless** [dônt′lis] *adj.* fearless.

**debut** [dā bū′, di-, dā′bū] *n.* a first public appearance.

**declaim** [di klām′] *v.* to recite or speak in a dramatic or artificial manner.

**declaration** [dek′lə rā′shən] *n.* something that is made known; announcement.

**declivity** [di kliv′ə tē] *n.* a downward slope.

**deduce** [di dōōs′, -dūs′] *v.* to conclude by reasoning from known facts.

**deface** [di fās′] *v.* to spoil the surface or appearance of.

**deference** [def′ər əns] *n.* respect.

**definitive** [di fin′ə tiv] *adj.* final; conclusive. — **definitively,** *adv.* — **definitiveness,** *n.*

**deflect** [di flekt′] *v.* to turn from a straight direction.

**degenerate** [di jen′ə rāt′] *v.* to fall to a lower condition.

**dejected** [di jek′tid] *adj.* sad; depressed.

**deliverance** [di liv′ər əns] *n.* the act of rescuing or freeing.

**delusion** [di lōō′zhən] *n.* a belief in something untrue or unreal.

**demigod** [dem′ē god′] *n.* a person who seems like a god.

**demote** [di mōt′] *v.* to lower in rank.

**denounce** [di nouns′] *v.* to attack; criticize.

**denude** [di nōōd′, -nūd′] *v.* to remove a covering; make bare.

**depend** [di pend′] *v.* ARCHAIC. to hang.

**deplete** [di plēt′] *v.* to reduce; use up.

**deplorable** [di plôr′ə bəl] *adj.* extremely bad.

**deprive** [di prīv′] *v.* to take away; keep from having.

**desecrate** [des′ə krāt′] *v.* to destroy the sacredness of.

**designation** [dez′ig nā′shən] *n.* a name.

**detachment** [di tach′mənt] *n.* the state of being apart or uninvolved.

**devotee** [dev′ə tē′] *n.* a strong supporter; ardent follower.

**dexterous** [deks′trəs, -tər əs] *adj.* skillful. — **dexterously,** *adv.*

**diffidence** [dif′ə dəns] *n.* lack of self-confidence; shyness.

**diffuse** [di fūz′] *v.* to spread out.

**dignitary** [dig′nə ter′ē] *n.* someone of high position or rank.

**diminutive** [di min′yə tiv] *adj.* tiny.

**dire** [dīr] *adj.* horrible; urgent; extreme. — **direst** [dīr′ist] superlative form of **dire.**

**discordant** [dis kôrd′ənt] *adj.* not in harmony or agreement.

**discount** [dis′kount′, dis kount′] *v.* to disregard; rule out.

**discourse** [dis′kôrs′] *n.* a long talk.

**discrepancy** [dis krep′ən sē] *n.* difference; disagreement.

**discrimination** [dis krim′ə nā′shən] *n.* unfair and inferior treatment of people.

**disheveled** [di shev′əld] *adj.* not well groomed; messy.

**disillusioned** [dis′i lōō′zhənd] *adj.* having lost one's faith, goals, or dreams.

**disinterested** [dis in′tris tid, -in′tər is-, -in′tə res′-] *adj.* 1. not having selfish motives. 2. not interested or concerned.

**dismantle** [dis mant′əl] *v.* to take apart.

**disparage** [dis par′ij] *v.* to speak of as having little value; belittle. — **disparagement,** *n.*

**disperse** [dis purs′] *v.* to scatter; cause to disappear.

**dispossess** [dis′pə zes′] *v.* to take away one's property.

**dissemble** [di sem′bəl] *v.* to disguise true facts or feelings.

**disseminate** [di sem′ə nāt′] *v.* to spread or distribute widely.

**dissolve** [di zolv′] *v.* to break up; end.

**dissuade** [di swād′] *v.* to persuade not to do something.

**distill** [dis til′] *v.* to cause to drip or ooze out.

**divert** [di vurt′, dī-] *v.* to amuse; entertain.

**divest** [di vest′, dī-] *v.* to take away from or off (someone).

**divine** [di vīn′] *v.* to guess.

**draft** [draft, drȧft] *n.* an amount of liquid or air that one drinks or breathes in.

**draught** [draft, drȧft] *n.* alternate spelling of **draft.**

**drove** [drōv] *n.* a crowd.

**dub** [dub] *v.* to make someone a knight by tapping him on the shoulder with a sword.

**dullard** [dul′ərd] *n.* a stupid person.


## E

**easement** [ēz′mənt] *n.* lack of worry; relief.

**eddy** [ed′ē] *n.* a water current moving in a circle.

**edifice** [ed′ə fis] *n.* a building.

**efface** [i fās′] *v.* to blot out; erase.

**ejaculate** [i jak′yə lāt′] *v.* to exclaim.

**elevation** [el′ə vā′shən] *n.* the surface of one side of a building.

**elocution** [el′ə kū′shən] *n.* the art of public speaking.

**elude** [i lōōd′] *v.* to get away from or avoid skillfully.

**emaciated** [i mā′shē ā′tid] *adj.* extremely thin.


---

at; āpe; cär; end; mē; it; īce; hot; ōld; fôrk; wood; fōōl; oil; out; up; ūse; turn; ə in ago, taken, pencil, lemon, circus; bat; chin; dear; five; game; hit; hw in white; joke; kit; lid; man; not; singer; pail; ride; sat; shoe; tag; thin; <u>th</u>is; very; wet; yes; zoo; zh in treasure; KH in loch, German ach; N in French bon; œ in French feu, German schön

---

*Glossary* **803**

**embankment** [em bangk'mənt] *n.* a long mound of earth, stones, etc., used to stop water or hold up a road.
**embellish** [em bel'ish] *v.* to add decorative details to.
**embody** [em bod'ē] *v.* to represent in a visible form.
**eminence** [em'ə nəns] *n.* a high area of land.
**endeavor** [en dev'ər] *v.* to try.
**engender** [en jen'dər] *v.* to cause.
**entrails** [en'trālz, -trəlz] *n.pl.* the organs inside the body.
**entreaty** [en trē'tē] *n.* a humble request.
**envisage** [en viz'ij] *v.* to imagine; picture.
**epic** [ep'ik] *adj.* long and detailed; impressive; heroic.
**erratic** [ə rat'ik] *adj.* unplanned; happening by chance.
**erroneous** [ə rō'nē əs] *adj.* incorrect.
**escarpment** [es kärp'mənt] *n.* a cliff or steep slope.
**essay** [e sā'] *v.* to try.
**ether** [ē'thər] *n.* a substance once thought to fill outer space.
**etiquette** [et'i kit, -ket'] *n.* the rules for correct manners and social behavior.
**evocative** [i vok'ə tiv] *adj.* bringing to one's mind a certain picture or memory.
**evolve** [i volv'] *v.* to develop or work out slowly.
**exemplary** [ig zem'plər ē, eg'zəm pler'ē] *adj.* setting an example; worthy of praise.
**exhortation** [eg'zôr tā'shən, ek'sôr-] *n.* strong advice or warning; urging.
**explicit** [eks plis'it] *adj.* clear; definite.
**exterminate** [iks tur'mə nāt'] *v.* to kill; wipe out.
**exultant** [ig zult'ənt] *adj.* joyful; rejoicing.

### F

**facilitate** [fə sil'ə tāt'] *v.* to make easier.
**fagot** [fag'ət] *n.* a pile of sticks tied together.
**fain** [fān] *adv.* ARCHAIC. gladly, willingly.
**farcical** [fär'si kəl] *adj.* ridiculous.
**fathom** [fath'əm] *v.* to figure out; understand.
**fatuous** [fach'ōō əs] *adj.* foolish.
**fawn** [fôn] *v.* to act humble; shower with attention and flattery.
**feasible** [fē'zə bəl] *adj.* able to be done; possible.
**featureless** [fē'chər lis] *adj.* without distinctive qualities or traits.
**feint** [fānt] *v.* to pretend to hit or attack.
**felted** [fel'tid] *adj.* covered with a soft, fuzzy substance like felt material.
**ferment** [*n.* fur'ment; *v.*, fər ment'] *n.* a state of great activity, excitement, or unrest. — *v.* to be in a state of great activity, excitement, or unrest.
**fervent** [fur'vənt] *adj.* full of intense feeling.
**fetter** [fet'ər] *v.* to tie or chain up.
**fidelity** [fi del'ə tē, fī-] *n.* faithfulness; loyalty.
**fissure** [fish'ər] *n.* a deep crack.
**fixity** [fik'sə tē] *n.* steadiness; lack of movement.
**flagstone** [flag'stōn'] *n.* flat pieces of stone used for paving.
**flail** [flāl] *v.* to swing one's arms; thrash around.
**flank** [flangk] *n.* the side.
**flaunt** [flônt, flänt] *v.* to show off; display.
**flay** [flā] *v.* to skin.
**fluent** [flōō'ənt] *adj.* smooth and flowing. — **fluently,** *adv.*
**flute** [flōōt] *n.* a groove.
**focal** [fō'kəl] **point** *n.* the center of attention.

**foliage** [fō'lē ij] *n.* the leaves of a plant.
**fondle** [fond'əl] *v.* to handle tenderly.
**forage** [fôr'ij, for'-] *n.* food for animals.
**forestall** [fôr stôl'] *v.* to prevent in advance.
**forfeit** [fôr'fit] *v.* to give up as a penalty.
**formidable** [fôr'mi də bəl] *adj.* causing fear or awe; of great size, strength, etc.
**founder** [foun'dər] *v.* to sink.
**fray** [frā] *v.* to become worn or weakened.
**freshet** [fresh'it] *n.* a stream.
**frivolity** [fri vol'ə tē] *n.* silliness; playfulness.
**frond** [frond] *n.* a leaf.
**fulsome** [fool'səm] *adj.* insultingly insincere.
**furl** [furl] *v.* to roll up.
**furtive** [fur'tiv] *adj.* secret.
**futility** [fū til'ə tē] *n.* uselessness; hopelessness.

### G

**garble** [gär'bəl] *v.* to mix up; distort.
**garish** [gār'ish] *adj.* unpleasantly bright; glaring.
**gaunt** [gônt] *adj.* thin and worn.
**gesticulation** [jes tik'yə lā'shən] *n.* a gesture.
**gild** [gild] *v.* to cover with gold or a gold color. — **gilt,** *adj.*
**goad** [gōd] *v.* to push; poke; urge.
**grandiloquent** [gran dil'ə kwənt] *adj.* using flowery and important-sounding but empty language.
**gravity** [grav'ə tē] *n.* seriousness.
**grope** [grōp] *v.* to feel around unsurely.
**grotesque** [grō tesk'] *adj.* strange; unnatural; ridiculous.
**guile** [gīl] *n.* slyness; craftiness; deceit. — **guileless,** *adj.*
**guttural** [gut'ər əl] *adj.* throaty; rasping.
**gyration** [jī rā'shən] *n.* a spinning or whirling motion.

### H

**habit** [hab'it] *n.* clothing.
**hale** [hāl] *adj.* strong and healthy.
**hallow** [hal'ō] *v.* to make holy.
**hew** [hū] *v.* to cut and shape with a knife or ax.
**hold** [hōld] *n.* the part of a ship below the decks where cargo is stored.
**homage** [hom'ij, om'-] *n.* a sign of honor or respect.
**hosannah** [hō zan'ə] *n.* a cry of praise and devotion.
**host** [hōst] *n.* an army.
**hover** [huv'ər, hov'-] *v.* **1.** to stay nearby; wait around. **2.** to hang in the air; fly around one spot. — *n.* the act of hovering.

### I

**ignominious** [ig'nə min'ē əs] *adj.* causing disgrace or dishonor. — **ignominiously,** *adv.*
**ill-omened** [il'ō'mənd] *adj.* destined to end badly; unlucky.
**illustrious** [i lus'trē əs] *adj.* famous; outstanding.
**imminent** [im'ə nənt] *adj.* about to happen; threatening.
**impale** [im pāl'] *v.* to stab or run through with a pointed stake or weapon.
**impart** [im pärt'] *v.* to give; tell; reveal.
**impassive** [im pas'iv] *adj.* not showing any feelings.
**impeccable** [im pek'ə bəl] *adj.* without fault; perfect.
**imperceptible** [im'pər sep'tə bəl] *adj.* extremely small or slow; not noticeable.
**imperious** [im pēr'ē əs] *adj.* ruling over harshly.

**804** *Glossary*

**impetuous** [im pech′ōō əs] *adj.* rushing into things without thinking.

**imprecation** [im′pri kā′shən] *n.* a curse.

**impregnable** [im preg′nə bəl] *adj.* that cannot be attacked, weakened, or questioned.

**impunity** [im pū′nə tē] *n.* freedom from punishment.

**inaudible** [in ô′də bəl] *adj.* not loud enough to be heard.

**incandescence** [in′kən des′əns] *n.* extreme brightness.

**incarcerate** [in kär′sə rāt′] *v.* to put in jail. — **incarceration,** *n.*

**incarnate** [in kär′nāt] *v.* to give a visible form to (a quality or idea).

**incessant** [in ses′ənt] *adj.* never stopping; constant. — **incessantly,** *adv.*

**incite** [in sīt′] *v.* to urge; persuade; spur on.

**incognito** [in′kog nē′tō, in kog′ni tō′] *adv.* using a false name; in disguise.

**incorrigible** [in kôr′ə jə bəl, -kor′-] *adj.* not capable of being corrected or improved.

**incredulous** [in krej′ə ləs] *adj.* not believing. — **incredulously,** *adv.*

**indolence** [ind′əl əns] *n.* laziness.

**ineffable** [in ef′ə bəl] *adj.* that cannot be put into words; indescribable.

**inert** [i nurt′] *adj.* not able to move.

**inextinguishable** [in′iks ting′gwi shə bəl] *adj.* not able to be put out.

**inextricable** [in eks′tri kə bəl, -iks trik′ə bəl] *adj.* that cannot be untangled or untied. — **inextricably,** *adv.*

**infectious** [in fek′shəs] *adj.* spreading easily to others.

**infest** [in fest′] *v.* to spread over; fill; overrun.

**infirmity** [in fur′mə tē] *n.* weakness.

**inflection** [in flek′shən] *n.* tone of voice.

**ingot** [ing′gət] *n.* a block of metal.

**ingratiating** [in grā′ shē ā ting] *adj.* done to win someone's good will.

**inherent** [in hēr′ənt, -her′-] *adj.* being an inseparable part or basic trait.

**inkling** [ingk′ling] *n.* a vague idea.

**inquisitive** [in kwiz′ə tiv] *adj.* questioning; curious.

**inscribe** [in skrīb′] *v.* to write or carve words on a surface.

**insensible** [in sen′sə bəl] *adj.* not aware.

**insinuating** [in sin′ū ā′ting] *adj.* so as to gain approval or confidence.

**insufferable** [in suf′ər ə bəl] *adj.* unbearable. — **insufferably,** *adv.*

**insuperable** [in sōō′pər ə bəl] *adj.* not able to be overcome or gone beyond.

**insurrection** [in′sə rek′shən] *n.* rebellion; revolt.

**integrity** [in teg′rə tē] *n.* the condition of being whole, unspoiled, or undamaged.

**intent** [in tent′] *adj.* showing concentration or effort; steady; fixed. — **intently,** *adv.*

**intercede** [in′tər sēd′] *v.* to ask for something in behalf of another person.

**intercession** [in′tər sesh′ən] *n.* **1.** a stepping in to help resolve differences between people. **2.** a prayer for another person.

**interlace** [in′tər lās′] *v.* to fit together as if woven or laced.

**interminable** [in tur′mi nə bəl] *adj.* endless.

**interval** [in′tər vəl] *n.* the difference in pitch between one note and another note higher or lower in the musical scale.

**intone** [in tōn′] *v.* to say or recite in a singsong way; chant. — **intonation,** *n.*

**intricate** [in′tri kit] *adj.* full of detail; complicated.

**introspective** [in′trə spek′tiv] *adj.* looking inward; examining one's own thoughts and feelings.

**intrusion** [in trōō′zhən] *n.* the act of pushing in without being invited.

**intuition** [in′tōō ish′ən, -tū-] *n.* the ability to know or be aware of something without consciously thinking about it.

**invariable** [in vār′ē ə bəl] *adj.* not changing; always the same. — **invariably,** *adv.*

**invigorate** [in vig′ə rāt′] *v.* to give energy to; make strong and lively.

**involuntary** [in vol′ən ter′ē] *adj.* done without choice or control. — **involuntarily,** *adv.*

**irrepressible** [ir′i pres′ə bəl] *adj.* not able to be held back or pushed down. — **irrepressibility,** *n.*

**irresolute** [i rez′ə lōōt′] *adj.* uncertain how to act; wavering. — **irresolution,** *n.*

**irreverency** [i rev′ər ən sē] *n.* something that shows a lack of respect.

**irruption** [i rup′shən] *n.* OBSOLETE. a bursting out, as of lava from a volcano: variation of **eruption**.


### J

**jaguar** [jag′wär, jag′ū är′] *n.* a large cat with a yellow or tan coat and black spots.

**jam** [jam] *v.* to make (radio signals, etc.) impossible to understand by interrupting with other signals. — *n.* a crowded group of things that blocks the way.

**jasmine** [jaz′min, jas′-] *n.* a plant with sweet-smelling yellow, white, or red flowers.

**judicial** [jōō dish′əl] *adj.* considering or judging carefully.

**judicious** [jōō dish′əs] *adj.* having good judgment; wise. — **judiciously,** *adv.*


### K

**kelp** [kelp] *n.* seaweed.

**knell** [nel] *n.* a slow ringing of a bell.


### L

**labyrinth** [lab′ə rinth′] *n.* a maze.

**lackey** [lak′ē] *n.* a servant.

**languid** [lang′gwid] *adj.* lacking liveliness and interest in things.

**languor** [lang′gər] *n.* lack of liveliness and interest in things.

**laudation** [lô dā′shən] *n.* praise.

**legend** [lej′ənd] *n.* something written or printed on an object; inscription.

---

at; āpe; cär; end; mē; it; īce; hot; ōld; fôrk; wood; fōōl; oil; out; up; ūse; turn; ə in ago, taken, pencil, lemon, circus; bat; chin; dear; five; game; hit; hw in white; joke; kit; lid; man; not; singer; pail; ride; sat; shoe; tag; thin; this; very; wet; yes; zoo; zh in treasure; KH in loch, German ach; N in French bon; œ in French feu, German schön

---

*Glossary* **805**

**legitimate** [li jit'ə mit] *adj.* having just cause; reasonable.

**leprosy** [lep'rə sē] *n.* a contagious disease that produces skin sores and deformities.

**lethargy** [leth'ər jē] *n.* great tiredness or sluggishness.

**levy** [lev'ē] *v.* to enlist.

**liberal** [lib'ər əl, lib'rəl] *adj.* not limited; broad.

**limber** [lim'bər] *adj.* bending easily. — **limberness,** *n.*

**list** [list] *v.* to tilt.

**listless** [list'lis] *adj.* tired and uninterested. — **listlessly,** *adv.*

**litter** [lit'ər] *n.* a stretcher for carrying a person.

**loophole** [lōōp'hōl'] *v.* to make holes in for shooting through.

**lucrative** [lōō'krə tiv] *adj.* paying well; profitable.

**ludicrous** [lōō'də krəs] *adj.* laughable; ridiculous.

**lumber** [lum'bər] *v.* to walk or move in a heavy, clumsy way.

**luminous** [lōō'mə nəs] *adj.* shining.

**lurid** [loor'id] *adj.* glowing.

**lusty** [lus'tē] *adj.* strong; vigorous. — **lustily,** *adv.*

**lute** [lōōt] *n.* a stringed instrument with a pear-shaped body.

## M

**mail** [māl] *n.* armor.

**maim** [mām] *v.* to disable by injuring or cutting off a part of the body; cripple.

**malign** [mə līn'] *adj.* evil.

**manifestation** [man'ə fis tā'shən] *n.* a showing or displaying.

**manipulate** [mə nip'yə lāt'] *v.* to operate with the hands.

**marrow** [mar'ō] *n.* the soft, fatty tissue inside bones.

**martial** [mär'shəl] *adj.* relating to war.

**meager** [mē'gər] *adj.* small; barely enough; low-quality.

**mediate** [mē'dē āt'] *v.* to settle differences; bring opposing sides together.

**menial** [mē'nē əl, mēn'yəl] *n.* a servant.

**meteorite** [mē'tē ə rīt'] *n.* a body from space that falls to earth.

**meticulous** [mi tik'yə ləs] *adj.* extremely concerned or careful about details.

**metropolis** [mi trop'ə lis] *n.* a large city.

**migrate** [mī'grāt] *v.* to move from one country or area to another.

**militancy** [mil'ə tən sē] *n.* willingness to fight or work actively for a cause.

**mill** [mil] *v.* to move around in a circular or purposeless way.

**mime** [mīm] *n.* the art of acting out situations and characters without words.

**minstrel** [min'strəl] *n.* a member of a group of performers who present a variety show consisting of songs and jokes.

**minute** [mī nōōt', -nūt', mi-] *adj.* extremely small.

**mirage** [mi räzh'] *n.* a condition in which the air seems to be moving in waves; an optical illusion.

**molest** [mə lest'] *v.* to bother; annoy.

**monogram** [mon'ə gram'] *n.* a design made up of two or more letters, such as initials.

**monolithic** [mon'ə lith'ik] *adj.* like a large structure carved from a single huge stone.

**monotone** [mon'ə tōn'] *n.* a single color.

**mortality** [môr tal'ə tē] *n.* the state of eventually having to die.

**mortar** [môr'tər] *n.* a cementlike mixture that is used to hold bricks together.

**muse** [mūz] *v.* to think; ponder.

**myriad** [mir'ē əd] *n.* an extremely large number.

**mystic** [mis'tik] *n.* a person who understands basic truths of existence through experiences beyond usual human perception and reasoning.

**mystify** [mis'tə fī'] *v.* to puzzle; bewilder.

## N

**namesake** [nām'sāk'] *n.* the person whom someone is named after.

**nebulous** [neb'yə ləs] *adj.* not clear; hazy.

**negation** [ni gā'shən] *n.* a statement or belief based on negative or destructive ideas.

**nettle** [net'əl] *v.* to annoy; irritate.

**nimble** [nim'bəl] *adj.* moving quickly and lightly.

**nocturnal** [nok turn'əl] *adj.* happening at night.

**noisome** [noi'səm] *adj.* having a bad smell.

**nominal** [nom'ən əl] *adj.* small; slight; unimportant.

**notoriety** [nō'tə rī'ə tē] *n.* the state of being famous or well known.

**novice** [nov'is] *n.* a beginner.

**nullify** [nul'ə fī'] *v.* to take away the value of; counteract; cancel out.

## O

**obese** [ō bēs'] *adj.* very fat.

**obliterate** [ə blit'ə rāt'] *v.* to wipe out; erase.

**obsequious** [əb sē'kwē əs] *adj.* overly humble, attentive, and obedient.

**obsolete** [ob'sə lēt', ob'sə lēt'] *adj.* no longer being used; outdated or old-fashioned.

**occult** [ə kult', ok'ult] *adj.* supernatural; magical.

**octave** [ok'tiv, -tāv] *n.* the interval between the first and eighth notes of a musical scale.

**ominous** [om'ə nəs] *adj.* suggesting future evil; threatening.

**omnipotence** [om nip'ət əns] *n.* unlimited power.

**opacity** [ō pas'ə tē] *n.* the state of not transmitting or reflecting light.

**oppress** [ə pres'] *v.* to weigh down; worry.

**oppression** [ə presh'ən] *n.* the state of being ruled over or kept down unfairly or cruelly.

**optical** [op'ti kəl] *adj.* relating to the sense of sight.

**orb** [ôrb] *n.* POETIC. an eye.

**orthography** [ôr thog'rə fē] *n.* spelling.

**ostensible** [os ten'sə bəl] *adj.* seeming to be; supposed.

**ovation** [ō vā'shən] *n.* enthusiastic applause.

**overtone** [ō'vər tōn'] *n.* something suggested or hinted; extra meaning.

**overture** [ō'vər choor', -chər] *n.* an offer to begin discussion.

## P

**pall** [pôl] *v.* to become boring; lose appeal.

**pallid** [pal'id] *adj.* pale; sickly.

**panic** [pan'ik] *n.* sudden, overwhelming fear not controlled by reason.

**parapet** [par'ə pit, -pet'] *n.* a wall, sometimes on top of a large mound of earth, to protect soldiers from attack.

**parasitic** [par'ə sit'ik] *adj.* living at another's expense.

**parley** [pär'lē] *n.* a conference or conversation.

**parody** [par'ə dē] *n.* an imitation.

**parry** [par'ē] *v.* to turn aside; fight off.

**paunch** [pônch, pänch] *n.* a belly that sticks out.

**peaked** [pēkt, pē'kid] *adj.* pale; sickly.

**peradventure** [pur'əd ven'chər] *adv.* ARCHAIC. perhaps.

**perambulate** [pər am'byə lāt'] *v.* to walk around.

**perceive** [pər sēv'] *v.* to see; observe.

**perceptible** [pər sep'tə bəl] *adj.* observable by the senses. — **perceptibly**, *adv.*

**percussion** [pər kush'ən] *n.* a sharp hitting of one thing against another.

**perdition** [pər dish'ən] *n.* hell.

**peremptory** [pə remp'tər ē] *adj.* not permitting argument or delay; commanding.

**periodicity** [pēr'ē ə dis'ə tē] *n.* the condition of happening repeatedly and regularly.

**personify** [pər son'ə fī'] *v.* to represent in the form of a person.

**pertinent** [purt'ən ənt] *adj.* related to what is being discussed; relevant.

**perverse** [pər vurs'] *adj.* refusing to agree with what is reasonable; stubborn; contrary.

**petulant** [pech'ə lənt] *adj.* in a bad mood; cranky; irritable.

**phaze** [fāz] *v.* to make uneasy; disturb; confuse: a variation of **faze**.

**phenomenon** [fə nom'ə non', -nən] *n.* a fact or happening that can be observed.

**phraseology** [frā'zē ol'ə jē] *n.* wording.

**piling** [pī'ling] *n.* a structure made of long pieces of wood, steel, etc., standing upright and supporting a dock or bridge.

**pinafore** [pin'ə fôr'] *n.* an apron worn over a dress.

**pivotal** [piv'ət əl] *adj.* around which something revolves; central.

**placid** [plas'id] *adj.* calm.

**plagiarist** [plā'jə rist] *n.* someone who presents another person's writing as his or her own.

**plaintive** [plān'tiv] *adj.* sad; sorrowful.

**plausible** [plô'zə bəl] *adj.* seeming on the surface to be true or reasonable.

**plebeian** [pli bē'ən] *adj.* a member of the lower class; common person.

**poignant** [poin'yənt] *adj.* emotionally moving.

**pompous** [pom'pəs] *adj.* overly proud and dignified.

**ponderous** [pon'dər əs] *adj.* heavy and clumsy. — **ponderously**, *adv.*

**portly** [pôrt'lē] *adj.* fat; stout.

**posterior** [pos tēr'ē ər, pōs-] *n.* the buttocks.

**precarious** [pri kar'ē əs] *adj.* not stable or secure. — **precariously**, *adv.*

**precincts** [prē'singkts'] *n.pl.* the surrounding area; neighborhood.

**preclude** [pri klo͞od'] *v.* to make impossible; rule out.

**predator** [pred'ə tər] *n.* an animal that kills other animals for food.

**predominate** [pri dom'ə nāt'] *v.* to be stronger or greater.

**presage** [pres'ij, pri sāj'] *v.* to give a sign or warning of (a future happening).

**probe** [prōb] *v.* to reach or press inward.

**procure** [prə kyoor'] *v.* to get; obtain.

**prodigious** [prə dij'əs] *adj.* very great; huge.

**prodigy** [prod'ə jē] *n.* an unusually talented person, particularly a child.

**progressive** [prə gres'iv] *adj.* believing in change and improvement of society.

**prominent** [prom'ə nənt] *adj.* noticeable; obvious.

**promontory** [prom'ən tôr'ē] *n.* a high point of land that juts out into the water.

**pronouncement** [prə nouns'mənt] *n.* a formal statement or declaration of opinion.

**propagation** [prop'ə gā'shən] *n.* increase in number; reproduction.

**proposition** [prop'ə zish'ən] *n.* a statement to be considered either true or false.

**prototype** [prō'tə tīp'] *n.* an original model or perfect example.

**protrude** [prō tro͞od'] *v.* to stick out.

**protuberance** [prō to͞o'bər əns, -tū'-] *n.* something that sticks out; bulge.

**prowess** [prou'is] *n.* extraordinary ability or skill.

**proximity** [prok sim'ə tē] *n.* nearness.

**Q**

**quadruped** [kwod'rə ped'] *n.* an animal with four feet.

**qualification** [kwol'ə fi kā'shən] *n.* the act of limiting or modifying.

**quell** [kwel] *v.* **1.** to quiet; calm. **2.** to put a stop to; bring under control.

**R**

**rabble** [rab'əl] *n.* a low class of people.

**ragtime** [rag'tīm'] *n.* a kind of American music, first developed in the late nineteenth century.

**rakish** [rā'kish] *adj.* carelessly stylish; dashing.

**ramification** [ram'ə fi kā'shən] *n.* a branching or spreading out.

**rampart** [ram'pärt', -pərt] *n.* a long mound or wall of earth, stones, etc.

**rancor** [rang'kər] *n.* strong hate or spite.

**rankle** [rang'kəl] *v.* to feel irritated or angry.

**ravishing** [rav'i shing] *adj.* causing joy; entrancing.

**rebuke** [ri būk'] *v.* to scold sharply.

**recalcitrant** [ri kal'sə trənt] *adj.* difficult to handle.

**recede** [ri sēd'] *v.* to move back or away.

**recess** [rē'ses, ri ses'] *n.* an inner or isolated place.

**recoil** [ri koil'] *v.* to pull or shrink back.

**recompense** [rek'əm pens'] *v.* to repay.

**recrimination** [ri krim'ə nā'shən] *n.* the accusing in return of one who has accused.

**recurrence** [ri kur'əns] *n.* repetition.

**redemptive** [ri demp'tiv] *adj.* making up for one's sins.

---

at; āpe; cär; end; mē; it; īce; hot; ōld; fôrk; wood; fo͞ol; oil; out; up; ūse; turn; ə in ago, taken, pencil, lemon, circus; bat; chin; dear; five; game; hit; hw in white; joke; kit; lid; man; not; singer; pail; ride; sat; shoe; tag; thin; this; very; wet; yes; zoo; zh in treasure; KH in loch, German ach; N in French bon; œ in French feu, German schön

---

*Glossary* **807**

**redress** [ri dres'] *v.* to make up for (a wrong); remedy. — **redresser**, *n.*

**redundant** [ri dun'dənt] *adj.* needlessly repetitive; wordy.

**reel** [rēl] *v.* to feel dizzy; stagger.

**repertoire** [rep'ər twär'] *n.* the works that a performer knows.

**repose** [ri pōz'] *n.* rest; sleep; relaxation.

**resin** [rez'in] *n.* a clear, yellowish or brown substance that oozes out of certain plants. — **resinous**, *adj.*

**respiratory** [res'pər ə tôr'ē, ri spīr'ə-] *adj.* related to breathing.

**retribution** [ret'rə bū'shən] *n.* repayment; punishment.

**retrieve** [ri trēv'] *v.* to get back.

**reverie** [rev'ər ē] *n.* a daydream.

**revoke** [ri vōk'] *v.* to give up; abandon; reject.

**rheum** [rōōm] *n.* a watery discharge, as from the eyes or nose.

**rite** [rīt] *n.* a religious or formal ceremony.

**ritualistic** [rich'ōō ə lis'tik] *adj.* like a religious or formal ceremony.

**roil** [roil] *v.* to move violently; be stirred up.

**roseate** [rō'zē it, -āt'] *adj.* reddish or pinkish; rosy.

**rout** [rout] *n.* a confused pulling back of troops; retreat.

**rubble** [rub'əl] *n.* rough or broken pieces of rock, etc. — **rubbly**, *adj.*

**rudiment** [rōō'də mənt] *n.* a beginning part or stage; basic principle or skill.

**rueful** [rōō'fəl] *adj.* showing regret.

**ruffed** [ruft] *adj.* having feathers or hairs sticking out from the neck.

**rustic** [rus'tik] *n.* a person from the country.

### S

**sac** [sak] *n.* a pouch inside an animal, often containing fluid.

**sacrilegious** [sak'rə lij'əs, -lē'jəs] *adj.* showing disrespect toward God or religion.

**salutation** [sal'yə tā'shən] *n.* a greeting.

**salvageable** [sal'vij ə bəl] *adj.* able to be saved or rescued.

**sanitarium** [san'ə tār'ē əm] *n.* an institution where invalids are treated and cared for.

**sapient** [sā'pē ənt] *adj.* wise; knowing; learned.

**sardonic** [sär don'ik] *adj.* bitter; ironic.

**scabbard** [skab'ərd] *n.* a case for the blade of a sword, etc.

**scallop** [skol'əp, skal'-] *n.* one of a continuous series of curves.

**scantling** [skant'ling] *n.* a small piece of lumber.

**score** [skôr] *n.* a group of twenty.

**scroll** [skrōl] *n.* a sheet of paper that is rolled up.

**scrupulous** [skrōō'pyə ləs] *adj.* paying strict attention to what is right; careful. — **scrupulously**, *adv.*

**scud** [skud] *v.* to be blown by the wind.

**scuttle** [skut'əl] *v.* to make holes in (a ship) and cause it to sink.

**sear** [sēr] *v.* to burn.

**segregation** [seg'rə gā'shən] *n.* the policy of separating people of different races.

**select** [si lekt'] *adj.* admitting only certain people, usually in a high social position.

**self-effacement** [self'i fās'mənt] *n.* the keeping of one-self in the background.

**self-evident** [self'ev'ə dənt] *adj.* obvious or apparent without needing to be proved.

**semblance** [sem'bləns] *n.* appearance; resemblance.

**sepulchral** [si pul'krəl] *adj.* like a tomb; gloomy.

**sequestered** [si kwes'tərd] *adj.* shut off from others; isolated.

**sever** [sev'ər] *v.* to cut off.

**sheaf** [shēf] *n.* a bundle.

**sheath** [shēth] *n.* a case for the blade of a knife, sword, etc.

**shunt** [shunt] *v.* to turn to the side.

**sidle** [sīd'əl] *v.* to move or sneak sideways.

**siegeworks** [sēj'wurks'] *n.pl.* MILITARY. a barricade set up by a force surrounding an enemy.

**signal** [sig'nəl] *adj.* noticeable; remarkable. — **signally**, *adv.*

**sinew** [sin'ū] *n.* a tough, cordlike tissue that connects a muscle to another part of the body; tendon.

**singular** [sing'gyə lər] *adj.* strange; remarkable.

**sinister** [sin'is tər] *adj.* threatening harm or evil.

**slovenly** [sluv'ən lē] *adj.* not thorough or precise; sloppy. — **slovenliness**, *n.*

**smite** [smīt], **smitten** [smit'ən], **smote** [smōt] *v.* to hit hard.

**solace** [sol'is] *v.* to comfort; console.

**solicitude** [sə lis'ə tōōd', -tūd'] *n.* concern.

**solstice** [sol'stis] *n.* either of two times during the year (**summer solstice** and **winter solstice**) when the sun is farthest from the equator.

**spawn** [spôn] *v.* to bring into existence; produce.

**speculative** [spek'yə lā'tiv, -lə tiv] *adj.* pondering; reflective.

**spew** [spū] *v.* to send out in a gush.

**spurn** [spurn] *v.* to push away scornfully.

**stagnant** [stag'nənt] *adj.* without movement or activity; dull.

**stalwart** [stôl'wərt] *adj.* strong; sturdy.

**stanch** [stônch, stänch] *v.* to stop or control.

**stark** [stärk] *adj.* sticking out or outlined sharply.

**statistics** [stə tis'tiks] *n.pl.* information relating to numbers or quantities collected and organized to explain a certain subject.

**stench** [stench] *n.* a very bad smell.

**stereotype** [ster'ē ə tīp', stēr'-] *n.* a fixed, simplified image of a person or group.

**stow** [stō] *v.* to store.

**strategist** [strat'ə jist] *n.* a person skilled in planning or scheming.

**strident** [strīd'ənt] *adj.* sharp and high-pitched; screeching. — **stridently**, *adv.*

**stringy** [string'ē] *adj.* lean; wiry.

**stupefy** [stōō'pə fī', stū'-] *v.* to astonish; bewilder. — **stupefaction** [stōō'pə fak'shən, stū'-], *n.*

**stymie** [stī'mē] *v.* to hold back; block; delay.

**suave** [swäv] *adj.* smooth and polite; poised.

**subjugation** [sub'jə gā'shən] *n.* the state of being ruled over or controlled.

**sublimity** [səb lim'ə tē] *n.* high rank or position.

**subordinate** [sə bôr'də nit] *n.* a person below another person in rank or power.

**subsequent** [sub'sə kwənt] *adj.* following.

**subservient** [səb sur'vē ənt] *adj.* not resisting; obedient.

**subside** [səb sīd'] *v.* to lessen; become quieter, calmer.

**808** *Glossary*

**substantive** [sub′stən tiv] *n.* a noun.
**succession** [sək sesh′ən] *n.* **1.** a number of things that follow one another; series. **2.** the order in which monarchs take over a throne, or the act of taking the throne.
**succor** [suk′ər] *n.* help or relief.
**suffice** [sə fīs′] *v.* to be enough.
**sully** [sul′ē] *v.* to dirty; soil; dishonor.
**summary** [sum′ər ē] *adj.* prompt; hasty. — **summarily** [sə mer′ə lē, sum′ər ə-], *adv.*
**sundries** [sun′drēz] *n.pl.* small, miscellaneous items.
**superlative** [sə pur′lə tiv] *adj.* supreme.
**suppliant** [sup′lē ənt] *adj.* asking or begging humbly.
**supplication** [sup′lə kā′shən] *n.* the act of asking humbly for something.
**surge** [surj] *v.* to swell or rush forward.
**surmount** [sər mount′] *v.* to be on top of.
**surreptitious** [sur′əp tish′əs] *adj.* secret, sneaking.
**sway** [swā] *n.* rule; power; authority.
**sweltering** [swel′tər ing] *adj.* extremely and uncomfortably hot.

## T
**tableau** [tab lō′] *n.* a scene or picture.
**taciturn** [tas′ə turn′] *adj.* preferring not to talk; silent.
**taint** [tānt] *n.* a hint of decay; stain; contamination.
**tankard** [tang′kərd] *n.* a large mug with a lid.
**tarry** [tar′ē] *v.* to linger.
**tedious** [tē′dē əs, tē′jəs] *adj.* boring and tiring.
**tenacious** [ti nā′shəs] *adj.* not giving up; stubborn.
**tenement** [ten′ə mənt] *n.* a house; residence.
**tentacle** [ten′tə kəl] *n.* a long, flexible part of some animals or plants.
**tepid** [tep′id] *adj.* lukewarm.
**terse** [turs] *adj.* short and to the point. — **tersely**, *adv.*
**testy** [tes′tē] *adj.* easily annoyed; irritable; impatient. — **testily**, *adv.*
**tether** [teth′ər] *v.* to tie or chain up.
**thickset** [thik′set′] *adj.* thick in build; stocky.
**thresh** [thresh] *v.* to thrash or toss around.
**tinct** [tingkt] *v.* OBSOLETE. to tint; color.
**transfigure** [trans fig′yər] *v.* to change the appearance of.
**transgression** [trans gresh′ən, tranz-] *n.* a sin.
**translucent** [trans lōō′sənt, tranz-] *adj.* letting light pass through.
**traverse** [trav′ərs, trə vurs′] *v.* to go over or across.
**tremolo** [trem′ə lō′] *n.* a wavering or trembling sound made on an instrument or by a singer.
**tremulous** [trem′yə ləs] *adj.* trembling; shaking.
**tribulation** [trib′yə lā′shən] *n.* suffering; misery.
**tumultuous** [too mul′chōō əs, tyoo-] *adj.* wild and noisy.
**turbulent** [tur′byə lənt] *adj.* moving wildly.

## U
**ulcer** [ul′sər] *n.* an open, oozing sore. — **ulcerous**, *adj.*
**ultimate** [ul′tə mit] *adj.* basic; fundamental.
**unalienable** [un āl′yə nə bəl, un ā′lē ə-] *adj.* that cannot be taken away.
**uncongenial** [un′kən jēn′yəl] *adj.* unpleasant; unfriendly.
**uncultivated** [un kul′tə vā′tid] *adj.* not refined or cultured.
**undermine** [un′dər mīn′] *v.* to weaken or injure.
**undulation** [un′jə lā′shən, -dyə-] *n.* a waving motion.

**unfeigned** [un fānd′] *adj.* not pretended; sincere.
**unformulated** [un fôr′myə lā′tid] *adj.* not expressed in a precise way.
**unhampered** [un ham′pərd] *adj.* not held back or weighed down.
**unmercenary** [un mur′sə ner′ē] *adj.* not motivated by a desire for money; not greedy.
**unsteadfast** [un sted′fast′, -fəst] *adj.* not firmly placed; unsteady.
**unsubstantial** [un′səb stan′shəl] *adj.* without substance or matter; unreal or imaginary.
**usurp** [ū surp′, ū zurp′] *v.* to take by force or without having the right.

## V
**variegated** [vār′ē ə gā′tid, vār′ə gā′-] *adj.* varied.
**vengeful** [venj′fəl] *adj.* wanting revenge.
**venom** [ven′əm] *n.* a poison produced by some insects and snakes.
**veracity** [və ras′ə tē] *n.* honesty.
**verge** [vurj] *v.* to be on the edge; border.
**veritable** [ver′i tə bəl] *adj.* true; real. — **veritably**, *adv.*
**vest** [vest] *v.* to give power or authority to.
**vestige** [ves′tij] *n.* a trace of something that is gone.
**veterinary** [vet′ər ə ner′ē, vet′rə-] *n.* an animal doctor: another word for **veterinarian**.
**vindicate** [vin′də kāt′] *v.* OBSOLETE. to get revenge for an injury or wrong done to (someone); avenge.
**vivacity** [vi vas′ə tē, vī-] *n.* liveliness.
**vivify** [viv′ə fī′] *v.* to make vivid or striking.
**volley** [vol′ē] *n.* the firing of a number of weapons at once.
**voluble** [vol′yə bəl] *adj.* speaking easily and rapidly; talkative. — **volubly**, *adv.*
**vortex** [vôr′teks] *n.* a whirling area of water that pulls things toward its center; whirlpool.
**vouchsafe** [vouch sāf′] *v.* to be kind enough to give.
**vulnerable** [vul′nər ə bəl] *adj.* easy to hurt or attack.

## W
**wake** [wāk] *n.* the track left behind a ship in the water.
**wan** [won] *adj.* **1.** pale; sickly. **2.** weak; faint. — **wanly**, *adv.*
**wary** [wār′ē] *adj.* guarding against danger; cautious; alert.
**writhe** [rīth] *v.* to twist; turn; squirm.
**wrought** [rôt] *v.* past tense and past participle of **work**. — **wrought up**. worked up; excited.

## Y
**yore** [yôr] *n.* time past.

## Z
**zenith** [zē′nith] *n.* the highest point; top; summit.

at; āpe; cär; end; mē; it; īce; hot; ōld; fôrk; wood; fōōl; oil; out; up; ūse; turn; ə in ago, taken, pencil, lemon, circus; bat; chin; dear; five; game; hit; hw in white; joke; kit; lid; man; not; singer; pail; ride; sat; shoe; tag; thin; this; very; wet; yes; zoo; zh in treasure; KH in loch, German ach; N in French bon; œ in French feu, German schön

*Glossary* **809**

# VOCABULARY REVIEW

In addition to the words listed in the Glossary and the words covered in the word study sections throughout this book, each of the following words is presented to help you prepare for standardized tests of verbal skills. The page numbers at the right tell where you can find these words treated in *Appreciating Literature*.

| | | | | | | |
|---|---|---|---|---|---|---|
| abutted | 20 | fluently | 44 | poverty | 662 |
| abyss | 309 | foundered | 309 | precluded | 75 |
| agitation | 44 | futility | 296 | prodigious | 332 |
| algae | 662 | gravity | 114 | prominent | 296 |
| allegiance | 44 | grotesque | 20 | prosperous | 44 |
| apologized | 129 | guttural | 114 | rebuking | 114 |
| archaic | 345 | hallowed | 332 | recess | 75 |
| assailed | 44 | ill-omened | 114 | redress | 75 |
| avowal | 154 | imminent | 133 | sank | 309 |
| bricklayer | 154 | incandescence | 662 | sea | 662 |
| chord | 662 | indigent | 662 | self-government | 326 |
| chuckled | 129 | infirmities | 133 | severed | 296 |
| compassion | 114 | ingratiating | 114 | ship | 309 |
| constrain | 154 | inherent | 326 | shouted | 129 |
| constrained | 154 | inkling | 114 | sighed | 129 |
| contracted | 114 | intently | 296 | singular | 20 |
| delusion | 133 | knots | 309 | solemn | 154 |
| denial | 154 | left | 309 | song | 662 |
| deprive | 296 | lethargy | 662 | speculative | 345 |
| depth | 309 | lucence | 662 | superior | 309 |
| designation | 154 | migrate | 133 | superlative | 309 |
| devotees | 332 | militancy | 332 | tenacious | 20 |
| discounted | 133 | mortar | 154 | thundered | 129 |
| distilled | 75 | negations | 326 | title | 154 |
| divesting | 114 | nominal | 20 | tremulous | 114 |
| estuaries | 326 | personified | 345 | tribulations | 332 |
| excitement | 662 | pessimist | 154 | ultimate | 345 |
| explicit | 345 | port | 309 | unstratified | 326 |
| fettered | 75 | | | | |

# INDEX OF TITLES BY THEME

This index groups all of the selections according to the themes that they address. Every selection is listed at least once; many are listed more than once. You may want to use this index to help students examine the presentation of a particular theme in different selections.

# INDEX OF SKILLS

Page numbers in boldface italics indicate entries in the Writing About Literature Handbook. Page numbers in italics indicate entries in the Literary Terms Handbook.

See the Table of Contents for list of complete *lessons* on Speaking and Listening Skills, Thinking Skills, Reading and Study Skills, and Writing Skills.

## LITERARY SKILLS

**812**  *Index of Skills*

in short story, 75
Inference, 350
Irony, 129, 133, 416, 612, *784, 796*
   dramatic, 416, **784**, *796*
   in novel, 612
   situational, 129, **784**, *796*
   verbal, 133, **784**, *796*

Legend, 575
Literal language, *796*
Local color, 167, *796*

Medieval romance, 579
Metaphor, 213, 215, 217, 289, **788**, *796*
   extended, 217
   implied, 215, 289
Meter, 192, *796*
Monologue, 235, 536, *796*
Mood, 58, 383, **774**, *797*
   in drama, 383
   in short story, 58
Moral, 613, *797*
Motif, 607

Narration, 225, 296, *797*
Narrative hook, 20, *797*
Narrator, 75, 612, *797*
   in novel, 612
   unreliable, 75
Nonfiction, 263, 346, **786**, *797*
Novel, 611, 612, *797*
   episodic, 612
Novella, 612

Octave, 241
Onomatopoeia, 200, **788**, *797*

Parable, 613, *797*
Parallelism, 194, 331, 346, *797*
Personification, 209, **788**, *798*
Persuasion, *798*
Petrarchan (Italian) sonnet, 241, *800*
Plot, 20, 134, 448, 612, **770**, *798*
   dramatic, 448
   in novel, 612
   in short story, 20
   structure, 20, 448, 612
   subplot, 612
Poem, 177
Poetry, 177, 181, 189, 222, 225, 231,
   235, 236, 244, 246, 249, **788**, *793,*
   *794, 796, 797, 798, 800*
   concrete, 244, *793*
   dramatic, 177, 222, 235, 249, *794*
   experimental, 177, 236, 246, 249
   lyric, 177, 222, 231, 249, *796*
   narrative, 177, 222, 225, 249, *797*
   patterns in, 236
   sound of, 189, 249
   speaker in, 181, 249, **788**, *800*
   traditional, 177, 236, 249
Point of view, 75, 82, 134, 612, **776**, *798*

first-person, 75, **776**, *798*
limited third-person, 82, **776**, *798*
   in novel, 612
   omniscient, 86, **776**, *798*
Prose, 177
Protagonist, *798*
Pun, *798*
Purpose, 263, 277, 290, 313, 346, **786**
   in autobiography, 277
   in essay, 290, 313
   in nonfiction, 263, 346, **786**

Quatrain, 239, *800*

Refrain, 194
Repetition, 194, 331, *798*
Resolution, 20, *798*
Rhyme, 192, 239, 250, 260, 261, *798*
   approximate, 192
   couplet, 239
   end, 250, *798*
   near, 192
   off, 192
   and rhythm, 260
   slant, 192, *799*
Rhyme scheme, 239, 241, *799*
Rhythm, 177, 192, 260, 261, **788**, *799*
Rising action, 20, *799*
Romance, 579, *799*

Satire, 663, 722, *799*
Scansion, *799*
Script, 354
Sensory language, 320, 346
Sestet, 241, *800*
Setting, 58, 68, 134, 383, 612, **774**, *799*
   and atmosphere, 58, **774**
   change of, 68
   in drama, 383
   in novel, 612
   in short story, 58, 68, 134
Shakespearean (English) sonnet, 239,
   241, *800*
Short story, 1, 149, 153, 166, 174, *799*
   elements of, 149, 166
   interaction of elements in, 166
   significant detail in, 174
   single effect of, 153
Simile, 211, 289, **788**, *799*
Soliloquy, 512, *799*
Sonnet, 236, 239, 241, *799, 800*
   Petrarchan, 241, *800*
   Shakespearean, 239, 241, *800*
Speaker of a poem, 178, 181, 249, **788**,
   *800*
Speeches, 331
Stage directions, 354, *800*
Staging, 354, 383, 432, 465, 536
   and character, 432
   Elizabethan, 465
   and setting, 383
   and theme, 536

Stanza, 177, 239, 241, *800*
Style, 263, *800*
Subplot, 612
Symbol, 114, 134, 175, 219, **782**, *800*
Symbolism, 219

Theme, 90, 98, 134, 536, 612, **780**, *800*
   in drama, 536
   implied, 90, 98
   in novel, 612
   in short story, 90, 98, 103, 134
   and staging, 536
   stated, 90
Thesis, implied, 339, *800*
Thesis statement, 339, **768**, *800*
Title, 134, 249, 263, 346
   in nonfiction, 263, 346
   in poetry, 249
   in short story, 134
Tone, 82, 134, 178, 186, 263, **778**, *800*
   in nonfiction, 263
   in poetry, 178, 186
   in short story, 82, 134
Topic sentence, **769**
Total effect, 134, 247, 253, 346, 459,
   569, 605, 661, 734, **790**
   in drama, 459, 569
   in heroic narrative, 605
   in nonfiction, 346
   in novel, 661, 734
   in poetry, 247, 253
   in short story, 134
Tragedy, 353, 462, 568, *800*
Tragic flaw, 568, *800*

Word choice, 178, 181, 249, *800*

## COMPOSITION SKILLS

### ANALYTICAL
Writing *about* the following:

Autobiography, 277, 281
Biography, 270
Character, 39, 44, 154, 460, 570, 662,
   **772**
   and tone, 154
Characters, comparing and contrasting,
   52, 662, **772**
Conclusion of a story, 133
Contrasting images, 207
Descriptive essay, 320, 323
Drama and fiction, 383
Dramatic poem, 235
Epic hero, 606
Essay, 296, 309, 313, 320, 323, 326,
   332, 339
   descriptive, 320, 323
   expository, 339
   narrative, 296, 309, 313
   persuasive, 326, 332

Fictional speaker, 183
Fiction and drama, 383
Imagery, 207, 213, 251
  and sound, 251
Irony, 129, *784*
Narrative essay, 313
Narrative poem, 230
Nonfiction, 349, *786*
Plot, 28, *770*
Poetry, 181, 194, 198, 206, 215, 217,
    227, 230, 233, 235, 239, 255, *788*
  dramatic, 235
  form in, 233
  and prose, 198
  sound of, 194
  speaker in, 181
Point of view, 75, *776*
Response to a story, 20
Response to nonfiction, 349
Rhythm and rhyme, 192
Setting, 58, 68, *774*
Sound and imagery, 251
Suspense, 150
Symbol, 114, 117, 345, *782*
Theme, 90, 99, 108, *780*
Title, 186
Tone, 86, 154, 289, *778*
  and character, 154
Total effect, 141, 167, 259, 570, 735,
    *790*
  in drama, 570
  in novel, 735
  in poetry, 259
  in short story, 141, 167
Two poems, 215
Verbs, 244

CREATIVE

Writing the following:

Advertisement, 167
Article, 108, 114, 606
Autobiographical incident, 277
Biographical sketch with anecdotes, 270
Character's speech, 460
Comparison/contrast, 345
Concrete poem, 244
Contrasts, 207
Description, 58, 68, 99, 117, 141, 192,
    206, 207, 251, 320, 323, 383

with contrasts, 207
of movement, 206
from a moving vantage point, 320
of an object, 58
of an ongoing event, 251
of a place, 68
of a process, 141
with rhythm, 192
with sensory language, 99
of a symbol, 117
from two perspectives, 323
Descriptions, contrasting, 383
Dialogue, 20, 52, 570
Diary entry, 133
Essay, 296, 309, 326, 339, 349
  autobiographical, 349
  expository, 339
  narrative, 296, 309
  persuasive, 326
Extended metaphor, 217
Fable, 90
Feature article, 114
Free verse, 198
Instructions for a camera, 662
Interview, 28
Letter, 39
Memoir, 289
Metaphor, 213, 217
  extended, 217
Monologue, 154
Narrative, 150, 309
New incident, 735
Newspaper article, 108, 606
Plot outline, 86
Poem, 181, 183, 186, 194, 198, 213,
    215, 227, 230, 233, 235, 239, 244,
    251, 255, 259
  with a comparison, 239
  concrete, 244
  from contrasting perspectives, 255
  describing an ongoing event, 251
  dramatic, 235
  about emotion, 233
  of farewell, 194
  in free verse, 198
  with metaphors, 213
  narrative, 227, 230
  as an object, 183
  about the past, 181

riddle, 215
  about a transformation, 259
  with unusual verbs, 186
Radio play, 75
Rhythm, 192
Riddle poem, 215
Speech, 44, 332, 460
  for a character, 460
  persuasive, 44, 332
Story for a child, 281
Supporting an opinion, 129
Traveler's journal entry, 313

## VOCABULARY SKILLS

### TEST-TAKING SKILLS

Analogies, 154, 309, 662
Antonyms, 114, 296, 332
Sentence completions, 44, 133, 326
Synonyms, 20, 75, 345

### WORD STUDY

Colloquial language, 232
Connotation, 200
Context clues, 99, 150, 320
Denotation, 200
Dialect, 606
Diction, 200
English words borrowed from French,
    460
Etymology, 39
Greek roots, 339
Hyphenated adjectives, 289
Inventive language, 246
Latin roots, 270
Middle English, 606
Midland dialect, 606
Noun-forming suffixes, 167
Precise verbs, 129
Prefixes, 167
Puns, 569
Roots, 270, 339
Slang, 735
Specific and concrete nouns, 188
Vivid modifiers, 227
Word choice, 200
Word origins, 39

# INDEX OF AUTHORS AND TITLES

E. Dickinson     William Faulkner     Tom Wolfe

Gerard M. Hopkins S.J.     Mark Twain     Rudyard Kipling

Gwendolyn Brooks     Randall Jarrell     Joseph Conrad

Stephen Spender     R. M. Rilke     C Brontë     Virginia Woolf

John Keats     Arthur Conan Doyle     Sidney Lanier

Yeats     Robert Burns     A Bradstreet     William Shakespeare

A Lincoln     Henry W. Longfellow     Marianne Moore

James Joyce     Fred'k Douglass     W Blake     J. Austen

Wallace Stevens     Robert Burns     Phillis Wheatley     Yeats

C Brontë     James Thurber     F Scott Fitzgerald